FINANCIAL

Third Edition

Accounting

A Critical Approach

JOHN FRIEDLAN

University of Ontario Institute of Technology

McGraw-Hill Ryerson

Connect. Learn. Succeed.

Financial Accounting: A Critical Approach
Third Edition

ISBN-13: 978-0-07-096760-1
ISBN-10: 0-07-096760-1

3 4 5 6 7 8 9 10 DOW 1 9 8 7 6 5 4 3 2 1

Printed and bound in the United States.

Care has been taken to trace ownership of copyright material contained in this text; however, the publisher will welcome any information that enables it to rectify any reference or credit for subsequent editions.

Vice-President and Editor-in-Chief: Joanna Cotton
Executive Sponsoring Editor: Rhondda McNabb
Executive Marketing Manager: Joy Armitage Taylor
Managing Editor, Development: Kelly Dickson
Developmental Editor: Rachel Horner
Senior Editorial Associate: Christine Lomas
Supervising Editor: Cathy Biribauer
Copy Editor: Julie van Tol
Proofreader: Rodney Rawlings
Team Lead, Production: Jennifer Hall
Inside Design: Michelle Losier
Composition: Kim Hutchinson, Cara Scime, First Folio Resource Group Inc.
Cover Design: Michelle Losier
Cover Photo: Media Bakery
Printer: RR Donnelley

Library and Archives Canada Cataloguing in Publication Data

Friedlan, John
    Financial accounting : a critical approach/John Friedlan.—3rd ed.

Includes index.
ISBN 978-0-07-096760-1

    1. Accounting--Textbooks. I. Title.

HF5636.F76 2010   657   C2009-905822-7

ABOUT THE AUTHOR

Many people travel to Italy to see the famous landmarks such as the Leaning Tower of Pisa, and the Sistine Chapel at the Vatican in Rome. But on a recent tour through Italy, accounting professor John Friedlan took a path less travelled: to two faces of accounting.

First, Friedlan and his family journeyed to the historic Tuscan city of Sansepolcro, near Florence, looking for the haunts of Luca Pacioli (1416–1517), a mathematician and teacher who is considered the "Father of Accounting." Pacioli is credited not with inventing accounting, but being first to codify it in a book. It was the method of record keeping used by Venetian merchants during the Italian Renaissance, known as the *double-entry bookkeeping system*.

Passing through the gates of the 16th-century walls into the oldest part of the city, Friedlan found the palazzo where Pacioli lived, although today it is a private residential apartment building and not open to visitors. Walking farther up the hill revealed a better clue, hidden under an archway: a frescoed portrait of Pacioli.

Soon Friedlan's first quest was realized: in a plaza not much bigger than his own office at the University of Ontario Institute of Technology in Oshawa, Ontario, stood a larger-than-life marble statue of Luca Pacioli.

Friedlan stood beside the statue for some time, posing for photos, probably the one person in Sansepolcro that day who knew that Pacioli's double-entry bookkeeping method was still in use around the world. One legend has Pacioli warning accountants they should not go to sleep at night unless the debits equalled the credits in their journals and ledgers. The visit in Sansepolcro ended with a celebration, an ice cream at one of the most famous gelato parlours in the country.

Several weeks went by before Friedlan would stumble across the other face of accounting, possibly at its most perverse. It was during a pilgrimage to the only Nazi death camp located inside Italy during the Second World War, the Risiera di San Sabba in Trieste. It is now a Holocaust shrine, to honour the approximately 5,000 people murdered there by 1945.

One of the exhibits at the museum was a yellowing income statement, typed by a German official at the time, showing the expenses and revenue entries calculating how much money, in Reichsmarks, it cost the Nazis to house a prisoner for nine months, including costs for the striped uniform and the food. It cost the regime two Reichsmarks for the gas used to kill the prisoner. Underneath, it showed the revenues from retrieval of the victim's gold teeth and other personal property.

Professor Friedlan has, since 2003, been Accounting Program Director in the Faculty of Business and Information Technology of the University of Ontario Institute of Technology. Before that he spent 13 years on the faculty of the Schulich School of Business at York University. In his classes, Friedlan challenges students to think critically about balance sheets, net income, and how accounting numbers can turn losses into profits, and vice versa.

A Montreal native, Friedlan originally wanted to be a scientist. After earning his Bachelor of Science at McGill University, he discovered that unlocking the mysteries of numbers was his true calling. He switched career paths and completed his M.B.A. at York University in 1978. Friedlan entered the working world as an auditor with Deloitte and Touche (then Deloitte, Haskins and Sells, Chartered Accountants) in Toronto and qualified as a CA two years later.

Friedlan gained real-world experience at Nabisco Brands, where he moved from bean counting to peanut counting as a manager with Planters Nuts. Next came a staff position with the Board of Examiners at the Canadian Institute of Chartered Accountants where he helped manage annual competency exams known as the Uniform Final Examination (UFE). In 1985, Friedlan moved to Seattle to pursue his Ph.D. at the University of Washington. After graduating in 1990, he returned to the classroom full time, this time as the teacher. In 1992, Friedlan was awarded Educator of the Year for undergraduates. He also won a Seymour Schulich Award for Teaching Excellence in 2000.

In his classes, Friedlan challenges students to think critically and to question the whys behind corporate financial reporting choices. His approach to teaching accounting stresses the mysteries and uncertainties of the discipline, and he encourages his students to be skeptical, to always question authority—a trait he learned first from his father, Irving, who handled the accounts for a carpet company in Montreal.

When not teaching undergraduates, Friedlan is a sought-after consultant, providing expert opinions to law firms engaged in civil lawsuits, and his specialized courses for lawyers have him teaching accounting in the boardrooms of Canada's top law firms. He has been a commentator on radio and television, including CTV's *Canada AM* and BNN (formerly Report on Business Television).

A lifelong runner, the Montreal native has been a loyal fan of *Star Trek*, Peter, Paul, and Mary, and the Montreal Canadiens. But Friedlan's favourite pursuits are listening to music everywhere, singing (badly), fiddling with his prized satellite radio, and playing basement hockey with his boys, Alex and Evan.

Friedlan lives with his wife, college professor and journalist Ellin Bessner, and their boys in Richmond Hill, Ontario.

BRIEF CONTENTS

CONTENTS

CHAPTER 3

The Accounting Cycle 88

CHAPTER 4

Income Measurement and the Objectives of Financial Reporting 169

CHAPTER 5

Cash Flow, Profitability, and the Cash Flow Statement 233

CHAPTER 9

Liabilities   477

CHAPTER 10

Owners' Equity   556

PREFACE

OBJECTIVES

Welcome to the third edition of *Financial Accounting: A Critical Approach*. I've written the book to provide an accessible and insightful introduction to the real nature of accounting information. My goal is to have any person who studies the book thoroughly become a sophisticated user of financial statements and possess a solid understanding of the accounting issues, controversies, and scandals that are reported in the business press. I'm proud that this book is written exclusively by a Canadian author. As Canada becomes an IFRS country, the relevance of a Canadian perspective is all the more important. Adaptations of foreign books will be less able to effectively capture the Canadian accounting environment.

The title of the book requires some explanation. The *Critical Approach* to financial accounting guides students to look critically at accounting information. The book emphasizes the importance of accounting information as a decision-making tool but also addresses the limitations, controversies, and problems with accounting and accounting information. Rather than accept the numbers in financial statements at face value, students learn that managers often choose from alternative acceptable ways of accounting for transactions and economic events and that these choices can have economic consequences for an entity's stakeholders and for the entity itself. Students also learn that accounting information provided by an entity can't be all things to all people. The information may be useful to some decision makers, but not to others. Students learn to critically evaluate whether the information is appropriate for the decisions *they* are making.

I was reminded recently of the importance of a critical approach to studying accounting. A student who had transferred from another university was struggling as he prepared for the mid-term exam. He said that he found the approach I use in introductory financial accounting quite challenging. He explained that at his previous university he was mainly asked to calculate, not to analyze and interpret information. After he left, I wondered how students' careers benefit from learning accounting from mainly a technical or procedural standpoint.

Many accounting textbooks classify themselves as having a "user" or a "preparer" orientation. In my view these classifications are artificial: a good introductory education in financial accounting requires elements of both. While the main purpose of this book is to make students literate readers of financial statements (a user orientation), it's difficult to understand financial statements without having some appreciation of how data are entered into an accounting system and converted into the information included in accounting reports. As a result, it's useful for introductory accounting students to have an understanding of basic bookkeeping (a preparer orientation). Without this familiarity, students will find it difficult to understand how and why accounting choices made by managers affect the financial statements.

Thus, while *Financial Accounting: A Critical Approach* is not primarily a book about how to do accounting, the "how to" part is fully covered. Chapter 3 explains how transactions and economic events are recorded and the data converted into financial statements. In the context of this book, understanding the procedural aspects of accounting is essential to understanding the relationship between transactions and economic events and the resulting financial statements.

One of the important features of *Financial Accounting: A Critical Approach* is the use of short, decision-oriented "mini-cases." The cases, and an approach for solving them, are first introduced in Chapter 4. Cases with solutions are provided as the Solved Problems in Chapters 4 through 12. Cases for assignment and exam purposes appear in the Appendix to the book. Additional cases are provided in Connect (**www.mcgrawhillconnect.ca**). Most of the cases place the student in the role of a user or interpreter of financial statements (what I call user-oriented cases). The cases serve three purposes: first, they help develop critical thinking and problem-solving skills; second, they help develop an appreciation of the context-specific nature of accounting; and third, they allow students to get "inside the heads" of preparers and users to understand how perspective affects the preparation and use of financial statements. Accounting comes to life as students are forced to think about alternative ways of accounting for transactions and economic events, and to consider the impact the different alternatives can have on decisions and economic outcomes.

Probably the most challenging aspect of writing the third edition was handling the dramatically changing Canadian accounting environment as we move from GAAP to IFRS and GAAP for Private Enterprises. The first challenge was how to orient the book. At the introductory level, GAAP for Private Enterprises and IFRS are very similar (like they say, "the devil is in the details"), so there's really not a big impact. I decided the main emphasis would be IFRS because public companies are the most visible, although there are many more private companies so there will likely be more users of GAAP for Private Enterprises. In places where there are significant differences between the two sets of standards I've included boxes called "Canadian GAAP for Private Enterprises." When using the book, you can be confident that, unless otherwise stated, GAAP for Private Enterprises and IFRS are the same for purposes of introductory accounting.

The second issue is that I wrote the book at a time when no Canadian companies are using IFRS or GAAP for Private Enterprises. As a result, most of the financial statement examples I use are from companies using GAAP. I've been careful to select examples that are in the spirit of IFRS, but some aspects or wording may not be exactly what IFRS statements will look like.

CHANGES IN THE THIRD EDITION

I've made some significant changes in the third edition. The table below summarizes the major revisions to the text.

- The chapters have been reoriented to reflect the changing Canadian accounting environment. IFRS is used in the main body of the text when accounting standards are discussed. Canadian GAAP for Private Enterprises boxes were added to explain significant difference between IFRS and GAAP for Private Enterprises.

- The approach to the accounting cycle in Chapter 3 is changed. In the third edition, the traditional journal entry T-account–trial balance approach has been integrated into the main body of the chapter instead of including it in an appendix. Some users of the book expressed a strong preference for the traditional approach and the revised presentation has been well received by reviewers.

- The chapter on Generally Accepted Accounting Principles (Chapter 5 in the second edition) has been removed. Presenting all that material in one chapter wasn't the best approach for introductory accounting, so the coverage of the topic has been reduced and integrated into other chapters as pedagogical boxes.

- There is no featured corporation. That approach was changed in the third edition because it is more effective to emphasize companies that demonstrated the issues I wanted to raise in each chapter.

- LIFO is not covered in the inventory chapter of this edition since it's no longer allowed by IFRS or GAAP for Private Enterprises. An Insight box has been included to identify and briefly explain LIFO since it's still in wide use in the U.S.

- All of the solved problems beginning in Chapter 4 are case analyses. This change will give readers more opportunity to learn how to analyze and interpret accounting information.

In this edition I changed the nature of the chapter-opening vignette. This time each chapter provides a feature on a Canadian accountant or user of financial statements. I think these stories provide a revealing and personal look into the lives and experiences of accounting professionals and people who use financial statements in their work. These vignettes were written by Canadian journalist Ellin Bessner (who is also my wife!). I hope you find them interesting and valuable.

In addition, many other minor changes have been added to improve the text. Many of the exercises and problems in the end-of-chapter material have been revised and many new problems and exercises added.

PEDAGOGICAL FEATURES OF *FINANCIAL ACCOUNTING: A CRITICAL APPROACH*

Besides the cases mentioned above, this text is full of other useful pedagogical tools.

- Learning Objectives and Summary of Key Points—The learning objectives at the beginning of each chapter focus students' attention on what they will learn. The summary at the end of each chapter outlines how each learning objective was addressed.

- Key Terms and Glossary—Key terms are printed in bold in the text and are listed with page references at the end of each chapter. The terms are defined in the text and appear with their definitions and a page reference in the glossary at the end of the book.

- Questions for Consideration—Each chapter contains a number of Questions for Consideration, providing opportunities for students to stop and think about what they have read so far in the chapter. The Questions for Consideration are designed as critical thinking questions requiring application of the material in the chapter. Solutions to these questions are provided.

- Knowledge Check—Each chapter contains a number of Knowledge Checks that give students a chance to stop and check their understanding of key points raised in the chapter. If a student can't answer the questions, they should go back and review the preceding sections. Solutions to the Knowledge Checks are provided on Connect.

- Insight boxes—Throughout the text, commentary on key points is provided in the Insight boxes. The Insight boxes provide additional details concerning the nature and interpretation of accounting information.

- Canadian GAAP for Private Enterprises boxes—Where appropriate these boxes highlight differences between IFRS and GAAP for Private Enterprises.

- Use of extracts from actual entities' financial statements—Many of the issues, concepts, and points raised in the book are demonstrated through extracts from the financial statements of actual entities, presented as they appeared in the entity's annual report. Students are able to see first-hand the presentation of the topic in a real-world setting.

- Solved Problems—Each chapter provides a detailed problem with a solution. Most of the solved problems are cases that should help students develop their analytical skills.

- Similar Terms list—This unique feature provides a list of accounting terms used in the text compared to other terms with essentially the same meaning that students may encounter in the media, in financial documents, and in accounting practice.

- Using Financial Statements—Each chapter's assignment material provides extensive extracts from an entity's financial statements and a series of questions that provide students with the opportunity to work with actual financial statement material and to apply the chapter content in a realistic context.

- Assignment material—Each chapter contains a large number of questions, exercises, and problems that provide students with the opportunity to apply the knowledge and skills they have gained from the chapter. Much of this material is keyed to the learning objectives in the text.

A NOTE ON COVERAGE

Financial Accounting: A Critical Approach provides considerable depth on a number of topics not normally covered in introductory accounting texts or courses. These topics include revenue recognition, leases, pensions, future income taxes (in an appendix), employee stock options, and consolidated financial statements. Coverage of revenue recognition is intended to introduce the concept of accounting choice and demonstrate the impact of different ways of reporting economic events on the financial statements. The other more complex topics are included because they are commonly reported in financial statements and often have large dollar amounts associated with them. If students are to make sense of the entire set of statements, they must have some familiarity and comfort with these topics, even if they tend to be complex. Some instructors may prefer not to cover some of the sections on leases, pensions, future income taxes, and investments in other companies. These topics can easily be skipped without having any impact on students' understanding of later chapters.

NAMES OF ENTITIES

Some readers may wonder about the origins of the names given to the entities used in the examples and end-of-chapter material. *Financial Accounting: A Critical Approach* provides names for more than 500 entities throughout the book and most are actual names of places in Canada!

SUPPLEMENTS

The supplements to support *Financial Accounting: A Critical Approach* have been completely revamped for the third edition. All are available within the instructor area of Connect at **www.mcgrawhillconnect.ca**. This exciting new package comprises the following elements:

Instructor's Manual The thoroughly updated Instructor's Manual includes learning objectives, chapter overviews, classroom icebreakers, active learning techniques, comprehensive lecture notes, writing assignments, and an assignment topic grid related to the coverage in the assignment material.

Computerized Test Bank The test bank contains more than 1,000 questions of the highest quality, varying in style and level of difficulty.

Microsoft® PowerPoint® Presentations With one presentation for every chapter of the text, instructors can guide their students through the text with ease. The slides have been adapted to fit the third edition, and the addition of figures and diagrams increases their visual appeal. The PowerPoint slides have been prepared by Athina Hall of the University of Ontario Institute of Technology.

Solutions Manual The fully revised Solutions Manual contains in-depth answers and step-by-step solutions for all assignment material included in the text.

For Students

Developed in partnership with Youthography, a Canadian youth research company, and hundreds of students from across Canada, McGraw-Hill Connect™ embraces diverse study behaviours and preferences to maximize active learning and engagement.

With McGraw-Hill Connect™, students complete pre- and post-diagnostic assessments that identify knowledge gaps and point them to concepts they need to learn. McGraw-Hill Connect™ provides students the option to work through recommended learning exercises and create their own personalized study plan using multiple sources of content, including a searchable e-book, multiple-choice and true/false quizzes, chapter-by-chapter learning goals, interactivities, personal notes, videos, and more. Using the copy, paste, highlight, and sticky note features, students collect, organize, and customize their study plan content to optimize learning outcomes.

For Instructors

McGraw-Hill Connect™ assessment activities don't stop with students! There is material for instructors to leverage as well, including a personalized teaching plan where instructors can choose from a variety of quizzes to use in class, assign as homework, or add to exams. They can edit existing questions and add new ones; track individual student performance—by question, assignment, or in relation to the class overall—with detailed grade reports; integrate grade reports easily with Learning Management Systems such as WebCT and Blackboard; and much more. Instructors can also browse or search teaching resources and text-specific supplements, and organize them into customizable categories. All the teaching resources are now located in one convenient place.

McGraw-Hill Connect™ — helping instructors and students <u>*Connect, Learn, Succeed!*</u>

SUPERIOR SERVICE

*i*Learning Sales Specialist

Your Integrated Learning Sales Specialist is a McGraw-Hill Ryerson representative with the experience, product knowledge, training, and support to help you assess and integrate any of the following products, technology, and services into your course for optimum teaching and learning performance. Whether it is using our test bank software, helping your students improve their grades, or putting your entire course online, your *i*Learning Sales Specialist is there to help you do it. Contact your local *i*Learning Sales Specialist today to learn how to maximize all of McGraw-Hill Ryerson's resources.

*i*Learning Services Program

McGraw-Hill Ryerson offers a unique *i*Learning Services package designed for Canadian faculty. Our mission is to equip providers of higher education with superior tools and resources required for excellence in teaching. For additional information, please visit **www.mcgrawhill.ca/highereducation/iservices**.

CourseSmart

CourseSmart brings together thousands of textbooks across hundreds of courses in an eTextbook format, providing unique benefits to students and faculty. By purchasing an eTextbook, students can save up to 50 percent on the cost of a print textbook, reduce their impact on the environment, and gain access to powerful Web tools for learning including full-text search, notes and highlighting, and email tools for sharing notes between classmates. For faculty, CourseSmart provides instant access for reviewing and comparing textbooks and course materials in their discipline area without the time, cost, and environmental impact of mailing print exam copies. For further details contact your *i*Learning Sales Specialist or go to **www.coursesmart.com**.

Course Management

Content cartridges are available for the course management systems WebCT and Blackboard. These platforms provide instructors with user-friendly, flexible teaching tools. Please contact your local McGraw-Hill Ryerson *i*Learning Sales Specialist for details.

ACKNOWLEDGMENTS

Many people contributed to the development of this book and I take this opportunity to thank them.

Many thanks to faculty reviewers who devoted significant time and effort to reading the manuscript as it developed and who provided valuable comments, suggestions, and criticisms, all of which served to make the book better:

Rick Bates, *University of Guelph*
Ann Clarke-Okah, *Carleton University*
Han Donker, *University of Northern British Columbia*
Ian Feltmate, *Acadia University*
Leo Gallant, *St. Francis Xavier University*
Sandy Hilton, *University of British Columbia*
Ferdinand Jones, *University of Ontario Institute of Technology*
Phillipe Levy, *McGill University*
David McConomy, *Queen's University*
Vanessa Oltmann, *Vancouver Island University*
Sandy Qu, *York University*
Amanda Wallace, *Nipissing University*
Peggy Wallace, *Trent University*

Thank you to the exceptional people who agreed to be interviewed for the opening vignettes of each chapter. I am flattered they were willing to be a part of this project:

Navdeep Bains
Katherine Chan
Ian Clarke
Hélène Fortin
Sheila Fraser
Craig Hannaford
Frances Horodelski
Christina Lovell
Robert Patterson
Mark Powell
Al Rosen
Robin Schwill

Thanks to Jenna Lasky, then a fourth-year accounting student at the University of Ontario Institute of Technology and now with Deloitte & Touche LLP, for the work she did on the solutions. Also, thank you to Susan Cohlmeyer and Robert Ducharme for their technical checks and comments, to Lois Leiff for providing editoral input, and to Ellin Bessner for writing the vignettes.

Various instructors assisted in preparing the set of supplements that accompany the book:

    Jane Bowen, *University of Ontario Institute of Technology* (Microsoft® PowerPoint® Presentations)
    Lynn de Grace, *McGill University* (Test Bank)
    Sandy Hilton, *University of British Columbia* (Connect)
    Alla Volodina, *York University* (Instructor's Manual)

I'd like to thank the many companies whose financial statement extracts are presented in the book. It would be very difficult to write a book like this without real-world examples of financial reporting.

The staff at McGraw-Hill Ryerson provided outstanding support to help develop and market the book and were a pleasure to work with. Many thanks to the entire team, specifically Rhondda McNabb, Sponsoring Editor; Rachel Horner, Developmental Editor; and Cathy Biribauer, Supervising Editor. Thanks also to Julie van Tol and Rodney Rawlings for their work on the copy editing and proofreading, respectively, of this book.

Finally, a special acknowledgment to Professor Al Rosen who helped shape and develop the way I think about and teach accounting. His contribution to this book is significant.

                    John Friedlan
                    Faculty of Business and Information Technology
                    University of Ontario Institute of Technology

THE ACCOUNTING ENVIRONMENT: WHAT IS ACCOUNTING AND WHY IS IT DONE?

LEARNING OBJECTIVES

After studying the material in this chapter you will be able to do the following:

▶ **LO 1** Define accounting and explain why it's important.

▶ **LO 2** Describe the accounting environment and understand that the accounting information an entity presents is affected by the accounting environment.

▶ **LO 3** Discuss how the interests of the people who prepare accounting information can conflict with the interests of those who use it.

▶ **LO 4** Explain what a critical approach to accounting is.

▶ **LO 5** Understand the purpose of accounting standards such as International Financial Reporting Standards (IFRS) and Generally Accepted Accounting Principles for Private Enterprises (GAAP) and be familiar with the different sets of accounting standards that are used in Canada.

▶ **LO 6** Understand that the main purpose of accounting is to measure economic activity and that accounting measurements can often be difficult and subjective.

Ian Clarke knows his job has perks that made his kids the envy of their school friends: access to tickets for every home game of the Toronto Maple Leafs, the Toronto Raptors, and the Toronto FC soccer club.

But as executive vice-president and CFO of the teams' parent company, Maple Leaf Sports & Entertainment (MLSE), Clarke is usually far too busy to attend games. Instead, the chartered accountant says he listens to the games while he works in his Toronto office at the Air Canada Centre.

—by Elin Bessner

Ian Clarke, CA
Executive Vice-President and Chief Financial Officer,
Maple Leaf Sports & Entertainment

Still, Clarke acknowledges that attending concerts by A-list celebrities like Tina Turner and signing pay cheques for star athletes like Jose Calderon, Chris Bosh, and Luke Schenn certainly ranks right up there in "cool" factor.

"We're in a fun business, so if you're not having fun here, you need to check your pulse!" Clarke quips.

Graduating from Concordia University in 1983 with a B. Comm. degree, Clarke was hired by Thorne Riddell in Toronto, a national accounting firm that later became KPMG. There, in the "bullpen" with other rookie accountants, Clarke got his start auditing clients such as Rogers Cantel, the precursor to Rogers Wireless; men's clothing retailer Grafton-Fraser; and, fatefully, Maple Leaf Gardens (MLG), which owned both the storied Toronto hockey arena and the hockey club. In 1990, MLG hired him away to become their controller.

Clarke credits working at a national accounting firm, especially "the discipline, the learning, the opportunity," for the launch of his corporate career. Clarke says, "I was fortunate because at an early age I got exposure to presidents and vice-presidents when [I was] doing interviews and asking them questions, [so] you can learn a lot about business."

Under Clarke's guidance MLG expanded, bought the Raptors, moved the Leafs into the new 19,000-seat Air Canada Centre, and changed its name to Maple Leaf Sports & Entertainment (MLSE). Forbes.com ranked the Leafs as the most valuable team in the NHL, worth $448 million ($US) in 2008. Besides the sports teams and arena, Clarke oversees two specialty television stations, merchandising, food concessions, and the Maple Leaf Square condominium and hotel complex.

Clarke says accounting is "one of the tools in my box of tools." It helps him to be analytical when making timely business decisions. Although he is responsible for governance, internal controls, financial statements, IT, and even firing people, Clarke admits he loves strategic planning the best.

"Preparing a financial statement or reading a financial statement, you get a lot from doing that. It tells you a story, but the real issue is what are you going to do with it?" Clarke says. "I think my challenge as an executive vice-president is to be a corporate leader, so what now turns my crank [are] the strategic elements of our business; where we're taking our business and growing."

This is why he advises students to consider accounting as a foundation for an exciting career in business or even politics, where they can be as passionate about their work as he still is. According to Clarke, "It gives you a great sense of reasoning, it gives you instant respect from people, and it just opens doors."

One such door enabled him to meet his childhood hero, former Boston Bruins defenceman Bobby Orr, not once but twice. The meetings left Clarke speechless, for once. "That was quite an amazing thing," he recalled. "I still believe he was the best player ever."

—E.B.

WHAT IS ACCOUNTING AND WHY DOES IT MATTER?

I have spent about 30 years in accounting education and I still get excited and passionate when I walk into a classroom to talk about the topic of the day. You may find this strange and surprising: How can anyone get excited about accounting? But there is a lot more to the subject than most people realize. Accounting is dynamic. It requires creativity. It can be controversial. Accounting matters! It's almost impossible to make good business decisions without relevant accounting information, and accounting information can be very relevant as well to personal decisions that people make in their day-to-day lives.

Some of the decisions that both business managers and individuals might use accounting information for are listed in Table 1.1. The details about how many of these decisions are made is what this book is going to explore.

TABLE 1.1 Business and Personal Decisions That Rely on Accounting Information
• Determine whether or not to buy a business and how much to pay.
• Calculate the amount of tax to pay.
• Evaluate whether to lend to a prospective borrower, and at what interest rate.
• Assess whether or not you can afford to borrow money.
• Decide if you can afford to go on vacation.
• Determine how to divide family assets in a divorce.
• Find out how much money you have in the bank.
• Determine how to invest money in a retirement savings plan.
• Determine bonuses earned by management.
• Evaluate whether to expand your business.
• Assess whether to make a product or to purchase it from an outside supplier.
• Evaluate how well managers have managed a business.
• Assess how well a business has performed.
• Determine if you should donate money to a particular charity (has the charity been managed well, is it using its money effectively?).
• Determine how much a business is worth.
• Evaluate how much regulated businesses should be allowed to charge for their goods and services.
• Evaluate if a government has provided effective and efficient financial management.
• Decide whether to make a major purchase like a computer or car.

Most people don't see accounting as it really is. Consider the following:

- *Accounting isn't a science.* Indeed, many people consider accounting more an art than a science.

- *Accounting isn't precise or exact.* Many estimates have to be made and uncertainty surrounds most accounting numbers.

- *Accounting doesn't provide the "right" answer.* There can be more than one reasonable answer for many accounting situations.

- *Accounting is flexible.*

- *Accounting requires judgment.*

As you work through the material in this book keep these statements in mind. There is no explanation for them here, but as you learn more about accounting you will gradually come to see they are true.

What Is Accounting?

Let's begin with some definitions. **Accounting** is a system for gathering data about an entity's economic activity, processing and organizing that data to produce useful information about the entity, and communicating that information to people who want to use it to make decisions (see Figure 1.1). The **entity** is an economic unit of some kind, such as a business, university, government, or even a person. Note that data and information aren't the same thing. *Data* are raw, unprocessed facts about an entity's economic activity that is entered into an accounting system. *Information* results from organizing and presenting the data in ways that make it useful for decision making by stakeholders.

FIGURE 1.1

The Accounting System

While this definition of accounting may seem straightforward, it's not. When designing an accounting system, accountants and managers have to make many decisions about what data should be gathered and how it should be organized. Communicating using accounting information presents the same complexities people face with any form of communication. Just as writers choose words to influence readers, accountants can use legitimate, alternative ways of reporting the economic activity of an entity to influence how people perceive financial information.

INSIGHT

Bookkeeping Is *Not* the Same as Accounting

It's important not to confuse accounting and bookkeeping. When most people think of accounting, what they are really thinking of is bookkeeping. For those of you who have taken an "accounting" course in the past, what you were probably studying was *bookkeeping*—the process of recording financial transactions and maintaining financial records. Bookkeeping is part of accounting, but only one part. *Accounting* involves the design and management of information systems, how to account for and report an entity's economic activity, and the analysis and interpretation of financial information.

financial = external stakeholders

managerial = internal

↳ effects of public vs private entities?

Accounting is often broken down into two subfields. The first, **financial accounting**, provides information to people who are *external* to an entity. External users include investors, lenders, taxation authorities (such as the Canada Revenue Agency), competitors, and many others. Usually 0such users don't have direct access to information about the entity and must rely on the entity to provide it. This book focuses on financial accounting.

The second subfield is **managerial accounting**, which addresses the information needs and decisions of the managers of an entity. Managerial accounting information assists in operating decisions such as price setting, expansion, evaluating which products are successful and which aren't, and determining the amount of a product that should be produced.

Why Does Accounting Matter?

Accounting matters because it has **economic consequences**—it affects people's wealth—and it can have an impact on the decisions they make. For example, suppose you owned a small business, and you could choose between two legitimate and legal ways to account for a particular transaction. One accounting method will result in paying less tax than the other. Which method would you choose? Almost everyone would choose the one that involves paying the least amount of tax. The economic consequence of your choice is that you keep more money and the government gets less. Choose the other accounting method and the economic consequence is that you have less money.

Does this example surprise you? In reality, accountants and managers can often choose among alternative ways of accounting for transactions and economic events, and often the method chosen has significant economic consequences. One of the main themes of this book is explaining the choices available to accountants and managers so that you can be a savvy user of accounting information and avoid unexpected negative economic consequences.

WHY DO PEOPLE NEED AND WANT ACCOUNTING INFORMATION?

More and better information allows for better decisions. Without information, a "decision" is nothing more than a guess. For example, suppose you wanted to take a vacation over the winter break. You see an advertisement in the newspaper promoting Aruba as a fabulous winter destination. Assuming you have never been to Aruba and know little about it, would you simply accept the advertisement's claims at face value? Most wouldn't. They would probably want to find out whether Aruba offered what they wanted from a winter vacation. They might ask friends and relatives if they know anything about Aruba, do research in the library or on the Internet, or consult with expert sources that specialize in travel information, such as a good travel agent or a guide published by an independent company. They would gather information until they were comfortable making a decision. Not all information is equal; in making a decision, you would generally give more weight to the information that is most reliable and most relevant to your needs.

What does a trip to Aruba have to do with accounting? To make good decisions, whether about a winter vacation or a business strategy, people need good information. Every day people make important decisions, both for themselves and on behalf of other entities: individuals decide how to invest their retirement money, bankers decide whether to lend money to struggling businesses. Table 1.1 lists other decisions people have to make.

 INSIGHT

The Cost-Benefit Trade-off

While more information leads to better decisions, there are limits. It's usually not possible or worthwhile to collect all the information available on a subject. First, gathering and analyzing information is costly and takes time. At some point the benefit isn't worth the cost. The concept of comparing the benefits of an action with its costs, and of taking the action only if the benefits are greater, is known as the **cost-benefit trade-off**. Information should be collected only if the benefit from it exceeds the cost of it. (For example, it's probably not worth the cost in time and money to call a hotel to find out the colour of its carpeting.) Second, there are limits to the amount of information people can effectively manage and process. Too much information or "information overload" can impair a person's ability to make decisions.

eg, 20 jams vs. 6

QUESTION FOR CONSIDERATION

Explain why a potential vacationer to Aruba would likely find travel information published by Aruba's government travel department less credible than information provided by an independent travel company.

Answer: The objective of the government travel department is to encourage people to visit the island. Its publications will likely emphasize the favourable qualities of the island and downplay or ignore negative ones. In contrast, an independent travel company's objective (if it's truly independent) should be to provide a useful service to its customers that will encourage them to use the company's services again (the company will make more money if it can generate repeat business). As a result, its information is less likely to be biased. This doesn't mean the information provided by Aruba's government travel department wouldn't be useful. It means that a user should recognize the probable bias, and its implications, when assessing the information.

reliability
? agendas/
vested
interests

Let's consider an example of how information can improve a business decision. Suppose you were approached by a recent acquaintance who asked you to lend a significant amount of your own money to her business. What would you want to know before you agree? Your first key question would probably be, "Will the company be able to pay back the money borrowed, plus interest?" A second question would be, "If the company were unable to pay me back, what resources does it have that I could take and sell to recover my money?"

This is where accounting comes in. In answer to the first question, accounting information might be helpful in telling you how well the corporation has performed in the past and how much cash the company has been able to generate. As an answer to the second question you might want a list of the resources the business owns and a list of other entities the corporation owes money to, so you can see what would be available to you if the loan weren't repaid. You can probably think of more examples. Of course, non-accounting information, perhaps about the people managing the corporation, might also be helpful in making your decision.

www.mcgrawhill
connect.ca

KNOWLEDGE CHECK

☐ What is accounting?

☐ What is meant by the statement "accounting has economic consequences"?

☐ What is the cost-benefit trade-off? Why is it usually not possible to collect all possible information that might be useful for making a decision?

☐ Explain the difference between data and information.

THE ACCOUNTING ENVIRONMENT

How an entity reports its economic activity in its financial statements or other type of accounting
report is influenced by the circumstances under which the activity is occurring. Accounting was
created to provide a record of economic activity and information useful in decision making, so it
makes sense that accounting should be responsive to the environment and the people using the
information. To say that all economic activity should be accounted for in the same way makes no
more sense than saying that everyone should live in the same type of house or drive the same type
of car. There are different types of houses and cars because people have different needs, dictated
by factors around them such as climate, family, wealth, and employment.

Therefore, before we start our examination of accounting information, we will explore
the accounting environment and consider the factors that can affect how an entity approaches
its financial reporting. There are four key components of the accounting environment: overall
environment, entities, stakeholders, and constraints. These components are displayed in Figure 1.2
and discussed in detail below.

Environment

The character of a county's institutions influence the way people there live their lives. Canada, for
example, is a constitutional democracy with a mixed economy and a legal system based on British
common law (the civil code in Quebec). The environment "umbrella" at the top of Figure 1.2
identifies some of the important factors that establish the structure of a society: political,
cultural, economic, competitive, regulatory, and legal parameters. The differences in these
between countries help to explain why accounting rules vary from country to country.

Entities

Entities are at the centre of the accounting environment because stakeholders are looking for
information about them and it's the entities that typically provide the accounting information
stakeholders need. There are three categories of business entities—corporations, proprietorships,
and partnerships—as well as not-for-profit organizations, governments, and individuals. Let's
take a brief look at some of the different types of entities.

Corporations A **corporation** is a separate legal entity created under the corporation laws of
either Canada, one of the provinces, or some other jurisdiction in the world. Corporations have
many of the same rights and responsibilities as individuals. For example, they must file tax returns,
can be sued, and can enter into contracts (to borrow money, to provide goods or services to a
customer, etc.).

Ownership in a corporation is represented by **shares**, and owners of shares are called
shareholders. Shares are issued to investors when a company is formed, and they can be issued
at any time during a corporation's life.

FIGURE **1.2**

The Accounting Environment

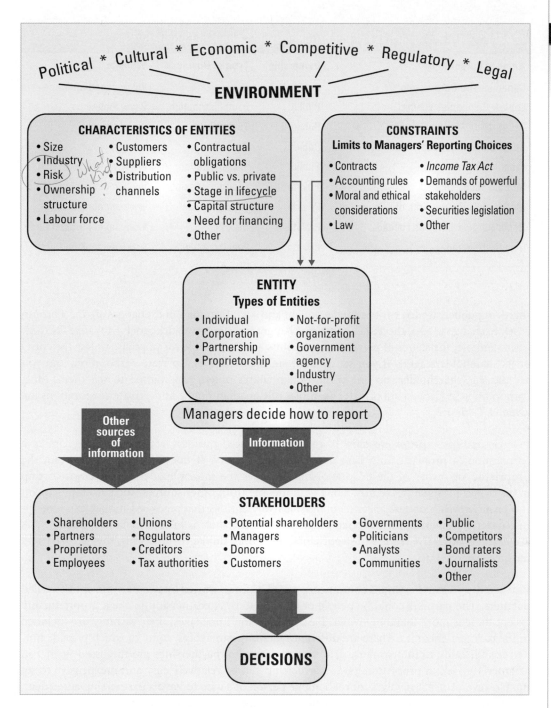

One of the most important features of a corporation is that it provides **limited liability** to its shareholders, which means that shareholders aren't liable for the obligations of the corporation or the losses it suffers. For example, if a corporation borrows money and is unable to repay the loan, the lender can't demand repayment from shareholders. Another attractive feature of corporations is that share ownership is easily transferred without affecting the corporation, which simply carries on business with new owners. For other types of entities, a transfer of ownership can be more difficult.

Shares of **public corporations** can be purchased by anyone interested in owning part of the entity. The shares are usually traded on a **stock exchange**—a place (physical or virtual) where the

TABLE 1.2	Examples of Public and Private Canadian Corporations		
Name of Corporation	**Ownership**	**Type of Business**	**Website**
Canadian Tire Corporation	Public	Retail	www.canadiantire.ca
Loblaw Companies Limited	Public	Food distribution	www.loblaw.ca
Research In Motion Limited	Public	Technology	www.rim.com
Royal Bank of Canada	Public	Bank	www.rbc.com
WestJet Airlines Ltd.	Public	Transportation	www.westjet.com
McCain Foods Limited	Private	Food processing	www.mccain.com
McDonald's Restaurants of Canada Ltd.	Private	Food services	www.mcdonalds.ca
Home Hardware Stores Limited	Private	Retail	www.homehardware.ca
Irving Oil Limited	Private	Fuel oil dealer	www.irvingoil.com

www.tsx.ca

shares of publicly traded entities can be bought and sold. Examples of exchanges are the Toronto Stock Exchange (TSX), the TSX Venture Exchange, and the New York Stock Exchange (NYSE).

In contrast, the shares of **private corporations** aren't available for purchase unless the entity or its shareholders agree. If you set up your small business as a private corporation, and you are the sole shareholder, no one could obtain shares unless you wanted to sell them. Most corporations in Canada are private. Examples of Canadian public and private corporations are given in Table 1.2.

Proprietorships A **proprietorship** is an unincorporated business with one owner. Unlike a corporation, a proprietorship isn't a separate legal entity. It doesn't pay taxes; instead, the **proprietor**, or owner of the proprietorship, includes the money made by the proprietorship in his or her personal tax return, along with income from other sources, such as employment. If a proprietorship doesn't meet its obligations, any entities that are owed money can attempt to recover it by seizing the proprietor's personal assets, such as his or her house, car, or bank account. An attractive feature of proprietorships is that, unlike corporations, they are easy and inexpensive to set up.

Partnerships A **partnership** is an unincorporated business owned by two or more entities called **partners**. The partners could be people or corporations. A partnership is like a proprietorship except there is more than one owner. Partnerships don't pay taxes; their earnings are included in the partners' incomes. There are different types of partnerships, some of which provide limited legal liability to the partners. (The different types of partnerships are discussed further in Chapter 10.) Like a proprietorship, a partnership can be relatively easy and inexpensive to set up. However, since it involves more than one person, it's wise to have a partnership agreement, which adds cost and complexity. The agreement is important, however, as it sets out the rights and responsibilities of the partners.

Not-for-Profit Organizations A large part of the Canadian economy isn't devoted to making money or profit. **Not-for-profit organizations** provide social, educational, professional, religious, health, charitable, and other services in Canadian communities and around the world. Examples are hospitals, charities, religious organizations, unions, clubs, daycare centres, and universities. Not-for-profit organizations can incorporate and provide members with limited liability. They are exempt from paying income taxes.

Governments Government plays a major role in the lives of Canadians. The various levels of government in Canada raise and spend hundreds of billions of dollars every year, and financial reporting by governments is an important source of accountability.

KNOWLEDGE CHECK

- ☐ Identify and describe the three types of business entities.
- ☐ Explain the differences between public and private corporations.
- ☐ What is a not-for-profit organization? Provide some examples.

Individuals *Individual* people are also accounting entities as they often have to produce information in quantitative form to meet the demands of everyday life. Consider the following examples:

- *Filing an income tax return.* Most individuals have to file a tax return every year with the **Canada Revenue Agency (CRA)**, the Canadian government agency responsible for administration and enforcement of federal tax laws, which means that information must be accumulated and organized to complete the return.

- *Keeping track of finances.* Accounting software is an easy-to-use accounting system designed to help people organize their finances.

- *Borrowing money from banks.* Banks may request financial information as part of the loan application.

- *Insuring homes and belongings.* To determine the amount of insurance needed, an individual lists his or her personal belongings and estimates a value for them.

- *Preparing budgets.* A student may want to estimate how much it will cost to attend university each year, and then plan monthly or weekly spending to ensure he or she has enough money to meet all financial needs for the year.

Others Although most of the common accounting entities have been identified above, there are other entities that may be of interest to people, depending on their needs. For example, some people may want data on a particular industry. While industries don't prepare financial statements, useful information can sometimes be obtained from sources such as trade associations, industry publications, public interest groups, and Statistics Canada.

Characteristics of Entities

No two entities are identical and, like people, each has characteristics that make it unique. Some characteristics are obvious; for example, an entity's size or industry. Canada has businesses in a vast range of industries, including natural resources, agriculture, finance, manufacturing, high technology, hospitality, and services, to name a few. But even though many companies may operate in an industry, there will still be differences among them. Some will be public and others private. They might be large or small, unionized or non-unionized. Each may do business in different markets. Figure 1.2 identifies some characteristics of entities. All these characteristics are important for understanding an entity—what it does, and how it accounts for its economic activity. We will explore many of these as we proceed.

Constraints

How an entity accounts for its economic activity and what information it reports aren't entirely up to the people who prepare the information (although they have a lot of influence over it). Often, the choices available are constrained by contracts, laws, accounting rules, and the information needs and demands of powerful stakeholders. Consider the following examples:

- The *Income Tax Act* defines how certain transactions and economic events must be accounted for in calculating the amount of income tax an entity must pay.

- Corporations must meet the requirements of the law they are incorporated under (such as the *Canada Business Corporations Act*).

- Some entities must agree to follow formal sets of accounting rules such as Generally Accepted Accounting Principles for Private Enterprises (GAAP) or International Financial Reporting Standards (IFRS).

- Companies that trade on Canadian stock exchanges must meet the requirements of the securities laws of their province and the rules of the stock exchange.

- Entities often enter voluntarily into contracts with other parties to do their accounting in a certain way.

- Above all, people involved in the accounting and financial reporting process have a responsibility to be ethical.

Stakeholders: Different Users, Different Decisions, Different Information

There are many groups and individuals that might be interested in, or "have a stake in," an entity. These interested parties are called **stakeholders**, and they include owners, lenders, taxation authorities, employees, governments, consumers, and regulators. (See Figure 1.2.) Of course, not every stakeholder will be interested in every entity—some entities will have many stakeholders, others very few. Each stakeholder has his or her own perspective and has specific decisions to make concerning an entity. An owner will be concerned about different things than a lender, who will in turn be concerned about different things than the public, the employees, or the government. Therefore, the information most useful to one stakeholder group might be different from what is most useful to another.

Many stakeholders don't have direct and unrestricted access to an entity's accounting system or the power to obtain specific information from management, so they have to rely on the information the entity provides. Ideally, each stakeholder would receive information tailored to his or her own needs; usually, however, the information provided is designed for the use of all stakeholders. Let's consider some of an entity's stakeholders and look at how accounting information can be useful to each of them.

Owners Often, the owners of a business don't manage it themselves and, thus, aren't involved in its day-to-day affairs (e.g., shareholders of public corporations). When the owners don't manage the business, they need information from it for purposes of evaluating how well their investment is doing, determining if management is doing a good job, assessing the effectiveness of business strategies, considering whether they should sell their interest in the entity, or deciding if the managers should be replaced.

Creditors A creditor is a stakeholder because it's owed money, goods, or services by an entity. Creditors need information to determine if an entity will be able to pay amounts owed and, in the event the entity doesn't pay, whether there are assets that might be taken and sold to recover the money owed.

Taxation Authorities In Canada, most individuals and corporations must file a tax return each year. The Canada Revenue Agency (CRA) requires taxpayers to calculate their taxes using methods consistent with the *Income Tax Act*, Canada's federal tax legislation. Provinces also have tax rules that must be followed. The CRA uses accounting information to assess the taxes owed by a business or individual.

Governments Governments use accounting information to decide whether certain entities should receive government support or subsidies. Accounting information can also have a political impact if, for instance, a company attracts the attention of politicians by making what the public perceives as "too much money."

Labour Unions Labour unions are concerned with the interests of their members and attempt to negotiate good wage and benefits packages with employers. Accounting information can provide insights to the union about how much an entity can afford to pay employees.

Communities/Public Interest Groups The lives of people are affected by the entities in their communities. For example, entities can be employers, taxpayers, or polluters. Accounting information provides citizens and community leaders with information regarding the entity and its impact in the community.

Donors to Charities Many Canadians donate money to charities. Donors would like to know their donations are being used mainly to achieve the goals of the charity and not excessively for administration and fundraising. Accounting information can be useful for assessing whether the money they donate will be put to good use.

Why Is It Important to Be Aware of the Accounting Environment?

From this discussion it should be clear that the accounting environment affects how an entity will and should account for its economic activity. The information needs of the stakeholders will also vary with the accounting environment so no single accounting report can suit all of them. An analogy may be useful in clarifying this point. Suppose your uncle, who is very busy, approaches you to help him choose a new car. What car would you suggest? You might encourage him to buy the car that appeals most to you, in the hope he will let you borrow it. However, if it's going to be suitable for your uncle, you will have to gather relevant information first. You will need to know how much he wants to spend, how big it should be, and how much importance he places on characteristics such as safety, style, colour, fuel economy, resale value, reliability, and so on. If you don't consider these factors, your uncle might say, "Nice car, but a two-seater sports car doesn't leave any room for the baby," or "I love the Rolls-Royce, but I only make $35,000 a year." In other words, deciding what car to recommend to your uncle involves considering his "environment."

This example illustrates how no single solution will be suitable for all because everyone's needs are different. Accounting is much the same. No one accounting report can provide the information every decision maker needs; accounting information has to be tailored. The people who prepare accounting information can often tailor information to suit needs by choosing among alternative accounting methods. (Sometimes the tailoring is for the benefit of the preparers themselves, as we will see!)

Stakeholders versus Preparers

You should understand that accounting information must be considered from two perspectives: stakeholders and preparers. **Preparers** (or managers of an entity) decide what, how, and when information is going to be presented in an entity's financial statements and other accounting reports. They are senior managers such as controllers, chief financial officers, and even chief executive officers. They aren't the people who physically prepare the information. It's essential to recognize that managers aren't neutral. Their personal interests and economic consequences may influence how they prepare accounting reports. Consider the following examples:

- Managers' bonuses are sometimes based on the numbers contained in accounting reports.

- Managers might own shares in a company so their wealth will be affected by the company's share price.

- Managers might lose their jobs if the company's performance isn't good enough.

- Selling prices of entities can be based on accounting information.

There is clearly potential for conflict here. Stakeholders want information that will be useful for their decision making. Managers have an interest in supplying useful information to them, but they are also motivated to act in their own interests. The danger is obvious because managers

conflict

have both the motivation and the ability to pursue their own interests using accounting information. They can do this because by its nature accounting is flexible, and managers must make choices that can affect the numbers and information in the financial statements.

We have to be very careful here not to jump to conclusions such as, "accounting information can't be trusted," "it's manipulated," or "it's not reliable or useful." Sometimes these reactions are valid, but for the most part they are overreactions. Accounting is a crucial source of information for decision making. What this means is that stakeholders must analyze and interpret the information carefully before reaching a decision. Paul Beeston, former president of the Toronto Blue Jays Baseball Club, former president and chief operating officer of Major League Baseball, and an accountant, characterized the situation well when he said:

> Anyone who quotes profits of a baseball club is missing the point. Under generally accepted accounting principles, I can turn a $4 million profit into a $2 million loss, and I can get every national accounting firm to agree with me.[1]

This flexibility means that the numbers reported in financial statements can vary depending on the choices the managers make and that a range of numbers can be considered "within the rules." This flexibility exists because the diversity of entities, stakeholders, and entity characteristics, along with the complexity of economic activity, requires flexibility—enough to allow information to be presented in a way that makes sense in the circumstances. Just as one type of car won't meet the needs of all drivers, one way of accounting won't meet the needs of all stakeholders, entities, and transactions. Indeed, it's sometimes difficult to say with certainty what the best way is to account for a transaction or economic event.

Even constraints don't eliminate flexibility and choice. GAAP and IFRS (common constraints) leave managers a great deal of latitude in deciding what, how, and when information is presented in statements. This issue is a major theme of this book, and we will return to it often.

www.mcgrawhill
connect.ca

✓ KNOWLEDGE CHECK

- ❑ What are stakeholders? Give examples and explain their "stake" in an entity.
- ❑ What are some of the reasons the personal interests of managers might influence how they prepare financial statements?
- ❑ Entities have different characteristics. Identify some of the characteristics that distinguish one entity from another.

The apparent conflict between stakeholders and managers creates a need for independent people who can examine the information provided by the managers, offering assurance to the stakeholders that the information follows certain stated principles. People who examine entities' financial information on behalf of external stakeholders are called **external auditors**, and their examination of an entity's information is called an **external audit**. Auditors examine the information in an entity's financial statements, as well as the data supporting it, to provide assurance the statements are fair representations of the entity's underlying economic activity and the accounting has been done in accordance with the designated set of accounting standards.

External auditors must be independent of the entities they audit. Independence means an auditor can't be involved in managing the entity, have an ownership interest in it, or participate in any type of relationship that will undermine the credibility of information. For example, if you were buying a used car and wanted to be sure it was in excellent condition, would you have more confidence in the opinion of the car dealer or in an independent mechanic? Clearly, the dealer has an interest in making you believe it's a good car since he will benefit from the sale, so his claims would be less credible.

Let's conclude this section with an example of the challenges accountants face. On December 15, 2014, a Toronto Blue Jays fan orders season tickets for the 2015 baseball season. The tickets cost $10,000 and the fan pays a $500 deposit when ordering them. The balance must be paid in full on February 28, 2015. The baseball games will be played from April through October, 2015. When do you think the Blue Jays should report they've sold these season tickets: when the tickets are ordered, December 15, 2014; when they're paid for, February 28, 2015; or when the games are actually played, April through October 2015? Arguments can be made for each of these, and accountants can actually disagree on when to report the sale. But while the accountants are scratching their heads figuring this out, the economic activity—receipt of the deposit, payment in full, and playing of the games—still occurs.

While the actual economic activity is unaffected by how the Blue Jays do their accounting, how the accounting is done can have economic consequences. When the sale is reported can affect the amount of tax the Blue Jays pay, the size of bonus the sales manager earns, perhaps the terms of a bank loan, and even the price of Rogers Communications Inc.'s (owner of the Blue Jays) shares.

INSIGHT

Accounting, Ethics, and Choice

This discussion of the accounting environment should make clear the potential for significant and frequent ethical dilemmas. Managers, auditors, and accountants continually face choices about what, how, and when information should be presented in an entity's financial statements and other accounting reports. These choices are often difficult and usually aren't a simple matter of being right or wrong. Economic activity is complex and deciding how to account for it requires careful judgment. Managers have an ethical and moral responsibility to provide information that is a reasonable representation of the entity's activity. But it's important to understand that intelligent, ethical, and responsible managers, auditors, and accountants can have legitimate differences of opinion about these things. The "right" answer isn't always obvious!

WHAT IS A "CRITICAL APPROACH" TO ACCOUNTING?

You may be wondering what I mean by "a critical approach" in the title of the book. "Critical" refers to critical thinking, which is applying high-level mental skills such as analysis, application, evaluation, explanation, inference, interpretation, judgment, and synthesis as a guide to decision making.

This first chapter shows how the world of accounting isn't nearly as straightforward as most people believe. The accounting environment is subtle, sophisticated, and complex. There are different kinds of entities with a wide variety of characteristics, and each entity can have many different stakeholders who have different information needs and interests. In addition, accounting information is prepared by an entity's managers, and their interests are often different from those of stakeholders. Also, measuring economic activity can be very difficult. A lot of judgment is required by the people preparing the accounting information, and accounting rules often allow different ways of measuring similar transactions or economic events. Add to this the fact that accounting has economic consequences and you should understand that using and working with accounting information is intellectually very challenging and demanding. One of the crucial lessons is that you, as a user of accounting information, can't just accept the numbers at face value; you will have to apply critical thinking skills to get the full story.

As a final comment, it should be remembered that while it's fine to develop strong critical thinking skills, you must have something to think critically about. It's easy to forget that there is a lot of knowledge to accumulate. The challenge is to accumulate the knowledge presented here and develop and apply your critical thinking skills to that knowledge. Figure 1.3 provides a pictorial view of knowledge and critical thinking.

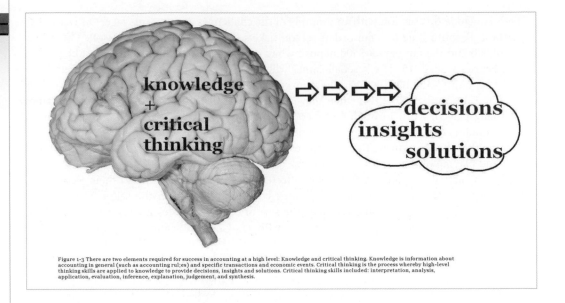

Figure 1-3 There are two elements required for success in accounting at a high level: Knowledge and critical thinking. Knowledge is information about accounting in general (such as accounting rul;es) and specific transactions and economic events. Critical thinking is the process whereby high-level thinking skills are applied to knowledge to provide decisions, insights and solutions. Critical thinking skills included: interpretation, analysis, application, evaluation, inference, explanation, judgement, and synthesis.

THE RULES OF THE GAME

One of the constraints I identified in the discussion of the accounting environment was formal sets of accounting rules or standards. In Canada there are two relevant sets of accounting standards:

a. **International Financial Reporting Standards (IFRS)** are mandatory for publicly accountable companies, while private companies can choose to use them.[2] IFRS are intended as a single set of globally accepted, high-quality accounting standards. They are produced by the International Accounting Standards Board and are used in over 100 countries in the world. IFRS became effective in Canada on January 1, 2011.

b. **Generally Accepted Accounting Principles for Private Enterprises (GAAP)** were developed for use by Canadian private companies. The objective of GAAP is to provide a simplified set of accounting principles that are appropriate for private businesses. Most private businesses have limited and identifiable external stakeholders who have the ability to request additional information about the entity.

There are no natural laws (like gravity) that define how accounting should be done so it's necessary to create rules of the game, or accounting standards, so preparers and stakeholders can understand what to expect from financial statements. IFRS and GAAP are the principles, conventions, practices, procedures, and rules that define acceptable accounting practices at a particular time. In other words, IFRS and GAAP provide bases for preparing financial statements.

Because accounting standards have been created to meet the information needs of stakeholders, they may differ depending on the characteristics of the entity, the situation, and the jurisdiction. In Canada, both GAAP and IFRS (which are similar but not identical) apply. The United States has its own set of standards, as do other countries.

How can this be? Shouldn't there be just one set of rules for everyone, everywhere? In reality, many things differ from one jurisdiction to another. Consider hockey, which isn't the same wherever it's played. Rules in the National Hockey League differ from those in games played under the authority of the International Ice Hockey Federation (such as the Olympics). For example, the size of the rink, penalties for fighting, calling of icing, and where the goaltender can go behind the net differ in each organization. Rules can also vary between minor professional and amateur leagues.

Just as hockey can be played with different rules, the same transactions and economic events can sometimes be legitimately accounted for differently. GAAP and IFRS are both flexible and each requires exercising of judgment by the managers who prepare the financial statements. The choices managers make when preparing statements can significantly affect the amounts reported in the financial statements.

GAAP and IFRS aren't necessarily the only or best bases for preparing financial statements. The measurements reported in GAAP or IFRS financial statements don't always provide the information a particular stakeholder requires. It's crucial for stakeholders to critically evaluate the relevance of any information for the decisions they have to make. Despite the usefulness of having a set of guidelines and rules for preparing financial statements, GAAP and IFRS aren't without flaws. To be a sophisticated user of financial information, you need to know and understand what GAAP and IFRS-based information tells you, how it can help you, and what its limitations are.

The two sets of standards are very similar as they are both based on the same set of concepts and principles, although their details can be different and they can result in different financial statements. For the purposes of this text, it's unnecessary to distinguish between IFRS and GAAP. This is appropriate for an introductory text because our objective is to provide the big picture, not to over-emphasize the details. In situations where the differences are important, IFRS will be addressed in the main part of the text and GAAP will be presented in an Insight box. Readers who are interested in more information about accounting standards can visit the websites of the International Accounting Standards Board (IASB) and the Canadian Institute of Chartered Accountants (CICA). The websites are indicated in the margin of the page.

www.iasb.org
www.cica.ca

Who Has to Follow IFRS and GAAP?

It's easy to get the impression that all Canadian entities have to follow either IFRS or GAAP. Public companies are required by law to provide audited financial statements prepared in accordance with IFRS. If a public company doesn't follow IFRS, securities regulators will intervene.

On the other hand, private companies, partnerships, and proprietorships don't have to follow GAAP or IFRS, although they can choose to. They might use IFRS or GAAP if there are external stakeholders—for example, creditors or others who aren't involved in the day-to-day management of the company—who rely on the financial statements for information. These stakeholders may demand financial statements prepared in accordance with an appropriate and understood set of accounting standards.

If there are no significant external stakeholders a private company might not use IFRS or GAAP, to simplify and reduce the cost of preparing financial statements. They might prepare their statements to meet the information needs of managers or owners, or to meet the requirements of the *Income Tax Act*.

INSIGHT

International Financial Reporting Standards The accounting world has gone global. Historically, most countries set their own accounting standards and, as a result, each country's standards are different. This approach makes sense because each country can set standards that reflect its accounting environment, for example, by addressing the issues facing important industries. In the 1970s companies were increasingly trying to raise money internationally by listing their shares on international stock exchanges. This created demand for a common set of accounting standards to make it easier for stakeholders in different countries to understand financial statements. In response, accountants in several countries, including Canada, formed the International Accounting Standards Committee (IASC) with the objective of developing accounting standards that could be used around the world.

In the 1990s, increasing globalization accelerated the push for international standards and the IASC was replaced by the International Accounting Standards Board (IASB), which is located in London, England, and is responsible for developing IFRS. Many countries around the world have adopted IFRS, including the countries in the European Union, Australia, and New Zealand.

Before 2011 setting accounting standards for Canadian public companies was the responsibility of the Accounting Standards Board (AcSB), part of the Canadian Institute of Chartered Accountants (CICA). Until the 1990s, Canada was satisfied to set its own accounting standards, but late in that decade the AcSB decided to harmonize Canadian standards with those of the United States. The rationale for this was that the U.S. was Canada's largest trading partner and many Canadian companies were listing on U.S. stock exchanges and trying to raise money in the U.S. In 2006 Canada changed course again and announced it would harmonize its standards with IFRS. On January 1, 2011 existing Canadian GAAP was replaced by IFRS. The AcSB remains responsible for setting standards for private companies.

PROFESSIONAL ACCOUNTANTS IN CANADA

In Canada there are three groups of professional accountants: Certified General Accountants (CGAs), Certified Management Accountants (CMAs), and Chartered Accountants (CAs). People with any of these designations have demonstrated that they have the knowledge, skills, and abilities required by the professional body, and that they have the expertise to practise accounting. Anyone who hires a professional accountant can be confident the person will be able to carry out their duties properly. Members of these designating groups have important responsibilities: to act in a professional, ethical, and competent manner at all times and to adhere to the code of conduct of their group.

Becoming a professional accountant isn't easy. Each professional body has its own requirements; but, in general, to earn an accounting designation it's necessary to

- obtain a university degree

- complete specific course requirements to learn the body of knowledge needed to be an effective practitioner

- pass the examinations administered by the professional body

- obtain experience on the job

ACCOUNTING IS FOR MEASUREMENT

Accounting is all about measuring economic activity. The information produced by an accounting system allows stakeholders to measure different attributes of an entity, such as

- performance

- efficiency

- performance of managers, and how much bonus they should receive

- how much it owes lenders

- how much it's worth

- tax obligation

But measurement isn't always straightforward. Some things, of course, are easy to measure and create little controversy: how tall you are, how much you weigh, or whether you did the calculations in a math problem correctly. Other measurements are very subjective and can give rise to a lot of controversy. Consider Olympic competitions in judged sports such as diving, gymnastics, or figure skating. Judges evaluating an athlete's performance don't always agree on scoring or ranking. Over the years there have been suggestions of bias among Olympic judges, and even some full-fledged scandals. It's also difficult to measure things like public opinion on an issue, an employee's job performance, a hospital patient's pain, even the quality of a term paper you wrote.

Accounting involves similar problems. Some things are easy to measure. For instance, there will be little controversy about how much cash an entity has at a certain point in time, or how much a building cost. Other accounting measurements, such as profit (as we'll see in a later chapter), are much more difficult.

Let's look at some examples of how accounting can be used for measuring. Suppose that you have a summer job in a mining town in northern Canada. You expect to earn enough money to pay for next year's tuition and a winter vacation with your friends. But after the first couple of months on the job, you look at your bank balance on the Internet and worry that you aren't saving enough. Fortunately, at the start of the summer you had decided to keep track of your spending in an accounting software package. An excerpt from your software for April and May is shown in Table 1.3.

TABLE 1.3	An Example of Basic Data in an Accounting System	
Money Spent during the Summer		
Date	**Purpose**	**Amount**
April 1	Rent	$300.00
•	•	•
•	•	•
•	•	•
April 13	Magazines	5.75
April 13	Entertainment	22.50
April 13	Groceries	44.85
•	•	•
•	•	•
•	•	•
May 17	Groceries	45.25
May 18	Entertainment	12.75
May 19	Miscellaneous	14.50
•	•	•
•	•	•
•	•	•
May 31	Clothes	47.99
May 31	Taxi	5.00

The list of transactions in your software is just raw data. To be useful, the data have to be processed, organized, and converted into information. Accounting software allows you to classify transactions into categories such as food, entertainment, and rent. Table 1.4 shows an example of how the software could organize the data so that it's easy to see how much money you made, how much you spent and on what, and how much you have left over.

TABLE 1.4	An Example of a Basic Accounting Report		
Summary of Earnings and Spending—April and May			
Amount earned (gross pay)	$5,258.88	
Amount withheld*	946.60	_____
Deposited in the bank (net pay)		$4,312.28
Amounts Spent		
Books, magazines, etc.	75.33	
Clothes	138.25	
Entertainment	221.55	
Groceries	327.58	
Local transportation	45.56	
Miscellaneous	99.98	
Rent	600.00	_____
Amount spent		1,508.25
Amount saved in April and May		$2,804.03

*Employers are required to withhold money from employees' pay for taxes, employment insurance, and Canada Pension Plan contributions. The amount earned before withholding is called *gross pay*. The amount after deductions is called *net pay*.

Next, consider how to use the information in Table 1.4. Your concern is that you're not saving enough money, so you might identify ways to reduce your spending. For example, you might go out less often or find less expensive forms of entertainment. You might consider working more hours. Notice that Table 1.4 helps you address your problem but doesn't actually tell you what to do. The decision maker (you, in this case) has to use the information to come up with a solution.

A crucial point is that you should organize the data according to what you or some other stakeholder wants to know. Table 1.4 doesn't tell you the type of entertainment you enjoyed, what groceries you bought, or what the miscellaneous items represent, so it might not be detailed enough for you. But if you didn't care how you spent your money, a statement like the one in Table 1.5 might suffice.

TABLE 1.5	An Example of a Basic Accounting Report

Summary of Earnings and Spending—April and May		
Amount earned (gross pay)	$5,258.88	
Amount withheld	946.60	
Deposited in the bank (net pay)		$4,312.28
Amount spent during April and May		1,508.25
Amount saved in April and May		$2,804.03

You should also recognize that your ability to extract information from an accounting system is limited to the data entered into it. That is, you couldn't see how much money you spent on soft drinks if you hadn't recorded soft drink spending separately. There is a cost to a more detailed breakdown of information: it takes more time to enter the data into the software.

That example demonstrates how accounting can organize and summarize data to provide useful information for solving a problem. Let's consider an example that looks at a different perspective on measurement.

Imagine you are a first-year university or college student who has just moved into a new apartment near the campus. You have furnished it with personal belongings and it has appliances supplied by the building's owner. You need to get insurance for the apartment, but how much coverage do you need? You want to have enough to protect your own things as well as things you're responsible for—the building owner's appliances. The insurance company needs to know how much coverage you require, and what type, so it can write a policy and set a premium. To estimate the amount of insurance you need, you go through the apartment and make a list of the items you want to insure (your list is shown in Table 1.6).

TABLE 1.6	Items in a Student's Apartment

Inventory of Apartment Contents			
Column 1	Column 2	Column 3	Column 4
Item	What it cost	What it would cost to replace	What it could be sold for
Television	$500	$650	$225
Computer	1,200	900	300
Furniture	3,200	3,800	1,700
Books	750	875	300
Clothes	1,600	1,950	300
Stereo	900	1,100	700
Jewellery	500	625	300
Appliances	2,100	2,600	1,400
Art	300	500	500
Other	1,000	1,200	750
Total	$12,050	$14,200	$6,475

Column 1 of Table 1.6 lists the contents of the apartment. You have to assign a value to each item so that you can "sum up" to a total. The total is important because if you don't know the worth of what you want to insure you may buy too little insurance, leaving you without enough coverage in the event of a fire or robbery. If you buy too much insurance you are wasting money on premiums, since the insurance company won't pay out more than the amount of the loss. (For example, if you have $50,000 of insurance coverage and everything you own is destroyed in a fire but is worth $10,000, the insurance company will pay you only $10,000.)

So what is the appropriate value to assign to each item? In Table 1.6 three different measurements of value have been given for each item, explained as follows:

- Column 2 gives the amount paid for each item.
- Column 3 shows the cost to replace the item with an equivalent, new item. (For example, the TV might be a ten-year-old model that is no longer made, so you would have to get something comparable that is available today.)
- Column 4 is the amount each item could be sold for (known as net realizable value).

Notice that the total of each column is different.

All these amounts represent valid measures of the items in your apartment, but which would be appropriate for determining the amount of insurance to purchase? That depends on your needs. If you want the insurance to return you to the situation you were in before the loss, Column 3 would be best (this is called *replacement cost insurance*). For example, if your television were stolen, replacement cost insurance would allow you to obtain an equivalent television. On the other hand, if you simply want compensation for the loss, Column 4 should be used. This would allow you the cash value of the items you lost. So if your ten-year-old television were stolen, your loss would be the market value of an identical ten-year-old TV. (The insurance company wouldn't get estimates of the worth of the specific items but would use a formula to estimate the extent to which they were used, based on the type of item and its age.)

There are two important points to note from the insurance example. First is the importance of measurement. To decide on the amount of insurance needed, it's necessary to come up with a measure of the total value of the items in the apartment. Secondly, there is often more than one way to measure the same thing. We have easily come up with three ways to measure, in dollars, the "value" of the items in an apartment. Which is best? That question can't be answered in absolute terms. Which is best depends on the situation and the needs of the decision maker.

INSIGHT

While most accounting reports use money as the basis for measurement, it's important to note that it isn't the only basis. Accounting and accountants can provide information in many different ways. For example, accountants might be involved in providing information on the amount of pollution a company produces or the effectiveness of a medical care system (mortality rates, utilization of beds and equipment, etc.). They might help develop measures of customer satisfaction or evaluate whether a government is getting value for the money it spends. These measurements aren't made in terms of money.

QUESTION FOR CONSIDERATION

A few months ago you borrowed $1,000 from an acquaintance and now you don't have the cash to pay back the loan. As repayment you have offered some of your personal belongings instead of cash. If the list in Table 1.6 represents your belongings, which measurement basis (which column) would be most appropriate for determining which items the acquaintance could reasonably take?

Answer: Column 4, what the items could be sold for, would be most appropriate. Since you owe $1,000, the acquaintance should be given items that would allow her to obtain the equivalent of $1,000 cash. She doesn't have to actually sell the items, just as long as they could be sold for $1,000.

Let's briefly consider an example showing a type of measurement problem that accountants face. Suppose you operate a business that offers credit (*credit* means that customers can buy now and pay later). A stakeholder would like to know how much you are currently owed by customers and how much you actually expect to collect. The first question is easy. You look at how much customers have promised to pay but that hasn't been collected yet. As long as your records are up to date this information will be readily available.

The second question is more challenging. How much you will actually collect depends on future events: customers actually paying. You can't know the answer for sure until some time in the future when a customer either pays or gives a definite indication it won't be paying. To provide the information now you'll have to make an estimate, an informed guess. You could base your estimate on a number of things: the proportion of the amount owed that has been collected in the past, your knowledge of your customers, and economic conditions. However, chances are your estimate won't be correct.

In sum, accounting is about measurement. The challenge for accountants is to develop appropriate ways of measuring aspects of economic activity that are difficult or even impossible to observe, and to make those measurements useful for stakeholders. Stakeholders have to realize that accounting measurements are a messy business. Many are inherently imprecise and uncertain, and the best way of accounting is often far from obvious. A large part of this book is devoted to helping you understand the complex nature of accounting measurement.

Solved Problem

Bayton Ltd.—Part 1

Bayton Ltd. (Bayton) operates garbage dumps in western Canada. The company purchases land from private owners, has the land zoned for a garbage dump, and then develops and operates the dump. The planning and development of the dumps is done in close cooperation with the local communities the dump will serve. Bayton doesn't provide garbage collection services; local governments or private contractors do that. The garbage collectors pay a fee to Bayton based on the weight of the garbage dumped.

Bayton is a privately owned corporation. It has 15 investors living all across Canada. The business is run by a team of professional managers who have considerable experience in the waste management business. Managers are paid a salary plus a bonus based on the company's performance, as measured by its accounting information. The company employs over 500 people, many of whom are unionized. Bayton has borrowed heavily from several banks and other lenders.

Required:

Identify all of the stakeholders in Bayton and explain their "stake" in the company. Not all the stakeholders are explicitly referred to in the scenario. You will have to think about the business situation carefully to identify others. (You may be able to identify stakeholders in addition to those in the Solution.)

Solution:

Stakeholders	Stake
1. Shareholders (owners)	The shareholders are Bayton's owners. Part of their wealth is invested in the company.
2. Lenders	Bayton owes the lenders money. The lenders are concerned about Bayton's ability to repay amounts owed to them.
3. Managers	Managers are interested in keeping their jobs and enhancing their reputations in the job market. In addition, part of the managers' compensation is based on the performance of Bayton.

4.	Canada Revenue Agency (CRA)	Bayton Ltd. is a taxpaying entity and the CRA is interested in ensuring it pays its taxes and complies with the *Income Tax Act*.
5.	People located in communities where dumps are or will be located	Garbage dumps are often unpopular neighbours. People living near existing dumps want to ensure the dumps are being managed responsibly and that Bayton will be able to carry out its obligations in the future. People living near prospective garbage dumps may want to take steps to prevent a dump from being set up near their homes.
6.	Government	Garbage dumps can be politically sensitive issues. Governments want to ensure that Bayton's garbage dumps don't cause political problems.
7.	Employees/unions	Bayton Ltd.'s employees rely on the company for their incomes. Unions negotiate contracts with Bayton Ltd. on behalf of their employees.
8.	Environmental regulatory agencies	Because of the potential environmental problems associated with Bayton's garbage dumps, many jurisdictions have regulatory agencies responsible for monitoring the company's waste management practices, ensuring compliance with government standards, and reporting to the government and public.
9.	Communities	Communities need to ensure reliable ways to dispose of their garbage. Bayton provides a solution for these communities.
10.	Garbage collection companies	Garbage collection companies require a place to dump the garbage they collect and must pay fees to do so.
11.	Environmental groups	Garbage dumps pose potentially serious environmental problems. Improper waste management practices can contaminate land and ground water. Private environmental groups monitor the dumps and the companies operating them.

Bayton Ltd.—Part 2

In 1974 Bayton paid $150,000 ($300 per hectare) for a 500-hectare piece of land it intended to develop into a garbage dump. For various reasons Bayton has not yet developed the land but Bayton's president has stated that it will do so at the appropriate time. Over the last two years there have been two transactions involving the sale of land located near Bayton's property. In the first transaction, which occurred 20 months ago, the land was sold for $825 per hectare. In the second transaction, which occurred three months ago, the land was sold for $730 per hectare.

Recently, a business person made an offer for Bayton's land of $690 per hectare or $345,000. The president of Bayton hired an independent appraiser to estimate the value of the land so he could assess the offer. The appraiser estimated the land was worth between $340,000 and $390,000. Two years ago, for the purpose of calculating property taxes, the local government where the land is located assigned it a value of $290,000. The president himself thinks that Bayton could sell the land for $410,000 if Bayton chose to sell it.

Required:

Identify and explain the different measurements of the value of Bayton's land. Discuss the usefulness of each measurement for determining whether a good price is being offered for the land.

Solution:

There are a number of different measurements available for valuing Bayton's land, none of which represents the actual current value of the land. The measurements are:

Measurement	Explanation	Usefulness
Cost: $150,000	The amount Bayton paid for the land.	Cost isn't useful for determining whether the price being offered is reasonable. There is no relationship between the amount Bayton paid in 1974 and the market value now. Cost isn't useful for most other decisions as well. It would be useful for determining the amount of tax that would have to be paid when the land is sold.

Property tax value: $290,000	The value assigned to the land by the local government for determining the property taxes.	Not very useful. The amount was determined two years ago, which makes it somewhat out of date. Also, it was determined for a very specific purpose and it isn't clear how it was determined, so its usefulness for non-property-tax purposes is difficult to assess.
Bayton's president's estimate: $410,000	The amount that Bayton's president thinks the company can sell the land for.	Could be useful depending on whether the president has good information on which to base his estimate. However, this estimate is the highest of all, which suggests the president may be influenced by his desire to get a high price for the land.
Independent appraiser's estimate: $340,000–$390,000	The price range that an independent appraiser estimated the land is worth.	The appraised value would be useful because it's a somewhat unbiased estimate of the land's current market value. However, the appraiser provided a range rather than an exact amount, which reduces usefulness. Also, the amount is an informed guess; it isn't based on the actual sale of the land.
Sale of nearby land: $412,500 based on the first sale (500 hectare × $825 per hectare) and $365,000 based on the second sale (500 hectare × $730 per hectare).	These amounts are calculated by multiplying Bayton's 500 hectares by the price per hectare paid in the transactions for the nearby land.	The sale prices for the nearby land is potentially useful but with limitations. They are useful because they are market prices for a similar commodity, and one of the transactions occurred fairly recently. However, there are three significant limitations: (1) though recent, the transactions don't necessarily represent the value today because market conditions may have changed; (2) the land may not be similar to Bayton's despite being nearby; and (3) the prices alone don't inform us about the circumstances surrounding the sales (the sellers may have required cash urgently and therefore could not wait to get a higher price).

SUMMARY OF KEY POINTS

▶ **LO 1** Accounting is a system for gathering data about an entity's economic activity, processing and organizing the data to produce useful information about the entity, and communicating the information to people who use it to make decisions. Communication is an important but often challenging part of the process. Effective decision making requires information and accounting is a crucial source of information. In addition, accounting matters because it has economic consequences for stakeholders.

▶ **LO 2** Accounting doesn't operate in a vacuum. You can't sensibly use or provide accounting information without considering the accounting environment, which includes the social, political, legal, cultural, and economic environment of a society; the types of entities and the characteristics of those entities; the different stakeholders that may have an interest in an entity; and the constraints that limit the accounting choices an entity can make. The diversity of the accounting environment makes it impossible for a single accounting report to be appropriate for all situations. Accounting reports must be tailored to suit the circumstances of an entity's accounting environment.

▶ **LO 3** An entity's stakeholders rely on the entity itself to provide accounting information. The managers of an entity who prepare the information aren't neutral. They may be influenced by their personal interests, and these interests may conflict with those of the stakeholders. Managers often have considerable leeway and choice in how they do their accounting, which makes it necessary for stakeholders to exercise a great deal of care to ensure they are aware of the choices managers made and the economic consequences of those choices.

▶ **LO 4** A critical approach to accounting refers to this book's emphasis on critical thinking; applying high-level mental skills such as analysis, application, evaluation, explanation, inference, interpretation, judgment, and synthesis to decision making. Economic activity can be complex so preparers need these skills to prepare accounting information and stakeholders need them to use it effectively.

▶ **LO 5** Accounting standards are the principles, conventions, procedures, and rules that define acceptable accounting practices and guide the preparation of financial statements in certain situations. In Canada, IFRS must be used by public companies while private companies can use a separate set of standards called GAAP for Private Enterprises. Most Canadian companies are private and not obliged to follow either standard. GAAP and IFRS are flexible and require managers to exercise judgment. The same transactions and economic events can sometimes be legitimately accounted for in different ways. The accounting choices managers make can significantly affect the amounts reported in the financial statements.

▶ **LO 6** Accounting is about measurement. Accountants face the challenge of developing appropriate ways of measuring aspects of economic activity that are difficult or even impossible to observe, and to make those measurements useful for stakeholders. There are often alternative ways of measuring the same thing and stakeholders must be aware of the methods being used and their economic consequences. Also, stakeholders have to realize that accounting measurements are inherently imprecise and uncertain, and it's often not obvious what, or if, there is a best way.

KEY TERMS

accounting, p. 3

Canada Revenue Agency (CRA), p. 9

corporation, p. 6

cost-benefit trade-off, p. 5

economic consequences, p. 4

entity, p. 3

external audit, p. 12

external auditors, p. 12

financial accounting, p. 4

Generally Accepted Accounting Principles for Private Enterprises (GAAP), p. 14

International Financial Reporting Standards (IFRS), p. 14

limited liability, p. 7

managerial accounting, p. 4

not-for-profit organization, p. 8

partner, p. 8

partnership, p. 8

preparer, p. 11

private corporation, p. 8

proprietor, p. 8

proprietorship, p. 8

public corporation, p. 7

share, p. 6

shareholder, p. 6

stakeholder, p. 10

stock exchange, p. 7

SIMILAR TERMS

The left column gives alternative terms that are sometimes used for the accounting terms introduced in this chapter, which are listed in the right column.

non-profit organization	**not-for-profit organization, p. 8**
stockholder	**shareholder, p. 6**
stock market	**stock exchange, p. 7**

ASSIGNMENT MATERIALS

Questions

Q1-1. Provide a definition of accounting that someone without a business background would understand.

Q1-2. Explain the difference between managerial and financial accounting.

Q1-3. Explain what economic consequences are. Why does accounting have economic consequences?

Q1-4. Explain how bookkeeping isn't the same as accounting.

Q1-5. Explain how accounting information could help you assess whether you could afford to borrow money.

Q1-6. Explain the difference between data and information.

Q1-7. Entities can have many different stakeholders. Explain why the same information may not be suitable or appropriate for all stakeholders.

Q1-8. Explain why the self-interests of preparers of accounting information can affect what information is reported to stakeholders and how it's reported.

Q1-9. Which of an entity's stakeholders do you think is most important? Explain.

Q1-10. Are employees of an entity also stakeholders? Explain.

Q1-11. What is a corporation? What are the attractive features of organizing a business as a corporation?

Q1-12. What is a proprietorship? How does a proprietorship differ from a corporation?

Q1-13. What is a publicly owned corporation? How does it differ from a privately owned corporation?

Q1-14. What is a not-for-profit organization? Give two examples. What is the purpose of each of the organizations you identified?

Q1-15. Why is information important for good decisions?

Q1-16. You're looking for a job. You're not completely sure what kind of job you want so you decided to contact several companies in different industries about a variety of jobs. You have prepared a two-page résumé (as recommended by your advisor) but you have modified it for each company and position you're applying for so that it emphasizes the experience, skills, and abilities you think will be most relevant for the prospective employer. All the information in each résumé is factual. You mention your approach to a friend who says she doesn't think it's ethical to have more than one résumé. How would you respond to your friend?

Q1-17. Explain the cost-benefit trade-off. What are its implications for decision making?

Q1-18. When you make a decision, should you collect all possible relevant information? What limits would you set on the information gathering?

Q1-19. Why is it important for stakeholders to understand that the managers of an entity are responsible for preparing accounting information?

Q1-20. What is an external audit of financial information and why is it important for many stakeholders of an entity?

Q1-21. What are Generally Accepted Accounting Principles for Private Enterprises (GAAP)?

Q1-22. What are International Financial Reporting Standards (IFRS)? Which Canadian entities must follow IFRS?

Q1-23. Which entities must follow GAAP and IFRS? Why would an entity that isn't required to follow GAAP or IFRS do so? If an entity doesn't follow GAAP or IFRS, how does it prepare its financial statements?

Exercises

E1-1. (**Consider the information relevant for making a decision, LO 2**) You meet a stranger on a street corner in Edmonton. She asks you for instructions on the best way to get from Edmonton to Ottawa. What would you tell her?

E1-2. (**Challenges with measurement, LO 6**) You have decided to sell your 2008, black, four door, manual transmission Honda Accord. The car has 130,000 kilometres on it and has been serviced on a regular basis. There is a small dent in the rear of the car and some minor scratching on the body. You don't like haggling so you would like to know the exact price you should sell the car for. Why will it be difficult to determine an exact price?

E1-3. (**Considering the stakeholders in a university or college, LO 2**) Consider the university or college you attend. Who are the stakeholders in your institution? Explain the interest or "stake" each has in the university. What types of decisions would each of these stakeholders have to make regarding the university? Explain what type of information would be useful to each of them?

E1-4. (**Assessing the credibility of information, LO 3**) You are looking to buy a new computer. You read an advertisement in a newspaper that describes Aylsham Computer Products Inc.'s (Aylsham) computer as the best value for the money for students. Based on this advertisement, would you purchase the computer? Why? What additional information would you require to decide whether to buy an Aylsham computer?

E1-5. (**Assessing the credibility of information, LO 3**) A chain of donut shops claims to have the world's best coffee. Do you believe the claim? Explain. How would one go about determining whether the chain had the world's best coffee?

E1-6. (**Consider the information relevant for making a decision, LO 2**) Your brother has just asked you to lend him $5,000 to help him buy a car. Would you lend him the money? How would you decide? What would you want to know before you made a final decision?

E1-7. (**Consider the information relevant for making a decision, LO 2**) Your cousin is in her last year of high school and is in the process of deciding which university to attend. Since you went through the process just a few years ago she has asked you to advise her on which university to attend. What would you tell your cousin? What questions would you ask her before you could provide an answer?

E1-8. (**Considering different ways of measuring, LO 6**) For each of the following situations, explain which method of valuing the item in question would be most useful:

Measurement method	Explanation of the method
Cost	What you paid for the item.
Replacement cost	What it would cost to replace the item with an identical item in the same condition.
Replacement cost new	What it would cost to replace the item with an identical item that is new.
Net realizable value	What the item could be sold for now.

a. You lost your accounting textbook and need to get another copy so you can study for the midterm exam.

b. You are planning to sell your textbooks from last year and want to estimate how much you will receive.

c. A photo album with irreplaceable pictures of your family was destroyed in a flood in your basement.

d. Your 2004 Ford Mustang was stolen and you are looking to get another one just like it.

e. You purchased a DVD player from a store that had a special sale offering to let you "use for a year and if you don't like it you can get your money back." You decide you don't like the DVD player.

E1-9.   **(Consider the different ways of measuring the attributes of a university, LO 6)** There are many attributes of an item you can measure. For a car, you could measure how fast it can go, its gas mileage, the number of doors it has, what you could sell it for, etc. Notice that only one of these measures is stated in terms of money. Now consider the university you attend. Identify six different attributes of your university and explain how you would measure each. How could measurement of each attribute be used? Which measure is best? Explain. Which measurements would be easy to make and which would be subjective? Explain. (Don't consider this question only from the perspective of a student.)

E1-10.   **(Consider different ways of organizing information, LO 6)** Your 99-year-old grandfather died recently and left you his beloved library of books. At the time of his death, your grandfather's library contained over 5,000 books. The books had been packed away in boxes, which have been delivered to you. After opening the boxes you realize the books were not organized in any particular way. You decide to build a library in your basement and organize and catalogue the books. What are some of the ways you could organize the library? What are the benefits and limitations of the different ways of organizing the books? What are the benefits of organizing the books at all?

E1-11.   **(Cost-benefit analysis, LO 1)** You are considering selling your car and replacing it with a smaller, more fuel-efficient model. The new car will cost you $19,000 including all taxes. Your existing car is fairly new, you bought it only six months ago, but you underestimated its operating costs. You estimate you can sell it for $14,700. The existing car uses 12 litres per 100 kilometres travelled while the new one is rated at 8 litres per 100 kilometres. The cost of insuring the new car will be $875 instead of the current $1,025, and you estimate that the cost of servicing the car will be about $225 instead of $350 per year. You drive approximately 22,000 kilometres per year and you expect to keep the car for five years. The current price of gas is $2.10 per litre. Is it worth it for you to buy the new car? Are there any considerations other than financial ones?

E1-12.   **(Cost-benefit analysis, LO 1)** You have the opportunity to buy a license to operate a food vending cart in a local park. The license would cost $1,000 per year. You expect to operate the cart each summer for the next four years, at which time you'll graduate from university and move on to other things. You aren't allowed to sell the license to someone else. You would also have to purchase a cart, which would cost $5,500. You estimate that after four years you would be able to sell the cart for about $1,200. You would have to work 11 hours per day seven days a week from May 15 to September 15. You estimate that on an average day you would be able to sell $250 of food and drinks and that the cost of the food and drinks you sell, along with condiments and other supplies (such as ice, straws, cutlery, cooking fuel) would be $150 per day. In addition, the annual maintenance cost for the cart would be about $750. Should you get into this business? What should you consider beyond the dollar and cents information that was provided? State any assumptions you make.

E1-13.   **(Take a first look at an annual report, LO 1, 2, 3, 6)** Choose a Canadian public company. (Your instructor can choose for you or could ask you to make your own choice.) Download the company's annual report from www.sedar.com or from the company's website and read through it, especially the section with the financial statements and notes. List seven questions that come to mind while reading the financial statements (or the annual report). Your questions should cover topics such as why particular information is reported or what it means.

Problems

P1-1.   (**Consider who should make accounting choices, LO 2, 3, 4, 6**) Figure 1.2 of the accounting environment and the chapter as a whole emphasized that it's the managers of an entity who choose the accounting methods an entity uses. Do you think the managers should have this responsibility or should it belong to someone else? Who else could possibly fulfill this task? Explain your answer fully.

P1-2.   (**Explain the reason stakeholders would want information about an entity, LO 2**) Consider the following stakeholders in an entity. Why would each want information about the entity? Explain.
  a. Members of a community group concerned about pollution by a local factory.
  b. A banker considering whether to lend money to a small business.
  c. Canada Revenue Agency (the federal government department responsible for tax collection).
  d. A shareholder in a company.
  e. A prospective employee being interviewed for a job.

P1-3.   (**Explain the reason stakeholders would want information about an entity, LO 2**) Consider the following stakeholders in an entity. Why would each want information about the entity? Explain.
  a. A person considering making a donation to a charity.
  b. The head of the CRTC (the regulatory agency responsible for the cable industry) determining whether a rate increase should be awarded to a cable company.
  c. A government minister evaluating whether to provide assistance to a business.
  d. The head of a labour union preparing for negotiations with management of a company.
  e. The president of a private corporation.

P1-4.   (**Identify the stakeholders in an entity and the decisions they make, LO 2**) Consider the following entities. Identify the stakeholders in each of the entities. What types of decisions would each of these stakeholders want to make?
  a. Bank of Montreal.
  b. Government of Canada.
  c. Princess Margaret Hospital.
  d. Irving Oil Limited.

P1-5.   (**Identify the stakeholders in an entity and the decisions they make, LO 2**) Consider the following entities. Identify the stakeholders in each of the entities. What types of decisions would each of these stakeholders want to make?
  a. A landscaping business owned and operated by two partners.
  b. A large, publicly owned company.
  c. A municipal minor hockey association.
  d. The government of a small Canadian city.

P1-6.   (**Consider the decisions stakeholders make and the nature of the information they require, LO 1, 2**) Consider the following decisions that a stakeholder of an entity might have to make. For each decision, identify the stakeholder who would likely be making the decision and indicate whether the decision would be considered a financial or managerial accounting decision. Remember that the classification as financial or managerial accounting depends on who the decision maker is. Explain your answers.
  a. The price a manufacturer's products should sell for.
  b. Whether to purchase the shares of a retail chain.
  c. Whether a corporation has paid an appropriate amount of tax.

P1-7.   (**Consider the decisions stakeholders make and the nature of the information they require, LO 1, 2**) Consider the following decisions that a stakeholder of an entity might have to make. For each decision, identify the stakeholder who would likely be making the decision and indicate whether the decision would be considered a financial or managerial accounting decision. Remember that the classification as financial or managerial accounting depends on who the decision maker is. Explain your answers.

a. Whether a local clothing store should open a store in a mall being built in an upscale suburb.

b. Whether a loan should be made to a small business.

c. Whether unionized employees should receive a significant wage increase.

P1-8. **(Considering the information needed to decide whether to invest in a business, LO 1, 2, 6)** A friend of yours has just called with "a great business opportunity." He is starting up a new ebusiness and needs money to purchase computer equipment. He says he is going to invest $10,000 in the business and wants to know whether you want to invest as well. Would you invest in the new ebusiness? Why or why not? What additional information would you want to have before making a decision?

P1-9. **(Considering the information needed to decide whether to invest in a business, LO 1, 2, 6)** A classmate of yours is thinking of starting a used-textbook business to service your campus. The university bookstore already operates such a business but your classmate thinks the prices are much higher than they should be. He has asked you to become a partner in the business, which he thinks is going to be very successful, by contributing $15,000. The money will be used to rent office space, advertise, and purchase books. Would you invest the $15,000? How would you decide? What additional information would you want to have before making a final decision?

P1-10. **(Considering the information needed to decide whether to invest in a business, LO 1, 2, 6)** Two of your friends own and operate a business that provides in-home technology services. The business helps people set up their computers and home theatres and helps solve technology related problems. They would like to hire two additional technicians to meet the increasing demand for their services, but they are short of the cash they need. Your friends have invited you to become a shareholder in the business by investing $20,000. Would you invest the $20,000? How would you decide? What additional information would you want to have before making a final decision?

P1-11. **(Classify and organize information so that it's useful for decision making, LO 1, 6)** Khaleel is a university student who is often short of cash. A month may pass and he has no idea where his money went. After suffering with this problem for several months, Khaleel decides to monitor his spending for the next month. He keeps his records using a software package. The summary of Khaleel's spending for the month follows:

Date	Amount	Purpose
Feb 4	$12.25	Starting balance (cash in wallet)
Feb 4	100.00	Cash from ATM
Feb 4	−22.50	Dinner and movie
Feb 6	−4.50	Photocopy of Steve's notes
Feb 6	−6.25	Lunch
Feb 10	−65.75	Book for course
Feb 11	−5.25	Snacks
Feb 12	50.00	Cash from ATM
Feb 12	−18.25	Date with Emily
Feb 15	−10.00	Long-distance phone card
Feb 17	−5.00	Contribution to charity drive
Feb 19	50.00	Cash from ATM
Feb 19	−22.50	Card and gift for Dad

Feb 20	−4.75	Overdue fees at library
Feb 20	−17.40	Share of phone bill for dorm room
Feb 21	15.00	Borrow from Lisa
Feb 21	−23.00	Food/drink for dorm room
Feb 24	50.00	Cash from ATM
Feb 24	−15.00	Pay Lisa back
Feb 27	−18.75	Partying after exam
Feb 28	$38.35	Amount remaining in wallet

Required:

Prepare a statement that organizes the information from the month's spending in a useful way. Explain why you organized the information the way that you did. How could you use the information if you were Khaleel?

P1-12. **(Classify and organize information so that it's useful for decision making, LO 1, 6)**
Mei is a university student who has been unable, so far, to find a summer job. While she has enough money to pay for school next year, she is concerned that she isn't managing her money as well as she could. She decides to monitor her spending for the next month to get an idea of where her money is going. She buys a small notebook and writes down the amount spent and the purpose of the spending. Mei's summary of her spending for July is shown below:

Date	Amount	Purpose
July 4	2.00	Starting balance (cash in purse)
July 4	160.00	Cash from ATM
July 4	−15.75	Partying with friends
July 6	−67.80	Clothes
July 6	−8.25	Lunch
July 10	−22.50	Novel
July 11	−8.50	Movie
July 12	60.00	Cash from ATM
July 12	−38.25	Software
July 15	−22.45	Gift for Mom's birthday
July 17	−3.00	Coffee with friends
July 19	80.00	Cash from ATM
July 19	−24.00	Drinks for party
July 20	−8.75	Snacks
July 20	−12.00	Taxi
July 20	−35.00	Monthly Internet access fee
July 21	−23.00	Cosmetics
July 21	100.00	Borrowed from Mom
July 24	40.00	Cash from ATM
July 24	−20.00	Tennis lesson
July 27	−125.00	Deposit for university courses in fall
July 31	7.75	Amount remaining in purse

Required:

Prepare a statement that organizes the information from the month's spending in a useful way. Explain why you organized the information the way that you did. How could you use the information if you were Mei?

P1-13.   **(Evaluate different ways of measuring the value of a house, LO 6)** Rajiv owns a home in suburban Ottawa. You obtain the following information about the home:

a. Purchase price in 1978	$175,000
b. Selling price of a similar house on another street last year	$625,000
c. Price offered (and turned down) for Rajiv's house two months ago	$575,000
d. What it would cost to rebuild the house (on the same land) if it were destroyed	$235,000

Required:

Explain how each of the measures of the "value" of Rajiv's house could be used by a decision maker. What decision would the person be making? How would the information be useful?

P1-14.   **(Evaluate different ways of measuring the value of a vintage automobile, LO 6)** Otto Collector owns a vintage 1925 Ford automobile. You obtain the following information about the car:

a. What Otto paid for the car in 1983	$29,000
b. Selling price of a similar car one year ago	$80,000
c. Price offered (and turned down) by Otto for his car last month	$95,000
d. What the car sold for new in 1925	$800

Required:

Explain how each of the measures of the "value" of Otto's car could be used by a decision maker. What decision would the person be making? How would the information be useful?

P1-15.   **(Consider the usefulness of audited information, LO 1, 2, 3)** For each of the following situations explain whether and why having an independent review of the information provided—that is, an audit—would be useful. Who would be an appropriate person to conduct the audit?

a. A charity states that it spends 85% of money raised providing services to the community.

b. A used car dealer says that a car you are interested in is in excellent condition.

c. A store's rent to the mall owner is $1,200 per month plus 5% of the amount of sales the store makes. For the year just ended, the store reports that its sales were $250,000.

d. The selling price of a business is based on the most recent profit of the company.

P1-16.   **(Consider the usefulness of audited information, LO 1, 2, 3)** For each of the following situations explain whether and why having an independent review of the information provided—that is, an audit—would be useful. Who would be an appropriate person to conduct the audit?

a. An individual files an income tax return with the Canada Revenue Agency in which she reports the amount of money her business earned during the previous year.

b. A proprietorship is managed by the proprietor. The proprietorship has not borrowed any money and has no stakeholders who are permitted to see its accounting information.

c. A private corporation that has borrowed large amounts of money from several banks.

d. A job applicant submits a résumé to a prospective employer outlining her employment history and educational background.

e. An electronics store states that it has "the lowest prices, guaranteed!"

P1-17.   **(Identify the characteristics of different entities, LO 2, 3)** Identify two distinct entities. These could be corporations, partnerships, proprietorships, not-for-profit organizations, or any other type of entity you are familiar with or can obtain information about. Identify the characteristics of each entity. (You can use the characteristics listed in Figure 1.2.) Explain how the entities differ.

P1-18. (**Identify the characteristics of different entities, LO 2, 3**) Identify two different corporations that are in a similar business. Identify the characteristics of each corporation. (You can use the characteristics listed in Figure 1.2). Explain how the corporations are similar and how they differ.

P1-19. (**Identify the stakeholders in an accounting partnership, LO 2, 3**) Bricket, Brack, and Bosh (BBB) is a small accounting firm in Oshawa, Ontario. The firm has four partners and ten other employees. All of the partners belong to professional accounting organizations. The firm provides accounting, tax, and consulting services to small- and medium-sized businesses in the community. When the firm does work for clients, the work is often used by third parties such as banks or prospective investors. For example, BBB might audit a client's financial statements, which are then given to the bank as part of a loan application. BBB is also part of a group of independent accounting firms in Ontario that will do work for clients of other firms in the group. For example, if BBB has a client that has an office elsewhere in Ontario, it might use the services of a firm in the group to do necessary work at that office.

Required:

Identify all of the stakeholders in Bricket, Brack, and Bosh and explain their "stake" in the partnership. Not all the stakeholders are explicitly referred to in the scenario. You will have to think about the business situation carefully to identify some of the stakeholders.

P1-20. (**Identify the stakeholders in a not-for-profit organization, LO 2, 3**) Safety House provides shelter and services to homeless and runaway youth in Vancouver. Safety House began in the early 1980s as a group home providing a safe haven to street children in the city but now provides additional services including a telephone support line, outreach programs, substance abuse programs, and other necessary community services. In recent years it has become an advocacy group for children, making government and the public aware of the problems faced by youth, as well as working with government and community social service agencies to improve the lives of children and families. Safety House is managed by people with experience in social services and it employs about 100 people who fill a wide range of roles. Safety House raises money from the public through a variety of fundraising programs and receives a significant amount of money from the provincial government.

Required:

Identify all of the stakeholders in Safety House and explain their "stake" in the organization. Not all the stakeholders are explicitly referred to in the scenario. You will have to think about the situation carefully to identify some of the stakeholders.

ENDNOTES

1. Andrew Zimbalist, *Baseball and Billions*, updated ed. (New York: Basic Books, 1994), p. 62.

2. The CICA defines publicly accountable companies as ones that have issued debt or equity securities that are traded in a public market, that are required to file financial statements with a securities commission, or that provide financial statements for the purpose of issuing any class of securities in a public market.

CHAPTER 2

FINANCIAL STATEMENTS: A WINDOW ON AN ENTITY

LEARNING OBJECTIVES

After studying the material in this chapter you will be able to do the following:

▶ **LO 1** Identify components that make up a set of general purpose financial statements, understand the information each statement provides, and prepare simple examples of them.

▶ **LO 2** Describe the accounting equation.

▶ **LO 3** Explain the nature of assets, liabilities, owners' equity, revenues, and expenses.

▶ **LO 4** Differentiate between accrual-basis and cash-basis accounting, and prepare simple income statements using each method.

▶ **LO 5** Use financial statement information to assess the liquidity, risk, and profitability of an entity.

Canada's 12th Auditor General, Sheila Fraser, has been called "the Mick Jagger of the accounting profession" and "Saint Sheila," and she has been described as having "the power of the Pope, the Queen, and the Dalai Lama."

But Fraser, who in 2001 was appointed to keep an eye on the books of the federal government, admits she didn't plan to be Canada's chief accountant.

Fraser took sciences and math at McGill University but soon found her courses "too theoretical." A bout of mononucleosis in her third semester prompted the switch to accounting, a move she says came about during frequent visits to her doctor.

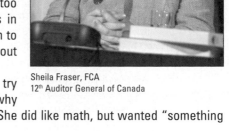

Sheila Fraser, FCA
12th Auditor General of Canada

"He said to me, 'Why don't you try accounting?' and I thought, 'Well, why not?'" Fraser recalled in an interview. She did like math, but wanted "something more applied."

Fraser earned her B.Comm. in 1972, her CA in 1974, and began working for a Montreal accounting firm, Clarkson Gordon (now Ernst & Young). There were few women in the profession, and she faced some "clients who would phone up and [said they] didn't want women, [but] the partners were…very supportive of us," Fraser recalled.

Being a woman in accounting has its advantages, Fraser explained, describing one of her first jobs, conducting an inventory count at Homelite in Pointe Claire, Quebec. The 21-year-old Fraser suffered initial feelings of panic.

"I remember having to go out there and wondering 'Oh my God! What am I going to do here?'" Fraser said, smiling.

But she got the count done, and discovered a secret to accounting success.

"I think women pay attention to detail [and] are also very good with people. In auditing, a lot of it is working with people and trying to get the information you need to figure things out. That's why women do well," Fraser said.

With 650 staff, the Office of the Auditor General is an independent body that tells lawmakers how well the government manages taxpayers' money and also how government departments, agencies, and Crown corporations are affecting the environment. Its reports have recommended many changes, from how

Transport Canada issues security clearances for airport employees to speeding up the delivery of spare parts to Canada's troops.

Fraser's highest profile audit began in 2002 when her office was asked to investigate contracts awarded to a Quebec ad agency for the government's sponsorship program. Her report touched off a wider audit and a royal commission inquiry, resulted in a jail term for the senior bureaucrat in charge, and likely cost the Liberals the 2006 election.

Although some politicians accused her of meddling in the affairs of state, Fraser insists she always tried to be fair and accurate. She maintains that the invoices for work of questionable value, which her auditors found, were exceptional and needed to be brought to Parliament's attention.

"Unfortunately at times there are serious consequences to audits, and that's when the political system takes over."

In the end, Fraser feels her job was "to make a change for Canadians and to make government management better." That mission earned her 900 long stemmed red roses sent one day by a Vancouver radio station.

"Everybody [in the Ottawa office] went home with a rose," she chuckled.

Being Auditor General of Canada was "the most amazing job," Fraser said, her face lighting up. "Besides," she quipped, "I don't have to do the spreadsheets anymore."

—E.B.

INTRODUCTION

The most familiar products of accounting and accountants are financial statements. The financial statements most people see are those published by public companies whose shares trade on stock exchanges. These companies are required to make this information available and anyone who is interested can easily obtain it. Virtually every business, government, and not-for-profit organization in Canada produces a set of financial statements at least once a year.

In this chapter we will explore the components of the financial statement package:

- balance sheet

- income statement and statement of comprehensive income

- statement of changes in equity or statement of retained earnings

- statement of cash flows

- notes to the financial statements

The objectives of this chapter are to familiarize you with the financial statement package and begin our investigation of how the information in financial statements can be used for decision making.

GENERAL PURPOSE FINANCIAL STATEMENTS

General purpose financial statements are prepared for use by all stakeholders and aren't necessarily tailored to meet the information needs of any particular stakeholder or purpose. In other words, **general purpose financial statements** are intended for no one in particular and for everyone in general. (The alternative to this are special purpose reports designed for a specific user and/or a specific use.) The focus of the discussion in this chapter will be the general purpose financial statements of Leon's Furniture Limited (Leon's). Leon's has been in the retail furniture business for nearly 100 years and has stores in every province. Leon's general purpose financial statements are shown in Exhibit 2.1.[1]

Every entity prepares a set of general purpose financial statements at least once a year, if for no other reason than the statements must be included with its tax return. It can also produce any number of special purpose reports. The published financial statements of public companies like Leon's are always general purpose and, because Leon's is a public company, must be prepared in accordance with IFRS.

Because general purpose financial statements aren't designed to meet the information needs of every stakeholder in every situation, it's important to consider the information carefully and critically. You must be aware of what the statements do and don't tell to use them effectively. You have to know the strengths and limitations of the information, what questions to ask, and when to look elsewhere for what you need.

LEON'S FINANCIAL STATEMENTS: AN OVERVIEW

Financial statements can be intimidating: What do the numbers mean? Where do they come from? What about all this unusual terminology? To familiarize you with financial statements and make you more comfortable looking at those of real companies, the following sections weave a general discussion of each financial statement with an examination of Leon's statements as examples. To begin, here are four points about Leon's statements you may have noticed when examining Exhibit 2.1:

1. Leon's financial statements are **consolidated**—they aggregate the financial information of more than one corporation into a single set of statements. They are prepared when a corporation controls (owns more than 50 percent of) other corporations and they are intended to give stakeholders information on all the companies in the group. We'll look at consolidated statements in more detail in Chapter 11.

EXHIBIT 2.1

Leon's Furniture Limited's Financial Statements

Consolidated Balance Sheets

As at December 31 (in thousands)	2008	2007
ASSETS		
Current		
Cash and cash equivalents	$ 39,483	$ 25,699
Marketable securities	83,194	102,013
Restricted marketable securities [note 8(d)]	16,598	14,567
Accounts receivable	30,291	33,684
Income taxes recoverable	2,037	–
Inventory	92,904	75,640
Future tax assets [note 7]	270	–
Total current assets	264,777	251,603
Prepaid expenses	1,490	1,282
Goodwill [note 14]	11,282	–
Intangibles [notes 6 and 14]	4,875	–
Other receivables	419	–
Future tax assets [note 7]	10,752	10,722
Property, plant & equipment, net [note 5]	219,813	211,619
	$ 513,408	$ 475,226
LIABILITIES AND SHAREHOLDERS' EQUITY		
Current		
Accounts payable and accrued liabilities	$ 95,247	$ 92,051
Income taxes payable	–	2,137
Customers' deposits	14,119	13,533
Dividends payable	4,952	4,949
Deferred warranty plan revenue	15,267	13,812
Future tax liabilities [note 7]	–	355
Total current liabilities	129,585	126,837
Deferred warranty plan revenue	21,712	19,124
Redeemable share liability [note 11]	285	180
Future tax liabilities [note 7]	8,468	7,080
Total liabilities	160,050	153,221
Shareholders' equity		
Common shares [note 12]	16,493	14,020
Retained earnings	338,960	307,068
Accumulated other comprehensive income [note 13]	(2,095)	917
Total shareholders' equity	353,358	322,005
	$ 513,408	$ 475,226

Commitments and contingencies [note 8]

See accompanying notes

EXHIBIT 2.1

(continued)
Leon's Furniture
Limited's Financial
Statements

Consolidated Statements of Income and Retained Earnings

Years ended December 31 (in thousands, except shares outstanding and earnings per share)

	2008	2007
Sales	$ 740,376	$ 637,456
Cost of sales	440,360	363,261
Gross profit	300,016	274,195
Operating expenses (income)		
Salaries and commissions	112,270	99,461
Advertising	33,752	32,008
Rent and property taxes	11,268	10,486
Amortization	16,253	14,034
Employee profit-sharing plan	4,321	4,200
Other operating expenses	46,447	39,251
Interest income, net	(4,836)	(4,695)
Other income	(13,595)	(11,573)
	205,880	183,172
Income before income taxes	94,136	91,023
Provision for income taxes (note 7)	30,746	32,529
Net income for the year	63,390	58,494
Retained earnings, beginning of year	307,068	276,037
Dividends declared	(26,873)	(19,828)
Excess of cost of share repurchase over carrying value of related shares (note 12)	(4,625)	(7,635)
Retained earnings, end of year	338,960	307,068
Weighted average number of common shares outstanding		
Basic	70,729,548	70,777,269
Diluted	72,817,871	73,403,200
Earnings per share		
Basic	$ 0.90	$ 0.83
Diluted	$ 0.87	$ 0.80
Dividends declared per share		
Common	$ 0.38	$ 0.2725
Convertible, non-voting	$ 0.14	$ 0.14

See accompanying notes

2. Financial statements are presented for two years. This provides stakeholders with benchmarks. It's very difficult to make sense of accounting information without something to compare with, such as other companies, the industry, performance in other years, and the economy in general. As we will discuss, making comparisons using accounting information can be very difficult and misleading, while not making comparisons makes accounting information difficult to interpret.

3. Financial statements cover a **fiscal year**—the 12-month period about which an entity provides information. Leon's fiscal year runs from January 1 to December 31. An entity can choose any 12-month period as its fiscal year. For example, Bank of Montreal's is November 1 to October 31.

4. Dollar amounts in the statements are rounded to the nearest thousand dollars. Leon's balance sheet reports cash of $25,699,000, but because the thousands are dropped, the actual amount of cash could be anywhere between $39,482,500 and $39,483,500. This presentation makes the statements less cluttered in appearance but assumes that rounding won't affect the decisions of any stakeholders. For example, ignoring the thousands isn't likely to affect whether an investor buys Leon's shares. Some companies round to the nearest million; for example, Air Canada, Rogers Communications Inc., and Royal Bank of Canada.

Consolidated Statements of Comprehensive Income

Years ended December 31 (in thousands)

	2008	Tax effect	
Net income for the year	$ 63,390	$ –	$ 63,390
Other comprehensive income, net of tax			
Unrealized losses on available-for-sale financial assets arising during the year	(2,671)	(454)	(2,217)
Reclassification adjustment for net gains and losses included in net income	(957)	(162)	(795)
Change in unrealized losses on available-for-sale financial assets arising during the year	(3,628)	(616)	(3,012)
Comprehensive income for the year	59,762	(616)	60,378

	2007	Tax effect	
Net income for the year	$ 58,494	$ –	$ 58,494
Other comprehensive income, net of tax			
Unrealized losses on available-for-sale financial assets arising during the year	(357)	(67)	(290)
Reclassification adjustment for net gains and losses included in net income	(1,428)	(243)	(1,185)
Change in unrealized losses on available-for-sale financial assets arising during the year	(1,785)	(310)	(1,475)
Comprehensive income for the year	56,709	(310)	57,019

See accompanying notes

Consolidated Statements of Cash Flows

Years ended December 31 (in thousands)

	2008	2007
Operating Activities		
Net income for the year	$ 63,390	$ 58,494
Add (deduct) items not involving an outlay of cash		
Amortization of property, plant & equipment	15,628	14,034
Amortization of intangible assets (note 6)	625	–
Amortization of deferred warranty plan revenue	(14,541)	(13,610)
(Gain) loss on sale of property, plant & equipment	(1,665)	5
Future income taxes	1,350	1,577
Gain on sale of marketable securities	(411)	(698)
Cash received on warranty plan sales	17,834	15,843
	82,210	75,645
Net change in non-cash working capital balances related to operations (note 10(a))	(12,482)	(7,112)
Cash provided by operating activities	69,728	68,533
Investing Activities		
Purchase of property, plant & equipment (note 10(c))	(22,668)	(23,404)
Proceeds on sale of property, plant & equipment	2,775	218
Purchase of marketable securities	(287,913)	(253,617)
Proceeds on sale of marketable securities	301,482	230,888
Decrease in employee share purchase loans (note 11)	2,626	2,286
Purchase of Appliance Canada Ltd.	(20,704)	–
Cash used in investing activities	(24,402)	(43,629)
Financing Activities		
Dividends paid	(26,870)	(19,671)
Repurchase of common shares (note 12)	(4,672)	(7,706)
Cash used in financing activities	(31,542)	(27,377)
Net increase (decrease) in cash and cash equivalents during the year	13,784	(2,473)
Cash and cash equivalents, beginning of year	25,699	28,172
Cash and cash equivalents, end of year	$ 39,483	$ 25,699

See accompanying notes

THE BALANCE SHEET

We'll begin our tour of the financial statements with an examination of the **balance sheet**, which is a summary of an entity's financial position at a point in time. A balance sheet is like a photograph—it captures the scene at a particular moment. The scene could be dramatically different the moment before or after the picture is taken. For example, Leon's balance sheet reports inventory (merchandise available to sell to customers) of $92,904,000 on December 31, 2008. It is possible that in early January 2009 Leon's could have purchased additional inventory that the December balance sheet wouldn't include.

Information about an entity's financial position can help stakeholders evaluate its financial health, assess its risk, and predict its future cash flows. When accountants talk about an entity's financial position they are referring to its assets, liabilities, and owners' equity. We can initially define these elements as follows:

- **Assets** are economic resources that provide future benefits to an entity.
- **Liabilities** are an entity's obligations.
- **Owners' equity** is the investment the owners have made in the entity.

Look at Leon's balance sheet in Exhibit 2.1 and find these three elements (Leon's calls its owners' equity shareholders' equity because the owners of a corporation are called shareholders).

The elements in a balance sheet are organized to conform to the **accounting equation**, which is the conceptual foundation of accounting. The accounting equation is

$$\text{Assets} = \text{Liabilities} + \text{Owners' Equity}$$

The left side of the equation represents the assets, the right side represents how those assets were financed. Assets can be financed by **creditors** (entities money is owed to), which results in liabilities, or by owners, resulting in owners' equity.

Leon's balance sheet can be expressed in terms of the accounting equation as follows:

Assets	=	Liabilities	+	Owners' (Shareholders') Equity
$513,408,000		$160,050,000		$353,358,000

Find these amounts in Leon's balance sheet (Exhibit 2.1). The two sides of the equation must always be equal, or in balance, which is why the statement is called the balance sheet. Notice that each of the elements in Leon's balance sheet is broken down into categories called accounts, which provide additional detail about an entity's financial position. For example, one of Leon's asset accounts is cash, which means that on December 31, 2008, it had $39,483,000 in cash.

INSIGHT

Accounting Terminology

Accounting terminology is sometimes confusing because different names are given to the same thing. For example, the balance sheet is often called the statement of financial position. Accounting standards are quite flexible when it comes to terminology. The list of Similar Terms at the end of each chapter will help sort things out.

The accounting equation as a tool for recording information in an accounting system is not unique to Canada, to IFRS or GAAP, or to any particular method of valuing balance sheet items. Recall the example in Chapter 1 where the contents of an apartment were valued in three different ways. The accounting equation can accommodate all of these ways, and others, of measuring assets.

All economic events entered into an accounting system are summarized in terms of the accounting equation; that is, each event is recorded based on its effect on assets, liabilities, and owners' equity. The equality between the left side and right side of the equation must be maintained for any event entered into an accounting system. For example, if an entity borrows $500 from a bank, its assets increase by $500 because it has additional cash. It also has a liability or obligation to repay the bank, so liabilities increase by $500 as well. Both sides of the accounting equation have increased by $500, so it remains in balance.

Now let's take a closer look at assets, liabilities, and owners' equity.

Assets

We can now expand our definition of assets. According to IFRS an asset must have the following characteristics:

- Provide a future benefit to the entity and it must be probable that the entity will enjoy the benefit. (If there is too much uncertainty about whether the entity will enjoy the benefit, there is no asset.) Note that when accountants speak of an asset having a future benefit they mean it will help the entity generate cash.

- Be controlled by the entity that will obtain the benefits. (This means the entity has the right to use the asset to make money).

- Be the result of a transaction or event that has already occurred.

- Be measurable.

Table 2.1 explains why some of the assets on Leon's balance sheet meet this definition.

Notice that the definition of an asset doesn't include a requirement for ownership. An entity only has to have control over the benefits of the item. For example, leased items are sometimes classified as assets because they can be used to make money even though they aren't owned.

INSIGHT

The Importance of Accounting Definitions

Definitions in accounting are crucial, so it's important to know and understand them. Applying a definition often helps to determine how to deal with an unfamiliar transaction or situation. Throughout the book you will be challenged to apply basic principles to solve accounting problems. It may sometimes seem that you're not prepared to solve a problem, but this is where your critical thinking skills come in.

TABLE 2.1	Why Are These Assets?	
Type of Asset	**What is it?**	**Why is it an asset?**
Cash	Money.	Future benefit: Cash can be spent to buy goods and services, pay debts, and pay dividends. Control: Leon's can use the cash however it wishes. Past transaction: Events in the past, such as a sale of furniture for cash, gave rise to the cash. Measurable: The amount of cash can be determined by counting.
Accounts receivable	Money owed to Leon's by customers who received goods and services but haven't paid for them yet.	Future benefit: Right to receive cash in the future. Control: The right to collect cash belongs to Leon's. Past transaction: Accounts receivable arise when goods are sold to customers on credit. Measurable: Measurable, but with uncertainty. The exact amount that will be collected isn't known because some customers may not pay.
Inventory	Merchandise that Leon's has available for sale to customers.	Future benefit: Leon's can sell the inventory to customers and receive cash. Control: Leon's owns the inventory and can determine how, when, where, and at what price it can be sold. Past transaction: The inventory was purchased in a transaction with the manufacturer. Measurable: The cost of the inventory can be determined from invoices.
Property, plant, and equipment	Includes land, buildings, equipment, furniture and fixtures, vehicles, computer hardware and software, and so on that allow Leon's to sell its merchandise to customers. Leon's doesn't sell these but uses them to operate the business.	Future benefit: A building provides a location to operate the business. Control: Leon's can use the building in any way it deems appropriate (sell, decorate, renovate, rent to others, etc.). Past transaction: A building would have been purchased from a previous owner or built to Leon's specifications. Measurable: The cost of the building can be determined from purchase documents or from construction cost details.

Missing assets: Not everything our intuition might tell us is an asset gets classified as one. For example, the Leon's brand name is known to most Canadians and most would agree it's valuable. Yet Leon's balance sheet doesn't report the brand name as an asset because its future benefit is very uncertain and difficult to measure. A brand name develops through advertising and promotion over time, and it's difficult to know at the time this money is spent whether it will give rise to a valuable brand name. As a result the amounts spent don't meet the definition of an asset. Other examples of items that aren't classified as assets when we might think they would be include human resources (an entity's employees), advertising, trademarks, and research. The implications of this for the balance sheet is that every asset of an entity may not be captured on it—the balance sheet isn't comprehensive.

Balance sheet measurements: When an asset is acquired, it's recorded at the transaction value—the amount paid. After acquisition, different measurements are used; inventory is usually reported at its cost; **capital assets** (property, plant, and equipment and intangible assets) can be reported, according to IFRS, at cost or market value; accounts receivable is an estimate of how much the entity expects to collect. We will return to measurement of balance sheet items many times in the book.

Current versus non-current assets: **Current assets** are used up, sold, or converted to cash within one year or one operating cycle. An **operating cycle** is the time it takes from the initial investment made in goods and services until cash is received from customers. Leon's will typically sell its inventory within one year, so its inventory is classified as current. The operating cycle of most businesses is a year or less but there are exceptions; for example, distillers and wineries age some products for more than a year but still classify them as current assets because the operating cycle is greater than one year.

In contrast, assets that won't be used up, sold, or converted to cash within one year or one operating cycle are classified as **non-current**. Leon's property, plant, and equipment are non-current assets because they will provide benefits for more than one year. Notice that non-current assets aren't specifically identified on Leon's balance sheet. If an asset isn't classified as current it's understood to be non-current.

? QUESTION FOR CONSIDERATION

Leon's balance sheet includes an account called prepaid expenses. This can include money spent to pay for an insurance policy in advance. For example, on December 15, 2014, an entity might pay $5,000 for insurance coverage for the period January 1, 2015, to December 31, 2015. Use the definition of an asset to explain why this insurance paid for in advance would be reported as an asset on December 31, 2014.

Answer: The prepaid insurance is reported as an asset because it meets the definition of an asset:

- Future benefit—the entity has the benefit of insurance coverage during 2015.
- Control—the policy provides the entity with insurance coverage on its property. The entity is entitled to recover any losses covered by the policy.
- Past transaction—the policy was purchased from an insurance company on December 15.
- Measurable—the amount paid for the policy is stated in the invoice from the insurance company. The amount and type of coverage is specified in the policy.

Liabilities

Liabilities are an entity's obligations to pay money or provide goods or services to suppliers, lenders, customers, and government. According to IFRS, a liability must

- be the result of a past transaction or economic event;
- require some kind of economic sacrifice to settle.

For example, if an entity borrows money from a bank it has a liability to repay the amount borrowed. The loan is the result of a transaction between the bank and the entity; the entity will have to "sacrifice" cash to repay the loan. Table 2.2 provides a description and explanation of some of Leon's liabilities.

Like assets, liabilities are classified on Leon's balance sheet as current and non-current. **Current liabilities** will be paid or satisfied within one year or one operating cycle. **Non-current liabilities** will be paid or satisfied in more than one year or one operating cycle. As was the case with assets Leon's doesn't specifically identify non-current liabilities on its balance sheet. If a liability isn't identified as current it's understood to be non-current.

💡 INSIGHT

It's important to understand that the assets, liabilities, and amounts reported on an entity's balance sheet are the result of applying accounting standards. If a different set of rules was used you would get a different balance sheet. Accounting information is a representation of an entity's economic activities. There are many different ways assets, liabilities, and other financial statement elements can be defined and measured, some allowed by IFRS and others not.

TABLE 2.2	Why Are These Liabilities?	
Type of Liability	**What is it?**	**Why is it a liability?**
Accounts payable and accrued liabilities	Amounts owed to suppliers for goods and services purchased on credit. Includes amounts owed to inventory suppliers, utilities, property owners, and employees, to name a few.	Obligation: Pay for goods and services provided by suppliers. Past transaction or economic event: The suppliers have provided the goods and services. Economic sacrifice: In most cases money must be paid to settle the liabilities.
Customers' deposits	Customers pay in advance for goods to be provided in future.	Obligation: Provide goods and services that have been paid for by customers but not yet delivered. Past transaction or economic event: Payment has been received from customers for goods or services. Economic sacrifice: Goods and services must be provided.
Income taxes payable	Amounts owed to government for income taxes.	Obligation: Pay governments for income taxes owed but not paid. Past transaction or economic event: Income taxes are based on income in earlier years. Economic sacrifice: Cash must be paid.
Deferred warranty plan revenue	Amounts paid to Leon's for extended warranty protection on merchandise.	Obligation: Provide warranty service to customers as required. Past transaction or economic event: Customers have purchased extended warranties. Economic sacrifice: Warranty service must be provided (parts and labour).
Dividends payable	Dividends that have been declared by the board of directors but not yet paid to shareholders. (Dividends are payments, usually in cash, by a corporation to its shareholders.)	Obligation: Pay shareholders dividends declared. Past transaction or economic event: Dividend has been declared by the board. Economic sacrifice: Cash must be paid.

Using Balance Sheet Information to Analyze Liquidity

The classification of assets and liabilities into current and non-current components is useful for assessing **liquidity**, which is the availability of cash or the ability to convert assets to cash to meet obligations. Liquidity is important to creditors who are expecting to be paid and to potential creditors who are considering extending credit. For example, a banker would want to assess the likelihood that a borrower will be able to repay a loan. Liquidity is also important to shareholders because a company that's unable to meet its obligations is at significant risk of going out of business.

Taken together, current assets and current liabilities provide important information about the liquidity of an entity. Current assets minus current liabilities is called **working capital**. The more working capital an entity has, the more current assets there are available to pay current liabilities. Negative working capital means the entity has more current liabilities than current assets and this could indicate liquidity problems, although that isn't always true. Leon's working capital on December 31, 2008 was

Working capital	=	Current assets	−	Current liabilities
$135,192,000	=	$264,777,000	−	$129,585,000

On that date, Leon's had over $135 million more current assets than current liabilities, which suggests that Leon's was in good shape to pay its current liabilities. Suppliers could confidently extend credit to Leon's because it had lots of working capital and lots of cash and marketable securities (which are easily converted to cash).

Another way of examining working capital is with a ratio. The ratio of current assets to current liabilities is called the **current ratio**, or **working capital ratio**, and is defined as

$$\text{Current ratio} = \frac{\text{Current assets}}{\text{Current liabilities}}$$

The current ratio gives the relative amount of current assets to current liabilities. The larger the ratio, the more current assets are available to meet current liabilities, which, on the surface at least, means the entity is more able to meet its obligations. Leon's current ratio on December 31, 2008 was

$$\begin{aligned} \text{Current ratio} &= \frac{\text{Current assets}}{\text{Current liabilities}} \\ &= \frac{\$264{,}277{,}000}{\$129{,}585{,}000} \\ &= 2.04 \end{aligned}$$

A current ratio of 2.04 means that for every dollar of current liabilities, Leon's has more than two dollars of current assets, which suggests the company will have little trouble meeting its obligations.

To make sense of accounting information, it's important to have benchmarks, such as a company's information over a number of years, information for similar firms, or industry averages. For example, examination of Leon's current ratio for the past six years shows a great deal of stability:

	Leon's Current Ratio on December 31,					
	2008	**2007**	**2006**	**2005**	**2004**	**2003**
Current ratio	2.04	1.98	1.73	1.90	1.90	1.86

Comparing Leon's with a similar company, such as The Brick (another large Canadian retail furniture chain), provides another perspective on Leon's liquidity. Table 2.3 provides liquidity information for Leon's and The Brick on December 31, 2008. Leon's liquidity position seems superior to The Brick's, as indicated by the higher current ratio and much larger amount of working capital, even though Leon's is a smaller company.

TABLE 2.3	Liquidity Information for Leon's and The Brick			
	Amounts on December 31, 2008			
	Current assets	**Current liabilities**	**Working capital**	**Current ratio**
Leon's	$264,777,000	$129,585,000	$135,192,000	2.04
The Brick	$296,029,000	$307,508,000	−$11,479,000	0.96

Different financial ratios will be introduced as we proceed through the book. There are no universal rules for evaluating ratios. For example, people sometimes learn that a "good" current ratio is 2:1, but different industries have different norms so a current ratio considered acceptable and reasonable in one industry could be a source of concern in another.

In general, making sense of financial information is usually not straightforward, and it can require a lot of detective work. The numbers in the financial statements can raise questions, but they will rarely provide answers. Stakeholders must analyze, assess, evaluate, and compare the information in financial statements to make sense of it. Calculating ratios is a part of the analysis and assessment of financial data, but it's often just a first step. After some preliminary investigation, it may be necessary to gather more information.

KNOWLEDGE CHECK

www.mcgrawhill
connect.ca

☐   Use Exhibit 2.1 to calculate Leon's working capital and current ratio on December 31, 2007.

Owners' Equity

Owners' equity is the amount owners have invested in an entity. In terms of the accounting equation, owners' equity represents the amount of the assets financed by the owners. Equivalent terms you may see in a financial statement include the following:

- **shareholders' equity**—owners' equity of a corporation

- **partners' equity**—owners' equity of a partnership

- *owner's* or *proprietor's equity*—owner's equity of a proprietorship

Owners' investments can be direct or indirect. Direct investments are made by purchasing shares of a corporation or units in a partnership, or by contributing money to a proprietorship. The investment is direct because the investors contribute their own assets directly to the entity. These investments are usually cash, but sometimes other assets can be invested. Indirect investment occurs when an entity's net income or profit isn't paid to the owners but is "reinvested" in the entity. The investment is indirect because investors don't choose to invest, and the decision to do so is made by the management or board of directors.

In a corporation's balance sheet the shareholders' equity section separates direct investments and the reinvestment of net income (see these terms in Leon's balance sheet in Exhibit 2.1):

- Direct investments by shareholders are reported in the common shares account (also called share capital or capital stock). The **common shares** account reflects the amount of money (or other assets) that shareholders have contributed to the corporation in exchange for shares.

- Reinvested net incomes are accumulated in retained earnings. **Retained earnings** is the sum of all the net incomes a corporation has earned since its inception, less dividends paid (there are some other adjustments but net income and dividends are the main items). **Dividends** are payments, usually in cash, by a corporation to its shareholders. If retained earnings is negative it's referred to as a **deficit**.

On its December 31, 2008, balance sheet (see Exhibit 2.1), Leon's reported shareholders' equity of $353,358,000. This is the total investment the shareholders have made in the company. Shareholders have made direct investments by purchasing $16,493,000 in common shares from the company and indirect investments of $338,960,000 in retained earnings. Shareholders' equity also includes $917,000 in an account called "accumulated other comprehensive income," which we'll discuss later in the chapter.

The Debt-to-Equity Ratio

Another common balance sheet analytical tool is the **debt-to-equity ratio**:

$$\text{Debt-to-equity ratio} = \frac{\text{Liabilities}}{\text{Shareholders' equity}}$$

This ratio is a measure of how an entity is financed—the higher the ratio, the more debt an entity is using relative to equity—and a measure of risk. More debt means more risk because, regardless of whether it's doing well or poorly the entity must make timely payments on its debt. Debt has a fixed cost associated with it called interest. **Interest** is the cost of borrowing money and is usually calculated as a percentage of the amount borrowed. For example, if an entity borrows $10,000 at a 10 percent interest rate the cost of the interest for the year would be $1,000 ($10,000 × 0.10). If an entity doesn't pay the interest and **principal** (the amount originally borrowed) the lenders can take legal action. In contrast, equity is less risky for an entity as there are no mandatory payments—it doesn't have to pay dividends at any time and shareholders can't take any action if they aren't paid.

Leon's debt-to-equity ratio on December 31, 2008 was

$$\text{Debt-to-equity ratio} = \frac{\text{Liabilities}}{\text{Shareholders' equity}} = \frac{\$160,050,000}{\$353,358,000} = 0.45$$

The ratio of 0.45 means Leon's is financed with about half as much debt as equity. In other words, for every \$1 invested by shareholders, \$0.45 is supplied by creditors. The 2008 ratio has changed very little from a year earlier when it was 0.48. A low debt-to-equity ratio is an indication of a strong balance sheet—the entity is low risk. Leon's liabilities are mainly operational, meaning they are incurred as a result of operating the business (obligations to suppliers, customers, and employees, for example), as opposed to the financing of it (Leon's has not borrowed any money). The company is at very little risk of getting into financial trouble as a result of being unable to meet its obligations.

This isn't to say that financing with debt is a bad thing—in fact, there are some very attractive reasons for doing so. Management must achieve the right balance between debt and equity when deciding how to structure the company's financing. Like the current ratio, average debt-to-equity ratios vary from industry to industry.

www.mcgrawhill
connect.ca

KNOWLEDGE CHECK

❑ Define the current ratio and explain what a decision maker would use it for.

❑ Define the debt-to-equity ratio and explain what a decision maker would use it for.

❑ Use the following information about Didzbury Inc. to calculate its current ratio and debt-to-equity ratio on December 31, 2014:
      Current assets, \$380,000
      Current liabilities, \$250,000
      Total liabilities, \$360,000
      Total shareholders' equity, \$180,000
                    (Answers: 1.52, and 2.0)

THE INCOME STATEMENT

If a balance sheet is like a photograph then an income statement is like a movie: it shows events over a period of time. The **income statement** is a "how did we do?" statement, measuring an entity's economic activity over a period of time, such as a year. Among the uses for an income statement are

- evaluating the performance of an entity and its management
- predicting future earnings and cash flows
- estimating the value of an entity
- determining the amount of tax that must be paid

The income statement can have significant economic consequences for entities and their stakeholders. For example,

- stock prices often change when a company announces its net income
- managers' bonuses are often based on net income
- net income is used to determine income taxes
- the selling price of a business can be based on net income

Measuring an entity's economic activity is more challenging than you might think. After all, how can the complex activities of an entity be reasonably reflected in an income statement? This is a question that we will devote considerable time to in the book.

There are different ways accountants measure an entity's activities. The two most common methods are cash accounting and accrual accounting.

- **Cash accounting** reports the cash flowing into and out of the entity. Under this method, economic performance represents the change in cash over the period.

- **Accrual accounting** measures an entity's economic activity rather than its cash flows.

We'll get a better sense of cash and accrual accounting with an example. Melissa Picard is a student entrepreneur who operates a small business called Melissa's Painting Business (MPB). During July, MPB had the following economic activity:

1. MPB started and completed seven painting jobs. It collected $2,500 for these jobs and was still owed $900 by one of its customers. The customer told Melissa she would pay her on August 15. MPB also collected $500 during July for jobs completed during June.

2. MPB paid $1,450 to people hired to paint and owed its employees $250 at the end of July. MPB will pay the amount owed in early August.

3. MPB purchased and used $1,550 of paint for the seven jobs undertaken in July. MPB has credit at the paint store so it didn't pay for any of the paint purchased in July, but it did pay $900 for paint it bought before July.

An income statement for the month of July prepared on the cash basis is shown in Table 2.4.

TABLE 2.4 Income Statement Prepared for MPB Using Cash Accounting	
Melissa's Painting Business **Income Statement** **For the Month Ended July 31**	
Revenue (cash collected) ($2,500 for the seven July jobs plus $500 for jobs completed in June)	$3,000
Less: Expenses (cash spent)	
For employees ($1,450 paid to employees in July)	(1,450)
For paint ($900 paid for paint purchased in previous months)	(900)
Net income (cash flow)	$ 650

Net income on the cash basis means that MPB had $650 more in cash at the end of July than at the beginning. Of course, MPB still has bills to pay (employees and paint) so Melissa can't spend the $650 however she'd like. In general, cash accounting is of limited usefulness for many stakeholders' decisions because it provides an incomplete measure of performance and economic activity.

In contrast, accrual accounting attempts to reflect a more complete picture of economic activity by capturing relevant economic events, not just cash flows. For example, it captures sales on credit whereas cash accounting doesn't. However, accrual accounting is a lot more complicated than cash accounting and requires much more judgment by managers, accountants, and stakeholders.

Two important definitions for measuring income under accrual accounting are

Revenue (or sales or sales revenue)—economic benefits earned by providing goods or services to customers.

Expenses—economic sacrifices made or costs incurred to earn revenue.

Under these definitions, revenue and expenses can be reported before, after, or at the same time as the related cash flow. A challenge of accrual accounting is determining when revenue and

TABLE 2.5	Income Statement Prepared for MPB Using Accrual Accounting

Melissa's Painting Business
Income Statement
For the Month Ended July 31

Revenue	$3,400
($2,500 for the six July jobs that were paid for, plus $900 for the July job that wasn't paid for by the end of July)	
Less: Expenses	
Employees	(1,700)
($1,450 paid for work done by employees in July plus $250 owed for work done in July.)	
Paint	(1,550)
($1,550 for paint purchased and used in July. This paint won't be paid for until later.)	
Equipment	(50)
Net income	$100

expenses occur, and when they should be reported in the income statement. MPB's income statement for the month of July using accrual accounting is shown in Table 2.5.

On the accrual income statement revenue reflects work done and money earned in July, not cash collected. Even though a customer hasn't paid as of the end of July the amount is still reported as revenue in July. On the other hand, the money collected for the June job isn't included in July's revenue because it has nothing to do with July's economic activity. The revenue for the June job would have been reported in June's income statement. The expenses include the cost of paint used and the cost of the work done by employees in July, regardless of when these expenses are paid. Expenses are the costs incurred to earn revenue in July—when the cash changed hands doesn't matter.

Expenses in the accrual income statement include $50 for equipment. MPB needs equipment (ladders, trays, scaffolding, etc.) to operate. Unlike paint that gets used up on one job, the equipment contributes to earning revenue over many periods and many jobs. As a result, under accrual accounting a portion of the cost of the equipment is expensed each month to reflect the economic sacrifice or "using up" of the equipment. The term **depreciation** describes the expensing of the cost of capital assets in a period.

The last line on the accrual statement is net income. What does accrual net income mean? It's more difficult to interpret than net income in the cash accounting income statement where the $650 bottom line simply represents how much more cash MPB had at the end of the month. In the accrual statement net income of $100 means that Melissa's business enjoyed a net economic gain of $100 during July because the economic benefits (revenue) exceeded the economic costs (expenses) by $100. Another way to interpret net income is that it corresponds with an increase in **net assets** (net assets equal assets − liabilities). For MPB, net income of $100 means assets − liabilities (or equity) increased by $100 in July as a result of its business activities. The increase could be due to more cash, more receivables, more of any other asset, or fewer liabilities.

It should be clear, even from this introductory discussion, that accrual accounting can be very tricky. With accrual accounting it's necessary to decide when economic activity occurs—when revenue and expenses happen and should be recorded in the accounting system. This accounting method is an important reason why accounting standards are flexible, why there are often valid alternatives for recording transactions and economic events, why judgment is so important in accounting, and why it's possible for managers to work within accounting standards to pursue their own interests.

Even though the income statement is always presented separately, it's really just part of the owners' equity section of the balance sheet. We could rewrite the accounting equation to reflect the current year's income statement (this equation ignores direct investments and dividends):

$$\text{Assets} = \text{Liabilities} + \text{Owner's equity at the beginning of the period} + \text{Revenue} - \text{Expenses}$$

or

$$\text{Assets} = \text{Liabilities} + \text{Owner's equity at the beginning of the period} + \text{Net Income}$$

Notice that net income in a period increases owner's equity, meaning the owner's investment in the entity or the owner's wealth increases. Also, since owner's equity equals assets minus liabilities, net income means net assets have increased.

? QUESTION FOR CONSIDERATION

Examine the two income statements that were prepared for Melissa's Painting Business in Tables 2.4 (cash basis) and 2.5 (accrual basis). Explain why revenue in the two statements is different.

Answer: With cash accounting, revenue is the cash collected from customers during a period. In contrast, with accrual accounting revenue represents amounts earned by providing goods and services to customers during the period, regardless of when the cash is collected. The difference between cash and accrual accounting for MPB is the $500 that was collected in July for the job done in June and the $900 owed at the end of July. Revenue on the cash basis includes the $500 from June and excludes the $900 owing at the end of July. Revenue on the accrual basis excludes the $500 from June and includes the $900 owing at the end of July. Both methods include the amounts for jobs completed and paid for in July.

Leon's Statement of Income (Income Statement)

For the year ended December 31, 2008, Leon's reported net income of $63,390,000 on its statement of income (Exhibit 2.1). This means revenues (economic benefits) exceeded all expenses (economic sacrifices) by $63,390,000 and shareholder wealth (as reflected by the equity section of the balance sheet) and net assets have increased. But is this amount of net income good news? That question must be answered in relation to benchmarks. Compared with 2007, Leon's 2008 net income increased by $4,896,000 or about 8.4 percent, so this is an improvement. But how did other similar businesses do? An 8.4 percent increase in net income wouldn't look as good if the average in the industry was 15 percent.

Besides net income itself Leon's statement of income includes important information about how it generated that net income. Consider the following:

- During fiscal 2008, Leon's sold $740,376,000 in goods and services (sales).

- Leon's reported several different types of expenses for the year ended December 31, 2008:

  ▸ **cost of sales** of $440,360,000—cost of inventory sold such as furniture, electronics, and extended warranties

  ▸ salaries and commissions of $112,270,000—amounts paid to employees

  ▸ advertising of $33,752,000

  ▸ rent and property taxes of $11,268,000—amounts paid for rent on stores, warehouses, and office space, or property taxes on owned property

  ▸ amortization (depreciation) of $16,253,000

  ▸ other operating expenses of $46,447,000—expenses not in other categories

These expenses, listed in the income statement under the heading "Operating expenses (income)" are the usual expenses an entity incurs in carrying out its main business activities. The term "income" in brackets refers to amounts that reduce expenses. Leon's reported $4,836,000 in interest income and $13,595,000 in other income in 2008, both amounts shown in brackets. The breakdown of operating expenses is very helpful for analyzing the company's performance. Throughout the book we'll examine different ways of analyzing this type of information.

Because Leon's is a corporation it must pay taxes. For fiscal 2008 Leon's reports an income tax expense of $30,746,000, which is deducted in the calculation of net income.

www.mcgrawhill connect.ca

KNOWLEDGE CHECK

During the summer, Hank operated a cart that sold hot dogs and cold drinks. At the end of the summer, Hank had collected $6,500 from customers and paid $3,300 to suppliers. At the end of the summer, Hank owed suppliers $500 and he was owed $200 by customers. The depreciation on his cart for the summer was $800.

❑ What was Hank's net income on a cash basis for the summer? (Answer: $3,200)

❑ What was his net income on an accrual basis? (Answer: $2,100)

❑ Why is depreciation an expense under accrual accounting?

Gross Margin and Gross Margin Percentage

A very useful tool for analyzing some companies' financial performance is **gross margin**, which is sales less cost of sales (remember that cost of sales is the cost of the inventory sold). The gross margin is then available for covering the other costs of operating the business and for providing profit to the owners. The higher a company's gross margin is, the better.

Gross margin can be useful as an analytical tool when expressed as a percentage of sales:

$$\text{Gross margin percentage} = \text{Gross margin} \div \text{Sales} \times 100 \text{ percent}$$

Gross margin percentage is the percentage of each dollar of sales that is available to cover other costs and return a profit to the entity's owners. If a company can increase its gross margin percentage (perhaps by increasing the selling price of its products) without decreasing sales or increasing other costs, its net income will increase. Using the gross margin percentage makes it easier to compare the performance of different entities and the same entity year to year.

www.leons.ca

Leon's identifies its gross margin (Leon's calls it gross profit) on its statement of income. The calculation of gross margin for 2008 is

Gross margin	=	Sales	−	Cost of sales
$300,016,000	=	$740,376,000	−	$440,360,000

This means that Leon's sold its furniture and appliances for $300,016,000 more than what they cost. From this, Leon's gross margin percentage can be calculated:

$$\text{Gross margin percentage} = \frac{\text{Sales} - \text{Cost of sales}}{\text{Sales}} \times 100\% = \frac{\text{Gross margin}}{\text{Sales}} \times 100\%$$

$$= \frac{\$740,376,000 - \$440,360,000}{\$740,376,000} \times 100\% = \frac{\$300,016,000}{\$740,376,000} \times 100\%$$

$$= 40.5\%$$

EXHIBIT 2.2

**Example of an
Uninformative
Income Statement**

Consolidated Statements of Earnings

53 weeks ended January 3, 2009 and 52 weeks ended December 29, 2007
(in thousands of dollars, except per share amounts)

	2008	2007
Sales	**$7,352,800**	$6,854,655
Operating expenses		
Cost of goods sold and other operating expenses (Note 2)	**6,215,011**	5,948,623
Amortization	**155,522**	131,124
Operating income	**982,267**	774,908
Interest expense (Note 4)	**51,125**	50,721
Earnings before income taxes	**931,142**	724,187
Income taxes (Notes 2 and 5)		
Current	**288,573**	246,290
Future	**(545)**	(4,989)
	288,028	241,301
Net earnings	**$ 643,114**	$ 482,886
Net earnings per common share (Note 13)		
Basic	**$ 1.95**	$ 1.41
Diluted	**$ 1.95**	$ 1.40

The accompanying notes are an integral part of these consolidated financial statements.

Leon's gross margin percentage in 2008 was 40.5 percent, which means that for every dollar of sales it has $0.405 to apply to costs other than the cost of sales, and to profit. Leon's gross margin percentage in 2007 was 43.0 percent (try to calculate this amount yourself), which is higher than in 2008. The 2008 decrease of 2.5 percent in gross margin percentage means that Leon's gross margin and net income decreased by $18,509,400 ($740,376,000 × .025) from what it would have been had the gross margin percentage been the same as in 2007.

Many companies are very secretive about their gross margins. They combine cost of sales with other expenses to hide information from competitors. Exhibit 2.2 provides an example of this type of highly aggregated income statement. For a real example of this format I suggest you download the 2008 annual report of the Shoppers Drug Mart Corporation (Shoppers).[2] The model in Exhibit 2.2 and Shoppers' income statement combine almost all of their expenses into a single line, making for a very uninformative presentation because of the lack of detail. These examples provide the minimum required by IFRS, which makes analysis difficult. Leon's statement of income is much more informative. IFRS requires separate disclosure of the cost of inventory expensed during the year, which provides the information to calculate the gross margin.

When assessing company performance, it's reasonable to compare gross margin percentages of similar businesses, but you can't meaningfully compare the gross margin percentages of different types of entities. Also, the percentage can't be calculated for some businesses, such as those offering services, as they don't have cost of sales.

? QUESTION FOR CONSIDERATION

In 2008, Leon's gross margin increased by $25,821,000 and its gross margin percentage decreased by 2.5 percent. What factors could give rise to these changes?

Answer:
An increase in gross margin could be due to three factors:
• an increase in the amount sold
• an increase in the selling price of the goods sold
• a decrease in the amount Leon's pays for the goods it sells

A decrease in the gross margin percentage would result from:
• a decrease in the selling price of the goods sold
• an increase in the amount Leon's pays for the goods it sells
• a change in the mix of products Leon's sold during the year, so that it sells more products with lower gross margin percentages

THE STATEMENT OF COMPREHENSIVE INCOME

Comprehensive income is an extension of net income. Over the years accounting standard setters decided to exclude certain types of economic events from the calculation of net income (the items went directly to owners' equity instead). The standard setters later decided there should be a measure that captures all transactions and economic events that involve non-owners and that affect equity (remember that revenue and expenses affect equity). This measure is called **comprehensive income** and is calculated as follows:

> Net income + Other comprehensive income = Comprehensive income

Other comprehensive income includes those transactions and economic events that involve non-owners and affect equity but are, for various reasons, excluded from the calculation of net income. Examine Leon's statement of comprehensive income in Exhibit 2.1. Notice that the first line of the statement is net income followed by two adjustments that are classified as other comprehensive income. Leon's comprehensive income for 2008 is $60,378,000 and other comprehensive income is −$3,012,000. Leon's provides a separate statement of comprehensive income but many companies combine their income statements and statements of comprehensive income into a single statement called the statements of comprehensive income.

Comprehensive income also affects the equity section of the balance sheet. Other comprehensive income is treated the same way that retained earnings is handled. In the equity section of the balance sheet, there is an account called *accumulated other comprehensive income*. The balance in this account on Leon's 2008 balance sheet is −$2,095,000 (find this amount on Leon's balance sheet in Exhibit 2.1). The amount of other comprehensive income for a period (on the statement of comprehensive income) is added to or subtracted from the amount of accumulated other comprehensive income (on the balance sheet) at the beginning of the period to get the end-of-period amount.

THE STATEMENT OF SHAREHOLDERS' EQUITY/ THE STATEMENT OF RETAINED EARNINGS

Companies that follow IFRS must provide a **statement of shareholders' equity**, which presents changes in each account in the equity section of the balance sheet during a period. Exhibit 2.3 provides the statement of changes in equity for WestJet Airlines Ltd.[3] Each section of the statement corresponds with an account in the equity section of WestJet's balance sheet, the equity section of which is provided at the bottom of Exhibit 2.3. Notice how the statement of equity shows how each equity account changed over the period.

In its 2008 financial statements Leon's hadn't yet adopted the IFRS requirement so it only provides a statement of retained earnings rather than a statement of shareholders' equity. Canadian GAAP for Private Enterprises only requires a **statement of retained earnings**, which summarizes the changes to retained earnings during a period. Leon's statement can be found at the bottom of its income statement in Exhibit 2.1. The calculation of retained earnings on December 31, 2008 extends from the net income line on the income statement.

Let's take a look at the transactions and economic events that affect Leon's retained earnings. Recall that retained earnings represents indirect investment by the owners of a corporation and equals the sum of an entity's net incomes over its life, less dividends paid. In equation form, changes to retained earnings can be expressed as

Retained earnings at the end of the year	=	Retained earnings at the beginning of the year	+	Net income for the year	−	Dividends declared during the year

Notice that in addition to net income and dividends Leon's also shows a reduction in retained earnings as a result of the company buying back shares from investors. I won't go into detail on this transaction now but recognize that occasionally events other than net income and dividends affect retained earnings.

EXHIBIT 2.3

WestJet Statement of Shareholders' Equity

Consolidated Statement of Shareholders' Equity

For the years ended December 31
(Stated in thousands of Canadian dollars)

	2008	2007
Share capital:		
Balance, beginning of year	$ 448,568	$ 431,248
Issuance of shares pursuant to stock option plans (note 8(b))	227	1,551
Stock-based compensation on stock options exercised (note 8(b))	11,181	20,040
Shares repurchased (note 8(b))	(7,091)	(4,271)
	452,885	448,568
Contributed surplus:		
Balance, beginning of year	57,889	58,656
Stock-based compensation expense (note 8 (e)(f))	13,485	19,273
Stock-based compensation on stock options exercised (note 8(b))	(11,181)	(20,040)
	60,193	57,889
Accumulated other comprehensive loss (note 12(c)):		
Balance, beginning of year	(11,914)	—
Change in accounting policy	—	(13,420)
Other comprehensive income (loss)	(26,198)	1,506
	(38,112)	(11,914)
Retained earnings:		
Balance, beginning of year	455,365	316,123
Change in accounting policy	—	(36,612)
Shares repurchased (note 8(b))	(22,329)	(16,979)
Net earnings	178,135	192,833
	611,171	455,365
Total accumulated other comprehensive loss and retained earnings	573,059	443,451
Total shareholders' equity	$ 1,086,137	$ 949,908

The accompanying notes are an integral part of the consolidated financial statements.

Consolidated Balance Sheet

As at December 31
(Stated in thousands of Canadian dollars)

	2008	2007
Shareholders' equity:		
Share capital (note 8(b))	452,885	448,568
Contributed surplus	60,193	57,889
Accumulated other comprehensive loss (note 12(c))	(38,112)	(11,914)
Retained earnings	611,171	455,365
	1,086,137	949,908

Finally, dividends aren't considered expenses when calculating net income. They are distributions of the shareholders' investment in the business back to the shareholders, not a cost of operating the business, and so aren't included in the calculation of net income. A dividend doesn't affect the overall wealth of a shareholder—it simply moves the wealth from the entity (which the shareholder owns) to the shareholder's bank account.

THE STATEMENT OF CASH FLOWS

Cash is crucial to the survival and success of any entity. It's needed to pay bills and meet obligations as they come due. As they say, cash is king! While accrual net income is an important indicator of performance, you can't forget cash. Cash and net income are not the same thing and no matter how large a company's net income, if it doesn't have the cash to meet its obligations it's in serious trouble.

The **statement of cash flows** shows how an entity obtained and used cash during a period and it provides information about how cash was managed. It's also an important source of information about an entity's liquidity. The statement of cash flows is another "how did we do?" statement but it measures "how we did" differently than the income statement.

The statement of cash flows reports three types of cash flows. Let's look at each type in detail.

1. **Cash from/used in operations** is the cash an entity generates from or uses in its regular business activities. For Leon's this is cash collected from customers through selling furniture, appliances, and electronics, as well as money spent to buy inventory and pay for advertising, employees, rent for stores, utilities, fuel for delivery vehicles—any money spent on the day-to-day operation of the business.

   For fiscal 2008, Leon's reported cash from operations (called cash provided by operating activities) of $69,728,000, which means that during this period Leon's regular business activities generated $69,728,000 in cash. This cash could be used for expansion, purchasing capital assets, paying dividends, and so on, without having to borrow or sell more shares. Notice that cash from operations is over $6 million higher than net income in 2008. Remember that under accrual accounting net income measures economic flows, not cash flows. That means that net income can include amounts that aren't cash flows, whereas cash from operations simply reflects the movement of cash.

2. **Cash from/used in investing activities** is cash spent buying and received from selling property, plant, and equipment; intangible assets; other long-term assets; and investments. Most of Leon's investing activity during 2008 was for the purchase and sale of marketable securities (investments that can be easily sold for cash). During 2008 Leon's spent $287,913,000 in cash purchasing marketable securities and received $301,482,000 in cash selling them. It also spent $22,668,000 in cash purchasing property, plant, and equipment and $20,704,000 in cash purchasing another company, Appliance Canada Ltd. Overall, Leon's had a net cash outflow of $24,402,000 for investing activities.

3. **Cash from/used in financing activities** is the cash an entity raises from and pays to equity investors and lenders. It includes cash borrowed or raised by issuing shares and cash paid for loan repayments, dividends, share repurchases, and sometimes loan interest. During fiscal 2008, Leon's had a net cash outflow from financing activities of $31,542,000, which included payment of $26,870,000 in dividends and $4,672,000 for repurchasing its common stock from shareholders.

Overall, what does Leon's statement of cash flows tell us? During 2008, Leon's generated cash from operations of $69,728,000 that it used to pay for property, plant, and equipment; purchase Appliance Canada; pay dividends; and buy back some of its common shares. With its internally generated cash Leon's was able to continue its expansion without having to borrow or sell shares to investors. Leon's also increased its cash holdings by $13,784,000 (calculated by adding together cash from operations, financing activities, and investing activities) during 2008.

THE RELATIONSHIP AMONG THE FINANCIAL STATEMENTS

It may not be clear from the discussion of the individual financial statements, but the statements are closely related. The relationships are shown for Cupar Inc.'s (Cupar) financial statements in Figure 2.1. At the top of Figure 2.1 is Cupar's balance sheet on December 31, 2012 and below it are *flow statements* showing changes during the period: the income statement, statement of comprehensive income, statement of shareholders' equity, and statement of cash flows for 2013. At the bottom of Figure 2.1 is Cupar's balance sheet on December 31, 2013. The flow statements capture the changes between the two balance sheets. Thus the statement of cash flows shows how the balance in the cash account on the balance sheet changed from December 31, 2012 to December 31, 2013. The statements of income and shareholders' equity provide information on changes in the equity section of the balance sheet from December 31, 2012 to December 31, 2013. The arrows in Figure 2.1 show how information flows from one statement to another.

The relationships among the statements are more extensive than cash and equity. Many transactions and economic events involve both the income statement and the balance sheet and any transaction that involves cash is included in the cash flows statement. Figure 2.1 only shows the amounts that are explicitly shown on more than one statement.

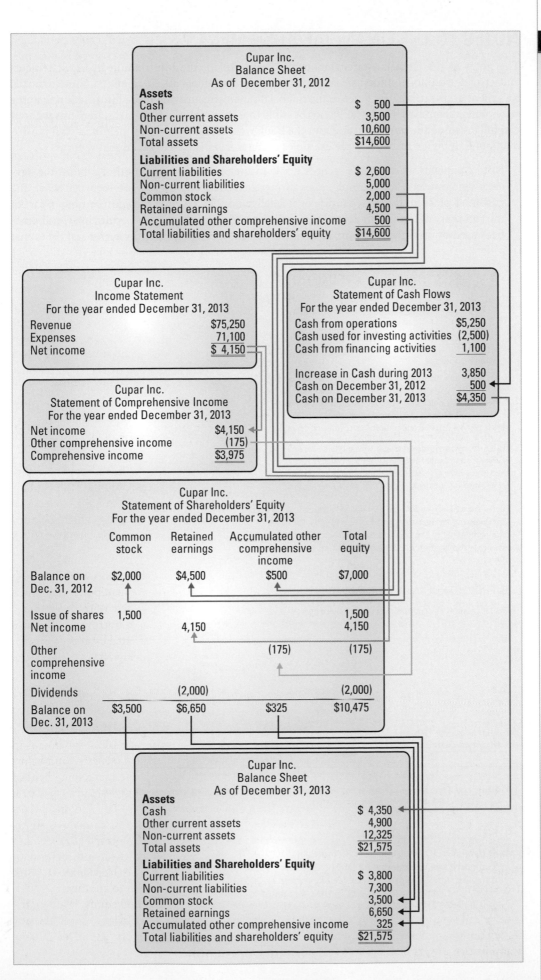

FIGURE 2.1

The Relationship among the Financial Statements

NOTES TO THE FINANCIAL STATEMENTS

The notes to the financial statements expand and explain the information in the statements and provide additional information that may help stakeholders assess an entity. Some financial statement users say that the notes to the financial statements provide more information than the statements themselves. It's certainly not possible to understand the financial statements without carefully reading the notes. Throughout the book we'll examine many of the notes. As an introduction, Exhibit 2.4 provides three examples of notes from Leon's 2008 annual report:[4]

- Note 1 explains when Leon's records a sale in the income statement (this is known as revenue recognition). For example, sales of merchandise to customers are recorded when the customer picks up the merchandise or it's delivered. The revenue recognition note is part of the summary of significant **accounting policies**, which are the methods, principles, and practices used by an entity to report its financial results. It has been mentioned several times that

Notes to the Consolidated Financial Statements

1. SUMMARY OF SIGNIFICANT ACCOUNTING POLICIES

Revenue recognition

Sales, net of any financing charges, are recognized as revenue for accounting purposes either when the customer picks up the merchandise ordered or when merchandise is delivered to the customer's home. Any payments received in advance of delivery are deferred and recorded as customers' deposits.

The Company recognizes extended warranty plan revenue and costs on a straight-line basis over the contract period. The service costs associated with the warranty obligations are expensed as incurred.

Leon's franchisees operate principally as independent owners. The Company charges each franchisee a royalty fee based on a percentage of the franchisee's gross sales. This royalty income is recorded by the Company on an accrual basis in other income.

5. PROPERTY, PLANT & EQUIPMENT

Property, plant & equipment consist of the following:

(in thousands)	2008			2007		
	Cost	Accumulated amortization	Net book value	Cost	Accumulated amortization	Net book value
Land	$ 63,956	$ –	$ 63,956	$ 63,117	$ –	$ 63,117
Buildings	171,546	87,480	84,066	171,553	80,120	91,433
Equipment	33,775	21,010	12,765	31,541	18,813	12,728
Vehicles	20,811	15,650	5,161	20,683	14,852	5,831
Computer hardware and software	11,731	9,489	2,242	9,994	8,835	1,159
Building improvement	73,239	21,616	51,623	55,387	18,036	37,351
	375,058	155,245	219,813	352,275	140,656	211,619

Included in the above balances are assets not being amortized with book values of approximately $7,150,000 [2007 – $13,263,000] due to construction-in-progress.

9. FRANCHISE OPERATIONS

As at December 31, 2008, a total of 27 franchises [2007 – 27] were in operation, representing 28 [2007 – 28] stores. Sales by franchise stores during the year ended December 31, 2008, on which the Company earns royalty income, amounted to approximately $209,848,000 [2007 – $195,925,000].

accounting rules, including IFRS, are flexible and often provide managers with different ways of accounting for a transaction or economic event. This note explains the accounting choices that managers have made and is crucial for understanding the financial statements and the impact of these choices on the amounts reported on the financial statements.

- Note 3 lists Leon's property, plant, and equipment. By examining this note a stakeholder gets an idea of the types of property, plant, and equipment owned by the company, the cost of the assets in each category, and how much has been amortized (depreciated). For example, Leon's reports buildings that cost $171,546,000, of which $87,480,000 has been depreciated.

- Note 9 provides information about Leon's franchise operations. A Leon's franchise allows someone to own and operate a Leon's store as their own business. Leon's receives fees, called royalties, from the franchise owner and provides support in return. The note says that the 28 franchise stores generated over $200 million in sales in 2008. This amount isn't included in the sales reported on Leon's income statement because it doesn't own these stores, but the royalties are included.

This section has provided only a brief introduction of the importance of reading and understanding the notes for effectively using an entity's financial statements. At this point I recommend that you obtain the complete annual report of Leon's, or of another company if you prefer, and read through the notes and tie the information to the financial statements themselves. You can obtain the annual reports of Canadian public companies at www.sedar.com.

www.sedar.com

 QUESTION FOR CONSIDERATION

You are a loan officer for a major bank and an executive from Leon's has come to ask for a $70,000,000 loan. What information on the balance sheet and statement of cash flows would be of interest to you?

Answer: As a banker your main concern is Leon's ability to repay the loan. You would be interested in whether Leon's has the cash flow to support the interest on the loan and to pay back the principal when it's due. If the interest rate on the loan were 8 percent Leon's would have to pay the bank $5,600,000 per year in interest. In 2008, Leon's had cash from operations of more than $69 million, which easily covers the interest cost. If you were confident that Leon's could continue to generate that much cash from operations each year you could assume that it would have little trouble paying the interest on the loan. You might also check Leon's debt-to-equity ratio to evaluate the risk of making the loan.

You would also be interested in knowing what other debts Leon's has. The liability section of the balance sheet shows no debt other than those that arise out of normal operations (amounts owed to suppliers, employees, etc.). Leon's hasn't borrowed any money from banks or other lenders. This makes Leon's a strong candidate for a loan.

USERS OF LEON'S FINANCIAL STATEMENTS

Leon's financial statements give us insights into the identity of some of the stakeholders of the company. From the information in the financial statements, we can surmise that there are a number of stakeholders:

- **Shareholders** Since Leon's is a public company traded on the TSX, shareholders are an important stakeholder group. Some of Leon's shareholders are small investors who don't have access to information other than what is publicly available.

EXHIBIT 2.5

**Example of a
Balance Sheet
Prepared in the
IFRS Format**

Consolidated annual balance sheet

Assets

In euro million	30.06.2007	30.06.2008
Net amounts		
Non-current assets		
Intangible assets	15,672	14,276
Goodwill	6,954	6,406
Property, plant and equipment	3,350	3,216
Biological assets	120	132
Non-current financial assets	242	290
Investments in associates	4	6
Deferred tax assets	1,678	1,444
NON-CURRENT ASSETS	28,020	25,770
Current assets		
Inventories	7,126	7,434
Operating receivables	2,456	2,292
Income taxes receivable	182	96
Other current assets	290	390
Current derivative instruments	102	38
Cash and cash equivalents	766	842
CURRENT ASSETS	10,924	11,092
TOTAL ASSETS	38,944	36,862

Liabilities

In euro million	30.06.2007	30.06.2008
Shareholders' equity		
Share capital	680	682
Share premium	4,106	4,130
Retained earnings and currency translation adjustments	6,134	6,350
Group net profit	1,662	1,680
Group shareholders' equity	12,580	12,840
Minority interests	336	354
TOTAL SHAREHOLDERS' EQUITY	12,916	13,194
Non-current liabilities		
Non-current provisions	1,068	934
Provisions for pensions and other long-term employee benefits	1,546	956
Deferred tax liabilities	4,652	4,256
Bonds	5,022	4,704
Non-current derivative instruments	146	418
Other non-current financial liabilities	7,876	6,106
TOTAL NON-CURRENT LIABILITIES	20,310	17,374
Current liabilities		
Current provisions	710	574
Operating payables	3,546	3,300
Income taxes payable	396	206
Other current liabilities	282	260
Other current financial liabilities	750	1900
Current derivative instruments	32	54
TOTAL CURRENT LIABILITIES	5,718	6,294
TOTAL LIABILITIES AND SHAREHOLDERS' EQUITY	38,944	36,862

- **Creditors** While Leon's hasn't borrowed money, it does owe a significant amount to various creditors as shown by accounts payable and accrued liabilities (a large proportion of the $95,247,000 is likely owed to suppliers of the merchandise Leon's sells in its stores). Some creditors will want to examine the financial statements as part of their assessment of how much credit they will offer Leon's.

- **Canada Revenue Agency** Leon's must file regular tax returns and the general purpose financial statements are required with the filing.

- **Competitors** Leon's is in a very competitive industry. Competitors such as The Brick will analyze the financial statements of Leon's to gain insight into how it's operating its business.

FORMAT OF GENERAL PURPOSE FINANCIAL STATEMENTS

There is no one right way to format financial statements. IFRS suggests (but doesn't require) a balance sheet format that is quite different from what Canadian companies have typically used—the arrangement used by Leon's (Exhibit 2.1) is typical. An example of the balance sheet format suggested by IFRS is seen in Exhibit 2.5. Notice that in contrast to the Leon's balance sheet non-current assets are at the top of the asset side and current assets at the bottom. On the liabilities and equity side, equity is at the top, followed by non-current liabilities, and then current liabilities. It's important to recognize that as long as the information you need is presented, statements can be reorganized to meet your requirements.

OTHER ACCOUNTING INFORMATION

In addition to the general purpose financial statements, accountants can prepare any type of report to satisfy the needs of stakeholders. The only limitations to this are the entity's willingness to provide the information and its availability in the accounting system (an accounting system can provide only information that's entered into it).

Accounting reports that are prepared to meet the needs of specific stakeholders or a specific purpose are called **special purpose reports**. For example, a creditor might want a statement of cash inflows and outflows, along with budgeted cash flows for the next year, to assess the borrower's ability to pay its debts. A property manager might want a statement of revenues from a retailer so that the appropriate amount of rent can be charged, if rent is based on the store's sales. The list of special purposes is endless. Normally, special purpose reports, even by public companies, aren't publicly available and they don't have to be prepared in accordance with IFRS.

Solved Problem

Snowflake's Snow Removal Company (SSRC)

Stan Snowflake recently started a new business clearing snow from residential driveways. Stan is a construction worker and while he tends to have a lot of work during the spring, summer, and fall, he doesn't usually work during the winter. Stan finds being idle quite frustrating so he decided that a snow removal business would be a good way to make some money and keep busy during the winter. As a result, he organized Snowflake's Snow Removal Company (SSRC), an unincorporated business. SSRC purchased a truck and offered snow removal for $250 for the entire winter, or for $50 per month for the five months SSRC would be operating (November through March). Ten people paid for the entire winter in October. Other people will pay monthly beginning in November. SSRC's balance sheet on October 31 is shown below.

Snowflake's Snow Removal Company
Balance Sheet
As at October 31

Assets		Liabilities and Owner's Equity	
Cash	$ 6,300	Bank loan	$ 5,000
Equipment	17,700	Accounts payable	6,500
		Services to be provided	2,500
			14,000
		Owner's equity	10,000
Total assets	$24,000	Total liabilities and owner's equity	$24,000

November and December were very busy for Stan and SSRC. There were a number of snowfalls, two of them quite heavy.

1. SSRC has 75 regular customers, 10 of whom paid in full in October. By the end of December, Stan had collected $5,600 from the customers who agreed to pay each month, and they owed $900. In addition, SSRC received $800 from people who stopped Stan on the street during heavy snowfalls and asked him to clean their driveway.

2. SSRC was so busy that Stan sometimes had to hire someone to help him do shovelling. He paid this person $450 for work done and owed her $100 at the end of December.

3. SSRC spent $700 on gas, oil, and service on the truck.

4. Stan estimates that the monthly depreciation of the truck and other equipment should be $700.

Required:

- Prepare income statements on the cash basis and the accrual basis for the two months ended December 31.

- Use the information from SSRC's balance sheet on October 31 to calculate the following amounts. Discuss the information provided by these results:

   a. working capital

   b. current ratio

   c. debt-to-equity ratio

Solution:

1.

Snowflake's Snow Removal Company
Income Statement
For the Two Months Ended December 31
(Prepared using the cash basis)

Revenue (cash collected)	$6,400
($5,600 from customers who pay monthly, plus $800 from people who stopped Stan on the street)	
Less: Expenses (cash spent)	
For employee ($450 paid for work done)	(450)
For oil, gas, and service ($700 for gas, oil, and service)	(700)
Net income (cash flow)	$5,250

Snowflake's Snow Removal Company
Income Statement
For the Two Months Ended December 31
(Prepared using the accrual basis)

Revenue	$8,300
($5,600 from customers who pay monthly, plus $900 owed by customers who pay monthly, plus $1,000 for the people who paid in advance [10 customers × $50 per month × 2 months]*, plus $800 from people who stopped Stan on the street)	
Less: Expenses	
For employee ($450 paid for work done, plus $100 owed)	(550)
For oil, gas, and service ($700 for gas, oil, and service)	(700)
Equipment depreciation (estimated at $700 monthly)	($1,400)
Net income	$5,650

*Even though customers paid in advance, SSRC earns the money on a monthly basis. Therefore, one-fifth of the advance payments should be recognized each month.

2. a. Working capital $=$ Current assets $-$ Current liabilities

($7,700) $=$ $6,300 $-$ $14,000

b. Current ratio $= \dfrac{\text{Current assets}}{\text{Current liabilities}} = \dfrac{\$6,300}{\$14,000} = 0.45$

c. Debt-to-equity ratio $= \dfrac{\text{Liabilities}}{\text{Owner's equity}} = \dfrac{\$14,000}{\$10,000} = 1.4$

The working capital calculation and current ratio show that SSRC has more current liabilities than current assets. This is a potential problem because if cash weren't forthcoming in the near future SSRC wouldn't be able to pay the bank or the truck dealer. However, on October 31 this wouldn't have been much of a concern because customers were expected to begin paying in November. The main concern on October 31 might have been signing up enough customers.

The debt-to-equity ratio indicates that SSRC has more liabilities than equity. It's not possible to tell whether this is a problem because there is no benchmark for comparison. However, the more debt an entity has, the more risk it faces. In this case, if SSRC isn't successful (if it didn't have enough paying customers), Stan would still be obliged to pay the bank and the truck dealer. SSRC probably doesn't have any major purchases left to make for the year, so it just has to concern itself with paying operating costs (wages, oil, gas, service) and using the remaining cash flow to pay debts and provide a profit to Stan.

SUMMARY OF KEY POINTS

▶ **LO 1** A set of general purpose financial statements includes the balance sheet, the income statement and statement of comprehensive income, the statement of retained earnings/statement of equity, the statement of cash flows, and the notes to the financial statements. The balance sheet summarizes the financial position of the entity—its assets, liabilities, and owners' equity—at a point in time. The income statement provides a measure of economic activity over a period. The statement of equity summarizes changes to equity over a period while statement of retained earnings summarizes the changes to retained earnings during a period. The statement of cash flows shows how cash during a period was obtained from and used for operating, investing, and financing activities. The notes to the financial statements expand and explain the information in the statements and provide additional information that may be helpful in assessing an entity. General purpose financial statements are designed to suit a broad set of users and uses and are usually prepared according to IFRS (or GAAP for Private Enterprises).

▶ **LO 2** The accounting equation is the conceptual foundation of accounting and is defined as

$$\text{Assets} = \text{Liabilities} + \text{Owner's equity}$$

All economic events entered into an accounting system must be summarized in terms of the accounting equation. The equality between of the equation must always be maintained.

▶ **LO 3** There are five basic elements in the financial statements: assets, liabilities, owners' equity, revenues, and expenses. Assets are economic resources that provide future benefits to an entity. Liabilities are an entity's obligations to pay debts or provide goods or services. Owners' equity represents the owners' investment in an entity. Owners' investments can be made directly by contributing assets to the entity or indirectly by reinvesting profits. Revenues represent economic benefits earned by providing goods and services to customers. Expenses are economic sacrifices made to earn revenue.

▶ **LO 4** The two most commonly used methods of accounting are the cash basis and the accrual basis. Cash accounting records only cash inflows and outflows. Under the cash basis revenues are recorded when cash is received and expenses are recorded when cash is paid. Accrual accounting attempts to measure economic activity rather than just cash flows. Under the accrual basis, revenues are economic benefits earned by providing goods or services to customers and expenses are economic sacrifices incurred to earn revenue. Accrual accounting is more complicated than cash accounting and it requires judgment by managers, accountants, and stakeholders.

▶ **LO 5** Obtaining and examining financial statements is often only the first step in evaluating an entity. Financial statement numbers can be analyzed to obtain additional insights. One of the analytical tools available to stakeholders is ratios. The current ratio (current assets ÷ current liabilities) provides information about an entity's liquidity. The debt-to-equity ratio (debt ÷ equity) gives an indication of an entity's risk, and the gross margin percentage (gross margin ÷ sales) gives an indication of an entity's profitability.

FORMULA SUMMARY

$$\text{Accounting equation: Assets} = \text{Liabilities} + \text{Owners' Equity}$$

$$\text{Working capital} = \text{Current assets} - \text{Current liabilities}$$

$$\text{Current ratio} = \frac{\text{Current assets}}{\text{Current liabilities}}$$

$$\text{Debt-to-equity ratio} = \frac{\text{Liabilities}}{\text{Owners' (shareholders') equity}}$$

$$\text{Gross margin} = \text{Sales} - \text{Cost of sales}$$

$$\text{Gross margin percentage} = \frac{\text{Gross margin}}{\text{Sales}} \times 100 \text{ percent}$$

KEY TERMS

accounting equation, p. 37

accounting policies, p. 54

accrual accounting, p. 45

asset, p. 37

balance sheet, p. 37

capital assets, p. 39

cash accounting, p. 45

cash from/used in financing activities, p. 52

cash from/used in investing activities, p. 52

cash from/used in operations, p. 52

common shares, p. 43

comprehensive income, p. 50

consolidated financial statements, p. 34

cost of sales, p. 47

creditor, p. 37

current asset, p. 39

current liability, p. 40

current ratio, p. 42

debt-to-equity ratio, p. 43

deficit, p. 43

depreciation, p. 46

dividend, p. 43

expense, p. 45

fiscal year, p. 35

general purpose financial statements, p. 33

gross margin, p. 48

gross margin percentage, p. 48

income statement, p. 44

interest, p. 43

liability, p. 37

liquidity, p. 41

materiality, p. 37

net assets, p. 46

non-current assets, p. 40

non-current liability, p. 40

operating cycle, p. 39

other comprehensive income, p. 50

owners' equity, p. 37, 43

partners' equity, p. 43

principal, p. 43

property, plant, and equipment, p. 39

retained earnings, p. 43

revenue, p. 45

shareholders' equity, p. 43

special purpose report, p. 57

statement of cash flows, p. 52

statement of retained earnings, p. 50

statement of shareholders' equity, p. 50

working capital, p. 41

working capital ratio, p. 42

SIMILAR TERMS

The left column provides alternative terms that are sometimes used for the accounting terms introduced in this chapter. The accounting terms are listed in the right column.

accrual basis of accounting	**accrual accounting, p. 45**
amortization	**depreciation, p. 46**
capital assets, fixed assets	**property, plant, and equipment, p. 39**
capital stock	**common shares, p. 43**
cash basis of accounting	**cash accounting, p. 45**
cash flow statement	**statement of cash flows, p. 52**
cash from operating activities	**cash from operations, p. 52**
common stock	**common shares, p. 43**
cost of goods sold	**cost of sales, p. 47**

depletion	**depreciation, p. 46**
gross profit	**gross margin, p. 48**
long-term assets, long-lived assets	**non-current assets, p. 40**
partners' equity (for a partnership)	**owners' equity, p. 37, 43**
sales, sales revenue	**revenue, p. 45**
share capital	**common shares, p. 43**
shareholders' equity (for a corporation)	**owners' equity, p. 37, 43**
statement of earnings, statement of income, statement of profit and loss, statement of operations	**income statement, p. 44**
statement of financial position	**balance sheet, p. 37**
stockholders' equity (for a corporation)	**owners' equity, p. 37, 43**

ASSIGNMENT MATERIALS

Questions

Q2-1.   What are the components of a complete financial statement package?

Q2-2.   Explain the difference between cash and accrual accounting.

Q2-3.   Do you think all entities should be required to use the same format for financial statements? Explain.

Q2-4.   What are general purpose financial statements? What problems does any individual stakeholder have with using general purpose statements?

Q2-5.   Why are the financial statements produced by public companies in Canada considered general purpose financial statements?

Q2-6.   The balance sheet has been compared to a photograph. Explain.

Q2-7.   Explain why net income calculated using cash accounting can be different from net income calculated using accrual accounting.

Q2-8.   Why is cash a crucial asset for an entity to have? What are the consequences of not having enough cash?

Q2-9.   Explain each of the following terms in your own words and give an example of each:
a. asset
b. liability
c. owners' equity
d. dividend
e. revenue
f. expense

Q2-10.   Define the following accounting measurements and explain how and why they would be used when evaluating an entity:
a. working capital
b. current ratio
c. debt-to-equity ratio
d. gross margin
e. gross margin percentage

Q2-11. Explain why each of the following would be classified as assets on an entity's balance sheet:
a. cash
b. rent paid for in advance
c. an oven in a restaurant
d. shares of other corporations owned by the entity

Q2-12. Explain why each of the following would be considered liabilities on an entity's balance sheet:
a. amounts owing to suppliers of inventory
b. advances received from customers for services to be provided in the future
c. bank loan

Q2-13. Under IFRS, money spent on research by companies in the biotechnology, pharmaceutical, high technology, and other industries isn't reported on the balance sheet as an asset. In your opinion, is the money companies spend on research an asset? Explain your thinking. Based on what you read in this chapter, why do you think money spent on research isn't considered an asset according to IFRS? What do you think the implications of this treatment of research costs are for stakeholders?

Q2-14. Explain the difference between common shares and retained earnings in the shareholders' equity section of a corporation's balance sheet.

Q2-15. What is comprehensive income? How does it differ from net income?

Q2-16. Explain the concept of liquidity. Why is evaluating liquidity important?

Q2-17. By law, distillers of Irish whiskey must age the whiskey for a minimum of three years, although the whiskey is often aged for a much longer time. If you were evaluating the liquidity of a distiller of Irish whiskey, how would you deal with the whiskey inventory?

Q2-18. Explain why net income results in an increase in owners' equity.

Q2-19. Explain why paying dividends results in a decrease in retained earnings of a corporation.

Q2-20. Why is knowing an entity's ability to generate cash flow so important to assessing the survival of the entity?

Q2-21. Virtually all entities prepare financial statements on an annual basis. For example, Leon's prepares its statements for a calendar year. Provide three reasons why entities report on an annual basis. In answering, consider the question from the point of view of the users of the information.

Q2-22. It's normal for entities to present financial statements for more than one year rather than for just the most recent year. Provide three reasons why it's useful for stakeholders to receive more than one year's financial statements.

Q2-23. Explain why different entities will organize the presentation of their financial statements in different ways (use different formats). For example, why would some companies present a lot of detail in their statements, whereas others might present as little as possible? In answering, consider different users and uses of the statements.

Exercises

E2-1. (**Accounting equation, LO 2**) For each of the following independent situations, fill in the shaded area with the appropriate dollar amount.

	Assets	=	Liabilities	+	Owners' Equity
Situation 1	$425,000				$189,000
Situation 2			$730,000		620,000
Situation 3	200,000		50,000		
Situation 4	420,000				350,000

E2-2.   (**Accounting equation, LO 2**) For each of the following independent situations, fill in the shaded area with the appropriate dollar amount. You are provided with assets and liabilities on December 31, 2013, owners' equity on January 1, 2013, and revenue and expenses for 2013.

	Assets on Dec. 31, 2013	=	Liabilities on Dec. 31, 2013	+	Owners' Equity on Jan. 1, 2013	+	Revenue in 2013	−	Expenses in 2013
Situation 1	$		$229,000		($75,000)		$210,000		$245,000
Situation 2	935,000				322,000		675,000		498,000
Situation 3	412,000		311,000		75,000				300,000
Situation 4	32,000		10,000		35,000		65,000		

E2-3.   (**Classification of balance sheet accounts, LO 1, 3**) Classify each of the following balance sheet accounts as a current asset, non-current asset, current liability, or non-current liability. Briefly explain your classification:
a. inventory
b. accounts payable that are usually paid within 60 days of receiving an invoice from a supplier
c. accounts receivable from customers that are usually paid within 30 days
d. machines used in a manufacturing facility
e. art work in the company's head office
f. a bank loan that the bank can ask the company to repay at any time
g. an account receivable that will be paid by the customer in two years
h. a loan that is to be repaid in full in three years

E2-4.   (**Prepare a statement of retained earnings, LO 1**) On December 31, 2013, Canmore Inc. (Canmore) reported retained earnings of $60,000. For the year ended December 31, 2014, Canmore had net income of $15,000 and paid dividends of $5,000.

Required:

Prepare a statement of retained earnings for Canmore for the year ended December 31, 2014.

E2-5.   (**Prepare a statement of comprehensive income, LO 1**) During the year ended December 31, 2013, Speers Ltd. had revenues of $4,500,000 and expenses of $3,750,000. In addition, the company had other comprehensive income of $75,000.

Required:

Prepare an income statement and a statement of comprehensive income for Speers Ltd. for the year ended December 31, 2013.

E2-6.   (**Prepare a statement of comprehensive income, LO 1**) During the year ended August 31, 2014, Vaughn Ltd. had revenues of $10,500,000 and expenses of $8,375,000. In addition, the company had other comprehensive income of $155,000.

Required:

Prepare an income statement and a statement of comprehensive income for Vaughn Ltd. for the year ended August 31, 2014.

E2-7.   (**Prepare a statement of retained earnings, LO 1**) Minden Corporation was incorporated on August 1, 2010, by five shareholders who each invested $50,000 in cash in exchange for common shares. Minden's year end is July 31. In its first year of business Minden had net income of $97,500. For its years ended July 31, 2012 and 2013, its second and third years of operation, Minden reported net income of $189,000 and $225,000, respectively. In its first year Minden didn't pay any dividends, but in fiscal 2012 it paid $25,000 in dividends and in 2013 it paid $40,000 in dividends.

Required:

Prepare a statement of retained earnings for the year ended July 31, 2013.

E2-8. (**Classification of cash flows, LO 1**) Classify each of the following cash flows as operating, financing, or investing activities:
a. cash paid for inventory
b. cash collected from customers
c. cash paid to suppliers
d. repayment of a bank loan
e. purchase of computer equipment for cash
f. sale of a building for cash
g. sale of common shares to investors for cash
h. cash spent to purchase advertising on radio

E2-9. (**Classification of cash flows, LO 1**) Classify each of the following cash flows as operating, financing, or investing activities:
a. wages paid to employees
b. cash paid to customers as refunds
c. cash paid for utilities
d. a new bank loan
e. purchase of used cars for cash by a used car dealer
f. purchase of new cars for cash by a taxi company
g. payment of a dividend to shareholders

E2-10. (**Prepare a balance sheet, LO 1, 3**) You have received the following alphabetical list of balance sheet accounts for Picton Corporation (Picton). Organize the accounts into Picton's balance sheet.

Accounts receivable	$ 35,000	Insurance paid for in advance	$ 10,000
Advances paid by customers		Inventory	85,000
for goods to be provided		Land	125,000
in the future	20,000	Loans made to the corporation	
Amounts owed to suppliers	75,000	by shareholders	50,000
Bank loan	100,000	Long-term debt	30,000
Capital stock	150,000	Retained earnings	80,000
Cash	12,000	Wages payable to employees	12,000
Furniture and fixtures	250,000		

E2-11. (**Complete statements of income and retained earnings, LO 1, 2**) Selkirk Corporation began operations in 2012. Its summarized financial statements are presented below. Fill in the shaded areas to complete the financial statements. Begin your work with 2012 and move forward from there.

	2014	2013	2012
Revenues	$478,000	$	$375,000
Expenses	327,000	290,000	
Net income		122,500	78,000
Retained earnings at the beginning of the year			0
Dividends declared during the year			10,000
Retained earnings at the end of the year	187,500	165,500	
Capital stock at the end of the year	180,000	150,000	
Liabilities at the end of the year	300,000		225,000
Assets at the end of the year		595,500	393,000

E2-12. (**Complete statements of income and retained earnings, LO 1, 2**) Sparwood Ltd. began operations in 2013. Its summarized financial statements are presented below. Fill in the shaded areas to complete the financial statements. Begin your work with 2013 and move forward from there.

	2015	2014	2013
Revenues	$130,000	$110,000	$
Expenses	105,000		82,000
Net income		(5,000)	8,000
Retained earnings at the beginning of the year			0
Dividends declared during the year		1,500	
Retained earnings at the end of the year	23,000		7,000
Common shares at the end of the year	21,000		15,000
Liabilities at the end of the year		7,000	5,000
Assets at the end of the year	50,500	25,000	

E2-13. (**Classification of cash flows, LO 1**) During 2014, Argentia Ltd. entered into the following cash transactions and indicate whether it's a cash inflow or outflow. Classify each transaction as operating, financing, or investing cash flows. Explain your thinking in each case.

  a. Inventory is purchased for $100,000.

  b. Dividends of $75,000 are paid to shareholders.

  c. $500,000 is borrowed from the bank.

  d. Office furniture is purchased for $20,000 to furnish the president's office.

  e. Four delivery trucks are sold for $22,500.

  f. Common shares are sold to investors for $500,000.

  g. Payments of $30,000 are collected from clients.

  h. Insurance for the next two years costing $8,000 is purchased.

E2-14. (**Prepare a statement of cash flows, LO 1**) You have been provided the following cash flow activities about Arcola Inc. for the year ended December 31, 2014. Organize this information into a statement of cash flows. Use Leon's statement in Exhibit 2.1 as a model. Be sure to provide a reconciliation to the cash balance on December 31, 2014:

• Cash balance on December 31, 2013	$28,000
• Cash balance on December 31, 2014	?
• Cash from operations	110,000
• Dividends paid to shareholders	25,000
• Sale of commons shares to new investors	200,000
• Purchase of new equipment	80,000
• Sale of land	35,000

E2-15. (**Prepare a statement of cash flows, LO 1**) You have been provided the following cash flow activities about Dugald Ltd. for the year ended December 31, 2015. Organize this information into a statement of cash flows. Use Leon's statement in Exhibit 2.1 as a model. Be sure to provide a reconciliation to the cash balance on December 31, 2015:

• New bank loan	$300,000
• Cash balance on December 31, 2014	125,000
• Cash balance on December 31, 2015	?
• Cash from operations	658,000
• Sale of computer equipment	125,000
• Purchase of marketable securities	480,000
• Repayment of mortgage	335,000

E2-16. **(Classifying items on the financial statements, LO 1, 3)** Name the financial statement (balance sheet, income statement, statement of shareholders' equity, statement of cash flows) on which each of the following items would appear. Some items may appear on more than one statement.
   a. Sales to customers
   b. Amounts owed to employees
   c. Land
   d. Retained earnings
   e. Cash spent to purchase new equipment
   f. Cash from financing activities
   g. Net income
   h. Amount borrowed from the bank

E2-17. **(Classifying items on the financial statements, LO 1, 3)** Name the financial statement (balance sheet, income statement, statement of shareholders' equity, statement of cash flows) on which each of the following items would appear. Some items may appear on more than one statement.
   a. Amounts owed by customers
   b. Depreciation expense
   c. Common shares
   d. Services owed to customers
   e. Delivery vehicles
   f. Cash from operations
   g. Dividends paid
   h. Cost of inventory sold to customers during the year

E2-18. **(Calculation of ratios, LO 5)** Below is a simplified balance sheet for Summerside Inc. (Summerside):

Summerside Inc.
Balance Sheet
As at December 31, 2014

Assets		Liabilities and shareholders' equity	
Current assets	$1,125,000	Current liabilities	$875,000
Non-current assets	3,125,000	Non-current liabilities	1,250,000
		Shareholders' equity	2,125,000
Total assets	$4,250,000	Total liabilities and shareholders' equity	$4,250,000

Required:

Calculate the following on December 31, 2014, using Summerside's balance sheet. Explain what each amount tells you.
   a. working capital
   b. current ratio
   c. debt-to-equity ratio

E2-19. **(Calculation of ratios, LO 1, 5)** Consider the following alphabetical list of income statement accounts for Sussex Ltd. (Sussex) for the year ended September 30, 2013:

Cost of sales	$34,000
Depreciation expense	22,500
General and administrative expense	139,000
Income tax expense	41,000
Interest expense	27,000
Marketing and promotion expense	15,000
Research expense	50,000
Revenue	495,000
Salaries and wage expense	97,500
Selling expense	35,000

Required:

    a. Prepare an income statement for Sussex for the year ended September 30, 2013.

    b. What is net income for the year?

    c. What is Sussex' gross margin for 2013?

    d. What is Sussex' gross margin percentage for 2013?

E2-20. **(Prepare income statements using cash and accrual accounting, LO 1, 4)** You have been provided the following information about Kedgwick Company, a small proprietorship, as of the end of its first year of operations. Assume that all supplies were used up at year end.

Cash collected from customers	$24,000
Amounts owing from customers	3,600
Amounts paid to suppliers	14,100
Amounts owing to suppliers	3,300

Required:

Calculate net income on the cash basis and on the accrual basis for Kedgwick Company. Explain why the cash basis and the accrual basis result in different amounts of income.

E2-21. **(Prepare income statements using cash and accrual accounting, LO 1, 4)** You have been provided the following information about Lunenberg Ltd. (Lunenberg) as of the end of its first year of operations.

Cash collected from customers	$206,500
Amounts owing from customers	19,600
Amounts paid to suppliers for business supplies	60,725
Amounts owing to suppliers for business supplies	14,175
Business supplies on hand at the end of the year	4,900
Amounts paid to employees for work done	30,625
Amounts owing to employees for work done	3,850
Advances paid to employees for work that will be done in the future	1,750
Depreciation of assets	7,000
Income taxes paid	13,125

Required:

Calculate net income on the cash basis and on the accrual accounting basis for Lunenberg. Explain why the cash basis and the accrual basis result in different amounts of income.

Problems

P2-1. **(Complete a set of financial statements, LO 1, 2, 3)** Below are three years of balance sheets, income statements, and statements of retained earnings for Auberndale Ltd.

Required:

a. Replace the missing information in the shaded areas with the appropriate amount. Begin your analysis with 2012 and work forward.
b. If you were a banker, would you lend Auberndale Ltd. $5,000,000? Explain your answer. What additional information would you require to make your decision whether to lend? Explain.

Auberndale Ltd. Balance Sheets As at December 31 (in thousands of dollars)			
	2014	**2013**	**2012**
Current assets			
Cash	$	$	$
Accounts receivable	11,067	9,996	8,925
Inventory	19,635	15,708	14,280
Prepaid assets	1,071	357	714
Total current assets	35,343		25,347
Land	4,463	4,463	
Plant and equipment	26,775	24,633	21,777
Accumulated depreciation		(11,067)	(9,639)
Other assets	1,643	2,925	3,656
Total non-current assets			20,256
Total assets	$	$	$
Current liabilities			
Accounts payable	$	$10,352	$8,211
Bank loan payable	1,193	3,084	1,428
Total current liabilities	11,903	13,436	
Mortgage payable	6,069		7,854
Total liabilities	17,972		17,493
Shareholders' equity			
Common shares			6,069
Retained earnings		26,226	
Total shareholders' equity	37,043	32,370	
Total liabilities and shareholders' equity	$	$52,871	$

Auberndale Ltd.
Income Statement
For the Year Ended December 31
(in thousands of dollars)

	2014	2013	2012
Sales revenue	$89,250	$	$73,185
Cost of goods sold		55,335	
Gross margin		24,990	
Expenses			
Selling	11,067	9,818	
Administrative	5,355		4,820
Depreciation	2,321	1,785	1,428
Interest	893	1,356	1,428
Total expenses		17,957	16,601
Income before income taxes	7,140	7,034	
Income taxes	2,714		2,057
Net income	$	$	$4,548

Auberndale Ltd.
Statement of Retained Earnings
For the Year Ended December 31
(in thousands of dollars)

	2014	2013	2012
Retained earnings, beginning of year	$	$	$17,850
Net income		4,578	
Dividends	393	393	
Retained earnings, end of year	$	$	$

P2-2. (**Preparing an income statement, LO 1, 3**) The junior accountant for Josselin Ltd. was asked to prepare an income statement and statement of comprehensive income for the year ended October 31, 2014. The accountant summarized the accounts he thought were necessary to prepare the statement but isn't sure how to proceed. Use the information provided by the junior accountant to prepare the income statement. Note that not all the information provided may be appropriate to use in the income statement.

Accounts payable	$210,000	Dividends payable	$75,000
Accounts receivable	510,000	Income tax expense	250,000
Advertising expense	195,000	Interest expense	185,000
Depreciation expense	425,000	Other comprehensive income	110,000
Property, plant, and equipment	1,870,000	Other expenses	215,000
Common shares	4,356,000	Salaries and wage expense	498,000
Cost of sales	3,200,000	Sales	6,500,000
Dividends	300,000	Selling, general, and administrative expense	725,000

P2-3. (**Prepare and interpret an income statement, LO 1, 4, 5**) You are provided with the following accounting information for Hanmer Ltd. (Hanmer), a retail electronics store, for the years ended December 31, 2012 and 2013:

	2013	2012
Advertising and promotion	$ 270,000	$ 250,000
Cost of inventory sold	1,200,000	1,040,000
General and administrative	321,000	301,000
Income tax	187,500	148,000
Miscellaneous	52,000	64,000
Rent	58,000	55,000
Salaries, wages, and commissions	485,000	450,000
Sales	3,160,000	2,851,000
Utilities	15,800	15,200

Required:

a. Prepare income statements for Hanmer for 2012 and 2013.

b. What was Hanmer's gross margin and gross margin percentage each year? In which year do you think Hanmer was more successful? Explain.

c. Suppose Hanmer had the same gross margin percentage in 2013 as it did in 2012. What would its gross margin and net income have been in 2013?

P2-4. (**Explaining assets, LO 3**) Explain why, according to IFRS, each of the following items would be considered an asset by a restaurant. If an item isn't an asset explain why not.

a. tables and chairs

b. advertisement in a local newspaper

c. money owed to the restaurant by its owner

d. rent paid in advance to the owner of the building

e. food left on people's plates when they finished eating

f. food to prepare meals

P2-5. (**Explaining assets, LO 3**) Explain why, according to IFRS, each of the following items would be considered an asset by a company that makes computers. If an item isn't an asset explain why not.

a. parts used to make the computers

b. a large sign outside the facility with the company's name

c. defective parts that must be disposed of

d. a building

e. insurance paid in advance for theft and fire on the facility

f. money owed by customers

P2-6. (**Explaining liabilities, LO 3**) Explain why each of the following items would be considered a liability by a restaurant:

a. wages owed to employees

b. bank loan

c. deposit received from a customer for catering a banquet later in the year

d. amounts withheld from employees' pay for income taxes.

P2-7. (**Prepare a balance sheet, LO 1, 3**) Andrea Reed is in her fourth year at a business school in Nova Scotia. Recently Andrea was asked by her brother Nathan to help him prepare a personal balance sheet. Nathan needed the balance sheet because he was applying for a scholarship at a prestigious art school and the school required the information to help it assess Nathan's financial need. Andrea sat down with Nathan to go over his situation and she obtained the following information:

a. Nathan has $844 in his bank account.

b. Nathan purchased a used car from his uncle three years ago. He paid $4,500 for the car and he thinks he should be able to use it for another two years.

c. Nathan is owed $750 for some decorating he did for a local social group's recent fundraising party.

d. Nathan owes $2,000 to a local bank for a job training program he took a couple of years ago. He must begin to pay back the money once he accepts a full-time job or in five years, whichever comes first.

e. About six months ago Nathan bought a computer from a local store. The computer cost $1,200 and he paid the seller $700 at the time he purchased it and he must pay $50 a month until the computer is paid for.

f. Nathan's personal property such as furniture, books, jewellery, etc. cost him about $6,000.

Required:

a. Use the information provided to prepare a balance sheet for Nathan. Provide an explanation for why you classified each item as you did (asset, liability, equity). The difference between assets and liabilities will give you Nathan's equity.

b. How do you think the balance sheet would help the art school assess whether Nathan should receive financial assistance?

c. What additional information do you think the school would want before making a decision to offer financial assistance?

P2-8. **(Prepare a balance sheet, LO 1, 3)** In addition to the information provided in P2-7, you also learn the following about Nathan's assets:

a. Nathan thinks the car could be sold for about $2,200.

b. A friend of Nathan recently offered him $1,000 for the computer.

c. Nathan is unlikely to receive more than $1,000 for his personal property.

Required:

a. Use the additional information along with the information provided in P2-7 to prepare a revised personal balance sheet for Nathan. Explain the choices you made in preparing the statement.

b. Compare your balance sheet with the one you prepared in P2-7. Which do you think would be more useful to the art school in assessing Nathan's need for financial assistance? Explain.

c. What problems arise when using market values of Nathan's assets instead of the cost? What are some of the benefits of using the cost of the assets? Is the balance sheet prepared using market value information more or less useful than the balance sheet prepared using the cost information?

P2-9. **(Prepare a balance sheet, LO 1, 3)** Louis Davis is a dentist with a practice in a small town in Manitoba. Recently, he separated from his wife and they are currently negotiating how they will divide their assets when their divorce proceedings conclude. As part of the process, Louis' lawyer has asked for a balance sheet for his dental practice to help value it. Louis has asked you to prepare the balance sheet. You gather the following information from Louis:

i.   Louis purchased all his equipment eight years ago when he started his practice. The total cost of all the equipment was $100,000. He expects to replace all the equipment in four years.

ii.   He purchased furniture and decorations for his office four years ago for $22,000. He expects the furniture and decorations to last for about ten years.

iii. Patients owe Louis $19,000.

iv.   Louis owes suppliers $12,000 for goods and services he purchased for his practice.

v.   The practice has $4,750 in its bank account.

vi.   Louis owes his staff $2,500. This amount will be paid on the next payday, in two weeks.

vii. Louis has a bank loan outstanding for $10,000.

viii. Louis keeps supplies he needs in his practice. The cost of the supplies he currently has on hand is $750.

Required:

   a. Use the information provided to prepare a balance sheet for Louis' dental practice. Provide an explanation for why you classified each item as you did (asset, liability, equity). The difference between assets and liabilities will give you Louis' equity.
   b. As a judge in this case, how would you use the balance sheet in deciding how to value Louis' practice?
   c. What additional information do you think you as judge might want before deciding how to value Louis' practice?

P2-10. **(Prepare a balance sheet, LO 1, 3)** In addition to the information provided in P2-9, you also learn the following about Louis' assets:
   i. Louis thinks that if he closed his practice he could sell his list of patients to another dentist for $125,000.
   ii. If Louis tried to sell his equipment he would receive about $25,000.
   iii. Louis would be unlikely to receive any money if he tried to sell the furniture and decorations.

Required:

   a. Use the additional information along with the information in P2-9 to prepare a revised personal balance sheet for Louis' dental practice. Explain the choices you made in preparing the statement.
   b. Compare your balance sheet with the one you prepared in P2-9. Which do you think would be more useful for valuing Louis' practice? Explain.
   c. What problems arise when using market values of Louis' assets instead of the cost? What are some of the benefits of using the cost of the assets? Is the balance sheet prepared using market value information more or less useful than the balance sheet prepared using the cost information?

P2-11. **(Prepare income statements using cash and accrual accounting, LO 1, 4, 5)** Belinda Bambrick recently began a business selling costume jewellery from a cart in a local mall. During November Belinda had cash sales to customers of $4,150, and $700 of credit sales. The cost of the merchandise sold during November was $1,750. All of the inventory sold during November was bought and paid for in October. In late November Belinda took delivery of new jewellery for which she paid $2,500 in cash. None of this new jewellery was sold in November. During November Belinda collected $1,000 that was owed from customers who purchased merchandise on credit in September and October. Belinda hired a friend to work on the cart when she wasn't able to do so. During November she paid the friend $850 cash, which included $150 owed for work done in October. At the end of November she owed the friend another $200 for work done in November. During November Belinda paid $500 cash to the mall manager to allow her to operate her cart during November and December. In early November she also took out a small ad in a local newspaper at a cost of $75. The ad will be for paid for in December.

Required:

Prepare income statements for Belinda's business for November using cash and accrual accounting. Explain why the two methods result in different amounts of income. Also calculate the gross margin for the business under the accounting methods.

P2-12. **(Prepare income statements using cash and accrual accounting, LO 1, 4, 5)**
Ali Grami operates a computer repair service from his home. During April he had the following activity:
   i.   Ali charged customers $7,200 for services he provided during April. He collected $6,300 of the amount charged.
   ii. He collected $1,350 for services provided in previous months.
   iii. A customer paid a $2,200 deposit for services Ali will provide later in the year.
   iv. Ali purchased goods for $1,600 that he used during the month. The goods will be paid for in 60 days.

v.   Ali paid $1,300 for goods purchased in previous months.

vi.   Ali has a part-time employee who earned $2,000 during April. The employee was paid $1,500 during the month and will receive the remainder in May. The employee also received $325 for work done in March.

vii. He purchased and paid for $800 of legal services during the month.

viii. Ali estimates depreciation of $500 for the month on his equipment, tools, and vehicle.

Required:

Prepare income statements for Ali's business for April using cash and accrual accounting. Explain why the two methods result in different amounts of income. Also calculate the gross margin for the business under the accounting methods.

P2-13. (**Correcting a balance sheet, LO 1, 3**) A friend of yours recently started a small business and he's prepared a balance sheet at the end of the first year end. He is puzzled because the balance sheet doesn't balance and he's not sure why not. Examine the balance sheet below and make any corrections needed. Your friend also said there were a couple of items he didn't know what to do with: deposits from customers (the cash received was included in the cash balance)—$1,000; furniture and fixtures—$9,000.

Balance Sheet as of September 30

Assets		Liabilities and shareholder's equity	
Cash	$4,000	Bank loan	$8,000
Accounts payable	2,100	Accounts receivable	1,200
Inventory	5,000	Common shares	4,000
Cash dividend paid	1,100	Net income	5,200

P2-14. (**Analyze financial information, LO 3, 5**) Below are the balance sheets and income statements for Penticton Inc. (Penticton) for 2013 and 2014.

Penticton Inc.
Balance Sheets
As of December 31

	2014	2013		2014	2013
Assets			**Liabilities and shareholders' equity**		
Cash	$ 12,500	$ 25,000	Bank loan	$ 250,000	$ 187,500
Accounts			Accounts payable	500,000	375,000
receivable	512,500	437,500	Goods to be provided		
Inventory	662,000	562,500	to customers	105,000	87,500
Equipment,			Long-term debt	625,000	375,000
furniture and					
fixtures (net of					
accumulated			Shareholders' equity		
depreciation)	1,785,500	1,325,000	Capital stock	650,000	625,000
Other non-			Retained earnings	1,043,000	950,000
current assets	187,500	250,000			
			Total liabilities and		
Total assets	$3,173,000	$2,600,000	shareholders' equity	$3,173,000	$2,600,000

Penticton Inc.
Income Statements
For the Years Ended December 31

	2014	2013
Revenue	$6,187,500	$4,812,500
Cost of goods sold	3,375,000	2,745,000
Selling, general, and administrative expenses	1,375,000	1,237,500
Depreciation expense	300,000	250,000
Interest expense	312,500	300,000
Tax expense	330,000	112,000
Net income	$ 495,000	$ 168,000

Required:

a. Calculate the following for Penticton for 2014 and 2013:
   i. working capital
   ii. current ratio
   iii. debt-to-equity ratio
   iv. gross margin
   v. gross margin percentage
b. Examine the balance sheets and income statements and explain why the amounts you calculated in (a) changed from 2013 to 2014.
c. Comment on Penticton's liquidity position on December 31, 2014. As a prospective lender of money to Penticton, what concerns would you have about its current liquidity position?
d. What could Penticton's management do to improve liquidity?

P2-15. **(Understanding the impact of transactions on financial ratios, LO 1, 5)** Victoria Ltd. (Victoria) is a small tool and die manufacturer in British Columbia. Victoria recently obtained financing from a local bank for an expansion of the company's facilities. The agreement with the bank requires Victoria's current ratio and debt-to-equity ratio be within ranges stated in the agreement. If the ratios fall outside of these ranges Victoria would have to repay the new loan immediately. At this time Victoria has a current ratio of 1.25 (based on current assets of $1.2 million and current liabilities of $960,000) and a debt-to-equity ratio of 1.6 to 1 (based on total liabilities of $2 million and total equity of $1.25 million). The chief financial officer of Victoria is concerned about the effect a number of transactions scheduled for the last few days of the year will have on the company's current ratio and debt-to-equity ratio.

Required:

Determine the effect that each of the following transactions will have on the initial current ratio and debt-to-equity ratio. Calculate what each ratio will be after each transaction takes place and state the effect each transaction has on the ratios (increase, decrease, or no effect). Treat each item independently.

	Transaction	Revised current ratio	Effect on the current ratio	Revised debt-to-equity ratio	Effect on the debt-to-equity ratio
	Example: Purchase equipment for $100,000. The equipment supplier will be paid in two years.	1.25	No effect	1.7 to 1	Increase
1.	Purchase inventory for $50,000 cash. The inventory won't be sold until after the year-end.				
2.	Bonuses of $60,000 cash are paid to senior managers. (This one is tricky. The bonus is an expense so be sure to consider the effect of the transaction on net income and the resulting impact on equity.)				
3.	Dividends of $50,000 are declared and will be paid after the year end. (Once the dividends have been declared they become a liability called dividends payable.)				
4.	Repayment of $150,000 on a long-term loan.				
5.	A $55,000 loan is arranged and the cash obtained. The loan must be repaid in 90 days.				

P2-16. (**Understanding the impact of transactions on financial ratios, LO 1, 5**) Longueuil Ltd. (Longueuil) is a small manufacturer of shirts in Québec. Longueuil recently obtained financing from a local bank for an expansion of the company's facilities. The agreement with the bank requires that Longueuil's current ratio and debt-to-equity ratio be within ranges stated in the agreement. If the ratios fall outside of these ranges Longueuil would have to repay the new loans immediately. At this time Longueuil has a current ratio of 1.5 (based on current assets of $900,000 and current liabilities of $600,000) and a debt-to-equity ratio of 1 to 1 (based on total liabilities of $1.2 million and total equity of $1.2 million). The chief financial officer of Longueuil is concerned about the effect a number of transactions that will be occurring in the last few days of the year will have on the company's current ratio and debt-to-equity ratio.

Required:

Determine the effect that each of the following transactions will have on the initial current ratio and debt-to-equity ratio. Calculate what each ratio will be after each transaction takes place and state the effect each transaction has on the ratios (increase, decrease, or no effect). Treat each item independently.

Transaction	Revised current ratio	Effect on the current ratio	Revised debt-to-equity ratio	Effect on the debt-to-equity ratio
Example: Purchase equipment for $200,000. The supplier of the equipment must be paid in six months.	1.1	Decrease	1 to 1.2	Increase
1. $25,000 owed by a customer is collected in cash.				
2. Sale of common shares to investors for $300,000 cash.				
3. Dividends of $50,000 are declared and paid in cash.				
4. A loan of $120,000 from a bank is arranged and the cash received. The loan must be repaid in 18 months.				
5. An $80,000 short-term bank loan is repaid.				
6. Merchandise is sold to a customer for $70,000. The customer must pay in two years. The inventory sold cost $30,000. (This one is tricky. Be sure to consider the effect of the transaction on net income and the resulting impact on equity.)				

P2-17.   (**Prepare financial statements from a list of accounts, LO 3, 4**) You have been provided with the following alphabetical list of accounts for Sudbury Ltd. for 2014. Use the information to prepare an income statement, statement of retained earnings, and statement of comprehensive income for the year ended December 31, 2014, and balance sheet as of December 31, 2014. You should be able to figure out how to treat accounts that have names that are unfamiliar to you by applying your understanding of the financial statements learned in this chapter.

Accounts payable	$17,600	Inventory	48,000
Accounts receivable	32,000	Investments in marketable securities	40,000
Accrued liabilities	7,360	Loan to customer	4,000
Accumulated depreciation	120,000	Loss due to fire	12,000
Accumulated other comprehensive income (on December 31, 2014)	4,250	Mortgage payable	200,000
Cash	4,000	Other comprehensive income	2,100
Common shares	240,000	Other current assets	1,600
Cost of sales	152,000	Other expenses	8,000
Current portion of mortgage payable	8,000	Other non-current assets	12,000
Deposits from customers	4,000	Patents	192,000
Depreciation expense	33,600	Plant, property, and equipment	320,000
Dividends	4,000	Prepaid assets	8,320
General and administrative expenses	44,000	Promotion and advertising expenses	12,000
Income tax expense	5,200	Research costs	122,000
Income taxes payable	3,200	Retained earnings at the beginning of the year	53,350
Income taxes recoverable from government	4,960	Salaries and wages expense	67,200
Interest expense	16,800	Salaries and wages payable	2,400
Interest revenue	3,520	Sales revenue	480,000

P2-18.   (**Prepare an income statement and balance sheet from a list of accounts, LO 3, 4**) You have been provided with the following alphabetical list of accounts for Thaxted Ltd. for 2014. Use the information to prepare an income statement for the year ended December 31, 2014, and balance sheet as of December 31, 2014. You should be able to figure out how to treat accounts that have names that are unfamiliar to you by applying your understanding of the financial statements learned in this chapter.

CL	Accounts payable	$26,250	Income taxes payable	$3,750
CA	Accounts receivable	27,500	Income taxes recoverable from government	2,250
CL	Accrued liabilities	5,000	Interest expense	70,000
N	Accumulated depreciation	375,000	Interest revenue	500
	Accumulated other comprehensive income	10,000	Inventory	42,500
	Advances to employees	1,250	Intangible assets	100,000
	Advertising expenses	47,500	Investments in the shares of other corporations (non-current)	60,000
	Depreciation expense	115,000	Long-term debt (non-current portion)	700,000
	Cash	5,000	Loss on lawsuit	45,000
	Cash sales to customers during 2014	112,500	Other comprehensive income	3,250
	Charitable donations made	50,000	Other expense	10,000
	Common shares	500,000	Other non-current assets	25,000
	Cost of sales	187,500	Prepaid insurance	1,000
	Credit revenue	725,000	Property, plant, and equipment	1,800,000
	Current portion of long-term debt	27,500	Retained earnings at the beginning of the year	366,000
	Deposits from customers	1,250	Selling expenses	67,500
	Dividends	12,500	Wages expense	110,000
	Income tax expense	75,000	Wages payable	1,750

P2-19. **(Evaluate the format of a balance sheet, LO 1)** Look at the balance sheet shown in Exhibit 2.5. Redo that balance sheet in the more traditional format used by Leon's. How does your statement differ from the one prepared by the company? Which statement is more informative? Should it make any difference to stakeholders how the balance sheet is formatted? Explain.

P2-20. **(Prepare a statement of cash flows, LO 4)** The Pas Ltd. was organized on August 1, 2013, with a cash investment of $2,000,000 by its shareholders. The Pas arranged a mortgage with a local lender for $600,000 and purchased a warehouse for $1,900,000. During its fiscal year ended July 31, 2014, The Pas collected $425,000 in cash from customers, paid $375,000 in cash for operating expenses, and paid $50,000 in cash dividends to its shareholders.

Required:

    a. Classify each of the cash flows described above as operating, investing, or financing.

    b. Organize the cash flows into a statement of cash flows.

    c. Explain what your statement of cash flows tells you that an income statement doesn't.

P2-21. **(Prepare a statement of cash flows, LO 4)** Markham Ltd. was organized on September 1, 2012, with a cash investment of $450,000 by its shareholders. Markham arranged a long-term loan with a local bank for $150,000 and purchased a small office building for $500,000. During its fiscal year ended August 31, 2013, Markham collected $600,000 in cash from customers, paid $360,000 in cash for operating expenses, and paid $80,000 in cash dividends to its shareholders.

Required:

    a. Classify each of the cash flows described above as operating, investing, or financing.

    b. Organize the cash flows into a statement of cash flows.

    c. Explain what your statement of cash flows tells you that an income statement doesn't.

P2-22. **(Explain whether and why an expenditure is an asset, LO 3)** Consider the following items:

    i. A large grocery store purchases land adjacent to the store for $300,000 so that it can expand its parking lot.

    ii. A company that operates call centres spends over $1 million per year providing training for staff so they can provide informed and courteous service to the people they speak with.

    iii. An auto parts manufacturer spends $200,000 to clear land to prepare it for construction of a new factory.

    iv. A metal fabricating shop is owed $25,000 by one of its customers. The customer recently filed for bankruptcy because it was unable to pay its debts.

    v. A student has paid university tuition totalling $15,000 to study business. The student plans to become a professional accountant in two years and hopes to open his own accounting practice within five years.

    vi. A major retailer is repeatedly found to have the most satisfied customers in its industry in surveys conducted by independent market research companies.

Required:

For each of the items explain whether and why it would be considered the following:

    a. an asset by a non-accountant (use your intuition, common sense, and judgment to decide whether the item in question should be considered an asset.)

    b. an asset according to IFRS (use the IFRS criteria that were discussed in the chapter.)

P2-23. **(Classify the effect of economic events on cash and accrual income, LO 3, 4)**
Consider the following economic events involving Leon's. Indicate whether Leon's would include each item in a calculation of net income using cash accounting and accrual accounting. Provide a brief explanation for your treatment:

	Economic Event	Net income on the cash basis	Net income on the accrual basis
	Example: Leon's sells merchandise to a customer for cash.	Yes, because cash is collected from a customer.	Yes, because a sale with a customer has been completed.
a.	Leon's sells merchandise to a customer on credit.		
b.	Leon's collects cash for goods that were sold last year.		
c.	Inventory Leon's paid for last year is sold in the current year.		
d.	Dividends are declared and paid to shareholders.		
e.	Leon's purchased and paid for inventory in the current period but the inventory is unsold as of the year-end.		
f.	Leon's depreciates a delivery truck.		

P2-24. **(Classify the effect of economic events on cash and accrual income, LO 2, 5)**
Indicate whether each of the following events would be included in a calculation of net income on the cash basis, the accrual basis, or both. Provide a brief explanation for your treatment:

	Economic Event	Net income on the cash basis	Net income on the accrual basis
	Example: An entity sells merchandise for cash.	Yes, because cash is collected from a customer.	Yes, because a sale with a customer has been completed.
a.	An entity receives a deposit from a customer for services that will be provided in the future.		
b.	An entity provides services to a customer this year that were paid for last year.		
c.	An advance is paid to an employee for work she will do in the future.		
d.	Supplies paid for last year are used this year to provide services to a customer.		
e.	Supplies are bought, paid for, and used this year to provide services to a customer.		
f.	A delivery truck is purchased for cash.		

P2-25. **(Prepare balance sheets using different asset values, LO 4)** In Chapter 1 you were asked to imagine you were a student needing insurance on your apartment and examined different ways of valuing the contents of the apartment. We identified three different ways of valuing the contents of the apartment. Table 1.6 from Chapter 1 is reproduced next. All the items on the list are owned by you, except for the appliances, which belong to the building.

Inventory of Apartment Contents			
Item	What it cost	What it would cost to replace	What it could be sold for
Television	$ 500	$ 650	$ 225
Computer	1,200	900	300
Furniture	3,200	3,800	1,700
Books	750	875	300
Clothes	1,600	1,950	300
Stereo	900	1,100	700
Jewellery	500	625	300
Appliances	2,100	2,600	1,400
Art	300	500	500
Other	1,000	1,200	750
Total	$10,650	$14,200	$6,475

In addition to the above, the following information is available:

Item	Amount
Student loans	$7,500
Loans from parents	3,000
Cash in bank	1,100
Owing from employer	800

Required:

a. Prepare three separate balance sheets using the information in each column above. Make sure to include the "other information" in each balance sheet.

b. Explain the benefits and limitations of each balance sheet to the people who might use them. Make sure to discuss specific stakeholders that might use each balance sheet.

c. Which balance sheet do you think would be appropriate under IFRS?

d. Which balance sheet do you think is best? Explain.

P2-26. **(Prepare a personal balance sheet, LO 1, 2, 3)** Make a list of your personal assets and liabilities and try to organize them into an accounting balance sheet format. Assign values to the assets and the liabilities. Answer the following questions about your balance sheet:

a. How did you determine your equity in your assets?

b. How did you decide what amount to assign to each asset and liability?

c. Did you include your education among your assets? Why or why not? If your personal balance sheet was being prepared according to IFRS would your education be included as an asset? Explain.

Using Financial Statements

High Liner Foods Incorporated (High Liner) is a processor and marketer of superior quality seafood products. It markets its products under the High Liner, Fisher Boy, FPI, Mirabel, Sea Cuisine, and Royal Sea brands to most major retail chain and club stores in North America and to restaurants and institutions for food service throughout North America.

The company began in 1899 with the founding of W.C. Smith & Company, a salt fish operation located in Lunenburg, Nova Scotia—the current home of its head office and one of the most modern and diversified food processing plants in the world.

High Liner is one of North America's largest marketers of prepared frozen seafood products.[5]

High Liner's consolidated balance sheets and statements of income, comprehensive income, changes in shareholders' equity, and cash flows, along with some extracts from the notes to the financial statements, are provided in Exhibit 2.6.[6] Use this information to respond to questions FS2-1 to FS2-11.

| EXHIBIT 2.6 High Liner Foods Inc.—Extracts from Financial Statements |

CONSOLIDATED BALANCE SHEETS

(in thousands of Canadian dollars)	Jan. 3, 2009	Dec. 29, 2007
ASSETS (notes 7 and 8)		
Current:		
Cash	$ 7,032	$ 7,064
Accounts receivable (note 4a)	63,873	68,662
Income tax receivable	45	2,414
Inventories (note 4b)	146,863	110,521
Prepaid expenses	1,782	1,712
Future income taxes (note 11)	1,533	1,302
Total current assets	221,128	191,675
Property, plant and equipment (note 6)	59,016	57,515
Other:		
Future income taxes (note 11)	833	1,677
Other receivables and sundry investments	133	66
Employee future benefits (note 14)	3,477	6,759
Intangible assets (notes 2 and 5)	24,065	–
Goodwill (notes 2 and 5)	30,767	–
Intangible assets and goodwill (notes 2 and 5)	–	42,762
	59,275	51,264
	$ 339,419	$ 300,454
LIABILITIES AND SHAREHOLDERS' EQUITY		
Current:		
Bank loans (note 7a)	$ 39,931	$ 61,280
Accounts payable and accrued liabilities (note 7b)	73,611	51,068
Income taxes payable	2,443	437
Current portion of capital lease obligations (note 8)	458	603
Total current liabilities	116,443	113,388
Long-term debt (note 8)	63,939	51,709
Long-term capital lease obligations (note 8)	513	259
Other long-term liabilities (note 2)	2,112	–
Employee future benefits (note 14)	563	4,227
Shareholders' Equity (see Statement of Changes in Shareholders' Equity):		
Preference shares (note 9)	–	50,270
Common shares (note 9)	109,787	58,800
Contributed surplus	364	490
Retained earnings	49,897	40,112
Accumulated other comprehensive loss (note 10)	(4,199)	(18,801)
	155,849	130,871
	$ 339,419	$ 300,454

FS2-1. Examine High Liner's balance sheet and confirm that the accounting equation equality holds in both years shown (Assets = Liabilities + Owners' Equity). Show your work.

FS2-2. What were High Liner's year ends in the last two fiscal years? Why aren't they the same? Do the different dates cause any problems for stakeholders who want to compare the two years of information High Liner provides? (To answer, look at the notes to the financial statements.)

FS2-3. Find the following information in High Liner's financial statements:
a. Sales for the year ended January 3, 2009.
b. Selling, general, and administrative expenses for the year ended January 3, 2009.
c. Total assets on January 3, 2009.
d. Long-term debt on January 3, 2009.

| EXHIBIT | 2.6 | (continued) High Liner Foods Inc.—Extracts from Financial Statements |

CONSOLIDATED STATEMENTS OF INCOME

For the fifty-three weeks ended January 3, 2009 (with comparative figures for the fifty-two weeks ended December 29, 2007)

(in thousands of Canadian dollars, except per share information)	Fiscal 2008	Fiscal 2007
Sales	$ 615,993	$ 275,391
Cost of sales (notes 4b and 17)	481,382	203,259
Distribution expenses (note 4b)	37,041	20,211
Gross profit	97,570	51,921
Commission income	625	33
Selling, general and administrative expenses (note 4b)	(65,513)	(39,809)
Foreign exchange loss	(1,234)	(170)
Business acquisition integration costs (note 2)	(4,879)	(1,286)
Amortization of intangible assets (note 2)	(1,383)	–
Interest expense:		
Short-term	(2,695)	(173)
Long-term	(3,768)	(212)
Other expense	(402)	(51)
Non-operating transactions	(84)	333
Income before income taxes and discontinued operations	18,237	10,586
Income taxes (note 11)		
Current	(3,002)	(2,505)
Future	(1,043)	(1,164)
Total income taxes	(4,045)	(3,669)
Income from continuing operations	14,192	6,917
Gain from discontinued operations; net of income tax (note 3)	–	372
Net income	$ 14,192	$ 7,289

CONSOLIDATED STATEMENTS OF COMPREHENSIVE INCOME

For the fifty-three weeks ended January 3, 2009 (with comparative figures for the fifty-two weeks ended December 29, 2007)

(in thousands of Canadian dollars)	Fiscal 2008	Fiscal 2007
Net income for the period	$ 14,192	$ 7,289
Other comprehensive income, net of future income taxes		
Unrealized foreign exchange gains (losses) on translation of self-sustaining foreign operations (net of nil income taxes)	9,093	(3,512)
Net gain (loss) on derivative financial instruments designated as cash flow hedges net of $3.6 million income tax expense (2007; $1.6 million income tax recovery)	7,045	(3,245)
Net (gain) loss on derivatives designated as cash flow hedges in prior periods transferred to net income in the current period net of $0.8 million income tax expense (2007; $0.6 million income tax recovery)	(1,536)	1,085
Change in gains and losses on derivatives designated as cash flow hedges	5,509	(2,160)
Other comprehensive income	14,602	(5,672)
Comprehensive income	$ 28,794	$ 1,617

e. Total current assets on January 3, 2009.

f. Dividends paid on common shares during the year ended January 3, 2009.

g. The amount High Liner spent on additions to property, plant, and equipment during 2009.

h. Comprehensive income for the year ended January 3, 2009.

i. The amount of cash raised by issuing equity during the year ended January 3, 2009.

j. The amount of accumulated other comprehensive loss on January 3, 2009.

FS2-4. Find the following information in High Liner's financial statements:

a. Net income for the year ended January 3, 2009.

b. Cost of sales for the year ended January 3, 2009.

EXHIBIT 2.6 (continued) High Liner Foods Inc.—Extracts from Financial Statements

CONSOLIDATED STATEMENTS OF CHANGES IN SHAREHOLDERS' EQUITY

For the fifty-three weeks ended January 3, 2009 (with comparative figures for the fifty-two weeks ended December 29, 2007)

(in thousands of Canadian dollars)	Series A Preference $	2nd Preference $	Non-Voting Equity $	Common $	Contributed Surplus	Retained Earnings	Accumlated Other Comprehensive Loss	Total
At December 30, 2006	$ –	$ 20,000	$ –	$ 28,106	$ 503	$ 36,204	$ (13,577)	$ 71,236
Issue of shares (notes 2 and 9)	30,270	–	–	30,270	–	–	–	60,540
Stock options exercised (note 9)	–	–	–	419	–	–	–	419
Stock options expense reclassified	–	–	–	5	(5)	–	–	–
Stock options expense credited	–	–	–	–	(8)	–	–	(8)
Adjustments on adoption of financial instruments, net of future income taxes	–	–	–	–	–	(98)	448	350
Other comprehensive loss	–	–	–	–	–	–	(5,672)	(5,672)
Net income	–	–	–	–	–	7,289	–	7,289
Common share dividends	–	–	–	–	–	(2,073)	–	(2,073)
Second preference share dividends	–	–	–	–	–	(1,210)	–	(1,210)
At December 29, 2007	30,270	20,000	–	58,800	490	40,112	(18,801)	130,871
Issue of shares (note 9)	–	–	530	–	–	–	–	530
Stock options exercised (note 9)	–	–	–	463	–	–	–	463
Stock options expense reclassified	–	–	–	126	(126)	–	–	–
Preference share conversion to Series A	19,966	(19,966)	–	–	–	–	–	–
Shares repurchased	–	(34)	(4)	(364)	–	–	–	(402)
Series A conversion to Non-voting equity	(50,236)	–	50,236	–	–	–	–	–
Other comprehensive income	–	–	–	–	–	–	14,602	14,602
Net income	–	–	–	–	–	14,192	–	14,192
Common share dividends	–	–	–	–	–	(3,244)	–	(3,244)
Second preference share dividends						(166)		(166)
Series A preference share dividend	–	–	–	–	–	(774)	–	(774)
Share issuance expenses						(223)		(223)
At January 3, 2009	$ –	$ –	$ 50,762	$ 59,025	$ 364	$ 49,897	$ (4,199)	$ 155,849

c. Other comprehensive income for the year ended January 3, 2009.

d. Cash on January 3, 2009.

e. Common shares on January 3, 2009.

f. Retained earnings on January 3, 2009.

g. Total liabilities on January 3, 2009 (this amount has to be calculated).

h. Total current assets on January 3, 2009.

i. Cash from operations for the year ended January 3, 2009 (this amount isn't named in the statements; you have to find it).

j. The amount of cash spent during the year ended January 3, 2009 to purchase a business.

k. The amount spent during the year ended January 3, 2009 repurchasing capital stock.

FS2-5. Use High Liner's financial statements to respond to the following:

a. Calculate the amount of working capital on January 3, 2009, and December 29, 2007.

b. Calculate the current ratio on January 3, 2009, and December 29, 2007.

c. By how much did working capital change between the end of fiscal 2007 and the end of fiscal 2008?

d. What does the information you calculated in (a) to (c) above tell you about High Liner's liquidity?

EXHIBIT **2.6** **(continued) High Liner Foods Inc.—Extracts from Financial Statements**

CONSOLIDATED STATEMENTS OF CASH FLOWS

For the fifty-three weeks ended January 3, 2009 (with comparative figures for the fifty-two weeks ended December 29, 2007)

(in thousands of Canadian dollars)	Fiscal 2008	Fiscal 2007
Cash provided by (used in) operations:		
Net income from continuing operations for the year	$ 14,192	$ 6,917
Charges (credits) to income not involving cash from operations:		
Depreciation and amortization	8,311	3,087
Stock compensation expense	(81)	135
Loss on asset disposals	448	89
Payments of employee future benefits in excess of expense	(523)	19
Future income taxes	1,043	1,164
Unrealized foreign exchange (gain) loss	475	(442)
Cash flow from continuing operations before changes in non-cash working capital:	23,865	10,969
Net change in non-cash working capital balances	3,464	(1,416)
Cash flows from operating activities of discontinued operations	–	375
	27,329	9,928
Cash provided by (used in) financing activities:		
Net change in current bank loans	(29,254)	53,760
Issuance of long term debt related to acquisition (notes 2 and 8)	–	53,625
Repayments of capital lease obligations	(519)	(418)
Dividends paid:		
Second Preference	(166)	(1,210)
Series A Preference	(774)	–
Common	(3,244)	(2,073)
Share issuance expenses	(323)	–
Repurchase of capital stock	(402)	–
Issue of equity shares	993	419
	(33,689)	104,103
Cash provided by (used in) investing activities:		
Purchase of property, plant and equipment	(4,671)	(3,019)
Proceeds of unwound foreign exchange contracts	7,436	–
Net expenditures on disposal of assets	(25)	(17)
Use of investment tax credits	1,368	1,516
Acquisition of business (2007; net of acquired cash of $1.0 million) (note 2)	2,000	(100,479)
Business acquisition costs (note 2)	(235)	(4,246)
Decrease in other receivables	(67)	(61)
Investing activities of discontinued operations	–	333
	5,806	(105,973)
Foreign exchange impact on cash	522	(1,234)
Change in cash during the year	(554)	8,058
Cash, beginning of year	7,064	240
Cash, end of year	$ 7,032	$ 7,064

NOTES TO CONSOLIDATED FINANCIAL STATEMENTS

January 3, 2009

1. Significant Accounting Policies

YEAR END

The Company's fiscal year end is on the Saturday closest to December 31. This results in a 53-week fiscal year every five to seven years. The 2008 fiscal year is a 53-week year while the 2007 fiscal year is a 52-week year.

FS2-6. Use High Liner's financial statements to respond to the following:

a. Calculate the debt-to-equity ratio on January 3, 2009, and December 29, 2007.

b. Explain why the debt-to-equity ratio changed from the end of fiscal 2007 to the end of fiscal 2008.

c. What comments can you make about High Liner based on your responses to (a) and (b) above?

EXHIBIT 2.6 (continued) High Liner Foods Inc.—Extracts from Financial Statements

6. Property, Plant and Equipment

($000)	Jan. 3, 2009	Dec. 29, 2007
Land	$ 2,630	$ 2,193
Buildings	40,160	38,471
Computers and electronic equipment	8,294	7,194
Machinery and equipment, other	66,571	55,073
Equipment under capital lease	1,532	2,542
	119,187	105,473
Less accumulated depreciation:		
Buildings	16,036	13,641
Computer and electronic equipment	5,847	4,620
Machinery and equipment, other	34,843	26,432
Equipment under capital lease*	516	1,180
	57,242	45,873
Investment tax credits	(2,929)	(2,085)
	$ 59,016	$ 57,515

8. Long Term Debt and Capital Lease Obligations

LONG TERM DEBT

($000)	Jan. 3, 2009	Dec. 29, 2007
Notes payable, due 2010 to 2012		
Series A at 6.31%	$ 17,250	$ 17,250
Series B at 6.012% (USD$31,058 in 2008 and 2007)	37,602	30,390
Series C at LIBOR plus 2.00% (USD$4,950 in 2008 and 2007)	5,992	4,843
Cross currency swap mark to market	3,765	(112)
Less financing charges	(670)	(662)
	$ 63,939	$ 51,709

CAPITAL LEASE OBLIGATIONS

($000)	Jan. 3, 2009	Dec. 29, 2007
Capital leases at 5.56% to 11.66% due 2009 to 2012	$ 971	$ 862
Less current installments	458	603
	$ 513	$ 259

As part of the Business Acquisition (see note 2), the Company entered into new long term funded debt as outlined above. All real property and equipment in its four production facilities and personal property including intellectual property are pledged as security. For the first 24 months of the term, only interest on the loans is payable. Repayments are based on a twelve-year amortization period, with the repaid balance due in full on December 20, 2012. The agreements include covenant requirements of debt coverage, defined cash flow to debt and debt to capitalization ratios. At January 3, 2009, the Company was in compliance with all convents associated with this debt.

The Series C tranche of debt shown above will be repaid if the Company sells one of its U.S. plants. Increases in amounts owing for long-term debt is due to the weakening of the Canadian dollar with relation to the U.S. dollar in 2008.

On December 20, 2007 the Company entered into a cross currency swap for the Series A note related to its U.S. operating entities to effectively convert both interest and principal payments to U.S. dollars. The effective interest rate on the Series A loan after taking into account the swap was 6.26%. The Company is using hedge accounting for this swap.

The principal payments required, in Canadian dollars, on long-term debt and capital leases in each of the next five fiscal periods are as follows:

CDN $000	Notes Payable
2009	$ –
2010	5,076
2011	5,076
2012	50,692
2013	–

FS2-7. Use High Liner's financial statements to respond to the following:
a. Calculate the gross margin for fiscal 2007 and 2008.
b. Calculate the gross margin percentage for fiscal 2007 and 2008.
c. Interpret your calculations in (a) and (b) above. What do they tell you about High Liner's performance? What additional information would you want to do a more thorough evaluation of High Liner's gross margin?

FS2-8. Examine the note to High Liner's financial statements that describes property, plant, and equipment. Describe the different types of property, plant, and equipment the company has.

FS2-9. Examine Note 8 to High Liner's financial statements entitled Long Term Debt and Capital Lease Obligations and respond to the following questions:
a. How much long-term debt did High Liner have on January 3, 2009?
b. How much of the Series B notes payable was outstanding on January 3, 2009. What was the interest rate on the Series B notes?
c. How much of its long-term debt will High Liner have to repay in fiscal 2009?
d. How does the information in the note help you evaluate High Liner's financial position better than only having the information on the balance sheet?

FS2-10. List five questions you would ask High Liner's management if you were considering lending money to the company. Your questions should pertain to information that you can't obtain from the financial statements.

FS2-11. Compare High Liner's balance sheet with Leon's. Describe how the composition of assets differs between the two companies. Given the different industries these two companies are in, does the difference make sense? Explain. In answering this question it may be helpful for you to calculate on a percentage basis what each asset represents as a proportion of total assets.

ENDNOTES

1. Extracted from Leon's Furniture Limited's 2008 Annual Report.

2. Available at Sedar.com.

3. Extracted from WestJet Airlines Ltd.'s 2008 Annual Report.

4. Extracted from Leon's Furniture Limited's 2008 Annual Report.

5. Adapted from High Liner Foods Incorporated website at http://www.highlinerfoods.com/inside.asp?cmPageID=79.

6. Extracted from High Liner Foods Incorporated 2008 Annual Report.

THE ACCOUNTING CYCLE

LEARNING OBJECTIVES

After studying the material in this chapter you will be able to do the following:

▶ **LO 1** Describe the purpose and nature of accounting information systems and the accounting cycle.

▶ **LO 2** Analyze transactions and economic events and prepare financial statements using an accounting equation spreadsheet.

▶ **LO 3** Understand that financial statements are affected by how managers choose to record transactions and economic events.

▶ **LO 4** Differentiate between the different types of adjusting journal entries and understand their purposes.

▶ **LO 5** Analyze transactions and economic events, record them using journal entries, post entries to T-accounts, and prepare and use the trial balance to prepare financial statements.

▶ **LO 6** Explain the purpose of closing journal entries and describe how to prepare them.

When RCMP Superintendent Craig Hannaford (ret'd) was chasing down suspects of white-collar crime and fraud, he usually wouldn't reveal he was a certified general accountant (CGA).

Hannaford says that in his nearly 25-year RCMP career, keeping his accounting designation secret helped him investigate some of the most famous Canadian corporate crooks, including Garth Drabinsky, the theatre mogul who took *Phantom of the Opera* to Broadway, and Alan Eagleson, the mastermind of Team Canada's 1972 hockey victory over Russia.

"I didn't even have it [the CGA] on my business cards," said Hannaford. "I preferred people to think that I was the classic bumbling cop...that really was maybe out of his depth...because I thought it gave me the advantage, when in fact I knew what was going on."

Craig Hannaford, CGA
Hannaford Partners Incorporated,
RCMP Superintendent (ret'd)

After completing a computer science degree from the University of Western Ontario, Hannaford graduated from the RCMP Academy in Regina, and was then posted to Manitoba and Ontario, working on white-collar and computer crime. Along the way, he completed his CGA designation and took a leave of absence to work at a forensic accounting firm in Toronto. He also became a certified fraud examiner.

"People have a classic sort of view of what accounting is and what an accountant is...basically somebody...in a little office somewhere poring over papers with a calculator or a spreadsheet," Hannaford acknowledged. "But you can have a very, very different career in accounting, a very dynamic career with accounting skills."

For Hannaford, that even meant tracking international criminals, once setting up a sting operation in Amsterdam with Dutch police to capture a Nigerian fraudster who'd been preying on victims in Canada and the United States. Now in private practice in Toronto, Hannaford helps companies in a variety of ways, including sniffing out embezzlers or investigating *Securities Act* violations.

He maintains that mopping up the perpetrators of fraud can't erase the trauma commercial crime brings for the victims.

"I've seen many lives devastated as a result of fraud cases so that's why I committed my life... to work in that whole field," Hannaford said.

In 2006, he co-founded Fraud Squad TV to produce and broadcast consumer fraud prevention tips on Canadian television networks and WebTV (www.fraudcast.ca). Hannaford provides advice about everything from how not to buy a fake Ferrari to protecting your identity on Facebook and MySpace.

"You can investigate these crimes usually [only] after people have lost their money, and generally there's no way to get money back for the victim of fraud, so prevention is 99 percent of the equation," Hannaford said.

And where should users of accounting information look to detect fraud in a Canadian entity's books?

Hannaford says it's usually something simple like journal entries that "goose up" the sales numbers of financial statements. Preparers must "document [their] reasons for doing that, particularly when these have an impact on the bottom line of the company's performance."

So whether it's the collapse of a telecommunications giant or a small company that doesn't make the headlines, he says most frauds come down to the same thing.

"The concepts are the same, the numbers are the same, the accounting principles are the same; it's just bigger dollars. The crooks are the same, the psychology is the same; it's just people trying to deceive."

—E.B.

INTRODUCTION

In Chapter 2 the different financial statements were introduced. In this chapter we examine the mechanics of accounting—how transactions and other economic events are recorded in an accounting system, and how the raw data are organized, processed, and converted into information that is useful to stakeholders.

Recording and processing transactions and economic events are essential parts of accounting. They provide the raw data used to produce the information needed by managers and stakeholders for decision making. But remember, the mechanics of accounting—bookkeeping—isn't accounting; it's only part of it. Learning the mechanics is useful for understanding the relationship between managers' accounting choices—their decisions about how to record transactions and economic events—and the impact of those choices on financial statements. This will help you become an effective and sophisticated user of financial statements.

Some readers may wonder if they need to know the mechanics of accounting if they don't want to be accountants. This is a good question. Users of accounting information don't have to be expert bookkeepers, but it's important to understand how accounting works so that you understand the relationship between accounting choices and the amounts reported in the financial statements.

Some students find a focus on accounting procedures attractive because there is little judgment, analysis, or evaluation required. These students are comfortable solving problems that have right answers. But this isn't learning accounting!

THE ACCOUNTING CYCLE: INTRODUCTION

The **accounting cycle** is the process of entering transaction and economic event data into an accounting system and then processing, organizing, and using it to produce information, such as financial statements. It's very difficult to understand and use data that aren't organized in a useful way. For example, you wouldn't know anything about your spending habits unless you recorded every purchase, organized each one by category, and determined the totals.

Figure 3.1, Panel A, provides an overview of an accounting system's role in capturing raw data, processing it, and producing financial statements and other financial information. Let's look at each step of the process. An entity is continuously involved in economic events. In many cases these are transactions with other entities, such as buying and selling assets, incurring and

FIGURE   3.1

Panel A—
Overview of
an Accounting
Information
System

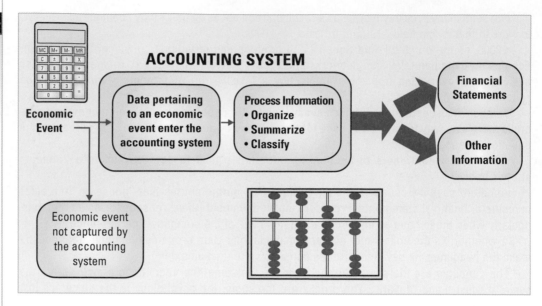

settling liabilities, and supplying goods and services to customers. Some economic events affect an entity but aren't the result of transactions involving it; for example, decisions by competitors and governments, technological changes, and economic conditions.

An accounting system is designed to capture relevant economic events affecting the entity. A relevant event must be entered into the accounting system in some way—it doesn't happen automatically—and judgment is required to decide if, when, and how the event is recorded. Figure 3.1, Panel A, shows that accounting systems aren't designed to capture all economic events. It's key that the accounting system gathers relevant data for providing information to meet the decision-making needs of the stakeholders and the reporting requirements of the entity.

In Canada, most entities base financial reporting on transactions that have already occurred. Once recorded, transaction values usually stay at that amount. For instance, if an entity buys a piece of land for $2,000,000, it's recorded at $2,000,000 and usually remains at that amount for as long as it's owned. If the value of the land increases, in most cases the increase wouldn't be recorded because the accounting systems of most Canadian entities aren't designed for this.

An accounting system is conceptually similar to a newspaper's editorial process (see Figure 3.1 Panel B). Each day the editors assign reporters to cover stories. Many newsworthy events take place in the world every day and it isn't possible to cover them all, so a newspaper will cover the stories the editors think are most relevant to its readers. If a story isn't covered, it can't appear in the newspaper.

This makes newspapers and financial reporting similar in two respects. First, a newspaper is a general purpose report—all readers get the same newspaper regardless of their interests or information needs, and it is designed for a wide range of readers. Second, newspapers have a "point of view"—they aren't neutral. The stories covered, how they are written, and the paper's editorial perspective all reflect the viewpoints of the publisher, editors, columnists, and reporters, and they are intended to influence, for example, the social or political agenda in a community. Similarly, financial statements are prepared from the managers' point of view. The accounting choices they make may be intended to have economic consequences for stakeholders; for example by increasing managers' bonuses, deferring taxes, or changing the selling price of a business.

Just as newspapers can't give a complete picture of what's going on in the world, accounting systems can't give a complete picture of the entity. Accounting systems can only provide information about transactions and economic events that have been entered into the system and organized in a way that makes them accessible.

FIGURE 3.1

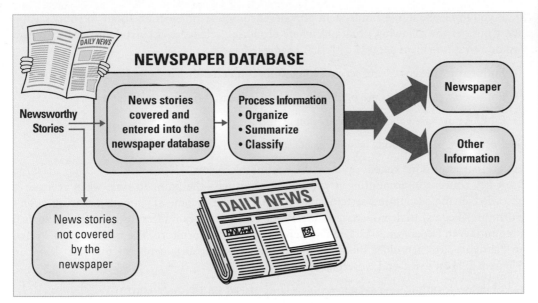

(continued)
Panel B—
Overview of
a Newspaper
Editorial Process

INSIGHT

Thinking of a Career in Accounting?

Many students enter university with the ambition of becoming professional accountants. Careers in accounting are challenging, satisfying, and rewarding, but to "make it" it's necessary to have the skills and abilities accountants require for success. The accounting profession believes that to be successful, accountants must be creative, comfortable with ambiguity, good critical thinkers and problem solvers, and they must possess strong quantitative, interpersonal, and communication skills, both written and oral.

Some students are attracted to accounting for the wrong reasons: they like the certainty, straightforwardness, and "right answers" of bookkeeping. Technical skills are important (as an accountant you have to know how to "do accounting") but that's only a small part of the skill set. So as you proceed through your introductory financial accounting course and ponder your career choices, keep in mind the things that accountants think are important for success in the profession.

ACCRUAL ACCOUNTING

In Chapter 2, I introduced accrual accounting as a method for measuring economic activity rather than using cash flows. Accountants believe that accrual accounting provides more relevant information to stakeholders than cash accounting does. Contrasting the two methods is a good way to explain accrual accounting. With cash accounting an economic event is recorded only when cash is exchanged: a sale is recorded when the customer pays cash, an expense when cash is paid to a supplier. Cash doesn't have to be exchanged when an economic event is recorded (although it may) with accrual accounting: inventory purchased on credit is recorded as an asset, and the obligation to pay the supplier is recorded as a liability. With accrual accounting, revenues and expenses can be recorded before, after, or at the same time cash changes hands. (Remember from Chapter 2 that revenue is economic benefits earned by providing goods or services to customers, and expenses are economic sacrifices made or costs incurred to earn revenue.)

If you think about it, a cash system provides incomplete information about an entity's activity. Consider the following situations where economic activity is occurring but a cash system wouldn't capture them because cash isn't changing hands:

- Entities provide goods and services to customers on credit.

- Entities have assets that are paid for before they are used (inventory, capital assets).

- Entities purchase goods and services on credit.

- Customers pay for goods or services before they receive them.

An accrual accounting system captures these economic events.

A key concept in accounting is **revenue recognition**—the point in time when revenue is recorded in the accounting system and reported in the income statement. Let's use Leon's Furniture (Leon's) to demonstrate how revenue recognition can differ under cash and accrual accounting. In December 2012, Leon's receives an order for furniture. The furniture is delivered in February 2013. Consider the three different payment arrangements for this sale shown in Figure 3.2. Leon's year-end is December 31:

- Situation 1: cash is received when the order is placed (in December 2012).

- Situation 2: cash is received on delivery of the goods to the customer (in February 2013).

- Situation 3: the customer takes advantage of a promotion whereby she doesn't have to pay for 12 months (in February 2014).

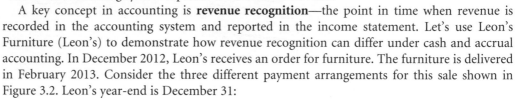

FIGURE 3.2 · Cash versus Accrual Accounting

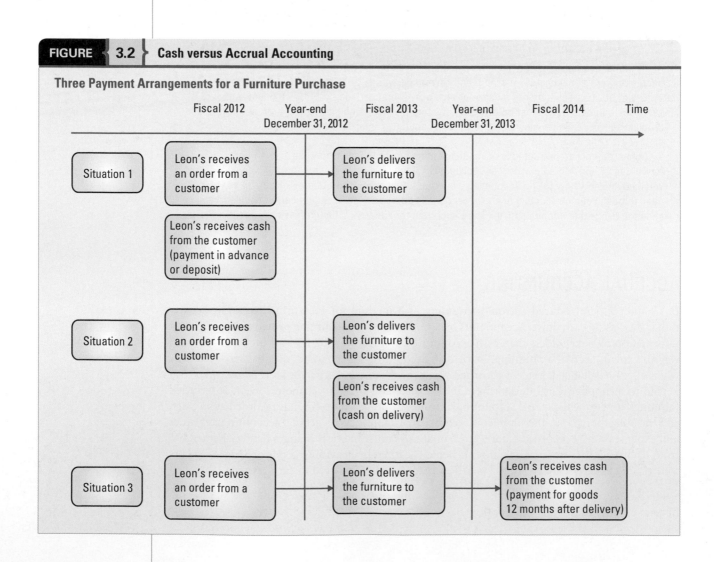

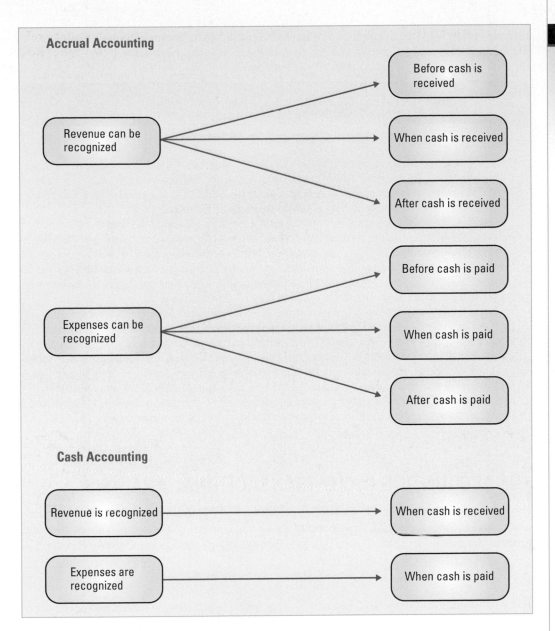

FIGURE **3.3**

Relationship between Revenue and Expense Recognition and Cash Flow

Delivery of goods to customers is typically (but not always) the economic event that triggers revenue recognition under accrual accounting, so Leon's would recognize revenue in fiscal 2013 in all three situations, regardless of when the cash is received. With cash accounting the sale would be recognized when cash is received, which is at a different time in each of the three situations.

A similar story exists for expenses. Under accrual accounting, accountants try to *match* expenses to revenue. With **matching**, expenses are recognized (recorded) in the same period as the revenue they helped earn is recognized. For the Leon's sale, the cost of the furniture sold would be expensed in the same period the revenue from the sale is recorded, regardless of when Leon's paid for the furniture. Matching is an important concept of accrual accounting. Associating economic benefits (revenues) and economic costs (expenses) is necessary if profit is to be a meaningful measure of performance. Figure 3.3 summarizes the relationship between revenue and expense recognition and cash flow under cash and accrual accounting.

While accrual accounting may provide more relevant information to stakeholders in many situations, it also requires judgment, which is subjective. With cash accounting it's obvious when a sale should be recognized—cash is received. With accrual accounting it isn't always obvious. Revenue is recognized when an entity enjoys an economic benefit, *but* someone has to decide when the benefit occurs. We will explore in Chapter 4 how managers decide when to recognize revenue and how to match expenses. For now, understand that revenue recognition and matching aren't always straightforward and can require the exercise of judgment.

INSIGHT

A Question of Timing

Sooner or later all transactions and economic events are reflected in the financial statements; it's mainly a matter of when. But the "when" matters a lot because it can have economic consequences for stakeholders and can influence the decisions they make. Under accrual accounting, it can be a matter of judgment when revenues and expenses are reported in the income statement.

Preparing financial statements only at the end of an entity's life would be much simpler for an accountant, because over the life of an entity accrual accounting and cash accounting provide the same results—there would be no decisions about when to recognize revenue and expenses. Indeed, many accounting scandals and controversies happen because financial statements are prepared periodically—monthly, quarterly, or annually—and judgment is often required in determining which period an economic event belongs to.

In the 15th and 16th centuries periodic income statements weren't important. At that time many business opportunities were operated as short-term ventures. Investors put money into a venture, like a trade voyage to the New World. The organizers purchased the necessary items, including a ship. At the end of the venture everything was sold off and the proceeds distributed among the investors. Income measurement during the trade voyage wasn't necessary and profit meant you received more than you invested. As business became more complex it was no longer possible or appropriate to sell all of a company's resources from time to time. But because stakeholders want to know how the entity is doing, the need for periodic statements of performance arose.

THE ACCOUNTING CYCLE: TRANSACTIONAL ANALYSIS

We are now going to examine the mechanics of accounting—the process of recording data about transactions and economic events in an accounting system and converting it into useful information like financial statements. At the heart of the process is the accounting equation introduced in Chapter 2:

$$\text{Assets} = \text{Liabilities} + \text{Owners' equity}$$

Every economic event is analyzed in terms of the accounting equation to determine the impact of the event on each element of the equation. The equality of the equation must be maintained with each entry to an accounting system. I will demonstrate the full accounting cycle in a straightforward, conceptual, and compact way using an *accounting equation spreadsheet*. The spreadsheet method clearly lays out the effect of transactions and economic events on the accounting equation and the process by which economic activity ultimately gets turned into financial statements. After that I will develop an approach to the accounting cycle that is a representation of the way accounting systems are structured in practice. Both of these methods apply the **double-entry bookkeeping** system in which each transaction or economic event is recorded in at least two places in the accounts. This system is necessary to keep the accounting equation in balance.

The Accounting Equation Spreadsheet and Journal Entries

In an accounting equation spreadsheet transactions and economic events are recorded to reflect their impact on the accounting equation. For example, if an entity borrows $10,000 from the bank, our analysis is that assets increase by $10,000 (the entity has more cash) and liabilities increase by $10,000 (money is owed to the bank). The effect could be shown in the following way:

Assets	=	Liabilities	+	Owners' equity
+$10,000		+$10,000		
(Cash increases)		(Bank loan increases)		

This represents a very basic accounting equation spreadsheet; each column represents one of the elements of the accounting equation and a row represents a transaction. To do this type of analysis you must answer each of the following questions:

1. Which elements of the accounting equation are affected—assets, liabilities, and/or owners' equity, including revenues and expenses?

2. How are the accounts affected—does the amount of each element increase or decrease?

3. By how much has each element increased or decreased?

Let's do some transactional analyses using this basic spreadsheet. It will be worthwhile to review the definitions of the financial statement elements (assets, liabilities, owners' equity, revenue, expenses) before proceeding. Consider the following transactions for Cheticamp Ltd. (Cheticamp):

Sells shares to investors for $50,000 cash.

- Purchases inventory and promises to pay the supplier $3,000 in 30 days.
- Provides services to a customer worth $1,100. The customer agrees to pay in 60 days.
- Collects $500 owed by a customer.
- Pays $2,000 owed to a supplier.
- Receives $2,500 from a customer for goods that will be delivered next month.

1. Cheticamp sells shares to investors for $50,000 cash.

Assets	=	Liabilities	+	Owners' equity
+$50,000	=		+	+$50,000
(Cash increases)				(Cash shares increases)

Explanation: Cheticamp received $50,000 from the investors so cash, an asset, increases. By purchasing shares the investors have made an equity investment in Cheticamp so owners' equity increases.

2. Cheticamp purchases inventory and promises to pay the supplier $3,000 in 30 days.

Assets	=	Liabilities	+	Owners' equity
+$3,000	=	+$3,000	+	
(Inventory increases)		(Accounts payable increases)		

Explanation: Cheticamp has received some inventory, which is an asset because it can be sold in the future to earn revenue. It didn't pay cash but promised to pay in 30 days so there is a liability to pay the supplier.

3. Cheticamp provides services to a customer worth $1,100. The customer agrees to pay in 60 days.

Assets	=	Liabilities	+	Owners' equity
+$1,100	=		+	+$1,100
(Accounts receivable increases)				(Revenue increases, Owners' equity increases)

Explanation: Services are provided to a customer, which represents an increase in revenue and an increase in owners' equity. The customer has agreed to pay in 60 days, which is an asset because it represents the right to receive the customer's money.

4. Cheticamp collects $500 owed by a customer.

Assets	=	Liabilities	+	Owners' equity
+$500	=		+	
(Cash increases)				
−$500				
(Accounts receivable decreases)				

Explanation: This transaction converts one asset into another. The entity received cash from a customer so assets increase. But assets also decrease because the customer has fulfilled its obligation to pay Cheticamp, which decreases asset accounts receivable.

5. Cheticamp pays $2,000 owed to a supplier.

Assets	=	Liabilities	+	Owners' equity
−$2,000	=	−$2,000	+	
(Cash decreases)		(Accounts payable decreases)		

Explanation: Cheticamp has fulfilled an obligation to a supplier by paying an amount owing so accounts payable decrease. The obligation is paid in cash so cash decreases.

6. Cheticamp receives $2,500 from a customer for goods that will be delivered next month.

Assets	=	Liabilities	+	Owners' equity
+$2,500	=	+$2,500	+	
(Cash increases)		(Unearned revenue increases)		

Explanation: Cheticamp has received cash in advance for providing goods to the customer. Cash increases since the cash was paid, but since the goods haven't been provided to the customer it's not appropriate in most cases to recognize revenue. Instead, Cheticamp has a liability to provide $2,500 of goods and services to the customer in the future.

In practice, an entity creates separate categories called **accounts** to reflect the different types of assets, liabilities, and owners' equity it has. Instead of a single column for each element of the accounting equation there will be many columns under each element, each representing a separate account. For example, an entity might have asset accounts for cash, accounts receivable, inventory, furniture, land, and any other assets the managers specify. The number and type of separate accounts an entity maintains are determined by the information managers need and want to have in their accounting system to meet their managerial and financial reporting needs. In general, a larger number of accounts provides more detailed information but at cost of making the accounting system more complicated and more costly to set up and run.

Cheticamp's transactions could be represented in a more detailed spreadsheet that breaks down assets, liabilities, and owners' equity into the different accounts (note that decreases in accounts are shown in parentheses):

	Assets			=	Liabilities		+	Owners' equity			
Transaction	Cash	Accounts receivable	Inventory		Accounts payable	Unearned revenue		Common shares	Retained earnings	Revenue	Expenses
1.	$50,000	$	$		$	$		$50,000	$	$	$
2.			3,000		3,000						
3.		1,100								1,100	
4.	500	(500)									
5.	(2,000)				(2,000)						
6.	2,500					2,500					

Before moving on to a detailed example, I'm going to introduce the method for entering transactions and economic events into an accounting system that is used in practice—journal entries. A **journal entry** describes how a transaction or economic event affects the accounting equation. A spreadsheet isn't very practical for an entity with large numbers of transactions in a year and hundreds or thousands of different asset, liability, and equity accounts. A journal entry accomplishes exactly the same thing as an entry to an accounting equation spreadsheet, but in a different format. The journal entry format showing the three key pieces of information appears below.

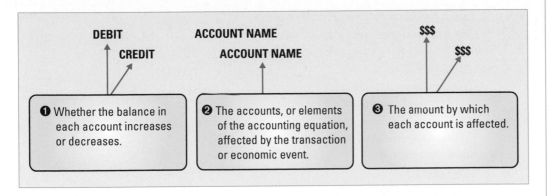

Account names in a journal entry correspond to the column headings on the spreadsheet. The terms **debit** and **credit** indicate whether the balance in the account has increased or decreased. These terms have very precise meanings in accounting and are defined as follows:

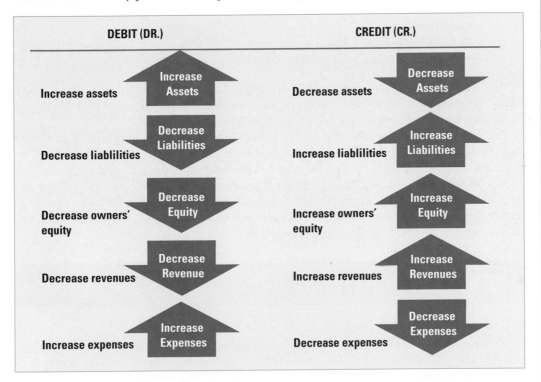

At first these terms may be confusing and cumbersome to work with. As you work with journal entries, what they mean will become second nature to you. In a journal entry the debits must equal the credits; if they don't the accounting equation won't balance.

Now we'll repeat the transactional analysis of six events that was done above for Cheticamp, only this time using journal entries. Notice that after each journal entry a brief explanation is provided.

1. Sells shares to investors for $50,000 cash.

2. Purchases inventory and promises to pay the supplier $3,000 in 30 days.

3. Provides services to a customer worth $1,100. The customer agrees to pay in 60 days.

4. Collects $500 owed by a customer.

5. Pays $2,000 owed to a supplier.

6. Receives $2,500 from a customer for goods that will be delivered next month.

1. Dr. Cash (asset +)   50,000
        Cr. Common shares (owners' equity +)   50,000
    To record the sale of shares for cash

2. Dr. Inventory (asset +)   3,000
        Cr. Accounts payable (liabilities +)   3,000
    To record the purchase of inventory on credit

3. Dr. Accounts receivable (asset +)   1,100
        Cr. Revenue (revenue +, owners' equity +)   1,100
    To record a sale on credit

4. Dr. Cash (asset +)   500
        Cr. Accounts receivable (assets −)   500
    To record collection of accounts receivable

5. Dr. Accounts payable (liabilities −)   2,000
        Cr. Cash (assets −)   2,000
    To record payment to a supplier

6. Dr. Cash (asset +)   2,500
        Cr. Unearned revenue (liabilities +)   2,500
    To record the deposit for goods to be delivered in future

After each account name shown above, the type of account (asset, liability, shareholders' equity, revenue, expense) and the direction of the change are shown. You may find this helpful for finding errors and making sure that your journal entries make sense.

Entering a transaction or economic event is a crucial step in the accounting process. Judgment must be exercised to determine if a transaction or event should be recorded, when it should be recorded, and how it should be accounted for (which elements of the accounting equation and specific accounts should be affected). Entries that occur frequently become routine and can be made by bookkeepers or clerks. However, an accountant must oversee the entry process to ensure that routine entries are done properly and that new and different transactions and economic events are carefully analyzed and interpreted.

INSIGHT

Debits and Credits

It's easy to fall into the trap of assigning qualities to debits and credits; for example, credits are good, debits are bad. While the term "credit" has positive connotations in ordinary language, it doesn't share that positive meaning in an accounting context. In accounting a credit means a decrease of an asset or an expense account or an increase to a liability, equity, or revenue account. A debit means an increase to an asset or an expense account or a decrease in a liability, equity, or revenue account. From the perspective of a journal entry, a debit amount is in the left-hand column and a credit amount is in the right-hand column. Also, the credit entry is indented.

www.mcgrawhill
connect.ca

KNOWLEDGE CHECK

A hot dog vendor operates a cart in an urban park. Prepare journal entries for the following transactions:

❑   The vendor sells food items to customers during a day for $425 cash.

❑   The vendor purchases a supply of condiments for $300 cash.

❑   The vendor pays $250 on his bank loan.

The Accounting Cycle—Example

Let's use the accounting equation spreadsheet and journal entries in a realistic business setting. In June 2014, two friends from business school, Filomena and Teresa, decide to open a small restaurant near the campus. They develop a business plan and set to work opening their restaurant, called Strawberries. They organize the business as a corporation for tax and legal liability purposes. They will use July and August to ready the restaurant and will open for business on September 1. Filomena and Teresa design their restaurant's accounting system to provide information needed to prepare tax returns and to evaluate the restaurant's performance. Thus, the accounting system will process mainly transactional information and historical costs. They will use this accounting equation spreadsheet:

			Assets			=	**Liabilities**	+		**Shareholders' equity**		
Transaction	Cash	Accounts receivable	Food, drinks, and supplies inventory	Prepaid rent	Renovations, equipment, and furniture		Bank loan	Accounts payable		Common shares	Retained earnings	Revenue	Expenses
Balance												
Transaction												
Balance												

The very top line of the spreadsheet states the accounting equation in the familiar format, with the difference that owners' equity is called shareholders' equity because Strawberries is a corporation and the owners of a corporation are called shareholders. Under each accounting equation element—asset, liability, and shareholders' equity—you find the various accounts making up the element. A transaction or economic event affecting an account will appear as a dollar amount in that account's column. Account decreases are shown in brackets. Note that only one column has been provided for each of revenue and expenses. In practice separate accounts would exist for each type of revenue and expense. The income statement details will be shown later.

To record transactions in the spreadsheet, we will follow these procedures:

- The row just under the account headings shows the balance in each account before the transaction under consideration is recorded in the spreadsheet.

- The transaction under discussion will be recorded in the next row and given a number for easy reference. This line is highlighted.

- The bottom row gives the balance in each account after the transaction is recorded. This row is the sum of the balance before the current transaction and the current transaction and that amount that will be carried forward to the next transaction.

For each transaction, the journal entry will also be provided.

The transactional analysis requires answering the following questions for each transaction and economic event (these are the same steps we examined earlier with step 2 as an additional step):

1. Which elements of the accounting equation are affected—assets, liabilities, and/or owners' equity, including revenues and expenses?

2. Which specific asset, liability, owners' equity, revenue, and expense accounts have been affected?

3. How are the accounts affected—does the amount of each account increase or decrease?

4. By how much has each specific asset, liability, owners' equity, revenue, and expense account increased or decreased?

Strawberries Transactions

1. On June 7, 2014, Filomena and Teresa set up a corporation called Strawberries Inc. They each contribute $20,000 to the corporation and receive 1,000 shares of Strawberries Inc. in return.

Transaction	Assets					=	Liabilities		+	Shareholders' equity			
	Cash	Accounts receivable	Food, drinks, and supplies inventory	Prepaid rent	Renovations, equipment, and furniture		Bank loan	Accounts payable		Common shares	Retained earnings	Revenue	Expenses
Balance													
1	$40,000									$40,000			
Balance	$40,000									$40,000			

    1. Dr. Cash (asset +)   40,000

          Cr. Common shares (shareholders' equity +)   40,000

          To record the sale of shares for cash

Strawberries Inc.'s cash (an asset) has increased by $40,000 because of Filomena and Teresa's contributions. The shares they received represent their ownership interest in Strawberries and result in an increase to common shares of $40,000. Notice the journal entry corresponds to entries on the spreadsheet: $40,000 debit to cash corresponds to $40,000 added to the cash column, $40,000 credit to common shares corresponds to $40,000 added to the common shares column. Also notice the debits equal the credits in the journal entry and in the spreadsheet the accounting equation is in balance because $40,000 was added to both sides.

2. Filomena and Teresa realize they will need more cash and take out a loan for $20,000 on July 4. Interest of $150 is due at the end of each month, beginning in September. Strawberries Inc. must begin paying back the loan in one year.

Transaction	Assets					=	Liabilities		+	Shareholders' equity			
	Cash	Accounts receivable	Food, drinks, and supplies inventory	Prepaid rent	Renovations, equipment, and furniture		Bank loan	Accounts payable		Common shares	Retained earnings	Revenue	Expenses
Balance	$40,000									$40,000			
2	$20,000						$20,000						
Balance	$60,000						$20,000			$40,000			

    2. Dr. Cash (asset +)   20,000

          Cr. Bank loan (liability +)   20,000

          To record the $20,000 bank loan

The bank loan increases Strawberries cash by $20,000 and creates a liability of $20,000—Strawberries owes the bank $20,000. As a result of the loan, cash and bank loan each increase by $20,000. The cost of borrowing the money, the interest, isn't recorded because under accrual accounting the cost of using money occurs with the passage of time. An interest expense will be recorded only after Strawberries has had the use of the money for a period of time.

3. Filomena and Teresa sign a two-year lease for space in a shopping centre and agree to pay $1,250 per month in rent beginning in September. Rent must be paid on the first day of each month with the first three months' rent due upon signing the lease. Filomena writes a cheque for $3,750.

Transaction	Cash	Accounts receivable	Food, drinks, and supplies inventory	Prepaid rent	Renovations, equipment, and furniture	Bank loan	Accounts payable	Common shares	Retained earnings	Revenue	Expenses
	Assets					**= Liabilities**		**+ Shareholders' equity**			
Balance	$60,000					$20,000		$40,000			
3	($3,750)*			$3,750							
Balance	$56,250			$3,750		$20,000		$40,000			

*Brackets indicate a decrease in the account balance.

> **3.** Dr. Prepaid rent (asset +)   3,750
> Cr. Cash (asset −)   3,750
> To record the prepayment of three months' rent

The $3,750 payment is an asset because it provides a future benefit—the right to use the location for three months beginning in September. This asset is called prepaid rent. As a result cash decreases by $3,750 and prepaid rent increases by $3,750.

The payment is treated as cash even though it was by cheque because a cheque is equivalent to cash. When a cheque is cashed the amount is removed from the bank account of the cheque writer. Also, even though the lease is for two years, only the amount paid is recorded as an asset. The right to use the location for two years at an agreed-upon price isn't recorded, even though having the lease is a benefit to Strawberries. This type of future benefit is usually not classified as an asset according to IFRS.

4. Filomena and Teresa undertake some renovations and do some plumbing and electrical work. The total cost of renovations is $15,000, all of which is paid in cash.

Transaction	Cash	Accounts receivable	Food, drinks, and supplies inventory	Prepaid rent	Renovations, equipment, and furniture	Bank loan	Accounts payable	Common shares	Retained earnings	Revenue	Expenses
	Assets					**= Liabilities**		**+ Shareholders' equity**			
Balance	$56,250			$3,750		$20,000		$40,000			
4	($15,000)				$15,000						
Balance	$41,250			$3,750	$15,000	$20,000		$40,000			

> **4.** Dr. Renovations, equipment, and furniture (asset +)   15,000
> Cr. Cash (asset −)   15,000
> To record the cost of renovating the restaurant

The renovations are an asset because they will contribute to the environment of the restaurant while it's in business—after all, a restaurant's ambiance is part of the attraction of dining out. The renovations were paid for in cash so cash decreases by $15,000 and renovations, equipment, and furniture increases by $15,000.

5. On August 10, Teresa buys equipment, furniture, dishes, and other necessary materials for $25,000. Half of the amount is paid in cash. The remainder must be paid to the supplier in 90 days.

Transaction	Cash	Accounts receivable	Food, drinks, and supplies inventory	Prepaid rent	Renovations, equipment, and furniture	Bank loan	Accounts payable	Common shares	Retained earnings	Revenue	Expenses
	Assets					**= Liabilities**		**+ Shareholders' equity**			
Balance	$41,250			$3,750	$15,000	$20,000		$40,000			
5	($12,500)				$25,000		$12,500				
Balance	$28,750			$3,750	$40,000	$20,000	$12,500	$40,000			

5. Dr. Renovations, equipment, and furniture (asset +)   25,000
  Cr. Cash (asset −)   12,500
  Cr. Accounts payable (liability +)   12,500
 To record the purchase of equipment and furniture

This transaction affects more than two accounts because the items were purchased partly for cash and partly on credit. As a result cash decreases by $12,500, the amount paid to the supplier, and there is a liability, accounts payable, to pay the supplier $12,500 in 90 days. Accounts payable are amounts owed to suppliers for goods or services purchased on credit and are usually current liabilities.

The items purchased are non-current assets because they will help Strawberries Inc. earn revenue over several years by providing the equipment to prepare meals, the dishes to serve meals on, and so on. They won't be used up, sold, or converted to cash within one year. The assets purchased are recorded at their cost of $25,000. The amount recorded is the full economic sacrifice made to acquire the assets; it doesn't matter that the full amount wasn't paid in cash at the time of purchase.

INSIGHT

Valuing Capital Assets

For the most part, capital assets (which for Strawberries is renovations, equipment, and furniture) are reported at cost. If the market value increases after it's purchased, no change is recorded in the accounting system. Under IFRS, companies can choose to value capital assets at net realizable value (the amount the asset could be sold for now), although research shows that few companies do. If an entity uses cost as the basis for valuing capital assets, the amount reported on the balance sheet doesn't provide any information about its market value.

6. As opening day approaches Strawberries hires a server and kitchen help, who will begin work when Strawberries opens. The restaurant purchases non-perishable food items and supplies for $900 and pays using its debit card. (A **debit card** allows a customer to pay for goods and services by transferring money directly from the customer's bank account to the vendor's bank account. Payment by debit card is equivalent to payment by cash.)

	Assets					=	Liabilities	+		Shareholders' equity		
Transaction	Cash	Accounts receivable	Food, drinks, and supplies inventory	Prepaid rent	Renovations, equipment, and furniture		Bank loan	Accounts payable		Common shares	Retained earnings	Revenue	Expenses
Balance	$28,750			$3,750	$40,000		$20,000	$12,500		$40,000			
6	($900)		$900										
Balance	$27,850		$900	$3,750	$40,000		$20,000	$12,500		$40,000			

6. Dr. Food, drinks, and supplies inventory (asset +)   900
  Cr. Cash (asset −)   900
 To record the purchase of inventory

The purchase for cash reduces Strawberries' cash by $900 and increases the food, drinks, and supplies inventory by $900. These purchases will contribute to meals for customers, so they are assets, and they will become expenses when they are used. The inventory is recorded at its cost.

The hiring of employees isn't recorded because they haven't done any work yet and Strawberries hasn't paid them. If the employees had worked or Strawberries had paid them, an entry would have been required. Under IFRS, these executory contracts aren't usually recorded in the accounting system. (An **executory contract** is an exchange of promises in which one party promises to supply goods or services and the other party promises to pay for them, but neither side has fulfilled its side of the bargain.)

7. During September, Strawberries purchases $12,000 of food and drinks to serve to customers. The food and drinks are paid for by debit card.

Transaction	Cash	Accounts receivable	Food, drinks, and supplies inventory	Prepaid rent	Renovations, equipment, and furniture	=	Bank loan	Accounts payable	+	Common shares	Retained earnings	Revenue	Expenses
			Assets			**=**	**Liabilities**		**+**	**Shareholders' equity**			
Balance	$27,850		$900	$3,750	$40,000		$20,000	$12,500		$40,000			
7	($12,000)		$12,000										
Balance	$15,850		$12,900	$3,750	$40,000		$20,000	$12,500		$40,000			

7. Dr. Food, drinks, and supplies inventory (asset +)	12,000	
Cr. Cash (asset −)		12,000

To record the purchase of food and drinks during September (In practice, each purchase of food and drinks would require a separate journal entry, but for the purpose of the example, all purchases are recorded in a single entry)

The food and drinks are classified as inventory because they will be used to prepare meals for customers. They will be expensed when used. Under accrual accounting, inventory is an asset until it's sold. Under a cash accounting system the purchase of food and drinks would be expensed when paid for. Cash decreases and food, drinks, and supplies inventory increases by $12,000.

8. During September Strawberries had sales of $17,900. Of these, $17,200 was for meals served in the restaurant and paid for by cash, credit card, or debit card and $700 was for a faculty party that was catered. Payment for the party is due in the middle of October.

Transaction	Cash	Accounts receivable	Food, drinks, and supplies inventory	Prepaid rent	Renovations, equipment, and furniture	=	Bank loan	Accounts payable	+	Common shares	Retained earnings	Revenue	Expenses
			Assets			**=**	**Liabilities**		**+**	**Shareholders' equity**			
Balance	$15,850		$12,900	$3,750	$40,000		$20,000	$12,500		$40,000			
8	$17,200	$700										$17,900	
Balance	$33,050	$700	$12,900	$3,750	$40,000		$20,000	$12,500		$40,000		$17,900	

8. Dr. Cash (asset +)	17,200	
Dr. Accounts receivable (asset +)	700	
Cr. Revenue (shareholders' equity +, revenue +)		17,900

To record sales for the month of September

All sales during the month are recorded as revenue. The amount owed for catering is an asset because it represents cash that will be received in the future, so $700 is recorded as accounts receivable, the usual account name for amounts owed by customers.

It isn't always obvious when revenue should be recorded. For example, did Strawberries enjoy an economic benefit from catering the faculty party when the order was received, when the event was catered, or when the cash was collected? Arguments can be made in support of each. Under IFRS and accrual accounting, it's not necessary to wait until cash is received to record a sale. On the other hand, IFRS encourage caution in deciding when to record a sale. If revenue is recorded too soon the financial statements could be unreliable. For example, if the faculty party was cancelled at the last minute and Strawberries had recorded the revenue when the order was received, revenue that never happened would be reported. In contrast, the only logical time to recognize revenue for the people who eat at Strawberries is when they pay at the end of their meals.

Although the $17,900 of sales was recorded on a single line on the spreadsheet and in a single journal entry, in fact a separate line would be added for each individual sale or each day's sales.

9, 10. At the end of September, Strawberries Inc. paid $525 for utilities and $925 in wages to its employees.

	Assets					=	Liabilities		+	Shareholders' equity			
Transaction	Cash	Accounts receivable	Food, drinks, and supplies inventory	Prepaid rent	Renovations, equipment, and furniture		Bank loan	Accounts payable		Common shares	Retained earnings	Revenue	Expenses
Balance	$33,050	$700	$12,900	$3,750	$40,000		$20,000	$12,500		$40,000		$17,900	
9	($525)												($525)*
10	($925)												($925)**
Balance	$31,600	$700	$12,900	$3,750	$40,000		$20,000	$12,500		$40,000		$17,900	($1,450)

*Utilities expense
**Wages expense

9, 10.	Dr. Utilities expense (shareholders' equity −, expenses +)	525	
	Dr. Wage expense (shareholders' equity −, expenses +)	925	
	Cr. Cash (asset −)		1,450
	To record the utilities and wages expenses for the month of September		

The utilities and wage payments are costs of operating the restaurant in September and represent expenses for the month. Since these expenses were paid in cash, cash decreases by $1,450. Notice in the spreadsheet that expenses are recorded as negative amounts (in brackets). This is done because expenses reduce shareholders' equity. Notice that both expenses were recorded as part of a single journal entry. Each expense could have also been recorded with a separate journal entry.

11. At the end of September, Strawberries Inc. pays the bank $150 interest for the loan.

	Assets					=	Liabilities		+	Shareholders' equity			
Transaction	Cash	Accounts receivable	Food, drinks, and supplies inventory	Prepaid rent	Renovations, equipment, and furniture		Bank loan	Accounts payable		Common shares	Retained earnings	Revenue	Expenses
Balance	$31,600	$700	$12,900	$3,750	$40,000		$20,000	$12,500		$40,000		$17,900	($1,450)
11	($150)												($150)*
Balance	$31,450	$700	$12,900	$3,750	$40,000		$20,000	$12,500		$40,000		$17,900	($1,600)

*Interest expense

11.	Dr. Interest expense (shareholders' equity −, expenses +)	150	
	Cr. Cash (asset −)		150
	To record the interest expense for the month of September		

The interest cost is a $150 expense. Cash decreases by $150 since it was paid in cash. If Strawberries hadn't made the interest payment at the end of September, it would still be recorded as an expense. Accrual accounting records as expenses any costs incurred to earn revenue during the period, regardless of when cash is paid. If Strawberries had the use of the bank's money during September but didn't pay the interest by the end of the month, it should expense the interest in that month and record a liability called interest payable (instead of a decrease in cash).

12. One of Strawberries' major operating costs is the food, drinks, and supplies used in preparing meals. At the end of September Teresa counted the food, drinks, and supplies inventory and found there were items costing $1,000 on hand. Because Strawberries had $12,900 of food, drinks, and supplies available during September and there was $1,000 left in inventory at the end of the month, this means that $11,900 ($12,900 − $1,000) was used.

Transaction	Assets					=	Liabilities		+	Shareholders' equity			
	Cash	Accounts receivable	Food, drinks, and supplies inventory	Prepaid rent	Renovations, equipment, and furniture		Bank loan	Accounts payable		Common shares	Retained earnings	Revenue	Expenses
Balance	$31,450	$700	$12,900	$3,750	$40,000		$20,000	$12,500		$40,000		$17,900	($1,600)
12			($11,900)										($11,900)*
Balance	$31,450	$700	$1,000	$3,750	$40,000		$20,000	$12,500		$40,000		$17,900	($13,500)

*Food, drinks, and supplies expense

12. Dr. Cost of sales (shareholders' equity −, expenses +)   11,900
    Cr. Food, drinks, and supplies inventory (asset −)   11,900
    To record the cost of food, drinks, and supplies used to provide meals to customers

An expense of $11,900 reflects the cost of food, drinks, and supplies used to earn revenue during September and the amount of food, drinks, and supplies inventory decreases by $11,900. By expensing the $11,900 we are *matching* the cost of the meals served to the revenue earned from providing those meals.

13. When Filomena paid $3,750 to the shopping centre owner the amount was recorded as an asset, prepaid rent. At the end of September, Strawberries has used up part of that asset. An asset that is used or consumed becomes an expense (another example of matching). This means the $1,250 ($3,750 ÷ 3) cost of September's rent can be matched to revenues earned in September. One month of prepaid rent has been used up so prepaid rent is reduced by $1,250 and there is a $1,250 rent expense for September. The remaining $2,500 balance in prepaid rent represents the right to use the space in the shopping centre in October and November, so it's still an asset.

Transaction	Assets					=	Liabilities		+	Shareholders' equity			
	Cash	Accounts receivable	Food, drinks, and supplies inventory	Prepaid rent	Renovations, equipment, and furniture		Bank loan	Accounts payable		Common shares	Retained earnings	Revenue	Expenses
Balance	$31,450	$700	$1,000	$3,750	$40,000		$20,000	$12,500		$40,000		$17,900	($13,500)
13				($1,250)									($1,250)*
Balance	$31,450	$700	$1,000	$2,500	$40,000		$20,000	$12,500		$40,000		$17,900	($14,750)

*Rent expense

13. Dr. Rent expense (shareholders' equity −, expenses +)   1,250
    Cr. Prepaid rent (asset −)   1,250
    To record the rent expense for September

14. During September Strawberries will have consumed some of its renovations, equipment, and furniture while operating its business. The renovations have future benefit as long as the restaurant occupies that particular location. As the lease period expires so do the benefits associated with the renovations. The equipment and furniture will eventually wear out, break down, or become obsolete.

	Assets					=	Liabilities		+	Shareholders' equity			
Transaction	Cash	Accounts receivable	Food, drinks, and supplies inventory	Prepaid rent	Renovations, equipment, and furniture		Bank loan	Accounts payable		Common shares	Retained earnings	Revenue	Expenses
Balance	$31,450	$700	$1,000	$2,500	$40,000		$20,000	$12,500		$40,000		$17,900	($14,750)
14					($1,042)								($1,042)*
Balance	$31,450	$700	$1,000	$2,500	$38,958		$20,000	$12,500		$40,000		$17,900	($15,792)

*Depreciation expense

14. Dr. Depreciation expense (shareholders' equity −, expenses +)   1,042
      Cr. Renovations, equipment, and furniture (asset −)   1,042
      To record the depreciation of renovations, equipment, and furniture

The renovations will be depreciated over two years, the period of Strawberries' lease. It's not possible to determine the renovations' contribution to revenue each month, so we will simply depreciate an equal amount of the cost each month: $625 ($15,000 ÷ 24 months). Depreciating an equal amount of the cost of an asset each period is called **straight-line depreciation**. Managers have some opportunity to exercise judgment here. If, for example, Strawberries has the option to renew its lease for another two years the managers could argue for depreciating over four years rather than two.

The equipment and furniture are handled in the same way. However, these assets can be moved to other locations, so their useful lives aren't limited to the term of the lease and an assumption must be made about how long they will provide benefits to Strawberries. We will assume the useful life of the equipment and furniture is five years (this is a simplification because it's likely the individual assets have a variety of useful lives) and depreciate it using the straight-line method over 60 months. The depreciation expense for September for the equipment and furniture should be $417 ($25,000 ÷ 60 months). Therefore, the depreciation expense for September is $1,042 ($625 + $417) and renovations, equipment, and furniture decreases by $1,042.

INSIGHT

Depreciation

Depreciation (or amortization) allocates the cost of a capital asset to expense over its useful life. It's also another example of matching. Since property, plant, and equipment (PPE) help an entity earn revenue, its cost should be matched to the revenue it helps earn. This type of matching can be hard to do; after all, how do a chair, an oven, or paint on a wall contribute to revenue? Still, the job has to be done, so accountants or managers estimate how long capital assets will be used (useful life) and choose a method for depreciating the cost.

Depreciation provides no information whatsoever about the change in the market value of capital assets. It's just the allocation of the cost to expense.

15. At the end of September, Filomena and Teresa decide to declare and pay a dividend of $0.50 per share, or $1,000 ($0.50 × 2,000 shares). They didn't pay themselves a salary in September, but they could have.

Transaction	Assets					=	Liabilities		+	Shareholders' equity			
	Cash	Accounts receivable	Food, drinks, and supplies inventory	Prepaid rent	Renovations, equipment, and furniture		Bank loan	Accounts payable		Common shares	Retained earnings	Revenue	Expenses
Balance	$31,450	$700	$1,000	$2,500	$38,958		$20,000	$12,500		$40,000		$17,900	($15,792)
15	($1,000)										($1,000)		
Balance	$30,450	$700	$1,000	$2,500	$38,958		$20,000	$12,500		$40,000	($1,000)	$17,900	($15,792)

15. Dr. Retained earnings (shareholders' equity –)   1,000
       Cr. Cash (asset –)   1,000
    To record the payment of a dividend of $0.50 per share

Retained earnings decreases when dividends are paid because some of the shareholders' investment is being returned to them. (Remember from Chapter 2 that retained earnings is the accumulated earnings of a business over its life, less dividends paid, and represents an indirect investment in the company by the owners.) Cash decreases by $1,000 because the dividend is paid in cash.

We have now accounted for all the transactions and other economic events that affected Strawberries in September 2014. All the activity is summarized in a single spreadsheet in Table 3.1. The table provides a separate account for each type of expense rather than aggregating all expenses into a single account. The beauty of the accounting equation spreadsheet for learning purposes is in how it simplifies preparation of the financial statements. The second row of the spreadsheet provides the names of the balance sheet and income statement accounts and the bottom row provides the amounts in each account at the end of the period. All you have to do to prepare the balance sheet and income statement is reorganize the information into an appropriate format. The statements for Strawberries are provided in Table 3.2.

Another attractive feature of the spreadsheet is that it's easy to see how the different ways of accounting for transactions and economic events affect the financial statements. For example, if we wanted to see how depreciating the equipment and furniture over 10 years instead of five would affect net income, we would just change the amount recorded for entry 14 and recalculate. If the equipment and furniture were depreciated over 10 years the expense would be $208 per month ($25,000 ÷ 120 months), the total depreciation expense for September would be $833 ($625 + $208), and net income would be $2,317, almost 10 percent more than our original calculation.

Notice that dividends aren't included in the calculation of net income. Net income represents the amount that is left for the owners after all other stakeholders (such as employees, lenders, and suppliers) have been considered, so payments of dividends aren't included. Also, the ending balance in the retained earnings account in Table 3.1 isn't the same as the amount on the balance sheet. If you add the balances in the revenue and expense accounts to retained earnings you will get the correct amount. (This process will be discussed later in this chapter in the section on closing entries.)

TABLE 3.1	Complete Accounting Equation Spreadsheet for Strawberries Inc.						
						=	**Liabilities**
		Assets					
Transaction	Cash	Accounts receivable	Food, drinks, and supplies inventory	Prepaid rent	Renovations, equipment, and furniture	Bank loan	Accounts payable
1	$40,000						
2	$20,000					$20,000	
3	($3,750)			$3,750			
4	($15,000)				$15,000		
5	($12,500)				$25,000		$12,500
6	($900)		$900				
7	($12,000)		$12,000				
8	$17,200	$700					
9	($525)						
10	($925)						
11	($150)						
12			($11,900)				
13				($1,250)			
14					($1,042)		
15	($1,000)						
Balance	**$30,450**	**$700**	**$1,000**	**$2,500**	**$38,958**	**$20,000**	**$12,500**

TABLE 3.2	Balance Sheet and Income Statement for Strawberries Inc.

Strawberries Inc.
Balance Sheet
As of September 30, 2014

Assets		Liabilities and Shareholders' equity	
Cash	$30,450	Bank loan	$20,000
Accounts receivable	700	Accounts payable	12,500
Food, drinks, and supplies inventory	1,000	Total liabilities	32,500
Prepaid rent	2,500	**Shareholders' equity**	
Renovations, equipment, and furniture	38,958	Common shares	40,000
		Retained earnings	1,108
		Total Shareholders' equity	41,108
		Total Liabilities and	
Total Assets	$73,608	Shareholders' equity	$73,608

Strawberries Inc.
Income Statement
For the Month Ended September 30, 2014

Sales		$17,900
Expenses		
Cost of sales	$11,900	
Rent	1,250	
Depreciation	1,042	
Wages	925	
Utilities	525	
Interest	150	
Total expenses		15,792
Net income		$ 2,108

+		Shareholders' equity							
	Common shares	Retained earnings	Sales	Cost of sales	Rent expense	Wages expense	Utilities expense	Depreciation expense	Interest expense
	$40,000								
			$17,900						
							($525)		
						($925)			
									($150)
				($11,900)					
					($1,250)				
								($1,042)	
		($1,000)							
	$40,000	($1,000)	$17,900	($11,900)	($1,250)	($925)	($525)	($1,042)	($150)

QUESTION FOR CONSIDERATION

Why does net income (revenue and expenses) affect retained earnings?

Answer: Revenue represents economic benefits earned by an entity from providing goods and services to customers and expenses are the economic sacrifices incurred to earn those benefits. Together they represent the net benefit or sacrifice for the entity, which belongs to the owners. As a result, when an entity has net income the owners' interest in the entity increases, which is reflected in the equity section, specifically in retained earnings, of the balance sheet. If an entity suffers a loss, equity decreases.

Now that we have prepared Strawberries Inc.'s balance sheet and income statement, what do we do with them? What do they tell us? In general, financial statements raise questions rather than provide definite answers. Strawberries' financial statements must be used with special care because they provide information for only the first month of operations. Nonetheless, a number of questions can be asked and observations made.

1. How well has Strawberries Inc. done? With only the first month's performance and nothing to compare it with, it's difficult to say. Perhaps if we had information about how restaurants do when they first begin operations we would have a better idea. After Strawberries has been operating for a few years we could compare its performance with other years or other restaurants. A stakeholder must be very cautious when making comparisons using the accounting information of different entities. Nonetheless, it isn't possible to make sense of accounting information without some benchmarks or bases for comparison.

2. Some analyses we can do suggest that Strawberries has done reasonably well in its first month:

- It has "turned a profit" of $2,108, which is a good start. It's very difficult to succeed in the restaurant business.

- The net income of $2,108 represents a return on equity of about 5 percent on Filomena and Teresa's $41,108 equity in Strawberries (return on equity = net income ÷ shareholders' equity = $2,108 ÷ $41,108). **Return on equity (ROE)** is a measure of the profitability of an entity and its effectiveness in using the assets provided by the owners to generate net income.

- Strawberries Inc.'s profit margin ratio (net income ÷ sales) is almost 12 percent, meaning that for every dollar of sales it earns $0.12. The **profit margin ratio** is a measure of how effective the entity is at controlling expenses and reflects the amount of income earned for each dollar of sales.

However, as I already pointed out, it's very difficult to draw conclusions from these statements without benchmarks or bases for comparison.

3. Why does Strawberries have so much cash? The new restaurant borrowed $20,000 from the bank, yet it has more than that amount in cash on September 30. It owes $12,500 to the restaurant supply company that it must repay in two months, so at this point it has the cash to meet that obligation. Should Strawberries reduce its bank loan? Or do Teresa and Filomena have plans for the money? Perhaps major purchases are still required. Certainly some of the cash will be needed to buy more food inventory.

4. While Strawberries seems to have a large cash balance, starting up and operating for a month consumed a lot of cash. Table 3.3 shows Strawberries' cash flow since it was incorporated. This statement was prepared by organizing the transactions in the cash column of the accounting equation spreadsheet.

TABLE 3.3 Strawberries Inc.'s Cash Flow		
Strawberries Inc. **Cash Flow Statement** **For the Period Ended September 30, 2014**		
Cash inflows		
Shareholders	$40,000	
Bank	20,000	
Sales	17,200	
Total cash inflows		$77,200
Cash outflows		
Renovations, furniture, and equipment	27,500	
Inventory	12,900	
Rent	3,750	
Utilities	525	
Wages	925	
Interest	150	
Dividends	1,000	
Total cash outflows		46,750
Net cash flow		$30,450

TABLE 3.4 Strawberries Inc.'s Cash from Operations		
Strawberries Inc. **Cash from Operations** **For the Period Ended September 30, 2014**		
Cash inflows from sales		$17,200
Cash outflows		
Inventory	12,900	
Rent	3,750	
Utilities	525	
Wages	925	
Interest	150	18,250
Net cash flow		($ 1,050)

The cash flow situation isn't nearly as favourable if you remember that $60,000 of this cash came from the bank and the owners. If we ignore these inflows, net cash flow is negative (cash inflows from sales − cash outflows = $17,200 − $46,750 = $−29,550), meaning Strawberries spent $29,550 more than it took in to get the restaurant up and running and for operating it in September.

Also, cash from operations (cash from or used by an entity's regular business activities) is −$1,050, which means that business operations used more cash than was generated. Cash from operations for Strawberries is shown in Table 3.4. This statement is also prepared using the cash column in Table 3.1. For this statement it's necessary to identify the operating cash flows and ignore non-operating ones (investment by owners, loans, purchases of equipment).

5. Strawberries' large cash balance means it can easily pay the accounts payable as well as purchase inventory, and it generally will be able to pay its debts as they come due. Strawberries' current ratio is 1.07 to 1 (current assets ÷ current liabilities = $34,650 ÷ $32,500), not usually considered to be very high. But the bank loan doesn't have to be paid for almost a year, suggesting the low current ratio isn't a significant problem yet.

6. The income statement doesn't tell us much about how Strawberries will perform in the future. The encouraging performance in the first month may be due to curiosity by local people who may not come back. Alternatively, next month may be even better as more people learn about the new restaurant. It isn't possible to predict what will happen based on the first month's performance of a restaurant.

In general, one of the limitations of general purpose financial statements is that they are prepared mainly on the basis of events that have already happened so they don't tell us very much about the future. Historical cost, transactional-based statements can sometimes be a starting point to predict the future. However, in the case of new entities such as Strawberries, or even for established entities facing significant change, the statements may not be very helpful for this.

KNOWLEDGE CHECK

www.mcgrawhill connect.ca

❑ What is depreciation and why are capital assets depreciated?

❑ What is the profit margin ratio and what does it mean?

❑ Describe the effect (increase or decrease) that debits and credits have on asset, liability, owners' equity, revenue, and expense accounts.

ADJUSTING ENTRIES

An entry into an accrual accounting system is usually triggered by a transaction—an exchange between the entity and an external party. In the Strawberries Inc. example most of the entries represented exchanges with outside parties (bankers, suppliers, and customers). But some economic events affecting an entity aren't transactions, and these events must sometimes be recorded in the accounting system; entries 12, 13, and 14 are examples. Entries to an accrual accounting system that aren't triggered by exchanges with outside entities are called **adjusting entries**. At the end of each reporting period managers identify events during the period that haven't been captured by the accounting system and make any necessary adjustments. Adjusting entries aren't required in a cash accounting system because recording is triggered only by the exchange of cash, which must involve an outside entity.

Adjusting entries are necessary in accrual accounting because recognition of revenues and expenses doesn't always correspond with cash flows. In Strawberries' case, Filomena signed a two-year lease in July and paid rent in advance for September, October, and November. As a result of that exchange we recorded an asset called prepaid rent. At the end of September some of that prepaid rent had been used up so we reduced the amount of prepaid rent and recorded a rent expense. This event didn't involve an exchange with another entity but the consumption of the prepaid rent had to be reflected in the accounting records.

Before we discuss adjusting entries in detail, note the following:

1. Adjusting entries are required because revenues and expenses can be recognized at times other than when cash is exchanged.

2. Every adjusting entry involves a balance sheet account and an income statement account.

3. Every adjusting entry is associated with a transactional entry that is recorded before or after the adjusting entry. A **transactional entry** is a journal entry triggered by an exchange with another entity.

4. Adjusting entries are required only when financial statements are prepared.

5. Adjusting entries never involve cash. If cash is part of the entry, it isn't an adjusting entry.

There are four types of adjusting entries. They are summarized Table 3.5.

TABLE 3.5	Four Types of Adjusting Entries				
Type	**Situation**	**Examples**	**Entry made in the current or previous period (Transactional Entry)**	**Entry made at the end of the current period (Adjusting Entry)**	**Entry made in the next period (Transactional Entry)**
Deferred expense/ prepaid expense	Cash is paid before the expense is recognized	Prepaid insurance Prepaid rent Capital assets	Dr. Asset Cr. Cash	Dr. Expense Cr. Asset	No entry
Deferred revenue	Cash is received before revenue is recognized	Deposits Subscriptions Advances Gift certificates	Dr. Cash Cr. Liability	Dr. Liability Cr. Revenue	No entry
Accrued expense/ accrued liability	Expense is recognized before cash is paid	Wages Utilities Interest payable	No entry	Dr. Expense Cr. Liability	Dr. Liability Cr. Cash
Accrued revenue/ accrued asset	Revenue is recognized before cash is received	Interest earned Royalties earned	No entry	Dr. Asset Cr. Revenue	Dr. Cash Cr. Asset

INSIGHT

Earnings Management

Managers are responsible for preparing an entity's accounting information, whether prepared in accordance with IFRS, GAAP, or on some other basis, and they are often able to choose how to account for, disclose, and present information about transactions and economic events. These choices can significantly impact the numbers in the financial statements and the information disclosed in the statements and the notes, which in turn can have significant economic consequences for stakeholders. Managers' use of accounting choices to achieve their own objectives is referred to as **earnings management**. While the term suggests a focus on net income, it also applies to choices made that affect any amounts reported in the financial statements, such as assets or liabilities, or disclosure in the notes.

We have already touched on how managers can manage earnings; for example, by choosing accounting policies, such as how to recognize revenue or depreciate capital assets, and in making accounting estimates such as the useful life of capital assets, the amount of accounts receivable that won't be collected, or the amount of sales that will be returned. This Insight box is intended to introduce the concept of earnings management and to put it on your radar screen as you work through the book. Each chapter will explain managers' opportunities to use accounting's inherent flexibility to make choices that affect the information reported in the financial statements and that may impose economic consequences for you.

Types of Adjusting Entries

1. Deferred Expense/Prepaid Expense Entities often purchase assets providing benefits for more than one period, including insurance policies, equipment, buildings, and patents. The terms **deferred expense** and **prepaid expense** refer to assets acquired in one period but not expensed, at least in part, until a later period or periods. This adjusting entry reduces the amount of the asset reported on the balance sheet and recognizes an expense for the portion of the asset that has been consumed in the period.

On January 5, 2014, Dahlia Ltd. (Dahlia) purchases three years of insurance coverage for $9,000 cash. The insurance covers the period January 1, 2014 to December 31, 2016. Dahlia's year-end is December 31.

When Dahlia purchases the insurance it makes the following journal entry:

Dr. Prepaid insurance (asset +)	9,000	
Cr. Cash (asset −)		9,000

To record the purchase of insurance for the period January 1, 2014, to December 31, 2016

This is a transactional entry because an exchange has taken place between Dahlia and the insurance company. The insurance is set up as an asset because the three years of coverage is a future benefit.

On December 31, 2014 an adjusting entry is needed because one year of the insurance coverage has been used up and should be expensed. The balance sheet on December 31, 2014 should report $6,000 of prepaid insurance for the remaining two years of coverage and there should be an insurance expense of $3,000 on the 2014 income statement to reflect the cost of insurance for the year. With no adjusting entry Dahlia's balance sheet would report $9,000 of prepaid insurance, implying three years of available coverage when there are only two, and expenses in 2014 would be understated by $3,000. On December 31, 2014, Dahlia should make this adjusting entry:

Dr. Insurance expense (expenses +, shareholders' equity −)	3,000	
Cr. Prepaid insurance (asset −)		3,000

To record the cost of insurance used in the year ended December 31, 2014
($9,000 ÷ 3 years of coverage = $3,000)

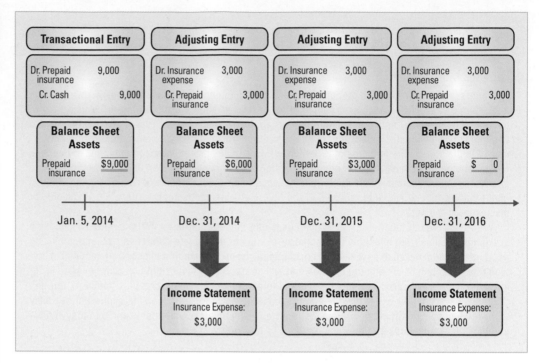

This is an adjusting entry because it isn't triggered by an exchange with another entity. It's assumed that the cost of the insurance is the same each year and the same adjusting entry is required on December 31, 2015 and 2016 to reflect the cost of insurance coverage and reduce the balance in the prepaid insurance account each year. The accounting impacts of the adjusting entries are shown in Figure 3.4.

Figure 3.4 shows the amount of prepaid insurance decreasing as the coverage is used up over time, and each year's expense matches the asset account's decrease. At the end of the life of the insurance policy on December 31, 2016 the amount of prepaid insurance on the balance sheet is zero.

If Dahlia's insurance policy came into effect on July 1, 2014 and ran until June 30, 2017, the adjusting entry would be a bit different. It would reflect that on December 31, 2014 only half of a year's insurance had been used and the expense was $1,500 ($3,000 ÷ 2):

> Dr. Insurance expense (expenses + shareholders' equity −)   1,500
>   Cr. Prepaid insurance (asset −)   1,500
> To record the cost of insurance used from July 1, 2014 to December 31, 2014
> ([$9,000 ÷ 3 years of coverage] × 1/2 year = $1,500)

Depreciation of capital assets is another type of this adjusting entry. Capital assets such as buildings, vehicles, machinery, computers, and furniture help earn revenue over more than one period so the cost must be expensed over the asset's life.

On January 2, 2013, Kaslo Ltd. (Kaslo) purchased a new delivery truck for $50,000 cash. Management estimates the truck will have a useful life of five years. Kaslo depreciates its trucks on a straight-line basis, which means it will expense an equal amount of the cost in each year of the asset's life. This adjusting entry would be recorded at the end of each year:

> Dr. Depreciation expense (expenses +, shareholders' equity −)   10,000
>   Cr. Accumulated depreciation (contra asset +)   10,000
> Adjusting entry to record depreciation of the truck
> (Cost of the asset ÷ estimated useful life = $50,000 ÷ 5 years = $10,000 per year)

The truck account isn't credited directly for the period's depreciation; the credit is made to accumulated depreciation. The accumulated depreciation account is referred to as a **contra-asset account**, which accumulates amounts deducted from a related asset. This makes information about

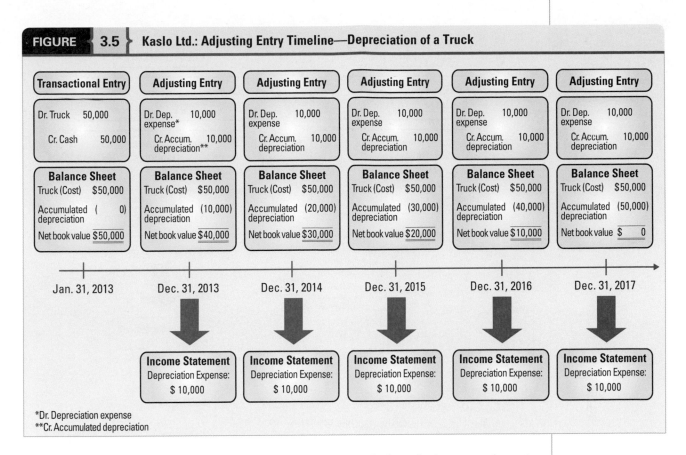

FIGURE 3.5 Kaslo Ltd.: Adjusting Entry Timeline—Depreciation of a Truck

the cost of an asset readily available from the accounting system, which can be important for various reasons, including for tax purposes. The balance in the accumulated depreciation account isn't meaningful by itself, but taken together the cost of capital assets less the accumulated depreciation gives the asset's **carrying amount**.

The accounting impact of the adjusting entries on Kaslo's financial statements is shown in Figure 3.5. Notice the balance in the truck account itself remains at $50,000 all the time. The accumulated depreciation increases by $10,000 each year, the amount of the annual depreciation expense and the carrying amount of the truck decreases by $10,000 each year.

KNOWLEDGE CHECK

www.mcgrawhill
connect.ca

Return to the Dahlia Ltd. example where Dahlia purchased its three-year insurance policy on July 1, 2012, for $9,000.

❑   What adjusting journal entries would be required on December 31, 2015 and 2016?

2. Deferred Revenue Sometimes an entity receives payment for goods or services before it recognizes the revenue. For example, a fan purchases tickets to a concert months before the show or a customer pays a deposit for delivery of goods some time later. If the entity recognizes revenue when the concert is performed or the goods are delivered it would record a liability when payment is received. The liability represents the obligation to provide the good or service the customer paid for. An adjusting entry is necessary when the revenue is recognized and the obligation is fulfilled.

On November 15, 2014 a traveller purchased a ticket for a January 18, 2015 flight from St. John's to Vancouver on Candiac Airlines Ltd. (Candiac) for $1,350. Candiac's year-end is December 31. When the passenger bought the ticket, Candiac made the following journal entry.

FIGURE 3.6

Candiac Airlines Inc.: Deferred Revenue Adjusting Entries

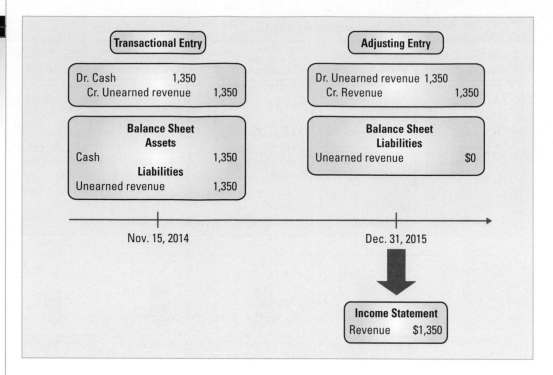

Dr. Cash (asset +)   1,350
    Cr. Unearned revenue (liability +)   1,350
To record cash received for a flight from St. John's to Vancouver on January 18, 2015

This is a transactional entry because it involves an interaction with an outside entity, the traveller. When Candiac received the payment revenue wasn't recognized because it had not provided the transportation. The unearned revenue liability represents Candiac's obligation to provide the trip on January 18, 2015. The amount is the payment received from the customer. **Unearned revenue** is a liability that is recorded when cash is received before revenue is recognized. When the traveller takes the trip, Candiac recognizes the revenue and makes the following adjusting entry:

Dr. Unearned revenue (liability −)   1,350
    Cr. Revenue (revenue +, shareholders' equity +)   1,350
To record revenue earned

This is an adjusting entry because it doesn't involve an outside entity. The accounting impact of this example is shown in Figure 3.6.

3. Accrued Expense/Accrued Liability This adjusting entry is needed when an entity has incurred an expense but an external event such as receipt of an invoice hasn't triggered the recording of the expense and related liability. An **accrued expense** is an expense recognized in the financial statements before a cash payment is made or an external event triggers an entry. Recognition of the expense gives rise to an **accrued liability** to pay for the expense. The accrued expense/accrued liability adjusting entry ensures that all costs of doing business in a period are expensed in that period and all liabilities are recorded. Note that no adjusting entry is required if the entity received an invoice or another external trigger. In that case, the expense and liability are recorded as a transactional entry, not an adjusting entry.

Every other Thursday, Babbit Inc. (Babbit) pays its employees for the two weeks ended the previous Friday. On June 27, 2013, employees were paid for the two weeks ended June 21. The next pay period runs from June 22 through July 5. Babbit's year-end is June 30. Because the year-end falls in the middle of a pay period an adjusting entry must record, or *accrue*, the wage expense for the last nine days of June and the liability for the wages owed on June 30. Even though the employees won't be paid until July 11, the amount earned from June 22 through July 5 should be expensed in fiscal 2013. Babbit would make the following adjusting entry on June 30, 2013, assuming employees earned $22,500 in the last nine days of June:

Dr. Wage expense (expenses +, shareholders' equity −)   22,500
    Cr. Accrued wages payable (liabilities +)   22,500
To accrue wage expense for the last nine days of June

The transactional entry is recorded on July 11 when the pay period ends and employees are paid:

Dr. Accrued wages payable (liabilities −)   22,500
Dr. Wage expense (expenses +, shareholders' equity −)   10,000
    Cr. Cash (assets −)   32,500
To record payment of wages for the last nine days of June and the first five days of July

The cash payment of $32,500 has two components:

a. Payment of $22,500 fulfills the liability recorded on June 30, 2013 for work expensed for the last nine days of June.

b. Payment of $10,000 for wages earned in the first five days of July. This amount is expensed in fiscal 2014.

The July 2013 entry is a transactional entry because completing the pay period and paying the employees triggers it. The balance sheet and income statement effects of this scenario are summarized in Figure 3.7.

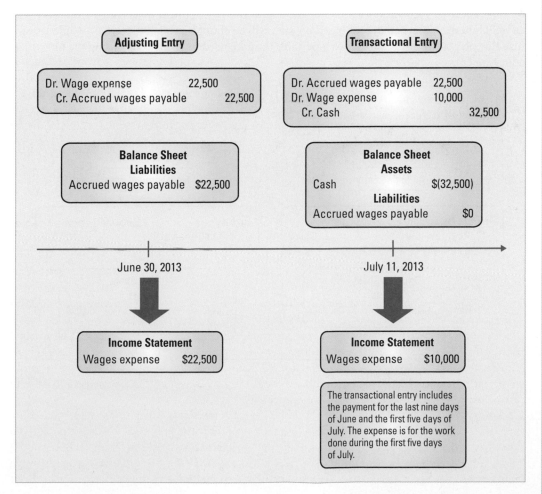

FIGURE 3.7

Babbit Inc.: Accrued Expense/ Accrued Liability Adjusting Entries

? QUESTION FOR CONSIDERATION

A sports fan buys tickets for a game. The game will be played in six months, which is in the team's next fiscal accounting year. When the fan purchases the ticket, the team records the following journal entry:

> Dr. Cash   xxx
> Cr. Unearned revenue   xxx

The team recognizes revenue from its games when the games are actually played. Explain why an adjusting entry is necessary to recognize revenue when the game is played.

Answer: The exchange between the fan and the team occurs when the fan pays for the tickets. There is no exchange between the fan and the team when the game is actually played so an adjusting entry is required to recognize revenue in that period.

4. Accrued Revenue/Accrued Asset **Accrued revenue** is revenue recognized before cash is received. The adjusting entry is required when an entity has earned revenue but there was no exchange with another entity to trigger the recording of it. A receivable (an asset) is also recorded to reflect the coming payment. For example, interest and royalties earned in a period might not be paid until a later period. An adjusting entry records the revenue in the period it's earned. This type of adjusting entry is recorded before the transactional entry.

Jalobert Ltd. (Jalobert) is a real estate company that owns a shopping mall in western Canada. Retail tenants pay rent based on the size of the store plus 2 percent of annual sales. The rent based on sales must be paid within 90 days of the end of the year. For the year ended December 31, 2014, Jalobert estimates that rent based on sales will be about $2,000,000. Jalobert would recognize this revenue in fiscal 2014 since it pertains to space used in 2014 by recording the following adjusting entry:

> Dr. Rent receivable (asset +)   2,000,000
> Cr. Rent revenue (revenue +, shareholders' equity +)   2,000,000
> To record accrual of rent revenue during 2014

FIGURE 3.8

Jalobert Ltd.: Accrued Revenue/ Accrued Asset Adjusting Entries

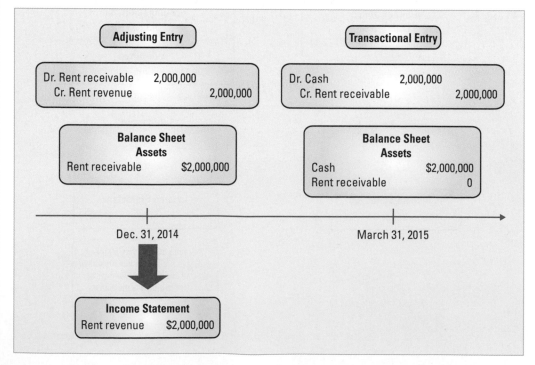

When payment is received on March 31, 2015, Jalobert would record the following transactional entry (we'll assume all the payments arrive at the same time and the $2,000,000 estimate was accurate):

Dr. Cash (asset +)	2,000,000	
Cr. Rent receivable (asset –)		2,000,000
To record cash received for rent revenue earned in 2014		

If the actual amount of revenue isn't the same as the estimate, Jalobert would correct the error in 2015. The effects on the balance sheet and income statement of this adjustment are summarized in Figure 3.8.

INSIGHT

Accounting Estimates

Adjusting entries and accrual accounting often require **accounting estimates** as the actual amounts are not known yet. In the Jalobert example, the amount of rent revenue earned from sales by the retail stores in the mall would be estimated when preparing the December 31, 2014 financial statements because the actual amount wouldn't be known until payment was received in March 2015. Estimates are imprecise because they are really educated guesses; it's very unlikely an estimate and the actual amount will be exactly the same. Most numbers in the financial statements rely to some extent on estimates.

Managers are responsible for making the estimates needed to prepare the financial statements and this requires judgment. Managers can use the inherent uncertainty in estimates to pursue their own interests and objectives, such as maximizing their bonuses, satisfying lenders so they keep lending money, and maximizing profits to keep investors happy.

THE FULL ACCOUNTING CYCLE, BEGINNING TO END

The accounting equation spreadsheet is a useful learning tool but not very practical for real-world use. A spreadsheet is difficult to manage if there are many accounts or transactions. In this section, I explain the mechanics of the accounting cycle as it operates in practice. We will work through the steps shown in Figure 3.9 using Strawberries Inc. as the example.

Preparing Journal Entries

As described earlier, a transaction or other economic event is initially recognized in the accounting system by a journal entry. These are recorded in the **general journal**, a chronological record of the entries to the accounting system also referred to as the book of original entry because events are first recorded in the accounting system there. It can be an actual book that entries are written in but is more likely an accounting software package. An example of a general journal is given in Figure 3.10, which shows three of Strawberries' journal entries.

Strawberries recorded the following transactional journal entries up to September 30, 2014. (These are the same entries that were developed earlier):

1.	Dr. Cash (asset +)	40,000	
	Cr. Common shares (shareholders' equity +)		40,000
	To record the sale of shares for cash		
2.	Dr. Cash (asset +)	20,000	
	Cr. Bank loan (liability +)		20,000
	To record the $20,000 bank loan		
3.	Dr. Prepaid rent (asset +)	3,750	
	Cr. Cash (asset –)		3,750
	To record the prepayment of three months' rent		

FIGURE 3.9 The Accounting Cycle

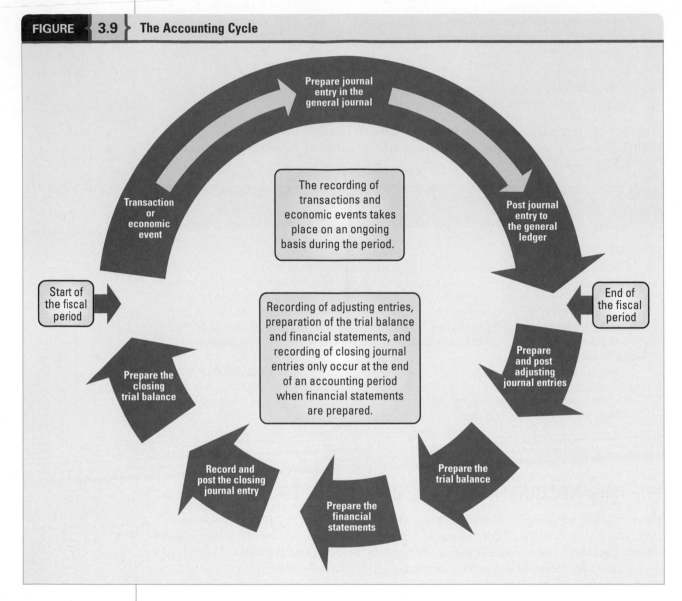

4. Dr. Renovations, equipment, and furniture (asset +)   15,000
    Cr. Cash (asset −)   15,000
To record the cost of renovating the restaurant

5. Dr. Renovations, equipment, and furniture (asset +)   25,000
    Cr. Cash (asset −)   12,500
    Cr. Accounts payable (liability +)   12,500
To record the purchase of equipment and furniture

6. Dr. Food, drinks, and supplies inventory (asset +)   900
    Cr. Cash (asset −)   900
To record the purchase of inventory

7. Dr. Food, drinks, and supplies inventory (asset +)   12,000
    Cr. Cash (asset −)   12,000
To record the purchase of food and drinks during September

8. Dr. Cash (asset +)   17,200
   Dr. Accounts receivable (asset +)   700
    Cr. Sales (shareholders' equity +, revenue +)   17,900
To record sales for the month of September

FIGURE 3.10

The General Journal

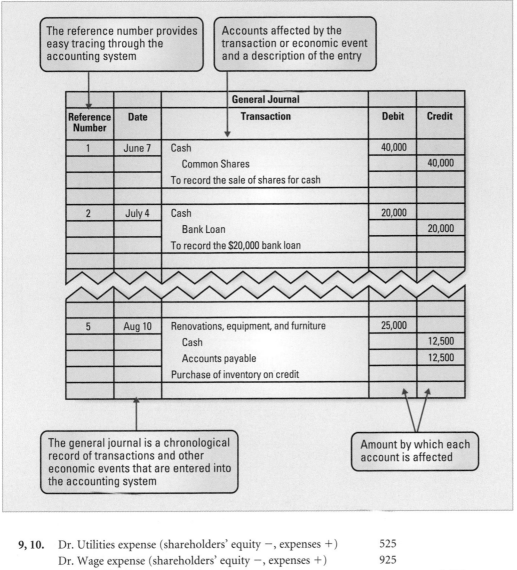

The reference number provides easy tracing through the accounting system

Accounts affected by the transaction or economic event and a description of the entry

Reference Number	Date	General Journal Transaction	Debit	Credit
1	June 7	Cash	40,000	
		Common Shares		40,000
		To record the sale of shares for cash		
2	July 4	Cash	20,000	
		Bank Loan		20,000
		To record the $20,000 bank loan		
5	Aug 10	Renovations, equipment, and furniture	25,000	
		Cash		12,500
		Accounts payable		12,500
		Purchase of inventory on credit		

The general journal is a chronological record of transactions and other economic events that are entered into the accounting system

Amount by which each account is affected

9, 10. Dr. Utilities expense (shareholders' equity −, expenses +)   525
Dr. Wage expense (shareholders' equity −, expenses +)   925
    Cr. Cash (asset −)   1,450
To record the utilities and wages expenses for the month of September

11. Dr. Interest expense (shareholders' equity −, expenses +)   150
    Cr. Cash (asset −)   150
To record the interest expense for the month of September

15. Dr. Retained earnings (shareholders' equity −)   1,000
    Cr. Cash (asset −)   1,000
To record the payment of a dividend of $0.50 per share

Post Journal Entries to the General Ledger

The next step in the accounting cycle is posting the journal entry to the general ledger. The **general ledger** is a record of all the entity's accounts. **Posting** a journal entry to the general ledger is the process of transferring each line of a journal entry to the corresponding account in the general ledger. Imagine the general ledger as a book in which each page represents a different account: a page for cash, a page for inventory, a page for sales, etc. Whereas a journal entry shows which accounts a transaction or economic event affects, a general ledger account shows the activity in each account over time. In the accounting equation spreadsheet each column represents a general ledger account.

FIGURE 3.11

The T-Account

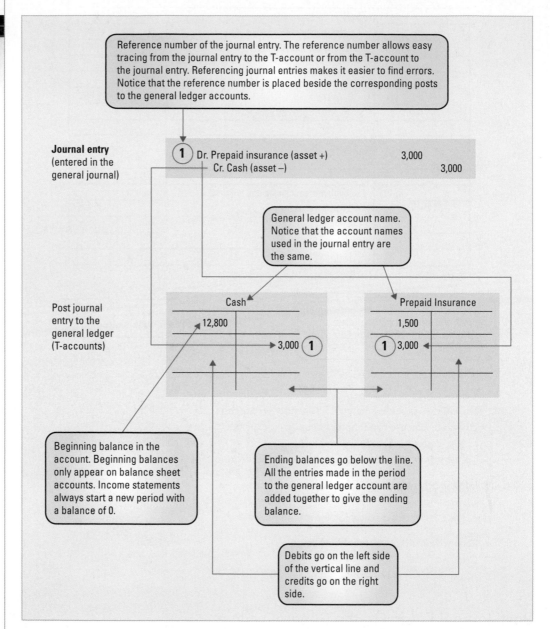

FIGURE 3.12

The Posting Process

Accounting textbooks use **T-accounts** to represent general ledger accounts. The name "T-account" reflects its shape, as you can see in the T-account shown in Figure 3.11. Note the following:

- Each T-account corresponds to a general ledger account. The name of the account is written on the horizontal line at the top.

- The vertical line separates the debits and credits made to the account—debits on the left, credits on the right.

FIGURE	3.13	T-accounts for Strawberries Inc.: Pre-adjusting Entry Postings to T-accounts

Cash

Bal	0		
1	40,000		
2	20,000		
3			3,750
4			15,000
5			12,500
6			925
7			12,000
8	17,200		
9			525
10			925
11			150
15			1,000

Accounts receivable

Bal	0	
8	700	

Food, drinks, and supplies inventory

Bal	0	
6	900	
7	12,000	

Prepaid rent

Bal	0	
3	3,750	

Renovations, equipment, and furniture

Bal	0	
4	15,000	
5	25,000	

Accumulated depreciation

Bal		0

Bank loan

Bal		0
2		20,000

Accounts payable

Bal		0
5		12,500

Common shares

Bal		0
1		40,000

Retained earnings

Bal		0
15	1,000	

Sales

Bal		0
8		17,900

Cost of sales

Bal	0	

Rent expense

Bal	0	

Wages expense

Bal	0	
6	925	

Depreciation expense

Bal	0	

Interest expense

Bal	0	
11	150	

Utilities expense

Bal	0	
9	525	

- The beginning balance, the balance in the account at the start of the period, is shown between the horizontal lines at the top of the T-account.

- The ending balance is shown below the horizontal line at the bottom.

- A debit balance at the beginning or end of the period is recorded on the left side of the vertical line. A credit balance at the beginning or end of the period is recorded on the right side.

- When a journal entry is posted to the T-accounts, debits are recorded on the left side of the vertical line and credits on the right side. If an account typically has a debit balance (assets, expenses), credits are subtracted from debits to calculate the ending balance. For accounts typically having a credit balance (liabilities, equity, revenue), debits are subtracted from credits.

The posting process is shown schematically in Figure 3.12.

T-accounts showing the postings of Strawberries transactions are given in Figure 3.13. The number on the left side of each line in each T-account corresponds to the number of the journal entry. This cross-referencing is important because it makes it easy to trace back from the general ledger account to the journal entry. The opening balance in all accounts is zero because Strawberries just started up. For ongoing businesses, opening amounts in the balance sheet T-accounts would be the ending amount from the previous period. Ending balances aren't shown in Figure 3.13 because we still have to make the adjusting and closing journal entries.

FIGURE 3.14 ▸ T-Accounts for Strawberries Inc.: Post-adjusting Entry Postings to T-Accounts

Cash		
Bal	12,800	
1	40,000	
2	20,000	
3		3,750
4		15,000
5		12,500
6		925
7		12,000
8	17,200	
9		525
10		925
11		150
15		1,000
Bal	30,450	

Accounts receivable		
Bal	0	
8	700	
Bal	700	

Food, drinks, and supplies inventory		
Bal	0	
6	900	
7	12,000	
12		**11,900**
Bal	1,000	

Prepaid rent		
Bal	0	
3	3,750	
13		**1,250**
Bal	2,500	

Renovations, equipment, and furniture		
Bal	0	
4	15,000	
5	25,000	
Bal	40,000	

Accumulated depreciation		
Bal		0
14		**1,042**
Bal		1,042

Bank loan		
Bal		0
2		20,000
Bal		20,000

Accounts payable		
Bal		0
5		12,500
Bal		12,500

Common shares		
Bal		0
1		40,000
Bal		40,000

Retained earnings		
Bal		0
15	1,000	
Bal	1,000	

Sales		
Bal		0
8		17,900
Bal		17,900

Cost of sales		
Bal	0	
12	**11,900**	
Bal	11,900	

Rent expense		
Bal	0	
13	**1,250**	
Bal	1,250	

Wages expense		
Bal	0	
6	925	
Bal	925	

Depreciation expense		
Bal	0	
14	**1,042**	
Bal	1,042	

Interest expense		
Bal	0	
11	150	
Bal	150	

Utilities expense		
Bal	0	
9	525	
Bal	525	

Prepare and Post Adjusting Journal Entries

Preparing journal entries and posting them to the general ledger is ongoing during a reporting period. The remaining steps in the accounting cycle occur at the end of a period when the entity prepares financial statements. At that time the managers examine the general ledger accounts and determine the adjusting entries that must be made. Many adjusting entries are automatic as they have to be made each period. Other adjustments don't occur regularly and managers must be careful to make sure these are also recorded. Strawberries' adjusting journal entries are shown below and the posting of them to the T-accounts are shown in bold in Figure 3.14.

12. Dr. Cost of sales (shareholders' equity –, expenses +)   11,900
      Cr. Food, drinks, and supplies inventory (asset –)   11,900
    To record the cost of food, drinks, and supplies used to provide meals to customers

13. Dr. Rent expense (shareholders' equity –, expenses +)   1,250
      Cr. Prepaid rent (asset –)   1,250
    To record the rent expense for September

14. Dr. Depreciation expense (shareholders' equity –, expenses +)   1,042
      Cr. Accumulated depreciation—renovations, equipment,
        and furniture (asset –)   1,042
    To record the depreciation of renovations, equipment, and furniture

Prepare the Trial Balance

The **trial balance** lists all the accounts in the general ledger with their balances. It ensures the debits equal the credits and provides a summary of the balances in each account. Unequal debits and credits mean there is an error that must be corrected. However, equal debits and credits don't mean the accounting has been done properly. It simply means that all journal entries and postings to the general ledger accounts were balanced. For example, if an entity purchases land and promises to pay in one year, the correct entry would debit land (asset) and credit payables (liability). If the accountant incorrectly debited cash instead of land, the debits and credits would balance but the account balances wouldn't be correct.

When preparing a trial balance, the accounts with debit balances in the general ledger (T-accounts) are placed in the left column of the trial balance, and accounts with credit balances are placed in the right column. Several trial balances are sometimes prepared at the end of a period, including before and after preparation of the adjusting entries and after the closing entry has been posted. Each trial balance helps ensure that the posting of the journal entries balances at each step.

Strawberries' trial balance is shown in Table 3.6. This trial balance was prepared after the adjusting journal entries had been entered and posted to the appropriate ledger accounts.

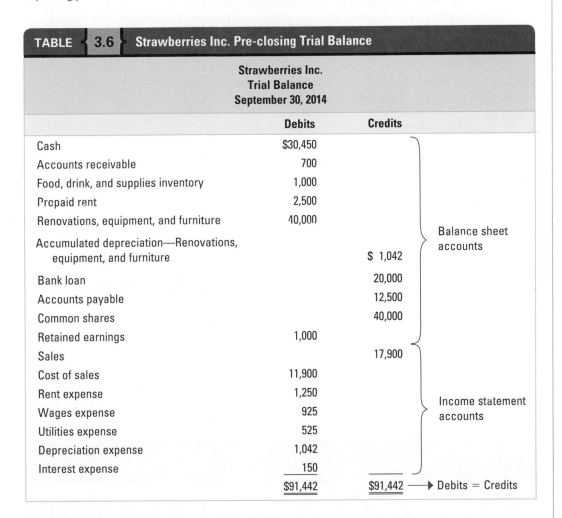

TABLE 3.6 Strawberries Inc. Pre-closing Trial Balance

Strawberries Inc.
Trial Balance
September 30, 2014

	Debits	Credits	
Cash	$30,450		
Accounts receivable	700		
Food, drink, and supplies inventory	1,000		
Prepaid rent	2,500		
Renovations, equipment, and furniture	40,000		Balance sheet accounts
Accumulated depreciation—Renovations, equipment, and furniture		$ 1,042	
Bank loan		20,000	
Accounts payable		12,500	
Common shares		40,000	
Retained earnings	1,000		
Sales		17,900	
Cost of sales	11,900		
Rent expense	1,250		
Wages expense	925		Income statement accounts
Utilities expense	525		
Depreciation expense	1,042		
Interest expense	150		
	$91,442	$91,442	→ Debits = Credits

Prepare the Financial Statements

The trial balance provides all the information required to prepare the balance sheet and income statement. To prepare these statements, the accounts in the trial balance have to be aggregated and organized into the format desired by the managers. (Trial balances will include every account an entity has whereas financial statements aggregate accounts. For example, an entity will have separate ledger accounts for each bank account but the balance sheet will only show a single cash amount.) At this point, retained earnings on the year-end balance sheet isn't known because the income statement accounts have not been closed (closing entries are described in the next section). Strawberries' balance sheet and income statement can be found in Table 3.2.

Prepare and Post Closing Journal Entries

The next step in the accounting cycle is preparing the closing journal entry, which sets all the income statement accounts to zero and transfers those amounts to owner's equity (retained earnings for corporations and owners' capital accounts for partnerships or proprietorships). All accounts on the income statement are **temporary accounts** because at the end of each period they are reset to zero and aren't carried forward to the next period. (In contrast, balance sheet accounts, which are called **permanent accounts**, carry forward from one period to the next.) The process of setting the income statement accounts to zero is called *closing* and is accomplished with **closing journal entries**. This simply involves recording a journal entry that is equal but opposite in amount to the ending balance in each account with "the other side of the entry" going to owners' equity. For example, if there is a $1,000,000 ending balance in sales, a debit to sales and a credit to owners' equity of $1,000,000 is recorded.

Closing the temporary accounts is necessary because an income statement reports results for a period of time. For example, an income statement might report revenues and expenses "For the Year Ended December 31, 2014." If the income statement accounts aren't closed on December 31, 2014, the revenue and expense accounts on December 31, 2015 would include amounts from 2014 and 2015, making it impossible to understand what amounts belonged to which year.

Here is Strawberries' September 30, 2014, closing journal entry:

16. Dr. Sales   17,900

Cr. Cost of sales		11,900
Cr. Rent expense		1,250
Cr. Wages expense		925
Cr. Utilities expense		525
Cr. Depreciation expense		1,042
Cr. Interest expense		150
Cr. Retained earnings		2,108

To close income statement accounts to retained earnings for the period ended September 30, 2014

Notice that for income statement accounts on Strawberries' trial balance there is an entry that is equal and opposite in amount to the ending balance. As a result, the income statement accounts have balances of zero and the balances have been "transferred" to retained earnings (notice the credit to retained earnings is equal to Strawberries' net income for the period—retained earnings increases by the amount of net income). Figure 3.15 shows the T-accounts after the closing entry has been posted (closing posts are shown in bold). The post-closing trial balance (the trial balance prepared after the closing entry has been posted) is shown in Table 3.7. Notice that the income statement accounts all have zero balances and the balance in retained earnings corresponds with the amount on the September 30, 2014, balance sheet.

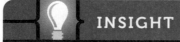

INSIGHT

Accounting Software

Some students may have had exposure to accounting software packages that don't seem to have the accounting cycle components described here. In fact, all the features discussed are present; they're just hidden in the background. Accounting software is designed to be friendly for use by non-accountants. For example, you might input information by completing an electronic form that doesn't require a journal entry. These software packages allow users to examine electronic versions of journals, ledgers, and trial balances.

FIGURE	3.15	T-Accounts for Strawberries Inc.: Post-closing Entry Postings to T-Accounts

Cash

Bal	12,800		
1	40,000		
2	20,000		
3		3,750	
4		15,000	
5		12,500	
6		925	
7		12,000	
8	17,200		
9		525	
10		925	
11		150	
15		1,000	
Bal	30,450		

Accounts receivable

Bal	0	
8	700	
Bal	700	

Food, drinks and supplies inventory

Bal	0		
6	900		
7	12,000	11,900	
12			
Bal	1,000		

Prepaid rent

Bal	0		
3	3,750		
13		1,250	
Bal	2,500		

Renovations, equipment, and furniture

Bal	0	
4	15,000	
5	25,000	
Bal	40,000	

Accumulated depreciation

Bal		0
14		1,042
Bal		1,042

Bank loan

Bal		0
2		20,000
Bal		20,000

Accounts payable

Bal		0
5		12,500
Bal		12,500

Common shares

Bal		0
1		40,000
Bal		40,000

Retained earnings

Bal		0
15	1,000	
16		2,108
Bal		1,108

Sales

Bal		0
8		17,900
Bal		17,900
16	17,900	
Bal		0

Cost of sales

Bal	0	
12	11,900	
Bal	11,900	
16		11,900
Bal	0	

Rent expense

Bal	0	
13	1,250	
Bal	1,250	
16		1,250
Bal	0	

Wages expense

Bal	0	
6	925	
Bal	925	
16		925
Bal	0	

Depreciation expense

Bal	0	
14	1,042	
Bal	1,042	
16		1,042
Bal	0	

Interest expense

Bal	0	
11	150	
Bal	150	
16		150
Bal	0	

Utilities expense

Bal	0	
9	525	
Bal	525	
16		525
Bal	0	

KNOWLEDGE CHECK

www.mcgrawhill connect.ca

☐ Identify and explain the four types of adjusting journal entries.

☐ Explain what accrued expense and accrued revenue are.

☐ What is a contra-asset account?

☐ What are closing journal entries and why are they necessary?

TABLE 3.7	Strawberries Inc. Post-Closing Trial Balance

Strawberries Inc.
Trial Balance
September 30, 2014

	Debits	Credits	
Cash	$30,450		
Accounts receivable	700		
Food, drink, and supplies inventory	1,000		
Prepaid rent	2,500		
Renovations, equipment, and furniture	40,000		
Accumulated depreciation—Renovations, equipment, and furniture		$ 1,042	Balance sheet accounts
Bank loan		20,000	
Accounts payable		12,500	
Common shares		40,000	
Retained earnings		1,108	
Sales		0	
Cost of sales	0		
Rent expense	0		
Wages expense	0		Income statement accounts
Utilities expense	0		
Depreciation expense	0		
Interest expense	0		
	$74,650	$74,650	→ Debits = Credits

 INSIGHT

Memorization

This is a challenging time to be studying accounting. Standards are changing rapidly as the world aligns itself with IFRS. At the same time, other sets of GAAP are being used for private companies. This rapidly changing world means that learning today's sets of rules may not prepare you to be an effective user of accounting information in the future. If you are only able to memorize rules your knowledge will be obsolete very quickly. If you understand accounting and can interpret rules, you will be much better positioned to adjust when the rules change.

Solved Problem

Child First Safety Ltd. (CFS) is a small business that provides safety advice and equipment to parents and daycare centres wanting a safe, childproofed environment for infants and toddlers. The company has been in business for approximately two years. CFS is 100 percent owned and operated by Yehuda Bigalli. Yehuda has never been much of a bookkeeper and his accounting system has tended to be a bag of business receipts, invoices, cancelled cheques (a cheque that has been cashed and returned by the bank), and so on. Last year an accountant friend organized the information and prepared financial statements. Yehuda used these for calculating his taxes and showing his bank. This year Yehuda comes to you for help instead. He gives last year's (October 31, 2013) balance sheet (Table 3.8) along with the information in the bag.

TABLE 3.8	Child First Safety Ltd. October 31, 2013, Balance Sheet

Child First Safety Ltd.
Balance Sheet
As of October 31, 2013

Assets		Liabilities and Shareholders' Equity	
Current assets		**Current liabilities**	
Cash	$ 12,800	Bank loan	$15,000
Accounts receivable	22,000	Accounts payable	49,000
Inventory	52,000	Taxes payable	5,000
	86,800	Unearned revenue	3,000
			72,000
Non-current assets		**Shareholder's equity**	
Property and equipment	24,000	Common Shares	15,000
Accumulated depreciation	(8,000)	Retained earnings	15,800
	16,000		30,800
Total assets	$102,800	Total liabilities and shareholder's equity	$102,800

You organize and summarize the data in the bag and determine the following:

1. On November 1, 2013, CFS purchased a two-year insurance policy for $3,000 cash.

2. During the year CFS sold safety equipment and advisory services to customers for $199,000: $140,000 for cash, the remainder on credit.

3. CFS purchased $65,000 of inventory during the year. All purchases were on credit.

4. CFS paid $62,000 during the year to suppliers for inventory purchases.

5. On November 15, 2013 CFS purchased a used car for $12,000 in cash. Yehuda uses the car for service calls and deliveries instead of using his personal vehicle. He estimates the car will last for four years.

6. During the year CFS paid Yehuda and a part-time sales person $70,000 in salary and commission.

7. During the year CFS collected $45,000 from customers for purchases they had made on credit.

8. On October 31, 2014 CFS paid interest of $900 for the year on its bank loan.

9. On October 31, 2014 CFS repaid $2,000 of its bank loan.

10. During the year CFS incurred other expenses of $20,000, all paid in cash.

11. CFS paid a dividend of $15,000 on September 15, 2014.

12. During the year CFS paid the $5,000 in taxes payable that was owing to the federal and provincial governments on October 31, 2013.

13. In November 2013 CFS supplied $3,000 of equipment to a large daycare centre. The daycare centre had paid in advance for the equipment in October 2013. The payment was reported as unearned revenue on the October 31, 2013, balance sheet.

TABLE 3.9 Child First Safety Ltd. Completed Spreadsheet

Transaction	Type of entry	Assets						=	Liabilities	
		Cash	Accounts receivable	Inventory	Prepaid insurance	Property and equipment	Accumulated depreciation		Bank loan	Accounts payable
Beginning Balance		12,800	22,000	52,000	0	24,000	(8,000)		15,000	49,000
1	Transactional	(3,000)			3,000					
2	Transactional	140,000	59,000							
3	Transactional			65,000						65,000
4	Transactional	(62,000)								(62,000)
5	Transactional	(12,000)				12,000				
6	Transactional	(70,000)								
7	Transactional	45,000	(45,000)							
8	Transactional	(900)								
9	Transactional	(2,000)							(2,000)	
10	Transactional	(20,000)								
11	Transactional	(15,000)								
12	Transactional	(5,000)								
13	Adjusting									
14	Adjusting									
15	Adjusting						(6,000)			
16	Adjusting			(72,000)						
17	Adjusting									
18	Adjusting				(1,500)					
Pre-closing Balance		7,900	36,000	45,000	1,500	36,000	(14,000)		13,000	52,000
19	Closing									
Ending Balance		7,900	36,000	45,000	1,500	36,000	(14,000)		13,000	52,000

14. At the end of the year CFS owed the part-time sales person $1,500 in salary and commissions. The amount owing will be paid in mid-November 2014.

15. Depreciation of property and equipment is $6,000, including the used car that was purchased on November 15, 2013.

16. The cost of the safety equipment sold during the year was $72,000.

17. CFS will have to pay $6,700 in income taxes for the 2014 fiscal year. No payments had been made with respect to the 2014 fiscal year as of October 31, 2014.

Required:

A. Use an accounting equation spreadsheet to record the economic activity for CFS during fiscal 2014. Make sure to include the adjusting and closing entries. Prepare the balance sheet as of October 31, 2014 and the income statement and the statement of retained earnings for the year ended October 31, 2014. Also discuss CFS's performance for the year ended October 31, 2014.

OR

B. Use the information provided about CFS to do the following:

a. Prepare all necessary transactional journal entries for the year ended December 31, 2014 and post each journal entry to the appropriate T-account.

c. Prepare and post adjusting journal entries to their appropriate T-accounts.

d. Prepare a trial balance as of December 31, 2014.

	Liabilities (cont.)		+		Shareholders' equity								
Salaries payable	Taxes payable	Unearned revenue		Common shares	Retained earnings	Sales	Cost of sales	Insurance expense	Salaries expense	Depreciation expense	Other expenses	Tax expense	Interest expense
0	5,000	3,000		15,000	15,800								
						199,000							
									(70,000)				
													(900)
											(20,000)		
					(15,000)								
	(5,000)												
		(3,000)				3,000							
1,500									(1,500)				
										(6,000)			
							(72,000)						
	6,700											(6,700)	
								(1,500)					
1,500	6,700	0		15,000	800	202,000	(72,000)	(1,500)	(71,500)	(6,000)	(20,000)	(6,700)	(900)
					23,400	(202,000)	72,000	1,500	71,500	6,000	20,000	6,700	900
1,500	6,700	0		15,000	24,200	0	0	0	0	0	0	0	0

e. Prepare a balance sheet for CFS as of December 31, 2014 and an income statement and statement of retained earnings for the year ended December 31, 2014.

f. Prepare the closing journal entry and post the closing entry to the appropriate T-accounts.

g. Prepare a trial balance as of December 31, 2014 after the closing entry has been prepared.

h. Discuss CFS's performance for the year ended October 31, 2014.

Solution—Approach A—Accounting Equation Spreadsheet

Table 3.9 provides the completed spreadsheet for the year ended October 31, 2014. Most of the entries should be clear, but note the following points:

- The first line of the spreadsheet, which is called "beginning balance," contains the values on the balance sheet on October 31, 2013. Remember that balance sheet accounts are permanent, so the ending balances in last year's balance sheet are the beginning balances in this year's. The income statement accounts all have beginning balances of zero because they are closed each year to retained earnings.

- The depreciation expense in item 15 is the portion of the cost of property and equipment that is matched to sales in fiscal 2014. The depreciation of the property and equipment is accumulated in a separate contra-asset account.

- Item 18 is tricky because the question doesn't specifically state that part of the prepaid insurance has to be expensed at year-end. This is typical of adjusting entries. Because adjusting entries are generated within the entity, the accountant or bookkeeper has to examine the accounts and decide when an adjusting entry is necessary.

- The balance sheet, income statement, and statement of retained earnings are shown in Table 3.10, following Approach B. The discussion of CFS's performance can also be found in Approach B.

Solution—Approach B

Prepare Journal Entries

1. Dr. Prepaid insurance (asset +)   3,000
      Cr. Cash (asset −)   3,000
   To record the purchase of insurance for two years

2. Dr. Cash (asset +)   140,000
   Dr. Accounts receivable (asset +)   59,000
      Cr. Sales (revenue +, shareholders' equity +)   199,000
   To record sales for the year

3. Dr. Inventory (asset +)   65,000
      Cr. Accounts payable (liability +)   65,000
   To record the purchase of inventory on credit

4. Dr. Accounts payable (liability −)   62,000
      Cr. Cash (asset −)   62,000
   To record the payment to suppliers for inventory purchased

5. Dr. Property and equipment (asset +)   12,000
      Cr. Cash (asset −)   12,000
   To record the purchase of a car

6. Dr. Salaries expense (expenses +, shareholders' equity −)   70,000
      Cr. Cash (asset −)   70,000
   To record salaries paid

7. Dr. Cash (asset +)   45,000
      Cr. Accounts receivable (asset −)   45,000
   To record collection of accounts receivable

8. Dr. Interest expense (expenses +, shareholders' equity −)   900
      Cr. Cash (asset −)   900
   To record the payment of interest on the bank loan

9. Dr. Bank loan (liability −)   2,000
      Cr. Cash (asset −)   2,000
   To record payment of principal on the bank loan

10. Dr. Other expenses (expenses +, shareholders' equity −)   20,000
       Cr. Cash (asset −)   20,000
    To record the payment of other expenses

11. Dr. Retained earnings (shareholders' equity −)   15,000
       Cr. Cash (asset −)   15,000
    To record the payment of a dividend

FIGURE 3.16 T-Accounts for Child First Safety Ltd.: Pre-adjusting Entry Postings to T-Accounts

Cash		
Bal	12,800	
1		3,000
2	140,000	
4		62,000
5		12,000
6		70,000
7	45,000	
8		900
9		2,000
10		20,000
11		15,000
12		5,000

Accounts receivable		
Bal	22,000	
2	59,000	
7		45,000

Inventory		
Bal	52,000	
3	65,000	

Prepaid insurance		
Bal	0	
1	3,000	

Property and equipment		
Bal	24,000	
5	12,000	

Accumulated depreciation		
Bal		8,000

Bank loan		
Bal		15,000
9		2,000

Accounts payable		
Bal		49,000
3		65,000
4	62,000	

Salaries payable		
Bal		0

Taxes payable		
Bal		5,000
12	5,000	

Unearned revenue		
Bal		3,000

Common shares		
Bal		15,000

Retained earnings		
Bal		15,800
11	15,000	

Sales		
Bal		0
2		199,000

Cost of sales		
Bal	0	

Insurance expense		
Bal	0	

Salaries expense		
Bal	0	
6	70,000	

Depreciation expense		
Bal	0	

Other expenses		
Bal	0	
10	20,000	

Tax expense		
Bal	0	
8	6,700	

Interest expense		
Bal	0	
8	900	

12. Dr. Taxes payable (liability −)   5,000
　　　Cr. Cash (asset −)   5,000
　　To record the payment of taxes payable

Post Journal Entries to the General Ledger

T-accounts are shown in Figure 3.16. For each balance sheet T-account, the beginning balance is the amount in the account on October 31, 2013. Remember that income statement accounts don't have beginning balances because they were set to zero on October 31, 2013, when the temporary accounts were closed.

FIGURE 3.17 T-Accounts for Child First Safety Ltd.: Post-adjusting Entry Postings to T-Accounts

Cash		
Bal	12,800	
1		3,000
2	140,000	
4		62,000
5		12,000
6		70,000
7	45,000	
8		900
9		2,000
10		20,000
11		15,000
12		5,000
Bal	7,900	

Accounts receivable		
Bal	22,000	
2		
7	59,000	45,000
Bal	36,000	

Inventory		
Bal	52,000	
3	65,000	
16		72,000
Bal	45,000	

Prepaid insurance		
Bal	0	
1	3,000	
18		1,500
Bal	1,500	

Property and equipment		
Bal	24,000	
5	12,000	
Bal	36,000	

Accumulated depreciation		
	Bal	8,000
	15	6,000
	Bal	14,000

Bank loan		
	Bal	15,000
9	2,000	
	Bal	13,000

Accounts payable		
	Bal	49,000
3		65,000
4	62,000	
	Bal	52,000

Salaries payable		
	Bal	0
	14	1,500
	Bal	1,500

Taxes payable		
	Bal	5,000
12	5,000	
	17	6,700
	Bal	6,700

Unearned revenue		
	Bal	3,000
13	3,000	
	Bal	0

Common shares		
	Bal	15,000
	Bal	15,000

Retained earnings		
	Bal	15,800
11	15,000	
	Bal	800

Sales		
	Bal	0
	2	199,000
	13	3,000
	Bal	202,000

Cost of sales		
Bal	0	
16	72,000	
Bal	72,000	

Insurance expense		
Bal	0	
18	1,500	
Bal	1,500	

Salaries expense		
Bal	0	
6	70,000	
14	1,500	
Bal	71,500	

Depreciation expense		
Bal	0	
16	6,000	
Bal	6,000	

Other expenses		
Bal	0	
10	20,000	
Bal	20,000	

Tax expense		
Bal	0	
17	6,700	
Bal	6,700	

Interest expense		
Bal	0	
8	900	
Bal	900	

Prepare and Post Adjusting Journal Entries

At the end of the period, the accounts are examined and any necessary adjusting entries are made. The adjusting entries are then posted to the corresponding general ledger accounts. The adjusting journal entries are shown below and posting of the adjusting entries to the T-accounts is shown in bold in Figure 3.17.

13. Dr. Unearned revenue (liability −)   3,000
        Cr. Sales (revenue +, shareholders' equity +)   3,000
    Adjusting entry to record recognition of revenue on merchandise paid for in advance

14. Dr. Salaries expense (expense +, shareholders' equity −)   1,500
        Cr. Salaries payable (liability +)   1,500
    Adjusting entry to accrue salaries owed but not paid

15. Dr. Depreciation expense (expenses +, shareholders' equity −) 6,000
    Cr. Accumulated depreciation (contra-asset +)   6,000
    Adjusting entry to record the depreciation of property and equipment

16. Dr. Cost of sales (expenses +, shareholders' equity −)   72,000
    Cr. Inventory (asset −)   72,000
    Adjusting entry to record cost of sales

17. Dr. Tax expense (expenses +, shareholders' equity −)   6,700
    Cr. Taxes payable (liability +)   6,700
    Adjusting entry to record income tax expense and accrue the liability for income taxes

18. Dr. Insurance expense (expenses +, shareholders' equity −)   1,500
    Cr. Prepaid insurance (asset −)   1,500
    Adjusting entry to record insurance used during the year

Prepare the Trial Balance

TABLE 3.10 Child First Safety Ltd. Trial Balance

Child First Safety Ltd.
Trial Balance
October 31, 2014

	Debits	Credits	
Cash	$ 7,900		
Accounts receivable	36,000		
Inventory	45,000		
Prepaid insurance	1,500		
Property and equipment	36,000		
Accumulated depreciation		$ 14,000	Balance sheet accounts
Bank loan		13,000	
Accounts payable		52,000	
Salaries payable		1,500	
Taxes payable		6,700	
Unearned revenue		0	
Common shares		15,000	
Retained earnings		800	
Sales		202,000	
Cost of sales	72,000		
Insurance expense	1,500		
Salaries expense	71,500		Income statement accounts
Depreciation expense	6,000		
Other expenses	20,000		
Tax expense	6,700		
Interest expense	900		
	$305,000	$305,000	→ Debits = Credits

Prepare the Financial Statements

The balances in the trial balance are used to prepare the financial statements, which are shown in Table 3.11. The financial statements are prepared before the closing entry because once the closing entry is made the balances in the income statement accounts will be zero. However, preparing the statements before the closing entry is made means that the ending balance in retained earnings isn't known from the trial balance.

TABLE 3.11	Child First Safety Ltd. Balance Sheet, and Income Statement and Statement of Retained Earnings

Child First Safety Ltd.
Balance Sheet
As of October 31, 2014

Assets		Liabilities and Shareholders' Equity	
Current assets		**Current liabilities**	
Cash	$ 7,900	Bank loan	$ 13,000
Accounts receivable	36,000	Accounts payable	52,000
Inventory	45,000	Salaries payable	1,500
Prepaid insurance	1,500	Taxes payable	6,700
	90,400		73,200
Non-current assets		**Shareholder's equity**	
Property and equipment	36,000	Common shares	15,000
Accumulated depreciation	(14,000)	Retained earnings	24,200
	22,000		39,200
Total assets	$112,400	Total liabilities and shareholder's equity	$112,400

Child First Safety Ltd.
Income Statement and Statement of Retained Earnings
For the Year Ended October 31, 2014

Sales		$202,000
Cost of sales		72,000
Gross margin		130,000
Expenses		
Insurance expense	$1,500	
Salaries expense	71,500	
Depreciation expense	6,000	
Other expenses	20,000	
Interest expense	900	
Total expenses		99,900
Income before taxes		30,100
Income tax expense		6,700
Net income		23,400
Retained earnings at the beginning of the year		15,800
Dividends		(15,000)
Retained earnings at the end of the year		$ 24,200

FIGURE 3.18 T-Accounts for Child First Safety Ltd.: Post-closing Entry Postings to T-Accounts

Cash

	Dr	Cr
Bal	12,800	
1		3,000
2	140,000	
4		62,000
5		12,000
6		70,000
7	45,000	
8		900
9		2,000
10		20,000
11		15,000
12		5,000
Bal	7,900	

Accounts receivable

	Dr	Cr
Bal	22,000	
2	59,000	
7		45,000
Bal	36,000	

Inventory

	Dr	Cr
Bal	52,000	
3	65,000	
16		72,000
Bal	45,000	

Prepaid insurance

	Dr	Cr
Bal	0	
1	3,000	
18		1,500
Bal	1,500	

Property and equipment

	Dr	Cr
Bal	24,000	
5	12,000	
Bal	36,000	

Accumulated depreciation

	Dr	Cr
Bal		8,000
15		6,000
Bal		14,000

Bank loan

	Dr	Cr
Bal		15,000
9	2,000	
Bal		13,000

Accounts payable

	Dr	Cr
Bal		49,000
3		65,000
4	62,000	
Bal		52,000

Salaries payable

	Dr	Cr
Bal		0
14		1,500
Bal		1,500

Taxes payable

	Dr	Cr
Bal		5,000
12	5,000	
17		6,700
Bal		6,700

Unearned revenue

	Dr	Cr
Bal		3,000
13	3,000	
Bal		0

Common shares

	Dr	Cr
Bal		15,000
Bal		15,000

Retained earnings

	Dr	Cr
Bal		15,800
11	15,000	
19		23,400
Bal		24,200

Sales

	Dr	Cr
Bal		0
2		199,000
13		3,000
Bal		202,000
19	202,000	
Bal		0

Cost of sales

	Dr	Cr
Bal	0	
16	72,000	
Bal	72,000	
19		72,000
Bal	0	

Insurance expense

	Dr	Cr
Bal	0	
18	1,500	
Bal	1,500	
19		1,500
Bal	0	

Salaries expense

	Dr	Cr
Bal	0	
6	70,000	
14	1,500	
Bal	71,500	
19		71,500
Bal	0	

Depreciation expense

	Dr	Cr
Bal	0	
15	6,000	
Bal		
19	6,000	6,000
Bal	0	

Other expenses

	Dr	Cr
Bal	0	
10	20,000	
Bal		
19	20,000	20,000
Bal	0	

Tax expense

	Dr	Cr
Bal	0	
17	6,700	
Bal		
19	6,700	6,700
Bal	0	

Interest expense

	Dr	Cr
Bal	0	
8	900	
Bal	900	
19		900
Bal	0	

Prepare and Post Closing Journal Entries

The closing journal entry for the year ended October 31, 2014 is

19.	Dr. Sales	202,000	
	Cr. Cost of sales		72,000
	Cr. Insurance expense		1,500
	Cr. Salaries expense		71,500
	Cr. Depreciation expense		6,000
	Cr. Other expenses		20,000
	Cr. Tax expense		6,700
	Cr. Interest expense		900
	Cr. Retained earnings		23,400

To close income statement accounts to retained earnings

T-accounts after the closing entry has been posted are presented in Figure 3.18.

Post-closing Trial Balance

The post-closing trial balance is in Table 3.12.

TABLE 3.12	Child First Safety Ltd. Trial Balance	

Child First Safety Ltd.
Post-closing Trial Balance
October 31, 2006

	Debits	Credits	
Cash	$ 7,900		
Accounts receivable	36,000		
Inventory	45,000		
Prepaid insurance	1,500		
Property and equipment	36,000		
Accumulated depreciation		$ 14,000	
Bank loan		13,000	Balance sheet accounts
Accounts payable		52,000	
Salaries payable		1,500	
Taxes payable		6,700	
Unearned revenue		0	
Common shares		15,000	
Retained earnings		24,200	
Sales		0	
Cost of sales	0		
Insurance expense	0		
Salaries expense	0		Income statement accounts
Depreciation expense	0		
Other expenses	0		
Tax expense	0		
Interest expense	0		
	$126,400	$126,400	→ Debits = Credits

How Did Child First Safety Ltd. (CFS) Do?

Since we have put these financial statements together on behalf of Yehuda, who doesn't seem too knowledgeable about the accounting information, we should probably give him some insights into what they say. We should warn Yehuda that the financial statements don't provide clear-cut answers to questions about an entity's situation, but they raise flags for further investigation.

1. As was the case with Strawberries Inc., our ability to analyze the performance of CFS is hampered by the absence of comparable income statement data. We do have the October 31, 2013, balance sheet for making comparisons between balance sheet accounts.

2. It can be difficult to evaluate the financial statements of an entity when the owner also manages the entity. One reason is that owner-managers are free to pay themselves any amount they choose and the payments can take different forms, including salary, dividends, and loans. Remember that only salary reduces net income so different combinations of payments will result in different net incomes. Often, an important objective of owner-managers of private corporations is to minimize the overall tax burden on themselves and their corporation.

3. Without knowing his share of the salaries expense, we can't make a conclusive statement about how well-paid Yehuda was this year, but it appears he had a reasonably good year. If we

assume that his share of the salaries expense was $45,000 (probably a reasonable assumption since the sales person was a part-time employee), Yehuda took home $60,000 in salary and dividends ($45,000 in salary + $15,000 in dividends). In addition, his business made money, so that also added to his wealth.

4. At first glance, CFS's liquidity position seems adequate. Its current ratio has been stable for the two years available (1.23 in 2014, 1.21 in 2013). We would need to compare these current ratios with other, similar businesses to get some perspective on the adequacy of this current ratio. Of some concern is the low amount of cash and receivables (current assets that are cash or will be cash very soon) relative to the liabilities that will require cash very soon (accounts payable, salaries payable, and taxes payable). If sales slow down there may be a cash problem since the sale of inventory generates cash. However, CFS's liquidity position was similar a year ago and the company seems to have managed.

5. CFS generated a return on equity of about 67 percent (net income ÷ average shareholders' equity), a very good return on investment. The profit margin for the year is 11.6 percent. This ratio is difficult to assess without some comparative data from similar businesses.

6. Compared with October 31, 2013, the amount of inventory on hand on October 31, 2014, has decreased, while the amount of accounts receivable has increased. Without comparable income statements to tell us how sales changed from fiscal 2013, it's difficult to interpret these changes. For example, the increase in accounts receivable could be due to higher sales, more generous credit terms being offered to customers to attract more business, customers paying more slowly than last year, or other reasons.

SUMMARY OF KEY POINTS

▶ **LO 1** The key to producing accounting information is having an accounting system that captures raw data and organizes, summarizes, and classifies it into a form that is useful for decision making. The information provided by an accounting system is limited by the data entered into it. The accounting cycle is the process by which data about economic events are entered into an accounting system, processed, organized, and used to produce information, such as financial statements.

▶ **LO 2** The accounting equation spreadsheet is used to demonstrate the full accounting cycle in a straightforward, conceptual, and compact way. The spreadsheet clearly lays out how transactions and economic events affect the accounting equation and how the economic activity ultimately gets turned into financial statements. Each column in the spreadsheet represents an account in the entity's records and each transaction or economic event is recorded on a separate row. Each entry to the spreadsheet must maintain the accounting equation. The ending balance in each column provides the information needed to prepare the balance sheet and income statement.

▶ **LO 3** Managers often have choices for how to record and report transactions and economic events. The choices managers make will affect the accounting numbers that are reported, which in turn may affect how the statements are interpreted and the decisions stakeholders make.

▶ **LO 4** Accrual accounting attempts to measure the economic activity of an entity. An entry into an accrual accounting system is usually triggered by a transaction—an exchange between the entity and an external party. Sometimes economic changes affecting the entity aren't triggered by transactions. Entries not triggered by exchanges with outside entities are called adjusting entries.
There are four types of adjusting entries:

1. Deferred expense/prepaid expense—cash is paid before an expense is recognized

2. Deferred revenue—cash is received before revenue is recognized

www.mcgrawhillconnect.ca

3. Accrued expense/accrued liability—an expense is recognized before cash is paid

4. Accrued revenue/accrued asset—revenue is recognized before cash is received

▶ **LO 5** The journal entry is the method used in practice to enter economic event information into the accounting system. Whenever a relevant transaction or economic event occurs, a journal entry is recorded. During the period journal entries are posted to T-accounts (general ledger accounts). At the end of the period adjusting entries are recorded and posted to T-accounts, the trial balance is prepared, and financial statements made. Finally, the closing journal entry is recorded and posted to T-accounts.

▶ **LO 6** At the end of each period the balances in the income statement, or temporary accounts, must be set to zero and the balances in those accounts transferred to owners' equity in the balance sheet. The balances in the income statement accounts are set to zero so that they can accumulate information about transactions and economic events that pertain only to the next period. This process is achieved by a closing journal entry.

FORMULA SUMMARY

Return on equity = Net income ÷ Average shareholders' equity

Profit margin ratio = Net income ÷ Sales

KEY TERMS

account, p. 96

accounting cycle, p. 89

accounting estimate, p. 119

accrued expense, p. 116

accrued liability, p. 116

accrued revenue, p. 118

adjusting entry, p. 112

carrying amount, p. 115

closing journal entry, p. 126

contra-asset account, p. 114

credit, p. 97

debit, p. 97

debit card, p. 102

deferred expense, p. 113

double-entry bookkeeping, p. 94

earnings management, p. 113

executory contract, p. 102

general journal, p. 119

general ledger, p. 121

journal entry, p. 96

matching (matching concept), p. 93

permanent accounts, p. 126

posting, p. 121

prepaid expense, p. 113

profit margin ratio, p. 110

return on equity (ROE), p. 110

revenue recognition, p. 92

straight-line depreciation, p. 106

T-account, p. 122

temporary accounts, p. 126

transactional entry, p. 112

trial balance, p. 125

unearned revenue, p. 116

SIMILAR TERMS

The left column gives alternative terms that are sometimes used for the accounting terms introduced in this chapter, which are listed in the right column.

deferred expense, deferred charge, deferred cost, deferred debit   **prepaid expense, p. 113**

nominal account   **temporary accounts, p. 126**

deferred revenue   **unearned revenue, p. 116**

ASSIGNMENT MATERIALS

Questions

Q3-1. Explain why much more judgment is required with accrual accounting than with cash accounting.

Q3-2. What are closing journal entries and why are they necessary? When do closing entries have to be prepared?

Q3-3. In 2014 Taymouth Inc. reported net income of $100,000. What would be the effect on retained earnings on Taymouth's 2014 balance sheet and on its 2015 income statement if it didn't record a closing journal entry?

Q3-4. Explain why adjusting entries are necessary in accrual accounting but not required when the cash basis of accounting is used.

Q3-5. Explain the difference between transactional journal entries and adjusting journal entries.

Q3-6. Identify the four types of adjusting entries and explain why each type is necessary.

Q3-7. For each type of adjusting entry explain the impact on assets, liabilities, owners' equity, revenue, expenses, and net income if the required adjusting entry were not made.

Q3-8. When do adjusting entries have to be made? Explain.

Q3-9. What do the terms *debit* and *credit* mean?

Q3-10. What is a contra-asset account? Why are contra-asset accounts used?

Q3-11. When a dividend is declared and paid by a corporation, a debit is made to retained earnings. Explain why.

Q3-12. A company sells merchandise on credit to a customer for $1,000. What is the impact on the balance sheet of the selling company and the customer? Explain.

Q3-13. Explain the difference between permanent and temporary accounts.

Q3-14. Consider the steps of the accounting cycle (recording of transactional and adjusting journal entries, posting of entries, preparation of the trial balance, and recording and posting of closing entries). Which step or steps requires the most judgment? Explain.

Q3-15. Why are dividends not treated as an expense?

Q3-16. What effect do revenue and expenses have on equity? Explain why.

Q3-17. If cash increases when a debit is made to the cash account, why does the bank credit your account when you make a deposit?

Q3-18. What is an executory contract? How do IFRS usually account for executory contracts?

Q3-19. Identify and explain the four things that must be known when a transaction is to be entered into an accounting system.

Q3-20. Why do entities divide assets, liabilities, and owners' equity into sub-accounts rather than accumulating data simply as assets, liabilities, and owners' equity?

Q3-21. How should an entity determine the number of accounts it should keep in its general ledger?

Q3-22. Why can managers sometimes choose among alternative ways of accounting for transactions and economic events when accrual accounting is used? What are the implications of these choices on the financial statements and to the users of financial statements?

Q3-23. Figure 3.1 (Panel A) shows that not every economic event affecting an entity is entered into the entity's accounting system. What do you think are the implications for financial statements and stakeholders of not having every economic event recorded in the accounting system?

www.mcgrawhillconnect.ca

Q3-24. Figure 3.1 (Panel A) shows that not every economic event affecting an entity is entered into the entity's accounting system. Give three examples of economic events that might affect an entity but not be recorded in the entity's accounting system.

Q3-25. Identify and explain the steps of the accounting cycle.

Q3-26. What is a T-account? Why are they used?

Q3-27. What does "posting" journal entries to the general ledger mean? Why are journal entries posted to the general ledger?

Q3-28. What is a trial balance and what is its purpose? Why doesn't a trial balance guarantee that your accounting is "correct"?

Q3-29. Why is it useful to cross-reference journal entries to the posting to the general ledger account (T-account)?

Q3-30. Explain how information recorded in the general journal (using journal entries) is organized differently from the information in the general ledger (posted from the general journal).

Exercises

E3-1. **(Types of events, LO 4)** For each of the events listed below, indicate whether the event will give rise to a transactional entry, an adjusting entry, or no entry in the accounting system. Assume the accounting system is designed to collect information on an accrual basis.
a. Depreciation of equipment.
b. Payment of an amount owing to a supplier.
c. Increase in the market value of land while it continues to be owned.
d. Recognition of revenue for work done in the current period but paid for in the previous period.
e. A competitor opens for business in the same neighbourhood.
f. Sale of merchandise to a customer on credit.
g. Earning of interest on an investment. The interest won't be paid until next year.
h. A customer pays in advance for work to be done next year.
i. Sale of land to a buyer in exchange for a promise to pay $1,000,000 in cash in two years.
j. Sale of company shares to new investors.
k. A hockey team signs a player to a long-term contract. The team will pay the player monthly.

E3-2. **(Creating transactions and economic events from accounting equation effects, LO 2, 5)** Below are pairs of changes that affect elements of the accounting equation. Give an example of a transaction or economic event that reflects each:
a. Asset increases, asset decreases
b. Asset increases, liability increases
c. Asset increases, shareholders' equity increases
d. Asset increases, revenue increases
e. Liability decreases, asset decreases
f. Asset decreases, expense increases
g. Liability decreases, revenue increases
h. Asset decreases, shareholders' equity decreases
i. Liability increases, expense increases
j. Asset decreases, revenue decreases (this one's a bit tricky)

E3-3. **(Preparing closing entries using spreadsheets and journal entries, LO 2, 4, 6)** Below is a summarized income statement for St. Bruno Inc. (St. Bruno).

St. Bruno Inc.
Income Statement for the Year Ended December 31, 2014

Revenue	$3,750,000
Expenses	2,900,000
Net income	$850,000

a. Prepare a spreadsheet and make the entry that is necessary to close the temporary accounts. Assume the balance in retained earnings on December 31, 2013 was $17,500,000.

b. Prepare the journal entry necessary to close the temporary accounts.

c. Explain why closing entries are necessary and when they should be recorded.

d. What would be the effect on net income in 2015 if St. Bruno Inc. forgot to prepare a closing entry in 2014?

E3-4. **(Preparing closing entries using spreadsheets and journal entries, LO 2, 4, 6)** Below is Niagara Falls Ltd.'s (Niagara Falls) summarized income statement for the year ended August 31, 2013, its first year in business.

Niagara Falls Ltd.
Income Statement for the Year Ended August 31, 2013
(in thousands of dollars)

Sales		$338,580
Cost of sales		114,300
Gross margin		224,280
Expenses		
Selling and marketing	$34,110	
General and administrative	23,175	
Research and development	14,513	
Depreciation	14,130	
Interest	6,750	
Total		92,678
Income before taxes		131,602
Income taxes		26,320
Net income		$105,282

a. Prepare a spreadsheet and make the entries necessary to close the temporary accounts.

b. Prepare the journal entry necessary to close the temporary accounts.

c. Explain why closing entries are necessary and when they should be recorded.

d. What would be the effect on net income in 2014 if Niagara Falls Ltd. forgot to prepare a closing entry in 2013?

E3-5. **(Impact of transactions on the accounting equation, LO 2, 5)** For each of the following transactions indicate the impact on the elements of the accounting equation:

a. Sale of land for cash.

b. Purchase of inventory on credit.

c. Sale of goods to a customer on credit.

d. Payment of an amount owing to a supplier.

e. Payment of rent in advance.

f. Receipt of cash from a customer for goods to be delivered in the future.

g. Sale of corporate shares for cash.

h. Receipt of an amount owing from a customer.

i. Payment of a dividend to shareholders.

E3-6.   (**Recognizing the effects of debits and credits, LO 5**) Indicate whether each of the following would be treated as a debit or a credit in a journal entry.

a. Increase in land.
b. Increase in bank loan.
c. Decrease in inventory.
d. Increase in revenues.
e. Increase in cost of goods sold.
f. Decrease in retained earnings.
g. Decrease in rent expense.
h. Decrease in accrued liabilities.

E3-7.   (**Identifying different types of adjusting entries, LO 4**) Refer to Table 3.5, which summarizes the different types of adjusting journal entries. For each of the following transactions involving Beulah Ltd. (Beulah) identify the type of adjusting entry required as a result of the event. Explain the reason for your choice.

	Type	Situation
Example	Deferred expense/prepaid expense	Beulah pays two years' rent in advance
a.	_____	Beulah hasn't paid or been billed for water used during the period.
b.	_____	Beulah is owed a licensing fee by a client with a licence to use Beulah's logo during the period. Payment hasn't been received.
c.	_____	Beulah received payment for services to be rendered in the future.
d.	_____	Beulah employees earned wages in the period that won't be paid until next period.
e.	_____	Beulah purchased new computer equipment. The estimated life of the equipment is four years.
f.	_____	Beulah earned interest on an investment. Payment isn't due to be received until next year.
g.	_____	Beulah paid for the right to use a retailer's name in an advertising campaign. The payment was made this year and the right to use the name begins next year.

E3-8.   (**Recording transactions using an accounting equation spreadsheet, LO 2**) Englee Ltd. (Englee) is a retail clothing store owned by Ned Englee. Set up an accounting equation spreadsheet and enter each of the following independent economic events into it.

a. Englee purchases new furniture and fixtures for the store for $100,000 cash.
b. Englee purchases new carpeting for $18,000. It pays $10,000 in cash and the remainder is payable in 90 days.
c. Englee purchases supplies for $900 cash.
d. Englee repays $5,000 on its bank loan.
e. Ned Englee pays $55,000 to purchase Englee common shares.
f. Englee receives an invoice from a local newspaper for advertising run the previous week. Englee pays the $500 owing immediately.
g. Englee sells merchandise to customers during the month worth $32,000 cash. The goods cost $15,000. (*Hint:* The company records the reduction in inventory and cost of sales at the time the sales are recorded.)
h. Englee sells merchandise worth $8,000 to a corporate executive. The merchandise cost $5,200. The customer promises to pay in 30 days. (*Hint:* The company records the reduction in inventory and cost of sales at the time the sale is recorded.)
i. Englee collects $5,000 that is due from a customer.
j. Englee pays a law firm a $4,500 deposit for legal service that will be provided next year.

E3-9. (Recording transactions using journal entries, LO 5) For each of the events described in Exercise E3-8, prepare the journal entry necessary to record the event. Create a T-account for each account you use and post the journal entries to the appropriate T-accounts.

E3-10. (Recording transactions using an accounting equation spreadsheet, LO 2) Feldstein and Partners (Feldstein) is a firm of accountants. Set up an accounting equation spreadsheet and enter each of the following independent economic events into the spreadsheet:

a. Feldstein completed an engagement for a client and sent an invoice for $5,000. The client is required to pay within 30 days.

b. Feldstein exchanges real estate owned by the partnership for a building. The real estate and building are each worth $425,000.

c. Feldstein pays $2,500 owed to a supplier of stationery.

d. Feldstein admitted a new partner to the partnership. The new partner paid $50,000 for an ownership interest.

e. Feldstein borrows $18,000 from the bank.

f. During the month Feldstein's employees earned $25,000 is salaries and wages. The amount owing will be paid early next month.

g. Feldstein hires a new accountant for the upcoming busy season. The new person will join the firm in two weeks.

h. Feldstein receives a $7,000 deposit from a client for services that will be provided next year.

i. Feldstein collects $3,700 owed by a client.

j. Feldstein donates $1,500 to a local charity.

E3-11. (Recording transactions using journal entries, LO 5) For each of the events described in Exercise E3-10, prepare the journal entry necessary to record the event. Create a T-account for each account you use and post each journal entry to the appropriate T-accounts.

E3-12. (Explaining journal entries, LO 4, 5) Provide a description of the event represented by each of the following journal entries.

a. Dr. Cash	1,000,000	
Cr. Building		1,000,000
b. Dr. Accounts receivable	20,000	
Cr. Revenue		20,000
c. Dr. Cash	7,500,000	
Cr. Common shares		7,500,000
d. Dr. Land	350,000	
Cr. Notes payable		350,000
e. Dr. Wages expense	8,500	
Cr. Wages payable		8,500
f. Dr. Unearned revenue	10,000	
Cr. Revenue		10,000
g. Dr. Accounts payable	15,000	
Cr. Cash		15,000
h. Dr. Rent expense	2,500	
Cr. Prepaid rent		2,500

E3-13. (Explaining journal entries, LO 4, 5) Provide a description of the event represented by each of the following journal entries.

a. Dr. Equipment	1,100,000	
Cr. Cash		350,000
Cr. Notes payable		750,000
b. Dr. Interest receivable	25,000	
Cr. Interest revenue		25,000
c. Dr. Cash	1,500,000	
Dr. Long-term receivable	3,500,000	
Cr. Land		5,000,000
d. Dr. Rent expense	5,000	
Cr. Prepaid rent		5,000

e. Dr. Sales	21,000	
Cr. Accounts receivable		21,000
f. Dr. Patent	250,000	
Cr. Common shares		250,000
g. Dr. Cash	35,000	
Cr. Revenue		25,000
Cr. Unearned revenue		10,000
h. Dr. Supplies expense	2,000	
Cr. Supplies inventory		2,000

E3-14. **(Recreating journal entries from T-account data, LO 5)** Use the information from the T-accounts below to create the related journal entries.

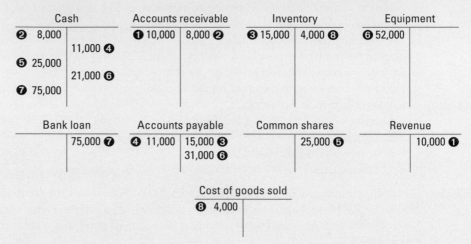

E3-15. **(Recording economic events in an accounting equation spreadsheet and preparing financial statements, LO 2, 4, 5, 6)** Fitness For All Ltd. is a new health club operating in a suburb of Winnipeg. The following transactions take place in September and October 2013:

i. September 1: Fitness For All Ltd. is incorporated. The owner pays $125,000 for 5,000 shares of company stock.

ii. September 3: Fitness For All Ltd. signs a three-year lease for space for the club. The owner pays $3,000 cash in rent for October and November.

iii. September 3-20: Renovations on the location are carried out at a cost of $20,000 cash. The expected useful life of the renovations is three years.

iv. September 21: Equipment worth $125,000 is purchased from a supplier. Fitness For All Ltd. pays $75,000 in cash and promises to pay the remainder in six months. The estimated life of the equipment is five years.

v. September 25: Supplies are purchased on credit for $5,000.

vi. During September and October: Memberships to the club are sold to 300 people at $350 per person per year. Members pay 50 percent immediately and promise to pay the remainder in 30 days. Fitness for All Ltd. records revenue when a new member joins.

vii. During September and October: Employees are paid wages of $10,000. At the end of October Fitness For All Ltd. owes employees $1,200.

viii. During September and October: Utilities costing $2,000 are paid.

ix. During September and October: Fitness For All Ltd. pays $2,700 toward the supplies purchased on credit on September 25.

x. During September and October: Fitness For All Ltd. collects $30,000 owed by members.

xi. During September and October: $3,900 of supplies is used.

Required:

a. Use an accounting equation spreadsheet to record the transactions that occurred during September and October.

b. Record all necessary adjusting entries (depreciation rent, supplies, and wages).

  c. Record the closing entry.
  d. Prepare the balance sheet as of October 31, 2013 and an income statement and statement of retained earnings for the period ending October 31, 2013.

E3-16. **(Recording adjusting entries, LO 2, 4, 5)** You are the accountant for Ilderton Ltd. (Ilderton). For each of the following situations prepare the required adjusting entries. Also show the related transactional entries and the date the entries would be made. Assume a December 31 year-end. This question can be done using an accounting equation spreadsheet or journal entries.
  a. On September 1 Ilderton purchases a building for $8,000,000 cash. The estimated life of the building is 20 years.
  b. As of December 31 Ilderton estimates it owes $1,200 to its electricity supplier for electricity used in December. The company won't be billed until early March.
  c. On July 10 Ilderton receives a $24,000 deposit for services to be provided over the next 18 months, beginning on August 1. The services provided are worth the same amount each month.
  d. Ilderton earns $5,000 per month in royalty revenue from another company that has rights to use one of its training programs. The full amount for the year must be paid on June 30 each year.
  e. On January 1, the office supplies account had a balance of $5,500. During the year office supplies costing $12,000 were purchased for cash. A count of office supplies on December 31 found supplies worth $2,100 on hand.

E3-17. **(Recording adjusting entries, LO 2, 4, 5)** You are the accountant for Halkirk Inc. (Halkirk). For each of the following situations prepare the necessary adjusting entries. Also show the related transactional entries and the date the entries would be made. Assume a July 31 year-end. This question can be done using an accounting equation spreadsheet or journal entries.
  a. During the year Halkirk's salespeople earned bonuses of $10,000 for the fiscal year just ended. The bonuses will be paid on September 1.
  b. Halkirk rents space in its building to a law firm for $1,000 per month. As of July 31, Halkirk hasn't received July's rent. The law firm has indicated that it will pay by the middle of August.
  c. Halkirk pays its salaried employees monthly, on the 15th of the month. On July 31 the company owes its employees $7,200.
  d. On April 1, Halkirk invested $50,000 in an investment account that pays interest of 4 percent per year, payable on March 31 and September 30.
  e. On November 1 Halkirk purchased a two-year computer maintenance service package for $12,000. The package provides same-day, on-site service for the company's computers.
  f. On February 15 Halkirk received $12,000 in advance for goods it will deliver over the next few months. As of July 31, 25 percent of the goods had been delivered.

E3-18. **(Recording adjusting entries, LO 4, 5)** The account balances before and after the adjusting entries have been made are presented below for a number of accounts. For each account, prepare the adjusting entry that gave rise to the change in the account balance and provide an explanation for each entry.

Account	Balance before adjusting entry	Balance after adjusting entry
Accumulated depreciation	$120,000	$160,000
Interest payable	0	10,000
Interest receivable	0	12,000
Prepaid rent	35,000	20,000
Supplies inventory	10,000	4,000
Unearned revenue	25,000	10,000
Wages payable	0	22,000

E3-19. **(Understanding the relationship between closing entries and the income statement, LO 6)** Below is the closing journal entry prepared by Bellburn Ltd. on December 31, 2014. Use the closing journal entry to prepare Bellburn Ltd.'s income statement for the year ended December 31, 2014.

Dr. Revenue	1,137,500	
Dr. Royalties	80,250	
Cr. Retained earnings		196,000
Cr. Salaries expense		218,750
Cr. Promotion and advertising expense		61,250
Cr. Depreciation expense		43,750
Cr. Cost of goods sold		468,750
Cr. General and administrative expense		56,000
Cr. Interest expense		21,875
Cr. Rent expense		31,500
Cr. Income tax expense		103,250
Cr. Other expense		16,625

E3-20. **(Evaluating the effect not recording adjusting entries has on net income, LO 4, 5)** For each of the following situations, indicate whether not recording the necessary adjusting entry will result in (i) an overstatement of net income (net income is higher than it would otherwise be), (ii) an understatement of net income (net income is lower than it would otherwise be), or (iii) no effect on net income. Briefly explain your conclusion.

a. Depreciation expense isn't recorded.

b. Interest is earned on a bond but the cash won't be received until next year. The interest earned isn't recorded.

c. A company receives a deposit from a customer for services that will be provided in the following year. When the services are provided in the following year the company doesn't make an adjusting entry.

d. A company purchases a two-year insurance policy on the first day of the year and records the purchase as prepaid insurance. At the end of the year no adjustment is made to reflect the portion of the policy that was consumed.

e. An entry to record interest on a loan that isn't payable until next month isn't recorded.

f. Wages are earned by employees in the last week of the year but won't be paid until next year. The wages earned aren't recorded.

E3-21. **(Evaluating the effect that not recording adjusting entries has on financial statement elements, LO 4, 5)** For each of the items described in E3-20 indicate how not recording the necessary adjusting entry will affect the following financial statement elements: assets, liabilities, owners' equity, revenues, and expenses. Will the impact be (i) an overstatement of each element, (ii) an understatement of each element, or (iii) no effect on each element. Briefly explain your conclusions.

E3-22. **(Using an accounting equation spreadsheet to determine the opening balance in an account, LO 2)** The chief financial officer of Afton Ltd. (Afton) is trying to determine the amount of cash the company had on hand one month ago on March 1, 2014. The company's computer system has lost the information. Use an accounting equation spreadsheet and the following information to determine the information the CFO requires. Afton Ltd. had a cash balance of $280,000 on March 31, 2014.

a. On March 15 Afton purchased equipment costing $100,000 by paying $45,000 in cash and promising to pay the remainder in 90 days.

b. On March 20 Afton made payments of $22,500 on its bank loan.

c. During March, Afton had sales of $393,000. $56,000 of the sales were for cash, the rest on credit.

d. During March, Afton collected $248,000 from customers who had made credit purchases and paid suppliers $202,000.

e. During March, Afton paid employees $72,000.

f. During March, Afton had other cash revenue of $10,000 and other cash expenses of $18,000.

E3-23.   (**Using an accounting equation spreadsheet to determine missing information, LO 2**) Use an accounting equation spreadsheet and the following information to determine the amount of credit sales to customers that occurred during November 2013:

a. On November 1, 2013 the balance in the accounts receivable account was $175,000.

b. During November 2013, $205,000 was collected from customers.

c. The balance in the accounts receivable account on November 30, 2013, was $190,000.

E3-24.   (**Using an accounting equation spreadsheet to determine missing information, LO 2**) Use an accounting equation spreadsheet and the following information to determine the amount paid to suppliers during June 2014:

a. On June 1, 2014, the balance in the accounts payable account was $50,000.

b. During June 2014, there were credit purchases from suppliers of $250,000.

c. The balance in the accounts payable account on June 30, 2014, was $60,000.

E3-25.   (**Correcting errors, LO 2, 3, 5**) Zhoda Ltd. (Zhoda) has been having problems with its bookkeeper. Recently errors have been observed in the bookkeeper's work. Examine each of the following items and make any journal entry necessary to correct the entries originally made. This question can also be answered using an accounting equation spreadsheet.

a. Zhoda received an advance for work to be done in the next fiscal year. The bookkeeper debited cash and credited revenue for $10,000.

b. Zhoda paid casual employees $2,000 at the end of the working day. The bookkeeper debited wages payable and credited cash.

c. Zhoda paid a dividend to shareholders of $50,000. The bookkeeper debited dividend expense and credited cash for $50,000.

d. Zhoda delivered $5,000 in merchandise to a customer who had already paid. The bookkeeper debited unearned revenue and credited accounts receivable.

E3-26.   (**Correcting errors, LO 2, 3, 5**) Examine the accounting errors described in Exercise E3-25. For each error explain the impact the error (and failure to correct the error) would have on the financial statements.

E3-27.   (**Correcting errors, LO 2, 3, 5**) Grosswerder Ltd. (Grosswerder) has been having problems with its bookkeeper. Recently errors have been found in the bookkeeper's work. Examine each of the following items and make any journal entry necessary to correct the entries originally made. This question can also be answered using an accounting equation spreadsheet.

a. Grosswerder received a $3,000 payment from a customer for goods previously delivered. The bookkeeper debited cash and credited revenue.

b. Grosswerder repaid $100,000 of its bank loan. The bookkeeper debited interest expense and credited cash.

c. Grosswerder sold shares to investors for $200,000. The bookkeeper debited cash and credited revenue for $200,000.

d. Grosswerder purchased a $1,500 insurance policy that would provide coverage in the next fiscal year. The bookkeeper debited insurance expense and credited cash.

E3-28.   (**Correcting errors, LO 2, 3, 5**) Examine the accounting errors described in Exercise E3-27. For each error explain the impact the error (and failure to correct the error) would have on the current year's financial statements.

E3-29.   (**Preparing a balance sheet and income statement using a trial balance, LO 5**) Below is Kuskonook Inc.'s (Kuskonook) December 31, 2014 trial balance that was prepared before the closing journal entry was recorded. Use the trial balance to prepare Kuskonook's balance sheet as of December 31, 2014 and the income statement for the year ended December 31, 2014. The accounts in the trial balance are listed alphabetically.

Kuskonook Inc.
Trial Balance
December 31, 2014

Account	Debit	Credit
Accounts payable	$	$150,000
Accounts receivable	93,750	
Accrued liabilities		13,500
Accumulated depreciation		618,750
Bank loan payable		112,500
Cash	18,750	
Common shares		937,500
Cost of sales	1,833,750	
Current portion of long-term debt		225,000
Depreciation expense	187,500	
Income tax expense	262,500	
Income taxes payable		11,250
Interest expense	135,000	
Interest payable		9,000
Inventory	168,000	
Land	562,500	
Loan receivable	36,000	
Long-term debt		1,575,000
Long-term loan receivable	82,500	
Miscellaneous expenses	136,500	
Patent	600,000	
Prepaid assets	13,500	
Capital assets	3,206,250	
Retained earnings		606,000
Revenue		4,312,500
Selling, general, and administrative expense	543,750	
Wages and salaries expense	712,500	
Wages and salaries payable		21,750
	$8,592,750	$8,592,750

E3-30. (Prepare a closing journal entry and a post-closing trial balance, LO 6) Use the information from the trial balance in E3-29 to prepare the closing journal entry and post-closing trial balance for Kuskonook Inc. for its December 31, 2014 year-end.

E3-31. (Record information in a simple spreadsheet and prepare a balance sheet, LO 1, 4, 5) In September 2015, Denis Sonin had a great idea to make some money. He decided he would sell holiday items in the local mall in the two months preceding Christmas. He set up a proprietorship he called Denis's Great Gifts, opened a bank account in the proprietorship's name, and deposited $10,000 of his savings into the account. He borrowed $7,000 from his grandmother, which he also deposited into the bank account. He promised his grandmother he would repay the money by the end of January. On October 15 he came to terms with the mall manager to rent a small store in a good location for two months ending December 31. He paid the rent of $2,000 for the two months in full on October 15. Next Denis purchased tables, shelving, and other materials he needed to operate his store for $3,000. He spent as little money as possible on these items because he wanted to provide the merchandise to customers at low prices and this meant keeping the store simple. In the last week of October Denis purchased merchandise to stock the store. He bought books, Christmas decorations, and other low cost items he thought would be popular. In total, Denis purchased merchandise costing $22,000. He paid the various suppliers $10,000 in cash and agreed to pay the rest in 30 days. He also purchased an advertisement in the community newspaper for $500 that would run in the first week of November. He paid for the advertisement on October 29.

Required:

    a. Use an accounting equation spreadsheet to record the economic activity of Denis's Great Gifts.

    b. Use the information from your spreadsheet to prepare a balance sheet for Denis as of October 31.

E3-32. **(Record transactions and prepare income statements, LO 1, 5)** Refer to the information in E3-31. Denis operated Denis's Great Gifts until December 31. In the two months he sold merchandise to customers for $52,000, all in cash, except for $1,200 that was owed by one customer. He sold all the inventory he originally purchased in October ($22,000) plus most of an additional $10,000 of inventory he purchased in early December. At the end of December there was about $600 of inventory unsold. As of the end of December he owed one of his suppliers $1,750. He paid the sales people he hired $3,000 in cash for their work and owed them $400 on December 31. He also incurred an additional $1,500 in advertising costs, all of which had been paid for as of the end of December. At the end of December he also owed about $500 for utilities and other miscellaneous costs that were incurred during November and December.

Required:

    a. Prepare income statements for Denis's Great Gifts for the period ending December 31 on the cash basis and on the accrual basis. (To do this question you will also have to complete the spreadsheet required in E3-31.)

    b. Explain why the two income statements are different.

    c. Prepare a balance sheet as of December 31, 2015.

    d. Assess the performance of Denis's business. Also discuss any issues surrounding Denis's inventory on December 31.

Problems

P3-1. **(Prepare adjusting entries, LO 2, 3, 4, 5)** For each of the following situations provide the necessary adjusting entries for Truax Ltd. (Truax) for the year ended December 31, 2014. (These situations are tricky. When preparing each adjusting entry compare what is recorded in the accounting system with what you think should be in the accounting system. Your adjusting entry should take the accounting system from "what is" recorded to "what should be" recorded.)

    a. On August 15, 2014, Truax received $180,000 as an advance for services to be rendered over the next 18 months. The services began on September 1, 2014, and will be provided equally each month of the contract. Truax Inc. recorded the transaction by debiting cash for $180,000 and crediting revenue for $180,000.

    b. On July 2, 2014 Truax purchased a two-year insurance policy for $15,000 cash. The company debited insurance expense for $15,000 and credited cash for $15,000.

    c. Truax owns the rights to market products that use the name and images of some well-known entertainers. It in turn licenses those rights to other companies. The arrangements require the licensees to pay a percentage of sales to Truax every six months, on October 1 and April 1. On April 1, 2014 Truax received a cheque from one of its licensees for $23,000 for the six months ending March 31, 2014. The accountant debited cash and credited revenue for $23,000.

P3-2. **(Prepare adjusting entries, LO 2, 3, 4, 5)** For each of the following situations provide the necessary adjusting entries for Carberry Inc. (Carberry) for the year ended December 31, 2013. (These situations are tricky. When preparing each adjusting entry, compare what is recorded in the accounting system with what you think should be in the accounting system. Your adjusting entry should take the accounting system from "what is" recorded to "what should be" recorded.)

a. On October 1, 2013, Carberry received $25,000 for goods it will produce and deliver to a customer. Carberry will deliver $5,000 of the goods each month beginning in November 2013. Carberry recorded the transaction by debiting cash and crediting revenue for $25,000.

b. On April 1, 2013, Carberry paid $25,000 cash for the right to use a vacant lot to store some of its equipment for the next two years. The company debited rent expense and credited cash for $25,000.

c. On February 15, 2013, Carberry received its quarterly natural gas bill covering the period November 1, 2012, to January 31, 2013. The accountant debited utilities expense—Natural Gas and credited cash for $2,400.

P3-3.   **(The effect of different lease arrangements on the financial statements, LO 3, 4, 5)** Liscomb Consulting is a partnership of business consultants located in Halifax. The company has been successful since it began business five years ago and the partners have decided to move into new offices. On August 20, 2013, the partners came to terms with a property owner and signed a three-year lease for space at a prestigious address. Liscomb occupied its new offices on September 1, 2013. Monthly rent is $1,000. For each situation below show what would appear on Liscomb's balance sheet and income statement if these statements were prepared on September 1, 2013 and on September 30, 2013. For each situation show all journal entries prepared in August and September 2013. Indicate whether each journal entry is a transactional or adjusting entry. Consider each situation separately.

a. On August 20, 2013 Liscomb pays the property owner rent for September and agrees to pay each month's rent on the first day of the month (so October's rent is due on October 1).

b. The property owner agrees to allow Liscomb to pay its rent in arrears so that the rent is due on the first day of the next month (so September's rent is due October 1, and so on).

c. The property owner agrees to allow Liscomb to pay its rent on the 15th of each month. The first month's rent is paid August 20 (so the payment on September 15 is for October).

d. The property owner agrees to allow Liscomb to pay its rent on the 15th of each month. The first month's rent is paid on September 15 (so the payment on September 15 is for September).

P3-4.   **(The effect of different lease arrangements on the financial statements, LO 3, 4, 5)** Kashabowie Properties Ltd. (Kashabowie) owns and operates several commercial real estate properties in Halifax. On August 20, 2014, Kashabowie signed a three-year lease with a consulting firm for space in one of its buildings. Monthly rent is $1,000. For each situation below show what would appear on Kashabowie's balance sheet and income statement if these statements were prepared on September 1, 2014, and on September 30, 2014. For each situation show all journal entries prepared in August and September 2014. Indicate whether each journal entry is a transactional or adjusting entry.

a. On August 20, 2014, Kashabowie receives the $1,000 rent payment for September. The lease agreement requires the consulting firm to pay each month's rent on the first day of the month (so October's rent is due on October 1).

b. Kashabowie agrees to allow the consulting firm to pay its rent in arrears so that its rent is due on the first day of the next month (so September's rent is due October 1 and so on).

c. Kashabowie agrees to allow the consulting firm to pay its rent on the 15th of each month. The first month's rent is paid on August 20 (so the payment on September 15 is for October).

d. Kashabowie agrees to allow the consulting firm to pay its rent on the 15th of each month. The first month's rent is paid on September 15 (so the payment on September 15 is for September).

P3-5. **(Determining missing information, LO 2, 4, 5)** Use the following information to calculate ending balance in accounts receivable. (This is a tricky question. All the information is relevant. Set up T-accounts or a spreadsheet to help.)

- Accounts receivable at the beginning of the period $125,000
- Revenue for the period (there are no cash sales) 750,000
- Unearned revenue at the beginning of the period 15,000
- Unearned revenue at the end of the period 12,000
- Cash collected—accounts receivable 705,000
- Cash collected—unearned revenue 16,000

P3-6. **(Understanding the effect of errors on the elements of the accounting equation, LO 4, 5)** For each of the following situations indicate whether assets, liabilities, equity, revenues, and expenses are overstated (too high), understated (too low), or unaffected by the error in the June 30, 2014 financial statements. Briefly explain why the effects occur and state any assumptions you make.

a. Employees are paid monthly on the 15th. No adjusting entry was made at the end of June. The employees will be paid $52,000 on July 15.

b. On March 15, 2014 $500 was received from a customer paying in advance for lawn care services that were to be provided from April to October 2014. The bookkeeper credited revenue for $500 when the cash was received. No adjusting entry was made on June 30, 2014.

c. On September 1, 2013 a company borrowed $1,000,000 from a private lender. The interest rate on the loan is 6 percent per year. Interest must be paid on August 31 and February 28 of each year. The loan principal must be paid in full on August 31, 2018. No adjusting entry was made by the borrower with respect to the loan and interest on June 30, 2014.

d. On January 3, 2014 a company purchased a new delivery truck for $35,000. The company estimates the truck will be used for five years. No adjusting entry was made at year-end.

e. On June 30, 2014 the bookkeeper made an entry to record revenue that was previously unearned. The adjustment recognized $12,000 of revenue instead of $21,000.

P3-7. **(Understanding the effect of errors on the elements of the accounting equation, LO 4, 5)** For each of the following situations, indicate whether assets, liabilities, equity, revenues, and expenses are overstated (too high), understated (too low), or unaffected by the error in the December 31, 2014 financial statements. Briefly explain why the effects occur and state any assumptions that you make.

a. A retail store pays rent to the mall owners of $36,000 per year (payable monthly) plus 2 percent of annual sales. The rent based on sales must be paid 90 days after the store's year-end. Estimated sales for fiscal 2014 are $550,000. No adjusting entry was made at year-end.

b. On December 15, 2013 a sports fan purchased seasons tickets for her city's baseball team's games for $4,000 cash. The baseball season begins in April and the team recognizes its revenue when the games are played. During 2014 no adjusting entries were recorded.

c. On June 30, 2014 a two-year insurance policy was purchased for $12,000 cash. The bookkeeper debited prepaid insurance for $9,000 when the policy was purchased. No adjusting entry was made at year-end.

d. An accounting firm provides service to a client over a six-month period beginning October 15, 2014. The client agreed to pay the $25,000 when the services had been fully provided in April 2015. No adjusting entry was made at year-end.

e. On December 31, 2014 bookkeeper incorrectly entered the entry for an accrued interest expense as $4,250 instead of $2,450.

P3-8. **(Effect of adjustments on financial ratios, LO 4, 5)** For each of the following adjusting entries state whether the entry increases, decreases, or has no effect on the following financial ratios: current ratio, debt-to-equity ratio, profit margin ratio, and return on equity. Assume the current ratio and debt-to-equity ratio are greater than one and the profit margin ratio and return on equity are less than one before each of the adjusting entries is considered.

a. Dr. Depreciation expense	220,000	
Cr. Accumulated depreciation		220,000
b. Dr. Insurance expense	15,000	
Cr. Prepaid insurance		15,000
c. Dr. Royalty receivable	102,000	
Cr. Royalty revenue		102,000
d. Dr. Unearned revenue	55,000	
Cr. Revenue		55,000
e. Dr. Wages expense	12,500	
Cr. Accrued wages payable		12,500

P3-9. **(Effect of adjustments on financial ratios, LO 4, 5)** Examine the adjusting entries provided in exercise P3-8. Indicate the impact that *not* making each of the entries would have on the following financial ratios: current ratio, debt-to-equity ratio, profit margin ratio, and return on equity. Assume the current ratio and debt-to-equity ratio are greater than one and the profit margin ratio and return on equity are less than one before each of the adjusting entries is considered.

P3-10. **(Using the accounting equation spreadsheet to record transactions and prepare financial statements, LO 1, 2, 4, 6)** Paul Byrne, a first-year student in a business program in Toronto, was approached by a friend offering to sell him his hot dog vending cart. The friend was going to be starting a permanent job in the summer so he no longer needed the cart. Paul decided to buy the cart as a way to make money to finance his education and learn how to manage a business at the same time.

Paul operated his business from late April, when the weather started to warm up, to early September. Paul was so busy running the business he had no time to keep any accounting records. So on September 10, after he had put away the cart until the next year, he sat down with all the data he had carefully collected in a shoebox throughout the summer. From the information in the shoebox he obtained the following:

a. On April 1 Paul opened a bank account in the name of his company Paul's Dogs and deposited $3,500 from his bank account into the account. Paul decided he would operate the business as a proprietorship. (Remember, in a proprietorship the owners' equity section of the balance sheet includes only a single account called owner's equity or owner's capital. This is different from a corporation where there will be a common shares account and a retained earnings account.)

b. Paul purchased the cart from his friend on April 8 for $2,400. He gave his friend $1,500 in cash and promised to pay him the rest at the end of the summer. The cart was already four years old and Paul's friend said it should be good for another three or four years, after which time it would probably be junk.

c. Paul took the cart to a repair shop and had the cart painted, serviced, and repaired. Paul paid the shop $700 in cash.

d. Paul went to city hall and obtained a licence to operate his cart in the city. It cost $750 and Paul paid with his debit card. The licence is valid for two years and expires at the end of the next calendar year.

e. During the summer Paul sold hot dogs and drinks for $22,750.

f. In late August Paul was asked to bring his cart to a softball tournament where he would be the official supplier of hot dogs to participants. The agreement was that Paul would keep track of the hot dogs and drinks he handed out to the players and send a bill to the tournament organizers. At the end of the tournament Paul delivered a bill for $1,615. The organizers said they would pay on September 20.

g. During the summer Paul bought hot dogs, buns, drinks, condiments, napkins, plastic cutlery, paper plates, and other supplies for $12,825. All of these items were paid for in cash.

h. At the end of the summer Paul had about $900 in non-perishable items stored in his basement at home (he had used $11,925 of the supplies he had bought).

i. On several days during the summer Paul was unable to operate the cart himself. On those days he hired his brother to do it. During the entire summer Paul paid his brother $1,655 cash. As of today Paul still owes him $115.

j. During the summer Paul incurred $1,400 in other expenses. All of these were paid in cash.

k. On August 15 Paul withdrew $4,500 from the business to pay for tuition and other school-related costs.

l. On September 5 Paul paid his friend the $900 he owed him.

Required:

a. Enter each of the transactions onto an accounting equation spreadsheet. You can use a computer spreadsheet program or create a spreadsheet manually, although the computer spreadsheet will probably be easier because you will be able to correct mistakes more easily. Create a separate column on the spreadsheet for each account.

b. Provide explanations for each of your entries. You should explain why you have treated the economic events as you have (that is, why you have recorded an asset, liability, etc.).

c. Prepare a balance sheet as of September 10 and an income statement for the period ended September 10 from your spreadsheet. Make sure to make a closing entry.

d. Explain why the financial statements you have prepared would be useful to Paul.

e. If Paul asked you for some feedback on his business from examining the financial statements, what would you be able to tell him?

P3-11. (**Following the steps of the accounting cycle, LO 1, 4, 5, 6**) Use the information provided in Problem P3-10 about Paul's Dogs to do the following:

a. Prepare all necessary journal entries until September 10.

b. Prepare T-accounts and post each journal entry to the appropriate T-account.

c. Prepare and post adjusting journal entries to their appropriate T-accounts. Adjusting entries are needed for the cart and the license.

d. Prepare a trial balance as of September 10.

e. Prepare a balance sheet for Paul's Dogs as of September 10 and an income statement covering the period until September 10.

f. Prepare the closing journal entry and post the closing entry to the appropriate T-accounts.

g. Prepare a trial balance as of September 10 after the closing entry has been prepared.

h. If Paul asked you for some feedback on his business from examining the financial statements, what would you be able to tell him?

P3-12. (**Using the accounting equation spreadsheet to record transactions and prepare financial statements, LO 1, 2, 4, 6**) We've Got Wheels, Inc. (Wheels) was formed on May 1, 2014 by two university friends who thought they could make money renting bikes and inline skates to visitors at a busy lake-front area near their homes. The friends thought the business would be a good way to spend their summer near the beach while making enough money to finance next year's university costs. If the business is successful the friends hope to operate it for as long as they attend university.

The two owners closed down Wheels for the year after the Labour Day weekend. It was a very hectic summer and they didn't have nearly as much time to have fun as they thought they would. They were also so busy that they didn't pay much attention to keeping any accounting records. They did, however, keep all the receipts, invoices, and deposit slips that accumulated over the summer.

It's now September 10. The owners have asked you to compile useful information about Wheels for them. After summarizing the data they provided, you have the following information for the summer of 2014:

i.   May 1: Each friend contributed $9,000 in cash to Wheels in exchange for stock in the company.

ii. May 5: Purchased 30 new and used bicycles for a total of $10,500. Wheels agreed to pay $6,000 immediately and the remainder on September 30, 2014. The owners think the bikes will last for at least three summers, after which time they will no longer be useful for the business.

iii. May 9: Obtained a permit to operate a business at the lake. The cost of the permit was $150 for the summer.

iv. May 10: Purchased 50 sets of inline skates and 50 sets of protective equipment for $6,750 in cash. The owners think that the most they will get out of this equipment is about two summers of use.

v.   During the summer: Wheels rented bicycles and skates to customers for $41,625 cash.

vi. During the summer: Purchased packaged snacks for $2,200 cash. At the end of the summer there was $450 of snacks left over. The snacks were sold to customers through the summer for $3,575 cash.

vii. During the summer: Purchased advertising on a local radio station. Advertising was paid for by cheque once an ad was played. Total amount spent during the summer was $1,500. Nothing was owing at the end of the Labour Day weekend.

viii. During the summer: Wheels provided inline skating lessons to children on behalf of the local Parks and Recreation Department. Wheels billed the department $3,500 for the lessons. As of September 10, $2,250 was still owed to Wheels. The amount owed is due on October 15.

ix. During the summer: Wheels incurred other expenses amounting to $12,500. All were paid in cash.

x.   During the summer: The owners took $7,500 each to meet their personal needs.

Required:

a. Enter each of the transactions onto an accounting equation spreadsheet. You can use a computer spreadsheet program or create a spreadsheet manually. Create a separate column on the spreadsheet for each account.

b. Provide explanations for each of your entries. You should explain why you have treated the economic events as you have (that is, why you have recorded an asset, liability, etc.).

c. Prepare a balance sheet as of September 10, 2014 and an income statement for the period ended September 10, 2014 from your spreadsheet. Make sure to make the closing entry.

d. Explain why the financial statements you have prepared would be useful to the owners of Wheels.

e. Compare Wheels' net income with the amount of cash that was generated by the business. Which is a better indicator of how Wheels did? Why are they different? (When looking at the cash flow consider the cash flows after the owners made their initial $18,000 investment.)

f. If Wheels' owners asked you to evaluate the financial statements for them, what would you be able to tell them?

P3-13. **(Following the steps of the accounting cycle, LO 1, 4, 5, 6)** Use the information provided in Problem P3-12 about We've Got Wheels, Inc. (Wheels) to do the following:

a. Prepare all necessary journal entries until September 10, 2014.

b. Prepare T-accounts and post each journal entry to the appropriate T-account.

c. Prepare and post adjusting journal entries to their appropriate T-accounts. Adjusting entries are needed for the bikes, inline skates and equipment, and the permit.

d. Prepare a trial balance as of September 10, 2014.

e. Prepare a balance sheet as of September 10, 2014 and an income statement for the period ended September 10, 2014 from your spreadsheet. Prepare the closing journal entry and post the closing entry to the appropriate T-accounts.

f. Prepare a trial balance as of September 10, 2014, after the closing entry has been prepared.

g. Compare Wheels' net income with the amount of cash that was generated by the business. Which is a better indicator of how Wheels did? Why are they different? (When looking at the cash flow, consider the cash flows after the owners made their initial $18,000 investment.)

h. If Wheels' owners asked you evaluate the financial statements for them, what would you be able to tell?

P3-14. **(Using the accounting equation spreadsheet to record transactions and prepare financial statements, LO 1, 2, 4, 6)** Superstar Ice Rinks Inc. (SIR) is a privately owned company owned by a group of investors headed by James T. Kirk, a retired professional hockey player. SIR owns three arenas in suburban areas near a large Canadian city, which it rents out to hockey leagues and individuals for recreational use. SIR's arenas also have a pro shop and food and beverage service.

SIR's balance sheet for June 30, 2013, the company's year-end, is shown below. SIR uses its financial statements for tax purposes, to show to the holders of the long-term debt that was used to finance the purchase of the arenas, and for the shareholders, particularly those who aren't involved in management.

Superstar Ice Rinks Inc.
Balance Sheet
As of June 30, 2013

Assets		Liabilities and Shareholders' equity	
Cash	$1,590,000	Bank loan	$180,000
Accounts receivable	50,000	Accounts payable	145,000
Inventory	168,000	Wages payable	17,000
		Taxes payable	92,000
Property, plant, and equipment	15,000,000	Interest payable	25,000
Accumulated depreciation	(3,900,000)	Unearned revenue	975,000
		Current portion of long-term debt	750,000
		Long-term debt	5,861,000
		Common shares	3,765,000
		Retained earnings	1,098,000
	$12,908,000		$12,908,000

It's now July 2014. SIR needs to prepare its financial statements for the year ended June 30, 2014. The following information has been obtained about the fiscal year just ended:

i.   During fiscal 2014 SIR purchased an existing arena for $3.75 million. The purchase was financed by $1.5 million of new long-term debt, SIR shares worth $1.0 million given to the previous owners of the arena, and the remainder in cash.

ii. During fiscal 2014 SIR earned $4,655,000 in revenue from renting ice. In addition the pro shop and restaurant earned $1,375,000 in revenue. Of these amounts $500,000 was on credit provided by SIR. During the year $491,000 was collected from customers who purchased on credit.

iii. Leagues renting ice time for the entire season are required to pay a deposit in May. The deposit is then recognized as revenue over the year as the ice is used by the league. In May 2014 SIR collected $1,045,000 in deposits from leagues.

iv. SIR has a $200,000 line of credit from a local bank. A line of credit means SIR can borrow up to $200,000 without additional approval from the bank.

v.   During the year SIR paid employees $850,000 in cash including the amount owing from the end of fiscal 2013. During the year employees earned $861,000.

vi. During fiscal 2014 SIR repaid $750,000 of its long-term debt. Next year SIR must repay $900,000 of the debt.

vii. During fiscal 2014 SIR paid lenders $450,000 in interest, including interest owed at the end of the previous year. No interest is owing at the end of fiscal 2014.

viii. During the year SIR purchased goods for sale in the pro shops and restaurants for $605,000, all purchased on credit. Suppliers were paid $600,000 during the year.

ix.   SIR purchased other goods and services (fuel for the Zamboni, utilities, maintenance, etc.) during the year costing $1,575,000, also on credit. These creditors received payments of $1,550,000 during the year.

x.   The products sold in the pro shops and food and drink sold in the restaurants during the year cost $612,000.

xi.   SIR incurred additional expenses during the year that cost $300,000 and were paid for in cash.

xii. During the year SIR paid the taxes it owed at the end of fiscal 2013. It also paid $51,000 in instalments on its 2014 income taxes. SIR estimates it owes an additional $33,500 in income taxes for 2014.

xiii. Depreciation for the year was $1,250,000.

xiv. During the year SIR traded ice time with a market value of $21,000 for services worth the same amount.

Required:

a.   Enter each of the transactions onto an accounting equation spreadsheet. You can use a computer spreadsheet program or create a spreadsheet manually. Create a separate column on the spreadsheet for each account. Make sure to prepare all adjusting entries and the closing entry. Indicate whether each entry is a transactional entry, an adjusting entry, or a closing entry.

b.   Provide explanations for each of your entries. You should explain why you have treated the economic events as you have (that is, why you have recorded an asset, liability, etc.).

c.   Prepare a balance sheet as of June 30, 2014 and an income statement for the year ended June 30, 2014 from your spreadsheet.

d.   SIR's non-management shareholders have asked you to analyze the company's financial position and performance. Write a report analyzing the information you prepared.

P3-15. **(Following the steps of the accounting cycle, LO 1, 4, 5, 6)** Use the information provided in Problem P3-14 about Superstar Ice Rinks Inc. (SIR) to do the following:

a.   Prepare all necessary journal entries for fiscal 2014.

b.   Prepare T-accounts and post each journal entry to the appropriate T-account.

c.   Prepare and post adjusting journal entries to their appropriate T-accounts.

d.   Prepare a trial balance as of June 30, 2014.

e.   Prepare a balance sheet for SIR as of June 30, 2014 and an income statement covering the period until June 30, 2014.

f.   Prepare the closing journal entry and post the closing entry to the appropriate T-accounts.

g.   Prepare an after-closing trial balance as of June 30, 2014.

h.   SIR's non-management shareholders have asked you to analyze the company's financial position and performance. Write a report analyzing the information you prepared.

P3-16. **(Using the accounting equation spreadsheet to record transactions and prepare financial statements, LO 1, 2, 4, 6)** Sundre Trucking Inc. (Sundre) is a small shipping company that carries goods between locations in western Canada and the northwestern United States. The Archer family of Tagish owns Sundre but professional managers manage it. One member of the Archer family serves as the chair of the board of directors. No other family members are actively involved with Sundre.

Sundre's balance sheet for the year ended December 31, 2013 is shown below. Sundre uses its financial statements for tax purposes, to show to the holders of the long-term notes that the company issued to finance the purchase of some of its trucks, and to provide information to the shareholders.

Sundre Trucking Inc.
Balance Sheet
As of December 31, 2013

Assets		Liabilities and Shareholders' equity	
Cash	$108,276	Accounts payable	$ 59,108
Accounts receivable	114,100	Taxes payable	21,000
Prepaid insurance	25,200	Wages payable	14,000
Capital assets	651,000	Customer deposits	37,800
Accumulated depreciation	(282,380)	Interest payable	16,660
		Long-term notes payable	196,000
		Common shares	112,000
		Retained earnings	159,628
	$616,196		$616,196

It's now January 2015. Sundre needs to prepare its financial statements for the year ended December 31, 2014. The following information has been obtained about the fiscal year just ended:

i. Shipping revenue for the year was $1,491,315. Sundre gives credit to all its customers and there were no cash sales during the year.

ii. Sundre purchased $385,000 worth of fuel during the year. All purchases were on credit. At the end of 2014 Sundre had not been billed for an additional $14,000 of fuel it purchased.

iii. Sundre incurred maintenance costs of $175,000 during 2014. At the end of 2014 Sundre owed mechanics $11,200.

iv. Sundre paid salaries and bonuses of $665,000 to employees, including the amounts owing on December 31, 2013. At December 31, 2014 Sundre owed employees $38,500.

v. During the year Sundre collected $1,505,000 from customers.

vi. Sundre paid its fuel suppliers $350,000 during 2014.

vii. During the year Sundre paid the taxes it owed at the end of 2013. It also paid $15,400 in instalments on its 2014 income taxes. Sundre estimates that it owes an additional $16,800 in income taxes for 2014.

viii. The deposits reported on the 2013 balance sheet pertained to customers who were perceived to be high risk and to whom Sundre wasn't prepared to offer credit. These customers were required to give deposits against shipping to be done during 2014. These customers used shipping services during 2014 in excess of the amount of the deposits. Sundre decided in 2014 to offer credit to these customers.

ix. Members of the Archer family sometimes use Sundre employees for personal work at their homes and cottages. Usually the work is done on weekends and the employees are paid at overtime rates. Sundre pays the employees' wages for the work done for the family members and accounts for the cost as a wage expense. The wages paid for work done on behalf of Archer family members was $15,400.

x. During 2014 Sundre purchased a new truck for $137,200 in cash.

xi. Depreciation expense for 2014 was $67,200.

xii. Prepaid insurance pertains to insurance on its truck fleet and premises. During 2014 it used $21,000 of insurance that was recorded as prepaid on December 31, 2013. In late 2014 Sundre purchased and paid $29,400 for insurance for 2015.

xiii. During the year Sundre paid $16,660 in interest to the holders of the long-term notes. Interest is paid annually on January 2. In addition to the interest payment Sundre paid $28,000 on January 2, 2014 to reduce the balance owed on the long-term notes. The interest rate on the notes is 7.5 percent.

xiv. Sundre paid $105,000 in cash for other expenses related to operating the business in fiscal 2014.

xv. Sundre paid dividends of $77,000 to shareholders.

Required:

a. Enter each of the transactions onto an accounting equation spreadsheet. You can use a computer spreadsheet program or create a spreadsheet manually. Create a separate column on the spreadsheet for each account. Make sure to prepare all adjusting entries and the closing entry. Indicate whether each entry is a transactional entry, an adjusting entry, or a closing entry.

b. Provide explanations for each of your entries. You should explain why you have treated the economic events as you have (that is, why you have recorded an asset, liability, etc.).

c. Prepare a balance sheet as of December 31, 2014 and an income statement for the year ended December 31, 2014 from your spreadsheet.

d. The North American economy is booming and there is a lot of work for shipping companies like Sundre. However, the competition is fierce and success and failure are defined by how efficient a company is and how well it services its customers. Sundre's managers would like to upgrade its fleet by adding two new trucks and making significant improvements to its existing vehicles. Based on your examination of the statements, what can you tell about Sundre that would be useful to your decision to lend it $125,000? Also, list five questions you might ask Sundre's management that would help you use the financial statements more effectively.

P3-17. **(Following the steps of the accounting cycle, LO 1, 3, 4, 6)** Use the information about Sundre Trucking Inc. (Sundre) provided in Problem P3-16 to do the following:

a. Prepare all necessary transactional journal entries for the year ended December 31, 2014.

b. Prepare T-accounts and post each journal entry to the appropriate T-account.

c. Prepare and post adjusting journal entries to their appropriate T-accounts.

d. Prepare a trial balance as of December 31, 2014.

e. Prepare a balance sheet for Sundre as of December 31, 2014 and an income statement and statement of retained earnings for the year ended December 31, 2014.

f. Prepare the closing journal entry and post the closing entry to the appropriate T-accounts.

g. Prepare an after-closing trial balance as of December 31, 2014.

h. The North American economy is booming and there is a lot of work for shipping companies like Sundre. However, the competition is fierce and success and failure are defined by how efficient a company is and how well it services its customers. Sundre's managers would like to upgrade its fleet by adding two new trucks and making significant improvements to its existing vehicles. Based on your examination of the statements, what can you tell about Sundre that would be useful to your decision to lend it $125,000? Also, list five questions you might ask Sundre's management that would help you use the financial statements more effectively.

P3-18. **(Using the accounting equation spreadsheet to record transactions and prepare financial statements, LO 1, 2, 4, 6)** Gary's Computer Maintenance Ltd. (GCML) is a small computer repair shop owned and operated by Gary Armstrong. Gary's wife Susan is a 50 percent shareholder in GCML but she isn't involved in the operations of the company. GCML has been in business for three years since being incorporated in 2010. Because he has been so busy recently and lacks expertise in financial matters, Gary has asked you to prepare the financial statements for GCML for 2013. Gary provides you with the company's balance sheet for the year ended December 31, 2012, and the following information about GCML's activities in the year.

Gary's Computer Maintenance Ltd.
Balance Sheet
As of December 31, 2012

Assets		Liabilities and Shareholders' equity	
Current assets		**Current liabilities**	
Cash	$ 9,000	Bank loan	$11,250
Accounts receivable	35,250	Accounts payable	19,500
Inventory	28,500	Taxes payable	2,250
	72,750	Interest payable	300
			33,300
Non-current assets		**Shareholders' equity**	
Equipment	16,500	Common shares	22,500
Accumulated depreciation	(7,500)	Retained earnings	25,950
	9,000		48,450
Total assets	$81,750	Total liabilities and shareholders' equity	$81,750

Information about GCML's activities during 2013:

i.   In August 2013 GCML signed a lease for a new shop on the main street in town. Monthly rent is $900. GCML paid six months' rent in advance when it signed the lease. The lease came into effect when GCML occupied the new shop on November 1, 2013. GCML paid rent of $7,500 in cash from January though October 2013 for its previous location.

ii.   During 2013 GCML earned revenues of $141,000. Credit sales accounted for $56,000 of the revenues earned.

iii.   GCML purchased equipment for $9,000 cash during 2013.

iv.   During 2013 GCML purchased inventory of parts and supplies for $39,000. All inventory purchases were on credit.

v.   During 2013 GCML collected $48,750 in amounts due from customers.

vi.   GCML paid suppliers $18,000 for inventory it purchased during 2013. It also paid $19,500 to suppliers for amounts owing on December 31, 2012.

vii.   On March 2, 2013 GCML borrowed an additional $6,000 from the bank.

viii.   During 2013 GCML paid cash dividends of $22,500 to its shareholders.

ix.   GMCL paid employees salaries of $38,750. In addition, Gary was paid a salary of $28,000. All salaries paid were for work done in 2013. At the end of 2013, GMCL owed employees $750.

x.   During 2013 GMCL incurred other expenses of $25,250, all paid in cash.

xi.   During the year, GCML paid the $2,250 in taxes payable that was owing to the federal and provincial governments on December 31, 2012.

xii.   In December 2013 GCML signed a number of one-year contracts to provide ongoing 24-hour service to customers' computers at their places of business. All of the contracts take effect in January 2014. The customers paid $7,500 in cash to GCML in December 2013 as deposits against future services to be provided.

xiii.   During 2013 GCML paid the bank $1,500 in interest. Of that amount, $1,200 pertained to 2013 and the remainder was owed to the bank from fiscal 2012. On December 31, 2013, GCML owed the bank $450 in interest, which will be paid in March 2014.

xiv.   On December 31, 2013 Gary counted the inventory of parts and supplies on hand. His count showed that there was $30,750 of inventory on hand. (Use this information to figure out how much inventory was used during 2013.)

xv.   Depreciation of equipment was $3,750.

xvi.   GCML will have to pay $2,400 in income taxes for the year. No payments had been made with respect to the fiscal 2013 year as of December 31, 2013.

Required:

a. Enter each of the transactions onto an accounting equation spreadsheet. You can use a computer spreadsheet program or create a spreadsheet manually. Create a separate column on the spreadsheet for each account. Make sure to prepare all adjusting entries and the closing entry. Indicate whether each entry is a transactional entry, an adjusting entry, or a closing entry.

b. Provide explanations for each of your entries. You should explain why you have treated the economic events as you have (that is, why you have recorded an asset, liability, etc.).

c. Prepare a balance sheet as of December 31, 2013 and an income statement for the year ended December 31, 2013 from your spreadsheet.

d. Gary is pleased with the performance of his business and he is considering opening a second location. He would like to get another investor to purchase an equity interest in GCML and operate the new location. Based on your examination of the statements, what can you tell about GCML that would be useful to your decision to purchase an equity stake in GCML? Also, list five questions you might ask Gary that would help you use the financial statements more effectively.

P3-19. **(Following the steps of the accounting cycle, LO 1, 3, 4, 6)** Use the information about Gary's Computer Maintenance Ltd. (GCML) provided in Problem P3-18 to do the following:

a. Prepare all necessary transactional journal entries for the year ended December 31, 2013.

b. Prepare T-accounts and post each journal entry to the appropriate T-account.

c. Prepare and post adjusting journal entries to their appropriate T-accounts.

d. Prepare a trial balance as of December 31, 2013.

e. Prepare a balance sheet for GCML as of December 31, 2013 and an income statement and statement of retained earnings for the year ended December 31, 2013.

f. Prepare the closing journal entry and post the closing entry to the appropriate T-accounts.

g. Prepare an after-closing trial balance as of December 31, 2013.

h. Gary is pleased with the performance of his business and he is considering opening a second location. He would like to get another investor to purchase an equity interest in GCML and operate the new location. Based on your examination of the statements, what can you tell about GCML that would be useful to your decision to purchase an equity stake in GCML? Also, list five questions you might ask Gary that would help you use the financial statements more effectively.

P3-20. **(Reconstructing adjusting entries, LO 2, 4, 5)** The first spreadsheet below provides the balances in Takhini Inc.'s accounts on December 31, 2014, before and after the adjusting entries have been made.

P3-20.

Transaction	Assets				=	Liabilities		
	Cash	Interest receivable	Supplies inventory	Advances to employees		Accounts payable	Customer desposits	Utilities Payable
Balance before adjusting entries	$30,000	$0	$22,000	$13,000		$8,000	$118,000	$0
Balance after adjusting entries	$30,000	$8,000	$10,000	$2,000		$8,000	$70,000	$5,000

P3-21.

Transaction	Assets					=	Liabilities		
	Cash	Inventory	Royalties receivable	Capital assets	Accumulated depreciation		Bank loan	Accounts payable	Salaries payable
Balance before adjusting entries	$50,000	$450,000	$0	$120,000	($44,000)		$58,000	$78,000	
Balance after adjusting entries	$50,000	$245,000	$17,800	$120,000	($69,000)		$58,000	$78,000	$12,000

Required:

Reconstruct the adjusting entries that were made to Takhini Inc.'s spreadsheet on December 31, 2014.

P3-21. (**Reconstructing adjusting entries, LO 2, 4, 5**) The second spreadsheet below provides the balances in Smithers Inc.'s accounts on May 31, 2015, before and after the adjusting entries have been made.

Required:

Reconstruct the adjusting entries that were made to Smithers Inc.'s spreadsheet on May 31, 2015.

P3-22. (**Evaluating the effect that not recording adjusting entries has on financial statements, LO 3, 4**) For each of the following economic events indicate the effect that *not* recording the necessary adjusting entry at year-end would have on the financial statements. Indicate whether not recording the required adjusting entry would result in:

i.   an overstatement of assets, liabilities, owners' equity, or net income,

ii. an understatement of assets, liabilities, owners' equity, or net income, or

iii. no effect on assets, liabilities, owners' equity, or net income.

Provide explanations for your conclusions and state any assumptions you make. Assume a December 31 year-end. To respond it's necessary to determine the required journal entry.

a. A sports fan bought and paid for a ticket to a game in the previous year. He attended the game in the current year. (Respond from the perspective of the sports team.)

b. On July 15 a company signed an agreement with another company allowing it use of some of its proprietary materials for the next three years in exchange for an annual fee of $100,000 payable on April 1 each year, beginning next year. The contract goes into effect on September 1 of this year. (Respond from the perspective of the company that is receiving the fee.)

c. A company uses electricity during December. It won't receive a bill from the utility until March of the next year. (Respond from the perspective of the company buying the electricity.)

d. On November 1 the company pays $12,000 for six months rent covering the period from November 1 through April 30. (Respond from the perspective of the company paying the rent.)

+				Shareholders' equity			
Common shares	Retained earnings	Revenue	Interest revenue	Supplies expense	Salaries expense	Utilities expense
$10,000	$12,000	$358,000			$115,000	$25,000
$10,000	$12,000	$406,000	$8,000	$12,000	$126,000	$30,000

Liabilities *cont.*		+			Shareholders' equity					
Unearned revenue	Interest payable	Common shares	Retained earnings	Revenue	Royalty revenue	Cost of goods sold	Salaries expense	Interest expense	Depreciation expense
$55,000		$50,000	$55,000	$258,000			$78,000		
$55,000	$6,000	$50,000	$55,000	$258,000	$17,800	$205,000	$90,000	$6,000	$25,000

P3-23. **(Evaluating the effect that not recording adjusting entries has on financial statements, LO 3, 4)** For each of the following economic events indicate the effect that *not* recording the necessary adjusting entry at year-end would have on the financial statements. Indicate whether not recording the required adjusting entry would result in:

(i)   an overstatement of assets, liabilities, owners' equity, or net income,

(ii) an understatement of assets, liabilities, owners' equity, or net income, or

(iii) no effect on assets, liabilities, owners' equity, or net income.

Provide explanations for your conclusions and state any assumptions you make. Assume a December 31 year-end. To respond it's necessary to determine the required journal entry.

a. A theatre production company sells season tickets to subscribers in advance of the theatre season. Subscribers receive a discount for paying in advance. The production company recognizes revenue when a show is performed. (Respond from the perspective of the production company.)

b. A customer made a $5,000 down payment last year for services that were provided in May of the current year. (Respond from the perspective of the customer.)

c. A retail store pays a percentage of its sales as rent to the property owner. The payment is made three months after its year-end, after the financial statements are released. (Respond from the property owner's perspective.)

d. A retail store pays a percentage of its sales as rent to the property owner. The payment is made three months after its year-end, when the financial statements are released. (Respond from the retail store's perspective.)

P3-24. **(Understanding the effect of different estimates on net income, LO 4)** In 2014 Otis Knight opened a small business that he called The Corner Coffee Cart. The Corner Coffee Cart sells a variety of coffee-based beverages from a portable cart. Otis purchased the cart for $12,000 cash when he began the business. All of The Corner Coffee Cart's transactions with suppliers and customers are for cash. At the end of 2014, Otis decided he wanted to get an idea about how well The Corner Coffee Cart performed in its first year. He assembled the following information:

i.   Sales to customers $22,000

ii. Cost of providing coffee to customers $13,000

From this information Otis concluded that he had made $9,000, which he was satisfied with. A friend who had recently taken an accounting course told Otis that his profit of $9,000 wasn't correct because he didn't depreciate the coffee cart. Otis asked his friend to help him calculate the "correct" amount of profit based on the friend's knowledge of accounting.

Required:

a. Why did Otis's friend tell Otis that his measure of profit was not correct without a depreciation expense for the cart? Do you agree with this?

b. If Otis assumes that the useful life of the cart is six years and he depreciates the cost of the cart using the straight-line method (an equal amount is expensed each year), what would The Corner Coffee Cart's net income for 2014 be? Assume that the cart would not have any value at the end of its life.

c. Calculate The Corner Coffee Cart's net income assuming that the cost of the cart is depreciated over three years. Calculate net income assuming the cost of the cart is depreciated over ten years. Assume straight-line depreciation in both cases.

d. What is the difference in The Corner Coffee Cart's net income using the three different periods for depreciating the cart in (b) and (c)?

e. How is your evaluation of how The Corner Coffee Cart performed during 2014 affected by using different periods for depreciating the cart?

f. Assume the different periods used for depreciating the cart simply represent different reasonable estimates of the cart's useful life. Is the actual performance of The Corner Coffee Cart really different even though the net income under each estimate is different? Explain.

g. What is the "correct" number of years over which to depreciate the cart?

Using Financial Statements

WestJet Airlines Ltd. (WestJet) was founded in 1996 by a team of Calgary entrepreneurs, headed by Clive Beddoe, as a Western Canadian regional carrier with three aircraft flying to five cities. Today, WestJet is Canada's leading high-value low-fare airline, offering scheduled service to 66 destinations in Canada, the United States, Mexico, and the Caribbean, with its fleet of 81 Boeing Next-Generation 737-series aircraft. WestJet is traded on the TSX under the symbols WJA and WJA.A.

WestJet's consolidated balance sheets, statements of earnings and comprehensive income, and retained earnings along with some extracts from the notes to the financial statements, are provided in Exhibit 3–1.[2]

Use this information to respond to questions FS3-1 to FS3-10.

FS3-1. Examine WestJet's balance sheets. Which accounts do you think would require adjustments at the year-end? Explain.

FS3-2. WestJet includes among its current liabilities $251,354,000 for "Advance ticket sales." Note 1(d) provides some additional information about this account.
   a. When does WestJet recognize its revenue?
   b. What does Advance Ticket Sales represent?
   c. Why is Advance Ticket Sales reported as a liability? Describe the circumstances that would give rise to an increase in this account.

EXHIBIT 3.1	WestJet Airlines Ltd.: Extracts from the Financial Statements

Consolidated Statement of Earnings

For the years ended December 31
(Stated in thousands of Canadian dollars, except per share amounts)

	2008	2007
Revenues:		
Guest revenues	$ 2,301,301	$ 1,899,159
Charter and other revenues	248,205	227,997
	2,549,506	2,127,156
Expenses:		
Aircraft fuel	803,293	503,931
Airport operations	342,922	299,004
Flight operations and navigational charges	280,920	258,571
Marketing, general and administration	211,979	177,393
Sales and distribution	170,605	146,194
Depreciation and amortization	136,485	127,223
Inflight	105,849	85,499
Aircraft leasing	86,050	75,201
Maintenance	85,093	74,653
Employee profit share	33,435	46,705
Loss on impairment of property and equipment (note 5)	—	31,881
	2,256,631	1,826,255
Earnings from operations	292,875	300,901
Non-operating income (expense):		
Interest income	25,485	24,301
Interest expense	(76,078)	(75,749)
Gain (loss) on foreign exchange	30,587	(12,750)
Gain (loss) on disposal of property and equipment	(701)	54
Loss on derivatives (note 11)	(17,331)	—
	(38,038)	(64,144)
Earnings before income taxes	254,837	236,757
Income tax expense: (note 7)		
Current	2,549	2,149
Future	74,153	41,775
	76,702	43,924
Net earnings	$ 178,135	$ 192,833

www.mcgrawhillconnect.ca

EXHIBIT ⟨ 3.1 ⟩ (continued) WestJet Airlines Ltd.: Extracts from the Financial Statements

Consolidated Balance Sheet

As at December 31
(Stated in thousands of Canadian dollars)

	2008	2007
Assets		
Current assets:		
Cash and cash equivalents (note 4)	$ 820,214	$ 653,558
Accounts receivable	16,837	15,009
Future income tax (note 7)	4,196	—
Prepaid expenses, deposits and other (note 12(a))	67,693	39,019
Inventory	17,054	10,202
	925,994	717,788
Property and equipment (note 5)	2,281,850	2,213,063
Other assets (note 12(a))	71,005	53,371
	$ 3,278,849	$ 2,984,222
Liabilities and shareholders' equity		
Current liabilities:		
Accounts payable and accrued liabilities	$ 249,354	$ 168,171
Advance ticket sales	251,354	194,929
Non-refundable guest credits	73,020	54,139
Current portion of long-term debt (note 6)	165,721	172,992
Current portion of obligations under capital lease	395	375
	739,844	590,606
Long-term debt (note 6)	1,186,182	1,256,526
Obligations under capital lease	713	1,108
Other liabilities (note 12(a))	24,233	11,337
Future income tax (note 7)	241,740	174,737
	2,192,712	2,034,314
Shareholders' equity:		
Share capital (note 8(b))	452,885	448,568
Contributed surplus	60,193	57,889
Accumulated other comprehensive loss (note 12(c))	(38,112)	(11,914)
Retained earnings	611,171	455,365
	1,086,137	949,908
Commitments and contingencies (note 10)		
	$ 3,278,849	$ 2,984,222

    d. What journal entry would be made to record an increase in advance ticket sales? (Alternative approach: Use an accounting equation spreadsheet to record an increase in advance ticket sales.)

    e. What circumstances would give rise to a decrease in advance ticket sales?

    f. What journal entry would be made to record a decrease in advance ticket sales? (Alternative approach: Use an accounting equation spreadsheet to record a decrease in advance ticket sales.)

FS3-3. WestJet includes among its current liabilities $73,020,000 for "Non-refundable guest credits." Note 1(e) provides some additional information about this account.

    a. What journal entry would WestJet record when a traveller makes the initial reservation? Remember that when a traveller pays for a ticket in advance of a flight the amount is credited to Advance Ticket Sales (see Note 1(d)). (Alternative

---

EXHIBIT 3.1 **(continued) WestJet Airlines Ltd.: Extracts from the Financial Statements**

(k) Deferred costs

Certain sales and distribution costs attributed to advance ticket sales are deferred in prepaid expenses, deposits and other on the consolidated balance sheet and expensed to sales and distribution in the period the related revenue is recognized.

(l) Property and equipment

Property and equipment is stated at cost and depreciated to its estimated residual value. Assets under capital lease are initially recorded at the present value of minimum lease payments at the inception of the lease.

Asset class	Basis	Rate
Aircraft, net of estimated residual value	Cycles	Cycles flown
Live satellite television included in aircraft	Straight-line	10 years/lease term
Ground property and equipment	Straight-line	3 to 25 years
Spare engines and parts, net of estimated residual value	Straight-line	20 years
Assets under capital lease	Straight-line	Term of lease
Buildings	Straight-line	40 years
Leasehold improvements	Straight-line	Term of lease

Aircraft are amortized over a range of 30,000 to 50,000 cycles. Residual values of the Corporation's aircraft range between $4,000 to $6,000.

Property and equipment are reviewed for impairment when events or changes in circumstances indicate that the carrying value may not be recoverable. When events or circumstances indicate that the carrying amount of property and equipment may not be recoverable, the long-lived assets are tested for recoverability by comparing the undiscounted future cash flows to the carrying amount of the asset or group of assets. If the total of the undiscounted future cash flows is less than the carrying amount of the property and equipment, the amount of any impairment loss is determined as the amount by which the carrying amount of the asset exceeds the fair value of the asset. The impairment loss is then recognized in net earnings. Fair value is defined as the amount of the consideration that would be agreed upon in an arm's length transaction between knowledgeable, willing parties who are under no compulsion to act.

(m) Maintenance costs

Maintenance and repairs, including major overhauls, are charged to maintenance expense as they are incurred.

Aircraft parts that are deemed to be beyond economic repair are disposed of and the remaining net book values of these parts are included in maintenance expense.

Recovery of costs associated with parts and labour covered under warranty are recognized as an offset to maintenance expense.

12. Additional financial information

(a) Balance sheet

		2008	2007
Prepaid expenses, deposits and other:			
Prepaid expenses		$ 26,521	$ 13,763
Short-term deposits	(i)	18,761	10,827
Deferred costs	(ii)	14,410	14,323
Foreign exchange derivative assets (note 11)		6,735	106
Other		1,266	—
		$ 67,693	$ 39,019

(ii) Deferred costs relate to certain sales and distribution expenses attributed to advance ticket sales.

For the year ended December 31, 2003

(i) Maintenance costs:

Costs related to the acquisition of an aircraft and preparation for service are capitalized and included in aircraft costs. Heavy maintenance ("D" check) costs incurred on aircraft are capitalized and amortized over the remaining useful service life of the "D" check.

All other maintenance costs are expensed as incurred.

---

approach: In each of parts (a) to (d), use an accounting equation spreadsheet to record the entry that would be made to record the transaction or economic event that is described.)

b. What adjusting entry is required if a traveller cancels his or her flight but WestJet grants the traveller a "guest credit"?

c. What journal entry would WestJet make if a traveller who has a travel credit calls to book another flight?

d. What journal entry would WestJet make if a traveller who has a guest credit allows it to expire without using it?

FS3-4. Read note 1(k) to WestJet's financial statements, which note explains how WestJet accounts for "Deferred Costs."

a. Where on WestJet's balance sheet are the deferred costs reported?

b. What amount of deferred costs is reported on WestJet's December 31, 2008 balance sheet?

c. What are the deferred costs?

    d. WestJet's treatment of the deferred costs can be considered an application of the matching principal. Explain.

    e. What journal entry would WestJet make to record the deferred costs? (Alternative approach: Use an accounting equation spreadsheet to record the entry WestJet would make to record the deferred costs.)

    f. What journal entry would WestJet make when it was time to expense the deferred costs? (Alternative approach: Use an accounting equation spreadsheet to record the entry WestJet would make when it was time to expense the deferred costs.

FS3-5. Note 1(m) explains that WestJet expenses all maintenance and repairs costs it incurs. Compare that note with a similar one from WestJet's 2003 annual report where it is explained that the company capitalizes some of the maintenance costs it incurs and expenses others. How do you think these different ways of accounting for maintenance and repairs would affect WestJet's financial statements? When answering consider how financial statements would differ under one accounting treatment versus the other. Would a different accounting treatment change the actual economic activity and performance of WestJet? How might the perceptions of users of the financial statements be affected by different accounting treatments?

FS3-6. Calculate the following ratios for WestJet for 2007 and 2008:
    a. profit margin
    b. return on equity (2008 only)
    c. current ratio
    d. debt-to-equity ratio

FS3-7. Prepare the closing journal entry that WestJet would make on December 31, 2008. (Alternative approach: Set up an accounting equation spreadsheet using WestJet's financial statements and record the closing entry WestJet would make on December 31, 2008.)

FS3-8. How much inventory does WestJet report on its December 31, 2008 balance sheet? Why do you think WestJet has so little inventory?

FS3-9. Compare WestJet's balance sheet and income statement with Leon's. Describe how the statements differ. Explain. In responding, consider the different types and relative amounts of assets, liabilities, revenues, and expenses reported on the statements. In answering this question consider current assets as a percentage of total assets, current liabilities as a percentage of total liabilities and shareholders' equity, and expenses as a percentage of revenues.

FS3-10. You are a supplier recently approached by WestJet's management to replace an existing supplier. Assess WestJet's liquidity. Would you be prepared to provide credit to WestJet? Explain your decision.

ENDNOTES

1. Summarized from WestJet Airlines Ltd.'s 2008 annual report and website at www.westjet.com.

2. Extracted from WestJet Airlines Ltd.'s 2008 annual report.

INCOME MEASUREMENT AND THE OBJECTIVES OF FINANCIAL REPORTING

LEARNING OBJECTIVES

After studying the material in this chapter you will be able to do the following:

▶ **LO 1** Explain and apply criteria for revenue recognition.

▶ **LO 2** Describe the critical-event and gradual approaches of recognizing revenue.

▶ **LO 3** Explain the effects that different approaches to recognizing revenue have on the income statement and on financial ratios.

▶ **LO 4** Describe expense recognition and the matching principle.

▶ **LO 5** (a) Understand how the constraints, economic facts surrounding a transaction or economic event, and managers' objectives of financial reporting affect the accounting choices made by an entity.

(b) Understand the reasons for, economic consequences to stakeholders of, and limitations to flexible accounting rules that give managers the opportunity to choose how they account for transactions and economic events.

▶ **LO 6** Apply an approach to solving accounting choice problems.

▶ **LO 7** Comprehend the qualitative characteristics of accounting information.

When Hélène Fortin shops for groceries at her Saint-Lambert, Quebec, supermarket she will occasionally splurge on a lottery ticket or two. She doesn't tell the cashier that she's the powerful chair of the board of directors of Loto-Québec.

"I'm even allowed to win," chuckled Fortin in a telephone interview, confident the system safeguards would prevent cheating to win a jackpot.

"There's no way I could influence the numbers," she said.

Appointed chair of the Quebec government's lottery agency in 2008, Fortin and her board wield influence in other ways; they oversee how well management runs the $3.8 billion operation with its weekly draws, four casinos, video lottery terminals, and

Hélène F. Fortin, CA
Partner, Demers Beaulne,
Chairwoman of the Board, Loto-Québec.

the Lotto Max and Lotto 6/49 contests. According to Fortin, it's more than simply verifying the financial statements and ensuring compliance with regulations.

"Once you have passed all the hurdles and they are complete and accurate, then…you start discussing the real stuff: Are revenues in line with what they thought it was going to be? Are goals achieved?" Fortin explained.

Now considered one of Quebec's most sought-after accountants, Fortin initially worked in clerical jobs because her parents couldn't afford to send her to university. One accounting class at secretarial school sparked her interest, though, prompting her to enrol in night school at Concordia University. She graduated first in her class with a bachelor of commerce in accounting, and then went on to a second degree in public accountancy from McGill. Her CA designation came in 1981, while working at Coopers and Lybrand (now PricewaterhouseCoopers).

She spent five years at printing giant Quebecor as the company expanded its empire into the United States. "I was in charge of acquisitions at a publicly listed company and I was pinching myself every day asking myself, 'Is this possible?,'" Fortin recalled.

Since 2008, she has been an audit partner for the Montreal accounting firm Demers Beaulne. She's sat on boards of the CBC, Concordia University, Hydro Quebéc, some private health care companies, and the Canadian Institute of Chartered Accountants.

Fortin says accountants are very valuable to boards of directors because they are trained to be disciplined, ethical, and to respect rules—qualities that she feels can prevent abuses of executive expense accounts.

"I keep saying to people, 'Let's avoid page 1 of *The Globe and Mail*, please!'" Fortin said. And while board members usually stay out of the day-to-day management of an entity, Fortin acknowledges there are times when accountants step in during a crisis, such as the 2005 lockout of CBC employees.

"Being an accountant does provide a way of explaining myself or a way of behaving that is very reassuring [to the managers]," Fortin said. "We inspire confidence on a board not only when we are discussing financial statements but issues in general, providing advice. It provides a way of thinking that ends up being a safe harbour for people who are more on the artistic side."

Fortin still makes time for mentoring accounting students, lecturing at McGill, Université du Québec, and HEC Montréal.

"It is a very diversified profession that can lead to various activities in pretty much any company, " she tells her students. "From pure accounting, to finance, tax, teaching, government, boards, public practice, you can reach top executive positions."

—E.B.

INTRODUCTION

We have now covered the fundamentals of accounting. In Chapters 1 to 3 we explored the accounting environment, became familiar with financial statements, and learned the basics of the accounting cycle. We can now begin our exploration of accounting information in depth. In the remainder of the book we will examine how economic events are reported (and not reported) in financial statements.

In the first part of this chapter we will explore revenue and expense recognition. The term *recognition* refers to when revenues and expenses appear in the income statement. There are different ways of recognizing revenues and expenses, and the methods chosen can affect the amounts reported in an entity's financial statements. Different recognition methods also affect many accounting and financial ratios—tools stakeholders often use to analyze financial statements. Managers must decide which methods to choose (remember from Chapter 1 that managers decide how to report accounting information). Chapter 4 provides some explanation of why alternative acceptable accounting methods are allowed, as well as some implications of allowing managers to choose the methods used.

The second part of this chapter examines the objectives of financial reporting. This material will help you understand factors influencing the accounting choices managers make and incentives encouraging them to pursue self-interests. Most often managers make accounting choices that are within the rules (such as IFRS or GAAP for private Canadian companies). But because the rules often allow managers to choose among acceptable alternatives, they can satisfy their own interests and still meet the rules. It's understandable that some readers may be uncomfortable with the ethical implications of this situation, but it's the reality of accounting. This material isn't intended to be a guide or encouragement to misuse accounting information. It's meant to help you understand and avoid being deceived by accounting information. For better or for worse, empirical evidence and casual observation suggest that when people have choices, the choices they make are the ones that are best for them. This applies in accounting too.[1]

However, an entity's managers are still responsible for supplying relevant and reliable information to stakeholders. This responsibility must be carried out to the highest ethical standards. Failure to do so has significant consequences for the economy, society, and stakeholders. Accounting scandals at Enron, WorldCom, Nortel, and Tyco have highlighted how managers can use accounting information unethically as well as what the consequences of unethical behaviour are. Some accounting controversies aren't clear violations of accounting rules but raise questions about management's intent when making accounting choices.

REVENUE RECOGNITION

When revenue recognition was introduced in Chapter 3, we learned that under accrual accounting revenue is an economic gain earned by an entity from providing goods or services to customers. But it isn't always obvious when an economic gain "happens," so someone has to decide what the economic event is that triggers revenue recognition. *When* revenue is recognized and *how* expenses are matched to revenue significantly impact the amounts reported in the financial statements, the value of financial ratios, and possibly a person's perception of how an entity is performing. Once you determine *when* revenue should be recognized, the journal entry to record it is straightforward:

> Dr. Cash (asset +) or Accounts receivables (asset +)   xxx
>   or Unearned revenue (liabilities −)
>   Cr. Revenue (revenue +, owners' equity +)   xxx
>   To record revenue

When revenue is recognized an income statement account for revenue is credited and a balance sheet account is debited. The entry to the balance sheet either increases assets (usually accounts receivable or cash) or decreases liabilities.

Conceptually, earning revenue is a continuous process. Any activity by an entity to make a good or service available or valuable to customers represents economic gain or revenue. For example, when Leon's Furniture Limited advertises, trains staff, displays merchandise in the store, or a salesperson spends time with a customer, economic value is created because Leon's merchandise is more attractive and available to customers. From an accounting standpoint, it's difficult to measure this continuous process so methods are required for reporting revenue in the income statement in a logical and rational way.

Accountants have devised two approaches for recognizing revenue. Each applies to different types of transactions—they aren't substitutes for one another. The first, the **critical-event approach**, identifies a point in the earnings process as the appropriate time to recognize revenue. That point is called the critical event. When the critical event occurs, 100 percent of the revenue is recognized. Before it occurs there is no revenue, and when it occurs all the revenue is recognized. Examples of critical events include delivery of goods to customers and collection of payment. The critical-event approach applies when goods are sold to a customer or a service is provided on a one-time basis (for example, having a computer repaired).

The second approach recognizes revenue gradually over a period of time; for example, services provided over a period, construction contracts, or interest earned, which occurs continuously over time. We can call this approach of recognizing revenue little by little over time the **gradual approach**.

The Critical-Event Approach

IFRS provides five criteria for identifying the critical event for recognizing revenue on the sale of goods:

1. Significant risks and rewards of ownership have been transferred from the seller to the buyer.

2. The seller has no involvement or control over the goods sold.

3. Collection of payment is reasonably assured.

4. The amount of revenue can be reasonably measured.

5. Costs of earning the revenue can be reasonably measured.

The first two we can call *performance* criteria, meaning the seller has done most or all of what it's supposed to do to be entitled to payment and the buyer has accepted the goods. Most of the time, but not always, performance has occurred when a customer purchases merchandise and takes delivery. Performance might not have occurred on delivery if

- The buyer has to resell the merchandise before the seller gets paid.

- The seller has to install the goods and installation is a significant part of the purchase.

The third criterion is collectability. The seller must have a reasonable expectation of being paid. If the seller doesn't have a reasonable expectation of being paid or can't make a reasonable estimate of how much won't be collected, revenue shouldn't be recognized. This doesn't mean the seller must expect to collect 100 percent of amounts owed. If the uncollectible amount can be estimated the revenue can be recognized and an expense recorded for the uncollected amount.

Criteria four and five deal with measurability. For revenue to be recognized the entity must be able to estimate the amount it has earned and the costs incurred to earn it. Often costs are incurred after the critical event and these must be recorded in the same period as the revenue. For example, warranty costs are incurred after the customer takes delivery of the merchandise. If the seller isn't able to estimate the warranty costs then revenue recognition should be delayed until the end of the warranty period.

These are the criteria according to IFRS. But remember, we are examining financial reporting with a critical eye so it's important not to think of these as the best or only possible criteria for recognizing revenue. We could probably come up with other ways that would suit the information needs of some stakeholders.

INSIGHT

Qualitative Characteristics

IFRS have what are called "qualitative characteristics," which are attributes financial statement information should have if it's to be useful to stakeholders. The qualitative characteristics are **understandability**, **comparability**, relevance, and reliability. This and one other Insight box in the chapter explain these characteristics.

Understandability

To be useful accounting information must be understood by stakeholders. But who is the target audience? Stakeholders range from very unsophisticated readers to highly skilled experts (e.g., financial analysts, pension fund managers). IFRS states that accounting information should be understood by a moderately skilled audience: people with a reasonable understanding of business and accounting and a willingness to study the information. This has implications for the information presented in financial statements as simpler information would have a wider audience, but financial statements directed at more sophisticated stakeholders could be more detailed and complex.

Comparability

Accounting numbers are very difficult to interpret in absolute terms so it's important for stakeholders to be able to compare the financial statements of an entity over time and with those of other entities. Comparisons are easier to make if the same accounting methods are used by an entity every period and by different entities. Different accounting methods make it difficult to know whether differences in the numbers are due to economic or accounting differences.

To help achieve comparability IFRS require that entities

- disclose their accounting policies (so stakeholders can identify differences in the accounting for similar transactions)
- disclose any changes to the accounting policies and their impact
- provide information about previous periods in their financial statements

Comparability is a worthwhile goal in principle but there are practical limits. Managers might impair comparability by making different choices for similar transactions and economic events. Comparability is also impaired if entities approach estimating differently. Entities must disclose their accounting policies but information about all estimates usually isn't available. Entities are allowed to change accounting policies if new policies result in better financial reporting.

One must use caution when comparing the financial information of different entities. You can't assume that different entities prepare their statements on the same basis. It's easier to compare an entity over time, but even then the basis for estimates may have changed or unusual events might have occurred.

The criteria provide guidance to managers, but they aren't hard and fast rules and require interpretation and judgment. Business transactions don't always fit into convenient categories. After all, at what point have the "significant rights and risks of ownership" been transferred? For criteria three through five, what does "reasonably" mean? These fairly vague terms provide flexibility for choosing when to recognize revenue. We will see later that this vagueness serves a purpose.

The criteria are fairly *conservative* because they tend to delay revenue recognition until fairly late in the revenue-generating process. This reduces the uncertainty surrounding the numbers in the financial statements, making the information more meaningful and reliable. Unreliable financial statement numbers aren't very useful for decision making. On the other hand, waiting until there is no uncertainty may not be useful either because stakeholders will receive the information too late to influence their decisions. For there to be no uncertainty revenue would have to be recognized very late—in most cases long after cash is collected and any post-transaction obligations (such as warranties) have been resolved. The IFRS criteria tend to reduce uncertainty but they don't eliminate it.

We can add one more criterion: the critical event selected should provide a reasonable and fair representation of the entity's activities, given the needs of the stakeholders. This means that after deciding on a revenue recognition point based on the above criteria the manager should assess whether the choice is reasonable and fair. If the manager believes the choice may be misleading or confusing, an alternative should be considered. As a matter of ethics, this criterion is pervasive and overriding. Remember that accounting information must, above all, provide useful information about an entity so stakeholders can make informed decisions. As our discussion proceeds, we will refer mainly to the first five criteria. However, this sixth criterion should always be kept in mind.

 KNOWLEDGE CHECK

www.mcgrawhill connect.ca

- ☐ What two approaches have accountants devised for recognizing revenue?
- ☐ What are the five criteria for recognizing revenue under IFRS? Explain each criterion.
- ☐ What is the "sixth" criterion for revenue recognition and why is it so important?

 QUESTION FOR CONSIDERATION

Evarts Ltd. (Evarts) is a retail store that sells clothing to men and women. Evarts has been in business for 15 years. Customers pay by cash or major credit card at the time they purchase and take their merchandise. Unused merchandise can be returned within 15 days. On occasion, Evarts replaces or repairs goods that are damaged or that customers are otherwise dissatisfied with beyond the 15 day return period. Evarts recognizes its revenue when the customer pays and takes the merchandise. Use the revenue recognition criteria to support when Evarts recognizes its revenue.

Answer: At the time of payment the revenue recognition criteria are clearly met. The amount of revenue is known since the customer has paid the agreed price. Most costs have been incurred by that time. The cost of the merchandise sold is known, as well as any other costs directly associated with the sale, such as the salesperson's commission. There are some uncertainties about costs, such as the cost of replacements and repairs, as well as of returns. However, these costs are likely small and, given the length of time Evarts has been in business, can be reasonably estimated. Collection isn't an issue since the customer pays when the goods are taken. The risks and rewards of ownership have transferred because the customer has the clothes and can use them as he or she chooses. Any damage is the responsibility of the customer. Evarts has no control over the clothes at all. While Evarts will accept responsibility for manufacturer's defects and certain repairs, it won't take goods back if a garment became stained or torn as a result of use by the customer. Notice that there are uncertainties (returns, exchanges, repairs) when Evarts recognizes its revenue, but these are normal, reasonable, and can be estimated.

Some Critical Events

Let's take a look at some of the critical events used in practice.

Delivery Delivery occurs when the buyer takes possession of the goods or receives the service (in a single exchange) being sold. Most retail, manufacturing, and service businesses use delivery as their critical event. There is too much uncertainty before delivery (it's usually unclear whether an exchange will take place), and recognizing revenue after delivery delays recognition beyond the transfer of the risks and rewards of ownership. However, there are exceptions as we will see. Exhibit 4.1 shows the revenue recognition notes for five Canadian companies in five different industries that use delivery as their critical event.

Indigo Books & Music Inc. is Canada's largest book retailer. As you would expect, Indigo recognizes revenue from in-store sales when customers make their purchases. Online sales are recognized when the goods are shipped. For its online business the five criteria are met on shipment because (a) the customer has paid (typically by credit card) so collection is assured, (b) the amount of revenue is known, (c) the cost of the product shipped along with associated costs (e.g., shipping costs) are known, (d) the risks and rewards of ownership have transferred, and (e) the merchandise is available to the customer to use and enjoy, and Indigo has no involvement or control since the product ordered has been sent to the customer. There are some uncertainties at shipment; for example, customers may return goods, wrong items might be shipped, and goods might be lost or damaged in transit. These costs can likely be estimated, so revenue can be reasonably recognized when the goods are shipped.

Aurizon Mines Ltd. is a gold mining company. It recognizes its revenue when bullion is delivered to customers. The note explains that title transfers to the purchaser at delivery, and

---

EXHIBIT 4.1

Revenue Recognition: Critical Events

Indigo Books & Music Inc. (Retailer)

Revenue recognition

The Company recognizes revenue when title passes to the customer. Revenue for retail customers is recognized at the point of sale and revenue for online customers is recognized when the product is shipped. The Company reports its revenues net of sales discounts and returns and is inclusive of amounts invoiced for shipping.

Aurizon Mines Ltd. (Gold mining company)

j)   Revenue Recognition

The Company recognizes revenue from gold and silver bullion sales when the bullion has been shipped and title has passed to the purchaser pursuant to a purchase arrangement from which collectability is reasonably assured.

Nexen Inc. (Oil and gas exploration and production company)

(o) **Revenue recognition**

Oil and gas

Revenue from the production of crude oil and natural gas is recognized when title passes to the customer. In Canada and the US, our customers primarily take title when the crude oil or natural gas reaches the end of the pipeline. For our other international operations, including the UK, our customers take title when crude oil is loaded onto tankers. When we produce

WestJet Airlines Ltd. (Air transportation service provider)

(d) **Revenue recognition**

(i)   Guest revenues

Guest revenues, including the air component of vacation packages, are recognized when air transportation is provided. Tickets sold but not yet used are reported in the consolidated balance sheet as advance ticket sales.

Source: Extracted from the 2008 annual reports of Indigo Books & Music Inc., Aurizon Mines Ltd., Nexen Inc., and WestJet Airlines Ltd.

the sales price is known. We can assume that the costs of production are known (there are likely few after delivery), and collection is reasonably assured. At delivery the customer has the gold to use as it requires.

Nexen Inc. explores for and produces oil and gas. Nexen recognizes its revenue when title passes to the customer (performance). In its Canadian operation title passes when oil and gas reaches the end of the pipeline.

WestJet Airlines Ltd. provides air transportation services. It recognizes its revenue when passengers actually travel, even though many people pay for their tickets in advance of their flight dates. This is consistent with the revenue recognition criteria since at the time of the journey WestJet provides what the passenger purchased. The other criteria are also met at this point: customers usually pay in advance so collection and the amount of revenue is known and the costs of operating the flight can be determined (wages, fuel, meals, etc.). WestJet records the following journal entry when a passenger books a trip:

Dr. Cash (asset +)	xxx	
Cr. Unearned revenue (liabilities −)		xxx
To record the purchase of a ticket in advance		

And this entry when the passenger travels:

Dr. Unearned Revenue (liabilities −)	xxx	
Cr. Revenue (revenue +, owners' equity +)		xxx
To recognize revenue		

Completion of Production   The revenue-recognition criteria can be met as soon as the product is produced, even if it hasn't been delivered to the customer, if the sale of the product is assured and the costs of selling and distributing it are minor. An example is a bill-and-hold arrangement, in which a customer orders merchandise but requests delivery at a later date (perhaps because of a lack of storage space). The seller can still recognize the revenue when the goods are produced if certain conditions are met, including: the buyer takes title to the goods and accepts billing, and if the goods are on hand and ready for delivery. Exhibit 4.2 provides the revenue recognition note for Supremex Income Fund, a manufacturer of envelopes and related products. The note explains the conditions Supremex must meet to recognize revenue before goods are delivered to the customer.

For many years it was common practice for Canadian mining companies to recognize revenue once the ore had been extracted from the ground and refined into the finished metal (gold or silver, for example). The principle was that, as there is a ready market for gold (selling the gold is never a problem), most of the effort in the process is completed once the refined gold is available for sale. Before IFRS were adopted in Canada the accounting rules changed so that mining companies were no longer allowed to use this approach and delivery was required before revenue could be recognized. IFRS is more flexible and may allow Canadian mining companies to recognize revenue when the finished metal is available for sale.

Let's look at an example of how a company would account for recognizing revenue on production. Manyberries Mines Ltd. (Manyberries) is a gold mining company. The company has

www.supremex.com
/en/index.asp

EXHIBIT 4.2

Supremex Income Fund: Bill-and-Hold Arrangement

SUMMARY OF SIGNIFICANT ACCOUNTING POLICIES

Revenue recognition

The Fund recognizes revenue when persuasive evidence of an arrangement exists, product delivery has occurred, pricing is fixed or determinable, and collection is reasonably assured. In addition, when the customer requests a bill and hold, revenue is recognized when the customer is invoiced for goods that have been produced, packaged and made ready for shipment. These goods are shipped within a specified period of time and are segregated from inventory which is available for sale, the risk of ownership of the goods is assumed by the customer, and the terms and collection experience on the related billings are consistent with all other sales.

Source: Extracted from Supremex Income Fund's 2008 annual report.

contracts with customers to purchase all of its production at $950 per ounce, so it recognizes its revenue when gold is refined and available for shipment. In May 2014, Manyberries produced 5,000 ounces of gold at a cost of $375 per ounce. To record the revenue at the time of production, Manyberries would make the following journal entry:

Dr. Inventory at market value (assets +)	4,750,000	
Cr. Revenue (revenue +, owners' equity +)		4,750,000
To recognize revenue on production of gold ($950 × 5,000)		
Dr. Cost of sales (expenses +, owners' equity −)	1,875,000	
Cr. Inventory at cost (asset −)		1,875,000
To record cost of gold sold ($375 × 5,000)		

These entries record the sale and increase the value of the inventory from its cost to its current market value. The inventory remains on the balance sheet since it's still on hand. When Manyberries actually delivers the gold to its customers it will make the following journal entry:

Dr. Accounts receivable (assets +)	4,750,000	
Cr. Inventory at market value (assets −)		4,750,000
To record delivery of gold to customer		

This entry only affects the balance sheet. It removes the inventory from the books (since it is delivered to the customer) and recognizes the amount owed by the customer. There is no change in the amount of assets, just the nature of the assets.

Revenue Recognition after Delivery In some situations revenue recognition is delayed until after goods have been delivered or services provided to customers. Delay is appropriate if the risk and rewards of ownership haven't transferred at the time of deliver or if there are significant uncertainties about costs, revenue, or collection. Remember, the appropriate time to recognize revenue is the moment that all of the criteria are met. Following are some examples of uncertainties that could delay recognizing revenue until after delivery:

- *Warranty costs* A **warranty** is a promise by a seller or producer of a product to correct specified problems with the product. If a company isn't able to make a reasonable estimate of its warranty costs it should wait until the end of the warranty period to recognize revenue. For example, a company gives a two-year warranty on a product that relies on a new technology. If the company can't make a reasonable estimate of the cost of providing the warranty service at the time of delivery, revenue recognition should be deferred until the warranty period ends because the costs required to earn the revenue can't be reasonably measured.

- *Returns* If a company can't estimate the amount of goods customers will return it should wait until the end of the return period to recognize revenue. For example, a company allows a new customer the right to return merchandise for 180 days. If the company isn't able to estimate the returns, revenue recognition should be delayed because the amount of revenue is unknown (estimated returns are deducted from sales).

- *Cash collection* The third criterion requires a reasonable expectation that payment will be received. If a reasonable estimate of the amount that will be collected isn't possible, collection becomes the critical event. For example, a business that sells on credit to high-risk customers (customers who have a high likelihood of not paying) might delay recognizing revenue until cash is collected.

For each of these cases it's important to understand that delaying revenue recognition results from too much uncertainty. If reasonable estimates can be made of warranty costs, returns, or uncollectible amounts, it's appropriate to recognize revenue at delivery.

Let's look at an example of recording revenue after delivery. Roblin Ltd. recently began marketing a new product that comes with an 18-month parts and service warranty. The product uses a new technology and the company is unable to estimate the cost of the warranty. As a result,

Roblin has decided to recognize revenue at the end of the warranty period. During 2014, Roblin sold $250,000 of the new product to customers for $400,000 and recorded the following entry:

Dr. Accounts receivable (assets +)	400,000	
Cr. Deferred gross margin (liabilities +)		150,000
Cr. Inventory (asset −)		250,000
To record shipment of goods to a customer		

Notice that this entry has no impact on the income statement. The amount owing by the customer is recorded (accounts receivable), but no revenue is recognized. The inventory is removed from the books since it has been shipped. The deferred gross margin is reported as a liability (something like unearned revenue) and represents the difference between the cost of the inventory and its selling price (this entry is necessary so the account receivable can be recognized without recognizing revenue). When the customers pay the amount owing, Roblin would record the following entry:

Dr. Cash (assets +)	400,000	
Cr. Accounts receivable (asset −)		400,000
To record receipt of payment		

Notice there is still no effect on the income statement. During the warranty period Roblin incurs costs for servicing the new product. The costs aren't expensed as incurred but are deferred (we don't expense them until the revenue is recognized so we can match) and included on the asset side of the balance sheet:

Dr. Deferred warranty expense (assets +)	40,000	
Cr. Cash (asset −)		40,000
To record the cost of warranty service (the credit could also be to accounts payable or parts inventory)		

At the end of the warranty period when the uncertainty about the warranty costs has been resolved, Roblin would make this entry:

Dr. Deferred gross margin (liabilities −)	150,000	
Dr. Cost of sales (expenses +, owners' equity −)	250,000	
Dr. Warranty expense (expenses +, owners' equity −)	40,000	
Cr. Revenue (revenue +, owners' equity +)		400,000
Cr. Deferred warranty expense (asset −)		40,000
To recognize revenue		

It's only at this point, when all the revenue criteria are met, that the income statement is affected. The revenue and expenses are recognized at the same time. Entries for recognition on cash collection or the end of the sales return period would be similar to these.

Another business arrangement where revenue is recognized after delivery is a **consignment sale**. In a consignment sale a producer/distributor transfers merchandise to another entity (the seller), which agrees to try to sell the merchandise. The seller pays the producer/distributor only when the goods are sold and any unsold merchandise can be returned to the producer/distributor. The producer/distributor recognizes revenue only when the seller sells the merchandise because it retains the risks and rewards of ownership until that time. Art galleries selling the work of artists operate on this principle, as the rights and risks of ownership of the art piece remain with the artist until the gallery sells the piece to a third party or returns it to the artist.

It's important to remember that the critical event selected for a transaction must meet all five revenue recognition criteria (if IFRS is a constraint). The earliest point when all five criteria are met is when revenue should be recognized. However, it's not always obvious when that point is. In some situations there may not be just one possible critical event. Circumstances surrounding a transaction may be ambiguous, allowing people to legitimately interpret the facts in different ways to support different critical events. When there is more than one possible critical event the entity's choice will be influenced by the entity's accounting environment—characteristics of the entity (industry, type of transactions, risk, etc.), constraints, stakeholder needs, and interests of the mangers (See Figure 1.1). Regardless of these other factors, the critical event selected must be supported by the revenue recognition criteria or whatever accounting standards are being followed.

Why Does It Matter When a Company Recognizes Revenue?

We can use an example to see the effects on the income statement of using different critical events for recognizing revenue. Escuminac Manufacturing Ltd. (Escuminac) makes sophisticated heavy equipment on a special-order basis to meet the specifications of each customer. Customers usually order equipment well in advance of when they need it and it's common practice in this industry for a manufacturer to store equipment it makes for several months before it's delivered. Customers usually make a payment to Escuminac when the contract to produce equipment is signed and then pay at milestones specified in the contract. In 2013 through 2015, the following dollar amounts of equipment were produced and delivered:

	2013	2014	2015
Produced by Escuminac	$10,000,000	$12,000,000	$8,000,000
Delivered to customers	$7,500,000	$11,500,000	$9,000,000

INSIGHT

Qualitative Characteristics—Relevance and Reliability

It should be self-evident that accounting information must be relevant to the people who use it. Information is **relevant** if it influences stakeholder decisions. Specifically, IFRS says that information is relevant if it helps stakeholders evaluate the impact of past, present, or future transactions and economic events, or if it confirms or corrects evaluations they made in the past. For example, lenders want to estimate future cash flows to determine whether an entity will be able to repay a loan. Shareholders may want to predict future earnings as a basis for predicting the stock price of public companies.

It's interesting to note that while accounting information is relevant if it helps make predictions, financial statements aren't themselves predictions. Stakeholders are expected to use financial statements as a basis for making their own predictions. This approach is probably effective for stable and established companies but for new entities and ones experiencing significant change, such as high-tech, Internet, and high-growth companies, the task can be difficult because historical financial statements may not provide a relevant basis for making predictions.

IFRS also says that accounting information should be reliable. **Reliable** information is representative of the entity's underlying economic activity and free of bias and material error. Information is free of bias (neutral) if it isn't designed to bias or manipulate stakeholders' decisions. While freedom from bias is definitely a desirable quality, research and casual observation of events reported in the media suggest that managers use their ability to make accounting choices to pursue their own interests and objectives.

Relevance and reliability are both necessary if information is truly going to be useful, but what happens if full measures of both characteristics can't be obtained? Stakeholders who can specify the information they receive from entities can deal with this trade-off in a way that satisfies their needs. However, most stakeholders have to rely on general purpose financial statements prepared using a set of standards like IFRS. The standard setters decide the trade-off between relevance and reliability for all users of the financial statements. By and large, IFRS shows a bias for reliability over relevance although in recent years more attention has been paid to relevance.

Without relevance and reliability financial statements aren't going to be very useful, but meeting those goals isn't always possible. For example, in Chapter 2 we saw examples of assets that aren't included in financial statements because their future benefits are too difficult to measure. It's important to recognize that real-world constraints introduce limits and trade-offs, and as a result it's essential for stakeholders to critically evaluate the information in financial statements to ensure that it satisfies their needs.

TABLE 4.1	Income Statements for Escuminac Manufacturing Ltd.						
	1. Revenue recognized when the equipment is produced			2. Revenue recognized when the equipment is delivered			
	2013**	2014	2015	2013	2014	2015	2016
Revenue*	$10,000,000	$12,000,000	$8,000,000	$7,500,000	$11,500,000	$9,000,000	$2,000,000
Production expenses	6,000,000	7,200,000	4,800,000	4,500,000	6,900,000	5,400,000	1,200,000
Gross margin	4,000,000	4,800,000	3,200,000	3,000,000	4,600,000	3,600,000	800,000
Other expenses (assumed)	3,000,000	3,000,000	3,000,000	3,000,000	3,000,000	3,000,000	0
Net income	$ 1,000,000	$ 1,800,000	$ 200,000	$ 0	$ 1,600,000	$ 600,000	$ 800,000
Financial Ratios							
Gross margin percentage	40.0%	40.0%	40.0%	40.0%	40.0%	40.0%	40.0%
Profit margin percentage	10.0%	15.0%	2.5%	0.0%	13.9%	6.7%	40.0%

*Results for 2016 are included for completeness since some of the equipment produced in 2015 wasn't delivered until 2016. No "other expenses" are reported in 2016 for comparability. Over the term of the contracts the amount of revenue, expenses, and net income reported aren't affected by the critical event chosen, but the timing of these elements is affected.

**Below are sample calculations for the amounts shown in the table. Calculations are shown for 2013 when revenue is recognized when the equipment is produced.
production expenses = 60% × revenue = 60% × $10,000,000 = $6,000,000
gross margin = revenue − production expenses = $10,000,000 − $6,000,000 = $4,000,000
other expenses = $3,000,000 (fixed amount)
net income = gross margin − other expenses − $4,000,000 − $3,000,000 = $1,000,000
gross margin percentage = gross margin/revenue − $4,000,000 ÷ $10,000,000 = 0.40 = 40%
profit margin = net income ÷ revenue = $1,000,000 ÷ $10,000,000 = 0.10 = 10.0%

Now let's look at Escuminac's financial results for the years 2013 to 2015. Two sets of income statements have been prepared and are shown in Table 4.1. The first set assumes production is the critical event for recognizing revenue and the second set assumes delivery is the critical event. Both statements assume the cost of producing the equipment, called *production expenses* in Table 4.1, is 60 percent of the revenue. These costs are expensed when the revenue is recognized, as required by matching. In addition, there are $3,000,000 of other costs, such as executive salaries, cost of support staff, and so on, that are expensed in the period the work is done. The example ignores income taxes.

The numbers in each set of income statements are different. In 2013, revenue is $10,000,000 using production as the critical event versus $7,500,000 using delivery. Net income in 2013 is $1,000,000 using production as the critical event and zero using delivery. Revenue and net income in 2014 and 2015 are also different with each critical event. The gross margin percentage is the same across years and critical events because it's assumed that production expenses were a constant percentage (60 percent) of revenue. The profit margin percentage differs across years and critical events because other expenses are a constant $3,000,000 per year.

The critical event used will also affect many of Escuminac's other financial ratios. For example, the current ratio (current assets ÷ current liabilities) will be different because the amount of accounts receivable, inventory, and liabilities will differ, as will the debt-to-equity ratio (debt ÷ equity).

Now we can consider some crucial questions. Which critical event for recognizing Escuminac's revenue is best? Which one reports the "right" amount of revenue? How do these different critical events affect Escuminac's stakeholders?

First, recognizing revenue on production or delivery are both potentially reasonable alternatives for Escuminac, depending on the details of the contracts between the company and its customers. Escuminac's business terms are an example of the bill-and-hold arrangement described earlier. Accounting standards provide guidance for recognizing revenue in situations like this, but ultimately managers and accountants must use professional judgment to interpret the terms of the contract and apply the accounting standard. Which critical event is *best* is a question that can't be answered. Assuming both can be supported by the revenue recognition criteria, the best or most appropriate critical event depends on the environment—the stakeholders, the managers, and the facts underlying the entity's economic transactions.

Which critical event reports the *right* amount of revenue and income? This is another question with no correct answer. The two critical events are different ways of measuring the same underlying economic activity. Both try to capture complex economic activity that occurs over time in a simple way. A critical event is a convenient way of overcoming the difficulty of measuring revenue as it's earned in an economic sense but it's also artificial. It's also important to remember that Escuminac is the same regardless of which critical event is selected: an entity's accounting choices don't change the underlying economic activities being reported.

The final question is, how are stakeholders affected by these alternative critical events? Using the 2013 data, here are some examples of the economic consequences for Escuminac's stakeholders of the different critical events:

- If the president's bonus is based on net income, her bonus will be higher if production is the critical event.

- Escuminac may pay less tax if revenue is recognized on delivery.

- Unionized employees might feel more confident about seeking wage increases if production is the critical event.

Indeed, many different contracts and agreements rely on accounting numbers, which makes accountants' measurement of things like revenue very important. So while an accounting choice doesn't affect an entity's underlying economic activity, it may have economic consequences for stakeholders.

More subtle is the effect the choices may have on the perceptions of stakeholders. Does a more "rosy" income statement make a company more attractive to investors and lenders? Do higher revenues and higher net incomes make stakeholders think managers have done a better job, even if the difference in the numbers is due to accounting choices, not real economic differences?

In summary, here are some of the important issues to keep in mind while you think about the Escuminac example:

1. An income statement doesn't show you what revenue or net income would have been under alternative critical events. That means the income statement you receive shapes your perceptions of the entity.

2. The managers choose the critical event for recognizing revenue. This means the self-interest of management (e.g. possibility of a higher bonus) can affect its choice.

3. The economic activity of an entity isn't affected by how or when it recognizes revenue. Regardless of which critical event Escuminac chooses, the same amount of equipment was produced each year, the same amount of equipment was delivered each year, and the same amount of cash was collected each year. What is affected is how the activities are accounted for and reported, and the different choices may have different economic consequences for stakeholders.

? QUESTION FOR CONSIDERATION

Suppose you are an investor who is interested in investing in a manufacturing company. Examine the two sets of income statements provided for Escuminac Manufacturing Ltd. in Table 4.1 and choose which set of statements represent a better investment. Explain your choice.

Answer: Were you fooled? The two financial statements represent exactly the same company, at exactly the same time, in exactly the same circumstances. The underlying economic activity of Escuminac isn't affected by the critical event chosen even though it affects how that economic activity is represented in the financial statements.

Google Inc.

Now let's look at a real example of how different revenue recognition methods can affect a company's financial statements. Google Inc. (Google) is well-known as the company that offers free online search services. In 2004, Google became a public company by offering its shares to investors (the shares were sold by the company itself and by its shareholders). When a company "goes public" it must file a document called a **prospectus** with the securities regulator. This is a legal document providing detailed information about a company offering its securities for public sale.

On July 12, 2004, Google filed a prospectus with the Securities and Exchange Commission (SEC) (the securities regulator in the United States). The income statements in that prospectus can be found in Panel A of Exhibit 4.3. Notice that for the year ended December 31, 2003, Google's revenue was $961,874,000, cost of revenues was $121,794,000, and net income was $105,648,000. Just two weeks later on July 26, 2004, Google filed an amended prospectus with the SEC. The income statements from that prospectus can be seen in Panel B of Exhibit 4.3. For the year ended December 31, 2003 Google's revenue had increased to $1,465,934,000 and cost of revenues had increased to $625,854,000. Net income was unchanged. In the space of two weeks Google's revenue increased by over $500,000,000, an increase of over 50 percent! What happened? A colossal error? An obvious fraud? No, it's nothing but accounting at work.

The dramatic change was the result of a change in how Google recognized its revenue. One of the ways Google makes money is by placing ads for advertisers on other entities' websites. Each time a Web user clicks on an ad, Google is entitled to payment from the advertiser and then must make a payment to the owner of the websites where the ad appeared. Suppose Google gets $1 each time an ad is clicked and pays $0.80 of it to the Web publisher on whose site the ad appears. For each click on the ad, how much revenue should Google recognize? Should it recognize $1 of revenue and $0.80 of expense for the payment? (This is called the gross method because the amount reported as revenue is the full amount owed by the advertiser.) Or should it simply recognize $0.20 in revenue? (This is the net method because the amount reported as revenue is the net amount earned by Google after deducting the amount owed to the Web publisher.)

In its July 12, 2004 prospectus Google used the net method for recognizing its revenue, whereas in the July 26 prospectus it switched to the gross method. By making this change revenues and cost of revenues increased by the same amount (this is why net income didn't change). No explanation was given. A possible reason is that Google wanted to use the same accounting method as its competitor, Yahoo. The key point is that Google's income statement looks quite different as a result of the change. While there is no effect on net income, there are significant effects on revenues, expenses, and financial ratios such as profit margin. In the July 12, 2004 prospectus Google's profit margin percentage for 2003 is 11.0 percent ($105,648,000/$961,784,000) while in the July 26, 2004 prospectus the profit margin percentage is 7.2 percent ($105,648,000/$1,465,934,000).

It's crucial to recognize that Google is the same company in the two prospectuses. Suddenly having an extra $500,000,000 of revenue changed nothing; Google's underlying economic activity is exactly the same. What has changed is the accounting representation of that economic activity.

Why Do Managers Have So Much Choice?

The discussions of Escuminac Manufacturing Ltd. and Google Inc. might make you wonder why managers are given so much power over reporting the information in financial statements. Can't rules be established to limit choices and effectively capture economic reality? Wouldn't it be easier if there was just one way to recognize revenue? Accounting standard setters and regulators often try to restrict or eliminate the accounting choices available to managers by issuing accounting standards that entities adhering to GAAP or IFRS must observe. However, while eliminating choice may make all financial statements consistent in when they recognize revenue, a consistent critical event may not result in comparable statements. Not all sale transactions are identical and the terms of sale can vary enough that the same critical event wouldn't make sense for every sale. For example, consider a producer who ships goods on consignment to the customer. The customer only pays if it sells the goods, which can be returned to the producer at any time without penalty. In another transaction the producer ships the goods to the customer on a final-sale basis.

Panel A—From the prospectus issued July 12, 2004

GOOGLE INC.
CONSOLIDATED STATEMENTS OF INCOME
(IN THOUSANDS, EXCEPT PER SHARE AMOUNTS)

	Year Ended December 31		
	2001	2002	2003
Net revenues	$86,426	$347,848	$961,874
Costs and expenses:			
Cost of revenues	14,228	39,850	121,794
Research and development	16,500	31,748	91,228
Sales and marketing	20,076	43,849	120,328
General and administrative	12,275	24,300	56,699
Stock-based compensation (1)	12,383	21,635	229,361
Total costs and expenses	75,462	161,382	619,410
Income from operations	10,964	186,466	342,464
Interest income (expense) and other, net	(896)	(1,551)	4,190
Income before income taxes	10,068	184,915	346,654
Provision for income taxes	3,083	85,259	241,006
Net income	$ 6,985	$ 99,656	$105,648

Extract from the notes to the financial statements:
Google AdSense is the program through which the Company distributes its advertisers' text-based ads for display on the Web sites of the Google Network members. The Company recognizes as revenues the fees charged advertisers net of the portion shared with its Google Network members under its AdSense program.

Panel B—From the prospectus issued July 26, 2004

GOOGLE INC.
CONSOLIDATED STATEMENTS OF INCOME
(IN THOUSANDS, EXCEPT PER SHARE AMOUNTS)

	Year Ended December 31		
	2001	2002	2003
Net revenues	$86,426	$439,508	$1,465,934
Costs and expenses:			
Cost of revenues	14,228	131,510	625,854
Research and development	16,500	31,748	91,228
Sales and marketing	20,076	43,849	120,328
General and administrative	12,275	24,300	56,699
Stock-based compensation (1)	12,383	21,635	229,361
Total costs and expenses	75,462	253,042	1,123,470
Income from operations	10,964	186,466	342,464
Interest income (expense) and other, net	(896)	(1,551)	4,190
Income before income taxes	10,068	184,915	346,654
Provision for income taxes	3,083	85,259	241,006
Net income	$ 6,985	$ 99,656	$ 105,648

Extract from the notes to the financial statements:
Google AdSense is the program through which the Company distributes its advertisers' text-based ads for display on the Web sites of the Google Network members. In accordance with Emerging Issues Task Force ("EITF") Issue No. 99-19, *Reporting Revenue Gross as a Principal Versus Net as an Agent*, the Company recognizes as revenues the fees it receives from its advertisers. This revenue is reported gross primarily because the Company is the primary obligor to its advertisers.

Source: Extracted from Google Inc.'s July 12, 2004 and July 26, 2004 prospectuses.

The goods can't be returned for any reason and must be paid for in full within 30 days. Does it make sense to use the same critical event in both cases? The transactions are different and the financial statements would probably be more informative if different critical events are used.

In theory, allowing choice for recognizing revenue and other accounting issues is sensible because the economic activities of the Canadian and world economies are too complex for precisely defined accounting rules that suit every situation. The challenge with accounting choice is ensuring that the people preparing accounting information provide the information most useful to stakeholders instead of focusing on their own interests. This is an ethical challenge faced by accountants and other financial professionals.

Consider this analogy. When preparing a résumé for a potential employer you would presumably try to highlight your strengths and downplay your weaknesses in the information you include. You wouldn't add false university degrees or work experience, but you would certainly organize the information and describe your accomplishments in ways that would put you in the best light. Further, if you were applying for several quite different jobs (perhaps in accounting, marketing, and finance), you might even prepare a different résumé for each job, with each one highlighting attributes most appropriate for that job.

Is it dishonest to give different résumés to different prospective employers if the information in each is truthful? Given the many ways a résumé can be written and organized, how would you describe the "right" way to prepare one? Should there be international rules dictating how every résumé should be prepared? In many ways preparing financial statements is the same. Most people have an honest desire to provide useful and relevant information to people using financial statements or résumés. At the same time, anyone preparing either of those documents will want to put him or herself in a good light. Without strict rules about the right way to prepare financial statements or résumés, a lot of power and judgment is given to the preparers. Strict rules reduce the power of and need for judgment by preparers, but it doesn't necessarily result in better, more useful information for users.

The Gradual Approach to Recognizing Revenue

The gradual approach recognizes revenue bit by bit over the entire earnings process rather than when a particular critical event occurs. The gradual approach is consistent with the conceptual nature of the revenue-earning process because it reflects earnings as a continuous rather than a one-time event. But as we discussed earlier, recording revenue gradually isn't practical in most situations. However, there are situations where the gradual method is practical or necessary for providing useful information to stakeholders. In these situations, the gradual approach isn't an *alternative* to the critical event approach; rather, it's the appropriate approach while the critical-event approach is not.

We have already considered one example of the gradual approach to revenue recognition. In Chapter 3 we examined how adjusting journal entries are made to accrue interest earned on investments such as bonds and bank accounts. These adjusting entries, called the accrued revenue/accrued asset type, are made so that the income statement will reflect interest earned to date even though cash hasn't been received and isn't owed as of the financial statement date. With this type of revenue there is no critical event triggering revenue recognition. Instead, the revenue is recognized in the same way it's earned, gradually over time.

The gradual approach is appropriate for delivery of services and long-term construction projects such as dams and large buildings. With a long-term contract, a single project takes place in more than one reporting period. If the critical-event approach is used, revenues and earnings would tend to be more erratic because economic activity occurring in more than one period would be reported at one point in time. Also, since the revenue recognition criteria usually lead to later rather than earlier revenue recognition, the early years of long-term contracts would have no revenue or income and the final year would have it all. As a result, stakeholders would not be receiving timely information about the entity's economic activity.

The Percentage-of-Completion Method A gradual-approach method used for recognizing revenue on service and long-term contracts is known as the **percentage-of-completion method**, which spreads revenues and expenses associated with a contract over the contract's life. This approach reduces the erratic reporting of revenues and earnings and provides useful economic information to stakeholders on a timelier basis.

To use the percentage-of-completion method it's necessary to have a way of determining how much revenue to recognize in each period. It's common to estimate based on the proportion of total costs incurred on the contract. You can do this by using the ratio of the actual costs incurred on the project during the period to the project's total estimated costs. Thus, the revenue recognized in a period is

$$\text{Revenue for the period} = \frac{\text{Cost incurred during the period}}{\text{Total estimated costs for the project}} \times \text{Estimated revenue for the project}$$

Note that it's necessary to estimate total revenues as well as total costs for the project when calculating the revenue that should be recognized in a period. In practice, the percentage-of-completion method is more complicated because the estimated total costs will vary from period to period. You could determine the percentage of completion in other ways; for example, the proportion of the physical work to be done (miles of a highway project completed) or achievement of specified milestones. The percentage-of-completion method is shown schematically in Figure 4.1.

If the Percentage-of-Completion Method Isn't Appropriate To use the percentage-of-completion method it's necessary to estimate the total costs that will be incurred over the contract, the amount of revenue that will be earned, and the percentage of the project that has been completed on the financial statement date. There also has to be a reasonable expectation of payment. If any of these requirements isn't met, IFRS requires entities to use the **cost-recovery**, or **zero-profit**, method. With this method revenue in a period is recognized up to the amount of costs incurred during the period (except for the last year of the project). In the final year of the contract the remaining revenue and expenses and all the profit are reported. In other words, no profit is reported until the final year of the contract (because revenue always equals expenses in the other years).

CANADIAN GAAP FOR PRIVATE ENTERPRISES

In Canada, when the percentage-of-completion method can't be used, Canadian GAAP for Private Enterprises requires entities to use the **completed-contract method**, which recognizes revenue in full when a contract is completed. No revenue is reported until the contract is complete and all expenses on the contract are deferred until the revenue is recognized, when they are expensed and matched to the revenue.

FIGURE 4.1

The Percentage-of-Completion Method

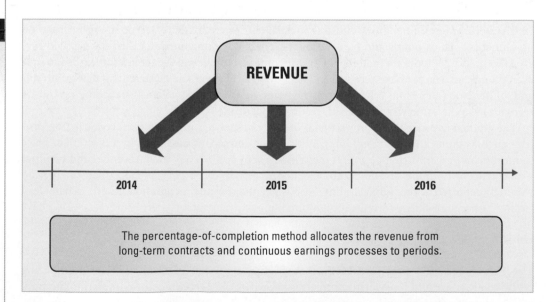

The percentage-of-completion method allocates the revenue from long-term contracts and continuous earnings processes to periods.

TABLE 4.2	Judique Construction Corporation: Amount of Revenue Recognized Using Percentage-of-Completion Method			
	Column A	Column B	Column C	Column D
Year	Cash payments by Hallam to Judique	Judique's estimated annual cost of building the factory	Percentage of project completed each year based on estimated costs	Amount of revenue recognized each year Calculated as: $\frac{\text{Year's cost}}{\text{Total estimates cost}} \times$ Total revenue
2014	$ 5,000,000			
2015	$10,000,000	$ 9,000,000	18.8%*	$14,063,000 $\left(\frac{\$9,000,000}{\$48,000,000} \times \$75,000,000\right)$
2016	$10,000,000	$18,000,000	37.5%*	$32,812,000 $\left(\frac{\$18,000,000}{\$48,000,000} \times \$75,000,000\right)$
2017	$10,000,000	$21,000,000	43.7%*	$32,812,000 $\left(\frac{\$21,000,000}{\$48,000,000} \times \$75,000,000\right)$
2018	$40,000,000			
Total	$75,000,000	$48,000,000	100%	$75,000,000

*The percentage of the project completed each year $= \dfrac{\text{Year's cost (Column B)}}{\text{Total estimate cost (total of Column B)}}$

Example of the Percentage-of-Completion and Zero-Profit Methods Let's look at an example comparing the percentage-of-completion and zero-profit methods. On December 15, 2014, Judique Construction Corporation (Judique) entered into a three-year contract to build a factory for Hallam Corp. (Hallam). Hallam agreed to pay $75,000,000 for the factory, from which Judique would pay all construction costs. Hallam paid $5,000,000 when it signed the contract and agreed to pay $10,000,000 on July 2 of each of the next three years. The final $40,000,000 is to be paid six months after the factory is completed. The expected completion date is August 1, 2017. Table 4.2 shows Judique's estimated annual costs and the amount of revenue that would be recognized each year using the percentage-of-completion method. Judique's year-end is December 31. It's important to recognize that cash flows and revenue and expense flows don't have to correspond. Revenue is recognized based on the proportion of the job that has been completed, not when payment is made.

Table 4.3 shows summarized income statements under the two methods for each year. For the zero-profit method the amount of revenue recognized in 2015 and 2016 is equal to the expenses incurred in each year. The total amount of revenue and expense under the two methods is the same. What differs is the amount that is reported in each period.

TABLE 4.3	Judique Construction Corporation: Percentage-of-Completion versus Zero-Profit Methods for Accounting for Long-Term Contracts								
	Judique Construction Corporation Income Statements (thousands of dollars)								
	Percentage-of-Completion Method					Zero-Profit Method				
	2014	2015	2016	2017	Total	2014	2015	2016	2017	Total
Income Statements										
Revenue	$0	$14,063	$28,125	$32,812	$75,000	$0	$9,000	$18,000	$48,000	$75,000
Expenses	0	9,000	18,000	21,000	48,000	0	9,000	18,000	21,000	48,000
Net income	$0	$ 5,063	$10,125	$11,812	$27,000	$0	$ 0	$ 0	$27,000	$27,000

The percentage-of-completion method gives some insight into Judique's economic activity. Over the term of the contract Judique earns revenue by building the factory. The percentage-of-completion method reflects this economic activity in the financial statements. A disadvantage of the percentage-of-completion method is that it allows managers some latitude in deciding how much revenue and income to report in each period. This latitude exists because complex estimates must be made to obtain the amount of revenue to be reported in a period.

The zero-profit method doesn't give much information about Judique's economic activity. If a company is involved in a small number of long-term contracts at any one time, the zero-profit method can produce wild fluctuations in earnings because profit is only reported when a contract is completed. This could be very misleading to stakeholders who are unaware of how Judique conducts its business.

Finally, the percentage-of-completion and zero-profit methods are not alternatives. IFRS requires the use of percentage-of-completion unless it isn't reasonably possible to do so.

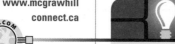

www.mcgrawhill
connect.ca

INSIGHT

Percentage-of-Completion versus Completed-Contract Methods for Tax Purposes

In Canada, the *Income Tax Act* allows companies to use the completed-contract method for tax purposes on contracts of less than 24 months, otherwise the percentage-of-completion method must be used. There is a tax advantage of using the completed-contract method because it delays payment of taxes until a contract is completed. The following example shows the tax benefit of the completed-contract method.

In 2014 Joynt Corp. (Joynt) signs a contract to renovate an office building. The work will be completed over three fiscal years beginning in July 2014 and finishing in May 2016. Joynt estimates that half the work will be done in 2015 and a quarter in each of 2014 and 2016. Joynt will be paid $900,000 for the job and will incur expenses of $360,000. Joynt's year-end is December 31 and it has a tax rate of 20 percent. Summarized income statements are shown in Table 4.4. If Joynt uses the percentage-of-completion method, it will report income in each of the three years and will have to pay taxes of $27,000 in 2014 and 2016 and $54,000 in 2015. If it uses the completed-contract method, it pays no tax in 2014 and 2015 because it doesn't report any income in those years, but it will pay $108,000 in taxes in 2016. Joynt pays the same amount of tax over the three years but it defers $81,000 of taxes until 2016 without any penalty by using the completed-contract method. This frees up a significant amount of cash for other purposes.

TABLE 4.4	Tax Benefits of Using the Completed-Contract Method

Joynt Corp. Income Statements						
	Percentage-of-Completion Method			Completed-Contract Method		
	Years Ended			Years Ended		
	2014	2015	2016	2014	2015	2016
Revenue	$225,000	$450,000	$225,000	$0	$0	$900,000
Expenses	90,000	180,000	90,000	0	0	360,000
Taxes	27,000	54,000	27,000	0	0	108,000
Net income	$108,000	$216,000	$108,000	$0	$0	$432,000

www.mcgrawhill
connect.ca

KNOWLEDGE CHECK

- ☐ What is the gradual approach to recognizing revenue?
- ☐ How do you determine the percentage of a project that has been completed?
- ☐ Under what circumstances is the zero-profit method used?
- ☐ Plato Inc. (Plato) recently entered into a three-year contract to build a small office building for a growing law firm. The law firm will pay Plato $7,000,000 for the building. Plato is required to pay all costs. Plato estimates its total cost of construction will be $5,200,000 with costs of $1,700,000 in the first year, $2,500,000 in the second year, and $1,000,000 in the third year. Assuming that Plato's cost estimates are correct, how much revenue will it recognize in each year of the contract using (1) the percentage-of-completion method and (2) the zero-profit method?

EXPENSE RECOGNITION

In accrual accounting a key concept for determining income is matching. According to the matching concept expenses are reported on the income statement in the same period as the revenue those expenses helped earn. The order is important: *expenses* are matched to *revenues*. First, revenue is recognized and then the costs incurred to earn that revenue are expensed. This process is generally the reverse of actual economic activity. Usually an entity first incurs the costs that will help generate revenues and then earns the revenue.

Matching makes sense, at least for some uses and users of accounting information. If the purpose of an income statement is to provide information about the economic activity (as opposed to cash flow) and performance of an entity, it makes sense to associate costs and benefits. If an entity sells a cell phone and the managers want to know how much better off it is because of the sale, it makes sense to subtract the cost of the phone, along with any other costs of selling it, from the revenue earned. Accrual accounting requires all costs to be matched to the revenue—regardless of whether cash was paid before, at the same time as, or after the revenue is recognized.

In a perfect accrual accounting world all costs would be matched to the related revenues. Practically speaking, it can't be done—many costs are difficult to match. Consider the costs a clothing store incurs to sell a pair of pants. The cost of the pants and the salesperson's commission are easy to match to the revenue from the sale. It's more difficult to match salespeople's hourly wages, rent and utilities for the store, advertising, furniture and fixtures in the store, and the CEO's salary. These are necessary costs of running the business, but what's their connection to the revenue from the sale of a single pair of pants? The fact is it's difficult to make a connection and therefore to match these costs to specific revenues.

When it's difficult or impossible to reasonably match costs to specific revenues, accountants don't try to force a match. Instead, these costs are expensed in the period they are incurred. Employees' wages, rent, utilities, and advertising are expensed when the employees do their work, when the space and utilities are used, and when the advertising is done. Costs expensed in the period they are incurred are called **period costs**. Costs that can be matched to specific revenues are called **product costs** and are expensed when the revenue they help generate is recognized. Product costs are usually accumulated in inventory on the balance sheet (or in some other balance sheet account) until the revenue is recognized. Some costs, like depreciation, are matched to revenue but usually no one is really sure what the relationship is between the amount expensed and the revenue earned. Note that the distinction between product costs and period costs isn't always clear, so a certain type of cost will not always be treated the same way.

Costs that have not yet been incurred must be estimated so they can be matched to revenues. For example, bad debts, returns, and warranty costs are usually incurred after revenue is recognized. Let's look at these situations in more detail:

- The bad-debt expense is an estimate of the amount owed by customers that won't be collected. Under accrual accounting, bad debts are a cost of selling on credit and should be expensed in the period the related sale is made.

- When merchandise is returned it represents revenue that never happened. As a result, an estimate of returns should be accrued in the period the related revenue is recognized.

- Warranty costs should be accrued when the revenue from the product or service under warranty is sold.

The difficult part of accounting for these costs is estimating how much they will be. Managers rely on historical information and their knowledge of the business and products to come up with estimates.

Matching can do strange things to the balance sheet. Earlier in this chapter, on pages 176 to 177, I gave the Roblin Ltd. example to demonstrate the journal entries required when recognizing revenue after delivery. (Look back at this example to refresh your memory.) You may have wondered why "deferred warranty expense" was an asset because there doesn't seem to be any future benefit associated with it. It's classified as an asset because of matching, which says the warranty cost should only be expensed when the revenue it helped earn is recognized. The problem is that deferring the expense forces the amount to show up as an asset (if you don't debit expense the only other place to debit in this situation is assets).

Some people think it's wrong to sacrifice balance sheet integrity to achieve matching. They argue that the most important thing is to classify an item as an asset only if it meets the definition of one. From this perspective the warranty costs should be expensed as incurred, which eliminates reporting them as assets. IFRS is moving toward reducing the focus on matching and the income statement and instead increasing the emphasis on the balance sheet. This doesn't mean matching will disappear but it does mean that where matching produces "strange" assets the costs associated with these assets will be expensed as incurred to maintain balance sheet integrity.

Finally, with all this talk about matching it's important to remember that not all stakeholders or uses of accounting information benefit from matching. For example, recognizing expenses as early as possible, regardless of matching, reduces the amount of income tax that has to be paid. Lenders might be more interested in cash flow information for assessing the liquidity of the entity, again regardless of matching. Always keep in mind that the usefulness of information to stakeholders has to be assessed. As a result, it shouldn't be said that a well-matched set of financial statements is the best way to present accounting information to all stakeholders or in all situations.

 INSIGHT

Important Accounting Concepts—Recognition

Throughout this chapter we have discussed the term "recognition" in the context of revenue and expense recognition. **Recognition** has a more general meaning in accounting: it refers to when any financial statement element—asset, liability, equity, expense, or revenue—is recorded. There are three conditions that must be met for an element to be recognized:

- The item under consideration meets the definition of an element—in other words it meets the definition of an asset, liability, equity, revenue, or expense, as the case may be.

- It's probable the economic cost or benefit associated with the element will occur. This means, for example an entity will probably enjoy the benefit associated with an asset.

- The element can be measured.

GAINS AND LOSSES

A gain or loss arises when an entity sells an asset it doesn't sell in the ordinary course of business and for an amount that is different from its carrying amount. For example, if an airline sells old aircraft or a bookstore sells furniture and fixtures or old computers a gain or a loss could arise.

Let's consider some possibilities for a company that owns land with a carrying amount of $500,000:

1. If the land was sold for $600,000, a gain of $100,000 would be reported on the income statement (selling price − carrying amount = $600,000 − $500,000 = $100,000).

2. If the land was sold for $425,000, a loss of $75,000 would be reported (selling price − carrying amount = $425,000 − $500,000 = − $75,000). The journal entries to record the gain and loss would be

  1. Dr. Cash   600,000
        Cr. Gain on sale of land (income statement)   100,000
        Cr. Land   500,000
    To record the gain on the sale of land

  2. Dr. Cash   425,000
        Dr. Loss on sale of land (income statement)   75,000
        Cr. Land   500,000
    To record the loss on the sale of land

In both cases the land account must be credited for $500,000, its carrying amount. The difference between the amount received and the cost of the land is the gain or loss. I have limited the examples here to the sale of land—an asset that isn't depreciated. Gains and losses also arise when assets that are depreciated are sold; we'll examine these in Chapter 8. In the meantime consider the following points about gains and losses:

1. The sale of incidental assets giving rise to gains and losses are presented differently in the income statement than is the sale of inventory. When inventory is sold the revenue and cost of the inventory are shown separately (revenue − cost of sales). When the sale of an incidental asset occurs the proceeds from the sale and the cost of the asset sold are shown net—only the gain or loss is shown.

2. It's important for gains and losses to be reported separately from revenues and expenses. Because gains and losses arise from the sale of assets that aren't the entity's main business, including them in revenues and expenses can be confusing and misleading to stakeholders. For example, a gain included in revenue will make revenues from the entity's main business activities greater than they really are, making it more difficult to predict future revenues or evaluate performance.

3. The amount of a gain or loss is affected by the accounting choices that impact the asset. Different accounting choices result in different carrying amounts and different gains and losses.

4. Proceeds from the sale of property, plant, and equipment should not be affected by the carrying amount. The amount a buyer pays for an asset is based on its economic value to the buyer, not its carrying amount. Sellers may be affected by the accounting effect of a potential sale because they may be concerned about the impact of the gain or loss on net income.

Exhibit 4.4 provides an example of how gains and losses are reported on the income statement. In its 2008 annual report Air Canada reported losses of $34 million in 2008 and gains of $19 million in 2007 from the disposal of assets and other activities. Notice how the gains and losses are disclosed separately. The exact presentation of gains and losses can vary from entity to entity but they should always be presented separately.

THE OBJECTIVES OF FINANCIAL REPORTING

Providing relevant information to stakeholders is the reason for financial accounting. There are a number of reasonable accounting treatments for transactions and other economic events, even under IFRS. The discussion of revenue recognition in this chapter highlights this idea. But how do managers decide which accounting methods to choose? Managers' choices are influenced by two factors: the information needs of stakeholders and their own self-interests, two factors that often conflict. The accounting choice that provides the "best" information to stakeholders (or at least to particular stakeholders) won't always be the one that best satisfies the managers' interests, which include maximizing their compensation, job security, increasing share price or the apparent value of the business, and so on.

Ideally, self-interest should not play a role in the accounting choices a manager makes, but given human nature self-interest can be a factor. In fact, there is considerable evidence that managers' accounting choices are influenced by self-interest (look at all the accounting scandals, for example). Given this reality, awareness of managers' motivation and ability to craft accounting information to serve their own interests and the economic consequences this behaviour can have on stakeholders is essential to any accounting education. Factors affecting accounting choice are shown in Figure 4.2. The figure builds on the accounting environment that was developed in Figure 1.1, and integrates managers' motivations, constraints they face, and objectives of financial reporting to show the financial statement effects of managers' motivations.

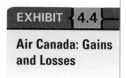

EXHIBIT 4.4

Air Canada: Gains and Losses

www.aircanada.ca

Consolidated Statement of Operations

For the year ended December 31 (Canadian dollars in millions except per share figures)		2008	2007*
Operating revenues			
Passenger		$ 9,713	$ 9,329
Cargo		515	550
Other		854	720
		11,082	10,599
Operating expenses			
Aircraft fuel		3,419	2,553
Wages, salaries and benefits		1,877	2,059
Airport and navigation fees		1,001	1,021
Capacity purchase with Jazz	Note 2d	948	537
Depreciation and amortization	Notes 3, 4, & 13	694	557
Aircraft maintenance		659	799
Food, beverages and supplies		314	319
Communications and information technology		286	277
Aircraft rent		279	323
Commissions		194	201
Other		1,450	1,458
		11,121	10,104
Operating income (loss) before under-noted item		**(39)**	**495**
Provision for cargo investigations	Note 17	(125)	-
Operating income (loss)		**(164)**	**495**
Non-operating income (expense)			
Interest income		57	94
Interest expense		(319)	(351)
Interest capitalized		37	108
Gain (loss) on capital assets	Note 3	(34)	19
Gain on financial instruments recorded at fair value	Note 15	92	26
Other		(3)	(18)
		(170)	(122)
Income (loss) before the following items		**(334)**	**373**
Non-controlling interest		(12)	(71)
Foreign exchange gain (loss)		(655)	317
Provision for income taxes			
Current	Note 7	(1)	(16)
Future	Note 7	(23)	(174)
Income (loss) for the year		$ (1,025)	$ 429

From Note 4 of Air Canada's 2007 financial statements (amounts in millions of dollars):

EXHIBIT 4.4

(continued)
Air Canada: Gains
and Losses

3. PROPERTY AND EQUIPMENT

During 2008:

- The Corporation received delivery of eight Boeing 777 aircraft. Three aircraft were financed with guarantee support from the Export-Import Bank of the United States ("EXIM") (Note 6). Five of the aircraft were financed under sale and leaseback transactions with proceeds of $708. The resulting gain on sale of $81 was deferred and is being recognized as a reduction to Aircraft rent expense over the term of the leases. The leases are accounted for as operating leases with 12 year terms, paid monthly.

- The Corporation recorded an impairment charge of $38 on its fleet of B767-200 aircraft due to the revised retirement date of the aircraft.

- The Corporation sold six Dash-8 aircraft for proceeds of $10 with a book value of $8, resulting in a gain on sale of $2.

- The Corporation sold an A319 aircraft for proceeds of $23 with a book value of $21, resulting in a gain on sale of $2.

During 2007:

- The Corporation sold an in-service aircraft for proceeds of $23 with a book value of $21, resulting in a gain on sale of $2 (loss of $2 net of tax).

- The Corporation sold a building to Aveos for proceeds of $28 which was equal to the carrying value of the asset (Note 18).

- A CRJ-100 aircraft owned by Air Canada and leased to Jazz was damaged beyond repair. As a result of insurance proceeds of $21, Air Canada recorded a gain on disposal of $14 ($10 net of tax).

- The Corporation sold one of its commercial real estate properties for net proceeds of $42 with a carrying value of $37, resulting in a gain on sale of $5 ($4 net of tax).

- The Corporation sold 18 parked aircraft for proceeds of $2 with a nil book value, resulting in a gain on sale of $2 ($1 net of tax).

Source: Extracted from Air Canada's 2008 annual report.

Manager self-interest is an important element in accounting choice, but even without this motivation managers still have choices to make, leaving stakeholders no assurance they will receive the information most useful for their decisions. There are many different stakeholders, each with different information needs, and an entity can prepare only one set of general purpose financial statements so some stakeholders might not be satisfied. (An entity can produce any number of special purpose reports but these are prepared only for powerful stakeholders who can demand information tailored to their needs.)

Let's consider an example of how the purpose of a set of financial statements can affect accounting choices. Ellin Bamboo owns and operates a small business, and its financial statements are prepared primarily for tax purposes. If choosing one accounting treatment over another reduces the amount of tax the company has to pay it makes sense to use the tax-lowering treatment. This isn't illegal, dishonest, or unethical. If the Canada Revenue Agency allows you to choose among alternatives, choosing the ones that work best for you make sense. If Ms. Bamboo can use, for example, the completed-contract method of revenue recognition for her business's long-term contracts, she should.

If Ms. Bamboo decides to sell her business, prospective buyers would want to examine the financial statements as part of their assessment of the business. Would the financial statements prepared for tax purposes be appropriate for this? No, because the financial statements prepared using the completed-contract method could misstate the economic activity of the business. The completed-contract method delays recognition of activity until a contract is completed, and this may understate the company's revenue and income. These financial statements may not fairly and reasonably reflect Ms. Bamboo's business even though they are perfectly acceptable for tax purposes. If they were used to set the price for Ms. Bamboo's business it's possible that Ms. Bamboo wouldn't receive a fair price for the business.

This example demonstrates that one set of financial statements may not satisfy all financial reporting objectives. But only one set of general purpose financial statements can be prepared so some stakeholders may have to be satisfied with statements that haven't been tailored to their specific needs. A manager's accounting choices will affect the usefulness of the financial statements to those stakeholders and may have economic consequences for them. Figure 4.2 lists some of the objectives of financial reporting that an entity can have. In the following sections we will look at these in detail.

FIGURE 4.2

Factors Influencing Managers' Accounting Choices

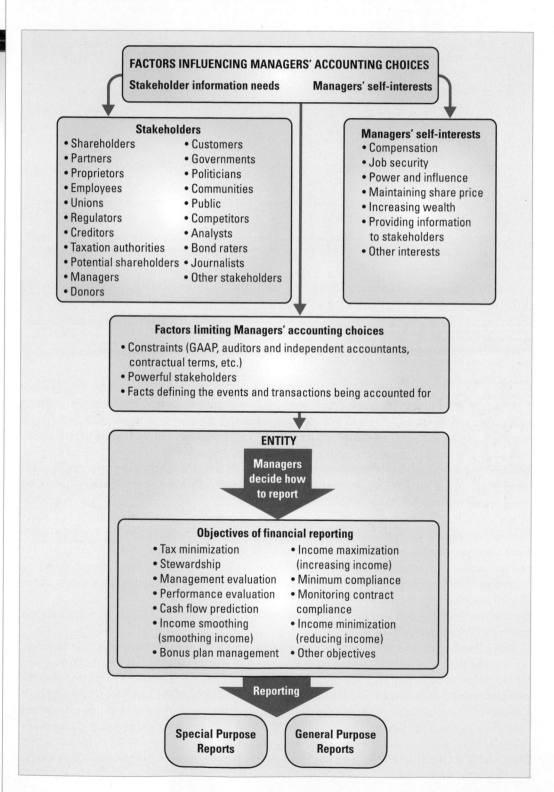

www.mcgrawhill
connect.ca

KNOWLEDGE CHECK

- ❏ Identify and explain the two factors that influence managers' accounting choices. Why do these two factors often conflict?

- ❏ What are some factors limiting the choices that managers can make?

Tax Minimization

Accounting information is used to determine the tax an entity pays and a business's general purpose financial statements must be filed with its tax return. (In the case of partnerships or proprietorships the general purpose financial statements must be filed along with the tax returns of the partners or proprietor.) *Tax minimization* means a taxpayer works within the tax laws to defer taxes or pay as little as possible. Pursuing this objective makes good economic sense because it keeps as much cash as possible in the hands of the entity for as long as possible. An entity's accounting choices impact the amount of tax it pays because the policies used in general purpose financial statements are often also used for tax purposes. Because tax savings are often not permanent but simply deferred to a later period, this objective is also called tax deferral.

Stewardship

Stewardship is responsibility for someone else's resources. For example, when an entity's owners don't manage it, managers act as stewards of the owners' resources. Stewardship relationships exist for all public companies and many private ones, between charities and their donors, and between governments and citizens. A stewardship objective is satisfied when reports to stakeholders inform them about how resources entrusted to others have been managed—have they been used efficiently, effectively, and satisfactorily? This information should allow the stakeholders to understand easily what has taken place during the reporting period. Stewardship is specifically identified in IFRS as an important objective of financial reporting.

Management Evaluation

Stakeholders often want to evaluate the performance of an entity's managers. Financial statements satisfying this objective provide information that reflects both the managers' decisions and the effects of those decisions on the entity's performance. The information should allow stakeholders to separate the effects of management's decisions from the effects of luck and other factors beyond management's control.

Performance Evaluation

Performance evaluation is similar to management evaluation but with a broader scope because it captures the overall performance of the entity. Stakeholders are interested in evaluating an entity's performance for many reasons: shareholders assess whether they should continue to invest, invest more, or divest; prospective lenders assess whether an entity is a worthwhile credit risk; or workers assess whether the entity can afford wage increases. For a charity performance evaluation may involve evaluating whether the organization is spending an appropriate proportion of the money it raises on the cause rather than on fundraising and administration.

Cash Flow Prediction

Many decisions stakeholders make are future oriented and an entity's future cash flows are especially important to this. Knowledge of future cash flows can help a lender evaluate a borrower's ability to pay back the interest and principal on a loan, assist an investor in estimating future dividends, or help a prospective buyer of a business evaluate whether the purchase price is reasonable. Prediction of future cash flows is explicitly identified in IFRS as one of the objectives of accounting information. However, information presented in accordance with IFRS in general purpose financial statements is historical—it reflects what *has already happened*, not what *will happen*. Stakeholders can use the financial statements as a basis for predicting the future cash flows but they need additional information to do so, such as future-oriented disclosures and accounting policies that correlate with future cash flows.

Monitoring Contract Compliance

Entities often enter into contracts requiring them to meet certain terms and conditions, including ones intended to limit the actions management can take. These are often stated in terms of financial statement numbers. For example, a lending agreement may require a borrower to maintain its current ratio above, or its debt-to-equity ratio below, a specified amount. Failure to meet these requirements could mean repaying or renegotiating the loan. Contracts include covenants restricting the behaviour of an entity so that, for example, a lender isn't exposed to unforeseen risks when making a loan, such as the entity taking on additional debt. When contract terms and conditions are based on financial statement numbers, the financial statements serve as tools for monitoring entity compliance with the terms of the contract.

Earnings Management

The objectives listed to this point look at things from the perspective of the stakeholders' information needs. In a perfect accounting world those needs would be met. However, managers might not want to fully cooperate with the needs of stakeholders. Instead, they might want stakeholders to evaluate performance favourably or make rosy predictions of future cash flows. This is where earnings management comes in; managers can use the flexibility in accounting to try to influence the decisions of stakeholders or affect the economic consequences to different stakeholders.

Earnings management was introduced in Chapter 3 where I gave the definition that managers, if given choices among *acceptable* alternative ways of accounting, will likely choose the ways that satisfy their own interests. This discussion of earnings management doesn't include fraud, just using the available legitimate accounting choices to their advantage. Also remember that the term earnings management applies to accounting choices by managers to affect *any* financial statement numbers with the intent of satisfying their self-interests.

As you proceed through this section remember that managing earnings through accounting choices has no impact on the underlying economic activity of the entity. Production, sales, expenditures, and collections are all assumed to be unaffected by the accounting methods used. However, different accounting choices may have economic consequences for stakeholders. In addition, it's also possible to manage earnings by timing transactions, which may have an impact on economic activity as well as economic consequences.

Now we will look at some of the reasons why managers manage their accounting information.

Managing Earnings to Reduce Income   It may come as a surprise but there are situations in which managers want to report lower earnings and make the entity not look so good. Companies in politically sensitive businesses may find themselves under pressure from politicians and citizens if they make "too much money". Managers can ease this pressure by making accounting choices that reduce what might otherwise be seen as excessive profits. Reducing income might also be a good strategy when an entity is looking for government support or subsidies. Lower reported earnings could also influence the outcome of labour negotiations by convincing workers and unions to accept lower wage settlements. Tax minimization is also a motivation for reducing income.

On an ongoing basis income can be reduced by recognizing revenue late in the earnings cycle and recognizing expenses early. Managers can significantly lower earnings in a particular period by taking a **big bath**, which is expensing a significant amount of assets in the current period that normally would have been depreciated or otherwise expensed in future periods. The benefit of a big bath is that while net income is lowered in the current period, it will be higher in future periods. Income will be higher in the years after a big bath because there are fewer expenses as they were recorded in the big-bath year. Big baths are sometimes seen when a company replaces its management. The new management blames poor current performance on the previous management, takes a big bath, and then takes the credit when earnings subsequently improve (even though the improvement is due, in part at least, to the bath).

Even not-for-profit organizations can benefit from this strategy. Although they don't operate to make a profit and, therefore, don't report earnings, they do report surpluses or deficits that reflect the amount by which their "revenues" are greater than or less than their "expenses." If the revenues of a not-for-profit organization exceed its expenses by a large amount contributors might doubt the organization's need and make their donations elsewhere.

Managing Earnings to Increase Income   At the other end of the spectrum are managers who make accounting choices that increase reported income. Situations in which managers might want to report higher earnings include the following:

- Managers may try to influence the stock price of publicly traded companies. There is a well-established relationship between earnings and stock prices, and managers might believe reporting higher earnings will have a positive effect on stock price.

- Before a private company is sold managers might make accounting choices that increase income to increase the selling price. Accounting information is crucial for determining the selling price and managing earnings may increase the amount of money sellers receive.

- Managers might manage accounting information to increase the likelihood of receiving a loan. Improved financial ratios may influence the risk assessment of the entity by lenders.

- By managing earnings upwards, managers may influence some stakeholders' perceptions about how well the entity and its managers are performing.

- Managers who have bonus plans based on net income or other accounting numbers might use accounting choices to increase their bonuses.

- Managers might manage earnings to avoid violating the terms of debt agreements or other kinds of contractual agreements.

Managing Earnings to Smooth Income   Earnings that fluctuate from period to period can indicate risk, and many managers prefer to avoid having stakeholders believe that their company is a risky investment. Research shows that the stock prices of public companies benefit from having smooth earnings. To reduce the perception of risk managers might take steps to smooth earnings over time.

It's important to understand that managers may be undermining the objectives of stakeholders by managing earnings. By their accounting choices managers might make an entity look less risky and, as a result, a prospective lender might overestimate future cash flows, underestimate risk, and thereby make a loan that it might not have made otherwise. Thus, by managing earnings, managers undermine the cash flow prediction objective of the prospective lender but help themselves achieve their objective of obtaining new financing.

Managing earnings is complex. Stakeholders have to be aware that managers have the ability to manage earnings and keep in mind the impact that different choices can have on financial statements.

Minimum Compliance

Managers sometimes provide only the minimum amount of information necessary to comply with reporting requirements. Minimum reporting requirements are defined in various pieces of federal and provincial legislation. All corporations are subject to the requirements of the *Canada Business Corporations Act* or the equivalent provincial corporations act. Public companies must also meet the requirements of the relevant provincial securities act and of any stock exchange the company's securities trade on. Relevant accounting standards also apply.

Some public companies will pursue minimum compliance if they are concerned about competitors getting information or if they aren't concerned about any negative stock market reactions to supplying limited information. Private companies may prepare minimum compliance statements if the shareholders are active in the entity and, therefore, have other sources of information or if there are special purpose reports for other stakeholders. By providing as little information as they are allowed managers make it difficult for stakeholders to effectively evaluate an entity and make good decisions. The financial statements of many retail companies appear to follow a minimum-compliance objective. Shoppers Drug Mart Corporaton's (Shoppers) 2008 income statement provides the minimum amount of information required. (You can find Shoppers' income statement at Sedar.com or on the company website. It wasn't possible to publish Shoppers' statement in this book.) The Shoppers 2008 statement reports only four lines of expenses: cost of goods sold and other operating expenses, amortization expense, interest expense, and income tax expense. Indeed, almost 95 percent of Shoppers' expenses are reported in cost of goods sold and other operating expenses. This presentation isn't very informative for decision making even though there is a bit more detail in the notes.

Is Accounting Information Relevant, Reliable, and Useful?

After reading this discussion of the different objectives of financial reporting, especially earnings management, you might conclude that accounting information can't be relied on or used for decision making. This isn't true. Accounting information is an absolutely essential source of information for most decisions regarding an entity and it would be a mistake to ignore it. The message you should take from this discussion is that accounting information must be analyzed and interpreted carefully before decisions are made. Understanding the nature of accounting information and the motivations of managers will help make you a more sophisticated user whose decisions are less likely to be affected by managers' accounting choices.

It's also important to recognize that accounting isn't different from other business disciplines or, for that matter, any other form of communication. Take advertising for example. When a company advertises a product it tries to make it attractive and desirable to consumers. Advertisers highlight the positive aspects and minimize or even ignore the negative ones. Sometimes advertising is considered misleading but most of the time it isn't. It's the responsibility of consumers to do their research to assure themselves they are getting what they bargained for. Accounting is no different.

INSIGHT

Can You Tell What Managers' Motivations Are?

A lot has been made of the importance of managers' motivations and objectives for understanding their financial reporting. To understand how an entity approached its financial reporting it's necessary to know the objectives of the managers. Unfortunately, managers aren't likely to be forthcoming about what their objectives of financial reporting are. They will justify their accounting choices in the context of relevant accounting rules and the economic facts surrounding the transaction. It may be possible to infer what manager's objectives are, but you can never tell for sure.

Reporting Impact

The objective of financial reporting chosen by an entity's managers can have a significant impact on the financial statements. The table below gives an indication of how managers with particular objectives in mind would approach the preparation of financial statements. The table isn't comprehensive but gives an idea of how different objectives might affect financial reporting.

Objective	Reporting Approach
Tax minimization	Recognize revenue as late as possible and recognize expenses as early as possible while complying with *Income Tax Act.*
Cash flow prediction	Choose accounting policies that correlate current earnings with future cash flows and provide extensive disclosure of information about future cash flows. Provide forecasts (not part of IFRS).
Minimum compliance	Provide the minimum amount of information in the financial statements and notes required by any constraints.
Performance evaluation	Associate economic costs and economic benefits. Separate items that are unusual, less likely to occur in future, and not the result of managerial decisions.
Stewardship	Provide historical, reliable information that will allow stakeholders to see how managers have managed entity resources over the reporting period.

 QUESTION FOR CONSIDERATION

Which objective of financial reporting is most important?

Answer: There is no "most important" objective of financial reporting. This question must be assessed in the context of each individual entity. For a small private company with few external stakeholders demanding information, income tax minimization is probably the most important objective. For a company urgently requiring a loan the most important objective is providing information that increases the likelihood of obtaining a loan—perhaps by reporting higher net income or providing detailed cash flow forecasts. For senior managers with a net income-based bonus plan the most important objective might be receiving a large bonus. From a stakeholder's perspective the most important objective is the one that satisfies that stakeholder's information needs.

CAN MANAGERS DO WHATEVER THEY WANT?

One could get the impression from our discussion that managers are completely unconstrained when they prepare their financial statements and that they can do whatever they want to accomplish their accounting objectives. This isn't true. There are, in fact, forces that limit managers accounting choices:

- accounting standards (GAAP, IFRS)
- laws (tax, securities, corporations laws)
- independent accountants and auditors who act on behalf of stakeholders to assess the accounting choices made by the managers
- contract terms

- the information demands of powerful stakeholders who may dictate accounting treatments and disclosures

- facts surrounding the economic event or transaction being accounted for

Note that not every constraint applies to every entity. For example, not all entities must follow IFRS or have contractual constraints. Only public companies have to adhere to securities laws and only corporations have to follow the corporations act.

Even companies not constrained by IFRS aren't really free to do whatever they want. Remember that accounting is a means of communication. If the people receiving the accounting information can't understand it, then it serves no purpose. Imagine receiving a set of financial statements prepared in a language you didn't understand!

Sometimes powerful stakeholders can make reporting demands on an entity. If an entity needs a loan a banker can demand special reports that meet the specific information needs of the bank. The entity isn't required to meet the demands of the bank, but the bank isn't required to lend money. Another example of a powerful stakeholder is a corporation's shareholder who owns a large proportion of the shares and, thus, may be able to demand special purpose reports that provide information not available in the general purpose report. A shareholder who controls the majority of the shares may be able to determine the objectives of the corporation and the accounting policies it uses. In contrast, a small shareholder in a public company would not be able to obtain information beyond what was in the general purpose financial statements.

The economic circumstances of transactions can also limit the choices managers have. Consider a vendor selling hot dogs for cash from a mobile cart on the street. No matter what the vendor's reporting objectives are, it's hard to imagine recognizing revenue at a time other than when a hot dog is exchanged for cash. On the other hand, in the case of Escuminac Manufacturing Ltd. (pages 178 to 180) there were two viable alternatives for recognizing revenue presented and other alternatives could be identified, especially if IFRS weren't a constraint. An entity not constrained by IFRS may have more accounting alternatives to choose from, but there still has to be a link between the economic circumstances and the choice made.

While constraints may reduce or eliminate choice in some circumstances it's rarely possible to limit completely by law or by contract all or even most of the accounting choices managers have. The economy is far too complex and dynamic to have rules for every possible situation.

SOLVING ACCOUNTING CHOICE PROBLEMS

So far this chapter has examined two important accounting topics: revenue and expense recognition and the objectives of financial reporting. In this section these two topics are linked as we develop a problem-solving technique to help you understand how managers make accounting choices and how stakeholders can both use and be limited by the information provided to them by entities.

Constraints, Facts, and Objectives

Before looking at the problem-solving approach, let's examine the factors that guide the accounting choices made by entities and that will form the central analytical tool for making these choices. The accounting choices made by managers are affected by three factors:

1. the *constraints* that formally limit the choices available to managers

2. the *facts* surrounding the transaction or economic event being accounted for

3. the *objectives* of financial reporting

The constraints, facts, and objectives that impact accounting choices are shown schematically in Figure 4.3.

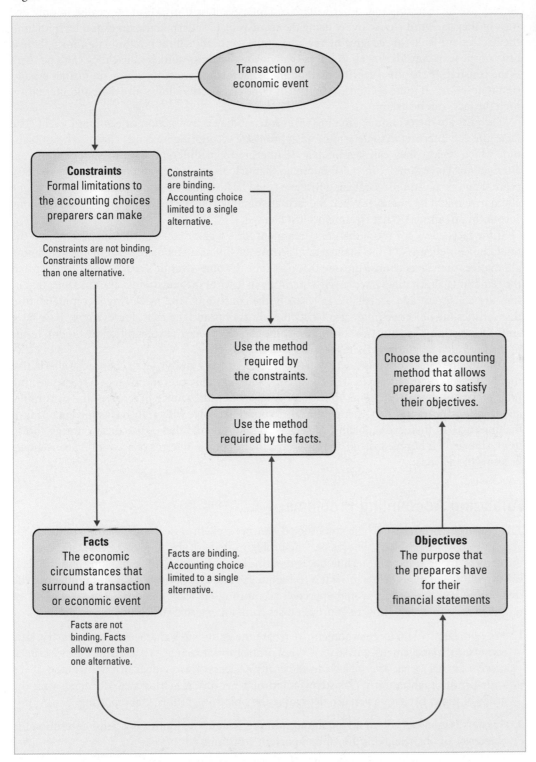

FIGURE **4.3**

The Impact of Constraints, Facts, and Objectives on Accounting Choices

Constraints are specific external limitations on the accounting choices managers can make. They include legal requirements, GAAP, IFRS, or the terms of contracts. Constraints can eliminate choice by requiring that a particular economic event or transaction be treated in only one way, or they can limit choice by reducing the set of available alternatives; for example, IFRS limit the choices available for recognizing revenue. If the constraints limit or eliminate choice there is little purpose in considering alternatives that violate the constraints because they can't be used. If the constraints require a specific method then that method must be used—no further evaluation is necessary. If there are no constraints, or if the constraints allow more than one alternative, then the facts can be examined.

The *facts* are the economic circumstances surrounding a transaction or economic event. The facts must be interpreted to determine an appropriate accounting method. They can be ambiguous, which means they can legitimately be interpreted in different ways to support different alternatives. For example, in the Escuminac Manufacturing Ltd. example (pages 178 to 180), more than one point for recognizing revenue could be justified. In some fact situations only one alternative might be possible. When the facts are binding (that is, they support one and only one accounting treatment), that treatment must be used.

If the facts allow for more than one treatment for a transaction or economic event then the final choice depends on the managers' *objectives* of financial reporting. From the remaining alternatives managers choose the one that best suits the objectives. It's crucial to remember that the remaining alternatives have survived scrutiny in light of the constraints and the facts; that is, they are consistent and acceptable in terms of the constraints and facts. Any recommendation that satisfies the objectives *must* also satisfy the constraints and the facts. For example, if we have an IFRS constraint, we must be able to justify the choice of revenue recognition method in terms of the revenue recognition criteria regardless of the objectives.

It should be clear from this discussion that managers don't always get to choose the alternative that best meets their objectives. The constraints and facts may prevent managers from selecting their preferred alternative. Being able to justify an accounting choice in terms of the constraints and facts is important for another reason: an accounting choice will rarely be justified in terms of the objectives of financial reporting. Managers will not say that they made an accounting choice to maximize their bonus. Instead, they will explain the choice in terms of accounting concepts—in terms of the facts.

Analyzing Accounting Problems

The constraints, facts, and objectives model can be used in a decision-making approach for accounting choice problems. Short cases and problems that ask you to make or evaluate accounting choices are an important technique used in this book to teach critical thinking and problem solving skills. The steps below provide a technique for addressing these cases and problems. The steps show how a manager would approach accounting-choice situations. These steps will be modified later to explain how to approach cases from an external stakeholder's perspective.

1. Assess the entity and its environment. What are the entity's key characteristics (industry, size, ownership, management, and so on)? What problems is it facing? What are the entity's crucial success factors (what are the keys to the entity's success)? How does it make money (if it's a for-profit organization)? This step is important because it helps you understand what the needs of the entity are so you can determine the objectives of financial reporting.

2. Create a framework for analyzing the accounting issues. The framework helps determine the objectives of financial reporting and important constraints:

   a. Identify the main stakeholders and the decisions they have to make.

   b. Based on the stakeholders and uses discussed in (a), identify the objectives of financial reporting that would serve the stakeholders.

   c. Rank the objectives in order of importance and explain the ranking. (The ranking is necessary so that the analysis can address the most important objective.)

d. Consider the accounting implications of the objectives, given your main objective(s). That is, you must understand how the objectives will affect accounting choices.

e. Identify any constraints that can limit or eliminate accounting choices.

Managers rank the objectives from their own perspective. They decide what is most important for the entity (and perhaps for themselves) and proceed accordingly. This step is crucial because it provides a basis for deciding among alternative accounting methods.

3. Identify the accounting issues. Some of the accounting problems an entity faces are clear. Other problems may be hidden and only detected through analysis and inference.

4. Rank the issues in order of importance and emphasize the more important ones in the analysis. More time and effort should be spent on the issues that are more complex and have the greatest impact on the entity.

5. Analyze each accounting problem:

a. Identify possible alternative accounting treatments.

b. Eliminate alternatives that violate the constraints. If the constraints allow only a single alternative, then the analysis is complete because the accounting treatment is determined by the constraints.

c. Analyze each alternative to determine whether the facts support it. This means you must use information about the transaction or economic event and relevant accounting rules/principles/concepts to provide support for the alternative. If an alternative can't be supported, it must be rejected. For example, analyzing a revenue recognition problem for an entity that is constrained by IFRS means applying the revenue recognition criteria discussed in this chapter. If the facts allow only for a single alternative then the analysis is complete because the accounting treatment is determined by the facts, even if the treatment isn't useful for achieving the objectives.

d. If any alternatives remain, choose the one that best suits the objective or objectives of financial reporting identified and ranked in step 2.

6. Link the solution for each accounting problem back to the framework by explaining why the solution addresses the main objectives. Sometimes you won't be able to provide a solution that serves the objective. That's okay. Explain why you weren't able to satisfy the objective.

When you work on cases there are some additional points to remember:

- Play your role. Make sure you understand what the role means so you can play it effectively. You could be asked to play the role of advisor to management or the board of directors, various stakeholder groups, arbitrator (a person who helps resolves disputes between parties), external auditor, or auditor for the Canada Revenue Agency. Write your response in role.

- State your assumptions. It's never possible to have all the information. Time, cost, and limitations on a person's ability to process information prevent this. As a result, it's necessary to make assumptions—to fill in the blanks—when information is missing. It's very important to recognize when you are making assumptions and to state them explicitly. Knowing when assumptions are being made and identifying what they are isn't always easy—it takes skill and practise to do it well.

- Cases rarely have one right answer. However, not having one right answer doesn't mean all answers are right—there are many wrong answers. The quality of a response depends on the weightings given to various factors, the assumptions made, and the interpretation of events. It's also possible to come up with a reasonable recommendation that is poorly supported. The quality and usefulness of a recommendation lie in the support provided for it, not in the recommendation itself.

When you are asked to play the role of an external stakeholder the approach is a bit simpler. It isn't necessary to consider all stakeholders and their objectives. As an external stakeholder you are only interested in your own objectives and information needs. Otherwise, the approach is the same as for all other roles.

The following solved problem shows an application of this decision-making approach. This solved problem and the one in Chapter 6 take a manager's (preparer's) perspective. The solved problems in Chapters 5, 7, 8, 9, 10, 11, and 12 take a user's perspective.

Solved Problem

Pizzazz Pizza Parlours Ltd. (PPPL) is a small chain of take-out/delivery pizza shops located in Atlantic Canada. The Pizzazz family owns the chain and until recently it was managed by several members of the family. Many other family members are passive shareholders who aren't involved in managing PPPL, including some who rely on the company for their incomes.

In early fiscal 2014 PPPL underwent a number of organizational and strategic changes. First, the family decided that instead of only owning pizza parlours themselves, PPPL would sell franchises to people interested in owning their own business. In a franchise arrangement an individual or company (the franchisee) would approach PPPL about purchasing the right to operate a Pizzazz Pizza Parlour in a particular area. The franchisee would pay PPPL a fee for the rights to own and operate a Pizzazz Pizza shop. The franchisee would also pay PPPL a percentage of the revenue it earned selling pizzas and buy certain supplies from PPPL. PPPL would help the franchisee find a good location; help it set up the shop; provide centralized purchasing, advertising, and order taking from customers; and provide business advice, training, and policy manuals.

The family members who were running the business realized they weren't qualified to manage the business they envisioned. As a result, PPPL's board of directors, which is made up mostly of members of the Pizzazz family, hired as president a person with many years of experience in the pizza industry. The new president signed an employment contract that entitles him to a salary plus a bonus based on net income. Some Pizzazzes remained as part of the new management team. One of the first actions taken by the new president was to arrange a large bank loan to finance the expansion of the company.

As of PPPL's year-end on August 31, 2014 PPPL's new strategy was developing nicely. Fourteen Pizzazz Pizza Parlour franchises had been sold, of which eight were already operating. The remaining six were expected to open by the end of December 2014. Franchises are sold for $70,000 each. A franchise owner pays PPPL $5,000 when the franchise agreement is signed, $15,000 when the restaurant opens, and $10,000 per year for five years on the anniversary of the opening of the pizza parlour. In addition, franchisees pay PPPL a royalty of 5 percent of sales and are required to purchase certain ingredients from PPPL or designated suppliers.

PPPL's 2014 fiscal year has just ended and it hasn't yet determined how to recognize revenue on the franchises it sells. You have been asked by PPPL's board of directors to prepare a report that responds to the following questions:

Required:

1. What businesses is PPPL in? How does it make its money? What do you think are some crucial success factors for PPPL's franchise business?

2. Who are the likely stakeholders of PPPL's financial statements? For what purposes will these stakeholders want the financial statements?

3. From the perspective of the board of directors of PPPL (which we will assume is responsible for approving major accounting policies used by PPPL), what are the possible objectives of financial reporting? Your response to question 2 should help answer this question. Which objective of financial reporting do you think is most important? Explain. How would you rank the remaining objectives? Are there any conflicts among the objectives?

4. Are there any constraints that limit the accounting choices that PPPL can make?

5. What are some possible alternatives for when PPPL could recognize the revenue from the sale of franchises? (You should be able to identify at least three different revenue recognition points.)

6. Do any of the revenue recognition points you identified in question 5 violate the constraints? Which of the alternatives can be justified and supported by the facts?

7. For each revenue recognition alternative you identify, calculate the amount of franchise fee revenue that would be recognized in the years ended August 31, 2014 and 2015.

8. Which revenue recognition method would you recommend PPPL use to recognize franchise fee revenue? Explain.

Solution:

1. PPPL is in three businesses:

   a. It owns and operates pizzerias making money by selling pizzas to customers.

   b. It sells franchise rights to people interested in operating their own Pizzazz Pizza Parlour, making money from the franchise fees and royalties paid by the franchisees.

   c. PPPL is also a supplier of ingredients to the franchised pizzerias, possibly making money by selling the ingredients at a profit.

   For the franchise business, the crucial success factors include:

   - Having strong management to run the company, especially during this period of strategic change. Strong management is crucial because the Pizzazz family doesn't feel it has the ability to manage the expansion of the business on its own.

   - Availability of financing for the franchising program. The franchise business requires cash because the pizzerias open before most of the cash is received from the franchises. For the expansion to continue successfully, credit must be available as required.

   - Capable people with adequate resources to buy and operate the franchises. The franchises must be successful so money will be available to pay debts and royalties to PPPL and to help attract new franchises in the future.

   - PPPL must successfully promote its name so that people will have a preference for eating Pizzazz Pizzas.

2. Possible stakeholders and uses of PPPL's financial statements:

Possible stakeholders	Decisions that will be assisted by the financial statements and how the information will help stakeholders make the decisions
Pizzazz family members	Pizzazz family members will have a number of uses that could be helped by financial statements:

   - They will want to evaluate the performance of the new president. Since the president's bonus is based on net income they will want the income statement to reflect the president's accomplishments.

   - Pizzazz family members, especially those who depend on PPPL for their incomes, will want information that allows them to assess the performance of PPPL and evaluate the amount of cash that will be available to pay dividends.

   - Family members who aren't involved in management will want information for stewardship purposes.

   - The board of directors may want to show the Pizzazz family members that PPPL is performing well.

Lenders and potential lenders	• Existing lenders will want to assess whether their loans are safe and check whether any restrictions (such as current-ratio or debt-to-equity ratio restrictions) have been violated.
	• Additional loans might be required if the franchising program continues. Potential lenders will want to assess PPPL's ability to generate the cash flows necessary to make interest and principal payments. They will also be interested in the market value of available collateral, which could be sold if PPPL were unable to pay back the loan. Potential lenders would want to know the terms of existing loans such as amounts already borrowed, the interest rate, repayment schedule, and collateral pledged to other lenders.
	• The company will want the financial statements to indicate to lenders that existing loans are and future loans would be secure, and that any restrictions have not been violated.
Canada Revenue Agency (CRA)	• The CRA will want to ensure PPPL complies with the *Income Tax Act*.
	• From PPPL's perspective, the company will want to pay as little tax as possible and still comply with the *Income Tax Act*.
New president of PPPL	• The president receives a bonus based on net income so he will want to see high net income.
	• From PPPL's perspective, the company would want the president to receive a fair bonus that reflects his contribution to the performance of the company.
Prospective franchise owners	• Prospective franchise owners may want to assess the financial position of PPPL to obtain some confidence the company is financially solid. If a franchise is purchased, but PPPL is unable to support it, the franchise owners' investment suffers. Depending on the level of sophistication, prospective franchise owners may want information about cash flows, the number of franchises sold and being negotiated, expansion plans, and information on the performance of operating franchises. PPPL is under no obligation to provide its financial statements to prospective franchisees unless it chooses to do so as part of its effort to sell franchises.
	• From PPPL's perspective, the company will want to give prospective franchise owners confidence it will be able to support its franchises and that a PPPL franchise is a good investment.
Suppliers	• Major suppliers may want assurances that PPPL will be able to pay for goods and services purchased. They will be interested in cash flows and liquidity.
	• From PPPL's perspective, the company will want to assure the suppliers that it's able to meet its obligations to pay for supplies. PPPL is under no obligation to provide its financial statements to suppliers, unless it chooses to do so.

3. From the analysis of the stakeholders and uses of accounting information a number of possible objectives emerge. Based on our analysis of the crucial success factors in part (1), the important stakeholders from PPPL's perspective are:

- prospective lenders, because additional loans will be required if PPPL continues to sell franchises;
- new franchise owners, who are key to PPPL's expansion strategy; and
- the president of PPPL, who has been hired to implement the new business strategy.

Of these three groups, the president is most important because PPPL's board chose him to lead the company in this phase of its development. To lose him at this stage would probably be a serious blow to PPPL's new strategy. A good president will be able to effectively manage the relationship with the bank and help attract good franchise owners.

Therefore, the objective of financial reporting should be ensuring that the financial statements reflect management performance and adequately compensate the president for his accomplishments—that is, the objective of management evaluation. The board would probably want to make sure that the net income of PPPL was a reasonable reflection of the president's actions so that he would receive a bonus he felt was fair. The needs of lenders would probably be satisfied by the statements used for management evaluation along with supplementary information on cash flows. While people who buy franchises are important stakeholders, PPPL would probably not be making financial statement information available to them.

Members of the Pizzazz family are also important and powerful stakeholders but their needs must be considered secondary to the stakeholders who are important to expanding PPPL. The board could provide special purpose reports to members of the family to satisfy their information needs.

Everything else being equal, all businesses want to pay as little tax as possible, and PPPL's need for cash makes the objective of tax minimization even more important. However, the need for strong management makes tax minimization a secondary objective.

Major suppliers could request financial information if they are to provide credit terms. It's possible PPPL may not need to provide this information

Note that there are conflicts among the objectives. In particular, the tax minimization objective, which suggests lower net income, conflicts with the management evaluation objective, which suggests "fair" or net income that is representative of the entity's underlying economic activity.

Comment: This ranking isn't the only one or the best one. Many other rankings are possible, reasonable, and supportable. However, any proposed ranking must be supported.

Comment: Had we examined the objectives from the perspective of the president of PPPL rather than from that of the board of directors, the primary objective might have been bonus maximization rather than management evaluation. The president's self-interest might have had a stronger influence since he would have been making accounting choices that directly affected his personal wealth.

4. There don't appear to be any statutory constraints stated in the question. PPPL is a private company and therefore its reporting responsibilities are limited. Some stakeholders may prefer audited, GAAP or IFRS-based financial statements, such as the bank, the shareholders who aren't involved in management, and prospective franchise owners. (PPPL could use Canadian GAAP for Private Enterprises as it isn't public or IFRS if it wanted to.) For purposes of preparing tax returns, PPPL will have to comply with the *Income Tax Act*. The lending agreement with the bank may have minimum requirements for accounting ratios, such as the current ratio or the debt-to-equity ratio, but without any information about these ratios it's not possible to make a reasonable assumption regarding specific amounts. Given the number of external stakeholders of the financial statements we will assume that IFRS will be a constraint.

5. Possible points for recognizing revenue from the sale of franchises include when
   - a franchise agreement is signed with a new franchise owner,
   - a franchised Pizzazz Pizza Parlour opens,
   - cash is collected from a franchise, or
   - full payment is received from a franchise.

6. Since it is assumed that IFRS will be followed, each revenue-recognition point must be evaluated in relation to the IFRS revenue-recognition criteria:
   - *When a franchise agreement is signed with a new owner of a franchise.* At the time of signing, PPPL has considerable work to do to help the new franchisee to get the shop up and

running. It seems clear that PPPL hasn't fulfilled its obligations so risks and rewards of ownership haven't really transferred at this point. On the other hand, a binding agreement is in place and the franchisee would have difficulty backing out of the deal if PPPL fulfilled its obligations. The amount of revenue is known when the contract is signed because the amount is specified in the contract. Costs are uncertain because PPPL still has work to do providing assistance to the franchisee. These costs may be fairly predictable, although at this stage PPPL has no history to base its estimates on and each new location may have unique aspects that affect PPPL's costs. Collection is a potential problem because payment depends on the success of the franchises and PPPL has no track record for evaluating how successful the franchised pizzerias will be so it's not clear how much will actually be collected from the franchisees. This alternative doesn't meet the revenue-recognition criteria.

- *When a franchised Pizzazz Pizza Parlour opens.* PPPL has probably performed as of this point since once a pizza parlour is open most of what PPPL agreed to has been done (though there are ongoing responsibilities). In addition, the franchise owner has an operating business at this point so one could argue that the risks and rewards of ownership are with the owners of the franchise restaurant. The amount of revenue is specified in the franchise agreement. Most costs are probably known at this time, although some cost uncertainty likely exists regarding the cost of the support that must be provided to the franchisee (especially given that PPPL is new to the franchising business), which may make estimating future costs difficult. Of course, at some point the support provided by PPPL can be considered paid for by the franchisees' royalties rather than from the initial franchise fee. Collection of the amounts owing is still an open question. At the time the pizza parlour opens the franchise will have paid $20,000 of the $70,000 franchise fee. The fact that PPPL is new to the business makes it difficult to estimate the amount that won't be collected. This alternative meets the five criteria provided that a reasonable estimate of the amounts that won't be collected from the franchises can be made.

- *When cash is collected from a franchise.* Restaurants are a notoriously risky business and franchises can fail. There is added concern in this case because PPPL doesn't have a track record of running a franchise operation. As a result, collection isn't a foregone conclusion. Waiting until cash is in hand is conservative but not unreasonable because collection may prove to be unpredictable. Except for the payment received when the franchise agreement is signed, recognizing revenue when cash is received meets the five criteria. The $5,000 received when the contract is signed would probably have to be deferred until the pizza parlour opened because if the opening doesn't go as planned PPPL might have to return the initial payment.

- *When full payment is received from a franchise.* This method is very conservative. It requires that there be significant and unpredictable costs in the later years of the contract, or that PPPL had not earned the revenue once a restaurant opened. The most likely reason for delaying revenue recognition for this long would be for tax purposes, something not allowed under the *Income Tax Act.*

Comment: *Observe from this analysis that reasonable arguments can be made for at least two of the revenue recognition points (opening and cash collection), because the facts surrounding the franchise arrangements are ambiguous and subject to interpretation. This is why managers often face situations where justifiable alternatives exist.*

7. Amount of revenue that would be recognized in the years ended August 31, 2014 and 2015, using each revenue recognition point:

- When a franchise agreement is signed with a new owner of a franchise

  Revenue in 2014: $980,000 (14 stores × $70,000 per store)
  Revenue in 2015: $0

- When a franchised Pizzazz Pizza Parlour opens

  Revenue in 2014: $560,000 (8 × $70,000)
  Revenue in 2015: $420,000 (6 × $70,000)

- When cash is collected from a franchise (except for the payment on signing of the franchise agreement, which must be recognized when the franchise restaurant opens)

  Revenue in 2014: $160,000 (8 × $20,000)
  Revenue in 2015: $200,000 (6 × $20,000 + 8 × $10,000)

- When full payment is received from a franchise

  Revenue in 2014: $0
  Revenue in 2015: $0

8. The analysis above supports using either the opening of a Pizzazz Pizza Parlour or collection of cash as acceptable points to recognize revenue. Because there is more than one alternative available after the constraints and the facts are addressed, consider the objectives of financial reporting. To satisfy the primary objective, management evaluation, revenue should be recognized when a franchised Pizzazz Pizza Parlour opens. While cash collection is a significant uncertainty in PPPL's earnings process, using cash collection as the basis for evaluating and rewarding the president would likely undermine the incentive value of the bonus plan because the bonus would be significantly delayed. While recognizing revenue when the store opens might make the president less selective in choosing franchise owners (he may focus more on making sure the franchises open rather than making sure that the franchisees are able to pay their debts), the disincentives override this problem. When a restaurant opens, the president has done his job of expanding the chain. At this point, the franchise owners have made a significant financial investment and would likely work hard to make sure that their restaurants succeed.

   Comment: This is one possible solution to this case. Other rankings of objectives, evaluations of alternatives, and recommendations are possible and acceptable provided they are well supported.

SUMMARY OF KEY POINTS

▶ **LO 1** To recognize revenue in a logical and rational manner we need criteria to guide the choice. Under IFRS the following five criteria are used:

1. Significant risks and rewards of ownership have been transferred from the seller to the buyer.

2. The seller has no involvement or control over the goods sold.

3. Collection of payment is reasonably assured.

4. The amount of revenue can be reasonably measured.

5. The costs required to earn the revenue can be reasonably measured.

   These criteria provide guidance to managers, but they are open to interpretation and require judgment. Additionally, overriding any criterion requires that the revenue recognition point selected provide a reasonable and fair representation of the entity's activities, given the needs of the people who are using the accounting information.

▶ **LO 2** Accountants have devised two approaches for recognizing revenue: the critical-event approach and the gradual approach. Under the critical-event approach an entity chooses a "critical event" in the earnings process that it considers an appropriate time to recognize revenue. When this critical event occurs 100 percent of the revenue is recognized. Under the gradual approach revenue is recognized gradually over a period of time. The gradual approach, often used by entities providing services or entering into long-term contracts, provides useful and timely information to stakeholders about long-term contracts.

▶ **LO 3** There are different ways and times that revenues and expenses can be recognized and the methods chosen can affect the amount of revenue, expense, and net income an entity reports. Different revenue and expense recognition methods also affect financial ratios. Even though the financial statements are affected by using different revenue and expense recognition methods, the underlying economic activity of the entity is the same regardless of the methods chosen.

▶ **LO 4** Accrual accounting requires that costs be matched to revenue—meaning expenses should be recognized in the same period as the revenue those expenses helped earn is recognized—whether the cash flow occurs before, at the same time, or after the revenue is recognized. Not all costs are easy to match to revenue. Costs expensed in the period they are incurred are period costs. Costs matched to specific revenues are product costs. Product costs are expensed when the revenue they help generate is recognized.

▶ **LO 5** Managers can often choose from a number of reasonable accounting treatments for transactions and other economic events, even under IFRS. Flexible accounting rules are needed because of the complexity of economic activity. Constraints, facts, and objectives relevant to the situation influence mangers' choice of accounting methods. Managers are influenced by their need to provide information to stakeholders and by their own self-interests.

▶ **LO 6** Managers must choose an appropriate accounting treatment when there are alternatives. Relevant constraints, facts, and objectives must be considered, and the problem-solving approach incorporating the following steps should be applied:

1. Assess the entity and its environment.

2. Create a framework for analyzing the accounting issues.

3. Identify the accounting problems.

4. Rank the problems in order of importance and emphasize the more important problems in the analysis.

5. Analyze the accounting problems.

6. Make a recommendation and explain why the recommendation is consistent with the main objectives.

▶ **LO 7** IFRS defines the qualitative characteristics accounting information should have if it's to be useful to stakeholders: understandability, comparability, relevance, and reliability.

KEY TERMS

big bath, p. 195

comparability, p. 172

completed-contract method, p. 184

consignment sale, p. 177

cost-recovery method, p. 184

critical-event approach, p. 171

gradual approach, p. 171

percentage-of-completion method, p. 184

period costs, p. 187

product costs, p. 187

prospectus, p. 181

recognition, p. 188

relevance, p. 178

reliability, p. 178

understandability, p. 172

warranty, p. 176

zero-profit method, p. 184

ASSIGNMENT MATERIALS

Questions

Q4-1. Can a single set of financial statements satisfy all objectives of financial reporting? Explain.

Q4-2. Explain the difference between period and product costs. How is each type of cost accounted for?

Q4-3. Explain the accounting term "revenue recognition."

Q4-4. How is the balance sheet affected when revenue is recognized? Explain your answer and give examples.

Q4-5. Explain why, under accrual accounting, revenue isn't always recognized when cash is received.

Q4-6. Do you think it's good or bad that entities have flexibility in choosing when to recognize revenue? Explain.

Q4-7. Why is the percentage-of-completion method not a good way for a restaurant to recognize revenue?

Q4-8. Does the percentage-of-completion method of recognizing revenue meet the revenue recognition criteria discussed in the chapter? Explain. How do accountants justify using the percentage-of-completion method for recognizing revenue on long-term contracts?

Q4-9. What effects do the objectives of financial reporting have on when an entity recognizes revenue? Explain.

Q4-10. What are constraints, facts, and objectives? How does each affect the accounting methods an entity uses? Why does each have to be considered when making an accounting choice?

Q4-11. What is the matching concept? Why is it relevant to revenue recognition?

Q4-12. Explain why recognizing revenue and expenses in different ways has no effect on the underlying economic activity of an entity.

Q4-13. Why can it be difficult for accountants to determine when revenue should be recognized under accrual accounting?

Q4-14. Why is determining when to recognize revenue more difficult under accrual accounting than under cash accounting?

Q4-15. Distinguish between the percentage-of-completion and the zero-profit (cost recovery) methods of revenue recognition. Which method requires the exercise of more judgment by managers? Explain.

Q4-16. Do you think that the managers of entities should be responsible for selecting the accounting methods and estimates that they use, or should that responsibility be given to an independent third party? Explain your view. Make sure you consider both sides of the argument.

Q4-17. Do you think accounting would be more useful and reliable if only a single method of revenue recognition were allowed, such as when cash is collected or when the goods or services are provided to the customer? Explain.

Q4-18. Identify and explain the five revenue-recognition criteria.

Q4-19. Does it matter how and when a company recognizes its revenue? Explain.

Q4-20. Under what circumstances should the zero-profit (cost recovery) method of revenue recognition be used instead of the percentage-of-completion method?

Q4-21. What are gains and losses? How do they arise? How are gains and losses reported in the financial statements?

Q4-22. Why are gains and losses usually shown separately from revenues and expenses from ordinary business activities? What are the implications to the users of the financial statements if gains and losses are included in revenues and/or expenses?

Q4-23. Identify and explain the two factors that influence the accounting choices that are made by the managers who prepare the financial statements.

Q4-24. Why does self-interest play a role in accounting choice? Should it, in an ideal world? Explain.

Q4-25. Why do managers have the opportunity to choose some of the accounting methods they use? Should managers have a choice? Explain.

Q4-26. Conceptually, why can the earning of revenue be considered to be a continuous process? In spite of the continuous conceptual nature of revenue, why is revenue usually recognized at a single instant in time?

Q4-27. Why isn't it possible to use the gradual approach to revenue recognition for sales of appliances by a retailer?

Q4-28. Explain what each of the following objectives of financial reporting means:
a. Tax minimization
b. Management evaluation
c. Minimum compliance
d. Cash flow prediction
e. Stewardship
f. Earnings management

Q4-29. What does it mean when accountants refer to recognizing revenue when a "critical event" occurs?

Q4-30. Why is it important for financial statements to be comparable? Why is it difficult to compare the financial statements of different entities?

Q4-31. Why is it important for financial statements to be relevant and reliable? If you had to choose between having information that was more relevant but less reliable or information that was more reliable but less relevant, which would you pick? Explain.

Q4-32. Explain the matching concept. Give some examples of matching. Why is matching important for financial accounting? Why is matching sometimes difficult to do in practice?

Exercises

E4-1. **(Classifying period and product costs, LO 4)** Oxbow Candy Company Ltd. (Oxbow) produces a range of candy products ranging from gum balls to chocolate bars to truffles for sale and distribution around the world. The company operates production facilities in North America, Europe, and Asia. For each of the costs described below state whether you would treat it as a product cost or a period cost. Explain your choices.
a. Amount paid to employees who work producing the candy.
b. Television and print advertising to promote Oxbow's latest candy sensation.
c. Depreciation of Oxbow's head office building in Montreal.
d. Commissions paid to salespeople who sell candy to distributors and retailers.

e. Sugar, milk, cocoa, and other materials that are used to produce candy.

f. Electricity and other utilities used in the production facilities.

g. Amounts paid for shipping candy to customers.

h. Salaries paid to head office staff and senior executives.

i. Amounts paid to research and develop new candy products.

E4-2.   **(Identify reasonable methods for determining the proportion of a long-term contract that has been completed, LO 2)** For each of the following long-term projects, provide a basis for estimating the percentage of the job that has been completed. The discussion in the text used the percentage of total estimated cost incurred during a year as the percentage completed. For this exercise identify bases other than cost for estimating the percentage completed.

a. Construction of a 20-floor building.

b. A three-year contract to provide 24/7 computer maintenance to a financial institution.

c. A contract to remove contaminated earth from around a factory that had been dumping toxic waste for many decades.

E4-3.   **(Recording journal entries for recording revenue at different critical events, LO 1, 2, 4)** Risteen Telephone Services Ltd. (Risteen) designs and installs telephone systems for commercial customers. For example, in December 2015 Risteen signed a contract with Yarm Telemarketing Systems Ltd. (Yarm) to design and install a phone system for Yarm's new call centre in New Brunswick. The following events pertain to the contract with Yarm:

i. December 13, 2015: The contract between Risteen and Yarm is signed. Yarm will pay $550,000 for the system that will cost Risteen $300,000 to design, produce, and install. The contract provides an 18-month warranty for any repairs or adjustments required. Yarm will pay within 90 days of the completed system installation.

ii. October 15, 2016: Installation of the system is completed.

iii. December 12, 2016: Warranty work costing $35,000 is performed.

iv. January 8, 2017: Risteen receives payment in full from Yarm.

v. April 15, 2017: Warranty expires.

Required:

Prepare the journal entries required for the above events assuming the following:

a. Revenue is recognized when the contract is signed.

b. Revenue is recognized when installation of the system is complete.

c. Revenue is recognized when cash is collected.

d. Revenue is recognized when the warranty period expires.

E4-4.   **(Identifying the objectives of financial reporting, LO 5, 6)** For each of the following entities, identify the objectives of financial reporting that the entity's managers might have. In answering, consider who the stakeholders might be and which stakeholder(s) would be most important to the managers. Explain how the objectives of financial reporting would influence the accounting choices made by the managers.

a. A public company planning to borrow a large amount of money to finance an expansion.

b. A not-for-profit curling club. Membership and usage fees, dining room charges, and pro shop sales are used to operate the club. Club members are elected to sit on the board of directors of the club.

c. A medium-sized, family-owned business. Many senior managers are family members but many shareholders (also family members) don't work for the company. The company has a large outstanding debt.

d. A barbershop operating as a proprietorship. The proprietor has a small business loan secured by her home.

e. The government of Canada.

E4-5.   (**Identifying the objectives of financial reporting, LO 5, 6**) For each of the following entities, identify the objectives of financial reporting that the entity's managers might have. In answering, consider who the stakeholders might be and which stakeholder(s) would be most important to the managers. Explain how the objectives of financial reporting would influence the accounting choices made by the managers.

a. A privately owned biotechnology company planning to sell shares to the public and become a public company. The money raised will be used to further develop a technology for the treatment of liver disease.

b. A public company that has been adversely affected by international competition and is trying to receive subsidies from government.

c. A community hospital.

d. A private company that recently hired a new CEO to turn the struggling company around. The CEO receives a small salary, a five percent ownership share in the company, and a bonus based on the company's performance.

e. A small consulting practice with a single shareholder who is also the only employee.

E4-6.   (**Determining when to recognize revenue, LO 1, 2**) For each of the following situations use the IFRS revenue-recognition criteria to determine when revenue should be recognized. Explain your reasoning.

a. A driver purchases $100 of gas for cash at a local Petro-Canada Station.

b. A hockey fan purchases season tickets for the Edmonton Oilers. The price includes tickets for the team's 41 home games plus exhibition games. Ticket buyers pay the full price of the tickets in the summer before the season begins and receive the tickets at the time of payment. Once purchased there are no refunds.

c. WestJet Airlines sells a ticket to a traveller for a trip next year. The traveller pays in full at the time of purchase, using his MasterCard. The ticket is refundable.

d. A parents' magazine sells a three-year subscription for $33. The subscriber makes the payment when she subscribes.

E4-7.   (**Determining when to recognize revenue, LO 1, 2**) For each of the following situations use the IFRS revenue-recognition criteria to determine when the interest revenue should be recognized. Explain your reasoning.

a. A lender makes a loan to a borrower with an excellent credit rating. Interest is paid annually and the principal must be paid in full in three years.

b. A lender makes a loan to a borrower. The borrower is now suffering serious financial problems and hasn't made interest payments for several months. Collection of interest and principal from this borrower is in doubt.

E4-8.   (**Determining when to recognize revenue, LO 1, 2**) A manufacturing company sells specialized parts to a new customer. The parts are made-to-order and they will have to be inspected and tested by the customer before the order is accepted. If the order fails the inspection the manufacturer will have to repair or replace the parts, which means making them again. Payment is due 30 days after the parts have been inspected and accepted. A credit check found that the customer has a good history of paying its bills in full and on time.

Required:

When should the manufacturing company recognize the revenue from the sale?

E4-9.   (**Determining when to recognize revenue, LO 1, 2**) Daphne's Catering Ltd. (DCL) provides catering services to people living in Saskatoon. DCL can provide meals for groups as small as two and as large as 500. In November 2013, DCL was approached by the executive director of a national accounting organization to cater a gala dinner at the organization's national convention to be held in August 2014. The parties signed a contract in December 2013 in which they agreed DCL would cater the function for a minimum of 250 people at a price of $110 per person (if fewer than 250 people attend, the organization will pay for 250). The organization paid a $5,000 deposit at the time the contract was signed. An additional $15,000 was paid on May 1, 2014. The dinner was held successfully on August 15, 2014, with 297 guests attending. The balance owing was paid to DCL on August 31, 2014. DCL's year-end is December 31.

Required:

    a. What are some of the possible points at which DCL could recognize the revenue from the gala dinner?

    b. Which revenue-recognition points can you support with the IFRS criteria? Explain.

E4-10. **(Determining when to recognize revenue, LO 1, 2)** Meteghan Electronics Ltd. (Meteghan) is a chain of consumer electronics stores. Meteghan sells a complete line of electronics products including audio, video, computers, and satellite radio, along with parts and service. Whenever a customer makes a purchase they are offered the opportunity to buy an extended warranty, which provides "free" parts and labour for three years beyond the one-year warranty provided by the manufacturer. The customer must purchase the extended warranty at the time the product is purchased. The warranty goes into effect when the manufacturer's warranty ends.

Required:

When should Meteghan recognize the revenue from its sale of extended warranties? Explain your answer.

E4-11. **(Determining when to recognize revenue, LO 1, 2)** Neidpath Inc. (Neidpath) owns a brand name and logo that are known throughout the world. Recently, Neidpath agreed to license the name and logo to a company that will use them on its products (the licensee products that don't compete with Neidpath's). The agreement requires the licensee to make an initial payment of $500,000 to Neidpath at the beginning of the contract plus a royalty of $1 for each item sold that has the name and/or logo on it. The royalty is to be paid within 30 days of the end of Neidpath fiscal year.

Required:

Explain how Neidpath should recognize the revenue from the licensing agreement. Consider the revenue from the initial fee and the royalty separately. Use the revenue recognition criteria to support your answer.

E4-12. **(Determining when to recognize revenue, LO 1, 2)** Wadena Ltd. (Wadena) is a retail store that sells tailored-to-measure suits for men and women. Wadena has been in business for 15 years. The process of making a suit takes two to three months. Customers come for an initial fitting and select the fabric and style they prefer. A minimum of two additional fittings are necessary as the garment is made. The average price for a Wadena suit is $3,000. Customers pay 50 percent of the price of the suit at the initial fitting and the remainder paid when the suit is complete and the customer takes it. One of the reasons for Wadena's success is its after-sales service. For as long as someone owns a suit, Wadena will repair or make alterations free of charge. Customers pay by cash or major credit card, although the store will accept cheques from customers it knows.

Required:

When should Wadena recognize the revenue for sale of a suit? Explain your answer.

E4-13. **(Determining when to recognize revenue, LO 1, 2)** Alma Books Ltd. (Alma) is a national chain of bookstores. Alma earns revenue in several different ways:

    a. Sale of books and magazines to customers in its stores—customers pay cash or use credit cards (Visa or MasterCard) to pay for their purchases.

    b. On-line sales—customers can browse for books on the company's Website and make purchases online using a credit card or PayPal. Alma ships the order as soon as it's available. Customers sometimes have to wait if an item isn't in stock.

c. Loyalty program—customers pay $20 per year for membership and receive discounts on their in-store or online purchases. Membership is for one year from the date of purchase.

d. Sale of gift cards—the cards, which can value from $5 to $500, allow customers to purchase items in the store or online without using their own cash. There are no service charges associated with the cards.

Required:

Use the five IFRS revenue recognition criteria to determine when revenue should be recognized for each source of revenue. Explain your reasoning.

E4-14. **(Calculating revenue using the percentage-of-completion and zero-profit methods, LO 2)** Whipporwill Ltd. (Whipporwill) is a small construction company in Alberta that recently signed a contract to build a recreation centre in a local community. The centre will have a swimming pool, arena, gym, fitness centre, and a small theatre. Whipporwill will receive $18,000,000 from the city for building the centre and will have to pay the costs of construction from that amount. Construction will begin in September 2014 and is expected to be completed in June 2016. Whipporwill's year-end is December 31. Whipporwill has estimated the construction costs for each year:

	2014	2015	2016	Total
Estimated costs	$1,500,000	$7,000,000	$4,400,000	$12,900,000

The town paid $3,000,000 when the contract was signed and will pay $5,000,000 on January 1, 2015, 2016, and 2017.

Required:

Calculate the amount of revenue and expense that Whipporwill would recognize in each year of the contract using the percentage-of-completion and zero-profit methods. Assume the actual costs incurred equal the estimated costs.

E4-15. **(The effect of using different ways of estimating the proportion of a long-term contract that has been completed on the amount of revenue recognized, LO 2, 3)** Hectanooga Ltd. (Hectanooga) is a large construction engineering company. In 2014, Hectanooga was awarded a contract by a provincial government to widen a 150 kilometre stretch of a major highway. Hectanooga will receive $187,000,000 for the work, from which it must pay the costs of construction. The company has agreed to complete the work by September 15, 2017. Information regarding the yearly progress of the contract measured in different ways is provided below:

	2014	2015	2016	2017	Total
Costs	$18,000,000	$42,000,000	$54,000,000	$29,000,000	$143,000,000
Number of kilometres completed during the year	16	55	51	28	150
Labour hours worked	145,000	292,000	307,000	222,000	966,000

Required:

Hectanooga's new vice-president of finance understands that there are different ways to calculate the percentage-of-completion of a project. The vice-president has asked you to calculate the amount of revenue that would be recognized in each year of the contract using three different methods of estimating the percentage completed:

a. Costs incurred

b. Number of kilometres of the highway completed during the year

c. Labour hours worked

The vice-president would also like you to explain how he should choose among the three methods and which method would provide the best indication of the progress of the project to external stakeholders.

E4-16. **(Understanding the impact of self-interest on decision making, LO 5)** Strathroy Ltd. (Strathroy) is a publicly traded newspaper publishing company. The newspaper industry has faced difficult times in recent years with declining circulation and advertising revenue, in part caused by competition from the Internet and other information sources. As a public company Strathroy has many different stakeholders with different goals and objectives for using the financial statements. The following are some of Strathroy's stakeholders:

a. Leaders of a union about to negotiate a new contract for its members.

b. A large supplier of newsprint negotiating a long-term contract to supply newsprint.

c. The CEO of the company who is paid a bonus based on the company's performance.

d. A financial analyst preparing a report for investors on Strathroy. The analyst's employer does investment banking work for Strathroy.

e. Strathroy's shareholders, including 40 percent of the shares that are owned by members of the family that founded the business 75 years ago.

Required:

Different stakeholders of an entity will view the entity's goals and objectives in different ways, in part (at least) influenced by their personal goals and objectives (self-interests). For each of the stakeholders listed above explain what the stakeholder would want to accomplish in its dealings with Strathroy. Explain how the interests of the identified stakeholder could conflict with the interests of other stakeholders.

E4-17. **(Accounting for gains and losses, LO 4)** For each of the following land sales, prepare the journal entry that would be recorded and indicate the amount of the gain or loss that would be reported. Assume that in each case the sale of land isn't a main business activity of the entity.

a. Land costing $2,750,000 is sold for $2,750,000.

b. Land costing $720,000 is sold for $525,000.

c. Land costing $1,000,000 is sold for $3,722,000.

E4-18. **(Explaining and understanding different roles that accounting problems can be viewed from, LO 5, 6)** Listed below are some of the roles that someone addressing accounting problems can have. The role can affect how the role-player approaches and analyzes an accounting problem. For each role listed below, explain the perspective the role brings to the analysis. (Example: an auditor for the Canada Revenue Agency examines accounting information to ensure an entity complies with the *Income Tax Act* and, as a result, pays an appropriate amount of tax.) In answering, consider the entity the person in the role is working for and the objectives of that entity, and apply these factors to explain how the role-player would approach providing advice on accounting problems.

a. Arbitrator. (An arbitrator is a person who helps resolve disputes between parties. In an accounting setting an arbitrator might be asked to resolve disagreements over the accounting choices an entity made when, for example, the selling price of the entity is based on net income.)

b. Advisor to management of the entity.

c. Advisor to the board of directors of the company.

d. External auditor.

e. Advisor to a prospective lender.

f. Advisor to a major shareholder who isn't involved in the day-to-day management of the entity.

E4-19. **(Choosing when to recognize revenue according to the objectives of financial reporting, LO 1, 2, 6)** Pisquid Ltd. (Pisquid) is a manufacturer of kitchen furniture. In November 2015, Pisquid received an order for 15,000 sets of specially designed furniture from a large retail chain. The contract guarantees the price the retailer will pay and the quantity it will buy from Pisquid. The furniture is to be delivered monthly, in equal quantities each month, beginning in March 2016 and continuing through August 2017. The retail chain is to pay Pisquid within 45 days of receiving each shipment. Because Pisquid had excess capacity in its plant when the contract was signed it decided to manufacture the full order as soon as it could. Pisquid began producing the furniture in January 2016 and completed making the 15,000 sets in November 2016.

Required:

a. Identify the different possible critical events that could be used to recognize revenue.
b. Which critical event would you recommend for recognizing revenue to satisfy the purposes of each of the following objectives? Explain. (In answering, don't consider the constraints and the facts.)
   i.   Tax minimization
   ii. Evaluation of management by outside shareholders
   iii. Income smoothing
   iv. Managing earnings to increase income
   v.   Cash flow prediction
c. Which of the revenue recognition methods that you identified in (a) satisfy the IRFS revenue recognition criteria? Explain.

E4-20. **(Assessing different ways of recognizing revenue, LO 1, 2, 5)** Valhalla Furniture Emporium Ltd. (Valhalla) sells poor-quality furniture at low prices. Customers take delivery of their furniture after making a down payment of 10 percent of the selling price. The customers agree to pay the balance owing in 36 equal monthly payments. Valhalla repossesses between 40 percent and 60 percent of the furniture sold because customers default on their payments. Repossessed furniture can be resold if it requires only minor repairs and cleaning. Some repossessed furniture is unsaleable and must be disposed of.

Required:

a. What are the possible points at which Valhalla could recognize revenue?
b. Explain what reporting objectives each revenue recognition point would satisfy?
c. Which revenue recognition points can you support with the IFRS criteria?

Problems

P4-1. **(Choosing a revenue recognition point to achieve an objective of financial reporting, LO 1, 2, 3, 5, 6)** For each of the following independent situations, recommend how you would want to recognize revenue if your reporting objective was to minimize taxes. Support your answer. (To respond you should identify alternative points for recognizing revenue and choose the one that best satisfies the objective of minimizing taxes and can be reasonably supported.)

a. A construction company signs a contract to build a warehouse for a food distribution company. The project is to take 18 months from the signing date and the company will receive $10,000,000. At the company's fiscal year-end 60 percent of the project has been completed.
b. An investment company purchases shares of publicly traded companies for its portfolio. During the year the market value of the portfolio increases from $2,300,000 to $3,745,000. None of the shares were sold during the year.

    c. A national bus company sells passes allowing passengers unlimited travel on the company's buses for 60 days from the day the pass is first used. Passes must be purchased at least 90 days before they are first used. Once purchased the passes aren't refundable.

    d. A law firm charges $10,000 per year to clients who wish to have legal advice available to them 24 hours a day, seven days a week. (The $10,000 fee is simply for the privilege of having a lawyer available all the time. These clients then have to pay the lawyer's hourly rate for the advice given.)

P4-2. **(Evaluating when to recognize revenue to try to achieve an objective of financial reporting, LO 1, 2, 3, 5, 6)** For each of the following independent situations, recommend how you would want to recognize revenue if you were the president of the company, you receive a significant bonus based on net income, and your financial reporting objective is to receive as high a bonus as is reasonably possible. Support your answer. (To respond you should identify alternative points for recognizing revenue and choose the one that best satisfies the objective of achieving a high bonus *and* can be reasonably supported.)

    a. A construction company signs a contract to build a warehouse for a food distribution company. The project is to take 18 months from the date the contract is signed and the company will receive $10,000,000. At the company's fiscal year-end 60 percent of the project has been completed.

    b. An investment company purchases shares of publicly traded companies for its portfolio. During the year the market value of the portfolio increases from $2,300,000 to $3,745,000. None of the shares were sold during the year.

    c. A national bus company sells passes allowing passengers unlimited travel on the company's buses for 60 days from the day the pass is first used. Passes must be purchased at least 90 days before they are first used. Once purchased the passes aren't refundable.

    d. A law firm charges $10,000 per year to clients who wish to have legal advice available to them 24 hours a day, seven days a week. (The $10,000 fee is simply for the privilege of having a lawyer available all the time. These clients then have to pay the lawyer's hourly rate for the advice given.)

P4-3. **(Determining when to recognize revenue, LO 1, 2, 5)** In December 2013 Salmo Ltd. (Salmo) received a large order from Richelieu Inc. (Richelieu), an established customer. The customer asked that the product be delivered in the second week of January 2014. During the last week of December Salmo's controller realized the company wouldn't meet its earnings target and as a result the company's senior managers would miss out on significant year-end bonuses. In an effort to meet the target the controller instructed the shipping department to ship Richelieu's order on December 30, rather than waiting until January 9, 2014, which would have met the customer's instructions. The controller figured the customer wouldn't mind receiving the product a few days early, even though the change in delivery date wasn't discussed with the customer. Because Salmo uses independent shipping companies to deliver its merchandise, it normally recognizes revenue when the goods are shipped.

Required:

When should Salmo recognize the revenue on the sale to Richelieu? Explain your answer.

P4-4. **(Determining when to recognize revenue, LO 1, 2, 5)** Naramata Software Corp. (Naramata) is a public company that provides software solutions to commercial customers around the world. Naramata has long been very popular among investors because it has consistently reported steadily growing income quarter after quarter. In addition to providing customer-designed software products it also sells a range of "off-the-shelf" products. Usually, with the purchase a software package a customer receives

18 months of technical support, online or by phone. In addition, Naramata promises to provide customers with free upgrades for any software they purchase for up to three years from the date of purchase. Naramata's CFO has been thinking about how the company recognizes its revenue from the sale of these off-the-shelf packages. He thinks the company is really selling three products (the package itself, the technical support, and free upgrades) not one and, accordingly, should recognize the revenue in three chunks. For example, if the customer pays $1,000 for a software package Naramata would recognize $750 immediately for the software, recognize $100 over 18 months for the technical support, and recognize $150 when upgrades become available.

Required:

What do you think of the CFO's proposal for recognizing revenue? Use the revenue recognition criteria to defend your answer. What do you think the CFO's motivation for proposing this new approach might be?

P4-5. **(Determining when to recognize revenue, LO 1, 2)** Good Health Magazine (GHM) is a monthly publication devoted to healthful living. The magazine is published monthly and can be purchased at newsstands for $5 a copy. The publisher delivers the magazine to newsstands at the beginning of the month and will accept up to 20 percent of an order as returns. From experience, GHM can make fairly good estimates of returns. Readers can also subscribe to the magazine for one, two, or three-year periods. With a subscription GHM mails the magazine to the subscriber each month, after payment in full for the subscription is received. The subscription price per copy is substantially lower than the newsstand price. GHM promises to refund any unused portion of the subscription. Historically, about 5 percent of customers ask for a refund.

Required:

Explain how GHM should recognize its revenue. Consider newsstand and subscription revenue separately. Be sure to use the revenue recognition criteria to support your answer.

P4-6. **(Observing the effects of different revenue recognition methods on financial ratios, LO 1, 2, 3, 4, 5)** On November 15, 2014 Desert Renovations Ltd. (Desert) signed a contract to renovate a 75-year-old building to be suitable to house the head office of a real estate company. Desert has provided you with the following information about the contract:

i. Desert expects the renovations to take three years.
ii. Desert will receive $10,000,000 for the renovations on the following schedule:
   • $2,500,000 when the contract is signed
   • $3,000,000 on September 1, 2015
   • $3,000,000 on June 1, 2016, the expected completion date of the project
   • $1,500,000 on January 15, 2017
iii. The total cost of the renovations is expected to be $6,500,000, incurred as follows:
   • 2014: $0
   • 2015: $2,400,000
   • 2016: $4,100,000
   • 2017: $0
iv. Other costs associated with the contract are $700,000 in each of 2015 and 2016. These costs are treated as period costs in the calculation of income.
v. Desert's year-end is December 31.

Required:

a. Calculate revenue, expenses, gross margin, and net income for each year using the following revenue recognition methods:

  i. Percentage-of-completion

  ii. Zero-profit

  iii. Cash collection (*Hint:* Match construction costs based on the proportion of cash collected in each year.)

 b. Calculate the gross margin percentage and the profit margin percentage for each year.

 c. Does it matter how Desert accounts for its revenue from the renovation contract? To whom does it matter and why?

 d. Is the actual economic performance of Desert affected by how it accounts for the revenue from the renovation contract? Explain.

P4-7. **(Observing the effects of different revenue recognition methods on financial ratios, LO 1, 2, 3, 5)** Thorsby Construction Ltd. (Thorsby) recently received a contract to do long-needed repairs on the major bridges leading to a large city. The bridges have stress fractures and other evidence of deterioration and the municipal and provincial government agreed to jointly finance repairs. The repairs to all the bridges are expected to take three years. Thorsby will receive $15 million in total for the work. A payment of $3 million will be made when the contract is signed on July 15, 2014 and $3.8 million on June 1, 2015. Thorsby will receive $6 million when the work is complete, expected to be in May 2016. A final payment of $2.2 million is to be made 90 days after the repairs are complete. Thorsby's year-end is July 31.

Thorsby expects to incur the following costs during each fiscal year for the work:

2014	2015	2016	2017	Total
$0	$6,000,000	$3,600,000	$0	$9,600,000

In addition, Thorsby expects to incur $1,200,000 in each of fiscal 2015 and 2016. These costs will be treated as period costs in the calculation of income.

Required:

 a. Calculate revenue, expenses, gross margin, and net income for each year using the following revenue recognition methods:

  i. Percentage-of-completion

  ii. Zero-profit

  iii. Cash collection (*Hint:* Match construction costs based on the proportion of cash collected in each year.)

 b. Calculate the gross margin percentage and the profit margin percentage for each year.

 c. Does it matter how Thorsby accounts for its revenue from the refitting contract? To whom does it matter and why?

 d. Is the actual economic performance of Thorsby affected by how it accounts for the revenue from the refitting contract? Explain.

P4-8. **(Observing the effects of different revenue recognition methods on financial ratios, LO 2, 3, 5)** Antler Manufacturing Ltd. (Antler) is a newly formed company specializing in the production of high-quality machine parts. Paul Wayne incorporated Antler on the understanding it would receive a large contract from his previous employer, Pocologan Inc. (Pocologan), to manufacture parts. Antler has rented the space and equipment it needs to operate. During Antler's first year of operations the following transactions and economic events take place:

  i. January 3, 2014: Paul Wayne contributes $500,000 cash in exchange for 100,000 common shares in Antler.

  ii. January 5, 2014: Antler borrows $250,000 from Pocologan. The loan carries an interest rate of 10 percent per year. No interest or principal needs to be paid until 2017.

  iii. January 8, 2014: Antler rents space and equipment to operate the business. Rent of $200,000 for two years is paid.

iv. January 10, 2014: Antler signs the contract with Pocologan. The contract requires Antler to manufacture and deliver $4,000,000 in parts over the period July 1, 2014 to December 31, 2016. The contract requires payment by Pocologan within 90 days of each delivery by Antler. The selling price of all parts is specified in the contract. Antler begins production of the parts immediately. Pocologan operates a just-in-time inventory system, which requires that Antler be ready to deliver parts within three hours of being notified by Pocologan that parts are required. As a result, Antler is required to keep an adequate supply of parts on hand to meet demand.

v. During 2014 Antler produced and delivered parts, and collected cash in the following amounts:

Selling price of parts produced during 2014	$1,400,000
Cost of parts produced during 2014	$840,000
Selling price of parts delivered to Pocologan during 2014	$900,000
Cost of parts delivered to Pocologan during 2014	$540,000
Cash collected from Pocologan during 2014	$525,000
Cost of parts that were paid for by Pocologan during 2014	$315,000

vi. All costs incurred to produce the parts were on credit. Of the $840,000 incurred to produce parts in 2014, $760,000 had been paid by December 31, 2014.

vii. During 2014 Antler incurred additional costs of $210,000, all on credit. As of December 31, 2014, $175,000 of these costs had been paid. Because these costs weren't directly related to the production of parts Antler plans to expense them in full in 2014. This amount doesn't include the amount paid for rent and the interest expense.

viii. Antler has a December 31 year-end.

Required:

a. Use an accounting equation spreadsheet or journal entries and T-accounts to record the transactions and economic events that occurred in 2014 for Antler. Complete this process separately for the following critical events for recognizing revenue:
   i.   Production
   ii. Delivery
   iii. Collection of cash

b. Prepare Antler's income statement for 2014 and its balance sheet as of December 31, 2014 using each of the three critical events (production, delivery, and collection of cash). Your income statements should show revenue, cost of goods sold, gross margin, other expenses, and net income.

c. Calculate the gross margin percentage, profit margin percentage, current ratio, and the debt-to-equity ratio for 2014 for each critical event.

d. Which method of revenue recognition in gives the best indication of Antler's performance and liquidity? Explain.

e. Does it matter how Antler recognizes revenue? To whom does it matter and why?

f. Is the actual economic performance of Antler affected by how it recognizes revenue? Explain.

P4-9.   **(Observing the effects of different revenue recognition methods on financial ratios, LO 2, 3, 5, 6)** Kinkora Manufacturing Ltd. (Kinkora) is a newly formed company specializing in the production of a new type of pizza oven. Adam Daniel organized Kinkora on the understanding that it would receive a large contract for pizza ovens from his previous employer, Cascumpec Inc. (Cascumpec), which was planning to renovate its chain of pizza restaurants. Cascumpec is one of the largest pizza restaurant chains in central Canada. Kinkora has rented the space and equipment it needs to operate its business. During Kinkora's first year of operations the following transactions and economic events took place:

- July 3, 2015: Adam Daniel contributes $100,000 cash in exchange for 100,000 common shares in Kinkora.
- July 5, 2015: Kinkora borrows $200,000 from Cascumpec. The loan carries an interest rate of 10 percent per year. No interest or principal must be paid until 2019.
- July 8, 2015: Kinkora rents space and equipment to operate the business. Rent of $100,000 for two years is paid.
- July 10, 2015: Kinkora signs the contract with Cascumpec. The contract requires that Kinkora manufacture and deliver $2,000,000 in pizza ovens over the period January 1, 2015, to June 30, 2018. The contract requires that Cascumpec pay within 90 days of delivery by Kinkora. The selling price of the pizza ovens is specified in the contract. Kinkora begins production of the pizza ovens immediately.
- During 2015 Kinkora produced and delivered pizza ovens, and collected cash in the following amounts:

Selling price of ovens produced during 2015	$650,000
Cost of ovens produced during 2015	325,000
Selling price of ovens delivered to Cascumpec during 2015	400,000
Cost of ovens delivered to Cascumpec during 2015	200,000
Cash collected from Cascumpec during 2015	230,000
Cost of ovens that were paid for by Cascumpec during 2015	115,000

- All costs incurred to produce the ovens were purchased on credit. Of the $325,000 incurred to produce ovens in 2015, $290,000 had been paid by June 30, 2015.
- During 2015 Kinkora incurred additional costs of $95,000, all on credit. As of June 30, 2015, $80,000 of these costs had been paid. Because these costs were not directly used in the production of ovens Kinkora plans to expense them in full in fiscal 2015. This amount excludes the amount paid for rent and the interest expense.
- Kinkora has a June 30 year-end.

Required:

a. Use an accounting equation spreadsheet or journal entries and T-accounts to record the transactions and economic events that occurred in 2015 for Kinkora. Complete this process separately for the following critical events for recognizing revenue:
   i. Production
   ii. Delivery
   iii. Collection of cash

b. Prepare Kinkora's income statement for the year ended June 30, 2015 and its balance sheet as of June 30, 2015 using each of the three critical events (production, delivery, and collection of cash). Your income statements should show revenue, cost of goods sold, gross margin, other expenses, and net income.

c. Calculate the gross margin percentage, profit margin percentage, current ratio, and the debt-equity ratio for fiscal 2015 for each critical event.

d. Which method of calculating the ratios in (c) gives the best indication of Kinkora's performance and liquidity? Explain.

e. Does it matter how Kinkora recognizes revenue? To whom does it matter and why?

f. Is the actual economic performance of Kinkora affected by how it recognizes revenue? Explain.

P4-10. **(Recognizing revenue in a bill and hold arrangement, LO 1, 4)** Josselin Inc. (Josselin) is a manufacturer of computer game consoles. The company's products are designed to the specifications of each customer. In 2014 Josselin entered into a number of bill-

and-hold arrangements with customers. Each arrangement is a bit different and management isn't sure when revenue should be recognized in each case. Provide a report to management explaining when you think revenue should be recognized for each arrangement (perhaps whether revenue should be recognized on production, delivery, or some other point). Josselin's year-end is December 31.

a. The customer signed a contract to purchase 100,000 consoles to meet expected increased demand for its products. The customer asked that the consoles be produced as soon as possible but not delivered until early the next year because of a shortage of space in its warehouse. The customer paid a deposit of 25 percent of the selling price and the contract states the customer must pay the agreed price in full for the consoles whether it needs them or not. The contract also specifies that 25,000 consoles are to be delivered on the 15th day of each of the first four months of 2015. Josselin completed production of the consoles in mid-December and they are awaiting shipment. The price has been agreed to and normal payment terms apply.

b. The customer ordered 50,000 consoles and paid a deposit of 30 percent of the selling price. The deposit must be refunded if the customer decides to cancel the order. The order can be cancelled at the option of the customer for any reason. The units ordered can be easily modified by Josselin and sold to other customers if need be. The contract also specifies that 12,500 consoles are to be delivered on the 15th day of each of the first four months of 2015. Josselin completed production of the consoles in mid-December and they are awaiting shipment. The price has been agreed to and normal payment terms apply.

c. To take advantage of some excess production capacity at its factory Josselin produced 200,000 consoles for one of its regular customers. The customer indicated in a conversation with Josselin's president that it was highly likely that the units would be needed but the customer would not make a commitment to purchase them. Josselin's management expects the units will be shipped to the customer by October of 2015 at the latest.

P4-11.   **(Evaluating when to recognize revenue, LO 1)** Pikwitonei Gallery Inc. (PGI) is a new art gallery in Vancouver specializing in Inuit and First Nations art. PGI signs agreements with artists to have their works displayed in the gallery. The agreement requires the parties to keep each work on display for a minimum of four months, after which the gallery can return the work to the artist or the artist can request PGI return the work. The artist doesn't receive any money from PGI unless a work is sold. If a work is sold PGI pays the artist the amount the work was sold for less a commission of 25 percent of the selling price. For example, PGI recently sold a work for $8,000, from which it paid the artist $6,000 and kept $2,000 as its commission.

Required:

When should Pikwitonei recognize its revenue and how much should it recognize? Explain your answer.

P4-12.   **(Evaluating when to recognize revenue, LO 1)** Fair Jewellers is a retail jewellery store. Fair offers a lay-away program allowing customers to make a down payment on an item in the store. The store holds the item for the customer until it's paid for in full. Customers are required to pay in full within 180 days of the down payment. Customers don't have to sign a formal agreement to pay for or purchase the selected item. If the customer fails to pay in full, the customer loses the down payment. If the merchandise is lost, damaged, or destroyed Fair must either refund the down payment or provide replacement merchandise. In the past about 8 percent of customers didn't complete the purchase and lost their down payments.

Required:

When should Fair Jewellers recognize its revenue from the lay-away sales? Also address how Fair should account for the deposits that are lost. Explain your answers.

P4-13. **(Evaluating when to recognize revenue and the objectives of financial reporting, LO 1, 5, 6)** In September 2013 the sole shareholder of Molanosa Ltd. (Molanosa) agreed to sell 100 percent of the shares of the company to Winona Ltd. The terms of the sale require Winona to pay the shareholder $1 million when the deal closes on February 15, 2014 plus two times net income for the year ended December 31, 2013. Winona also agreed to pay an additional $100,000 if net income for 2013 exceeds $200,000. You are Winona's CFO and you have just received Molanosa financial statements for 2013, which shows net income for the year of $207,900. Further investigation showed that in late December 2013 Molanosa made a $20,000 shipment of goods to a new customer. Molanosa had been in negotiations with the new customer for some time and the final agreement was an important step in its planned expansion into western Canada. The terms of the sale are unusual in that they allow the customer to return any and all of the goods shipped at any time up until March 1, 2014. The customer isn't required to pay for the goods until March 31, 2014. Molanosa normally recognizes revenue when goods are delivered to the customer and normally provides 30 days to pay. Molanosa recognized the sale to the new customer in 2013.

Required:

Prepare a report to Winona's CFO analyzing Molanosa's sale to the new customer. Your report should include an evaluation of the appropriateness of Molanosa's accounting for the sale and an assessment of why it might have entered into this transaction and why it might have accounted for it this way.

P4-14. **(Considering how to recognize expenses, LO 4, 5, 6)** Duthil Ltd. is a small public company that publishes a variety of newsletters and magazines. The CEO and founder of Duthil owns 35 percent of the shares of the company with the remainder owned by public investors. Duthil makes money through the sale of subscriptions and individual issues of its magazines and newsletters (revenue is recognized when a publication is mailed to a subscriber or an individual issue is sold) and through the sale of advertising in the publications. In late 2014 Duthil conducted a campaign to increase subscriptions. The company engaged a telemarketing firm to call potential subscribers in the desired demographic group. The cost of the campaign was $66,000. As a result of the campaign several hundred new subscriptions were obtained. The subscriptions will come into effect in fiscal 2015 and will generate about $75,000 for the year. All the new subscriptions are for one year but management expects that approximately 50 percent of those subscriptions will be renewed for the next year and then for each year after that approximately 75 percent of the subscribers will renew. Duthil's year-end is December 31.

Required:

a. Who are of Duthil's stakeholders and what use do they have for the financial statements?

b. What objectives of financial reporting might Duthil's management consider when preparing the financial statements? Explain.

c. How would you recommend the objectives be ranked? Explain.

d. Prepare a report to Duthil's management explaining how to account for the costs incurred to increase the number of subscribers. In your answer, be sure to consider your responses to (a), (b), and (c) above. Also consider whether the costs incurred should be considered an asset or an expense when incurred, and if considered an asset when incurred, over what period the asset should be expensed. Explain your response.

P4-15. (**Evaluating objectives of financial reporting and recommending how to recognize revenue, LO 1, 2, 6**) Notigi Mines Ltd. (Notigi) is a mining venture that recently began operations in northern Manitoba. The mine has been under development for the last two years and will produce its first shipments of refined metal before the end of the current fiscal year. Two senior executives who have extensive mining experience manage the mine. The mine is owned by a syndicate of twenty investors, mainly professionals such as accountants, doctors, lawyers, and dentists who live in various locations in western Canada.

Notigi extracts ore from the ground and ships it to another company for processing into refined metal. The processing company then returns the refined metal to Notigi for sale and shipment to buyers. Notigi has already entered into long-term contracts with several buyers to purchase virtually all of the mine's production at prices specified in the contract. Any production not covered by the long-term contracts can easily be sold at prevailing prices in the open market.

Required:

a. What do you think Notigi's objectives of accounting might be? Explain.
b. How would you rank the objectives? Explain.
c. When would you recommend that revenue be recognized on the sale of the refined metal? Explain your recommendation. Make sure that you consider the constraints, facts, and objectives in your answer.

P4-16. (**Evaluating objectives of financial reporting and recommending how to recognize revenue, LO 1, 2, 5**) Opeongo Construction Ltd. (Opeongo) is a recently formed company that builds commercial and industrial buildings in the Ottawa area. All of Opeongo's common stock is owned by five people: Adam and Nikki, a brother and sister who operate the company; two cousins of Adam and Nikki who live and work in Vancouver; and a wealthy aunt who is retired and lives in Europe. Opeongo borrowed money from the bank to cover the costs of starting the business. All the money initially borrowed from the bank has been spent.

In October 2013, Opeongo won a contract to build a warehouse in suburban Ottawa. This will be its first large job. The warehouse will take about 18 months to build and construction is scheduled to begin in late March 2014. Opeongo will receive $1.96 million to build the warehouse. The contract specifies the following payment schedule:

• On commencement of construction	$ 100,000
• On the first day of each month beginning with the month after construction begins ($70,000 per month for 18 months)	1,260,000
• On completion of construction	400,000
• 90 days after the purchaser takes possession of the warehouse	200,000
• Total	$1,960,000

From this amount Opeongo has to pay the costs of construction, which it estimates to be about $1,500,000. Construction costs are expected to be incurred evenly over the construction period. Opeongo's year-end is December 31.

Required:

a. What do you think Opeongo's objectives of accounting could be? Explain.
b. How would you rank the objectives? Explain.
c. What different revenue recognition methods could Opeongo consider for the warehouse project? How much revenue would be recognized in 2013, 2014, and 2015 under the different methods you identified? Show your work.

d. When would you recommend that revenue be recognized on the warehouse construction project? Explain your recommendation. Make sure that you consider the constraints, facts, and objectives in your answer.

P4-17. (**Considering when to recognize revenue, LO 1, 2, 5, 6**) Teslin Inc. (Teslin) is a medium-sized manufacturer of plastic storage containers. Teslin is a private corporation that is owned entirely by a single shareholder, Rima Ishtiaque. Ms. Ishtiaque isn't involved in the day-to-day management of Teslin but she speaks regularly with Teslin's president, Mr. Krajden. Mr. Krajden is compensated with a salary plus a bonus based on Teslin's net income.

On October 1, 2013 Teslin signed a $1,000,000 contract with the Government of Canada to design and manufacture storage containers for all the tax dollars it collects from Canadians. The storage containers must be delivered by April 1, 2015. The government will pay $250,000 on April 1, 2014, $250,000 on January 15, 2015, and the balance 30 days after all the containers have been delivered. Teslin plans to begin production of the containers in early 2014. Teslin plans to ship 10 percent of the contracted containers per month beginning in September 2014. The contract stipulates that Teslin pay a penalty of $20,000 per week if the containers aren't completely delivered by April 1, 2015. Teslin had to borrow $300,000 from the bank to finance the project. Teslin expects to earn $225,000 from this contract.

You have been hired by Mr. Krajden to provide advice to him on how to recognize revenue on the contract with the government. Teslin's year-end is December 31.

Required:

a. Who are the possible users of Teslin's financial statements and what use do they have for the statements?
b. What objectives of financial reporting would you suggest that Mr. Krajden consider when preparing Teslin's financial statements? Explain.
c. How would you advise Mr. Krajden to rank the objectives? Explain.
d. What critical events for recognizing the revenue on the government contract can you identify? Explain.
e. When would you recommend that Teslin recognize the revenue on the contract? Make sure to consider the constraints, facts, and objectives when responding.

P4-18. (**Evaluating when a partnership of lawyers should recognize revenue, LO 1, 2, 3, 5, 6**) Elnora and Partners is a recently formed partnership of lawyers. The partnership has ten partners (all of whom are practising lawyers) and 15 associate lawyers (lawyers who work for the partnership but who aren't partners), along with 12 other employees. The partnership's financial statements will be used to determine the following:

- The amount of income tax each partner pays (remember, partners, not the partnership, pay income tax).
- The amount of money paid to each partner, based on the net income of the partnership.
- The amount a new partner pays to join the partnership and the amount a departing partner is paid for his or her partnership interest. In addition, the financial statements are provided to the bank because the partnership has a large line of credit available to it.

The partnership's September 30 year-end has just passed and the managing partner of the firm has asked for your advice on how to recognize revenue. The managing partner provides you with the following information on how the partnership generates revenue:

i. Some clients are billed at the completion of a case, based on the number of hours lawyers worked on the case. (Each lawyer has an hourly billing rate.) Lawyers keep track of the time they spend on each case and report the number of hours each month to the accounting department, which keeps track of the hours spent on each case by each lawyer. The amount actually billed to a client may differ from the actual charges generated by the lawyers who worked on the case. (That is, the amount billed may differ from the number of hours worked multiplied by the hourly billing rate.) The final amount billed is based on the judgment of the partner in charge of the case. Clients have 60 days from receipt of their bill to pay.

ii. Some clients pay only if their cases are successful. The partnership receives a percentage of the settlement if the client wins the case. It can be difficult to determine whether a client will win a case and the amount that will be received if the client does win. Many of these cases can take years to resolve.

iii. Some clients pay amounts called retainers, which are amounts paid to the partnership before services are provided. The retainer is used to pay for legal services as they are provided. If the amount of retainer isn't used by the end of the year, the remaining amount is applied against future years' legal services.

iv. Clients who wish to have legal advice available to them 24 hours a day, seven days a week, pay a fee of $10,000 per year for the service. (The $10,000 fee is simply for the privilege of having a lawyer available all the time. These clients also have to pay the lawyer's hourly rate for the advice given.)

Required:

a. What are the possible objectives of financial reporting? Explain each objective that you identify. Are there any conflicts among the objectives? Explain.

b. Rank the objectives in order of importance. Explain your ranking.

c. When should the partnership recognize its revenue? Explain your recommendations fully. Make sure to discuss constraints, facts, and objectives in your answer.

P4-19. **(Selecting and justifying revenue-recognition alternatives to suit the objectives of financial reporting, LO 2, 3, 5, 6)** Eyebrow Technologies Ltd. (Eyebrow) is a Canadian-owned developer of computer hardware and software. Eyebrow is owned by 20 private investors, most of whom aren't involved in the day-to-day management of the company. Eyebrow has borrowed extensively from banks, and management believes additional loans will be required in the near future. Senior executives own a small number of Eyebrow's shares and are compensated with a salary plus a bonus based on the performance of the company.

Eyebrow is completing development of a new product. The product combines a modification of Eyebrow's existing computer hardware with a newly developed proprietary software program. The new product is targeted at firms in the financial services industry (firms such as Canadian banks, mid- to large-sized trust companies, and insurance companies). The design of the product requires that customers purchase both Eyebrow's hardware and software (a customer can't purchase only the software and the hardware isn't useful without the software).

The new product (hardware and software) sells for $325,000. Eyebrow has 12 firm orders for the new product. In January 2014 Eyebrow shipped the computer hardware component to the 12 customers. The software will be provided to customers when it's completed in May 2014. The software was originally expected to be ready in February 2014 but unexpected programming problems delayed its completion. Eyebrow now expects to complete testing and debugging of the software in time to meet the May shipping date. Costs of the product include the hardware, software development, and marketing, sales, and administrative costs.

Customers have already paid 25 percent of the cost of their orders. They will pay an additional 60 percent 30 days after the product is delivered and operating, and the balance six months after that.

Eyebrow's year-end is February 28.

Required:

    a. Identify the stakeholders who would have an interest in the financial information of Eyebrow. Explain each stakeholder's interest in the information (i.e., why would they want it?).

    b. Identify possible objectives of financial reporting that Eyebrow's management might have. Explain why each objective might be relevant.

    c. Identify possible critical events that Eyebrow could use to recognize the revenue on the new product. (In answering this question, consider whether the new product is really two products instead of one.)

    d. Select two of the stakeholders and recommend a revenue and expense recognition policy to Eyebrow's management that might satisfy the information needs of each of the two stakeholders. (*Note:* You should come up with two *different* policies, one for each stakeholder.) Fully explain your choices by justifying them in terms of the constraints, facts, and objectives.

Using Financial Statements

TIM HORTONS INC.

Everybody in Canada knows Tim Hortons. Tim Hortons Inc. develops, operates, and franchises quick-service restaurants in the United States and Canada. It primarily offers premium coffee, home-style soups, sandwiches, baked goods, and donuts. As of December 28, 2008, Tim Hortons and its franchisees operated 2,917 restaurants in Canada and 520 restaurants in the United States. The company was founded in 1964 and is based in Oakville, Canada. Tim Hortons trades on the NYSE and TSX (THI).[2]

Tim Hortons' consolidated balance sheet and statements of operations, along with some extracts from the notes to the financial statements, are provided in Exhibit 4.5. Use this information to answer questions FS4-1 to FS4-11.

FS4-1. Examine the information in Exhibit 4.5. In what currency are the amounts in the financial statements stated? According to what accounting principles are Tim Hortons' financial statements prepared? Why do you think the company uses this combination of accounting principles and currency? Do you think it's important to know the accounting principles and currency used to prepare the financial statements? Explain.

FS4-2. Read the note to Tim Hortons' financial statements called "Use of Estimates." Why do you think this note is included in the statements? How does it help stakeholders? What does the note caution stakeholders? Do you think Tim Hortons' financial statements would be more relevant and reliable if there were no estimates? Explain. What estimates are mentioned in the note?

FS4-3. Read the note called "Gift Certificates and Cash Cards" in Exhibit 4.5. What is the TimCard program and how does it work? Why do you think Tim Hortons implemented this program? What journal entry does Tim Hortons record when a customer purchases a TimCard? When does Tim Hortons recognize revenue on the TimCard? What journal entry would be recorded when revenue is recognized? On December 28, 2008 how much had customers paid on their TimCards that they had not yet used? How do you know? What is the accounting concern when people lose or misplace their TimCards?

FS4-4. How many different ways does Tim Hortons make money? How does it recognize the revenue for each way?

FS4-5. Many people buy Tim Hortons gift certificates as gifts for friends and family. What journal entry does Tim Hortons record when someone buys a gift certificate? When

| EXHIBIT | 4.5 | Tim Hortons Inc.: Extracts from the Financial Statements |

TIM HORTONS INC. AND SUBSIDIARIES
Consolidated Balance Sheet
(in thousands of Canadian dollars)

	As at	
	December 28, 2008	December 30, 2007
Assets		
Current assets		
Cash and cash equivalents	$ 101,636	$ 157,602
Restricted cash and cash equivalents (note 1)	62,329	37,790
Accounts receivable, net (note 5)	159,505	104,889
Notes receivable, net (note 6)	22,615	10,824
Deferred income taxes (note 7)	19,760	11,176
Inventories and other, net (note 8)	71,505	60,281
Advertising fund restricted assets (note 9)	27,684	20,256
Total current assets	465,034	402,818
Property and equipment, net (note 10)	1,332,852	1,203,259
Notes receivable, net (note 6)	17,645	17,415
Deferred income taxes (note 7)	29,285	23,501
Intangible assets, net (note 11)	2,606	3,145
Equity investments (note 12)	132,364	137,177
Other assets	12,841	9,816
Total assets	$1,992,627	$1,797,131
Liabilities and Stockholders' Equity		
Current liabilities		
Accounts payable (note 13)	$ 157,210	$ 133,412
Accrued liabilities		
Salaries and wages	18,492	17,975
Taxes	25,605	34,522
Other (note 13)	110,518	95,777
Advertising fund restricted liabilities (note 9 and note 14)	47,544	39,475
Current portion of long-term obligations	6,691	6,137
Total current liabilities	366,060	327,298
Long-term obligations		
Term debt (note 14)	332,506	327,956
Advertising fund restricted debt (note 9 and note 14)	6,929	14,351
Capital leases (note 17)	59,052	52,524
Deferred income taxes (note 7)	13,604	16,295
Other long-term liabilities	74,072	56,624
Total long-term obligations	486,163	467,750
Commitments and contingencies (note 18)		
Stockholders' equity		
Common stock, (US$0.001 par value per share), Authorized: 1,000,000,000 shares, Issued: 193,302,977 (note 19)	289	289
Capital in excess of par value	929,102	931,084
Treasury stock, at cost: 11,754,201 and 6,750,052 shares, respectively (note 19)	(399,314)	(235,155)
Common stock held in trust, at cost: 358,186 and 421,344 shares, respectively (note 19)	(12,287)	(14,628)
Retained earnings	677,550	458,958
Accumulated other comprehensive loss	(54,936)	(138,465)
Total stockholders' equity	1,140,404	1,002,083
Total liabilities and stockholders' equity	$1,992,627	$1,797,131

does Tim Hortons recognize revenue on the sale of gift certificates? On December 28, 2008 how much in gift certificates were outstanding? How do you know? What is the accounting concern when people lose or misplace their gift certificates?

FS4-6. An accounting problem with gift certificates and TimCards is not all of them get used. Sometimes they will get lost or forgotten. How should Tim Hortons account for money paid for gift certificates and TimCards that will never be used? Should it be recognized as revenue and if so, when? What is one of the challenges of dealing with this issue from an accounting perspective?

FS4-7. How does Tim Hortons account for its advertising costs? Why do you think it uses this approach? Do you agree with the approach? Explain.

| EXHIBIT 4.5 | (continued) Tim Hortons Inc.: Extracts from the Financial Statements |

TIM HORTONS INC. AND SUBSIDIARIES
Consolidated Statement of Operations
(in thousands of Canadian dollars, except per share data)

	Year ended		
	December 28, 2008	December 30, 2007	December 31, 2006
Revenues			
Sales	$1,348,015	$1,248,574	$1,072,405
Franchise revenues			
Rents and royalties	601,870	553,441	503,375
Franchise fees	93,808	93,835	83,769
	695,678	647,276	587,144
Total revenues	2,043,693	1,895,850	1,659,549
Costs and expenses			
Cost of sales	1,180,998	1,099,248	941,947
Operating expenses	216,605	201,153	182,332
Franchise fee costs	87,486	87,077	76,658
General and administrative expenses (note 3 and note 20)	130,846	119,416	113,530
Equity (income) (note 12)	(37,282)	(38,460)	(35,236
Asset impairment and related closure costs (note 4)	21,266	—	—
Other expense (income), net	208	2,307	1,102
Total costs and expenses, net	1,600,127	1,470,741	1,280,333
Operating income	443,566	425,109	379,216
Interest (expense)	(24,558)	(24,118)	(22,253
Interest income	4,926	7,411	11,671
Affiliated interest (expense), net	—	—	(7,876
Income before income taxes	423,934	408,402	360,758
Income taxes (note 7)	139,256	138,851	101,162
Net income	$ 284,678	$ 269,551	$ 259,596

NOTE 1 SUMMARY OF SIGNIFICANT ACCOUNTING POLICIES

Use of estimates

The preparation of Consolidated Financial Statements in conformity with U.S. GAAP requires management to make assumptions and estimates. These assumptions and estimates affect the reported amounts of assets and liabilities and the disclosure of contingent assets and liabilities as of the date of the Consolidated Financial Statements and the reported amounts of revenues and expenses during the reporting periods. Estimates and judgments are inherent in, but not limited to the following: the estimation of the collectibility of royalty and other franchise related revenue; legal obligations; income taxes; insurance liabilities; various other commitments and contingencies; valuations used when assessing potential impairment of assets and other intangibles; inventory valuations; gift certificate and cash card breakage; property and equipment, including the estimation of the useful lives of property and equipment and other long-lived assets; and, valuations associated with estimating stock-based compensation expenses. While management applies its judgment based on assumptions believed to be reasonable under the circumstances and at the time, actual results could vary from these assumptions or had different assumptions been used. The Company evaluates and updates its assumptions and estimates based on new events occurring, additional information being obtained or more experience being acquired.

FS4-8. How many Tim Hortons restaurants were in operation on December 28, 2008? How many were franchises and how many were operated by the company? How many franchises were opened and closed in each of the last three years? How has the number of company-operated restaurants changed over the last three years? What does this tell you about Tim Hortons' strategy for making money?

FS4-9. Examine Note 22 to Tim Hortons' financial statements and respond to the following questions:
   a. What is segmented financial information and why do you think it's provided (consider how it will help you as a stakeholder)?
   b. What segments does Tim Hortons provide information about?

EXHIBIT 4.5 (continued) Tim Hortons Inc.: Extracts from the Financial Statements

Gift certificates and cash cards

In 2007, the Company introduced the TimCard quick pay cash card program. Customers can prepay for future purchases at participating Tim Hortons restaurants or over the internet by reloading a dollar value onto their TimCard through cash or credit card, when and as needed. A TimCard entitles the holder to use the value for purchasing product only and the amounts generally are nonrefundable and not redeemable for cash. TimCard holders are not entitled to any interest, dividends or returns on prepaid amounts. There are no expiration dates on the cash cards and the Company does not charge any service fees that cause a decrease to customer balances.

Cash collected from the loading of the TimCard and interest earned thereon are recorded as Restricted cash and cash equivalents on the Consolidated Balance Sheet since these funds have been designated for use only by the cash card program to honour outstanding obligations. Changes in the Restricted cash and cash equivalents balances have been classified as an operating activity on the Consolidated Statement of Cash Flows. The restricted cash and cash equivalents balances at December 28, 2008 and December 30, 2007 represent the prepaid amounts not yet redeemed by customers. The outstanding customer obligations for both TimCards and gift certificates are recorded in Accrued liabilities, Other (see Note 13) on the Consolidated Balance Sheet. Since the inception of the program, interest on the restricted cash and cash equivalents has been contributed by the Company to the Company's advertising and promotion funds to help offset costs associated with this program.

While the Company will honour all cash cards presented for payment, the Company may, based on historical review after the program has been in place for some time, determine the likelihood of redemption to be remote for certain card balances due to, among other factors, long periods of inactivity. In these circumstances, to the extent management determines there is no requirement for remitting card balances to government agencies under unclaimed property laws, the obligation for any such card balances may be transferred to the Company's advertising and promotion funds. No such amounts were recognized in 2008 or 2007.

In addition to the TimCard program, the Company has gift certificates available in certain locations for a limited time. The Company will continue to honour outstanding gift certificates. When a customer uses a gift certificate or a TimCard to purchase product at a Company-operated restaurant, the Company recognizes the revenue from the sale of the product. When a customer uses a gift certificate or TimCard at a franchised restaurant, the Company recognizes revenues, in the form of rents and royalties, arising from the sale of the product. The Company recognizes income on unredeemed gift certificates ("gift certificate breakage") when it can determine that the likelihood of the gift certificate being redeemed is remote and that there is no legal obligation to remit the unredeemed gift certificate value to relevant jurisdictions. The Company determines gift certificate breakage based on historical redemption patterns. Once the breakage rate is determined, it is recognized over a seven-year time period which is the estimated life of a gift certificate. Insignificant amounts have been recognized as a reduction in cost of sales in fiscal 2008, 2007 and 2006.

Revenue recognition

The Company operates warehouses in Canada to distribute coffee and other dry goods and refrigerated and frozen products to its extensive franchise system. Revenues from distribution sales are recorded when the product is delivered to the franchisee or, in certain cases, when the product is delivered to a third party distributor. Revenues from Company-operated restaurants are recognized upon tender of payment at the time of sale. Royalty revenues are recognized in the month earned and are normally collected within the month or shortly thereafter. Rental revenue, excluding contingent rent, is recognized on a straight-line basis. Contingent rent is recognized in the month earned. Franchise fees are collected at the time of sale, resale, or renovation of the franchised restaurant. The timing of revenue recognition for sales, and franchise revenues (rents and royalties and franchise fees) does not involve significant estimates and assumptions. See also discussion of "Franchise operations" below for further information regarding franchise revenues.

Franchise operations

The Company's Tim Hortons restaurants are predominantly franchised. The Company grants franchise license or operator agreements to independent operators who in turn pay franchise fees and other payments, which may include payments for equipment, royalties and, in most cases, rents for each restaurant opened. Franchise fees are collected at the time of sale or resale of the franchise. Franchise fees and equipment sales are generally recognized as income when each restaurant commences operations and payment is received from the franchisee unless the franchisee is participating in the Company's franchise incentive program (see below). Royalties, based on a percentage of monthly sales, are recognized as income on the accrual basis.

> ### EXHIBIT 4.5 (continued) Tim Hortons Inc.: Extracts from the Financial Statements
>
> The following progression outlines the Company's franchised locations and system activity for each of the years 2006 through 2008:
>
> | | 2008 | 2007 | 2006 |
> |---|---|---|---|
> | **Franchise Restaurant Progression** | | | |
> | Franchise restaurants in operation – beginning of year | 3,149 | 2,952 | 2,790 |
> | Franchises opened | 265 | 192 | 184 |
> | Franchises closed | (36) | (17) | (30) |
> | Net transfers within the franchised system (primarily resales) | 25 | 22 | 8 |
> | Franchise restaurants in operation – end of year | 3,403 | 3,149 | 2,952 |
> | Company-operated restaurants | 34 | 72 | 95 |
> | Total systemwide restaurants[1] | 3,437 | 3,221 | 3,047 |
>
> ---
>
> [1] Includes various types of standard and non-standard restaurant formats with varying restaurant sizes and menu offerings as well as self-serve kiosks, which serve primarily coffee products and a limited selection of donuts. Collectively, the Company refers to all of these units as "systemwide restaurants."
>
> *Advertising costs*
>
> Advertising costs are expensed as incurred with the exception of media development costs, which are expensed in the month that the advertisement is first communicated (see Note 9).
>
> **NOTE 13 ACCOUNTS PAYABLE AND ACCRUED LIABILITIES—OTHER**
>
> Included within other accrued liabilities are the following obligations as at December 28, 2008 and December 30, 2007:
>
> | | 2008 | 2007 |
> |---|---|---|
> | | (in thousands) | |
> | Gift certificate obligations | $ 12,960 | $25,147 |
> | Cash card obligations | 62,882 | 37,784 |
> | Other accrued liabilities | 34,676 | 32,846 |
> | | $110,518 | $95,777 |
>
> Other accrued liabilities include accrued rent expense, deposits, and various equipment and other accruals. The carrying amount of Accounts payable and Accrued liabilities approximates fair value due to the short-term nature of these balances.

c. How much sales and revenue did Tim Hortons earn in Canada and the U.S. in each of the last three fiscal years? How much operating income was reported from each country? What is the operating profit margin percentage in each segment in each year? Evaluate the performance in each country.

d. Why do you think Tim Hortons is paying so much attention to the U.S. market?

FS4-10. Examine Tim Hortons' income statement. What were Tim Hortons' total revenues and net income in each of the last three years? Explain how Tim Hortons earns each of the types of revenue it reports in its income statement. Which type of revenue is growing fastest? How are revenues growing as compared with net income? What explains the difference in the growth of the two?

FS4-11. What are warehouse sales (look at the revenue recognition note)? Who are the customers for warehouse sales? How much in warehouse sales did Tim Hortons report in 2008?

EXHIBIT ❮ 4.5 ❯ (continued) Tim Hortons Inc.: Extracts from the Financial Statements

NOTE 22 SEGMENT REPORTING

The Company operates exclusively in the food-service industry and has determined that its reportable segments are those that are based on the Company's methods of internal reporting and management structure. The Company's reportable segments are the geographic locations of Canada and the U.S. As set forth in the table below, there are no amounts of revenues shown between reportable segments.

The table below presents information about reportable segments:

	Year ended					
	December 28, 2008	% of total	December 30, 2007	% of total	December 31, 2006	% of total
Revenues						
Canada	$1,879,799	92.0%	$1,741,372	91.9%	$1,518,737	91.5%
U.S	163,894	8.0%	154,478	8.1%	140,812	8.5%
	$2,043,693	100.0%	$1,895,850	100.0%	$1,659,549	100.0%
Segment Operating Income (Loss)						
Canada	$ 507,006	105.5%	$ 467,884	101.0%	$ 410,582	99.6%
U.S[1]	(26,488)	(5.5)%	(4,804)	(1.0)%	1,736	0.4%
Reportable segment operating income ...	480,518	100.0%	463,080	100.0%	412,318	100.0%
Corporate charges[2]	(36,952)		(37,971)		(33,102)	
Consolidated Operating Income	443,566		425,109		379,216	
Interest, Net	(19,632)		(16,707)		(18,458)	
Income Taxes	(139,256)		(138,851)		(101,162)	
Net Income	$ 284,678		$ 269,551		$ 259,596	

Revenues consisted of the following:

	Year ended		
	December 28, 2008	December 30, 2007	December 31, 2006
	(in thousands)		
Sales			
Warehouse sales	$1,173,738	$1,067,106	$ 894,817
Company-operated restaurant sales	38,327	56,161	69,897
Sales from restaurants consolidated under FIN 46R	135,950	125,307	107,691
	1,348,015	1,248,574	1,072,405
Franchise revenues			
Rents and royalties	601,870	553,441	503,375
Franchise fees	93,808	93,835	83,769
	695,678	647,276	587,144
Total revenues	$2,043,693	$1,895,850	$1,659,549

Source: Extracted from Tim Hortons Inc.'s 2008 10K. The statements and information regarding Tim Hortons set forth herein are part of and/or include: (i) excerpts from financial statements included in reports filed by Tim Hortons Inc. with the U.S. Securities and Exchange Commission (SEC) and the Canadian securities administrators that have been reproduced with permission but not endorsed or confirmed by Tim Hortons, and (ii) other data and information generated by third parties unaffiliated with Tim Hortons Inc. in connection with its financial results and/or other information. Accordingly, Tim Hortons Inc. makes no representation or warranty as to, and expressly disclaims responsibility regarding, the accuracy or completeness of any of the information related to Tim Hortons, or the inquiries, analysis or interpretation regarding any such information, that is described above and/or otherwise included herein. This information should not be relied upon for purposes of trading in securities of Tim Hortons or otherwise. You may find current financial and other information prepared by Tim Hortons Inc. at its investor relations website at www.timhortons-invest.com, or as filed with the SEC and the Canadian securities administrators at www.sec.gov and www.sedar.com, respectively.

ENDNOTES

1. For a fascinating look at how people respond to incentives, see the book *Freakonomics* by Steven D. Levitt and Stephen J. Dubner, published in 2005 by HarperCollins.

2. Adapted from Yahoo! Finance Canada at http://ca.finance.yahoo.com/q/pr?s=THI and Tim Hortons Inc.'s website at http://www.timhortons.com/ca/en/about/index.html.

CHAPTER 5

CASH FLOW, PROFITABILITY, AND THE CASH FLOW STATEMENT

LEARNING OBJECTIVES

After studying the material in this chapter you will be able to do the following:

▶ **LO 1** Understand the importance of cash flow and distinguish cash from operations and net income.

▶ **LO 2** Describe the cash cycle.

▶ **LO 3** Read and interpret the cash flow statement.

▶ **LO 4** Explain how cash flow information can be manipulated and how accrual accounting policy choices affect the cash flow statement.

Navdeep Singh Bains, Liberal Member of Parliament for Mississauga-Brampton South, says there's never been an accountant sitting as prime minister of Canada.

But Bains, who's been called a "rising star," has parlayed his certified management accountant designation into a role in Ottawa's corridors of power.

"We look at deficit projections, we look at the economists' numbers.... then we look at our program costing and we try to prioritize that, and if you don't have a good appreciation for the numbers, especially now because everything's accrual accounting ... those terminologies and phraseologies would turn most politicians' heads, but for me it makes a lot of sense," Bains said.

Navdeep Singh Bains, CMA
Member of Parliament

Born in 1977, Bains was first elected in 2004, then the youngest MP in the House of Commons. Re-elected twice more, he was Parliamentary Secretary to former Prime Minister Paul Martin, and later, in Opposition, was his party's critic for International Trade, Public Works, Treasury Board and Natural Resources.

In 2009, Liberal leader Michael Ignatieff appointed Bains to develop the party's policy platform, an experience Bains called "very exciting": it meant travelling the country, listening to Canadians' views, and delving into such areas as aboriginal issues, arctic sovereignty, and the economic recession.

"My approach to designing the platform [was] very systematic and I think some of that organizational discipline, the way of dealing with getting all this information and putting it in a manner that makes sense, ... goes back to some of the training that I had in accounting," Bains said.

In 2006, Bains garnered national attention for questioning how Conservative party officials reported money earned at 2005 election campaign fundraisers. In his view, the donations should have been disclosed as revenue to Elections Canada, with proper receipts issued to donors. That was not done.

Bains acknowledges that, initially, he found his accounting courses at York University a "struggle". But eventually, he caught on.

"I realized very quickly that there was a lot of flexibility within the rules and creativity of how you can display numbers, and make a convincing argument," Bains said. " I find it very satisfying being able to balance a balance sheet, for example, and to be able to look at a balance sheet and say, 'Ah that makes sense to me.'"

After graduating from York in 1999, Bains completed his MBA at the University of Windsor in 2001 and his CMA in 2003. That led to jobs as a financial analyst at Nike and Ford of Canada.

Now Bains works with a national government budget where annual revenues are "roughly $250 billion," by his estimate.

Bains uses his accounting training for more then just pure number crunching; he uses "soft skills" too—everything from making proactive telephone calls before a meeting to informal discussions with managers over morning coffee.

"It's the way of working, ... with a bunch of people that may agree or may disagree," he explained. "So you have to find a way to bring them together, make them focus on the objective at hand and to accomplish that goal."

While most Canadian politicians start out as lawyers, only time will tell if Canada's top job will someday be held by an accountant. Bains' advice to accounting students?

"Accounting skills are very transferable and so the objective is to learn those skills, and then have a very open mind. You don't have to fall for the traditional track. Build that base and the sky's the limit."

—E.B.

INTRODUCTION—CASH IS KING!

Cash is king. If an entity has enough cash it can pay its bills and weather any storm. Without it, business quickly grinds to a halt. If an entity is short of cash, suppliers may stop supplying and employees may stop working. Remember, it's cash, not income or revenue that pays the bills.

In the first four chapters of this book most of our attention has been on developing an understanding of accrual accounting. Accrual measures provide important information about an entity. But make no mistake, cash and cash flow are ignored at your peril. A business can survive quite nicely without showing a profit, provided it has adequate cash inflows or reserves. But an entity that can't generate enough cash, regardless of how profitable it is, will eventually find itself in trouble because it will be unable to meet its financial obligations. Clearly, focusing only on earnings can give a misleading picture of how an entity is doing.

In this chapter we will explore the importance of cash flow and liquidity. We will discuss the cash cycle, the process of investing in resources that will generate cash for the entity. Most of the chapter will be devoted to understanding and interpreting the cash flow statement. (We won't cover preparing the cash flow statement. Readers who are interested can visit the text website at www.mcgrawhillconnect.ca.)

THE CASH CYCLE

Being in business costs money. An entity usually has to spend money before collecting cash from customers. There is almost always a lag between the expenditure of cash and the receipt of cash. For example, if Leon's Furniture Limited opens a new store it would buy or rent an appropriate building, design, decorate and equip it, stock it with inventory, hire and train employees, and so on. Once operating, the store continually purchases and displays new inventory. Most of the time furniture is sold long after Leon's paid for it. Even a relatively simple business such as street hot dog vending requires an upfront investment for equipment and supplies before business begins. The cycle of investing cash in resources, providing goods or services to customers using those resources, and collecting cash from customers is called the **cash cycle**. The cash cycle is shown in Figure 5.1.

It's important to notice in Figure 5.1 that an entity expends cash to purchase resources before it collects any cash from customers. Also notice the cash cycle is partially self-sustaining—the cash generated from customers finances the purchase of new resources that will produce future sales. Cash also enters the cycle from equity investments and loans. These cash injections are needed when, for example, business expands or the cost of inputs increase. Cash leaves the cycle to repay loans, buy capital assets, and pay dividends to shareholders.

FIGURE   5.1

The Cash Cycle

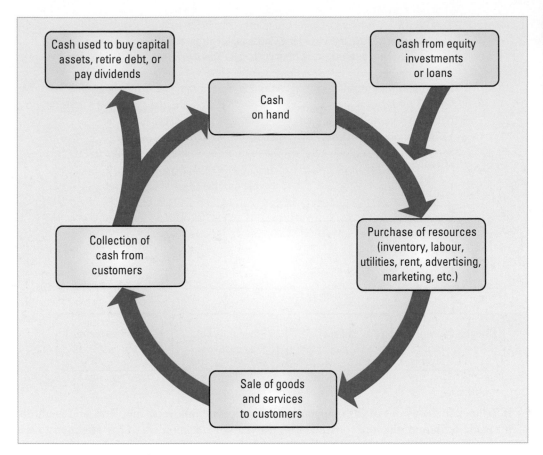

The cash cycle in Figure 5.1 shows all investment, including capital assets, needed to operate a business. A shorter-term view of the cash cycle ignores capital assets and focuses on the investment of cash in operating inputs such as inventory and cash received from customers. The delay between the expenditure of cash and the receipt of cash is called the **cash lag**. We'll examine the cash lag by looking at an example using some numbers (see Figure 5.2). First, here are some relevant definitions:

- **inventory conversion period**—average length of time between receiving inventory from a supplier and selling it to a customer

- **payables deferral period**—average number of days between receipt of goods or services from a supplier to payment of the supplier

- **receivables conversion period**—average length of time between delivery of goods to a customer and receipt of cash

- **inventory self-financing period**—average number of days between date inventory is paid for and the date it's sold to a customer

Yellowknife Corp. (Yellowknife) is a distributor of outdoor clothing and equipment. It purchases merchandise from different manufacturers and sells it to retailers. From Figure 5.2 we can see Yellowknife's inventory conversion period (180 days), receivables conversion period (40 days), payables deferral period (30 days), and inventory self-financing period (190 days).

Figure 5.2 shows that 220 days pass from the time Yellowknife receives inventory from a manufacturer to when it receives cash from a customer. For 30 days Yellowknife doesn't have to pay for its inventory—suppliers finance the purchases by providing credit. For the remaining 190 days, Yellowknife's cash is tied up in inventory (inventory self-financing period). This means that Yellowknife must use cash on hand, borrow money, or get money from owners to pay for the inventory it has on hand. The more inventory Yellowknife carries or the longer it has to self-finance it, the more cash it needs. Similarly, the longer customers take to pay for purchases, the more cash is tied up.

FIGURE 5.2

The Cash Lag for Yellowknife Corp.

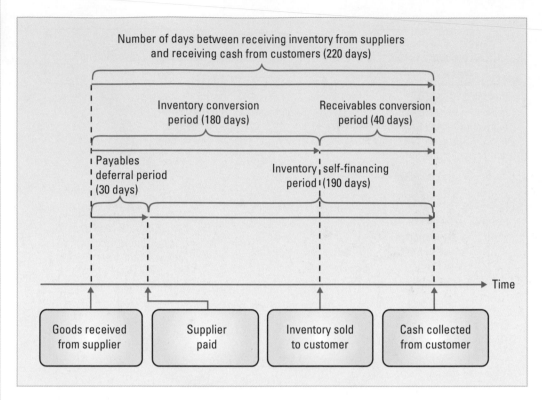

FIGURE 5.2

The Cash Lag for Yellowknife Corp.

If Yellowknife runs out of cash, operations will stop as employees, suppliers, and creditors aren't paid. Because of the dire consequences, it's vital for stakeholders to pay attention to the entity's cash position. An entity might have a bright future but to get there it has to survive its present. When examining an entity's financial statements it's necessary to consider the cash it has on hand, the cash it can obtain from external sources, and its ability to generate cash from business activities. We'll look at some tools for examining liquidity later in the chapter.

INSIGHT

The Length of the Cash Lag

This varies from business to business and depends on many factors. Credit terms with suppliers and customers vary—the less time suppliers give an entity to pay and the more time an entity gives its customers, the longer the lag. The nature of the business is important. Companies with lengthy manufacturing processes will have money tied up in inventory for a longer time than wholesalers of fresh fruits and vegetables that have to sell inventory very quickly. The cash lag for many service businesses will be short because there isn't any inventory to contend with. Understanding how long an entity has its cash tied up in operations is crucial for understanding its ability to generate cash it needs to operate.

If the future were perfectly predictable few entities would face liquidity problems. Liquidity problems occur because things don't always go according to plan. For example, a clothing store manager must order merchandise months before the clothes will be sold. When making buying decisions the manager must predict customers' tastes and the economic conditions to ensure availability of appropriate merchandise, in the right quantities, to sell at the right price. But many things can go wrong. If there is a downturn in the economy or the manager made bad buying decisions, sales will be poor and the clothing store will have less cash coming in than expected and more cash will be tied up in the unsold inventory. Even so, creditors, including the suppliers of the merchandise, still have to be paid.

KNOWLEDGE CHECK

www.mcgrawhill
connect.ca

Ushta Ltd. manufactures auto parts. The company purchases materials from suppliers and stores them in a warehouse, holding them for an average of 30 days until using them in the manufacturing process. The manufactured parts are held for an average of 15 days until they are sold and shipped to customers. Ushta pays its suppliers 40 days after receiving the goods, and customers pay 30 days after delivery. Calculate the following for Ushta and explain the cash implications of the inventory self-financing period:

- ❑ payables deferral period
- ❑ inventory self-financing period
- ❑ inventory conversion period
- ❑ receivables conversion period
- ❑ number of days between receiving inventory from suppliers and receiving cash from customers

Growing businesses often face liquidity problems. Expansion and growth are positive times for businesses, but poor planning and excessive optimism can lead to serious cash shortages. Consider a successful restaurant that decides to expand. Expansion requires upfront capital costs to renovate the new space and purchase furniture, fixtures, and equipment. Ongoing operating costs will increase with expansion as well: additional rent, increased utilities costs, more staff, and more inventory. What happens if customers don't come to the new location in the numbers expected? Many of the higher operating costs still have to be paid. If loans were obtained to finance the upfront costs, interest must be paid. If cash inflows are inadequate to meet the cash requirements of the business, financial distress could result.

Example: Cash Flow Scenarios at Peabody Corp.

Let's look at an example demonstrating the cash flow problems an entity can face and the differences between earnings and cash flow. Peabody Ltd. (Peabody) began operations on January 1, 2014. Peabody purchases various types of candy in bulk from producers, packages the candy, and sells it to corporate customers. The corporate customers use the packaged candy as gifts for customers, suppliers, and employees. Peabody must maintain an inventory of candy and packaging so it can fill customer orders quickly. The following information is available about Peabody's operation:

- All inventory purchases are for cash because suppliers aren't ready to extend credit to the new company.

- Customers have up to 90 days to pay for their purchases. Assume that customers always pay in the quarter after they make their purchases.

- Inventory on hand at the start of a quarter is based on management's forecast of sales for the quarter. All purchases of inventory are made on the first day of each quarter.

- Markup on its product is 100 percent. (Candy costing Peabody $100 is sold to customers for $200.)

- Operating costs, other than the cost of product sold, are $12,000 per quarter. These costs are paid in cash during the quarter.

- Shareholders contributed $40,000 in cash when the company was organized.

- Inventory costing $16,000 was purchased when operations began.

- Sales by quarter for 2014 were:

1st Quarter	2nd Quarter	3rd Quarter	4th Quarter	Total sales in 2014
$20,000	$24,000	$27,500	$31,500	$103,000

Peabody's quarterly income statements for 2014 are shown in Table 5.1. Information about Peabody's inventory purchases and accounts receivable are shown in Table 5.2.

The income statements show that Peabody suffered a loss of $2,000 in the first quarter, broke even in the second quarter, and made profits in the third and fourth quarters. For the entire year Peabody made a small profit of $3,500. Table 5.2 shows that Peabody's sales are growing and so is the amount of inventory it has on hand. This is an important point—as sales increase it's necessary to carry more inventory to meet customer demand, and more inventory means more cash is required to purchase it. Accounts receivable represents cash owed to Peabody but not available now. Like it does for inventory, growth means more accounts receivable and more cash not currently available for use.

Now let's consider Peabody's cash flow statements for 2014. These are provided in Table 5.3.

Peabody's cash flow statements tell a different story than the income statements. During 2014, Peabody expended considerably more cash than it collected, and at year-end most of the $40,000 it began operations with was gone. In every quarter cash flow was negative, and for the entire year Peabody had negative cash flow of $37,450. In contrast, net income was $3,500. Why the difference? As a new business, Peabody had to purchase a large amount of inventory, but the buildup in inventory isn't reflected in net income because only goods sold are expensed in an accrual income statement. However, the buildup of inventory did use cash. In addition, Peabody gives customers 90 days to pay. If it had required cash payment on delivery there would have been an additional $31,500 in cash at the end of 2014—the amount of accounts receivable at year-end.

TABLE 5.1 Peabody Ltd.: Quarterly Income Statements for 2014

Peabody Ltd.
Quarterly Income Statements for 2014

	1st Quarter	2nd Quarter	3rd Quarter	4th Quarter	Total 2014
Sales	$20,000	$24,000	$27,500	$31,500	$103,000
Cost of sales	10,000	12,000	13,750	15,750	51,500
Other costs	12,000	12,000	12,000	12,000	48,000
Net income	$ (2,000)	$ 0	$ 1,750	$ 3,750	$ 3,500

TABLE 5.2 Peabody Ltd.: Inventory Information for 2014

Peabody Ltd.
Inventory and Accounts Receivable Information for 2014

	1st Quarter	2nd Quarter	3rd Quarter	4th Quarter	Total 2014
Inventory					
Beginning inventory	$ 0	$ 6,000	$ 7,200	$ 8,250	$ 0
+ Purchases	16,000	13,200	14,800	16,950	60,950
− Cost of sales (inventory sold)	10,000	12,000	13,750	15,750	51,500
= Ending inventory	$ 6,000	$ 7,200	$ 8,250	$ 9,450	$ 9,450
Accounts Receivable					
Beginning accounts receivable	$ 0	$20,000	$24,000	$27,500	$ 0
+ Sales	20,000	24,000	27,500	31,500	103,000
− Collections	0	20,000	24,000	27,500	71,500
= Ending accounts receivable	$20,000	$24,000	$27,500	$31,500	$ 31,500

The fact that Peabody couldn't buy on credit lengthened the inventory self-financing period and made things worse.

If a stakeholder focused on the income statement and ignored the cash flow statement, Peabody's performance would look positive despite that it had just about run out of cash. If in late 2014 Peabody had to make a $5,000 cash payment, it couldn't have. This highlights how earnings and cash flow can differ dramatically, and how important it is to pay attention to both.

Now let's look at Peabody again to see how cash is affected under different operating scenarios about inventory purchases and credit terms offered to customers. The income statements are unaffected in both new scenarios.

Scenario 1: Peabody decides it needs more variety in inventory and buys $1,000 more inventory per quarter. Inventory information is shown in Table 5.4 and quarterly cash flow information in Table 5.5.

TABLE 5.3 Peabody Ltd.: Quarterly Cash Flow Statements and Cash Flow Balances for 2014

Peabody Ltd.
Quarterly Cash Flow Statements for 2014 and Quarterly Cash Balances

	1st Quarter	2nd Quarter	3rd Quarter	4th Quarter	Total 2014
Collections*	$ 0	$20,000	$24,000	$27,500	$ 71,500
Disbursements**	28,000	25,200	26,800	28,950	108,950
Net cash flow	(28,000)	(5,200)	(2,800)	(1,450)	(37,450)
Beginning cash balance	40,000	12,000	6,800	4,000	40,000
Ending cash balance	$12,000	$ 6,800	$ 4,000	$ 2,550	$ 2,550

*Collections equal the amount of sales in the previous quarter. Assume 100% of amounts are collected.
**Disbursements equal the amount spent purchasing inventory plus $12,000 per month in other costs.

TABLE 5.4 Peabody Ltd.: Inventory Information for 2014

Peabody Ltd.
Inventory Information for 2014—Scenario 1

	1st Quarter	2nd Quarter	3rd Quarter	4th Quarter	Total 2014
Beginning inventory	$ 0	$ 7,000	$ 9,200	$11,250	$ 0
+ Purchases	17,000	14,200	15,800	17,950	64,950
− Cost of sales (inventory sold)	10,000	12,000	13,750	15,750	51,500
= Ending inventory	$ 7,000	$ 9,200	$11,250	$13,450	$13,450

*Accounts receivable information is the same as in Table 5.2.

TABLE 5.5 Peabody Ltd.: Quarterly Cash Flow Statements and Cash Flow Balances for 2014

Peabody Ltd.
Quarterly Cash Flow Statements for 2014 and Quarterly Cash Balances—Scenario 1

	1st Quarter	2nd Quarter	3rd Quarter	4th Quarter	Total 2014
Collections*	$ 0	$20,000	$24,000	$27,500	$ 71,500
Disbursements**	29,000	26,200	27,800	29,950	112,950
Cash flow	(29,000)	(6,200)	(3,800)	(2,450)	(41,450)
Beginning cash balance	40,000	11,000	4,800	1,000	40,000
Ending cash balance	$11,000	$ 4,800	$ 1,000	$ (1,450)	$ (1,450)

*Collections equal the amount of sales in the previous quarter. Assume 100% of amounts are collected.
**Disbursements equal the amount spent purchasing inventory plus $12,000 per month in other costs.

TABLE	5.6	Peabody Ltd.: Inventory Information for 2014

Peabody Ltd.
Accounts Receivable Information for 2014—Scenario 2

	1st Quarter	2nd Quarter	3rd Quarter	4th Quarter	Total 2014
Beginning accounts receivable	$ 0	$ 6,667	$ 8,000	$ 9,167	$ 0
+ Sales	20,000	24,000	27,500	31,500	103,000
− Collections**	13,333	22,667	26,333	30,167	92,500
= Ending accounts receivable	$ 6,667	$ 8,000	$ 9,167	$10,500	$ 10,500

*Inventory information is the same as in Table 5.2.
**Collection in a quarter equals two-thirds of the sales in that quarter plus accounts receivable at the beginnings of the quarter (the uncollected portion of accounts receivable from the previous quarter is collected in the current quarter).

TABLE	5.7	Peabody Ltd.: Quarterly Cash Flow Statements and Cash Flow Balances for 2014

Peabody Ltd.
Quarterly Cash Flow Statements for 2014 and Quarterly Cash Balances—Scenario 2

	1st Quarter	2nd Quarter	3rd Quarter	4th Quarter	Total 2014
Collections*	$13,333	$22,667	$26,333	$30,167	$ 92,500
Disbursements**	28,000	25,200	26,800	28,950	108,950
Cash flow	(14,667)	(2,533)	(467)	1,217	(16,450)
Beginning cash balance	40,000	24,333	22,800	22,333	40,000
Ending cash balance	$25,333	$22,800	$22,333	$23,550	$ 23,550

*Collections equal the amount of sales in the previous quarter. Assume 100% of amounts are collected.
**Disbursements equal the amount spent purchasing inventory plus $12,000 per month in other costs.

Under this scenario Peabody runs out of cash in the fourth quarter and actually has negative cash of $1,450 at the end of the year. The cash shortfall occurs because there is $4,000 more cash invested in inventory at the end of 2014 than under the original scenario. Suppliers are paid in cash so Peabody would have needed a source of money, perhaps from the owners or a bank loan, to pay them.

Scenario 2: Peabody allows customers 30 days (instead of 90) to pay for their purchases. As a result, two-thirds of a quarter's sales are collected during the quarter and the remainder is collected in the next quarter. Accounts receivable information is shown in Table 5.6 and quarterly cash flow information in Table 5.7:

Because it collects amounts owed by customers much more quickly in this scenario, Peabody ends 2014 with $23,550 in cash (compared with $2,550 in the original scenario).

There are some important points that should be taken from this discussion.

- Cash and net income can be dramatically different things. Each provides useful and different information. (A lot more will be said about this issue later in the chapter and throughout the book.)

- The cash cycle and the cash lag are important concepts for understanding the cash and liquidity positions of entities.

- As businesses grow they usually need more cash to fund operations.

- Many factors and events can affect an entity's liquidity. Scenarios 1 and 2 were management decisions, but often the circumstances are out of management's control; for example, declining sales (caused by a recession or changing consumer tastes), customers who don't pay or take too long to pay, or unexpected expenditures.

- It's management's responsibility to manage an entity's cash and liquidity. An external stakeholder must monitor the entity to ensure it has adequate cash and liquidity to survive and operate successfully.

INSIGHT

Basic IFRS Assumptions

In this Insight box, I introduce the four basic assumptions that underlie contemporary accounting and IFRS.

Unit of Measure

The **unit-of-measure assumption** states that the economic activity of an entity can be effectively reported in terms of a single unit of measure, namely money. This is usually the Canadian dollar in Canada, although some Canadian companies, for example Research In Motion Limited, use the U.S. dollar.

A single unit of measure allows diverse information to be aggregated and summarized. Otherwise, it wouldn't be possible to calculate sums like total assets, total liabilities, or net income. It's like adding apples, pears, and oranges together—it can't be done without designating a common unit of measure; in this case, fruit.

There are drawbacks to a single unit of measure:

- Information about the individual items being measured is lost. For example, cost of goods sold reported as a single dollar amount on the income statement doesn't indicate the quantity or type of inventory that was sold.
- Characteristics not easily measured in terms of dollars aren't accounted for. For example, intellectual and human capital and social costs are typically not reported.
- In Canada, the changing purchasing power of the dollar over time caused by inflation is ignored.

Entity Concept

The **entity concept** assumes an entity of interest (corporation, partnership, proprietorship, a division of a corporation, etc.) can provide information that is separate from the information of owners or other entities. Transactions and economic events that don't pertain to the entity of interest should be excluded, but this doesn't always occur. For example, in some proprietorships and private corporations the personal transactions of the owners are included with the entity's business activities. When expenses and revenues that aren't relevant are included in financial statements, stakeholders can come to inappropriate decisions and conclusions.

Going Concern

For accounting purposes, a **going concern** is an entity that will be continuing its operations for the foreseeable future. It's expected to complete its current plans, use its existing assets in the ordinary course of business, and meet its obligations as they come due. In the absence of evidence to the contrary it's normally assumed an entity is a going concern.

If the going-concern assumption doesn't apply—for example, because an entity is going out of business or because it's a short-term venture, such as a summer business set up by a student—the approach to financial reporting changes. Inventory and capital assets usually valued at historical cost are valued on a liquidation basis—the amount that will be received from their immediate sale. Liabilities are valued at the amount they will be settled for. Also, when an entity isn't a going concern all assets and liabilities are classified as current because they are expected to be liquidated or settled in the short term.

Periodic Reporting

The **periodic-reporting assumption** states that meaningful financial information about an entity can be provided for periods of time that are shorter than the entity's life, such as annually or quarterly. Accounting would be much easier if entities only had to prepare financial information at the end of their life because then everything about their activities would be certain—no estimates or accounting policy decisions would be needed. But by waiting until the end of an entity's life, information wouldn't be provided to stakeholders on a timely basis. At a minimum, financial statements are prepared annually, although some stakeholders, for example banks, may require more frequent reports, and stock exchanges and securities commissions usually require public companies to produce quarterly reports.

However, reporting periodically has many problems. When the life of an entity is broken into smaller pieces, it can be difficult to determine in which periods revenues, expenses, assets, and liabilities should be reported. The periodic reporting requirement is at the heart of many accounting problems and controversies.

THE CASH FLOW STATEMENT: OVERVIEW

The discussions of the cash cycle and the differences between cash and accrual accounting lead to an important conclusion: financial statement users need to pay attention to cash and cash flow. Cash flow information is found in a set of general purpose financial statements in the **cash flow statement**. It's also known as the statement of cash flows or the statement of changes in financial position.

The cash flow statement is necessary because the income statement doesn't give a complete picture of an entity's resource flows. The income statement reports economic flows but doesn't distinguish liquidity. This means that an income statement treats a cash expense the same as a non-cash expense (such as depreciation) or a cash sale the same as a credit sale. The income statement also doesn't reflect financing transactions or investment in long-term assets. The cash flow statement helps fill these gaps by providing stakeholders with information about the historical changes in an entity's cash position.

The statement of cash flows and related notes of WestJet Airlines Ltd. (WestJet) given in Exhibit 5.1 will be the focus of our discussion. The cash flow statement groups cash flows into three categories: cash from operations, cash from financing activities, and cash from investing activities:

1. **Cash from operations (CFO)** is the cash an entity generates or uses in its day-to-day business activities. WestJet's cash inflows from operations include amounts received from passengers who buy tickets, proceeds from sales of inflight goods and services, and amounts received from sales of vacation packages. Cash outflows from operations include payments to employees and for fuel, maintenance, ground services, and marketing.

2. **Cash from financing activities** is the cash an entity raises from and pays to equity investors and lenders. WestJet's financing activities include the addition and repayment of long-term debt and the sale of common shares.

3. **Cash from investing activities** is the cash an entity spends on buying capital assets and other long-term assets and the cash it receives from selling those assets. WestJet's investing activities include cash spent and received from the purchase and sale of airplanes.

Examples of the types of cash flows in each category are shown in Figure 5.3 (page 246).

It may seem like an obvious and unnecessary question, but what is cash? Notice that near the bottom of WestJet's statement of cash flows the term "Cash and cash equivalents" is used. In a cash flow statement, cash and cash equivalents includes the following:

- Cash on hand and cash in bank accounts.

- Short-term liquid investments—investments easily converted to a known amount of cash, with little risk that the amount of cash to be received will change. Short term usually means investments maturing within three months. Examples include guaranteed investment certificates, term deposits, commercial paper, money market funds, and government treasury bills. Equity investments can't be classified as cash equivalents because their market values fluctuate.

- Certain types of bank loans such as bank overdrafts and lines of credit where the loans are part of the entity's day-to-day cash management. (A **bank overdraft** is a liability to the bank created when an entity writes cheques for amounts exceeding the balance in its bank account. For example, if an entity has $20,000 in its bank account and it writes cheques on the account for $30,000, the account will be overdrawn by $10,000. The $10,000 is treated as a liability. A **line of credit** is a prearranged loan that can be drawn on as required by an entity.)

EXHIBIT 5.1

WestJet Airlines
Ltd.: Statement
of Cash Flows,
Statement of
Earnings, and
Related Notes

Consolidated Statement of Cash Flows

For the years ended December 31
(Stated in thousands of Canadian dollars)

	2008	2007
Operating activities		
Net earnings	$ 178,135	$ 192,833
Items not involving cash:		
Depreciation and amortization	136,485	127,223
Amortization of other liabilities	(937)	(897)
Amortization of hedge settlements	1,400	1,400
Unrealized loss on derivative instruments (note 11)	6,725	—
Loss on disposal of property, equipment and aircraft parts (note 5)	1,809	32,773
Stock-based compensation expense (note 8(e)(f))	13,485	19,273
Future income tax expense	74,153	41,775
Unrealized foreign exchange loss (gain)	(34,823)	13,813
Change in non-cash working capital (note 12(b))	84,154	112,872
	460,586	541,065
Financing activities		
Increase in long-term debt	101,782	141,178
Repayment of long-term debt	(179,397)	(156,516)
Decrease in obligations under capital lease	(375)	(356)
Increase in other assets	(4,135)	(20,897)
Shares repurchased (note 8(b))	(29,420)	(21,250)
Issuance of common shares (note 8(b))	227	1,551
Change in non-cash working capital	(4,111)	(3,000)
	(115,429)	(59,290)
Investing activities		
Aircraft additions	(114,470)	(191,437)
Aircraft disposals	84	1,975
Other property and equipment additions	(90,663)	(24,639)
Other property and equipment disposals	172	13,819
Change in non-cash working capital	5,147	—
	(199,730)	(200,282)
Cash flow from operating, financing and investing activities	145,427	281,493
Effect of exchange rate on cash and cash equivalents	21,229	(5,452)
Net change in cash and cash equivalents	166,656	276,041
Cash and cash equivalents, beginning of year	653,558	377,517
Cash and cash equivalents, end of year	$ 820,214	$ 653,558
Cash interest paid	$ (76,604)	$ (75,712)
Cash taxes received (paid)	$ (2,305)	$ 10,623

Bank overdrafts and lines of credit can be included in the definition of cash when they are used as pools of cash for short-term financing of operations. For example, seasonal businesses will use their lines of credit to finance an inventory buildup before the busy period. Cash collected from sales in the busy period is then used to pay back the bank. When bank overdrafts and amounts borrowed on a line of credit are included in the definition of cash and cash equivalents, the total of these is subtracted from the amount of cash and cash equivalents to determine the amount of cash an entity has.

EXHIBIT 5.1

(continued)
WestJet Airlines
Ltd.: Statement
of Cash Flows,
Statement of
Earnings, and
Related Notes

Consolidated Statement of Earnings

For the years ended December 31
(Stated in thousands of Canadian dollars, except per share amounts)

	2008	2007
Revenues:		
Guest revenues	$ 2,301,301	$ 1,899,159
Charter and other revenues	248,205	227,997
	2,549,506	2,127,156
Expenses:		
Aircraft fuel	803,293	503,931
Airport operations	342,922	299,004
Flight operations and navigational charges	280,920	258,571
Marketing, general and administration	211,979	177,393
Sales and distribution	170,605	146,194
Depreciation and amortization	136,485	127,223
Inflight	105,849	85,499
Aircraft leasing	86,050	75,201
Maintenance	85,093	74,653
Employee profit share	33,435	46,705
Loss on impairment of property and equipment (note 5)	—	31,881
	2,256,631	1,826,255
Earnings from operations	292,875	300,901
Non-operating income (expense):		
Interest income	25,485	24,301
Interest expense	(76,078)	(75,749)
Gain (loss) on foreign exchange	30,587	(12,750)
Gain (loss) on disposal of property and equipment	(701)	54
Loss on derivatives (note 11)	(17,331)	—
	(38,038)	(64,144)
Earnings before income taxes	254,837	236,757
Income tax expense: (note 7)		
Current	2,549	2,149
Future	74,153	41,775
	76,702	43,924
Net earnings	$ 178,135	$ 192,833

1. **Summary of significant accounting policies**

(i) **Cash and cash equivalents**

Cash and cash equivalents consist of cash and short-term investments that are highly liquid in nature and have a maturity date of three months or less.

4. **Cash and cash equivalents**

As at December 31, 2008, cash and cash equivalents includes bank balances of $98,998 (2007 – $37,395) and short-term investments of $721,216 (2007 - $616,163). Included in these balances, as at December 31, 2008, the Corporation has US-dollar cash and cash equivalents totaling US $56,920 (2007 – US $59,843).

As at December 31, 2008, cash and cash equivalents includes total restricted cash of $10,748 (2007 - $2,357). Included in this amount is $6,062 (2007 – $nil), representing cash held in trust by WestJet Vacations, a wholly owned subsidiary of the Corporation, in accordance with regulatory requirements governing advance ticket sales for certain travel-related activities; $4,222 (2007 – $2,069) for security on the Corporation's facilities for letters of guarantee; and, in accordance with U.S. regulatory requirements, US $381 (2007 – US $295) in restricted cash representing cash not yet remitted for passenger facility charges.

In Note 1(i) WestJet provides its definition of cash and cash equivalents (see Exhibit 5.1). Note 4 discloses the amount of cash ($98,998,000) and short-term investments classified as cash equivalents ($721,216,000) the company had on December 31, 2008. So while the cash flow statement explains more than just the changes in cash, the statements also provide information on the amount of cash WestJet has.

12. Additional financial information

(a) Balance sheet

		2008		2007	
Prepaid expenses, deposits and other:					
Prepaid expenses		$	26,521	$	13,763
Short-term deposits	(i)		18,761		10,827
Deferred costs	(ii)		14,410		14,323
Foreign exchange derivative assets (note 11)			6,735		106
Other			1,266		—
		$	67,693	$	39,019
Other assets:					
Aircraft-related deposits	(iii)	$	68,492	$	51,754
Other			2,513		1,617
		$	71,005	$	53,371
Other liabilities:					
Deferred gains	(iv)	$	5,270	$	6,139
Unearned revenue	(v)		—		3,000
Lease return costs	(vi)		3,508		1,292
Long-term fuel derivative liability (note 11)			14,487		—
Other			968		906
		$	24,233	$	11,337

(i) Short-term deposits include deposits relating to aircraft fuel, other operating costs and short-term US-dollar deposits.

(ii) Deferred costs relate to certain sales and distribution expenses attributed to advance ticket sales.

(iii) Aircraft-related deposits include long-term deposits with lessors for the lease of aircraft and long-term US-dollar deposits, which relate to purchased aircraft.

(iv) Deferred gains from the sale and leaseback of aircraft, net of amortization, which are being deferred and amortized over the lease term with the amortization included in aircraft leasing. During the year ended December 31, 2008 the Corporation recognized amortization of $869 (2007 - $868).

(v) Unearned revenue relates to the BMO Mosaik® AIR MILES® MasterCard® credit card for future net retail sales and for fees on newly activated credit cards. During the year ended December 31, 2008 the Corporation recognized the remaining $3,000 (2007 - $3,000).

(vi) Included in other liabilities is an estimate pertaining to lease return costs on its aircraft under operating leases. During the year ended December 31, 2008, the Corporation increased the liability by $2,216 (2007 – $185) due to the addition of further leased aircraft and a revision to the existing estimate with $nil (2007 – $nil) incurred on the settlement of these obligations.

(b) Supplementary cash flow information

	2008		2007	
Net change in non-cash working capital from operations:				
Increase in accounts receivable	$	(1,828)	$	(2,364)
Decrease in income taxes recoverable		—		13,820
Increase in prepaid expenses and deposits (i)		(22,045)		(8,292)
Increase in inventory		(6,852)		(2,002)
Increase in accounts payable and accrued liabilities (ii)		43,373		47,014
Increase in advance ticket sales		56,425		46,186
Increase in non-refundable guest credits		18,881		13,631
Other non-cash items		(3,800)		4,879
	$	84,154	$	112,872

(i) Excludes $6,735 (2007 – $106) for unrealized current portion of foreign exchange derivatives.
(ii) Excludes $37,811 for unrealized current portion of fuel derivatives.

Source: Extracted from WestJet Airlines Ltd.'s 2008 annual report.

EXHIBIT 5.1

(continued)
WestJet Airlines
Ltd.: Statement
of Cash Flows,
Statement of
Earnings, and
Related Notes

FIGURE 5.3

Examples of Cash Flows

Examples of Cash Flows by Category	
Cash from Operations	
Cash inflows	**Cash outflows**
Amounts received from customers	Payments for inventory
Tax refunds	Payments to other suppliers
Interest received*	Payments to employees
Dividends received*	Taxes paid
	Interest paid*
	Dividends paid*
Cash from Investing Activities	
Cash inflows	**Cash outflows**
Sale of capital assets	Purchase of capital assets
Collection of principal on loans made by the entity	Loans made to other entities
Proceeds from the sale of securities held for investment by the entity (i.e., stocks and bonds)	Purchase of securities of other entities made for investment purposes
Interest received*	Cash expended and capitalized as intangible assets (e.g., pre-opening costs, oil and gas exploration costs)
Dividends received*	
Cash from Financing Activities	
Cash inflows	**Cash outflows**
Proceeds from the sale of shares to investors	Dividends paid to shareholders*
	Interest paid*
Proceeds from the issuance of debt to investors	Repurchase of the entity's shares from investors
Amounts received from bank loans	Repayment of debt principal
	Repayment of bank loans

*Under IFRS, entities can choose to classify interest and dividends received as cash from operations or cash from investing activities and interest and dividends paid as cash from operations or cash used for financing activities.

? QUESTION FOR CONSIDERATION

Quick Motors Ltd. (Quick) sells new cars and services cars. Classify the following cash flows of the business as operating, investing, or financing. Explain your reasoning

a. *purchase of a number of cars and vans for resale for $375,000 cash*
b. *purchase of a courtesy van for customer drop off and pick up for $40,000 cash*
c. *sale of a car to a customer for $32,000 cash*
d. *repayment of a $500,000 bank loan used to renovate the showroom*
e. *sale of old furniture and computers for $25,000 cash*
f. *sale of infrequently sold auto parts inventory to a dealer specializing in parts for older cars*
g. *sale of cars used by its salespeople to a charitable organization, which is given 12 months to pay for the cars*

Answer:

a. Operating: Cars and vans are Quick's inventory, so sales of these are its business and an operating item

b. Investing: This van won't be resold but is a capital asset generating revenue by providing convenience to customers

c. Operating: Quick's business is selling cars. Cash received from a sale is an operating item.

d. Financing: Repayment of a loan is a financing activity

e. Investing: Quick's business is cars, not furniture or computers. Furniture and computers support the sale of vehicles

f. Operating: Sale of auto parts is a regular business activity of a car dealership

g. None: No cash is involved in this transaction so it doesn't appear on the cash flow statement

UNDERSTANDING THE CASH FLOW STATEMENT: SPECIFIC ACTIVITIES

This section will focus on understanding the cash flow statement. Its main emphasis will be the cash from operations section because it's more difficult to understand than cash from investing or financing activities. The different categories are explained graphically in Figure 5.4.

Cash from Financing and Investing Activities

Cash flows from financing and investing activities are straightforward. The financing activities section reports cash transactions involving the financing accounts on the balance sheet. Financing involves transactions with lenders and equity investors and includes bank loans, mortgages, bonds, notes, long-term debt, and preferred and common shares. Financing activities include cash inflows from the issuance of debt and equity and cash outflows for the repayment of debt, the repurchase of shares, and the payment of dividends. Most people would consider interest payments to be a financing activity since it's a cost of borrowing, but IFRS allows entities to choose to classify interest payments as either financing or operating activities.

WestJet's statement of cash flows shows that in 2008 it repaid $179,397,000 in long-term debt and spent $29,420,000 repurchasing its common shares from investors (this means WestJet bought its own shares back from shareholders). In addition, the company was able to raise $101,782,000 in cash by issuing new long-term debt to investors. Overall, WestJet had a net cash outflow from financing activities of $115,429,000, which means it spent $115,429,000 more on financing activities than it raised.

The items in the investing activities section show money spent by buying and received from selling assets that help earn revenue over more than one year. This includes plant, property, and equipment; intangible assets; and investments in the equity and debt of other companies.

WestJet's 2008 statement of cash flow shows that it spent $114,470,000 in cash purchasing new airplanes and $90,663,000 purchasing other property, plant, and equipment. WestJet had little in the way of cash coming in from investing activities. Overall, WestJet spent $199,730,000 more on investing activities than it received.

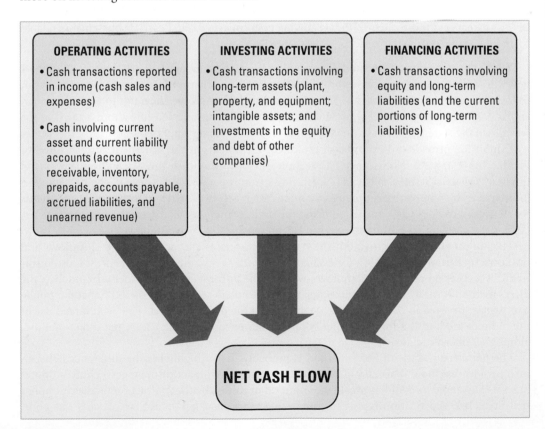

FIGURE 5.4

Classification of Cash Flows

In essence, these two sections reorganize the information on the balance sheet to reflect the cash flows related to investing and financing activities. However, if this is all the cash flow statement did there would be little benefit to having it at all; stakeholders could simply reorganize the information themselves. In fact, the financing and investing activities sections provide additional information by not combining positive and negative changes in the related balance sheet accounts. For example, WestJet reports separate financing activities for "increase in long-term debt" and "repayment of long-term debt" and separate investing activities for "aircraft additions" and "aircraft disposals." It's sometimes very difficult, if not impossible, to determine these more detailed changes from the balance sheet and notes.

One final point about the cash flow statement is that it only reports transactions involving cash. This may seem obvious but it's important. Consider a company that borrows $100,000 from the bank to buy equipment. The cash flow statement reports $100,000 of financing activities (the bank loan) and $100,000 of investing activities (the equipment purchase). But suppose the company finances the $100,000 equipment purchase directly with the equipment manufacturer. The company receives the equipment and promises to pay the manufacturer $100,000 later. This transaction isn't reported in the cash flow statement because no cash is involved. These two arrangements are essentially the same but they are accounted for differently in the cash flow statement. Similarly, if transactions partially involve cash only the cash portion is reported in the cash flow statement. It's important to understand from this that the cash flow statement doesn't reflect all activity in the financing and investing accounts on the balance sheet. IFRS does, however, require disclosure of non-cash transactions in the notes.

Cash from Operations

Cash from operations (CFO) is the cash an entity generates and consumes in its ordinary, day-to-day operations. For example, WestJet's cash inflows from operations include cash from air travel sales, drinks sold during flights, and excess baggage fees, while cash outflows include cash payments for labour, fuel, maintenance, ground services, marketing, and interest.

There are two ways that CFO can be presented in a cash flow statement:

1. The **indirect method** reconciles net income to CFO by adjusting net income for non-cash amounts and for operating cash flows not included in the calculation of net income.

2. The **direct method** reports CFO by showing cash collections and cash disbursements related to operations during the period.

WestJet uses the indirect method. If you look at WestJet's statement of cash flows in Exhibit 5.1 you will see that the starting point for calculating CFO is net earnings (net income) for the year, followed by a series of adjustments. These adjustments reconcile net earnings to a cash number. In fiscal 2008, WestJet had CFO of $460,586,000. (CFO is an untitled line about a third of the way down the statement of cash flows, just before the financing activities section.)

Exhibit 5.2 provides an example of the direct method from the statement of cash flows of Stantec Inc. (Stantec). Notice the CFO section lists operating cash inflows and outflows from different sources (Stantec calls CFO "Cash flows from operating activities"). The presentation looks like an income statement prepared on the cash basis. In Note 19 to its financial statements Stantec also provides CFO calculated using the indirect method. Compare the two approaches. CFO is the same under both methods, but the presentation is very different.

The appeal of the direct method is that it reports sources and amounts of cash inflows and outflows, important information for evaluating an entity's liquidity and solvency. It's also intuitive as it focuses on an entity's cash flows, which is the purpose of the statement. In practice, the direct method is rarely used. *Financial Reporting in Canada* reports that of 200 Canadian public companies surveyed in 2007, only one, Stantec, used the direct method.[1] The widespread use of the indirect method is a bit surprising because IFRS encourages the use of the direct method, although it doesn't require it.

The popularity of the indirect method is probably that it highlights the difference between income and cash flow. This allows stakeholders to see the impact of managers' choices on net income. Stakeholders could, however, be confused or misled by the indirect method as it implies that items like depreciation represent sources of cash, when they're not (we discuss this point further below). The only cash flow information with the indirect method is CFO itself. The two methods are compared schematically in Figure 5.5.

Now we'll examine the indirect method of calculating CFO in detail because it's so widely used and can be difficult to understand. Broadly, when reconciling from net income to CFO there are two types of adjustments that must be made. The first removes transactions and economic events that are included in the calculation of net income but have no effect on cash flow.

Think of net income as a combined set of red and blue balls; the red balls are transactions involving cash and the blue balls are non-cash transactions. If you mix the balls together, the mix reflects all transactions—cash and non-cash. If you had to show only information on cash transactions you would take out the blue balls. In effect, you are removing the blue balls that you previously added in.

A common example of this type of adjustment is depreciation expense. Depreciation doesn't involve cash—it's just allocating the cost of a depreciable item to expense over its life. Since net

EXHIBIT 5.2

Stantec Inc.:
Statement of
Cash Flows

Stantec

Consolidated Statements of Cash Flows

Years ended December 31 (In thousands of Canadian dollars)	2008 $	2007 $	2006 $
CASH FLOWS FROM (USED IN) OPERATING ACTIVITIES			
Cash receipts from clients	1,222,566	940,085	816,846
Cash paid to suppliers	(276,862)	(259,493)	(221,056)
Cash paid to employees	(737,931)	(565,803)	(467,766)
Dividends from equity investments	150	450	450
Interest received	1,857	6,496	6,292
Interest paid	(6,597)	(4,271)	(7,665)
Income taxes paid	(50,037)	(33,656)	(37,588)
Income taxes recovered	6,884	3,691	3,876
Cash flows from operating activities (note 19)	160,030	87,499	93,389

19. Cash Flows From Operating Activities

Cash flows from operating activities determined by the indirect method are as follows:

(In thousands of Canadian dollars)	2008 $	2007 $	2006 $
CASH FLOWS FROM OPERATING ACTIVITIES			
Net income for the year	29,017	69,279	60,182
Add (deduct) items not affecting cash:			
Depreciation of property and equipment	25,405	19,038	15,604
Amortization of intangible assets	10,679	3,702	6,132
Impairment of goodwill and intangible assets	58,369	-	-
Future income tax	(5,731)	(5,159)	(2,242)
Gain on dispositions of investments and property and equipment	(520)	(1,085)	(1,238)
Stock-based compensation expense	5,118	3,452	2,224
Provision for self-insured liability	12,470	6,153	6,329
Other non-cash items	(3,445)	(2,135)	(994)
Share of income from equity investments	(160)	(292)	(285)
Dividends from equity investments	150	450	450
	131,352	93,403	86,162
Change in non-cash working capital accounts:			
Accounts receivable	23,987	20,848	(14,117)
Costs and estimated earnings in excess of billings	21,305	(25,067)	23,029
Prepaid expenses	2,499	1,715	(269)
Accounts payable and accrued liabilities	(20,088)	(11,106)	(3,958)
Billings in excess of costs and estimated earnings	2,728	3,485	4,590
Income taxes payable/recoverable	(1,753)	4,221	(2,048)
	28,678	(5,904)	7,227
Cash flows from operating activities	160,030	87,499	93,389

Source: Extracted from Stantec Inc.'s 2008 annual report.

FIGURE 5.5

Comparison of
the Direct and
Indirect Methods
of Calculating
Cash from
Operations

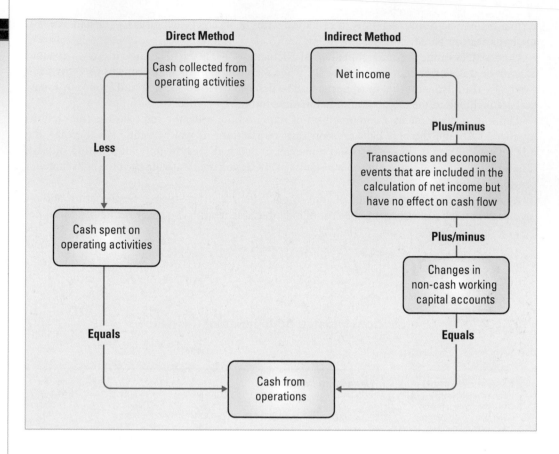

income includes depreciation, a non-cash expense, it needs to be removed when reconciling from net income to CFO. The same is true for any transaction or economic event that doesn't involve cash. Because depreciation is a non-cash expense subtracted in the calculation of net income, adding the amount back to net income will eliminate it.

Let's consider an example. Here is the income statement of Moose Jaw Company (Moose Jaw):

Moose Jaw Company
Income Statement
For the Year Ended December 31, 2014

Revenue	$35,000
Expenses	18,000
Depreciation expense	8,000
Net income	$ 9,000

All of Moose Jaw's revenues and expenses are in cash except for depreciation. All of its cash flows are operating cash flows. If you were asked to calculate Moose Jaw's cash from operations it would be a simple matter of subtracting expenses from revenue since these were all cash transactions:

Revenue (all cash)	$35,000
Expenses (all cash)	18,000
Cash from operations	$17,000

The depreciation expense would be ignored because it doesn't involve cash. CFO calculated using the direct method would have this appearance.

The difference between net income and CFO is simply the amount of the depreciation expense. To calculate Moose Jaw's CFO using the indirect method we adjust net income by adding back the depreciation that was expensed when calculating net income in the first place:

Net income	$ 9,000
Add: Depreciation expense	8,000
Cash from operations	$17,000

The thinking is straightforward. If a non-cash item is subtracted when calculating net income (as depreciation is) then it must be added back when reconciling from net income to CFO. Similarly, if a non-cash item is added when calculating net income then it must be subtracted when reconciling from net income to CFO. When we calculate CFO using the direct approach, we ignore these non-cash items and simply prepare a statement that reflects only operating cash inflows and outflows.

? QUESTION FOR CONSIDERATION

A friend suggests that an entity can increase its CFO by increasing its depreciation expense. The friend reasons that because non-cash expenses such as depreciation are added back to net income when calculating CFO using the indirect method, a larger depreciation expense will result in more CFO. Evaluate your friend's suggestion.

Answer: While depreciation is added back to net income when calculating CFO using the indirect method, the amount of depreciation expensed has no effect on CFO. Depreciation is added back to net income because it's a non-cash expense deducted in the calculation of net income. Whether the depreciation expense is large or small has no effect on cash from operations because you would add back the same amount that was subtracted when calculating net income.

A list of non-cash items that must be adjusted for when calculating CFO using the indirect method is provided in Figure 5.6. (Some of the items on the list won't be discussed in detail until later in the book.) Understanding this type of adjustment is important. Many people who use the cash flow statement ask why depreciation (or writeoffs, gains, and losses) is on the cash flow statement when it has no effect on cash. The preceding discussion explains why.

The second type of adjustment for calculating CFO using the indirect method adjusts accrual revenues and expenses so only cash flows are reflected. Revenues and expenses are recognized on an accrual basis, which means they can have cash and non-cash components. Remember the cash flows associated with revenues and expenses can occur before, after, or at the same time as recognition on the income statement. We can convert accrual revenues and expenses to cash by adjusting for changes over a period in the non-cash working capital accounts on the balance sheet (such as accounts receivable, inventory, prepaids, accounts payable, wages payable, and accrued liabilities). You can see this type of adjustment on WestJet's statement of cash flows in Note 12(b) in Exhibit 5.1. The total shown in Note 12(b) can be found in the calculation of CFO in the statement of cash flows on the line named "Decreases in non-cash working capital."

FIGURE 5.6	Non-Cash Items and Their Treatment in CFO Calculation Using the Indirect Method	
Expense	**Description**	**Treatment (Add to or subtract from net income when reconciling net income to CFO)**
Depreciation/amortization	Allocation of the cost of a capital asset to expense over the asset's life.	Add
Gains	The amount by which the selling price of an asset is greater than its net book value.	Subtract
Losses	The amount by which the selling price of an asset is less than its net book value.	Add
Future (deferred) income taxes	Difference between how taxes are calculated for accounting purposes versus how they are calculated for the taxation authorities. Future income taxes will be discussed later in the book.	Add or subtract
Writeoffs and writedowns of assets	Occurs when an asset's book value is decreased to reflect a decline in market value that is not supported by a transaction.	Add

INSIGHT

Adjusting for Gains and Losses

The treatment of gains and losses when calculating CFO using the indirect method can be confusing. When an asset (not inventory) is sold, a gain or loss is reported on the income statement if the selling price is different from its carrying amount. The gain or loss is the difference between the carrying amount of the asset and the selling price; it's not cash. The cash from the sale is an investing activity. Net income, however, includes the gain or loss. The reconciliation from net income to CFO removes the gain or loss so that a non-cash event is not included in CFO (gains are subtracted, losses added). If they weren't removed there would be a double count (i.e., the same amount would be included twice in the statement) because CFO would include the gain or loss and the full amount of the proceeds would be reported as an investing activity—the total would be different from the amount of cash actually received.

For example, Rife Inc. (Rife) sells land with a carrying amount of $10,000 for $25,000 cash. This is the only transaction Rife has for the year. The gain on the sale of the land is $15,000 ($25,000 − $10,000) and net income is also $15,000, since the sale is Rife's only transaction. CFO is

Cash from operations:	
Net income	$15,000
Less: Gain on sale of land	15,000
Cash from operations	$ 0

Cash from investing activities:	
Sale of land	$25,000

Consider the journal entry for the sale:

Dr. Cash	25,000	
Cr. Land		10,000
Cr. Gain		15,000

The cash flow statement only reflects transactions that affect cash. In this case cash increased by $25,000, which is reported as an investing activity. If the gain wasn't subtracted from net income when reconciling to CFO, CFO would be $15,000 and cash from investing activities would be $25,000, for total inflow of $40,000. This is clearly wrong, since Rife only received $25,000.

KNOWLEDGE CHECK

In 2015, Baltic Ltd. (Baltic) reported net income of $16,000, based on revenues of $100,000; expenses other than depreciation of $70,000; depreciation of $6,000; and a loss on the sale of a piece of land of $8,000. All revenues and expenses (other than depreciation) were for cash.
Calculate Baltic's CFO for 2015 using the indirect method.

Converting accrual net income to CFO is quite straightforward. Understanding why the adjustments are made is less obvious. First, let's look at the mechanics. Figure 5.7 shows the adjustments that must be made when reconciling from net income to CFO. The box in Figure 5.7 entitled "Adjustments for non-cash transactions" represents the first type of adjustment we discussed above. The second type of adjustment is for the changes in the non-cash current operating accounts on the balance sheet. When using the indirect method, increases in current operating asset accounts such as accounts receivable, inventory, and prepaids are subtracted from net income and decreases are added back. Increases in current operating liability accounts such as accounts payable, wages payable, and accrued liabilities are added to net income and

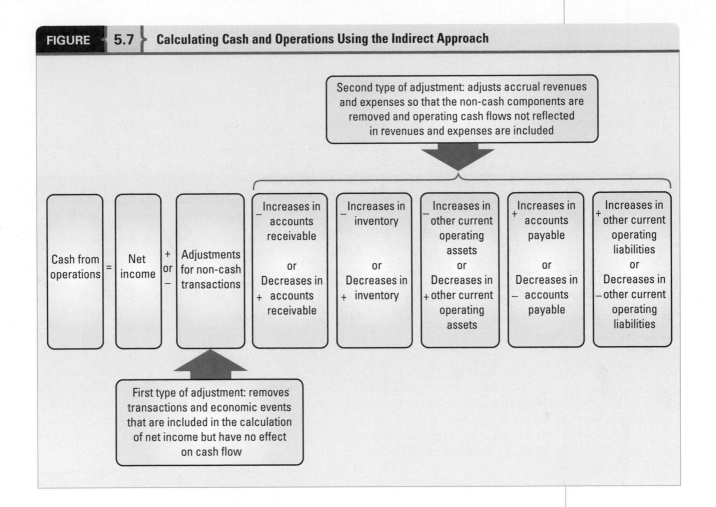

FIGURE 5.7 | Calculating Cash and Operations Using the Indirect Approach

decreases are subtracted. At this point take another look at WestJet's statement of cash flows and Note 12(b) in Exhibit 5.1 to see this type of adjustment.

What is the connection between accrual revenues and expenses, non-cash working capital accounts on the balance sheet, and cash flows? The connection is that the non-cash part of a revenue or expense is included in a non-cash current operating account on the balance sheet. Consider the following scenarios:

- A sale is made on credit doesn't involve cash but an account receivable is recorded. When cash from the sale is collected there is no income statement effect and accounts receivable decreases.

- Purchase of insurance coverage for a future period means cash is expended but there is no expense until the coverage is in effect. The amount paid for the policy is reported as prepaid insurance.

We will show these effects with three examples. The first looks at cash collections and revenue; the second at cash disbursements and wage expense; and the third at cash flow associated with inventory, accounts payable, and cost of goods sold. We will use the accounting equation spreadsheet method introduced in Chapter 3 to show the cash implications for each example. This method is useful because the cash flow column in the spreadsheet provides all the information we need to understand cash flows.

Example 1: Kamloops Inc. Consider the information for Kamloops Inc. in Table 5.8 and the partial accounting equation spreadsheet in Table 5.9. The spreadsheet summarizes the entries that would have been made in 2015 regarding revenue, cash, and accounts receivable. Examine the spreadsheet to see how these entries affected revenue comparison with cash.

TABLE 5.8	Kamloops Inc.: Financial Information			
		Kamloops Inc. Information about the Year 2015		
Cash on December 31, 2014	$ 70,000	Cash on December 31, 2015	$566,000	
Accounts receivable on December 31, 2014	60,000	Accounts receivable on December 31, 2015	89,000	
Sales during 2015	525,000	Collections from customers in 2015	496,000	

TABLE 5.9	Kamloops Inc.: Partial Accounting Equation Spreadsheet		
	Kamloops Inc. Partial Spreadsheet for 2015		
	Cash	Accounts receivable	Revenue
Balance on December 31, 2014	70,000	60,000	
During 2015—revenue		525,000	525,000
During 2015—collection of receivables	496,000	(496,000)	
Balance on December 31, 2015	566,000	89,000	525,000

From the cash column of the spreadsheet you can see that $496,000 of cash was collected in 2015 while revenue was $525,000. Why the difference? There are two reasons: (a) there was $60,000 of receivables outstanding at the end of 2014 that were collected in 2015 (this is cash inflow in 2015 but not revenue) and (b) there was $89,000 of sales in 2015 that were uncollected at the end of the year (this is revenue in 2015 but not cash inflow). The effect of these can be shown by the following equation:

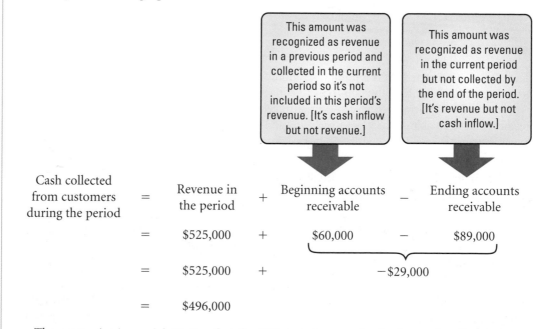

The next point is crucial. Notice that the difference between beginning and ending accounts receivable ($60,000 − $89,000 = −$29,000) is the same as the difference between cash collected during 2015 and revenue in 2015 ($496,000 − $525,000 = −$29,000). This isn't a coincidence! When accounts receivable increase it means the amount of credit sales in the year that are uncollected as of the year-end is greater than the amount of cash collected from credit sales recognized in a previous year. As a result, revenue will be greater than cash collected by the amount of the difference. When accounts receivable decrease, the opposite is true. This is why an increase in accounts receivable is deducted from net income when calculating CFO using the indirect method and why a decrease is subtracted.

TABLE 5.10	Yoho Ltd.: Financial Information		
Yoho Ltd. Information about the Year 2013			
Cash on December 31, 2012	$98,000	Cash on December 31, 2013	$ 5,000
Wages payable on December 31, 2012	13,000	Wages payable on December 31, 2013	8,000
Wage expense for 2013	88,000	Wages paid to employees during 2013	93,000

TABLE 5.11	Yoho Ltd.: Partial Accounting Equation Spreadsheet		
Yoho Ltd. Partial Spreadsheet for 2013			
	Cash	Wages payable	Wage expense
Balance on December 31, 2012	98,000	13,000	
During 2013—wage expense		**88,000**	(88,000)
During 2013—wages paid to employees	**(93,000)**	(93,000)	
Balance on December 31, 2013	5,000	8,000	**(88,000)**

Example 2: Yoho Ltd. For this example we will examine cash spent to pay employee wages. Consider the information about Yoho Ltd. in Table 5.10 and the partial accounting equation spreadsheet in Table 5.11. The spreadsheet summarizes the entries that would have been made in 2013 regarding wage expense, cash, and wages payable. Examine the spreadsheet to see how these entries affected the wage expense account compared with the cash account.

The same logic applied in example 1 applies here. The difference between the wage expense in 2013 and cash spent on wages during 2013 ($88,000 − $93,000 = $ −5,000) is the same as the decrease in wages payable in 2013 ($8,000 − $13,000 = $ −5,000). Once again, this isn't a coincidence. A decrease in wages payable means that the entity paid employees more during the year than it expensed in wages. Therefore, the wage expense is less than cash paid. So when calculating CFO using the indirect method, a *decrease* in wages payable over the period is subtracted from net income. The relationship is reversed if wages payable increased in which case an increase would be added to net income. The relationship can be shown in the form of an equation:

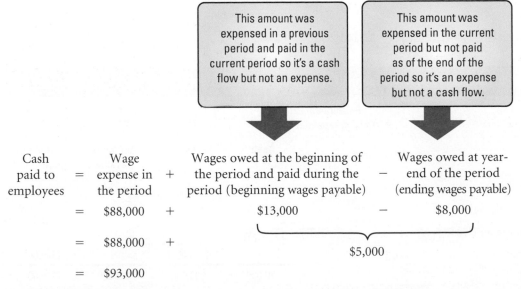

So for Yoho we should subtract $5,000 from net income when calculating CFO using the indirect method because $5,000 more cash was paid in wages in 2013 than was expensed.

Example 3: Rollingdam Ltd.   For the third example we will examine cash paid for inventory. Consider the following information about Rollingdam Ltd. (Rollingdam) in Table 5.12 and the partial accounting equation spreadsheet in Table 5.13. The spreadsheet summarizes the entries that would have been made in 2014 regarding cost of goods sold, cash, inventory, and accounts payable. Examine the spreadsheet to see how these entries affected cost of goods sold in comparison with cash. This example is a bit more complicated because cash spent for inventory involves two balance sheet accounts, inventory and accounts payable, not just one. The example assumes accounts payable pertains only to inventory purchases.

First, remember that inventory isn't expensed until it's sold. This is important because if you buy inventory but don't sell it, you're spending money but there is no effect on the income statement. If inventory is paid for in cash when purchased, a decrease in inventory means less cash is spent on inventory in the year than the amount expensed as cost of goods sold (because you are using inventory purchased in previous periods). Therefore, a decrease in inventory should be added to net income when calculating CFO using the indirect method, and an increase in inventory should be subtracted.

Of course, inventory is usually purchased on credit. A decrease in accounts payable means that the entity paid more for inventory during the year than it expensed to cost of goods sold. Therefore, the cost of goods sold is less than cash paid so a decrease in accounts payable should be subtracted from net income when calculating CFO. Similarly, an increase in accounts payable should be added to net income.

From Table 5.13 we see the amount Rollingdam's spent on inventory in 2014 was $55,000 less than its cost of goods sold ($270,000 − $325,000 = −$55,000). We can also see that inventory decreased by $25,000 ($100,000 − $125,000) and accounts payable increased by $30,000 ($90,000 − $60,000). If we add the decrease in inventory and the increase in accounts payable ($25,000 + $30,000) we come up with the same $55,000 difference.

TABLE 5.12	Rollingdam Ltd.: Financial Information		
Rollingdam Ltd. **Information about the Year 2014**			
Cash on December 31, 2013	$340,000	Cash on December 31, 2014	$ 70,000
Inventory on December 31, 2013	125,000	Inventory on December 31, 2014	100,000
Accounts payable on December 31, 2014	60,000	Accounts payable on December 31, 2013	90,000
Payments made to inventory suppliers during 2014	270,000	Inventory purchased during 2014 (All inventory is purchased on credit)	300,000
Cost of goods sold during 2014	325,000		

TABLE 5.13	Rollingdam Ltd.: Partial Accounting Equation Spreadsheet			
Rollingdam Ltd. **Partial Spreadsheet for 2014**				
	Cash	**Inventory**	**Accounts payable**	**Cost of goods sold**
Balance on December 31, 2013	340,000	125,000	60,000	
During 2014—inventory purchases		300,000	300,000	
During 2014—payments made for inventory	**(270,000)**		**(270,000)**	
During 2014—cost of goods sold		(325,000)		**(325,000)**
Balance on December 31, 2014	70,000	100,000	90,000	(325,000)

The methods described in this section are intended to help you understand the workings of the calculation of CFO using the indirect method. They also enable use of balance sheet and income statement information to calculate CFO using the direct method. We will do this in the next section.

www.mcgrawhill
connect.ca

KNOWLEDGE CHECK

You are provided with the following information about Ituna Inc. (Ituna) for 2014. Use this information to calculate the amount that net income would be adjusted by (how much would be added to or subtracted from net income) when reconciling from net income to CFO using the indirect method.

Ituna Inc. Information about the Year 2014			
Inventory on December 31, 2013	$ 8,500	Inventory on December 31, 2014	$5,600
Accounts payable on December 31, 2013	6,200	Accounts payable on December 31, 2014	4,900
Cost of goods sold during 2014	47,250		

INTERPRETING AND USING THE CASH FLOW STATEMENT

WestJet's Statement of Cash Flows

We've done a fairly thorough job looking at what's in WestJet's statement of cash flows but we haven't talked about what it means. WestJet's cash flow statement (Exhibit 5.1) shows that during fiscal 2008 it generated CFO of $460,586,000. CFO is cash that can be used for paying dividends, acquiring assets, paying-off liabilities, financing expansion, and so on. CFO is valuable because it provides cash internally—it isn't necessary to go to lenders or prospective shareholders. WestJet's CFO means that ordinary business activities produced enough cash to meet its operating requirements with over $460 million left to apply to other purposes. In 2008 WestJet used its CFO to purchase additional aircraft ($114,470,000) and other property and equipment ($90,663,000) and reduce its debt load ($77,615,000) by repaying more debt than it incurred. It also increased its cash reserves by $166,656,000, leaving the company with cash and equivalents of $820,214,000 on December 31, 2008. These reserves give WestJet **financial flexibility** because it has resources to react and adjust to threats and opportunities. For example, if fuel prices increased dramatically and unexpectedly or if there was a significant decline in air travel WestJet's ability to operate wouldn't be threatened.

WestJet's 2008 CFO is $80,479,000 lower than in 2007. It takes some work to figure out why because the indirect method doesn't make things clear. But we can use the information provided to get an idea of what took place. We can use the skills we developed in the previous section to construct a cash flow statement using the direct method. We will calculate cash collected from customers and cash expenses in 2007 and 2008 for this. This approach will be rough as not all the necessary information is provided, but it may give some insight as to why operating cash flows declined.

First we can calculate cash collections by adjusting revenue on the income statement: subtract the increase in accounts receivable and add the increases in advance ticket sales and non-refundable guest credits. Remember that the last two accounts are unearned revenue accounts—amounts received but not recognized as revenue because the customers haven't taken their trips. The information for this calculation is available from WestJet's statement of earnings and Note 12(b) (see Exhibit 5.1):

Cash collected from customers in 2008	=	Revenue	−	Increase in accounts receivable	+	Increase in advance ticket sales	+	Increase in non-refundable guest credits
	=	$2,549,506,000	−	$1,828,000		$56,425,000		$18,881,000
	=	$2,622,984,000						

During 2008 WestJet collected $2,622,984,000 in cash from customers. For 2007 cash collections were $2,184,609,000 (try this calculation yourself).

For expenses we will start with the expenses on the income statement except for depreciation and gains and losses (which are non-cash). We will adjust these by adding and subtracting changes in inventory, prepaids, and accounts payable like we did in examples 2 and 3 in the previous section. Changes in these accounts are in Note 12 of WestJet's cash flow statements. We won't be able to determine the cash spent for each expense category because the financial statements don't provide enough detail:

TABLE 5.14   WestJet Airlines Ltd.: Estimated Cash Expenses

Expenses:	2008	2007
Aircraft fuel	$ 803,293	$ 503,931
Airport operations	342,922	299,004
Flight operations and navigational charges	280,920	258,571
Marketing, general, and administration	211,979	177,393
Sales and distribution	170,605	146,194
Inflight	105,849	85,499
Aircraft leasing	86,050	75,201
Maintenance	85,093	74,653
Employee profit share	33,435	46,705
Taxes expense	2,549	2,149
Interest expense	76,078	75,749
Interest income	(25,485)	(24,301)
	$2,173,288	$1,720,748
Add: Increase in prepaids	22,045	8,292
Add: Increase in inventory	6,652	2,002
Deduct: Increase in accounts payable and accrued liabilities	(43,373)	(47,014)
Deduct: Decrease in taxes receivable		(13,820)
Deduct: Stock-based compensation expense (this is a non-cash item found in WestJet's cash flow statement)	(13,485)	(19,273)
Other adjustments	15,342	1,063
Estimated cash expenses	$2,160,469	$1,651,998

TABLE 5.15   WestJet Airlines Ltd.: Estimated Cash from Operations Using the Direct Method

	2008	2007	Difference
Cash collections	$2,622,984	$2,184,609	$438,375
Cash expenses (except interest and taxes)	2,081,560	1,586,909	494,651
Interest paid	76,604	75,712	892
Taxes paid	2,305	(10,623)	12,928
Cash from operations	$ 462,515	$ 532,611	$ (70,096)

Some comments on this analysis:

- Cash from operations isn't the same as is the statement of cash flow. This is because there isn't enough information to do a complete analysis. We're pretty close (within about $2 million in 2008 and within about $8 million in 2007).

- The analysis shows that the decrease in cash from operations from 2007 to 2008 is mainly due to the increase in cash expenses. WestJet's cash collections increased by $438,375,000 in 2008 but cash expenses (excluding interest and taxes) increased by $494,651,000.

- There was a significant increase in the amount of prepaids in 2008, which increased the amount of cash spent. This was offset by the significant increase in accounts payable and accrued liabilities.

- We can separate interest and taxes paid because these are provided in the statement of cash flows (at the bottom). These amounts are subtracted from the total in Table 5.14 to get the cash expenses in Table 5.15.

- This analysis may look complicated but it's really the same as what we did in the examples in the previous sections. Most of the adjustments are captured in the changes in inventory, prepaids, and account payable and accrued liabilities.

- This is a useful analysis because it gives information about the actual amounts of cash going in and out of the entity for different purposes. This information isn't available from the indirect method.

INSIGHT

Liquidity versus Solvency

Stakeholders often use financial statements to assess an entity's liquidity and solvency. Liquidity is a short-term concept that refers to the availability of cash or the ability to convert assets to cash. It's important for evaluating whether an entity can meet its current obligations. Cash, investments in the shares of public companies, and accounts receivable (usually) are liquid. Land, buildings, equipment, and intangible assets are usually not very liquid because it can be difficult to convert them to cash quickly.

Solvency refers to an entity's viability in the long-term and its ability to pay its debts as they come due. An entity might be insolvent if its liabilities are greater than its assets or if it's unable to pay its debts. An entity with $1 million in cash may be liquid, but with a $2 million loan coming due in two years and no ability to generate additional cash it would be considered insolvent.

Other Issues

CFO, especially if it's regular and predictable, is an important source of liquidity because it represents a reliable source of cash for meeting obligations. The cash flow statement provides other valuable information about an entity's solvency by indicating whether it will be able to pay liabilities when they mature. In Chapter 2 the current ratio was introduced as a commonly used measure of liquidity. There are limits to the current ratio because it's static—it's based only on balance sheet elements. The cash flow statement, the CFO in particular, provides a different view of liquidity because it shows cash generated over time. Another measure of an entity's ability to meet its short-term obligations is the operating cash flows to current liabilities ratio:

$$\text{Operating cash flows to current liabilities ratio} = \frac{\text{Cash from operations}}{\text{Average current liabilities}}$$

This ratio indicates whether an entity is generating enough cash from operations to meet its current liabilities. A ratio less than one indicates CFO isn't adequate to meet current liabilities and cash may have to be obtained from other sources or the rate of cash expenditure slowed. WestJet's operating cash flows to current liabilities ratio is

$$\frac{\text{Cash from operations}}{\text{Average current liabilities}} = \frac{\$460,586,000}{\$665,225,000}$$
$$= 0.69$$

This means that WestJet doesn't generate enough cash from operations to cover its average current liabilities for the year. The ratio for 2007 was 1.03. In fact, WestJet's 2008 ratio is actually better than this because about 43 percent of its current liabilities are unearned revenue (obligations to provide air travel to customers who paid in advance), which are obligations to provide services, not cash. If we adjust current liabilities for these accounts the ratio becomes a healthier 1.22. For 2007 the adjusted ratio was 1.75. Like most ratios, it's important to evaluate the operating cash flows to current liabilities ratio in relation to benchmarks such as other airlines and over a number of years for WestJet.

Because CFO is an important source of cash, negative CFO is cause for concern. Negative CFO means that simply operating the business uses cash so the entity must have sources of cash to make up the shortfall. In the short run, negative CFO can be covered by drawing on cash reserves, using available lines of credit, borrowing or raising equity capital, or selling assets. Negative CFO is a significant problem in the longer term because external sources of cash aren't inexhaustible.

Negative CFO isn't necessarily bad news. Entities just starting up or in a growth phase often have negative CFO because growth requires investment in current assets such as inventory and accounts receivable. Also, a new or expanding business doesn't reach its maximum sales capacity immediately, and many operating costs have to be incurred regardless of the level of sales; for example, salaries and wages, rent, advertising and promotion, insurance, and interest. As a result, a business may have negative CFO while sales are increasing. Growth and expansion often also go hand-in-hand with cash outflows for additional capital assets. Debt and equity investors may be willing to provide cash to new or growing businesses with good prospects. On the other hand, companies may have difficulty raising cash if lenders and equity investors think they are "throwing good money after bad." Lenders will demand higher interest rates to compensate for the risk of lending to a struggling company and equity investors won't pay very much for the shares of companies offering not much promise of a reasonable return on their investment.

Another way of considering an entity's cash flow is by examining its **free cash flow**, which is defined as

Free cash flow = CFO − Capital expenditures

An entity must regularly spend on capital assets to maintain its ability to operate. Equipment, buildings, furniture and fixtures, computers, and other capital assets must be replaced as they become old or obsolete. Free cash flow is the cash available after s have been made. (A **capital expenditure** is money spent to purchase capital assets.) Free cash flow is available for use at managements' discretion; for example, to acquire new companies, expand, reduce debt, or buy back shares. WestJet's free cash flow for 2008 is

Free cash flow = CFO − Capital expenditures
= $460,586,000 − $199,730,000
= $260,856,000

There are eight different combinations of cash flows from operations, investing activities, and financing activities that an entity can have and each one tells a different story. For example, one would expect a new, fast-growing company to have negative CFO, cash inflows from financing activities, and cash outflows for investing activities because it would be spending cash on growth and would need to raise financing to cover the CFO shortfall and purchase needed capital assets.

A stable, mature entity might have positive CFO, negative cash from investing activities (it would be investing in capital assets, presumably replacing assets as required), and negative cash from financing activities (it would be paying down debt and/or paying dividends). A summary of different cash flow patterns is provided in Figure 5.8.

Patterns of the components of cash flow for several Canadian firms are shown in Figure 5.9. There are some things to notice in this table:

- Second Cup reports a net loss but has positive CFO. Net losses don't automatically mean a cash flow problem, but it will if they continue.

- Timberwest reports a sizable net income but negative CFO. This situation highlights the importance of not ignoring the cash flow statement. Net income doesn't automatically imply liquidity.

FIGURE 5.8

Cash Flow Patterns

	Cash from Operations	Cash from Investing Activities	Cash from Financing Activities	
1	+	+	+	Entity is building its cash reserves by generating positive cash from operations, selling capital assets and/or investments, and raising capital by issuing debt and/or equity. This is an uncommon pattern—a very liquid entity, possibly looking for acquisition.
2	+	+	−	Entity is using CFO and cash from the sale of capital assets/investments to reduce debt or pay owners. Perhaps a still successful but contracting industry (need to reduce capacity) or entity has excessive debt that must be retired.
3	+	−	+	Entity is using CFO and cash from borrowing and/or sale of equity to expand. This is indicative of a successful growing entity.
4	+	−	−	Entity is using CFO to buy capital assets and reduce debt or pay owners. This may be a mature, successful entity that isn't investing (all) its cash in maintaining operating capacity or growth.
5	−	+	+	Entity's negative CFO is being covered by selling capital assets and/or long-term investments and by borrowing or from equity investments. Entity may be downsizing but investors seem willing to invest.
6	−	+	−	Entity is financing operating cash flow shortages and debt retirement and/or payments to shareholders by selling capital assets and/or investments. Lack of operating success and sell-off of assets suggests downsizing, perhaps in a declining industry.
7	−	−	+	Entity is growing as indicated by negative CFO (increasing inventories and accounts receivable) and increasing investment in capital assets. Lenders and/or owners are providing capital to finance the growth.
8	−	−	−	Entity is using existing cash reserves to finance operations, purchase capital assets or long-term investments, and reduce debt and/or pay equity investors. This is not sustainable because cash reserves will eventually be exhausted and the entity won't be able to operate.

Source: Adapted from M.T. Dugan, B.E. Gup, and W.D. Samson, "Teaching the Statement of Cash Flow," *Journal of Accounting Education,* Volume 9, 1991, pages 35–52.

FIGURE   5.9

Cash Flow
Patterns of
Selected
Canadian
Corporations

Company and year-end	Net income (000)	Cash from operations (000)	Investing activities (000)	Financing activities (000)	Net change in cash (000)
The Second Cup Limited December 27, 2008	$ (1,626)	$ 10,383 +	$ 201 +	$ (12,201) −	$ (1,617)
Shoppers Drug Mart Corporation January 3, 2009	565,212	478,989 +	(664,566) −	194,556 +	8,979
Timberwest Forest Corp. December 31, 2008	235,300	(94,400) −	9,400 +	108,700 +	29,600
WestJet Airlines Ltd. December 31, 2008	178,135	460,586 +	(199,730) −	(115,429) −	166,656
Air Canada December 31, 2008	(1,025,000)	(102,000) −	190,000 +	(116,000) −	(28,000)
Azure Dynamics Corporation December 31, 2008	(38,867)	(33,403) −	(1,232) −	24,276 +	(10,359)

+ Indicates a net cash inflow.
− Indicates a net cash outflow.
Cash from operations + cash from investing activities do not necessarily add to the net change in cash
because of adjustments not included in the table.

CANADIAN GAAP FOR PRIVATE ENTERPRISES

IFRS and Canadian GAAP for Private Enterprises (GAAP) are quite similar on the cash flow statement,
although there are some differences:

• GAAP doesn't require a cash flow statement provided the required cash flow information is available from the other financial statements and the notes. IFRS don't provide this option. This means that while cash flow statements will always be available in the annual reports of public companies, they may not be included in the financial statements of private companies.

• GAAP requires interest paid and collected that is reported in the income statement to be classified as CFO while IFRS allows entities to classify interest payments as CFO or financing activities and interest received as CFO or investing activities.

Let's take a further look at the cash flow statements of Azure Dynamics Corporation (Azure) a Canadian start-up company. **Start-up** or **development-stage** companies are those in the process of developing their products and markets and have not yet begun their planned business activity. Azure has developed electric and hybrid electric power train drive technology for commercial vehicles. It was founded in 1999 to commercialize technology developed by a research company. A start-up technology company needs cash to develop its product so you would expect to see negative CFO and cash from investing activities and positive cash from financing activities. Since its founding Azure has never made a profit and as of December 31, 2008 had accumulated negative retained earnings of $136,731,000. Total revenue since its inception is only $20,831,000. Yet Azure has managed to raise almost $150 million, including over $24 million in 2008 from shareholders to finance the development of its products and markets. Exhibit 5.3 provides Azure's statements of cash flow for the years ended December 31, 2002 through 2008. Operations have consumed a huge amount of cash while trying to bring the company's product to market. Azure has only survived because equity investors have been willing to purchase shares when they were offered.

So far we have focused on the cash flow statements of businesses. Cash flow is also a relevant topic for governments and not-for-profit organizations. Exhibit 5.4 shows the statement of cash

EXHIBIT 5.3 **Azure Dynamics Corporation: Statements of Cash Flow**

Azure Dynamics Corporation Statements of Cash Flow December 31,								
	2008	2007	2006	2005	2004	2003	2002	Total
Cash flows from operating activities								
Net loss for the period	($38,867)	($30,235)	($23,434)	($21,896)	($8,198)	($3,833)	($5,285)	($131,748)
Adjustments for:								
Depreciation of property and equipment	1,005	931	780	661	270	199	194	4,040
Amortization of intangible assets	1,414	1,431	1,749	1,591				6,185
Unrealized foreign currency losses	525	(450)	(245)	170				0
Accretion expense on convertible debentures						74		74
Amortization of deferred financing costs						88		88
Lease termination							458	458
Common shares issued in exchange for services					28	25		53
Loss on disposal of assets	0	214						214
Stock option compensation expense	711	967	1,696			131		3,505
Deferred share units compensation expense	184	826		1,618	497			3,125
	(35,028)	(26,316)	(19,454)	(17,856)	(7,403)	(3,316)	(4,633)	(114,006)
Changes in non-cash working capital items (Note 16)	1,625	(2,809)	(5,232)	(362)	(381)	(653)	(670)	(8,482)
Movement due to exchange impact		88	(24)	(76)				(12)
Total cash flows from operating activities	(33,403)	(29,037)	(24,710)	(18,294)	(7,784)	(3,968)	(5,303)	(122,488)
Cash flows from financing activities								
Issuance of common shares (net of costs)	24,342	27,858	31,905	26,287	15,696	9,953	5,877	141,918
Alternative Investment Market listing costs					(1,000)			(1,000)
Capital Assurance Agreement costs					(965)			(965)
Convertible debentures funds received (net of costs)						2,009		(2,009)
Issuance of special warrants								0
Repayment of obligations under capital lease	(26)					(10)	(12)	(48)
Repayment of long term debt								0
Principle payments on notes payable	(40)	(36)	(54)	(42)				(172)
Movement due to exchange impact			4	(374)				(370)
Total cash flows from financing activities	24,276	27,822	31,855	25,871	13,731	11,952	5,865	141,372
Cash flows from investing activities								
Acquisition of property and equipment	(1,089)	(1,278)	(820)	(864)	(598)	(46)	(138)	(4,833)
Acquisition of intangible assets	(143)	(172)	(97)	(71)	(203)	(60)	(60)	(806)
Changes in restricted cash	0	(473)		(698)				(1,171)
Cash acquired from acquisition of subsidiary, net of costs				365				365
Changes in loans to employees					92	167	14	273
Movement due to exchange impact		(154)	238					84
Total cash flows from investing activities	(1,232)	(2,077)	(679)	(1,268)	(709)	61	(184)	(6,088)
Increase (decrease) in cash and cash equivalents	(10,359)	(3,292)	6,466	6,309	5,238	8,045	378	12,785
Exchange impact on cash held in foreign currency	29	233	5	99				366
Cash and cash equivalents, beginning of period	24,133	27,192	20,721	14,313	9,075	1,031	652	652
Cash and cash equivalents, end of period	$13,803	$24,133	$27,192	$20,721	$14,313	$9,075	$1,031	$13,803

Source: Extracted from Azure Dynamics Corporation's 2002–2008 annual reports.

EXHIBIT 5.4

Government
of Canada:
Statements of
Cash Flow

GOVERNMENT OF CANADA
Statement of Cash Flow
(in millions of dollars)
For the Year Ended March 31

	2005	2006	2007	2008
OPERATING ACTIVITIES—				
ANNUAL SURPLUS	**1,463**	**13,218**	**13,752**	**9,597**
Items not affecting cash—				
Share of annual profit in enterprise Crown corporations and other government business enterprises	-4,853	-5,041	-5,336	-4,256
Amortization of tangible capital assets	3,696	3,904	3,807	3,954
Net loss or gain (-) on disposal of tangible capital assets, including adjustments	317	-149	99	-576
Change in inventories and prepaid expenses	414	-431	-509	132
Change in pension and other liabilities	-1,090	116	5,136	6,107
Change in foreign exchange accounts	3,442	44	-3,351	1,879
Net change in other accounts	5,163	-3,192	-1,508	5,194
Cash provided by operating activities	**8,552**	**8,469**	**12,090**	**22,031**
CAPITAL INVESTMENT ACTIVITIES—				
Acquisition of tangible capital assets	-4,619	-4,046	-4,789	-5,957
Proceeds from disposal of tangible capital assets	144	146	202	440
Cash used by capital investment activities	**-4,475**	**-3,900**	**-4,587**	**-5,517**
INVESTING ACTIVITIES—				
Enterprise Crown corporations and other government business enterprises—				
Equity transactions	1,669	2,012	2,602	2,436
Loans and advances issued	-142	-198	-3,713	-5,052
Loans and advances repayments	334	331	3,894	435
Other loans, investments and advances issued	-8,218	-6,861	-16,969	-6,571
Other loans, investments and advances repayments	6,866	5,182	16,475	6,883
Cash provided or used (-) by investing activities	**509**	**466**	**2,289**	**-1,869**
TOTAL CASH GENERATED OR REQUIRED (-) BEFORE FINANCING ACTIVITIES	**4,586**	**5,035**	**9,792**	**14,645**
FINANCING ACTIVITIES—				
Canadian currency borrowings issued	335,682	363,824	369,354	343,755
Canadian currency borrowings repayments	335,969	-366,123	-373,886	-366,493
Foreign currencies borrowings issued	13,608	15,859	11,586	11,099
Foreign currencies borrowings repayments	-17,864	-18,061	-15,299	-11,973
Cash used by financing activities	**-4,543**	**-4,501**	**-8,245**	**-23,612**
NET INCREASE OR DECREASE (-) IN CASH	**43**	**534**	**1,547**	**-8,967**
CASH AT BEGINNING OF YEAR	**20,572**	**20,615**	**21,149**	**22,696**
CASH AT END OF YEAR	**20,615**	**21,149**	**22,696**	**13,729**

Source: Extracted from the Public Accounts of Canada, 2008, Volume I.

flow for the Government of Canada for the years ended March 31, 2005 through 2008. The statement has the same structure as those of profit-oriented entities. In fiscal 2008 the Canadian Government generated CFO of $22.031 billion. In fiscal 2007 CFO was $12.090 billion. The CFO numbers show that the government has been generating huge cash surpluses, which can be used to reduce taxes, reduce debt, and invest in programs that the Canadian people would value. The financing section shows that in fiscal 2008 Canada reduced its national debt by $23.612 billion. The statement shows that the federal government chose to use its CFO along with some of its cash reserves to reduce the country's debt. The financial situation began to change in 2009 as Canada began to run deficits and increase borrowing in response global financial problems.

MANIPULATING CASH FLOW INFORMATION AND THE EFFECT OF ACCRUAL ACCOUNTING CHOICES ON THE CASH FLOW STATEMENT

Throughout the book we have discussed how managers can use the alternative accounting methods and judgment that are part of accrual accounting to manage financial statement numbers. Some people suggest that an attractive aspect of cash accounting and the cash flow statement is that they can't be managed or manipulated the way accrual information can be.

This conclusion isn't true. Cash information can't be manipulated in the same way as accrual information, where managers decide when to recognize revenue and expenses, but it can be manipulated and perhaps in a way that is even more dangerous to the entity. Cash information is "cleaner" in the sense that a transaction has an impact on cash flow only if cash is involved, and as a result managers can't exercise any judgment on the accounting for cash *once a transaction involving cash has occurred*. However, managers can manipulate cash flow by influencing the timing of cash flows.

Managers can alter the timing of cash flows by reducing "discretionary" spending on research and development, advertising and promotion, marketing, or maintenance. These spending reductions increase CFO but they may or may not be in the interests of the entity. Take the following examples:

- Reducing maintenance spending on equipment would increase CFO in the short term but could contribute to higher costs in the future. The equipment may eventually require more costly maintenance or even need replacing sooner than if it had been properly maintained. Poorly maintained equipment could also reduce the efficiency of operations or the quality of the goods produced, which would increase costs and reduce revenues.

- Cutting research and development and advertising, marketing, and promotion would increase CFO in the current period but have negative longer-term consequences.

- Increasing CFO by delaying payments to suppliers could affect suppliers' willingness to offer credit in future.

- Increasing cash flow by selling capital assets or other long-term assets would increase cash from investing activities but it could result in the disposal of assets that could generate revenue and profit.

- Selling the entity's accounts receivable to a third party that takes responsibility for collection is a legitimate way to raise cash and would significantly increase CFO in the period the receivables were sold.

Of course, in all these examples it's difficult to be sure whether management is making good decisions or desperately trying to conserve cash, which makes understanding the cash flow statement numbers more difficult.

Cash flow statement users can overcome the difficulty of preparers who manage the timing of their cash flows by examining cash flow statements for a number of periods. Many of these manipulations are simply moving cash flows among periods, which an alert user can observe by carefully examining a number of cash flow statements.

Accounting policy choices don't affect the cash flows associated with a transaction. For example, how the revenue is recognized doesn't affect when cash is collected. However, the accounting choice may have other cash flow implications. For example, an accounting choice could affect the amount of tax an entity pays or the bonus the managers receive.

Solved Problem

This solved problem is another case analysis that will help you to learn and develop the problem-solving skills introduced in Chapter 4. In this case, a student operating a small business comes to you for an explanation for the business's poor cash position despite a good net income. You should attempt to solve the case on your own before reading the solution.

TRENDY T-SHIRTS INC.

In spring 2014 Simon Francis decided that instead of working for someone else during the summer, he would start a business of his own to finance his education. He would design and sell t-shirts to the residents and many vacationers in the area near where he lived.

Simon incorporated a company called Trendy T-Shirts Inc. (Trendy). He decided he would operate the business out of a modified van Trendy purchased. The van would allow him to move around so he could be where the customers were. Simon used his own computer to create t-shirt designs and purchased equipment to print the designs on the shirts. To start up the business, Simon invested $6,000 of his own money and borrowed $10,000 from his parents. His parents told him they had to be repaid within three years.

Simon thought that Trendy's first year in business was successful. He earned enough money to pay for his schooling and take a nice vacation during the winter. In fact, Simon thought Trendy was so successful he expanded in 2015. For 2015 Simon bought some additional equipment and a second van that was operated by an employee. He also increased the number of designs and the quantity of t-shirts he produced because the previous summer he had run short of shirts. Trendy financed the purchase of the second van and the equipment with a bank loan he quickly repaid out of operating cash flows.

It's now October 2015 and Trendy has ceased operations for the year. Simon feels very satisfied with the performance of his business for the year—a net income of $14,250 for the year ended September 30, 2015. However, when Simon got around to looking at Trendy's bank statements (he hadn't bothered to look at them over the summer because he was so busy) he was shocked to see that there was only $2,820 in the bank. There isn't enough money to pay for school, take another vacation, or repay the remaining bank loan. Trendy's cash flow statements for the last two years (shown in Exhibit 5.5) confirmed his fears—there isn't enough cash to meet his needs—and Simon can't figure out why.

Required:

a. Use the cash flow statement to explain to Simon how his business can be successful but not give him enough cash to meet his needs. Be sure to consider Trendy's activities and Simon's decisions in both 2014 and 2015.

b. Simon is thinking about going to the bank to borrow $10,000 that would be paid to him as a dividend. If you were the banker, would you lend money to Trendy? Explain.

EXHIBIT 5.5	Cash Flow Statements for Trendy T-Shirts Inc.

Trendy T-Shirts Inc.
Cash Flow Statement for the Years Ended October 31

	2015	2014
Operations		
Net income	$14,250	$ 9,430
Add: Amortization expense	8,100	3,250
Less: Increase in inventory	3,510	1,250
Cash from operations	18,840	11,430
Financing		
Loan from parents	(6,000)	10,000
Bank loan	7,500	
Van and equipment loan	(18,000)	
Van and equipment loan repayment	18,000	
Common stock issued		6,000
Dividends paid		(12,500)
Investing		
Purchase of van	17,000	11,000
Purchase of equipment	2,200	2,250
Increase in cash	1,140	1,680
Cash balance at the beginning of the year	1,680	0
Cash balance at the end of the year	$ 2,820	$ 1,680

Solution:

Part (a)

Report to Simon Francis regarding the performance of Trendy T-Shirts Inc.

Dear Simon:

I am writing to help clarify your confusion regarding Trendy T-Shirts Inc.'s cash position compared with its accrual accounting performance. Your business performed well in 2015—earning an income of $14,250—but your cash position is poor—only $2,820 is on hand at the end of the year before paying yourself a dividend. To explain, it is important to understand the difference between accrual accounting and cash flow. Accrual accounting reflects economic flows and economic activity, not just cash and the change in cash. As a result, the amount of income you report does not necessarily match your business's cash flow.

During 2014 Trendy generated cash from operations—the cash an entity generates from selling t-shirts—of $11,430, which could be used for paying off debts, paying dividends, expanding operations, making investments in equipment, and so on. This amount was different from your net income of $9,430 for two reasons. First, in the calculation of net income, a depreciation expense of $3,320 was deducted. This is not cash that was spent; it is simply part of the cost of the van and equipment deducted in calculating net income. The idea is to expense part of the cost of these assets each year because they contribute to your business over many years. (Note that Trendy did spend $13,250 in cash on the van and equipment in 2014. I will have more to say about this shortly.) The second difference between cash from operations and net income was the $1,250 investment in inventory you had at the end of the 2014 season. This inventory had been paid for by the end of 2014 but it had not been expensed because it had not been sold. This means that you had $1,250 in cash tied up in t-shirts you could sell in 2015.

A similar analysis can be provided for 2015. Your cash from operations in 2015 was $18,840, a fair bit higher than in 2014. Trendy's income statement reported $8,100 in non-cash depreciation expense and an additional $3,510 was invested in inventory that was unsold at end of the year. The bottom line is your business is generating decent cash flow. So why do you not have enough cash on hand to meet your needs?

There are several reasons. First, you have spent a significant amount of money purchasing assets that will help you make money over an extended period of time; that is, the vans and equipment. So, while your business is generating cash, you have invested a significant amount of money to get your business going. These cash outlays are required when a business starts up or expands. In your first two years, Trendy spent $32,450 on assets. If you do not expand in future years these assets will contribute to sales without costing you any cash.

Second, Trendy has $4,760 in cash invested in inventory, which seems like a lot. Does this amount represent plain t-shirts or ones that have designs? If it is the latter, will these shirts be saleable? Do designs go out of style? If the inventory cannot be sold the income of your business may, in fact, be overstated because the cost of unsaleable inventory should be expensed. If the inventory is shirts without designs then they can be used in future, although it seems like a lot of money to be tied up in items that can be easily purchased at any time. If possible, you might return the t-shirts to free up some cash.

Third, in 2014 Trendy paid a $12,500 dividend, probably one it couldn't afford. In 2014 Trendy was able to pay for the van and equipment ($13,250) and for the dividend ($12,500) by generating cash from operations ($11,430), borrowing ($10,000), and from your own investment ($6,000). But by paying the dividend there was little cash left to finance to expansion. Had Trendy not expanded, paying the dividend probably would not have been a problem.

In 2015 operations generated most of the cash ($18,840) needed to pay for the second van and some additional equipment ($19,200), although a short-term loan ($18,000) was needed to bridge the cash shortage at the beginning of the year. A $7,500 bank loan was used mainly to repay your parents. The problem in 2015 was that Trendy spent about the same amount of money as it generated from all sources. There was nothing left over to pay a dividend. In contrast, the amount of money spent in 2014 before paying the dividend was significantly less than the amount generated from operations and financing activities. However, your dividend in 2014 was paid for by borrowing from your parents and from the money you invested in Trendy to start with, not with cash from operations.

This should be a short-term problem for you. Assuming that your business continues to be as successful as it has been, and if you control your inventory, Trendy should be generating about $20,000 a year in cash from operations. Assuming you don't expand further, that amount will allow you to pay off your $7,500 bank loan in 2016 and have plenty of cash available for your own needs. In the meantime, you will have to find an alternative source of cash to meet your personal needs this year. Perhaps you can borrow from your parents again or obtain a personal bank loan.

Part (b)

As a banker, I would give serious consideration to providing a $10,000 loan to Trendy on the basis of its operations. Trendy generates a lot of cash and it would be able to support a loan—both the interest and principal—assuming it continues to perform as it did in 2015. That said, t-shirts can be a risky business; what is popular one year might not be popular in the next. On the other hand, over the years, t-shirts have enjoyed sustained popularity so this mitigates some of the risk. Even if the business contracted by 25 percent there would still be adequate cash flow to repay the loan plus interest. Trendy has its two vans and the equipment along with the inventory to use as collateral for a loan. It is not clear, however, how much cash those items would raise if they had to be sold. I would need an estimate of what they are worth.

It is a significant concern that Trendy does not need the cash for the business. Assuming no additional purchases of capital assets are required (no additional expansion is indicated) and little cash is needed for working capital (for example, to purchase inventory and supplies), the main purpose of the loan would be to allow Trendy to pay a dividend. If that is the case, the amount of equity that Simon would have in the business would be $7,180 (initial equity investment + net incomes − dividends = $6,000 + $9,430 + $14,250 − $12,500 − $10,000 [assuming the bank loan of $10,000]). This would be in comparison with liabilities of $21,500 ($4,000 + $7,500 + $10,000 [assuming the bank loan and dividends of $10,000]). This represents a relatively small amount of equity relative to debt (debt-to-equity ratio = $21,500/$7,180 = 2.99). If Simon neglects his business for some reason in the future or chooses not to continue in business, our bank and the other lenders stand to lose much more than Simon does (although Simon's parents will lose $4,000 of their money).

All told, I would be inclined to recommend a loan to Trendy. The business has been able to generate cash in the past and stands to do so in the future. I recommend that, if any assets have not been secured against the other bank loan, we should take those assets as security against our loan. In addition, we should obtain personal guarantees from Simon and his parents, if possible. This will provide the bank with additional protection.

Finally, the terms of the loan should prevent Trendy from purchasing additional equipment until the bank loans have been reduced or paid off. This is necessary because additional purchases will use up cash from operations and reduce or eliminate cash needed to pay off the bank loan. Additional purchases will also result in a repetition of the current situation where Simon is not able to draw enough cash from Trendy to meet his personal needs. In addition, further expansion may add to the bank's risk since future demand for Trendy's products isn't known, and it is not clear whether Simon will be able to effectively manage an expanded business.

INSIGHT

"What if" Scenarios

Notice that the banker's response in part (b) focuses on what will happen, not on what has happened. This is very important to keep in mind. Historical information can sometimes be a useful basis for predicting future cash flows (and earnings), but the future will usually not be the same as the past. As a result, the bank must consider "what if" scenarios. What if sales decrease? What if profit margins decrease? This type of assessment allows the banker to evaluate the risks faced. Also recognize that the banker's response is only one of many possible ones. For example, some bankers might decline to make the loan because it's for personal rather than business reasons. That conclusion would be fine but it would still have to be supported by a similar type of analysis as in part (b).

SUMMARY OF KEY POINTS

▶ **LO 1** Cash is king. Without adequate cash or cash flow an entity won't be able to operate because it won't be able to pay its bills. If an entity can't generate enough cash from its business activities to meet its needs it will have to raise cash by borrowing, selling shares, or selling assets. Stakeholders sometimes don't give enough attention to cash flow when evaluating an entity. The standard measure of performance under accrual accounting, earnings, isn't designed to reflect flows of cash. Cash flow isn't a better or worse measure than earnings is; it's just a different measure of performance than earnings, and each has its role to play.

▶ **LO 2** The cycle cash is the process of how an entity begins with cash, invests in resources, provides goods or services to customers using those resources, and then collects cash from customers. Entities usually have to invest cash in resources before cash is received from customers—there is almost always a lag between the expenditure of cash and the receipt of cash.

▶ **LO 3** The cash flow statement provides information about an entity's historical cash flows. Cash flows in the cash flow statement are grouped into three categories: cash from operations (CFO), cash from investing activities, and cash from financing activities. CFO can be calculated and reported in two ways on the cash flow statement. The indirect method reconciles from net income to CFO by adjusting for non-cash amounts and for operating cash flows not included in the calculation of net income. The direct method reports CFO by showing cash collections and cash disbursements related to operations during the period.

▶ **LO 4** Some people argue that one of the attractions of cash accounting over accrual accounting is that cash accounting can't be managed or manipulated. Cash accounting information can't be manipulated in the same way as accrual information, where managers must decide when to recognize revenue and expenses. However, managers can manipulate cash information by influencing the timing of cash flows.

FORMULA SUMMARY

$$\text{Operating cash flows to current liabilities ratio} = \frac{\text{Cash from operations}}{\text{Average current liabilities}}$$

$$\text{Free cash flow} = \text{CFO} - \text{Capital expenditures}$$

KEY TERMS

bank overdraft, p. 242

capital expenditure, p. 260

cash cycle, p. 234

cash flow statement, p. 242

cash from financing activities, p. 261

cash from investing activities, p. 261

cash from operations (CFO), p. 261

cash lag, p. 235

development-stage company, p. 262

direct method (of calculating cash from operations), p. 248

entity concept, p. 241

financial flexibility, p. 257

free cash flow, p. 260

going-concern assumption, p. 241

indirect method (of calculating cash from operations), p. 248

inventory conversion period, p. 235

inventory self-financing period, p. 235

line of credit, p. 242

payables deferral period, p. 235

periodic-reporting assumption, p. 241

receivables conversion period, p. 235

start-up company, p. 262

unit-of-measure assumption, p. 241

SIMILAR TERMS

The left column gives alternative terms that are sometimes used for the accounting terms introduced in this chapter, which are listed in the right column.

statement of cash flows, statement of changes in financial position

cash flow statement, p. 242

cash flow from operating activities

cash from operations, p. 261

ASSIGNMENT MATERIALS

Questions

Q5-1. Explain the difference between cash accounting and accrual accounting.

Q5-2. Why is the cash flow statement included in the general purpose financial statement package? Explain your answer fully.

Q5-3. Explain each of the following:
a. Payables deferral period
b. Inventory self-financing period
c. Inventory conversion period
d. Receivables conversion period

Q5-4. What is cash from operations? How is information about cash from operations useful to stakeholders?

Q5-5. Explain the difference between liquidity and solvency. Which is more important to an entity? Is it possible for an entity to be liquid but not solvent or solvent but not liquid? Explain.

Q5-6. Why is it important for stakeholders to be aware of an entity's liquidity? What are the consequences of not having adequate liquidity? Explain.

Q5-7. Which should be more important to a shareholder of a company, cash flow or net income? Explain your answer.

Q5-8. Why is depreciation added back to net income when cash from operations is calculated using the indirect method?

Q5-9. Why are losses added back to and gains subtracted from net income when cash from operations is calculated using the indirect method?

Q5-10. What does it mean when an entity has negative cash from operations? What circumstances can result in this? Why is it cause for concern? Is it necessarily bad news for an entity? Explain.

Q5-11. Which should be more important to the management of an entity, cash flow or income? Explain your answer.

Q5-12. Explain the three types of cash flows reported in a cash flow statement. Give examples of each type and explain the classification of each example.

Q5-13. New businesses frequently fail because of poor cash flow. Explain why you think new businesses have this problem.

Q5-14. What are the two methods for calculating and reporting cash from operations? Explain how each arrives at cash from operations. As a user of financial statements, which method of calculating cash from operations would you prefer to see in a cash flow statement? Explain.

Q5-15. How is interest paid classified in a cash flow statement prepared in accordance with Canadian GAAP for private companies? Does this treatment make sense? Explain.

Q5-16. IFRS allows managers to choose how to classify interest paid in the cash flow statement. What are the alternative classifications allowed? What is the impact on the cash flow statement of these alternatives? What is the impact on the income statement? Which treatment do you prefer? Explain.

Q5-17. What information does the cash flow statement provide to stakeholders that isn't in the income statement?

Q5-18. What is the cash cycle? Describe the cash cycle for a wine maker.

Q5-19. An entity has a very profitable year, yet its cash flow and cash from operations are negative. Explain how this can happen.

Q5-20. An entity reports a loss for the year. Explain how the entity could have positive cash flow and positive cash from operations in that year.

Q5-21. What does the term "cash" in the cash flow statement refer to? Explain.

Q5-22. Why does an increase in accounts receivable imply a decrease in cash from operations? Explain.

Q5-23. Why does a decrease in inventory imply an increase in cash from operations? Explain.

Q5-24. How is it possible for managers to manipulate the information in the cash flow statement?

Q5-25. What type of manipulation of accounting information do you think is more likely to cause operational problems for an entity: the manipulations done with accrual accounting or the manipulations done with cash accounting? Explain your answer.

Q5-26. Managers often receive bonuses based on the net income of the entities they manage. Do you think it would be better to use cash from operations as a basis to award bonuses rather than net income? Explain your answer.

Q5-27. What objectives of financial reporting does the cash flow statement serve? Explain.

Q5-28. One way for a biotechnology, software, or other high-technology company to increase cash from operations would be to reduce spending on research. Explain why reducing spending on research (which is expensed when incurred according to IFRS) would increase cash from operations. Explain why reducing spending on research is potentially a serious problem for these types of entities. Respond by discussing the business implications of reducing spending on research.

Q5-29. In a recent negotiation between labour and management of a major corporation, management argued that the company's low earnings made it imprudent to grant the requested wage increase. The labour union disagreed and argued that the company had ample resources to meet the wage demands of the union. What do you think might have been the basis of the union's argument? Do you think that it's adequate to base the ability of a company to grant a wage increase only on net income? Explain.

Q5-30. Give examples of the circumstances that could cause cash flow problems for an automaker.

Q5-31. Explain why growing companies sometimes face cash flow problems.

Q5-32. Identify and explain the four assumptions that underlie IFRS accounting.

Q5-33. Explain why the periodic reporting assumption is the cause of many of the problems and controversies that face the accounting professions today.

Q5-34. Explain what accountants mean when they speak of a going concern. What are the implications for financial reporting of an entity not being a going concern? Do you think these implications make sense? Explain.

Q5-35. What unit of measure is typically used in the financial statements of Canadian companies? What are the some of the benefits and drawbacks of using the Canadian dollar as the unit of measure?

Exercises

E5-1. **(Calculating the cash lag, LO 2)** Dickens Tailor Shop (Dickens) makes tailored-to-measure suits, jackets, and pants for men and women. Customers who are interested in purchasing this clothing make an appointment with one of Dickens' tailors, at which time the customer decides on the style of clothing, selects an appropriate fabric, and is measured by the tailor. Dickens keeps a large selection of fabrics so customers can see the actual fabric their clothing will be made from. A bolt of fabric is, on average, held in inventory for five months before it's used to make a garment. Dickens pays for its fabric 45 days from the time it's received from a supplier. The time from a customer's first appointment to the completion and delivery of the garment is, on average, 35 days. Customers receive an invoice when the garment is delivered and payment is received from the customer, on average, 15 days from the time of delivery.

Required:

Calculate the following for Dickens Tailor Shop:
a. Payables deferral period
b. Inventory self-financing period
c. Inventory conversion period
d. Receivables conversion period
e. Number of days between receiving inventory from suppliers and receiving cash from customers

E5-2. **(Determining the effect of credit policy on cash flow, LO 2)** You are provided the following information about McPherson Inc.:

Sales by quarter for 2015 were

1st Quarter	2nd Quarter	3rd Quarter	4th Quarter	Total
$105,000	$124,000	$125,000	$155,000	$509,000

- Accounts receivable at the beginning of the 1st quarter were $45,000. McPherson gives its customers 60 days to pay for purchases.
- Assume sales and collections occur evenly over each quarter.

Required:

a. How much cash will McPherson collect in each quarter of 2015 and for the entire 2015?
b. If McPherson changed its credit policy so customers had to pay in 90 days how much would it collect in each quarter and for the entire 2015 (assume beginning accounts receivable is $127,500)?

E5-3. **(The effect of depreciation on cash from operations, LO 1, 3)** In 2015 Anyox Ltd. (Anyox) reported net income of $150,000. All revenues and expenses were in cash, except for a $22,000 depreciation expense.

Required:

a. Calculate cash from operations for Anyox in 2015.
b. Suppose that instead of a $22,000 depreciation expense in 2015 Anyox expensed $33,000 for depreciation. Assume that all other revenues and expenses remained the same. What would Anyox's net income be in 2015? What would its cash from operations be in 2015? Explain the reasons for any differences or similarities in your answer for when the depreciation expense was $22,000 and when it was $33,000.

E5-4. **(The effect of asset writedowns on cash from operations, LO 1, 3)** In the year ended December 31, 2013 Hexham Inc. (Hexham) reported net income of $3,200,000, which included a writedown* of $1,000,000 of company assets. During 2013 accounts receivable increased by $250,000, inventory decreased by $175,000, and accounts payable decreased by $90,000. Depreciation expense in 2013 was $410,000.

Required:

a. What journal entry did Hexham make to record the writedown of the assets?
b. Calculate cash from operations using the indirect method.
c. Suppose that at the last minute, Hexham's management decided to delay writing down the assets:
   i. What would Hexham's net income be in 2013?
   ii. What would Hexham's cash from operations be in 2013?
d. Explain the differences you found between the net income Hexham originally reported and the net income you calculated under c(i).
e. Explain the differences you found between the cash from operations numbers you calculated under (b) and (c)(ii).

*A writedown is a reduction in the carrying amount of an asset to some measure of its market value. It's achieved by debiting an expense and crediting the asset.

E5-5. **(Classifying transactions for a cash flow statement, LO 3)** Classify each of the following transactions and economic events as an operating, investing, or financing cash flow; a cash equivalent; or whether the item has no effect on cash flow. Also, indicate whether each item increases or decreases cash.
a. Merchandise is sold on credit.
b. Suppliers of inventory are paid in cash.
c. Accounts receivable are collected from customers.
d. Sale of shares of a public company.
e. Inventory is purchased on credit.
f. Interest is paid on a bond.
g. Equipment is depreciated.
h. Equipment is purchased for cash.
i. Payment is made to a law firm for services rendered.
j. Cash is obtained from a lender in exchange for a long-term note payable.
k. A bank loan is repaid.
l. Cash dividends are paid to shareholders.
m. Purchase of a government of Canada treasury bill that matures in one month.
n. Purchase of a guaranteed investment certificate that matures in three years.
o. Land is purchased. The seller of the land takes back a mortgage.
p. Inventory is sold for cash.

E5-6. **(Classifying transactions for a cash flow statement, LO 3)** Lasky and Partners (Lasky) is a small accounting firm. For each of the following, specify whether the item should be classified as an operating, financing, or investing cash flow, whether the item represents a cash inflow or outflow, and the amount of the transaction. Explain your reasoning.
a. Collected $5,000 from a client for services rendered.
b. Purchased new laptop computers for the accountants for $26,000 cash.
c. Repaid a $50,000 loan from the bank.
d. Depreciation expense for the year was $55,000.
e. Sold some old office furniture for $4,500. The gain on the sale was $1,000.
f. Paid employees $76,000 cash in wages for the period.
g. Admitted a new partner to the firm. The new partner contributed $100,000 in capital to the firm to become a partner.
h. Provided services to a client and the client was billed $8,700. The client is expected to pay in 60 days.

E5-7. **(Classifying transactions for a cash flow statement, LO 3)** Basanti Oil Inc. (Basanti) is a privately owned oil exploration and production company. For each of the following specify whether the item should be classified as an operating, financing, or investing cash flow, whether the item represents a cash inflow or outflow, and the amount of the transaction. Explain your reasoning.

a. Sold oil produced from its wells for $500,000.

b. Sold some drilling equipment for $175,000 cash. There was a loss of $54,000 on the sale.

c. Purchased drilling rights from the government for $250,000 cash. The rights allow the company to explore and drill for oil in a particular part of the province for the next 10 years.

d. Paid $12,000 to a service company for maintenance on some of its drilling equipment.

e. Owes the federal government $210,000 in income taxes. The amount will be paid next year.

f. Paid a dividend of $100,000 to its shareholder.

g. Paid interest on its outstanding bank loan of $20,000.

E5-8. (**Determining missing information, LO 3**) Calculate the missing information (indicated by shaded areas) from the following cash flow statements:

Cash from (used by)	Company 1	Company 2	Company 3	Company 4	Company 5
Operations	$	$72,000	$	$50,000	($72,000)
Investing activities	(30,000)	(45,000)	11,500	(24,500)	
Financing activities	8,000	(27,000)	(25,000)		90,000
Net increase (decrease) in cash	(45,000)		13,000	9,000	60,000

E5-9. (**Calculating cash from operations, LO 3**) You are provided the following information about Joggins Inc. (Joggins) for 2015:

Net income	$222,000
Accounts receivable on January 1, 2015	595,000
Accounts receivable on December 31, 2015	520,000
Inventory on January 1, 2015	975,000
Inventory on December 31, 2015	910,000
Accounts payable on January 1, 2015	640,000
Accounts payable on December 31, 2015	595,000
Depreciation expense for 2015	310,000

Required:

Calculate cash from operations for Joggins for 2015. Provide a brief explanation for the difference between net income and cash from operations.

E5-10. (**Calculating cash from operations, LO 3**) You are provided the following information about Pubnico Ltd. (Pubnico) for fiscal 2015:

Net income	$ 585,000
Accounts receivable on July 1, 2014	195,000
Accounts receivable on June 30, 2015	250,000
Inventory on July 1, 2014	775,000
Inventory on June 30, 2015	955,000
Accounts payable on July 1, 2014	450,000
Accounts payable on June 30, 2015	490,000
Unearned revenue on July 1, 2014	1,000,000
Unearned revenue on June 30, 2015	250,000
Depreciation expense for the year 2014	200,000

Required:

Calculate cash from operations for Pubnico for fiscal 2015. Provide a brief explanation for the difference between net income and cash from operations.

E5-11. (**Organize information into a cash flow statement, LO 3**) Use the following information to prepare a well-organized cash flow statement for Quesnel Ltd. for the year ended December 31, 2014. Use the information to calculate net income for the year.

Cash and cash equivalents at the beginning of the year	$ 52,000
Cash and cash equivalents at the end of the year	68,000
Increase in prepaids	3,000
Decrease in taxes payable	4,500
Depreciation	75,000
Dividends	22,000
Decrease in accounts payable	12,200
Increase in accounts receivable	18,000
Decrease in inventory	33,000
Issuance of common shares	80,000
Issuance of long-term debt	125,000
Gain on the sale of land	14,000
Net income	?
New bank loans	250,000
Proceeds from the sale of land	168,000
Purchase of property, plant, and equipment	275,000
Retirement of long-term debt	165,000
Purchase of long-term investments	50,000

E5-12. (**Adjustments to net income when using the indirect method of calculating cash from operations, LO 3**) Tracadie Inc. (Tracadie) uses the indirect method to calculate and report cash from operations in its cash flow statement. For each of the following items indicate whether the item would be added to net income, deducted from net income, or not be relevant when calculating cash from operations.
a. Loss on the sale of office furniture from Tracadie's executive offices.
b. Dividends paid.
c. Purchase of a building.
d. Increase in accounts payable.
e. Decrease in inventory.
f. Sale of land.
g. Decrease in accrued liabilities.
h. Increase in long-term debt.
i. Gain on the sale of equipment used by Tracadie to provide its services.
j. Increase in accounts receivables.
k. Depreciation expense.

E5-13. **(Calculate cash from operations using the indirect method, LO 1, 3)** Consider the following non-cash current operating account information of Yahk Ltd. (Yahk):

	2015	2014		2015	2014
Accounts receivable	$ 88,000	$ 77,500	Accounts payable	$410,000	$450,500
Inventory	312,500	285,500	Wages payable	38,500	30,000
Prepaids	12,000	20,000	Taxes payable	75,000	85,000
			Interest payable	42,750	32,500
Total current operating assets	$412,500	$383,000	Total current operating liabilities	$566,250	$598,000

Yahk's net income for 2015 was $57,000. In addition, Yahk reported a depreciation expense of $70,000 and a gain on sale of equipment of $33,000.

Required:

　　a. Calculate cash from operations for Yahk using the indirect method and prepare the cash from operations section of Yahk's cash flow statement.

　　b. Explain why cash from operations is different from net income in 2015.

E5-14. **(Calculate cash collections, LO 3)** In its April 30, 2015 financial statements, Ebbsfleet Inc. (Ebbsfleet) reported a beginning accounts receivable balance of $110,000 and an ending accounts receivable balance of $92,000. Ebbsfleet reported sales for the year ended April 30, 2015, of $975,000. All sales are on credit.

Required:

Calculate the amount of cash Ebbsfleet collected from customers during fiscal 2015.

E5-15. **(Calculate cash payments, LO 3)** In its May 31, 2014 financial statements, Maloneck Ltd. (Maloneck) reported that it had inventory of $65,000 and accounts payable of $54,000 on May 31, 2013, and inventory of $59,000 and accounts payable of $72,000 on May 31, 2014. Maloneck's income statement for the year ended May 31, 2014, reported cost of goods sold of $525,000.

Required:

Calculate the amount of cash that Maloneck paid to suppliers for purchases of inventory during fiscal 2014. Assume that accounts payable pertain only to the purchase of inventory on credit.

E5-16. **(Calculate cash payments made for interest, LO 3)** In its August 31, 2016 financial statements, Pitquah Corp. (Pitquah) reported interest payable on August 31, 2015 of $7,500, and interest payable on August 31, 2016 of $2,500. Pitquah's income statement reports interest expense of $35,000.

Required:

Calculate the amount of cash Pitquah paid in interest in fiscal 2016.

E5-17. **(Calculate cash collections, LO 3)** In its November 30, 2014 financial statements, Matapedia Inc. (Matapedia) reported a beginning accounts receivable balance of $3,225,000 and an ending accounts receivable balance of $3,392,000. The company also had unearned revenue at the beginning of fiscal 2014 of $345,000 and a $275,000 of unearned revenue on November 30, 3014. Matapedia reported sales for the year ended November 30, 2014, of $27,400,000. All sales are on credit.

Required:

Calculate the amount of cash Matapedia collected from customers during fiscal 2014.

E5-18. **(Impact of the sale of land, LO 1, 3)** Willems Ltd. (Willems) owns a piece of land that cost $10,000. Willems recently sold the land for $25,000. The buyer paid $5,000 in cash and will pay the remainder in 14 months.

Required:

a. What is the gain or loss on the sale of the land?
b. What is the effect of the sale on Willems' cash?
c. How would this transaction affect the cash flow statement? Respond assuming Willems uses (i) the indirect method of calculating CFO and (ii) the direct method of calculating CFO.
d. What would be the effect on CFO if the gain or loss was adjusted for, if Willems used the indirect method?
e. Discuss how the sale of the land is accounted for in the cash flow statement? Can you think of other ways that the transaction could be presented? Which approach do you think is best? Explain.

Problems

P5-1. **(Calculating missing information about balance sheet accounts, LO 3)** The following general equation can be used to determine missing information about balance sheet accounts:

Ending balance in the account	=	Beginning balance in the account	+	Transactions and economic events that increase the balance in the account	−	Transactions and economic events that decrease the balance in the account

Use the equation to determine the missing information in each of the following independent situations. For each case assume that the year-end is December 31. You can also use an accounting equation spreadsheet to determine the missing information.

a. On January 1, 2013 Ewart Ltd. (Ewart) had $450,000 of inventory on hand. During 2013 Ewart sold $1,520,000 of inventory and purchased $1,330,000 of inventory. How much inventory did Ewart have on December 31, 2013?
b. Peno Inc. (Peno) had $1,500,000 and $1,750,000 of accounts receivable and on January 1 and December 31, 2014 respectively. During 2014 Peno collected $4,900,000 from customers. What amount of credit sales did Peno make during 2014?
c. Noir Inc. (Noir) capitalizes certain development costs and amortizes them over five years. On January 1, 2013 the balance in Noir's development cost account on the balance sheet was $333,000 and on December 31, 2013 the balance was $422,000. During 2013 the amortization expense for development costs was $62,000. What amount of development costs did Noir capitalize during 2013? Assume that Noir doesn't have a separate contra-asset account for accumulating amortization for this account.
d. On December 31, 2014 Hythe Ltd. (Hythe) owed its employees $121,000. During 2014 Hythe's employees earned $1,400,000 and were paid $1,320,000. How much did Hythe owe its employees on December 31, 2013?
e. Cadzow Inc. (Cadzow) purchases all of its inventory on credit. On January 1, 2013 Cadzow had $2,000,000 of inventory on hand and on December 31, 2013 it had $1,600,000 of inventory. Cost of goods sold during 2013 was $9,200,000. The balances in Cadzow's accounts payable account on January 1, 2013 and December 31, 2013 were $1,700,000 and $1,400,000 respectively. How much did Cadzow pay its suppliers during 2013?

P5-2.   (**Calculating missing information about balance sheet accounts, LO 3**) The following general equation can be used to determine missing information about balance sheet accounts:

Ending balance in the account	=	Beginning balance in the account	+	Transactions and economic events that increase the balance in the account	−	Transactions and economic events that decrease the balance in the account

Use this equation to determine the missing information in each of the following independent situations. For each case assume that the year-end is June 30. You can also use an accounting equation spreadsheet to determine the missing information.

a. On June 30, 2015, Zincton Ltd. (Zincton) reported $75,000 of prepaid rent. During fiscal 2015 Zincton had a rent expense of $525,000 and paid $600,000 to the owners of the property it rented. How much prepaid rent did Zincton report on July 1, 2014?

b. Winsloe Inc. (Winsloe) had $500,000 and $425,000 of accounts receivable on July 1, 2014 and June 30, 2015 respectively. During fiscal 2015 Winsloe had $3,750,000 in credit sales. How much cash did Winsloe collect from customers during fiscal 2015?

c. Union Inc. (Union) capitalizes its store opening costs and amortizes them over five years. On July 1, 2014 Union had $125,000 in unamortized store opening costs and on June 30, 2015 the balance was $285,000. During fiscal 2015 the amortization expense for store opening costs was $30,000. What amount of store opening costs did Union capitalize during fiscal 2015? Assume that Union doesn't have a separate contra-asset account for accumulating amortization for this account.

d. On July 1, 2014 Sawbill Ltd. (Sawbill) had unearned revenue $1,275,000. During fiscal 2014 Sawbill received $975,000 in advances from customers and recognized $1,445,000 of unearned revenue as revenue. How much unearned revenue did Sawbill have June 30, 2015?

e. Otter Inc. (Otter) purchases all of its inventory on credit. On July 1, 2014 Otter had $250,000 of inventory on hand and on June 30, 2015 it had $310,000 of inventory. Cost of goods sold during fiscal 2015 was $1,375,000. On July 1, 2014 the balance in Otter's accounts payable account was $215,000 and during fiscal 2015 Otter paid suppliers $1,510,000. How much did Otter owe its suppliers on June 30, 2015?

P5-3.   (**Inferring cash flow patterns, LO 1, 3**) Pasadena Ltd. (Pasadena) is a small manufacturing company. During 2015 Pasadena has been struggling because of a slow down in the overall economy and in the industry it supplies parts to. Sales are down significantly but the company has been unable to reduce many of its operating costs. To generate cash Pasadena has been forced to sell off some land it owns at a loss. Even so, cash reserves have decreased by 50 percent. Management has decided to delay all but essential capital expenditures until business conditions have improved. Pasadena also had to repay a large bank loan that came due during the year. Despite extensive negotiations with a number of banks, the company was unable to refinance the loan, although it was able to raise some cash by selling shares to existing shareholders. Pasadena didn't pay dividends during the year.

Required:

What pattern of cash flows would you expect to see if you examined Pasadena's cash flow statement for 2015? That is, would you expect operating, investing, and financing cash flows to be positive or negative? Explain your answer fully. Be sure to make reference to business conditions faced by the company.

P5-4.   (**Inferring cash flow patterns, LO 1, 3**) Killam Inc. operates a growing chain of discount retail stores. In 2014 Killam opened three new stores and now has five in total. Further expansion is planned for the future. Opening a new store requires significant investment in furniture and fixtures, inventory, advertising and promotion, and staff training. Killam financed the new stores through bank borrowing and equity investment by shareholders.

Required:

What pattern of cash flows would you expect to see if you examined the Killam cash flow statement for 2014? That is, would you expect operating, investing, and financing cash flows to be positive or negative? Explain your answer fully. Be sure to make reference to business conditions faced by the company.

P5-5. **(Interpreting cash flow patterns, LO 1, 3)** Viewmont Inc. is a small manufacturing company. You have been presented with the following summarized information from Viewmont Inc.'s cash flow statement:

Cash from operations	$(1,247,500)
Cash from investing activities	(3,675,000)
Cash from financing activities	5,098,000

Required:

Examine the cash flow pattern for Viewmont Inc. What does the pattern say about the situation the company finds itself in? (That is, consider what type of circumstances would give rise to a situation in which CFO and investing activities would be negative and financing activities would be positive.)

P5-6. **(Interpreting cash flow patterns, LO 1, 3)** You have been presented with the following summarized information from Inverness Ltd.'s cash flow statement:

Cash from operations	$5,354,000
Cash from investing activities	(1,580,000)
Cash from financing activities	2,500,000

Required:

Examine the cash flow pattern for Inverness Ltd. What does the pattern say about the situation that the company finds itself in? (That is, consider what type of circumstances would give rise to a situation in which CFO and financing activities would have net cash inflows and investing activities would have a net cash outflow.)

P5-7. **(Interpreting cash flow patterns, LO 1, 3)** You have been presented with the following summarized information from Dunvegan Ltd.'s cash flow statement:

Cash from operations	$4,250,000
Cash from investing activities	(2,450,000)
Cash from financing activities	(1,610,000)

Required:

Examine the cash flow pattern for Dunvegan Ltd. What does the pattern say about the situation that the company finds itself in? (That is, consider what type of circumstances would give rise to a situation in which CFO would have a net cash inflow and investing and financing activities would have net cash outflows.)

P5-8. **(Analyzing cash flows, LO 2)** Simpson Ltd. (Simpson) imports novelty items from Asian manufacturers and sells them to retailers. The company began operations at the beginning of 2015. The following information is available about Simpson's operation:

- Simpson's suppliers allow it 30 days to pay for purchases. Assume purchases are made evenly throughout the year.

- Simpson allows customers 60 days to pay for their purchases. Assume sales occur evenly throughout the year.

- Simpson has a markup on its product of 100 percent. (If a customer purchases merchandise that costs Simpson $1 the customer pays $2.)

- Operating costs, other than the cost of product sold, are $40,000 per quarter. These costs are paid in cash during the quarter.

- Simpson began operations with $100,000 in cash contributed by its shareholders.

- Quarterly information for 2015:

	1st Quarter	2nd Quarter	3rd Quarter	4th Quarter	Total
Sales	$160,000	$180,000	$210,000	$250,000	$800,000
Inventory purchases	$200,000	$110,000	$125,000	$100,000	$535,000

Required:

a. Prepare income statements for each quarter of 2015 and for the entire year. (*Hint:* Use the fact that Simpson has a 100 percent markup to calculate cost of goods sold.)

b. Calculate the amount of inventory on hand at the end of each quarter and the end of the year.

c. Calculate the amount of accounts receivable at the end of each quarter and the end of the year.

d. Calculate the amount of accounts payable at the end of each quarter and the end of the year.

e. Calculate the amount of cash on hand at the end of each quarter and the end of the year. What was the net cash flow for each quarter and the year?

f. Explain the difference between net income and net cash flow during 2015. Evaluate Simpson's liquidity during 2015. What could be done to improve Simpson's liquidity?

g. What would net income be if Simpson gave customers 90 days to pay? What would net cash flow be? Discuss your results compared with when customers had 60 days to pay.

P5-9. **(Organize information into a cash flow statement, LO 3)** Use the following alphabetical list of information to prepare a well-organized cash flow statement for Winkler Ltd. for the year ended July 31, 2015. The bookkeeper who prepared the information wasn't sure about exactly what information to provide to you so there may be information that should not be included in the cash flow statement.

Accounts payable	$ 560,000
Cash and cash equivalents at the beginning of the year	1,250,000
Cash and cash equivalents at the end of the year	1,619,400
Decrease in accounts receivable	98,000
Decrease in net bank loans	85,000
Decrease in taxes payable	35,600
Depreciation	1,150,000
Dividends declared but not paid	225,000
Dividends paid	1,000,000
Increase in cash	369,400
Increase in accounts payable	78,000
Increase in inventory	101,000
Increase in prepaids	9,000
Issuance of common shares	888,000
Issuance of long-term debt	175,000
Loss on the sale of capital assets	125,000
Net income	485,000
New bank loans	325,000
Proceeds from the sale of property, plant, and equipment	758,000
Property, plant, and equipment	13,420,000
Purchase of long-term investments	422,000
Purchase of capital assets	900,000
Repayment of bank loans	410,000
Retirement of long-term debt	1,100,000
Shares exchanged for capital assets	300,000
Writedown of assets	265,000

P5-10. **(Calculating cash from operations, LO 1, 3, 4)** You are provided with the following balance sheet information and summarized income statement for Rivulet Inc.:

Rivulet Inc. Current Operating Assets and Liabilities as of December 31, 2014 and 2015					
	2015	2014		2015	2014
Accounts receivable	$310,000	$252,500	Accounts payable	$480,000	$542,500
Inventory	687,500	787,500	Accrued liabilities	122,500	80,000

Rivulet Inc. Income Statement for the Year Ended December 31, 2015	
Revenue	$2,487,500
Cost of goods sold	1,330,000
Gross margin	1,157,500
Other expenses	980,000
Depreciation expense	537,500
Gain on sale of capital assets	(62,500)
Net loss	(297,500)

All sales are credit sales. Accounts payable pertains exclusively to the purchase of inventory and accrued liabilities pertains exclusively to other expenses.

Required:

a. Prepare Rivulet's cash from operations section of the cash flow statement using the indirect method.

b. Calculate these amounts:
   i. cash collected from customers
   ii. cash paid to suppliers of inventory
   iii. cash paid for other expenses

Use this information to prepare Rivulet's cash from operations section of the cash flow statement using the direct method.

c. Do you think the direct method or indirect method provides more useful information to stakeholders? Explain. What information is available when the direct method is used that isn't available when the indirect method is used?

d. Explain the difference between net income and cash from operations. Why did Rivulet have a loss on its income statement but positive cash from operations?

e. What are the implications of having a loss on the income statement but positive cash from operations?

P5-11. **(Calculating cash from operations using both the direct and indirect methods, LO 1, 3)** You are provided the following balance sheet information and summarized income statement for Katrime Ltd.:

Katrime Ltd.
Current Operating Assets and Liabilities as of May 31, 2013 and 2014

	2014	2013		2014	2013
Accounts receivable	$320,250	$208,500	Accounts payable	$294,000	$236,250
Inventory	673,500	424,500	Wages payable	54,000	63,750
Prepaid insurance	54,000	26,250			

Katrime Ltd.
Income Statement for the Year Ended May 31, 2014

Revenue	$1,235,750
Cost of goods sold	551,625
Gross margin	684,125
Wages expense	249,750
Depreciation expense	31,875
Insurance expense	22,500
Other expenses	103,125
Loss on sale of capital assets	20,625
Net income	$ 256,250

All sales are credit sales. Accounts payable pertains exclusively to the purchase of inventory. Other expenses were fully paid in cash during the year.

Required:

a. Prepare Katrime's cash from operations section of the cash flow statement using the indirect method.

b. Calculate these amounts:
   i. cash collected from customers
   ii. cash paid to suppliers of inventory
   iii. cash paid to employees

Use this information to prepare Katrime's cash from operations section of the cash flow statement using the direct method.

c. Do you think the direct method or indirect method provides more useful information to stakeholders? Explain. What information is available when the direct method is used that isn't available when the indirect method is used?

d. Explain the difference between net income and cash from operations. Why did Katrime have a profit on its income statement but negative cash from operations?

e. What are the implications of showing a profit on the income statement but negative cash from operations?

P5-12. **(Interpreting the cash flow statement, LO 1, 3)** Ramea Environmental Insulation Ltd. (Ramea) manufacturers a low-cost, highly efficient insulation for use in buildings. The company is private and has one shareholder. The product was invented about seven years ago and was introduced to the market soon after. Sales grew slowly in the first few years but increasing awareness among builders and homeowners and higher heating costs have caused sales to increase dramatically over the last few years. The company has been unable to keep up with customer demand and is concerned it will lose business to competitors, even those with inferior products. Ramea's sales have increased over the last few years by almost 600 percent and profits have increased from $75,000 in 2011 to $1 million in the year ended December 31, 2015. Despite its success, Ramea is using up cash very quickly and management is worried that it won't have enough to operate successfully. You have been provided with Ramea's cash flow statements for the years ended December 31, 2014 and 2015. Prepare a report to management explaining the reasons for the company's cash problems despite its profitability. Management has also asked for any suggestions you might have to improve the situation.

Required:

Prepare the report.

Ramea Ltd.
Statement of Cash Flows
For the Years Ended December 31,

	2015	2014
Net income	$1,000,000	$875,000
Items not affecting cash: Depreciation	325,000	260,000
	1,325,000	1,135,000
Changes in non-cash working capital accounts		
Accounts receivable	(455,000)	(260,000)
Inventory	(683,000)	(377,000)
Prepaids	9,100	(19,500)
Accounts payable and accrued liabilities	127,500	162,500
	323,600	641,000
Financing activities		
Issue of long-term debt	1,300,000	0
Bank loans	552,500	650,000
Repayment of long-term debt	(292,500)	(292,500)
Issue of shares	0	1,950,000
Dividends paid	(230,000)	(130,000)
	1,330,000	2,177,500
Investing activities		
Purchase of property, plant, and equipment	(2,950,000)	(1,625,000)
	(2,950,000)	(1,625,000)
Increase in cash and cash equivalents	(1,296,400)	1,193,500
Cash and cash equivalents, beginning of year	1,388,500	195,000
Cash and cash equivalents, end of year	$92,100	$1,388,500

P5-13. **(Interpreting the cash flow statement, LO 1, 3)** Kitwanga Furniture Ltd. (Kitwanga) is a manufacturer of high-quality traditional wood furniture. Kitwanga sells its furniture to retailers and distributors mainly in Canada and the United States, although about 8 percent of its business is in Europe and Asia. The company has been very successful since it was founded in 1953, but in the last few years Kitwanga's performance has deteriorated significantly in the face increasing operating costs, international competition, and currency problems. Management is concerned that the company is in financial distress and heading for serious problems that will threaten its survival. Some of Kitwanga's shareholders have approached you for advice about the company's status. They have provided you with Kitwanga's most recent cash flow statements and have asked you to prepare a report that addresses the prospects for the company.

Required:

Prepare the report.

Kitwanga Furniture Ltd.
Statement of Cash Flows for the Years Ended July 31,

Operations	2014	2013
Net loss	($972,800)	($1,808,800)
Items not affecting cash		
Depreciation	529,150	589,000
Losses on disposal of assets	209,000	427,500
Writedown of assets	285,000	180,500
	50,350	(611,800)
Changes in non-cash working capital accounts		
Accounts receivable	395,200	459,800
Inventory	285,000	171,000
Prepaids	161,500	191,900
Accounts payable and accrued liabilities	(167,200)	(209,000)
	724,850	1,900
Financing activities		
Issue of short-term debt	1,020,000	427,500
Repayment of short-term debt	(445,000)	
Bank loans	807,500	950,000
Repayment of long-term debt	(855,000)	(855,000)
Dividends paid	(1,900,000)	(1,900,000)
	(1,372,500)	(1,377,500)
Investing activities		
Purchase of property, plant, and equipment	(136,800)	(22,800)
Proceeds from sale of property, plant, and equipment	1,805,000	921,500
Purchase of long-term investments	(1,187,500)	(161,500)
	480,700	737,200
Decrease in cash and cash equivalents	(166,950)	(638,400)
Cash and cash equivalents, beginning of year	264,100	902,500
Cash and cash equivalents, end of year	$97,150	$264,100

P5-14. **(Preparing and interpreting financial statements, LO 1, 3)** Souvenirs-On-The-Go Ltd. (Souvenirs-On-The-Go) is a mobile souvenir stand that moves around the city to be "where the action is." Souvenirs-On-The-Go was started this summer by Evan Shayne as a way to earn money in the summer months to help pay for his education. Evan registered his corporation and contributed $15,000 of his savings to the company in exchange for shares. Souvenirs-On-The-Go borrowed $7,000 from Evan's parents to provide additional cash and purchased a used cart for $15,000 cash. If it's successful, Evan hopes to operate Souvenirs-On-The-Go for four years, until he graduates from university. Souvenirs-On-The-Go obtained a municipal vending license for $500 that allows the cart to operate in designated areas around the city. The license is valid for two years.

Over the summer, Souvenirs-On-The-Go sold $22,400 in souvenirs, all for cash. It purchased $12,200 worth of souvenirs, including $1,800 in souvenirs that weren't paid for by the end of the summer. Souvenirs-On-The-Go incurred $1,050 of maintenance and repairs on the cart and $3,100 of miscellaneous expenses during the summer. As of the end of the summer, the maintenance and repairs had been fully paid for and $500 of the miscellaneous expenses was still owed to the suppliers, and unsold souvenirs costing $2,200 remained. However, Evan thinks he will be able to sell them next summer. Also, Souvenirs-On-The-Go owes Evan's parents $600 in interest.

Required:

The summer is now over and Evan is back at school. Evan hasn't had a chance to evaluate the performance of Souvenirs-On-The-Go and he has asked you to prepare an income statement, balance sheet, and cash flow statement for the summer just ended. Use the financial statements you prepared to assess the financial situation of Souvenirs-On-The-Go. Your assessment should consider information from all of the financial statements. (To prepare the cash flow statement, identify Souvenirs-On-The-Go cash transactions and organize them into the different categories [operating, investing, financing].)

P5-15. **(The effect of accrual accounting policies on the cash flow statement, LO 5)** The chief accountant of Phidias Publications Ltd. (Phidias) is thinking about how accrual accounting policy choices affect the cash flow statement. Phidias publishes a number of newspapers in mid-sized Canadian communities. One of the key success factors of the newspaper business is the circulation of the papers. Phidias spends a significant amount of money recruiting and maintaining subscribers. The accountant thinks that sound arguments could be made for both expensing the cost of recruiting and maintaining subscribers when they are incurred, and capitalizing the costs and amortizing them over a number of years.

The accountant has prepared the following cash flow statement, which is complete except for how to account for the cost of recruiting and maintaining subscribers. During 2015 Phidias spent $54,000 on this.

Phidias Publications Ltd.
Cash Flow Statement for the Year Ended December 31, 2015

Cash from operations		
Cash collected from customers and advertisers	$938,400	
Cash paid to employees	(450,000)	
Cash paid to suppliers	(362,000)	
Cash paid in interest	(20,800)	
Cash from operations		$105,600
Cash from investing activities		
Proceeds from sale of capital assets	44,000	
Purchase of capital assets	(120,000)	
Cash from investing activities		(76,000)
Cash from financing activities		
Dividends paid	(30,000)	
Repayment of bank loan	(70,000)	
Proceeds of long-term debt	130,000	
Cash from financing activities		30,000
Unclassified—recruiting and maintaining subscriber costs		(54,000)
Cash generated during the year		5,600
Cash on hand on December 31, 2014		18,500
Cash on hand on December 31, 2015		$24,100

Required:

  a. Present arguments for and against the two proposed accounting treatments for the cost of recruiting and maintaining subscribers.
  b. Explain the effect of the two accounting alternatives on Phidias' income statement.
  c. Complete Phidias' cash flow statement assuming that cash spent on recruiting and maintaining subscribers is expensed when incurred.
  d. Complete Phidias' cash flow statement assuming that cash spent on recruiting and maintaining subscribers is capitalized and amortized over three years.
  e. Discuss the difference between the statements you prepared in (c) and (d) above. What are the implications of the different treatments to the underlying cash flow and liquidity of Phidias?
  f. Which cash flow statement do you think the managers of Phidias would prefer? Explain.

P5-16. **(Accrual and cash flow information analysis, LO 1, 3)** In December 2014 Alexander Bedlam organized Soldit Properties Ltd. (Soldit), a company that sells real estate on behalf of clients. Alexander exchanged $40,000 in cash for 1,000 common shares of Soldit. When business actually began in January 2015 Alexander was very busy—so busy that he didn't bother keeping any records. At the end of the month Alexander noticed that he had less than the $40,000 in cash that he started business with. He didn't understand how he could have been so busy and still have lost money. Alexander has come to you for help to understand his situation. From your conversation with Alexander you obtain the following information:

  i. During the month, five properties were sold with a sales value of $1,200,000. Soldit earns a commission of five percent of the sales value of the property.
  ii. Sales assistants sold three of the five properties sold in January. These three properties had a total sales value of $800,000. Sales assistants receive a commission of four percent of the sales value of the properties they sell.
  iii. The commission on one of the properties hasn't been received. The client owes Soldit $16,000.
  iv. During January Soldit made the following payments in cash:

Salaries	$ 4,400
Commissions to sales assistants	32,000
Down payment on car	6,000
Rent	2,400
Purchase of computer, fax, and copier	4,000
Utilities	1,000

  v. Soldit has taken delivery of the car and the computer, fax, and copier. The price of the car was $40,000 and the price of the computer, fax, and copier was $10,000.

Required:

  a. Prepare an income statement for the month of January for Soldit.
  b. Prepare a cash flow statement for January for Soldit. (To prepare the statement, organize the amounts into the different cash flow categories.)
  c. How did Soldit perform in January? How should Alexander interpret these two statements? Did Soldit perform as badly as Alexander seems to think? Explain your answer.

P5-17. **(Interpreting the cash flow statement, LO 1, 3)** Anna Malover is a full-time veterinarian who started her own business five years ago. Anna felt that the market for doggie fashions had a lot of promise, based on her clients' complaints about fashionable doggie clothes being so hard to find. She decided to start a business to design, make, and sell a line of high-fashion doggie clothes including hats, booties, sweaters, and coordinating accessories under the name Doggie Duds.

  Anna wanted to continue her career as a full-time veterinarian and hired a full-time manager to manage Doggie Duds on a day-to-day basis. Anna has never been involved in the daily operations of the company, relying on periodic meetings with the manager and the company's annual financial statements. Since the business started, it has grown to be the number-one provider of dog clothes and accessories in the country, with seven stores across Ontario and Quebec. Anna has come to rely on the cash flow generated by Doggie Duds to support her lifestyle and usually pays herself a significant cash dividend each year.

After seeing the cash flow statement for 2013, Anna was very disappointed that the cash balance had decreased for the first time since the business began. As a result, she fired the manager for his poor performance and hired a new manager, Hue Gego, to "turn around" the company in 2014. Anna offered Hue a bonus based on the increase in total cash from 2013 to 2014.

It's now January 2015. Upon seeing the 2014 financial statements, Anna is very pleased with her decision, noting that cash increased significantly during the year. As a result, Anna was able to increase her dividend for the year to $90,000.

Doggie Duds Inc.
Cash Flow Statement for the Years Ended December 31,

	2014	2013
Operations		
Net income	$116,020	$133,500
Add: Depreciation expense	27,600	25,300
Less: Gain on sale of land*	150,000	0
Cash from operations	(6,380)	158,800
Financing		
Repayment of bank loan**	0	(85,000)
Dividends	(90,000)	(50,000)
Investing		
Sale of land	200,000	0
Purchase of new computer system***	0	(40,000)
Increase (decrease) in cash	103,620	(16,200)
Cash balance at the beginning of the year	22,200	38,400
Cash balance at the end of the year	$125,820	$ 22,200

*In 2011, Doggie Duds purchased for $50,000 a vacant lot beside one of its stores for future expansion. As of 2014, the land was still vacant and it was sold in 2014 for $200,000.
**In 2012, Doggie Duds borrowed $85,000 from the bank to open its seventh store. The loan was fully repaid in 2013. Doggie Duds has an additional loan of $250,000 still outstanding. The full balance is due on December 31, 2015.
***In 2013, Doggie Duds replaced its aging computer system with a new system that includes integrated sales, accounting and inventory tracking systems, and state-of-the-art registers in all stores. The system is expected to last five years.

Required:

a. Who are the users of the Doggie Duds financial statements? What will they be using the statements for? Discuss the possible objectives of financial reporting for Doggie Duds.

b. Do you think that Anna was justified in firing the manager based on poor performance in 2013? Why or why not?

c. Do you think that the company performed as well as Anna thinks in 2014? Why or why not?

d. Do you think it's wise of Anna to offer a bonus based on the overall increase in cash? Why or Why not?

Note: This question was written by Angela Kellett of the University of Ontario Institute of Technology and is used with permission.

P5-18.   **(Comparing the direct and indirect methods of calculating CFO, LO 1, 3)** Examine the cash flow statements provided by Stantec Inc. and shown in Exhibit 5.2. Stantec provides calculations of CFO using both the direct and indirect methods. How do the two cash flow statements differ? What information does each statement provide that the other doesn't? Which do you think provides more useful information to stakeholders?

Using Financial Statements

MAGNOTTA WINERY CORPORATION

www.magnotta.com

Magnotta Winery Corporation (Magnotta) is Ontario's third-largest winery and the only company of its kind in Canada licensed to produce and sell wine, beer, and distilled products. With over 3,000 awards to date for product excellence, Magnotta is Canada's most award winning winery. The company makes wine under the VQA label using grapes grown on its own 180 acres of vineyards in Ontario's Niagara Peninsula. Certain grapes are reserved for the production of icewine, which is made from grapes picked during winter. The company owns a 351-acre vineyard in Chile's Maipo Valley. It uses some of the produce of that vineyard for its own wines and sells the rest to Chilean wineries. The company also brews premium beers under the Magnotta name. Through its Festa Juice subsidiary, Magnotta produces juice used for home-based wine production.[2] Magnotta's consolidated balance sheets and statements of cash flows and earnings, along with extracts from the notes to the financial statements, are provided in Exhibit 5.6. Use this information to respond to questions FS5-1 to FS5-12.

EXHIBIT 5.6 ▸ Magnotta Winery Corporation: Extracts from Financial Statements

MAGNOTTA WINERY CORPORATION

CONSOLIDATED BALANCE SHEETS

January 31, 2009 and 2008

		2009		2008
ASSETS				
Current assets:				
Cash and cash equivalents	$	–	$	344,231
Accounts receivable		260,800		285,995
Inventories (note 2)		27,847,603		25,108,695
Income taxes receivable		465,620		1,918
Future income taxes (note 8)		4,453		51,208
Prepaid expenses and deposits		247,038		240,526
		28,825,514		26,032,573
Property, plant and equipment (note 3)		21,092,890		21,141,229
Winery licenses		251,516		251,516
	$	50,169,920	$	47,425,318
LIABILITIES AND SHAREHOLDERS' EQUITY				
Current liabilities:				
Bank indebtedness (note 4)	$	5,881,325	$	5,536,786
Accounts payable and accrued liabilities		1,137,033		704,514
Current portion of long-term debt (note 5)		784,920		850,027
		7,803,278		7,091,327
Long-term debt (note 5)		6,616,380		7,238,694
Future income taxes (note 8)		826,832		932,046
Shareholders' equity:				
Share capital (note 6)		6,961,617		6,961,617
Notes receivable for share capital (note 9(b))		(232,500)		(348,750)
Other paid-in capital		210,000		210,000
Retained earnings		27,984,313		25,340,384
		34,923,430		32,163,251
Commitments (note 12)				
	$	50,169,920	$	47,425,318

MAGNOTTA WINERY CORPORATION
CONSOLIDATED STATEMENTS OF EARNINGS, COMPREHENSIVE INCOME AND RETAINED EARNINGS
Years ended January 31, 2009 and 2008

	2009	2008
Net sales	$ 24,046,671	$ 23,391,225
Cost of goods sold, excluding amortization of property, plant and equipment	14,172,992	13,158,084
Amortization of property, plant and equipment (production)	511,764	651,794
Total cost of goods sold	14,684,756	13,809,878
Gross profit	9,361,915	9,581,347
Expenses:		
Selling, administration and other	4,400,094	3,949,054
Amortization of property, plant and equipment (non-production)	698,676	644,992
Interest:		
Long-term debt	449,700	535,152
Bank indebtedness	184,714	327,228
	5,733,184	5,456,426
Earnings before income taxes	3,628,731	4,124,921
Income taxes (recovery) (note 8):		
Current	1,043,261	1,553,228
Future	(58,459)	(85,566)
	984,802	1,467,662
Net earnings and comprehensive income	2,643,929	2,657,259

FS5-1. What amounts does Magnotta report in its January 31, 2009, and January 31, 2008, statements of cash flow for each of the following?
  a. Cash provided by (used for) operating activities.
  b. Cash provided by (used for) investing activities.
  c. Cash provided by (used for) financing activities.

FS5-2. Examine Magnotta's statements of cash flows. Explain and interpret the information in the statement and discuss what it tells you about Magnotta.

FS5-3. What method does Magnotta use to calculate cash flows from operating activities? How can you tell?

FS5-4. Magnotta's statement of cash flows uses the term cash and cash equivalents.
  a. What does Magnotta include in its definition of cash equivalents?
  b. Does it make sense to include cash and cash equivalents in a statement of cash flow, or would using cash only make better sense? Explain your answer.
  c. How much cash and cash equivalents does Magnotta have on January 31, 2008 and 2009? Is the amount of cash on hand a concern? Explain.

FS5-5. Compare Magnotta's net earnings and cash from operations in 2008 and 2009. Why are the amounts in each year different? In general, why are net income and cash from operations different?

MAGNOTTA WINERY CORPORATION
CONSOLIDATED STATEMENTS OF CASH FLOWS
Years ended January 31, 2009 and 2008

	2009	2008
Cash provided by (used in):		
Operations:		
Net earnings	$ 2,643,929	$ 2,657,259
Items not involving cash:		
Amortization of property, plant and equipment	1,210,440	1,296,786
Future income taxes	(58,459)	(85,566)
Unrealized foreign exchange loss	76,032	14,173
Change in non-cash operating working capital:		
Accounts receivable	25,195	110,402
Inventories	(2,738,908)	(2,348,128)
Income taxes receivable/payable	(463,702)	(178,708)
Prepaid expenses and deposits	(6,512)	39,616
Accounts payable and accrued liabilities	432,519	(86,051)
	1,120,534	1,419,783
Financing:		
Decrease in long-term debt	(763,453)	(659,198)
Repayment of notes receivable for share capital	116,250	116,250
Increase (decrease) in bank indebtedness	344,539	(74,078)
	(302,664)	(617,026)
Investments:		
Purchase of property, plant and equipment	(1,162,101)	(669,022)
Increase (decrease) in cash and cash equivalents	(344,231)	133,735
Cash and cash equivalents, beginning of year	344,231	210,496
Cash and cash equivalents, end of year	$ –	$ 344,231
Supplemental cash flow information:		
Interest paid	$ 730,822	$ 880,324
Income taxes paid	1,506,963	1,731,936

1. SIGNIFICANT ACCOUNTING POLICIES:

(b) Cash and cash equivalents:

Cash and cash equivalents include cash on deposit, amounts deposited in money market funds and term deposits maturing within 90 days of acquisition and are valued at cost plus accrued interest, which approximates fair value.

11. FINANCIAL INSTRUMENTS AND RISK MANAGEMENT:

(b) Liquidity risk:

Liquidity risk is the risk that the Company will not be able to meet its financial obligations when they come due. The Company manages liquidity risk by monitoring sales volumes and cash receipts to ensure sufficient cash flows are generated from operations to meet the liabilities when they become due. Management monitors consolidated cash flows on a weekly basis, quarterly through forecasting and annually through the budget process. The Company believes its current cash flow from operations will continue to meet current and foreseeable financial requirements.

Source: Extracted from Magnotta Winery Corporation's 2008 annual report.

FS5-6. Use the information in Exhibit 5.6 to prepare a statement that shows cash from operations calculated using the direct method. Your statement should show the amount of cash collected from customers, the amount paid to suppliers, and the amounts paid in interest and taxes.

FS5-7. What pattern of cash flows does Magnotta have (are operating, financing, and investing cash flows positive or negative)? What does this pattern tell you about the circumstances of Magnotta's business?

FS5-8. Why is depreciation added back to net income when calculating CFO using the indirect method? How much did Magnotta expense for amortization (depreciation) in 2009? What would Magnotta's net earnings have been if its amortization expense for 2009 was $1,500,000? What would have been its CFO? Explain your results.

FS5-9. How much did Magnotta expense for interest in 2008 and 2009? How much did it pay in interest to lenders? Why might these amounts be different?

FS5-10. Explain how Magnotta's non-cash working capital accounts affected cash flows from operating activities during 2009. Explain changes in non-cash working capital account CFO.

FS5-11. Calculate Magnotta's free cash flow for the years ended January 31, 2008 and 2009. What does the free cash flow tell you about Magnotta?

FS5-12. You are analyst for an investment company. Use the information provided to prepare a report evaluating Magnotta's liquidity. Do you think the company has a strong liquidity position? Explain.

ENDNOTES

1. Andrée Lavigne, CA, Diane Paul, CA, John Tang, CA, Jo-Ann Lempert, CA, Hélène Marcil, CA, and Louise Overbeek, CA, *2008 Financial Reporting in Canada, 33rd Edition*, 2008.

2. Adapted from Magnotta Winery Corporation's website at http://www.magnotta.com/About.aspx and from Yahoo! Finance at biz.yahoo.com/ic/113/113319.html.

CHAPTER 6

CASH, RECEIVABLES, AND THE TIME VALUE OF MONEY

LEARNING OBJECTIVES

After studying the material in this chapter you will be able to do the following:

▶ **LO 1** Discuss how cash is accounted for in financial statements and recognize the importance of cash management and internal controls over cash.

▶ **LO 2** Explain the concept of the time value of money and its relevance to accounting, and do some basic time value of money calculations.

▶ **LO 3** Describe accounting for receivables and uncollectible amounts.

▶ **LO 4** Analyze and interpret information for evaluating the liquidity of an entity and understand how managers can use accounting estimates to create hidden reserves to manage earnings.

On the morning of Tuesday May 12, 2009, Canadian hardware retailer RONA Inc. released its first-quarter results: a loss of $2.5 million or 2 cents a share. At her desk in the Toronto television studios of Business News Network, anchor woman Frances Horodelski combed through RONA's official press release and the accompanying 30 pages of financial statements before she went on the air to tell viewers what the results meant for investors.

Frances Horodelski, CFA
Television Journalist—Business News Network

"In investing, those numbers are all that matters," Horodelski said in an interview. "If [the company] can't generate profits from what they are doing or selling, BlackBerrys or nails, it doesn't matter, that's what you have to look at."

After a career analyzing stocks and stock markets at Bay Street giants including RBC Dominion Securities and ScotiaMcLeod, Horodelski is able to look through a company's rosy public relations spin. She credits that ability, in part, to the accounting courses she took for her designation as a chartered financial analyst.

"A lot of people who are investing never read the notes [to the financial statements], but that's where all the good stuff can be found, and all the details, and all the off balance sheet things that are referred to," Horodelski explained. "Because accounting is not just the numbers, it's the decisions as to how those numbers are presented, what things you might do in terms of depreciation rates, for example, and all within the realm of legality but it makes a big difference how you treat it for taxes."

A political science and political philosophy major, Horodelski "fell into" investing while working at the investment wing of Crown Life Insurance (now Canada Life). While at first she admits she didn't know the difference between a stock and a bond, she soon learned how markets worked. Her CFA accounting courses would eventually come in very handy.

"Getting some instruction in that was very useful in how you value companies and value markets and aggregates," she said. "So it was a very useful base for what I ultimately did, [which] was picking stocks and managing portfolios."

At BNN, where she appears on shows such as Market Morning and Stock Sense, Horodelski spans what she calls the "intimate connection" between

accounting and the investment world. She reads reams of reports prepared by accountants, where they are analysts who work with investment dealers, portfolio managers, or corporate CFOs. She always looks at a company's fundamentals, and then interviews key players, including CEOs, to ask why a stock might be up 100 percent in two months.

"Decisions CFOs and accountants make, that's where the fun is; to find out why those decisions were made and the implications of them," she said.

Horodelski unwinds from the stress of her on-air television job by competing in walking marathons, which she explains have taken her to Mount Kilimanjaro, Athens, and Ottawa. But the woman the *Toronto Star* once called a member of "the Bank of Nova Scotia's investment Dream Team" admits she gets her biggest thrill watching the trading day.

"I really like investing in companies; it's so exciting," she said.

—E.B.

INTRODUCTION

So far we have examined accounting and accounting information from a broad perspective. In the remaining chapters we will delve more deeply into the accounting used for the major components of the financial statements. Don't be misled by these chapters' apparent focus on the balance sheet. The financial statements are all closely linked and accounting choices affecting one will invariably impact the others. Therefore, our discussion will cover the effect of accounting information on the income statement and the cash flow statement as well as on the balance sheet.

In this chapter we will examine some of an entity's most liquid assets: cash and receivables. Cash, of course, is the most liquid and is vital for the effective operation and survival of an entity. Yet, accounting for cash isn't always as straightforward as counting the money in your pocket. Receivables are amounts owed to the entity, usually by customers. Our examination of receivables will show the effect of estimates on the values of assets on the balance sheet and the amount of income an entity reports.

The chapter also introduces a powerful tool used in accounting and financial analysis—"time value of money," which recognizes that money received today is more valuable than the same amount of money received sometime in the future.

CASH

We discussed the importance of cash and cash flow at length in Chapter 5. This chapter will cover some of the accounting issues of cash. Accounting for cash is relatively straightforward and doesn't generate much controversy, although there are some twists and turns you should be aware of.

www.transalta.com

Exhibit 6.1 shows the asset side of TransAlta Corporation's (TransAlta) December 31, 2008, and 2007 balance sheets.[1] TransAlta is a power generation and wholesale marketing company, generating electricity from coal, natural gas, water, geothermal energy for customers in Canada, the U.S., and Australia.[2] TransAlta reported cash and cash equivalents of $50 million and $51 million on December 31, 2008 and 2007, respectively. The cash is all the money in bank accounts and safes throughout the organization. Cash equivalents are short-term investments easily and quickly converted into a known amount of cash. Cash equivalents include treasury bills, guaranteed investment certificates (GICs), commercial paper, and money market funds. Short-term investments typically must mature within three months to be classified as a cash equivalent. Cash equivalents exclude equity investments such as common and preferred shares because their prices fluctuate daily, which means the amount of cash received from selling them is only certain once they are sold.

Sometimes an entity's cash is restricted because of a legal or contractual obligation to use it in a specified way. On TransAlta's December 31, 2007 balance sheet (Exhibit 6.1) there was $242.4 million of restricted cash classified as a non-current asset. Note 12 explains that this cash is held as security for a subsidiary's obligation and can't be used for day-to-day purposes. Restricted cash isn't a liquid asset and isn't included in cash and cash equivalents in the cash flow statement.

Sometimes an entity reports no cash on its balance sheet. For example, Rogers Communications Inc.'s (Rogers) reported no cash and cash equivalents on its December 31, 2008 and 2007, balance sheets (Exhibit 6.2).[3] This doesn't mean Rogers has no cash at all. As was explained in Chapter 5,

| EXHIBIT | 6.1 | Transalta Corporation: Consolidated Balance Sheets |

Consolidated Balance Sheets

Dec. 31 (in millions of Canadian dollars)	2008	2007
Assets		(Restated, Note 2)
Current assets		
Cash and cash equivalents (Note 7)	$ 50	$ 51
Accounts receivable (Notes 7, 8, and 31)	542	546
Prepaid expenses	6	9
Risk management assets (Notes 7, 9, and 10)	200	93
Future income tax assets (Note 6)	3	40
Income taxes receivable	61	49
Inventory (Note 11)	51	30
	913	818
Restricted cash (Notes 7 and 12)	–	242
Investments (Note 13)	–	125
Long-term receivables (Notes 6 and 14)	14	6
Property, plant, and equipment (Note 15)		
Cost	9,919	8,593
Accumulated depreciation	(3,898)	(3,476)
	6,021	5,117
Assets held for sale, net (Note 16)	–	29
Goodwill (Notes 17 and 32)	142	125
Intangible assets (Note 18)	213	209
Future income tax assets (Note 6)	248	303
Risk management assets (Notes 7, 9, and 10)	221	122
Other assets (Note 19)	43	61

8. Accounts Receivable

As at Dec. 31	2008	2007
Gross accounts receivable	$ 599	$ 592
Allowance for doubtful accounts (Note 31)	(57)	(46)
Net accounts receivable	$ 542	$ 546

The change in allowance for doubtful accounts is outlined below:

Balance, Dec. 31, 2007		$ 46
Change in foreign exchange rates		11
Balance, Dec. 31, 2008		$ 57

12. Restricted Cash

Restricted cash is comprised of debt service funds that are legally restricted, and require the maintenance of specific minimum balances equal to the next debt service payment, and amounts restricted for capital and maintenance expenditures.

The change in restricted cash is outlined below:

Balance, Dec. 31, 2007		$ 242
Amount returned to TransAlta		(248)
Change in foreign exchange rates		6
Balance, Dec. 31, 2008		$ –

During 2008, a subsidiary closed its position under a credit derivative agreement. The investment in notes held in trust as security for the subsidiary's obligation of $245 million under this agreement was returned to the subsidiary.

14. Long-Term Receivables

In 2008, the Corporation received a notice of reassessment from the federal taxation authority relating to the disposal of the transmission business in the 2002 taxation year (Note 6). The Corporation is in the process of challenging this reassessment. Since it is anticipated that the dispute will not be resolved within one year, any prepayment transfers and cash paid are recorded as a long-term receivable.

The Corporation has a right to recover a portion of future asset retirement costs. The estimated present value of these payments has also been recorded as a long-term receivable.

cash and cash equivalents can be shown net of certain types of bank loans, such as overdrafts (or advances as Rogers calls them) and lines of credit, when these loans are used as part of the day-to-day cash management (see the definition at the bottom of Exhibit 6.2). If the cash and cash equivalents are greater than the bank advances, the net amount is a current asset. If the reverse is true, as was the case for Rogers in 2008 and 2007, the net amount appears on the balance sheet as a current liability. Including bank advances in the definition of cash and cash equivalents makes it impossible to know how much cash Rogers actually has and affects the calculation of the current ratio.

EXHIBIT 6.2	Rogers Communications Inc.: Current Assets and Liabilities

CONSOLIDATED BALANCE SHEETS
(IN MILLIONS OF CANADIAN DOLLARS)

December 31, 2008 and 2007	2008	2007
Assets		
Current assets:		
Accounts receivable, net of allowance for doubtful accounts of $163 (2007 - $151)	$ 1,403	$ 1,245
Other current assets (note 9)	442	304
Future income tax assets (note 7)	446	594
	2,291	2,143
Liabilities and Shareholders' Equity		
Current liabilities:		
Bank advances, arising from outstanding cheques	$ 19	$ 61
Accounts payable and accrued liabilities	2,412	2,260
Current portion of long-term debt (note 14)	1	1
Current portion of derivative instruments (note 15(d))	45	195
Unearned revenue	239	225
	2,716	2,742

Cash and cash equivalents (deficiency) are defined as cash and short-term deposits, which have an original maturity of less than 90 days, less bank advances.

? QUESTION FOR CONSIDERATION

Why is it important for an entity to disclose that some of its cash is restricted?

Answer: It is normally assumed cash is a liquid asset available for use as needed by management. Restricted cash has been set aside for a specific use; therefore, it isn't available to meet the liquidity needs of the entity. Stakeholders will be interested in restricted cash because it could affect their evaluation of the entity's liquidity.

IS A DOLLAR A DOLLAR?

Chapter 5 introduced the unit-of-measure assumption, a fundamental IFRS accounting concept requiring that financial statement information be measurable and stated in monetary units, such as Canadian dollars. A dollar of cash reported on a balance sheet means a dollar in hand. But is a dollar always worth a dollar? In fact, a dollar's value isn't constant over time. While the face value of a dollar stays the same, what a dollar can buy and its value relative to other currencies will change.

The Effect of Changes in Purchasing Power

If you hide $10,000 under your mattress your IFRS financial statements will always show $10,000 in cash, *but* as time passes you will be less and less well off. Why? Over time **inflation**—a period when, on average, prices in the economy are rising—reduces the purchasing power of cash. If prices are rising you can buy fewer goods and services with your money as time passes, which means the purchasing power of your money is declining even though the face value stays the same. The reverse is true with **deflation**, a period when, on average, prices in the economy are falling. Deflation is a far less common phenomenon than inflation.

Using Canada's inflation rate, $10,000 hidden at the beginning of 2000 would purchase at the end of 2008 what $8,246 would have purchased in 2000. In other words, while the number of dollars you had would be the same in 2000 and 2008, you would be able to buy fewer goods and services in 2008 than in 2000.

Canadian companies use the "nominal dollar" as the unit of measure for financial reporting, which means no adjustment is made for changes in purchasing power. IFRS requires adjustments for entities in countries considered to be hyperinflationary, but this isn't a problem in Canada. A decrease in purchasing power could be reflected in financial statements by recording a loss. If an entity held $10,000 cash over a period where purchasing power decreased by 10 percent, a loss of $1,000 would be reported on the income statement. By doing this, the financial statements would reflect the cost of holding cash.

The Effect of Changing Prices of Foreign Currencies

Canada is a trading nation. Much of its economic activity involves transactions with entities in foreign countries and in foreign currencies. Many Canadian companies have operations in other countries. Transactions involving foreign currencies and foreign operations can impact an entity's financial statements, including the amount of cash it reports.

For example, Quarry Ltd. (Quarry) has a U.S. dollar bank account. Because of the unit-of-measure assumption all amounts reported in the financial statements must be stated in a single currency. If Quarry's unit of measure is Canadian dollars, its U.S. cash must be stated in Canadian dollars. Since **exchange rates** of currencies fluctuate, the number of Canadian dollars that a U.S. amount represents will vary. (The exchange rate is the price to buy one currency, stated in terms of another currency.)

Suppose that on December 31, 2015, Quarry had US$1,000,000 and the exchange rate was $1.10—that is, US$1 could be exchanged for Cdn$1.10. For its financial statements, Quarry must report its US$1,000,000 as $1,100,000 of Canadian cash (exchange rate × amount of foreign currency = $1.10 × US$1,000,000). The Cdn$1,100,000 is reported even though the money is still actually in U.S. dollars. If one year later, on December 31, 2016, Quarry's U.S. bank account still had US$1,000,000 but the exchange rate was $1.15, Quarry would report $1,150,000 of Canadian cash.

Thus, when exchange rates change, the number of Canadian dollars reported change even though the amount of the foreign currency stays the same. The change in the exchange rate from December 31, 2015, to December 31, 2016, causes Quarry to report $50,000 more in Canadian dollars, even though the amount of U.S. dollars hadn't changed.

CASH MANAGEMENT AND CONTROLS OVER CASH

It would be easy to conclude that the more cash an entity has, the better; but that's not quite true. Having too little cash, of course, is a potential threat to the survival of an entity. But having too much cash can be a problem as well. While holding cash provides insurance against the unexpected, it's an unproductive asset—it doesn't make money. At best, cash in an interest bearing account or other liquid investments earns a very small return—far less than what could be earned if the cash were invested in the business. Businesses unable to find productive use for cash would probably be best off returning the surplus to shareholders, who could find more effective investments for their money, or using it to retire outstanding liabilities. But a crucial question when examining an entity's financial position is how much surplus cash is too much? In late 2008 a global liquidity crisis played havoc with the world economy. Banks weren't lending so companies without significant cash reserves were in serious trouble. Cash management is a key function of an entity's management. Stakeholders use financial statement information to assess whether an entity is maintaining adequate reserves of liquidity and evaluate management's stewardship of the liquidity.

Management has the important stewardship responsibility of developing and maintaining adequate internal controls. **Internal controls** ensure an entity achieves its objectives. In an accounting context internal controls address the reliability the accounting system's information and protect an entity's assets from loss, theft, or inappropriate use. For example, a retail store may place alarm devices on more expensive inventory items. These devices are an internal control that helps prevent theft. In general, poor internal controls can lead to significant losses.

External stakeholders should be concerned that an entity's internal controls are adequate. Without them, stakeholders can't rely on the financial statements for decision making or be confident that management is protecting assets from theft or misuse. Canadian public companies must annually disclose the results of senior managers' assessment of the company's internal control over financial reporting. These controls provide assurance of the reliability of financial statement information produced by an entity's accounting system. Any weaknesses identified in the design or effectiveness of internal controls must be described in the annual report, along with plans to resolve the problems. These requirements don't apply to private companies.

Cash is an important asset for an entity to control. It's attractive to thieves because it's easy to hide and it can't be identified once it's stolen. Entities that handle a lot of cash—such as retail stores, casinos, arcades, and laundromats—need special internal controls to protect their cash.

There are many ways cash can be stolen, in addition to being physically taken. Weak internal controls might allow an employee to write cheques to non-existent suppliers and then cash the cheques him- or herself, pay a supplier more than is actually owed, or alter records to cover up a cash theft.

There are many controls that could limit the likelihood that cash will be stolen. One of the most important and effective controls over cash and other assets is **segregation of duties**, which means ensuring that people who handle an asset are not also responsible for record keeping for that asset. If duties aren't segregated, an employee could steal assets and cover up the theft with fictitious entries to the accounting records. For example, consider a person who receives cheques from customers and deposits them in the bank, and who is also responsible for recording the deposit in the accounting system. That person might deposit some of cheques in his or her own bank account and cover up the theft with a journal entry writing off accounts receivable in the amount stolen.

An important internal control tool for cash used by management is the **bank reconciliation**, which explains differences between an entity's accounting records and its bank account. Readers who are interested in learning about the bank reconciliation and how to prepare it can visit the text website at www.mcgrawhillconnect.ca.

www.mcgrawhill
connect.ca

✓ KNOWLEDGE CHECK

- ❑ How is it possible for an entity to have too much cash?
- ❑ What are internal controls? Why are they important for an entity to have?
- ❑ How does IFRS deal with the effect that inflation has on the purchasing power of money? What is the economic impact of inflation on the purchasing power of money?

? QUESTION FOR CONSIDERATION

You purchased a vending machine selling a variety of drinks in a busy suburban mall as an investment. As owner, you are responsible for stocking the machine with drinks, collecting the cash, and maintaining the machine, and you've hired someone living near the mall to take care of these things for you. Explain why internal controls are important in this situation and why hiring one person to handle all those tasks represents weak internal controls. What internal controls would help protect you?

Answer: Internal controls are important to protect your assets—in this case, the drinks and the cash. Because you have hired someone to stock the machine and collect the cash, it's possible your employee could steal the drinks, the cash, or both. Without proper controls, it would be difficult to know whether your employee was stealing.

The easiest way to ensure that cash or drinks aren't stolen is to do the jobs yourself. If you can't, control would be stronger if different people stocked the machine and collected the cash (segregation of duties). This way, you could compare the number of drinks sold as reported by the person stocking the machine with the cash received from the person collecting the cash. Sales and cash collections that didn't match would indicate a problem.

If you must use the same person for both stocking and collection, it's important to keep control of the inventory. Controlling the inventory means that your employee would only use inventory supplied by you, so you would know the number of drinks going into the machine and, therefore, the amount of cash you should receive. This is a weak control because there is nothing to prevent the person from buying drinks, placing them in the machine, and keeping the cash from those sales. This kind of theft is very difficult to detect. Another possible control is an electronic counter, not accessible to your employee, to keep track of the number of drinks sold. This also would allow you to compare the number of drinks sold with the cash collected, but you would have to inspect the machine from time to time to check the counter.

THE TIME VALUE OF MONEY

Would you rather receive $1,000 today or $1,000 a year from now? The answer should be easy: It's better to have cash now rather than the same amount of cash later. Here are some reasons why:

1. Having the money sooner allows you to earn a return on the money. By having the money now and investing in a one-year investment certificate paying 4 percent interest per year, your $1,000 would turn into $1,040 in a year. By waiting a year to receive the $1,000 you would lose the opportunity to earn that $40.

2. By getting the money today, you can spend and enjoy it now. A person is likely to prefer having a plasma TV or taking a holiday sooner rather than later, or at least having the option of doing so.

3. As explained earlier, inflation causes the purchasing power of money to decline over time. With inflation of 2 percent, $1,000 received in a year will only buy what $980 would buy today.

4. Getting the money sooner reduces the likelihood that you aren't going to be paid.

However you look at it, it should be clear you're ahead if you get your money sooner. This doesn't mean people will never decide to receive their money later rather than sooner. However, the delay should come with a price. The concept that people prefer to receive money sooner rather than later is known as the **time value of money**. While conceptually it makes sense that money today is better than the same amount of money in the future, how do you choose among different amounts that can be received at different times? For example, suppose you won a contest that allowed you to choose among receiving $10,000 today, $4,000 at the end of each of the next three years, or $14,000 in three years. Which would you choose?

It's hard to decide by just looking at these three alternatives, but there is a powerful tool for evaluating this choice and other business and accounting problems involving cash flows occurring at different times. Valuing cash flows occurring at different times can be viewed from two perspectives: the future value and the present value. The **future value (FV)** of cash flows is the amount of money you will receive in the future by investing today at a given interest rate. The **present value** of cash flows is the value today of money that will be received in the future.

Future Value

Money in a bank account growing over time is an application of the future value concept. If you put $1,000 in a bank account paying interest of 5 percent per year, in one year you will have earned $50 in interest and your bank account will have $1,050 in it. The amount of interest earned is calculated by multiplying the amount in your bank account by the interest rate: $1,000 $\times$ 0.05 = $50. The amount of money in the bank account at the end of the year is calculated by multiplying the amount in the account by one plus the interest rate $(1 + r)$: $1,000 $\times$ 1.05 = $1,050. In time-value-of-money terms, the future value of $1,000 invested at 5 percent for one year is $1,050.

If you leave your $1,050 in the bank for another year and continue to receive interest at 5 percent per year, at the end of the second year you will have $1,102.50 ($1,050 $\times$ 1.05). During the second year you will have earned $52.50 of interest ($1,050 $\times$ 0.05). You earned more than $50 in interest in the second year because of **compound interest**—interest earned on the principal amount and on interest accumulated in previous periods. In the second year interest wasn't only earned on the original $1,000, but also on the $50 in interest earned in the first year. In time value of money terms, the future value of $1,000 invested at 5 percent for two years is $1,102.50. (If the interest was only calculated on the initial investment of $1,000, the interest every year would be $50. Interest paid or earned only on the principal amount is called **simple interest**.)

The formula for calculating the future value of an investment made today is:

$$FV_{n,r} = (1 + r)^n \times \text{Amount invested}$$

FV (future value) is the amount you will receive in the future for an amount invested for n periods at an interest rate of r per period. This formula incorporates the compounding of interest. We can use the formula to calculate the future value of an investment of $1,000 at 5 percent for two years:

$$
\begin{aligned}
FV_{2,0.05} &= (1 + 0.05)^2 \times \$1,000 \\
&= 1.1025 \times \$1,000 \\
&= \$1,102.50
\end{aligned}
$$

This is the same amount that we calculated earlier.

You could find out how much you would have if you invested $1,000 at 8 percent for 25 years:

$$
\begin{aligned}
FV_{n,r} &= (1 + r)^n \times \text{Amount invested} \\
FV_{25,0.08} &= (1 + 0.08)^{36} \times \$1,000 \\
&= 6.84848 \times \$1,000 \\
&= \$6,848.48
\end{aligned}
$$

The future value technique is very useful and powerful. There are many questions that can be answered by using it. Let's look at a couple of examples.

Example 1: The Mayos In 2015, Mr. and Mrs. Mayo received $2,500 from Mr. Mayo's parents as a gift in honour of the birth of their first daughter, Ellin. Mr. and Mrs. Mayo plan to invest the money to help pay for Ellin's university education. They would like to know how much Ellin will receive if they invest the $2,500 in a 20-year investment certificate that earns 6 percent interest per year.

$$
\begin{aligned}
FV_{n,r} &= (1 + r)^n \times \text{Amount invested} \\
FV_{20,0.06} &= (1 + 0.06)^{20} \times \$2,500 \\
&= \$8,017.84
\end{aligned}
$$

Therefore, Ellin will receive $8,017.84 when the investment certificate matures in 2035. In this example the periods are years, but periods could be days, weeks, months, or anything else. However, the interest rate selected must be appropriate to the period used in the analysis (that is, you would use the annual interest rate only if you were measuring the periods in years).

Example 2: Ms. Secretan Ms. Secretan recently purchased a new car to replace her rusting 13-year-old vehicle. She arranged a $35,000, three-year loan at 0.5 percent per month from the bank to pay for the car, interest compounded monthly. Under the terms of the loan, Ms. Secretan doesn't have to make any payments until the end of the three-year term, at which time she must pay the bank the principal and interest in full. Ms. Secretan would like to know how much she will have to pay in three years when the loan must be repaid.

$$
\begin{aligned}
FV_{n,r} &= (1 + r)^n \times \text{Amount invested} \\
&= FV_{36,0.05}\,(1 + 0.005)^{36} \times \$35,000 \\
&= \$41,883.82
\end{aligned}
$$

Ms. Secretan will have to pay the bank $41,883.82 in three years. Because the loan is compounded monthly, the number of periods is 36 months, not three years. If three years at an interest rate of 6 percent was used the answer would be different.

KNOWLEDGE CHECK

www.mcgrawhill
connect.ca

❑   What reasons explain why it is better to have money today than in the future?

❑   What is the difference between simple and compound interest?

❑   What is the formula used to determine the future value $1 invested today?

? QUESTION FOR CONSIDERATION

Your aunt recently won $100,000 in a lottery and she has come to you for advice on investing her money. She wants to invest for ten years and then retire. Your aunt is only interested in investments she considers safe so she has narrowed her choice to two investments with large banks: a ten-year investment certificate with an interest rate of 8 percent calculated annually and a ten-year certificate with interest calculated and compounded at the rate of 4 percent every six months (this means that there are 20 six-month investment periods at 4 percent rather than 10 one-year investment periods at 8 percent).

Which investment would you recommend to your aunt? Explain your answer. Make sure to explain why the quantitative result you obtain occurs.

Answer: Your aunt would be better off with the investment that has 4 percent interest calculated and compounded every six months. Quantitatively,

$$\text{Investment 1:} \quad FV_{n,r} = (1 + r)^n \times \text{Amount invested}$$
$$FV_{10,0.08} = (1 + 0.08)^{10} \times \$100,000$$
$$= \$215,892$$

$$\text{Investment 2:} \quad FV_{n,r} = (1 + r)^n \times \text{Amount invested}$$
$$FV_{20,0.04} = (1 + 0.04)^{20} \times \$100,000$$
$$= \$219,112$$

Investment 2 is more attractive because compounding occurs more often. Even though the interest rate appears to be the same for both investments more interest is earned with Investment 2. For example, in the first year, your aunt earns 8 percent on $100,000 with Investment 1. But with Investment 2, she earns 4 percent on $100,000 in the first half of the first year ($4,000) and then 4 percent on $104,000 in the second half ($4,160) of that year, which gives a total of $8,160 of interest in the first year. The effect of the more frequent compounding builds over the life of the investment.

Present Value

The present value technique looks at what cash received in the future is worth today. This is another very powerful tool for comparing alternative cash flow arrangements. Consider the $1,102.50 you had in your bank account after two years invested at 5 percent per year (this is the example that introduced the discussion of future values). The question asked in a present value analysis is, "At an interest rate of 5 percent, what is today's equivalent of the $1,102.50 you will receive in two years?" Another way of posing the question is, "How much would you pay or invest today to receive $1,102.50 in two years if the interest rate was 5 percent?" Based on the earlier example, you should guess that the present value of $1,102.50 to be received in two years at 5 percent is $1,000. This result can be confirmed by using the following formula:

$$PV_{n,r} = \frac{1}{(1 + r)^n} \times \text{Amount to be received or paid}$$
$$PV_{2,0.05} = \frac{1}{(1 + 0.05)^2} \times \$1,102.50$$
$$= \$1,000$$

In this formula n is the number of periods and r is the interest rate. Note that the term discount rate is often used instead of interest rate in a present value analysis. The **discount rate** is the rate used to calculate the present value of future cash flows. Present value is nothing more than the amount that would be received in the future less the interest that would be earned on the money over the investment period.

What the calculation tells us is that at a discount rate of 5 percent, having $1,000 now is equivalent to receiving $1,102.50 in two years. In other words, if you were offered a choice between $1,000 now or $1,102.50 in two years and your discount rate was 5 percent, you would be indifferent—the two amounts are equally valuable to you. However, if you were offered $1,100 in two years instead, you would prefer the $1,000 now. And if you were offered $1,110 in two years you would prefer the $1,110 to $1,000 now. Remember when I introduced the time-value-of-money concept I explained that people would accept money later rather than sooner, but only at a price. That price is a larger amount of money.

Suppose that instead of using a discount rate of 5 percent to determine the present value of $1,102.50 to be received in two years you decide that 7 percent is the appropriate discount rate. What is the present value of the $1,102.50 in this case?

$$PV_{2,0.07} = \frac{1}{(1 + 0.07)^2} \times \$1,102.50$$
$$= \$962.97$$

In other words, if your discount rate was 7 percent the present value of $1,102.50 to be received in two years is $962.97. This means you would be willing to pay no more than $962.97 today to receive $1,102.50 in two years. Having to pay anything more than $962.97 would be too much. To put it another way, you would prefer receiving any amount more than $962.97 today rather than $1,102.50 in two years. Anything less than $962.97 today would make $1,102.50 in two years preferable. At a discount rate of 7 percent you would be indifferent between $1,102.50 in two years and $962.97 today.

It's important to recognize the key role the discount rate plays in determining the present value. The higher the discount rate, the lower the present value of a future amount. This corresponds to the future-value effect whereby the higher the interest rate paid on an investment, the more money received in the future. Discount rate selection is somewhat subjective and many considerations go into the choice, including risk and expected inflation. Further discussion about determining the discount rate is beyond the scope of this book.

Let's look at two examples of the present value technique.

Example 3: Luiz DeSilva Luiz DeSilva has decided to give his new nephew a gift of a university education. Luiz estimates that it will cost $150,000 for a four-year education at a good school, including tuition and living expenses, when his nephew is ready for university in 18 years. Luiz has an investment opportunity that will earn 8 percent per year. How much must Luiz invest today to have the $150,000 required in 18 years? In other words, what is the present value of $150,000 to be received in 18 years using a discount rate of 8 percent?

$$PV_{n,r} = \frac{1}{(1 + r)^n} \times \text{Amount to be received or paid}$$

$$PV_{18,0.08} = \frac{1}{(1 + 0.08)^{18}} \times \$150,000$$

$$= \$37,537.35$$

Therefore, if Luiz invested \$37,537.35 today at 8 percent, his nephew would have \$150,000 in 18 years to pay for his university education.

Example 4: Quyon Ltd. Quyon Ltd. (Quyon) recently purchased a machine for \$500,000. The purchase agreement allows Quyon to pay for the machine in three years with no interest. What would be the equivalent price if Quyon had to pay for the machine in cash today if the appropriate discount rate was 6 percent? In other words, what is the present value of \$500,000 to be paid in three years using a discount rate of 6 percent?

$$PV_{n,r} = \frac{1}{(1 + r)^n} \times \text{Amount to be received or paid}$$

$$PV_{3,0.06} = \frac{1}{(1 + 0.06)^3} \times \$500,000$$

$$= \$419,809.64$$

Therefore, \$419,809.64 is the current cash equivalent of paying \$500,000 in three years at a discount rate of 6 percent.

? QUESTION FOR CONSIDERATION

You have the option of receiving \$1,000 today, \$1,500 in four years, or \$1,700 in six years. Which would you choose? Assume a discount rate of 6 percent. Explain your choice.

Answer: To answer the question it's necessary to compare the present values of each of the cash flows and select the one with the highest present value because it's the most valuable. Note that the present value of a cash flow to be received or paid now is always the actual amount of the cash flow, regardless of the discount rate:

Option 1: $PV_{n,r} = \frac{1}{(1 + r)^n} \times \text{Amount to be received or paid}$

$$PV_{0,0.06} = \frac{1}{(1 + 0.06)^0} \times \$1,000$$

$$= \$1,000$$

Option 2: $PV_{4,0.06} = \frac{1}{(1 + 0.06)^4} \times \$1,500$

$$= \$1,188.14$$

Option 3: $PV_{6,0.06} = \frac{1}{(1 + 0.06)^6} \times \$1,700$

$$= \$1,198.43$$

Option 3 is the best one because it has the largest present value.

TABLE 6.1	Option 4: Calculation of Present Value		
Calculation of Present Value of Option 4 (Receive $250 per year for six years, beginning one year from now, at a discount rate of 6 percent)			
Cash received	Amount of cash received	Discount factor $\dfrac{1}{(1 + r)^n}$	Present value of cash flow
Now	$ 0		
In one year	250	0.9434	$ 235.85
In two years	250	0.8900	222.50
In three years	250	0.8396	209.90
In four years	250	0.7921	198.02
In five years	250	0.7473	186.82
In six years	250	0.7050	176.25
Totals		4.9174	$1,229.34

Discounting, another term for determining the present value of a future cash flow, is a very powerful tool because it allows comparisons of cash flows received at different times and in different amounts. So far, we have looked at simple situations involving a single cash flow sometime in the future. The present-value technique can be used in more complex situations. Let's add a fourth option to the three prizes offered in the previous Question for Consideration. Option 4 is that you could receive $250 per year for six years, beginning in one year. How would option 4 stack up against receiving $1,700 in year six, the best option of the first three?

This calculation is a bit more complicated but the concepts and approach are the same. Option 4 requires determining the present value of a series of six cash flows occurring at different times. The calculation of the present value of this series of cash flows is shown in Table 6.1.

Since the present value of the cash flows in option 4 is the largest of the four offered, it should be selected.

Present Value of an Annuity

For option 4 in the example above you would receive a $250 payment at the end of each of the next six years. A series of equal cash flows (inflows or outflows) made at equally spaced time intervals is known as an **annuity**. To calculate the present value of the series of six $250 payments you would do the following:

1. Find the discount rate for each of the six years.

2. Multiply the cash flow in each year by the appropriate discount rate to determine the present value of the cash flow in each year.

3. Add up the present values from each year to get the present value of the entire series of cash flows.

We followed these three steps in Table 6.1. The present value of an annuity can also be calculated using the following equation:

$$PV_{n,r} = \sum \left[\frac{1}{(1 + r)^n} \right] \times \text{Amount to be received or paid in each period}$$

$$= \frac{1}{r} \times \left[1 - \frac{1}{(1 + r)^n} \right] \times \text{Amount to be received or paid in each period}$$

Applying this formula to option 4 gives the following:

$$\text{PV of an annuity}_{n,r} = \frac{1}{r} \times \left[1 - \frac{1}{(1 + r)^n}\right] \times \text{Amount to be received or paid in each period}$$

$$\text{PV of an annuity}_{6,0.06} = \frac{1}{0.06} \times \left[1 - \frac{1}{(1 + 0.06)^6}\right] \times \$250$$

$$= \$1,229.33$$

This is the same amount that we calculated in Table 6.1. Note that the n in this formula refers to the number of periods for which the cash flow will be received.

The formula can only be used if the following conditions are met:

- The cash flow is the same in each year.

- The same discount rate is applied to each year's cash flow.

- The cash flow occurs in every year beginning one year from the present.

If *any* of these conditions isn't met the formula doesn't apply and the individual cash flows must be evaluated on a year-by-year basis. Let's look at an example of an annuity.

Example 5: Tuttle Inc. Tuttle Inc. (Tuttle) can invest in a business opportunity paying $5,000,000 at the end of each of the next five years. Assuming the appropriate discount rate is 12 percent, what is the present value of the payments Tuttle would receive by investing in the opportunity? What is the maximum amount that Tuttle should pay to invest in the business opportunity? The answer can be obtained by applying the formula for the present value of an annuity.

$$\text{PV of an annuity}_{n,r} = \frac{1}{r} \times \left[1 - \frac{1}{(1 + r)^n}\right] \times \text{Amount to be received or paid in each period}$$

$$\text{PV of an annuity}_{5,0.12} = \frac{1}{0.12} \times \left[1 - \frac{1}{(1 + 0.12)^5}\right] \times \$5,000,000$$

$$= \$18,023,881$$

The present value of a series of $5,000,000 payments to be received at the end of each of the next five years at a discount rate of 12 percent is $18,023,881. This means that Tuttle would pay no more than $18,023,881 to invest in this business opportunity. By paying $18,023,881, Tuttle is earning exactly 12 percent on its investment, which is what it requires (that's why the 12 percent discount rate is used). If Tuttle had to pay more than $18,023,881 it would earn less than 12 percent, which wouldn't be acceptable.

Discounting is relevant for a number of accounting issues. For example, if a company makes sales on credit where payment isn't due for a long time and no interest is charged on the debt, discounting helps determine how much revenue should be recognized. Discounting is also relevant for many liabilities, such as leases, pensions, and other long-term obligations. Later in this chapter, we will examine an accounting application of the time value of money.

KNOWLEDGE CHECK

❑ What is the formula used to determine the present value of $1 to be received sometime in the future?

❑ What is the present value of $100 to be received in ten years if the discount rate is 9 percent? ($42.24)

❑ What is an annuity?

A famous professional athlete recently signed a one-year contract with his team for $15,000,000. Because the team was having financial problems, the athlete agreed to accept the $15,000,000 in equal payments of $750,000 over the next 20 years. The team stated at a press conference that the $15,000,000 justly rewarded the best player in the game with the highest one-year salary in the history of the sport, exceeding the previous high salary of $9,500,000.

Do you agree with the team's statement that the salary is the highest in the history of the sport? Explain your answer. Assume a discount rate of 10 percent and that payments are received at the end of each year.

Answer: If the previous high salary of $9,500,000 was paid in one year, the $15,000,000 salary is nowhere near the previous high. The present value of a series of $750,000 payments received over 20 years is

$$PV_{n,r} = \frac{1}{r} \times \left[1 - \frac{1}{(1+r)^n} \right] \times \text{Amount to be received or paid}$$

$$\text{PV of an annuity}_{20,0.10} = \frac{1}{0.10} \times \left[1 - \frac{1}{(1+0.10)^{20}} \right] \times \$750,000$$

$$= \$6,385,173$$

Because the payments on the contract are spread over 20 years, the present value of the athlete's salary is $6,385,173. Receiving $750,000 over 20 years is equivalent to receiving $6,385,173 today. In nominal dollar terms, the athlete is receiving more money than any athlete before him. However, comparing the present value of the payments made under different contracts is a more legitimate way of comparing the contracts.

RECEIVABLES

Receivables are amounts owing to an entity. Usually these amounts will be received in cash, but goods and services can also be receivable. Most receivables result from selling goods and services to customers on credit. These are usually called *accounts receivable*. Receivables can also represent amounts owing by shareholders and employees (shareholder/employee loans receivable), tax refunds (taxes receivable), amounts owing from investments (interest and dividends receivable), proceeds due from the sale of capital assets, and so on. Receivables are usually current assets, but if an amount owing is to be received in more than a year it would be classified as non-current. Our discussion will focus on accounts receivable because these are the most common and significant receivables reported on financial statements, but the concepts generally apply to all types of receivables.

Accounts receivable arise when revenue is recognized but payment isn't received. As discussed in Chapter 4, the journal entry to record a credit sale is

Dr. Accounts receivable (asset +)	xxx	
Cr. Revenue (revenue +, owners' equity +)		xxx

When the customer pays the amount owed, the journal entry recorded is

Dr. Cash (asset +)	xxx	
Cr. Accounts receivable (asset −)		xxx

Accounts receivable are essentially loans to customers. Most businesses would probably prefer to do business on a cash basis because selling on credit lengthens an entity's cash cycle and introduces the risk that amounts owed won't be collected. There are also costs to administer the credit program—doing credit checks, processing billings and collections, and pursuing customers that don't pay. However, selling on credit is the normal, practical way of doing business in non-retail transactions.

For most retail businesses, credit is offered through major credit cards such as MasterCard and Visa, but credit can be an important and lucrative business in the retail industry. Companies such as Sears Canada, Home Depot, Canadian Tire, and Hudson's Bay Company offer their own credit cards to their customers and earn interest from customers who don't pay for purchases within the allowed period of time.

Financial statements prepared in accordance with IFRS report receivables at their net realizable value (NRV)—the estimated amount that will be collected. When a company sells on credit, a number of events can reduce the amount actually collected:

- Customers might not pay what they owe due to financial problems, disputes over whether the goods or services were delivered or acceptable, or simply because they are dishonest.

- Some customers may demand refunds or price reductions if they aren't satisfied with the goods or services provided.

- Customers may receive a discount if they pay their bills early. For example, an entity may offer a customer a 2 percent discount if the amount owed is paid within 10 days. Thus, if the customer owes $1,000, only $980 has to be paid if payment is made within 10 days. After 10 days the full amount must be paid.

Under accrual accounting, bad debts, returns, and discounts are costs of doing business in the period the revenue is recognized and the effect of these items is to reduce net income (by reducing sales or increasing expenses) and reduce accounts receivable. Importantly, management won't know the amount of bad debts, returns, and discounts at the end of a period when financial statements are being prepared so management has to make estimates.

Reporting receivables at NRV makes sense for many stakeholders. NRV is most useful for cash flow prediction and liquidity analysis because it represents the amount of cash that will likely be received. For the stewardship and management evaluation objectives, knowing the actual amount owed by customers and the estimated amount that will be collected are useful for assessing how well receivables, credit and collection, returns, and discounts are being managed.

Return to Exhibit 6.1 and examine the information about TransAlta's receivables on the face of the balance sheet and in Notes 8 and 14. TransAlta reported accounts receivable of $542 million and $546 million on December 31, 2008 and 2007 respectively. These are the amounts TransAlta expects to collect from customers. Note 8 shows that at end of 2008 the company had gross accounts receivable of $599 million and estimated $57 million to be uncollectible (allowance for doubtful accounts). TransAlta also reported income taxes receivable of $61 million on December 31, 2008, meaning the company is expecting to receive money from the government because it paid too much in income taxes. Finally, notice that TransAlta reports long-term receivables as non-current assets on December 31, 2008 and 2007. These will be discussed later in the chapter.

www.transalta.com

When a customer makes a purchase using a credit card such as Visa or MasterCard the amount isn't reported as accounts receivable. The credit card receipt is equivalent to cash; in most cases the money is transferred electronically to the merchant's bank account. The account receivable belongs to the credit card company. The merchant pays a fee for being able to accept the credit cards for payment. For example, a $100 purchase made using a MasterCard might cost a business 1 percent of the charged amount, or $1. When the merchant receives payment from the bank it would receive $99 instead of $100.

A credit card transaction could be recorded in two ways. First, it could simply record the sale in the amount of the cash received. For a $100 sale with a service charge of $1 the journal entry would be

Dr. Cash (asset +)	99	
Cr. Revenue (revenue +, owners' equity +)		99

To record the sale of goods using a credit card at the net amount

Second, it could record the sale at the amount the customer agreed to pay and create a separate account for the service charge. In this case, the journal entry would be

Dr. Cash (asset +)	99	
Dr. Credit card service fee (expense +, owners' equity −)	1	
Cr. Revenue (revenue +, owners' equity +)		100
To record the sale of goods using a credit card at the gross amount		

This entry provides information about the cost of allowing customers to use credit cards. With the first entry this information is lost. Also, with the second approach the amount of revenue reported isn't affected by how the customer paid—$100 of revenue would be recorded regardless of whether the customer paid by cash, cheque, or credit card.

INSIGHT

For private companies that don't follow IFRS or Canadian GAAP for Private Enterprises, the amount reported for accounts receivable could represent gross receivables, net receivables, or receivables net of some estimates (such as bad debts) but not others (such as returns). A stakeholder must be very careful to understand exactly what is represented by the reported numbers. This is especially true for financial statements prepared primarily for tax purposes. Estimates such as returns and discounts can't be deducted when calculating taxable income so a preparer might not include these estimates in the financial statements. For tax purposes an allowance for uncollectible amounts can be deducted.

Accounting for Uncollectible Receivables

A cost of doing business on credit is that some customers don't pay what they owe and this cost must be accounted for. Accounting for uncollectible receivables must address two effects. First, an expense must be recorded to reflect the cost of amounts not collected. Second, accounts receivable must be decreased by the estimated uncollected amount so the balance sheet reflects the amount that will be collected.

The easiest way to account for uncollectible receivables, or bad debts, is to simply write off the receivable when it becomes clear that a customer won't be paying. In this approach, known as the **direct writeoff method**, an amount owing from a customer is removed from the list of receivables and an expense recorded when management decides it won't be collected. The journal entry would be

Dr. Bad debt expense (expense +, owners' equity −)	xxx	
Cr. Receivables (assets −)		xxx

For example, in September 2015 the management of Killowen Inc. (Killowen) decided that $10,000 owed to it by Fredericton Ltd. wouldn't be paid. The amount had been in dispute for 18 months and management decided that pursuing the matter further wasn't worthwhile. Killowen has a December 31 year-end. If Killowen used the direct writeoff method, it would make the following journal entry in September 2015 when management decided the $10,000 wouldn't be collected:

Dr. Bad debt expense (expense +, owners' equity −)	10,000	
Cr. Accounts receivable (assets −)		10,000
To write off an uncollectible account receivable		

The direct writeoff method is simple and straightforward, but it isn't good matching. In the example, the expense for the bad debt would be recognized over the 18 months after the sale had occurred. Matching requires the cost of bad debts to be expensed in the period when the related revenue is recognized. In other words, if Killowen is using accrual accounting it shouldn't wait until it decides a customer isn't going to pay. Another problem with the direct writeoff method is that it's easily manipulated because management can pick and choose exactly when to write off accounts receivable.

If we are going to match and expense bad debts in the period in which the related revenue is recognized, an obvious question is, "How do we know which accounts to write off?" Answer: We don't know. If we knew at the time of the transaction that a customer wasn't going to pay, we wouldn't have offered them credit. Under accrual accounting, an estimate of the amount that won't be collected is made without knowing which specific receivables won't be collected.

There are two methods used to estimate the cost of bad debts:

1. the percentage-of-receivables method

2. the percentage-of-credit-sales method

With either method, the following adjusting journal entry is made each period to account for bad debts:

Dr. Bad debt expense (expense +, owners' equity −)   xxx
    Cr. Allowance for uncollectible accounts (contra-asset +)   xxx

The bad debt expense is a cost of selling on credit. The **allowance for uncollectible accounts** is a contra-asset account to accounts receivable or another receivables account representing the amount of receivables management estimates won't be collected. A contra-asset account is used as it's impossible to identify the specific receivables that won't be collected when the estimate is made. The accounts receivable account is a listing of the amount owed by each customer. An extract from the detailed list for Killowen Inc. is presented in Table 6.2. Taken together, accounts receivable and allowance for uncollectible accounts provide an estimate of the NRV of accounts receivable.

TABLE 6.2	Killowen Inc.: Selected Accounts Receivable
Killowen Inc. **Accounts Receivable Ledger** **December 31, 2015**	
Customer	**Account balance**
Charlottetown Inc.	$ 31,200.05
Dartmouth Ltd.	157,000.10
Fredericton Ltd.	25,000.92
Gander Inc.	38,500.68
Moncton Ltd.	22,250.25
Saint John Inc.	117,410.41
St. John's Ltd.	57,200.09
Total	$1,194,000.00

The Percentage-of-Receivables Method With the **percentage-of-receivables method**, managers estimate at the end of the period the amount of receivables that won't be collected. The managers determine the amount that should be in the allowance for uncollectibles account at the end of the period and the amount of debit or credit needed to bring the allowance account to bring it to the desired balance. The focus is on estimating the NRV of the ending balance of receivables. The bad debt expense isn't calculated directly—it's simply "the other side of the journal entry" required to adjust the allowance account.

For example, Killowen Inc.'s management estimates that $71,500 of its ending accounts receivable of $1,194,000 on December 31, 2015, won't be collected. The balance in the allowance account before the end-of-period adjusting entry is recorded is a credit of $5,000. (The reason why there might be a balance in the allowance account before the adjusting entry is made will be made clear shortly.) To bring the allowance account to the desired credit balance of $71,500, a credit of $66,500 is required. The following journal entry is recorded:

Dr. Bad debt expense (expense +, owners' equity −)   66,500
    Cr. Allowance for uncollectible accounts (contra-asset +)   66,500
To record the bad debt expense for 2015

This focus on calculating the balance in the allowance account is why the percentage-of-receivables method is called a *balance sheet approach*. The effect on the accounts involved can be seen in Table 6.3.

The NRV of Killowen's accounts receivable is $1,122,500 ($1,194,000 − $71,500). There is a balance in the allowance account before the adjusting entry is made on December 31, 2015 because management's estimate of the amount of receivables it wouldn't collect during 2015 wasn't correct—the estimate, which was made on December 31, 2014 was $5,000 too high. This isn't surprising. An estimate is a prediction of the future and it's unlikely to be exact. When the adjusting entry is made management is making an educated guess of the amount of receivables that won't be collected. The actual amount will only be known long after the period ends. As we will see later in this chapter, managers can use estimates as a way of managing financial statement numbers to achieve their reporting objectives.

How does management estimate the amount of receivables that won't be collected? One way is to use an **aging schedule**—a technique that estimates uncollectible accounts receivable based on the length of time they have been unpaid. Current receivables are ones that are due within the period the entity allows customers to pay. If the entity allows customers to pay within 30 days, receivables that have been outstanding for 30 days or less are current. The remaining receivables are then classified by how long overdue they are.

TABLE 6.3	Killowen Inc.: Accounts Receivable, Allowance for Uncollectible Accounts, and Bad Debt Expense		
Killowen Inc. **December 31, 2015**			
	Accounts receivable	**Allowance for uncollectible accounts**	**Bad debt expense**
Balances on December 31, 2015, before adjusting entry	$1,194,000	$ (5,000)	
Adjusting entry		(66,500)	66,500
Ending balances on December 31, 2015	1,194,000	(71,500)	66,500

Management uses historical information about the proportion of each category of receivables that hasn't been collected in the past, along with current knowledge of factors that might cause those historical percentages to change, to estimate the amount of current accounts receivable that won't be collected. Typically, the older a receivable is the less likely it is to be collected. Note that historical information might be helpful for making a prediction but you can't assume the future will be the same as the past. Circumstances such as an economic slowdown or a change in the credit terms an entity offers can weaken the relationship between the past and the future. An aging schedule for Killowen is shown in Table 6.4.

TABLE 6.4	Killowen Inc.: Aging Schedule				

Killowen Inc.
Aging Schedule
December 31, 2009

	Current	1 to 30 days overdue	31 to 90 days overdue	Over 90 days overdue	Total
Amount	$950,000	$125,000	$72,000	$47,000	$1,194,000
Percentage estimated to be uncollectible	1%	4%	40%	60%	
Amount estimated to be uncollectible	$9,500	$5,000	$28,800	$28,200	$71,500

Based on the aging schedule, Killowen would report gross accounts receivable of $1,194,000, less an allowance for uncollectible accounts of $71,500. Information about bad debts and uncollectible accounts receivable can be used by stakeholders to assess the efficiency and effectiveness of an entity's credit and collection policies as well as the valuation of the receivables. Companies following IFRS must disclose all changes to the allowance account during the year, so stakeholders can understand the estimates being made.

Exhibit 6.3 provides information from the management discussion and analysis section of the 2008 annual report of Gildan Activewear Inc. (Gildan), a marketer and manufacturer of activewear, socks, and underwear.[4] Panel A shows an aging schedule for accounts receivable on October 5, 2008, Gildan's year-end. Panel B shows fiscal 2008's reconciliation of the allowance for doubtful accounts, the bad debt expense, and amount of accounts receivable written off during the year. Panel C explains Gildan's approach to estimating bad debts; notice the emphasis on judgment. From this information it appears Gildan is effective in managing its receivables, with only about 1.3 percent estimated to be uncollectible. Of course, this evaluation would be better with comparative information, but 2008 is the first time Gildan provided this information.

The aging schedule isn't only an internal device for calculating uncollectible receivables. Banks will usually require this schedule if the receivables are security for a loan and/or the maximum amount to be borrowed is a percentage of receivables. Banks usually won't accept receivables more than 90 days old as security because they have a high risk of being uncollectible.

 KNOWLEDGE CHECK

www.mcgrawhill
connect.ca

You have been given the following list of aged accounts receivable for Onward Inc. (Onward) on December 31, 2014:

Current	$175,000
1–30 days overdue	32,000
31–60 days overdue	12,500
61–90 days overdue	5,700
Over 90 days overdue	2,300

Onward's management estimates that it will collect 98 percent of the current accounts receivable, 94 percent of the receivables 1–30 days overdue, 80 percent of those 31–60 days overdue, 65 percent of those 61–90 days overdue, and 30 percent those more than 90 days overdue. Onward uses the percentage-of-receivables method for estimating bad debts. There is a credit balance of $1,025 in allowance for uncollectible accounts on December 31, 2014, before the adjusting entry is made.

Required:

❑ How much of each category of accounts receivable does Onward not expect to collect?

❑ Prepare the journal entry that Onward should make on December 31, 2014, to record the bad debt expense.

EXHIBIT 6.3

Gildan Activewear Inc.: Receivables Aging and Reconciliation of the Allowance for Doubtful Accounts

Panel A—Aging Schedule on October 5, 2008

(in $ millions)

	October 5, 2008
Not past due	186.0
Past due 0-30 days	15.7
Past due 31-120 days	5.1
Past due 121-180 days	2.3
Past due over 180 days	–
Trade receivables	209.1
Less allowance for doubtful accounts	(2.8)
Total trade receivables	206.3

Panel B—Reconciliation of the Allowance for Doubtful Accounts for Fiscal 2008

(in $ millions)

Balance as at September 30, 2007	2.0
Bad debt expense	4.5
Write-off of accounts receivable	(4.0)
Increase due to acquisition of Prewett	0.3
Balance as at October 5, 2008	2.8

Allowance for Doubtful Accounts

Trade accounts receivable consists of amounts due from our normal business activities. We maintain an allowance for doubtful accounts to reflect expected credit losses. We provide for bad debts based on collection history and specific risks identified on a customer-by-customer basis. A considerable amount of judgment is required to assess the ultimate realization of accounts receivable and the credit-worthiness of each customer. Furthermore, these judgments must be continuously evaluated and updated. Uncollected accounts are written off through the allowance for doubtful accounts. We are not able to predict changes in the financial condition of our customers, and if circumstances related to our customers' financial condition deteriorate, our estimates of the recoverability of our trade receivables could be materially affected and we may be required to record additional allowances. Alternatively, if we provide more allowances than we need, we may reverse a portion of such provisions in future periods based on our actual collection experience.

Percentage-of-Credit-Sales Method Managers can estimate the bad debt expense by using a percentage of credit sales recognized in the period. This is called the **percentage-of-credit-sales method**. The logic is that some portion of credit sales won't be collected in each period, and that amount is the bad debt expense. Cash sales are not considered because, of course, they are 100 percent collected. Again, management bases its estimate on the historical collection rate of credit sales and knowledge of any changes that might cause it to change. If Killowen had credit sales of $9,375,000 during 2015 and management estimated that 0.8 percent wouldn't be collected, the adjusting journal entry on December 31, 2015, would be

Dr. Bad debt expense (expenses +, owners' equity −)   75,000
    Cr. Allowance for uncollectible accounts (contra-asset +)   75,000
To record the bad debt expense for 2015

Unlike the percentage-of-receivables method, which takes a balance sheet approach, the percentage-of-credit-sales method follows an *income statement approach*. Its focus is the bad debt expense, an income statement account. The credit to the allowance account isn't calculated directly. This method gives a better matching of costs and benefits because the amount expensed is directly related to the amount of credit sales recognized in the period. Because this method focuses on the income statement, the estimate of the NRV of accounts receivable may not be as accurate as with the percentage-of-receivables approach.

In any year, the estimated bad debts won't equal the actual amount of uncollected receivables—that's the nature of estimates. However, the annual bad debt estimate may sometimes be consistently too high or too low; that is, the percentage of credit sales used doesn't reflect the actual amount of bad debts incurred each year. Management may not be changing or aware of the need to change the assumptions for estimating bad debts in response to a change in the environment. If the bad debt expense is consistently too high a credit balance builds up in the allowance account and net accounts receivable will be understated (the amount reported will be lower than what is likely to be collected). The opposite is true if the bad debt expense is consistently too low. Eventually, an adjusting entry will be needed to put the allowance account in line with the actual economic situation.

CANADIAN GAAP FOR PRIVATE ENTERPRISES

Canadian GAAP for Private Enterprises doesn't require disclosure of the details of the allowance for doubtful accounts, so stakeholders only know the NRV of accounts receivable, which makes analysis difficult. Some external stakeholders, such as banks, have the power to request additional information on things such as changes to allowance for uncollectible accounts.

Writing Off Receivables We have examined methods for estimating uncollectible amounts. But what happens when we finally know who isn't going to pay? For both estimation methods the receivable is removed from the receivables listing when a specific item is identified as being uncollectible. A credit to accounts receivable reduces the balance in the account. The allowance account is reduced by a debit to it because the specific uncollectible account identified is now a reality instead of an estimate, and the amount is transferred from the "estimate account" (uncollectibles) to the "actual account" (receivables).

When Killowen Inc.'s management decides the $10,000 owing from Fredericton Ltd. isn't going to be collected, it would make the following entry:

Dr. Allowance for uncollectible accounts (contra-asset −)   10,000
    Cr. Accounts receivable—Fredericton (asset −)   10,000
To write off a $10,000 account receivable from Fredericton Ltd.

This entry writes off, or removes from the accounting records, the account receivable from Fredericton Ltd. If we examined the accounts receivable ledger in Table 6.2 after the writeoff, we would find that Fredericton's amount owing is $15,000.92 instead of $25,000.92. A writeoff has no effect on the net amount of accounts receivable (accounts receivable − allowance for uncollectibles). This can be seen by comparing Killowen's receivables before and after the writeoff of the $10,000 owed by Fredericton. The comparison is shown in Table 6.5. The allowance and accounts receivable both decrease by $10,000, but net accounts receivable remains the same.

TABLE 6.5	Killowen Inc.: Accounts Receivable before and after Writeoff	
	Before writeoff	**After writeoff**
Accounts receivable	$1,194,000	$1,184,000
Less: Allowance for uncollectible accounts	71,500	61,500
Accounts receivable, net	$1,122,500	$1,122,500

Recognize that writing off an account receivable has no effect on the income statement. The income statement effect occurs when the adjusting entry to record the bad debt expense and the adjustment to allowance for uncollectible accounts is made.

Comparison of the Methods Three methods for addressing the problem of accounting for uncollectible amounts—direct writeoff, percentage-of-receivables, and percentage-of-credit sales—have been discussed. Under accrual accounting, the direct writeoff method isn't acceptable because it doesn't match expenses to revenues. The two estimation methods are used in practice and both provide a bad debt expense and report accounts receivable at NRV. These methods require management judgment to determine the amount of the bad debt expense, the balance in the allowance account, and the decision to write off a specific account receivable. This need for judgment makes estimating bad debts a tool managers can use to "manage the numbers" in the financial statements.

Returns Adjustments to the financial statements for estimated returns (goods sold but expected to be returned by customers) must also be made. Like uncollectible amounts, estimated returns are recorded in a contra-asset account (contra-accounts receivable). Unlike uncollectibles, returns aren't reported as an expense but are netted against revenue (accumulated in a contra-revenue account). Revenue reported on the income statement is normally shown after estimated returns have been deducted, so a stakeholder doesn't see the amount of returns (which could be useful information). If estimated sales returns aren't recorded, accounts receivable and revenue will be overstated. For example, if Killowen estimated that $5,000 of its credit sales were going to be returned it would record the following journal entry:

Dr. Sales return (contra-revenue)	10,000	
Cr. Allowance for sales returns (contra asset +)		10,000
To record estimate sales returns		

Long-Term Receivables

Receivables aren't always current assets. Amounts owing from customers or others can be due in more than one year or operating cycle. Receivables due in more than a year or operating cycle are classified as long-term assets. TransAlta's balance sheet in Exhibit 6.1 shows long-term receivables of $14 million on December 31, 2008. Note 14 in the exhibit explains how the company can recover certain costs related to retiring assets and that the amount owing is recorded at the present value of the amount to be received.

When payment isn't due for a long time, or if it's spread out over a long period, then the time value of money becomes a consideration. If interest isn't being paid on the long-term receivable or if the interest rate charged is below the market rate, the amount of revenue recognized and the receivable will be too high if the time value of money is ignored.

Let's look at an example. On December 31, 2015 Winnipeg Inc. (Winnipeg) sold goods to Regina Ltd. (Regina) for $200,000. Because of Regina's financial difficulties, Winnipeg agreed to accept payment in full in two years, on January 2, 2018. Regina isn't required to pay interest. Regina's owners have personally guaranteed the debt so Winnipeg is confident it will receive its money and recognized the revenue when the goods were shipped.

How much revenue should Winnipeg recognize when the goods are shipped and how should it account for the receivable? Clearly, Winnipeg hasn't earned $200,000 because the present value of the money it will receive in two years is less than $200,000. Assuming a discount rate of 8 percent we can calculate the present value of $200,000 to be received in two years:

$$PV_{n,r} = \frac{1}{(1 + r)^n} \times \text{Amount to be received or paid}$$

$$PV_{2,0.08} = \frac{1}{(1 + 0.08)^2} \times \$200,000$$

$$= \$171,468$$

If we consider the time value of money, Winnipeg should recognize $171,468 of revenue in 2015 for the sale to Regina. The journal entry Winnipeg would make in 2015 is

Dr. Long-term receivable (asset +)   171,468
    Cr. Revenue (revenue +, shareholders' equity +)   171,468
To record the sale of goods to Regina Ltd.

You're probably wondering how we can record a receivable for $171,468 when Winnipeg will be receiving $200,000 in 2018. The difference between the amount Winnipeg recognizes as revenue in 2015 and the cash it will receive in January 2018 is interest. Even though Winnipeg and Regina agreed there wouldn't be any interest in their deal, accountants would argue the interest is really there but hidden. So from an accountant's perspective there is a sale for $171,468 and

TABLE 6.6   Winnipeg Inc.: Long-Term Receivables

	Cash	Current accounts receivable	Long-term receivable	Revenue	Interest revenue	Journal entry	
December 31, 2015 (transactional entry)			171,468	171,468		Dr. Long-term receivable 171,468 Cr. Revenue 171,468	Recognition of revenue on sale of goods to Regina Ltd.
Ending balance sheet December 31, 2015			**171,468**				
December 31, 2016 (adjusting entry)			13,717		13,717	Dr. Interest expense 13,717 Cr. Long-term account receivable 13,717	Recognition of interest revenue earned in 2016. Interest is calculated based on the receivable on December 31, 2015. The interest is added to the long-term receivable account. Interest earned = $171,468 × 0.08. Amounts are rounded to the nearest dollar.
Ending balance sheet December 31, 2016			185,185				
December 31, 2017 (adjusting entry)			14,815		14,815	Dr. Interest expense 14,815 Cr. Long-term account receivable 14,815	Recognition of interest revenue earned in 2018. Interest earned = $185,185 × 0.08.
December 31, 2017 (adjusting entry)		200,000	(200,000)			Dr. Accounts receivable 200,000 Cr. Long-term account receivable 200,000	To reclassify the receivable as current.
Ending balance sheet December 31, 2017		**200,000**					
January 2, 2018	200,000	(200,000)				Dr. Cash 200,000 Cr. Accounts receivable 200,000	Collection of the $200,000 from Regina Ltd.

$28,532 in interest ($200,000 − $171,468). Over the two-year period Winnipeg will recognize interest revenue and increase the long-term receivable by the amount of the interest revenue. Winnipeg's journal entry each year would be

> Dr. Long-term receivable (asset +)   xxx
>   Cr. Interest revenue (revenue +, shareholders' equity +)   xxx
>   To accrue interest revenue on the long-term receivable from Regina Ltd.

The effect on the accounts involved in the sale to Regina are shown in Table 6.6.

When the time value of money is considered, the sale to Regina is equivalent to selling the goods for $171,468 cash on the transaction date and then earning $28,532 in interest by financing the sale. Over the two years $200,000 of revenue is recognized but the timing and type of revenue changes. Table 6.6 shows that Winnipeg recognizes interest revenue each year, but because it won't be paid until 2018 the amount accrued each year is added to the long-term receivable. Winnipeg's December 31, 2017 balance sheet reports a $200,000 receivable, the amount Regina originally agreed to pay. The amount is classified as a current asset because it's then due within one year.

If Regina was paying interest at the market rate, it would be unnecessary to discount the cash flow. The revenue and receivable would be set up at $200,000 in 2015 and the interest revenue would be recorded each year.

FINANCIAL STATEMENT ANALYSIS ISSUES

Earnings Management—Hidden Reserves

In principle, errors in estimates aren't a major concern. Predicting the future is difficult, so no one should expect management to get the estimates "right" each time (or anytime, for that matter). But if managers' errors are biased, that is always higher or always lower than the actual amount in the end then amounts in the financial statements can be significantly misstated. Making biased estimates (have intentional "errors") allows managers to manage earnings.

Hidden reserves are undisclosed accounting choices by which managers can manage earnings and other financial information with the intention of satisfying their self-interests. Using hidden reserves is an abuse of accounting information; it undermines the usefulness and credibility of financial statements. While hidden reserves are inappropriate, the suspected use of them makes it important for stakeholders to understand them. A simple example will show how management can manage earnings by using accounting estimates to move profits from one period to another through the allowance for uncollectible accounts and bad debt expense.

In 2015, Discovery Ltd. (Discovery), a public company, enjoyed its most successful year ever. Its performance exceeded the expectations of management, investors, and stock market watchers. Sales in 2015 were $50,000,000 and net income should have been $3,000,000. However, in late 2015 managers realized that 2016 would be less successful and they feared the poorer performance in 2016 would have a negative effect on Discovery's stock price and the managers' bonuses.

For its December 31, 2015 financial statements, Discovery's management decided to increase the allowance for uncollectible accounts to 4.5 percent of the ending balance of accounts receivable. Historically, Discovery had used 3 percent of year-end accounts receivable to estimate its allowance for uncollectibles, which had proven to be a reasonable estimate. Management justified the change by arguing it was concerned about the collectibility of a number of receivables so a more cautious (conservative) allowance was appropriate. Because IFRS tends to be conservative in nature and accounting estimates can be very difficult for auditors to verify, you have a situation that managers can use to their advantage. (There will be more said about conservative accounting in the next chapter.) By increasing the percentage-of-receivables that was expected to be uncollectible, Discovery increased its bad debt expense in 2015 from $405,000 to $607,500 and decreased net income by $202,500. Table 6.7 shows the activity in Discovery Ltd.'s accounts if it were creating a hidden reserve.

As expected, in 2016 Discovery's performance wasn't as strong as in 2015. Sales declined to $47,000,000. During 2016, $405,000 of accounts receivable were written off (which turned out to be 3 percent of the December 31, 2015 accounts receivable). At the end of 2016 management decided that the receivables it was "concerned" about a year earlier were no longer a problem and, accordingly, Discovery would return to its usual 3 percent estimate. Because only $405,000 of accounts receivable had to be written off during 2016 there was a credit balance of $202,500 in the allowance account before the 2016 adjusting entry. For the allowance account to have the desired balance of $397,500 at the end of 2016 (representing 3 percent of the 2016 year-end accounts receivable—$13,250,000 × 0.03), it needed to be increased (credited) by $195,000 making the bad debt expense for 2016 only $195,000. These entries can be seen in Table 6.7.

Table 6.8 shows income statements and accounts receivable information comparing when Discovery creates a hidden reserve and when it doesn't. By using a hidden reserve, Discovery is able to report a profit increase of $207,500 from 2015 to 2016, an increase of over 7 percent

TABLE 6.7   Discovery Inc.: Account Activity Showing How Hidden Reserves Can Be Used to Manipulate Earnings

The zero balance in the allowance account means that during 2015 the exact amount of the estimate of bad debts made at December 31, 2016 was written off during 2015.

The pre-adjusting balance in the bad debt expense account is zero because the account would have been closed at the end of 2015 and no entries would be made to the account until the adjusting entries were made.

	Cash (B/S)	Accounts receivable (B/S)	Allowance for doubtful accounts (B/S)	Revenue (I/S)	Bad debt expense (I/S)
31/12/15 (pre-adjusting entries)		13,500,000	0		0
31/12/15 adjusting entries			(607,500)		(607,500)
31/12/15 (final)		13,500,000	(607,500)		(607,500)*
During 2016					
Sales		47,000,000		47,000,000	
Collections	46,845,000	(46,845,000)			
Bad debts written off		(405,000)	405,000		
31/12/16 (pre-adjusting balances)		13,250,000	(202,500)		
31/12/16 adjusting entries			(195,000)		(195,000)
31/12/16 (final)		13,250,000	(397,500)		(195,000)[1]

The balance in allowance for doubtful accounts is equal to 4.5% of closing accounts receivable.

During 2016 management writes off $405,000 in receivables that it decides are uncollectible.

*The balance in the bad debt expense account would become zero when the closing entry is made. The closing entry isn't shown in this example.

The amount that must be added to the allowance account for it to have the desired balance of 3% of year-end accounts receivable at the end of 2016. By making too large an estimate of uncollectibles in 2015, the expense required in 2016 is lower than it would have been.

TABLE 6.8	Discovery Ltd.: Extracts from Financial Statements			
Discovery Limited **Extracts from the December 31, 2015 and 2016,** **Financial Statements (in thousands)**				
	No hidden reserves		**Using hidden reserves**	
	2015	**2016**	**2015**	**2016**
Revenue	$50,000	$47,000	$50,000	$47,000
Expenses (except bad debts)	46,595	43,800	46,595	43,800
Bad debt expense	405	397.5	607.5	195
Net income	$ 3,000	$ 2,802.5	$ 2,797.5	$ 3,005
Accounts receivable	$13,500	$13,250	$13,500	$13,250
Allowance for uncollectible accounts	405	397.5	607.5	397.5

instead of a decrease of $197,500, and a positive earnings trend rather than a negative one. Note that total income over the two years is the same under either scenario but by altering the allowance for uncollectible accounts, Discovery is able to shift income from 2015 to 2016.

This example is set up to makes the problem, motivation, and effect of the uncertainty of accounting estimates transparent. It allows you to see how management can use the uncertainties to achieve its reporting objectives. In reality, it's hard to see these hidden choices so it's difficult to know anything unusual is occurring. This is why these types of manipulations are called hidden reserves.

You might be wondering how managers can get away with behaviour that is clearly unethical, violates the spirit of fair presentation of the financial statements, and, as a result, is inconsistent with IFRS. One reason is that it can be difficult to evaluate the reasonableness of estimates. As long as an estimate falls within a reasonable range and managers can provide a satisfactory explanation for it, a change can be difficult to quarrel with. After all, management knows the entity best so is best able to make estimates, and is responsible for the financial statements. Additional disclosures of estimates (for example the reconciliation of changes to the allowance account provided by Gildan Activewear in Panel B of Exhibit 6.3) are very helpful.

It is important to emphasize that the problem shown in the example isn't that the estimate of uncollectibles changed. The problem is with the motivation for the change. For financial statement information to be useful it must reflect current economic circumstances. If there is legitimate concern about the collectibility of receivables then increasing the allowance for uncollectibles is appropriate. Unfortunately, it's difficult to tell whether management is providing information or satisfying its self-interests.

 INSIGHT

Hidden Reserves

Are hidden reserves a real problem? Back in the late 1990s Arthur Levitt, then chairman of the U.S. Securities and Exchange Commission, commenting on the problems with financial reporting, said, "Companies stash accruals in 'cookie jar' reserves during the good economic times and reach into them when necessary in the bad times."[5]

Mr. Levitt's comments highlight the problem of entities using the flexibility available in GAAP to manage the information reported in their financial statements. While many years have passed since Mr. Levitt made his comment, examples continue to arise of managers using hidden reserves to manage the earnings of their companies. The hidden reserve is a problem all stakeholders should be aware of.

The allowance for the uncollectible accounts estimate is only one of many available to management for creating hidden reserves. Estimates for sales returns and warranty liabilities can also be used. The use of hidden reserves isn't limited to public companies. Managers of private companies might also want to have a "rainy day" fund.

Current and Quick Ratios

In this chapter we have examined two of an entity's most liquid assets—cash and receivables. We will discuss one other liquid asset, investments in shares and debt of other companies, in Chapter 11. In Chapter 2 we examined the current ratio, an indicator of whether an entity had adequate resources to meet its current obligations. A problem with the current ratio is that all current assets included in the numerator may not be liquid.

Exhibit 6.4 provides the balance sheets and statements of income from the 2008 annual report of Magna International Inc. (Magna), the Canadian-based global automotive supplier.[6] Among Magna's December 31, 2008 current assets are $1.647 billion of inventory and $115 million of prepaid expenses. Inventory often converts to cash relatively slowly (look back at the discussion of the cash lag in Chapter 5), calling into question whether inventory is truly a liquid asset. For example, Magna's inventory includes $605 million of raw materials and supplies (see Note 7 in Exhibit 6.4). Raw materials are the inputs Magna uses to produce auto parts and it can be many months before the parts are produced, sold, and paid for by customers. While some inventory can be sold quickly and considered liquid (for example gold and silver), in many cases it isn't a liquid asset. Prepaid expenses, for instance, include amounts paid in advance for insurance, rent, or services to be received in the future. Prepaids represent cash already spent so they won't be converted to cash in the ordinary course of business.

To compensate for these problems, the **quick** or **acid test** ratio is a stricter test of liquidity. It's stricter because it excludes less liquid assets. The quick or acid test ratio is defined as

$$\text{Quick ratio} = \frac{\text{Quick assets}}{\text{Current liabilities}} = \frac{\text{Cash} + \text{Cash equivalents} + \text{Marketable securities} + \text{Receivables}}{\text{Current liabilities}}$$

Quick assets are assets that are cash or can be realized in cash fairly quickly. Marketable securities are investments such as shares and debt of public companies (particularly investments in public companies). Magna's quick ratio for 2008 is

$$\text{Quick ratio} = \frac{\$5,589,000,000}{\$5,093,000,000} = 1.10$$

| EXHIBIT 6.4 | Magna International Inc.: Balance Sheets and Income Statements |

MAGNA INTERNATIONAL INC.
Consolidated Balance Sheets

[U.S. dollars in millions]

As at December 31,

	Note	2008	2007
ASSETS			
Current assets			
Cash and cash equivalents		$ 2,757	$ 2,954
Accounts receivable		2,821	3,981
Inventories	7	1,647	1,681
Income taxes receivable	11	11	—
Prepaid expenses and other		115	154
		7,351	8,770
Investments	8, 15	194	280
Fixed assets, net	3, 9	3,701	4,307
Goodwill	3, 10	1,160	1,237
Future tax assets	11	182	280
Other assets	12	601	469
		$ 13,189	$ 15,343
LIABILITIES AND SHAREHOLDERS' EQUITY			
Current liabilities			
Bank indebtedness	14	$ 909	$ 89
Accounts payable		2,744	3,492
Accrued salaries and wages		448	544
Other accrued liabilities	13	835	911
Income taxes payable	11	—	248
Long-term debt due within one year	14	157	374
		5,093	5,658
Deferred revenue		31	60
Long-term debt	14	143	337
Other long-term liabilities	15	423	394
Future tax liabilities	11	136	252
		5,826	6,701
Shareholders' equity			
Capital stock	17		
Class A Subordinate Voting Shares			
[issued: 2008 – 111,879,059; 2007 – 115,344,184]		3,605	3,708
Class B Shares			
[convertible into Class A Subordinate Voting Shares]			
[issued: 726,829]		—	—
Contributed surplus	18	67	58
Retained earnings	17	3,357	3,526
Accumulated other comprehensive income	17, 19	334	1,350
		7,363	8,642
		$ 13,189	$ 15,343

The ratio means that for every dollar of current liabilities, Magna has $1.10 of quick assets. Assessing whether this is a reasonable ratio involves comparison. Magna's quick and current ratios for 2003 through 2008 and industry ratios for those years are provided in Table 6.9:

| TABLE 6.9 | Magna International Inc. and Its Industry, 2003–2008: Current and Quick Ratios |

	2008	2007	2006	2005	2004	2003
Magna: Current ratio	1.44	1.55	1.48	1.50	1.55	1.56
Magna: Quick ratio	1.10	1.23	1.15	1.17	1.18	1.21
Industry: Current ratio	1.62	1.79	1.42	1.57	1.40	1.48
Industry: Quick ratio	1.13	1.36	1.01	1.19	0.95	1.08

| EXHIBIT 6.4 | (continued) Magna International Inc.: Balance Sheets and Income Statements |

MAGNA INTERNATIONAL INC.
Consolidated Statements of Income and Comprehensive (Loss) Income

[U.S. dollars in millions, except per share figures]

Years ended December 31,

	Note	2008	2007	2006
Sales		$ 23,704	$ 26,067	$ 24,180
Costs and expenses				
Cost of goods sold		20,982	22,599	21,211
Depreciation and amortization		873	872	790
Selling, general and administrative	8, 16, 19	1,319	1,461	1,360
Interest income, net	14	(62)	(62)	(14)
Equity income		(19)	(11)	(13)
Impairment charges	3	283	56	54
Income from operations before income taxes		328	1,152	792
Income taxes	11	257	489	264
Net income		71	663	528
Other comprehensive (loss) income:	19			
Net realized and unrealized (losses) gains on translation of net investment in foreign operations		(881)	727	193
Repurchase of shares	17	(32)	(181)	—
Net unrealized losses on cash flow hedges		(102)	(8)	—
Reclassification of net (gains) losses on cash flow hedges to net income		(1)	1	—
Comprehensive (loss) income		$ (945)	$ 1,202	$ 721

7. INVENTORIES

Inventories consist of:

	2008	2007
Raw materials and supplies	$ 605	$ 663
Work-in-process	166	204
Finished goods	228	248
Tooling and engineering	648	566
	$ 1,647	$ 1,681

Tooling and engineering inventory represents costs incurred on separately priced tooling and engineering services contracts in excess of billed and unbilled amounts included in accounts receivable.

Both Magna's current and quick ratios have been fairly stable for the last six years, suggesting no emerging liquidity problems. Magna's ratios are also similar to the industry averages, indicating its liquidity is within the expected range. Of course, current and quick ratios are only two indicators of liquidity. Others, such as the ability to generate cash from operations, should be considered as well.

Figure 6.1 shows current and quick ratios for a number of Canadian industries for the years 2005–2008, as well as the industry seven-year average (2002–2008).[7] Notice the wide variation in both ratios across the industries and the variation over time within some of the industry. This table emphasizes the importance of using appropriate benchmarks for ratio analysis. There are no norms that apply to all firms in all industries.

| FIGURE 6.1 | Current and Quick Ratios for a Number of Canadian Industries |

	Current ratio					Quick ratio				
	2008	2007	2006	2005	7-year average	2008	2007	2006	2005	7-year average
Automotive & Components	1.62	1.79	1.42	1.57	1.63	1.13	1.36	1.01	1.19	1.19
Biotechnology	3.01	5.46	3.85	6.20	6.34	2.53	4.88	3.24	5.61	5.88
Computers and Electronic Equipment	2.39	2.87	3.10	2.99	2.79	1.54	1.82	2.16	2.09	2.04
Food and Staples Retailing	1.32	1.10	1.15	1.27	1.22	0.50	0.47	0.51	0.42	0.50
Gold	2.94	4.15	4.04	3.81	4.72	1.87	2.92	3.20	2.77	3.66
Media	1.48	1.82	2.02	1.60	1.55	1.17	1.46	1.57	1.21	1.21
Oil, Gas, and Consumable Fuels	1.42	2.23	2.16	3.61	3.12	1.16	2.01	1.89	3.45	2.75
Paper and Forest Products	1.93	2.09	2.13	1.97	2.00	0.73	0.88	1.12	0.99	0.96
Retailing	2.34	2.28	2.15	2.26	2.22	0.98	0.93	0.74	0.80	0.82
Software	2.00	3.69	2.70	2.39	2.47	1.84	3.53	2.54	2.24	2.31
Telecommunications Services	0.64	0.76	0.67	0.64	0.71	0.43	0.52	0.44	0.37	0.45
Transportation	1.01	1.08	1.09	1.10	1.10	0.81	0.86	0.86	0.90	0.87

Accounts Receivable Turnover Ratio

An important responsibility of management is to effectively manage the entity's credit program. The **accounts receivable turnover ratio** is useful for assessing information about an entity's liquidity and how well credit is managed. The ratio is defined as

$$\text{Accounts receivables turnover ratio} = \frac{\text{Credit sales}}{\text{Average accounts receivable}}$$

For receivables, *turnover* means the number of times in a period they are incurred and collected. An accounts receivable turnover ratio of eight means the entity collects its receivables eight times a year. Since credit sales typically aren't reported, total sales are used instead. Magna's average for fiscal 2008 is calculated using accounts receivable on December 31, 2007 and 2008. The ratio provides information on how quickly the entity collects its receivables and it therefore provides insight on both liquidity and management's handling of its stewardship responsibilities over its credit program. The higher the ratio, the more quickly cash is being collected from customers (thereby shortening the cash lag). Average accounts receivable is calculated by adding the balances in the accounts receivable account at the beginning and end of the year and dividing by two.

A more intuitive measure can be obtained by dividing the accounts receivable turnover ratio into 365 to give the **average collection period of accounts receivable**—the number of days, on average, it takes to collect receivables. The ratio is defined as

$$\text{Average collection period of accounts receivable} = \frac{365}{\text{Accounts receivable turnover ratio}}$$

Table 6.10 shows the accounts receivable turnover ratio and the average collection period of accounts receivable for Magna for 2003 to 2007.

TABLE 6.10	Magna International.: Accounts Receivable Turnover Ratio and Average Collection Period of Accounts Receivable			
For the year ended December 31,	Sales (000)	Average accounts receivable (000)	Accounts receivable turnover ratio	Average collection period of accounts receivable
2008	$23,704,000	$3,401,000	6.97	52.4
2007	26,067,000	3,805,000	6.85	53.3
2006	24,180,000	3,532,500	6.85	53.3
2005	22,811,000	3,356,000	6.80	53.7
2004	20,653,000	2,945,500	7.01	52.1
2003	15,345,000	2,354,500	6.52	56.0

Table 6.10 shows that Magna's accounts receivable turnover ratio was quite stable over the six years, indicating that management is in control of receivables. Additional information would be helpful for evaluating these results. For example, the credit terms Magna offers its customers are very important. Our interpretation of the results would be different depending on whether Magna allowed customers 30 or 60 days to pay. Things look very good if Magna allows 60 days but there is plenty of room for improvement if normal credit terms are 30 days. There are some caveats to using this ratio:

- First, correctly applying the ratio requires credit sales, but most financial statements don't report credit and cash sales separately. For entities with significant cash sales (such as retail businesses) using total sales can make the ratio difficult to interpret, especially if the proportion of cash sales varies.

- Second, if an entity operates in a number of different industries or offers different credit terms to different customers the ratio will be affected by the proportion of sales in each business.

- Third, using the year-end accounts receivables balances to calculate average receivables may not provide a good estimate of the year's average. Ratios of businesses that are highly seasonal will be sensitive to how average receivables is calculated.

Despite these limitations the accounts receivable turnover ratio is a useful tool for assessing an entity's credit management and liquidity. The limitations may make it difficult to compare different entities but examining an entity's trends may be a reasonable way to apply this tool. Changes in the ratio will raise questions for further investigation but won't likely provide any definitive answers.

Solved Problem

The solved problem in this chapter will build on the problem-solving skills developed in Chapter 4. Some of the issues raised in this and similar questions may have actual rules prescribed by IFRS. However, at this stage it isn't necessary for you to be aware of the rules. Instead, apply the principles you have learned to come up with sensible responses to accounting issues. Consider the principles and basic definitions developed in the book so far. When reviewing the problem, keep in mind that the objective is to provide a well-reasoned and well-supported set of recommendations that address the accounting issues faced by the entity in the context of the role you are assigned.

Savoy Health Club Ltd.

Fred Irving, the founder, owner, and operator of the Savoy Health Club Ltd. (Savoy or "the club") recently agreed in principle to sell Savoy to Jim Floor. The parties have agreed in principle to a purchase price equal to five times net income for the year ended June 30, 2015. The deal cannot be finalized until Jim Floor receives the June 30, 2015 financial statements and accepts them. In the event that Jim Floor doesn't accept the financial statements, outstanding accounting issues can be submitted to an independent arbitrator for resolution. Until the agreement in principle was signed, Savoy's financial statements were prepared exclusively for tax purposes. Fred Irving is in the process of finalizing the June 30, 2015 financial statements but he is unsure about how to account for a number of issues.

Fred Irving has hired you to prepare a report explaining appropriate accounting treatments for the issues he is concerned about. Fred wants full explanations and justifications for the recommendations you make so he can explain them to Jim Floor and to the arbitrator, if necessary. Your discussions with Fred Irving provide the following information:

1. People join the club by paying a one-time initiation fee of $600. Provincial legislation requires that health clubs allow members to pay their initiation fees in equal instalments over 12 months, which most new members do. Historically, between 30 percent and 35 percent of people who join the club stop paying their initiation fees sometime during the year.

   In addition, members must pay a monthly fee of $80, either on the first day of each month or as a single payment on the renewal date of their contract, in which case they receive a $160 discount. (Members sign a one-year contract each year.) Approximately 40 percent of members pay in a lump sum at the start of the year. Some members who pay their monthly fees each month stop paying sometime during the year.

2. During fiscal 2015 the club began selling passes allowing non-members to participate in aerobics classes. Passes for individual classes are $8 each, or monthly passes can be purchased for one month ($70), three months ($200), or six months ($375). A monthly pass allows the holder 15 classes per month, but only in the month for which it was issued. Aerobics instructors receive $1.50 for each participant in their classes.

3. Normal maintenance work on some of the athletic equipment has been delayed for the last two months due to scheduling problems with the contractor. The work will cost about $4,000 and is now scheduled for July 2015.

4. The club pays monthly rent of $3,000. Rent is paid six months in advance on October 1 and April 1.

5. Fred Irving has never taken a salary.

Required:

Prepare the report requested by Fred Irving.

Comment: As you examine this solution it's important to remember that there is no single right answer to this question. There are many wrong answers, but more than one good answer. Good answers are well supported, consistent, and have the role well played. The answer below is prepared as a report to Fred Irving. Comments on the answer, which aren't part of the report itself but provide some additional explanation, are shown in italics.

Solution:

Mr. Fred Irving
2334 Piché St.
Bordeaux, Québec

Dear Mr. Irving:

Attached is the report you requested recommending accounting treatments for unresolved items in the financial statements of Savoy Health Club Ltd. In preparing this report I have attempted to provide reasonable, justified alternatives for the outstanding accounting issues. There is often more than one reasonable choice for treating accounting problems. In these situations, I have attempted to choose the alternative that serves the objective of increasing net income, thereby increasing the selling price of Savoy.

In previous years, Savoy's financial statements were prepared primarily for income tax purposes and presumably the accounting choices made served to legitimately reduce Savoy's tax burden. Financial statements prepared for tax purposes meet the requirements of the Income Tax Act but are often not appropriate for determining the selling price of a business as they are designed to defer taxes and therefore tend to understate income. Using such statements for determining the selling price of Savoy will unfairly reduce the proceeds you receive.

Financial statements prepared for determining the selling price of a business should provide a reasonable representation of the ongoing earning ability of the business. Because these financial statements will be used by Mr. Jim Floor, the prospective buyer of Savoy, and potentially by an arbitrator, it is important to use a recognized standard as the basis for preparing the statements. Accordingly, I recommend using International Financial Reporting Standards (IFRS). While IFRS are not necessarily the best criteria for setting the selling price of a business, they are widely known and recognized. It is possible that the buyer will reject some of the accounting choices you incorporate into the financial statements and you may have to concede some issues to come to an agreement. However, all recommendations made in this report are supportable in terms of IFRS, fairness, and accrual accounting.

If you have any questions, please contact me.

Yours truly,

John Friedlan, CA

Comment: *The letter to Fred Irving, the person who engaged the accountant, lays out the accountant's perspective in pursuing the engagement. The letter is an important part of effective role-playing and provides a vehicle for discussing the constraints, facts, and objectives relevant to the case. The objective of preparing financial statements for determining the selling price of Savoy is clearly the most important objective. The accountant's perspective in the report is to work within the constraints and the facts, but, when possible, serving the client's objective of getting a good price for Savoy. Clearly, Savoy's financial statements to date aren't appropriate for the intended purpose. Using them would be unfair to Mr. Irving. Some might contend that it isn't appropriate to change accounting methods because consistency would be violated. However, because the objectives of financial reporting have changed, the change in accounting approach is justifiable. As a result, the accountant should advise Mr. Irving to make accounting choices that produce a fair price for the sale of his business. This isn't to imply that the managers will intentionally misstate the financial statements. Rather, when there are legitimate alternatives, they will select the more favourable. It's reasonable to assume that the other parties will take a similar position— that Jim Floor will argue for accounting treatments that will tend to lower the selling price of Savoy. The solution recommends using IFRS but GAAP for Private Enterprises would also be appropriate.*

REPORT TO FRED IRVING

Terms of Reference

You have asked me to prepare a report recommending appropriate accounting treatments for a number of issues that must be resolved before presenting the financial statements of Savoy

Health Club Ltd. (Savoy) to Mr. Jim Floor, who has agreed in principle to purchase Savoy from you. The financial statements, specifically net income, will be used to determine the final selling price of Savoy. I understand that if Mr. Floor does not accept the financial statements as presented to him, you and Mr. Floor will attempt to resolve any differences through negotiations, followed by arbitration if necessary.

My objective in preparing this report is to come up with reasonable and justified treatments for the accounting problems that will result in an income measure that reflects normalized earnings (earnings that can reasonably be expected to repeat in future years). International Financial Reporting Standards will be the basis for my evaluation of the accounting issues.

Comment: Materiality will be low in this situation. Each dollar change in net income has a five-dollar effect on the price of Savoy. That is, if an accounting choice results in a $1,000 increase in net income, the selling price of Savoy increases by $5,000. Also, disclosure can't be used to resolve any accounting issues. Because the selling price depends on net income, measurement of all accounting events is necessary for them to be relevant.

Issues

Revenue Recognition   There are three revenue recognition issues that must be addressed: initiation fees, monthly membership fees, and aerobics fees, as follows:

1. *Initiation fees*   There are three possible ways the initiation fees could be recognized:
   (i)   when the membership agreement is signed
   (ii) when cash is collected
   (iii) over the life of the membership

Under IFRS, there are five criteria that must be met if revenue is to be recognized. There is no uncertainty about revenues and costs once the contract is signed. New members sign contracts agreeing to pay the $600 initiation fee, so the amount of revenue is known when someone joins. The costs of recruiting new members include advertising, salespeople, promotions, office space for meeting with prospective members, and so on. There are no costs after someone joins, except perhaps the cost of collecting amounts owed.

The key question in this analysis is what is Savoy providing in exchange for the initiation fee. If the fee represents the right to be a member and actual usage requires additional fees, it can be argued that revenue can be recognized when the agreement is signed. Alternatively, if the initiation fee is really part of the cost of ongoing membership then recognizing revenue over the life of the membership is appropriate.

In my opinion, the initiation fee is clearly separate from the monthly fee and simply represents the "right to belong." In other words, by signing a membership contract a person earns the right to use the club, provided the monthly fee is paid. As such, Savoy has delivered what has been promised when the contract is signed (subject to collectibility).

Collectibility is an issue because most people do not pay their initiation fees in full and 30 to 35 percent stop paying. Revenue can be recognized as long a reasonable estimate of the uncollectible amount can be made. If a reasonable estimate cannot be made then recognizing revenue when cash is collected makes sense. In my opinion, the 30 to 35 percent range provides a reasonable basis for an estimate and the historical range is not unreasonably large.

I recommend that the initiation fee revenue be recognize when a member signs a contract. An allowance for uncollectible amounts should be set up within the 30 to 35 percent range. At that point, cash has been paid or is owing and Savoy has provided a right to membership. The monthly membership fees cover the actual usage of the facility.

Comment: The most difficult revenue recognition issue is initiation fees because other alternatives for recognizing the revenue can be defended. For example, a case can be made for recognizing revenue when cash is collected or over the life of the membership. The method I recommended is the best one for Mr. Irving and it's consistent with IFRS. Mr. Floor may object on the basis that the approach makes him pay for uncertain revenue. The key to doing a good job on these types of analyses is to identify a valid accounting alternative that is, when possible, consistent with the interest of your client, and well supported.

2. *Monthly membership fees* Monthly fees should be recognized during the month they pertain to. The monthly fee entitles members to use the club for a period of time. This means that revenue is earned as time passes. Therefore, revenue should be accrued to reflect portions of monthly membership fees earned as of the financial statement date. This accounting approach should be used regardless of whether a member pays monthly or at the start of the year. If the member pays in full on the renewal date of the contract, the amount paid should be treated as unearned revenue and an adjusting entry should be prepared to recognize the appropriate amount of revenue when the financial statements are prepared.

There are no legitimate alternatives for recognizing revenue for the monthly fees. Revenue is earned as members have access to the club. The amount of revenue is known because the monthly fee is set in the contract signed by the member. Costs of earning the revenue are known because these are the costs of operating the club. Collection may be an issue for some members, although it should be possible to make an estimate of the amounts that will not be collected, based on past experience.

Comment: Accounting for the monthly membership fees is an example of a situation where the facts dictate the accounting method. It would be desirable from Mr. Irving's point of view to recognize revenue earlier, say when a member signs the annual contract, because this would place more revenue in the current period. However, these choices wouldn't be appropriate under IFRS (our constraint) because the service has not yet been provided (the facts).

3. *Aerobics fees* Non-members can attend aerobics classes at the club by purchasing passes for individual classes or monthly passes that entitle a person to attend 15 aerobics classes per month. Payment is made when the pass is purchased. Clearly, revenue is earned when a person attends a class. The service being provided is an aerobics class, and it is difficult to argue that revenue is earned at any other time. The fee earned by the instructor should be matched to the revenue when it is recognized. If a pass holder does not attend all the allowable aerobic sessions, the unused amount should be recognized at the end of the month since the right to attend classes expires at that point.

Comment: The timing of aerobics fee revenue is also dictated by the facts. An alternative might be to recognize revenue when passes are purchased but under the IFRS criteria point of purchase is too early because the service being purchased hasn't been provided when a pass is purchased. Considerable effort is still required to put on the aerobics class.

Maintenance Costs Maintenance ensures that the equipment lives up to its operating potential. Without it the useful life of the equipment will be shorter than expected. While regularly scheduled maintenance is necessary for proper operation of the equipment and for customer satisfaction, management judgment determines whether maintenance is required at a point in time. It is senseless from a business perspective to do maintenance unless it is required.

In this case we must rely on management's judgment that maintenance was not required at the time and therefore should not be included as an expense in the income statement in the current period. This is not a situation where an expense should be accrued, such as a good or service consumed but not billed (such as electricity costs), nor is it an expense that should be matched to revenue recognized in the current period but that will not be incurred until a future period (such as a warranty expense). This is an independent transaction that has not taken place. IFRS are a transactions-based accounting system. Since there has been no transaction, it is inappropriate under IFRS to accrue the maintenance costs.

Comment: Strictly speaking, the maintenance expense should be recorded when it is incurred. There are many uncertainties surrounding this cost, including the amount and whether it will be incurred (perhaps Mr. Floor will decide, should he buy Savoy, that this particular service call isn't necessary). Since IFRS record transactions and economic events that have happened, it's easy to make a case that these maintenance costs should not be accounted for in 2015.

However, as the accountant explained in the letter to Mr. Irving, the financial statements should be a reasonable representation of the ongoing and continuing earning ability of the business. After all, Mr. Floor is buying future earnings and future cash flows. Maintenance is an ongoing and regular cost of operating a health club. By excluding this particular maintenance cost in fiscal 2015, net income is overstated in relation to ongoing and continuing earnings. So, while the treatment proposed by the accountant is consistent with IFRS, we can question whether it's fair. The accountant's choice is consistent with Mr. Irving's objectives and with the constraints, and perhaps with the facts, and therefore is a reasonable recommendation. Mr. Floor and the arbitrator may see things differently. This demonstrates some of the practical limitations of using IFRS for setting the price of a business.

Rent Clearly, rent should be accrued on a monthly basis. Rent expense should reflect the cost of the space used during the period in question because it is only that cost that contributed to earning revenue. Savoy paid $18,000 to the property owner on April 1, 2015 to cover rent for April 1 to September 30, 2015. A rent expense of $9,000 should be accrued in the June 30, 2015, income statement.

Comment: This is a clear application of accrual accounting. The rent should be expensed in the period when the space was used, regardless of when the cash is expended.

Owner's Salary The owner's salary is a non-existent expense. Over the life of the business, Mr. Irving never took a salary so it is inappropriate to include it in the calculation of net income. Historical cost financial statements are intended to be representations of what happened. If a salary for Mr. Irving is included it means that the statements would include something that did not happen.

Comment: The issue here is whether the selling price should include a cost of management. An owner-manager has the option of removing money from the company as salary or dividend (a question that has significant tax implications), or not at all. From an entity standpoint, the financial statements don't reflect all the costs of operating Savoy because the cost of management is a part of the cost. The method and amount of compensation received by an owner-manager can distort net income for purposes of setting the price of Savoy because the owner-manager can choose to pay himself as much or as little as he wishes. There is no simple solution to this issue. The treatment recommended by the accountant is consistent with IFRS and is the best choice to achieve Mr. Irving's objectives. Ultimately, this issue, along with the accounting for the maintenance cost, may be better resolved through negotiations.

SUMMARY OF KEY POINTS

▶ **LO 1** Cash reported on the balance sheet often includes cash equivalents, which are short-term investments that can be converted into a known amount of cash easily and quickly. Good management requires that there be enough cash available to meet obligations, but not so much as to result in the inefficient use of the entity's resources.

Protecting the entity's assets is an important management responsibility. Internal controls are mechanisms ensuring an entity achieves its objectives. In an accounting context, internal controls work to make information produced by the accounting information system reliable and protect an entity's assets from loss, theft, or inappropriate use.

The amount of cash reported on the balance sheet represents the face value of an entity's cash and doesn't reflect changes in the purchasing power of the money. Also, because financial statements are stated in a single currency, cash held in foreign currencies must be translated into Canadian dollars so it can be reported on the balance sheet.

▶ **LO 2** The time value of money is the concept that cash received in the future isn't worth as much as the same amount of cash today. The future value of cash flows is the amount of money you will receive in the future by investing it today at a given interest rate. The present value of cash flows is the equivalent value today of money that will be received in the future. Present and future value analyses are valuable tools for comparing the values of cash flows that occur at different times and in different amounts. Present value is commonly used as a basis for valuing certain assets and liabilities.

▶ **LO 3** Receivables are amounts owing to an entity. Under accrual accounting, receivables should be valued at their net realizable value (NRV). This means that uncollectibles, discounts, and returns can reduce the amount of cash the entity will actually realize. There are three ways to account for uncollectible amounts:

- direct writeoff method
- percentage-of-receivables method
- percentage-of-credit-sales method

The percentage-of-receivables and percentage-of-credit-sales methods are accrual methods that attempt to match the cost of offering credit to customers to the revenue in the period. The direct writeoff method doesn't match costs and revenues. The three methods can lead to different bad debt expenses in a given year, although over the life of an entity the amount expensed will be the same.

▶ **LO 4** Hidden reserves are undisclosed accounting choices used to manage earnings and other financial information with the intention of satisfying the self-interests of the managers.

The current ratio has limitations because some current assets aren't very liquid. The quick or acid test ratio is sometimes used to overcome this problem by including only liquid assets in the numerator. The accounts receivable turnover ratio and the average collection period of accounts receivable provide information on how well management is managing the entity's credit program and on the entity's liquidity.

FORMULA SUMMARY

$$\text{Quick ratio} = \frac{\text{Quick assets}}{\text{Current liabilities}} = \frac{\text{Cash + Cash equivalents + Marketable securities + Receivables}}{\text{Current liabilities}}$$

$$\text{Accounts receivables turnover ratio} = \frac{\text{Credit sales}}{\text{Average accounts receivable}}$$

$$\text{Average collection period of accounts receivable} = \frac{365}{\text{Accounts receivable turnover ratio}}$$

KEY TERMS

SIMILAR TERMS

The left column gives alternative terms that are sometimes used for the accounting terms introduced in this chapter, which are listed in the right column.

interest rate   **discount rate, p. 302**
allowance for doubtful accounts,
    allowance for bad debts   **allowance for uncollectible accounts, p. 309**

ASSIGNMENT MATERIALS

Questions

Q6-1.   What is meant by "internal control"? Why are strong internal controls important to an entity?

Q6-2.   What is meant by "segregation of duties"? Why is it important for internal control purposes that people who physically handle an asset aren't also responsible for accounting for the asset?

Q6-3.   Why is cash considered an unproductive asset?

Q6-4.   How is it possible that an entity can have too much cash?

Q6-5.   You are examining the financial statements of a company you are interested in investing in. The company reports a negative balance in the cash account (the cash account on the balance sheet is reported as a negative amount on the asset side of the balance sheet). How would you interpret the negative balance in the cash account?

Q6-6.   In August 2012 you received a birthday gift of $500 in cash from a generous uncle. Your uncle wanted you to have the money so that you could enjoy yourself as you were beginning your studies at university. Unfortunately, you lose the $500 in your very messy room in your residence hall. In June 2016 when you graduate, you find the $500 when you clean out your room to move out. With respect to the $500, are you as well off on the day you found the $500 as you were on the day you received it? Explain your answer.

Q6-7.   The unit of measure used in Canadian financial statements is the *nominal* dollar. What is a nominal dollar? What real economic costs are ignored by using a nominal dollar as the unit of measure, rather than using a unit of measure that takes into consideration the changing purchasing power of a dollar?

Q6-8.   What does it mean when cash on an entity's balance sheet is classified as restricted? What are the implications of restricted cash for interpreting the financial statements?

Q6-9.   Why is an amount of cash today more valuable than the same amount of cash in the future?

Q6-10.   What is the difference between compound interest and simple interest? Would you receive more interest from an investment that pays compound interest or from one that pays simple interest? Explain.

Q6-11.   Which investment would be more attractive: 8 percent per year compounded annually or 8 percent per year compounded quarterly? Explain.

Q6-12.   Explain the terms *present value* and *future value*. Give an example of when each measurement would be appropriate.

Q6-13.   What is a "receivable"? How are receivables classified and valued on a balance sheet? What are some of the different types of receivables that an entity can report?

Q6-14. How are the current and quick ratios affected by how an entity recognizes revenue? Explain. Is an entity's liquidity affected by how it recognizes revenue? Explain.

Q6-15. What is the relationship between an account receivable and the income statement? What is the relationship between an account receivable and the revenue recognition criteria discussed in Chapter 4?

Q6-16. What are some of the benefits and drawbacks to a business of offering credit terms to customers? Would a business prefer to do business in cash or on credit? Explain.

Q6-17. Why is the amount reported on a balance sheet for receivables usually not the same as the sum of the amounts that customers and other people who owe the entity money have promised to pay?

Q6-18. You are a bank manager. The owner of a small business has come to see you about a loan. He presents you with the financial statements of his business. The accounts receivable are reported at the amount customers have promised to pay. The owner says he writes off bad debts once he decides the amount won't be collected. Do you have any concerns about how the receivables are reported on the balance sheet? Explain.

Q6-19. Explain why, when an entity uses the percentage-of-receivables or percentage-of-credit-sales method of accounting for bad debts, a writedown of a receivable has no effect on the income statement.

Q6-20. A small business has used the same percentage of end of year accounts receivable to calculate the allowance for doubtful accounts and the bad debt expense for the last eight years. What are the problems and financial statement consequences of the business' approach?

Q6-21. What are the three methods for accounting for uncollectible amounts from customers? Explain each method.

Q6-22. Why is the direct writeoff method of accounting for bad debts not appropriate in accrual accounting?

Q6-23. Why is the percentage-of-credit-sales method of accounting for bad debts referred to as an income statement approach, whereas the percentage-of-receivables method is referred to as a balance sheet approach?

Q6-24. If an entity uses the percentage-of-credit-sales method of accounting for uncollectible accounts, what are the effects on the financial statements if the entity consistently uses too low a percentage of credit sales for estimating bad debts? What are the effects on the financial statements if it consistently uses too high a percentage? Consider the effects on both the income statement and the balance sheet.

Q6-25. What is an aging schedule? How is the aging schedule used for calculating the bad debt expense?

Q6-26. How does management decide what percentage of receivables or what percentage of credit sales should be used to calculate the bad debt expense and the balance in the allowance for uncollectibles account? Is this a subjective or objective decision? Explain.

Q6-27. How does management decide when to write off an account receivable or some other receivable? Is this an objective or subjective decision? Explain. How can management use the judgment required to decide when to write off a receivable to affect the numbers in the financial statements? Explain.

Q6-28. Verlo Ltd. recently made a $100,000 sale to a customer. Terms of the sale agreement permit the customer to pay the $100,000 in two years. The customer doesn't have to pay any interest. The revenue recognition criteria were met at the time of delivery of the product and so Verlo Ltd. recognized $100,000 of revenue. Evaluate Verlo Ltd.'s accounting for this sale.

Q6-29. What is a hidden reserve? Why would management create hidden reserves? Why is it possible for managers to create hidden reserves? Why is the existence of hidden reserves a problem for users of financial statements?

Q6-30. What is the quick ratio? How does the quick ratio differ from the current ratio? What would be a better measure of liquidity for a jewellery store, the quick ratio or the current ratio? Explain. Which would be the better measure of liquidity for a mine holding a large inventory of gold bullion? Explain.

Q6-31. Explain why the accounts receivable turnover ratio is useful for evaluating the liquidity of an entity.

Exercises

E6-1. (**Classifying cash on the balance sheet, LO 1**) For each of the following items, explain whether the amount described should be included in "Cash and cash equivalents" on Jelly Inc.'s (Jelly) December 31, 2014, balance sheet:
a. $10,000 kept in the safe in the CEO's office for emergencies.
b. An investment certificate that will pay $10,000 plus accrued interest on the date it is cashed. The certificate can be cashed at any time by Jelly.
c. A line of credit from the bank that Jelly uses to provide working capital on an as needed basis. On December 31, 2014, Jelly had borrowed $120,000 from the line of credit.
d. $41,000 owed by a shareholder. The amount is to be paid on January 2, 2015.
e. A guaranteed investment certificate that matures on July 15, 2016. Jelly will receive $11,000 when the certificate matures.
f. $250,000 seized by a foreign government as part of a dispute over a transaction with a company in the foreign country.
g. $22,300 in Jelly's chequing account at the bank.
h. $25,000 in post-dated cheques. The cheques can be cashed on February 21, 2015.
i. $10,000 held by Jelly's lawyer for purposes of paying a particular supplier when equipment ordered is delivered. The supplier required that the lawyer hold the money so that it would be assured of payment. The equipment is due to be delivered in February 2015.
j. £3,000 (British pounds) held in an account at a major British bank.
k. Shares in a public company traded on the Toronto Exchange.

E6-2. (**Calculating future values and the effect of compounding, LO 2**) Calculate the future value in each of the following situations. (*Hint:* The interest rates are stated in annual amounts.)
a. Invest $25,000 at 5 percent for eight years.
b. Invest $25,000 at 5 percent for eight years, compounded semi-annually.
c. Invest $25,000 at 5 percent for eight years, compounded quarterly.
d. Invest $25,000 at 5 percent for eight years, compounded monthly.

E6-3. (**Calculating future values, LO 2**) Calculate the future value in each of the following situations:
a. An investor purchases a long-term investment for $100,000 that pays 4 percent interest per year for nine years, compounded semi-annually. How much will the investor receive when the investment matures?
b. Marcel borrows $60,000 at 7 percent to buy a new luxury car. Interest and principal must be paid in full in three years. How much will Marcel have to pay the lender in three years?
c. A 50-year-old woman invests $10,000 into her registered retirement saving plan. She purchases an investment certificate that pays 5 percent per year for 15 years. How much will she have in her plan when the certificate matures?

    d. Brenda invests $25,000 in a money market fund. If the fund earns 2 percent per year, compounded quarterly, how much will she have at the end of five years?

E6-4. **(Calculating present values, LO 2)** Answer the following questions:
- a. Present value of $1,000,000 to be received in eight years at a discount rate of 10 percent.
- b. Present value of the following series of cash payments: $10,000 to be received in one year, $20,000 in two years, and $30,000 in three years, at a discount rate of 8 percent.
- c. Present value of the following series of cash payments: $30,000 to be received in one year, $20,000 in two years, and $10,000 in three years, at a discount rate of 8 percent.

E6-5. **(Calculating present values, LO 2)** Answer the following questions. Provide explanations for each:
- a. If your discount rate is 12 percent would you prefer $10,000 today or $20,000 in five years?
- b. A customer purchases $32,000 of goods. The goods will be paid for in cash in four years. How much revenue should be recorded on the date the goods are delivered, assuming a discount rate of 5 percent?
- c. If your discount rate is 18 percent what would be the maximum amount you would pay for cash flows of $20,000 in two years, $30,000 is four years and $50,000 in six years?
- d. A "zero coupon bond" is a type of long-term debt that pays no interest but pays a single amount on the date the bond matures. Your broker offers you a zero coupon bond that will pay $10,000 in 15 years. How much would you pay for the bond today, if your discount rate is 8 percent?
- e. Would you pay $100,000 to receive $30,000 in one year, $50,000 in two years, and $70,000 in three years? Assume your discount rate is 20 percent.
- f. At what discount rate would you be indifferent between $1,000 today and $1,610.51 in five years?

E6-6. **(Calculating the present value of annuities, LO 2)** Answer the following questions. Explain your answers:
- a. You can purchase a series of cash flows of $10,000 for 25 years for a payment of $100,000 today. If your discount rate is 8 percent would you make the investment?
- b. You decide to purchase a new car. The dealer offers 12 percent interest on a five-year car loan. Monthly payments will $400. What is the equivalent cash price today for the new car? (*Hint:* The monthly interest rate is the annual interest rate divided by 12.)
- c. An investor can purchase an investment that pays interest of $1,000 per year for 12 years as well as paying the investor $10,000 at the end of the 12th year. If the appropriate discount rate for an investment of this type is 6 percent, what is the maximum amount the investor should pay for the investment? (When answering, remember that calculating an annuity only applies to equal payments. In this question, the present value of the additional $10,000 received in the tenth year must be determined separately.)
- d. A professional athlete recently signed a 13-year contract paying him $9.5 million a season. What is the present value of the contract at the time it is signed? Assume the annual salary is paid at the end of each season and the appropriate discount rate is 10 percent.
- e. You have the option of receiving $500,000 today or $50,000 a year for 30 years, beginning one year from now. If your discount rate is 9 percent, which would you choose?

E6-7. **(Calculating the future value, present value, and present value of annuities, LO 2)** Use the tools introduced in the chapter to answer the following questions. You have to decide which tool to use in each case. Explain your conclusions. In all cases assume the interest or discount rate is 10 percent:

a. A company sells a piece of equipment to a customer for $250,000. The company agrees to accept payment in full in five years. The agreement between the parties specifies that the buyer won't be charged interest. How much revenue should the company recognize for this sale?

b. A contest advertises that the winner will get $5,000,000 paid in equal instalments of $250,000 a year for 20 years, with the first payment being made one year from the date the contest winner is announced. What is the "real" value of the prize?

c. Mr. Insulacco purchased an investment certificate for $10,000 in honour of the birth of his niece. How much will Mr. Insulacco's niece receive when the certificate matures in eight years?

d. An investor has the opportunity to invest in one of three investments. In each case the investor must invest $10,000. The first investment will pay the investor $35,000 at the end of year 5. The second investment will pay the investor $2,000 in one year, $4,000 in two years, $6,000 in three years, $8,000 in four years, and $10,000 in five years. The third alternative will pay the investor $6,000 at the end of each of the next five years. Which investment would you recommend?

e. An investor purchases a $10,000 investment certificate that pays compounded semi-annual interest. How much will the investor receive when the certificate matures in 10 years?

f. An investor has the opportunity to receive $5,000 per year for the next 25 years. What is the most the investor should pay for this investment?

g. You are offered a choice of receiving $1,000 today or $1,500 in three years. Which alternative would you prefer?

E6-8. **(Basic journal entries, LO 3)** Prepare the journal entries necessary to record the following transactions and economic events for Sahali Ltd. (Sahali):

a. During 2015 Sahali had cash sales of $175,000 and credit sales of $625,000.

b. During 2015 $405,000 of accounts receivable were collected.

c. Management estimated that 5 percent of credit sales wouldn't be collected.

d. During 2015 Sahali wrote off $34,000 of accounts receivables.

E6-9. **(Journal entries for accounts receivable, LO 3)** In early 2014 Pugwash Ltd. (Pugwash) delivered a large order of goods to Ripon Inc. (Ripon), a new customer. In compliance with company policy, Pugwash did a credit check on Ripon and decided to provide it with a credit limit of $7,000. Ripon's order was for $9,500 so $2,500 was paid when the goods were delivered. Due to financial problems Ripon wasn't able to pay the amount owing to Pugwash and in September the amount owing was written off. In December, Pugwash received a cheque from Ripon for the amount owing along with a letter of apology for the delay in paying the invoice.

Required:

a. Prepare the journal entry to record the sale to Ripon.

b. Prepare the journal entry to record the writeoff of the receivable from Ripon. Assume Pugwash estimates its bad debt expense using the percentage of credit sales method.

c. Prepare the journal entry that would be recorded when Pugwash received the cheque from Ripon in December.

E6-10. **(Writing off an account receivable, LO 3)** Malagash Ltd. (Malagash) recently learned that a major customer would be permanently shutting down its operations within 30 days. The reason for the shut-down isn't clear but Malagash's management assumes there are financial problems underlying the decision. As of Malagash's year-end it isn't clear whether it will receive any of the $50,000 owed to it by the customer. Despite the uncertainty regarding collection, Malagash's management decided it would write off the $50,000 receivable in the current fiscal year.

Required:

    a. Prepare the journal entry that Malagash would prepare if it were using the direct writeoff method of accounting for uncollectible amounts. What would be the effect on net income of the entry?

    b. Prepare the journal entry that Malagash would prepare if it were using the percentage-of-credit-sales method of accounting for uncollectible amounts. What would be the effect on net income of the entry?

    c. Prepare the journal entry that Malagash would prepare if it were using the percentage-of-receivables method of accounting for uncollectible amounts. What would be the effect on net income of the entry?

    d. Why do you think that Malagash decided to write off the receivable in the current fiscal year, even though it didn't know whether it would be paid or not? In answering consider accounting principles and the objectives of accounting.

E6-11. **(Accounting for long-term receivables, LO 2, 3)** On May 31, 2015, Namaka Ltd. (Namaka) sold specialized heavy equipment to Audy Inc. (Audy) for $25,000,000. The sale agreement required that Audy pay $7,000,000 to Namaka on May 31, 2015, and then $6,000,000 on each of May 31, 2016, 2017, and 2018. Namaka decided to recognize the sale of the equipment in the year ended May 31, 2015.

Required:

    a. How much revenue should Namaka recognize as a result of its sale of the office building to Audy? Prepare the journal entry that Namaka should prepare to record the sale. Assume a discount rate of 14 percent.

    b. How much interest revenue will be reported on Namaka's income statement for the years ended May 31, 2016, 2017, and 2018, as a result of the sale to Audy? Prepare the journal entry that should be prepared each year to record the interest revenue.

    c. How much would be reported as receivable from Audy on Namaka's balance sheet for the years ended May 31, 2015, 2016, 2017, and 2018? How would the receivable be classified on each year's balance sheet? Explain your answer.

    d. Suppose Namaka insisted on recognizing $25,000,000 as revenue in 2015. What would be the implications for stakeholders? Why might Namaka's management want to report the full $25,000,000 immediately?

E6-12. **(Calculating accounts receivable, LO 3)** Use the following information to calculate accounts receivable on July 31, 2015, and the amount of accounts receivable written off in 2015:

	July 31,	
	2015	**2014**
Accounts receivable	$?	$ 175,000
Allowance for uncollectible accounts	(10,500)	(9,200)
Revenue recognized during 2015*	725,000	
Collections of accounts receivable during 2015	742,000	
Bad debt expense for 2015	10,000	
Amount of accounts receivable written off during 2015	?	
*Assume all sales are on credit.		

E6-13. (Calculating accounts receivable, LO 3) Use the following information to calculate accounts receivable on December 31, 2016 and the amount of cash received from customers in 2016 for services to be provided during 2017:

	December 31,	
	2016	**2015**
Accounts receivable	$?	$227,650
Allowance for uncollectible accounts	(13,250)	(14,223)
Unearned revenue	110,500	88,850
Revenue recognized during 2016*	1,758,000	
Collections of accounts receivable during 2016	1,595,000	
Bad debt expense for 2016	12,000	
Amount of accounts receivable written off during 2016	12,973	
Cash received from customers in 2016 for services to be provided during 2017	?	

*Includes recognition of revenue classified as unearned in previous periods. All other revenue is on credit.

E6-14. (Calculating the bad debt expense and the allowance for uncollectible accounts, LO 3) You are provided with the following information about Nyanza Corp.:
  i.   Accounts receivable on December 31, 2015 = $287,500.
  ii. Sales during the year ended December 31, 2015 = $3,758,000 (all sales are on credit).
  iii. Accounts receivable written off during 2015 = $108,250.
  iv. Balance in Allowance for uncollectible accounts on December 31, 2014 = $112,500.
  v. Historically, an average of 1.5 percent of credit sales has been uncollectible.

Required:

Calculate Nyanza's bad debt expense for the year ended December 31, 2015, and the allowance for uncollectible accounts on December 31, 2015. Prepare the journal entry required to record the bad debt expense.

E6-15. (The effect of errors on net income, LO 3) Capstick Ltd. (Capstick) uses the percentage-of-credit-sales method of estimating the bad debt expense. Since 2011 Capstick has used too low a percentage in calculating the bad debt expense each year. In 2015 management realized the error and decided to make an adjusting entry to correct it. Credit sales every year from 2011 through 2015 were $1,200,000. Capstick determined the bad debt expense using 1.5 percent of revenue as the basis of its estimate each year. Management decides it will use 1.75 percent beginning in 2016 (and should have done since 2011). Capstick has written off $21,000 of accounts receivable each year from 2011 through 2015. The credit balance in the allowance account on January 1, 2011 (the first day of Capstick's fiscal year) was $21,000.
  a. What bad debt expense did Capstick record in each year from 2011 to 2015?
  b. What was the effect on net income each year of using too low a bad debt expense estimate?
  c. What was the balance in the allowance account at the end of each year?
  d. What effect does correcting the error have on net income in 2015?
  e. Prepare the journal entry that Capstick would make in 2015 to correct the error and leave an appropriate balance in the allowance account. Assume the adjusting entry to correct the error is made after the entry to record the 2015 bad debt expense.

E6-16. (Comparing the percentage-of-receivables and percentage-of-credit-sales methods, LO 3) The following information has been obtained about Elzevir Inc. (Elzevir) for 2014. The information was obtained before any year-end adjusting entries were made.

Elzevir's year-end is March 31:

Accounts receivable on March 31, 2014	$ 800,000
Credit sales for the year ended March 31, 2014	7,525,000
Allowance for uncollectible accounts on March 31, 2014 (debit balance)	9,750

Required:

    a. Calculate the bad debt expense that Elzevir would record for the 2014 fiscal year, assuming that management expects that 4.5 percent of year-end accounts receivable won't be collected. What would be the balance in allowance for uncollectible accounts on March 31, 2014? Prepare the journal entry to record the bad debt expense.

    b. Calculate the bad debt expense that Elzevir would record for the 2014 fiscal year, assuming that management expects that 0.5 percent of credit sales during fiscal 2014 won't be collected. What would be the balance in allowance for uncollectible accounts on March 31, 2014? Prepare the journal entry to record the bad debt expense.

    c. What would your answers in (a) and (b) be if the balance in allowance for uncollectible accounts on March 31, 2014 (before any year-end adjusting entries), was a credit of $9,750? Explain any differences you find.

E6-17. **(Using an aging schedule to calculate the bad debt expense, LO 3)** Pipestone Ltd. (Pipestone) uses an aging schedule to estimate the amount of receivables that won't be collected. Pipestone allows its customers up to 30 days to pay amounts owed. Any receivable outstanding for more than 30 days is considered overdue. Based on historical information management estimates that it will collect 98 percent of current accounts receivable, 92 percent of receivables overdue by between 1 and 30 days, 80 percent of receivables overdue by between 31 and 60 days, 50 percent of receivables overdue by between 61 and 90 days, and 25 percent of receivables overdue by more than 90 days. Management has provided you with the following aged receivable schedule:

Account age	Balance on January 31, 2014
Current	$625,000
1–30 days overdue	95,000
31–60 days overdue	58,000
61–90 days overdue	41,000
More than 90 days overdue	82,000

The balance in allowance for uncollectible accounts before the period-end adjusting entry is made is a credit of $7,300.

Required:

    a. What amount of ending accounts receivable is estimated to be uncollectible on January 31, 2014?

    b. Prepare the journal entry required to record the bad debt expense for Pipestone for the year ended January 31, 2014.

E6-18. **(Compute the accounts receivable turnover ratio and the average collection period for accounts receivable, LO 4)** The following information was obtained from Acamac Corp.'s (Acamac) 2016 financial statements:

Sales (all sales are on credit)	$7,450,000
Accounts receivable on March 31, 2016	1,110,000
Accounts receivable on March 31, 2015	1,050,000

Required:

a. Calculate Acamac's accounts receivable turnover ratio for 2016.
b. Calculate the average collection period for accounts receivable during 2016.
c. Is Acamac's average collection period for 2016 reasonable? What information would you require to answer this question? Explain.

E6-19. **(Correcting the balance in Allowance for Uncollectible Accounts, LO 3)** Trilby Inc. (Trilby) uses the percentage-of-credit-sales method for estimating its bad debt expense. The percentage that Trilby uses is based on historical information. Trilby's management hasn't revised the percentage for several years, a period during which a number of environmental and business factors have changed. Trilby's management recently realized that over the last three years the percentage of credit sales that the company used was too high. As a result, the balance in allowance for uncollectible accounts is $53,000 higher than it would have been had a better estimate of bad debts been used each year.

Required:

a. Prepare the adjusting journal entry that Trilby must make to have an appropriate balance in allowance for uncollectible accounts.
b. What is the effect of the error in estimating bad debts in each of the years the error is made? What is the effect of the adjusting entry on net income? Answer the question by comparing the reported net income with what net income would have been had the error not been made and the adjusting entry not required.
c. What is the impact of this error and the adjusting entry on the users of the financial statements? Explain fully.

E6-20. **(Identifying quick assets, LO 4)** Which of the following assets would you classify as quick assets for purposes of calculating the quick ratio? Explain your reasoning.
a. Prepaid rent
b. Account receivable due to be paid in 16 months
c. Current portion of a long-term note receivable
d. Delivery truck
e. Investment certificate maturing in 12 months
f. Dividends receivable
g. Inventory of gold bars
h. Income taxes receivable
i. Accounts receivable
j. Inventory of gravel
k. Post-dated cheques—the cheques can be cash 45 days after the year-end
l. Shares in TransAlta Corporation
m. Term deposit maturing in one month
n. Shares in a privately owned corporation

E6-21. **(Compute current and quick ratios, LO 4)** Following are the balance sheets for the years ended June 30, 2015 and 2014, for Seahorse Inc.:

Seahorse Inc. Balance Sheets As of June 30					
Assets	**2015**	**2014**	**Liabilities and shareholders' equity**	**2015**	**2014**
Current assets			*Current liabilities*		
Cash and cash equivalents	$ 76,000	$ 84,000	Accounts payable	$140,000	$139,000
Accounts receivable	190,000	116,000	Accrued liabilities	24,000	38,000
Inventory	220,000	196,000	Unearned revenue	20,000	24,000
Prepaids	16,200	15,000	Current portion of long-term debt	90,000	120,000
Current assets	502,200	411,000	Current liabilities	274,000	321,000
Equipment (net)	745,800	820,000	Long-term debt	220,000	310,000
			Capital stock	330,000	250,000
			Retained earnings	424,000	350,000
Total assets	$1,248,000	$1,231,000	Total liabilities and shareholders' equity	$1,248,000	$1,231,000

Required:

a. Calculate the current ratio and the quick ratio on June 30, 2014 and 2015.
b. Assess the change in the liquidity position of Seahorse Inc.
c. Can you think of any circumstances where a significant increase in the quick ratio could be an indicator of a deteriorating liquidity position?

E6-22. **(Working with the accounts receivable turnover ratio, LO 4)** During 2014 Oderin Inc. (Oderin) reported revenue of $1,178,000. Oderin's accounts receivable turnover ratio for 2014 was 6.32. What was Oderin's average amount of accounts receivable during 2014? What was Oderin's average collection period for accounts receivable during 2014?

E6-23. **(Working with the accounts receivable turnover ratio, LO 4)** During 2015 Hemlo Inc. (Hemlo) reported revenue of $3,250,000. During 2015 the average collection period for accounts receivable was 38 days. Accounts receivable at the end of 2016 was 10 percent greater than at the end of 2015. What was Hemlo's average accounts receivable for 2016?

E6-24. **(Interpreting accounts receivable turnover, LO 4)** Agassiz Inc. (Agassiz) provides commercial cleaning services. The company picks up items needing cleaning and returns them to the business within 48 hours. Agassiz invoices customers monthly and requires payment within 30 days. Over the last few years the company has been growing fairly rapidly. You are provided with the following information about Agassiz:

	2015	2014	2013	2012
Accounts receivable—June 30	$ 95,200	$ 82,400	$ 59,650	$48,750
Revenue—year ended June 30	788,000	675,000	582,000	

Required:

You are the bank manager responsible for Agassiz's loan. You have decided to have a look how well the company has been managing its receivables in light of its recent growth. Calculate Agassiz's accounts receivable turnover ratio and the average collection period for accounts receivable and use the information to prepare a report analyzing the situation.

Problems

P6-1.   (**Thinking about internal controls, LO 1**) For the following two scenarios, describe what you think are the weaknesses in the internal controls and explain the implications of the weaknesses:

a. The administrative assistant to the corporate controller keeps a cash box with up to $500 of company money in her desk so that she can pay for incidental expenses as they occur: couriers, reimbursements for expenditures on behalf of the company, food ordered for meetings and people who work late, and so on. The cash is kept in a locked box in a locked drawer in the administrative assistant's desk. The cash in the box is replaced when the administrative assistant tells the corporate controller that more is required. The administrative assistant has been with the company for over 20 years and is highly respected and trusted by all members of senior management.

b. Because of its small size, Hochelaga Ltd. has only one person, Mathew Jordan, in its accounting department. For accounts payable, Mr. Jordan is responsible for ensuring that goods and services that have been ordered are received, authorizing payments to suppliers, preparing cheques, and entering transactions into the accounting system. He also prepares the bank reconciliation. The owner of the company signs all cheques and frequently reviews Mr. Jordan's work. The owner is often out of the country on business, sometimes for up to two weeks. Office staff are always aware of when the owner will be returning.

P6-2.   (**Thinking about internal controls, LO 1**) For the following two scenarios, describe what you think are the weaknesses in the internal controls and explain the implications of the weaknesses:

a. Trustees of a local school board are given credit cards by the board for charging amounts pertaining to their responsibilities. Statements come to the board office and are reviewed by a staff person who approves them for payment. Occasionally, a trustee will be asked to explain a charge not clearly related to the trustee's work. Trustees are also entitled to receive reimbursement for travel, including $0.50 per kilometre travelled in their own cars. To receive reimbursement a trustee must submit a form indicating the number of kilometres travelled. Trustees usually submit a travel form every six to eight months.

b. Day & Night is a local convenience store. It is owned and operated by the Verrato family. Most of the time a member of the family is in the store but for about 20 hours a week an employee is the only person working. The employee's main responsibility is to ring up customer purchases on the cash register and collect cash (credit cards aren't accepted). Other duties include stocking shelves and keeping the store clean, as well as locking up the store at the end of the day. A family member takes cash from the register to the bank, usually the next day.

P6-3.   (**Interpreting current and quick ratio data, LO 4**) Refer to Figure 6.1. Why do you think retailing businesses have such a large difference between their quick ratios and their current ratios? To answer, think about what the balance sheet of a retail business would look like, particularly the types of current assets that it has.

P6-4.   (**Time value of money calculations, LO 2**) For each of the following situations, do the calculations necessary to make a decision:

a. A company sells land and a building for $22 million. The buyer agrees to pay $5 million cash when title to the property transfers, $3 million at the end of each of the next four years and $5 million at the end of the fifth year. The buyer and seller agree the financing provided by the seller will be interest-free. At a discount rate of 14 percent, what is the selling price if the time value of money is considered?

b. Today is January 1, 2014. An investor deposits $1,000 in a savings account that guarantees 5 percent interest per year compounded annually. She also deposits $1,000 in the account on January 1 of each of the next four years (2015–2018) under the same terms. How much will she have on December 31, 2018 of the fifth year?

c. An aunt of yours is planning to retire and would like her income to be secure. She said she was approached by a company that offered her annual payments of $50,000 for 20 years, paid in equal semi-annual instalments, beginning one year from the date she enters the program. Your aunt would pay $500,000 to participate in the program. If an appropriate discount rate is 8 percent, should your aunt participate in the program? What is the maximum amount she should pay?

d. A woman wants to save for a dream vacation. She estimates the vacation will cost $50,000. If she has $15,000 to invest today, how many years will she have to invest for until she has enough for the trip if the appropriate discount rate is 5 percent? Calculate to the nearest full year.

e. The present value of $10,000 to be received in five years is $7,472. What is the discount rate?

P6-5.   (**Analyzing changes to credit policy, LO 3, 4**) Magundy Inc. (Magundy) imports high-end merchandise from Europe and distributes it to retailers across eastern Canada. Magundy has tended to be very conservative in managing its operations. In late 2014 the shareholders of Magundy decided that they weren't satisfied with the performance and growth of the company, and replaced the president with a younger, more aggressive person whom they believed would be better able meet their performance and growth objectives.

In early 2015 the new president decided that Magundy had been too cautious in granting credit to customers and he implemented a new credit policy that significantly increased the number of retailers who would be able carry Magundy's merchandise. The new president thought the new credit policy would increase sales significantly, which would meet the objectives of the owners. The new credit policy allowed businesses that were considered higher credit risks (customers that were more likely to not pay their debts) to obtain credit from Magundy. The new credit policy also allowed all customers more time to pay Magundy for purchases.

By the end of 2015, it appeared that the new president's strategy was working. Sales during the year had increased 20 percent over the previous year, to $2,395,000.

Required:

You have been asked by the shareholders to prepare a report evaluating certain aspects of Magundy's performance during 2015. Your report should consider the following:

a. What should be Magundy's bad debt expense for 2015? In previous years Magundy calculated its bad debt expense based on 2 percent of credit sales during the year. Explain your answer.

b. How would you expect Magundy's accounts receivable turnover ratio to change from 2014 to 2015? Explain.

c. How would the new credit strategy affect Magundy's liquidity?

d. Do you think the new president's credit strategy is a good one? What are the risks and benefits of the new strategy?

P6-6.   (**Comparing the effects of different methods of accounting for bad debts, LO 3**) You have obtained the following information about Eskasoni Inc. (Eskasoni) from its 2014 annual report:

i.   Eskasoni's year-end is November 30.

ii.   Sales for the year ended November 30, 2014, were $3,750,000; 78 percent of sales are credit sales.

iii.   The balance in accounts receivable on November 30, 2014, was $386,000.

iv.   The balance in allowance for uncollectible accounts on November 30, 2013, was $20,800.

v.   During fiscal 2014, Eskasoni wrote off $23,000 of accounts receivable.

vi.   The bad debt expense can be estimated as 0.75 percent of credit sales or 5 percent of year-end accounts receivable.

vii.   Net income for the year ended November 30, 2014, including all revenues and expenses except for the bad debt expense, was $75,000.

Required:

a. Determine the bad debt expense for the year ended 2014, assuming that Eskasoni used:
   i. the direct-writeoff method for accounting for uncollectible accounts.
   ii. the percentage-of-credit-sales method for accounting for uncollectible accounts.
   iii. the percentage-of-receivables method for accounting for uncollectible accounts.

b. What would be the balance in allowance for uncollectible accounts on November 30, 2014 using the three methods identified in (a)?

c. Prepare the journal entry required to record the bad debt expense under each of the three methods identified in (a).

d. What would net income be in 2014 under each of the three methods in (a)?

e. Explain why the three methods in (a) provide different bad debt expenses.

f. Which method of determining the bad debt expense and the allowance for uncollectible accounts is best? Explain.

P6-7. (**Comparing the effects of different methods of accounting for bad debts, LO 3**) You have obtained the following information about Dogwood Inc. (Dogwood) from its 2015 annual report:

   i. Dogwood's year-end is April 30.

   ii. Sales for the year ended April 30, 2015 were $1,275,000; 90 percent of sales are credit sales.

   iii. The balance in accounts receivable on April 30, 2015 was $222,500.

   iv. The balance in allowance for uncollectible accounts on April 30, 2014 was $22,950.

   v. During fiscal 2015 Dogwood wrote off $19,700 of accounts receivable.

   vi. The bad debt expense can be estimated as 2 percent of credit sales or 11 percent of year-end accounts receivable.

   vii. Net income for the year ended April 30, 2015, including all revenues and expenses except for the bad debt expense, was $112,000.

Required:

a. Determine the bad debt expense for the year ended 2015, assuming that Dogwood used:
   i. the direct-writeoff method for accounting for uncollectible accounts.
   ii. the percentage-of-credit-sales method for accounting for uncollectible accounts.
   iii. the percentage-of-receivables method for accounting for uncollectible accounts.

b. What would be the balance in allowance for uncollectible accounts on April 30, 2015 using the three methods identified in (a)?

c. Prepare the journal entry required to record the bad debt expense under each of the three methods identified in (a).

d. What would net income be for 2015 under each of the three methods in (a)?

e. Explain why the three methods in (a) provide different bad debt expenses.

f. Which method of determining the bad debt expense and the allowance for uncollectible accounts is best? Explain.

P6-8. (**Observing the effect of errors in estimating the bad debt expense and the allowance of uncollectible accounts on the financial statements, LO 3, 4**) Since 2011 Kyuquot Inc. (Kyuquot) has estimated that its bad debt expense would be approximately 2 percent of credit sales each year. During 2012 a number of changes took place in the company's finance department that significantly reduced the effectiveness of its internal controls over credit granting and receivables collection. As a result, in 2013 uncollectibles increased to about 3 percent of credit sales. However, the accounting department never bothered to increase the 2 percent rate that had been implemented in 2011.

The following information is also available about Kyuquot's receivables and bad debts:
  i. Kyuquot's year-end is December 31.
  ii. The balance in Kyuquot's allowance account on January 1, 2011, was $40,000.
  iii. Credit sales and writeoffs by year and accounts receivable on December 31 of each year were:

Year	Credit sales made during the year	Writeoffs during the year	Accounts receivable on December 31*
2011	$1,500,000	$45,000	$526,000
2012	1,650,000	48,750	562,000
2013	1,860,000	56,200	614,000
2014	2,100,000	63,950	672,000
2015	2,390,000	70,500	752,000
2016	2,600,000	77,800	806,000

*Accounts receivable is the gross amount, before deducting the allowance for doubtful accounts.

Required:

a. Calculate the bad debt expense Kyuquot's accounting department would have made in each year from 2011 through 2016.

b. Calculate the balance in allowance for uncollectible accounts on December 31 of each year, after the adjusting entry recording the bad debt expense for the year recorded.

c. Examine the balance in the allowance account over the period from 2011 through 2016. Explain what is happening to the allowance account as a result of using a percentage of credit sales that is consistently too high. (To answer it may help to look at the balance in the allowance account as a percentage of accounts receivable.)

d. What is the effect on income each year of using a percentage of credit sales that is consistently too small? Explain.

e. What is the net amount of accounts receivable (accounts receivable − allowance for uncollectibles) on Kyuquot's balance sheet on December 31, 2016? Does the amount on the balance sheet represent the net realizable value of the accounts receivable on December 31, 2016? Explain.

f. What would the balance in the allowance account be on December 31, 2016 after the adjusting entry for bad debts is made if Kyuquot expensed 3 percent of credit sales as bad debts beginning in 2013?

g. Suppose that in 2016 management become aware of the error it was making estimating bad debts each year by using 2 percent of credit sales instead of 3 percent. What journal entry would Kyuquot have to make to reduce the balance in the allowance account to the amount calculated in (f)? What would be the effect of this journal entry on net income in 2016? What are some of the implications of these errors on users of the financial statements?

P6-9. (**The effect of transactions on ratios, LO 3, 4**) Indicate whether each of the following transactions and economic events will increase, decrease, or have no effect have on the current ratio, quick ratio, accounts receivable turnover ratio, and the average collection period of accounts receivable. Assume that the current and quick ratios are greater than 1.0 before each of the items is considered.
  1. Credit sale.
  2. Recording a new long-term receivable.
  3. Cash sale.
  4. Writing off an uncollectible account.
  5. Recording the bad debt expense.

6. Collection of accounts receivable.
7. Purchase of inventory on credit.
8. A new short-term bank loan.
9. Reclassification of a long-term receivable as current (because it will come due within 12 months).
10. A GIC classified as a cash equivalent matures and cash is received from the bank.

P6-10. (**Determine missing information, LO 4**) Use the information provided to determine the values for the missing information (indicated by shaded boxes):

Current assets on December 31, 2015 = $ 235,000

Current liabilities on December 31, 2015 = $_____

Current ratio on December 31, 2015 = _____

Quick assets on December 31, 2015 = $183,750

Quick ratio on December 31, 2015 = 1.05

Accounts receivable on December 31, 2015 = $85,200

Accounts receivable on December 31, 2014 = $87,500

Revenues (all on credit) during 2015 = $_____

Accounts receivable turnover ratio for 2015 = _____

Average collection period of accounts receivable for 2015 = 47 days

P6-11. (**Determine missing information, LO 4**) Use the information provided to determine the values for the missing information (indicated by shaded boxes):

Current assets on December 31, 2015 = $275,000

Current liabilities on December 31, 2015 = $ _____

Current ratio on December 31, 2015 = 1.5

Quick assets on December 31, 2015 = $ 140,000

Quick ratio on December 31, 2015 = _____

Accounts receivable on December 31, 2015* = $_____

Accounts receivable on December 31, 2014 = $_____

Revenues (all on credit) during 2015 = $ 585,000

Accounts receivable turnover ratio for 2015 = 6.50

Average collection period of accounts receivable for 2015 = _____

*Accounts receivable on December 31, 2015 is 10 percent greater than on December 31, 2014.

P6-12. (**The effect of transactions and economic events on ratios, LO 3, 4**) Complete the table below by indicating whether the transactions or economic events would increase, decrease, or have no effect on the financial ratios in the period they occur. Assume the entity uses an accrual method for estimating the bad debt expense and the allowance for uncollectibles. Also assume the current and quick ratios are greater than one before each of the events occurs.

	Current ratio	Quick ratio	Accounts receivable turnover ratio	Average collection period of accounts receivable	Debt-to-equity ratio	Profit margin ratio
Writeoff of an account receivable						
Collection of a previously written off account receivable						
Collection of an account receivable						
Recording the bad debt expense						
Sale of merchandise on credit; payment due in three years						
Purchase of inventory for cash						
Purchase of inventory on credit						

P6-13. (**The effect of transactions on ratios, LO 3, 4**) For the year ended December 31, 2015 Alpena Inc. (Alpena) had revenues of $750,000, of which 80 percent were on credit. Its accounts receivable turnover ratio for 2015 was 8.39. Accounts receivable on December 31, 2014 was $68,000. Calculate the effect on the average collection period of accounts receivable and the accounts receivable turnover ratio if the following additional transactions occurred during 2015. Consider the effect of each transaction or economic event separately.

a. Alpena, which uses the percentage-of-credit-sales method of estimating the bad debt expense, wrote off an additional $500 of accounts receivable.
b. Alpena collected an additional $8,000 of accounts receivable from customers.
c. Alpena recognized additional cash revenue of $12,500.
d. Alpena recognized additional credit revenue of $12,500.
e. Alpena recorded an additional bad debt expense of $1,000.

P6-14. (**Accounting for long-term receivables, LO 2, 3**) On July 31, 2016 Romanace Ltd. (Romanace) agreed to sell Youbou Inc. (Youbou) $12,000,000 of specialized equipment for use at its newly developed mine site in northern Manitoba. Because the mine hasn't begun production, the parties agreed that Youbou would pay for the equipment on August 6, 2018, at which time the mine would be generating the cash flow needed to pay Romanace. Despite the fact Romanace wouldn't be receiving its cash for two years it decided to recognize the revenue from the sale during the year ended July 31, 2016. The agreement between Romanace and Youbou states that Youbou doesn't have to pay any interest on the amount owed. The market rate of interest for an arrangement of this type is 10 percent.

Required:

a. How much revenue should Romanace recognize in the year ended July 31, 2016, for the sale to Youbou? Prepare the journal entry that Romanace should prepare to record the sale.
b. What amount would be reported on Romanace's July 31, 2016 balance sheet for accounts receivable as a result of the sale to Youbou? How would the receivable from Youbou be shown on the balance sheet? Explain your answer.
c. How much interest revenue should Romanace report on its July 31, 2017 and 2018 income statements as a result of the sale to Youbou? Prepare the journal entry that Romanace would make to record the interest revenue each year. What amount would be shown as receivable from Youbou on Romanace's July 31, 2017 and 2018

balance sheets? How would the receivable from Youbou be classified on the balance sheet each year?

d. What journal entry would Romanace make when it received payment in full on August 6, 2018?

e. Suppose that instead of being an interest free arrangement Youbou agreed to pay 10 percent interest per year, payable on July 16 each year. What amount of revenue should Romanace recognize in fiscal 2016?

P6-15. **(Using an aging schedule to calculate the bad debt expense, LO 3)** Examine the following information about Weyakwin Inc. (Weyakwin):

i. Ending balance in allowance for uncollectible accounts on April 30, 2014 = $102,000 (credit balance).

ii. Accounts receivable written off during the year ended April 30, 2015 = $97,000.

iii. Aging schedule for accounts receivable outstanding on April 30, 2015:

Account age	Balance on April 30, 2015	Percent estimated to be uncollectible
Current	$432,000	1.25%
1–30 days overdue	168,000	4.50
31–60 days overdue	90,000	12.00
61–120 days overdue	60,000	50.00
More than 120 days overdue	90,000	80.00

Required:

a. What amount of closing accounts receivable is estimated to be uncollectible on April 30, 2015?

b. Prepare the journal entry required to record the bad debt expense for Weyakwin for the year ended April 30, 2015.

c. What are some possible explanations for the change in the allowance account between April 30, 2014, and April 30, 2015?

P6-16. **(Correcting the balance in Allowance for Uncollectible Accounts, LO 3)** Trilby Inc. (Trilby) uses the percentage-of-credit-sales method for estimating its bad debt expense. The percentage Trilby uses is based on historical information. Trilby's management hasn't revised the percentage for several years, a period during which a number of environmental and business factors have changed. Trilby's management recently realized that over the last three years the percentage of credit sales the company has been using is too high. As a result, the balance in allowance for uncollectible accounts is $53,000 higher than it would have been had a better estimate of bad debts been used each year.

Required:

a. Prepare the adjusting journal entry that Trilby must make to have an appropriate balance in allowance for uncollectible accounts.

b. What is the effect of the error in estimating bad debts in each of the years the error was made? What is the effect of the adjusting entry on net income? Answer the question by comparing the reported net income with what net income would have been had the error not been made and the adjusting entry not required.

c. What is the impact of this error and the adjusting entry on the users of the financial statements? Explain fully.

P6-17. **(Managing accounts receivable, LO 4)** A financial analyst is comparing the credit management of two companies, Zealand Inc. (Zealand) and Manotick Ltd. (Manotick). The two companies are in the same industry, but operate in different parts of the country. They don't compete because their services can only be provided in their local markets. Through conversations with representatives of each of the companies the analyst learned that Zealand gives its customers 45 days to pay invoices while Manotick gives 60 days. The analyst obtained the following information about each company:

Zealand Inc.	2015	2014	2013	2012	2011
Revenue	$1,405,560	$1,326,000	$1,300,000	$1,250,000	
% Credit sales	85.0%	82.0%	83.0%	80.0%	
Accounts receivable at year-end	$184,100	$162,410	$153,250	$139,165	$125,000
Manotick Ltd.	2015	2014	2013	2012	2011
Revenue	$1,518,967	$1,446,635	$1,404,500	$1,325,000	
% Credit sales	70.0%	71.0%	68.0%	72.0%	
Accounts receivable at year-end	$212,120	211,910	$195,188	$208,200	$196,000

Required:

a. Calculate the accounts receivable turnover ratio for Zealand and Manotick for 2012–2015.
b. Calculate the average collection period of accounts receivable for Zealand and Manotick for 2012–2015.
c. Which company is doing a better job managing its receivables? Explain.

P6-18. **(Creating hidden reserves, LO 4)** The president of Remo Ltd. (Remo) wants to use hidden reserves to "save" income for a year when the company isn't performing very well. To accomplish this objective the president instructed the accounting department to overestimate the bad debt expense each year. Instead of using the historical norm of 1.5 percent of credit sales, the president suggested using 1.75 percent of credit sales. Remo commenced this "policy" in 2012 and it has continued through 2016, a period in which Remo has been very successful. The following information about Remo is available:

	2012	2013	2014	2015	2016
Credit sales	$2,527,000	$3,158,750	$3,632,563	$4,286,424	$4,929,387
Net income, excluding the bad debt expense	$232,484	$315,875	$345,093	$398,637	$443,645
Accounts receivable writeoffs	$31,500	$37,905	$47,381	$54,488	$64,296

The credit balance in Remo's allowance for uncollectible accounts on January 1, 2012, was $31,500.

Required:

a. Prepare a table that shows
   i. Remo's bad debt expense from 2012 through 2016 using the 1.5 percent rate.
   ii. Remo's bad debt expense from 2012 through 2016 using the 1.75 percent rate.
   iii. The allowance for uncollectible accounts at the end of each year using each of the estimates.
   iv. Net income for each year using each of the two estimates.
b. How could the president of Remo justify using the 1.75 percent rate for estimating bad debts?
c. In 2017 Remo's net income fell slightly and the president was concerned about a negative response from shareholders and creditors. He was especially concerned that Remo was planning to approach new equity investors to invest in Remo.

Credit sales during 2017 were $5,191,000 and net income for the year, excluding the bad debt expense, was $441,410. At this point the president "recognized" the error that had been made over the previous five years and decided it was time to correct it. The president instructed the accounting department to reduce the balance in the allowance account to the level that would have existed had Remo used 1.5 percent of credit sales as the basis of calculating the bad debt expense each year.

    i. What journal entry would be prepared to reduce the balance in the allowance account to the desired level?

    ii. What would be the effect on net income of making this journal entry?

d. Why are hidden reserves a serious problem that undermines the integrity and usefulness of accounting information?

P6-19. **(Interpreting bad debts for a bank, LO 3, 4)** Zbaraz Bank Ltd. (Zbaraz) lends money to borrowers around the world. The major areas of concern to management and stakeholders are what's called the *loan loss provision* (which is equivalent to the bad debt expense for non-banking companies) and the *allowance for loan losses* (which is equivalent to the allowance for uncollectible accounts for non-banking companies). You are provided with the following information about Zbaraz loan situation:

Zbaraz Bank Ltd. Allowance for Loan Losses			
	2013	**2012**	**2011**
Beginning balance	$17,615,000	$17,770,000	$18,450,000
Loan losses (writeoffs of loans)			
Consumer loans	5,425,000	5,115,000	3,805,000
Canadian commercial loans	770,000	1,315,000	1,175,000
International commercial loans	330,000	195,000	75,000
Total	6,525,000	6,625,000	5,055,000
Loan loss recoveries			
Consumer loans	1,110,000	1,155,000	710,000
Canadian commercial loans	775,000	580,000	905,000
International commercial loans	135,000	300,000	495,000
Total	2,020,000	2,035,000	2,110,000
Loan loss provision	?	?	?
Ending balance	$17,500,000	$17,615,000	$17,770,000

a. Calculate the loan loss provision for Zbaraz for 2011, 2012, and 2013.

b. Examine the information about Zbaraz's loan losses and the loan loss provision you calculated in (a). Interpret and discuss any trends that you see in the data.

c. At the end of 2010, Zbaraz had a total of $835,555,000 of loans in its portfolio and reported on its balance sheet. The loan portfolio was broken down as follows:

Consumer loans	$370,545,000
Canadian commercial loans	322,350,000
International commercial loans	142,660,000
Total	$835,555,000

Which of the categories of loans is the most risky? Explain. Given the risk of that category, why does Zbaraz lend to this group?

d. The portfolio of loans could be further broken down in countries loaned to, industries, purpose of the consumer loan (car loan, home renovation loan, etc.), and so on. What additional information would you want about Zbaraz's loan portfolio as a stakeholder in the bank? Explain your answer.

Using Financial Statements

McGRAW-HILL RYERSON LIMITED

McGraw-Hill Ryerson Limited (MHR) publishes and distributes educational and professional products in both print and non-print media. These products are designed to fulfill the individual needs of customers by providing effective and innovative educational and learning solutions. Product offerings include text and professional reference books, multimedia tools, and teaching, assessment, support, and monitoring solutions. The company is committed to providing Canadians with material of the highest quality for their education and enjoyment.

www.mcgrawhill.ca

The company is structured on a market-focused basis and operates in three primary market areas through the following revenue divisions:

- Higher Education Division: postsecondary education, including universities, community, and career colleges.

- School Division: secondary and elementary schools.

- Professional Division: retailers (online and bricks and mortar), wholesalers, libraries, professionals.

McGraw-Hill Ryerson is a public company trading on the TSX under the symbol MHR, operated independently, in close cooperation with its majority shareholder, The McGraw-Hill Companies, Inc.[8]

EXHIBIT	6.5	McGraw-Hill Ryerson: Extracts from Financial Statements

Balance Sheets
McGraw-Hill Ryerson Limited. Incorporated under the laws of Ontario

(In Thousands of Dollars)

As at December 31	2008	2007
Assets		
Current		
Cash and cash equivalents	43,856	35,646
Accounts receivable [net of allowance for sales returns of $6,986; 2007 - $7,206] [note 10]	14,285	14,489
Due from parent and affiliated companies [note 2]	1,827	1,870
Inventories [note 4]	7,082	7,717
Prepaid expenses and other	296	354
Future tax assets [note 7]	2,263	2,390
Total current assets	69,609	62,466
Capital assets, net [note 5]	16,048	17,247
Other assets, net [note 6]	16,540	14,365
Future tax assets [note 7]	623	582
	102,820	94,660
Liabilities and Shareholders' Equity		
Current		
Accounts payable and accrued charges	10,721	10,821
Dividends payable	13,976	—
Income taxes payable	359	972
Due to parent and affiliated companies [note 2]	5,669	5,454
Total current liabilities	30,725	17,247
Employee future benefits [note 8]	2,026	1,983
Total liabilities	32,751	19,230
Commitments [note 9]		
Shareholders' equity		
Share capital		
Authorized 5,000,000 common shares		
Issued and outstanding 1,996,638 common shares	1,997	1,997
Retained earnings	68,072	73,433
Total shareholders' equity	70,069	75,430
	102,820	94,660

EXHIBIT 6.5 **(continued) McGraw-Hill Ryerson: Extracts from Financial Statements**

Statements of Income, Comprehensive Income, and Retained Earnings

(In Thousands of Dollars—except Per Share Data)

Years ended December 31	2008	2007
Revenue		
Sales, less returns	91,485	89,778
Other	3,065	2,754
	94,550	92,532
Expenses		
Operating [notes 2 and 4]	37,613	37,324
Editorial, selling, general and administrative [notes 3 and 13]	33,030	34,355
Amortization – prepublication costs	6,206	5,788
Amortization – capital assets	1,349	1,368
Employee future benefits [note 8]	99	(2,777)
Foreign exchange loss	345	644
	78,642	76,702
Income before income taxes	15,908	15,830
Provision for income taxes [note 7]		
Current	5,320	5,021
Future	86	849
	5,406	5,870
Net income and comprehensive income for the year	10,502	9,960

MHR's consolidated balance sheets, statements of income, and statements of cash flow, along with extracts from the notes to the financial statements are provided in Exhibit 6.5.[9] Use this information to respond to questions FS6-1 to FS6-10.

FS6-1. Find or determine the following amounts in MHR's financial statement information:
  a. Cash and equivalents on December 31, 2008.
  b. Net amount of accounts receivable on December 31, 2008.
  c. Gross amount of accounts receivable on December 31, 2008.
  d. Allowance for doubtful accounts on December 31, 2008.
  e. Allowance for estimated returns on December 31, 2008.
  f. Returns received from customers during 2008.
  g. Cash from operations for 2008.
  h. Revenue for 2008.

FS6-2. How much does MHR report on its balance sheet for accounts receivable on December 31, 2008? What does that amount represent (how would you explain its meaning to a novice user of financial statements)? How much do MHR's customers actually owe it on December 31, 2008? Why are the two amounts different?

FS6-3. Use the information provided in Exhibit 6.5 to make a complete assessment of MHR's liquidity position. Discuss the liquidity on December 31, 2008 and compare it with its liquidity on December 31, 2007. Assume MHR had accounts receivable on December 31, 2006, of $17,948,000.

FS6-4. Calculate MHR's current and quick ratios, and the amount of working capital on hand on December 31, 2008 and 2007. Using the current and quick ratios, the amount of working capital, and the information in the statements of cash flow, provide an assessment of MHR's liquidity position.

EXHIBIT 6.5 (continued) McGraw-Hill Ryerson: Extracts from Financial Statements

Statements of Cash Flows

(In Thousands of Dollars)

Years ended December 31	2008	2007
Operating Activities		
Net income for the year	10,502	9,960
Add (deduct) non-cash items		
Amortization – prepublication costs	6,206	5,788
Amortization – capital assets	1,349	1,368
Employee future benefits	43	(2,838)
Future income taxes	86	849
	18,186	15,127
Net change in non-cash working capital balances related to operations [note 12]	381	2,444
Cash provided by operating activities	18,567	17,571
Investing Activities		
Pre-publication costs	(8,320)	(7,423)
Additions to capital assets	(150)	(256)
Cash used in investing activities	(8,470)	(7,679)
Financing Activities		
Dividends paid to shareholders	(1,887)	(7,757)
Cash used in financing activities	(1,887)	(7,757)
Net increase in cash during the year	8,210	2,135
Cash and cash equivalents, beginning of year	35,646	33,511
Cash and cash equivalents, end of year	43,856	35,646

1 SUMMARY OF SIGNIFICANT ACCOUNTING POLICIES

Cash and cash equivalents

The Company considers all highly liquid instruments with a maturity date of ninety days or less at the date of acquisition to be cash equivalents.

Allowance for doubtful accounts and sales returns

The accounts receivable reserve methodology is based on historical analysis and a review of outstanding balances. A significant estimate for the Company is the allowance for sales returns, which is based on the historical rate of return and current market conditions.

Revenue recognition

The Company recognizes revenue for product sales, net of estimated returns, when the products are shipped to customers, which is also when title passes to the customer.

Other revenue is comprised mainly of rental income, interest, copyright/translation fees and other miscellaneous income, and is recognized as earned on a monthly basis.

FS6-5. Examine the significant accounting policy note on the allowance for doubtful accounts and sales returns. Explain why these allowances are important. What are the challenges that managers face in determining the amount of these allowances? What journal entries are required to record the allowances? What would the impact on the financial statements be if these allowances weren't recorded? What journal entry would be recorded when a customer returns books to MHR? How could MHR's managers use these accounts to create hidden reserves?

EXHIBIT ⟨ 6.5 ⟩ (continued) McGraw-Hill Ryerson: Extracts from Financial Statements

Use of estimates

The preparation of financial statements in accordance with Canadian generally accepted accounting principles requires management to make estimates and assumptions that affect the reported amounts of assets and liabilities and disclosure of contingent assets and liabilities at the date of the financial statements and the reported amounts of revenue and expenses during the reporting period. Actual results may differ from those estimates.

10 FINANCIAL INSTRUMENTS

As at December 31,	2008	2007
Accounts receivable	21,677	22,081
Less: Allowance for doubtful accounts	(406)	(386)
Less: Allowance for estimated returns	(6,986)	(7,207)
Accounts receivable as reported	14,285	14,489

	2008	2007
Allowance for doubtful accounts, beginning of year	386	390
Add: Provision booked to expense	24	104
Less: Write-offs	(4)	(108)
Allowance for doubtful accounts, end of year	406	386

	2008	2007
Allowance for estimated returns, beginning of year	7,207	7,013
Less: Returns received from customers	(6,621)	(7,013)
Add: Provision for current year sales	6,400	7,207
Allowance for estimated returns, end of year	6,986	7,207

The following table sets forth the age of trade receivables that are not overdue as well as an analysis of overdue amounts:

As at December 31,	2008	2007
Not overdue	84%	88%
Past due for more than one day but not more than three months	14%	11%
Past due for more than three months	2%	1%

The Company's five largest customers make up approximately 29% [2007 - 33%] of the accounts receivable balance and approximately 14% [2007 - 14%] of net sales.

Liquidity risk arises through the excess of financial obligations over available financial assets due at any point in time. The Company's objective in managing liquidity risk is to maintain sufficient readily available reserves in order to meet its liquidity requirements at any point in time. The Company achieves this by maintaining sufficient cash and cash equivalents and through the availability of funding from committed credit facilities. As at December 31, 2008, the Company was holding cash and cash equivalents of $43,856 and had undrawn lines of credit available to it of $6,500. As the majority of the Company's cash and cash equivalents are held by one bank in Canada there is a concentration of credit risk. This risk is managed by performing a periodic review of the credit status of our financial institution.

FS6-6. Read the significant accounting policy note on the use of estimates. Why is this note included in the financial statements and why is it important?

FS6-7. How does MHR recognize revenue? How much revenue did MHR recognize in 2008? What adjustments were required to revenue in 2008 to arrive at the amount reported on the income statement? What is the gross amount of sales that MHR recorded in 2008? What accounts are affected when MHR records a sale?

FS6-8. Calculate MHR's accounts receivable turnover ratio for the years ended December 31, 2008 and 2007 (assume account receivable on December 31, 2006, was $17,948,000). What is the average collection period of accounts receivable for the two years? Do the accounts receivable turnover ratio and the average collection period indicate that MHR is managing its receivables well? Explain.

FS6-9. What amount of MHR's December 31, 2008 accounts receivable are not overdue? What amount is overdue three months or less? What amount is overdue more than three months? Compare the percentages of overdue receivables on December 31, 2008 with the percentages on December 31, 2007. Assess the change over the year.

FS6-10. What are sales returns and why is it necessary to have an allowance for them? How does accounting for the allowance affect the financial statements? What was MHR's allowance on December 31, 2008? What journal entry did MHR make to record the provision for returns in 2008? How much merchandise did customers return in 2008? What journal entry did MHR make to record returns during 2008? How good an estimate did MHR's management make in 2007 for returns in 2008?

ENDNOTES

1. Extracted from TransAlta Corporation's 2008 annual report.

2. Extracted from TransAlta Corporation's website, http://www.transalta.com/transalta/webcms.nsf/AllDoc/6BC91FA6BF1556AE87257157004FAB9D?OpenDocument (accessed January 1, 2009).

3. Extracted from Rogers Communications Inc.'s 2008 annual report.

4. Extracted from Gildan Activewear Inc.'s 2008 annual report.

5. Arthur Levitt, speech to the Financial Executives Institute, New York, New York, November 16, 1998, quoted at the United States Securities and Exchange Commission website, http://www.sec.gov/news/speech/speecharchive/1998/spch227.htm (accessed April 18, 2002).

6. Extracted from Magna International Inc.'s 2008 annual report.

7. Industry data extracted from 2009 Industry Reports published by the Financial Post.

8. Adapted from McGraw-Hill Ryerson Limited 2008 annual report.

9. Extracted from McGraw-Hill Ryerson Limited 2008 annual report.

CHAPTER

7

INVENTORY

LEARNING OBJECTIVES

After studying the material in this chapter you will be able to do the following:

▶ **LO 1** Understand the nature, purpose, and importance of inventory to an entity.

▶ **LO 2** Distinguish between the perpetual and periodic methods of inventory control.

▶ **LO 3** Distinguish among the different cost formulas used to account for inventory and cost of sales, and understand the impact the different cost formulas have on the amounts reported in the financial statements.

▶ **LO 4** Explain the lower of cost and market rule.

▶ **LO 5** Recognize the issues, choices, and effects on the financial statements of using market values instead of cost for valuing inventory.

▶ **LO 6** Discuss the relationship between inventory accounting policy and income tax.

▶ **LO 7** Analyze and interpret inventory information in financial statements.

Robert Patterson was working in war-torn Sarajevo in 1997, in the aftermath of a long siege by Serb troops loyal to the former Yugoslav government. Patterson, a Canadian accountant, was attached to an American government charity and overseeing $250 million in post-war reconstruction loans.

Plenty of small- and medium-sized enterprises (SMEs) were eager to get their share of that loan money, but few had solid business plans or reliable financial forecasts. Patterson, a CA since 1977, had to improvise.

The old library at Warsaw University of Technology, photo by Jacek Surma.

"You'd just take the back of an envelope and you'd work backwards; you'd reconstruct financial statements," Patterson recalled. He'd ask the businessmen what they were selling and who they were buying from. "That was the beauty of it because you could see the economic reality, the balance sheet was a stock in time, and you could see it and kick the tires," he said.

Although he calls his work with the U. S. Agency for International Development (USAID) one of his most satisfying projects, Patterson has also spent two decades as a consultant to banks in emerging and transition markets, including India, Russia, Kazakhstan, Vietnam, Romania and China.

His message to bankers in countries that are slowly moving away from their communist traditions to a market economy: Use accounting before lending money to SMEs.

"From a banking point of view, you get the numbers, what do the numbers say? How is this company doing? Is it viable? And could I, based on taking a good hard look at the financial statements, come up with a vision of the future, their debt servicing capacity in the future, a forecast?"

Patterson grew up in Ottawa and obtained his bachelor of commerce and a master's degree in economics from Queen's University. After receiving his CA designation while working at Price Waterhouse (now PricewaterhouseCoopers), he was hired by the Toronto Dominion bank as a credit officer.

"The accounting helped a lot," Patterson said. "They perceived me as something special and they plunked me in training at Bloor Street and Spadina Avenue. It was a tough branch. That's where the action was. I had a great year and I loved it."

Although he eventually worked his way up to TD's corporate head office in Toronto, Patterson says he always preferred direct contact with customers. So,

after losing his job during the recession in 1990, he volunteered abroad with CESO (Canadian Executive Service Organization). He started in Poland and never left.

Now based in Poland, where he also teaches accounting courses at Warsaw's University of Technology, Patterson says a chartered accountant, or "Biegly rewident" in Polish, is seen there as a highly respected professional, although there are relatively few for a country with the population about the size of Canada's (15,000 CAs for 38 million people in Poland, compared with 74,000 CAs in Canada).

Patterson says having a CA after his name became a "means to an end."

"It's a business skill. It's not about compliance," he explained. "That's what makes accounting interesting. They're the ones with the intellectual horsepower. They're calling the shots. Accounting rules."

—E.B.

INTRODUCTION

For many entities, inventory is the business. What's a clothing store without clothes or a car dealership without cars? What's an appliance manufacturer without the parts to build the appliances or a fast food outlet without burgers, fries, or the ingredients to make pizza? In each case, it's the inventory that is directly responsible for revenue generation. Many service businesses also require inventory to provide their services to customers. Painters require paint. Lawn care companies require fertilizer.

Accounting for inventory can be surprisingly tricky. Our exposure to accounting for inventory so far has been straightforward—we record the inventory at cost and then expense the cost when it's sold. But the real world isn't always that simple. Imagine a company with thousands of identical units of inventory that didn't all cost the same amount. In many cases we don't know the cost of the particular unit that was sold. However, we still have to determine a cost for the inventory sold so we can prepare an income statement and balance sheet. This is a challenge accountants face: how to determine the value of inventory on hand and the cost of inventory sold when we don't know the cost of the specific inventory sold or used.

This chapter examines inventory accounting issues and how the resolutions of those issues affect financial statement numbers. The chapter also discusses a number of other issues that will broaden your perspective of accounting information. I have already pointed out that historical cost, transaction-based accounting isn't the only way to account, although it's the dominant method in Canada. In this chapter we'll take a quick look at non-cost-based methods for accounting for inventory to see how financial statements would be affected by using alternatives to cost. We will also discuss the close link between accounting and tax. We have already identified tax minimization as an important objective of financial reporting. Here we'll see how the Canadian income tax system affects accounting choices and financial reporting by entities.

WHAT IS INVENTORY?

Inventory is assets held for sale or assets used to produce goods that will be sold as part of the entity's normal business activities. It can also include materials and supplies used to provide a service to customers. The type of inventory carried depends on what an entity does. Consider inventory in the following businesses:

Business	Inventory
Pizza shop	Pizza ingredients, drinks, dipping sauces, pizza boxes, napkins, plastic utensils, paper cups and plates
Winery	Wine available for sale, aging wine, supplies needed to make wine (grapes, sugar, yeast), other supplies (bottles, labels, corks)
Land development and home builder	Homes completed or under construction, developed and undeveloped land
Forest products company	Lumber, panels, pulp, paper, logs, wood chips, processing materials and supplies

We can learn a lot about the nature of a business from the composition of its balance sheet. For example, Indigo Books & Music Inc.'s inventory is 66.2 percent of current assets and 45.5 percent of total assets (see Table 7.1). Indigo requires a huge inventory in its stores and warehouses to meet the demands of in-store and online customers, but because its stores are rented rather then owned it doesn't have a lot of investment in property and equipment, and because it's a retail business, accounts receivable are low (retail customers mainly pay by cash or major credit cards). Magna International Inc., an auto parts manufacturer, also has a huge investment in inventory (see Table 7.1), but it has even larger investments in accounts receivable (its sales are on credit) and property, plant, and equipment (land, buildings, machinery, and equipment used to manufacture its products). In contrast, WestJet Airlines Inc., a service company, needs very little inventory to run its business. WestJet's inventory of spare parts, fuel, and supplies is only 1.8 percent of current assets and 0.5 percent of total assets. Table 7.1 shows the dollar value of the inventory of eight companies in different industries, along with the proportion of current assets and total assets the inventory is.

Many entities have different categories of inventory, and information about these can be disclosed on the balance sheet or in the notes. Companies that manufacture or process inputs into finished goods can break inventory down into three subcategories:

www.canfor.com
www.highlinerfoods.com
www.indigo.ca
www.loblaw.ca
www.magna.com
www.magnotta.com
www.westjet.com
www.timhortons.com

1. **Raw materials** The inputs into the production process. For example, raw materials inventory for a furniture manufacturer includes wood used to build the furniture.

2. **Work-in-process** or **WIP** Inventory that is partially completed on the financial statement date. For a car manufacturer, a partially completed car would be classified as WIP inventory.

3. **Finished goods** Inventory that has been completed and is ready for sale. Also, one entity's inventory is another's equipment, and one entity's finished good is another's raw material. For example, the ovens used to bake bread are equipment for the bakery but finished goods inventory to the company that makes ovens. The flour and sugar used to make bread are the bakery's raw materials but finished goods for the flour mill and the sugar refiner.

TABLE 7.1	Amount of Inventory In Different Companies			
Company	Type of business	Dollar value of inventory	Inventory as a percentage of current assets	Inventory as a percentage of total assets
Canfor Corporation	Forest products	$ 404,900,000	37.5%	12.7%
Highliner Foods Incorporated	Food processing	146,863,000	66.4	43.3
Indigo Books & Music Inc.	Retail	221,767,000	66.2	45.5
Loblaw Companies Limited	Grocery retail	2,188,000,000	55.3	15.6
Magna International Inc.	Auto parts maker	1,647,000,000	22.4	12.5
Magnotta Winery Corporation	Winery	27,847,603	96.6	55.5
Tim Horton's Inc.	Fast food service	71,505,000	15.4	3.6
WestJet Airlines Ltd.	Airline	17,054,000	1.8	0.5

WHAT DOES IFRS SAY?

There are some important questions about accounting for inventory:

- How should inventory be measured in financial statements?

- What costs should be included in inventory?

- How should inventory costs flow through the inventory account on the balance sheet to cost of goods sold on the income statement?

- What information should be disclosed?

Generally, IFRS require inventory to be valued at cost on the balance sheet. When the net realizable value (NRV) of inventory is less than cost, inventory should be written down to its NRV. (NRV is the amount an asset could be sold for now, less selling costs.) This is known as the lower of cost and market rule. There are some industries that always record inventory at NRV. These topics will be discussed later in the chapter.

The cost of inventory usually includes more than the amount paid to the supplier. For inventory that's purchased (for example, inventory acquired by retailers and wholesalers for sale to customers, and raw materials purchased by manufacturers and processors), cost includes all costs incurred to ready the inventory for sale or use: purchase price of the inventory, import duties and other taxes, shipping and handling, and any other costs directly related to the purchase of the inventory.

For manufacturers and processors, determining the cost of inventory is tricky. A manufacturer uses a combination of purchased raw materials, workers, and other assets (for example, machinery and equipment) to produce finished goods. The cost of inventory should include all the costs incurred to produce the finished inventory. IFRS require that the cost of inventory include the cost of materials used plus the cost of labour directly used to produce the product, plus an allocation of overhead incurred in the production process. **Overhead** is the costs in a manufacturing process other than direct labour and direct materials. Overhead costs can be very difficult to associate directly with the product being made.

Without going into too much detail let's consider how this costing process works. Consider a small shop that makes handcrafted wood furniture. A skilled worker uses wood, fabric, glue, and nails to make a chair. Clearly, the cost of the materials and the amount the worker is paid while making the chair are included in the cost of inventory. But there are other costs: machines to do some of the work, rent for the facility where the work is done, and heat and light for this facility. Others work in the facility; people supervise our skilled worker, clean up the shop, maintain the equipment, prepare the furniture for shipping, and so on. These other costs, things other than the cost of materials and skilled labour that builds the chair, are considered part of overhead and must be included in the cost of inventory. Accountants must find ways of attaching these overhead costs to the furniture produced. Keep in mind that most production facilities produce more than one product. The furniture shop will produce different types of tables and chairs along with other kinds of furniture, so the allocation problem is even more complex.

KNOWLEDGE CHECK

www.mcgrawhill
connect.ca

Again consider the small shop making handcrafted wood furniture. According to IFRS, which of the following costs would be included in the cost of inventory and which would not? Briefly explain your answers.

- ❑ amount paid to shipping company that delivered a shipment of fabric for a custom order of furniture

- ❑ salary paid to the accountant in the facility

- ❑ cost of varnish used to finish a set of bookcases

- ❑ shop floor supervisor who ensures all projects are proceeding as planned

Even though IFRS require all production costs, including overhead, to be included in the cost of inventory, they don't provide specific directions for determining which costs and how much of them should be included. As a result, different entities can determine the cost of inventory differently, which impairs comparability. IFRS do state that costs not related to producing the inventory and readying it for sale are to be excluded. These costs include storage, administration (head-office costs), selling and marketing, and waste.

Keep in mind that entities that don't have to follow IFRS might approach things differently. For example, an entity's whose main objective is to minimize taxes might expense as much of its overhead costs as it can as it's incurred, within the rules of the *Income Tax Act*, to defer taxes.

PERPETUAL AND PERIODIC INVENTORY CONTROL SYSTEMS

There are two systems for keeping track of or "controlling" transactions affecting inventory in an accounting system: perpetual inventory systems and periodic inventory systems. A **perpetual inventory control system** keeps an ongoing tally of purchases and sales of inventory, and the inventory account is adjusted to reflect changes as they occur. When inventory is purchased or sold the inventory records are immediately debited or credited to record the change. When inventory is sold, cost of sales is debited immediately. A perpetual system can determine cost of sales at any time.

On December 31, 2014, Telkwa Ltd. (Telkwa) had $20,000 of inventory on hand. During 2015 it purchased $100,000 of new inventory and had sales of $210,000. Cost of sales for 2015 was $95,000. On December 31, 2015, Telkwa had inventory of $25,000. The following journal entry records the purchase of inventory in a perpetual inventory control system:

Dr. Inventory (asset +)	100,000	
Cr. Accounts payable (liability +) or Cash (asset −)		100,000
To record the purchase of inventory using a perpetual inventory control system		

When inventory is sold, Telkwa would record the following journal entries:

Dr. Cash (asset +) or Accounts receivable (asset +)	210,000	
Cr. Revenue (revenue +, owners' equity +)		210,000
To record the sale of inventory		

Dr. Cost of sales (expense +, owners' equity −)	95,000	
Cr. Inventory (asset −)		95,000
To record the sale of inventory in a perpetual inventory control system and the corresponding cost of sales		

With a perpetual system the cost of the inventory sold is known when the sale occurs and is recorded at that time. Because recording cost of sales occurs when the actual exchange with the customer takes place, the entry is a transactional entry.

With a **periodic inventory control system** the inventory account isn't adjusted whenever a transaction affects inventory. Inventory purchases aren't recorded directly to inventory but are accumulated in a separate purchases account. The balance in inventory at the end of a period is determined by actually counting the inventory, not from the accounting system. With a periodic system, cost of sales is determined indirectly using the following equation:

Cost of sales = Beginning inventory + Purchases − Ending inventory

The beginning and ending inventory balances are known from the inventory counts and the amount of purchases are available from the purchases account. Because it's necessary to count the inventory to calculate cost of sales, it isn't possible to determine cost of sales from the accounting system before the end of a period.

The following journal entry records the purchase of inventory in a periodic inventory control system:

Dr. Purchases (expense +)   100,000

    Cr. Accounts payable (liability +), Cash (asset −)   100,000

To record the purchase of inventory in a periodic inventory control system (*Note:* The purchases account is an expense account.)

When inventory is sold Telkwa would make the following journal entry:

Dr. Cash (asset +)   210,000

    Cr. Revenue (revenue +, owners' equity +)   210,000

To record the sale of inventory (This entry is the same as with the perpetual system. The sale transaction isn't affected by the inventory control system being used.)

No entry records cost of sales until the end of the period after the inventory has been counted. Because the recording of cost of sales isn't triggered by an external transaction (it isn't triggered by the sale), it's an adjusting entry. Telkwa's cost of sales for 2015 would be calculated as follows:

$$\text{Cost of sales} = \text{Beginning inventory} + \text{Purchases} - \text{Ending inventory}$$
$$= \$20,000 + \$100,000 - \$25,000$$
$$= \$95,000$$

The following adjusting entry is necessary so that $25,000 of inventory is reported on Telkwa's December 31, 2015, balance sheet and $95,000 of cost of sales is reported on its 2015 income statement:

Dr. Cost of sales (expenses +)   95,000

Dr. Inventory (assets +)   5,000

    Cr. Purchases (expenses −)   100,000

To record cost of sales for 2015

www.mcgrawhill connect.ca/

KNOWLEDGE CHECK

❑ Describe the three subcategories of inventory usually reported in the financial statements of manufacturing firms.

❑ Describe the two inventory control systems used to keep track of inventory transactions. How do the two differ?

❑ Trenche Ltd. provides you with the following information about its inventory:

Inventory on December 31, 2013	$ 175,000
Purchases during 2014	1,245,000
Inventory on December 31, 2014	210,000

Trenche uses a periodic inventory control system. Use this information to calculate Trenche's cost of sales for 2014.

Internal Control

A perpetual inventory control system doesn't eliminate the need for counting the inventory from time to time. Sales aren't the only way inventory is consumed; it can be stolen, lost, damaged, or destroyed. A perpetual system only accounts for the cost of inventory actually sold and only a physical count will determine inventory consumed in other ways.

For example, if $5,000 of inventory had been stolen during the year, the perpetual inventory records would show $5,000 more inventory than there actually is because the theft wouldn't be recorded (thieves don't usually report their activities). If the inventory wasn't counted the inventory amount on the balance sheet would be overstated by $5,000 and expenses would be understated by $5,000. (Stolen inventory is an expense in the period the theft occurs or is discovered.) Differences between the accounting records and the count can also be due to errors in recording transactions. After the count the accounting records should be adjusted to correspond with the actual amount of inventory on hand.

Counting inventory is valuable for internal control. Differences between the count and the accounting records allow management to identify inventory "shrinkage," allowing them to investigate its cause and implement a plan for reducing or eliminating the problem. For example, if management discovered that inventory was being stolen it could consider steps to better protect it from theft. Information about inventory theft could help stakeholders assess how well management is fulfilling its stewardship responsibilities, but information on stolen inventory is rarely, if ever, reported in financial statements. It is usually included in cost of sales.

With a periodic inventory control system it isn't possible to determine whether any theft has taken place as there are no records to compare with the physical count. Therefore, the cost of stolen items is included, by default, in cost of sales. More important, it isn't possible to tell from the accounting records that there is a problem with stolen inventory. This is a weakness of a periodic system. A periodic system doesn't allow for as effective control over inventory as a perpetual system. The choice between a periodic and perpetual inventory control system is thus an internal control issue, not an accounting issue. Managers choose between periodic and perpetual inventory control systems based on the costs and benefits of the two systems.

INVENTORY VALUATION METHODS

Now we'll discuss how the amount of ending inventory and cost of sales is determined each period. So far, we've assumed the actual cost of a unit of inventory when it's used or sold is known so cost of sales is simply debited and inventory credited for the amount. In fact, the actual cost is often not known. Consider an oil refinery that purchases oil daily on the world market at the prevailing price and stores it in large storage tanks. The price of oil fluctuates day-to-day, even minute-to-minute, so each storage tank will contain oil purchased at many different prices. What is the cost of a barrel of oil removed from the tank to produce gasoline and other petroleum products? It's impossible to know. Once oil of different prices is mixed together the cost of the individual amounts of oil is lost and it isn't possible to determine the cost of gasoline produced from a barrel of the oil.

Inventories of nails, lumber, seeds, tennis balls, chocolate bars, and plastic furniture—inventory that is relatively low in cost and homogeneous (the items are virtually identical)—have the same problem. Tracking the cost of individual items requires identifying the cost of each individual nail, seed, or tennis ball, which would be difficult, costly, and impractical. But to determine cost of sales for a period and the amount of ending inventory it's necessary to assign a cost to the inventory used or sold.

To solve the problem, accountants have developed methods called *cost formulas* that move costs through the inventory account to cost of sales without regard for the actual physical movement of the inventory. By using a cost formula the balance sheet cost of inventory may not be the actual cost of the physical items in inventory and cost of sales may not be the actual cost of the physical units received by customers.

There are three cost formulas allowed by IFRS:

1. first-in, first-out (FIFO)
2. average cost
3. specific identification

If the inventory is homogeneous or interchangeable then average cost or first-in, first-out (FIFO) inventory cost formulas are used. IFRS don't state a preference between the two. IFRS require specific identification for inventory items that aren't interchangeable. For example, each car on a dealer's lot has distinctive features that distinguish it from most of the other ones on the lot so one car isn't necessarily a replacement for another. In addition, each car has a vehicle identification number (VIN).

Before these cost formulas are described in detail, keep the following points in mind:

- The method used has no effect on the underlying economic activity of the entity but, like other accounting choices, it may affect the amounts reported on the balance sheet and income statement, so there may be economic consequences.

- Cost formulas allocate cost between ending inventory and cost of sales. The sum of ending inventory and cost of sales is always the same, but different cost formulas allocate the cost differently.

- Cost formulas are a way to move costs from the balance sheet to the income statement in a logical and understandable way. A formula's cost flow doesn't necessarily reflect or affect the physical flow of inventory.

- Cost isn't the only basis for valuing inventory. There are methods that use measures of current market value to value inventory, such as replacement cost and net realizable value. In most cases these methods aren't acceptable according to IFRS because they aren't based on cost. (These methods will be examined later in the chapter.)

QUESTION FOR CONSIDERATION

Thessalon Inc. (Thessalon) manufactures gumballs. Its most popular product is a one-quarter-inch gumball that comes in six colours. This is the gumball size commonly found in dispensers in stores, malls, and so on, as well as in candy stores. Thessalon can have as many as 1,000,000 of these gumballs in inventory at a point in time, depending on the time of year. Once they are made the gumballs are stored in large containers that hold up to 50,000 gumballs. The gumballs are then packaged into smaller containers for shipment to customers. The cost of gumballs can vary because some of the inputs used in their production are commodities whose price can vary from day to day.

Why is it unlikely that Thessalon would know the exact cost of any particular order of one-quarter-inch gumballs? Why is it likely that Thessalon would use a cost formula to determine the value of its inventory and its cost of sales?

Answer: With the cost of gumballs varying because of changing input prices and the vast number of gumballs on hand at any time, it's impossible to determine the cost of any particular gumball under the current storage arrangement unless each gumball were given an identifying mark allowing Thessalon's management to determine its cost. This would be impractical and costly. Because Thessalon is unable to identify the cost of individual gumballs, it's impossible to determine the cost of an order. However, Thessalon needs to have a cost associated with the gumballs sold so that net income and the value of ending inventory can be determined. This is where a cost formula becomes useful. The large amount of low-cost, identical inventory makes using a cost formula cost-effective and practical for Thessalon, rather than trying to determine the exact cost of the gumballs sold.

First-In, First-Out (FIFO)

Under **first-in, first-out (FIFO)** the cost associated with the inventory that was purchased or produced first is the cost expensed first. For raw materials used in a manufacturing process the cost associated with the raw materials purchased first is the cost charged to the production process first. With FIFO, the cost of inventory reported on the balance sheet represents the cost of the inventory most recently purchased or produced. The inventory cost that has been on hand for the least amount of time is the inventory cost that will still be on hand at the end of the period. The oldest costs are the first ones matched to revenue.

We can conceptualize FIFO by imagining a warehouse with new purchases of inventory entering the warehouse from a loading dock at the back while customers buy and receive the inventory at the front of the warehouse as shown in Figure 7.1. New inventory purchases coming into the warehouse "push" the inventory purchased earlier toward the front of the warehouse.

FIGURE 7.1

FIFO Inventory
System

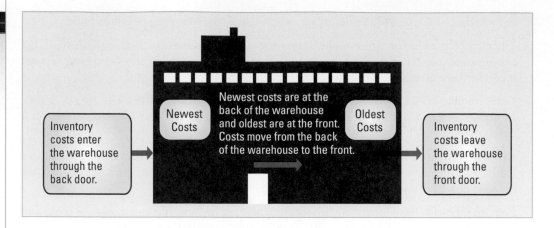

The inventory gradually moves from the back of the warehouse to the front where it can be sold to customers. The result is that the "oldest" costs (those that entered the accounting system first) are expensed first, while the "newest" costs (those associated with the most recently acquired inventory) remain in inventory at the end of the period. This conceptualization uses a physical flow of goods through a warehouse to show how costs move through a FIFO inventory system, but remember that the cost formulas address the flow of costs, not the physical flow of goods.

Average Cost

With the **average cost method**, the average cost of the inventory on hand during the period is calculated, and that average is used to determine cost of sales and ending inventory. It doesn't attempt to distinguish between units of inventory with different costs or make assumptions about when costs move from inventory to cost of sales (as FIFO does). Instead, the average cost method simply assumes all inventory units have the same cost, and the cost of individual units of inventory is lost.

We have to conceptualize the average cost inventory cost formula differently than we did with FIFO. The refinery discussed earlier purchases crude oil at market prices and stores it in storage tanks. All the crude oil purchased at different prices is mixed in the tank so the cost of each litre drawn is an average of the prices that went into the tank in the first place.

Specific Identification

The **specific identification method** assigns the actual cost of a particular unit of inventory to that unit of inventory. Unlike average cost and FIFO, when specific identification is used the physical flow of inventory matches the flow of costs in the accounting system. As a result, the inventory cost reported on the balance sheet is the actual cost of the specific items that are in inventory, and cost of sales is the actual cost of the specific items sold during the period. The specific identification method is suitable for more expensive inventory that is unique (such as works of art or some types of jewellery) or for inventory with relatively distinguishable individual units (such as cars, major appliances, and home entertainment equipment, which have individual serial numbers). As mentioned above, IFRS recommend this method for inventories that aren't interchangeable.

www.mcgrawhill
connect.ca

KNOWLEDGE CHECK

☐ What are cost formulas and why are they necessary for inventory accounting?

☐ Identify and explain the three cost formulas allowed by IFRS.

Specific identification provides some opportunity for managers to manipulate financial statement information. If there are identical items with different costs in inventory, managers could choose to sell the items that would have a desired effect on the financial statements. For example, a car dealer may have two of the same model car with the same features but purchased for different amounts. Selling the more expensive car will lower net income and selling the less expensive model will result in a higher net income. By choosing the "appropriate" unit of inventory, the dealer can help achieve an objective of financial reporting. FIFO and average cost don't allow for this type of income management.

Comparison of the Different Cost Formulas

Now that the cost formulas have been explained, let's examine an example to see the effects they have on the financial statements. Information about the purchases and sales of inventory made by Woolchester Inc. (Woolchester) during October 2014 is shown in Table 7.2. We will use this information and a periodic inventory control system to calculate ending inventory on October 31, 2014 and the cost of sales and the gross margin for October 2014. We will also see that cash flow isn't affected by the choice of inventory cost formula and control method.

TABLE 7.2	Woolchester Inc.: Purchases and Sales of Inventory		
Woolchester Inc. Information about the Purchases and Sales of Inventory during October 2014			
	Number of units	**Price per unit**	**Total**
Inventory balance on September 30, 2014	0	$ 0	$ 0
Purchases:*			
October 3	100	50	5,000
October 15	125	55	6,875
October 25	75	59	4,425
Sales:**			
October 8	80	125	10,000
October 20	130	125	16,250

*All purchases of inventory are made for cash.
**All sales are for cash.

FIFO These transactions are accounted for using FIFO in Table 7.3. On October 31 Woolchester has to make the adjusting entry to record cost of sales and inventory used during the period. We determine the costs that should be expensed for October by looking at the units and costs available for sale during the month in the order the inventory was purchased. Woolchester had the following inventory on hand, in order of acquisition, during October:

- 100 units at $50
- 125 units at $55
- 75 units at $59

To record the cost of selling 210 units during October, Woolchester would expense the cost associated with the 100 units at $50 each and the cost associated with 110 units at $55 each. Under FIFO, the total cost of sales for October would be $11,050. Ending inventory would contain the costs associated with the remaining 15 units at $55 and the 75 units at $59 each. It's important to note that if Woolchester had a beginning inventory balance at the start of October, the costs associated with that inventory would be expensed first under FIFO.

Average Cost When the average cost method is used, the average cost of the inventory available for sale is determined when the entry that records cost of sales is made. The average cost is then applied to the inventory sold and the inventory on hand at the end of the period.

The entries for Woolchester for October using average cost periodic are shown in Table 7.4. The table shows

- The average cost per unit of inventory available for sale during October is $54.33 ([(100 units @ $50) + (125 units @ $55) + (75 units @ $59)] ÷ 300 units).
- Cost of sales for October is $11,409.30, the product of the average cost and the number of units sold ($54.33 × 210).
- Ending inventory is $4,890.70, the product of the average cost and the number of units on hand at the end of October ($54.33 × 90). The $54.33 is also the cost associated with each of the 90 units of inventory on hand at the start of the next period.

TABLE 7.3	Woolchester Inc.: Inventory Transactions—FIFO				
Woolchester Inc. **Inventory Transactions for October 2014 Using FIFO Periodic**					
		Cash	Inventory*	Revenue	Cost of sales
October 3	Purchase 100 units @ $50	$(5,000)	$ 5,000		
October 8	Sell 80 units @ $125	10,000		$10,000	
October 15	Purchase 125 units @ $55	(6,875)	6,875		
October 20	Sell 130 units @ $125	16,250		16,250	
October 25	Purchase 75 units @ $59	(4,425)	4,425		
October 31	Inventory expensed for October 2014: 100 units @ $50 + 110 units @ $55		(11,050)		$(11,050)
October 31	**Ending balances**	$ 9,950	$ 5,250	$26,250	$(11,050)
	Remaining in inventory: 15 units @ $55 = $ 825 75 units @ $59 = $4,425				

*For clarity, in this table purchases are made directly to the inventory account instead of to purchases.

TABLE 7.4	Woolchester Inc.: Inventory Transactions—Average Cost				
Woolchester Inc. **Inventory Transactions for October 2014 Using Average Cost Periodic**					
		Cash	Inventory*	Revenue	Cost of sales
October 3	Purchase 100 units @ $50	$(5,000)	$ 5,000		
October 8	Sell 80 units @ $125	10,000		$10,000	
October 15	Purchase 125 units @ $55	(6,875)	6,875		
October 20	Sell 130 units @ $125	16,250		16,250	
October 25	Purchase 75 units @ $59	(4,425)	4,425		
October 31	Cost of sales for October 2014: 210 units @ $54.33		(11,409.30)		$(11,409.30)
	Average cost $$= \frac{[(100 \text{ units @ } \$50) + (125 \text{ units @ } \$55) + (75 \text{ units @ } \$59)]}{300 \text{ units}}$$ = $54.33				
October 31	**Ending balances**	$ 9,950	$ 4,890.70	$26,250	$(11,409.30)
	Remaining in inventory: 90 units @ $54.33 = $ 4,890.70				

*For clarity, in this table purchases are made directly to the inventory account instead of to purchases.

If the perpetual system of inventory control was used the results for average cost will be different. The inventory control system doesn't affect the amounts with FIFO or specific identification. The mechanics of periodic and perpetual systems are essentially the same, but with a perpetual system the cost of sales and changes to inventory are calculated with each transaction, whereas with a periodic system these calculations are only done at the end of the period.

Specific Identification   When the specific identification method is used the flow of costs and the physical flow of the inventory are the same: cost of sales is the cost of the actual units of inventory sold and the balance in inventory at the end of the period is the actual cost of the units still on hand. As a result, the amount of inventory at the end of the period and cost of sales for the period depends on which units are sold. With FIFO and average cost, ending inventory and cost of sales aren't affected by which physical units are sold.

Woolchester's entries for October using specific identification appear in Table 7.5. With specific identification the cost of the actual units is tracked. During October we'll assume that Woolchester sold the following units:

- October 8 sale: 80 units at $50
- October 20 sale: 12 units at $50 and 118 at $55 units for $7,090
- Ending inventory: 8 units at $50, 7 at $55 units, and 75 at $59 units for $5,210

The units sold during October are shown graphically in Figure 7.2.

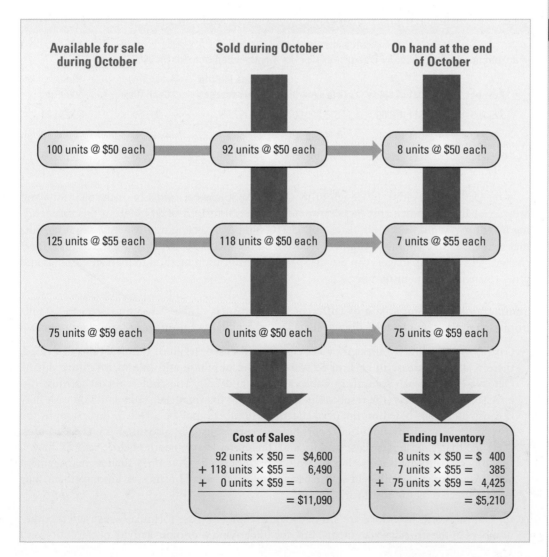

FIGURE 7.2

Woolchester Inc.: Specific Identification— Units Sold

TABLE 7.5	Woolchester Inc.: Inventory Transactions—Specific Identification

Woolchester Inc.
Inventory Transactions for October 2014 Using Specific Identification

			Cash	Inventory	Revenue	Cost of sales
October 3		Purchase 100 units @ $50	$(5,000)	$ 5,000		
October 8		Sell 80 units @ $125	10,000		$10,000	
October 15		Purchase 125 units @ $55	(6,875)	6,875		
October 20		Sell 130 units @ $125	16,250		16,250	
October 25		Purchase 75 units @ $59	(4,425)	4,425		
October 31		Inventory expensed for October 2014: 80 units @ $50 ⎫ + 12 units @ $50 ⎬ +118 units @ $55 ⎭		(11,090)		$(11,090)

October 31	**Ending balances**
	Remaining in inventory: 8 units @ $50 = $ 400 ⎫
	                          7 units @ $55 = $ 385 ⎬
	                         75 units @ $59 = $4,425 ⎭
			$ 9,950	$ 5,210	$26,250	$(11,090)

TABLE 7.6	Woolchester Inc.: Summary of Inventory Information Under the Cost Formulas

Woolchester Inc.
Summary Information on Inventory Transactions for the Month Ended October 31, 2005

	Revenue	Cost of sales	Gross margin	Gross margin percentage	Cash flow	Ending inventory
FIFO	$26,250	$11,050.00	$15,200.00	57.9%	$9,950	$5,250.00
Average cost	26,250	11,409.30	14,840.70	56.5	9,950	4,890.70
Specific identification	26,250	11,090.00	15,160.00	57.8	9,950	5,210.00

If on October 20, either by design or by chance, Woolchester sold 124 of the $55 units and only six of the $50 units, cost of sales would be $11,120 instead of $11,090. In this case, ending inventory would be $5,180 instead of $5,210. Simply by changing the actual physical units that were given to customers, amounts reported on the income statement and the balance sheet change. This is how managers can use the specific identification method to manage earnings and other financial statement numbers.

Summary of the Comparison of Different Cost formulas Table 7.6 summarizes the results from each of the cost formulas discussed above and highlights a number of important points:

- Cash flow isn't directly affected by the cost formula used. In all of the situations described, there is a net increase in cash of $9,950 from the purchase and sale of inventory during October (see the cash column in Tables 7.3, 7.4, and 7.5). The choice of cost formula can have secondary effects (the result of measurements in the financial statements) on cash flow because outcomes based on financial statement numbers may be affected. For example, the cost formula used for financial reporting purposes is usually also used for tax purposes. Methods that yield higher cost of sales and, therefore, lower income before tax will have a smaller cash outflow because less tax will have to be paid. Outcomes such as management bonuses, compliance with debt covenants, and selling prices of businesses, among others, may also be affected by the cost formula used.

- Cost of sales and inventory are affected by the choice of cost formula, which affects other numbers in the financial statements. But, the underlying economic activity of the entity isn't affected. This means that the number of units sold and purchased during the period and the number of units in inventory at the end of the period are the same regardless of the cost formula used.

- Because the amounts reported for inventory and cost of sales differ under each cost formula, many other financial accounting measures and ratios are also affected. For example, gross margin, gross margin percentage net income, return on assets and return on equity, profit margin, current ratio, and debt-to-equity ratio will vary. Again, the underlying economic activity of the entity isn't affected but the representation of the activity is affected, which may alter the perceptions, interpretations, and inferences of stakeholders and may have economic consequences (taxes, bonuses, etc.).

- The sum of cost of sales and ending inventory in each case is $16,300. This isn't a coincidence. The different cost formulas affect the balance sheet and income statement allocation of the cost of inventory available for sale during a period but they don't affect the total amount.

- When inventory prices are rising, FIFO cost of sales will always be lower than average cost method cost of sales and FIFO gross margin and net income will always be higher.

- The different cost formulas provide different results only if the cost of inventory is changing. If the cost of inventory remains constant over a period of time all the methods will yield the same results.

QUESTION FOR CONSIDERATION

Table 7.6 shows that cost of sales and gross margin are different with different cost formulas, but cash flow is the same for each. Explain why this is the case.

Answer: The cost formulas are accounting methods for allocating the cost of inventory between the balance sheet and the income statement. They are accrual accounting concepts that involve economic flows, not necessarily cash flows. The cost formula an entity selects has no effect on the amount of cash it pays to suppliers of inventory or for the inputs used to produce inventory. The actual amount of cash paid isn't affected by accrual accounting choices made by the preparers of the financial statements. Therefore, cost of sales and gross margin will change with the cost formula, but cash flows will remain the same. Alternative cost formulas may affect secondary cash flows, such as income tax and bonuses to managers.

WHICH METHOD IS BEST?

As stated earlier, IFRS require the specific identification method when units of inventory aren't interchangeable. Most entities don't have inventories that justify using specific identification so they have to choose between FIFO and average cost. IFRS don't recommend one method over the other and offer no guidance on how to choose between them. Entities may use more than one cost formula but the same formula should be used for similar inventories with the same use to the entity. FIFO and average cost are both widely used in Canada. *Financial Reporting in Canada* (33rd Edition) reported that of 129 companies that disclose their cost formulas, 81 used average cost (either alone or along with other methods), 53 used FIFO (either alone or along with other methods) and six used specific identification, but for some of its inventory only.[1]

It's difficult to provide strong conceptual support for either one of these methods, which is probably why both are acceptable. In many cases an entity will choose the method used by other similar entities for comparability. Ultimately, what we have to pay attention to is the impact the two methods will have on the financial statements and be aware that companies can use different methods.

When FIFO is used, the inventory costs reported on the balance sheet are most current—they are associated with the inventory purchased or produced most recently. This provides as close an approximation of the replacement cost of the inventory as is possible while still valuing the inventory at cost. (Replacement cost is the amount it would cost to replace inventory, or any asset, at current prices.) Stakeholders who are interested in predicting future cash flows might find a FIFO valuation useful because it gives the most current indication of what it would cost to replace the inventory at current prices. *When prices are rising*, the reported amount for ending inventory will be higher with FIFO than with average cost because the newest (higher) costs are in inventory. As a result, the current ratio will be higher with FIFO when prices are rising. The higher balance sheet valuation could be beneficial if, for example, the size of an entity's bank loan is related to the amount of inventory (e.g., the bank will lend $0.30 for each $1 of inventory).

On the income statement the costs associated with the oldest inventory are expensed to cost of sales first under FIFO. This means the cost of sales is less current—the most current cost of inventory isn't being matched to the current revenue. As a result, gross margin and net income are poorer indications of actual economic performance than when a more current measure of cost of sales is used. This effect could be misleading to a stakeholder attempting to predict future profitability. Future profitability is based on what inventory will cost in the future, not what it cost in the past. If inventory costs are rising and the entity can't raise prices to offset the increase in costs, the gross margin calculated under FIFO isn't as good an indicator of future performance. Consequently, stakeholders who base predictions on an income statement based on FIFO might overestimate future profitability.

Average cost provides a balance sheet measure of inventory that isn't as current as FIFO provides, but cost of sales is more current than with FIFO. In periods when inventory costs are rising, the effects of using FIFO versus average costs are summarized in Table 7.7:

TABLE 7.7	Impact of Using FIFO versus Average Cost When Prices Are Rising						
	Ending inventory	Current ratio	Current assets	Total assets	Liabilities	Cost of Sales	Net income
FIFO	Higher	Higher	Higher	Higher	No effect	Lower	Higher
Average cost	Lower	Lower	Lower	Lower	No effect	Higher	Lower

FIFO is appealing because in many cases it corresponds with the physical flow of goods. It approximates the specific identification method, where the actual costs of items sold are matched to the revenue recognized. Good inventory management may require that the oldest inventory be sold to customers first, such as with perishable goods.

Because average cost yields an income figure that is lower than FIFO when prices are rising, companies with a tax minimization objective would choose average cost over FIFO. Private companies often prefer average cost because the tax minimization objective is most important, although some private firms may wish to maximize net income to satisfy lenders or because of an upcoming sale of shares.

INSIGHT

Last-In, First-Out (LIFO)—Another Cost Formula

There is a fourth cost formula—**last-in, first-out** or **LIFO**, which first expenses the costs associated with the inventory purchased or produced most recently. With LIFO the cost of inventory reported on the balance sheet represents the cost of old, sometimes very old, inventory. Because the cost of the newest inventory is expensed first under LIFO, the cost of the older inventory won't be expensed for a long time if new inventory is being purchased. On the income statement, the cost of inventory sold represents the most recent costs. Notice that the impact of LIFO is the opposite of that of FIFO.

LIFO isn't allowed under IFRS and can't be used in Canada for tax purposes. In the United States LIFO can be used both for financial reporting purposes and for tax purposes. If a U.S. company chooses to use LIFO for tax purposes it must also use it for financial reporting purposes. This means that in periods when inventory prices are rising, a company will have accept lower net income for financial reporting purposes to get the tax benefit. The fact that LIFO is widely used in the U.S. suggests that many companies consider tax reduction an important objective as they are prepared to report lower earnings in their general purpose financial statements for this.

THE LOWER OF COST AND MARKET RULE

In the fashion business what's popular today might be virtually unsaleable in a couple of months. A clothing chain buys a large supply of fashionable styles for the 2013 fall season, but when the spring 2014 merchandise arrives it may still have fall inventory left that will be hard to sell at the full retail price. From a business standpoint, it makes sense to sell those fall fashions for whatever it can get—even if it's for less than their cost.

But how should the chain account for items that can't be sold for more than they cost? According to IFRS, inventory on hand at the end of a period must be evaluated according to the **lower of cost and market (LCM) rule**, which requires inventory to be recorded at its **net realizable value (NRV)** if NRV is less than cost. NRV is the amount the entity would receive from selling the inventory, less any additional costs to complete production of the product and less costs to complete the sale.

If the NRV of inventory is less than its cost the inventory must be written down to NRV. The amount of the writedown is the difference between the inventory's cost and its NRV, and it's reported as a loss or expense on the income statement in the period the impairment is identified, not when the inventory is sold. Remember that if inventory is written down, it's still on hand and can be sold. What has changed is its carrying amount (the carrying amount will be its NRV, not its cost). A **writedown** is a reduction in the carrying amount of inventory (or another asset) to some measure of market value, and it's achieved by debiting an expense and crediting the asset. When an asset is written down to zero, the event is referred to as a **writeoff**.

If inventory is written down the following journal entry is recorded:

> Dr. Cost of sales or inventory loss (expenses +, owner's equity −)   xxx
>   Cr. Inventory (asset −)   xxx
> To record a writedown of inventory

This journal entry reduces the balance in inventory on the balance sheet, increases expenses, and decreases net income. The writedown could be disclosed on a separate line on the income statement or included in cost of sales with disclosure in the notes. That some entities would only disclose a writedown in the notes emphasizes how important reading the notes is. If a writedown isn't disclosed at all (it's buried in cost of sales and not disclosed in the notes), a stakeholder's ability to interpret the financial statements is impaired. A writedown might distort the gross margin and without adequate disclosure a stakeholder wouldn't understand why the gross margin percentage might have changed from previous years. Information about the nature and amount of inventory writedowns helps stakeholders assess management performance and predict future earnings.

IFRS require a writedown to be reversed if the NRV of inventory increases in a subsequent period. In this situation, inventory that was previously written down is written back up to its original cost (it wouldn't be written up above its original cost).

The LCM rule is an application of the accounting concept of conservatism, which requires that measurements in financial statements should ensure that assets, revenues, and net income aren't overstated and that liabilities and expenses aren't understated. Conservatism is discussed in detail in the next Insight box.

Let's consider an example showing how the LCM rule is applied. Sangree Ltd. (Sangree) carries three inventory items. Information about the cost and NRV of Sangree's inventory on December 31, 2014 is shown in Table 7.8.

The LCM rule is applied by comparing the cost and NRV for each item of inventory and using the lower amount to determine the inventory's value. For items 1 and 3, NRV is lower than cost, so NRV is used and included in column 6, while for item 2 cost is lower than NRV so cost is used. The total of column 6 is the amount that will appear on the balance sheet for inventory. Since the inventory is recorded at cost, a writedown of $5,200 ($145,500 − $140,300) is required. Column 7 shows the amount by which items 1 and 3 must be written down by. Sangree would make the following journal entry to record the inventory writedown:

> Dr. Cost of sales or inventory loss (expense +, shareholders' equity −)   5,200
>   Cr. Inventory (asset −)   5,200

TABLE 7.8	Sangree Ltd.: Inventory Information						
			Sangree Ltd. Inventory Information on December 31, 2014				
	1	2	3	4	5	6	7
	Number of units	Cost per unit	NRV* per unit	Total cost	Total NRV	Lower of cost and NRV	Amount of writedown required
Item 1	10,000	$7.23	$6.92	$ 72,300	$ 69,200	$ 69,200	$3,100
Item 2	5,000	4.24	4.48	21,200	22,400	21,200	0
Item 3	10,000	5.20	4.99	52,000	49,900	49,900	2,100
Total				$145,500	$141,500	$140,300	$5,200

*NRV equals selling price less cost to complete the sale.

To record the writedown of inventory to market value

Now let's suppose that in the first quarter of 2015 the market for inventory item 3 recovers and at the end of the quarter its NRV was $7 per unit. Let's also assume that Sangree still had 4,000 of the units on hand on December 31 at the end of the first quarter. Because NRV has increased, Sangree should reverse the writedown recorded for the 4,000 units still on hand. The remaining 4,000 item 3s were written down by a total of $840 (4,000 units × $0.21 ($5.20 − $4.99)) so the following entry is made to reverse the writedown:

Dr. Inventory (asset +)   840
    Cr. Cost of sales or inventory loss (expense −, shareholders' equity +)   840
To reverse the writedown of inventory

Two things to notice about the reversal are (a) it only applies to inventory that was previously written down, in this case only inventory that was on hand on December 31, 2014 and (b) inventory is only written back up to its cost—even though the NRV at the end of the third quarter was $7, the inventory is only written up to $5.20, its original cost.

In the example, Sangree applied the LCM rule on an item-by-item basis. The rule could also have been applied on the inventory as a whole, in which case the total cost would have been compared to the total NRV. Using this approach, the amount of the writedown required would be $4,000 ($145,500 − $141,500). Notice that the approach used can affect the amount of the writedown and the value of ending inventory. In most situations IFRS require that cost and NRV be compared on an item-by-item basis.

Now let's consider an actual example. In the third quarter of fiscal 2009 (quarter ended December 31, 2008), Saputo Inc. (Saputo), a Canadian-based manufacturer and distributor of dairy and grocery products, took an $18,489,000 writedown of its inventory. Exhibit 7.1 provides extracts from Saputo's 2009 third-quarter report.[2] Notice the writedown isn't shown on the income statement. It's included in "cost of sales, selling and administrative expenses." You have to read the notes to find out about it.

There are many circumstances that can cause the NRV of inventory to decline. Changes in fashion styles have already been mentioned, and other reasons include

- technological change (for example, the selling price of last year's leading-edge computer equipment will usually fall dramatically when faster and more powerful computers come on the market)

- damaged goods

- fluctuations in commodity markets (e.g., lumber, minerals)

EXHIBIT 7.1

Saputo Inc.:
Inventory
Writedown

CONSOLIDATED STATEMENTS OF EARNINGS
(in thousands of dollars, except per share amounts)
(unaudited)

	For the three-month periods ended December 31		For the nine-month periods ended December 31	
	2008	2007	2008	2007
Revenues	$ 1,517,457	$ 1,277,037	$ 4,332,911	$ 3,792,754
Cost of sales, selling and administrative expenses	1,391,802	1,140,081	3,926,993	3,404,211
Earnings before interest, depreciation, impairment and income taxes	125,655	136,956	405,918	388,543
Depreciation and impairment of fixed assets (Note 5)	34,090	19,669	79,447	59,607
Operating income	91,565	117,287	326,471	328,936
Interest on long-term debt	5,573	4,494	15,004	14,218
Other interest, net	3,212	1,468	7,226	5,499
Earnings before income taxes	82,780	111,325	304,241	309,219
Income taxes	25,021	29,307	94,491	96,230
Net earnings	$ 57,759	$ 82,018	$ 209,750	$ 212,989
Earnings per share (Note 9)				
Net earnings				
Basic	$ 0.28	$ 0.40	$ 1.02	$ 1.03
Diluted	$ 0.28	$ 0.39	$ 1.01	$ 1.02

4 — Inventories

The following table presents the components of the inventories:

	December 31, 2008	March 31, 2008
Finished goods	$ 361,893	$ 322,550
Raw materials, work in process and supplies	230,438	211,136
	$ 592,331	$ 533,686

The amount of inventories recognized as an expense for the three- and nine-month periods ended December 31, 2008, is $1,251,182,000 and $3,541,368,000 respectively.

The Company recorded a write-down of inventory of $18,489,000 which was recognized as an expense in the current quarter. The carrying amount of inventory at net realizable value is $76,974,000.

INSIGHT

Conservatism/Prudence

One of the most prominent accounting concepts used under GAAP/IFRS is conservatism. (IFRS uses the term **prudence** to represent this concept.) **Conservatism** requires that measurements in financial statements should be made to ensure that assets, revenues, and net income aren't overstated and that liabilities and expenses aren't understated. Another way of explaining conservatism is, "anticipate no profit, but anticipate all losses." Conservatism doesn't mean there should be a deliberate understatement of assets, revenues, and net income or a deliberate overstatement of liabilities and expenses, but the uncertainty surrounding many economic events makes caution in measurements and estimates necessary. Some examples of conservatism include the following:

- The lower of cost and market rule used for inventory.
- Capital assets written down if impaired.
- Losses recorded as soon as they are identified but gains must be realized before recognizing.
- Intangible assets not reported as assets unless purchased.
- Research costs expensed as incurred.
- Revenue recognized late in the earnings process.
- Market values of many assets not recorded in the financial statements.
- Big baths.
- Managers cautious when making estimates.

continued...

INSIGHT CONT.

The reasons for conservatism in accounting aren't entirely clear. A possible explanation is that the managers who are responsible for an entity's financial statements tend to be optimistic about the prospects for the entities they manage, or that they have incentives to act in their self-interest when making accounting choices. Conservatism can serve to dampen the effects of managerial optimism and self-interest.

Some of the examples of conservatism make sense. If capital assets or inventory aren't written down when impaired then the future benefits associated with these assets would be less than the amount reported on the balance sheet.

An important issue with conservatism is its asymmetry—standards applied to economic events that increase income and assets are different than those of events that decrease them. If the market value of assets increases, the gains are typically not recognized until the assets are sold and the increases in value realized. (IFRS allows increases in the market value of capital assets to be recorded in certain circumstances, but this option isn't widely used at this point.) Also, when assets are written down, the historical cost, transactions-based approach to valuation isn't being followed. This isn't necessarily a bad thing, but an effect of conservatism. Conservatism also violates comparability because cost isn't being applied from period to period.

It's noteworthy that IFRS is currently considering removing conservatism as a concept from its accounting standards.

One of the problems with conservatism is that conservative choices today can result in an opposite effect in later periods. For example, in 2015 Carcajou Ltd. (Carcajou) purchased computer equipment for $210,000. Carcajou's management decides to depreciate the equipment over three years. Carcajou's summarized income statements for the years ended December 31, 2015, 2016, and 2017 are shown in Panel A of Table 7.9. If, instead, Carcajou's management made a more conservative estimate of the equipment's life and chose to depreciate it over two years, net income in the first two years would be lower than when the three-year depreciation period is used, a more conservative result (see Panel B of Table 7.9). However, in 2017 net income is much higher because there is no depreciation expense. Over the three years the depreciation expense and net income are the same, but they are distributed differently.

TABLE 7.9 Carcajou Ltd.: Income Statements

Panel A

Carcajou Ltd.
Income Statements for the Years Ended December 31

	2015	2016	2017	Total
Revenue	$750,000	$800,000	$825,000	$2,375,000
Expenses	620,000	660,000	680,000	1,960,000
Depreciation of computer equipment*	70,000	70,000	70,000	210,000
Net income	$ 60,000	$ 70,000	$ 75,000	$ 205,000

*Computer equipment cost $210,000 and is depreciated over three years.

Panel B

Carcajou Ltd.
Income Statements for the Years Ended December 31

	2015	2016	2017	Total
Revenue	$750,000	$800,000	$825,000	$2,375,000
Expenses	620,000	660,000	680,000	1,960,000
Depreciation of computer equipment*	105,000	105,000	0	210,000
Net income	$ 25,000	$ 35,000	$145,000	$ 205,000

*Computer equipment cost $210,000 and is depreciated over two years.

Managers can use conservatism to pursue their self-interests by managing financial statement measurement. Applying conservatism requires judgment by the managers, and these judgments can be highly subjective and open to abuse.

KNOWLEDGE CHECK

❑ In times of rising prices, which inventory cost formula will provide the highest inventory valuation and the highest net income? Which will provide the lowest inventory valuation and net income? Explain.

❑ What is the lower of cost and market (LCM) rule, and why is it used?

❑ Explain the accounting concept of conservatism.

VALUING INVENTORY AT OTHER THAN COST

Cost isn't the only way inventory can be valued for financial reporting purposes. For many stakeholders, market-based valuation methods could provide relevant information for decision making, but because of conservatism, inventory usually isn't recorded at market value under IFRS, as doing so would mean recognizing revenue or gains before it's sold.

We have seen that inventory is valued at market when cost is greater than NRV, but this is a special situation. When market value accounting is used for inventory the market value is always used, regardless of the cost of the inventory. Market value measures that can be used for inventory are net realizable value (what you can sell it for) and **replacement cost**—what it would cost to replace.

When inventory is valued at replacement cost, the amount reported on the balance sheet is what it would cost the entity to replace the inventory on hand on the balance sheet date. At the time inventory is purchased or manufactured, the cost and replacement cost are the same. After that, the cost to buy or make the same item can change. For example, during 2014, Stellarton Ltd. (Stellarton) purchased inventory for $1,000. None of this inventory was sold by the end of 2014, and on December 31, 2014, (Stellarton's year-end) it had a replacement cost of $1,100. Stellarton would make the following journal entry to record the change in the replacement cost:

Dr. Inventory (assets +)	100	
Cr. Holding gain (income statement +, owner's equity +)		100
To record the increase in the replacement cost of inventory		

The change in the replacement cost of the inventory from the date it was purchased to either the date it was sold or the end of the period is called a **holding gain or loss**—the change in the value of inventory while an entity owns or "holds" it. This entry increases the amount recorded for inventory on the balance sheet and recognizes a gain on the income statement. The gain represents the economic benefit of owning something that has become more valuable (a loss would be an economic loss due to a decrease in value). This approach is different from IFRS accounting where gains are recognized only when the inventory is actually sold.

Returning to the Stellarton example, suppose that during 2015 Stellarton sold the inventory for $2,500. The following journal entries would be recorded:

Dr. Cash (assets +)	2,500	
Cr. Revenue (income statement +, owner's equity +)		2,500
To record the sale of inventory		

Dr. Cost of sales (expenses +, owner's equity −)	1,100	
Cr. Inventory (asset −)		1,100
To record cost of inventory sold		

If holding gains weren't recognized, there would be no journal entry in 2014 and the following entries would be recorded in 2015 (this is what is done under IFRS):

Dr. Cash (assets +)   2,500
    Cr. Revenue (income statement +, owner's equity +)   2,500
To record the sale of inventory

Dr. Cost of sales (expenses +, owner's equity −)   1,000
    Cr. Inventory (asset −)   1,000
To record cost of inventory sold

With replacement cost accounting there is income of $100 in 2014 and $1,400 in 2015, and with IFRS there is no income in 2014 but $1,500 in 2015. The effects on the financial statements are shown in Figure 7.3. Information about holding gains and losses can help stakeholders assess how well inventory is being managed and predict future cash flows.

Valuing inventory at its NRV is equivalent to recognizing the revenue and profit from the sale of the inventory before it is sold. Revenue is recognized for the NRV of the inventory and the cost is expensed at the same time. However, because the inventory hasn't actually been sold, the debit of the sale journal entry is to inventory rather than accounts receivable. As a result, the inventory is reported at NRV on the balance sheet. We examined this approach in Chapter 4 when we discussed recognizing revenue at the time of production. Look back at Manyberries Mines Ltd. example on pages 175–176 and notice how the journal entry results in the gold being recorded at NRV.

By recording the inventory at NRV stakeholders get an idea of the amount of cash that will be realized from the sale of the inventory. This is useful information for predicting cash flows. Of course, estimating the selling price of inventory can be difficult in many situations. As well, it's possible that not all inventory will be sold so there is a danger of recognizing gains that will never be realized. This approach can make sense if the selling price is known because there is a contract to sell the inventory or if there is a market that virtually guarantees the ability to sell (for example, gold and oil can always be sold at market prices). IFRS do allow certain types of inventory to be valued at NRV, including agricultural and forest products, and refined natural resources.

FIGURE 7.3

Stellarton Ltd.: Effect of Holding Gains on the Financial Statements

Replacement Cost Accounting	Traditional (IFRS) Accounting
Stellarton Ltd. **Balance Sheet** **December 31, 2014** Inventory $1,100	**Stellarton Ltd.** **Balance Sheet** **December 31, 2014** Inventory $1,000
Stellarton Ltd. **Income Statement** **December 31, 2014** Holding gain $100 Net income $100	**Stellarton Ltd.** **Income Statement** **December 31, 2014** Net income $ 0
Stellarton Ltd. **Income Statement** **December 31, 2015** Sales $2,500 Cost of sales 1,100 Net income $1,400	**Stellarton Ltd.** **Income Statement** **December 31, 2015** Sales $2,500 Cost of sales 1,000 Net income $1,500

INVENTORY DISCLOSURES IN FINANCIAL STATEMENTS

IFRS require that the following information be disclosed about inventory:

- accounting policies adopted, including cost formula used
- carrying amount (book value) of inventories
- carrying amount of inventories carried at fair value less costs to sell (NRV)
- amount of inventory expensed during the period
- amounts of any inventory writedowns and reversals of writedowns
- circumstances that led to the reversal of a previous writedown
- carrying amount of inventories pledged as security for liabilities

EXHIBIT 7.2

Inventory Disclosures Panel A— Ballard Power Systems Inc.

www.ballard.com

BALLARD POWER SYSTEMS INC.
Consolidated Balance Sheets
December 31,
(Expressed in thousands of U.S. dollars)

	2008	2007
Assets		
Current assets:		
Cash and cash equivalents	$ 54,086	$ 49,340
Short-term investments	31,313	96,234
Accounts receivable (notes 5 & 16)	18,856	18,963
Inventories (note 6)	10,402	14,859
Prepaid expenses and other current assets	1,434	1,740
Current assets held for sale (note 3)	-	105
	116,091	181,241
Property, plant and equipment (note 7)	38,755	42,906
Intangible assets (note 8)	3,726	4,303
Goodwill	48,106	48,106
Investments (note 9)	1,765	3,250
Long-term assets held for sale (note 3)	-	16,286
Other long-term assets	-	2,599
	$ 208,443	$ 298,691

1. Significant accounting policies:

(i) Inventories:

Inventories are recorded at the lower of cost and net realizable value. The cost of inventories is based on the first-in first-out principle, and includes expenditures incurred in acquiring the inventories, production or conversion costs and other costs incurred in bringing them to their existing location and condition. In the case of manufactured inventories and work in progress, cost includes materials, labor and appropriate share of production overhead based on normal operating capacity. Costs of materials are determined on an average per unit basis. Net realizable value is the estimated selling price in the ordinary course of business, less the estimated costs of completion and selling expenses. In establishing the appropriate inventory obsolescence, management estimates the likelihood that inventory carrying values will be affected by changes in market demand, technology and design, which would make inventory on hand obsolete.

6. Inventories:

	2008	2007
Raw materials and consumables	$ 6,632	$ 9,497
Work-in-progress	1,891	3,371
Finished goods	1,879	1,991
	$ 10,402	$ 14,859

In 2008, changes in raw materials and consumables, finished goods and work-in-progress recognized as cost of product and service revenues amounted to $25,948,000 (2007 - $21,252,000; 2006 – $13,677,000). In 2008, the write-down of inventories to net realizable value amounted to $745,000 (2007 - $1,375,000; 2006 - $2,301,000). There were no reversals of write-downs in 2008, 2007 or 2006. Write-downs and reversals are included in either cost of product and service revenues, or research and product development expense, depending on the nature of inventory.

EXHIBIT 7.2

(continued)
Inventory
Disclosures
Panel B—
Genesis Land
Development Corp.

www.genesisland.com

Genesis Land Development Corp.
Consolidated Balance Sheets
As at December 31, 2008 and 2007

	2008 $	2007 $
Assets		
Real estate held for development and sale (note 6)	285,574,479	221,264,426
Amounts receivable (note 8)	29,498,202	47,587,450
Other operating assets (note 9)	45,100,539	22,564,452
Future income taxes (note 10)	778,245	-
Cash and cash equivalents	4,502,984	11,007,142
	365,454,449	302,423,470

3.   SIGNIFICANT ACCOUNTING POLICIES

(c) Real estate held for development and sale

Land under development, land held for future development and housing projects under development are recorded at the lower of cost and estimated net realizable value on a project specific basis. An impairment loss is recognized to the extent that the carrying value of a project exceeds the fair value of that project. Cost includes land acquisition costs, other direct costs of development and construction, interest on debt used to finance specific projects, property taxes and legal costs. Fair value is estimated using comparisons of recent sales of similar or adjacent lands in the same geographic area. Land acquisition costs are prorated to a phase of a project on an acreage basis.

6.   REAL ESTATE HELD FOR DEVELOPMENT AND SALE

	2008 $	2007 $
Land held for future development	130,026,407	118,622,917
Land under development	123,124,339	84,262,693
Housing projects under development	38,425,004	18,765,688
	291,575,750	221,651,298
Less write-down	(6,001,271)	(386,872)
	285,574,479	221,264,426

During the year ended December 31, 2008, interest of $7,189,000 (2007 - $2,742,000) and other carrying costs of $961,000 (2007 - $1,038,000) were capitalized to land held for future development. Of the land held for future development at December 31, 2008, $43,539,000 (2007 - $46,125,400) is held in limited partnerships controlled by Genesis (see note 7(a)). Of the land under development at December 31, 2008, $22,260,000 (2007 - $25,275,000) is held in limited partnerships controlled by Genesis, and $5,129,000 (2007 - $NIL) is held in the variable interest entity (see note 7(b)).

In Exhibit 7.2 are three examples of the type of information about inventory that appears in financial statements.[3]

- Panel A provides information about Ballard Power Systems Inc.'s (Ballard) inventory. Ballard develops, makes, sells, and services clean energy hydrogen fuel cells parts. The company balance sheet for the year ended December 31, 2008 reports inventory of $10,402,000, representing 5 percent of total assets. This single number reports the entire inventory held by Ballard; however, additional information is available in the notes to the financial statements. From Note 1(i) we learn that Ballard values its inventory at the lower of cost and NRV and uses FIFO as its cost formula. The note explains the costs included in purchased and manufactured inventories, defines NRV, and describes how Ballard determines which inventory is obsolete. Note 6 provides a breakdown of inventory into categories (raw materials and consumables, work-in-progress, and finished goods), the amount of inventory expensed during the year ($25,948,000), the amount of inventory writedown to NRV ($745,000), and the amount writedowns reversed (none). The note also explains where in the income statement the writedowns are included.

- Panel B provides information about Genesis Land Development Corp. (Genesis), a Calgary-based real estate company that develops planned communities. Real estate development companies have inventory, but it isn't usually called that in the financial statements. Genesis' balance sheet has an account called "Real estate held for development and sale," which is its inventory. The accounting for this asset is described in Note 3c which explains that properties held for development or construction and held for sale are valued at the lower of cost and net realizable value. The note also describes the costs that are included in the account. Note 6 shows the components of the real estate held for development and sale account. Genesis doesn't state a cost formula because specific identification is likely used; each house or building is unique and identifiable so it's possible and appropriate to keep track of each separately.

 CANADIAN GAAP FOR PRIVATE ENTERPRISES

Canadian GAAP for Private Enterprises and IFRS are very similar with respect to accounting for inventory, although there are some differences that we don't discuss here.

INVENTORY AND THE SERVICES INDUSTRY

For the most part in this chapter the discussion of inventory has focused on entities that sell physical goods to customers. A large part of the Canadian economy is made up of entities providing services. Examples of service businesses include banks, insurance companies, hotels, professional services (e.g., accountants and lawyers), and airlines. The not-for-profit sector also provides many services in the Canadian economy; for example, hospitals. One characteristic of service businesses is that they don't have inventory to offer customers—their services can't be stored. An empty seat on a plane or an empty hotel room can't be saved for when there is more demand. An hour of an accountant's or lawyer's time can't be stored for the busy season.

However, if you examine the balance sheet of a service provider such as an accounting firm, you would find a kind of inventory. The costs the firm has accumulated by providing services to clients represents its inventory. For example, the firm's accounting records would accumulate the cost of employee and partner time spent on an engagement. Travel costs, administration costs, supplies, printing, and any other costs incurred to provide services to the client would be recorded as assets until the revenue earned from the client is recognized, at which time the accumulated costs would be expensed and matched to the revenues. Accumulation of costs by client engagement is important for internal control purposes so that management can have information to base billings, and to assess the profitability of different engagements.

INVENTORY ACCOUNTING AND INCOME TAXES

The accounting choices made by managers frequently have tax implications. Often, as we have discussed, managers must choose among accounting alternatives that can lower the entity's tax burden or achieve some other objective of financial reporting. In situations where the *Income Tax Act* doesn't specify a treatment, the method used for financial reporting purposes will often be used for tax purposes. Inventory accounting choice is one such situation. The *Income Tax Act* isn't very specific about how to account for inventory for tax purposes so entities will usually use the inventory accounting methods selected for the general purpose financial statements. This means that these accounting choices can have a bearing on the amount of tax an entity pays.

The Canada Revenue Agency (CRA) suggests that the cost formula used for financial reporting purposes should also be used for tax purposes. While, in principle, using different methods for financial reporting and tax is allowed, using different methods might raise a red flag that encourages the CRA to investigate. This doesn't mean that the CRA will automatically accept the method being used for financial reporting purposes. It states that "the method used for income tax purposes should be the one that gives the truer picture of the taxpayer's income."[4] Even if the method used for financial reporting purposes is acceptable according to IFRS, the CRA can challenge the choice if it believes that the method isn't the one that "gives the truer picture of taxpayer income."

The definition of cost for tax purposes is similar to that used for accounting purposes. The CRA explains that cost for inventories of merchandise purchased for resale or of raw materials acquired for a manufacturing process, means laid-down cost. Laid-down cost includes invoice cost, customs and excise duties, transportation and other acquisition costs, and storage costs where they are significant.[5]

Entities are also allowed to use the lower of cost and market rule for inventory valuation purposes. If the fair market value of inventory at the end of a year is less than its cost then the taxpayer can use fair market value. This treatment allows the taxpayer to reduce income by writing down the value of inventory to fair market value (NRV).

The CRA requires that methods used to account for inventory for tax purposes be applied consistently from period to period. A method used for tax purposes can only be changed with the permission of the Minister of National Revenue. The minister will usually approve a change if the new method proposed by the taxpayer (a) is a more appropriate way of determining income, (b) will be used for financial reporting purposes, and (c) will be used consistently in future years.[6] Restrictions on an entity's ability to change how it accounts for inventory limits changes made simply to avoid tax.

FINANCIAL STATEMENT ANALYSIS ISSUES

For many businesses, inventory management is a crucial managerial responsibility. Management's effectiveness and efficiency in managing inventory can have a significant impact on company performance. Managing inventory requires careful balance as carrying too much or too little inventory can be costly. The more inventory an entity has, the more cash is tied up and unavailable for other purposes. On the other hand, too little inventory may mean an entity runs out of the products customers need. This means a loss of revenue for that particular transaction. Worse, the customer and the stream of revenue it would have generated may be permanently lost. Thus, the consequence of not carrying enough inventory is a decline in revenue. If a manufacturing company runs out of inventory required for its production process, the entire production process may be forced to stop, which would be very costly.

The **inventory turnover ratio (ITO)** provides information on how efficiently inventory is being managed by measuring how quickly the entity is able to sell its inventory. The inventory turnover ratio is defined as

$$\text{Inventory turnover ratio} = \frac{\text{Cost of sales}}{\text{Average inventory}}$$

Average inventory can be calculated by summing the amount of inventory at the beginning and the end of the period and dividing by two. A better measure can be obtained by using quarterly or monthly data if they are available. This is especially important for seasonal businesses. Many retail businesses have their lowest amount of inventory after the Christmas season and the highest amount in the period leading up to Christmas.

The ITO indicates the number of times during a period the entity is able to purchase and sell its stock of inventory. Usually, a higher ITO ratio is better because it indicates the entity can sell or "turn over" the inventory more quickly. It also indicates the inventory is more liquid as it's sold more quickly and cash is realized sooner than with slower-moving inventory. A lower ITO may indicate that inventory isn't selling or is slow moving because it's obsolete or there is low demand for it. In deteriorating economic periods an entity's ITO should decrease because it will have too much inventory (the amount of inventory increases while sales and cost of sales decrease). On the other hand, a decreasing ITO could indicate that inventory is being built up in anticipation of increasing sales.

As with other financial ratios, it isn't possible to make sense of the inventory turnover ratio in absolute terms. The ratio must be considered in comparison with those of other, similar entities, or for a particular entity over time. Inventory turnover ratios can vary significantly from industry to industry.

Another way of looking at the efficiency of inventory management is obtained by dividing the ITO into 365 to give the **average number of days inventory on hand**, which indicates the number of days it takes an entity to sell its inventory. The average number of days inventory on hand is defined as

$$\text{Average number of days inventory on hand} = \frac{365}{\text{Inventory turnover ratio}}$$

A company improves its efficiency by reducing the average number of days it holds its inventory.

If an entity has many types of inventory, the ITO ratio can be difficult to interpret because the different inventories may turn over at different rates. The ITO ratio calculated using the aggregate total reported on the balance sheet will just be an average of the turnover ratios of all the different types of inventory.

Let's look at the ITO and the average number of days of inventory on hand for Leon's Furniture Limited (Leon's) for 2000 through 2008 to see if we can find any trends in the data. The information is presented in Table 7.10.

TABLE 7.10	Leon's Furniture Ltd.: Inventory Turnover Ratio 2000–2008 (in thousands of dollars)								
	2000	**2001**	**2002**	**2003**	**2004**	**2005**	**2006**	**2007**	**2008**
Inventory	$49,171	$51,079	$55,047	$58,841	$71,279	$72,644	$74,733	$75,640	$92,904
Cost of goods sold	$234,798	$248,445	$261,265	$267,323	$295,241	$323,629	$341,403	$363,261	$440,360
Inventory turnover ratio	4.75	4.96	4.92	4.69	4.54	4.50	4.63	4.83	5.23
Average number of days inventory on hand	76.8	73.6	74.1	77.8	80.4	81.2	78.8	75.6	69.8

The calculation of the 2008 ITO and average number of days inventory on hand is as follows:

$$\text{Inventory turnover ratio} = \frac{\text{Cost of sales}}{\text{Average inventory}}$$

$$= \frac{\$440,360,000}{(\$75,640,000 + \$92,904,000)/2}$$

$$= 5.23$$

$$\text{Average number of days inventory on hand} = \frac{365}{\text{Inventory turnover ratio}}$$

$$= \frac{365}{5.23}$$

$$= 69.8 \text{ days}$$

Over the period shown Leon's ITO has been relatively stable, ranging from a low of 4.50 in 2005 to a high of 5.23 in 2008. The average number of days has ranged from 69.8 to 81.2 days. There are no trends in the data, with the ITO decreasing steadily from 2001 through 2005, then increasing in 2006, and decreasing again in 2007. There are many possible reasons for Leon's year-to-year changes in ITO; more inventory may be needed to meet the demands of customers and the competition, or the mix of inventory may be changing (each category of Leon's inventory may not have the same turnover ratio).

To calculate the ITO ratio in Table 7.10, I used cost of goods sold from the income statement. This is reasonable since most of cost of sales would be the cost of inventory. Beginning in 2008, in compliance with IFRS, Leon's began disclosing the cost of inventory sold during the period in the notes to the financial statements (see Note 3(a) in Leon's 2008 annual report). The cost of inventory sold is slightly less than cost of goods sold. For 2008, cost of inventory sold was $430,347,000, and $355,175,000 in 2007. By using these amounts, the ITO for 2008 was 5.11 and 4.72 for 2007. The differences from the amounts shown in Table 7.10 are small in this case, but the new disclosures allow for more appropriate calculations. I used cost of goods sold in Table 7.10 so the numbers would be comparable.

In Table 7.11 Leon's inventory information is compared with The Brick's, another large furniture retailer.

TABLE 7.11 Leon's versus The Brick: Inventory Turnover Ratio				
	2005	2006	2007	2008
Leon's				
Inventory turnover ratio	4.50	4.63	4.83	5.23
Average number of days inventory on hand	81.2	78.8	75.6	69.8
The Brick				
Inventory turnover ratio	4.08	3.95	3.87	3.71
Average number of days inventory on hand	89.5	92.4	94.3	98.4

The table shows that Leon's turns its inventory over faster than The Brick, whose turnover has gotten worse over the years shown while Leon's has improved. All things being equal, Leon's has a distinct competitive advantage because it manages its inventory more efficiently, meaning it has less cash tied up in inventory.

Another point to note is that a company's management of its inventory affects the ratios and how they are interpreted. For example, many companies use an approach called **just-in-time** (JIT) inventory management. In a JIT inventory system a manufacturer orders materials or produces parts or finished goods only when they are required. In a non-JIT system a company maintains stocks of inventory for use in production or for sale. A company that uses JIT inventory should have lower amounts of inventory and a higher ITO than companies that don't use JIT. With less inventory and faster ITO the impact of different cost formulas will be less significant. You may discuss JIT inventory systems in detail in your managerial accounting course, but for now the point is to recognize that ratios can be affected by many different management decisions.

Like other information in the financial statements, information about inventory and cost of sales raises questions without necessarily providing answers. For example, the existence of inventory doesn't mean that it can be sold. Suppose that at the end of a year you notice that the amount of inventory reported on the balance sheet had increased significantly from previous years. How can that change be interpreted? If sales had increased along with inventory we might conclude that inventory has increased to support the increased level of sales. If there was no increase in sales we could conclude that management was building up inventory in anticipation of an expansion or to reflect anticipated sales growth. On the other hand the increase might reflect over-purchasing or obsolete inventory that had not yet been written off.

INSIGHT

It should be clear from the discussion of the different inventory cost formulas that financial analysis and financial ratios for an entity will be affected by the cost formula used. This means it may be difficult to compare firms in an industry if the amount of inventory and cost of sales differ because they are using different cost formulas or treating similar costs differently. The different treatments can affect the inventory turnover ratio, current ratio, gross margin, and profit margin, to name a few. It's important to remember that while the various accounting methods affect our accounting measures, they don't affect the concept that is being measured. Whether a company uses FIFO or average cost doesn't alter its actual liquidity or profitability.

A Banker's View of Inventory

When an entity borrows money, the lender commonly requests collateral in the event the borrower can't repay the loan. Inventory seems like a sensible asset to use as collateral but, generally, banks don't welcome it because inventory can be difficult to dispose of. After all, if the borrower can't sell the inventory, how will a bank sell it? What would a bank do with large quantities of toasters, shirts, or machine-tooled dies? Generally, banks recover as little as five or ten cents for each dollar of inventory that is reported on the balance sheet if the borrower can't repay a loan.

All the same, many businesses require financing for their inventory. This is especially true for seasonal businesses. Consider a company that produces Christmas decorations. The company would build up its inventory during the year until it began shipping its products as the holiday season approached. Most seasonal businesses won't have a stockpile of cash available to self-finance the inventory buildup so they rely on bank credit to finance this, and banks will lend against inventory, despite their concerns. However, when a bank lends against inventory, it generally expects the loan to be repaid in full at the end of the entity's operating cycle. In other words, inventory loans aren't permanent. In contrast, when accounts receivable is the collateral, the amount borrowed can remain outstanding permanently, based on the amount of receivables the entity has.

Solved Problem

In 2010, Naomi Krajden developed a computer game called Zordef of the Deep (Zordef). The game was a big hit among Naomi's friends and they suggested it might be successful commercially. At first Naomi tried to market Zordef online on her website. However, it quickly became obvious that this approach wasn't going to work. In the six months Naomi tried to distribute the game on her own she managed to sell only 154 copies.

In mid-2011 Naomi had a chance meeting with a marketing representative with Wonder Software Ltd. (WS), a company that produces computer software. WS is a privately owned corporation with its head office near Ottawa. Naomi demonstrated Zordef to the representative and he offered to bring it to WS's executives for evaluation. After testing and discussions WS offered to market Zordef. Naomi and WS agreed that Naomi would transfer title to the game to WS in exchange for 30 percent of the net income earned on sales of the game. The contract between the parties stipulated that WS could deduct appropriate, reasonable expenses in determining net income. Zordef of the Deep was released in November 2012.

Games of this type have lives of about three years. Most sales are generated in the first few months and they then tail off quickly. Sales of Zordef in the ten months ended August 31, 2013, were $838,000. WS estimates that sales of Zordef for the 12 months ending August 31, 2014, will be about $420,000 and perhaps $100,000 in the 12 months after that. WS recently presented Naomi with an income statement for the ten months ended August 31, 2013 and a cheque for $18,000. The income statement and additional information obtained from WS is shown below:

Zordef of the Deep Computer Game
Statement of Income for the Ten Months Ended August 31, 2013

Sales (Note 1)		$838,000
Cost of goods sold (Note 2)	$304,000	
Selling and administrative costs (Note 3)	252,000	
Packaging design costs (Note 4)	97,000	
Advertising (Note 5)	85,000	
Product development costs (Note 6)	32,000	
Taxes	8,000	778,000
Net Income		$ 60,000

Notes:

1. Revenue is recognized when shipped to the customer. The sales figure is net of an allowance for doubtful accounts and returns.

2. Cost of goods sold includes production costs of the game. Approximately $154,000 represents direct costs of production (labour and materials) and an allocation of $115,000 of overhead costs, including depreciation of plant and equipment, supervisory staff, quality control staff, and so on. Also included is $15,000 for games that had to be discarded because they were damaged or not usable and $20,000 for the estimated payment to Naomi.

3. Selling and administrative costs include commissions paid to salespeople, an allocation of salespeople's salaries and an allocation of general office overhead. A special charge of $50,000 was levied against Zordef of the Deep to account for senior management's time spent on the game.

4. The charge represents money spent to develop packaging for Zordef of the Deep. The packaging was designed by an outside agency and the charge represents the full amount paid for the design.

5. The company spent $40,000 directly advertising and promoting Zordef of the Deep to consumers and retailers. The remaining amount is an allocation of the overall corporate advertising budget that includes promotion of the WS full product line.

6. Before Zordef was brought to market WS made modifications to the program. The cost represents the time of WS's programmer charged at the prevailing market rate. This is the rate WS charges outsiders who contract WS to do programming.

Naomi Krajden is disturbed that, despite the amount of sales of the game, the profit figure is very low and she doesn't think she is being dealt with fairly. She has asked you to prepare a report examining the accounting methods used by WS in calculating Zordef's net income. The report will be used in negotiations with WS and potentially in any legal action taken by Naomi.

Required:

Prepare the report to Naomi Krajden.

Comment: This case takes an aggressive stance on behalf of Naomi Krajden. The response argues that only incremental costs should be charged to Zordef. Other approaches are possible and legitimate. WS would likely disagree strongly with this approach and the negotiations would go from there.

Ms. Naomi Krajden
11242 Joseph Casavant
Montreal, Quebec

Dear Naomi:

I have reviewed the financial statements you have been given by Wonder Software Ltd. (Wonder) that shows the profitability of your Zordef of the Deep game, which you sold to Wonder in exchange for 30 percent of the profits. It appears from the information disclosed in the statement that Wonder has done its best to charge as many expenses to the product as possible, presumably with the purpose of minimizing the net income earned by the game and thereby minimizing the payments to you. This is a good strategy for Wonder since it keeps more cash in the company but bad for you because you get paid less.

Comment: The role is important. You are advising Naomi Krajden who believes she has been disadvantaged by the accounting done by Wonder Software. This means your response should focus on looking out for the best interests of Naomi.

There are many ways accounting can be done. Often there are reasonable alternative methods that can be justified in a situation. In my analysis below I will recommend alternative accounting treatments that are in your interests but can be reasonably justified. I will not bind myself to generally accepted accounting principles (GAAP) or International Financial Reporting Standards (IFRS). I do not think that limiting choices to GAAP/IFRS will always provide an economically sound alternative. The basis of my approach will be that the only costs that should be charged to Zordef are additional costs Wonder incurred by adding Zordef to its product line. I will argue that allocated costs should not be included. This approach can be called an incremental cost approach. This is, of course only one approach to this situation and Wonder will likely use alternatives to make their case. While I am confident the positions I take are compelling, it is important to recognize that good arguments can be made for the alternatives.

It is not always possible to definitively resolve the controversy without additional information. In these situations I will identify the additional information that is required and why it is required.

1. Revenue recognition describes the point in time an entity records a sale. It is appropriate for Wonder to recognize revenue when the programs are shipped. It is really the only reasonable time available. It is reasonable to allocate the bad debt expense since it is likely very difficult to attribute the costs directly to the sales of individual products. Returns should be based on estimated returns of Zordef. However, the bases for allocating the costs and estimating returns should be reviewed to ensure they are reasonable and are applied correctly (so that Zordef is not overcharged).

2. The $154,000 of direct materials and labour can be reasonably charged to Zordef since they are costs incurred to produce the product. The allocation of overhead is consistent with IFRS but is not, in my opinion, appropriate in this situation. The only overhead costs that should be allocated to Zordef are incremental ones—new costs that were incurred because of the introduction of Zordef. From the information provided, it does not appear that new costs were incurred because of Zordef. The $15,000 for production problems should be excluded in the determination of your profit share since it pertains to management and production inefficiencies. There is no reason why you should bear this cost. It is also completely inappropriate to include your profit share in the Zordef statement. Your payment represents a share of the profit, not a cost of the product. Therefore, Zordef's net income should be increased by $150,000.

    In the event my recommendations above are not accepted (through negotiation or a legal ruling), it will be necessary to verify the amounts allocated to Zordef. It will be necessary to find out the method used to allocate costs and to assess its reasonableness and to determine whether the method has been properly applied. These steps are necessary because Wonder has incentives to overstate the costs allocated to Zordef.

3. As described in point 2, allocated costs should not be included in the Zordef income statement. Unless a case can be made for incremental general and admin costs, these should not be charged to Zordef. The $50,000 senior management charge is not appropriate since Zordef is being charged for the work senior managers are supposed to do. In addition, there may be double counting with the allocation of the general and admin plus the $50,000 for senior management. Only the sales commissions represent a legitimate charge. Therefore expenses must be decreased by $50,000 plus the allocated portion of general office overhead.

4. The cost of developing packaging for Zordef should be charged against Zordef. However, the full amount of the cost was expensed in fiscal 2013. Since Zordef will be sold in fiscal 2014 and 2015 it is appropriate that some of the cost of the packaging be charged against revenue in those years. This is known as matching. If the Zordef income statement is to reflect the actual performance of the product then it makes economic sense to match costs attributable to sales to the revenue. Instead, Wonder has fully expensed the cost in 2013, which lowers income in the current period and reduces the payment to you. The packaging could be allocated on a straight-line basis over the three years of the expected product life. This treatment will reduce expenses by about $65,000 in the current year.

5. The $40,000 of direct advertising costs should be charged against Zordef since they are direct costs. The remaining costs should not be charged because they are not direct costs and there was likely no increase in the overall advertising budget because of the addition to Zordef. Therefore, expenses should decrease by $45,000.

6. It is unreasonable to charge Zordef for costs that were not incurred by Wonder. Zordef should be charged the actual cost incurred to pay the programmers to do the modifications. If the programmers are on salary and did not get paid more or overtime as a result of Zordef, this is not an incremental cost and should not be charged to Zordef at all. Charging the market rate for the services provided by in-house programmers does not in any way reflect the economic cost to Wonder for the programming. I suggest that your initial position should be that unless incremental programming costs were incurred there should be no charge to Zordef, and in negotiations you can back off to the actual cost of the programmers' time.

Without complete information it is not possible to determine the exact net income to present to Wonder. However, based on the analysis above, net income should increase by a minimum of $310,000 (which may increase with additional information) and increase the payment to you by $93,000.

Please contact me if you have any questions.

SUMMARY OF KEY POINTS

▶ **LO 1** Inventory is goods available for sale by an entity, or goods that will be used to produce goods that will be sold. It can also include materials used in supplying a service to customers. According to IFRS, inventory is valued at the lower of cost and net realizable value, where cost includes all costs incurred to purchase or make the products and get them ready for sale to customers. For inventory that's purchased, cost should include all the costs incurred to ready the inventory for sale or use. For manufacturers and processors, cost of inventory should include the cost of materials used plus the cost of labour directly used to produce the product plus an allocation of overhead incurred in the production process.

▶ **LO 2** There are two types of inventory control systems for keeping track of inventory transactions: perpetual systems and periodic systems. A perpetual inventory control system keeps an ongoing tally of purchases and sales of inventory, and the inventory account is adjusted to reflect changes as they occur. With a periodic inventory control system, the balance in the inventory account at the end of period is determined by counting the inventory on hand and calculating cost of sales indirectly using the equation, cost of sales = beginning inventory + purchases − ending inventory. The choice between a periodic and perpetual inventory control system is an internal control issue, not an accounting one.

▶ **LO 3** Accountants don't usually keep track of the costs associated with individual items of inventory. Instead, they use cost formulas to move costs from inventory to cost of sales, without regard for the actual physical flow of the inventory. There are three cost formulas currently in use in Canada: FIFO, average cost, and specific identification. The choice of cost formula doesn't directly affect the cash flow of the entity, but the amounts reported on the balance sheet and the income statement can be significantly different depending on the cost formula used.

▶ **LO 4** According to IFRS, inventory on hand at the end of a period must be reported at the lower of cost and net realizable value (NRV). If the NRV of inventory at the end of a reporting period is lower than its cost, the inventory must be written down to its NRV. The amount of a writedown is expensed in the period of the writedown. The LCM rule is an application of conservatism. Inventory that has been written down can be written back up to its original cost (but not higher than that).

▶ **LO 5** Historical cost, transactions-based accounting isn't the only accounting model available. For many users of financial statements, alternative valuation methods such as replacement cost or net realizable value can provide useful information for decision making. These alternative methods aren't generally used in Canada for inventory because of conservatism and a general preference for reliability over relevance (but are allowed for certain types of inventory).

▶ **LO 6** Managers often make accounting choices that have tax implications. When the *Income Tax Act* doesn't specify a treatment, the method used for financial reporting purposes will often be used for tax purposes. The Canada Revenue Agency suggests that the cost formula used for financial reporting purposes should also be used for tax purposes. Entities can apply the lower of cost and market rule for tax purposes. The CRA requires that methods used to account for inventory be applied consistently.

▶ **LO 7** Management's effectiveness and efficiency in managing inventory can have a significant impact on entity performance. Managing inventory requires careful balance as carrying too much or too little can be costly. The inventory turnover ratio and the average number of days inventory on hand provide information on how efficiently and effectively inventory is being managed. A low or decreasing inventory turnover ratio can indicate that inventory isn't selling or is slow moving because it's obsolete or there is low demand. Generally, a higher inventory turnover ratio indicates better management of inventory.

FORMULA SUMMARY

$$\text{Inventory turnover ratio} = \frac{\text{Cost of sales}}{\text{Average inventory}}$$

$$\text{Average number of days inventory on hand} = \frac{365}{\text{Inventory turnover ratio}}$$

KEY TERMS

average cost method, p. 362

average number of days inventory on hand, p. 379

conservatism, p. 371

finished goods inventory, p. 356

first-in, first-out (FIFO), p. 361

holding gain or loss, p. 373

inventory, p. 355

inventory turnover ratio (ITO), p. 378

just-in-time (JIT) inventory, p. 380

last-in, first-out (LIFO), p. 368

lower of cost and market (LCM) rule, p. 369

net realizable value (NRV), p. 369

overhead, p. 357

periodic inventory control system, p. 358

perpetual inventory control system, p. 358

prudence, p. 371

raw materials inventory, p. 356

replacement cost, p. 373

specific identification method, p. 362

work-in-process inventory (WIP), p. 356

writedown, p. 369

writeoff, p. 369

SIMILAR TERMS

The left column gives alternative terms that are sometimes used for the accounting terms introduced in this chapter, which are listed in the right column.

prudence   **conservatism**, p. 371

ASSIGNMENT MATERIALS

Questions

Q7-1. Describe the type of inventory you would expect each of the following entities to have:
   a. Shoppers Drug Mart Corporation (drug store)
   b. Holiday Inn (hotel)
   c. Barrick Gold Corporation (gold mining company)
   d. York Central Hospital (hospital)
   e. Toyota Motor Corporation (car maker)
   f. Brick Brewing Corp. (beer maker)
   g. Burger King Corporation (fast-food chain)

Q7-2. For each of the following entities, describe what would be included in raw materials, work-in-process, and finished goods inventory:
   a. computer producer (company assembles computers from parts it buys from various manufacturers)
   b. producer of frozen French fries
   c. wood-furniture maker
   d. grower of trees (trees often take many years to mature before they are available for sale)
   e. miner and refiner of gold

Q7-3. Explain the concept of conservatism.

Q7-4. Why do making conservative accounting choices today sometimes result in non-conservative effects in later periods?

Q7-5. Explain why it isn't possible to calculate cost of goods sold when a periodic inventory control system is used if the inventory isn't counted.

Q7-6. Explain and give examples of the following types of inventory:
   a. raw materials
   b. work-in-process
   c. finished goods
   d. supplies

Q7-7. Why is it not possible to determine the amount of inventory that was stolen during a period when a periodic inventory control system is used?

Q7-8. Explain the difference between periodic and perpetual inventory control systems. Which do you think is the better system to use? Why?

Q7-9. Why is it often necessary to use a cost formula for valuing inventory and determining cost of sales? Why can't the actual cost of the goods sold be used to calculate cost of sales in these situations?

Q7-10. Regardless of the cost formula being used (FIFO, average cost, specific identification), the sum of cost of sales plus ending inventory will be the same. Explain why.

Q7-11. Explain why a FIFO inventory system gives higher inventory valuation and lower cost of sales than average cost when prices are rising.

Q7-12. Explain how costs flow through the following cost formulas: FIFO versus average cost versus specific identification.

Q7-13. What is the lower of cost and market rule? Why is it used? What is meant by the term "market" in lower of cost and market?

Q7-14. Why might it be difficult to actually determine the NRV of inventory when applying the lower of cost and market rule? Provide some examples of when determining NRV might be difficult.

Q7-15. What is a holding gain? How are holding gains accounted for when traditional historical cost, transactions-based accounting is used?

Q7-16. Under historical cost, transactions-based accounting model, are holding gains and losses always treated the same way? Describe the difference in the accounting treatment used for each and explain the reason for the difference.

Q7-17. Why is it necessary to count inventory when a perpetual inventory control system is used? Explain. Why is it necessary to count inventory when a periodic inventory control system is used? Explain.

Q7-18. Explain how the specific identification method of valuing inventory works. Why do most entities not use this method? Under what circumstances is the method useful? Why does this method sometimes make it easy to manipulate the financial statements?

Q7-19. Why is the choice of the inventory cost formula important for tax purposes? Explain.

Q7-20. Why is it not possible to satisfy a tax minimization objective and an income maximization objective when selecting the inventory cost formula that an entity should use?

Q7-21. Onslow Ltd. (Onslow) is a small public company trading on a Canadian stock exchange. Onslow's managers have a bonus plan that is based on net income and the managers believe that the amount of reported earnings is important for maintaining the company's stock price. Assume that whether Onslow uses FIFO or average cost will have a significant effect on reported earnings (FIFO earnings being higher) and the amount of assets it reports on its balance sheet. Discuss the issues that Onslow's management must consider when choosing between FIFO and average cost.

Q7-22. Does it matter which cost formula an entity uses if the price it pays for its inventory is stable? Explain.

Q7-23. How does the choice of cost formula affect financial ratios such as the inventory turnover ratio and the current ratio? Does the choice have any effect on the actual rate at which an entity's inventory turns over or the entity's actual liquidity? Explain.

Q7-24. What is inventory turnover? What does it tell a stakeholder about how the entity is managing its inventory? What could be some reasons for a decreasing inventory turnover ratio? What could be some reasons for an increasing inventory turnover ratio?

Q7-25. Which cost formula for valuing inventory is best? Explain.

Q7-26. Explain why the cash spent on inventory isn't affected by the cost formula used.

Exercises

E7-1. **(Effect of an error on the financial statements, LO 2)** Ayr Inc. (Ayr) uses a periodic inventory control system. During Ayr's inventory count on December 31, 2014, $100,000 of the inventory was counted twice, in error. Ayr reported inventory of $750,000 on December 31, 2013, and during the year it purchased $2,000,000 of inventory. What effect would the counting error have on net income for the year ended December 31, 2014, and on the amount of inventory reported on the balance sheet on December 31, 2014? Explain your answer.

E7-2.   **(Determine cost of units sold and cost of units remaining in inventory using different cost formulas, LO 2, 3)** The following information is provided for Badger Inc. (Badger):

Badger Inc. Inventory Information for October 2014		
	Number of units purchased	Price paid per unit
Purchased on October 8, 2014	30,000	$3.00
Purchased on October 17, 2014	21,150	3.25
Purchased on October 25, 2014	23,300	3.50

On October 31, 2014, Badger sold 61,100 units of inventory to customers.

Required:

Identify which inventory costs would be expensed in October 2014 and which costs would be in inventory on October 31, 2014 using the average cost and FIFO cost formulas. Assume Badger had no inventory on hand at the beginning of October.

E7-3.   **(Calculating cost of sales and ending inventory using different cost formulas, LO 3)** You are provided the following information about Chetwynd Ltd. (Chetwynd) for June 2015. Assume that Chetwynd uses a periodic inventory system and that during June the company sold 500 units of inventory:

Date	Description	Number of units	Cost per unit	Total cost
June 1	Opening inventory	300 units	$ 8	$ 2,400
June 12	Purchase	350 units	9	3,150
June 22	Purchase	450 units	10	4,500
	Total	1,100 units		$10,050

Required:

Calculate cost of goods sold and ending inventory on June 30, 2015, for Chetwynd using the average cost and FIFO cost formulas. How many units of inventory are on hand at the end of June under each cost formula?

E7-4.   **(Calculating cost of sales and ending inventory using different flow assumptions, LO 3)** You are provided the following information about Klemtu Inc. (Klemtu) for April 2014. Assume that Klemtu uses a periodic inventory system and that during April the company sold 100,000 units of inventory:

Date	Description	Number of units	Cost per unit	Total cost
April 1	Opening inventory	70,000 units	$2.50	$ 175,000
April 13	Purchase	42,200 units	2.60	109,720
April 21	Purchase	23,700 units	2.70	63,990
	Total	135,900 units		$348,710

Required:

Calculate cost of goods sold and ending inventory on April 30, 2014, for Klemtu using the average cost and FIFO cost formulas. How many units of inventory are on hand at the end of June under each cost formula?

E7-5. (**Calculating cost of sales and ending inventory using average cost and FIFO cost formulas, LO 2, 3**) Information is provided for Olds Ltd. below.

Date	Purchases	Sales	Balance
December 31, 2013			5,500 units @ $5.50
January 5, 2014	4,400 units @ $6		
January 8, 2014		3,100 units @ $11	
January 15, 2014	5,400 units @ $6.50		
January 20, 2014		6,500 units @ $12	
January 22, 2014	5,000 units @ $6.75		
January 29, 2014		4,200 units @ $12.50	
January 31, 2014			6,500 units @ $

Required:

Calculate cost of goods sold and ending inventory for Olds Ltd. using the average cost and FIFO cost formulas.

E7-6. (**Classifying different types of inventory, LO 1**) Whonock Tailors Ltd. (Whonock) is a manufacturer of high-quality men's and women's clothing. Indicate whether Whonock would classify the costs associated with each of the following items as inventory and, if it should be classified as inventory, whether it would be considered raw materials, work-in-process, finished goods, or supplies. Provide a brief explanation for each classification.
a. thread
b. partially completed suits
c. reusable containers for packing clothing for shipment
d. sewing machines
e. pins and needles
f. fabric
g. clothing awaiting shipment on the loading dock
h. storage containers for accessories (buttons, etc.) used in the making of clothing

E7-7. (**Classifying different types of inventory, LO 1**) Quesnel Inc. (Quesnel) is a coffee shop that sells brewed coffee and beans, as well as baked goods made on the premises. For each of the following items indicate whether Quesnel should classify the items as inventory and, if it should be classified as inventory, whether it would be considered raw materials, work-in-process, finished goods, or supplies. Provide a brief explanation for each classification.
a. paper cups for take-out
b. china cups and plates for eating in
c. brooms and mops
d. plastic wrap to package baked goods
e. coffee beans
f. pans for cooking baked goods
g. flour, sugar, eggs, chocolate
h. cleaning supplies (soap, disinfectant, etc.)

E7-8.   **(Classifying different types of inventory, LO 1)** For each of the following, explain whether the asset can be classified as inventory on the entity's balance sheet. This is a tricky question that requires some careful thought:

Entity	Asset
a. bank	cash
b. equipment rental store	chain saw
c. farm	cows
d. commercial real estate developer	shopping centre

E7-9.   **(Using the specific identification cost formula to account for inventory, LO 3)** Explain which of the following businesses would likely use the specific identification cost formula to account for its inventory and which would use FIFO or average cost:
a. jewellery store
b. aircraft manufacturer
c. bookstore
d. computer store
e. fruit store

E7-10.   **(Calculating cost of sales and ending inventory using the average cost and FIFO cost formulas when prices are stable, LO 2, 3)** The following information is provided for Exlou Ltd. (Exlou):

	Number of units	Purchase price per unit	Selling price per unit
Inventory on hand on January 1, 2014	60,000	$25	
Inventory purchases during 2014	280,000	25	
Inventory purchases during 2015	310,000	25	
Sales during 2014	300,000		$45
Sales during 2015	290,000		45

Required:

a. Calculate ending inventory on December 31, 2014 and 2015, and cost of sales and gross margin for the years ended December 31, 2014 and 2015 for Exlou using FIFO and average cost. Assume that Exlou uses a periodic inventory control system.
b. Explain the results you obtained in (a). Do you find anything unusual about the amounts you calculated for ending inventory, cost of sales, and gross margin under each of the cost formulas?

E7-11.   **(Manipulating income with specific identification, LO 3)** Baddeck Antiques Ltd. (Baddeck) sells rare antiques to discriminating clients. Over the years Baddeck has acquired four essentially identical vases from one of the ancient dynasties in China. The cost of the vases is as follows:

Vase A	$14,200
Vase B	8,950
Vase C	17,150
Vase D	12,250

Recently, a customer purchased one of the vases for $32,000.

Required:

a. If Baddeck wanted to minimize its profit on this sale, which of the vases would it have sold to the customer? Calculate gross margin and ending inventory at the end of the period.

b. If Baddeck wanted to maximize its profit on this sale, which of the vases would it have sold to the customer? Calculate gross margin and ending inventory at the end of the period.

c. What is the impact on ending inventory of your choices in (a) and (b)? Under what circumstances might Baddeck's management want to maximize profit? Under what circumstances might it want to minimize profit? In reality, would it be possible for Baddeck's management to have the opportunity to manage the financial statements in this way? Explain.

E7-12. **(Calculating inventory turnover ratio and the average number of days inventory on hand, LO 7)** You are provided with the following information about Kepenkeck Inc. (Kepenkeck):

Cost of sales for the year ended November 30, 2014	$7,250,000
Inventory balance on November 30, 2013	$2,300,000
Inventory balance on November 30, 2014	$2,150,000

Required:

a. Calculate Kepenkeck's inventory turnover ratio for the year ended November 30, 2014.

b. What is the average length of time it took Kepenkeck to sell its inventory in 2014?

c. Is Kepenkeck's inventory turnover ratio satisfactory? What would you need to know to fully answer this question?

E7-13. **(Lower of cost and market, LO 4)** Massawippi Inc. (Massawippi) uses the lower of cost and market rule to value its inventory. Massawippi's inventory on February 28, 2014 had a cost of $2,750,000 and a NRV of $2,200,000.

Required:

a. By how much should Massawippi's inventory be written down?

b. Prepare the journal entry Massawippi should prepare to record the writedown.

c. What amount should be reported for inventory on Massawippi's February 28, 2014, balance sheet?

E7-14. **(Lower of cost and market, LO 4)** Wolf Ltd. (Wolf) uses the lower of cost and market rule to value its inventory. Wolf's inventory on December 31, 2014 had 100,000 units of inventory on hand with a total cost of $780,000 and a NRV of $700,000. On March 31, 2015, 30 percent of the inventory that was on hand at the end of December was still in inventory. On March 31, 2015 the NRV per unit had recovered 75 percent of the amount written down in December.

Required:

a. By how much should Wolf's inventory be written down in 2014?

b. Prepare the journal entry Wolf will prepare to record the writedown in 2014.

c. What amount should be reported for inventory on Wolf's December 31, 2014 balance sheet?

d. By how much should Wolf's inventory be written up on March 31, 2015?

e. Prepare the journal entry needed to write up the inventory.

f. What amount should be reported for inventory on Wolf's March 31, 2015 balance sheet? Assume no new inventory was purchased in the first quarter of 2015.

E7-15. **(Working with the inventory turnover ratio and the average number of days inventory on hand, LO 7)** Use the information provided in each row to calculate the missing values (shaded boxes). Each row is an independent situation.

	Cost of sales	Average inventory	Inventory turnover ratio	Average number of days inventory on hand
a.	$ 558,950	$ 125,250		
b.	10,500,000			159.4
c.		250,000	11.00	
d.		9,850,000		68.5

E7-16. **(Identifying and calculating holding gains and losses, LO 5)** For each of the following situations, indicate whether the event gives rise to a holding gain or a loss. Explain your answer.
   a. In 1995, a land development company purchased raw land for later development for $5,000,000. In 2014 development of the land had not yet begun. The company had recently received an offer for the land of $14,000,000.
   b. In November 2013 a jeweller purchased $10,000 of gold for making jewellery. In May 2014 when the jeweller sold the jewellery made from the gold, the same amount of gold would have cost $9,000.
   c. In March 2015 a company purchased a large supply of lumber for $200,000. By the end of the year, the market price of the lumber had doubled because of high demand in the U.S.

E7-17. **(Compute missing information, LO 2)** Complete the following table by calculating the missing values (shaded boxes).

	Dec. 31, 2013	Dec. 31, 2014	Dec. 31, 2015	Dec. 31, 2016
Beginning inventory	$370,000	$	$	$
Purchases	875,000	945,000		1,300,000
Ending inventory		425,000	400,000	480,000
Cost of sales	900,000		1,225,000	

E7-18. **(The effect of different cash flow assumptions on liquidity, LO 3, 7)** The balances in the current asset and liability accounts for Feeder Ltd. (Feeder) are provided below. The balances for inventory are provided using the FIFO and average cost formulas.

Cost formula	Inventory balance on December 31, 2014
FIFO	$222,500
Average cost	311,500

Account	Account balance on December 31, 2014
Cash	$ 40,000
Accounts receivable	167,000
Prepaid assets	25,000
Bank loan	175,000
Accounts payable and accrued liabilities	225,000

Required:

    a. Calculate Feeder's current ratio on December 31, 2014, using the two cost formulas.

    b. How do you explain the results you obtained in (a)?

    c. How do the different results you obtained in (a) affect your analysis of Feeder Ltd.'s liquidity?

    d. Which current ratio provides the best measure of Feeder's liquidity? Explain.

E7-19. **(Effect of transactions and economic events on ratios, LO 4, 7)** Complete the following table by indicating whether the transactions or economic events would increase, decrease, or have no effect on the financial ratios listed. Assume that the current ratio is greater than 1.0 and the quick ratio less than 1.0 before considering the effect of each transaction or economic event.

	Current ratio	Quick ratio	Gross margin percentage	Inventory turnover ratio	Profit margin percentage	Debt-to-equity ratio
a. Inventory is written down						
b. Inventory costing $5,000 is sold on credit for $11,000						
c. Inventory is lost						
d. Inventory is written up following a writedown in the previous period						
e. Inventory is purchased for cash						

E7-20. **(Recording inventory transactions, LO 2, 4)** For each of the following transactions and economic events, prepare the necessary journal entries. Provide a brief explanation for each journal entry and state any assumptions you make.

    a. Inventory costing $20,000 is purchased on credit.

    b. Inventory costing $15,000 is written off because it has become unsaleable.

    c. Inventory costing $10,000 is sold to a customer for $22,000 cash. The entity uses a periodic inventory control system.

    d. Inventory costing $8,000 is sold to a customer on credit for $20,000, with the amount due in 30 days. The entity uses a perpetual inventory control system.

    e. Management discovers that the NRV of its inventory is $200,000 and its cost is $215,000.

    f. A supplier is paid $5,000 for inventory purchased on credit.

    g. Inventory on hand was written down in the previous period by $50,000. The NRV of that inventory has since increased by $30,000. All inventory from the previous period is still on hand.

E7-21.   (**Inventory cost formulas when prices are falling, LO 3, 4**) Azilda Inc. (Azilda) operates in a part of the computer industry where the cost of inventory has been falling recently. The cost of inventory purchased by Azilda over the last year is summarized below. Azilda values its inventory at the lower of cost and net realizable value. Assume that purchases are made at the start of a month before any sales occur during that month.

Date	Quantity	Cost per unit	Selling price per unit
Purchases			
Opening inventory	175	$760	
October 1, 2014	360	720	
January 2, 2015	270	688	
April 1, 2015	210	648	
July 2, 2015	425	620	
Sales			
October–December, 2014	405		$1,368
January–March, 2015	290		1,296
April–June, 2015	215		1,240
July–September, 2015	395		1,112

Required:

a. Calculate cost of sales for the year ended September 30, 2015 and ending inventory on September 30, 2015 for Azilda using the average cost and FIFO cost formulas.
b. Which cost formula is most attractive for an accounting objective of income maximization?
c. Which cost formula is most attractive for an accounting objective of tax minimization?
d. Compare the relative values under the two cost formulas of ending inventory and cost of sales in this situation versus a situation where prices are rising. What is different between the two situations?
e. Apply the lower of cost and market rule to the year-end inventory. Assume that Azilda's selling costs for inventory are $300 per unit.

E7-22.   (**Inventory cost formulas and taxes, LO 3, 6**) Sayabec Ltd.'s (Sayabec) purchases for 2015 were

Date	Quantity purchased	Cost per unit
March 1	35,000	$8.25
June 4	41,000	8.75
September 9	25,000	9.00
December 4	20,000	9.30

The beginning balance in inventory on January 1, 2015 was 46,000 units with a cost of $8 per unit. The inventory count on December 31, 2015 found that there were 39,000 units on hand at the end of the year. Sayabec uses a periodic inventory control system. During 2015 Sayabec had revenues of $2,984,000 and expenses other than the cost of sales and taxes of $1,525,000. Sayabec pays taxes equal to 18 percent of its income before taxes.

Required:

    a. Prepare income statements for 2015 for Sayabec using FIFO and average cost. Your income statements should show the amount of taxes the company has to pay for the income it earned in 2015. Taxes are calculated by multiplying income before taxes (revenue − all expenses except taxes) by the tax rate.

    b. Which method would you recommend that Sayabec use if its primary objective of financial reporting is to minimize taxes? Explain your answer.

    c. What are possible explanations as to why Sayabec would choose not to use the method you recommended in (b)?

E7-23. **(Considering the impact of valuing inventory at replacement cost, LO 5)** Kapuskasing Inc. (Kapuskasing) imports widgets from China for sale in the Canadian market. You are provided with the following information about Kapuskasing's inventory for 2014:

Beginning inventory	10,000 units @ $8.25 per unit
Purchases during 2014	95,000 units @ $8.80 per unit
Sold during 2014	90,000 units for $18 when the replacement cost per unit was $9
Ending inventory	15,000 units with replacement cost of $9.25 per unit

In addition, Kapuskasing incurred $125,000 in other costs to operate its business. The company's year-end is December 31.

Required:

    a. Prepare an income statement for Kapuskasing for 2014. Show the gross margin and net income for the year on your income statement. Assume that Kapuskasing uses FIFO to account for its inventory.

    b. Prepare an income statement for Kapuskasing for 2014 assuming that it values its inventory at replacement cost. Prepare the journal entries you require to record the ending inventory at replacement cost at the end of 2014.

    c. What amount would be reported on the December 31, 2014 balance sheet for inventory if

        i. Kapuskasing uses FIFO to value its inventory?

        ii. Kapuskasing uses replacement cost to value its inventory?

    d. Explain the differences between the two income statements you prepared. How would a stakeholder interpret these income statements?

E7-24. **(Examining conservatism, LO 4)** Anvil Ltd. (Anvil) follows IFRS when preparing its financial statements. For each of the following independent situations, explain how Anvil should account for the transaction or economic event. Explain your reasoning. In each case, provide the journal entry that Anvil should prepare.

    a. A piece of equipment purchased for $25,000 was destroyed in an accident during initial installation. The equipment had not yet been depreciated.

    b. Inventory with a cost of $100,000 has gone out of style and it will have to be sold at a discount. Management estimates that Anvil will be able to sell the inventory for $60,000.

    c. Equipment used by one of the divisions of Anvil has become technologically obsolete because there is a new generation of equipment that is more efficient and produces higher quality output. Anvil's existing equipment can still be used (it still functions) but is used infrequently because of the lower quality output it produces.

    d. Last year Anvil loaned $300,000 to a biotechnology company. Last week, the biotechnology company announced it was bankrupt and would be liquidating all of its assets and going out of business. Anvil expects to receive nothing from the biotechnology company for the loan.

Problems

P7-1. **(Calculating cost of sales and ending inventory using average cost and FIFO cost formulas, LO 1, 2, 3)** Adamo Limited (AL) is a wholesaler of machine parts. Jacob Avery, an employee of AL, recently purchased AL from the original owner, Mr. Adam, who is retiring. Mr. Avery has come to you for advice on how to calculate ending inventory and cost of goods sold. He has asked you to explain your reasoning for any choices you make. Mr. Avery provided you with the following example of his inventory costs using Part 17592a.

Inventory Information for Part 17592a				
	Number of units	Date of purchase/sale	Cost per unit	Selling price per unit
Opening inventory	150 units	Various	$4.00	
Purchase	100 units	Nov. 10	4.50	
Sale	200 units	Nov. 12		$11.00
Purchase	175 units	Nov. 20	4.70	
Sale	340 units	Nov. 22		11.00
Purchase	180 units	Nov. 25	4.95	

Required:

Calculate ending inventory as at November 30 and cost of goods sold for Part 17592a for November. Provide the explanations requested by Mr. Avery.

P7-2. **(The impact of cost formulas on ratios, LO 3, 7)** Cardigan Corp. (Cardigan) and Huskisson Ltd. (Huskisson) are small distribution companies. They are identical in every respect—amount of sales, quantity of inventory sold, number of employees. Everything is the same except that Cardigan uses FIFO as its cost formula and Huskisson uses average cost.

Balance Sheets as of December 31, 2015		
	Cardigan (FIFO)	Huskisson (Average cost)
Assets		
Cash	$ 45,250	$ 45,250
Accounts receivable	389,000	389,000
Inventory	1,107,750	823,725
Other current assets	35,200	35,200
Total current assets	1,577,200	1,293,175
Property, plant, and equipment (net)	2,150,000	2,150,000
Total assets	$3,727,200	$3,443,175
Liabilities and Owners' equity		
Bank loan	$ 210,500	$ 210,500
Accounts payable	855,000	855,000
Other current liabilities	68,250	68,250
Total current liabilities	1,133,750	1,133,750
Long-term debt	545,000	545,000
Other non-current liabilities	52,500	52,500
Total liabilities	1,731,250	1,731,250
Capital stock	420,000	420,000
Retained earnings	1,575,950	1,291,925
Total liabilities and owners' equity	$3,727,200	$3,443,175

Income Statements for the Year Ended December 31, 2015		
	Cardigan (FIFO)	Huskisson (Average cost)
Revenue	$11,585,000	$11,585,000
Cost of sales	7,778,800	8,062,825
Gross margin	3,806,200	3,522,175
Other expenses	2,220,000	2,220,000
Net income	$ 1,586,200	$ 1,302,175

You also learn that on December 31, 2014, the balances in inventory for the two companies were

Ending Inventory Balances on December 31, 2014		
	Cardigan (FIFO)	Huskisson (Average cost)
Inventory	$1,002,855	$749,910

Required:

a. Calculate the following ratios for each of the two companies:
   i. current ratio
   ii. quick ratio
   iii. inventory turnover ratio
   iv. average number of days inventory on hand
   v. gross margin percentage
   vi. profit margin percentage
b. Which company has the strongest liquidity position?
c. Which company is the most profitable?
d. Which company manages its inventory most effectively?
e. The two companies' bankers lend money based on the amount of accounts receivable and inventory on hand. Which company will be able to obtain the largest loan? From the banks' point of view, is the company that receives the largest loan the best credit risk? Explain.

P7-3. **(The impact of cost formulas on ratios, LO 3, 7)** Weybridge Corp. (Weybridge) and Kennetcook Ltd. (Kennetcook) are small retail stores. They are identical in every respect—amount of sales, quantity of inventory sold, number of employees. Everything is the same except that Weybridge uses FIFO as its cost formula and Kennetcook uses average cost.

Income Statements For the Year Ended December 31, 2014		
	Weybridge (FIFO)	**Kennetcook (Average cost)**
Revenue	$831,000	$831,000
Cost of sales	586,951	634,288
Gross margin	244,049	196,712
Other expenses	169,400	169,400
Net income (loss)	$ 74,649	$ 27,312
Assets		
Cash	$ 14,220	$ 14,220
Accounts receivable	44,100	44,100
Inventory	184,625	137,288
Other current assets	7,350	7,350
Total current assets	250,295	202,958
Property, plant, and equipment (net)	263,725	263,725
Total assets	$514,020	$466,683
Liabilities and Owners' equity		
Bank loan	$ 22,500	$ 22,500
Accounts payable	132,125	132,125
Other current liabilities	11,375	11,375
Total current liabilities	166,000	166,000
Long-term debt	45,850	45,850
Other non-current liabilities	8,750	8,750
Total liabilities	220,600	220,600
Capital stock	35,000	35,000
Retained earnings	258,420	211,083
Total liabilities and owners' equity	$514,020	$466,683

You also learn that on December 31, 2013, the balances in inventory for the two companies:

Ending Inventory Balances on December 31, 2013		
	Weybridge (FIFO)	**Kennetcook (Average cost)**
Inventory	$164,000	$127,084

Required:

a. Calculate the following ratios for each of the two companies:
  i.   current ratio
  ii. quick ratio
  iii. inventory turnover ratio
  iv. average number of days inventory on hand
  v.   gross margin percentage
  vi. profit margin percentage
b. Which company has the strongest liquidity position?
c. Which company is most profitable?
d. Which company manages its inventory most effectively?

e. The two companies' bankers lend money based on the amount of accounts receivable and inventory on hand. Which company will be able to obtain the largest loan? From the banks' point of view, is the company that receives the largest loan the best credit risk? Explain.

P7-4. (**Recommending inventory accounting policies, LO 1, 2, 3, 4, 6**) Tesseralik Inc. (Tesseralik) is a small private manufacturing company that makes inexpensive laptop computers. Tesseralik is owned by three brothers who converted their interest in computers into a business. All three brothers are involved in the management of the company. The company is relatively free of debt, with only a small bank loan that is personally guaranteed by the brothers. Tesseralik purchases all component parts from independent manufacturers and assembles them into the laptops.

The company has been successful because it has been able to provide a good-quality product at a low price. Management searches extensively to find the lowest-cost components that meet its quality standards. Tesseralik employs 14 people, mainly assemblers who put together the computers. The major costs incurred are the cost of labour and parts for the computers. There is, as well, a significant amount of both fixed and variable overhead incurred by the business. While the company has been successful, it's often short of cash.

Required:

Prepare a report to Tesseralik's management recommending accounting policies for inventory. Your report should fully explain your recommendations.

P7-5. (**Recommending inventory accounting policies, LO 1, 2, 3, 4, 6**) Howser Ltd. (Howser) is a Canadian manufacturer of wooden shingles. Howser purchases lumber from saw mills and manufactures the shingles in one of its two factories. The shingles are used in house construction, mainly in the southern and western United States. Howser is owned by 20 investors, not all of whom are involved in the day-to-day management of the company. The professional management team receives salary plus bonuses based on company performance as compensation. Howser has a large loan outstanding from the bank. The amount of the loan is based on accounts receivable and inventory outstanding on the last day of each calendar month. Howser has usually borrowed the maximum amount allowable under the borrowing agreement. Howser pays surplus cash (cash that isn't required for operations and is available after paying of debts) out to its shareholders.

Required:

Prepare a report to Howser's management recommending accounting policies for inventory. Your report should fully explain your recommendations.

P7-6. (**Considering the effect of inventory errors, LO 1, 2, 7**) Abney Ltd. (Abney) is a small manufacturing company. During the fiscal year just ended, a number of errors were made in accounting for inventory. For each of the following errors indicate their effect on the financial statement elements and ratios shown in the table below. Indicate whether the financial statement element or ratio would be overstated (higher than it would have been had the error not occurred), understated (lower than it would have been had the error not occurred), or not affected by the error. Abney uses a periodic inventory control system. The ratios before considering the adjustments are shown in brackets in the following table.
a. Some of the inventory in Abney's warehouse was not counted during the year-end inventory count.
b. Certain costs that are normally expensed as incurred were included in inventory.
c. The purchase of some inventory on credit was not recorded (both the inventory and the payable) but the inventory was included in the year-end inventory count.

d. Damaged inventory that can't be sold was included in the year-end inventory balance.
e. Some inventory was included in the inventory count even though it was shipped to a customer before year-end. Revenue is recognized when merchandise is shipped to customers.

	Net income	Cost of sales	Total assets	Owners' equity	Current ratio [1.65]	Inventory turnover ratio [4.3]	Debt-to-equity ratio [1.25]
a.							
b.							
c.							
d.							
e.							

P7-7. **(Considering the effect of inventory errors, LO 1, 2, 4, 7)** Cariboo Ltd. (Cariboo) is a distributor of imported products. In the fiscal year just ended a number of errors were made in accounting for inventory. For each of the following errors indicate their effect on the financial statement elements and ratios shown in the following table. Indicate whether the financial statement element or ratio would be overstated, understated, or not affected by the error. Cariboo uses a periodic inventory control system. The ratios before considering the adjustments are shown in brackets in the table.

a. Some inventory was accounted for as sold even though it wasn't shipped as of the end of the year. The inventory wasn't included in the inventory count.
b. Certain costs that are normally included in the cost of inventory were expensed as incurred.
c. The NRV of previously written down inventory recovered but wasn't written back up.
d. Obsolete inventory (it can't be used) was included in the year-end inventory amount.

	Net income	Cost of sales	Total assets	Owners' equity	Current ratio [1.31]	Inventory turnover ratio [2.4]	Debt-to-equity ratio [0.52]
a.							
b.							
c.							
d.							

P7-8. **(Determining the amount of inventory on hand when a periodic inventory control system is used, LO 2, 7)** On March 24, 2015 Ahousat Inc. (Ahousat) suffered a flood that destroyed its entire inventory of Persian rugs. Ahousat uses a periodic inventory control system and as a result doesn't keep track of the amount of inventory that has been sold. Ahousat last counted its inventory on December 31, 2014, its year-end. At that time there was $1,800,000 of inventory on hand. Ahousat's records indicate that sales from January 1 to March 24, 2015 were $1,480,000 and that during that time additional inventory was purchased for $1,300,000. Ahousat's usual gross margin on its sales of rugs is 60 percent.

Required:

Ahousat has insurance that covers it fully for the flood losses, except for a $50,000 deductible. Prepare a report to Ahousat's management that computes the amount of the loss that should be claimed from the insurance company. Explain any factors that management should be aware of that would change the amount of the claim.

P7-9. **(Determining the amount of inventory on hand when a periodic inventory control system is used, LO 2, 7)** On February 19, 2015 Exploits Inc.'s (Exploits) entire inventory was stolen in a daring daylight robbery. The thieves held warehouse personnel at gunpoint while they methodically loaded trucks with the contents of the warehouse. There were no injuries.

Exploits is fully insured against theft and so must file a claim with its insurance company for the loss suffered. Because Exploits uses a periodic inventory control system, it doesn't know for certain the amount of inventory that was stolen. However, from your discussions with company personnel you have learned that Exploits has two categories of inventory. Category one inventory usually generates a gross margin of 60 percent while the category two usually generates a gross margin of 40 percent. Sales of category one since the company's year-end on October 31, 2014 were $425,000. Sales of category two over the same time period were about $877,500. During the period since the year-end, Exploits purchased $162,500 of category one inventory and $400,000 of category two inventory. The financial records show that on October 31, 2014 there was $225,000 of category one inventory and $500,000 of category two inventory on hand.

Required:

Prepare a report to Exploits' management that computes the amount of the loss that should be claimed from the insurance company as a result of the robbery. Explain any factors that management should be aware of that would change the amount of the claim.

P7-10. **(Lower of cost and market, LO 4, 7)** Tumbell Corp. (Tumbell) reports its inventory at the lower of cost and net realizable value. Tumbell has five inventory categories. You are provided with the following cost and NRV information about each category:

Inventory category	Cost	Net realizable value
Category 1	$ 67,050	$ 94,500
Category 2	132,300	126,000
Category 3	88,290	132,750
Category 4	100,800	90,000
Category 5	207,900	294,000
Total	$596,340	$737,250

Required:

a. What amount should Tumbell report on its balance sheet for inventory?
b. What is the amount of writedown that is required?
c. Record any journal entries required to account for the writedown.

P7-11. **(Lower of cost and market, LO 4, 7)** Wolverine Corp. (Wolverine) reports its inventory at the lower of cost and NRV. Wolverine has five inventory categories. You are provided with the following cost and NRV information about each category on December 31, 2014, Wolverine's year-end:

Category	Number of units	Cost per unit	NRV per unit	Total cost	Net realizable value
Category 1	7,502	$ 6.25	$ 5.37	$ 46,888	$ 40,286
Category 2	18,455	6.94	14.90	128,078	274,980
Category 3	15,750	11.60	9.52	182,700	149,940
Category 4	8,275	8.90	20.54	73,648	169,969
Category 5	16,120	5.22	11.48	84,146	185,058
Total				$515,460	$820,233
*Note: Totals have been rounded.					

You later receive the following information about Wolverine's inventory on March 31, 2015, the end of the company's first quarter:

Category	Total number of units	Number of units that were on hand on December 31, 2014	Cost per unit	NRV per unit	Total cost	Net realizable value
Category 1	8,525	3,001	$ 6.25	$ 7.37	$ 53,281	$ 62,829
Category 2	16,588	4,614	6.94	16.80	115,121	278,678
Category 3	14,700	7,875	11.60	9.60	170,520	141,120
Category 4	9,150	1,490	8.90	18.00	81,435	164,700
Category 5	15,900	4,836	5.22	12.10	82,998	192,390
Total					$503,355	$839,717

*Note: Totals have been rounded.

Required:

a. What amount should Wolverine report on its balance sheet for inventory on December 31, 2014?
b. What is the amount of writedown required on December 31, 2014?
c. Record any journal entries required on December 31, 2014 to account for the writedown.
d. Are any adjustments needed to inventory on March 31, 2015? Describe and explain any adjustments required and prepare any journal entries that are needed.
e. What amount should Wolverine report on its balance sheet for inventory on March 31, 2015?

P7-12. **(Determine the amount of inventory lost due to theft, LO 1, 2)** Wekusko Ltd. (Wekusko) is a wholesaler of electronic equipment that it imports from Asia. Recently, the manager of Wekusko's warehouse in Winnipeg became concerned that a significant amount of goods were being stolen from the warehouse. He wanted to know the extent of the problem so he could take remedial steps, if necessary. He spoke with the company accountant who told him that if he would count the inventory on hand she could give him an idea of how much inventory was being stolen.

The manager closed the warehouse and had the inventory counted. The warehouse manager advised the accountant there was $2,088,888 of inventory on hand on the date of the count. The manager also told the accountant that since the last year-end, goods costing $14,250 had been damaged and had to be thrown away. The accountant examined the financial records pertaining to the Winnipeg warehouse and found that since the last year-end, goods costing $1,750,000 had been purchased and stored in the warehouse and goods costing $2,248,400 had been shipped to customers. The inventory count at the end of the previous reporting period reported inventory of $2,775,800.

Required:

a. Estimate the amount of electronic equipment that might have been stolen from the Winnipeg warehouse.
b. Is it possible to conclude with certainty the amount you calculated in (a) was due to theft? Explain.
c. Why was it necessary to count the inventory to estimate the amount of inventory that was stolen?

P7-13. **(Determine the amount of inventory shrinkage, LO 1, 2)** Magyar Ltd. (Magyar) is a large retail clothing store. Recently, the store manager became concerned about the amount theft and she wanted an idea of how much was being stolen so she could decide whether it was worthwhile to install theft-prevention equipment. The accountant told the manager that if she counted the inventory on hand he could give her an idea of the amount of inventory being stolen.

The manager had the inventory counted after store closing one Sunday. According to the count there was $255,000 of inventory on hand. The manager also told the accountant that since the year-end the store had purchased $198,000 of inventory, had sales of $450,000, and returned $27,500 of merchandise suppliers. At the last year-end Magyar had $325,000 of inventory. The gross margin that Magyar usually earns is 52 percent.

Required:

a. Determine the amount of clothing that might have been stolen from the store.
b. Is it possible to conclude with certainty that the amount you calculated in (a) was due to theft?
c. Why was it necessary to count the inventory to estimate the amount of inventory that was stolen?
d. If Magyar had used a perpetual inventory control system would a count of the inventory have been required to provide the manager with the information she required?

P7-14. **(Consider the effect of different inventories on the inventory turnover ratio, LO 7)**
Xena Inc. (Xena) is an importer of gift items from Europe and Asia. Xena classifies its inventory into three categories: porcelain figurines, toys, and linens. Over the years Xena has found that the success of the three categories has tended to vary, sometimes quite significantly, although, fortunately for the company, poor performance of one category seems to be offset by success in another. On its balance sheet and income statement Xena doesn't break down its inventory, sales, and cost of sales into the three categories.

For its years ended October 31, 2013 and 2014 Xena reported inventory of $668,000 and $693,200 respectively. For the fiscal year ended October 31, 2014 Xena reported sales of $3,137,600 and cost of sales of $1,541,800. However, the following breakdown of inventory, sales, and cost of sales has been made available to you:

Category	Inventory balance on October 31, 2013	Inventory balance on October 31, 2014	Sales for the year ended October 31, 2014	Cost of sales for the year ended October 31, 2014
Porcelain figurines	$234,000	$255,200	$1,380,000	$552,000
Toys	270,000	202,000	1,108,400	665,200
Linens	164,000	236,000	649,200	324,600

Required:

a. Calculate the gross margin percentage, inventory turnover ratio, and the average number of days inventory on hand for the year ended October 31, 2014 using the aggregated amounts reported for inventory, sales, and cost of sales on Xena's balance sheet and income statement.
b. Calculate the gross margin, inventory turnover ratio, and the average number of days inventory on hand for the year ended October 31, 2014 for each category of inventory that Xena carries.
c. What are the implications of the results you obtained in parts (a) and (b) of the question?
d. How is your ability to analyze Xena affected by the aggregated information presented in the company's balance sheet and income statement versus the information that was made available to you? Explain fully.

P7-15. **(Consider the effect of different inventories on the inventory turnover ratio, LO 7)**
Herschel Inc. (Herschel) is a small chain of convenience stores. Herschel classifies its inventory into three categories: perishable items, packaged goods, and household items. On its balance sheet and income statement, Herschel doesn't break down its inventory, sales, and cost of sales into three categories.

For its years ended December 31, 2013 and 2014 Herschel reported inventory of $568,000 and $742,600 respectively. For the fiscal year ended December 31, 2014 Herschel reported sales of $5,955,000 and cost of sales of $4,737,500. However, the following breakdown of inventory, sales, and cost of sales has been made available to you:

Category	Inventory balance on October 31, 2013	Inventory balance on October 31, 2014	Sales for the year ended October 31, 2014	Cost of sales for the year ended October 31, 2014
Perishable items	$ 42,500	$ 36,250	$2,020,000	$1,700,000
Packaged goods	155,000	260,100	1,700,000	1,402,500
Household items	370,500	446,250	2,235,000	1,635,000

Required:

a. Calculate the gross margin percentage, inventory turnover ratio, and the average number of days inventory on hand for the year ended December 31, 2014 using the aggregated amounts reported for inventory, sales, and cost of sales on Herschel's balance sheet and income statement.

b. Calculate the gross margin percentage, inventory turnover ratio, and the average number of days inventory on hand for the year ended December 31, 2014 for each category of inventory that Herschel carries.

c. What are the implications of the results you obtained in parts (a) and (b)? How is your ability to analyze Herschel affected by the aggregated information presented in the company's balance sheet and income statement versus the information that was made available to you? Explain fully.

P7-16. **(Cost formulas, LO 2, 3, 4, 6)** The purchase and sale of inventory by Yearly Inc. (Yearly) during the year ended November 30, 2015 is summarized below. Assume that purchases are made on the first day of each quarter and sales on the last day of each quarter. Yearly pays for all its inventory in cash when it's delivered.

Economic event	Quantity	Purchase price per unit	Selling price per unit
Opening inventory	52,500	$16.50	
Purchases—first quarter	42,000	16.95	
Purchases—second quarter	57,750	18.15	
Purchases—third quarter	99,750	18.70	
Purchases—fourth quarter	36,750	19.25	
Sales—first quarter	68,250		$30.25
Sales—second quarter	52,500		30.25
Sales—third quarter	115,500		32.20
Sales—fourth quarter	26,250		32.20

Required:

a. Determine cost of sales for the year ended November 30, 2015 and ending inventory on November 30, 2015 using FIFO and average cost, assuming that Yearly uses a periodic inventory control system.

b. How much cash was spent on inventory during 2015 under each cost formula? Is the amount of cash spent on inventory under each cost formula the same or different? Explain.

c. Which cost formula would you recommend if Yearly's objective was to minimize taxes? Explain.

d. Which cost formula would you use if you were Yearly's CEO and your bonus were based on net income? Explain.

e. Which cost formula would you recommend if the amount of Yearly's bank loan was a percentage of inventory? Explain.

f. Yearly uses the lower of cost and net realizable value to value its inventory. Suppose that on November 30, 2015 the NRV of Yearly's inventory plummeted to $6.25 per unit. What would you do under each cost formula?

g. Does it matter which cost formula Yearly uses? Explain fully.

P7-17. **(Cost formulas, LO 2, 3, 4, 6)** The purchase and sale of inventory by Ripple Inc. (Ripple) during the year ended April 30, 2014 is summarized below. Assume that sales are made on the first day of each quarter and purchases are made on the last day. Ripple pays for all its inventory in cash when it's delivered.

Economic event	Quantity	Purchase price per unit	Selling price per unit
Opening inventory	187,500	$17.90	
Purchases—first quarter	225,000	22.75	
Purchases—second quarter	127,500	26.00	
Purchases—third quarter	175,000	27.60	
Purchases—fourth quarter	200,000	24.05	
Sales—first quarter	170,000		$45.00
Sales—second quarter	220,000		45.00
Sales—third quarter	137,500		45.00
Sales—fourth quarter	167,500		45.00

Required:

a. Determine cost of sales for the year ended April 30, 2014, and ending inventory on April 30, 2014 using FIFO and average cost, assuming that Ripple uses a periodic inventory control system.

b. How much cash was spent on inventory during 2014 under each cost formula? Is the amount of cash spent on inventory under each cost formula the same or different? Explain.

c. Which cost formula would you recommend if Ripple's objective was to minimize taxes? Explain.

d. Which cost formula would you use if you were Ripple's CEO and your bonus was based on net income? Explain.

e. Which cost formula would you recommend if the amount of Ripple's bank loan was a percentage of inventory? Explain.

f. Ripple uses the lower of cost and net realizable value to value its inventory. Is it necessary to make any adjustments to inventory on April 30, 2014 to ensure compliance with the lower of cost and NRV rule? Explain.

g. Does it matter which cost formula Ripple uses? Explain fully.

P7-18. **(Analyzing inventory problems, LO 7)** Champlain Books Ltd. (Champlain) is a small independent book seller in a Canadian city. Book selling is a tough, competitive business but Champlain has managed to succeed by providing good service, offering hard-to-find book titles, and building a loyal clientele. The owner of the store, Sam Champlain, has been concerned recently about the store's performance, mainly a declining cash balance, despite increasing sales. Sam has asked you to look at the store's performance over the last five years to see if you can see any problems he should address. He has provided you with the following information:

Champlain Books Ltd.
Selected Financial Information for the Year Ended December 31,

	2015	2014	2013	2012	2011	2010
Sales	$378,931	$367,894	$362,457	$355,350	$345,000	$
Cost of sales	263,756	253,612	249,127	242,342	234,600	
Gross margin	115,175	114,282	113,330	113,008	110,400	
Inventory	118,686	110,921	104,643	99,470	93,840	91,024

Required:

Examine the information provided to you by Sam Champlain and from your analysis prepare a report explaining any problems you identify and the consequences of the problems. Provide possible explanations and solutions that might resolve the problems.

P7-19.   **(Analyzing inventory problems, LO 7)** Pincher Creek Mountain Equipment Ltd. (PCME) is an importer and national distributor of high-quality outdoor clothing and equipment. PCME has exclusive Canadian distribution rights for many of the products it purchases from manufacturers. The company orders merchandise throughout the year but must bring in stock in anticipation of the needs of retailers. Retailers place orders several months in advance of the delivery date and PCME must in turn place orders with the manufacturers. However, PCME must assess to what extent it should order more or less inventory than retailers ordered and how much of new products it should bring in. PCME must keep adequate inventory on hand because it's too time consuming and costly to make special orders in most cases (for example, if a retailer decided that more of a particular item was needed it wouldn't make sense in most cases for PCME to make the order). PCME normally gives its customer 60 days from the date of delivery to pay. The economy has deteriorated over the last few months. You have been provided with the following extracts from PCME's financial statements:

Pincher Creek Mountain Equipment Ltd.
Selected Financial Information for the Year Ended December 31,

	2014	2013	2012	2011
Sales	$6,430,225	$6,095,000	$5,750,000	$
Cost of sales	3,440,170	3,382,725	3,162,500	
Gross margin	2,990,055	2,712,275	2,587,500	
Cash	$ 115,000	$ 220,000	$ 250,000	$ 215,000
Accounts receivable	1,613,236	1,216,567	1,116,505	1,095,000
Inventory	1,985,000	1,352,000	1,003,000	875,000
Other current assets	35,000	27,000	32,000	31,000
Short-term bank loan	1,000,000	750,000	525,000	450,000
Accounts payable and accrued liabilities	2,758,000	1,850,000	1,585,000	1,385,000

Required:

You have been asked to evaluate PCME's liquidity from the information provided. (Be sure to use evaluation tools that have been introduced in this chapter as well as one from previous chapters.) Explain factors that could have given rise to your findings. Consider the following issues in your report:
- What are the possible ways that PCME could increase the inventory turnover ratio? Do you think these ways could be reasonably achieved?
- How would an improvement affect the liquidity of the company? Explain.
- Why is the ITO an important indicator of liquidity?

Using Financial Statements

RONA INC.

RONA Inc. (RONA) is the largest distributor and retailer of hardware, home renovation, and gardening products in Canada. It operates a network of over 680 corporate, franchise, and affiliate stores of various sizes and formats. With over 27,000 RONA employees across Canada, the store network generates over $6.3 billion in annual retail sales. RONA's mission is to offer the best service and the right product at the right price to North American consumers of housing and home improvement products. RONA is listed on the TSX under the symbol RON.[7]

www.rona.com

RONA's consolidated balance sheets and statements of earnings and cash flows, along with extracts from the notes to the financial statements and extracts from management's discussion and analysis, are provided in Exhibit 7.3.[8] Use this information to respond to questions FS7-1 to FS7-10.

FS7-1. What amount of inventory did RONA report on its December 28, 2008, balance sheet? What proportion of current assets and what proportion of total assets did inventory comprise? What do you think is included in RONA's inventory? Do you think the inventory can be considered liquid? Explain.

FS7-2. Describe the accounting policies that RONA uses to account for its inventory. What does the term "net realizable value" mean? How would RONA know the net realizable value of the inventory in its stores?

FS7-3. What was the cost of inventory sold by RONA in 2008 and 2007? How much was expensed in each year? Why do the amounts differ? Calculate RONA's gross margin and gross margin percentage for 2008 and 2007.

FS7-4. During fiscal 2007 and 2008 RONA reported inventory writedowns. What is a writedown and why was it necessary for RONA to write down some of its inventory? What was the amount of the writedowns? Where is it reflected in the income statement? What impact does it have on RONA's cash flow? Explain. What impact did the writedown have on gross margin for fiscal 2008? What journal entry would RONA have made in 2008 to record the writedown? Do you think inventory writedowns are a major problem in a business like RONA's? Explain.

FS7-5. Examine the operating activities section of RONA's cash flow statement and Note 7 to the financial statements. What was RONA's cash flow from operations in 2008? Why was cash from operations so different from net income in 2008? By how much did RONA's inventory change in 2008? What was the impact of the change in inventory on cash from operations? Explain why the change has that effect. Do you think RONA will be able to decrease inventory by similar amounts next year? Explain.

FS7-6. Calculate RONA's inventory turnover ratio and the number of days inventory on hand for 2008 and 2007. (The amount of inventory sold in 2008 and 2007 isn't in the income statement—you have to look in the notes for it). Assume RONA's inventory at the end of fiscal 2006 was $790,496,000. Evaluate the change in turnover over the two-year period.

FS7-7. Read the extracts from RONA's Management Discussion and Analysis.

a. What has RONA's management identified as a strategic objective with respect to inventory? Why is this objective desirable? How would RONA's success in achieving this objective impact profitability and inventory turnover? Explain why.

b. Did RONA accomplish this strategic objective in 2008? Explain why. Calculate RONA's inventory turnover ratio and the number of days inventory on hand for 2008, and 2007. (The amount of inventory sold in 2008 and 2007 isn't in the income statement—you have to look in the notes for it.) Assume RONA's inventory at the end of fiscal 2006 was $790,496,000.

EXHIBIT 7.3 RONA Inc.: Extracts from Financial Statements

CONSOLIDATED FINANCIAL STATEMENTS

Consolidated Balance Sheets
December 28, 2008 and December 30, 2007
(In thousands of dollars)

	2008	2007
Assets		
Current assets		
Cash	$ 12,345	$ 2,866
Accounts receivable (Note 9)	234,027	237,043
Income taxes receivable	6,046	5,684
Inventory (Note 4)	763,239	856,326
Prepaid expenses	33,104	24,249
Derivative financial instruments (Note 21)	1,089	1,168
Future income taxes (Note 6)	13,800	12,279
	1,063,650	1,139,615
Investments (Note 10)	10,186	11,901
Fixed assets (Note 11)	875,634	816,919
Fixed assets held for sale (Note 12)	34,870	–
Goodwill	454,889	454,882
Trademarks (Note 13)	3,797	4,145
Other assets (Note 14)	38,466	32,349
Future income taxes (Note 6)	24,681	22,635
	$2,506,173	$2,482,446
Liabilities		
Current liabilities		
Bank loans (Note 15)	$ 8,468	$ 19,574
Accounts payable and accrued liabilities	422,318	421,446
Derivative financial instruments (Note 21)	2,180	1,067
Future income taxes (Note 6)	4,854	3,650
Instalments on long-term debt (Note 16)	15,696	34,239
	453,516	479,976
Long-term debt (Note 16)	478,475	602,537
Other long-term liabilities (Note 17)	28,571	24,526
Future income taxes (Note 6)	23,998	23,781
Non-controlling interest	29,098	26,420
	1,013,658	1,157,240
Shareholders' equity		
Capital stock (Note 19)	426,786	421,194
Retained earnings	1,053,166	892,967
Contributed surplus	12,563	11,045
	1,492,515	1,325,206
	$2,506,173	$2,482,446

CONSOLIDATED FINANCIAL STATEMENTS

Consolidated Earnings
Years ended December 28, 2008 and December 30, 2007
(In thousands of dollars, except earnings per share)

	2008	2007
Sales	$4,891,122	$4,785,106
Earnings before the following items (Note 5)	377,101	400,207
Interest on long-term debt	28,106	28,270
Interest on bank loans	2,134	3,329
Depreciation and amortization (Notes 11, 13 and 14)	108,091	90,901
	138,331	122,500
Earnings before income taxes and non-controlling interest	238,770	277,707
Income taxes (Note 6)	73,541	88,130
Earnings before non-controlling interest	165,229	189,577
Non-controlling interest	5,030	4,488
Net earnings and comprehensive income	$ 160,199	$ 185,089
Net earnings per share (Note 25)		
Basic	$ 1.39	$ 1.61
Diluted	$ 1.37	$ 1.59

| EXHIBIT | 7.3 | (continued) RONA Inc.: Extracts from Financial Statements |

CONSOLIDATED FINANCIAL STATEMENTS

Consolidated Cash Flows
Years ended December 28, 2008 and December 30, 2007
(In thousands of dollars)

	2008	2007
Operating activities		
Net earnings	$ 160,199	$ 185,089
Non-cash items		
Depreciation and amortization	108,091	90,901
Derivative financial instruments	1,192	(2,483)
Future income taxes	(1,733)	1,894
Net loss (gain) on disposal of assets	(2,796)	1,041
Compensation cost relating to stock option plans	1,518	2,082
Non-controlling interest	5,030	4,488
Other items	3,465	3,158
	274,966	286,170
Changes in working capital items (Note 7)	75,336	(9,361)
Cash flows from operating activities	350,302	276,809

3. Accounting policies

Accounting estimates

The preparation of financial statements in accordance with Canadian generally accepted accounting principles requires management to make estimates and assumptions that affect the amounts recorded in the financial statements and notes to financial statements. Significant estimates in these consolidated financial statements relate to the valuation of accounts receivable, inventory, long-term assets, goodwill, store closing costs, income taxes as well as certain economic and actuarial assumptions used in determining the cost of pension plans and accrued benefit obligations. These estimates are based on management's best knowledge of current events and actions that the Company may undertake in the future. Actual results may differ from those estimates.

Inventory valuation

Inventory is valued at the lower of cost and net realizable value. Cost is determined using the weighted average cost method.

Vendor rebates

The Company records cash consideration received from vendors as a reduction in the price of vendors' products and reflects it as a reduction to cost of goods sold and related inventory when recognized in the consolidated statements of earnings and consolidated balance sheets. Certain exceptions apply where the cash consideration received is either a reimbursement of incremental selling costs incurred by the reseller or a payment for goods or services delivered to the vendor, in which case the rebate is reflected as a reduction of operating expenses.

4. Inventory

For the year ended December 28, 2008, $3,571,962 of inventory was expensed in the consolidated results ($3,542,605 as at December 30, 2007). This amount includes an inventory write-down charge of $46,752 ($48,883 as at December 30, 2007).

7. Cash flow information

The changes in working capital items are detailed as follows:

	2008	2007
Accounts receivable	$ (6,518)	$ 11,801
Inventory	94,455	(18,451)
Prepaid expenses	(8,916)	(3,740)
Accounts payable and accrued liabilities	(4,495)	13,700
Income taxes (receivable) payable	810	(12,671)
	$75,336	$ (9,361)

FS7-8. Why is careful management of inventory so important for a company like RONA?

FS7-9. Read the financial statement note that discusses accounting estimates. What important information for readers does this note provide? Why is it important for stakeholders to understand this note? What are some estimates that RONA's management must make when preparing the financial statements? What type of estimates do you think RONA's management has to make with respect to inventory?

| EXHIBIT 7.3 | (continued) RONA Inc.: Extracts from Financial Statements |

Strategic plan phase one

There are four major projects in this initial phase.

2. Optimize the Supply Chain

Inventories. Reduce inventory levels on a comparable basis and improve inventory turns (which improve profitability by reducing the cost of holding inventory).

> Comparable inventories were reduced $118 million at year end 2008 compared to 2007 (excluding new stores and acquisitions) resulting in lower operating and financing costs. Including new stores and acquisitions, inventories were reduced by $93 million.

The loss of inventory, or shrinkage, is an example of the level of detail needed in terms of cost control in order to become best performer in the retail industry. The reasons for shrinkage are many: products can get broken, stolen, or damaged.

Inventory

Management annually reviews inventory movement in order to establish the obsolescence reserve required to cover potential losses associated with obsolete or low-turnover inventory.

Source: Extracted from RONA Inc.'s 2008 annual report.

FS7-10. A problem frequently faced by retail businesses like RONA is the loss of inventory or inventory shrinkage. What are the possible ways that inventory in a RONA store could "shrink"? Is shrinkage bad for RONA? Why? What would the impact of inventory shrinkage be on the following ratios: current ratio, gross margin percentage, inventory turnover ratio, and profit margin?

ENDNOTES

1. Andree Lavigne, Diane Paul, John Tang, Jo-Ann Lempert, Helene Marcil, and Louise Overbeek, *Financial Reporting in Canada 2008*, 33rd Edition (Federal Publications Inc., 2008).

2. Extracted from Saputo Inc.'s 2009 third-quarter report.

3. Panel A extracted from Ballard Power Systems Inc.'s 2008 annual report; Panel B extracted from Genesis Land Development Corp.'s 2008 annual report.

4. Interpretation Bulletin IT473R, "Inventory Valuation" (Canadian Customs and Revenue Agency, December 21, 1998); http://www.cra-arc.gc.ca/E/pub/tp/it473r/ it473r-e.html.

5. Ibid.

6. Ibid.

7. Adapted from RONA Inc.'s website at http://www.rona.ca.

8. Extracted from RONA Inc.'s 2008 annual report.

CHAPTER 8

CAPITAL ASSETS

Canada's most outspoken forensic accountant, L.S. "Al" Rosen, says he first learned the world has crooks as a toddler in Vancouver, after someone stole his brand new tricycle. Some years later, on the same street, Rosen recalls noticing a shady con artist trying to sell unnecessary brickwork repairs to vulnerable widows.

L.S. (Al) Rosen FCA, FCMA
Forensic Accountant

"That sticks with you," said Rosen, in an interview at his Toronto office where the veteran chartered accountant and his staff at Rosen & Associates unearth evidence used to prosecute companies for fraud.

A commerce graduate from the University of British Columbia, Rosen went on to complete his MBA and PhD at the University of Washington. As a freshly minted CA, Rosen's employer, the accounting firm now known as KPMG, sent him out to audit a bank, where his team discovered one of the tellers had been stealing money and then fiddling with the books "to make it appear everything was OK," he recalled.

That same week, while auditing the books at another company, he noticed an unexpected $1 million had been added to the cash accounts.

"It was one of those overnight loans because they wanted to have a nice balance sheet that showed more cash, and I said, 'Hmmmm, that's interesting,'" Rosen recalled.

Those two incidents in one week didn't set him immediately on the path to becoming a forensic accountant. Rosen worked for 20 years in public practice with big accounting firms, became an advisor to three federal auditors general, and taught legions of students at several North American universities, including York University's Schulich School of Business in Toronto.

"For really good students who want to have a career in accounting, it's important they not only learn the technical material that's taught in the classroom, but also that they sit there expressing great skepticism," he said.

Rosen's private forensic practice is located in a building directly across the street from the Toronto Stock Exchange. That's fitting for the prolific author and commentator who once said more than half the companies listed on the country's benchmark stock index, known then as the TSE 300, pushed the envelope in their accounting practices.

Over the years, Rosen has predicted trouble at Cott Beverages, The Loewen Group, Teleglobe Canada, Nortel, and Canada's popular income trusts ("a complete Ponzi fraud") well before their financial problems garnered news headlines.

"My talents lie best in the area of going after these people, and let's face it, there are a lot of scumbags around that I don't particularly like, so if you can straighten them out so much the better," Rosen said.

Now in his seventies, Rosen admits he can't retire because there is still so much work to do. He regularly testifies at government-related hearings, even sending case files to elected politicians, all the while pushing for lawmakers to create a strong national securities regulator with the power to go after swindlers.

Meanwhile, Rosen even places under the microscope the other tenant on the same floor in his office tower: the Office of the Superintendent of Financial Institutions. It is the government's watchdog for chartered banks, insurance companies, and some pension plans. Their findings often are rosier than the reports in Rosen's investigations of banks' accounting practices.

"We bother them," joked Rosen, adding that conversations in the elevator often sputter to a halt when "Rosen's boys" get on.

—E.B.

INTRODUCTION—WHAT ARE CAPITAL ASSETS?

Capital assets are resources that contribute to earning revenue over more than one period by helping an entity produce, supply, support, or make available the goods or services it offers to its customers. Unlike inventory, these assets aren't bought and sold in the ordinary course of business (although they are sometimes bought and sold), but they are essential to any type of entity. In this chapter we will examine three categories of capital assets: property, plant, and equipment; intangibles; and goodwill. These categories are described in Table 8.1:

TABLE 8.1	Categories of Capital Assets	
	Definition	**Examples**
Property, plant, and equipment	Tangible assets used to produce or supply goods or services to customers, rented to customers, or used for administrative purposes	Land, buildings, equipment, vehicles, computers, furniture and fixtures, money spent to find and develop natural resources
Intangible assets	Capital assets without physical substance	Patents, copyrights, trademarks, brand names, computer software, customer lists, broadcast rights, licences, movies
Goodwill	An intangible asset that arises when one business acquires another and pays more than the fair value of the net assets purchased	

Property, plant, and equipment (PPE) are **tangible assets** because they have physical substance; for example, land, buildings, equipment, and furniture. **Intangible assets** lack physical substance. They can be ideas, rights, or images, like patents, copyrights, brands, trademarks, and software. PPE and intangibles both can have very long lives—like land, which lasts forever, or buildings, which can last for decades. Or they can have relatively short lives—like computer hardware and software. I'll explain goodwill later.

Virtually all entities need some capital assets. Indigo Books & Music Inc.'s capital assets include furniture and fixtures for its stores, the cost of renovating and decorating stores, and computer equipment. Magna International Inc. has land, buildings, and equipment to operate its manufacturing facilities. The amount and percentage of different categories of capital assets for different companies are shown in Table 8.2. In examining Table 8.2, you might be surprised that Loblaw, a retail grocery chain, has such a larger proportion of PPE than Indigo. Both are in the retail business but Loblaw owns its land and buildings whereas Indigo doesn't.

TABLE 8.2	Amount of Capital Assets in Different Companies						
Company	Type of business	Dollar value of property, plant, and equipment	Dollar value of intangibles	Dollar value of goodwill	Property, plant, and equipment as a percentage of total assets	Intangibles as a percentage of total assets	Goodwill as a percentage of total assets
BCE	Communications	$19,407,000,000	$6,394,000,000	$5,659,000,000	48.9%	16.1%	14.3%
Canfor Corporation	Forest products	1,798,500,000		85,700,000	56.2	0.0	2.7
Corus Entertainment Inc.	Media and entertainment	73,562,000	717,473,000	797,854,000	3.6	35.3	39.2
High Liner Foods Incorporated	Food processing	59,016,000	24,055,000	30,767,000	17.4	7.1	9.1
Indigo Books & Music Inc.	Retail	72,137,000	16,299,000	27,523,000	14.8	3.3	5.6
Loblaw Companies Limited	Grocery retail	8,045,000,000		807,000	57.5	0.0	0.0
Magna International Inc.	Auto parts maker	3,701,000,000		1,160,000,000	28.1	0.0	8.8
Magnotta Winery Corporation	Winery	21,092,890	251,516		42.0	0.5	0.0
Tim Hortons Inc.	Fast food service	1,332,852,000	2,606,000		66.9	0.1	0.0
WestJet Airlines Ltd.	Airline	2,281,850,000			69.6	0.0	0.0

Some of an entity's capital assets don't appear on its balance sheet even though most people, including accountants, would agree they have future benefits. Traditional accounting sometimes has difficulty with certain types of capital assets, especially intangibles. For example, many software and biotechnology companies don't report the software and pharmaceuticals they develop as assets. Some of the aircraft flown by airlines aren't reported because they're leased. Many companies' brand names aren't recorded. The investments that entities make in their employees rarely appear as assets.

www.bce.ca
www.canfor.com
www.corusent.com
www.highlinerfoods.
com
www.indigo.ca
www.loblaw.ca
www.magna.com
www.magnotta.com
www.timhortons.com
www.westjet.com

MEASURING CAPITAL ASSETS AND LIMITATIONS TO HISTORICAL COST ACCOUNTING

Most companies following IFRS use historical cost to account for their capital assets. With historical cost, all costs incurred to acquire an asset and get it ready for use are **capitalized**—recorded on the balance sheet as an asset—and this amount forms the basis of its valuation, most of the time. For example, a piece of land purchased in 1953 for $25,000 would be reported on the 2014 balance sheet at $25,000, even if the market value of the land may have increased to $1,000,000.

One has to wonder about the usefulness of historical cost information. How useful is it today to know that land cost $25,000 when it was purchased in 1953? Historical cost accounting's purpose is to match the cost of capital assets to revenue earned over the life of the asset. But for making projections or other future-oriented decisions it's difficult to understand how the historical cost of capital assets, which are sometimes very old, can be useful.

There are three alternatives to historical cost accounting for capital assets: net realizable value (NRV), replacement cost, and value-in-use. Each alternative provides different information to stakeholders and has shortcomings of its own. None is ideal for all uses. These methods are summarized in Figure 8.1.

NRV is the amount received from selling an asset after the selling costs are deducted. This amount is more useful than historical cost to a bank, for example, which usually requires an appraisal of a property when an entity asks for a mortgage loan. NRV gives a current estimate of the amount that would be received if the property had to be sold. It's less objective and less reliable than historical cost because the amount is an estimate and isn't supported by a transaction. For many capital assets, obtaining a reasonable estimate of the NRV is difficult because used and even new capital assets aren't bought and sold very often. Also, today's NRV doesn't say anything about what the asset could be sold for in the future—it's only an estimate of the current NRV.

Replacement cost is the amount that would have to be spent to replace a capital asset. It can be the cost of a new, identical item, or it can be the cost of an equivalent one if, for example, the existing asset is no longer available. Most capital assets have to be replaced from time to time and information on the timing and amounts involved in replacement would be very useful for predicting cash flows. Like NRV, replacement cost is less objective than historical cost because there is no transaction supporting the amount and obtaining replacement costs can be very difficult for some assets, especially if they don't exist anymore. Also, today's replacement cost doesn't say anything about the cost when the asset is actually replaced.

Another method of valuing capital assets is **value-in-use**, which is the net present value of the cash flow the asset will generate or save over its life (IFRS refers to value-in-use as **entity-specific value**). For example, value-in-use for an apartment building is the present value of rents, less operating costs over the remaining life of the building, plus the amount the building could be sold for at the end of its life. Value-in-use is relevant for many purposes, including for investors trying to figure out the value of a business. However, value-in-use has severe practical limitations. First, individual assets rarely generate cash on their own but instead they interact with other assets to generate cash flows. For example, what is the value-in-use of a computer that contributes to the development of some software? Second, estimating the future cash flows of an asset or group of assets can require many assumptions, making the estimate very unreliable.

Historical cost also has its uses, although not for future-oriented decisions. It can be used by stakeholders interested in evaluating historical performance, such as calculating return on investment. Historical cost information is also useful for stewardship and tax purposes.

FIGURE 8.1

Ways to Measure Capital Assets

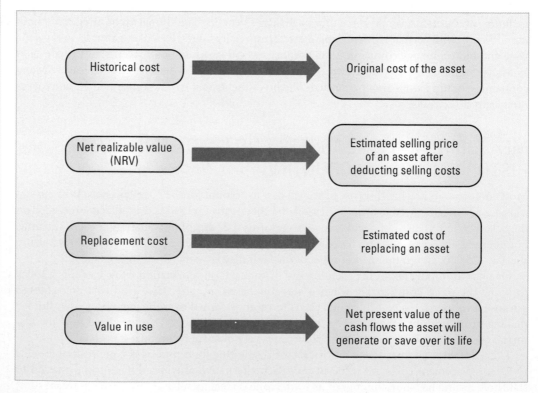

QUESTION FOR CONSIDERATION

For each of the following situations, specify which measurement basis—historical cost, NRV, replacement cost, or value-in-use—is most appropriate for the purpose described. Provide a brief explanation for each choice.

a. *Determine the amount of fire insurance needed for a building.*

b. *Determine the value of the assets of an entity going out of business.*

c. *Evaluate the price that should be paid for a business.*

Solution:

Situation	Measurement basis	Explanation
a. Determine the amount of fire insurance needed for a building.	Replacement cost	Fire insurance is intended to allow the insured to replace a building destroyed by fire. Therefore, the replacement cost of the building is the appropriate measurement basis.
b. Determine the value of the assets of an entity going out of business.	NRV	An entity that is going out of business will likely be looking to sell its assets to satisfy its creditors and/or allow the owners to receive cash from the liquidation. NRV gives the current selling prices of assets.
c. Evaluate the price that should be paid for a business.	Value-in-use	The value of a business is the present value of the future net cash flows that will be obtained from operating it.

WHAT IS COST?

When a capital asset is acquired it's always recorded on the balance sheet at cost. Cost should include all the costs incurred to purchase (or build) the asset and get it ready for use. Amounts that can be included are the purchase price; architectural design and engineering fees; taxes; delivery costs; transportation insurance costs; duties, testing, and preparation charges; installation costs; and legal costs, as well as any and all costs related to getting the asset up and running. Employee costs to ready the asset for use, including wages, should also be capitalized. Costs that aren't necessary or related to the acquisition, such as repairs or unnecessary work caused by poor planning, should not be capitalized.

Interest can be capitalized until an asset is ready for use, after which it is expensed. Capitalizing interest is most common when an entity is building an asset itself. For example, an entity using its own employees to build an extension to its warehouse capitalizes the interest incurred to finance the project up until it's complete and ready for use. Determining whether certain costs should be capitalized can be difficult, and treatment of the costs requires judgment. This need for judgment introduces the possibility that different managers will account for similar costs differently. Any time ambiguity exists, managers' choices may be influenced by self-interest. For example, if tax minimization is an entity's main objective, it may expense as much and as many of the costs of acquiring the asset as it reasonably can. On the other hand, if the entity prefers to maximize current income it will capitalize as much as it can to defer expensing the costs. Figure 8.2 provides a graphic example of the costs that could be included in the cost of a new machine.

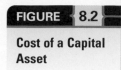

FIGURE 8.2

Cost of a Capital Asset

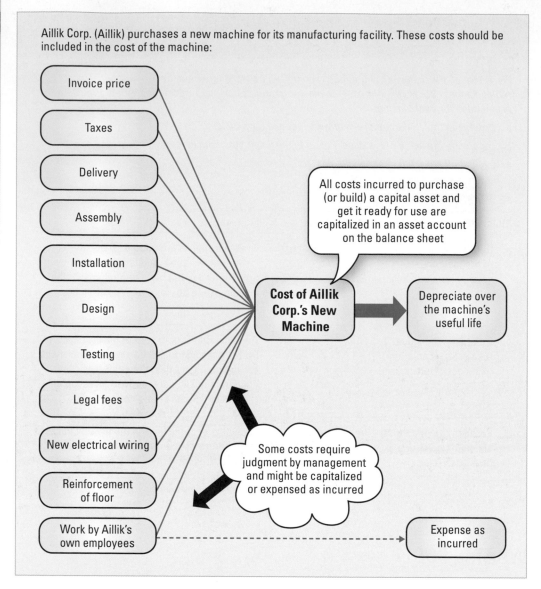

Aillik Corp. (Aillik) purchases a new machine for its manufacturing facility. These costs should be included in the cost of the machine:

- Invoice price
- Taxes
- Delivery
- Assembly
- Installation
- Design
- Testing
- Legal fees
- New electrical wiring
- Reinforcement of floor
- Work by Aillik's own employees

Cost of Aillik Corp.'s New Machine

All costs incurred to purchase (or build) a capital asset and get it ready for use are capitalized in an asset account on the balance sheet

Depreciate over the machine's useful life

Some costs require judgment by management and might be capitalized or expensed as incurred

Expense as incurred

Sometimes expenditures are made that improve an existing capital asset. This type of investment is called a **betterment**, which increases the future benefit associated with a capital asset, perhaps by increasing the asset's useful life or improving its efficiency or effectiveness. In other words, the betterment stands to make the entity more profitable. Because betterments provide future benefits, the cost is capitalized and depreciated over the remaining life of the asset.

In contrast, expenditures enabling an asset to do what it's designed to do are considered **repairs** or **maintenance** and should be expensed when incurred. Changing a car's oil regularly doesn't make the car better—it allows it to operate as intended by the manufacturer. On the other hand, the cost of rebuilding an engine so that it's more powerful and efficient should be capitalized, as the vehicle can now do more work (carry heavier loads) and use less fuel, both of which benefit the entity.

While some expenditures can easily be classified as betterments or maintenance, the treatment isn't always obvious. As a result, managers' choices may be motivated by their reporting objectives. If management is most concerned with the current bottom line it will be inclined to capitalize as much of the outlays as possible. Treating an expenditure as a betterment spreads the cost over a number of years because it's capitalized and depreciated over the remaining life of the asset. Treating it as a repair or maintenance increases expenses and reduces income by the full amount of the expenditure in the period in which it's incurred. Generally, expenditures on existing capital assets are much more likely to be repairs or maintenance than betterments.

QUESTION FOR CONSIDERATION

Meadow Inc. (Meadow) recently acquired a new computer server for its head-office network. The server had a list price of $50,000 but the head of the computing department negotiated a price of $46,900. Taxes were $7,035 and delivery was $2,000. Replacing the cables in the offices to meet the needs of the new server cost $8,000. A planning error by Meadow's management made it necessary for most of the cabling work to be redone, which cost an additional $2,100. Installing the server was $3,000, but once it was installed, management realized that the ventilation wasn't adequate. Moving and reinstalling the server cost an additional $2,600. Meadow purchased a three-year insurance policy for the server for $3,600.

Calculate the amount that should be capitalized for the purchase of the new server. Also, indicate which cost items shouldn't be included in the capitalized amount. Explain your reasoning.

Solution:

Cost	Amount capitalized	Explanation
Purchase price	$46,900	The only price that is relevant is the amount actually paid. The list price doesn't matter.
Taxes	7,035	Taxes are a part of the cost of the server.
Delivery	2,000	Delivery costs are necessary to get the server ready for use.
Cabling	8,000	Cabling costs are necessary to get the server ready for use. The server can't do its job without adequate cabling.
Cabling required due to error	Not capitalized	The additional costs were incurred due to a mistake. They weren't required to get the server ready for use and don't add anything to the value of the server. These costs should be expensed when incurred.
Installation	3,000	Installation costs are necessary to get the server ready for use. It can't serve its purpose if it isn't installed.
Reinstallation	Not capitalized	Reinstallation was required because of poor planning. The cost wasn't necessary and doesn't provide future benefit.
Insurance	Not capitalized	Insurance isn't a cost to get the server ready for use. It is insurance protection for the server when it's operating. It should be recorded as a prepaid asset and expensed as it's used.
Total amount to be capitalized for acquisition of the server	$66,935	

Basket Purchases and Componentization of Assets

Sometimes an entity will purchase a "basket" or bundle of assets at a single price where the prices of individual assets won't be known. Basket purchases raise the problem of how to allocate the total cost among the assets in the bundle. Good accounting requires that the purchase price be allocated in proportion to the market values of each of the assets. The allocation is important because the different assets in the bundle may be accounted for differently, and different allocations will result in different financial statement effects (as we will see below).

For example, suppose that Pockwock Ltd. (Pockwock) purchases land and a building for $25,000,000. If the land was worth 40 percent of the total cost and the building 60 percent, the journal entry would be

Dr. Land (asset +)	10,000,000	
Dr. Building (asset +)	15,000,000	
Cr. Cash (asset −)		25,000,000

To record the basket purchase of land and building

In practice, it's difficult to know exactly what the market values of the land and building are as separate assets. Consequently, as long as the amount assigned to each is reasonable, managers have the flexibility to make the allocation as it suits their reporting objectives. If the main concern is minimizing taxes, managers will allocate more of the cost to the building because buildings can be deducted to reduce taxes whereas land can't. If management is more concerned about increasing net income it could allocate more of the cost to land, which isn't depreciated.

If Pockwock obtained an independent appraisal estimating the value of the land at between $9,000,000 and $12,000,000, it could justifiably assign any amount between those two values to the land. If Pockwock's reporting objective was minimizing tax it would allocate $9,000,000 of the purchase price to land and $16,000,000 to the building. This would maximize the amount of expense, thereby permanently reducing the tax Pockwock would have to pay. The downside is that net income would be lower. If instead management wanted to minimize the effect on income, it would allocate $12,000,000 to the cost of the land and $13,000,000 to building, which would minimize the amount to be depreciated.

The choice being made here isn't arbitrary. Both treatments can be justified because they are within the range of the independent appraisal. A reader might be suspicious of any management choice in these circumstances, but it's important to keep in mind that it's usually not possible to know what the "truth" is. The actual individual market values of the land and building can't be known unless they are sold separately. The portion of cost assigned to each asset is an informed estimate.

In a related issue, IFRS requires **componentization** of assets. When an item of property, plant, and equipment is made up of parts or components for which different useful lives or depreciation methods are appropriate, IFRS requires each component to be accounted for separately. For example, the engines, fuselage, electronics, seats, etc. of an airplane have different useful lives, and the cost of the plane is allocated among the components and depreciated separately. Because this asset is usually purchased for a single price, management has to decide how to allocate the cost among the components. As a result, management has some flexibility here, and that can be used to achieve reporting objectives.

DEPRECIATION

Most capital assets get used up. A machine, a mine, even an idea doesn't last forever. The machine no longer produces goods effectively and has to be updated. The resource in the mine is exhausted and the patent for the idea expires. Because capital assets get used up while helping to earn revenue, it makes sense for the cost to somehow be matched to the revenues they help earn. Expensing the cost of a capital asset is conceptually the same as expensing the cost of inventory when it's sold or salaries when the work is done. It's an application of matching. The hard part is figuring out how to do it. Because capital assets contribute to revenue indirectly and over more than one period, the cost must be expensed in a reasonable way over the life of the asset.

Different terms are used for the process of allocating the cost of a capital asset to expense over time. IFRS uses the term **depreciation** for the process of allocating the cost of property, plant, and equipment to expense and **amortization** for intangible assets. A third term, **depletion**, is used for natural resources. In practice, however, these terms are used interchangeably and inconsistently. The categories of capital assets and the terms applied to each are summarized in Figure 8.3.

As mentioned, the hard part about expensing the cost of a capital asset is figuring out a way of doing it. There is little authoritative or specific guidance. IFRS say the cost of an asset less its **residual value** (the amount that would be received today from selling the asset if it was at the end of its useful life) should be depreciated or amortized over its useful life in a "systematic" way. There are many questions: What is a systematic way of depreciating the cost? What is the useful life? What is the residual value?

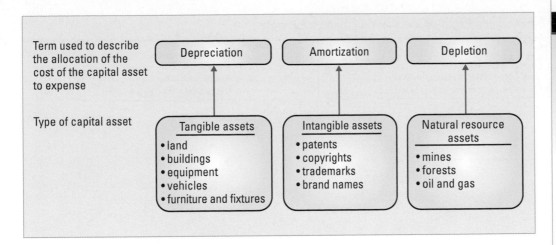

FIGURE 8.3

Summary of Types of Capital Assets and Terms Used to Describe the Allocation of the Cost

Managers must use their knowledge and judgment to answer these questions, and stakeholders must recognize there are different reasonable treatments. Any choice within a reasonable range is likely acceptable. For example, could anyone strongly argue that the useful life of a car is three, five, or seven years? An asset doesn't come with a tag advising owners how long it will last or what its residual value is. The useful life, residual value, and how an asset contributes to earning revenue depend on how it's used, what it's used for, and how it's cared for.

There are two main reasons why capital assets are depreciated: physical use and obsolescence. Physical use refers to the effects that passage of time, wear and tear, and exposure to the elements have on the capital asset's ability to help earn revenue. As a machine gets older and is used, it will break down more often, use more energy to operate, and produce less and lower-quality output. Eventually, the machine must be replaced.

Assets become obsolete because of changes in technology and shifts in the business environment. Most computers purchased three or more years ago can probably still do what they did when they were new. However, these computers may now be too slow, lacking memory or multimedia capabilities, or unable to handle some software applications. They have less to contribute to the money-making activities of the business than state-of-the-art equipment would. Advances in technology have rendered most of those computers obsolete.

Not all assets are depreciated. Land is usually not depreciated because it doesn't wear out or become obsolete. The buildings on a piece of land will come and go but the land will always be there. An exception to this treatment is land mined for its natural resources. In that case, the cost of the land is expensed as the land is mined because it's "used up" as the resource is removed. Intangible assets aren't amortized when there are no factors limiting their useful lives. For example, the licenses bought by wireless companies for the right to use airwaves for wireless communications aren't amortized. Goodwill also isn't amortized.

Depreciation and Market Values

Depreciation allocates the cost of a capital asset to expense. The carrying amount of the asset (cost less depreciation to date) isn't an estimate of its market value. Resist the temptation to think that it is.

Depreciation Methods

Now let's look at how capital assets are depreciated. Several methods are generally accepted in Canada. Each method allocates the cost of a capital asset to expense in a different way and, as a result, each will provide a different net income and carrying amount in each year of the asset's life. These methods can be grouped into three major categories:

1. straight-line
2. accelerated
3. usage-based

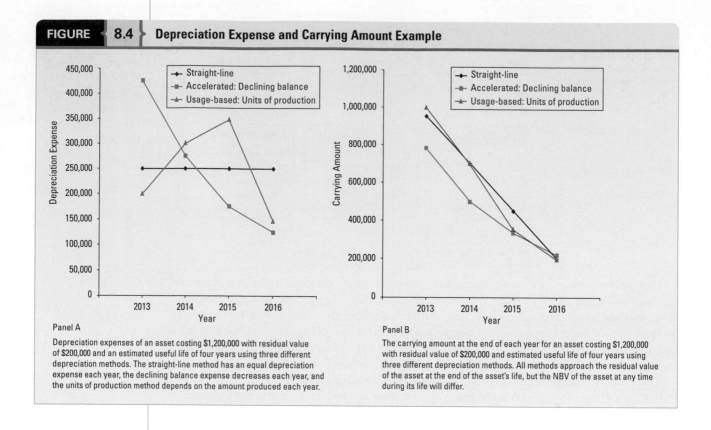

FIGURE 8.4 Depreciation Expense and Carrying Amount Example

Panel A

Depreciation expenses of an asset costing $1,200,000 with residual value of $200,000 and an estimated useful life of four years using three different depreciation methods. The straight-line method has an equal depreciation expense each year, the declining balance expense decreases each year, and the units of production method depends on the amount produced each year.

Panel B

The carrying amount at the end of each year for an asset costing $1,200,000 with residual value of $200,000 and estimated useful life of four years using three different depreciation methods. All methods approach the residual value of the asset at the end of the asset's life, but the NBV of the asset at any time during its life will differ.

At the beginning of fiscal 2013 Vermilion Corp. (Vermilion) purchased equipment for $1,200,000. Management estimated a residual value of $200,000 and a useful life of four years. Panel A of Figure 8.4 plots the annual depreciation expense over the useful life of the asset under each of the three methods. The decline of the asset's carrying amount under each method is shown in Panel B. Refer to Figure 8.4 when you study the following discussion of each method.

When the asset is purchased, the following journal entry is made:

Dr. Capital assets—equipment (assets +)   1,200,000
    Cr. Cash (assets −) or Liability (liability +)   1,200,000
To record the purchase of a capital asset

Under any depreciation method the following journal entry will be made each period to record the depreciation expense:

Dr. Depreciation expense (expense +, owners' equity −)   xxx
    Cr. Accumulated depreciation (contra-asset +)   xxx
To record the depreciation expense and the increase in the accumulated
depreciation account for the year

The depreciation expense is the portion of the equipment's cost that is matched to revenues earned during the period. The credit entry reduces the carrying amount of the equipment on the balance sheet. Notice that the credit is to a contra-asset account, not to the equipment account itself. Recall from Chapter 3 that a contra-asset account accumulates reductions in a related asset account. That means the equipment remains in its account at full cost while depreciation accumulates in the contra-asset accumulated depreciation account. The carrying amount of the equipment equals the amount in the equipment account less the amount in the accumulated depreciation account.

Figure 8.5 shows the relative use of the different depreciation methods in Canada, as reported in *Financial Reporting in Canada 2008*, 33rd Edition.[1] Straight-line depreciation is by far the method most commonly used by public companies in Canada.

Depreciation method	Number of firms	Percentage of firms in the sample using the method (%)*
Straight-line	182	94%
Accelerated: Declining balance	43	22
Usage-based: Unit of production	58	30
Other	1	0

*Results are from 2007 annual reports. Percentages add up to more than 100% because some firms use more than one depreciation method.

FIGURE 8.5

Use in Canada of Different Depreciation Methods for Plant, Property, and Equipment

Straight-Line Depreciation This method is straightforward and simple to use, which makes it appealing. With **straight-line depreciation**, the depreciation expense is the same in each period, implying that the contribution to revenue generation by the capital asset is the same each period. This assumption is probably not entirely valid because over time the capability of most assets declines, repairs and maintenance increase, and sales tend to vary. However, since it's so difficult to estimate the asset's contribution in each period, this approach is reasonable (or as reasonable as any other). The equation for calculating depreciation using the straight-line method is

$$\text{Depreciation expense} = \frac{\text{Cost} - \text{Estimated residual value}}{\text{Estimated useful life}}$$
$$= \frac{\text{Depreciable amount}}{\text{Estimated useful life}}$$

The **depreciable amount** is the amount of a capital asset that will be depreciated. For Vermilion's machine, the depreciable amount is $1,000,000 ($1,200,000 − $200,000) and the annual depreciation expense is $250,000 ($1,000,000 ÷ 4 years).

$$\text{Depreciation expense} = \frac{\$1,200,000 - \$200,000}{4 \text{ years}}$$
$$= \$250,000 \text{ per year}$$

Figure 8.6 shows the depreciation schedule for the life of the asset.

The annual depreciation expense equals $1,000,000 ÷ 4

Carrying amount equals column 1 − column 2

	Balance Sheet			Income statement
	Column 1	Column 2	Column 3	Column 4
Year	Cost	Accumulated depreciation on December 31	Carrying amount on December 31 (cost − depreciation)	Depreciation expense for the year ended December 31
2013	$1,200,000	$ 250,000	$1,000,000	$ 250,000
2014	1,200,000	500,000	700,000	250,000
2015	1,200,000	750,000	450,000	250,000
2016	1,200,000	1,000,000	200,000	250,000
Total				$1,000,000

FIGURE 8.6

Depreciation Schedule Using Straight-Line Depreciation

The annual depreciation expense will change as estimates of the asset's useful life and residual value change. If we changed the estimated useful life to five years and the residual value to $150,000, the annual depreciation expense becomes $210,000. If everything else stays the same, these changes will result in net income being $40,000 higher in each of the first four years compared with our original estimates. These changes have no direct economic impact on the entity, but they may affect the outcome of contracts based on net income and other financial statement measures. This example shows how management's estimates may influence perceptions of the entity, affect decisions a stakeholder makes, and have economic consequences. As we will discuss in the appendix to this chapter, the choice of depreciation method has no tax implications.

Accelerated Depreciation **Accelerated depreciation** methods allocate more of the cost of a capital asset to expense in the early years of its life and less in the later years. When an asset's revenue-generating ability is greater in the early part of its life, an accelerated method of depreciation makes sense. Accelerated depreciation is appropriate for assets sensitive to obsolescence, such as computers, and assets that clearly lose efficiency and/or effectiveness over time. Look at Figure 8.4 to see the pattern of accelerated depreciation in graphic form.

The most common accelerated depreciation method used in Canada is the **declining balance** method. This method applies a depreciation rate to the carrying amount of the asset at the beginning of the period to calculate the depreciation expense. That is,

> Depreciation expense = [(Cost − Accumulated depreciation) at the beginning of the period] × Rate
> = Carrying amount at the beginning of the period × Rate

Because a fixed rate is being applied to a declining balance, an asset is never depreciated to zero. This is one of the reasons why the residual value is usually ignored with this method.

The depreciation schedule for Vermilion's equipment is shown in Figure 8.7. A rate of 35 percent is applied to this asset. The depreciation expense in the first year is $420,000 ($1,200,000 × 0.35). In the second year, it's $273,000 ([$1,200,000 − $420,000] × 0.35). Notice how the depreciation expense decreases each year. You can also see that at the end of year 4 only $985,793 of the cost has been depreciated. Since the residual value of the equipment is $200,000, the remaining $14,207 would also be expensed in year 4.

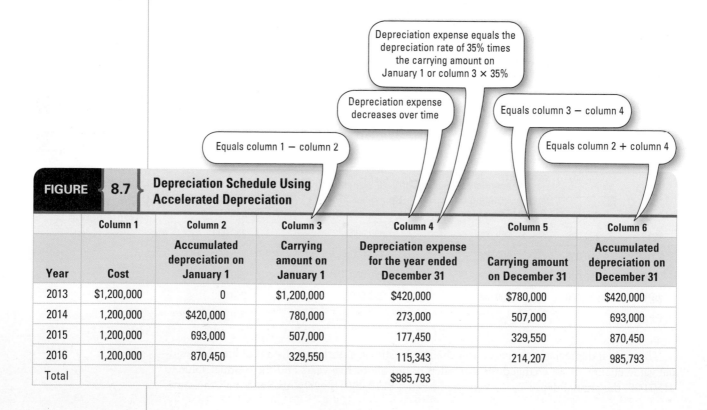

	Column 1	Column 2	Column 3	Column 4	Column 5	Column 6
Year	Cost	Accumulated depreciation on January 1	Carrying amount on January 1	Depreciation expense for the year ended December 31	Carrying amount on December 31	Accumulated depreciation on December 31
2013	$1,200,000	0	$1,200,000	$420,000	$780,000	$420,000
2014	1,200,000	$420,000	780,000	273,000	507,000	693,000
2015	1,200,000	693,000	507,000	177,450	329,550	870,450
2016	1,200,000	870,450	329,550	115,343	214,207	985,793
Total				$985,793		

FIGURE 8.7 Depreciation Schedule Using Accelerated Depreciation

Equals column 1 − column 2

Depreciation expense decreases over time

Depreciation expense equals the depreciation rate of 35% times the carrying amount on January 1 or column 3 × 35%

Equals column 3 − column 4

Equals column 2 + column 4

For managers who are concerned about their company's level of income, accelerated depreciation is less attractive than straight-line depreciation because in the first years of an asset's life the depreciation expense is larger, which makes net income lower. In later years, however, the accelerated depreciation expense is lower than with straight-line depreciation and net income will be higher. This effect can be seen in the plots in Panel A of Figure 8.4. However, if an entity is growing and continually purchasing and replacing capital assets, the depreciation expense using straight-line depreciation will almost always be lower than with declining balance. If an entity isn't growing, declining balance eventually produces lower depreciation expenses.

There are other accelerated depreciation methods, but these are rarely used in Canada and will not be discussed.

Usage-Based Depreciation: Unit of Production If an asset's consumption can be readily associated with its use and not to the passage of time or obsolescence, then a usage-based depreciation method can be used. One of the more common usage-based methods is unit of production. To use the **unit-of-production** method, the manager must be able to estimate the number of units that the asset will produce over its life. The year's depreciation expense is the proportion of units produced in the year to total estimated units to be produced over the asset's life. In our example, if the asset's estimated production over its useful life is 200,000 units and 40,000 are produced in the first year, the depreciation expense in the first year would be

$$\text{Depreciation expense} = \frac{\text{Number of units produced in the period}}{\text{Estimated number of units produced over the asset's life}} \times (\text{Cost} - \text{Estimated residual value})$$

$$= \frac{40,000 \text{ units}}{200,000 \text{ units}} \times (\$1,200,000 - \$200,000)$$

$$= \$200,000$$

The depreciation schedule using this method is shown in Figure 8.8. Note that it's assumed the asset's actual lifetime production will equal the estimated production. In practice, this assumption will often not be true.

The proportion of estimated total output produced in the year. Equals column 4 ÷ total of column 4

Equals the depreciable amount ($1,000,000) times column 4

	Balance Sheet					Income Statement
	Column 1	Column 2	Column 3	Column 4	Column 5	Column 6
Year	Cost	Accumulated depreciation	Carrying amount	Percentage of total production in year	Production	Depreciation expense
1	$1,200,000	$ 200,000	$1,000,000	20%	40,000	$ 200,000
2	1,200,000	500,000	700,000	30	60,000	300,000
3	1,200,000	850,000	350,000	35	70,000	350,000
4	1,200,000	1,000,000	200,000	15	30,000	150,000
Total				100%	200,000	$1,000,000

FIGURE 8.8

Depreciation Schedule Using Unit-of-Production Depreciation

There are other measures of asset use. For example, the number of kilometres a delivery truck travels and the number of hours that equipment runs are possibilities. There are a number of difficulties with applying a depreciation method based on actual use:

- It's difficult to make a reasonable estimate of the capacity of many assets, but the estimate is crucial for determining the depreciation expense for a period. For example, estimating that a truck will travel 200,000 kilometres rather than 150,000 will have a significant effect on the depreciation expense.

- Usage-based depreciation isn't appropriate for many types of assets. For example, this method doesn't work well for buildings or office equipment as there is no obvious unit of measurement that could be applied.

If reasonable measures of usage can be obtained, the usage-based depreciation methods result in good matching; there is a direct association between the amount of depreciation and the consumption of the asset. Unfortunately, the difficulties described above limit the usefulness of the method.

Figure 8.5 does show wide use of the unit-of-production method in Canada: 30 percent of the firms surveyed. This is because the method is common in natural resource industries such as mining, oil and gas, and forestry. In these industries it's possible to estimate the amount of resource available. The estimated amount is the basis for depreciating the costs of discovering and developing the mine, oil and gas reserve, or forest (costs such as the purchase of the land or land rights, finding the resource, and developing it).

Comparing Methods

We'll now expand the Vermilion example to see of how different depreciation methods affect the financial statements. Vermilion has no capital assets other than the machine it purchased in 2013. Table 8.3 shows summarized income statements, year-end capital assets, and total assets for the years 2013 through 2016 using the three different depreciation methods. Note the following when examining Table 8.3:

- Vermilion began operations in 2013 with $1,500,000 in cash.
- Vermilion's revenues and expenses, other than the depreciation expense, are identical regardless of the method of depreciaton.
- The tax expense is based on the actual rules stated in the *Income Tax Act* and is the same under all three methods.
- The undepreciated portion of the equipment under the declining balance method is fully expensed in 2016.
- All production is sold in the year it's produced.

Notice the significant effect the depreciation method has on Vermilion's net income, net capital assets, and total assets. In 2013, for example, net income ranges from a loss of $117,936 to a profit of $102,064. What does this tell a stakeholder? Is Vermilion doing well, as suggested by the $102,064 profit, or poorly, as indicated by the loss? These questions aren't easy to answer because while the numbers are different in each income statement the underlying economic position of Vermilion is the same. Accounting choices affect the appearance of the statements but not the underlying economic activity.

While income in individual years differs under the three depreciation methods, notice that total net income for the four years is the same for all the methods (see Panel E of Table 8.3). The cumulative income statements highlight the fact that the different accounting choices affect the timing of revenues and expenses but not the totals.

Does this mean that accounting choice doesn't matter? It can matter very much, but whether it does or not depends on who is using the financial statements, how they're being used, and for what reason. Only the most unsophisticated financial statement user would likely be misled by a company's depreciation policy. Research shows that changing depreciation methods to report a higher income doesn't result in a higher stock price. However, if a contract depends on the financial statement numbers, the depreciation method could make a difference.

If Vermilion's managers had a bonus plan based on net income, they might prefer unit-of-production depreciation because their bonus would be higher in the first year. If a loan was needed, managers might be reluctant to use the declining balance method because of the loss it produces in the first year. The managers may believe that lenders are less willing to invest in an unprofitable entity. For tax purposes, none of these methods is appropriate because the *Income Tax Act* specifies how depreciation must be calculated (as will be discussed in the appendix to this chapter).

TABLE 8.3   Vermilion Corp.: Summarized Financial Statement Information Using Three Different Depreciation Methods

Panel A	Vermilion Corp. 2013		
	Straight line	35% declining balance	Unit of production
Revenue	$ 680,000	$ 680,000	$ 680,000
Expenses	360,400	360,400	360,400
Depreciation expense	250,000	420,000	200,000
Operating income	69,600	(100,400)	119,600
Taxes	17,536	17,536	17,536
Net income	$ 52,064	($ 117,936)	$ 102,064
Equipment (at cost)	1,200,000	1,200,000	1,200,000
Accumulated depreciation	(250,000)	(420,000)	(200,000)
Equipment (net)	950,000	780,000	1,000,000
Total assets	$1,552,064	$1,382,064	$1,602,064

Panel B	Vermilion Corp. 2014		
	Straight line	35% declining balance	Unit of production
Revenue	$1,020,000	$1,020,000	$1,020,000
Expenses	540,600	540,600	540,600
Depreciation expense	250,000	273,000	300,000
Operating income	229,400	206,400	179,400
Taxes	21,264	21,264	21,264
Net income	$ 208,136	$ 185,136	$ 158,136
Equipment (at cost)	1,200,000	1,200,000	1,200,000
Accumulated depreciation	(500,000)	(693,000)	(500,000)
Equipment (net)	700,000	507,000	700,000
Total assets	$1,760,200	$1,567,200	$1,760,200

Panel C	Vermilion Corp. 2015		
	Straight line	35% declining balance	Unit of production
Revenue	$1,190,000	$1,190,000	$1,190,000
Expenses	630,700	630,700	630,700
Depreciation expense	250,000	177,450	350,000
Operating income	309,300	381,850	209,300
Taxes	53,452	53,452	53,452
Net income	$ 255,848	$ 328,398	$ 155,848
Equipment (at cost)	1,200,000	1,200,000	1,200,000
Accumulated depreciation	(750,000)	(870,450)	(850,000)
Equipment (net)	450,000	329,550	350,000
Total assets	$2,016,048	$1,895,598	$1,916,048

Panel D	Vermilion Corp. 2016		
	Straight line	35% declining balance	Unit of production
Revenue	$ 510,000	$ 510,000	$ 510,000
Expenses	270,300	270,300	270,300
Depreciation expense	250,000	129,550	150,000
Operating income	(10,300)	110,150	89,700
Taxes	3,428	3,428	3,428
Net income	($ 13,728)	$ 106,722	$ 86,272
Equipment (at cost)	1,200,000	1,200,000	1,200,000
Accumulated depreciation	(1,000,000)	(1,000,000)	(1,000,000)
Equipment (net)	200,000	200,000	200,000
Total assets	$2,002,320	$2,002,320	$2,002,320

Panel E	Vermilion Corp. 2013–2016		
	Straight line	35% declining balance	Unit of production
Revenue	$3,400,000	$3,400,000	$3,400,000
Expenses	1,802,000	1,802,000	1,802,000
Depreciation expense	1,000,000	1,000,000	1,000,000
Operating income	598,000	598,000	598,000
Taxes	95,680	95,680	95,680
Net income	$ 502,320	$ 502,320	$ 502,320
Equipment (at cost)	1,200,000	1,200,000	1,200,000
Accumulated depreciation	(1,000,000)	(1,000,000)	(1,000,000)
Equipment (net)	200,000	200,000	200,000
Total assets	$2,002,320	$2,002,320	$2,002,320

Revenue and expenses (except for depreciation) are the same under all three methods.

Net income varies significantly from method to method because the depreciation expense is different under each method.

The carrying amount of the equipment, accumulated depreciation, and the amount of total assets at the end of the year depend on the depreciation method used.

Over Vermilion's four-year life, the income statements are identical.

KNOWLEDGE CHECK

Dragon Ltd. (Dragon) is a small, privately owned company. A professional manager manages the company, and the shareholders aren't involved in day-to-day management. Recently Dragon began to manufacture products it had previously purchased and sold to its customers.

☐   What decisions must Dragon's manager make regarding the accounting for the new equipment before she can calculate the depreciation expense for the current year?

☐   Using the following assumptions, calculate each year's depreciation expense and ending balance in accumulated depreciation expense using the straight-line, declining balance, and unit-of-production depreciation methods. For declining balance use a rate of 50 percent.

     i.   The cost of buying and getting the equipment operating was $800,000 ($750,000 cost + $50,000 in delivery, set-up, and ancillary costs).

     ii.   The residual value of the equipment is estimated to be $80,000.

     iii.   The useful life of the equipment is three years.

     iv.   The equipment will produce 20,000 units in the first year, 32,000 in the second year, and 28,000 units in the third year.

☐   Prepare the journal entries that would be required for each of the three years for the straight-line method.

INSIGHT

Depreciation: An Arbitrary Allocation?

Practically speaking, no depreciation method can be justified over all others because in almost all cases it's impossible to know how a capital asset contributes to earning revenue. Indeed, some people have argued that the choice of depreciation method is arbitrary—one method of depreciation can't be proven to be superior to any other. It can also be difficult to estimate the useful life of an asset or its residual value with any precision. As long as an estimate is reasonable under the circumstances, it's acceptable. As a result, managers have considerable leeway in choosing the depreciation methods, useful lives, and residual values for their entity's capital assets. Their decisions can be influenced by their knowledge of how the assets are actually used, the methods used by other firms in the industry, the information needs of stakeholders, and their own interests.

Summary

In summary, there are some depreciation issues to be aware of:

1. There are a number of different, acceptable methods of depreciating capital assets, with little restriction on which can be used. None of the methods stand out clearly as the best.

2. Because it's difficult to estimate the useful life or residual value of an asset, there will be variation in managers' choices. Estimates depend on how the asset is used and how it's cared for, and these can be difficult to figure out from financial statements.

3. As a result of points 1 and 2, managers can make choices that serve their reporting objectives.

4. Depreciation has no effect on cash flow.

5. Managers' choices can have economic consequences; for example they will affect contracts such as management bonuses and debt covenants that depend on accounting measurements.

Because of these issues, similar entities might use different depreciation methods and make different assumptions regarding useful life and residual value. As a result, comparability of financial statements can be impaired. Stakeholders must pay careful attention to the entities' accounting choices so they can understand whether differences between them reflect actual differences in economic activity or simply differences in how the accounting is done.

Figure 8.9 shows the useful lives of the capital assets of three Canadian airlines: Air Canada, Transat A.T. Inc., and WestJet. All use straight-line depreciation, but notice the differences in the useful lives of the assets. Air Canada depreciates its planes over 20 to 25 years, Transat over 5 to 10 years, and WestJet on the number of cycles (takeoffs and landings). While there might be economic reasons for the differences, they may simply reflect different judgments by management. These methods are significantly different and as a result the comparability of the financial statements is impaired.

Category of asset	Company		
	Air Canada	WestJet	Transat A.T.
Aircraft and flight equipment	20–25 years	Cycles*	5–10 years
Spare engines and related parts	20–25 years	20 years	Cycles*
Buildings	40–50 years	40 years	35 years
Leaseholder improvements	Lesser of the lease term or five years	Term of lease	Term of lease
Ground and other equipment	3–25 years	5–25 years	

*Cycles are the number of takeoffs and landings a plane makes.

FIGURE 8.9

Differences in Depreciation Policies and Estimates among Canadian Airlines

VALUING CAPITAL ASSETS AT MARKET VALUE

So far our discussion has assumed that entities will account for their capital assets at cost. Most entities do use cost but IFRS provides the option of valuing certain capital assets at market value. Property, plant, and equipment can be reported at market value if the market value can be measured reliably. Intangibles can be valued at market if there is an active market for them. Intangibles tend to be unique so this requirement makes revaluation of them very unusual. A taxi licence or tradable pollution rights are examples of intangibles that could meet the requirement.

Let's demonstrate the accounting with an example. At the beginning of 2014 Restoule Ltd. purchased a building with an estimated life of 25 years for $5 million. On December 31, 2014 and 2015 Restoule recorded depreciation expenses of $200,000 ($5,000,000 ÷ 25 years) and on December 31, 2015 the building had a carrying amount of $4,600,000 ($5,000,000 − [$200,000 × 2]). At the end of 2015 Restoule elects to value the building at its market value of $6 million. By revaluing the building at market, the carrying amount on December 31, 2015 becomes $6,000,000. The revaluation could be presented on Restoule's balance sheet in two ways:

	Gross method	Proportional method
Building (gross carrying amount)	$6,000,000	$6,521,739*
Accumulated depreciation	0	521,739
Carrying amount	$6,000,000	$6,000,000

*To obtain the gross amount of the building multiply the original cost by the new carrying amount ÷ the old carrying amount or $5,000,000 × ($6,000,000 ÷ $4,600,000).

The gross method simply records the asset at its revalued amount and eliminates accumulated depreciation. With the proportional method, the ratio of accumulated depreciation to gross carrying amount of the asset must be the same before and after the revaluation, and the carrying amount must equal the market value. At the time of the revaluation, Restoule's building was 8 percent depreciated ($400,000 ÷ $5,000,000) so after the revaluation accumulated depreciation must be 8 percent of the gross carrying amount of the building and the carrying amount must be $6,000,000. These requirements mean the gross carrying amount at the end of 2015 must be $6,521,739, and accumulated depreciation $521,739. The key point is that the building is reported on the balance sheet at $6 million, its market value.

Since assets increased by $1,400,000 ($6,000,000 − $4,600,000), another adjustment is needed to keep the accounting equation in balance. This adjustment is reported in "other comprehensive income" in the statement of comprehensive income and as "accumulated other comprehensive income – revaluation surplus" in the equity section of the balance sheet. Restoule's statement of comprehensive income and the equity section of its balance sheet might appear as follows (all numbers shown are assumed except for the increase in the value of the building):

Restoule Ltd. Statement of Comprehensive Income For the Year Ended December 31, 2015	
Net income	$5,300,000
Other comprehensive income—revaluation surplus	1,400,000
Comprehensive income	$6,700,000

Restoule Ltd. Balance Sheet—Shareholders' Equity As of December 31, 2015	
Common shares	$17,250,000
Retained earnings	35,550,000
Accumulated other comprehensive income – revaluation surplus	1,400,000
Total shareholders' equity	$54,200,000

If instead the market value of Restoule's building decreased to $4 million at the end of 2015, the carrying amount on the balance sheet would become $4,000,000. However, the decrease in value would be reported as a loss on the income statement (not in other comprehensive income), and there would be no accumulated other comprehensive income – revaluation surplus account on the balance sheet. In other words, losses are recognized on the income statement while gains are included in other comprehensive income, not in the calculation of net income, because they aren't realized.

IFRS requires that revaluations be done often enough so the difference between the carrying amount and market value isn't significant. It also requires an entity to account for similar assets in the same way. Treatment of changes in valuation after the first one can get complicated, so I'll leave coverage of that to a higher-level accounting course.

Evidence shows that very few companies have elected to use the market value approach for valuing capital assets. An exception is the real estate business, where many companies value their real estate holdings at market.

CANADIAN GAAP FOR PRIVATE ENTERPRISES

Canadian GAAP for Private Enterprises doesn't allow valuation of capital assets at market value.

Financial Statement Disclosure

Companies that adhere to IFRS are required to disclose the following information about their capital assets:

- measurement basis for determining the carrying amount (cost or market value)
- depreciation method and useful lives of each major category of capital assets
- gross carrying amount accumulated depreciation at the beginning and end of the period
- a reconciliation of the carrying amount at the beginning and end of the period
- depreciation expense

Consolidated Statements of Financial Position

As at December 31   in millions of US dollars except share amounts

Notes		2008	2007
	Assets		
	Current assets		
	Cash and cash equivalents	$ 276.8	$ 719.5
Note 3	Accounts receivable	1,189.9	596.2
Note 4	Inventories	714.9	428.1
Note 5	Prepaid expenses and other current assets	79.2	36.7
Note 6	Current portion of derivative instrument assets	6.4	30.8
		2,267.2	1,811.3
Note 6	Derivative instrument assets	11.5	104.2
Note 7	Property, plant and equipment	4,812.2	3,887.4
Note 8	Investments	2,750.7	3,581.5
Note 9	Other assets	288.7	210.7
Note 10	Intangible assets	21.5	24.5
Note 10	Goodwill	97.0	97.0
		$ 10,248.8	$ 9,716.6

Consolidated Statements of Operations and Retained Earnings

For the years ended December 31   in millions of US dollars except per-share amounts

Notes		2008	2007	2006
Note 19	Sales	$ 9,446.5	$ 5,234.2	$ 3,766.7
	Less: Freight	324.9	346.1	255.8
	Transportation and distribution	132.4	124.1	134.1
Note 20	Cost of goods sold	4,081.8	2,882.8	2,374.8
	Gross Margin	4,907.4	1,881.2	1,002.0
Note 21	Selling and administrative	188.4	212.6	158.4
Note 22	Provincial mining and other taxes	543.4	135.4	66.5
	Foreign exchange (gain) loss	(126.0)	70.2	(4.4)
Note 23	Other income	(333.5)	(125.5)	(94.0)
		272.3	292.7	126.5
	Operating Income	4,635.1	1,588.5	875.5
Note 24	Interest Expense	62.8	68.7	85.6
	Income before Income Taxes	4,572.3	1,519.8	789.9
Note 25	Income Taxes	1,077.1	416.2	158.1
	Net Income	3,495.2	1,103.6	631.8

Note 2 BASIS OF PRESENTATION

Asset Impairment

The company reviews both long-lived assets to be held and used and identifiable intangible assets with finite lives whenever events or changes in circumstances indicate that the carrying amount of such assets may not be fully recoverable. Determination of recoverability is based on an estimate of undiscounted future cash flows resulting from the use of the asset and its eventual disposition. Measurement of an impairment loss for long-lived assets and certain identifiable intangible assets that management expects to hold and use is based on the fair value of the assets, whereas such assets to be disposed of are reported at the lower of carrying amount or fair value less costs to sell.

Goodwill impairment is assessed at the reporting unit level at least annually (in April), or more frequently if events or circumstances indicate there may be an impairment. Reporting units comprise business operations with similar economic characteristics and strategies and may represent either a business segment or a business unit within a business segment. Potential impairment is identified when the carrying value of a reporting unit, including the allocated goodwill, exceeds its fair value. Goodwill impairment is measured as the excess of the carrying amount of the reporting unit's allocated goodwill over the implied fair value of the goodwill, based on the fair value of the assets and liabilities of the reporting unit.

EXHIBIT 8.1

(continued)
Potash Corporation of Saskatchewan Inc.: Disclosures about Capital Assets

Note 7 PROPERTY, PLANT AND EQUIPMENT

Property, plant and equipment (which includes certain mine development costs and pre-stripping costs) are carried at cost. Costs of additions, betterments, renewals and interest during construction are capitalized.

Maintenance and repair expenditures that do not improve or extend productive life are expensed in the year incurred.

Certain mining and milling assets are depreciated using the units-of-production method based on the shorter of estimates of reserves or service lives. Pre-stripping costs are amortized on a units-of-production basis over the ore mined from the mineable acreage stripped. Other asset classes are depreciated or amortized on a straight-line basis as follows: land improvements 5 to 40 years, buildings and improvements 6 to 40 years and machinery and equipment (comprised primarily of plant equipment) 20 to 40 years.

	Cost	2008[1] Accumulated Depreciation and Amortization	Net Book Value
Land and improvements	$ 321.6	$ 58.1	$ 263.5
Buildings and improvements	950.2	235.8	714.4
Machinery and equipment	5,842.2	2,160.3	3,681.9
Mine development costs	224.8	72.4	152.4
	$7,338.8	$2,526.6	$4,812.2

[1] See change in accounting policy (Note 2).

	Cost	2007 Accumulated Depreciation and Amortization	Net Book Value
Land and improvements	$ 248.9	$ 53.9	$ 195.0
Buildings and improvements	647.9	220.5	427.4
Machinery and equipment	5,074.5	1,937.3	3,137.2
Mine development costs	196.8	69.0	127.8
	$ 6,168.1	$ 2,280.7	$ 3,887.4

Depreciation and amortization of property, plant and equipment included in cost of goods sold and in selling and administrative expenses was $313.2 (2007 – $279.8; 2006 – $226.3). The net carrying amount of property, plant and equipment not being amortized at December 31, 2008 because it was under construction or development was $1,433.0 (2007 – $608.8).

During 2008, the company recorded no impairment charge (2007 – $NIL; 2006 – $6.3) relating to property, plant and equipment. Interest capitalized to property, plant and equipment during the year was $42.9 (2007 – $21.8; 2006 – $19.1).

The opening balance of pre-stripping costs at January 1, 2008 was $33.4 (2007 – $28.5), additions during 2008 were $27.4 (2007 – $24.8) and amortization was $23.6 (2007 – $19.9), for a balance at December 31, 2008 of $37.2 (2007 – $33.4).

Acquiring or constructing property, plant and equipment by incurring a liability does not result in a cash outflow for the company until the liability is paid. In the period the related liability is incurred, the change in operating accounts payable on the Consolidated Statements of Cash Flow is typically reduced by such amount. In the period the liability is paid, the amount is reflected as a cash outflow for investing activities. The applicable net change in operating accounts payable that was reclassified from (to) investing activities on the Consolidated Statements of Cash Flow in 2008 was $61.9 (2007 – $59.8; 2006 – $(2.6)).

Note 10 INTANGIBLE ASSETS AND GOODWILL

Intangible Assets

Intangible assets relate primarily to production and technology rights and computer software. Finite-lived intangible assets are amortized on a straight-line basis over their estimated useful lives as follows: production and technology rights 25 to 30 years and computer software up to 5 years.

Goodwill

All business combinations are accounted for using the purchase method. Identifiable intangible assets are recognized separately from goodwill. Goodwill is carried at cost, is not amortized and represents the excess of the purchase price and related costs over the fair value assigned to the net identifiable assets of a business acquired.

	2008	2007
Intangible assets – net of accumulated amortization of $31.8 (2007 – $27.9)	$ 21.5	$ 24.5
Goodwill – net of accumulated amortization of $7.3 (2007 – $7.3)	$ 97.0	$ 97.0

Other than goodwill, the company has not recognized any intangible assets with indefinite useful lives. Total amortization expense relating to finite-lived intangible assets for 2008 was $3.9 (2007 – $6.1; 2006 – $6.9). Amortization expense in each of the next five years calculated upon such assets held as at December 31, 2008 is estimated to be $3.9 for 2009, $3.4 for 2010, $1.0 for 2011, $0.8 for 2012 and $0.8 for 2013.

Substantially all of the company's recorded goodwill relates to the nitrogen segment.

www.potashcorp.com

Exhibit 8.1 provides an example of capital asset disclosure for Potash Corporation of Saskatchewan Inc. (Potash), an integrated producer of fertilizer, industrial, and animal feed products.[2] Potash's balance sheets only provide a small part of the capital asset story, showing only the net amount (cost less accumulated depreciation) of the company's PPE, goodwill, and intangible assets. The notes must be examined to get the full story about these assets.

The following information is provided about capital assets:

- net amount of PPE, goodwill, and intangibles (balance sheet)

- depreciation expense (Note 7)

- amortization expense (Note 10)

- depreciation methods and rates for PPE (Note 7)

- how PPE is accounted for (Note 7)

- nature and accounting for goodwill (Note 10)

- accounting for intangible assets, identification of intangibles with indefinite lives (these aren't amortized), amortization method and periods, and impairment testing (Note 10)

- approach to impairment testing of PPE, intangibles, and goodwill (Note 2)

- cost, accumulated depreciation, and carrying amount of each category of PPE (Note 7)

- accumulated amortization and carrying amount of intangibles and goodwill (Note 10)

Potash's financial statements provide some context for understanding the accounting it uses for capital assets. The information doesn't give an idea about whether the accounting methods are reasonable or appropriate. That insight comes from familiarity with the business. Managers have considerable discretion for deciding how to present details about their entities' capital assets, and Potash provides fairly detailed information about theirs. Potash's method of presenting the accounting policy and detail about the asset category in a single note rather than splitting then into a significant accounting policies note and an asset category note is unusual.

? QUESTION FOR CONSIDERATION

Some people argue that depreciation of the cost of capital assets is arbitrary. Explain.

Solution: The purpose of depreciation is to match the cost of capital assets to the revenues they help generate. But what is the relationship between a delivery vehicle and revenue, a lawn mower and revenue, a computer and revenue, or a machine and revenue? Clearly, these capital assets make contributions to earning revenue, but it's impossible to know exactly what they are. Nevertheless, accrual accounting requires that capital assets be depreciated, so it's necessary to develop methods to do this. As a result, different depreciation methods can be justified in terms of the facts, as long as they are reasonable. It's impossible to argue that one method allocates the cost of capital assets to expense better than any other method. In other words, the choice is arbitrary.

INTANGIBLE ASSETS

Intangible assets, including knowledge assets or intellectual capital, are capital assets with no physical qualities. Intangible assets can't be seen, touched, or felt like a machine, building, or table, but they are often crucial to the success of an entity. Intangible assets include patents, copyrights, trademarks, franchise rights, brand names, customer lists, software, licences, movies, human resources, and goodwill.

Accounting for intangible assets under IFRS is similar to accounting for property, plant, and equipment, although there are differences, as we'll see. Generally, to be recognized as an intangible asset, an item must meet the following conditions:

- It must be separately identifiable (be able to sell or license it).

- It must have future benefits.

- The future benefits must be controlled by the entity.

- The cost must be reliably measurable.

- Alternatively, an intangible asset can be recognized if it represents a contractual or legal right.

Consolidated balance sheets

As at August 31
(in thousands of Canadian dollars)

	2008	2007
Assets (note 8)		
Current		
Cash and cash equivalents	19,642	33,347
Accounts receivable (notes 3 and 24)	157,440	151,380
Income taxes recoverable	1,615	–
Prepaid expenses and other	10,135	10,921
Program and film rights	131,301	125,068
Future tax asset (note 13)	9,593	13,518
Total current assets	329,726	334,234
Tax credits receivable	21,952	16,875
Investments and other assets (note 4)	93,086	17,492
Property, plant and equipment (note 5)	73,562	78,342
Program and film rights	103,163	90,687
Film investments (note 6)	80,819	66,593
Deferred charges	–	4,100
Broadcast licenses (note 15)	533,491	532,812
Goodwill (note 15)	797,854	795,832
	2,033,653	1,936,967

Note 2. Significant accounting policies

Program and film rights

Program and film rights represent contract rights acquired from third parties to broadcast television programs, feature films and radio programs. The assets and liabilities related to these rights are recorded when the license period has begun and all of the following conditions have been met: (i) the cost of the rights is known or reasonably determinable; (ii) the program material is accepted by the Company in accordance with the license agreement; and (iii) the material is available to the Company for airing. Long-term liabilities related to these rights are recorded at the net present values of future cash flows, using an appropriate discount rate. These costs are amortized over the contracted exhibition period as the programs or feature films are aired. Program and film rights are carried at the lower of cost less accumulated amortization and net recoverable amount.

Amortization of program and film rights is included in direct cost of sales, general and administrative expenses and has been disclosed separately in the consolidated statements of cash flows.

Broadcast licenses and goodwill

The cost of acquiring media broadcasting, production/distribution and publishing businesses is allocated to the fair value of related net identifiable tangible and intangible assets acquired. Net identifiable intangible assets acquired consist primarily of broadcast licenses. The excess of the cost of acquiring these businesses over the fair value of related net identifiable tangible and intangible assets acquired is allocated to goodwill.

Broadcast licenses are considered to have an indefinite life based on management's intent and ability to renew the licenses without substantial cost and without material modification of the existing terms and conditions of the license.

Broadcast licenses and goodwill are tested for impairment annually or more frequently if events or changes in circumstances indicate that they may be impaired. The Company has selected August 31 as the date it performs its annual impairment test.

If these criteria aren't met the costs involved must be expensed when incurred.

Intangible assets are amortized over their useful lives. However, if the period it is expected to provide benefits over is not limited, the intangible is considered to have an indefinite life and doesn't have to be amortized. For example, Exhibit 8.2 shows the accounting treatment of two of Corus Entertainment Inc.'s intangible assets.[3] Program rights that meet certain criteria are amortized over the period that Corus is allowed to broadcast the programs. Broadcast licenses aren't amortized because management believes these have indefinite lives as the company intends and is able to renew them.

Like property, plant, and equipment, an entity can elect to value intangibles at cost or fair value, but fair value can only be used if there is an active market for it, to provide a value. The accounting treatment of intangible assets, particularly internally generated ones, is one of the greatest challenges currently facing the accounting profession. In the "new economy" of the 21st century, entities invest significant resources in the creation of knowledge assets and intellectual capital that they use rather than sell. Regardless of how valuable they might be, costs associated with internally generated brands, customer lists and loyalty, information, and similar types of items, as well as training costs, advertising and promotion costs, and so on must be expensed as incurred. The accounting for intangible assets that are purchased is significantly different. When an intangible asset is purchased, in most situations it's recorded at cost, classified as an asset on the balance sheet, and amortized over its useful life (or treated as having an indefinite life). The accounting for purchased versus internally developed intangible assets is compared in Figure 8.10.

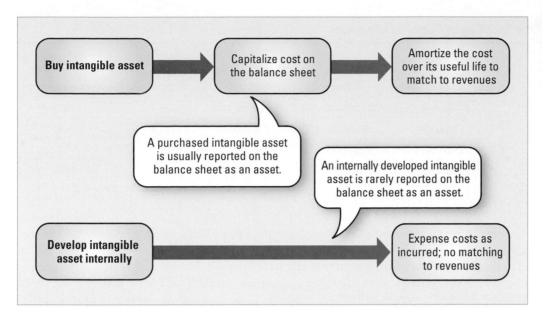

FIGURE 8.10

Accounting for Purchased versus Internally Developed Intangible Assets

It's difficult to argue that internally generated intangibles aren't assets, at least conceptually. There is no doubt that these investments provide an expectation of future benefits. Without ongoing research, technology companies would quickly become worthless as their products became obsolete. Successful brand names, customer lists, and skilful personnel clearly provide future benefits to an entity. There are reasons why contemporary accounting fails to recognize knowledge assets and intellectual capital. One is that IFRS's recognition criteria states that for an item to be recognized as an asset there must be probable future benefits associated with it. It's very uncertain if there will be a future benefit to expenditures on these asset types. Measurability is also a problem since the relation between an expenditure and a future benefit is often unclear. Another part of the problem is that many knowledge assets are developed internally by entities over time and in many or most cases it isn't at all clear that a valuable resource will ultimately emerge. In contrast, most tangible capital assets are purchased in a completed form—ready or almost ready for use.

The fact that investments in knowledge assets are expensed when they are incurred has significant implications for the financial statements. For instance, matching is violated as a major cost associated with earning revenues isn't being matched to the revenue it helps generate. For example, a pharmaceutical company will expense all expenditures in developing a new drug. By the time the new drug has been developed, tested, and approved by Health Canada and other regulators around the world, many years will have passed. When the drug finally makes it to market, most of the costs incurred to develop it have been expensed. What does profit mean if many of the costs incurred to earn the revenues aren't reported in the period the revenues are recognized? Clearly, net income won't be the performance measure we typically think it is. This is similar to expensing the cost of a retailer's inventory when it's purchased rather than when it's sold.

Many financial ratios are adversely affected by the accounting treatment used for knowledge assets. Gross margin, profit margin, return on assets (net income ÷ total assets), return on equity (net income ÷ shareholders' equity), and many others are distorted as a result of the accounting used for intangibles. Research has shown that return on assets and return on equity would both tend to be higher if knowledge assets were capitalized.

Let's look at Research In Motion Limited's (RIM) spending on research and development (R&D) to get an idea of the magnitude of the issue. RIM is the designer and maker of the BlackBerry wireless device. In the year ended February 28, 2009 RIM spent $684,702,000 on research and development, representing 36.2 percent of net income for the year and 6.2 percent of revenue. (RIM spent $359,828,000 and $236,173,000 in 2008 and 2007 respectively on R&D.) These investments develop the products and technologies of the future, but the amounts are being expensed as incurred, not when the products are ultimately sold. If RIM's investment in R&D has future benefit, there is a clear and significant mismatching of revenues and expenses

FIGURE 8.11	R&D Spending by Canadian Companies				
	Net income (000s)	Revenues (000s)	R&D expense (000s)	R&D as a percentage of net income	R&D as a percentage of revenue
Research In Motion Limited*	$1,892,616	$11,065,186	$ 684,702	36.2%	6.2%
Magna International Inc.*	663,000	26,067,000	675,000	101.8	2.6
BCE	3,926,000	17,866,000	1,260,000	32.1	7.1
Biovail Corporation*	195,539	842,818	118,117	60.4	14.0

*U.S. dollars.

resulting in net income and assets being lower than they should be. If the $1,339,590,000 that RIM spent on research and expensed in 2006 through 2009 had been capitalized instead of expensed, total assets and net income would have been significantly higher than reported. For example, if RIM capitalized its R&D spending and amortized it over three years, net income in fiscal 2009 would have been about $249 million or 13 percent higher. Figure 8.11 provides information on the amount and impact of R&D spending by four Canadian companies. Notice the significant impact that R&D spending has on net income.

Another way to consider assets missing from the balance sheet is to compare the book value of the equity of a company (the amount in the equity section of its balance sheet) and the market value of its equity (the price on the stock market of the company's shares times the number of shares outstanding). On December 31, 2008, the book value of Google Inc.'s equity was US$28,238,862,000 whereas the market value of equity was US$96,952,969,903 ($307.65 per share times 315,140,484 shares outstanding). The huge $69 billion difference between the book value and market value of equity is at least in part due to the fact that Google's balance sheet doesn't report the full value of many of its intangible assets, such as its technology. Another example: Coca-Cola is one of the best-known brand names in the world, yet if you examine its balance sheet there is no mention of this valuable asset. On December 31, 2008, the book value of Coca-Cola's shareholders' equity was US$20.472 billion whereas the market value of its equity was almost US$105 billion, a difference of over $84 billion. A large measure of this difference is likely due to the missing value of the Coca-Cola brand name.

Goodwill

Most intangible or knowledge assets, regardless of how they are accounted for, can be identified. An entity will own a patent, a copyright, a franchise, a licence, and so on. Goodwill, probably the most commonly seen intangible asset on balance sheets, is different: it doesn't really represent anything in particular. To understand this point, we need to understand how goodwill arises.

Goodwill arises when one company purchases all or a majority of the shares of another company and pays more for it than the fair value of the assets and liabilities of the purchased company. The purchaser must determine the market value of each asset and liability on the purchase date. **Goodwill** is the amount paid over and above the fair market value (fair value) of the purchased entity's identifiable assets and liabilities on the date of purchase. That is,

Goodwill = Purchase price − Fair value of identifiable assets and liabilities purchased

Identifiable assets and liabilities are tangible and intangible assets and liabilities that can be specifically identified. Identifiable assets include cash, inventory, land, buildings, patents, copyrights, and research and development.

For example, assume that Rushoon Inc. (Rushoon) purchased 100 percent of the outstanding shares of Molanosa Ltd. (Molanosa) for $12,000,000. The fair of Molanosa's identifiable net assets (assets − liabilities) on the date of the purchase was $10,500,000. The goodwill that arose as a result of the purchase of Molanosa's shares by Rushoon is

$$\begin{aligned} \text{Goodwill} &= \text{Purchase price} - \text{Fair value of identifiable net assets} \\ &= \$12{,}000{,}000 - \$10{,}500{,}000 \\ &= \$1{,}500{,}000 \end{aligned}$$

Why would Rushoon pay $1,500,000 more than the fair value of the Molanosa's identifiable net assets? What does the goodwill actually represent? Well, it's hard to be sure because goodwill is a residual—the amount left over after the identifiable net assets have been valued. It's assumed that if a purchaser paid more than the fair value of the identifiable assets and liabilities for a company, the extra amount paid is for something of value, even if it isn't clear exactly what. Goodwill is often attributed to things such as management ability, location, synergies created by the acquisition, customer loyalty, reputation, and benefits associated with the elimination of a competitor—all things that should lead to higher profits but are very difficult to specifically identify and measure. Of course, it's also possible the buyer paid too much. However, it would probably be imprudent for a manager to admit that too soon after the purchase!

It's interesting to note that assets such as management skill, location, reputation, and so on that are considered goodwill all existed before a company is purchased. However, internally generated goodwill never appears on the balance sheet. Goodwill is recognized only when one company purchases another. Because of conservatism, reliability, and measurement issues, the costs of generating goodwill internally are expensed when incurred.

IFRS say that goodwill isn't amortized. Instead, management must estimate the fair value of the goodwill each year to determine if it's impaired. If the fair value is less than the carrying amount, the goodwill must be written down to its fair value. The writedown amount is expensed in the income statement in the year. IFRS provide guidelines for estimating the fair value of goodwill. However, because of its nature, the estimate is very subjective and requires judgment, so management has considerable leeway in deciding the timing and amount of any writedown.

Goodwill can represent a significant proportion of a company's assets. Return to Table 8.2 and notice that goodwill represented over 39 percent of Corus Entertainment Inc.'s assets and over 14 percent of BCE's assets. Goodwill on the balance sheet doesn't tell stakeholders very much. It provides information about the amount that was spent for an investment, but nothing about what the goodwill represents, or if it represents anything at all. Stakeholders can only speculate as to whether it represents a wise expenditure of company resources.

? QUESTION FOR CONSIDERATION

Why is it difficult to say for sure what goodwill is? Do you think goodwill meets the definition of an asset under IFRS? (See Chapter 2 for the criteria for an asset.)

Solution: It's difficult to say for sure what goodwill is because it's a residual—the amount left over after identifiable assets and liabilities have had fair values assigned to them. Therefore, it's not possible to determine what the goodwill reported on the balance sheet represents. Also, other than faith in IFRS's requirement to estimate the fair value of goodwill, it isn't possible to know whether an entity's goodwill really has any future benefit because it's hard to assess future benefit if you don't know what it is you are assessing.

In Chapter 2 the following criteria for an asset were identified:
- Provide a future benefit to the entity that it's probable the entity will enjoy.
- Be controlled by the entity that will obtain the benefits.
- Be the result of a transaction or event that has already occurred.
- Be measurable.

The first and fourth criteria pose the biggest problems. If we don't really know what goodwill is, how can we be reasonably sure there is a future benefit and reasonably measure it? The second criterion is met since the buying entity controls the company that was purchased so it will control the goodwill. The third criterion is met because goodwill is recorded only when another company is purchased. Goodwill is measurable when it's purchased, although very imprecisely since the goodwill itself isn't measured—it's the portion of the purchase price not assigned to specific assets and liabilities. One can question whether the cost of goodwill can actually be determined.

SALE OF CAPITAL ASSETS

In Chapter 4 we discussed the gains and losses that arise on the sale of capital assets. When an entity sells an asset not usually sold in the ordinary course of its business for an amount that's different from its carrying amount, a gain or a loss arises. In Chapter 4 the examples were limited to situations where land, an asset that isn't depreciated, was sold. In this section, we look at depreciable assets.

When a depreciable asset is sold, the cost of the asset and its accumulated depreciation must both be removed from the books. A gain or loss arises when the asset is sold for an amount that is different from its carrying amount. If the amount received is greater than the carrying amount, a gain is recorded. If the amount received is less than the carrying amount, there is a loss.

Let's look at an example. At the beginning of 2008, Ycliff Inc. (Ycliff) purchased equipment for $1,200,000. Management estimated the equipment would have a residual value of $200,000 and useful life of 10 years. Ycliff depreciated the equipment on a straight-line basis. At the end of 2014 the carrying amount of the asset was $500,000:

Cost	$1,200,000
Accumulated depreciation	
([$1,200,000 − $200,000] ÷ 10 × 7 years)	700,000
Carrying amount	$ 500,000

In 2015, one-quarter of the way through the year, Ycliff sold the equipment for $400,000 in cash. Since the sale occurred one-quarter of the way into 2015, a depreciation expense of $25,000 is necessary for 2015. (The depreciation expense to the date of sale of the asset is required at the time of sale. Otherwise, the depreciation expense will be understated and the gain or loss on sale will be misstated.)

Dr. Depreciation expense (expense +, shareholders' equity −)	25,000	
Cr. Accumulated depreciation (contra-assets +)		25,000

To record the part-year depreciation expense for equipment sold during 2015
([($1,200,000 − 200,000) ÷ 10] × 0.25)

On the date of the sale, accumulated depreciation on the equipment was $725,000 ($700,000 + $25,000) and the carrying amount was $475,000 ($1,200,000 − $725,000). The journal entry to record the sale is as follows:

Dr. Cash (asset +)	400,000	
Dr. Accumulated depreciation (contra-asset −)	725,000	
Dr. Loss on sale of equipment		
(income statement −, shareholders' equity −)	75,000	
Cr. Equipment (asset −)		1,200,000

To record the sale of equipment at a loss

The journal entry removes the cost of $1,200,000 and the accumulated depreciation of $725,000 from the books. The gain or loss is equal to the proceeds from the sale of the asset, less its carrying amount. In the example,

Proceeds from sale	$400,000
− Carrying amount	− 475,000 ($1,200,000 − $725,000)
Loss	($ 75,000)

In this scenario, there is a loss because the sale proceeds are less than the carrying amount. It's interesting that the amount of gain or loss on the sale of a capital asset is simply a function of how the asset is accounted for. We should assume that the selling price of a capital asset is fixed—that is, the amount a buyer pays for the asset isn't affected by its carrying amount. The amount of gain or loss is determined by the carrying amount, which was determined by the amount capitalized for the asset in the first place and the amount of depreciation that has accumulated over its life.

EXHIBIT 8.3

North American Palladium Ltd.: Presentation of a Loss on Disposal of Capital Assets

North American Palladium Ltd.
Consolidated Statements of Operations, Comprehensive Loss and Deficit
(expressed in thousands of Canadian dollars, except share and per share amounts)

Year ended December 31	2008	2007	2006
Revenue – before pricing adjustments	$ 148,428	$ 201,367	$ 145,819
Pricing adjustments:			
Commodities	(38,633)	8,756	11,674
Foreign exchange	15,696	(14,191)	1,707
Revenue – after pricing adjustments – Note 18	125,491	195,932	159,200
Operating expenses			
Production costs	115,037	124,921	112,458
Inventory pricing adjustment – Note 4	3,875	144	–
Smelter treatment, refining and freight costs	19,325	22,444	15,438
Amortization – Note 6(b)	36,026	46,908	30,103
Asset impairment charge – Note 6(c)	90,000	–	–
Insurance recovery – Note 14	(13,800)	–	–
Loss on disposal of equipment	2,466	–	194
Asset retirement costs	321	1,010	554
Total operating expenses	253,250	195,427	158,747
Income (loss) from mining operations	(127,759)	505	453
Other expenses			
General and administration	7,666	7,773	6,734
Exploration	23,070	12,138	11,831
Interest and other financing costs – Note 19	3,443	18,633	15,647
Foreign exchange loss (gain)	971	(8,422)	1,759
Investing Activities			
Additions to mining interests	(40,691)	(15,346)	(19,384)
Proceeds on disposal of mining interests	302	–	–
	(40,389)	(15,346)	(19,384)

Consolidated Statements of Cash Flows
(expressed in thousands of Canadian dollars)

Year ended December 31	2008	2007	2006
Investing Activities			
Additions to mining interests	(40,691)	(15,346)	(19,384)
Proceeds on disposal of mining interests	302	–	–
	(40,389)	(15,346)	(19,384)

www.napalladium.com

If, for example, Ycliff depreciated the equipment over 12 years instead of ten, the carrying amount of the equipment would have been $595,833 ($1,200,000 − {[($1,200,000 − $200,000) ÷ 12] × 7.25}) and the loss would have been $195,833 ($400,000 − $595,833). Any changes affecting the carrying amount of an asset will change the amount of gain or loss reported (assuming the selling price is a constant). In some cases, a manager's decision to sell an asset may be affected by the amount of any gain or loss. For example, if an entity requires higher net income to meet the requirements of a loan covenant, the manager may be unwilling to sell a capital asset at a loss or may sell one to generate a gain.

Exhibit 8.3 shows the financial statement presentation of a loss on the disposal of capital assets. In 2008, North American Palladium Inc. (Palladium), which explores and mines for platinum group metals, reported a loss of $2,466,000 on the disposal of equipment.[4] The equipment was sold for $302,000 (see the investing section of Palladium's statements of cash flow in Exhibit 8.3). The separate disclosure (rather than including the amount in revenue or other production costs) is important because it allows stakeholders to see the impact of transactions that aren't a main part of the company's business.

www.mcgrawhill
connect.ca

KNOWLEDGE CHECK

Suppose that in the Ycliff example the company had sold the equipment for $750,000 instead of $400,000.

☐ How much depreciation would be recorded on the asset for 2015?

☐ What would be the gain or loss that Ycliff would report for the sale of the equipment in 2015?

☐ Prepare the journal entry required to record the sale.

IMPAIRMENT OF CAPITAL ASSETS

Sometimes the value of capital assets becomes impaired. Impairment means that the carrying amount of a capital asset is greater than its future benefits. Examples of impaired capital assets include a building destroyed by fire, a plant that is no longer productive, and reductions in the earnings expected from a mine. When capital assets become impaired they should be written down to their fair value. A writedown reduces the carrying amount of the capital asset and reduces income.

According to IFRS, a capital asset is impaired if its recoverable amount is less than its carrying amount. **Recoverable amount** is the greater of the net realizable value (NRV) less cost to sell and value-in-use (defined as the present value of the asset's future cash flows). If an asset is impaired, the amount of the writedown equals

Carrying amount − Recoverable amount

Under IFRS, writedowns of capital assets can be reversed if the recoverable amount increases in a later period, except for writedowns of goodwill.

Note that capital assets aren't evaluated for impairment in the same way as inventory, which uses the lower of cost and market rule. For inventory, cost is compared with NRV at the end of each period, and if NRV is less than cost, the inventory must be written down. The assessment of capital assets takes a longer-term perspective—cash flows over the entire life of an asset are considered, not a short-term measure of market value. A short-term decline in NRV or a short-term reduction in net cash flows isn't enough to trigger the writedown of a capital asset.

Let's consider the example of Overflow Ltd. (Overflow), which owns a small office building. The building is recorded at its cost of $12,000,000 less accumulated depreciation of $5,000,000. In recent years the neighbourhood has deteriorated and as a result the rents Overflow can obtain have declined. Management now estimates the building will generate net cash flows with a present value of $5,000,000 (this is the value-in-use) over its remaining life. In addition, an independent real estate appraisal estimated the NRV of the building to be $2,500,000. Since the value-in-use is greater than NRV, we use the value-in-use as the recoverable amount. Since the recoverable amount is less than the carrying amount, Overflow must write down the building to its recoverable amount of $5,000,000, a writedown of $2,000,000 ($7,000,000 − $5,000,000).

Dr. Loss due to impairment of building
  (income statement −, shareholders' equity −)   2,000,000
    Cr. Accumulated depreciation (contra-asset +)   2,000,000
  To write down the building to its recoverable amount

The writedown is credited to accumulated depreciation, which decreases the carrying amount of the asset. Notice from the journal entry that cash isn't affected. A writedown decreases the carrying amount of assets, but cash isn't involved.

While the rules for determining whether a capital asset is impaired are clear, actually determining the impairment is very subjective and requires a lot of judgment in deciding the timing and amount of a writedown. For many assets the future cash flows, present value of future cash flows, and NRV are highly uncertain. There is ample evidence that managers will time writedowns of capital assets to accomplish reporting objectives.

For example, managers might write down capital assets as part of a big bath (introduced in Chapter 4) when the company is facing hard times. During a big bath assets are written down, resulting in large expenses now, but paving the way for higher earnings in the future because there will be fewer assets to depreciate (assets written off in the big bath don't have to be depreciated in the future). A company must be able to justify a big bath—assets can't be written off on the whim of management, but management can usually provide a "reasonable" justification, particularly if the company isn't performing well and with the help of conservatism.

CANADIAN GAAP FOR PRIVATE ENTERPRISES

According to Canadian GAAP for Private Enterprises, a capital asset is impaired if the undiscounted net cash flow the asset is expected to generate over its remaining life, including its residual value, is less than its carrying amount. When this condition exists, the carrying amount of the asset is compared with its net realizable value (NRV). If the NRV is greater than the carrying amount, the asset is written down to its NRV. GAAP doesn't allow writedowns to be reversed if the NRV increases in a later period.

DOES THE WAY CAPITAL ASSETS ARE ACCOUNTED FOR AFFECT THE CASH FLOW STATEMENT?

It may come as a surprise, but how certain expenditures are accounted for can affect the cash flows reported in the cash flow statement. Accounting choices don't affect the actual amount of cash entering and leaving an entity, but they can affect how cash flows are classified. An expenditure that is capitalized appears as an investing activity in the cash flow statement. If that same expenditure is expensed when incurred, it's included in cash from operations (CFO).

Suppose that in 2013, Balaclava Ltd. (Balaclava) spends $1 million in cash on the development of a new product. If the expenditure is capitalized, Balaclava records an intangible asset called new product development costs. If the company amortizes the development costs over four years there will be an annual amortization expense of $250,000 in 2013 through 2016. If instead Balaclava expenses the new product costs when incurred (the decision to capitalize or expense product development costs requires a lot of judgment) there would be an expense of $1 million in 2013.

Panel A of Table 8.4 provides summarized income statements for Balaclava Ltd. for 2013 and 2014, for both capitalizing and expensing the new product development costs. These income statements assume that revenues and expenses other than the amortization expense are cash. If the expenditure is capitalized, net income is reduced by $250,000 in 2013 through 2016, the amount of the amortization expense, because the $1,000,000 is being amortized over four years. If the product development costs are expensed when incurred, income is reduced by $1,000,000 in 2013 and there is no income statement effect in the following years.

Panel B of Table 8.4 provides summarized cash flow statements for Balaclava Ltd. for 2013 and 2014 under the two scenarios. If the $1,000,000 is capitalized, the outlay is classified as an investing activity and the $250,000 amortization expense is added back to net income in the calculation of CFO using the indirect method. If the cost is expensed in full in 2013, it's classified as CFO. (With this alternative the cost doesn't appear explicitly in the cash flow statements because it's in the calculation of net income.)

Notice how the accounting choice affects the cash flow statement. In 2013 there is a $9,000,000 overall increase in cash under both methods, but CFO is $10,000,000 when the product development costs are capitalized and $9,000,000 when they are expensed as incurred. If the costs are capitalized, investing activities are $1,000,000, whereas if the costs are expensed there are no investing activities. In 2014 CFO and investing activities are the same under both alternatives because the only financial statement impact of the new product development costs is amortization, which has no effect on cash.

Even the cash flow statement, a statement designed to neutralize the effects of accounting choices by managers, is affected by accounting choices. In evaluating CFO, a stakeholder has to consider the accounting policies used by similar companies as some will capitalize certain outlays while others will expense them, which impairs comparability.

TABLE 8.4 Balaclava Ltd.

Panel A: Summarized Income Statements

Balaclava Ltd.
Income Statement for the years ended December 31, 2013 and 2014

	December 31, 2013		December 31, 2014	
	Capitalize	Expense	Capitalize	Expense
Revenues	$25,000,000	$25,000,000	$25,000,000	$25,000,000
Expenses	15,000,000	15,000,000	15,000,000	15,000,000
Amortization of product development costs	250,000		250,000	
Product development expense		1,000,000		
Net Income	$ 9,750,000	$ 9,000,000	$ 9,750,000	$10,000,000

Panel B: Summarized Cash Flow Statements

Balaclava Ltd.
Cash Flow Statements for the Years Ended December 31, 2013 and 2014

	December 31, 2013		December 31, 2014	
	Capitalize	Expense	Capitalize	Expense
Cash Flow Operations				
Net income	$ 9,750,000	$9,000,000	$ 9,750,000	$10,000,000
Add back:				
Amortization of product development costs	250,000	0	250,000	0
Cash from operations	10,000,000	9,000,000	10,000,000	10,000,000
Investing activities:				
Product development	1,000,000	0	0	0
Increase in cash	$ 9,000,000	$9,000,000	$10,000,000	$10,000,000

INSIGHT

Why Accounting Choice?

It's difficult for accounting students to understand why there is so much choice available to managers. Accounting choice is a double-edged sword. It allows managers to present information in ways that are useful to stakeholders, but it also provides them the means to achieve their own reporting objectives. It isn't always possible for stakeholders to see how the managers are using flexible accounting rules. This is a danger stakeholders face.

The issue of dealing with accounting policy choice has no easy answer. A system that allows choice opens itself up for abuse by managers. A system with no choice reduces the likelihood for abuse but may render financial statements useless by not allowing accounting choices that reflect an entity's actual economic activity. IFRS allow a lot of choice and emphasize the exercise of judgment. Stakeholders should recognize the opportunity for abuse and use accounting information cautiously. Thus far, we have seen the effect the choice of revenue recognition method, inventory cost formula, and depreciation method, along with many estimates managers make, have on the financial statements. With these choices alone, a wide range of numbers could appear in an entity's financial statements, all representing the identical underlying economic activity.

Accounting plays a very important role in communicating information about an entity. For the efficient and effective operation of the economy, it's essential that managers and any external accountants (including auditors) behave ethically. If stakeholders can't use accounting information with confidence, the costs of doing business will increase and economic performance will decline.

FINANCIAL STATEMENT ANALYSIS ISSUES

Despite the importance of capital assets to many entities, there are limits to the insights about an entity that can be gained from analyzing historical cost information about them. First, as we discussed earlier, the usefulness of historical cost information about capital assets for many decisions is questionable. Second, even under IFRS there is extensive choice for how to account for capital assets, and how it's done significantly affects the numbers in the financial statements. The following policy and estimate choices will affect expenses, net income, assets and retained earnings, and any ratios that depend on these measures:

- what costs get capitalized
- depreciation method used
- estimates of useful life and residual value
- existence of unrecorded assets (especially intangible assets)
- impairment of capital assets

With that in mind, a ratio often used to measure the performance and operating efficiency of an entity is **return on assets (ROA)**, defined as

$$\text{Return on assets} = \frac{\text{Net income} + \text{After-tax interest expense}}{\text{Average total assets}}$$

The numerator is a measure of how the entity has performed—in this case, net income with the after-tax interest expense added back. After-tax interest expense is the cost of interest after taking into consideration the fact the government picks up part of the cost of borrowing because interest is deductible for tax purposes. That is, if an entity incurs $10,000 in interest and its tax rate is 25 percent, the actual cost of interest is $7,500 ($10,000 × [1 − tax rate] = $10,000 × [1 − 0.25]) as the entity pays $2,500 less in taxes because the interest expense is deductible. After-tax interest expense is added back so the ROA is independent of how the assets are financed. If the interest expense isn't deducted, the ROA would be affected by the amount of debt the entity had.

The denominator is the investment—in this case the entity's investment in assets. It can be expressed as average assets for the year, or year-end assets. Both the numerator and denominator introduce some problems. In addition to being affected by management's accounting choices, the ratio will also be affected by when the assets were purchased. Assets purchased at different times will have different costs. As a result, comparing the ROA of different entities must be done with a great deal of caution.

This ratio can be thought of in the same way as a bank account. The denominator—the investment or the assets invested—is the amount of money in your bank account. The numerator—the return—is the interest that the bank pays you over the year. The return on assets is the interest rate the bank account earned. If you invested $1,000 in a bank account and over the following year the bank paid you $50 in interest, your return would be 5 percent ($50 ÷ $1,000).

ROA is a measure of how efficiently an entity uses its assets to generate a profit. A company can improve its ROA in two ways: lower its asset base or increase its profits. For example, if a company is able to reduce its inventory or increase its accounts receivable turnover without affecting profits, ROA will increase. If an entity has capital assets it isn't using, selling them will increase its ROA.

As an example we'll look at WestJet Airlines Ltd. (WestJet). Relevant information from WestJet's financial statements for the period 2004 through 2008 is summarized in Table 8.5. ROA is shown in the last row:

TABLE 8.5 WestJet Airlines Ltd.: Return on Assets

	2008	2007	2006	2005	2004	2003
Net income	$178,135,000	$192,833,000	$114,676,000	$24,001,000	($17,168,000)	
Interest expense	76,078,000	75,749,000	70,196,000	55,496,000	44,109,000	
Tax expense	76,702,000	46,137,000	49,805,000	27,974,000	1,192,000	
Tax rate	30.1%	19.3%	30.3%	53.8%	−7.5%	
Total assets	$3,278,849,000	$2,984,222,000	$2,726,527,000	$2,213,092,000	$1,877,354,000	$1,476,858,000
ROA	7.39%	8.89%	6.62%	2.43%	1.80%	

The calculation of ROA for 2008 is as follows:

$$\text{Return on assets} = \frac{\text{Net income} + \text{After-tax interest expense}}{\text{Average total assets}}$$
$$= \frac{\$178,135,000 + [\$76,078,000 \times (1 - 0.301)]}{(\$3,278,849,000 + \$2,984,222,000)/2}$$
$$= \frac{\$231,313,522}{\$3,131,535,500}$$
$$= 7.39\%$$

The tax rate is calculated by dividing the tax expense by income before taxes:

$$\text{Tax rate} = \frac{\text{Tax expense}}{\text{Income before taxes (Net income} + \text{Tax expense)}}$$
$$= \frac{\$76,702,000}{\$178,135,000 + \$76,702,000}$$
$$= 30.1\%$$

TABLE 8.6	Comparison of Return on Assets for Canadian Airlines and the Transportation Industry					
	2008	**2007**	**2006**	**2005**	**2004**	**5-year average**
WestJet Airlines Ltd.	7.39%	8.89%	6.62%	2.43%	1.80%	5.43%
Transat A.T. Inc.	(3.47)	8.45	7.64	7.19	10.18	6.00
Air Canada	(6.24)	5.73	3.17	3.32		1.50
Transportation industry average	8.26	9.30	8.37	17.65	−3.51	8.01

WestJet's ROA for the period shown was low in the first two years but improved in 2006 through 2008. Comparisons can also be made with other companies. Table 8.6 shows ROA for three airlines and for a group of companies in the transportation industry (which includes airlines, railways, and shipping companies).[5]

WestJet outperformed the other airlines in 2007 and 2008 but didn't perform as well as its competitors in 2004 and 2005. WestJet didn't meet the overall industry average in four of the five years, and its five-year average is well below that of the industry and slightly below Transat's.

To illustrate the effect of policy choices on financial statement analysis, we will examine how using different depreciation methods affects two financial ratios, profit margin and ROA, for Vermilion Corp. Vermilion's financial statements are found in Table 8.3. For simplicity, we assume that Vermilion incurred no interest expense and total assets at the beginning of 2013 are $1,500,000. The two ratios are calculated using straight-line and declining balance depreciation. The results are shown in Table 8.7.

Observe how different the ratios are in each year. For example, in 2013 the profit margin with straight-line depreciation is 7.7 percent while with declining balance it's −17.1 percent. The ROA using straight-line depreciation ranges from a low of −0.7 percent to a high of 13.6 percent, while for declining balance the lowest value is −17.1 percent and the highest is 19 percent.

TABLE 8.7	Vermilion Inc.: Effect of Straight-Line and Declining Balance Depreciation Methods on Profit Margin and ROA				
		2013	**2014**	**2015**	**2016**
Profit margin	Straight line	7.7%	20.4%	21.5%	−2.7%
	Declining balance	−17.3	18.2	27.6	20.9
Return on assets	Straight line	3.4	12.6	13.6	−0.7
	Declining balance	−8.2	12.6	19.0	5.5

While the different accounting choices don't affect an entity's economic situation, ratios can paint a variety of pictures. The conclusions we draw about an entity will vary with accounting choices so we need to be aware of the impact of these. Financial analysis must be based on an understanding of the accounting choices that went into the financial statements. If comparisons are being made between entities, or for a particular entity over time, it's important to ensure that like things are being compared.

Solved Problem

This chapter's solved problem is a case analysis in an unusual setting. It gives readers an opportunity to apply the material covered thus far in the book. The case is challenging and readers should not be discouraged if they struggle in places. Take the time to do a complete and thorough analysis before reading the solution.

High-Tech Industries Inc.

High-Tech Industries Inc. (Hi-Tech) develops and manufactures highly sophisticated technical equipment for mining companies and has gained a worldwide reputation for the quality and reliability of its products. For many years, High-Tech was the only company in this market but recently a number of competitors have entered the industry. All these competitors have been supported by their national governments. In the last three years, High-Tech has seen its profits and its margins decline drastically in the face of the new competition. In its most recent fiscal year, High-Tech reported a loss of $42,000,000.

The management of High-Tech has approached government officials for financial support to "level the playing field" with its competitors. High-Tech has suggested that without adequate support it may be forced to move some or all of its operations to another country and it has asked for immediate subsidies of between $50 and $75 million.

A government committee is examining whether High-Tech should receive government funding. While the government itself and many members of the committee seem to support High-Tech, there is at least one member of the committee who strongly believes that governments should not be subsidizing private businesses. The dissenting committee member has asked you to evaluate whether High-Tech's financial information provides a reasonable picture of its financial position. Your report will be used to present the dissenting member's side of the story to the committee, so it's important that you clearly detail any problems that you identify with the accounting information. Your report should also discuss alternative treatments for the problems you identify and consider the quantitative impact of them.

The committee member has supplied you with the information in Figure 8.12.

Required:

Prepare the report requested by the dissenting committee member.

Comment: This is another user-oriented case. Your task is to assist the committee member by providing an analysis of the income statement that supports the committee member. The role requires you to identify areas where the accounting used by High-Tech doesn't reasonably indicate a need for government support. In other words, you must assess whether High-Tech's income statement is appropriate for the stated purpose.

The report should make clear that High-Tech has incentives to understate its performance and it should identify situations where High-Tech has taken advantage of accounting to make its situation look poor. The report must establish some criteria for assessing High-Tech's performance. It could be cash flow (low income doesn't necessarily mean poor liquidity or financial problems), it could be accrual income adjusted for unusual items, or some other measure of performance. Some criteria are necessary so that there is a context for interpreting financial statements.

An important aspect of this case is that IFRS (and GAAP) have no role to play. It might be necessary for High-Tech to prepare IFRS financial statements, but these statements may not provide the information needed for the intended purpose. Because of IFRS's rules, it's possible that High-Tech's income statement doesn't reasonably reflect its need for a subsidy. Remember that managers preparing the financial statements may be constrained by IFRS but stakeholders may adjust and modify financial statements to whatever form they please. If IFRS's rules don't provide information that is appropriate, then those rules shouldn't be followed. This doesn't imply a free-for-all. Any basis of accounting must be supported and supportable. Each choice must be well explained and justified so that it will be convincing to other committee members and to High-Tech's representatives.

| FIGURE 8.12 | Additional Information about High-Tech Industries Inc. |

1. High-Tech is a private company. Normally its financial statements are not publicly available, but to support its position High-Tech has provided the government committee with a summarized income statement for its 2014 fiscal year.

High-Tech Industries Inc.
Summarized Income Statement for the Year Ended October 31, 2014

Revenue		$225,000,000
Cost of sales		106,000,000
Gross margin		119,000,000
Expenses:		
Salaries and benefits	$59,000,000	
Selling, general, marketing, and administration	25,000,000	
Loss on sale of technology	22,000,000	
Research and development	40,000,000	
Depreciation and amortization	15,000,000	161,000,000
Net loss		($ 42,000,000)

2. High-Tech normally uses the percentage-of-completion method for recognizing revenue on its long-term contracts.

3. In 2014 the company entered into a large contract with an Asian company to develop a unique type of mining equipment. Work has begun on the project and it's expected to be completed in 2016. Because of economic problems in the Asian country, High-Tech will recognize revenue on a zero-profit basis for this contract. Management believes there is a higher than normal probability that the customer will be unable to pay in full for the equipment.

   The contract should generate $33,000,000 in revenue and incur estimated costs of $17,000,000. To date $6,900,000 of costs have been incurred and the customer has already made payments of $7,000,000 to High-Tech. In addition, High-Tech expensed the costs of obtaining the contract in its 2014 income statement.

4. The majority shareholder of High-Tech owns a company that provides testing and other consulting advice to High-Tech. During 2014, High-Tech paid $18,000,000 to that company.

5. In 2011 High-Tech purchased the rights to a technology developed by a British company. The technology proved not to be useful to High-Tech and in 2014 it sold those rights to another company at a loss of $22,000,000.

6. High-Tech invests heavily in research and development. These expenditures have been increasing significantly in each recent year and the trend is expected to continue. Research and development costs are expensed when they are incurred.

Solution:

Report on High-Tech Industries Inc.

I have examined the income statement and explanatory information provided by High-Tech Industries Inc. In my opinion, that statement is not appropriate for evaluating the economic condition of High-Tech for the purpose of determining whether it should receive a government subsidy.

The statement tends to understate the actual economic performance of the company because of the measurement conventions used. The statement takes a conservative approach to reporting and includes at least one item that is not representative of ongoing performance. In addition, the statement is not a good indication of whether High-Tech actually needs cash. The statement is prepared on what is known as accrual accounting, which measures economic flows rather than cash flows.

The usual basis for preparing financial statements in Canada is Canadian GAAP for Private Enterprises or IFRS, and it appears that High-Tech followed this. While IFRS provide a useful set of standards for preparing financial statements, they are not useful for all decisions in all situations. In the case of High-Tech, application of IFRS served to understate its income in the current period, as IFRS are inherently conservative. In my analysis below, I suggest treatments that may deviate from IFRS as those treatments do not give a reasonable view of the economic situation of the company. Overall, I will use accrual accounting as the basis for evaluating High-Tech's performance, although not necessarily IFRS-based accrual accounting. I think it is also important to assess High-Tech's liquidity.

My review of the statements assesses the information provided. However, there is considerable additional information that would be very useful for assessing High-Tech. Thus, my conclusions are only preliminary. Additional information that should be requested includes: comparative financial statements, cash flow statements, balance sheets, and notes to the financial statements. I have provided my analysis in the absence of a more complete set of information so you can participate in the upcoming committee meeting in an informed way.

Use of Zero-Profit Method

The impact of the zero-profit method is to reduce income by deferring profits to 2016 when the contract is completed. There is no theoretical problem with using different revenue recognition methods for different contracts, provided that the facts justify the different treatments. That is, the circumstances surrounding the contract with the Asian country must be such that the revenue or costs are difficult to reasonably estimate or collection of cash is questionable.

In this situation, it does not appear that the zero-profit method is justified. High-Tech contends that cash collection is quite uncertain, but High-Tech has already collected $7,000,000, which suggests willingness and ability to pay. Therefore, there does not seem to be good reason to deviate from the percentage-of-completion method. Since the contract spans three years, I suggest using the percentage-of-completion method and recognizing one-third of the revenue and related expenses in 2014. This treatment will add almost $6.5 million $\left(\text{[\$33,000.000} - \text{\$17,000,000]}\right.$ $\times \left.\dfrac{\$6,900,000}{\$17,000,000}\right)$ to income during the year. (The exact amount may change pending additional information on the amount of work done through the end of 2014.)

Related-Party Transactions

High-Tech does business with a company owned by it's majority shareholder. These "related-party transactions" are a concern because the shareholder could influence the terms of transactions between the companies. If the services provided have an actual market value of $18,000,000 and were required by High-Tech, then recording them at their transaction value is acceptable. However, it is impossible to determine what the market value of the services actually is. The majority shareholder is in a position to overstate the value of the services provided, with the purpose of understating High-Tech's income to make its financial situation look worse. There are no negative economic consequences to the major shareholder because she has an economic interest in both transacting entities. It is necessary to know extensive details on the services provided to High-Tech and even to confirm the actual existence of them. I recommend that these costs be completely removed from the income statement until additional information is provided. This treatment will reduce the reported loss by $18,000,000.

Loss on Sale of Purchased Technology

During 2014 High-Tech sold technology at a significant loss, which represented more than half of the reported net loss for the year. A number of issues arise from this loss:

- The loss is likely not to recur in future periods. Therefore, if everything else stayed exactly the same as this year, the loss in 2015 would be $20,000,000 instead of $42,000,000.

- The loss is an accounting loss, not a cash loss. High-Tech paid for this technology a few years ago and the sale does not leave the company out of pocket in the current period. In fact, by selling the technology it is actually $22,000,000 better off in a cash sense.

- When did the economic loss actually occur? While the loss was realized in 2014, the actual economic loss may have been suffered in a previous period, which means the loss should have been recognized earlier.

- Should taxpayers be subsidizing a company for its poor decisions?

I recommend that this loss be disregarded when evaluating the company's income statement. Instead, the analysis should focus on earnings before non-recurring items. This treatment would reduce High-Tech's loss by $22,000,000.

Research and Development Costs

Research and development (R&D) is an investment by an entity in future revenue-generating resources. Standard accounting practice (IFRS) expenses research and most development costs when they are incurred. While no one would dispute that R&D is, conceptually, an asset, the future benefits associated with these expenditures are highly uncertain, which is why they are expensed. By expensing R&D currently, High-Tech understates its current income because expenses are not being matched to the revenues they will help earn, presumably sometime in the future.

It makes better sense to capitalize the R&D costs and amortize them over some (probably short) period of time (say four years). That means that only $10,000,000 of the year's expenditures should be expensed this year. This adjustment will increase income by $30,000,000. However, for consistency, R&D expensed in previous years should be capitalized and amortized. Given that R&D spending is increasing, the net effect of these adjustments will be to increase income in the current period. However, it is not possible to state an amount that should be amortized in the current period.

Summary

Net income as reported	($42,000,000)
Add:	
Adjustment to percentage-of-completion method	5,000,000
Loss on sale of technology	22,000,000
Non-arm's-length transactions	18,000,000
Research and development costs	30,000,000
Deduct: Amortization of previous years' R&D	?
Revised net income	$33,000,000

Revised net income shows that High-Tech was profitable in 2014. Even with additional adjustments for R&D amortization and for the related-party transactions, income will likely be positive. This approach is also more representative of its ongoing economic performance.

Please contact me if you have any questions about my report and if you require assistance at the upcoming hearing.

Comment: A good analysis should have included the following:

- *effective role playing*

- *an indication of a basis for evaluating whether High-Tech should receive a subsidy*

- *a solid discussion of the accounting issues and recommendations on appropriate treatments*

- *an attempt to quantify the impact of the proposed accounting changes*

Remember that this analysis represents only one approach. Different ones are possible. The preceding problem is intended to give an idea how this case could be approached, not to serve as the definitive answer.

SUMMARY OF KEY POINTS

▶ **LO 1** Most companies using IFRS use historical cost to account for their capital assets. There are three alternatives to historical cost for valuing capital assets: net realizable value, replacement cost, and value-in-use. A main objection to these alternatives is that the measures aren't as reliable as historical cost. None of these measurement bases is ideal for all purposes. IFRS provides entities with the option of valuing certain capital assets at market value.

▶ **LO 2** The cost of an asset reported on an entity's balance sheet should include all the costs associated with purchasing the asset and getting it ready for use. Costs incurred by employees of the purchasing entity, including wages, should also be capitalized. Costs incurred to improve an existing asset should be capitalized and depreciated whereas costs incurred to maintain an asset should be expensed when incurred.

▶ **LO 3** The process of allocating the cost of a capital asset to expense over time to reflect its use is known as depreciation. IFRS say the cost of an asset, less its residual value, should be depreciated over its useful life in a "systematic" way. There are three major methods of depreciation: straight-line, accelerated, and usage-based. All of the methods result in the same amount of depreciation over the life of the asset. Only the timing of the expense is affected. Different depreciation methods don't affect an entity's cash flow, but the method used can have economic consequences because of the effect on financial statement numbers.

▶ **LO 4** Intangible assets, including knowledge assets and intellectual capital, are capital assets that have no physical substance. Most internally generated intangible assets aren't reported as assets on the balance sheet because the recognition criteria for assets aren't met. Instead, the money spent developing intangible assets is expensed when incurred. Expensing investments in knowledge assets and intellectual capital when they are incurred has significant implications for the financial statements, including violation of the matching principle, and impairs the meaningfulness of net income.

▶ **LO 5** When a depreciable asset is sold, the cost of the asset and the accumulated depreciation associated with it must be removed from the accounting records. If the proceeds received on disposal are different from the asset's carrying amount, a gain or loss is reported on the income statement. The amount of the gain or loss is a function of how the capital asset is accounted for.

   Sometimes situations arise that impair the value of capital assets. A capital asset is impaired when its recoverable amount is greater than its carrying amount. When a capital asset is impaired it must be written down to its recoverable amount. Management has considerable discretion in deciding the timing and amount of a writedown because determining the impairment is very subjective.

▶ **LO 6** How expenditures on capital assets are accounted for affects presentation of cash flows reported in the cash flow statement. Accounting choices don't affect the actual amount of cash that enters and leaves an entity, but they can affect the amount reported as cash from operations (CFO) and investing activities. If an expenditure is capitalized, the outlay is reported in the cash flow statement as an investing activity. If that same expenditure is expensed when incurred, the expenditure is included in CFO.

▶ **LO 7** Despite the importance of capital assets to many entities, there are limits to the insights about an entity that can be gained from analyzing the historical cost information about them in the financial statements. Despite the limitations, return on assets is a ratio often used to measure the performance and operating efficiency of an entity.

▶ **LO 8** (Appendix). *The Income Tax Act* (ITA) uses the term capital cost allowance (CCA) to describe depreciation for tax purposes. The mechanics of CCA are the same as they are for financial accounting—the cost of capital assets is somehow expensed over time—but the ITA is very detailed about the method and rate that must be used for each type of asset. For most assets, the ITA requires the declining balance method, though straight line is used for some assets. There is no choice or discretion available to the managers—the rules in the ITA must be followed exactly.

APPENDIX: DEPRECIATION AND TAXES

The *Income Tax Act* (ITA) is very specific about how capital assets can be depreciated for tax purposes. The ITA uses the term **capital cost allowance (CCA)** to describe depreciation for tax purposes. The mechanics of CCA are the same for tax as they are for financial accounting—the cost of capital assets is somehow expensed over time—but the ITA is very detailed about the method and rate that must be used for each type of asset. For most assets, the ITA requires the declining balance method, though straight line is required for some assets. Examples of CCA classes are provided in Figure 8.13. There is no choice or discretion available to the managers—the rules in the ITA must be followed exactly. Managers can do whatever they please for financial reporting purposes, but when the entity's income tax return is prepared, the depreciation expense in the general purpose financial statements is replaced with CCA.

FIGURE 8.13	Examples of CCA Classes and Rates	
CCA class	**Example**	**CCA rate**
Class 1	Buildings acquired after 1987.	4% declining balance
Class 7	Canoes, boats, and other vessels, including their furniture, fittings, or equipment.	15% declining balance
Class 10	Automobiles, vans, trucks, buses, computers, and system software.	30% declining balance
Class 16	Automobiles for lease or rent, taxicabs, and coin-operated video games or pinball machines.	40% declining balance

While the CCA rules would be acceptable for financial reporting purposes for many assets, in some cases they might not satisfy the IFRS requirement that depreciation must be done in a systematic way. The government might use the ITA to achieve policy objectives. For example, the government might try to encourage investment by allowing entities to expense certain assets quickly. This treatment is fine for tax purposes, but may not achieve the matching objective.

Another example is the **half-year rule**, which requires an entity to deduct for tax purposes, in the year an asset is purchased, only one-half the otherwise allowable amount of CCA. If an entity purchases a vehicle for $20,000, it should be allowed to deduct 30 percent of the cost for tax purposes, or $6,000 ($20,000 × 0.3), in the first year (vehicles are a CCA class that allows a 30 percent declining balance rate). The half-year rule requires the entity to deduct only $3,000 ($20,000 × 0.3 × 0.5). The half-year rule prevents entities from getting the full tax benefit from a new capital asset if the asset is purchased late in the year. While this treatment may satisfy the policy objectives of the government, it doesn't really satisfy some of the basic concepts of IFRS, such as matching.

 INSIGHT

It's easy to make the mistake of thinking that a depreciation policy that minimizes income for financial reporting purposes will minimize taxes. However, depreciation for financial reporting purposes is irrelevant for tax. If an entity uses different methods and rates for financial reporting than those specified in the ITA, an adjustment is required when preparing the entity's tax return. Some companies will use the CCA methods for financial reporting, especially private companies that use their financial statements mainly for tax purposes, to reduce their bookkeeping costs. The irrelevance of depreciation for tax purposes contrasts with the ITA treatment of inventory. Because the ITA doesn't specify how to account for inventory for tax purposes, the accounting method selected for the general purpose financial statements is usually used for tax purposes.

FORMULA SUMMARY

$$\text{Depreciation expense (straight line)} = \frac{\text{Cost} - \text{Estimated residual value}}{\text{Estimated useful life}}$$

$$\text{Depreciation expense (declining balance)} = \text{Carrying amount at the beginning of the period} \times \text{Rate}$$

$$\begin{array}{c}\text{Depreciation expense} \\ \text{(unit of production)}\end{array} = \frac{\text{Number of units produced in the period}}{\begin{array}{c}\text{Estimated number of units} \\ \text{produced over the asset's life}\end{array}} \times (\text{Cost} - \text{Estimated residual value})$$

$$\text{Goodwill} = \text{Purchase price} - \text{Fair value of identifiable assets and liabilities purchased}$$

$$\text{Return on assets} = \frac{\text{Net income} + \text{After-tax interest expense}}{\text{Average total assets}}$$

$$\text{Tax rate} = \frac{\text{Tax expense}}{\text{Income before taxes (Net income} + \text{Tax expense)}}$$

KEY TERMS

accelerated depreciation, p. 422

amortization, p. 418

betterment, p. 416

capital asset, p. 412

capital cost allowance, p. 449

capitalize, p. 413

componentization, p. 418

declining balance, p. 422

depletion, p. 418

depreciable amount, p. 421

depreciation, p. 418

entity-specific value, p. 414

goodwill, p. 434

half-year rule, p. 449

identifiable assets and liabilities, p. 434

intangible asset, p. 412

maintenance, p. 416

recoverable amount, p. 438

repair, p. 416

residual value, p. 418

return on assets (ROA), p. 441

straight-line depreciation, p. 421

tangible asset, p. 412

unit-of-production depreciation, p. 423

value-in-use, p. 414

SIMILAR TERMS

The left column gives alternative terms that are sometimes used for the accounting terms introduced in this chapter, which are listed in the right column.

fixed asset, long-lived asset   **capital asset, p. 412**

knowledge asset, intellectual capital   **intangible asset, p. 412**

diminishing balance   **declining balance, p. 422**

entity-specific value   **value-in-use, p. 414**

ASSIGNMENT MATERIALS

Questions

Q8-1. Describe the types of capital assets you would expect each of the following entities to have:

    a. grocery store   b. university
    c. fast food restaurant   d. bank branch
    e. car dealership   f. arena

Q8-2. What is an intangible asset? How do intangible assets differ from tangible ones? Give examples of each.

Q8-3. Why do intangible assets often not appear on the balance sheet? Under what circumstances will intangible assets be reported on the balance sheet?

Q8-4. What is goodwill? How does it arise?

Q8-5. Why are capital assets depreciated?

Q8-6. What characteristics distinguish capital assets from inventory?

Q8-7. What effect does depreciation have on an entity's cash flow? Why is depreciation added back to net income when the indirect method of calculating cash from operations is used?

Q8-8. Academic research has shown that the stock price of a public company isn't affected by the depreciation method an entity uses. Why do you think this is the case? Does the depreciation method an entity uses ever matter? Explain.

Q8-9. Why is the depreciation of the cost of an asset considered arbitrary?

Q8-10. Why is the selection of a depreciation method not a concern if tax minimization is the main objective of financial reporting?

Q8-11. Why is accounting for knowledge assets and intellectual capital such a difficult problem under IFRS?

Q8-12. To make room for new equipment that it was installing, Sandwich Inc. had to knock down a wall. The cost of knocking down the wall was $32,000. While the installation was in progress another wall was accidentally knocked down. The cost of replacing that wall was $44,000. Which, if any, of these costs should be capitalized? Explain.

Q8-13. Explain why repairs are expensed whereas betterments are capitalized.

Q8-14. An uncle of yours explains that depreciation is important because it ensures that money is set aside for replacing the capital assets that are being used up. What is your response to your uncle?

Q8-15. What effect does a writedown of capital assets have on cash flow? Explain.

Q8-16. What is a writedown of a capital asset? Why are writedowns required? How does the approach to writing down capital assets differ from the approach used for writing down inventory?

Q8-17. For each business identified below, explain how the capital asset contributes to generating revenue by the business:

Business	Asset
a. house painting	ladders
b. bank	banking machine
c. shopping centre	parking lot
d. bowling alley	bowling pins
e. restaurant	tables and chairs
f. auto parts manufacturer	fork lift

Q8-18. Why does judgment by the managers who prepare financial statements play such an important role in determining an entity's depreciation expense? Be specific.

Q8-19. You are the accountant for a restaurant. The restaurant has recently started a home delivery service and purchased a car to make deliveries. You have to prepare the year-end financial statements for the restaurant and have to decide how to depreciate the car. What useful life and residual value would you assign to the car? Explain your decision fully and discuss the factors you considered. Assume the restaurant prepares its financial statements in accordance with IFRS. The car cost $24,000.

Q8-20. Explain how accounting policies can affect the cash from operations an entity reports when we know that different accounting policies have no effect on cash flow.

Q8-21. Explain the following bases for valuing capital assets. Provide examples of how each might provide useful information to a user:
a. historical cost
b. replacement cost
c. net realizable value
d. value-in-use

Q8-22. Company A owns a world-renowned trademark, but it doesn't appear on its balance sheet. Company B owns a world-renowned trademark, which is valued on the company's balance sheet at $125,000,000. Explain why this difference might arise.

Q8-23. Wisdom Inc. tries to use very conservative accounting methods. For example, it tends to make conservative estimates of the useful lives of capital assets (shorter lives rather than longer ones) and residual value (lower estimates of residual value).
a. What is the impact of these conservative accounting policies on income? Explain.
b. How could these conservative policies have unconservative effects when Wisdom Inc. disposes of capital assets? Explain.

Q8-24. What is capital cost allowance? How does capital cost allowance differ from depreciation for financial reporting purposes?

Q8-25. Define and explain the use of the following terms. Provide examples of when each would be used:
a. amortization
b. depreciation
c. depletion

Q8-26. Is it possible for an entity to use a capital asset that is completely depreciated? Explain. What would be the carrying amount of such an asset?

Q8-27. Esk Ltd. (Esk) recently purchased a fully equipped restaurant at an auction for $500,000. The restaurant included all the equipment, furniture, and fixtures. The building itself is rented. Now Esk must allocate the purchase price to the items purchased. Explain how Esk should allocate the purchase price to the specific items. Why is it necessary for the purchase price to be allocated to the specific items? What motivations might influence the allocations that Esk makes?

Exercises

E8-1. **(Accounting for acquisition costs, LO 2)** A restaurant purchases some used kitchen equipment. For each of the following, explain whether the expenditure would be capitalized or expensed:
a. The equipment cost $58,000, plus $2,900 in GST. $30,000 was paid in cash with the remainder due in 90 days.
b. Some of the equipment required repairs before it could be used. The repairs cost $9,200.

c. Soon after the equipment was delivered, some was damaged because some kitchen staff didn't know how to use it properly. Additional repairs costing $2,000 were required.

d. The restaurant had to hire people to help rearrange the kitchen so the new equipment would fit. The work cost $2,500.

E8-2. **(Straight-line depreciation, LO 2, 3, 5)** Roxana Inc. (Roxana) recently purchased a new stamping machine for its workshop. The cost of the machine included cost, $225,000; taxes, $28,000; delivery, $12,000; installation, $5,000; and testing, $22,000. Roxanna's management expects to use the machine for eight years, at which time it will be replaced. Management uses straight-line depreciation on assets of this type and estimates the machine has a residual value of $25,000.

Required:

a. Prepare the journal entry to record the purchase of the new machine.

b. Prepare a depreciation schedule showing the depreciation expense for each of the eight years Roxana expects to keep the machine and the carrying amount of the machine at the end of each year. Assume that the machine was purchased midway through the fiscal year and only a half-year's depreciation is to be expensed in the first year.

c. Suppose the machine sold at the end of the third year for $75,000. Prepare the journal entry to record the sale and any other journal entries required with respect to the display cases in the third year.

E8-3. **(Accelerated depreciation, LO 2, 3, 5)** Examine the information provide in E8-2 and respond to parts (a), (b), and (c) assuming Roxanna will use declining balance depreciation at a rate of 40 percent for the stamping machine.

E8-4. **(Accelerated depreciation, LO 2, 3, 5)** In early 2014, Jupitagon Ltd. (Jupitagon) purchased new computer equipment. Jupitagon does cutting-edge graphic design work and requires highly sophisticated computer hardware and software. The new equipment cost $320,000 plus $38,400 in sales taxes, $25,000 for installation, $20,000 for training employees, and $45,000 for a three-year service contract on the equipment. In addition, the company spent $50,000 to prepare a room to house the equipment.

Jupitagon's management expects to be able to use the computer equipment for about five years, although with the passage of time the equipment will likely be less useful for more sophisticated work because better equipment becomes available very quickly. Accordingly, management has decided to depreciate the equipment using the declining-balance method at a rate of 40 percent per year. Management estimates the equipment's residual value to be $30,000 and its useful life five years.

Required:

a. Prepare the journal entry to record the purchase of the new equipment.

b. Prepare a depreciation schedule showing the depreciation expense for each of the five years Jupitagon expects to use the computer equipment and the carrying amount of the equipment at the end of each year.

c. Suppose the computer equipment was sold at the end of 2016 for $75,000. Prepare the journal entry to record the sale and any other journal entries required with respect to the computer equipment in 2016. Assume that year-end adjusting entries had not been made when the sale occurred.

E8-5. **(Straight-line depreciation, LO 2, 3, 6)** Examine the information provide in E8-4 and respond to parts (a), (b), and (c) assuming that Jupitagon Ltd. will use straight-line depreciation for the computer equipment.

E8-6. **(Unit-of-production depreciation, LO 2, 3, 6)** Grindstone Corp. (Grindstone) produces fad toys for children. In 2014, Grindstone purchased a new stamping machine to produce the latest fad toy. The machine cost $100,000 plus taxes of $13,000, and delivery and installation of $12,000. Grindstone's management estimates that the market for the toy is about 600,000 units and demand will last no more than three years.

Management expects that it will be able to produce and sell 320,000 units in 2014, 210,000 units in 2015, and 70,000 units in 2016. Once the fad dies, the machine won't be useful for any purpose and will have to be sold for scrap, about $4,000. Grindstone will use unit-of-production depreciation for the machine.

Required:

   a. Prepare the journal entry to record the purchase of the new machine.

   b. Prepare a depreciation schedule showing the depreciation expense for each year and the carrying amount of the machine at the end of each year.

   c. Suppose that at the end of 2015, Grindstone's management realized the fad had died more quickly than expected and there was no more demand for the toy. Prepare the journal entry to record the sale and any other journal entries required with respect to the machine in 2015. Assume that Grindstone produced and sold 75,000 units in 2015 and received $2,000 from a scrap dealer for the machine.

E8-7. **(Straight-line depreciation, LO 2, 3, 5)** Examine the information provide in E8-6 and respond assuming that Grindstone will use straight-line depreciation for the machine.

E8-8. **(Accelerated depreciation, LO 2, 3, 5)** Examine the information provide in E8-6 and respond assuming that Grindstone will use declining balance depreciation at a rate of 50 percent for the machine. Evaluate the appropriateness of the rate Grindstone will use to depreciate the machine.

E8-9. **(Accounting for a basket purchase, LO 2)** In January 2015, Bath Inc. (Bath) purchased an office building on a one hectare piece of land in Saskatoon for $6,000,000. An appraiser valued the land at $1,375,000. The building is eight years old and Bath's management expects it to last for another 12 years, after which time it will have to be demolished. Management has decided to use straight-line depreciation.

Required:

Prepare the journal entries that Bath would make to record the purchase of the land and building. What entry would be made to record the depreciation expense for the year ended December 31, 2015?

E8-10. **(Determining the gain or loss on the sale of land, LO 5)** In 2010 Chin Corp. purchased a piece of land for $4,500,000. In 2015 the land was sold for $3,000,000.

Required:

Prepare the journal entries necessary to record the purchase and sale of Chin Corp's land.

E8-11. **(Determining the gains or loss on the sale of capital assets, LO 5)** For each of the following situations, calculate any gain or loss that would arise on the sale of the asset and prepare the journal entries that would be required at the time of the sale. Assume that in each case the assets were depreciated on a straight-line basis and that a full year's depreciation was expensed in the year the asset was purchased. All sale transactions occur in the fiscal year ended December 31, 2014.

   a. Machinery purchased in 2006 for $96,000 is sold on June 30, 2014 for $21,000. When the machinery was acquired it was estimated to have a 12-year life and residual value of $12,000.

   b. A building purchased in 2004 for $12,000,000 is sold on April 30, 2014 for $9,000,000. When the building was purchased it was estimated to have a 20-year life and a residual value of $1,000,000.

   c. Office furniture purchased in 2011 for $24,000 is sold on December 31, 2014 for $8,000. When the furniture was purchased it was estimated to have a five-year life and a residual value of $4,000.

E8-12. **(Classifying capital assets, LO 4)** Indicate whether the following assets would be considered tangible or intangible. Explain your reason for the classification.
   a. Exclusive licence to use a professional sport's team's logo on certain clothing items
   b. Clothing designs
   c. Clothing manufactured using the designs
   d. Equipment used to manufacture clothing
   e. Patent for a process to water proof clothing
   f. Chemicals used to waterproof clothing

E8-13. **(Calculation of goodwill, LO 4)** On December 31, 2015, Resolute Inc. (Resolute) purchased 100 percent of the common shares of Uno Ltd. (Uno) for $32,000,000. At the time of the purchase, Resolute's management made the following estimates of the fair values of Uno's assets and liabilities:

Assets	$47,000,000
Liabilities	18,000,000

Required:

Calculate the amount of goodwill that Resolute would report on its December 31, 2015 consolidated balance sheet as a result of its purchase of Uno.

E8-14. **(Calculate the amount of goodwill, LO 4)** On April 15, 2014, Cashtown Inc. (Cashtown) purchased 100 percent of the common shares of Shakespeare Ltd. (Shakespeare) for $48,000,000. At the time of the purchase, Cashtown's management made the following estimates of the fair values of Shakespeare's assets and liabilities:

Current assets	$21,000,000
Tangible capital assets	49,000,000
Patents	11,500,000
Current liabilities	13,250,000
Long-term debt	29,750,000

Required:

   a. Calculate the amount of goodwill that Cashtown recorded when it purchased Shakespeare on April 15, 2014.
   b. In fiscal 2018, management determined that the goodwill associated with the purchase of Shakespeare was impaired and that it should be written down to $2,500,000. Prepare the journal entry that Cashtown would make to record the impairment of the goodwill. What amount would be reported on the fiscal 2018 balance sheet for goodwill and what expense would be reported in the income statement?

E8-15. **(Calculation of gains and losses on sale of capital assets, LO 3, 5)** On July 4, 2013, Vroomanton Inc. (Vroomanton) purchased new equipment for its print shop. Vroomanton's accountant determined that the capital cost of the equipment was $240,000. The accountant also estimated that the useful life of the equipment would be six years and the residual value $18,000. Assume that Vroomanton took a full year of depreciation for the equipment in the year ended June 30, 2014.

Required:

   a. Prepare a depreciation schedule for the new equipment, assuming the use of straight-line depreciation. Set up your depreciation schedule like Figure 8.6 in the chapter.
   b. Prepare a depreciation schedule for the new equipment assuming the use of declining-balance depreciation using a depreciation rate of 40 percent. Set up your depreciation schedule like Figure 8.7 in the chapter.

c. Assume that on June 30, 2017, after the depreciation expense had been recorded for the year, Vroomanton sold the equipment for $33,000. Prepare the journal entry that is required to record the sale assuming that
   i. The depreciation schedule in (a) was used.
   ii. The depreciation schedule in (b) was used.
d. Explain the reason for the different income statement effects for the journal entries you recorded in (c).

E8-16.   **(Preparing depreciation schedules, LO 3)** In July 2014, Savory Inc. (Savory) purchased new equipment for $450,000. Savory's management estimates that the equipment's useful life will be five years and that its residual value will be $45,000. Savory's year-end is June 30.

Required:

a. Prepare a depreciation schedule for each year of the new piece of equipment's life using
   i.   straight-line depreciation
   ii. declining balance depreciation (35 percent)
   iii. unit-of-production method

   Your depreciation schedule should show the depreciation expense for each year and the carrying amount of the equipment and accumulated depreciation at the end of each year. For the unit-of-production method, assume that 15 percent of the production is produced in fiscal 2014 and 2015, 20 percent in 2016, and 25 percent in 2017 and 2018.
b. Which method do you think Savory's managers would prefer if they have a bonus based on the company's net income? Explain.

E8-17.   **(Repairs and maintenance, or betterments, LO 2)** For each of the following independent items, indicate whether the expenditure should be capitalized or expensed. Provide your reasoning.
a. An apartment building improves the insulation in the roof and walls to decrease heat loss.
b. Potholes in the parking lot of a shopping mall are patched.
c. The floor of a workshop is reinforced so that it can support heavier equipment.
d. The walls of accounting firm are painted.
e. The carpets in a law office are cleaned.
f. The equipment in a factory is inspected, cleaned, and lubricated.
g. Staff is sent on a training program to develop their customer service skills.
h. Refrigeration equipment at a hockey arena is replaced with a new, more efficient unit.
i. The damaged engine of a delivery truck is replaced with an identical used engine purchased from a parts dealer.

E8-18.   **(Choosing a depreciation period, LO 3)** Wandby Inc. (Wandby) owns a building on land it leases from a local municipality. The 28-year land lease was part of an arrangement signed in 1999 that allowed Wandby to operate a business that employed local people without having to incur the cost of buying land. Wanby's building was constructed in 2000 and was expected to have a life of 25 years. In the current year, 2014, Wandby added an extension to the building. The extension cost $1.5 million and the builder said it should be usable for 20 to 25 years. Wandby's management has stated that it has no plans to renew the land lease and will not continue the business beyond the lease period. The lease agreement requires that Wandby return the land to the condition it was in at the inception of the lease (before 1999 the land was a park).

Required:

How should Wandby depreciate the extension (method, useful life, and residual value)? Explain your answer fully.

E8-19. **(Determine the cost of a capital asset, LO 2)** The Smooth Rock Falls Resort (Smooth) is a luxury hotel and spa in Atlantic Canada. Recently, Smooth built a new restaurant on its grounds. The new restaurant is an expansion of the existing main building and was built by Holyrood Construction Inc. (Holyrood). The following costs were incurred to build the restaurant:

a. Building permits	$ 2,000
b. Design costs	48,000
c. Redesign costs required to make changes that Smooth wanted after construction began	5,000
d. Cost of digging the foundation	35,000
e. Cost to remove and reconstruct the wall of the existing building where the new restaurant will be attached	26,000
f. Amount paid to Holyrood for construction of the restaurant	350,000
g. Damage and repairs to an adjacent property caused when heavy equipment was brought onto the site to do the excavation	22,000
h Cost of meals served to workers	2,000
i. Penalties paid to Holyrood because Smooth didn't want construction to be done on certain regular working days	9,000
j. Special electrical wiring for the sound system	15,000

Required:

Determine the amount that should be capitalized as part of the cost of the restaurant. Explain your reasoning for including or excluding each item in the capitalized cost.

E8-20. **(Effect of transactions and economic events on ratios, LO 4, 5, 7)** Complete the table below by indicating whether the transactions or economic events would increase, decrease, or have no effect on the financial ratios listed in the period they occur. Assume the current ratio is greater than 1.0 before considering each of the situations.

	Return on assets	Profit margin percentage	Current ratio	Debt-to-equity ratio	Gross margin percentage
a. Writedown of a machine.					
b. Reduce the estimated life of a building by five years.					
c. Expense R&D costs. Costs were incurred in cash.					
d. Capitalize development costs. Costs were incurred in cash and depreciation will begin in a future period.					

E8-21. **(Effect of transactions and economic events on ratios, LO 4, 5, 7)** Complete the table below by indicating whether the transactions or economic events would increase, decrease, or have no effect on the financial ratios listed in the period they occur. Assume the current ratio is greater than 1.0 before considering each of the situations.

	Return on assets	Profit margin percentage	Current ratio	Debt-to-equity ratio	Gross margin percentage
a. Sale of a building. The buyer promises to pay in full in three years. The carrying amount of the building is less than the selling price.					
b. A company following IFRS owns a factory with a carrying amount of $25 million. The value-in-use of the factory is estimated to be $37 million and the NRV less cost to sell is $21 million.					
c. An intangible asset was acquired for cash and it was determined that no factors limit its useful life.					
d. A company that follows IFRS decides that it will account for its land at market. It determines that the value of its land has increased from $1 million to $4 million.					

E8-22. **(Effect of transactions and economic events on accounting measures, LO 4, 5, 6, 7)** Complete the following table by indicating whether the transactions or economic events would increase, decrease, or have no effect on the financial ratios listed in the period they occur.

	Net income	Gross margin	Total assets	Owners' equity	Cash from operations	Cash from (used in) investing activities	Total cash flow
a. Writedown of equipment.							
b. Sell a building for cash. The carrying amount of the building is greater than the selling price.							
c. Increase the estimated useful life of equipment by two years.							
d. Expense R&D costs. Costs were incurred in cash.							
e. Capitalize R&D costs. Costs were incurred in cash and depreciation will begin in a future period.							

E8-23. (**Evaluating the effect of the sale of a capital asset, LO 5, 6**) In 2010, Triangle Corporation purchased a piece of heavy equipment for $725,000. The equipment was estimated to have an eight-year life and it was depreciated on a straight-line basis. In 2014 (after four years of depreciation was recorded) the equipment was sold for $300,000 in cash. What journal entry would be made to record the sale of the equipment? How would the sale be reflected in the cash flow statement? Would there be any effect on the calculation of cash from operations?

E8-24. (**Impact of capital asset transactions on the cash flow statement, LO 6**) For each of the following items, indicate whether it would appear on the cash flow statement as cash from operations, an investing cash flow, or a financing cash flow, or that it would not have an effect on cash flows:
a. Loss on the sale of furniture and fixtures
b. Purchase equipment in exchange for a long-term note payable
c. Purchase of a patent for cash
d. Depreciation expense
e. Proceeds from the sale of land
f. Research costs
g. Writedown of equipment
h. Capitalization of development costs

E8-25. (**CCA versus depreciation, LO 8, Appendix**) On January 3, 2014, Goglin Inc. (Goglin) purchased a corporate aircraft to transport executives to the company's construction projects across the county. The aircraft cost $2,225,000, which was capitalized for accounting and tax purposes. Goglin's aircraft is classified as class 9, which has a CCA rate of 25 percent declining balance. Goglin's year-end is December 31.

Required:

a. What is the maximum amount of CCA that could be claimed for tax purposes in 2014? Explain.
b. What is the maximum amount of CCA that could be claimed for tax purposes in 2015? Explain.
c. If Goglin decides to depreciate the equipment on a straight-line basis over 15 years, what would the depreciation expense be in 2014?
d. How does the useful life estimated by Goglin's management affect the amount of CCA that can be claimed? Explain.
e. Why are the amounts calculated in (a) and (c) likely different? Explain.

E8-26. (**Revaluing capital assets to market LO 3**) Maniwaki Ltd. (Maniwaki) is a small public company located in eastern Canada. Maniwaki's management has decided to report its land and building at market as allowed by IFRS for its December 31, 2015 year-end. The land was acquired 20 years ago for $1,000,000. The building was built eight years ago at a cost of $7,500,000. The building is being depreciated over 20 years on a straight-line basis with a residual value of zero. A recent appraisal valued the land at $3,500,000 and the building $6,500,000. Assume that Maniwaki's net income for 2015 was $4,750,600 and common shares and retained earnings on December 31, 2015 were $8,000,000 and $14,000,000 respectively.

Required:

a. What amount would Maniwaki report on its December 31, 2015 balance sheet for land and building if it carries them at market value?
b. If Maniwaki uses the proportional method to present is capital assets what would be the balance in the accumulated depreciation account for the building on December 31, 2015?
c. How would the change in the value of the land and building be reported in the income statement and balance sheet in 2015?
d. What do you think are the benefits and problems for stakeholders of a company reporting its capital assets at market value?

Problems

P8-1. **(Interpreting a writedown, LO 4, 5, 7)** Fiscal 2014 was an outstanding year for Esterhazy Inc. (Esterhazy). For a variety of reasons, the company's sales surged and net income was going to exceed financial analysts' expectations by more than 20 percent or $13,000,000. Esterhazy's management recognized that the high earnings for the year were due to some unusual business circumstances and weren't likely to be repeated in the foreseeable future.

Before finalizing its financial statements, Esterhazy's management evaluated the company's assets and determined that several were overvalued. As a result, Esterhazy's assets were written down by a total of $12,000,000 so that the assets wouldn't be overstated on the balance sheet. All of the assets written down were being depreciated and their remaining useful lives ranged between five and eight years. Esterhazy is a public company that is traded on a Canadian stock exchange.

Required:

a. Explain the effect of the writedown on the 2014 financial statements as well as the implications for subsequent years' financial statements.
b. Explain how users of the financial statements would be affected by the writedown and how the financial statements should be interpreted as a result of recording the writedown.
c. Why do you think Esterhazy chose to write down the assets?
d. Does it matter that Esterhazy wrote down these assets? Explain.

P8-2. **(Interpreting a writedown, LO 4, 5, 7)** In fiscal 2014, Plumas Technologies Inc. (Plumas) purchased a company that owned a technology Plumas believed was extremely valuable for its future success. Plumas paid $900,000,000 for the company. Among the assets that Plumas obtained by purchasing the company was "technologies under development" that Plumas estimated to have a fair value of $350,000,000. This means that Plumas estimated that the technologies under development would generate net revenues of at least $350,000,000.

Plumas decided to expense the technologies under development in full in fiscal 2014. As an alternative, Plumas could have treated the technologies under development as an asset and amortized them over 10 years. Plumas is a public company that is traded on a Canadian stock exchange.

Required:

Explain the effect on the current year's financial statements, as well as the implications for future years' financial statements, of fully expensing the technologies under development. Also, explain how users of the financial statements would be affected by how Plumas accounted for the acquired technologies and how the financial statements should be interpreted as a result of how the acquired technologies were accounted for. Why do you think Plumas chose to account for the technologies in the way it did?

P8-3. **(Determining cost, LO 2)** Mr. Bogan operates a dairy farm in Québec. Recently, one of his cows gave birth to a female calf that will eventually join the dairy herd that produces the milk Mr. Bogan sells. When the calf was born, Mr. Bogan had the veterinarian check the calf. At first the calf drinks its mother's milk, but later it will graze on grass in the pasture. During the winter, the calf will eat hay that Mr. Bogan grows on another part of his farm. Eventually the calf will be a milk-producing cow.

Required:

a. How would you report the dairy herd on Mr. Bogan's farm's balance sheet? Explain.
b. What cost will appear on the farm's balance sheet for the new calf when she is old enough to produce milk? Explain.

c. From what you've learned about accounting for capital assets, what are the problems that exist for accounting for the dairy herd and the new calf? How would you recommend the herd and new calf be accounted for? Consider this question from the point of view of a banker and a prospective buyer of the farm.

P8-4.   (**Repairs, maintenance, and betterments, LO 2**) In March 2010, Hazlet Inc. (Hazlet) purchased a storage building for $760,000. The building was estimated to have a useful life of 10 years and no residual value. In April 2016, Hazlet paid $280,000 to reinforce the building. By doing so, Hazlet extended its life by five years. In July 2016, part of the floor collapsed and had to be replaced to make the building usable. The work cost $25,000. Hazlet's year-end is February 28.

Required:

a. Provide the journal entry to record the purchase of the building in March 2010.
b. How would you account for the reinforcement done on the building in April 2016? Explain your reasoning.
c. How would you account for the work done in July 2016? Explain.
d. What effect would the events in (b) and (c) have on Hazlet's depreciation expense?
e. What would be the depreciation expense in each year of the equipments life, assuming that Hazlet uses straight-line depreciation?

P8-5.   (**Calculate missing information, LO 2, 3, 5**) Use the following information and determine the carrying amount of the property, plant, and equipment of June Inc. (June) on September 30, 2015, the company's year-end. (An accounting equation spreadsheet, journal entries, or T-accounts may help you answer this question.)
   i.   On October 1, 2014, the cost of June's property, plant, and equipment was $4,750,000 and the accumulated depreciation was $1,450,500.
   ii. During fiscal 2015, June sold equipment with a cost of $365,000 at a loss of $90,000. June received $105,000 in cash.
   iii. During fiscal 2015, June sold land for $417,500 cash, which generated a gain for accounting purposes of $120,000.
   iv. During fiscal 2015, property, plant, and equipment was purchased for $210,000 cash, plus a long-term note payable of $155,000.
   v.   During fiscal 2015, June wrote down equipment by $112,000.
   vi. June recorded a depreciation expense of $725,000 for fiscal 2015.

P8-6.   (**Calculate missing information, LO 2, 3, 5**) Use the following information and determine the carrying amount of the property, plant, and equipment of Ziska Ltd. (Ziska) on July 1, 2014, the first day of its 2015 fiscal year. (An accounting equation spreadsheet, journal entries, or T-accounts may help you answer this question. *Hint:* You are calculating the account balance at the beginning of the year.)
   i.   On June 30, 2015, the cost of Ziska's property, plant, and equipment was $550,000 and the accumulated depreciation was $175,000.
   ii. During fiscal 2015, Ziska purchased property, plant, and equipment for $127,000 in cash plus $50,000 in notes payable.
   iii. During fiscal 2015, Ziska sold property, plant, and equipment for $50,000. The property, plant, and equipment had accumulated depreciation of $175,000 and Ziska recognized a gain of $35,000.
   iv. During fiscal 2015, Ziska sold land for $68,000 cash, which produced a loss of $12,000.
   v.   During fiscal 2015, Ziska wrote down property, plant, and equipment by $22,000.
   vi. Ziska recorded a depreciation expense of $66,000.

P8-7.   (**Comparing income statements, LO 2, 3, 7**) You have been provided with the following financial statements of two companies Aguanish Ltd. (Aguanish) and Lanigan Inc. (Lanigan).

	Aguanish Ltd. Income statement for the year ended December 31, 2014	Lanigan Inc. Income statement for the year ended December 31, 2014
Sales	$1,275,000	$1,275,000
Cost of sales	465,000	465,000
Selling, general, and administrative expenses	375,000	375,000
Depreciation expense	210,000	325,000
Interest expense	52,000	52,000
Income tax expense	51,000	51,000
Net income	$ 122,000	$ 7,000

The two companies are identical in every respect, except for how they account for their capital assets. Aguanish depreciates its assets on a straight-line basis while Lanigan depreciates its assets using the declining balance method.

Required:

a. Examine the financial statements of the two companies. Which would be a better investment? Explain.

b. Why do you think the two companies would use different depreciation methods?

c. Does it matter that the companies use different depreciation methods? Explain.

P8-8. (**Effect of capitalizing versus expensing R&D costs, LO 3, 4, 6, 7**) Utopia Inc. (Utopia) is a biotechnology company located in Montréal. Utopia has successfully marketed a number of products since it went public three years ago. Biotechnology is a highly competitive industry and a company's decline in the marketplace is no further away than a competitor's dramatic scientific breakthrough. To remain competitive, companies must invest heavily in research and development to ensure they have a pipeline of new medicines to bring to market.

Utopia prepares its financial statements in accordance with IFRS, so it expenses all research costs and any development costs that don't meet the criteria for capitalization. To date, none of Utopia's development costs have met the criteria for capitalization. The following information has been summarized from Utopia's financial statements:

Utopia Inc. Extracts from Financial Statements					
	2016	2015	2014	2013	2012
Summarized from the income statement					
Revenue	$3,984,750	$2,488,750	$1,677,500	$467,500	$ 13,750
Expenses*	1,793,000	1,194,600	855,250	552,750	412,500
R&D expenditures	2,475,000	1,925,000	1,100,000	412,500	275,000
Net loss	(283,250)	(630,850)	(277,750)	(497,750)	(673,750)
Summarized from the balance sheet					
Total assets	6,943,750	6,179,250	5,802,500	1,787,500	770,000
Total liabilities	2,708,063	2,224,530	2,030,875	750,750	346,500
Total shareholders' equity	4,235,687	3,954,720	3,771,625	1,036,750	423,500
Summarized from the cash flow statement					
Cash from operations	343,750	(495,000)	(225,500)	(385,000)	(825,000)
Cash expended on investing activities	(550,275)	(679,250)	(2,942,500)	(962,500)	(522,500)

*Includes all expenses incurred by Utopia except for research and development.

Required:

    a. Recalculate net income for 2014 through 2016 assuming that R&D costs were capitalized and expensed over three years using straight-line amortization.

    b. What would total assets be at the end of 2014 through 2016 if R&D costs were capitalized and amortized over three years?

    c. What would shareholders' equity be at the end of 2014 through 2016 if R&D costs were capitalized and amortized over three years?

    d. What would cash from operations and cash expended on investing activities be if R&D costs were capitalized and amortized over three years?

    e. What would the following ratios be assuming that (1) R&D costs were expensed as incurred and (2) R&D costs were capitalized and amortized over three years? Assume that Utopia didn't have an interest expense over the period 2012–2016.

       i.   return on assets

      ii. debt-to-equity ratio

     iii. profit margin percentage

    f. How would your interpretation of Utopia differ depending on how R&D costs are accounted for? Which accounting approach do you think is more appropriate? Explain. Your answer should consider the objectives of the stakeholders and the managers who prepare the accounting information, as well as the accounting concepts discussed throughout the book.

P8-9. **(Effect of capitalizing versus expensing R&D costs, LO 3, 4, 6, 7)** Florze Software Inc. (Florze) is a software development company located in Kanata, Ontario. Software is a highly competitive industry and the life of a software product is usually quite short. To remain competitive, companies must invest heavily in research and development to keep their existing products up to date and to develop new ones. Florze expenses all research costs and any development costs that don't meet the criteria for capitalization. Florze has never capitalized any development costs. The following information has been summarized from Florze's financial statements:

Florze Software Inc. Extracts from Financial Statements					
	2017	**2016**	**2015**	**2014**	**2013**
Summarized from the income statement					
Revenue	$4,491,900	$2,805,500	$1,891,000	$ 527,000	$ 449,500
Expenses*	2,052,975	1,631,375	1,402,750	1,061,750	1,042,375
R&D expenditures	1,743,750	1,356,250	775,000	290,625	193,750
Net income (loss)	695,175	(182,125)	(286,750)	(825,375)	(786,625)
Summarized from the balance sheet					
Total assets	4,892,188	4,353,563	4,088,125	1,259,375	542,500
Total liabilities	2,005,798	1,523,748	1,226,438	365,219	135,625
Total shareholders' equity	2,886,390	2,829,815	2,861,687	894,156	406,875
Summarized from the cash flow statement					
Cash from operations	232,500	(387,500)	(116,250)	(542,500)	(1,162,500)
Cash expended on investing activities	(697,500)	(542,500)	(2,712,500)	(775,000)	(441,750)

*Includes all expenses incurred by Florze except for research and development.

Required:

    a. Recalculate net income for 2015 through 2017, assuming that R&D costs were capitalized and amortized over three years using straight-line amortization.

    b. What would total assets be at the end of 2015 through 2017 if R&D costs were capitalized and amortized over three years?

c. What would shareholders' equity be at the end of 2015 through 2017 if R&D costs were capitalized and amortized over three years?

d. What would cash from operations and cash expended on investing activities be for 2015 through 2017 if R&D costs were capitalized and amortized over three years?

e. What would the following ratios be assuming that (1) R&D costs were expensed as incurred and (2) R&D costs were capitalized and expensed over three years? Assume that Florze didn't have an interest expense over the period 2013–2017.
    i.   return on assets
    ii. debt-to-equity ratio
    iii. profit margin percentage

f. How would your interpretation of Florze differ depending on how R&D costs are accounted for? Which accounting approach do you think is more appropriate? Explain. Your answer should consider the objectives of the stakeholders and the managers who prepare the accounting information, as well as the accounting concepts discussed throughout the book.

P8-10. (**Recommending a depreciation policy, LO 2, 3, 7**) Early in 2013, Mr. Peribonka purchased a machine for $100,000 to produce a new gadget he designed. Mr. Peribonka invested $70,000 of his own money to buy the machine and borrowed the remainder from the bank. Mr. Peribonka figures the machine will last five years after which it will be worthless. He has sold 30,000 gadgets this year and thinks he can sell 75,000 in 2014; 110,000 in 2015 and 2016; and 40,000 in 2017.

Mr. Peribonka needs to prepare financial statements for the year ended December 31, 2013. He needs the statements for tax purposes, the bank, and for his own information. He has most of the information put together but he isn't sure what to do about depreciation and has come to you for advice.

Required:

Provide the advice Mr. Peribonka has requested. Explain in detail your thinking, your alternatives, and your recommendations.

P8-11. (**Impaired asset, LO 3, 5**) In January 2010, Coaticook Inc. (Coaticook) purchased a patent for a pharmaceutical designed to help bald people to grow hair. The drug behind the patent was considered revolutionary at the time and Coaticook's management thought that purchasing the patent would provide it with a product that would reinvigorate sales and the company's stock price. Coaticook purchased the patent for $125 million. At the time of the purchase, the patent had 10 years left before it expired and it was being amortized on a straight-line basis. At purchase, management estimated the patent would generate an average of $22 million in net revenue (revenue less the cost of producing and selling the drug) per year over its remaining life. In 2010 and 2011, net revenues significantly exceeded expectations, but in mid-2012 a competing product came to market that was more effective than Coaticook's product, with fewer side effects. As a result, management slashed its estimate of the net revenues by 50 percent. A present value analysis of the estimated future cash flows produced an estimated fair value of the product in mid-2012 of $42 million. Management thinks it might be able to sell the patent for about $7 million.

Required:

Coaticook's management has approached you for advice on how it should account for, if at all, the change in market conditions for its product. Management would like you to fully explain your reasoning and to provide any journal entries required to deal with the problem. They would also like your opinion on what effect this information will have on the company's stock price and on its performance for the year.

P8-12. (**Effect of a recording error on the financial statements, LO 2, 3, 6, 7**) In 2011, Zumbro Ltd. (Zumbro) purchased a forklift for $28,000. In error, Zumbro's bookkeeper recorded the purchase as an expense rather than classifying it as an asset. The error went unnoticed until late in 2014, when the forklift was sold for $6,000 and no record could be found of it in the accounts.

Required:

a. Show the entry that Zumbro's bookkeeper made to record the purchase of forklift. Show the entry that should have been made.

b. Zumbro uses straight-line depreciation for its vehicles and the useful life assigned to forklifts is five years with a $5,000 residual value. What would have been the effect of the error on net income and total assets (amount and direction of the error) in 2011, 2012, and 2013?

c. What would be the effect of the error on net income and total assets (amount and direction of the error) in 2014, the year the forklift was sold?

d. What would be the effect of the error on the cash flow statement in each of years 2011 through 2014?

e. Assuming the error is material, what would the implications of this error be for users of the financial statements? Explain.

P8-13. **(Effect of a recording error on the financial statements, LO 2, 3, 6, 7)** Sifton Financial Ltd. (Sifton) is a small financial institution operating in western Canada. In 2014, Sifton purchased a new computer system for its head office for $1,120,000 (including installation), all of which was capitalized. The system is being depreciated on a declining balance basis at 25 percent per year. Because of errors made by Sifton's management, significant changes had to be made to the wiring in the building and to the special room housing the system. The extra work added $275,000 to the cost of the system and is included in the $1,120,000 cost.

Required:

a. How should the cost of the extra work be accounted for? Explain.

b. What would be the effect of capitalizing the cost of the extra work instead of expensing it on net income and total assets (amount and direction of the error) in 2014, 2015, and 2016? Explain your reasoning.

c. What would be the effect of capitalizing the cost of the extra work instead of expensing it on the cash flow statement in each of years 2014 through 2016?

d. Assuming the effect is material, what would be the implications of capitalizing the cost of the extra work instead of expensing it for users of the financial statements? Explain.

P8-14. **(Effect of accounting on business decisions, LO 5, 7)** Judge Ltd. (Judge) operates a small chain of auto supply shops. The company has been in business for many years and for most of that time it was owned and operated by the Judge family. In recent years Judge has been in financial difficulty and management has been turned over to a team of professional managers. The managers own 10 percent of Judge's shares and the Judge family owns the remainder. Judge has agreed to a number of strict accounting-based covenants with its creditors, including that Judge's debt-to-equity ratio not go above 1.5:1 at the end of any quarter over the term of either its bank loan or long-term debt. If the covenant is violated, all loans become payable in full in 30 days.

Judge owns a piece of land and a building that was one of its shops but hasn't been used for four years. The building is in very poor condition and isn't in a very good part of town. Judge hasn't been able to find a tenant or a buyer in over two years. The land and building have a carrying amount of $3,370,000 and Judge has now received an offer of $2,000,000 for them. The offer is attractive, especially because it would provide some urgently needed cash. The offer expires on June 30, 2015, the last day of Judge's fiscal year, and it's not likely to be renewed.

It's now June 27, 2015. Judge's management estimates that net income for the year will be about $450,000. Management also projects that on June 30, 2015 current liabilities will be $1,150,000 and long-term debt will be $3,350,000. Capital stock on June 30, 2015 will be $1,600,000 and retained earnings on June 30, 2014 was $1,450,000.

You have been asked by Judge's president to prepare a report discussing all the business and accounting issues relevant to the land and building.

Required:

Prepare the report requested by Judge's president.

P8-15. **(Effect of accounting on business decisions, LO 2, 3, 5)** Togo Ltd. (Togo) and Fairfax Inc. (Fairfax) are small property development companies. Ms. Bessnerdium owns 60 percent of the shares of each company and the rest are owned by separate consortiums of investors in the cities where the companies own properties. Togo owns several small apartment buildings in Ottawa and Fairfax owns a number of apartments in Windsor. Recently, Togo and Fairfax traded buildings. Fairfax received from Togo a building that had a cost of $3,765,000 and accumulated depreciation of $1,950,000, and Togo received from Fairfax a building that had a cost of $4,720,000 and accumulated depreciation $1,425,000. Both buildings were appraised by independent appraisers, who estimated that the market value of each building was between $9,500,000 and $10,500,000.

Required:

a. Prepare the journal entries that Fairfax and Togo would have to make to record the exchange of the buildings.
b. What would be the effect of the exchange on each company's financial statements in the year of the exchange? Explain.
c. What would be the effect of the exchange on each company's financial statements in the year following the transactions? Explain.
d. Why do you think Fairfax and Togo entered into the exchange?
e. Do you think the accounting treatments you prescribed in (a) make sense? Provide arguments to support and oppose the accounting treatment you prescribed.
f. If you were responsible for setting accounting standards, how would you require companies in the situation of Fairfax and Togo to account for these transactions? Explain your reasoning.

P8-16. **(Basket purchase, LO 2, 3, 8)** Quabbin Corp. (Quabbin) is a small manufacturing company in Regina. It's owned by five shareholders, two of whom manage the company. The other three are silent investors who invested when the company was struggling financially. Quabbin has significant borrowings from the bank and it anticipates it will have to request a large increase in its line of credit in the next few months.

Recently, Quabbin purchased some land, a building, and a number of pieces of used equipment from a bankrupt company. The total cost of the bundle of goods was $7,500,000. For accounting purposes Quabbin estimates the building will last about 15 years and the equipment should last about seven years. It's expected that neither the building nor the equipment will have any residual value. For tax purposes, CCA on the building can be charged at 4 percent per year on a declining balance basis. CCA on the equipment is 30 percent per year, declining balance. CCA can't be claimed on land.

The land, building, and equipment were appraised by Quabbin to ensure it was getting a good deal. The land was appraised at between $1,600,000 and $2,500,000, the building at between $2,950,000 and $3,450,000, and the equipment at between $2,000,000 and $2,750,000.

You have been asked for advice by Quabbin's controller about how to account for the purchase. The controller has requested that you explain your recommendation fully so that he can in turn explain the situation to the managers. Your report should also provide the journal entry that Quabbin would make to record its purchase.

Required:

Prepare the report.

P8-17. (**Preparing depreciation schedules, LO 2, 3, 4, 5**) In July 2013, Yreka Platinum Mines Inc. (Yreka), a public company, began operation of its new platinum mine. Geologists estimate that the mine contains about 825,000 ounces of platinum. Yreka incurred the following capital costs in starting up the mine:

Exploration and development	$225,000,000
Mine extraction equipment	115,000,000
Buildings	35,000,000

The exploration and development costs were incurred to find the mine and prepare it for operations. The extraction equipment should be useful for the entire life of the mine and could be sold for $10,500,000 when the mine is exhausted in 10 years. The buildings are expected to last much longer than the life of the mine, but they will not be useful once the mine is shut down. The production engineers estimate the following year-by-year production for the mine:

2014	45,000 oz.
2015	90,000
2016–2021	100,000
2022	75,000
2023	15,000

Yreka's year-end is June 30.

Required:

a. Show the journal entries necessary to record the purchase of the extraction equipment and the construction of the buildings.

b. Prepare depreciation schedules using the straight-line, declining balance (20 percent per year), and unit-of-production methods for the three types of capital costs.

c. Which method would you recommend that Yreka use to depreciate its capital assets? Explain. Do you think the same method should be used for each type of capital asset? Explain.

d. The mine is viable as long as the cash cost of extracting the platinum remains below the price Yreka can obtain for its platinum. If the price falls below the cash cost of extraction, it may be necessary to close the mine temporarily until prices rise. What would be the effect on depreciation if the mine were temporarily shut down?

e. Under some circumstances it may become necessary to shut the mine permanently. How would you account for the capital assets if the mine had to be shut down permanently? Show the journal entries you would make in regard to the capital assets in this event. State any assumptions you make.

P8-18. **(Observing the effects of accounting choices on the cash flow statement, LO 4, 6)**
Barkway Inc. (Barkway) is in the process of finalizing its cash flow statement for 2014. The statement has been completely prepared except for the new product development costs that the controller hasn't decided how to account for. Preliminary net income, *before* accounting for the development costs, is $325,000. The product development costs for the year are $375,000. Based on the controller's interpretation of the relevant accounting standards, an argument could be made for either capitalizing the costs or expensing them. Barkway's preliminary cash flow statement is shown below (the product development costs aren't reflected in the cash flow statement):

Barkway Inc. Cash Flow Statement for the Year Ended August 31, 2014	
Cash from operations	
Net income	$
Add: Depreciation	208,125
Add: Net decrease in non-cash working capital	147,875
Add: Loss on sale of capital assets	118,125
Cash from operations	
Investing activities	
Proceeds from the sale of capital assets	275,625
Purchase of capital assets	(551,250)
Cash from (used for) investing activities	
Financing activities	
Increase in long-term debt	421,875
Repayment of mortgage loan	(140,625)
Dividends	(56,250)
Cash from (used for) financing activities	
Change in cash during 2014	
Cash and equivalents, beginning of the year	123,750
Cash and equivalents, end of the year	

Required:

a. Complete the cash flow statement (shaded boxes) assuming that
   i. the new product development costs are capitalized and depreciated
   ii. the new product development costs are expensed as incurred
   Assume that if the product development costs are capitalized it isn't necessary to depreciate any of the costs in 2014.
b. Compare the two cash flow statements. How is your evaluation of Barkway influenced by them?
c. How are the balance sheet and income statement affected by the different accounting treatments for the new product development costs?
d. If Barkway's management received bonuses based on net income, which treatment for the product development costs do you think they would prefer? Explain.

P8-19. **(Observing the effects of accounting choices on the cash flow statement, LO 4, 6)** Juskatla Ltd. (Juskatla) is in the process of finalizing its cash flow statement for 2015. The statement has been completely prepared except for some costs that the controller isn't sure whether to classify as repairs or betterments. Normally relatively minor, this year these costs were significant and the classification will have an impact on the financial statements. The preliminary net loss, *before* accounting for the repairs/betterments, is $125,000. The repair/betterment costs for the year are $225,000. The nature of the costs is ambiguous so the controller will likely be able to classify them as either repairs or betterments. The costs aren't reflected in the preliminary cash flow statement shown below:

Juskatla Ltd. Cash Flow Statement for the Year Ended April 30, 2015	
Cash from operations	
Net loss	$
Add: Depreciation	330,000
Less: Gain on sale of capital assets	47,500
Less: Net increase in non-cash working capital	110,000
Cash from operations	
Investing activities	
Proceeds from the sale of capital assets	202,000
Purchase of capital assets	(862,000)
Cash from (used for) investing activities	
Financing activities	
Increase in long-term debt	650,000
Repayment of long-term loan	(487,000)
Sale of common stock	682,000
Cash from (used for) financing activities	
Change in cash during 2015	
Cash and equivalents, beginning of the year	200,000
Cash and equivalents, end of the year	$

Required:

a. Complete the cash flow statement (shaded boxes) assuming that
   i. the costs are treated as betterments
   ii. the costs are treated as repairs
   Assume that if the costs are treated as betterments, it will be necessary to depreciate $30,000 in 2015.

b. Compare the two cash flow statements. How is your evaluation of Juskatla influenced by them?

c. How are the balance sheet and income statement affected by the different accounting treatments for the repairs/betterments?

d. Assuming that the controller is correct in her belief that the costs can be reasonably classified as either repairs or betterments, what factors would you advise the controller to consider in making her decision? Explain.

P8-20. **(Understanding the relationship between the balance sheet and the cash flow statement, LO 2, 6)** Albanel Ltd. (Albanel) is a manufacturing company. On December 31, 2013, Albanel reported property, plant, and equipment, net of accumulated depreciation, of $4,750,000. Below is Albanel's cash flow statement for the year ended December 31, 2014.

Albanel Ltd.	
Cash Flow Statement for the Year Ended December 31, 2014	
Net income	$275,000
Depreciation expense	310,000
Gain on sale of land	(75,000)
Gain on sale of equipment	(32,000)
Loss on sale of building	110,000
Increase in non-cash working capital	(70,000)
	518,000
Investing Activities	
Purchase of land and building	(487,000)
Purchase of equipment	(315,000)
Proceeds from sale of building	780,000
Proceeds from sale of land	225,000
Proceeds from sale of equipment	100,000
	303,000
Financing Activities	
Repayment of long-term debt	(800,000)
Increase in cash during the year	21,000
Cash at beginning year	82,000
Cash at end of year	$103,000

Required:

a. What were the carrying amounts of the property, plant, and equipment Albanel sold during 2014?

b. What amount would Albanel report for property, plant, and equipment, net of accumulated depreciation, on its December 31, 2014, balance sheet?

P8-21. **(Evaluating and interpreting the effects of a writedown, LO 4, 5)** Mildmay Ltd. (ML) is a public company that manufactures machine parts. In its most recent financial statements, ML wrote down $131,000,000 of its assets, which it will continue to use. The new president and CEO of ML announced that the writedowns were the result of competitive pressures and poor performance of the company in the last year. They were reported separately in ML's income statement as a "non-recurring" item—ones that "result from transactions or events that aren't expected to occur frequently over several years, or don't typify normal business activities of the entity." Mildmay doesn't include the writeoff in its calculation of operating income.

ML's summarized income statement for the year ended December 31, 2014, is (amounts in millions of dollars):

Revenue		$469
Operating expenses		
Cost of goods sold	$353	
Depreciation	65	
Selling, general, and administrative costs	62	480
Operating income		(11)
Other expenses		
Non-recurring item	131	
Interest expense	25	
Income tax expense	(40)	116
Net income		($127)

The writedowns will reduce the depreciation expense by $16,500,000 per year for each of the next eight years. After the announcement and release of the income statement, analysts revised their forecasts of earnings for the next three years to

Year ended December 31, 2015	$11,000,000
December 31, 2016	35,000,000
December 31, 2017	71,000,000

Required:

a. What would net income be in each of 2014 through 2017 had ML not written off the assets and continued to depreciate them? Assume that the operations of ML don't change regardless of the accounting method used.
b. Why do you think the new management might have made the decision to write off the assets?
c. As an investor trying to evaluate the performance and predict future profitability, what problems do asset writedowns of this type create for you? Consider how the writeoff is reflected in the income statement and use the ML case as a basis for your discussion.

P8-22. (**Case analysis, uses concepts from the book so far**) Wanda's Fashions is a small tailor's shop located in the centre of a medium-sized community. The shop is owned and operated by Wanda who alters clothing, tailors clothing to the specification of customers, and carries a line of ready-made clothing that she designs and makes herself. Wanda also makes all the uniforms worn by the employees of her brother Wendel's businesses. Wanda has been in business for over 20 years and has a list of over 200 people who use her services regularly, both for tailoring new clothes and for repairing and altering clothes.

The store owns several sewing machines, pressing equipment, mannequins, and furniture and fixtures in the showroom portion of the store. There is also a large sign in front of the store. All capital assets are depreciated using the rates required by the *Income Tax Act*. Wanda has a large quantity of fabrics in stock so she can provide selection to customers who wish to have clothes made for them.

Wanda operates the store on her own. She has two tailors who work for her part-time, based on how busy she is. Her children, Wendy and Webster, sometimes work in the store when it's busy. Webster also helps his mother do alterations and some of the tailoring. The children aren't paid for their work but Wanda pays for their university tuition fees and last year bought them a car.

The shop is located in a three-storey building owned by Wanda and her husband Willie. In addition to Wanda's shop, the building houses three other storefront businesses (a fruit store, a butcher shop, and a video store) and has two businesses and three apartments on the second floor. Each of the tenants (except Wanda's Fashions) pays a monthly rent. Wanda, Willie, and their children live on the third floor of the building.

Wanda and Willie prepare a single set of financial statements for tax purposes. The statements encompass all income and expenses generated by the business activities (all of which are unincorporated), including Wanda's Fashions, building operations, and some of Willie's unincorporated business ventures.

Wolfgang Wondergarment has expressed interest in purchasing Wanda's shop. Wolfgang is an experienced tailor who arrived in Canada three years ago. He has been working as a tailor for a major chain but he feels he is ready to have his own business. He will be meeting with Wanda next week to discuss the sale. Wanda has indicated that she will provide any information that is required.

Required:

Wolfgang Wondergarment has asked you for help in preparing for the meeting. Wolfgang would like a report outlining the information that should be requested from Wanda, including questions and concerns he should have about the financial statements that Wanda will show him. Wolfgang believes that Wanda's accountant (actually her cousin Wesley) will be present, so Wolfgang wants full explanations of what is needed and why it's required.

Using Financial Statements

ROGERS COMMUNICATIONS INC.

◇ROGERS™

Rogers Communications Inc. (Rogers) is a major Canadian communications and media company with three primary lines of business. Rogers Wireless is a wireless voice and data communications services provider. Rogers Cable offers cable television, high-speed Internet, and telephone services for residential and business customers, and operates a retail distribution chain offering Rogers branded wireless and home entertainment products and services. Rogers Media controls broadcast, specialty print, and online media assets with businesses in radio and television broadcasting, televised shopping, magazine and trade journal publication, and sports entertainment.[6]

Rogers' statements of income and extracts from the balance sheets, statements of cash flows, and notes to the financial statements are provided in Exhibit 8.4.[7] Use this information to respond to questions FS8-1 to FS8-11.

FS8-1. Find or determine the following from the information provided about Rogers:
   a. What amount of property, plant, and equipment does Rogers report on its December 31, 2008 balance sheet?
   b. What amount of goodwill does Rogers report on this balance sheet?
   c. What amount of plant and equipment was written down during fiscal 2008?
   d. What amount did Rogers expense for depreciation and amortization during 2008?
   e. What is the cost and carrying amount (net book value) value of Rogers' network equipment on December 31, 2008?
   f. Over what period is Rogers depreciating its computer equipment and software?
   g. How much cash did Rogers spend on the purchase of property, plant, and equipment in 2008?
   h. Over what period is Rogers amortizing the Fido brand name?
   i. What amount of its broadcast licences did Rogers write down in 2008?
   j. How much was Rogers' amortization expense for brand names, subscriber bases, baseball player contracts, roaming agreements, dealer networks, wholesale agreements, and marketing agreements in 2008?

FS8-2. What was Rogers' net income for fiscal 2008? What was its cash from operations (CFO)? How do you explain the large difference between the net loss and CFO? Based on your assessment of net income and CFO, did Rogers have a good year or a bad year in 2008? Based on the information provided, are you concerned about Rogers' liquidity position? Explain.

FS8-3. What amount of property, plant, and equipment does Rogers report on its December 31, 2008 balance sheet? What does the amount on the balance sheet represent (how would you explain what the amount means to a novice user of financial statements)? What proportion of Rogers' assets are capital assets? Why do you think the proportion and amount is so large? (When you answer, consider the nature of the business.) What was the net realizable value of Rogers' property, plant, and equipment on December 31, 2008?

FS8-4. What was the cost and carrying amount (net book value) of Rogers' leasehold improvements on December 31, 2008? How does Rogers depreciate its leasehold improvements? Why do you think it depreciates the leasehold improvements this way?

FS8-5. One of Rogers' businesses is video rental in its Rogers Video stores and by mail. Read Note 2k to Rogers' financial statements. How does Rogers account for the DVDs and games it rents? Why do you think it accounts for these items this way (it isn't typical of "inventory")? Why do think it uses the six-month period for these items?

FS8-6. How much goodwill did Rogers report on December 31, 2008? How did the goodwill arise? How does Rogers amortize its goodwill? By how much did Rogers write down its goodwill in 2008? Why was the writedown necessary? What was the impact of the goodwill writedown on cash flow? Explain. How much new goodwill did Rogers add in 2008? What was the largest source of the new goodwill?

EXHIBIT 8.4 Rogers Communications Inc.: Extracts from the Financial Statements

◆ ROGERS

CONSOLIDATED BALANCE SHEETS
(IN MILLIONS OF CANADIAN DOLLARS)

December 31, 2008 and 2007

	2008	2007
Assets		
Current assets:		
Accounts receivable, net of allowance for doubtful accounts of $163 (2007 - $151)	$ 1,403	$ 1,245
Other current assets (note 9)	442	304
Future income tax assets (note 7)	446	594
	2,291	2,143
Property, plant and equipment (note 10)	7,898	7,289
Goodwill (note 11(b))	3,024	3,027
Intangible assets (note 11(c))	2,761	2,086
Investments (note 12)	343	485
Derivative instruments (note 15(d))	507	—
Other long-term assets (note 13)	269	295
	$ 17,093	$ 15,325

CONSOLIDATED STATEMENTS OF INCOME
(IN MILLIONS OF CANADIAN DOLLARS, EXCEPT PER SHARE AMOUNTS)

Years ended December 31, 2008 and 2007

	2008	2007
Operating revenue (note 3(b))	$ 11,335	$ 10,123
Operating expenses:		
Cost of sales	1,303	961
Sales and marketing	1,334	1,322
Operating, general and administrative	4,569	4,251
Stock option plan amendment (note 19(a)(i))	—	452
Integration and restructuring (note 6)	51	38
Depreciation and amortization	1,760	1,603
Impairment losses on goodwill, intangible assets and other long-term assets (notes 11(a) and 13)	294	—
Operating income	2,024	1,496
Interest on long-term debt	(575)	(579)
Debt issuance costs (note 14(a))	(16)	—
Loss on repayment of long-term debt (note 14(f))	—	(47)
Foreign exchange gain (loss)	(99)	54
Change in fair value of derivative instruments	64	(34)
Other income (expense), net	28	(4)
Income before income taxes	1,426	886
Income tax expense (recovery) (note 7):		
Current	3	(1)
Future	421	250
	424	249
Net income for the year	$ 1,002	$ 637

CONSOLIDATED STATEMENTS OF CASH FLOWS
(IN MILLIONS OF CANADIAN DOLLARS)

Years ended December 31, 2008 and 2007

	2008	2007
Cash provided by (used in):		
Operating activities:		
Net income for the year	$ 1,002	$ 637
Adjustments to reconcile net income to net cash flows from operating activities:		
Depreciation and amortization	1,760	1,603
Impairment losses on goodwill, intangible assets and other long-term assets	294	—
Program rights and Rogers Retail rental amortization	146	92
Future income taxes	421	250
Unrealized foreign exchange loss (gain)	65	(46)
Change in fair value of derivative instruments	(64)	34
Loss on repayment of long-term debt	—	47
Stock option plan amendment	—	452
Stock-based compensation expense (recovery)	(100)	62
Amortization of fair value increment on long-term debt and derivatives	(5)	(6)
Other	3	10
	3,522	3,135
Change in non-cash operating working capital items (note 20(a))	(215)	(310)
	3,307	2,825
Investing activities:		
Additions to property, plant and equipment ("PP&E")	(2,021)	(1,796)
Change in non-cash working capital items related to PP&E	40	(20)
Acquisition of spectrum licences	(1,008)	—
Acquisitions, net of cash and cash equivalents acquired	(191)	(537)
Additions to program rights and CRTC commitments	(150)	(67)
Other	(7)	(18)
	(3,337)	(2,438)

EXHIBIT 8.4	(continued) Rogers Communications Inc.: Extracts from the Financial Statements

2. SIGNIFICANT ACCOUNTING POLICIES

(E) DEPRECIATION:
PP&E are depreciated over their estimated useful lives as follows:

Asset	Basis	Rate
Buildings	Mainly diminishing balance	5% to 6²/₃%
Towers, head-ends and transmitters	Straight line	6²/₃ % to 25%
Distribution cable and subscriber drops	Straight line	5% to 20%
Network equipment	Straight line	6²/₃% to 33¹/₃%
Wireless network radio base station equipment	Straight line	12¹/₂% to 14¹/₃%
Computer equipment and software	Straight line	14¹/₃% to 33¹/₃%
Customer equipment	Straight line	20% to 33¹/₃%
Leasehold improvements	Straight line	Over shorter of estimated useful life and lease term
Equipment and vehicles	Mainly diminishing balance	5% to 33¹/₃%

(K) INVENTORIES AND ROGERS RETAIL RENTAL INVENTORY:
Inventories are primarily valued at the lower of cost, determined on a first-in, first-out basis, and net realizable value. Rogers Retail rental inventory, which includes videocassettes, DVDs and video games, is amortized to its estimated residual value. The residual value of Rogers Retail rental inventory is recorded as a charge to operating expense upon the sale of Rogers Retail rental inventory. Amortization of Rogers Retail rental inventory is charged to cost of sales on a diminishing-balance basis over a six-month period.

(P) GOODWILL AND INTANGIBLE ASSETS:
(i) Goodwill:
Goodwill is the residual amount that results when the purchase price of an acquired business exceeds the sum of the amounts allocated to the tangible and intangible assets acquired, less liabilities assumed, based on their fair values. When the Company enters into a business combination, the purchase method of accounting is used. Goodwill is assigned, as of the date of the business combination, to reporting units that are expected to benefit from the business combination.

Goodwill is not amortized but instead is tested for impairment annually or more frequently if events or changes in circumstances indicate that the asset might be impaired. The impairment test is carried out in two steps. In the first step, the carrying amount of the reporting unit, including goodwill, is compared with its fair value. When the fair value of the reporting unit exceeds its carrying amount, goodwill of the reporting unit is not considered to be impaired and the second step of the impairment test is unnecessary. The second step is carried out when the carrying amount of a reporting unit exceeds its fair value, in which case, the implied fair value of the reporting unit's goodwill, determined in the same manner as the value of goodwill is determined in a business combination, is compared with its carrying amount to measure the amount of the impairment loss, if any.

(ii) Intangible assets:
Intangible assets acquired in a business combination are recorded at their fair values. Intangible assets with finite useful lives are amortized over their estimated useful lives and are tested for impairment, as described in note 2(q). Intangible assets having an indefinite life, being spectrum and broadcast licences, are not amortized but are tested for impairment on an annual or more frequent basis by comparing their fair value to their carrying amount. An impairment loss on an indefinite life intangible asset is recognized when the carrying amount of the asset exceeds its fair value.

Intangible assets with finite useful lives are amortized on a straight-line basis over their estimated useful lives as follows:

Brand name – Rogers	20 years
Brand name – Fido	5 years
Brand name – Citytv	5 years
Subscriber bases	2¼ to 4²/₃ years
Roaming agreements	12 years
Dealer networks	4 years
Marketing agreement	5 years

The Company tested goodwill and intangible assets with indefinite lives for impairment during 2008 and recorded a writedown of $154 million related to the goodwill of the conventional television reporting unit and $75 million related to the Citytv broadcast licence (note 11(a)). No impairment of goodwill and intangible assets with indefinite lives was recorded in 2007.

FS8-7. What are intangible assets? How much of intangible assets did Rogers report on its December 31, 2008 balance sheet? What are the largest categories of Rogers' intangible assets? How are these intangible assets amortized? Why are some of Rogers' intangible assets not amortized? By how much did Rogers write down its intangible assets in 2008? Why were the writedowns necessary?

FS8-8. What is the cost and carrying amount (net book value) of the brand names Rogers reports in its financial statements? How are Rogers' brand names amortized? Why do you think Rogers amortizes its brand names but not some of its other intangible assets? Why does Rogers report brand names on its balance sheet but many other entities don't? How does Rogers determine the amount to report for its brand names? By how much did Rogers write down its brand names in 2008?

EXHIBIT 8.4 (continued) Rogers Communications Inc.: Extracts from the Financial Statements

(N) PROPERTY, PLANT AND EQUIPMENT:

PP&E are recorded at cost. During construction of new assets, direct costs plus a portion of applicable overhead costs are capitalized. Repairs and maintenance expenditures are charged to operating expenses as incurred.

The cost of the initial cable subscriber installation is capitalized. Costs of all other cable connections and disconnections are expensed, except for direct incremental installation costs related to reconnect Cable customers, which are deferred to the extent of reconnect installation revenues. Deferred reconnect revenues and expenses are amortized over the related estimated service period.

(Q) IMPAIRMENT OF LONG-LIVED ASSETS:

The Company reviews long-lived assets, which include PP&E and intangible assets with finite useful lives, for impairment annually or more frequently if events or changes in circumstances indicate that the carrying amount may not be recoverable. If the sum of the undiscounted future cash flows expected to result from the use and eventual disposition of a group of assets is less than its carrying amount, it is considered to be impaired. An impairment loss is measured as the amount by which the carrying amount of the group of assets exceeds its fair value.

The Company tested long-lived assets with finite useful lives for impairment during 2008 and recorded a write-down of $51 million related to the Citytv CRTC commitments asset (note 13) and $14 million related to the Citytv brand name (note 11(a)(ii)). No impairment was recorded in 2007.

10. PROPERTY, PLANT AND EQUIPMENT

Details of PP&E are as follows:

	2008			2007		
	Cost	Accumulated depreciation	Net book value	Cost	Accumulated depreciation	Net book value
Land and buildings	$ 762	$ 156	$ 606	$ 662	$ 133	$ 529
Towers, head-ends and transmitters	1,179	705	474	998	566	432
Distribution cable and subscriber drops	4,874	2,802	2,072	4,562	2,542	2,020
Network equipment	5,320	2,805	2,515	4,749	2,393	2,356
Wireless network radio base station equipment	1,459	876	583	1,250	770	480
Computer equipment and software	2,424	1,730	694	2,068	1,518	550
Customer equipment	1,260	787	473	1,068	614	454
Leasehold improvements	349	193	156	316	175	141
Equipment and vehicles	825	500	325	754	427	327
	$ 18,452	$ 10,554	$ 7,898	$ 16,427	$ 9,138	$ 7,289

Depreciation expense for 2008 amounted to $1,456 million (2007 — $1,303 million).

PP&E not yet in service and, therefore, not depreciated at December 31, 2008 amounted to $853 million (2007 - $614 million).

11. GOODWILL AND INTANGIBLE ASSETS

(A) IMPAIRMENT:

(i) Goodwill:

In the fourth quarter of 2008, the Company determined that the fair value of its conventional television reporting unit was lower than its carrying value. This primarily resulted from weakening of industry expectations in the conventional television business and declines in advertising revenues. As a result, the Company recorded a goodwill impairment charge of $154 million related to its conventional television reporting unit, which is included in the Company's Media operating segment.

(B) GOODWILL:

A summary of the changes to goodwill is as follows:

	2008	2007
Opening balance	$ 3,027	$ 2,779
Acquisition of Outdoor Life Network (note 4(a)(i))	31	—
Acquisition of Aurora Cable (note 4(a)(ii))	56	—
Acquisition of channel m (note 4(a)(iii))	48	—
Other acquisitions and adjustments	9	(6)
Adjustments to Citytv purchase price allocation (note 4(b)(ii))	7	264
Reduction in valuation allowance for acquired future income tax assets	—	(10)
Impairment charge on conventional television reporting unit (note 11(a)(i))	(154)	—
	$ 3,024	$ 3,027

FS8-9. How does Rogers account for its property, plant, and equipment? How does it account for expenditures on repairs and maintenance? Why do you think it accounts for these expenditures this way?

EXHIBIT 8.4 **(continued) Rogers Communications Inc.: Extracts from the Financial Statements**

(C) INTANGIBLE ASSETS:
Details of intangible assets are as follows:

	Cost prior to impairment losses	Accumulated amortization	Impairment losses (note 11(a)(ii))	Net book value	Cost	Accumulated amortization	Net book value
				2008			**2007**
Indefinite life:							
Spectrum licences	$ 1,929	$ —	$ —	$ 1,929	$ 921	$ —	$ 921
Broadcast licences	164	—	75	89	147	—	147
Definite life:							
Brand names	437	158	14	265	437	116	321
Subscriber bases	999	900	—	99	1,046	790	256
Roaming agreements	523	181	—	342	523	138	385
Dealer networks	41	41	—	—	41	32	9
Wholesale agreement	13	13	—	—	13	13	—
Marketing agreement	52	15	—	37	52	5	47
Advertising bookings	6	6	—	—	—	—	—
Baseball player contracts	—	—	—	—	120	120	—
	$ 4,164	$ 1,314	$ 89	$ 2,761	$ 3,300	$ 1,214	$ 2,086

During 2008, broadcast licences increased by $17 million as a result of acquisitions and decreased by $75 million to reflect impairment of the carrying amount of the Citytv broadcast licence (note 11(a)(ii)).

During 2008, brand names decreased by $14 million to reflect impairment of the carrying amount of the Citytv brand name (note 11(a)(ii)).
Amortization of brand names, subscriber bases, baseball player contracts, roaming agreements, dealer networks, wholesale agreements and marketing agreement amounted to $280 million for the year ended December 31, 2008 (2007 - $282 million).

FS8-10. How much cash did Rogers spend on property, plant, and equipment during 2008? Why is the amount spent not necessarily the same amount as additions to the property, plant, and equipment account? How does Rogers account for purchases of new plant and equipment on its balance sheet? What method(s) does Rogers use to depreciate its property, plant, and equipment? What was Rogers' depreciation expense for property, plant, and equipment in 2008? How much depreciation had been accumulated against property, plant, and equipment on December 31, 2008? Why does Rogers depreciate its property, plant, and equipment (aside from the fact it's required by IFRS)?

FS8-11. What was Rogers' return on assets for the year ended December 31, 2008 and 2007? Assume Rogers' total assets on December 31, 2008 were $14,105,000,000?

ENDNOTES

1. Andree Lavigne, Diane Paul, John Tang, Jo-Ann Lempert, Helene Marcil, and Louise Overbeek, *Financial Reporting in Canada 2008*, 33rd Edition (Toronto: Federal Publications Inc., 2008).

2. Extracted from Potash Corporation of Saskatchewan Inc.'s 2008 annual report.

3. Extracted from Corus Entertainment Inc.'s 2008 annual report.

4. Extracted from North American Palladium Ltd.'s 2008 annual report.

5. Data obtained from "Financial Post Industry Report," Financial Post website, http://www.fpdata.finpost.com/suite/autologreports.asp (accessed March 2009).

6. Adapted from Rogers Communications Inc.'s website at http://www.rogers.com.

7. Extracted from Rogers Communications Inc.'s 2008 annual report.

Fans of the Canadian rock band Hedley have accountant Katherine Chan to thank, in part, when they buy the group's CDs or attend one of its concerts.

Chan, a certified general accountant, is manager of Internal Financial Reporting at Hedley's music label, Universal Music Canada (UMC), the domestic wing of the world's largest music label. Her job is to oversee the financial analysis of UMC's deals with Canadian musicians.

Canadian rock band Hedley

"We basically run a few numbers based on sales estimates, how much they think they need to spend for marketing, and then we send that back with the results and some recommendations, if we can, and then they go from there," said Chan, in an interview at UMC's Toronto headquarters.

In the case of Hedley's third album, Chan also tracked expenses such as advances to the band to rent recording studios, as well as sales of CDs, digital song downloads, and merchandise such as t-shirts.

While Chan suggests it's the folks in marketing and A&R (artists and repertoire) who have more influence on whether to risk money on an artist, the company does rely on Chan's financial data to make those calls.

It's a career that is a perfect fit for a self-professed music lover who has "way too many" CDs cluttering her Toronto home.

"That's the beauty of it, that I can tie together what I enjoy about accounting with an industry that I find so exciting," Chan said.

Katherine Chan, CGA
Manager of Internal Financial
Reporting, Universal Music Canada

Chan completed her bachelor of commerce degree from the University of Toronto, and first worked for a private accounting firm, then in real estate with a bank, and later as a corporate accountant at a property management firm. She joined UMC as a financial analyst in 2000 and obtained her CGA designation in 2005. She credits the training with helping her advance to her current, more senior position.

"Being able to see a full [accounting] cycle from sales all the way down to EBITDA (earnings before interest, taxes, depreciation, and amortization), [including] what does sales affect, the manufacturing costs, our royalty expenses, our copyright expenses, that sort of thing, ...seeing all the pieces fall into place and understanding it...helps because being able to see the big picture is key," Chan explained.

Her accounting training also helped her develop the ability to talk to clients, even international stars, including KISS vocalist and bass player Gene Simmons. He came to UMC in 2008 to discuss his Simmons Records label, and then stayed on to chat with back-office staff, including Chan.

"Everyone…brought their KISS dolls and all their paraphernalia and he signed them all. He was just fantastic," said Chan, who prizes her photo taken with Simmons.

As she works on Universal Music Canada's annual budget forecasts, Chan spends nearly a month each summer gathering data on overhead, margin items, and sales forecasts from all departments. But her responsibilities are more strategic then simply presenting the numbers to the chief financial officer; ultimately it will help UMC decide whether to continue to support its roster of musicians, including Jann Arden, The Tragically Hip, Sam Roberts, and Sarah Harmer.

"Anyone can really crunch the numbers, use a spreadsheet, use an accounting system, but to be able to communicate the results, or do analysis, is important because without that [they] can't make any decisions," Chan said. "You have to be able to interpret it, see the meaning, understand implications, that's key."

—E.B.

INTRODUCTION: WHAT ARE LIABILITIES?

Liabilities are obligations—to provide cash, goods, or services to customers, suppliers, employees, governments, lenders, and anyone else an entity "owes something to." Liabilities can be classified as current—for example, wages owed to employees or payments that must be made to suppliers for recently delivered goods or services—or long-term; for example, Rogers Communications Inc. has US$350 million in notes that don't have to be paid until 2038. Many liabilities are straightforward to understand and measure; for example, amounts owed to suppliers and creditors can be traced back to invoices or loan agreements. Other liabilities are very complex. There are also obligations that aren't recorded on the balance sheet at all.

Liabilities are a significant part of most entities' balance sheets. While not all companies use debt to finance their operations, virtually all will have some liabilities simply because not all purchases are for cash. Table 9.1 shows the amount and proportion of liabilities of a number of Canadian companies. Notice how much the ratio of liabilities to assets varies. Magnotta Winery Corporation finances its assets with about 30 percent debt whereas for WestJet Airlines it's about 67 percent debt. The relative amount of current liabilities also varies. Most of Indigo's liabilities are current, it has very little long-term debt, while Corus Entertainment Inc. has few current liabilities.

TABLE 9.1	Amount of Liabilities in Different Companies				
Company	Type of business	Dollar amount of current liabilities	Dollar amount of non-current liabilities	Liabilities as a proportion of assets	Current liabilities as a proportion of total liabilities
BCE	Communications	$6,227,000,000	$16,125,000,000	56.4%	27.9%
Canfor Corporation	Forest products	548,900,000	1,156,700,000	53.3	32.2
Corus Entertainment Inc.	Media and entertainment	196,026,000	860,622,000	52.0	18.6
High Liner Foods Incorporated	Food processing	116,443,000	67,127,000	54.1	63.4
Indigo Books & Music Inc.	Retail	206,321,000	10,929,000	52.6	95.0
Loblaw Companies Limited	Grocery retail	3,230,000,000	4,925,000,000	58.3	39.6
Magna International Inc.	Auto parts maker	5,093,000,000*	733,000,000*	44.2	87.4
Magnotta Winery Corporation	Winery	7,091,327	8,170,740	30.4	46.5
Tim Horton's Inc.	Fast food service	366,060,000	486,163,000	42.8	43.0
WestJet Airlines Ltd.	Airline	739,844,000	1,452,868,000	66.9	33.7

*U.S. dollars.

An entity's liquidity and solvency is assessed using information about its liabilities. Liabilities are claims on an entity's cash and other resources, so stakeholders may need to know whether there are adequate resources to meet these claims. In the longer term, they need to assess whether an entity will be able to meet its obligations as they come due (in other words, is the entity solvent). Liabilities are usually not negotiable—they have to be paid regardless of whether an entity is doing well or poorly. If an entity can't meet its obligations it will likely face legal and/or economic consequences.

The IFRS definition of a liability is straightforward: liabilities are obligations arising from past transactions or economic events that require the sacrifice of economic resources to settle. But don't be deceived by the simplicity of this definition. Accounting for some liabilities involves applying very complex rules; accounting for leases, pensions, and future income taxes are among the most difficult accounting topics.

Let's apply the IFRS definition to three different obligations.

1. An amount owed to a supplier for inventory purchased—an account payable.
   - Obligation: The entity must pay for the inventory purchased from the supplier.
   - Past transaction or economic event: The supplier has provided the inventory.
   - Economic sacrifice: The supplier has to be paid, most likely with cash.

2. A customer pays in advance for a service to be delivered at a later date—unearned revenue.
   - Obligation: The entity must provide the goods or services already paid for by the customer.
   - Past transaction or economic event: The customer has paid.
   - Economic sacrifice: The entity must provide the paid-for goods or services.

3. A customer is given a two-year warranty on a purchased item—an accrued liability/provision.
   - Obligation: Provide warranty service as required to the customer.
   - Past transaction or economic event: Purchase of the warrantied item by the customer.
   - Economic sacrifice: Warranty service must be provided.

You should be able to apply this definition to each type of liability we examine in the chapter to understand why it's considered a liability.

In principle, liabilities should be valued at their present value. (Suggestion: Review time value of money in Chapter 6.) For many liabilities, the timing and amount of the cash flows are known, and in other cases it's possible to estimate them. It's also possible to identify an appropriate rate for discounting the cash flows associated with liabilities. Long-term liabilities are valued at the present value of the cash flows they will pay. However, not all liabilities are discounted to their present value. Current liabilities aren't discounted because the impact is usually immaterial. (That is, the present value of an account payable to be paid in 30 days would almost be the same as the undiscounted amount.) Also, liabilities that don't represent an actual amount of money to be paid aren't discounted; for example, unearned revenue isn't discounted because it represents an obligation to deliver goods and services, not cash.

CURRENT LIABILITIES

Current liabilities are obligations that will be satisfied in one year or one operating cycle. Information about current obligations is important for assessing the short-term liquidity of an entity. As mentioned, current liabilities are usually not discounted to their present value. In this section, we will look at a number of different types of current liabilities and discuss the issues that affect accounting for them.

Bank and Other Current Loans

Loans are reported as current liabilities if the amount must be repaid within the next year or operating cycle. **Demand loans** must be repaid whenever the lender requests repayment. They are classified as current because of the lender's right to call the loan at any time, even though they rarely demand repayment and the loans remain on the books for a long time. Entities can also have short-term borrowing arrangements to meet day-to-day operating needs. A **line of credit** from a lender allows an entity to borrow up to a specified maximum amount whenever it requires the money. A line of credit is only classified as a liability if money is actually borrowed.

Accounts Payable

Accounts payable are amounts an entity owes to suppliers for goods and services. Goods and services include anything the entity uses in the course of its operations, including inventory, supplies, utilities, cleaning services, and labour. We have seen numerous examples of recording and settling of accounts payable throughout this book. Measuring the amount of accounts payable is usually not difficult because the recording is triggered by an invoice from the supplier. On most balance sheets, accounts payable is highly aggregated, capturing all amounts owed to suppliers.

Collections on Behalf of Third Parties

Most entities act as tax collectors for various government taxation authorities. For example, when we purchase merchandise in a store, the GST (goods and services tax) or the HST (harmonized sales tax), and provincial sales tax in some provinces, is added to the purchase price. Employers withhold amounts from their employees' pay for income taxes, employment insurance, and Canada or Québec Pension Plans. Employers also withhold amounts for items such as employee shares of benefits, union dues, pension plan contributions, and charitable donations.

The money withheld doesn't belong to the entity. The amounts must be sent to the appropriate government agency, union, pension plan, and so on, and a liability reflects the obligation. For example, suppose a shopper in Alberta buys a plasma TV at Future Shop for $2,200. In addition to charging $2,200 for the TV, Future Shop also collects $110 of GST. This entry would be made to record the sale (assuming the purchase paid for in cash):

Dr. Cash (assets +)	2,310	
Cr. Revenue (revenue +, shareholders' equity +)		2,200
Cr. GST payable (liabilities +)		110
To record the sale of merchandise and collection of GST		

The $110 is a liability because the money doesn't belong to Future Shop; it belongs to the government. When Future Shop remits the money to the government, it would make the following entry:

Dr. GST payable (liabilities −)	110	
Cr. Cash (assets −)		110
To record remittance of GST to the government		

Amounts collected on behalf of third parties are usually not disclosed separately but would be included in accounts payable.

Income Taxes Payable

Canadian businesses pay tax on their income to both the federal and provincial governments. Most businesses pay instalments based on the estimated amount of tax they will owe for the year. A corporation pays taxes on its income and must file a tax return within six months of its fiscal year-end. An unincorporated business's income is included in the proprietor or partner's tax return. In an entity's financial statements, the amount of income taxes owed is accrued. The amount accrued is the difference between the estimated amount of income tax for the year and the amount already paid.

Dividends Payable

Dividends payable is an obligation to pay the corporation's shareholders a dividend that has been declared. Once the board of directors has declared a dividend, the amount of the dividend is classified as a liability until it's paid.

Accrued Liabilities and Provisions

An accrued expense and liability are recorded (with an adjusting journal entry) when an entity incurs an expense with no external event such as receipt of an invoice to trigger recording it. A **provision** is similar to this, except there is more uncertainty about the timing and amount of the liability. Examples of accrued liabilities and provisions include

- wages and salaries for employees unpaid at the end of a period (accrued liability)

- interest costs incurred but not payable until a later period (accrued liability)

- goods and services acquired but not invoiced (and not recorded) (accrued liability)

- warranty liabilities (provision)

- liabilities for affinity programs (e.g., airline frequent flyer programs) (provision)

- liabilities to redeem coupons (e.g., discount coupons for grocery products, Canadian Tire money) (provision)

All of these examples require the entity's managers to determine the amount of the expense and associated liability. Accrued liabilities can be estimated fairly accurately. For example, accrued wages and salaries can be based on the number of hours worked or proportion of salary earned from the end of the last pay period to the end of the reporting period.

Provisions are more difficult to estimate. For example, managers must estimate the average cost of warranty service. For frequent flyer programs, it's necessary to estimate the number of outstanding miles that will be redeemed and the cost of the rewards the customer will receive. For coupon distributions, it's necessary to estimate the coupon redemption rate. In all of these examples there is the potential for significant errors. Accrued liabilities and provisions can have non-current as well as current components. Carmakers, for instance, offer warranties of three or more years on their vehicles. The warranty cost must be estimated for each year.

Exhibit 9.1 provides an example of warranty provision disclosure for Bombardier Inc.[1] Note 2 explains how the warranty is accounted for and how the estimate is made. The first part of Note 12 breaks down accounts payable and accrued liability amounts from the balance sheet into their component parts and shows that the product warranties provision on January 31, 2009, is $931 million. The second part of the note shows the changes to the warranty provision over the year. Notice that the ending balance is affected by the expense for the year, the impact of changes in estimates, and cash paid to meet warranty obligations.

BOMBARDIER INC.

CONSOLIDATED BALANCE SHEETS

As at January 31

(In millions of U.S. dollars)

	Notes	2009[1]	2008[1]
Liabilities			
Accounts payable and accrued liabilities	12	$ 6,988	$ 6,919
Advances and progress billings in excess of related long-term contract costs		2,072	2,791
Advances on aerospace programs		2,991	2,926
Fractional ownership deferred revenues		573	631
Long-term debt	13	3,952	4,393
Accrued benefit liabilities	25	992	1,066
Derivative financial instruments	3	1,194	276
		18,762	19,002
Shareholders' equity		2,544	3,118
		$ 21,306	$ 22,120

2. SUMMARY OF SIGNIFICANT ACCOUNTING POLICIES
Product warranties

A provision for warranty cost is recorded in cost of sales when the revenue for the related product is recognized. The cost is estimated based on a number of factors, including the historical warranty claims and cost experience, the type and duration of warranty coverage, the nature of products sold and in service and counter-warranty coverage available from the Corporation's suppliers.

The Corporation reviews its recorded product warranty provisions quarterly and any adjustment is recorded in cost of sales.

12. ACCOUNTS PAYABLE AND ACCRUED LIABILITIES

Accounts payable and accrued liabilities were as follows as at January 31:

	2009	2008
Trade accounts payable	$ 2,243	$ 2,079
Accrued liabilities	1,048	1,251
Sales incentives[1]	1,001	1,011
Product warranties	931	1,041
Payroll-related liabilities	438	496
Income and other taxes	113	213
Non-controlling interest	66	66
Interest	61	77
Provision for repurchase obligations	59	82
Severance and other involuntary termination costs	43	37
Other	985	566
	$ 6,988	$ 6,919

[1] Comprised of provision for credit and residual value guarantees and trade-in commitments, as well as other related provisions and liabilities in connection with the sale of aircraft (see Note 26 – Commitments and contingencies). The carrying value of related liabilities in connection with the sale of aircraft is $190 million as at January 31, 2009 ($268 million as at January 31, 2008). The amount contractually required to be paid for these liabilities is $232 million as at January 31, 2009 ($318 million as at January 31, 2008).

Product warranties – Product warranties typically range from one to five years, except for aircraft structural warranties that extend up to 20 years.

Changes in the product warranty provision were as follows for fiscal years 2009 and 2008:

	BA	BT	Total
Balance as at January 31, 2007	$ 291	$ 694	$ 985
Current expense	107	335	442
Changes in estimates	(28)	(69)	(97)
Cash paid	(85)	(287)	(372)
Effect of foreign currency exchange rate changes	-	83	83
Balance as at January 31, 2008	285	756	1,041
Current expense	95	279	374
Changes in estimates	-	(63)	(63)
Cash paid	(100)	(202)	(302)
Effect of foreign currency exchange rate changes	-	(119)	(119)
Balance as at January 31, 2009	$ 280	$ 651	$ 931

INSIGHT

Accounting Estimates

Estimating is integral to accounting. Simply because some amounts are difficult to estimate doesn't mean they shouldn't be made, or that they don't provide useful information to stakeholders. It is, however, important to be aware that estimates are imprecise and that they do affect financial statement numbers. In addition, because the actual amounts are uncertain, difficult-to-estimate accruals are attractive for earnings management. Remember in Chapter 6 we discussed how managers can use hidden reserves to manage earnings. Managers can also use estimates of warranty costs or coupon usage in this way. For example, to smooth their income over time, managers could make slightly higher warranty or coupon expenses in years where net income was higher (to lower income) and make slightly lower warranty or coupon expenses in years where net income was lower (to increase income). Management can do this because it's very difficult to be precise with many of the estimates that must be made.

Unearned Revenue

When an entity receives cash in advance of providing goods or services, it has an obligation to provide those goods or services. Since cash is in hand but revenue has not been recognized, a liability for the amount received is required. Examples of unearned revenue include

- advance rent payments received by a property owner
- deposits for future goods and services
- tickets purchased for upcoming sporting events, concerts, and the theatre
- gift cards

For example, on December 4, 2014, Mr. Wayne purchased a $100 gift card at Dromore Books Ltd. (Dromore) for his daughter. The gift card entitles the holder to purchase books worth up to $100 but can't be exchanged for cash. Dromore would make the following entry to record the sale:

EXHIBIT 9.2

Indigo Books & Music Inc.: Accrued Liabilities

www.chapters.indigo.ca

Indigo Books & Music Inc.
Consolidated Balance Sheets

(thousands of dollars)	As at March 28, 2009	As at March 29, 2008 (Restated – Note 3)
LIABILITIES AND SHAREHOLDERS' EQUITY		
Current		
Accounts payable and accrued liabilities (notes 2 and 14)	233,353	193,323
Deferred revenue	11,612	10,350
Income taxes payable	344	–
Current portion of long-term debt (notes 6 and 12)	2,734	2,648
Total current liabilities	248,043	206,321

Gift cards

The Company sells gift cards to its customers and recognizes the revenue as the gift cards are redeemed. The Company also recognizes revenue from unredeemed gift cards (gift card breakage) if the likelihood of the gift card being redeemed by the customer is considered to be remote. The Company determines its average gift card breakage rate based on historical redemption rates. Once the breakage rate is determined, the resulting revenue is recognized over the estimated period of redemption, commencing when the gift cards are sold, based on historical redemption patterns. Gift card breakage is included in revenues in the Company's consolidated statements of earnings.

The Company recorded $4.6 million in gift card breakage in fiscal 2009, and $2.9 million in gift card breakage in fiscal 2008. As at March 28, 2009, the provision for unredeemed gift card liability is $34.5 million (March 29, 2008 – $32.7 million) and is included in accounts payable and accrued liabilities.

| Dr. Cash (assets +) | 100 | |
| Cr. Unearned revenue—gift card (liabilities +) | | 100 |

To record the sale of a gift card on December 4, 2014

When Mr. Wayne's daughter uses the gift card, Dromore would make the following entry:

| Dr. Unearned revenue—gift card (liabilities −) | 100 | |
| Cr. Revenue (revenue +, shareholders' equity +) | | 100 |

To record the use of a $100 gift card

Since the gift card can be used at any time, the liability is classified as current even though it might not be used in the next year. An interesting problem with gift cards is how to deal with the fact that not all gift cards sold will be redeemed. Exhibit 9.2 shows how Indigo Books & Music deals with this problem.[2] Indigo estimates the amount of gift cards that won't be redeemed (called breakage) and includes the amount in revenue (the journal entry debits liabilities and credits revenue). The estimated breakage recorded for 2009 was $4.6 million. The liability for gift cards on March 28, 2009 was $34.5 million and is included in accounts payable and accrued liabilities.

Disclosure

IFRS' disclosure requirements for current liabilities are quite general and the financial statements of public companies show a wide variation in classification and detail provided. Current liabilities must be segregated by main class (i.e., bank loans, accounts payable and accrued liabilities, taxes payable, unearned revenue, current portion of long-term debt, and so on). Detailed disclosure on provisions, similar to Bombardier's in Exhibit 9.1, is also required. Most entities segregate current and non-current liabilities, although IFRS allows entities to present assets and liabilities in order of liquidity without classifying them as current or non-current.

Many entities present highly aggregated information in their accounts payable. For example, in Exhibit 9.2, Indigo includes virtually all operating current liabilities in accounts payable and accrued liabilities. In contrast, Bombardier breaks down its accounts payable and accrued liabilities in the notes to the financial statements (see Exhibit 9.1). This more detailed breakdown allows more insight into the operation of the business and better calculation of certain ratios.

www.mcgrawhill connect.ca

KNOWLEDGE CHECK

❑ According to IFRS, what is the definition of a liability?

❑ What is a current liability? Why might stakeholders want to know the amount of current liabilities?

❑ Explain why amounts owing to employees should be considered a liability.

BONDS AND OTHER FORMS OF LONG-TERM DEBT

Debt is amounts borrowed and owed by an entity. Debt can be long-term (**non-current**) or current. Exhibit 9.3 provides information about the long-term debt of WestJet Airlines Ltd. On December 31, 2008, WestJet reported long-term debt of $1,351,903,000, of which $165,721,000 was classified as current because it was due to be repaid within the next year.[3] Many entities use long-term debt to finance their businesses. WestJet uses debt mainly to finance aircraft purchases.

Debt comes in all shapes and sizes. Money can be borrowed from banks. Debt can be issued to the public at large or to private organizations such as insurance companies or pension funds. Borrowers can provide receivables, inventory, equipment, buildings, or land to lenders as collateral for loans. The **collateral** is protection for the lenders should the borrower not repay the loan. In that event, the lenders get the collateral or the proceeds from its sale. The interest rate can be fixed or it can vary with changes in interest rates in the economy. The interest rate of a **variable-rate loan** varies with market conditions while the rate of a **fixed-rate loan** doesn't change. The period the debt is outstanding can be long or short. In sum, a debt arrangement will include whatever terms the borrowers and lenders agree on. Note 6 in Exhibit 9.3 describes the terms of WestJet's long-term debt.

The following are examples of debt instruments:

- **bond**—a formal borrowing arrangement in which a borrower agrees to make periodic interest payments to lenders as well as repay the principal at a specified time in the future

- **debenture**—a bond with no collateral provided to the lenders

- **mortgage**—a loan that provides the borrower's property as collateral

- **note payable**—a formal obligation signed by the borrower, promising to repay a debt

In this section we will focus our attention on bonds, but other forms of debt have similar characteristics.

An entity can be financed either through debt and equity. Equity represents ownership in the entity while debt is borrowings that have to be repaid. Each form of financing has a number of advantages and disadvantages. Interest on debt is tax deductible, which means the actual cost of borrowing is lower than the interest rate stated in the loan. (The tax deductibility of interest will be explained later in the chapter.) However, debt holders don't have a say in the entity's management; only equity investors (the owners) do. Debt is riskier for the issuing entity because the interest and principal payments have to be made as specified in the loan agreement regardless of how well the entity is doing. Defaulting on these payments (failing to make them when they are due) can have significant and costly economic and legal consequences for an entity. On the other hand, debt is less risky for investors because debt investors must be fully repaid before equity investors get anything if an entity goes out of business. Because debt is less risky for investors, it's a less costly way to finance an entity (the higher the risk investors face, the higher the return they expect).

| EXHIBIT 9.3 |
| **WestJet Airlines Ltd.: Long-Term Debt** |

www.westjet.com

consolidated balance sheet

As at December 31
(Stated in thousands of Canadian dollars)

	2008	2007
Liabilities and shareholders' equity		
Current liabilities:		
Accounts payable and accrued liabilities	$ 249,354	$ 168,171
Advance ticket sales	251,354	194,929
Non-refundable guest credits	73,020	54,139
Current portion of long-term debt (note 6)	165,721	172,992
Current portion of obligations under capital lease	395	375
	739,844	590,606
Long-term debt (note 6)	1,186,182	1,256,526
Obligations under capital lease	713	1,108
Other liabilities (note 12(a))	24,233	11,337
Future income tax (note 7)	241,740	174,737
	2,192,712	2,034,314
Shareholders' equity:		
Share capital (note 8(b))	452,885	448,568
Contributed surplus	60,193	57,889
Accumulated other comprehensive loss (note 12(c))	(38,112)	(11,914)
Retained earnings	611,171	455,365
	1,086,137	949,908
Commitments and contingencies (note 10)		
	$ 3,278,849	$ 2,984,222

EXHIBIT 9.3

(continued)
WestJet Airlines Ltd.: Long-Term Debt

6. Long-term debt

		2008	2007
Term loans – purchased aircraft	(i)	$ 1,331,083	$ 1,389,888
Term loan – flight simulator	(ii)	7,265	23,325
Term loans – live satellite television equipment	(iii)	1,740	3,621
Term loan – Calgary hangar facility	(iv)	9,648	10,054
Term loan – Calgary hangar facility	(v)	2,167	2,630
		1,351,903	1,429,518
Current portion		165,721	172,992
		$ 1,186,182	$ 1,256,526

(i)   52 individual term loans, amortized on a straight-line basis over a 12-year term, each repayable in quarterly principal instalments ranging from $668 to $955, including fixed interest at a weighted average rate of 5.32%, maturing between 2014 and 2020. These facilities are guaranteed by Ex-Im Bank and secured by one 800-series aircraft, 38 700-series aircraft and 13 600-series aircraft.

(ii)   Term loan repayable in monthly instalments of $95, including floating interest at the bank's prime rate plus 0.88%, with an effective interest rate of 4.38% as at December 31, 2008, maturing in 2011, secured by one flight simulator.

(iii)   14 individual term loans, amortized on a straight-line basis over a five-year term, repayable in quarterly principal instalments ranging from $29 to $42, including floating interest at the Canadian LIBOR rate plus 0.08%, with a weighted average effective interest rate of 2.82% as at December 31, 2008, maturing between 2009 and 2011. These facilities are for the purchase of live satellite television equipment and are guaranteed by the Ex-Im Bank and secured by certain 700-series and 600-series aircraft.

(iv)   Term loan repayable in monthly instalments of $108, including interest at 9.03%, maturing April 2011, secured by the Calgary hangar facility.

(v)   Term loan repayable in monthly instalments of $50, including floating interest at the bank's prime rate plus 0.50%, with an effective interest rate of 4.00% as at December 31, 2008, maturing April 2013, secured by the Calgary hangar facility.

The net book value of the property and equipment pledged as collateral for the Corporation's secured borrowings was $2,012,915 as at December 31, 2008 (2007 – $2,028,548).

Future scheduled repayments of long-term debt are as follows:

2009	$ 165,721
2010	165,034
2011	177,557
2012	163,279
2013	162,740
2014 and thereafter	517,572
	$ 1,351,903

Held within the special-purpose entities, as identified in note 1, significant accounting policies, are liabilities of $1,332,859 (2007 – $1,393,526) related to the acquisition of the 52 purchased aircraft, which are included above in the long-term debt balances.

10. Commitments and contingencies

(c) Letters of credit

The Corporation has available two facilities with a Canadian chartered bank for a total of $15,000 (2007 – $15,000) for letters of guarantee. As at December 31, 2008, letters of guarantee totaling $12,222 (2007 – $9,950) have been issued. The facilities are secured by a general security agreement, an assignment of insurance proceeds and $4,222 (2007 – $2,069) of restricted cash.

(d) Operating line of credit

During the year ended December 31, 2008, the Corporation signed a three-year revolving operating line of credit with a syndicate of three Canadian banks. The line of credit is available for up to a maximum of $85 million commencing May 1, 2009 subject to various customary conditions precedent being satisfied, and will be secured by the Corporation's new Campus facility. The line of credit will bear interest at prime plus 0.50% per annum, or a bankers acceptance rate at 2.0% annual stamping fee or equivalent and will be available for general corporate expenses and working capital purposes. The Corporation is required to pay a standby fee of 15 basis points, based on the average unused portion of the line of credit for the previous quarter, payable quarterly and commencing on August 1, 2009. As at December 31, 2008, no amounts were drawn on this facility.

11. Financial instruments and risk management

(a) Fair value of financial assets and financial liabilities (continued)

The fair values of financial assets and liabilities, together with carrying amounts, shown in the balance sheet as at December 31, 2008 and 2007, are as follows:

		2008		2007	
		Carrying amount	Fair value	Carrying amount	Fair value
Asset (liability)					
Cash and cash equivalents	(i)	$ 820,214	$ 820,214	$ 653,558	$ 653,558
Accounts receivable	(i)	16,837	16,837	15,009	15,009
Foreign exchange options	(ii)	862	862	—	—
Cash flow hedges:					
Foreign exchange forward contracts	(iii)	5,873	5,873	106	106
Fuel derivatives	(iv)	(52,298)	(52,298)	—	—
US-dollar deposits	(v)	24,309	24,309	22,748	22,748
Accounts payable and accrued liabilities	(vi)	(211,543)	(211,543)	(168,171)	(168,171)
Long-term debt	(vii)	(1,351,903)	(1,515,487)	(1,429,518)	(1,473,997)
		$ (747,649)	$ (911,233)	$ (906,268)	$ (950,747)
Unrecognized loss			$ (163,584)		$ (44,479)

EXHIBIT 9.3

(continued)
WestJet Airlines
Ltd.: Long-Term
Debt

[vii] The fair value of the Corporation's fixed-rate long-term debt is determined by discounting the future contractual cash flows under current financing arrangements at discount rates obtained from the lender, which represent borrowing rates presently available to the Corporation for loans with similar terms and remaining maturities. As at December 31, 2008, rates used in determining the fair value ranged from 2.08% to 2.58% (2007 – 4.52% to 4.61%). The fair value of the Corporation's variable-rate long-term debt approximates its carrying value as it is at a floating market rate of interest.

Characteristics of Bonds

A bond is a formal borrowing arrangement in which a borrower agrees to make periodic interest payments to the lenders and to repay the principal at a specified time in the future. The essentials of a bond are as follows:

- **face value**—the amount the bondholder will receive when the bond matures

- **maturity date**—the date on which the borrower has agreed to pay back the principal (the face value of the bond) to the bondholders

- **coupon rate**—the percentage of the face value the issuer pays to investors each period

A bond with a $1,000 face value, annual coupon rate of 10 percent, and maturity of September 15, 2020, pays the bondholder $100 per year in interest and will repay the $1,000 principal on September 15, 2020.

The **proceeds** of a bond—the amount the issuer receives from the sale of the bond—isn't necessarily the same as its face value. The proceeds are determined by the appropriate **effective interest rate**—the real or market rate of interest required by investors to invest in the bond. If the coupon rate is different from the effective interest rate, the bond selling price must allow investors to earn the effective interest rate. If the coupon rate is lower than the effective interest rate, the bond is sold at a discount and the proceeds are less than the face value. If the coupon rate is greater than the effective interest rate, the bond is sold at a premium and the proceeds are greater than the face value. Only if the coupon rate and effective interest rate are the same will the proceeds equal the face value.

A bond can have features in addition to the basic ones described above, but these are bells and whistles added on to meet the needs of the lenders and borrowers. The additional features come at a price—a change in the interest rate. If a feature is beneficial to investors, the issuing entity should be able to offer a lower interest rate. If a feature is beneficial to the issuing entity, then investors will require a higher interest rate. Following are some examples of features bonds can have:

- **Callable bond**—the bond issuer has the option to repurchase the bond from investors at a time other than the maturity date. This feature is attractive to the issuer because if interest rates fall, the issuer can call the bond and make another issue at a lower interest rate. That isn't attractive to investors as they lose an investment paying a higher-than-market rate of interest. A callable bond will offer a higher market interest rate than an equivalent bond without the call feature.

- **Convertible bond**—may be exchanged by the investor for other securities of the issuing entity, such as common stock.

- **Retractable bond**—gives investors the option of cashing in the bond before the maturity date, under certain conditions.

A bond agreement can also impose restrictions on the issuer's activities. These restrictions are intended to reduce the investor's risk and, thus reduce the cost of borrowing. Many restrictions are stated in accounting terms; for example, a maximum debt-to-equity ratio or a minimum current ratio. Restrictions may prohibit the payment of dividends if retained earnings falls below a certain amount. Violating restrictive covenants can have significant economic consequences for the entity, including an increase in the interest rate on the debt, an increase in the collateral required, additional covenants, or immediate repayment of the bond. Because violating restrictive covenants is costly, managers will take steps, including operating decisions or accounting choices, to avoid it.

Pricing of Bonds

The present value tools discussed in Chapter 6 are used in determining the price of a bond or other long-term debt. The price of a bond is equal to the present value of the cash flows that will be paid to the investor, discounted at the effective interest rate. The effective interest rate of a bond is determined by market forces and depends on the bond's risk; the riskier the bond, the higher the effective interest rate. The risk for bond investors is whether they will receive their interest and principal.

Let's consider an example of the pricing of long-term debt. Bardal Ltd. (Bardal) plans to issue a bond to raise about $5,000,000 to finance a major expansion. The bonds have a face value of $5,000,000 and will be issued on October 1, 2015. They will carry a coupon rate of 9 percent, with interest paid semi-annually on March 31 and September 30 of each year, and will mature in five years, on September 30, 2020. Each semi-annual interest payment will be $225,000 ($5,000,000 × 0.09 × 1/2). For a bond of this type (risk, features, maturity), the effective interest rate is 10 percent. Therefore, the discount rate used to value the cash flows from this bond is 10 percent. (This is important! The appropriate discount rate is the effective interest rate, not the coupon rate on the bond.) Bardal's year-end is September 30. The cash flows that will be generated by the bond are shown in Figure 9.1.

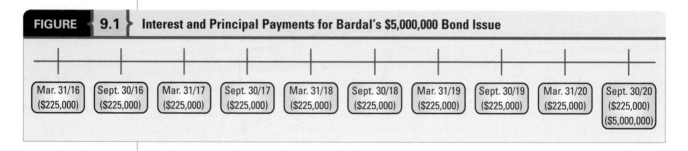

FIGURE 9.1 **Interest and Principal Payments for Bardal's $5,000,000 Bond Issue**

Mar. 31/16	Sept. 30/16	Mar. 31/17	Sept. 30/17	Mar. 31/18	Sept. 30/18	Mar. 31/19	Sept. 30/19	Mar. 31/20	Sept. 30/20
($225,000)	($225,000)	($225,000)	($225,000)	($225,000)	($225,000)	($225,000)	($225,000)	($225,000)	($225,000) ($5,000,000)

The proceeds from this bond issue is the present value (discounted at 10 percent) of (a) a series of 10 semi-annual payments of $225,000 and (b) a payment of $5,000,000 on September 30, 2020, the maturity date of the bond. The semi-annual interest payments are a little twist on our discussion in Chapter 6. Instead of discounting the interest payments at 10 percent over five years, we use a 5 percent discount rate over ten six-month periods. We use the formula for the present value of an annuity to calculate the present value of the interest payments:

$$\text{PV of an annuity}_{n,\,r} = \frac{1}{r} \times \left[1 - \frac{1}{(1+r)^n} \right] \times \text{Amount to be paid in each period}$$

$$\text{PV of an annuity}_{10,\,0.05} = \frac{1}{0.05} \times \left[1 - \frac{1}{(1+0.05)^{10}} \right] \times \$225,000$$

$$= \$1,737,390$$

We also have to calculate the present value of the principal that will be repaid on September 30, 2020. We use the formula for the present value of a single payment to be received in the future:

$$PV_{n,r} = [1 + r]^n \times \text{Amount to be paid in each period}$$
$$PV_{10, 0.05} = \frac{1}{(1 + 0.05)^{10}} \times \$5,000,000$$
$$= \$3,069,566$$

The proceeds from the bond is the sum of these two present value calculations:

Proceeds from bond issue	=	Present value of interest payments	+	Present value of principal repayment
	=	$1,737,390	+	$3,069,556
	=	$4,806,946		

Once the terms of the bond have been set (coupon rate, maturity, other features), the proceeds are a function of the effective interest (discount) rate that is used. If we assume the effective interest rate appropriate for Bardal's bond is 8 percent instead of 10 percent, the proceeds could be calculated:

$$\text{PV of an annuity}_{n,r} = \frac{1}{r} \times \left[1 - \frac{1}{(1 + r)^n}\right] \times \text{Amount to be paid in each period}$$
$$\text{PV of an annuity}_{10, 0.04} = \frac{1}{0.04} \times \left[1 - \frac{1}{(1 + 0.04)^{10}}\right] \times \$225,000$$
$$= \$1,824,952$$

$$PV_{n,r} = [1 + r]^n \times \text{Amount to be paid in each period}$$
$$PV_{10, 0.04} = \frac{1}{(1 + 0.04)^{10}} \times \$5,000,000$$
$$= \$3,377,821$$

Proceeds from bond issue	=	PV of interest payments	+	PV of principal repayment
	=	$1,824,952	+	$3,377,821
	=	$5,202,773		

If we repeat the calculation using an effective interest rate of 9 percent, the same rate as the coupon rate on the bond, the proceeds would be $5,000,000. Try that calculation on your own to prove it! This result isn't a coincidence. When the effective interest rate and the coupon rate of a bond are the same, the proceeds and the face value of the bond will be the same.

Accounting for Bonds

Now that we've seen how bonds are priced in the marketplace, let's look at how we account for them. We will continue with the example of Bardal's $5,000,000 bond offer. We will examine the three scenarios we used for pricing the bonds: (i) when the effective interest rate is the same as the coupon rate on the bond, (ii) when the effective interest rate is greater than the coupon rate, and (iii) when the effective interest rate is less than the coupon rate.

Scenario 1: Selling Bonds at Face Value When the effective rate of interest is the same as the coupon rate, the bonds sell at their face value and Bardal will receive $5,000,000 from the offering. Bardal would make the following journal entry on October 1, 2015 to record the issue of the bonds:

Dr. Cash (asset +)	5,000,000	
Cr. Long-term debt—bonds (liability +)		5,000,000
To record the issue of bonds on October 1, 2015		

On March 31 and September 30 of each year from 2015 through 2020, Bardal would make the following journal entry to record the payment of interest and the interest expense:

Dr. Interest expense (expense +, shareholders equity −)	225,000	
Cr. Cash (asset –)		225,000
To record the interest expense on the $5,000,000 bond offering		

On September 30, 2020, when the bond matures, Bardal would make the following journal entry to derecognize the bond. **Derecognition** occurs when a bond or other liability is removed from the balance sheet; in this case, when the bond is retired by paying the principal to the investors.

Dr. Long-term debt—bonds (liability −)	5,000,000	
Cr. Cash (asset −)		5,000,000
To record derecognition of the bonds on September 30, 2020		

The accounting in this scenario is straightforward. The bonds were reported as a $5,000,000 non-current liability on Bardal's balance sheet, but on the September 30, 2019, balance sheet they would be reclassified as a current liability because the bond would be payable in the next fiscal year. The income statement would show an interest expense of $450,000 (2 × $225,000) each year over the life of the bond.

Scenario 2: Selling Bonds at a Discount In this scenario the effective interest rate for Bardal's bonds is greater than the coupon rate. Investors expect a return of 10 percent on a bond like Bardal's, but Bardal's coupon rate is only 9 percent. As a result, Bardal has to sell its bonds for less than their face value so that investors can earn the 10 percent effective interest rate. Recall that the price for Bardal's bond with an effective interest rate of 10 percent is $4,806,946. This means investors earn a 10 percent return by investing $4,806,946 for ten $225,000 semi-annual interest payments plus a $5,000,000 payment at the end of five years. (If Bardal tries to sell the bond for more than $4,806,946 no one will buy it.)

When bonds are sold for less than their face value, they are said to have been sold at a **discount**. The discount is the difference between the face value of the bonds and the proceeds, in this case $193,054 ($5,000,000 − $4,896,946). The discount is recorded in a contra-liability account. Bardal would make the following entry that to record the issue of its bonds:

Dr. Cash (asset +)	4,806,946	
Dr. Bond discount (contra-liability +)	193,054	
Cr. Long-term debt—bonds (liability +)		5,000,000
To record the issue of bonds on October 1, 2015, at a discount		

The carrying amount of the bonds, the face value of the bonds less the bond discount, is the net present value of bonds discounted using the effective interest rate. The discount can be thought of as interest that investors must receive to earn the effective rate of interest and represents compensation for the low coupon rate. The discount of $193,054 is amortized over the life of the bonds and each period's portion is reported on the income statement as part of the interest expense.

The bonds might be reported on Bardal's October 1, 2015 balance sheet shown in Panel A of Table 9.2. Panel A and the journal entry above treat the discount as a contra-liability account, which would be netted against the face value of the bonds, to report the carrying amount of the bonds on the liability side of the balance sheet.

TABLE 9.2	Methods of Reporting Bond Discount

Panel A—Discount reported as a contra-liability account

Bardal Ltd. Extracts from the October 1, 2015, Balance Sheet	
Long-term debt—Bonds payable	$5,000,000
Unamortized discount on October 1, 2015	193,054
Carrying amount of long-term debt—Bonds payable	$4,806,946

Panel B—Discount reported as "other assets"

Bardal Ltd. Extracts from the October 1, 2015, Balance Sheet			
Non-current assets:		Non-current liabilities:	
Other assets	$193,054	Long-term debt—Bonds payable	$5,000,000

Alternatively, the discount is included on the asset side of the balance sheet and reported as a deferred charge or other assets. The deferred charge represents interest paid in advance. In this approach the bonds would be shown at their face value on the liability side of the balance sheet and the discount would appear separately on the asset side. This approach is shown in Panel B of Table 9.2.

There are two methods for amortizing the discount: straight-line method and effective interest method. IFRS requires the effective interest method. The key point to understand is that the discount is amortized over the life of the bond and becomes part of the interest expense. To demonstrate, I'll use the straight-line method because the effective interest method is more complicated; the mechanics of it are shown briefly in the Insight box below. With the straight-line method, the discount is spread evenly over the life of the bond. For the Bardal bond discount, $38,611 ($193,054 ÷ 5 years) would be amortized each year, or $19,306 when each semi-annual interest payment is made. The entry made each semi-annual period would be

        Dr. Interest expense (expense +, shareholders equity −)   244,305
            Cr. Bond discount (contra-liability −)   19,305
            Cr. Cash (asset −)   225,000

Notice that the interest expense has two components: the cash payment of $225,000 and the amortization of the bond discount of $19,305. The interest expense at each semi-annual payment is $244,305, but each cash payment is only $225,000. With the effective interest method, the amount amortized each period would be different, but the concept is the same.

At maturity, Bardal would derecognize the bond with the same entry as in Scenario 1. The discount would be completely amortized by then. Table 9.3 shows how the discount decreases over the life of the bond and how the carrying amount of the bond increases, reaching its face value at maturity.

TABLE 9.3	Amortization of Bond Discount and Carrying Amount of Bonds			
Issue date	Bond discount at the beginning of the period	Discount amortized	Bond discount at the end of the period	Carrying amount of the bond
October 1, 2015	$193,054			$4,806,946
March 31, 2016	193,054	$19,305	$173,749	4,826,251
September 30, 2016	173,749	19,305	154,443	4,845,557
March 31, 2017	154,443	19,305	135,138	4,864,862
September 30, 2017	135,138	19,305	115,832	4,884,168
March 31, 2018	115,832	19,305	96,527	4,903,473
September 30, 2018	96,527	19,305	77,222	4,922,778
March 31, 2019	77,222	19,305	57,916	4,942,084
September 30, 2019	57,916	19,305	38,611	4,961,389
March 31, 2020	38,611	19,305	19,305	4,980,695
September 30, 2020	19,305	19,305	0	5,000,000

Note: Numbers sometimes don't add up exactly due to rounding.

INSIGHT

Effective Interest Method

Under the effective interest method, the amortization of a bond discount or premium in a period is calculated using the following formulas:

$$\text{Interest expense for the period} = \text{Carrying amount of bond during the period} \times \text{Effective interest rate}$$

$$\text{Discount amortization for the period} = \text{Interest expense for the period} - \text{Interest payment}$$

By using the effective interest rate method, the period's interest expense as a percentage of the carrying amount is constant over the life of the bond. That is, interest expense ÷ carrying amount of the bond, is constant. For the Bardal bond, the amount of the discount amortized for the six months ended March 31, 2016, is:

$$\text{Interest expense for the period} = \$4,806,946 \times 5\%(10\% \times \tfrac{1}{2})$$
$$= \$240,347.30$$

$$\text{Discount amortization for the period} = \$240,347.30 - \$225,000$$
$$= \$15,347.30$$

If we divide the interest expense by the carrying amount of the bond, you get 0.05 or 5% ($240,347.30 ÷ $4,806,946). If you do the same calculation using the straight-line method, the answer is 5.08%. With the straight-line method the interest expense as a percentage of the carrying amount of the bond decreases over the life of the bond because the interest expense remains constant while the carrying amount increases.

KNOWLEDGE CHECK

www.mcgrawhill
connect.ca

On January 1, 2014, Krydor Inc. (Krydor) issued a two-year, $1,000,000 bond with a 10 percent coupon, with interest paid annually on December 31. The bond matures on December 31, 2020. The effective interest rate for this bond is 11 percent.

❑ What price will Krydor sell the bond for?

❑ What journal entry will Krydor make to record the issue of the bond?

❑ Record journal entries that would be made on December 31, 2014 and 2019, to record the interest expense for the year (use straight-line method).

❑ What journal entry will Krydor make when the bond is derecognized and the investors are repaid the principal? Don't include the interest portion of the entry.

Scenario 3: Selling Bonds at a Premium In this scenario, the bonds are sold to investors for more than their face value; that is, the bonds are sold at a **premium**. This will happen when the coupon rate is greater than the effective rate of interest for a bond of that type. When Bardal's bond had a coupon rate of 9 percent and the effective interest rate was 8 percent (4 percent semi-annually), it sold for $5,202,773 and had a premium of $202,773 ($5,202,773 − $5,000,000). The premium is the difference between the proceeds and the face value of the bonds. Bardal would make this entry to record the issue of the bonds at a premiums:

Dr. Cash (asset +)	5,202,773	
Cr. Bond premium (contra-liability +)		202,773
Cr. Long-term debt—bonds (liability +)		5,000,000
To record the issue of bonds on October 1, 2015 at a premium		

Accounting for a premium is the same as for a discount, except that the bond premium account carries a credit balance (for a discount its a debit balance) and the amortization of the premium decreases the interest expense (instead of increasing it, as with a discount). When investors pay a premium for a bond, they are, in effect, repaying in advance the interest they will collect that is over and above the amount required by the effective interest rate.

As with a discount, a premium is amortized over the life of the bonds using the straight-line method or effective interest method. Using the straight-line method, $40,554 of the premium would be amortized each year, or $20,277 when each semi-annual interest payment is made. This entry would be made each semi-annual period:

Dr. Interest expense (expense +, shareholders' equity −)	204,723	
Dr. Bond premium (contra liability −)	20,277	
Cr. Cash (asset −)		225,000

At maturity, Bardal would make the same entry to derecognize the bond as in Scenario 1. The premium would be completely amortized by then. Table 9.4 shows how the premium decreases over the life of the bond and how the carrying amount of the bond decreases, reaching its face value at maturity.

TABLE 9.4	Amortization of Bond Premium and Carrying Amount of Bonds			
Issue date	Bond discount at the beginning of the period	Premium amortized	Bond premium at the end of the period	Carrying amount of the bond
October 1, 2015	$202,773			$5,202,773
March 31, 2016	202,773	$20,277	$182,496	5,182,496
September 30, 2016	182,496	20,277	162,218	5,162,218
March 31, 2017	162,218	20,277	141,941	5,141,941
September 30, 2017	141,941	20,277	121,664	5,121,664
March 31, 2018	121,664	20,277	101,387	5,101,387
September 30, 2018	101,387	20,277	81,109	5,081,109
March 31, 2019	81,109	20,277	60,832	5,060,832
September 30, 2019	60,832	20,277	40,555	5,040,555
March 31, 2020	40,555	20,277	20,277	5,020,277
September 30, 2020	20,277	20,277	0	5,000,000

Other Comments In any period, the straight-line and effective interest methods give different measurements for the interest expense, carrying amount of bonds, and unamortized amounts of discounts and premiums. If the difference between the straight-line and effective interest methods is small (not material), the straight-line method can be used, even if IFRS is a constraint.

INSIGHT

Some Perspective on Technical Complexity

Accounting can be very complex; some liability topics are especially so. The effective interest method is an example. It's important to put this complexity in perspective at this point in your accounting studies. The emphasis in this book is for you to understand what the numbers in financial statements mean, so you can use them intelligently and effectively. To this end, the details of how premiums and discounts are amortized is less important than understanding how the price of bonds is determined, why premiums and discounts arise, and the impact premiums and discounts have on the interest expense.

Accruing Interest on Long-Term Debt

What happens if an entity's year-end isn't the same as the date the interest is paid? With accrual accounting it's necessary to accrue the interest expense at the end of the period so the cost of borrowing is recognized in the appropriate period, even though the interest isn't paid until later. This is the accrued expense/accrued liability adjusting entry we discussed in Chapter 3.

If we assume Bardal's year-end is December 31 instead of September 30, an adjusting entry is made on December 31 of each year of the bond's life to accrue the interest expense for October 1 to December 31. We'll use the facts from Scenario 1 to show this adjusting entry. For the period October 1 through December 31, 2017, Bardal incurs three months of interest costs that should be matched to the 2017 fiscal year, so on December 31, 2017, the following adjusting entry is required:

Dr. Interest expense (expense +, shareholders' equity −)   112,500
   Cr. Interest payable (liability +)   112,500
The amount is one-quarter of the interest cost for a year ($450,000 × 0.25)

On March 31, 2018, when Bardal actually pays interest, it would record the following entry:

Dr. Interest expense (expense +, shareholders' equity −)   112,500
Dr. Interest payable (liability −)   112,500
    Cr. Cash (asset −)   225,000

This entry records the following information:

1. the interest expense for the first three months of fiscal 2018
2. the reduction in the interest payable liability that was accrued on December 31, 2017
3. the payment of interest earned by investors from October 1, 2017 through March 31, 2018 (part of the payment is for interest expensed in fiscal 2017 and part is being expensed in fiscal 2018)

Early Retirement of Debt

Entities sometimes retire their long-term debt before it matures. For example, lower market interest rates can make it worthwhile to retire existing high-interest-rate debt and then issue new debt at a lower rate. This can be done relatively easily, if the debt includes an option for the issuer to redeem it. Alternatively, an entity could repurchase its debt on the open market, if it's publicly traded.

Accounting for the early retirement of debt requires any unamortized discount or premium to be removed from the books—the remaining unamortized premium or discount is included in full in the income statement when the debt is retired. A gain arises if the cost of retiring the debt is less than its carrying amount, and a loss occurs if the cost of retiring the debt is greater than its carrying amount.

For example, on December 31, 2014 Aklavik Ltd. (Aklavik) retired its bonds by paying $1,250,000 to investors. The bonds had a face value of $1,000,000 and there was an unamortized discount of $58,000 at the time the bonds were retired. Aklavik would record the following journal entry to derecognize (retire) the bonds (note: this entry assumes that the interest expense for the period ended December 31, 2014 was recorded before the bonds were retired):

December 31, 2014

Dr. Long-term debt—bonds (liability −)   1,000,000
Dr. Loss on redemption of bond
    (income statement +, shareholders' equity −)   308,000
        Cr. Bond discount (contra-liability−)   58,000
        Cr. Cash (asset −)   1,250,000
To record the early retirement of bonds on December 31, 2014

A similar approach would be used if there was an unamortized premium recorded on the date the bonds were retired. If there was no unamortized discount or premium, the gain or loss would be the difference between the face value of the bonds and the amount paid to retire them.

Disclosure

The balance sheet itself usually only reveals the total amount of long-term debt outstanding and the amount that is maturing within the next year. The totals might provide some information about the riskiness of the entity, but stakeholders need more information to estimate future cash flows, funding requirements, and earnings, and to evaluate the management and stewardship of the entity.

Return to Exhibit 9.3 and examine WestJet's long-term borrowing. The table at the beginning of Note 6 groups long-term borrowing by purpose. The vast majority of the borrowing is for purchasing aircraft. The footnotes below the table describe the terms of the loans. For example, footnote (ii) describes the terms of the $7,265,000 term loan for the flight simulator:

- Repayable in monthly instalments of $95,000.
- An interest rate of prime plus 0.88 percent and an effective interest rate on December 31, 2008, of 4.38 percent.
- Matures in 2011.
- Secured by one flight simulator.

The table near the end of Note 6 discloses the principal repayments WestJet is scheduled to make in each of the next five years and thereafter on its long-term debt. This information is important for assessing future cash flows, cash requirements, and financing needs. According to this disclosure, WestJet is scheduled to repay about the same amount in each of the next five years.

Note 10 on commitments and contingencies describes credit resources available to WestJet. Note 10(c) explains that the company has $15,000,000 available from Canadian chartered banks for letters of credit. A **letter of credit** is a guarantee from a bank that a customer will pay amounts owed to a seller. On December 31, 2008, letters of credit of $12,222,000 had been issued, meaning that the banks had guaranteed payment for purchases of $12,222,000. The letters of credit are secured by a general agreement against company assets (which means that bank has a broad claim against company assets, an insurance policy, and $4,222,000 in restricted cash).

Note 10(d) describes the terms of an operating line of credit WestJet arranged during 2008. It provides up to $85 million in borrowing beginning on May 1, 2009, secured against its new office building. It's a source of liquidity that isn't reflected in the financial statements until the money is actually borrowed. The note describes the interest rate that applies, the allowable purposes for the money (general expenses and working capital), and that WestJet must pay 0.15 percent per quarter on the unused portion of the line of credit.

Most public companies provide similar disclosure about their long-term liabilities, though the extensiveness will vary. Private companies may provide less information than what WestJet does because stakeholders don't require, or managers don't wish to provide, the information. However, powerful stakeholders may request additional detail on liabilities.

Fair Value of Debt

Under IFRS, bonds and other forms of long-term debt are valued at the present value of the cash payments to investors, discounted using the effective (market) interest rate on the date the bond is issued. Interest rates change over the life of a bond, which changes the market value of the bond (if interest rates go up the market value decreases and vice versa), but financial statements don't reflect the change. By ignoring changes in interest rates, financial statements don't reflect real economic gains and losses on long-term debt.

For example, if interest rates increase after a bond is issued, the issuer's interest cost is then lower than the new market interest rate. The effect of having to pay less than the going market interest rate is to decrease in the market value of the liability. (Remember, when the discount rate increases, the present value of a given series of cash flows decreases. As a result, an increase in the effective interest rate decreases the value of the bond.) This can be thought of as an economic gain because the entity now has less debt and is therefore better off. The journal entry to record a decrease in the market value of debt would be

> Dr. Long-term debt (liability −)   xxx
>   Cr. Gain on decrease in market value of long-term debt
>   (income statement +, shareholders' equity +)   xxx
> To record a decrease in the market value of long-term debt

An alternative would be to credit the gain to other comprehensive income. The opposite logic applies if interest rates decrease. In that case, an entity would be paying a higher-than-market interest rate and as a result, the present value of the debt would increase and the entity would suffer an economic loss.

These gains and losses are not recognized under IFRS, but disclosure of the market value of debt must be made in the notes to the financial statements. For example, in Exhibit 9.3, Note 11 shows that the fair value of WestJet's long-term debt on December 31, 2008, was $1,515,487,000 versus a book value (carrying amount) of $1,351,903,000. This represents a loss of $163,584,000 that isn't reflected in the financial statements. The footnote to the table in Note 11 explains the calculation of the fair value of the debt.

? QUESTION FOR CONSIDERATION

Because of an increase in competition in the industry, a respected bond-rating agency recently downgraded its rating on Quaw Inc.'s (Quaw) corporate bonds, which means that the bonds are considered more risky. What do you think the effect of the downgrade would be on the carrying amount of Quaw's bonds? What do you think the impact would be on the market value of the bonds? Explain your answers.

Answer: The carrying amount would be unchanged and the amount of interest Quaw would have to pay would be the same until the bond matured. IFRS doesn't allow an entity's own bonds to be recorded at market value, so changes in the effective rate of interest don't affect the carrying amount. The downgrade causes the effective rate of interest of the bonds to increase and the market value of the bonds to fall, so that investors will receive the rate of return they require.

LEASES

Suppose an entity needs a new truck, but doesn't have the money to pay for it so borrows from a bank. When an asset purchase is financed this way, the balance sheet will show the truck as an asset and the bank loan as a liability. Now suppose the entity finds someone with a truck who will let the entity use it for a few years in exchange for payment. In this case, what should appear on the balance sheet? This is the issue of leasing. A **lease** is a contract in which one entity, the lessee, agrees to pay another entity, the lessor, a fee for the use of an asset. A **lessee** is the entity that leases an asset from its owner and a **lessor** is the entity that leases assets it owns to other entities. In a lease, the lessor owns the asset but the lessee has certain rights and obligations defined in the lease agreement.

Leasing is a very common way for entities to obtain the use of assets without actually buying and owning them. For example, airlines often lease airplanes. On December 31, 2008, WestJet had a fleet of 76 aircraft of which 24 were leased and Air Canada leased 129 of its fleet of 200 planes. There are a number of reasons why entities might prefer to lease assets instead of buying them:

- With a lease, an entity doesn't have to obtain separate financing for the purchase. This can be important when there already is a lot of debt and lenders such as banks are reluctant to lend more.

- Leasing allows for financing of 100 percent of the cost of the asset. Lenders will often lend only a portion of a purchase amount.

- Leases can provide flexibility to lessees. For example, a lease agreement could allow the exchange of leased computer equipment for more up-to-date equipment during the term of the lease. This gives the lessee some protection from technological obsolescence.

- Leasing is attractive for entities that don't need certain assets continuously. For example, a company may require heavy equipment only at certain stages of a project. A lease allows the entity to use the equipment without the cost of owning assets that are idle for significant amounts of time.

Leasing has accounting implications. Before accounting standards for leasing were introduced, creative managers were able to use leases to do **off-balance-sheet financing**—when an entity incurs an obligation without reporting a liability on its balance sheet. Initially, accounting rules required a lessee to simply record a lease or rent expense when payment to the lessor was paid or payable. The lessee could have use of the leased asset in much the same way a purchaser would, but neither the leased asset nor the lease liability had to be reported on the balance sheet.

Off-balance-sheet financing allows an entity the benefit of a liability without the balance sheet consequences, such as a higher debt-to-equity ratio. This can be attractive to entities that are in danger of violating debt-to-equity covenants or for simply limiting the amount of debt the entity appears to have. Also, since the debt-to-equity ratio is a measure of an entity's risk, off-balance-sheet financing makes an entity appear less risky. Of course, an entity's risk isn't affected by the accounting treatment, but the tools for measuring it are.

As leasing became more common, accounting standard setters recognized that many of these leasing contracts were actually purchases in disguise. Rules were established requiring leased assets and associated liabilities to be reported on the lessee's balance sheet if the lease resulted in the transfer of the risks and rewards of ownership to the lessee. Effectively, a lease transaction is accounted for in the same way as a purchase, if certain criteria were met.

There are two categories of leases: capital or finance leases and operating leases. A **finance** or **capital lease** transfers the risks and rewards of ownership to the lessee. At the beginning of a capital lease the leased asset and a liability are recorded on the lessee's balance sheet at the present value of the lease payments to be made over the life of the lease. The leased asset is accounted for in the same way as an owned asset, including being depreciated over its useful life (or the term of the lease if its shorter than the useful life). In most cases, the lessor treats the lease as a sale, removes the leased asset from its books, and reports a receivable equal to the present value of lease payments to be received. For a lessee, a lease should be classified as a capital lease if any of the following three criteria are met:

1. It's likely that the lessee will get ownership of the asset by the end of the lease.

2. The lease term is long enough that the lessee receives most of the economic benefits of the asset.

3. The present value of the lease payments is equal to most of the fair value of the leased asset.

Deciding if any of these criteria are met is a matter of professional judgment. IFRS doesn't provide any quantitative guidelines, so there are no rules for managers and accountants to follow.

If the risks and rewards of ownership aren't transferred to the lessee but are retained by the lessor, then it is an **operating lease**. With an operating lease, the lessee doesn't record the leased assets or the associated liability on its balance sheet. Instead, the lessee recognizes an expense when a payment to the lessor is paid or payable, and the lessor recognizes revenue from the lease when payments are received or receivable. When a lease is classified as an operating lease, the lessee has off-balance-sheet financing.

Let's look at an example to see how lease accounting works. On December 31, 2014, Outram Inc. (Outram) signed an agreement to lease 200 computers from Cheekye Computer Leasing Corp. (Cheekye) for its new head office and distribution centre in Edmonton. The lease was for four years and Outram agreed to pay Cheekye $80,000 on December 31 of each year, beginning in 2015. Outram took delivery of the computers on January 1, 2015. At the end of the lease, Outram can purchase the computers for $1 each. Outram is responsible for maintaining, repairing, and insuring the computers. If Outram had purchased the computers they would have cost $265,000. Outram's year-end is December 31.

Let's apply the criteria to this lease arrangement:

- Outram is likely to gain title of the computers at the end of the lease because it can purchase them for $1 each. At such a low price, Outram would certainly purchase them if they could still be used or if they could be sold for more than $1.

- We don't know the useful life of these computers, but it's hard to imagine they'd have a life much longer than four years. Given the nature of computer equipment, it's reasonable to conclude that Outram will derive most of the economic benefits from them.

- Outram pays $80,000 a year for four years under the terms of the lease. The present value of a series of four payments of $80,000 beginning in 2015 is $253,589 ($1/0.10 \times [1-1/(1 + 0.10)^4] \times \$80,000$), assuming a discount rate of 10 percent, so the present value of the lease payments is over 95 percent ($253,589 \div \$265,000$) of the purchase price of the computers and very close to the fair value of the equipment.

Outram should account for this as a capital lease because it appears that all three criteria are met. Remember, if any of the criteria are met the lease would be accounted for as a capital lease. Outram should capitalize an amount equal to the present value of the lease payments it will make over the life of the lease, which is $253,589. The journal entry to record the acquisition of the computers by a capital lease is

Dr. Assets under capital lease (asset +)   253,589
    Cr. Lease liability (liability +)   253,589
    To record the acquisition of 200 computers under a capital lease

After the initial recording of the leased asset and lease liability, the asset and liability are accounted for separately. (The accounting effects are summarized in the complicated-looking Table 9.5.) Leased capital assets are accounted for in much the same way as any capital asset—depreciated over their useful lives. Depreciation does present some interesting issues, though. If the term of the capital lease is shorter than the useful life of the asset and the lessee isn't likely to take title of the asset at the end of the lease, the asset should be depreciated over the term of the lease.

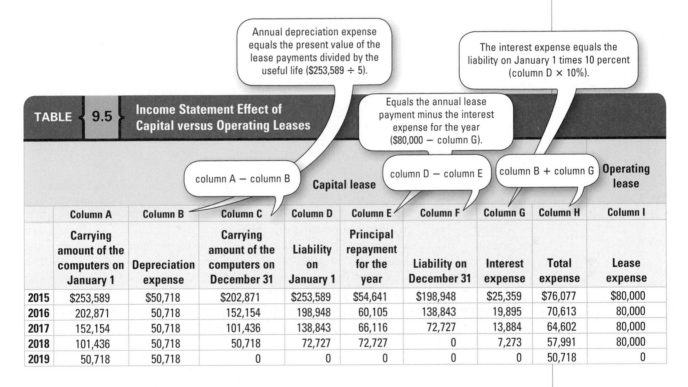

TABLE 9.5 Income Statement Effect of Capital versus Operating Leases

Annotations:
- Annual depreciation expense equals the present value of the lease payments divided by the useful life ($253,589 ÷ 5). → Column B
- Equals the annual lease payment minus the interest expense for the year ($80,000 − column G). → Column F
- The interest expense equals the liability on January 1 times 10 percent (column D × 10%). → Column G
- column A − column B → Column C
- column D − column E → Column F
- column B + column G → Column H

	Column A	Column B	Column C	Column D	Column E	Column F	Column G	Column H	Column I
			Capital lease						Operating lease
	Carrying amount of the computers on January 1	Depreciation expense	Carrying amount of the computers on December 31	Liability on January 1	Principal repayment for the year	Liability on December 31	Interest expense	Total expense	Lease expense
2015	$253,589	$50,718	$202,871	$253,589	$54,641	$198,948	$25,359	$76,077	$80,000
2016	202,871	50,718	152,154	198,948	60,105	138,843	19,895	70,613	80,000
2017	152,154	50,718	101,436	138,843	66,116	72,727	13,884	64,602	80,000
2018	101,436	50,718	50,718	72,727	72,727	0	7,273	57,991	80,000
2019	50,718	50,718	0	0	0	0	0	50,718	0

Since Outram will likely own the computers at the end of the lease, depreciating them over an estimated five-year life is reasonable (although it does seem a bit long for computers). If Outram uses straight line depreciation, the annual depreciation expense will be $50,718 ($253,589 ÷ 5, column B), assuming no residual value. The carrying amount of the computers on January 1 and December 31 of each year is shown in columns A and C respectively (the carrying amount of the computers decreases by $50,718 each year, the amount of the depreciation expense). The journal entry to record the depreciation expense each year is

Dr. Depreciation expense (expense +, shareholders' equity −) 50,718
    Cr. Accumulated depreciation (contra-asset +)   50,718
    To record the depreciation of leased computers

The interest expense is calculated by multiplying the liability outstanding at the beginning of the year by the interest rate. Lease agreements typically don't state the interest rate so the rate has to be assumed. Here we use the same rate, 10 percent, that was used to calculate the present value of the lease payments. Remember though, the interest rate will affect the financial statements numbers and managers have some flexibility in choosing the rate.

Throughout 2015, Outram's liability was $253,589 (column D), so the interest expense for 2015 is $25,359 ($253,589 × 0.10, column G). The portion of the $80,000 payment that's not for interest is repayment of principal that reduces the liability. In 2015, the liability is reduced by $54,641 ($80,000 − $25,359, column E), so the liability on December 31, 2015, is $198,948 ($253,589 − $54,641, column F). For 2016, the interest expense is calculated on the $198,948 liability that is outstanding for the entire year.

Over time the interest portion of the annual payment decreases and the principal portion increases. This happens because, as the liability decreases, less interest is paid and more of the payment is applied to the liability. This effect can be seen in columns D, E, and G of Table 9.5. The journal entry to record the lease payment in 2015 is

Dr. Interest expense (expenses +, shareholders' equity −)	25,359	
Dr. Lease liability (liability −)	54,641	
Cr. Cash (asset −)		80,000
To record the lease payment to Cheekye for 2015		

Notice in Table 9.5 that the carrying amount of the computers (column C) and the associated liability (column F) on December 31 are different from each other in each year. This is expected because the asset and liability are accounted for separately after the initial recording of the lease.

If Outram accounted for the lease as an operating lease, entries would only be required when a payment was made or became payable. In that case, the following entry would be made on December 31, 2015 through 2018:

Dr. Lease expense (expense +, shareholders' equity −)	80,000	
Cr. Cash (asset −)		80,000
To record the annual payment to Cheekye for the computers leased under an operating lease		

The annual lease expense for Outram under an operating lease is shown in column I of Table 9.5.

Whether a lease is classified as operating or capital affects many numbers in the financial statements. With a capital lease, total assets and liabilities will be higher than under an operating lease, and expenses can be different (as can be seen by comparing columns H and I in Table 9.5). These differences can affect many different ratios used in financial analysis. For example, with a capital lease, total assets will be greater so ROA will be lower (though the exact impact will depend on how net income is affected). With an operating lease, as mentioned earlier, an entity's debt-to-equity ratio will be lower because there are fewer liabilities.

Let's look at an example to see the effect of leasing on financial ratios. Consider the information about Outram's lease of computers shown in Table 9.5. Assume the following:

a. Outram's 2015 net income before considering costs related to the lease was $425,000.

b. Outram's interest expense for 2015, before considering lease interest was $50,000.

c. Total assets on December 31, 2014, before considering the effect of the lease were $2,250,000.

d. Total assets on December 31, 2015, before considering the effect of the lease was $2,500,000.

e. Outram's tax rate is 20 percent (the amount of tax Outram pays isn't affect by the classification of the lease).

Outram's ROAs for 2015 using each of the two leasing arrangements are

	Capital lease	Operating lease
Total assets, December 31, 2014	$2,503,589[1]	$2,250,000[2]
Total assets, December 31, 2015	2,702,871[3]	2,500,000[2]
Net income for fiscal 2015	348,923[4]	345,000[5]

[1] $2,250,000 + $253,589 (carrying amount of the computers on December 31, 2014—from column B in Table 9.5).
[2] Total assets aren't affected when the lease is classified as an operating lease.
[3] $2,500,000 + $202,871 (carrying amount of the computers on December 31, 2015—from column B in Table 9.5).
[4] $425,000 − $76,077 (lease related expenses—column H in Table 9.5).
[5] $425,000 − $80,000 (lease expense—column I in Table 9.5).

$$\text{ROA} = \frac{\text{Net income} + \text{After-tax interest expense}}{\text{Total assets}}$$

$$\text{ROA}_{\text{capital lease}} = \frac{\$348,923 + (\$75,359 \times (1 - 0.2))}{\frac{(\$2,702,871 + \$2,503,589)}{2}}$$

$$= 15.7\%$$

$$\text{ROA}_{\text{operating lease}} = \frac{\$345,000 + (\$50,000 \times (1 - 0.2))}{\frac{(\$2,500,000 + \$2,250,000)}{2}}$$

$$= 16.2\%$$

The ROA with a capital lease is slightly lower than with an operating lease because average total assets are greater, but the numerator is also larger because of the related interest expense.

IFRS require extensive disclosure about an entity's lease transactions. For operating leases, an entity should disclose in the notes the minimum lease payments in each of the next five years. For capital leases, an entity should disclose the amount of assets it has under capital leases, along with accumulated depreciation associated with those assets, and information about capital lease liabilities.

In Exhibit 9.3 you can see the information about capital lease liabilities on WestJet's balance sheet. On December 31, 2008, WestJet had current capital lease obligations of $395,000 and non-current ones of $713,000. Exhibit 9.4 provides the following disclosures about its leases:[4]

- Accounting policies applied to capital leases are shown in Notes 1(l) and (n).

- Note 5 shows the carrying amount of assets under capital lease. There are $792,000 of leased assets included in property, plant, and equipment on the December 31, 2008, balance sheet.

- Note 10(b) gives a breakdown of the payments to be made for operating leases in each of the next five years and thereafter. This is important information because it gives insight into the amount of off-balance-sheet financing the company has.

Is off-balance-sheet financing an issue stakeholders should be concerned with? The table in Note 10(b) of Exhibit 9.4 shows that WestJet has contracts representing obligations to spend $1,736,950,000 that isn't reflected on the balance sheet. On a present value basis, that represents between $500 million and $1 billion of off-balance-sheet liabilities (depending on the discount rate used), which increases WestJet's debt load by 20 to 45 percent!

This isn't a situation unique to WestJet. Many companies have significant off-balance-sheet obligations. For example, Magna International Inc. had US$1.826 billion in operating lease commitments on December 31, 2008. Clearly, it's very important to pay attention to these off-balance-sheet obligations to get a complete view of an entity's situation. In general, one has to wonder whether IFRS should recognize all these items on the balance sheet in order to achieve a complete picture of a company's obligations.

1. Summary of significant accounting policies

(l) Property and equipment

Property and equipment is stated at cost and depreciated to its estimated residual value. Assets under capital lease are initially recorded at the present value of minimum lease payments at the inception of the lease.

Asset class	Basis	Rate
Aircraft, net of estimated residual value	Cycles	Cycles flown
Live satellite television included in aircraft	Straight-line	10 years/lease term
Ground property and equipment	Straight-line	3 to 25 years
Spare engines and parts, net of estimated residual value	Straight-line	20 years
Assets under capital lease	Straight-line	Term of lease
Buildings	Straight-line	40 years
Leasehold improvements	Straight-line	Term of lease

(n) Leases

The Corporation classifies leases as either a capital lease or an operating lease. Leases that transfer substantially all of the benefits and risk of ownership to the Corporation are accounted for as capital leases. Assets under capital leases are depreciated on a straight-line basis over the term of the lease. Rental payments under operating leases are expensed as incurred.

The Corporation provides for asset retirement obligations to return leased aircraft to certain standard conditions as specified within the Corporation's lease agreements. The lease return costs are accounted for in accordance with the asset retirement obligations requirements and are initially measured at fair value and capitalized to property and equipment as an asset retirement cost.

5. Property and equipment

2008	Cost	Accumulated depreciation	Net book value
Aircraft	$ 2,394,098	$ 402,095	$ 1,992,003
Ground property and equipment	157,223	83,648	73,575
Spare engines and parts	86,728	17,099	69,629
Buildings	40,028	6,828	33,200
Leasehold improvements	12,019	5,692	6,327
Assets under capital lease	2,482	1,690	792
	2,692,578	517,052	2,175,526
Deposits on aircraft	23,982	—	23,982
Assets under development	82,342	—	82,342
	$ 2,798,902	$ 517,052	$ 2,281,850

10. Commitments and contingencies

(b) Operating leases and commitments

The Corporation has entered into operating leases and commitments for aircraft, land, buildings, equipment, computer hardware, software licences and satellite programming. As at December 31, 2008, the future payments, in Canadian dollars and when applicable the US-dollar equivalents under operating leases and commitments are as follows:

	US dollar	CAD dollar
2009	$ 121,909	$ 165,777
2010	156,114	201,458
2011	175,610	220,324
2012	181,594	226,104
2013	171,008	212,758
2014 and thereafter	547,870	710,529
	$ 1,354,105	$ 1,736,950

As at December 31, 2008, the Corporation is committed to lease an additional 15 737-700 aircraft and five 737-800 aircraft for terms ranging between eight and 10 years in US dollars. These aircraft have been included in the table totals.

KNOWLEDGE CHECK

☐ Explain the difference between capital and operating leases. How does each affect the financial statements?

☐ On January 1, 2014, a company enters into a 10-year lease for some equipment. The lease requires annual payments of $25,000 on December 31 of each year. If the appropriate discount rate for the lease is 7 percent, how much would be recorded on the balance sheet for the equipment if the lease was classified as a capital lease?

QUESTION FOR CONSIDERATION

Explain why companies might prefer to have their leases classified as operating leases instead of capital leases. Explain why and how companies are able to arrange their leases to satisfy this preference under IFRS.

Answer: The disadvantage of a capital lease is that a liability equal to the present value of the lease payments must be reported on the balance sheet. This increases the amount of debt reported, which may affect the entity's perceived risk and perceived ability to carry additional debt. Measurements such as the debt-to-equity ratio increase when leases are capitalized, which may have economic consequences if there exists a covenant limiting the debt-to-equity ratio, or similar measures. Operating leases, on the other hand, have no effect on liabilities. They allow the entity to keep its lease liabilities "off the balance sheet."

A lease is classified as a capital lease if the benefits and risks of ownership are transferred to the lessee. IFRS don't clearly define benefits and risks of ownership, but they provide criteria for guiding managers, so judgment plays an important role in determining the classification.

CANADIAN GAAP FOR PRIVATE ENTERPRISES

Canadian GAAP for Private Enterprises provides quantitative guidelines to help managers classify leases. A leased asset to be used by the lessee for more the 75 percent of its useful life or a present value of lease payments that is greater than 90 percent of the fair value of the asset indicate a capital lease. These guidelines are often interpreted as rules by managers. As a result, classifying a lease according to Canadian GAAP for Private Enterprises requires less judgment than IFRS.

A private company might choose not to follow Canadian GAAP for Private Enterprises for leases. It may make sense for small businesses to avoid the complexities of lease accounting if their stakeholders don't require it.

PENSIONS AND OTHER POST-RETIREMENT BENEFITS

As part of their compensation packages, many employees receive pensions and other benefits after they retire. A **pension** is income provided after retirement. Pensions are provided to Canadians by employers, by government, through the Canada and Québec Pension Plans, and through savings in registered retirement savings plans (RRSPs). Retired employees can also receive benefits such as extended medical (medical costs not covered by a provincial health plan), dental, vision, and prescription coverage. Employee pensions and other post-retirement employee benefits are negotiated between an employer and its employees.

Post-retirement benefits are an extremely important issue in Canada, for both economic and accounting reasons. The amounts involved in benefit plans give an idea of their economic significance. Table 9.6 gives the fair value of the assets in a number of Canadian companies' benefit plans and the estimated benefits that employees are entitled to as of the end of their 2008 fiscal years. Notice that for all of the companies shown, except Telus Communications Inc., the benefits promised exceed the value of the assets in the plans, sometimes by huge amounts (like over $2 billion for BCE Inc.). This means the plans are underfunded—there aren't enough assets to meet the current obligations to the employees.

Accounting for pensions and post-retirement benefits is complex and the information reported in the financial statements can be confusing. Most of the issues in pension and post-retirement benefits accounting are beyond the scope of this book. However, because of the subject's economic significance and its prominence in many entities' financial statements, an introduction to it is appropriate.

TABLE 9.6	Benefit Plan Information for Some Large Canadian Companies		
Company	Fair value of benefit plan assets	Estimated benefit obligation	Unfunded amount (difference between plan assets and estimated benefits)
BCE Inc.	$11,510,000,000	$13,602,000,000	($2,092,000,000)
Canadian Pacific Railway Limited	3,070,000,000	4,738,000,000	(1,668,000,000)
Husky Energy Inc.	110,000,000	132,000,000	(22,000,000)
Loblaw Companies Limited	1,079,000,000	1,484,000,000	(405,000,000)
Magna International Inc.	176,000,000	250,000,000	(74,000,000)
Royal Bank	5,867,000,000	7,529,000,000	(1,662,000,000)
Telus Communications Inc.	5,688,000,000	5,307,000,000	381,000,000

Employees earn their benefits while they are working even though they receive them after they retire. In effect, instead of giving full compensation in cash while working, the employer funds a pension plan that provides benefits to employees after retirement. The benefits are part of employees' compensation so the cost is expensed over the employee's working career. In other words, it's a question of matching.

There are two types of pension plans: defined-contribution plans and defined-benefit plans. In a **defined-contribution plan** the employer makes contributions to the plan as specified in the pension agreement with the employees. For example, the employer's contribution might be a percentage of each employee's wage or salary. Employees often make contributions as well. The pension benefits an employee receives depend on the amount contributed to the plan by the employer and the employee and on the performance of the investments in the pension plan.

Accounting for defined-contribution plans is fairly straightforward. The employer's contribution is the pension expense for the year. A pension liability is reported on the employer's balance sheet if the full contribution isn't made by the end of the period. For example, under its defined-contribution pension plan, Nojack Ltd. (Nojack) is required to contribute $250,000 to the plan in 2014. On December 15, 2014, Nojack's treasurer wrote a cheque for $200,000 to the plan. The remaining $50,000 is to be paid in 2015. The entry that Nojack would make to record its contribution in 2014 is

> Dr. Pension expense (expense +, shareholders' equity −)   250,000
>   Cr. Cash (asset −)   200,000
>   Cr. Pension liability (liability +)   50,000
> To record the contribution to the employee defined-contribution pension plan for 2014

The $50,000 pension liability would be reported on Nojack's December 31, 2014 balance sheet.

In a **defined-benefit plan** the employer promises to provide employees with specified benefits in each year they are retired. For example, a defined-benefit plan might provide employees with a pension equal to 2.5 percent of the final year's salary for each year worked for the entity. An employee who worked for 30 years and had a salary in the last year of $125,000 would receive an annual pension of $93,750 ($125,000 × 0.025 × 30 years).

The crucial difference between defined-contribution and defined-benefit plans is risk. With a defined-benefit plan employers bear the risk because they promise specified benefits to employees, regardless of how the investments in the pension plan perform. If there isn't enough money in the plan to pay the pensions, the employer must make up the difference. In a defined-contribution plan, on the other hand, the employer only promises a contribution. The pension the retired employee receives depends on the performance of the pension fund. As a result, the employee bears the risk.

With a defined-benefit pension plan, there are two decisions an entity must make. The first is the accounting question—what should the annual pension expense be? The second is the funding question—what should be the annual contribution to the plan be? The pension expense and the amount contributed are often separate calculations, and the amounts don't have to be, and usually aren't, the same.

Determining the amount to expense and the amount to fund are complex present-value problems. The objective of a defined-benefit plan is to provide an employee with regular payments of a specified amount (an annuity) for the rest of the employee's life after retirement. The calculation itself is relatively straightforward, but the assumptions required are difficult. For example, consider the employee described previously who is to receive an annual pension of $93,750. Conceptually, the pension plan must have enough money on hand when the employee retires to purchase an annuity that will pay the employee $93,750 a year for life. If the employee is expected to live for 15 years after retirement and the appropriate discount rate is 8 percent, the plan would need $802,451.13 ($1/0.08 \times [1 - 1/(1 + 0.08)^{15}] \times \$93,750$) to purchase an annuity that guaranteed an annual payment of $93,750 for 15 years. Two crucial assumptions have been made: the number of years that the employee would live after retirement and the appropriate discount rate. If either of these assumptions changes, the amount that must be available in the retirement year to purchase the annuity would change, possibly dramatically.

We also have to determine the amount to invest in the pension plan each year over the employee's working life so the $802,451 will be in the plan when the employee retires. Then consider that we have to figure this out for an entire workforce, and the process becomes very complicated. The whole exercise is dependent on a set of assumptions:

- the number of years employees will work for the employer

- the number of employees who will qualify for benefits

- the number of employees who will die before they retire

- the age at which employees will retire

- the salary employees will earn in the year or years on which the pension is based

- the number of years employees will live after retirement

- the return the money in the pension fund will earn (the higher the expected return, the less money that needs to be invested in the pension fund by the employer)

Now remember that funding pension plans and calculating pension expenses is based on events that will take place over the many years until an employee retires—20, 25, 30, or even more years into the future! These assumptions and the time span involved make pension accounting complex.

Accounting for other post-retirement benefits (other than pensions) is similar to the accounting for pensions. However, unlike pensions, companies aren't required to fund non-pension post-retirement benefits, and most pay for these benefits as they occur. The obligations can be significant and will likely grow as the number of retired employees grows.

An example of pension and benefits disclosure is provided in Exhibit 9.5 for Saputo Inc., the manufacturer and distributor of dairy and grocery products.[5] The numbered references below refer to the relevant parts of Exhibit 9.5.

❶ The significant accounting policy for employee future benefits explains how the company accounts for its employee future benefits.

❷ The $196,170,000 is the pension benefits that have been promised to employees. The $12,684,000 is the amount promised for other benefits.

❸ The value of the assets in the pension plan is $192,060,000. The difference between ❸ and ❹ is the amount by which the pension plan and other benefit plans are underfunded. Important: The assets and obligations of the pension fund itself don't appear in Saputo's balance sheet. The pension fund is a separate entity.

❹ This is the accounting asset or liability that is reported on the balance sheet. The amounts are the result of complex accounting rules about determining the pension and benefit expense each year.

❺ These are the amounts expensed in Saputo's income statement for the year.

❻ These assumptions went into the calculations. They are very important because the results are only as good as the underlying assumptions. By disclosing them, stakeholders can assess whether they are reasonable.

1. SIGNIFICANT ACCOUNTING POLICIES

Employee future benefits

❶ The cost of pension and other post-retirement benefits earned by employees is actuarially determined using the projected benefit method prorated on services and using estimates of expected return on plan assets, which is based on market-related value, rates of compensation increase, retirement ages of employees and expected health care costs and other post retirement benefits. Current service costs are expensed in the year. In accordance with generally accepted accounting principles, past service costs and the excess of the net actuarial gains or losses related to defined benefit pension plans over 10% of the greater of the benefit obligation or fair value of plan assets are amortized over the expected average remaining service period of active employees entitled to receive benefits under the plans. The Company uses five-year asset smoothing to determine the defined benefit pension costs. In the case where a plan restructuring entails both a plan curtailment and settlement of obligations from the plan, the curtailment is recorded before the settlement. The average remaining service period of active participants covered by the pension plans is 11.5 years.

16. EMPLOYEE PENSION AND OTHER BENEFIT PLANS

The Company provides benefit and defined contribution pension plans as well as other benefit plans such as health insurance, life insurance and dental plans to be eligible employees and retired employees.

Under the terms of the defined benefit pension plans, pensions are based on years of service and the average salary of the last employment years or the career salary. Contributions paid by employees and contributions by the Company are based on recommendations from independent actuaries. Actuarial valuations were performed in December 2006 and July 2007. The measurement date of pension plan assets and liabilities is December 31.

The defined contribution pension plans entitle participating employees to an annual contribution giving right to a pension.

Plan assets are principally comprised of shares of Canadian and foreign companies (53%), fixed income investments (43%) and cash and short-term investments (4%).

FINANCIAL POSITION OF THE PLANS

	2008		2007	
	Defined benefit pension plans	Other benefit plans	Defined benefit pension plans	Other benefit plans
Changes in accrued benefit obligations				
Benefits obligation at beginning of year	$ 199,938	$ 13,143	$ 200,370	$ 13,001
Addition during the year	-	588	-	-
Current service cost	7,756	224	7,096	256
Interest cost	10,361	667	10,339	658
Benefits paid	(12,690)	(1,368)	(14,612)	(1,144)
Actuarial (gains) losses	(8,805)	(278)	(3,225)	406
Foreign currency gain	(390)	(292)	(30)	(34)
❷ Benefits obligation at end of year	196,170	12,684	199,938	13,143
Changes in fair value of plan assets				
Fair value of plan assets at beginning of year	193,146	-	175,819	-
Actual return on plan assets	657	-	19,254	-
Employer contributions	10,101	1,196	11,563	944
Employee contributions	1,125	172	1,150	200
Benefits paid	(12,690)	(1,368)	(14,613)	(1,144)
Foreign currency loss	(279)	-	(27)	-
❸ Fair value of plan assets at end of year	192,060	-	193,146	-
Funded status				
Deficit, end of year	(4,111)	(12,684)	(6,792)	(13,143)
Unamortized actuarial losses	65,903	2,223	67,104	2,251
Unamortized past service cost	963	201	1,081	231
Valuation allowance	(573)	-	(181)	-
Unamortized transitional obligation	(7,593)	973	(8,749)	1,169
Asset (liability) as at the measurement date	54,589	(9,287)	52,463	(9,492)
Employer contributions made from the measurement date to the end of the year	1,650	85	1,863	62
❹ Net asset (liability) recognized in the balance sheet	$ 56,239	$ (9,202)	$ 54,326	$ (9,430)

Information about pensions and other post-retirement benefits is important to many stakeholders. These benefits can represent very significant obligations to an entity and may even affect its solvency. Increasingly, entities are questioning their ability to meet the commitments they have made to their employees and some have attempted to reduce the size of their commitments. Stakeholders want to assess the impact benefits have on the entity's ability to survive, compete, and be profitable. Employees and retired employees would clearly have an interest in information about the benefit plans since it affects the quality of their lives after retirement. The pension plan's condition provides information about an entity's cash flow requirements.

Most defined benefit pension plans present an accrued benefits obligation in excess of plan assets.

EMPLOYEE BENEFIT PLANS EXPENSE

	2008		2007	
	Pension plans	Other benefit plans	Pension plans	Other benefit plans
Defined benefit plans				
Employer current service cost	$ 6,631	$ 52	$ 5,946	$ 56
Interest cost on benefits obligation	10,361	667	10,339	658
Actual return on plan assets	(657)	-	(19,254)	-
Acturial (gains) losses	(8,805)	(278)	(3,225)	406
Unadjusted benefits (income)/expense before taking into account the long-term nature of the cost	7,530	441	(6,194)	1,120
Difference between expected return and actual return on plan assets	(12,765)	-	6,538	-
Difference between amortized past service costs and plan amendments for the year	115	31	115	31
Difference between net actuarial loss recognized and actual actuarial loss on benefits obligation	13,858	636	8,608	(140)
Transitional obligation amortization	(1,156)	196	(1,156)	196
Defined benefit plan expense before valuation allowance	7,582	1,304	7,911	1,207
Valuation allowance	392	-	181	-
❺ Defined benefit plan expense	7,974	1,304	8,092	1,207
Defined contribution plan expense	12,733	-	11,929	-
Total benefit plan expense	$ 20,707	$ 1,304	$ 20,021	$ 1,207

For the year ended March 31, 2008, the Company's total expense for all its employee benefits plans was $22,011,000 ($21,228,000 in 2007) and the total Company contributions to the employee benefits plans was $24,030,000 ($24,436,000 in 2007).

Weighted average assumptions

To determine benefits obligation at the end of year:				
Discount rate	5.61%	5.44%	5.26%	5.35%
Rate of compensation	3.50%	3.50%	3.50%	3.50%
❻ To determine benefit plans expense:				
Discount rate	5.26%	5.35%	5.26%	5.31%
Expected long-term rate of return on plan assets	7.30%	N/A	7.31%	N/A
Rate of compensation increase	3.50%	3.50%	3.50%	3.50%

For measurement purposes, a 6.6% to 9% annual rate of increase was used for health, life insurance and dental plan costs for the year 2009 and this rate is assumed to decrease gradually to 6% in 2013. In comparison, during the previous year, a 7% to 10% annual rate was used for the year 2008 and that rate was assumed to decrease gradually to 5.1% in 2012.

EXHIBIT 9.5

(continued) Saputo Inc.: Pension and Other Benefit Plan Disclosures

There is one final point about pension accounting. The complexity of the assumptions required to calculate the pension expense cause managers to exercise considerable judgment. Some critics contend that some managers have made unrealistic assumptions and that by doing so they have significantly understated the pension expense and pension liability.

CONTINGENCIES

Suppose an entity realizes that it might incur a gain or a loss as the result of an event. But the amount of that gain or loss, or even if there will be one at all, is uncertain and won't be known until some future event occurs. What, if anything, should the impact on the financial statement be?

For example, in 2013, Rosyth Ltd. (Rosyth) was sued for $10,000,000. As of the end of fiscal 2014, the case had not been resolved so the amount (if anything) Rosyth will ultimately have to pay is unknown. The lawsuit could be accrued, disclosed in the notes, or ignored for financial reporting purposes. If accrued, the financial statements will reflect the economic impact of the lawsuit, but does it make sense to accrue contingencies that have a low probability of being realized; for example, a frivolous lawsuit launched by a disgruntled employee? Recognition would impact the financial statements, but would it result in reasonable representation of the company's economic situation? It's not known what the cost will actually be, even though the suit is for $10,000,000. After all, just because someone sues you for $10,000,000 doesn't mean they're

Consolidated Financial Statements
2008

17. CONTINGENCIES, GUARANTEES AND INDEMNITIES

Contingencies
Investigations by Competition Authorities Relating to Cargo

The European Commission, the United States Department of Justice and the Competition Bureau in Canada, among other competition authorities, are investigating alleged anti-competitive cargo pricing activities, including the levying of certain fuel surcharges, of a number of airlines and cargo operators, including the Corporation. Competition authorities have sought or requested information from the Corporation as part of their investigations. The Corporation is cooperating with these investigations, which are likely to lead, or have led, to proceedings against the Corporation and a number of airlines and other cargo operators in certain jurisdictions including in the European Union where all formal procedural steps preceding a decision have been completed. The Corporation is also named as a defendant in a number of class action lawsuits that have been filed before the United States District Court and in Canada in connection with these allegations.

During 2008, the Corporation recorded a provision of $125 as a preliminary estimate. This estimate is based upon the current status of the investigations and proceedings and the Corporation's assessment as to the potential outcome for certain of them. This provision does not address the proceedings and investigations in all jurisdictions, but only where there is sufficient information to do so. Management has determined it is not possible at this time to predict with any degree of certainty the outcome of all proceedings and investigations. Additional material provisions may be required.

Pay Equity

The Canadian Union of Public Employees ("CUPE"), which represents the Corporation's flight attendants, has a complaint before the Canadian Human Rights Commission where it alleges gender-based wage discrimination. CUPE claims the predominantly female flight attendant group should be paid the same as the predominantly male pilot and mechanics groups because their work is of equal value. The complaint dates from 1991 but has not been investigated on the merits because of a legal dispute over whether the three groups work in the same "establishment" within the meaning of the Canadian Human Rights Act. On January 26, 2006, the Supreme Court of Canada ruled that they do work in the same "establishment" and sent the case back to the Canadian Human Rights Commission, which may now proceed to assess the merits of CUPE's complaint. On March 16, 2007, the Canadian Human Rights Commission referred the complaint against the Corporation for investigation. The Corporation considers that any investigation will show that it is complying with the equal pay provisions of the Canadian Human Rights Act; however, management has determined it is not possible at this time to predict with any degree of certainty the final outcome of the Commission's investigation.

Other Contingencies

Various other lawsuits and claims, including claims filed by various labour groups of Air Canada are pending by and against the Corporation and provisions have been recorded where appropriate. It is the opinion of management that final determination of these claims will not have a significant material adverse effect on the financial position or the results of the Corporation.

going to get $10,000,000. On the other hand, ignoring an event like this deprives stakeholders of important information about risks the entity faces and could open entities and their auditors to lawsuits for failing to provide important information. Disclosure provides information about existence and significance but don't affect the financial statement numbers, so outcomes such as bonus payments or covenants that depend on financial statement numbers aren't affected.

IFRS identifies economic events called **contingent liabilities**, which have the following characteristics:

- a possible obligation whose existence has to be confirmed by a future event beyond the control of the entity (for example, a judge's ruling in a lawsuit)

- an obligation with uncertainties about the probability that payment will be made or about the amount of payment (it doesn't meet the definition of a provision)

A contingent liability isn't recognized in the financial statements but is disclosed in the notes, unless the probability of having to pay is remote. If it's recognized, it's classified as a provision (discussed earlier in the chapter).

A contingent asset is an asset whose existence is uncertain. Contingent assets aren't recognized in the financial statements, but they are disclosed in the notes if realization is probable (IFRS defines probable as "more likely than not"). If realization of the asset becomes virtually certain, the asset is recognized in the financial statements and no longer referred to as a contingent asset. Application of these accounting standards requires considerable judgment because it's necessary to estimate the probability of a contingency being realized and its amount.

Exhibit 9.6 provides extracts from Air Canada's contingency note from its 2008 annual report.[6] The first two items describe specific contingent liabilities relating to an investigation about cargo-pricing services and to a pay equity dispute. The third item under "Other Contingencies" refers to other claims and lawsuits against and by the company that, regardless of outcome, aren't expected to have a materially adverse affect. Many companies provide a general statement of this kind disclosing the existence but not the details of contingencies believed to be minor.

COMMITMENTS

A **commitment** is a contractual agreement to enter into a future transaction. Agreements committing an entity to future purchases of goods or services aren't reported as liabilities, according to IFRS. These arrangements are called executory contracts. When neither party to a contract has performed its part of the bargain, then neither the liability to pay nor the asset representing the good or service to be received is recorded. For example, it's common in professional sports for athletes to sign long-term, high-value, guaranteed contracts. Neither the liability to pay the athlete nor the team's right to the athlete's services are reported on the team's balance sheet. Signing the contract doesn't trigger recognition of the liability; performance by the athlete does. Once the athlete has played (assuming that he or she wasn't paid in advance) a liability for wages can be set up.

The IFRS approach isn't the only way of accounting for executory contracts. An alternative would be to record the asset and liability associated with the contract (perhaps only when it isn't possible for either party to cancel the contract). For example, in December 2014 Chopaka Inc. (Chopaka) signed a contract to purchase $400,000 of lumber for construction of new homes. The lumber is to be delivered over the period March through October 2015. The contract isn't cancellable by either Chopaka or the supplier. Under IFRS, this contract would not be reflected in the financial statements. However, if executory contracts were recognized, Chopaka would report a $400,000 asset representing the lumber to be delivered and a $400,000 liability to pay for the lumber when it's delivered. There are no income statement effects of this treatment, but it increases assets and liabilities. There is no effect on working capital (current assets − current liabilities), but the current ratio (current assets ÷ current liabilities) is affected if the ratio isn't equal to 1.0.

While IFRS generally don't allow for recognition of executory contracts, information about an entity's significant commitments can be important to stakeholders, so disclosure of them is appropriate. If Chopaka followed IFRS, it might disclose its contract to purchase lumber. This decision is a judgment call made by the managers.

EVENTS AFTER THE REPORTING PERIOD/ SUBSEQUENT EVENTS

What happens if a significant economic event occurs after the end of an entity's fiscal year? Strictly speaking, events that didn't occur during the reporting period should be ignored. On the other hand, any information that is potentially useful to stakeholders should be provided on a timely basis, and IFRS recognizes this. An **event after the reporting period**, or **subsequent event**, is an economic event that occurs after an entity's year-end but before the financial statements are released to stakeholders.

There are two subsequent event categories:

1. events that provide information about circumstances that existed at the year-end
2. events that happened after the end of the period

For the first type of subsequent event, the financial statements are adjusted to reflect the new information. The new information allows managers to make better estimates than they could at the financial statement date. Here are some examples of subsequent events that could lead to adjustments to the financial statements:

- A customer files for bankruptcy after the year-end; the estimated uncollectible accounts receivable might be adjusted.

- Sale of inventory after the end of the period; this could provide information about the NRV of the inventory at year-end.

- Settlement of a lawsuit after the year-end; a liability could be accrued rather than just disclosed in the notes.

No information about these adjustments is disclosed in the notes. The information is used to revise the numbers in the statements.

The second type of subsequent event is events that took place after the end of the period and are unrelated to circumstances that existed at year-end. These events only appear in the notes—the financial statements aren't adjusted. Of course, many events occur after the year-end and virtually none of them are disclosed as subsequent events. What should be disclosed isn't well defined. IFRS say that events that will have a significant or material effect on the entity should be disclosed. Ultimately, what constitutes a subsequent event of either type is a matter of judgment, and in many cases managers have flexibility as to whether and how an event occurring after the year-end will be reported in the financial statements.

For public companies, most events of any consequence would be disclosed to the public by newspaper reports or press releases long before the financial statements are released. For private companies, especially those that get little public attention, disclosure of the second type of event would much more likely be "news" to stakeholders.

Information about subsequent events, regardless of how a stakeholder learns about them, is useful for forecasting future earnings or cash flows. Exhibit 9.7 provides some examples of subsequent event disclosures. The examples are for the acquisition of another company, arranging additional credit, and declaration of a dividend.[7]

EXHIBIT 9.7

Examples of Subsequent Event Notes

www.corusent.com
www.enbridge.com
www.canadabread.ca

Corus Entertainment Inc.

Note 26. Subsequent event

On September 2, 2008, the Company announced that it had completed the acquisition of Canadian Learning Television ("CLT") effective September 1, 2008. The acquisition cost was approximately $75,000, including customary closing adjustments. The CRTC approved the acquisition on August 22, 2008 and the Company took over ownership and operation of CLT on September 1, 2008.

Enbridge Inc.

31. SUBSEQUENT EVENT

In January, 2009, the Company secured incremental credit of $225 million from its banking group for an existing credit facility established in December 2008. The new commitments provide additional liquidity and increase the total credit facilities to $8.8 billion.

Canada Bread Company Limited

23. SUBSEQUENT EVENT

On February 23, 2009, the Company declared a dividend of $0.06 per share, payable to shareholders of record as of March 10, 2009, on April 1, 2009.

INSIGHT

Debt and Taxes

Earlier, we briefly discussed the tax implications of debt. Entities are allowed to deduct interest when calculating taxable income. (**Taxable income** is the measure of income, as defined by the *Income Tax Act*, that is used to calculate the amount of tax an entity must pay.) This means the actual cost of borrowing money is less than the amount paid to the lender. In effect, taxpayers pay for part of the cost of borrowing. The **after-tax cost of borrowing** is the interest rate an entity pays after taking into consideration the savings that come from being able to deduct interest in the calculation of taxable income. It is calculated using the following formula:

After-tax cost of borrowing = Stated interest rate × (1 − Tax rate)

Estmere Inc. (Estmere) has a $10,000,000 long-term bond outstanding that has an interest rate of 11.5 percent. Estmere pays the bondholder $1,150,000 in interest on December 31 of each year, and its tax rate is 40 percent. Estmere's after-tax cost of borrowing is as follows:

$$After\text{-}tax\ cost\ of\ borrowing = Stated\ interest\ rate \times (1 - Tax\ rate)$$
$$= 11.5\% \times (1 - 0.4)$$
$$= 11.5\% \times 0.6$$
$$= 6.9\%$$

Since Estmere is able to reduce its income by $1,150,000 each year because it can deduct the interest cost, it has to pay $460,000 ($1,150,000 × 0.4) less tax than it would if the cost of borrowing weren't deductible.

FINANCIAL STATEMENT ANALYSIS ISSUES

Analyzing an entity's liabilities provides important information about its financial situation and its prospects, and it can also provide insight into its financial management. For example, creditors can obtain information allowing them to assess the amount they would be willing to lend the entity; the terms of the loan, including interest rate and amount and type of collateral; and restrictive covenants. In addition, the evaluation of liabilities provides important information about an entity's liquidity. We looked at tools for evaluating liquidity in previous chapters. Below, tools for analyzing risk, capital structure, and the ability to carry debt are discussed.

Debt-to-Equity Ratio

The debt-to-equity ratio is a measure of the amount of debt relative to equity an entity uses for financing. The ratio gives an indication of the entity's risk and ability to carry more debt. More debt makes an entity riskier. As explained earlier in the chapter, debt is riskier for an entity because interest and principal payments on debt must be made regardless of how well the entity is doing. An entity that has relatively little debt (compared with industry norms) is able to assume more.

It's important to recognize that debt isn't necessarily a bad way to finance an entity. Debt is less costly than equity and interest on debt is tax deductible whereas dividends paid to shareholders aren't. However, debt becomes more risky for lenders as the amount of it increases because the likelihood of non-payment increases with the amount of debt. As a result, debt becomes costlier for borrowers because lenders are paid higher interest rates as compensation for accepting more risk. An entity should have a balance between debt and equity, but the appropriate mix depends on the nature of the entity. The debt-to-equity ratio is an important tool for evaluating an entity's debt load and its capital structure. (**Capital structure** is the term used to describe how an entity is financed. It's the amount of debt and equity the entity has.)

The debt-to-equity ratio is defined as

$$\text{Debt-to-equity ratio} = \frac{\text{Total liabilities}}{\text{Total shareholder's equity}}$$

WestJet's debt-to-equity ratio on December 31, 2008 is calculated as

$$= \frac{\$2,192,712,000}{\$1,086,137,000}$$
$$= 2.02$$

WestJet's debt-to-equity ratio of 2.02 means it has $2.02 of liabilities for every $1 of equity. Is that too much? It isn't possible to answer without a context. Determining whether a ratio is too high depends on many factors, including industry and circumstances. Entities that have highly reliable cash flows can carry more debt because they can be confident that the cash flows will be available to make interest and principal payments. WestJet's ratio has been stable since 2004 (see Table 9.7); before 2004 it increased significantly as WestJet borrowed heavily to finance growth. The ratios of Air Canada and Air Transat are provided in Table 9.7 for comparison. Note that in the period shown, Air Canada went through significant financial crises that resulted in the company filing for bankruptcy protection.

TABLE 9.7 Debt-to-Equity Ratios of Canadian Airlines[8]

Debt-to-equity ratio	2008	2007	2006	2005	2004	2003	2002	2001	2000	1999
WestJet	2.02	2.14	2.38	2.30	2.18	1.54	1.20	0.77	0.86	0.97
Air Canada*	13.91	3.85	5.34	8.61	—	−2.66	−4.24	−10.49	29.76	8.25
Air Transat	2.70	2.88	2.24	1.62	1.67	1.96	2.97	3.52	1.94	1.67

*Air Canada's debt-to-equity ratio is negative in some years because equity was negative in those years.

Interest Coverage Ratio

The **interest coverage ratio** is one of a number of coverage ratios that measure an entity's ability to meet its fixed financing charges. In particular, the interest coverage ratio indicates how easily an entity can meet its interest payments from its current income. The interest coverage ratio is defined as

$$\text{Interest coverage ratio} = \frac{\text{Net income} + \text{Interest expense} + \text{Income tax expense}}{\text{Interest expense}}$$

The larger the ratio, the more able the entity is to meet its interest payments. The ratio is limiting in that it ignores the fact that entities have financing charges other than interest. These include debt repayment and payments on operating leases. This ratio can be modified to include these other charges, but the interest coverage ratio is appropriate to this introductory discussion.

The interest coverage ratio for WestJet for the year ended December 31, 2008, is calculated as

$$\text{Interest coverage ratio} = \frac{\text{Net income} + \text{Interest expense} + \text{Income tax expense}}{\text{Interest expense}}$$
$$= \frac{\$178,135,000 + \$76,078,000 + \$76,702,000}{\$76,078,000}$$
$$= 4.35$$

The interest coverage ratio of 4.35 means that WestJet's income before taxes and interest expense covers its interest costs over four times. Of course, earnings and cash flows can be volatile and coverage ratios can change dramatically from period to period. Also, net income isn't cash.

TABLE 9.8 Interest Coverage Ratios for Canadian Airlines										
Interest coverage ratio	2008	2007	2006	2005	2004	2003	2002	2001	2000	1999
WestJet	4.35	4.15	3.34	1.94	0.64	4.91	12.77	12.46	18.95	11.22
Air Canada	n.m.*	2.66	1.04	1.42	—	n.m.	n.m.	n.m.	0.47	2.59
Air Transat	n.m.	15.32	12.33	8.42	13.46	n.m.	1.98	n.m.	6.18	5.49
Transportation Industry Average	5.55	13.23	9.06	6.97	11.01	6.23	6.81	8.41	5.55	13.23

*n.m. means the ratio isn't measurable, usually because of negative income.

WestJet's interest coverage ratio for the period 1999 through 2008 is shown in Table 9.8, along with the ratios for Air Canada, Air Transat, and the averages for the transportation industry (which includes three railroads, a helicopter company, Air Transat, and WestJet).[9] WestJet has consistently had a higher ratio than Air Canada but a much lower one than Air Transat, in the last five years (except in 2008 when Air Transat had a loss).

THE IMPACT OF OFF-BALANCE-SHEET LIABILITIES

So far in this chapter we have encountered a number of off-balance-sheet liabilities. Leases, pensions, contingencies, and commitments can give rise to obligations not classified as liabilities on the balance sheet, even if the entity is in compliance with accounting standards. In this section we'll look at the impact that off-balance-sheet liabilities can have on the balance sheet.

Exhibit 9.8 provides the commitments and contingencies note from WestJet's 2008 financial statements and a table of contractual obligations taken from the management discussion and analysis.[10] Refer also to the liabilities and shareholders' equity side of WestJet's 2008 balance sheet in Exhibit 9.3. On December 31, 2008, WestJet reported liabilities of $2,192,712,000. In addition, it had commitments to spend $1,266,452,000 on new aircraft and satellite television systems between 2009 and 2013, and $1,736,950,000 in operating leases and other items from 2009 forward. Discounting these amounts using a rate of 20 percent gives a present value for these off-balance-sheet items of about $1,378,000,000, which would increase liabilities on December 31, 2008, to $3,750,712,000—an amount almost 62 percent greater than the amount actually reported. As a result, the debt-to-equity ratio (total liabilities ÷ shareholders' equity) would increase from 2.02 to 3.29. There are some important points to keep in mind when thinking about this analysis:

- The off-balance-sheet items have a significant effect on an important measure of capital structure and risk, and it's important to consider them when analyzing the financial statements. Misleading conclusions can be drawn if they aren't considered. If an entity makes extensive use of operating leases, liabilities and the debt-to-equity ratio will be understated.

- Off-balance-sheet obligations can impair comparability if companies use different approaches to acquiring assets (purchase versus lease).

- WestJet's accounting for these off-balance-sheet items is legitimate and appropriate.

- WestJet's actual risk isn't affected by including the off-balance-sheet items in a debt-to-equity analysis but risk measurement is affected.

10. Commitments and contingencies

(a) Purchased aircraft and live satellite television systems

As at December 31, 2008, the Corporation is committed to purchase 24 737-700 aircraft for delivery between 2010 and 2013. The remaining estimated amounts to be paid in deposits and purchase prices for the 24 aircraft, as well as amounts to be paid for live satellite television systems on purchased and leased aircraft in Canadian dollars and the US-dollar equivalents, are as follows:

	US dollar	CAD dollar
2009	$ 50,919	$ 62,019
2010	107,672	131,144
2011	124,419	151,542
2012	461,047	561,555
2013	295,724	360,192
	$ 1,039,781	$ 1,266,452

The Corporation has yet to pursue financing agreements for the remaining 24 purchased aircraft included in the above totals. The next purchased aircraft delivery is not expected until September 2010.

(b) Operating leases and commitments

The Corporation has entered into operating leases and commitments for aircraft, land, buildings, equipment, computer hardware, software licences and satellite programming. As at December 31, 2008, the future payments, in Canadian dollars and when applicable the US-dollar equivalents under operating leases and commitments are as follows:

	US dollar	CAD dollar
2009	$ 121,909	$ 165,777
2010	156,114	201,458
2011	175,610	220,324
2012	181,594	226,104
2013	171,008	212,758
2014 and thereafter	547,870	710,529
	$ 1,354,105	$ 1,736,950

As at December 31, 2008, the Corporation is committed to lease an additional 15 737-700 aircraft and five 737-800 aircraft for terms ranging between eight and 10 years in US dollars. These aircraft have been included in the table totals.

The Corporation signed a six-year agreement with Bell ExpressVu to provide satellite programming. The agreement commenced in 2004 and can be renewed for an additional four years. The minimum commitment amounts associated with this agreement have been included in the table totals.

On December 19, 2008, the Corporation signed an agreement with Sabre Airline Solutions Inc. (Sabre) for Sabre to provide WestJet with a licence to access and use its reservation system, SabreSonic. The term of the agreement will continue for a period of five years. The minimum contract amounts associated with the reservation system have been included in the table totals.

From WestJet's Management Discussion and Analysis

($ in thousands)	Total	2009	2010	2011	2012	2013	Thereafter
Long-term debt repayments	$ 1,351,903	$ 165,721	$ 165,034	$ 177,557	$ 163,279	$ 162,740	$ 517,572
Capital lease obligations[1]	1,179	444	698	37	—	—	—
Operating leases and commitments[2]	1,736,950	165,777	201,458	220,324	226,104	212,758	710,529
Purchase obligations[3]	1,266,452	62,019	131,144	151,542	561,555	360,192	—
Total contractual obligations	$ 4,356,484	$ 393,961	$ 498,334	$ 549,460	$ 950,938	$ 735,690	$ 1,228,101

[1] Includes weighted average imputed interest at 5.29 per cent totaling $71.
[2] Included in operating leases are US-dollar operating leases primarily related to aircraft. The obligations of these operating leases in US dollars are: 2009 – $121,909; 2010 – $156,114; 2011 – $175,610; 2012 – $181,594; 2013 – $171,008; 2014 and thereafter $547,870.
[3] Relates to purchases of aircraft, live satellite television systems and winglets. These purchase obligations in US dollars are: 2009 – $50,919; 2010 – $107,672; 2011 – $124,419; 2012 – $461,047; 2013 – $295,724.

Solved Problem

The solved problem for this chapter is another example of a user-oriented case. This case will give you more experience with and exposure to situations where you have to work with the financial statements provided. The purpose is learning to look critically at what is done and to apply your knowledge to satisfy your client.

Benito Corp.

In October 2014, the Benito family sold its 100 percent interest in Benito Corp. (BC) to a corporation wholly owned by the Nampa family. Because the two families couldn't agree on an exact selling price, the contract of purchase and sale required that the purchaser pay an amount equal to two times BC's audited net income before taxes for the fiscal year ended September 30, 2015. When BC was purchased, the Nampa family replaced the company's senior management. The new CEO of BC is the son of the head of the Nampa family, Shayne Nampa. Shayne has explained that acquiring BC is an important step in the growth the Nampa family's corporate holdings and an important objective is to minimize the tax that must be paid.

On October 25, 2015, Ellin Benito approached you for advice. She explained that the Benito family had received BC's financial statements and they were very concerned about some aspects of them. They believe that Shayne Nampa isn't acting in good faith and is trying to cheat the Benito family of money that is rightfully owed to them. Ms. Benito has asked you for a detailed report analyzing aspects of the financial statements the Benito family find questionable. She would like thorough explanations of the issues and recommendations of alternative treatments you think are more appropriate. Ms. Benito wants you to provide clear explanations and support for your positions so she will be able to explain her concerns when she meets Mr. Nampa. The outstanding items are described below:

a. During fiscal 2014 (before BC was sold), BC management began planning to offer its products online. Shayne Nampa continued the development of the new ebusiness and expects that it will be launched mid-way through fiscal 2016. Through the end of fiscal 2015, BC spent $476,000 developing the new ebusiness. Costs were incurred for website design, market surveys, and so on. The costs incurred in 2014 had been capitalized but BC expensed the full amount in fiscal 2015.

b. In May 2015, BC signed a contract with Fong Inc. for a large order of specially designed products. Fong Inc. didn't want to take delivery until the order was complete, so BC agreed to deliver the products in September 2015. Representatives of Fong Inc. monitored production to ensure all finished goods met Fong Inc.'s specifications. Fong Inc. agreed to pay BC as production proceeded and as a result, by August 2015 Fong Inc. had paid 80 percent of the agreed price. The remaining 20 percent was to be paid on final delivery. The products were ready for shipping in the first week of September 2015. However, Ms. Benito learned from a BC employee that BC requested and obtained permission to delay shipping until mid-October. The products were finally delivered on October 13, 2015 and revenue was recognized at that time. Fong Inc. normally recognizes revenue on delivery.

c. During fiscal 2015, BC significantly wrote down the carrying amount of some of the company's manufacturing equipment. The notes to the financial statements explained that, upon review, the equipment was becoming obsolete and, as a result, the carrying amount exceeded the net recoverable amount, so the equipment was written down to its recoverable amount. The equipment is still being used on the main production line of BC's manufacturing facility.

Required:

Prepare the report requested by Ellin Benito.

REPORT TO ELLIN BENITO ON THE SEPTEMBER 30, 2015, FINANCIAL STATEMENTS OF BENITO CORP.

Dear Ms. Benito:

Thank you for engaging me to examine the September 30, 2015 financial statements of Benito Corp. (BC). Based on the information you provided, it appears that Shayne Nampa is using International Financial Reporting Standards (IFRS) to his advantage and to your detriment. You may find it surprising, but IFRS is quite flexible and often requires judgment, and managers can sometimes use that to their own economic benefit. Since the final selling price for Benito Corp. depends on the company's income for fiscal 2015, it is in Mr. Nampa's interest to report as low a net income as he can justify. I will look at each of the issues in turn:

New ebusiness: BC expensed all the costs incurred ($476,000) for its proposed ebusiness in fiscal 2015. This has the effect of reducing the selling price by $952,000 ($476,000 × 2). By expensing the amount rather than treating it as an asset, management is saying that the money spent has no future benefit, or that the future benefit is very uncertain. BC can use conservatism to justify expensing these costs since, according to IFRS, it is not acceptable to overstate assets. However, IFRS doesn't mean that you can write off any costs incurred. If there is a case supporting a future benefit for the amounts spent then it is appropriate to capitalize the costs and amortize them when revenue is being earned; that is, match the costs to the revenue. The key question is, what are the revenue prospects for the new ebusiness? Mr. Nampa is continuing with development, which suggests that he thinks it will be successful. If there is reasonable evidence that the investment will be recovered from its operation, then it is appropriate to capitalize the costs. It is not possible to provide a definitive conclusion at this point, but it is also not necessary to accept the treatment used in BC's financial statements.

Comment: IFRS can often be reasonably interpreted in different ways. Just because the managers who prepared the financial statements have made certain choices doesn't mean you shouldn't or can't question those choices. To serve the needs of your client, you need to consider alternative ways of accounting. However, it's essential that you provide valid support for your alternative. An alternative shouldn't be proposed just because it's better for your client. It should be proposed because it's better for your client and it can be supported with the constraints and facts.

Sale to Fong Inc.: It is my opinion that BC rearranged the terms of the contract with Fong Inc. to avoid recognizing the revenue in fiscal 2015. BC normally recognizes revenue on delivery, and by delaying delivery until after the year-end it was able to defer this revenue and income. This delay violates the spirit of the agreement made with the Benito family. As of September 30, 2015, all the conditions necessary for recognizing revenue had been achieved: production was complete, Fong representatives were satisfied that the goods met specifications, the goods were ready for shipment, and 80 percent of the agreed price had been paid. In essence, the risks and rewards of ownership had been transferred even though BC had physical custody of the goods. Delivery had not occurred, but the delay was at BC's request. Revenue should be recognized on the Fong sale in the year ended September 30, 2015.

Comment: This situation is an excellent example of how acceptable accounting according to IFRS leads to an undesirable outcome for a stakeholder. The revenue recognition criteria are designed to discourage entities from recognizing their revenue too early. For the sale of BC, the conservative nature of the criteria serves the purposes of the new owners. Further, revenue should be recognized at the earliest time revenue recognition is achieved; in the sale to Fong that would be in September 2015. Further, simply following IFRS doesn't automatically make a treatment appropriate in the circumstances. From the information provided, it's clear that BC modified the terms of the contract to reduce income and the amount it would pay the Benito family. As an advisor to Ms. Benito, it's appropriate to call into question the structure of and accounting for the transaction.

Writedown of manufacturing equipment: By writing down the equipment, BC lowers its income and reduces the payment to the Benito family. According to IFRS, assets should be written down when the recoverable amount is less than their carrying amount. Because determining both impairment and net recoverable amounts are subjective decisions, writedowns are very subjective and managers have some leeway in deciding when to record them. However, BC is still using the equipment on its main production line, which suggests that it isn't obsolete. I suggest that you contest the writedown on two grounds. First, the equipment is still in use on the main production line, calling its impairment into question. Second, writedowns are highly subjective and somewhat arbitrary. I think a case can be made that out-of-the-ordinary events like writedowns should not be part of the determination of the selling price of BC since they are not an actual operating cost. The terms of your contract may work against you on this point, but I think it is worthwhile pursuing.

Again, thank you for using my services. If you have any questions, please do not hesitate to contact me.

Sincerely,

John Friedlan, CA

SUMMARY OF KEY POINTS

▶ **LO 1** Liabilities are obligations to provide cash, goods, or services to customers, suppliers, employees, governments, lenders, and any other creditors. According to IFRS, liabilities are obligations arising from past transactions or economic events, that an entity must sacrifice economic resources to satisfy. In principle, liabilities should be valued at their present value, and in many cases they are. However, there are some exceptions.

▶ **LO 2** Current liabilities are obligations that will be satisfied in one year or one operating cycle. Information about current obligations is important for assessing the short-term liquidity of an entity. Current liabilities are usually not discounted to their present value. There are many different types of current liabilities, including loans, accounts payable, collections on behalf of third parties, accrued liabilities, and unearned revenue.

▶ **LO 3** A bond is a formal borrowing arrangement in which a borrower agrees to make periodic interest payments to the lenders, as well as to repay the principal at a specified time in the future. The essential characteristics of a bond are its face value, maturity date, and coupon rate. The price of bonds and other long-term debt is determined by discounting the interest and principal payments to investors using the effective interest rate.

If a bond's coupon rate is different from the effective interest rate, a premium or discount arises, which is amortized over the life of the debt. The amount amortized each period is included in the interest expense for the period. Once long-term debt is recorded, its value isn't adjusted for changes in market interest rates. If the end of the reporting period doesn't correspond with the date interest payments are made, the interest expense and interest payable must be accrued. When debt is retired early, any premium or discount must be removed from the books immediately, and a gain or a loss may arise from this.

▶ **LO 4** A lease is a contractual arrangement whereby a lessee agrees to pay a lessor a fee in exchange for the use of an asset. There are two types of leases: capital leases and operating leases. A capital lease transfers the risks and rewards of ownership to the lessee. Assets associated with a capital lease are capitalized on the balance sheet of the lessee, along with a liability equal to the present value of the lease payments to be made over the life of the lease. An important accounting and reporting benefit of capital leases is that they overcome the problem of off-balance-sheet financing. If the risks and rewards of ownership aren't transferred to the lessee, then it's an operating lease. Under an operating lease, the lessee recognizes an expense when the payment to the lessor is paid or payable. The assets and related liabilities don't appear on the lessee's balance sheet.

▶ **LO 5** A pension provides income to a person after retirement. Employees earn their pensions and other post-retirement benefits while they are working, even though they receive the benefits after they retire. There are two types of pension plans: defined contribution and defined benefit. Accounting for defined-contribution plans is relatively straightforward, but accounting for defined-benefit plans is complex because it's necessary to estimate and accrue the cost of benefits that will be received many years in the future. The pension asset or liability doesn't provide information about the condition of the pension plan—its ability to meet the obligations to retirees. It's simply the difference between the accounting measure of the pension expense and the amount funded.

▶ **LO 6** A contingent liability is a possible obligation whose existence has to be confirmed by a future event that isn't in the control of the entity, or it's an obligation with uncertainties about the probability that payment will be made or the amount of payment (it doesn't meet the definition of a provision). A contingent liability isn't recognized in the financial statements but it is disclosed in the notes, unless the probability of having to pay is remote.

A commitment is a contractual agreement to enter into a transaction in the future. Agreements that commit an entity to purchase goods or services in the future aren't reported as liabilities, according to IFRS. Significant commitments should be disclosed in the notes to the financial statements.

A subsequent event is an economic event that occurs after an entity's year-end, but before the financial statements are released to stakeholders. When a subsequent event provides additional information about circumstances that existed at the year-end, the financial statements should be adjusted to reflect the new information. Subsequent events unrelated to circumstances at year-end should only be disclosed in the notes to the financial statements if they are material or significant.

▶ **LO 7** Analysis of an entity's liabilities can provide important information about its financial situation and prospects. This analysis can also provide insight into the financial management of the entity. Two tools for analyzing liabilities are the debt-to-equity ratio and the interest coverage ratio. In addition, the evaluation of liabilities provides important information about an entity's liquidity.

▶ **LO 8** (Appendix) Future income taxes arise because the accounting policies used to prepare general purpose financial statements are sometimes different from the rules entities must follow to determine the amount of income tax they must pay. The differences that give rise to future income taxes are temporary and eventually reverse. Future income taxes don't represent money owed to or owed by the government.

APPENDIX: FUTURE INCOME TAXES/DEFERRED INCOME TAXES

Perhaps one of the most confusing and misunderstood topics in accounting is *future income taxes* or *deferred income taxes* (you'll see both terms used in financial statements). Table 9.9 shows the future income tax asset or liability of four Canadian companies. With numbers this big it's important to understand where they come from and what they mean.

TABLE 9.9	Future Income Tax Assets and Liabilities of Some Canadian Companies			
Company	**Future income tax asset**	**Percentage of total assets**	**Future income tax liability**	**Percentage of total liabilities**
Indigo Books & Music	$49,995,000*	11.9%		
Encana Corporation**			US$6,919,000,000	28.5%
Magna International Inc.**	US$601,000,000	4.6%	US$136,000,000	2.3%
WestJet Airlines Ltd.	$4,196,000	1.2%	$241,740,000	11.0%

*Indigo reports $6,745,000 in current and $43,250,000 in non-current future income tax assets.
**Encana and Magna report in U.S. dollars but follow Canadian accounting standards.

Future income taxes have two sides. They appear as assets and liabilities on the balance sheet and they are reported on the income statement as part of the income tax expense. Examine WestJet's income statement in Exhibit 9.9 and notice that the *income tax expense* is split into two parts: current expense and future expense.[11] The current expense is the income taxes WestJet must pay now—the amount calculated on WestJet's tax return and cash paid or is currently payable to government. For the year ended December 31, 2008, WestJet had to pay income taxes of $2,549,000 and its future income tax expense was $74,153,000. WestJet's income tax expense for 2008 was $76,702,000 ($2,549,000 + $74,153,000). Also look at WestJet's balance sheet in Exhibit 9.3 and notice the future income tax liability of $241,740,000.

EXHIBIT 9.9 WestJet Airlines Ltd.: Income Statement

consolidated
statement of earnings

For the years ended December 31
(Stated in thousands of Canadian dollars, except per share amounts)

	2008	2007
Revenues:		
Guest revenues	$ 2,301,301	$ 1,899,159
Charter and other revenues	248,205	227,997
	2,549,506	2,127,156
Expenses:		
Aircraft fuel	803,293	503,931
Airport operations	342,922	299,004
Flight operations and navigational charges	280,920	258,571
Marketing, general and administration	211,979	177,393
Sales and distribution	170,605	146,194
Depreciation and amortization	136,485	127,223
Inflight	105,849	85,499
Aircraft leasing	86,050	75,201
Maintenance	85,093	74,653
Employee profit share	33,435	46,705
Loss on impairment of property and equipment (note 5)	—	31,881
	2,256,631	1,826,255
Earnings from operations	292,875	300,901
Non-operating income (expense):		
Interest income	25,485	24,301
Interest expense	(76,078)	(75,749)
Gain (loss) on foreign exchange	30,587	(12,750)
Gain (loss) on disposal of property and equipment	(701)	54
Loss on derivatives (note 11)	(17,331)	—
	(38,038)	(64,144)
Earnings before income taxes	254,837	236,757
Income tax expense: (note 7)		
Current	2,549	2,149
Future	74,153	41,775
	76,702	43,924
Net earnings	$ 178,135	$ 192,833

The first thing to recognize is that future income taxes have nothing to do with the amount of income tax an entity has to pay. **Future income tax assets and liabilities** and the **future income tax expense** arise because the accounting methods used to prepare general purpose financial statements are sometimes different from the methods used to calculate the income tax an entity must pay. When the *Income Tax Act* (ITA) specifies how an entity must account for particular transactions and economic events, that method must be used for tax purposes, but a different accounting method can be used for financial reporting purposes.

There are many revenues and expenses that are ultimately fully recognized for both tax and financial reporting purposes, but recognition happens at different times. These differences in timing are called **temporary differences** and they give rise to future income taxes. **Permanent differences** are revenues and expenses recognized for tax purposes but not for financial reporting purposes, or recognized for financial reporting purposes but not for tax purposes. These are referred to as permanent because they never reverse. Examples of temporary and permanent differences are shown in Table 9.10.

TABLE 9.10	Temporary and Permanent Differences between Tax and Financial Reporting		
Issue	**Type of difference**	**Tax**	**Financial reporting**
Depreciation of assets	Temporary	CCA (capital cost allowance) at prescribed rates	Depreciate in a "systematic" way over an asset's useful life
Revenue recognition	Temporary	Percentage of completion for contracts lasting more than two years	Completed-contract or zero-profit methods allowed if consistent with the facts
Warranty costs	Temporary	Deduct when the warranty cost is incurred	Accrue the expense when the revenue is recognized
Discounts and premiums on long-term debt repaid	Temporary	Recognized when the principal is repaid	Amortized over the term of the debt
Pension costs	Temporary	Deduct when money contributed to the pension fund	Expense based on accounting estimate of the pension obligation
Capital gains	Permanent	50 percent of capital gains and losses are taken into income for tax purposes	100 percent of capital gains and losses are taken into income for financial reporting purposes
Meals and entertainment expenses	Permanent	Only 50 percent of the amount spent is deductible for tax purposes	100 percent is expensed for financial reporting purposes
Interest and penalties on late payment of taxes	Permanent	Not deductible for tax purposes	Expensed for financial reporting purposes

Future income taxes arise because certain assets and liabilities are measured differently for tax and financial reporting purposes. The amount of future income tax associated with an asset or liability at a point in time is calculated using the following formula (this is the amount that would appear on the balance sheet at the end of a period):

$$\text{Future income tax}_{\text{end of period}} = \left[\begin{array}{c} \text{Tax basis of an} \\ \text{asset or liability} \end{array} - \begin{array}{c} \text{Accounting basis of} \\ \text{an asset or liability} \end{array} \right] \times \text{Tax rate}$$

The tax basis of an asset or liability is its carrying amount for tax purposes. For a capital asset, the tax basis would be the cost of the asset less the amount of capital cost allowance deducted since it was acquired. The accounting basis of an asset or liability is the carrying amount for financial reporting purposes. It's the amount reported on a general purpose balance sheet.

The amount of future income tax expense for a period related to an asset or liability is calculated as follows:

$$\text{Future income tax expense} = \text{Future income tax}_{\text{end of period}} - \text{Future income tax}_{\text{beginning of period}}$$

This process is repeated for every asset and liability for which there is a difference between the tax basis and accounting basis, to obtain the future income tax amounts on the balance sheet and income statement.

To see how this works, we'll examine a common source of temporary differences: CCA versus depreciation expense. For tax purposes, a company must follow the CCA rules in the ITA, while for financial reporting purposes depreciation is calculated to match the cost of capital assets to the revenues they help earn.

On January 1, 2013, Askilton Inc. (Askilton) purchased a new machine for $200,000. For tax purposes the machine has a CCA rate of 30 percent declining balance. For accounting purposes, management is depreciating the machine straight line over ten years with no residual value. Askilton's tax rate is 20 percent. Table 9.11 compares the tax and financial reporting bases for Askilton's machine, and shows the calculation of future income tax amounts.

TABLE 9.11		Comparison of Tax Basis and Accounting Basis for Askilton Inc.'s Machine						
	Tax			**Financial reporting**				
	Tax basis, January 1 [1]	CCA for the year [2]	Tax basis, December 31 [3]	Accounting basis [carrying amount], January 1 [4]	Depreciation expense [5]	Accounting basis [carrying amount], December 31 [6]	Tax basis – Accounting basis [7]	Future income tax asset (liability) [8]	Future income tax expense [9]
2013	$200,000	$30,000	$170,000	$200,000	$20,000	$180,000	($10,000)	($ 2,000)	(2,000)
2014	170,000	51,000	119,000	180,000	20,000	160,000	(41,000)	(8,200)	(6,200)
2015	119,000	35,700	83,300	160,000	20,000	140,000	(56,700)	(11,340)	(3,140)

[1] Tax basis of the asset at the beginning of the year: equals the tax basis at the end of the previous year.

[2] Amount of CCA for the year: equals the tax basis at the beginning of the year times 30%, except for 2013 where the amount is $200,000 × 30% × 50% (half-year rule).

[3] Tax basis of the asset at the end of the year: equals the tax basis at the beginning of the year, less CCA for the year.

[4] Accounting basis of the asset at the beginning of the year: equals the accounting basis at the end of the previous year.

[5] Depreciation expense for the year (cost ÷ useful life [$200,000 ÷ 10 years]).

[6] Accounting basis of the asset at the end of the year: equals the accounting basis at the beginning of the year less the depreciation expense for the year.

[7] Column [3] − column [6]: difference between the tax basis and accounting basis for the machine at the end of the year.

[8] Column [7] × tax rate (20%): future income tax liability associated with the machine at year-end.

[9] Amount by which the future income tax liability changed during the year: The balance in the future income tax liability account on December 31, 2013 is ($2,000). The required balance on December 31, 2014 is ($8,200). To reach the required balance an adjustment of ($6,200) is needed. In journal entry terms, a credit to future income tax liability and a debit to future income tax expense for $6,200 are needed.

Table 9.12 shows situations giving rise to future income tax assets and liabilities. In the case of Askilton's machine (an asset), the tax basis of the machine is less than the accounting basis (column 1 < column 3) on December 31 of each year, so there is a future income tax liability. What the future income tax liability means is that more of the cost of the machine has been expensed for tax purposes than for financial reporting purposes (the amount of CCA claimed is greater than the amount of depreciation expensed on the machine).

TABLE 9.12		Tax Basis, Accounting Basis, and Future Income Tax Balance	
			Future income tax balance
Tax basis of an asset	>	Accounting basis of an asset	Asset
Tax basis of an asset	<	Accounting basis of an asset	Liability
Tax basis of a liability	>	Accounting basis of an liability	Liability
Tax basis of a liability	<	Accounting basis of an liability	Asset

The other piece of the puzzle is the amount of tax Askilton has to pay. Calculating taxes can be very complicated and won't be discussed here. To show the presentation in the financial statements we'll assume the following:

	Income before taxes	Current income tax expense
2013	$65,000	$10,000
2014	78,000	9,400
2015	70,000	11,460

The income tax expense in Askilton's income statement would be reported as shown in Table 9.13. (It's assumed that the only source of future income taxes is Askilton's machine.) Financial statements must disclose the current and future portions of the income tax expense. The amount can be shown in the income statement as in Table 9.13 or in the notes to the financial statements. The balance sheet presentation is shown in Table 9.14.

TABLE 9.13	Financial Statement Presentation of Future Income Taxes		
Askilton Inc. **Income Statement Extracts** **December 31,**			
	2013	**2014**	**2015**
Income before taxes	$65,000	$78,000	$70,000
Income tax expense:			
Current expense	10,000	9,400	11,460
Future expense (benefit)	2,000	6,200	3,140
	12,000	15,600	14,600
Net income	$53,000	$62,400	$55,400

TABLE 9.14	Financial Statement Presentation of Future Income Taxes		
Askilton Inc. **Extracts from the Balance Sheet** **December 31,**			
	2013	**2014**	**2015**
Non-current liabilities:			
Future income taxes	$2,000	$8,200	$11,340

A simpler approach to accounting for income taxes is called the taxes payable method, in which the tax expense equals the amount of tax an entity must pay for the year. There are no future income taxes with this method because temporary differences are ignored. In general, the taxes payable approach makes earnings more variable, which can make an entity look riskier. Askilton's tax expense using the taxes payable method is shown in Table 9.15.

TABLE 9.15	Net Income Calculated Using the Taxes Payable Method		
Askilton Inc. **Extracts from the Income Statement** **December 31,**			
	2013	**2014**	**2015**
Income before taxes	$65,000	$78,000	$70,000
Income tax expense	10,000	9,400	11,460
Net income	$55,000	$68,600	$58,540

Believe it or not, the Askilton example is a straightforward one. In practice things can get a lot more complicated. But here we're interested in a basic understanding of what future income taxes tell us. Here are some points to consider:

- Look at WestJet's income statement in Exhibit 9.9 and notice the company paid only $2,549,000 in tax—that's a remarkably low tax rate of 1 percent. WestJet's actual tax rate is about 31 percent (see Exhibit 9.10).[12] Stakeholders could get the wrong impression about how much tax WestJet has to pay if they only consider the current income tax expense. The low tax rate is due (in part) to temporary differences. Eventually, over WestJet's life, those temporary differences will reverse and WestJet will pay higher taxes.

- The temporary differences giving rise to future income taxes are often not very temporary. For example, if an entity is growing the temporary differences due to differences between the CCA deducted and the depreciation expensed will usually grow as well, resulting in a future income tax liability that increases year after year. This is why capital-intensive businesses often have huge future income tax liabilities.

- Future income tax liabilities aren't discounted. As a result, amounts reported on the balance sheet are overstated because the time value of money is ignored. If future income tax balances won't decrease for a long time, some of them can actually be relatively small in present value terms.

- Future income taxes are affected by the accounting policies used. For example, changing the method of depreciation or the useful life of an asset will change the amount of future income taxes but not the amount of taxes paid.

- Future income taxes have long been misinterpreted and abused. Every now and then the media or politicians point to future or deferred income tax liabilities as evidence that corporations aren't paying "their fair share" of taxes. This interpretation is wrong as future income taxes don't represent money owed to government—they are the result of differences between financial reporting and tax. If entities used the taxes payable method, future income taxes would disappear but they would pay exactly the same amount of income tax.

- Only the current portion of the income tax expense on the income statement represents a current cash flow. The future portion represents a non-cash accrual. As a result, future income tax accounting reduces the association between earnings and cash flows.

Finally, have a look at Exhibit 9.10 for an example of the disclosures about income taxes provided in the notes to the financial statements. In the note WestJet discloses the following information:

❶ The tax rate that WestJet's income is subject to.

❷ The expected income tax expense (tax rate times income accounting income before taxes).

❸ Permanent differences between tax and financial reporting explaining why the income tax expense isn't equal to the tax rate times income for accounting purposes.

❹ Sources of the future income tax asset and liability. Most of the liability is timing differences associated with plant and equipment (CCA versus depreciation expense).

EXHIBIT 9.10   WestJet Airlines Ltd.: Income Taxes

7.   Income taxes

The provision for income taxes differs from that which would be expected by applying the combined federal and provincial statutory rates. A reconciliation of the difference is as follows:

	2008	2007
❶ Earnings before income taxes	$ 254,837	$ 236,757
❷ Income tax rate	31.30%	33.99%
Expected income tax provision	79,764	80,474
Add (deduct):		
Non-deductible expenses	2,097	1,728
❸ Non-deductible stock-based compensation	4,218	6,542
Effect of tax rate changes	(9,540)	(44,811)
Other	163	(9)
Actual income tax provision	$ 76,702	$ 43,924

The Corporation has included in its reconciliation an amount of $9,540 (2007 – $44,811) for the effect of tax rate changes. This amount reflects the impact of certain federal and provincial corporate income tax rate reductions enacted in 2008 and 2007, changes to the timing around when the Corporation expects certain temporary differences to reverse and differences between current statutory rates used in the reconciliation and future rates at which the future income tax liability is recorded.

The components of the net future tax liability are as follows:

		2008	2007
Future income tax liability:			
Property and equipment		$ (305,623)	$ (261,879)
Deferred partnership income		(34,741)	(17,420)
Future income tax asset:			
Share issue costs		13	79
Net unrealized loss on effective portion of derivatives designated in a hedging relationship		11,346	—
Non-capital losses		91,461	104,483
		$ (237,544)	$ (174,737)
The net future tax liability is presented on the consolidated balance sheet as follows:			
Future income tax	Current assets	4,196	—
Future income tax	Long-term liability	(241,740)	(174,737)
		$ (237,544)	$ (174,737)

The Corporation has recognized a benefit of $314,384 (2007 – $352,298) for non-capital losses which are available for carry forward to reduce taxable income in future years. These losses will begin to expire in the year 2014.

CANADIAN GAAP FOR PRIVATE ENTERPRISES

Companies that follow Canadian GAAP for Private Enterprises can choose to use the taxes payable method.

FORMULA SUMMARY

$$\text{PV of an annuity}_{n,\,r} = \frac{1}{r} \times \left[1 - \frac{1}{(1+r)^n} \right] \times \text{Amount to be paid in each period}$$

$$PV_{n,r} = \frac{1}{(1+r)^n} \times \text{Amount to be paid in each period}$$

$$\text{Proceeds from bond issue} = \text{Present value of interest payments} + \text{Present value of principal repayment}$$

$$ROA = \frac{\text{Net income} + \text{After-tax interest expense}}{\text{Total assets}}$$

$$\text{After-tax cost of borrowing} = \text{Stated interest rate} \times (1 - \text{Tax rate})$$

$$\text{Debt-to-equity ratio} = \frac{\text{Total liabilities}}{\text{Total shareholder's equity}}$$

$$\text{Interest coverage ratio} = \frac{\text{Net income} + \text{Interest expense} + \text{Income tax expense}}{\text{Interest expense}}$$

$$\text{Future income tax}_{\text{end of period}} = \left(\begin{array}{c} \text{Tax basis of an} \\ \text{asset or liability} \end{array} - \begin{array}{c} \text{Accounting basis of} \\ \text{an asset or liability} \end{array} \right) \times \text{Tax rate}$$

$$\text{Future income tax expense} = \text{Future income tax}_{\text{end of period}} - \text{Future income tax}_{\text{beginning of period}}$$

KEY TERMS

after-tax cost of borrowing, p. 511

bond, p. 485

callable bond, p. 487

capital lease, p. 498

capital structure, p. 511

collateral, p. 484

commitment, p. 509

contingent liability, p. 508

convertible bond, p. 487

coupon rate, p. 487

debenture, p. 485

debt, p. 484

defined-benefit plan, p. 504

defined-contribution plan, p. 504

demand loan, p. 479

derecognition, p. 490

discount (on debt), p. 490

effective interest rate, p. 487

event after the reporting period, p. 509

face value of a bond, p. 487

finance lease, p. 498

fixed-rate loan, p. 485

future income tax assets and liabilities, p. 519

future income tax expense, p. 519

interest coverage ratio, p. 512

lease, p. 497

lessee, p. 497

lessor, p. 497

letter of credit, p. 496

line of credit, p. 480

maturity date of a bond, p. 487

mortgage, p. 485

non-current debt, p. 484

note payable, p. 485

off-balance-sheet financing, p. 497

operating lease, p. 498

pension, p. 503

permanent differences, p. 519

premium (on debt), p. 493

proceeds, p. 487

provision, p. 481

retractable bond, p. 487

subsequent event, p. 509

taxable income, p. 511

temporary differences, p. 519

variable-rate loan, p. 485

SIMILAR TERMS

The left column gives alternative terms that are sometimes used for the accounting terms introduced in this chapter, which are listed in the right column.

long-term debt **non-current debt, p. 484**

deferred income taxes **future income taxes, p. 519**

security **collateral, p. 484**

event after the reporting period **subsequent event, p. 509**

ASSIGNMENT MATERIALS

Questions

Q9-1. What happens to the market value of a bond if the effective interest rate decreases after the bond is issued? Explain. How is the change in the effective interest rate reflected in the financial statements?

Q9-2. Explain the following terms as they relate to bonds:
a. effective rate of interest
b. coupon rate
c. maturity date
d. proceeds
e. face value

Q9-3. What are off-balance-sheet liabilities? What is the attraction of keeping liabilities off-balance-sheet? How do off-balance-sheet liabilities affect stakeholders' ability to interpret financial statements? Why is it possible to keep some liabilities off-balance-sheet?

Q9-4. Hyannis Inc. has recently arranged financing for its planned expansion. The $5,000,000 bank loan is secured against inventory, receivables, and certain capital assets while the second loan for $2,000,000 is unsecured. Which loan would you expect to have a higher interest rate? Explain.

Q9-5. Use the definition of a liability to explain why taxes payable is a liability.

Q9-6. Why would recording an "interest-free" loan at its face value result in the overstatement of net income?

Q9-7. What are bond discounts and premiums? Why are bonds sometimes sold at a discount or premium?

Q9-8. What are restrictive covenants? Why are restrictive covenants sometimes included as part of debt agreements? How does a borrower benefit from a restrictive covenant? Why would a borrower prefer to avoid having restrictive covenants in loan agreements, assuming no changes in the other terms of the loan?

Q9-9. How do bond discounts and premiums affect an entity's interest expense? Explain.

Q9-10. Why do gains and losses arise when an entity redeems its bonds before they mature? How are the gains and losses calculated?

Q9-11. Explain the difference between a capital lease and an operating lease. Explain how each type of lease is accounted for and the effect each has on the balance sheet and income statement.

Q9-12. What amount is reported on a lessee's balance sheet at the start of a lease for a leased asset and the associated liability? Why do the amounts reported for the asset and liability differ for balance sheets prepared after the start of the lease?

Q9-13. What is a subsequent event? How are subsequent events accounted for?

Q9-14. What is a commitment? How are commitments accounted for?

Q9-15. Distinguish between a defined-benefit pension plan and defined-contribution pension plan. Which plan is more attractive for employees? Explain. Which plan is less risky for employers? Explain.

Q9-16. According to IFRS, what is a contingent liability? How does IFRS require contingent liabilities to be accounted for? What happens if a contingent liability becomes measurable?

Q9-17. What is an accrued liability? What is a provision? Distinguish among an accrued liability, provision, and account payable? Under what circumstances are accrued liabilities and provisions required?

Q9-18. Because it's so difficult to estimate the cost of providing defined-benefit pensions to employees, it would make more sense, and result in more accurate financial statements, to simply expense pension costs as employees receive their pension. Discuss this statement. In your discussion address relevant accounting concepts and the impact of the proposed approach on the financial statements.

Q9-19. What is a current liability? Why is it important to know the amount of current liabilities an entity has?

Q9-20. Why is the current portion of long-term debt classified separately as a current liability? What would be the impact on users of the financial statements if the current portion wasn't reported separately?

Q9-21. What is the interest coverage ratio? What information does the interest coverage ratio provide?

Q9-22. What is a liability? According to IFRS, what are the characteristics of a liability? Do you think these characteristics capture every obligation an entity has? Explain.

Q9-23. Why do managers sometimes have incentives to understate liabilities? What are the implications for the financial statements of understating liabilities? Provide examples of how managers can understate their entities' liabilities.

Q9-24. What are the characteristics of debt that make it risky? Why do these characteristics make debt risky?

Q9-25. Why are long-term liabilities such as bonds valued for financial reporting purposes at their present value, but capital assets aren't?

Q9-26. What is the relationship between the coupon rate and effective interest rate when a bond is sold at a discount? What is the relationship when a bond is sold at a premium?

Q9-27. Why is the actual cost of borrowing usually lower than the stated rate of interest that the borrower pays to a lender such as a bank? Can you think of a situation where the actual cost of borrowing wouldn't be lower than the stated rate of interest?

Q9-28. Describe defined-contribution and defined-benefit pension plans. How are they different and how are they the same?

Q9-29. Why are the assets in a pension plan not reported on the balance sheet of the entity sponsoring the pension plan? Does this treatment result in an understatement of the sponsoring entity's assets?

Q9-30. What is unearned revenue? Why is it considered a liability?

Q9-31. Identify and explain the criteria that IFRS provide to assist in the classification of leases. What are the problems and benefits of providing preparers of the financial statements with these criteria?

Q9-32. In its most recent balance sheet, Vosburg Inc. reported a debt-to-equity ratio of 1.85 to 1. This ratio has increased slightly from the previous year when the ratio was 1.55 to 1. Assess Vosburg Inc.'s debt-to-equity ratio and the change in the ratio over the last year.

Q9-33 (Appendix).   A labour union leader said at a recent rally that there would be plenty of money for health care, education, and other social programs if governments simply collected the future income taxes that corporations owe and report on their balance sheets. A friend of yours asked you, in response to the union leader's comments, how it is that businesses can avoid paying their taxes whereas working people cannot.

Required:

Respond to your friend.

Q9-34 (Appendix).   What are future income taxes and what circumstances cause them to appear on an entity's balance sheet?

Q9-35 (Appendix).   Distinguish the future income tax method of accounting for income taxes from the taxes payable method.

Q9-36 (Appendix).   Entities that use future income tax accounting show two components of the income tax expense: the current expense and the future expense. Explain these two components.

Exercises

E9-1.   **(Determining the proceeds from a bond, LO 3)** On July 15, 2014, Dyce Inc. (Dyce) will be making a $6,000,000 bond issue to public investors. The bond matures in six years on July 14, 2020, has a coupon rate of 6 percent, and pays interest annually on July 14. Determine how much Dyce will receive in proceeds from its bond if the effective interest rate when the bond is issued is

a. 5 percent
b. 6 percent
c. 7 percent

E9-2. **(Determining the proceeds from a bond, LO 3)** On December 1, 2013, Koidern Inc. (Koidern) will be making a $10,000,000 bond issue to public investors. The bond matures in ten years on November 30, 2023 and pays interest annually on November 30. The effective interest rate on December 1, 2013 is expected to be 7 percent. How much will Koidern receive in proceeds from its bond if the coupon rate on the bond is
  a. 6 percent
  b. 7 percent
  c. 8 percent

E9-3. **(Preparing journal entries, LO 3)** Provide the journal entries needed for each of the following situations:
  a. Ajax Ltd. borrows $100,000 from its bank. The bank deposits the money in Ajax's bank account.
  b. Arborg Inc. arranges a $1,000,000 mortgage on its new office building. The lender pays the money directly to the seller of the building. The first payment on the mortgage is $5,535, of which $3,750 is for interest.
  c. Barrhead Corp. borrowed $250,000 in the short-term market. Two days later the company repaid $250,070 to the lender.

E9-4. **(Accruing interest expense, LO 3)** For each of the following situations record the adjusting journal entry that would be required at year-end to accrue the interest expense. In each case assume that the year-end is December 31:
  a. On September 1, a company borrowed $500,000 from a bank at an interest rate of 4 percent per year, payable on March 31 and September 30.
  b. On June 1, a company issued a $6,000,000 bond that pays interest of 7 percent per year, payable annually on May 31.
  c. On May 1, a company issued a $1,000,000 note that pays interest of 9 percent per year, payable quarterly on January 31, April 30, July 31, and October 31.
  d. On July 2, a company borrowed $8,000,000 from a pension fund at an interest rate of 8 percent per year, payable monthly, on the last day of the month.

E9-5. **(Accounting for gift cards, LO 2, 7)** Juno Boutique Inc. (Juno) operates a chain of fashion boutiques. In 2013, Juno began offering gift cards for sale to customers. The cards can be exchanged for any merchandise in Juno's stores, but they can't be redeemed for cash. During 2013, gift cards worth $112,000 were sold. By the end of the year, $65,000 of the gift cards had been redeemed by customers who purchased merchandise that cost Juno $37,000.

Required:

  a. Prepare the journal entry required to record the sale of the gift cards.
  b. Prepare the journal entry required to record the redemption of the gift cards.
  c. How would the unused gift cards be reported in Juno's financial statements?
  d. What effect does the sale of gift cards have on Juno's current ratio?

E9-6. **(Accounting for gift cards, LO 2, 7)** Neepawa Sports Inc. (Neepawa) operates sporting goods stores in several medium-sized cities in western Canada. For several years Neepawa has offered gift cards for sale as a convenient gift option for customers. The cards can be exchanged for any merchandise in Neepawa's stores but can't be redeemed for cash. At the beginning of 2014, Neepawa had $215,000 in its unredeemed gift card liability account. During 2014, gift cards worth $542,000 were sold and $389,000 were redeemed to purchase merchandise costing $178,000. Neepawa estimates that about 5 percent of outstanding gift cards outstanding at the end of the year won't be redeemed.

Required:

> a. For the year ended December 31, 2014, prepare all journal entries (transactional and adjusting) Neepawa must make.
> b. How would the unused gift cards be reported in Neepawa's financial statements?
> c. What effect does the sale of gift cards have on Neepawa's current ratio? What impact does using a gift card have on the current ratio?

E9-7. **(Classifying liabilities, LO 2, 3)** How would each of the following items be classified on Atluck Grocery Store Corp.'s (Atluck) September 30, 2014 balance sheet? Explain your reasoning.

> a. On June 15, 2014, Atluck purchased new refrigeration equipment for the store for $110,000, of which $50,000 is due on October 31, 2014 and the remainder on February 1, 2016.
> b. On July 6, 2014, a customer paid $3,100 in advance for catering to be provided at a community gathering to be held on Thanksgiving 2014.
> c. On August 5, 2014, Atluck obtained a $25,000 demand loan from the bank.
> d. During the fourth quarter of fiscal 2014, GST of $50,000 was collected on sales to customers.
> e. Atluck has a $250,000, 20-year mortgage on its land and building. The mortgage requires equal annual payments of $29,365.
> f. Atluck accrued $4,800 for utilities in the September 30, 2014 balance sheet.

E9-8. **(Valuing liabilities, LO 1, 3)** On March 31, 2014 Etzikom Inc. (Etzikom) purchased a corporate jet from the manufacturer for $1,460,000. Etzikom paid $200,000 in cash to the manufacturer and received a three-year, $1,260,000, interest-free loan for the remainder of the purchase price. The terms of the loan require Etzikom to pay the manufacturer $420,000 on March 31 of each of the next three years, beginning on March 31, 2015. Assume a discount rate of 7 percent when responding to the following questions.

Required:

> a. Prepare the journal entry that Etzikom should make to record the purchase of the jet. Explain the amount you have recorded for the jet on the balance sheet.
> b. Prepare the journal entries that Etzikom should make on March 31, 2014 through 2017 to record payments on the loan.
> c. How much should Etzikom report as a liability for the loan on its balance sheet on March 31, 2014 through 2017?
> d. Could Etzikom record the liability at $1,260,000 on March 31, 2014? What are the problems of accounting for the liability this way?

E9-9. **(Collections on behalf of third parties, LO 2)** For the following two independent situations, prepare the journal entry that Durrell Ltd. (Durrell) should record. Record the entry for both the amounts collected or withheld and for the remittances.

> a. During November 2014, Durrell sold and delivered $145,000 of services to customers. In addition, customers were charged and paid 5 percent GST. Durrell remits the GST it collects from customers on the tenth day of the following month.
> b. During November, Durrell's employees earned $42,000. From this amount Durrell withheld $13,000 for income taxes, $4,105 for Canada Pension Plan (CPP), $1,860 for Employment Insurance (EI), $750 in union dues, $1,450 for employee contributions to the company pension plan, $1,000 for long-term disability insurance, and $200 in contributions to local charities. Durrell remits the withholdings on the tenth day of the following month.

E9-10.   (**Classifying liabilities as current and non-current, LO 2**) The accountant of Hantsport Ltd. (Hantsport) is currently preparing the December 31, 2014 financial statements. She has asked you to help her classify the following items:

    a. During December 2014, Hantsport withheld $4,000 from employees for their contributions to the company pension plan. The company is required to remit the contributed amount to the pension fund manager within 10 days of collection.

    b. As of the end of December Hantsport owed suppliers $68,000 for inventory purchases during November and December 2014.

    c. The company has a $50,000 note payable coming due in March. Hantsport has arranged a three-year, $50,000 loan from the bank that will be used to repay the loan.

    d. Hantsport has received $10,000 in advances for goods that will be delivered during 2015.

    e. Hantsport has $100,000 outstanding with a private lender. $25,000 is scheduled to be repaid in 2015.

    f. Hantsport declared a $120,000 cash dividend on December 21, 2014. The dividend is to be paid on January 15, 2015.

    g. Hantsport has a $300,000 loan from the bank that has been outstanding for three years. The bank can demand repayment at anytime.

Required:

Classify each of the items as a current or non-current liability (note that some may classified partially as current and partially as non-current). Provide your reasoning for each item.

E9-11.   (**Accounting entries for a defined-contribution pension plan, LO 5**) Iskut Inc. (Iskut) provides its employees with a defined-contribution pension plan. Each year the company is required to contribute $1,000 to an investment fund for each employee. In the year ended December 31, 2014, Iskut contributed $200,000 on behalf of its 230 employees.

Required:

    a. What journal entry would Iskut make to record the contribution to the pension plan?

    b. What other entries would be necessary? Explain. What would appear on the balance sheet with respect to the pension plan on December 31, 2014?

E9-12.   (**Accounting entries for a defined-benefit pension plan, LO 5**) Brigus Corp. (Brigus) provides its employees with a defined-benefit pension plan. The plan was instituted three years ago. During the year ended March 31, 2014, Brigus contributed $150,000 to the plan. An evaluation of the plan as of the end of fiscal 2014 found that contributions of $250,000 were required in 2014 to have enough money in the plan to provide the benefits promised to employees when they retire.

Required:

    a. What journal entry would Brigus have made in fiscal 2014 to record the cash it contributed to the pension plan?

    b. How much pension liability should be reported on Brigus' balance sheet on March 31, 2014? Explain what this amount represents.

E9-13.   (**Classifying transactions and economic events, LO 6**) Classify the following transactions and economic events for Floral Ltd. (Floral) as commitments, subsequent events, or contingencies. Some may fit more than one classification. Indicate how each should be reflected in the December 31, 2014 financial statements and explain your reasoning. In responding, consider the usefulness of the information to different stakeholders.

a. On January 15, 2015, Floral announced it had acquired a major competitor for cash and Floral shares.

b. In October 2013, Floral was sued for $5 million by a disgruntled former senior executive. The case is expected to go to trial in mid-2015. → contingent

c. In August 2014, Floral signed a three-year agreement with a customer to supply certain goods and services. The goods and services will be supplied at market prices at the time and the agreement can be cancelled by the customer with 90 days notice. The agreement will make the customer one of Floral's largest customers.   commitment

d. In May 2014, Floral guaranteed a $1,000,000 bank loan made to Nokomis Inc., a company owned by one of Floral's shareholders. Floral is responsible for paying the principal and any outstanding interest in the event that the company is unable to make its payments. On January 5, 2015, Nokomis Inc. filed for bankruptcy.   commitment?

E9-14. (**Classifying transactions and economic events, LO 6**) Classify the following transactions and economic events for Moonbeam Ltd. (Moonbeam) as commitments, subsequent events, or contingencies. Some may fit more than one classification. Indicate how each should be reflected in the December 31, 2014 financial statements and explain your reasoning. In responding, consider the usefulness of the information to different stakeholders.

a. In January 2015, a company that Moonbeam was suing for damages for breaching a contract made an offer of $500,000 to settle the case. Moonbeam agreed to accept the offer. Payment was received on January 21, 2015.

b. In May 2014, Moonbeam launched a $10 million lawsuit against a company for breach of contract. The suit is expected to reach the courts by mid-2015. Moonbeam's lawyers believe the company has a good chance of winning the suit.

c. On November 15, 2014, Moonbeam decided to construct a new head office building for $3.5 million. The board of directors allocated funds for the project and contracts are being finalized with construction contractors. The project is scheduled to begin in September 2015.

d. On January 18, 2015, one of Moonbeam's warehouses burned to the ground.

E9-15. (**Interest-free loans, LO 1, 3**) On December 31, 2014, Hecla Inc. (Hecla) purchased heavy equipment from a dealer. The dealer, through the manufacturer, financed the purchase by giving Rowena a three-year, $300,000 interest-free loan. Under the terms of the loan, Rowena is required to pay $100,000 on December 31 of each of the next three years. Assume the market rate of interest on financing of this type is 6 percent.

Required:

a. How much should Rowena report as a liability for the loan on its balance sheet on December 31, 2014 through 2017? What would the interest expense be each year?

b. Why isn't it appropriate to record the liability initially at $300,000? What are the consequences for the financial statements of recording the liability at this amount?

E9-16. (**Accounting for bonds, LO 3**) On November 1, 2014 Nordin Inc. (Nordin) issued a $24,000,000 bond with a 4 percent coupon rate and a maturity date of October 31, 2021. Interest is paid annually on October 31. The effective interest rate for a bond of this type on November 1, 2014 was 3.5 percent. Nordin's year-end is October 31.

Required:

a. What will be the proceeds from the bond issue?

b. Prepare the journal entry to record the issue of the bond on November 1, 2014.

c. Prepare an amortization schedule using the straight-line method for any premium or discount that arose on issue of the bond.

d. Prepare the journal entry required to record the interest expense on October 31, 2015, 2017, and 2019.

e. Prepare the journal entry required to record the retirement of the bond on maturity.

E9-17. **(Accounting for bonds, LO 3)** On September 1, 2015, Yone Ltd. (Yone) issued a $50,000,000 bond with a 6 percent coupon rate and a maturity date of August 31, 2030. Interest is paid semi-annually on March 1 and August 31. The effective interest rate for a bond of this type on September 1, 2009 was 7 percent. Yone's year-end is August 31.

Required:

    a. What will be the proceeds from the bond issue?

    b. Prepare the journal entry to record the issue of the bond on September 1, 2015.

    c. Prepare an amortization schedule using the straight-line method for any premium or discount that arose on issue of the bond.

    d. Prepare the journal entry required to record the interest expense on March 1 and August 31, 2016, 2021, and 2026.

    e. Prepare the journal entry required to record the retirement of the bond on maturity.

E9-18. **(Accounting for bonds, LO 3)** On January 2, 2015, Jura Corp. (Jura) issued a $78,000,000 bond with a 5 percent coupon rate and a maturity date of December 31, 2024. Interest is paid annually on December 31. The effective interest rate for a bond of this type on January 2, 2015 was 5 percent. Jura's year-end is December 31.

Required:

    a. What will be the proceeds from the bond issue?

    b. Prepare the journal entry to record the issue of the bond on January 2, 2015.

    c. Prepare an amortization schedule using the straight-line method for any premium or discount that arose on issue of the bond.

    d. Prepare the journal entry required to record the interest expense on December 31 of each year over the life of the bond.

    e. Prepare the journal entry required to record the retirement of the bond on maturity.

E9-19. **(Early retirement of bonds, LO 3)** In fiscal 2014, Ruthilda Inc. (Ruthilda) decided to exercise its option to redeem its outstanding bond issue before the maturity date in 2021. The bonds had a face value of $25,000,000 and Ruthilda paid $25,750,000 to redeem them. The bonds were originally issued at a premium of $1,500,000 and at the time the bonds were redeemed, $900,000 of the premium had been amortized.

Required:

    a. Prepare the journal entry to record the early retirement of the bonds.

    b. What would be the entry if Ruthilda was able to redeem the bonds on the open market at a cost of $23,500,000?

    c. What is the economic significance of a gain or loss on the redemption of bonds? How do you think the gain or loss should be reported in the financial statements? Explain. In responding, consider the information needs of the stakeholders.

E9-20. **(Early retirement of bonds, LO 3)** In fiscal 2013, Hurette Inc. (Hurette) decided to exercise its option to redeem its outstanding bond issue before they matured in 2020. The bonds had a face value of $80,000,000 and Hurette paid $83,000,000 to redeem them. The bonds were originally issued at a discount of $2,500,000 and at the time the bonds were redeemed $1,000,000 of the discount had been amortized.

Required:

    a. Prepare the journal entry to record the early retirement of the bonds.

    b. What would be the entry if Hurette were able to redeem the bonds on the open market at a cost of $78,500,000?

    c. What is the economic significance of a gain or loss on the redemption of bonds? How do you think the gain or loss should be reported in the financial statements? Explain. In responding, consider the information needs of users of the financial statements.

E9-21. (**Cost of borrowing, LO 3**) For each of the following situations, determine the entity's after-tax cost of borrowing:

a. A corporation has a $2,500,000 bank loan with an interest rate of 4 percent. The corporation has a tax rate of 30 percent.

b. A small business has a three-year, $500,000, 5 percent note payable with a supplier. The small business has a tax rate of 15 percent.

c. A charity, which doesn't have to pay tax, has a $25,000 bank loan at the prime lending rate plus 2.5 percent. For the year just ended the prime lending rate was 2.5 percent.

d. How is an entity's after-tax cost of borrowing affected by its tax rate? Is it more desirable for an entity to have a higher tax rate so that it can lower its after-tax cost of borrowing? Explain.

E9-22. (**Accounting for leases, LO 4**) On February 1, 2014, Flatwater Ltd. (Flatwater) signed a four-year lease for computer equipment. The terms of the lease require Flatwater to make annual lease payments of $120,000 on January 31, commencing in 2015. The interest rate that applies to the lease is 7 percent.

Required:

a. Assume Flatwater's lease was accounted for as an operating lease:
   i.   What amount would be recorded as an asset for the leased equipment on February 1, 2014?
   ii. Prepare the journal entries that would have to be made in fiscal 2015 and fiscal 2017 to account for the lease.

b. Assume Flatwater's lease was accounted for as a capital lease:
   i.   What amount would be recorded as an asset for the computer equipment on February 1, 2014?
   ii. What journal entry would be required on February 1, 2014?
   iii. What journal entries would be required on January 31, 2015 to record the lease payment?
   iv. What journal entry would be required on January 31, 2015 to record the depreciation of the computer equipment (assume straight-line depreciation and no residual value)?
   v.   What would be the carrying amount of the computer equipment and the lease liability on Flatwater's January 31, 2015 and 2017 balance sheets?

E9-23. (**The effect of interest rates on capital leases, LO 4**) On June 1, 2015, Grumbler Corp. (Grumbler) signed a ten-year lease for five small airplanes. The lease requires Grumbler to make annual lease payments of $500,000 on May 31 of each year beginning in 2016. The lease is to be treated as a capital lease.

Required:

a. Indicate the amount that would be recorded for airplanes and for the lease liability on June 1, 2015, assuming the appropriate interest rate for the lease was
   i.   7 percent
   ii. 9 percent
   iii. 11 percent

b. Indicate the annual depreciation expense for the airplanes, assuming straight-line depreciation over 10 years and assuming the appropriate interest rate for the lease was
   i.   7 percent
   ii. 9 percent
   iii. 11 percent

    c. Indicate the interest expense pertaining to the lease in the fiscal year ended May 31, 2016, assuming the appropriate interest rate for the lease was

      i. 7 percent

      ii. 9 percent

      iii. 11 percent

E9-24. **(The effect of bond transactions on the cash flow statement, LO 3)** Wivenhoe Ltd. (Wivenhoe) includes a cash flow statement in the financial statement package it prepares for the bank. Wivenhoe uses the indirect method for calculating cash from operations. For each of the following items, indicate whether it would be reported in Wivenhoe's cash flow statement as an operating, financing, or investing activity. Indicate how each item would be shown in reconciling from net income to cash from operations using the indirect method.

    a. Amortization of a bond premium.

    b. Proceeds from the issue of a bond.

    c. Interest payment to lenders.

    d. Repayment of a bond on maturity.

    e. Gain on early retirement of a bond.

    f. Amortization of a bond discount.

E9-25. **(Lease accounting and financial ratios, LO 4, 7)** Zeballos Inc. (Zeballos) has arranged to lease new equipment for its distribution centre. The terms of the lease require Zeballos to pay $300,000 per year for the next six years. The interest rate for the lease is 8 percent. The lease comes into effect on December 31, 2014, the last day of the current fiscal year and the first payment is to be made on that day. Subsequent payments are due on December 31 of each year through 2019. Zeballos has provided you with the following balance sheet information on December 31, 2014, before accounting for the new lease.

Current assets	$ 785,000
Non-current assets	5,255,000
Current liabilities	621,000
Non-current liabilities	4,250,000
Shareholders' equity	1,169,000

Required:

    a. Calculate the current ratio and debt-to-equity ratio for Zeballos, assuming the lease is accounted for as an operating lease (ignore the effect of the lease payments).

    b. Calculate the current ratio and debt-to-equity ratio for Zeballos, assuming the lease is accounted for as a capital lease (ignore the effect of the lease payments).

    c. Which calculations provide a better representation of Zeballos' liquidity and underlying risk? Explain.

    d. Does it matter how Zeballos accounts for its lease (IFRS notwithstanding)? Explain.

E9-26. **(Accounting for bonds, LO 3)** On June 1, 2014, Joffre Inc. (Joffre) issued a $75,000,000, 15-year bond with a 6 percent coupon rate. Proceeds from the bond issue were $73,950,000. Interest is to be paid annually on May 31. Joffre's year-end is December 31. Assume that Joffre uses the straight-line method to amortize any bond premiums or discounts.

Required:

    a. Prepare the journal entry to record the issue of the bond on June 1, 2014.

    b. Prepare the journal entry to accrue the interest expense on December 31, 2014.

    c. Prepare the journal entry to record the payment of interest to bondholders on May 31, 2015.

E9-27. **(Future income taxes, LO 8)** Use the following information to calculate the balance in the future income tax account for a machine owned by the entity:

Cost of the machine when it was purchased	$350,000
Total amount of CCA deducted since purchase	52,500
Total amount of depreciation expensed since purchase	70,000
Tax rate	15%

E9-28. **(Future income taxes, LO 8)** Use the following information to calculate the balance in the future income tax account for a building owned by the entity:

Cost of the machine when it was purchased	$2,500,000
Total amount of CCA deducted since purchase	1,771,125
Total amount of depreciation expensed since purchase	1,000,000
Tax rate	30%

E9-29. **(Future income taxes, LO 8)** For the fiscal year ended November 30, 2014, Vibank Ltd. (Vibank) has income before taxes of $1,700,000. Vibank's tax return shows taxable income of $1,850,000 for that year. The tax basis of Vibank's assets exceeded the accounting basis by $600,000 on November 30, 2014 and the balance in the future income tax account on November 30, 2013 was a credit of $225,000. All temporary differences pertain to non-current assets. Vibank has a tax rate of 30 percent.

Required:

a. What amount should Vibank report for future income taxes on its November 30, 2014 balance sheet?
b. What is Vibank's net income for fiscal 2014?
c. What would Vibank's net income be if it used the taxes payable method?
d. Explain the difference between (b) and (c).
e. Prepare the journal entry required to record Vibank's income tax expense for fiscal 2014.

E9-30. **(Future income taxes, LO 8)** For the fiscal year ended December 31, 2014, Rossland Ltd. (Rossland) has income before taxes of $325,000. Rossland's tax return shows taxable income of $275,000 for that year. The accounting basis of Rossland's assets exceeded the tax basis by $75,000 on December 31, 2014 and the balance in the future income tax account on December 31, 2013 was a credit of $10,000. All temporary differences pertain to non-current assets. Rossland has a tax rate of 15 percent.

Required:

a. What should Rossland report for future income taxes on its December 31, 2014 balance sheet?
b. What is Rossland's net income for fiscal 2014?
c. What would Rossland's net income be if it used the taxes payable method?
d. Explain the difference between (b) and (c).
e. Prepare the journal entry required to record Rossland's income tax expense for fiscal 2014.

E9-31. **(The effect of different depreciation methods on future income taxes, LO 8)**
Caycuse Inc. (Caycuse) has just completed its first year of operations on December 31, 2014. The company owns a single asset that cost $150,000. For tax purposes Caycuse can deduct $22,500 in CCA in calculating its taxable income in 2014. Assume that Caycuse's tax rate is 12 percent.

Required:

    a. Determine the future income tax asset or liability on December 31, 2014, if Caycuse depreciates its asset on a straight-line basis over 10 years.

    b. Determine the future income tax asset or liability on December 31, 2014, if Caycuse depreciates its asset on a straight-line basis over five years.

    c. Determine the future income tax asset or liability on December 31, 2014, if Caycuse depreciates its asset on a declining balance basis at 30 percent per year.

    d. Determine the future income tax asset or liability on December 31, 2014, if Caycuse depreciates its asset using the same basis used for tax purposes.

    e. According to the IFRS characteristics for determining whether a liability exists, is a future income tax liability really a liability? Should a future income tax asset be considered an asset? How would you interpret the future income tax assets or liabilities that you calculated in parts (a) through (d) above?

Problems

P9-1. **(Determining whether certain economic events are liabilities, LO 1)** Explain whether each of the following would be considered a liability according to IFRS (using the criteria from the chapter) on December 31, 2014. Intuitively, would you consider each of these items a liability, regardless of how it's accounted for according to IFRS? Explain.

    a. A company pays a licensing fee to use a sports team's logo on its clothing line. The fee is 5 percent of sales of items with the logo. During 2014 $2.4 million of the items were sold. The fee must be paid on April 30, 2015.

    b. A company will pay for goods it received by providing services to the customer instead of cash.

    c. The cost of closing a landfill when it's full. Significant costs will have to be incurred to ensure that it meets government standards. The landfill is expected to close in 15 years.

P9-2. **(Determining whether certain economic events are liabilities, LO 1)** Explain whether each of the following would be considered a liability according to IFRS (using the criteria from the chapter) on December 31, 2014. Intuitively, would you consider each of these items a liability, regardless of how it's accounted for according to IFRS? Explain.

    a. An airline allows passengers who didn't use their non-refundable tickets to redeem them for transportation within one year of the missed flight.

    b. A $1,000,000 loan from a shareholder that bears no interest and has no scheduled repayment date.

    c. An accounting firms signs a two-year contract in December 2014 with a janitorial company to clean its offices every night. The contract begins January 1, 2015 and the accounting firm will pays for the service on the first of each month.

www.mcgrawhillconnect.ca

P9-3.   (**Effect of transactions and economic events on ratios, LO 2, 3, 4, 6, 7, 8**) The president of Oskelaneo Ltd. (Oskelaneo) wants to know the effect a number of transactions and economic events will have on several financial measures for the company's fiscal year ended September 30, 2014. Complete the following table by indicating whether the listed transactions or economic events would increase, decrease, or have no effect on the financial measures listed. Explain your reasoning and state any assumptions that you make. Consider each item independently.

Ratio/amount before taking the transaction/economic event into account	Debt-to-equity ratio	Current ratio	Interest coverage ratio	Cash from operations	Return on assets
	1.3:1	1.67	3.98	$650,000	5.6%
a. Oskelaneo paid amounts owing to employees.					
b. Oskelaneo entered into a new capital lease.					
c. Oskelaneo recorded a future income tax expense and corresponding liability due to temporary differences associated with new equipment.					
d. Oskelaneo received cash from a customer for services it will provide in February 2015.					
e. Oskelaneo retired a bond early and recognized a loss of $25,000 (the bond retired was classified as a non-current liability).					
f. Oskelaneo paid $1,000,000 to settle a lawsuit that was launched three years ago. The amount was accrued in the financial statements in fiscal 2013.					

P9-4.   (**Effect of transactions and economic events on ratios, LO 3, 4, 5, 6, 7, 8**) The president of Ruskin Inc. (Ruskin) wants to know the effect a number of transactions and economic events will have on several financial measures for the company's fiscal year ended April 30, 2014. Complete the following table by indicating whether the listed transactions or economic events would increase, decrease, or have no effect on the financial measures listed. Explain your reasoning and state any assumptions that you make. Consider each item independently.

Ratio/amount before taking the transaction/economic event into account	Debt-to-equity ratio 0.7:1	Current ratio 0.85	Interest coverage ratio 4.21	Cash from operations $1,750,000	Return on assets 7.6%
a. Ruskin signed a contract to purchase raw materials beginning in 2015 at an agreed-to price.					
b. Ruskin repaid a bond that was classified as a current liability.					
c. Ruskin provided services to a customer that were paid for in the previous fiscal year.					
d. Ruskin made the annual payment on its capital leases on April 25, 2014.					
e. Ruskin arranged a new operating lease.					
f. Ruskin paid $1,000,000 to settle a lawsuit that was launched three years ago. The lawsuit has not been recognized in the financial statements.					

P9-5. **(Buy or lease?, LO 4)** Senior Living Ltd. (SLL) is a not-for-profit organization that operates the publicly owned nursing homes in a large Canadian city. SLL obtains operating funds from grants from the government, donations, and payments by residents of the homes (if they are able to pay). Recently, management decided to buy several ambulances for emergencies and to take residents to doctor's appointments. As a not-for-profit organization, SLL doesn't pay income taxes or claim capital cost allowance on its capital assets. The ambulances would have useful lives of about four years. They would cost $200,000 if purchased and could be sold for about $25,000 after four years. To complete the purchase, SLL would have to borrow about $100,000 from the bank for three years at 7 percent. Management is also considering the possibility of leasing the ambulances. The proposed lease would be for four years with monthly payments of $5,500. At the end of the lease the ambulances would remain the property of the lessor.

Required:

Prepare a report to management that explains fully whether SLL should buy or lease the ambulances.

P9-6. **(Impact of covenants, LO 3, 7)** In late 2014, Bedeque Ltd. (Bedeque) arranged to borrow $1,300,000 from a local bank to provide $325,000 in needed working capital and $975,000 to finance the purchase of some new equipment. However, the terms of a previous loan require that the company maintain a current ratio greater than 1.5 and a debt-to-equity ratio of less than 1. If either of these restrictions isn't met the loan would have to be repaid within 30 days. The previous loan agreement also states that for Bedeque to pay dividends, retained earnings must be greater than $1,700,000 after the dividend.

Bedeque's controller has asked you to figure out how the new loan will affect the restrictions on the December 31, 2014 balance sheet. Bedeque's shareholders are expecting a dividend in early 2015 so the controller also wants to know how much can be paid. The controller has provided you with a projected balance sheet for December 31, 2014. The balance sheet takes into consideration all expected economic activity through the end of the year (including the closing entry), except for the impact of the new loan.

		Bedeque Inc. Projected Balance Sheet as of December 31, 2014	
Current assets	$ 900,000	Current liabilities	$ 750,000
Non-current assets	6,562,500	Non-current liabilities	1,875,000
		Capital stock	2,500,000
		Retained earnings	2,337,500
Total assets	$7,462,500	Total liabilities and shareholders' equity	$7,462,500

Required:

Prepare a report that provides the information the controller wants. Explain your findings and reasoning.

P9-7. (**Accounting for possible unexpected warranty costs, LO 6**) Nouvelle Ltd. (Nouvelle) is a privately owned industrial-products manufacturer located in Sherbrooke, Québec. The president of Nouvelle owns 25 percent of the shares of the company and three investors who aren't active in managing the company own the rest. The company has a large demand loan outstanding. The terms of the loan require that Nouvelle maintain a current ratio of greater than 1.5 and a debt-to-equity ratio of 1.25 to 1 or less. Nouvelle's senior executives have an employment contract that entitles them to share a bonus pool equal to 10 percent of the company's net income. The financial statements are also used for tax purposes.

On December 21, 2014, Nouvelle's quality control engineer presented a report to the president where she expressed concern about problems with a new product line. The engineer believes these new products were rushed into production with some technical flaws that haven't been corrected. The engineer says service calls required on the new products are about 20 percent higher than other company products and she expects repairs will increase dramatically once the products have been used by customers for more than 2,500 hours, which should occur 12 to 18 months from the date of purchase. She estimates that the cost of repairing these products will be $1,500,000 higher than the amount originally budgeted. To date, repair costs on the new product line are about $125,000 higher than budgeted. The engineer bases her concerns on extensive tests she has carried out in the quality control laboratory.

Nouvelle's product design engineer, who was responsible for developing the products, has stated flatly that there are no technical flaws and that the increase in service calls is reasonable for a new product line.

On December 15, 2014, Nouvelle's vice-president of finance provided the president with the following estimates of the December 31, 2014 financial statements:

Net income	$ 1,270,000
Current assets	11,150,000
Current liabilities	9,100,000
Non-current liabilities	28,750,000
Shareholders' equity	31,400,000

Required:

Prepare a report to Nouvelle's president discussing the accounting and financial reporting issues regarding treatment of the concerns raised by the quality control engineer. Your report should identify alternative ways to treat the possible future costs and explain the implications of the alternatives. The president would also like your supported recommendations on what should be done.

P9-8. **(Assessing debt load, LO 3, 6, 7)** Lintlaw Ltd. (Lintlaw) recently released its December 31, 2015 financial statements. In a press release announcing the results, Lintlaw's management proudly stated that the company had maintained its debt load well below the industry average of 2.5 to 1. Lintlaw's summarized balance sheet for the years ended December 31, 2014 and 2015, along with extracts from the notes to the financial statements are provided below.

Required:

Assess Lintlaw's debt position. Do you think management should be as proud of its financial situation as it is? Explain your thinking.

Lintlaw Ltd. Balance Sheets for the Years Ended December 31 (in thousands of dollars)					
	2015	**2014**		**2015**	**2014**
Cash	$ 175	$ 138	Accounts payable and accrued liabilities	$ 910	$ 850
Accounts receivable	375	360	Current portion of long-term debt	100	100
Inventory	650	605		1,010	950
Other	175	155	Long-term debt	600	700
	1,375	1,258	Other non-current liabilities	125	138
				1,735	1,788
Property, plant, and equipment (net)	985	1,005			
Intangible assets (including goodwill)	875	925	Capital stock	900	900
			Retained earnings	600	500
				1,500	1,400
Total assets	$3,235	$3,188	Total liabilities and shareholders' equity	$3,235	$3,188

Extracts from Lintlaw's financial statements:
- The company leases most of its production equipment. The leases are generally for four to five years and all are classified as operating leases. Minimum annual lease payments for the next five years are

2016	$375,000
2017	390,000
2018	405,000
2019	425,000
2020	400,000

- The company has long-term binding commitments to purchase supplies from a Korean company. The commitments require a minimum purchase of $500,000 for the next three years.
- On January 15, 2016, the company signed an agreement to borrow $750,000 from a local bank. The annual interest rate on the loan will be 6 percent for a term of three years. The loan comes into effect on February 19, 2016.

P9-9. **(Accounting for frequent travel plans, LO 1, 2, 6, 7)** Intercity Bus Lines (Intercity) is a Canadian company that provides bus transportation between communities throughout Canada. In recent years, bus travel and the company's revenues have declined significantly and it's looking for ways to build its customer base. The marketing manager has observed that frequent flyer programs are very successful for airlines and has suggested a similar program for Intercity. She suggests that for every mile of travel on an Intercity bus a traveller would receive one point. The points could be redeemed for travel on Intercity buses. She proposes that levels be established; for example, for 500 points a customer might receive a trip of 250 miles or less.

At a recent planning meeting, Intercity's CFO raised some questions about the frequent travel programs. He wondered if there would be any impact on the company's financial statements. After the meeting, the CFO asked you to prepare a report discussing the proposed program and the financial reporting impact it would have. He asked you to consider the following:

- Would frequent travel points be considered liabilities?
- If they are liabilities, how are they measured?
- What effect would the plan have on the financial statements and should management be concerned about these impacts?
- What types of concerns should management have in operating such a program?

Required:

Prepare the report requested by the CFO.

P9-10. (**Accounting for a rebate promotion, LO 1, 2, 6**) Urling Inc. (Urling) is a small public company that produces packaged consumer foods. Urling began operations about 22 years ago and has been a public company for eight years. The company is managed by professional managers, who own about 10 percent of Urling's stock. About 30 percent of the shares are owned by members of the family who originally founded the company and the rest are widely held by private and institutional investors. Urling stock has struggled in recent years. The company has failed to meet earnings targets for the last two fiscal years. For the current fiscal year, management has projected earnings of $2,500,000, which is about a 2 percent increase from last year.

Recently, Urling introduced a new line of upscale frozen entrées to satisfy the tastes and lifestyles of busy baby boomers. For the first time, Urling's management decided to promote sales by offering rebates to customers. In the past, the company had promoted its products through advertising and in-store price reductions. The new promotion entitles customers to a $5 rebate if they purchase four entrées and mail in the UPC labels from the packages. Urling used special packaging highlighting the promotion, provided in-store signs, and advertised it in newspaper and magazines. Since the promotion began several months ago, approximately 250,000 entrées have been sold and sales of an additional 70,000 are expected by year-end. Approximately 1,500 customers have already mailed in their requests for rebates.

Because Urling has never used this type of promotion before, its marketing manager isn't sure how to account for it. The marketing manager has indicated that the number of rebate claims can be very difficult to estimate, especially because it's a new promotion and a new product. The manager has indicated that the number of claims can range between 2 percent and 25 percent of the product sold. Urling's controller has projected that net income before accounting for the new promotion will be about $2,555,000. Because projected earnings are so close to the forecast, the president is quite uneasy about the effect the new promotion will have.

Required:

a. Prepare a report to Urling's president outlining the accounting issues and problems with the new rebate promotion. Provide recommendations on how the promotion should be accounted for and provide support for your recommendations that can be used in any discussions with the company's auditors. Indicate how the rebate promotion will be reported in the financial statements.

b. Prepare a journal entry that will account for the rebate promotion in the current fiscal year.

P9-11. (**Accounting for a possible loss, LO 6**) Hoselaw Ltd. (Hoselaw) is a privately owned manufacturing company in eastern Ontario. The company is owned by five shareholders, three of whom aren't active in management of the business. The company has a large demand loan outstanding at the bank.

The government recently informed Hoselaw's management that seepage from a dumpsite on its property might have polluted the ground water used by a local community. The company has denied responsibility but the community has launched a $2,000,000 lawsuit against Hoselaw to compensate it for additional costs of obtaining fresh water and for cleaning up the contamination. The lawyers for the community and the company have met to discuss possible settlement terms, but little progress has been reported. Hoselaw's net income over the last five years has averaged $725,000 and its assets, as reported on the most recent balance sheet, have a carrying amount of $3,750,000.

Required:

Prepare a report to Hoselaw's president discussing the issues surrounding how to account for the environmental incident and the lawsuit. Your report should include a discussion of the alternative accounting treatments available and the implications of each.

P9-12. **(Accounting for a possible loss, LO 6)** In February 2011, Paul Willow slipped on ice in the parking lot of the Frontier Hotel and Resort (Frontier) suffering a fractured ankle and a third-degree concussion. Mr. Willow has been unable to work since the accident, has difficulty walking, and suffers serious headaches. Mr. Willow contends that his fall was due to the negligence of Frontier because of its failure to keep the parking lot free of ice and is suing for $5 million for loss of income and pain and suffering. As of December 31, 2012 (Frontier's year-end), the lawsuit has not been settled. Frontier's lawyers believe that the company will probably lose the lawsuit if it goes to trial. They think that Frontier stands to lose at least $1 million.

Frontier is a family-owned business but no family members are involved in management of the resort. The financial statements are used by the members of the Frontier family, by its banker, and for tax purposes. In January 2014, the lawsuit was finally settled with Frontier paying Mr. Willow $2.34 million.

Required:

a. Prepare a report to Frontier's president explaining the accounting issues that must be considered in deciding how to account for the lawsuit in the December 31, 2012 financial statements. Provide a recommendation on how the lawsuit should be accounted for and explain your reasoning fully.

b. What are the accounting issues that would have to be considered when the December 31, 2013 financial statements are prepared?

P9-13. **(Accounting for leases, LO 4)** Vista Inc. (Vista) is a new manufacturing company that was formed in January 2014, to supply certain specialized machine parts to a large public company. Vista's managers decided to arrange long-term leases for the company's equipment, rather than to arrange financing and buy the equipment. Had Vista purchased the equipment, it would have cost about $1,500,000. Instead, Vista signed an eight-year lease for the equipment in January 2014 that required it to make annual payments of $225,000 on December 31, the company's year-end. At the end of the lease, Vista has the option to purchase the equipment at its fair market value at the time. However, Vista's management thinks it's unlikely it will exercise the option because after eight years the equipment will likely be technologically out of date. The interest rate appropriate for this lease is 10 percent.

On December 31, 2014, Vista had total liabilities (before accounting for the lease obligation) of $1,200,000, capital stock of $750,000, and income before lease-related expenses and taxes of $540,000. Vista's tax expense for 2014 is estimated to be $60,000 (including the effect of the lease).

Required:

    a. What are some of the reasons that Vista might have leased rather than purchased the equipment?

    b. Should the lease be accounted for as a capital lease or an operating lease? Explain.

    c. What journal entry would be required when the lease agreement was signed if the lease was considered a capital lease? What entry would be required if it was classified as an operating lease?

    d. Prepare a schedule showing the principal and interest components of each annual payment over the life of the lease, assuming the lease is treated as a capital lease. Prepare the journal entries that Vista would make on December 31, 2014 and December 31, 2017 to record the lease payment. What would the entries be if the lease were classified as an operating lease?

    e. What amount would be reported on Vista's balance sheet for the machinery when the lease was signed in January 2014? What does this amount represent?

    f. Over what period of time should the equipment be depreciated? Explain. Prepare the journal entry to record the depreciation expense for the year ended December 31, 2014. Assume Vista uses straight-line depreciation.

    g. How would Vista's debt-to-equity ratio be affected by accounting for the lease as a capital lease? Compare the debt-to-equity ratio on December 31, 2014, when the lease is classified as a capital lease versus an operating lease.

    h. Compare the effect on the income statement of classifying the lease as a capital lease versus an operating lease. Make the comparison for the years ended December 31, 2014 and 2017, and in total over the term of the lease.

    i. What steps could Vista take to have the lease classified as an operating lease? Why might Vista prefer that classification?

    j. For purposes of determining a bonus for Vista's managers, do you think it's more appropriate to treat the lease as a capital lease or an operating lease? In answering, focus on determining management's bonus, not how IFRS would require the lease to be classified.

P9-14. **(Accounting for leases, LO 4)** On May 1, 2015, Isachsen Inc. (Isachsen) signed a five-year lease with an office supply company to supply Isachsen with all required office equipment over the lease period. Had Isachsen purchased the office equipment, it would have cost about $175,000. The lease requires Isachsen to make annual lease payments of $55,000 on May 1 of each year. Isachsen made the first payment on May 1, 2015. At the end of the lease Isachsen will own the equipment. Isachsen's management believes the office equipment will be useful for between six and eight years. The interest rate appropriate for this lease is 10 percent.

    On April 30, 2016, Isachsen had total liabilities (before accounting for the lease obligation) of $1,000,000, capital stock of $200,000, and retained earnings of $380,000. Isachsen's income before lease related-expenses and taxes for the year ended April 30, 2016 was $210,000. Isachsen's tax expense for fiscal 2016 is estimated to be $40,000 (including the effect of the lease).

Required:

    a. What are some of the reasons that Isachsen might have leased rather than purchased the office equipment?

    b. Should the lease be accounted for as a capital lease or an operating lease? Explain.

    c. What journal entry would be required when the lease agreement was signed if the lease was considered a capital lease? What entry would be required if it were classified as an operating lease?

    d. Prepare a schedule showing the principal and interest components of each annual payment over the life of the lease, assuming the lease is treated as a capital lease. Prepare the journal entries that Isachsen would make on May 1, 2016 and May 1, 2017 to record the lease payment. What would the entries be if the lease was classified as an operating lease?

e. What amount would be reported on Isachsen's balance sheet for the equipment when the lease was signed in May 1, 2015? What does this amount represent?

f. Over what period of time should the equipment be depreciated? Explain. Prepare the journal entry to record the depreciation expense for the year ended April 30, 2016. Assume Isachsen uses straight-line depreciation.

g. How would Isachsen's debt-to-equity ratio be affected by accounting for the lease as a capital lease? Compare the debt-to-equity ratio on April 30, 2016 when the lease is classified as a capital lease versus an operating lease.

h. Compare the effect on the income statement of classifying the lease as a capital lease versus an operating lease. Make the comparison for the years ended April 30, 2016 and 2017, and in total over the term of the lease.

i. What steps could Isachsen take to have the lease classified as an operating lease? Why might Isachsen prefer that classification?

j. Suppose you were considering buying all the shares of Isachsen. Which balance sheet and income statement would be more useful to you in assessing the company—statements where the lease was classified as a capital lease or as an operating lease?

P9-15. **(Effect of inaccurate accruals, LO 7)** In 2014, Ogoki Ltd. announced a major restructuring of its operations. The restructuring was in response to several years of poor performance and declining net income, the result of increased competition from Asia. The company announced it would be downsizing its production facilities and reducing its workforce by 20 percent. Management estimated that the cost of reducing the workforce would be about $75 million. The reduction in the workforce and the related costs are to take place in 2015.

In 2015, Ogoki carried out its restructuring. When it was completed, the actual cost of reducing the workforce was $50 million. All of these costs were related to severance packages paid to and retraining of employees. Ogoki's year-end is December 31.

Required:

a. Provide the journal entry that Ogoki would make in 2014 to record the estimated cost of reducing the workforce. Why do you think the entry would be made in 2014 when the reduction in the workforce was to actually take place in 2015? How would the amount be shown on the income statement? Explain.

b. What entry would be made to record the $50 million in cash costs incurred in 2015 to reduce the workforce. What effect would this entry have on the income statement in 2015? Explain.

c. What additional entry or entries would be needed in 2015 to adjust for the fact that management estimated the cost of reducing the workforce to be $75 million while the actual cost proved to be only $50 million? What is the effect of this difference on the financial statements in 2014 and 2015? Provide some possible explanations for the error in the estimate in 2014. When answering, consider the managers' financial reporting objectives.

P9-16. **(The effects of buying versus leasing on the financial statements, LO 4)** Winterton Rail Ltd. (Winterton) is considering obtaining some new locomotives. The purchase price of the locomotives is $82,014,121. Winterton is considering whether it should purchase the locomotives or lease them from the manufacturer. If Winterton buys the locomotives, it would borrow the full purchase price from a large institutional lender and repay the loan by making an annual payment of $10,000,000 on the last day of each of the next 18 years. If Winterton leases the locomotives, it would make annual lease payments of $10,000,000 to the manufacturer on the last day of each of the next 18 years.

Required:

    a. Prepare the journal entries Winterton would make if it borrowed the money and purchased the locomotives.

    b. Prepare the journal entries Winterton would make when the lease agreement is signed if it leased the locomotives and the lease was considered a capital lease.

    c. Prepare the journal entries Winterton would make when the lease agreement is signed if it leased the locomotives and the lease was considered an operating lease.

    d. Compare the three alternatives in (a), (b), and (c). Explain the similarities and differences among them. Under what circumstances might one of the alternatives be preferred over the others? Explain.

P9-17. **(Lease accounting and financial ratios, LO 4, 7)** Uphill Corp. (Uphill) operates amusement arcades throughout Atlantic Canada. Uphill's summarized balance sheet on March 31, 2014 is shown below.

    The non-current liabilities of $215,000 include a $120,000 term note that matures in 2020. The terms of the note stipulate that Uphill must maintain a current ratio greater than 1.4 and a debt-to-equity ratio of less than 1.5. If either of these covenants is violated, the term note becomes payable immediately.

    In January 2014, management decided, in response to declining revenues, to upgrade the quality of the games in the arcades, many of which were no longer popular with the young people who are Uphill's primary customers. Uphill arranged a 10-year lease for new games from an equipment manufacturer. The terms of the lease require annual payments of $35,000. A key condition of the lease is that it allows Uphill to replace up to 25 percent of the leased arcade games each year with newer games carried by the lessor. The lease goes into effect on April 1, 2014.

Uphill Corp. Balance Sheet as of March 31, 2014			
Assets:		Liabilities and shareholders' equity:	
Current assets	$ 85,000	Current liabilities	$ 49,000
Capital assets and other non-current assets	435,000	Non-current liabilities	215,000
			264,000
		Shareholders' equity	256,000
Total assets	$520,000	Total liabilities and shareholders' equity	$520,000

Required:

    a. Calculate the current ratio and debt-to-equity ratio on March 31, 2014.

    b. Calculate the current ratio and debt-to-equity ratio on April 1, 2014, if the new lease is accounted for as an operating lease.

    c. Calculate the current ratio and debt-to-equity ratio on April 1, 2014, if the new lease is accounted for as a capital lease. Assume that the appropriate interest rate that should be applied to the lease is 9 percent. Assume the first payment is due on April 1, 2014.

    d. You are Uphill's controller. The president of the company has just informed you of his plan to lease the new arcade equipment. Write a memo to the president raising any concerns you have with the plan and providing advice and recommendations on how he should proceed.

P9-18. **(Accounting for bonds, LO 3)** On May 1, 2014, Kuldo Inc. (Kuldo) issued a $25,000,000 bond with a 6.5 percent coupon rate and a maturity date of April 30, 2019. Interest will be paid semi-annually on April 30 and October 31. Kuldo's year-end is December 31. The effective interest rate for a bond of this type on May 1, 2014 was 5 percent.

Required:

    a. What will be the proceeds from the bond issue?

    b. Prepare the journal entry to record the issue of the bond on May 1, 2014.

    c. Prepare an amortization schedule using the straight-line method for any premium or discount that arose from the issue of the bond.

    d. Prepare the journal entry required to accrue the interest expense and interest payable on December 31, 2016. Make the entry assuming straight-line amortization.

    e. Prepare the journal entry required to record the interest expense on April 30, 2017. Assume Kuldo uses the straight-line amortization method.

    f. Prepare the journal entry required to record the retirement of the bond on maturity. Include the interest expense and amortization of any bond premium or discount in the entry.

    g. Assume that Kuldo's bond agreement allowed it to redeem the bond on April 30, 2017 for $27,000,000. Prepare the journal entry required to record early retirement of the bond.

    h. Assume the role of a shareholder in Kuldo. How would you interpret the gain or loss that would be reported on Kuldo's income statement as a result of the early retirement of the bond? Explain.

P9-19. **(Accounting for bonds, LO 3)** On August 1, 2014, Quilty Inc. (Quilty) issued a $3,500,000 bond with a 7 percent coupon rate and a maturity date of July 31, 2022. Interest will be paid semi-annually on July 31 and January 31. Quilty's year-end is December 31. The appropriate interest rate for a bond of this type on August 1, 2014 was 7.5 percent.

Required:

    a. What will be the proceeds from the bond issue?

    b. Prepare the journal entry to record the issue of the bond on August 1, 2014.

    c. Prepare an amortization schedule using the straight-line method for any premium or discount that arose from the issue of the bond.

    d. Prepare the journal entry required to accrue the interest expense and accrued interest payable on December 31, 2015.

    e. Prepare the journal entry required to record the interest expense and the payment to investors on January 31, 2016.

    f. Prepare the journal entry required to record the retirement of the bond on maturity. Include the interest expense and amortization of any bond premium or discount in the entry.

    g. On July 31, 2019, Quilty was able to buy back all the outstanding bonds on the open market for $2,850,000. Prepare the journal entry required to record early retirement of the bond.

    h. Do you think that the decision to buy back the bonds early was a good one? Explain.

P9-20. **(Future income taxes, LO 8)** Rougemont Inc. (Rougemont) is a small print and photocopy shop that began operations in 2014. Rougemont purchased equipment for $100,000 to begin operations. For accounting purposes, Rougemont is depreciating the equipment on a straight-line basis over eight years, with no residual value. For tax purposes, the asset is in a CCA class that allows Rougemont to deduct 20 percent of the capital cost of the asset on a declining-balance basis. Because of the half-year rule, Rougemont can deduct only one-half of the allowable amount (10 percent) of the cost in 2014. Rougemont has an income tax rate of 16 percent and its income before depreciation and taxes is $140,000 in each year from 2014 through 2016. Rougemont has no temporary differences between tax and financial reporting except for the difference between depreciation and CCA on the equipment, and there are no permanent differences.

Required:

      a. Calculate Rougemont's taxable income in 2014 through 2016.

      b. Calculate the amount of income tax that Rougemont must pay in 2014 through 2016.

      c. Calculate the accounting and tax bases of the equipment in 2014 through 2016.

      d. Calculate the future tax asset or liability that would be reported on Rougemont's balance sheet at the end of 2014 through 2016.

      e. Prepare the journal entry that Rougemont would make each year to record its income tax expense in 2014 through 2016.

      f. Calculate Rougemont's net income in 2014 through 2016.

      g. What would Rougemont's net income be in 2014 through 2016 if it used the taxes payable method?

      h. As a banker, which measure of net income is more useful to you? Explain.

Using Financial Statements

ALIMENTATION COUCHE-TARD INC.

www.couchetard.com/
home.html

Alimentation Couche-Tard Inc. (Couche-Tard) is a Canadian convenience store operator with a network of over 2,000 stores in Canada and more than 3,000 stores in the U.S. Over 3,600 of the total number are company-operated and the rest operate under an affiliate program. The company sells fuel in 65 percent of its company-operated stores. The stores are primarily operated under the Couche-Tard and Mac's trademarks in Canada and the Circle K trademark in the U.S. In addition to the North American Couche-Tard network, there are approximately 3,500 Circle K–licensed stores in other parts of the world.[13]

Couche-Tard's consolidated balance sheets and statements of earnings as well as extracts from the statements of cash flows and notes to the financial statements from its 2009 annual report are provided in Exhibit 9.11.[14] Use this information to respond to questions FS9-1 to FS9-8.

FS9-1. Use the information in Exhibit 9.11 to respond to the following questions:

      a. What amount of current liabilities did Couche-Tard have on April 27, 2008 and April 26, 2009? What amount of non-current liabilities did it have?

      b. How much did Couche-Tard owe in salaries and related benefits on April 27, 2008 and April 26, 2009?

      c. What was Couche-Tard's debt-to-equity ratio on April 27, 2008 and April 26, 2009? Interpret the ratios you calculated.

      d. Which liabilities on Couche-Tard's balance sheet are valued at their present value?

      e. What was Couche-Tard's interest coverage ratio in 2009?

      f. Calculate Couche-Tard's current and quick ratios on April 27, 2008 and April 26, 2009. What is your assessment of the company's liquidity? What other factors might you consider in assessing the company's liquidity?

      g. What is Couche-Tard's cash from operations for 2008 and 2009? Why is cash from operations so different from net earnings?

FS9-2. What is a contingent liability? How are contingent liabilities accounted for? Describe the information Couche-Tard provides about its contingent liabilities. Do you find this information useful? Explain.

FS9-3. The following questions pertain to Couche-Tard's long-term debt:

      a. How much long-term debt was outstanding on April 26, 2009? How much of that long-term debt was classified as current? What does it mean when long-term debt is classified as a current liability? What is the purpose of classifying long-term debt as current?

      b. How much did Couche-Tard have outstanding from its term revolving operating credit agreements on April 26, 2009? How much of the amount is in Canadian

EXHIBIT 9.11 Alimentation Couche-Tard Inc.: Extracts from the Financial Statements

CONSOLIDATED BALANCE SHEETS
as at April 26, 2009 and April 27, 2008
(in millions of US dollars (Note 2))

	2009	2008
	$	$
Assets		
Current assets		
Cash and cash equivalents	173.3	216.0
Accounts receivable (Note 10)	225.4	251.7
Inventories (Note 11)	400.3	444.5
Prepaid expenses	8.5	8.3
Future income taxes (Note 7)	37.0	24.7
	844.5	945.2
Property and equipment (Note 12)	1,789.4	1,748.3
Goodwill (Note 13)	384.8	402.6
Trademarks and licenses	172.0	170.3
Other assets (Note 14)	60.7	53.3
Future income taxes (Note 7)	4.5	0.9
	3,255.9	3,320.6
Liabilities		
Current liabilities		
Accounts payable and accrued liabilities (Note 15)	758.1	842.7
Income taxes payable (Note 7)	26.3	18.6
Current portion of long-term debt (Note 16)	3.9	1.2
Future income taxes (Note 7)	0.7	-
	789.0	862.5
Long-term debt (Note 16)	745.3	841.0
Deferred credits and other liabilities (Note 17)	259.0	253.8
Future income taxes (Note 7)	136.6	109.6
	1,929.9	2,066.9
Shareholders' equity		
Capital stock (Note 18)	329.1	348.8
Contributed surplus	17.7	15.6
Retained earnings	932.6	775.0
Accumulated other comprehensive income	46.6	114.3
	1,326.0	1,253.7
	3,255.9	3,320.6

CONSOLIDATED STATEMENTS OF EARNINGS
For the years ended April 26, 2009, April 27, 2008 and April 29, 2007
(in millions of US dollars (Note 2), except per share amounts)

	2009	2008	2007
	$	$	$
Revenues	15,781.1	15,370.0	12,087.4
Cost of sales (excluding depreciation and amortization of property and equipment and other assets as shown separately below)	13,344.5	13,146.5	10,082.9
Gross profit	2,436.6	2,223.5	2,004.5
Operating, selling, administrative and general expenses (note 6)	1,848.8	1,738.9	1,512.4
Depreciation and amortization of property and equipment and other assets (Note 6)	183.0	172.5	133.8
	2,031.8	1,911.4	1,646.2
Operating income	404.8	312.1	358.3
Financial expenses (Note 6)	36.2	54.6	48.0
Earnings before income taxes	368.6	257.5	310.3
Income taxes (Note 7)	114.7	68.2	113.9
Net earnings	253.9	189.3	196.4

dollars and how much is in U.S. dollars? What were the effective interest rates in 2009 and 2008 on the Canadian and U.S. portions of the loans? Why do you think Couche-Tard has both Canadian and U.S. dollar loans? What types of restrictions are on these loans?

c. How much did Couche-Tard have outstanding from its subordinated unsecured debt on April 26, 2009? When does this debt mature? What is the interest rate on the debt?

d. What was Couche-Tard's interest expense in 2007, 2008, and 2009? How much interest did Couche-Tard pay in those years? Why are the interest expense and the amount of interest paid different?

EXHIBIT ⟨9.11⟩ (continued) Alimentation Couche-Tard Inc.: Extracts from the Financial Statements

CONSOLIDATED STATEMENTS OF CASH FLOWS

For the years ended April 26, 2009, April 27, 2008 and April 29, 2007
(in millions of US dollars (Note 2))

	2009	2008	2007
	$	$	$
Operating activities			
Net earnings	253.9	189.3	196.4
Adjustments to reconcile net earnings to net cash provided by operating activities			
Depreciation and amortization of property and equipment and other assets, net of amortization of deferred credits	161.4	151.8	114.4
Future income taxes	32.0	19.0	21.7
Loss (gain) on disposal of property and equipment and other assets	2.8	(0.9)	(3.8)
Deferred credits	9.4	13.3	30.5
Other	13.3	24.2	13.1
Changes in non-cash working capital (Note 9)	30.0	(36.9)	30.7
Net cash provided by operating activities	502.8	359.8	403.0
Financing activities			
Net (decrease) increase in long-term debt	(116.5)	(14.3)	513.0
Repurchase of Class A multiple voting shares and Class B subordinate voting shares	(99.5)	(101.3)	-
Cash dividends paid	(24.1)	(25.6)	(19.5)
Interest rate swap early termination fees received (note 22)	9.4	-	-
Issuance of shares	1.8	4.7	1.1
Repayment of long-term debt	-	-	(167.2)
Net cash (used in) provided by financing activities	(228.9)	(136.5)	327.4
Effect of exchange rate fluctuations on cash and cash equivalents	(20.0)	11.4	-
Net (decrease) increase in cash and cash equivalents	(42.7)	74.3	(189.8)
Cash and cash equivalents, beginning of year	216.0	141.7	331.5
Cash and cash equivalents, end of year	173.3	216.0	141.7

4. Accounting policies

Rent expense

The Company accounts for capital leases in instances when it has acquired substantially all the benefits and risks incident to ownership of the leased property. The cost of assets under capital leases represents the present value of minimum lease payments and is amortized on a straight-line basis over the lease term. Assets under capital leases are presented under Property and equipment in the consolidated balance sheet.

Leases that do not transfer substantially all the benefits and risks incident to ownership of the property are accounted for as operating leases. When a lease contains a predetermined fixed escalation of the minimum rent, the Company recognizes the related rent expense on a straight-line basis over the term of the lease and, consequently, records the difference between the recognized rental expense and the amounts payable under the lease as deferred rent expense. The Company also receives tenant allowances, which are amortized on a straight-line basis over the term of the lease or useful life of the asset, whichever is shorter.

Environmental costs

The Company provides for estimated future site remediation costs to meet government standards for known site contaminations when such costs can be reasonably estimated. Estimates of the anticipated future costs for remediation activities at such sites are based on the Company's prior experience with remediation sites and consideration of other factors such as the condition of the site contamination, location of sites and experience with contractors that perform the environmental assessments and remediation work.

Asset retirement obligations

Asset retirement obligations relate to estimated future costs to remove underground motor fuel storage tanks and are based on the Company's prior experience in removing these tanks, estimated tank useful life, lease terms for those tanks installed on leased properties, external estimates and governmental regulatory requirements. A discounted liability is recorded for the fair value of an asset retirement obligation with a corresponding increase to the carrying value of the related long-lived asset at the time an underground storage tank is installed. To determine the initial recorded liability, the future estimated cash flows have been discounted at rates of 9.0% and 10.0%, representing the Company's credit-adjusted risk-free rates at the time the costs have been estimated and revised. The amount added to property and equipment is amortized and an accretion expense is recognized in connection with the discounted liability over the remaining life of the tank or lease term for leased properties.

Guarantees

A guarantee is defined as a contract or an indemnification agreement contingently requiring a company to make payments to a third party based on future events. These payments are contingent on either changes in an underlying or other variables that are related to an asset, liability, or an equity security of the indemnified party or the failure of another entity to perform under an obligating agreement. It could also be an indirect guarantee of the indebtedness of another party. Guarantees are initially recognized at fair value and subsequently revaluated when the loss becomes likely.

6. Supplementary information relating to the consolidated statements of earnings

Financial expenses			
Interest on long-term debt	37.4	58.2	54.0
Interest income	(1.2)	(3.6)	(6.0)
	36.2	54.6	48.0

7. Income taxes

	2009	2008	2007
	$	$	$
Current income taxes	82.7	49.2	92.2
Future income taxes	32.0	19.0	21.7
	114.7	68.2	113.9

The principal items which resulted in differences between the Company's effective income tax rates and the combined statutory rates in Canada are detailed as follows:

	2009	2008	2007
	%	%	%
Combined statutory income tax rate in Canada [a]	30.90	31.66	32.02
Impact of tax rate changes	0.12	0.32	0.30
Other permanent differences	0.10	(1.65)	1.20
Effective income tax rate before unusual income tax expense (reversal)	31.12	30.33	33.52
Unusual retroactive income tax (reversal) expense [b]	-	(3.84)	3.19
Effective income tax rate	31.12	26.49	36.71

[a] The Company's combined statutory income tax rate in Canada includes the appropriate provincial income tax rates.

[b] On June 9, 2006, the Government of Québec adopted Bill 15 in the National Assembly of Québec, regarding amendments to the Taxation Act and other legislative provisions. As a result, in 2007, the Company has recorded an unusual retroactive income tax expense of $9.9. During fiscal year 2008, the Company reversed this unusual income tax expense following an agreement with the taxing authorities.

The components of future income tax assets (liabilities) are as follows:

	2009	2008
	$	$
Short-term net future income tax assets		
Expenses deductible during the next year	22.8	22.1
Loss deductible during the next year	13.8	-
Revenues taxable during the next year	(6.5)	-
Deferred credits	1.5	0.4
Other	4.7	2.2
	36.3	24.7
Long-term net future income tax liabilities		
Property and equipment	(110.8)	(69.5)
Trademarks and licences	(58.5)	(53.8)
Deferred credits	17.6	19.7
Asset retirement obligations	12.7	14.0
Goodwill	(11.0)	(7.7)
Expenses deductible in future years	8.2	7.2
Non-capital losses	2.6	2.9
Unrealized exchange gain	(0.8)	(19.3)
Other	7.9	(2.2)
	(132.1)	(108.7)

9. Supplementary information relating to the consolidated statements of cash flows

Cash flows relating to interest and income taxes are detailed as follows:

	2009	2008	2007
	$	$	$
Interest paid	34.2	59.5	50.6
Income taxes paid	66.1	89.0	57.7

15. Accounts payable and accrued liabilities

	2009	2008
	$	$
Accounts payable and accrued expenses	510.3	618.0
Sales and other taxes payable	124.3	95.6
Salaries and related benefits	64.5	60.9
Deferred credits	13.7	18.6
Environmental costs	9.5	10.0
Other	35.8	39.6
	758.1	842.7

EXHIBIT 9.11 (continued) **Alimentation Couche-Tard Inc.: Extracts from the Financial Statements**

16. Long-term debt

	2009	2008
	$	$
US dollar term revolving unsecured operating credit A, maturing in September 2012 [a]	229.4	460.0
Canadian dollar term revolving unsecured operating credit A, maturing in September 2012 (Cdn$28.6 in 2009 and Cdn$41.0 in 2008) [a]	23.6	40.3
US dollar term revolving unsecured operating credit B, maturing in September 2012 [a]	110.6	-
Canadian dollar term revolving unsecured operating credit B, maturing in September 2012 (Cdn$21.4) [a]	17.7	-
Subordinated unsecured debt, at amortized cost [b]	351.7	334.7
Note payable, secured by the assets of certain stores, 8.75%, repayable in monthly instalments, maturing in 2019	4.5	4.7
Obligations related to buildings and equipment under capital leases, rates varying from 0.53% to 12.54% (9.00% to 12.54% in 2008), payable on various dates until 2019	11.7	2.5
	749.2	842.2
Current portion of long-term debt	3.9	1.2
	745.3	841.0

(a) Term revolving unsecured operating credits A, B and C:

As at April 26, 2009, the Company has credit agreements consisting of three revolving unsecured facilities of initial maximum amounts of $650.0 (Operating credit A), $310.0 (Operating credit B) and $40.0 (Operating credit C) each, with initial terms of five years, 51 months and 42 months respectively, that can be extended each year by one year at the request of the Company with the consent of the lenders. The credit facilities are available in the following forms:

- A term revolving unsecured operating credit, available i) in Canadian dollars, ii) in US dollars, iii) in the form of Canadian dollar bankers' acceptances, with stamping fees and iv) in the form of standby letters of credit not exceeding $50.0 or the equivalent in Canadian dollars, with applicable fees. Depending on the form and the currency of the loan, the amounts borrowed bear interest at variable rates based on the Canadian prime rate, the bankers' acceptance rate, the US base rate or the LIBOR rate plus a variable margin;

- An unsecured line of credit in the maximum amount of $50.0, available in Canadian or US dollars, bearing interest at variable rates based, depending on the form and the currency of the loan, on the Canadian prime rate, the US prime rate or the US base rate plus a variable margin.

Stand by fees, which vary based on a leverage ratio and on the utilization rate of the credit facilities, apply to the unused portion of the credit facilities. Stamping fees, standby letters of credit fees and the variable margin used to determine the interest rate applicable to amounts borrowed are determined according to a leverage ratio of the Company.

Under the credit agreements, the Company must maintain certain financial ratios and respect certain restrictive provisions.

As at April 26, 2009, the weighted average effective interest rate is 1.10% (3.51% in 2008) for the US dollar portion and 1.24% for the Canadian dollar portion (4.21% in 2008). In addition, Cdn$1.0 (Cdn$0.7 in 2008) and $18.3 ($17.9 in 2008) are used for standby letters of credit. As at April 26, 2009 and April 27, 2008, the available line of credit was unused and the Company was in compliance with the restrictive provisions and ratios imposed by the credit agreement. As at April 26, 2009, operating credit C was unused.

(b) Subordinated unsecured debt:

Subordinated unsecured debt of a nominal amount of $350.0, maturing December 15, 2013, bearing interest at a nominal rate of 7.5% (effective rate of 7.56% (8.23% in 2008)). Since December 15, 2008, the Company has the option for early repayment at a premium.

The Subordinated unsecured debt agreement imposes restrictions on certain transactions.

Instalments on long-term debt for the next fiscal years are as follows:

	Obligations related to buildings and equipment under capital leases	Other loans denominated in US dollars	Other loans denominated in Canadian dollars
	$	$	Cdn$
2010	3.7	0.3	-
2011	3.4	0.3	-
2012	2.4	0.3	-
2013	2.1	340.3	50.0
2014	1.4	350.4	-
2015 and thereafter	0.7	2.8	-
	13.7		
Interest expense included in minimum lease payments	2.0		
	11.7		

EXHIBIT 9.11 (continued) Alimentation Couche-Tard Inc.: Extracts from the Financial Statements

17. Deferred credits and other liabilities

	2009	2008
	$	$
Deferred gain on sale and leaseback transactions	101.3	97.7
Asset retirement obligations [a]	42.5	39.0
Deferred rent expense	20.4	16.1
Deferred branding costs	16.5	17.9
Provision for workers' compensation	16.5	11.5
Provision for site restoration costs	14.2	10.7
Deferred credits	10.2	17.1
Accrued pension benefit liability	9.8	10.4
Other liabilities	27.6	33.4
	259.0	253.8

[a]   The total undiscounted amount of estimated cash flows to settle the asset retirement obligations is approximately $127.5 and is expected to be incurred over the next 40 years. Should changes occur in estimated future removal costs, tank useful lives, lease terms or governmental regulatory requirements, revisions to the liability could be made.

The reconciliation of the Company's liability for the asset retirement obligations related to the removal of its underground motor fuel storage tanks is as follows:

	2009	2008
	$	$
Balance, beginning of year	48.8	45.1
Liabilities incurred	0.4	0.6
Liabilities settled	(2.5)	(1.4)
Accretion expense	3.8	4.0
Business acquisitions	1.4	0.3
Revision of estimations	-	0.1
Effect of exchange rate fluctuations	(1.0)	0.1
Balance, end of year	50.9	48.8

Of the total liability recorded in the consolidated balance sheets as at April 26, 2009 and April 27, 2008, $42.5 and $39.0, respectively, are included in Deferred credits and other liabilities and the remainder is included in Accounts payable and accrued liabilities.

23. Contractual obligations

Minimum lease payments

As at April 26, 2009, the Company has entered into operating lease agreements expiring on various dates until 2031 which call for aggregate minimum lease payments of $1,542.8 in the United States and of Cdn$775.5 in Canada for the rental of commercial space, equipment and a warehouse. Several of these leases contain renewal options and certain sites are subleased to franchise holders. The minimum lease payments for the next fiscal years are as follows:

	United States	Canada
	$	Cdn$
2010	134.4	88.2
2011	128.3	76.6
2012	123.4	68.0
2013	115.6	59.7
2014	102.4	50.6
2015 and thereafter	938.7	432.4

Purchase commitments

The Company has concluded agreements to acquire, during the next fiscal year, equipment which call for aggregate payments of Cdn$0.8.

Moreover, the Company has entered into various product purchase agreements that require it to purchase minimum amounts or quantities of merchandise and motor fuel annually. The Company has generally exceeded such minimum requirements in the past and expects to continue doing so for the foreseeable future. Failure to satisfy the minimum purchase requirements could result in termination of the contracts, change in pricing of the products, payments to the applicable providers of a predetermined percentage of the commitments and repayments of a portion of rebates received.

| EXHIBIT 9.11 | (continued) Alimentation Couche-Tard Inc.: Extracts from the Financial Statements |

24. Contingencies and guarantees

Contingencies

Various claims and legal proceedings have been initiated against the Company in the normal course of its operations. In management's opinion, these claims and proceedings are unfounded. Management estimates that any payments resulting from their outcome are not likely to have a substantial negative impact on the Company's results and financial position.

Guarantees

Sublease agreements

The Company entered into a number of agreements to sublease premises to third parties. Under some of these agreements, the Company retains ultimate responsibility to the landlord for payment of amounts under the lease agreements should the sublessees fail to pay. The total future lease payments under such agreements are approximately $2.2 and their fair value is not significant. Historically, the Company has not made any significant payments in connection with these indemnification provisions.

26. Subsequent event

On May 28, 2009, the Company acquired 43 corporate stores in the Phoenix, Arizona region, United-States from ExxonMobil Corporation (ExxonMobil). The land and buildings of ten of these sites are leased. As per the agreement, ExxonMobil also transferred to Couche-Tard the "*On the Run*" trademark rights in the United Sates as well as 450 franchised stores operating under this trademark in the United States.

e. How much is scheduled to be repaid to lenders in each of the next five years? In examining the scheduled repayments do you have any concerns? Explain.

FS9-4. The following questions pertain to Couche-Tard's income taxes:

a. What amount did Couche-Tard report as its income tax expense in the years ended April 27, 2008 and April 26, 2009? What portion was classified as a current expense and what portion was a future income tax expense? How much did Couche-Tard owe government for income taxes on April 26, 2009? How much did the company actually pay in income taxes to government during 2009? Why is this amount different from the current income tax expense?

b. What amount does Couche-Tard report on its April 27, 2008 and April 26, 2009 balance sheet for future income taxes? What do these amounts represent? What is the largest source of future income tax liabilities?

c. What was Couche-Tard's combined statutory income tax rate in 2007, 2008, and 2009? What is Couche-Tard's actual (effective) income tax rate based on the income tax expense in 2007, 2008, and 2009? What is Couche-Tard's tax rate based on its current income tax expense in 2007, 2008, and 2009?

FS9-5. The following questions pertain to Couche-Tard's contractual obligations (commitments):

a. What is a commitment and how are they accounted for? What types of commitments has Couche-Tard entered into? Are the disclosures about Couche-Tard's commitments important? Explain.

b. Suppose the operating lease payments reported in Note 23 were to be reported as capital leases:

i. What would be the journal entry on April 27, 2009 to record these leases as capital leases, assuming the leases went into effect on that date? Assume a discount rate of 7 percent and assume the payments to be made "thereafter" are evenly distributed over 2015 through 2024.

ii. What effect would classifying these leases as capital leases have on Couche-Tard's debt-to-equity ratio? Explain and show your calculations.

iii. Do you think that treating all leases as capital leases gives a better indication of an entity's debt load? Explain.

FS9-6. What is a guarantee? Describe the nature of the guarantees that Couche-Tard has? Under what circumstances are guarantees reported as liabilities? If a guarantee isn't reported as a liability, why are they reported in the notes to the financial statements? Is information about guarantees useful to stakeholders? Explain.

FS9-7.   What is a subsequent event and why are they reported in financial statements? Describe the subsequent event Couche-Tard reported in its 2009 statements. What is the relevance of this event to stakeholders? Do you think the event when reported in the financial statement would be "news" to any stakeholder who was very interested in Couche-Tard? Explain.

FS9-8.   What is an "asset retirement obligation" and why does Couche-Tard have them? What is Couche-Tard's asset retirement obligation on April 26, 2009? Where is this amount reported in the financial statements (be careful when looking for the answer)? When will Couche-Tard fulfill this obligation? Do you think it's easy or difficult to determine the amount of this obligation? Explain. Do you think information about the asset retirement obligation is important and useful to stakeholders? Explain.

ENDNOTES

1. Extracted from Bombardier Inc.'s fiscal 2009 annual report.

2. Extracted from Indigo Books & Music Inc.'s fiscal 2009 annual report.

3. Extracted from WestJet Airlines Ltd.'s 2008 annual report.

4. Ibid.

5. Extracted from Saputo Inc.'s 2008 annual report.

6. Extracted from Air Canada's 2008 annual report.

7. Extracted from the 2008 annual reports of Corus Entertainment Inc., Enbridge Inc., and Canada Bread Company Limited.

8. Data obtained from "Financial Post Industry Report," at the *Financial Post* website, http://www.fpdata.finpost.com/suite/autologreports.asp (accessed March 2009).

9. Ibid.

10. Extracted from WestJet Airlines Ltd.'s 2008 annual report.

11. Ibid.

12. Ibid.

13. Adapted from Alimentation Couche-Tard Inc.'s website at http://www.couchetard.com/home.html.

14. Extracted from Alimentation Couche-Tard Inc.'s 2009 annual report.

CHAPTER
10

OWNERS' EQUITY

I f Chris Lovell had her way, accounting would be a mandatory subject in all Canadian high schools. Lovell, a certified general accountant, teaches accounting and other business and information technology topics to high school students in Whitby and Bowmanville, Ontario. How does she make accounting relevant to teenagers who'd rather be posting their journal entries to Facebook?

She tells them this: "Everyone eventually, if they're not going to be working in a business, they'll be owning their own business, so these courses are important."

Lovell brings her nearly two decades working on Bay Street in Canada's financial district right into the classroom. Raised in Toronto, she joined the CIBC directly after high school, where her strength in math was an asset in performing various accounting tasks in the bank's real estate division. She obtained her CGA in 1994 when she worked preparing the financial statements at Confederation Life Insurance (now Aetna). Later, as a senior associate in tax for PricewaterhouseCoopers, Lovell relied on her accounting training when working with insurance company clients.

Chris Lovell, CGA
Teacher

"What's important is being extremely resourceful, using your strong analytical skills and being an independent and critical thinker," Lovell recalled of one her first client audits. Admitting to being "terrified" on that case, she quickly discovered clients don't "sit there and hold your hand." Getting the job done forced her to ask questions and probe in order to get the information she needed to prepare the numbers the client eventually entered on his federal income tax return.

Now she finds her teenage students asking her for tax advice and reacting with surprise when she explains what happens to their wages.

"I tell them, 'Once you get over a certain threshold, over 45 cents of every dollar goes to taxes,' and we get into a lot of interesting conversations," Lovell said.

In her classes, students learn to prepare basic financial statements and how to make sure the credits and debits balance.

"Kids really struggle with creating a spreadsheet," Lovell said. "They know Facebook and all the fun things, but not things they need to get them a job."

But her students also discuss more sophisticated topics including accounting scandals and ethics.

"Accounting isn't just putting together a set of financial statements; you also want them to understand what the purpose of the financial statements is and who uses them."

While raising her two children, Lovell began spending more and more time away from the corporate boardroom and more time volunteering in schools, often as treasurer of the parent council and mentoring students in classroom activities. She decided to use her business background to obtain a bachelor of commerce degree from the University of Ontario Institute of Technology in 2007, then a teaching degree from York in 2008.

"I love teaching, I love being in a classroom," Lovell enthused.

Calling her accounting training "a tool that opened up other doors," Lovell finds it fulfilling when one of her students displays an aptitude for the accounting profession.

"I tell them, 'Every business needs an accountant, there will always be jobs for you.'"
—E.B.

INTRODUCTION

Entities finance their assets from two sources: debt and equity. These two sources of financing are seen in the structure of the accounting equation:

$$\text{Assets} = \text{Liabilities} + \text{Owners' (shareholders') equity}$$

Liabilities represent assets financed by debt and equity represents assets financed by the owners. Owners' investments can be direct or indirect. Direct investment is purchasing an ownership interest from an entity in exchange for cash or other assets. Indirect investments occur when an entity reinvests the profits it earns into its own activities, instead of distributing them to owners as dividends or distributions.

The accounting equation provides another view of equity: equity as the residual interest of owners. The accounting equation can be rearranged as follows:

$$\text{Assets} - \text{Liabilities} = \text{Owners' (shareholders') equity}$$

Equity can be viewed as what is left over after the entity's assets have been used to satisfy the creditors. As we will see, the equity section of the balance sheet represents the owners' interest as measured by accountants; it doesn't represent the market value of the entity.

CORPORATIONS, PARTNERSHIPS, AND PROPRIETORSHIPS

We will begin the discussion with a look at the different types of entities in our economy. Our focus throughout most of the book has been on corporations, so let's begin there. A corporation is a separate legal and taxable entity. The owners of a corporation are its shareholders. One of the main attractions of a corporation is the limited liability provided by its corporate status. Shareholders aren't liable for the corporation's obligations and losses beyond the amount they have invested.

This limited liability is especially important for public companies, where most shareholders have little involvement in the management and operation of the entity. If the owner of 1,000 shares of a large public corporation was liable for obligations the corporation couldn't meet—for example, paying off a bank loan—that shareholder would probably be reluctant to invest. After all, how many people would want to hold stock in public companies if it included the risk of losing their savings, cars, or houses?

In some circumstances, shareholders might agree to waive the limited liability protection of a corporation. For example, lenders often demand that the shareholders of smaller, private corporations personally guarantee to repay amounts borrowed by the corporation in the event it isn't able to repay.

Corporations divide the shareholders' equity section of their balance sheets into four categories:

Share capital	Money and other assets from the purchase of shares by shareholders directly from the corporation. Represents direct investments by shareholders.
Contributed surplus	A catch-all category that captures equity transactions not included in the other categories.
Retained earnings	Accumulated earnings not distributed to the shareholders. Represents indirect investment by shareholders.
Accumulated other comprehensive income	Accumulated amounts reported as other comprehensive income.

It's important to separate direct and indirect investment on the balance sheet because the shareholders need to know whether the money distributed to them is due to the profits earned by the corporation or if it's just a return of the money they invested. A dividend paid because the corporation has been profitable shares the success of the corporation with the shareholders. A dividend paid from amounts directly invested simply returns the money the shareholders have invested. (Investments that use investors' money to provide returns to the investor are known as Ponzi schemes. Financial statements showing where the payouts are coming from can help expose them.)

Proprietorships and, generally, partnerships aren't incorporated and don't pay income taxes. A proprietorship's income is included in the personal tax return of the proprietor and the income of a partnership is divided among the partners who include it in their tax returns. Partnerships and proprietorships don't have limited legal liability, which means that partners and proprietors are personally liable for any obligations a partnership or proprietorship is unable to meet. **Limited partnerships** provide limited liability protection to some partners. There are two types of partners in a limited partnership:

- **Limited partners** have the same limited liability protection as they would if the entity was a corporation—they aren't personally liable for the debts and obligations of the partnership.

- **General partners** don't have limited liability and are liable for all debts and obligations of the partnership. A limited partnership must have at least one general partner.

Limited partnerships are useful when a partnership is preferred but some of the investors aren't actively involved and not prepared to accept the risk associated with unlimited liability. Limited partners can't be involved in the management of the partnership or they risk losing their limited liability. There are tax benefits associated with using limited partnerships.

Another form of partnership, commonly used by professionals such as accountants and lawyers, is the **limited liability partnership (LLP)**. A LLP is an ordinary partnership where partners aren't personally liable for claims against the firm arising from negligence or other forms of malpractice by other partners. The assets of the partnership are at risk but not the personal assets of an innocent partner. If you look at the websites of Canadian accounting and law firms, you will see that most have "LLP" after their names.

Most accounting for partnerships and proprietorships isn't very different from that of corporations. There are no legal requirements that partnerships or proprietorships use IFRS or Canadian GAAP for Private Enterprises, although these could be used if, for example, a lender demanded it. Publicly traded partnership units prepare financial statements in accordance with IFRS.

The equity sections of partnerships' and proprietorships' balance sheets are structured differently from those of corporations. For example, Exhibit 10.1 shows the balance sheet, statement of partners' equity, and Note 5 of the financial statements of 2100 Bloor Street West Limited Partnership (2100 Bloor), a limited partnership that operates a retirement home, senior citizens apartment complex, and commercial complex.[1]

In the equity section of 2100 Bloor's balance sheet, there is a single line called partners' equity. The statement of partners' equity provides additional detail about the partners' capital. Notice that the partners' direct investment isn't separated from the retained earnings of the partnership, as it is in a corporation. In a partnership, an equity account is kept for each partner showing the capital contributed, portion of the earnings that is attributable to, and drawings made by each partner. (Drawings are amounts taken out of the partnership.) This breakdown by partner isn't shown in 2100 Bloor's statement of partners' equity, but information is broken out for limited and general partners.

2100 Bloor Street West Limited Partnership
Balance Sheets

December 31	2008	2007
Assets		
Cash	$ 2,324,762	$ 1,492,734
Accounts receivable	193,395	109,137
Prepaid supplies and expenses	57,259	553,792
Deferred charges (Note 2)	132,900	109,765
Retirement home property (Note 1)	17,954,758	18,370,785
	$ 20,663,074	$ 20,636,213
Liabilities and Partners' Equity		
Accounts payable and accrued liabilities	$ 1,144,663	$ 1,000,533
Tenant deposits	554,728	562,708
Long term debt (Note 3)	14,545,880	13,491,947
	16,245,271	15,055,188
Partners' equity (Note 4)	4,417,803	5,581,025
	$ 20,663,074	$ 20,636,213

Statements of Partners' Equity

For the years ended December 31, 2008 and 2007

	Limited Partners	General Partner	2008 Total	2007 Total
Balance, beginning of year	$ 5,581,015	$ 10	$ 5,581,025	$ 5,776,577
Net income for the year	1,259,128	-	1,259,128	1,881,873
Distributions	(2,422,350)	-	(2,422,350)	(2,077,425)
Balance, end of year	$ 4,417,793	$ 10	$ 4,417,803	$ 5,581,025

Financial Statement Note

4. Partners' Equity

630 units of limited partnership interest were issued in 1985 for a total consideration of $9,450,000. The Initial Limited Partner and the General Partner contributed $10 each. Income of the Partnership is allocated .005% each to the General Partner and the founding Limited Partner. All other income and 100% of the losses are allocated to the Limited Partners in their proportionate shares.

An example of a statement of partners' equity with a column for each partner is shown in Table 10.1.

TABLE 10.1	Statement of Partners' Equity for a Partnership with Three Partners			
Statement of Partners' Equity **For the year ended December 31, 2014**				
	Partner 1	Partner 2	Partner 3	Total
Capital on January 1, 2009	$85,000	$117,000	$49,000	$251,000
Share of net income	22,000	31,000	15,000	68,000
Withdrawals	(15,000)	(8,000)	(6,000)	(29,000)
Capital on December 31, 2009	$92,000	$140,000	$58,000	$290,000

www.cancer.ca
www.heartstroke.ca

Not-for-profit organizations (NFPO) are economic entities whose objective is to provide services, not to make a profit. NFPOs don't have owners or ownership shares that can be traded or sold. Any "net income" earned by the NFPO is reinvested in the organization. Because NFPOs aren't organized to earn a profit, it isn't appropriate to use the term net income when discussing them. Usually the "bottom line" on an NFPO's statement of operations (the term sometimes used for an NFPO's "income statement") is called the excess of revenues over expenses. This terminology indicates that the NFPO produced revenues greater than expenses, or vice versa.

For NFPOs such as charities, revenues shouldn't be thought of in the same way as revenues earned by a business. For charities, revenues come from donations, contributions, and grants and the money is spent providing services to people in need, not to earn revenue. For example, the Canadian Cancer Society provides support to cancer patients across Canada. The services are paid for by contributors to the Cancer Society, not by patients. Thus, the relationship that exists between expenses and revenues in a for-profit organization doesn't exist for many NFPOs.

Because an NFPO doesn't have owners, it won't have an owners' or shareholders' equity section in its balance sheet. However, the difference between assets and liabilities must somehow be referred to on the balance sheet. Different NFPOs use different terms; for example, the Heart and Stroke Foundation of Ontario refers to its "equity" as *net assets*, while the Canadian Cancer Society uses the term *resources*.

Most Canadian universities are not-for-profit organizations. The University of Ontario Institute of Technology's (UOIT) statement of financial position and statement of operations are presented in Exhibit 10.2.[2] Accounting for NFPOs is somewhat specialized and we won't go into detail here. However, notice the net assets section of Exhibit 10.2. These are resources obtained by the university from sources other than creditors. UOIT classifies its net assets—its assets less its liabilities—into the following categories:

- *invested in capital assets*: the amount UOIT has invested in capital assets, less the amount financed by long-term debt and capital contributions

- *internally restricted*: funds whose use has been restricted by the university; in this case for academic and research purposes

- *endowments*: donations to the university; only income generated from endowed funds can be used, not the principal donated

- *unrestricted*: resources that can be used in whatever way UOIT chooses

Notice that the bottom line of UOIT's statement of operations is called "excess of revenue over expenses." Also notice the sources of UOIT's revenue: almost $49 million from government grants and donations. In a business, revenue comes from the customers who buy the business's goods and services. About 47 percent of UOIT's revenue comes from government. The students who benefit from their university education provide about 24 percent of revenue.

EXHIBIT 10.2

University of Ontario Institute of Technology: Financial Statements

UNIVERSITY OF ONTARIO INSTITUTE OF TECHNOLOGY
Statement of Financial Position
March 31, 2009

		2009		2008
ASSETS				
CURRENT				
Cash (Note 8)	$	16,089,436	$	-
Restricted cash and cash equivalents (Note 15)		1,148,529		466,498
Grants receivable		9,861,956		12,112,577
Other accounts receivable		7,645,012		4,422,855
Inventories		217,642		268,192
Prepaid expenses and deposits		749,923		581,116
		35,712,498		17,851,238
INVESTMENTS (Note 5)		8,843,291		8,634,799
CAPITAL ASSETS (Note 6)		302,014,106		272,510,905
OTHER ASSETS (Note 7)		6,831,815		6,831,815
TOTAL ASSETS	$	353,401,710	$	305,828,757
LIABILITIES				
CURRENT				
Bank indebtedness (Note 8)	$	-	$	2,108,786
Accounts payable and accrued liabilities		23,622,940		12,556,190
Deferred revenue (Note 11)		13,296,608		30,985,602
Current portion of other long term debt (Note 10)		3,961,989		3,153,237
Current portion of long term debenture debt (Note 9)		3,298,903		3,098,963
		44,180,440		51,902,778
OTHER LONG TERM DEBT (Note 10)		2,610,505		2,535,865
LONG TERM DEBENTURE DEBT (Note 9)		205,387,336		208,686,238
DEFERRED CAPITAL CONTRIBUTIONS (Note 12)		115,888,227		57,015,123
		368,066,508		320,140,004
NET ASSETS				
UNRESTRICTED		(1,134,380)		(25,419,280)
ENDOWMENTS		10,136,818		8,956,835
INVESTED IN CAPITAL ASSETS (Note 13)		(29,132,854)		(1,978,521)
INTERNALLY RESTRICTED (Note 14)		5,465,618		4,129,719
		(14,664,798)		(14,311,247)
Contingencies and Contractual Commitments (Note 20)				
Guarantees (Note 21)				
TOTAL LIABILITIES AND NET ASSETS	$	353,401,710	$	305,828,757

EXHIBIT 10.2

(continued)
University of
Ontario Institute
of Technology:
Financial
Statements

UNIVERSITY OF ONTARIO INSTITUTE OF TECHNOLOGY
Statement of Operations
For the year ended March 31, 2009

	2009		2008
REVENUE			
Grants	$ 56,313,091	$	45,683,200
Donations	3,762,578		3,288,116
Student tuition fees	27,020,704		23,490,051
Student ancillary fees	12,042,906		10,552,327
Other income	12,047,937		10,689,838
Amortization of deferred capital contributions	2,022,217		2,349,496
Interest revenue	238,739		492,013
	113,448,172		96,545,041
EXPENSES			
Salaries and benefits	51,257,801		43,479,556
Supplies and expenses	32,613,349		30,844,866
Cost of goods sold	1,869,519		1,701,325
Professional fees	491,010		335,528
Interest expense	14,411,118		14,048,214
Amortization of capital assets	14,305,413		13,046,966
Unrealized loss on investments	33,496		27,259
	114,981,706		103,483,714
EXCESS OF EXPENSES OVER REVENUE	$ (1,533,534)	$	(6,938,673)

CHARACTERISTICS OF EQUITY

Unlike debt, equity offers no promises. When a corporation borrows money, the rate of interest, the timing of payments, and other terms of the loan are usually laid out in a contract. If the corporation is unable to meet the terms of the contract, it faces potentially significant economic and legal consequences. In contrast, a shareholder isn't entitled to dividends or any other type of payments, and return of principal isn't guaranteed. The rights of shareholders come after those of debt holders. If a corporation goes bankrupt, the debt holders must be paid what they are owed before shareholders receive anything. From the corporation's standpoint, issuing equity is less risky than debt because equity doesn't commit the corporation to any payments at any time. The corporation has more flexibility to manage, particularly through difficult times.

However, there are drawbacks to issuing equity, for both the corporation and its existing shareholders. New shareholders have a voice in the corporation—not necessarily a say in its day-to-day affairs, but certainly the right to be heard on certain issues. New shareholders dilute the power of existing ones. Consider a small business operated by a single entrepreneur who needs money for expansion and finds an investor willing to invest in exchange for a 50 percent interest in the corporation. The new shareholder owns 50 percent of the corporation and is able to participate in the key decisions of the company, so the entrepreneur can no longer act alone. Also, dividends aren't deductible for tax purposes, which raises the cost of equity relative to debt. Dividends aren't expensed for accounting purposes as they aren't a cost of doing business—they are a distribution of company assets to the shareholders. Interest payments, in contrast, are expensed in the calculation of net income and are deductible for tax.

When a corporation is formed, it must file articles of incorporation with the appropriate government agency. The articles of incorporation define the terms of reference of the new corporation. Any changes to these terms of reference must be approved by the shareholders. The articles of incorporation define the types and characteristics of the shares the corporation can issue. The maximum number of each type of share that can be issued is the **authorized capital stock** of the corporation.

EXHIBIT 10.3

**Leon's Furniture
Limited: Equity
Information**

Consolidated Balance Sheets

LIABILITIES AND SHAREHOLDERS' EQUITY	2008	2007
Current		
Accounts payable and accrued liabilities	$ 95,247	$ 92,051
Income taxes payable	–	2,137
Customers' deposits	14,119	13,533
Dividends payable	4,952	4,949
Deferred warranty plan revenue	15,267	13,812
Future tax liabilities [note 7]	–	355
Total current liabilities	129,585	126,837
Deferred warranty plan revenue	21,712	19,124
Redeemable share liability [note 11]	285	180
Future tax liabilities [note 7]	8,468	7,080
Total liabilities	160,050	153,221
Shareholders' equity		
Common shares [note 12]	16,493	14,020
Retained earnings	338,960	307,068
Accumulated other comprehensive income [note 13]	(2,095)	917
Total shareholders' equity	353,358	322,005
	$ 513,408	$ 475,226

Commitments and contingencies [note 8]

Consolidated Statements of Income and Retained Earnings

	2008	2007
Net income for the year	63,390	58,494
Retained earnings, beginning of year	307,068	276,037
Dividends declared	(26,873)	(19,828)
Excess of cost of share repurchase over carrying value of related shares [note 12]	(4,625)	(7,635)
Retained earnings, end of year	338,960	307,068
Weighted average number of common shares outstanding		
Basic	70,729,548	70,777,269
Diluted	72,817,871	73,403,200
Earnings per share		
Basic	$ 0.90	$ 0.83
Diluted	$ 0.87	$ 0.80
Dividends declared per share		
Common	$ 0.38	$ 0.2725
Convertible, non-voting	$ 0.14	$ 0.14

12. COMMON SHARES

On June 27, 2007, the Company completed a four-for-one split of its common shares. All current figures and comparative figures reflect the stock split retroactively.

The Company's common shares consist of the following:

(in thousands)	2008	2007
Authorized		
Unlimited common shares		
Issued		
70,745,139 common shares [2007 – 70,713,532]	$ 16,493	$ 14,020

12. COMMON SHARES (continued)

During the year ended December 31, 2008, 197,980 convertible, non-voting, series 1998 shares [2007 – 411,748] and 229,427 convertible, non-voting, series 2002 shares [2007 – 103,116] were converted into common shares with a stated value of approximately $871,000 [2007 – $1,812,000] and $1,649,000 [2007 – $741,000], respectively.

During the year ended December 31, 2008, the Company repurchased 395,800 [2007 – 599,600] of its common shares on the open market pursuant to the terms and conditions of Normal Course Issuer Bid at a net cost of approximately $4,672,000 [2007 – $7,706,000]. All shares repurchased by the Company pursuant to its Normal Course Issuer Bid have been cancelled. The repurchase of common shares resulted in a reduction of share capital in the amount of approximately $47,000 [2007 – $71,000]. The excess net cost over the average carrying value of the shares of approximately $4,625,000 [2007 – $7,635,000] has been recorded as a reduction in retained earnings.

Exhibit 10.3 provides equity information about Leon's Furniture Limited.[3] Note 12 shows that Leon's has authorized an unlimited number of common shares. This means that Leon's board of directors can issue new shares whenever new capital is required, without consulting the shareholders. Other companies have a limit on the number of shares that can be issued—for example, High Liner Foods Inc. has 200 million shares authorized.

The number of shares that have been distributed to shareholders is the **issued shares** of the corporation. The **outstanding shares** of a corporation are the number of shares currently in the hands of shareholders. The number of shares outstanding may differ from the number of shares issued because shares are sometimes repurchased by a corporation and held for resale. On December 31, 2008 Leon's had 70,745,139 common shares outstanding.

Corporation or company acts are federal and provincial laws that govern companies incorporated in particular jurisdictions. For example, the *Canada Business Corporations Act* is the federal legislation governing federally incorporated companies. These laws give shareholders certain rights and privileges, regardless of whether their investments are large or small. For example, a corporation's shareholders are entitled to attend its annual general meeting, where they can ask questions. Shareholders can usually vote on the composition of the board of directors, the appointment of auditors, amendments to the corporation's articles of incorporation, and other matters. For smaller shareholders, the annual general meeting of a public company may be the only place their voices can be heard.

Even though every shareholder has the right to attend the annual meeting, smaller shareholders have a limited ability to exert any influence. For example, a shareholder who owns 1,000 shares of BCE Inc. owns about 0.00012 percent of the votes. BCE had 803,056,958 shares outstanding on December 31, 2008.

www.mcgrawhill
connect.ca

KNOWLEDGE CHECK

❑ What is a not-for-profit organization (NFPO)? Why don't NFPOs have "owners' equity"?

❑ What characteristics distinguish equity from debt?

❑ Explain the terms *authorized capital stock* and *outstanding shares*.

Common and Preferred Shares

Broadly speaking, there are two types of shares a corporation could issue: common and preferred. Because these shares can have various features added to them, many different varieties of shares are possible.

Common Shares **Common shares** represent residual ownership in an entity. Common shareholders are entitled to whatever earnings and assets are left after obligations to debt holders and preferred shareholders have been satisfied. For example, consider a one-year venture into which common shareholders invest $50,000 and creditors lend $50,000 at 10 percent interest for the year. If the venture earned $25,000 before interest, the creditors would receive $5,000 plus the $50,000 principal amount. The common shareholders would get the rest—$20,000 ($25,000 − $5,000). The creditors are entitled only to the loan principal plus interest. They don't share in the profits. On the other hand, common shareholders are the last ones to be satisfied. If the venture earned $7,000, the common shareholders would receive only $2,000 ($7,000 − $5,000).

Common shares don't have a specified dividend associated with them. Boards of directors declare dividends at their own discretion. A corporation has no obligation to pay a dividend at any time and the board can eliminate or reduce dividends if it so chooses. Public companies don't like to cut their dividends because it suggests the company is in serious trouble and usually the share price falls dramatically as a result.

There can be more than one class of common shares. Some corporations issue common shares with different voting rights and different dividends. For example, Rogers Communications Inc. has two classes of common shares, Class A voting common shares and Class B non-voting common shares. The Class A common shares are multiple voting shares that have 50 votes per share while the Class B shares have no votes. This difference in voting power allows the Rogers family to control the company without owning more than 50 percent of the company's common shares, an arrangement fairly common in Canada; other examples include Bombardier Inc., CanWest Global Communications Corp., and Magna International Inc.

Some shares have a **par value**—a value assigned to each common share in the articles of incorporation. The *Canada Business Corporations Act* and the corporations acts of a number of provinces don't permit par value shares, so they are quite rare in Canada (shares that don't have a par value are called **no par value shares**). The financial statement impact of par value shares is that the selling price of the share is split between the common shares account (credited for the par value of the shares issued) and contributed surplus (credited for rest).

While equity is usually sold for cash, it doesn't have to be. An investor can exchange property or expertise for an equity interest. In this situation, the challenge is determining the amount that should be recorded for the property received and the shares issued. This is problematic for private companies since their shares aren't actively traded. In situations where the market value of the shares or property isn't available, estimates or appraisals have to be made, in which case a wide range of valuations is possible.

Preferred Shares   **Preferred shares** are shares with rights that must be satisfied before those of common shareholders. Their dividends must be paid before any are paid to common shareholders and if the corporation is liquidated, preferred shareholders' claims to assets are satisfied before those of common shareholders. Preferred shares often have characteristics of debt, such as specifying a dividend payment. However, unlike debt holders, preferred shareholders can't take any action against the corporation if the dividend isn't paid. Dividends on preferred shares aren't guaranteed, and if the management decides that it won't pay a dividend then the preferred shareholders are out of luck.

There are various types of preferred shares:

- **Cumulative** Dividends not paid on the preferred shares in current or previous years must be paid before the common shareholders can receive any dividends.

- **Convertible** Shareholders can exchange preferred shares for a specified number of common shares for each preferred share that they convert.

- **Redeemable** The issuer can repurchase the preferred shares from the shareholders if it chooses, according to specified terms.

- **Retractable** Shareholders can require the issuer to purchase the preferred shares from them, if they choose, according to specified terms.

- **Participating** The amount of the preferred share dividend increases above the stated amount if certain conditions are met. The amount is often tied to the dividend paid on the common shares.

One of the attractions of preferred shares is that investors can expect to receive periodic payments (as they would with debt), but preferred dividends are taxed at a lower rate than interest. On the other hand, corporations can't deduct preferred dividends for income tax purposes. Private companies sometimes use preferred shares for tax and estate-planning purposes.

INSIGHT

Treasury Stock

In most jurisdictions in Canada, shares that are repurchased must be retired or cancelled immediately, meaning the shares no longer exist. In some jurisdictions in Canada, and in other countries, entities are allowed to own shares that were previously sold to investors and repurchased but not retired. These are called **treasury stock**. Treasury stock can't vote or receive dividends but it's available for resale by the entity.

Preferred shares are known **hybrid securities**, a category of securities with characteristics of both debt and equity. (Convertible debt, debt that can be converted to equity, is another example.) IFRS require hybrid securities to be classified according to their economic nature, not simply by what they are called. Applying this accounting standard is complicated and beyond the scope of this book. Generally, the classification depends on whether a security has a mandatory payment associated with it and has to be repaid or converted by contract or at the option of the security holder.

The journal entry to record issuance of preferred shares is similar to the one made to record issuance of common shares. The credit is made to a preferred shares account instead of the common shares account.

Share Repurchases

Sometimes a corporation will buy its own common shares from the shareholders. For example, during 2008, Leon's repurchased 395,800 of its common shares for $4,672,000 (see Note 12 in Exhibit 10.3). Also notice in Leon's statement of retained earnings in Exhibit 10.3 that, as a result of the repurchase, retained earnings is decreased by $4,625,000, the difference between the average price paid per share by investors and the repurchase price per share. The journal entry would be

Dr. Retained earnings ($-$)	4,625,000	
Dr. Common shares (shareholders' equity $-$)	47,000	
Cr. Cash (assets $-$)		4,672,000
To record the repurchase of 395,000 common shares		

Why an entity repurchases its shares isn't entirely clear, but some explanations have been suggested and investigated:

- If an entity has excess cash, repurchasing shares is a way of distributing the cash to investors without establishing a precedent of paying regular or higher dividends.

- It increases the earnings per share (net income ÷ average number of common shares outstanding during the period) and should increase share price, assuming the operating activity of the entity isn't affected by the repurchase, because ownership is divided among fewer shares.

- A way for management to communicate to the market that it thinks the market is understating the value of its shares.

When an entity repurchases its shares there is no effect on the income statement. The accounting for share repurchases reduces the amount of cash and the amount in shareholders' equity.

INSIGHT

Exchanges between Investors

www.tsx.ca

Remember that an entry is made in the accounting records only when an entity issues shares to or repurchases shares from shareholders. For public companies, the vast majority of purchase and sale transactions of shares takes place between individual investors in the secondary market; for example, on the Toronto Stock Exchange (TSX). The entity whose shares are being exchanged isn't a party to these transactions and the transactions have no financial statement effect.

That isn't to say that an entity's managers aren't keenly interested in its share price. The entity's share price can have an effect on the managers' wealth (their compensation is sometimes related to share price and they are often shareholders), on their job prospects (managers of entities whose share price isn't doing well will sometimes be fired or may have fewer opportunities in the job market), and because market price provides information about how the entity is perceived.

RETAINED EARNINGS, DIVIDENDS, AND STOCK SPLITS

Retained Earnings

Retained earnings represents the accumulated earnings of an entity less all dividends paid to shareholders over its entire life. Retained earnings can be thought of as profits that have been reinvested in the entity by the shareholders. It represents an indirect investment by shareholders—indirect because investors don't decide for themselves to make the investment. While net income or loss and dividends are the most common economic events affecting retained earnings, some others are shown in Table 10.2 while still others are beyond the scope of this book.

TABLE 10.2 Transactions and Economic Events That Affect Retained Earnings	
Economic event	**Description**
Net income or net loss	A measure of how the owners' wealth has changed over a period.
Dividends	Distributions of earnings to shareholders.
Correction of errors	Accounting errors made in a previous period should be corrected retroactively.
Retroactive application of an accounting policy	When an entity changes an accounting policy, the financial statements are restated as if the new accounting policy had always been used.
Share retirement	When an entity repurchases its shares from shareholders and pays more than the average price shareholders paid for them.

Correction of errors affects retained earnings when an error made in a previous period is discovered. The prior years' financial statements are restated so they appear in their corrected form. For example, in 2012 Auld Ltd. (Auld) purchased land for $700,000. The cost of the land was incorrectly expensed instead of capitalized. The error wasn't discovered until 2014. To correct the error, Auld would make the following journal entry in 2014:

Dr. Land (assets +)	700,000	
Cr. Retained earnings (shareholders' equity +)		700,000
To correct an error in accounting for the purchase of land in 2012		

The credit to retained earnings is required because when the land was incorrectly expensed in 2012, net income was reduced by $700,000 (tax effects are ignored). At the end of 2012, retained earnings was $700,000 lower than it should have been because the land should have been capitalized, not expensed. The entry shown above restates retained earnings with the balance as it would have been had the error not occurred.

Changes in accounting policy are discussed later in this chapter, but when an entity changes an accounting policy, the financial statements are restated so that it appears as if the entity has always been using the new accounting policy. This means that current amounts in balance sheet accounts, including retained earnings, must be restated to reflect the new accounting policy.

Throughout the book I have emphasized that managers have considerable latitude, even under IFRS, in deciding how to account for many transactions and economic events. The effects of these differences accumulate in retained earnings. Over an entity's entire life, retained earnings won't be affected by different accounting choices, but at any point retained earnings can vary significantly, depending on the accounting choices made.

Dividends

Dividends are distributions of a corporation's earnings to its shareholders. They are discretionary and must be declared by the board of directors. Dividends are declared on a per share basis and every share of a specific class must receive the same dividend. If, for example, an entity has a single class of common shares, it isn't possible to pay some of the shareholders a dividend and not others. Once a dividend is declared, it's classified as a liability on the balance sheet until it's paid.

Corporations don't have an unlimited ability to pay dividends, and there are legal limitations against paying them. The *Canada Business Corporations Act* prohibits payment of dividends if it's reasonable to believe the corporation would be unable to pay its liabilities as a result. There can also be contractual restrictions, such as a lending agreement, against paying dividends For example, TransCanada Pipelines Limited (TCPL) states that some of its preferred share and debt securities limit its ability to declare dividends on preferred and common shares (see Exhibit 10.4).[4]

EXHIBIT 10.4

TransCanada Pipelines Limited: Restrictions on Dividends

> **NOTE 17   COMMON SHARES**
> **Restriction on Dividends**
> Certain terms of the Company's preferred shares and debt instruments could restrict the company's ability to declare dividends on preferred and common shares. At December 31, 2008, approximately $1.7 billion (2007 – $1.5 billion) was available for the payment of dividends on common and preferred shares.

For accounting purposes, there are three important dates pertaining to dividends:

- **date of declaration**: The date when the board of directors of a corporation declares a dividend.

- **date of record**: The registered owner of shares on the date of record receives the dividend. If a shareholder sells shares after the date of declaration but before or including the date of record, the new shareholder is entitled to receive the dividend. If a shareholder sells shares after the date of record, the previous shareholder receives the dividend.

- **date of payment**: The date when the dividends are actually paid to shareholders.

There are three types of dividends: cash, property, and stock.

Cash Dividends These are the most common form of dividend. A **cash dividend** is a cash payment from the corporation to its shareholders. People sometimes say that dividends are "paid out of retained earnings." This means retained earnings will decrease when dividends are paid. However, if an entity doesn't have cash or access to cash, it can't pay a cash dividend no matter how much retained earnings there is.

Let's look at an example. On December 15, 2014 Bankeir Inc. (Bankeir) declared a $0.10 quarterly dividend on its common shares and a $0.25 quarterly dividend on its preferred shares. On the date of declaration, Bankeir had 500,000 common shares and 250,000 preferred shares outstanding. It paid the dividend on January 12, 2015. The company's year-end is December 31. The following journal entries are required to record the declaration and payment of the dividends:

December 15, 2014

Dr. Retained earnings (shareholders' equity −)	112,500	
Cr. Dividend payable on common shares (liability +)		50,000
Cr. Dividend payable on preferred shares (liability +)		62,500

To record the declaration of a $0.25 per preferred share
and $0.10 per common share dividend on December 15, 2014

January 12, 2015

Dr. Dividend payable on common shares (liability −)	50,000	
Dr. Dividend payable on preferred shares (liability −)	62,500	
Cr. Cash (asset −)		112,500

To record payment of the preferred and common share
dividends on January 12, 2015

The first entry records the reduction of retained earnings and the liability to pay the preferred and common share dividends. The second entry records the cash payment to the shareholders and removes the liabilities from the balance sheet. Bankeir's December 31, 2014 balance sheet would report the dividends payable on the preferred and common shares as current liabilities.

Property Dividends **Property dividends** are paid with property instead of cash. In theory, the payment can be any property the entity has: inventory, capital assets, investments, etc. In practice, for public companies or for private companies with many shareholders, property dividends are impractical. Since every share of the same class must receive the same dividend, the entity must have property that can be distributed equally. One type of property that can be readily used for this is shares of a corporation owned by the issuing entity (not its own shares).

If an entity pays a property dividend, the dividend is recorded at the property's market value on the date the dividend is declared. If the market value of the property isn't equal to its carrying amount on that date, a gain or loss is reported on the income statement. For example, Drook Corp. (Drook) decided to distribute the shares it owned of Rylstone Inc. (Rylstone) as a dividend. The carrying amount of the shares was $5,000,000 and their market value on the date the dividend was declared was $7,200,000. The journal entries that Drook would make to record the property dividend are

Dr. Investment in Rylstone (assets +)	2,200,000	
Cr. Gain on disposal of investments		
(income statement + shareholders' equity +)		2,200,000
To record the gain on the shares of Rylstone being distributed to		
shareholders as a property dividend		
Dr. Retained earnings (shareholders' equity −)	7,200,000	
Cr. Property dividend payable (liability +)		7,200,000
To record the declaration of a property dividend		
Dr. Property dividend payable (liability −)	7,200,000	
Cr. Investment in Rylstone (assets −)		7,200,000
To record payment of the property dividend		

The first entry adjusts the value of the property to its market value on the date the dividend was declared. Because the market value of the dividend was greater than its carrying amount, a gain is recognized on the income statement. The second entry records the declaration of the dividend. The amount of the property dividend is the market value of the property on the date the dividend is declared. The third entry records the actual payment of the dividend—Drook's shareholders receive the actual shares of Rylstone when the dividend is paid.

Stock Dividends In a **stock dividend,** shareholders receive company shares as the dividend. The number of shares received depends on how many shares a shareholder owned on the date of declaration. For example, if Hylo Ltd. (Hylo) declared a 5 percent stock dividend, a shareholder that owned 1,000 shares would receive 50 shares of Hylo stock and now have 1,050 shares of Hylo stock. If Hylo had 100,000 shares outstanding before the stock dividend, there would be 105,000 afterwards. Each shareholder would own exactly the same proportion of Hylo before and after the dividend. The market price of Hylo's shares should fall by 5 percent as a result because nothing about the entity has changed except for the number of shares outstanding. Thus, the value of Hylo is spread over a larger number of shares (and the value of each share is less), but the total value of Hylo's shares should be the same.

A stock dividend decreases retained earnings and increases common shares, but there is more than one acceptable method of assigning an amount to the shares distributed. The shares can be valued at either their market value just before they are issued or the board of directors can assign a value to the shares; for example, the average amount paid by shareholders for the shares already outstanding.

Returning to the Hylo example, suppose that Hylo declared and distributed its stock dividend on June 23, 2014, when the market price of its common shares was $10. It would make the following entry if it valued the shares at their market value:

Dr. Retained earnings (shareholders' equity −)	50,000	
Cr. Common shares (shareholders' equity +)		50,000
To record declaration and distribution of a 5 percent stock dividend		

The form of the journal entry would be the same if a different value was assigned to the share, only the amount would change. Note that no matter how the shares are valued, only the shareholders' equity section of the balance sheet is affected. There is no effect on assets, liabilities, or the income statement.

Stock Splits

A **stock split** divides an entity's shares into a larger number of units, each with a smaller value. A stock split is really nothing more than a big stock dividend. A **reverse stock split** reduces the number of shares. A stock split might split an entity's existing shares two for one, which means that a shareholder that previously had 1,000 shares would have 2,000 after the split. A three-for-two split means that a shareholder with 1,000 shares would have 1,500 after the split. In a one-for-two reverse stock split a shareholder who had 1,000 shares would have 500 after the split.

Unlike a stock dividend, there is no accounting effect of a stock split—the amounts in the retained earnings and common shares accounts are unchanged. No journal entries are required to record a stock split. The number of shares outstanding changes, so any measurements based on the number of shares will change. For example, if an entity's shares split three for one, retained earnings will be unchanged, but earnings per share will be one-third of what it was before the split.

Various explanations have been offered for stock dividends and splits. One is that it allows shareholders to received "something" when the entity is unable or unwilling to pay a cash dividend. Another explanation is that it lowers the price of a stock into a range that makes it accessible to more investors. Some companies don't split their stock even though the price of their common shares is very high. For example, Berkshire Hathaway Inc.'s (the company run by Warren Buffet) shares have traded at prices near $100,000 per share and the company has specifically rejected calls to split its stock to lower the price.

www.mcgrawhill
connect.ca

 KNOWLEDGE CHECK

☐ What are retained earnings? Why is retained earnings considered an indirect investment in an entity?

☐ What economic events affect retained earnings?

☐ What is a stock dividend? Is an investor better off when he or she receives a stock dividend?

 INSIGHT

The reality is that both stock splits and stock dividends are a bit of sleight of hand. Neither has any real economic significance—they merely divide the entity into a different number of pieces. In other words, there are more pieces of pie, not more pie. Stock dividends and stock splits have no effect on the assets, liabilities, or net income of an entity, and they don't change the underlying value of a shareholder's interest in an entity. There is no evidence to suggest that shareholders are better off after a stock dividend or split than they were before.

QUESTION FOR CONSIDERATION

Several years ago a friend of yours received 1,000 shares of a public company as a gift from her uncle. Recently, the company shares split four for one and now she has 4,000 shares. Your friend isn't sure what this means, but she is concerned that the shares that were trading for $104 per share before the split are now trading for around $26 per share.

Explain the meaning of a stock split and its economic significance to your friend. Should she be concerned about the decrease in the share price?

Answer: A stock split is the division of a company's shares into a larger number of units, each with a smaller value. A stock split doesn't really have any economic significance. It is like cutting a pie into six pieces, and then cutting it into 12 pieces when you realize that you will have more than six guests. You have the same amount of pie, just more pieces. One slice from a pie cut into six pieces is the same as two pieces of a pie cut into 12 pieces if the pies are the same size.

The same is true for a stock split. You have 4,000 shares instead of 1,000, but there are also four times as many shares outstanding. You own exactly the same percentage of the outstanding shares. The decrease in the share price makes perfect sense because after the split each share represents 25 percent of what it did before the split. The market value of your shares is the same before and after the split. Before the split the shares were worth $104,000 (1,000 × $104), and after the split they were worth $104,000 (4,000 × $26).

ACCUMULATED OTHER COMPREHENSIVE INCOME

Comprehensive income was introduced in our initial examination of the financial statements in Chapter 2. Over the years, accounting standard setters excluded certain transactions and economic events from the calculation of net income and these were included in equity directly. **Comprehensive income** was created to be an all-inclusive measure of performance capturing all transactions and economic events, even ones excluded from the calculation of net income, that don't involve owners. Comprehensive income is

> Net income
> + Other comprehensive income
> Comprehensive income

Comprehensive income has two components: net income as it is usually calculated and **other comprehensive income**, which is revenues, expenses, gains, and losses that aren't included in the calculation of net income. There are only a few events classified as other comprehensive income:

- gains and losses on cash flow hedges
- gains and losses on certain investment securities (discussed in Chapter 11)
- gains and losses from translation of companies owned that are stated in foreign currencies
- gains from writing up property, plant, and equipment (discussed in Chapter 8)

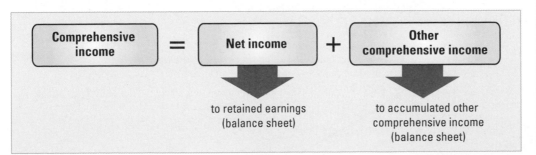

FIGURE 10.1

Comprehensive Income

EXHIBIT 10.5

WestJet Airlines Inc.: Equity Information

consolidated balance sheet

As at December 31
(Stated in thousands of Canadian dollars)

	2008	2007
Shareholders' equity:		
Share capital (note 8(b))	452,885	448,568
Contributed surplus	60,193	57,889
✳ Accumulated other comprehensive loss (note 12(c))	(38,112)	(11,914)
Retained earnings	611,171	455,365
	1,086,137	949,908
Commitments and contingencies (note 10)		
	$ 3,278,849	$ 2,984,222

consolidated statement of shareholders' equity

For the years ended December 31
(Stated in thousands of Canadian dollars)

	2008	2007
Share capital:		
Balance, beginning of year	$ 448,568	$ 431,248
Issuance of shares pursuant to stock option plans (note 8(b))	227	1,551
Stock-based compensation on stock options exercised (note 8(b))	11,181	20,040
Shares repurchased (note 8(b))	(7,091)	(4,271)
	452,885	448,568
Contributed surplus:		
Balance, beginning of year	57,889	58,656
Stock-based compensation expense (note 8(e)(f))	13,485	19,273
Stock-based compensation on stock options exercised (note 8(b))	(11,181)	(20,040)
	60,193	57,889
Accumulated other comprehensive loss: (note 12(c))		
Balance, beginning of year	(11,914)	—
Change in accounting policy	—	(13,420)
◈ Other comprehensive income (loss)	(26,198)	1,506
✳	(38,112)	(11,914)
Retained earnings:		
Balance, beginning of year	455,365	316,123
Change in accounting policy	—	(36,612)
Shares repurchased (note 8(b))	(22,329)	(16,979)
Net earnings	178,135	192,833
	611,171	455,365
Total accumulated other comprehensive loss and retained earnings	573,059	443,451
Total shareholders' equity	$ 1,086,137	$ 949,908

Examine the shareholders' equity section of WestJet's balance sheet in Exhibit 10.5 and notice the account called "accumulated other comprehensive loss." In the same way retained earnings accumulates net incomes over an entity's life, **accumulated other comprehensive income** (or **loss**) accumulates other comprehensive incomes. When the books are closed, the amount of other comprehensive income is added to accumulated other comprehensive income in the equity section, as shown in Figure 10.1.

Exhibit 10.5 shows information about comprehensive income in WestJet Airlines Inc.'s financial statements.[5] Note the following as you examine the exhibit:

- WestJet's consolidated statement of comprehensive income provides the items that are included in other comprehensive income for the year. Other comprehensive income for 2008 was ($26,198,000) as designated by the ◈.

- The consolidated statement of shareholders' equity provides a reconciliation for the year for the accumulated other comprehensive loss account. The balance in this account on December 31, 2008, is ($38,112,000). This is the amount that appears on the balance sheet and is designated by the ✱.

- Other comprehensive income is closed to accumulated other comprehensive loss on the balance sheet.

- Note 12(c) provides the components of accumulated other comprehensive loss on December 31, 2008.

EXHIBIT 10.5

(continued) WestJet Airlines Inc.: Equity Information

consolidated statement of comprehensive income

For the years ended December 31
(Stated in thousands of Canadian dollars)

	2008	2007
Net earnings	$ 178, 135	$ 192,833
Other comprehensive income, net of taxes:		
Amortization of hedge settlements to aircraft leasing	1,400	1,400
Net unrealized gain on foreign exchange derivatives under cash flow hedge accounting		
(net of tax of ($3,097); 2007 – $nil)	7,224	88
Reclassification of net realized (gains) losses on foreign exchange derivatives to net earnings		
(net of tax of $1,357; 2007 – $nil)	(3,197)	18
Net unrealized loss on fuel derivatives under cash flow hedge accounting		
(net of tax of $13,086)	(31,625)	—
◈	(26,198)	1,506
Total comprehensive income	$ 151,937	$ 194,339

12. **Additional financial information (continued)**

(c) Accumulated other comprehensive loss

	Amortization of hedge settlements	Cash flow hedges – foreign exchange derivatives	Cash flow hedges – fuel derivatives	Total
Balance as at January 1, 2007	$ —	$ —	$ —	$ —
Change in accounting policy	(13,420)	—	—	(13,420)
Amortization of settlements	1,400	—	—	1,400
Unrealized gain on derivatives	—	88	—	88
Realized loss on derivatives	—	18	—	18
Balance as at December 31, 2007	(12,020)	106	—	(11,914)
Amortization of settlements	1,400	—	—	1,400
Unrealized gain (loss) on derivatives	—	10,321	(44,711)	(34,390)
Tax on unrealized portion	—	(3,097)	13,086	9,989
Realized gain on derivatives	—	(4,554)	—	(4,554)
Tax on realized portion	—	1,357	—	1,357
✱ Balance as at December 31, 2008	$ (10,620)	$ 4,133	$ (31,625)	$ (38,112)

CONTRIBUTED SURPLUS

There is one more account in the equity section we need to mention: contributed surplus. **Contributed surplus** captures equity transactions that don't fit into the other equity accounts:

* amounts paid for company shares in excess of the par value

* receipt of donated assets

* equity component of some hybrid securities

* repurchase of shares for more than the average per share cost

* employees' stock-based compensation (discussed later in the chapter)

In the equity section of WestJet's balance sheet in Exhibit 10.5, contributed surplus of $60,193,000 is reported. The statement of shareholders' equity shows that the changes to contributed surplus during 2008 were due to stock-based compensation.

STATEMENT OF SHAREHOLDERS' EQUITY

The statement of shareholders' equity provides a summary of changes during a year in each of an entity's equity accounts. This statement captures the impacts we have discussed in each of the preceding sections. Exhibit 10.5 provides WestJet's statement of shareholders' equity.

ACCOUNTING CHANGES—POLICIES AND ESTIMATES

Consistency in applying accounting choices is an important principle. If an entity changed its accounting on a whim, the integrity and usefulness of the financial statements would be undermined and it would be much more difficult for users to understand and interpret the statements. However, this doesn't mean an entity can never change its accounting. New accounting standards implemented in IFRS might require a change. Or an entity may decide that the facts underlying certain transactions have changed or the reporting objectives of the entity have changed, making a different way of accounting appropriate. IFRS allow changes in accounting policies only if they make financial statement information more relevant and reliable. Of course, whether information is more relevant and reliable is a judgment call.

There are two types of accounting changes—changes in policies and changes in estimates. **Accounting policies** are methods an entity selects for financial reporting. They include the revenue recognition method, inventory cost formula, and capitalization policies. **Accounting estimates** are judgments about uncertain future events that managers must make to complete accrual accounting financial statements. Accounting estimates include the useful lives and residual values of capital assets, bad debt expenses, warranty expenses, and many more. We've discussed these often in the book.

What happens if an entity decides to change an accounting policy or estimate? The two types of changes are dealt with differently. If a company changes an accounting policy—for example, switching from FIFO to average cost to the straight-line method—the change is applied retroactively. That is, previous years' financial statements are restated as if the new accounting method had always been used. This treatment also means that retained earnings has to be restated to adjust for the difference between the old and new methods.

A change in accounting estimate is treated differently. If management decides an accounting estimate has to be revised—for example, if the initial estimate of an asset's useful life was too long—the change is reflected from the time of management's decision. Previous years aren't revised.

Let's look at an example. In 2010, Aubigny Ltd. (Aubigny) purchased an asset for $48,000. Management used straight-line depreciation and assumed a zero residual value and a useful life of eight years. In each of years 2010, 2011, and 2012, Aubigny expensed $6,000 for depreciation ($48,000 ÷ 8 years). In 2013, it became clear the asset would only last for six years. As a result, Aubigny would have to depreciate the undepreciated cost of the asset over three years rather than five. The $30,000 ($48,000 − $18,000) carrying amount of the equipment at the begin-

EXHIBIT 10.6

Accounting Policy Changes

www.potashcorp.com
www.chaptersindigo.ca

Panel A—Potash Corporation of Saskatchewan Inc.

Note 2 BASIS OF PRESENTATION (CONTINUED)

Change in Accounting Policy

Inventories

Effective January 1, 2008, the company adopted the Canadian Institute of Chartered Accountants ("CICA") Section 3031, "Inventories", which replaces Section 3030 and harmonizes the Canadian standard related to inventories with International Financial Reporting Standards ("IFRSs"). This standard provides more extensive guidance on the determination of cost, including allocation of overhead; narrows the permitted cost formulas; restricts the classification of spare and replacement parts as inventory; requires impairment testing; requires the reversal of writedowns when circumstances which caused the writedown no longer exist; and expands the disclosure requirements to increase transparency. This standard has been applied prospectively. Accordingly, comparative amounts for prior periods have not been restated. The adoption of this standard resulted in a reclassification of certain spare and replacement parts to property, plant and equipment. The effects of the adjustment were to decrease inventory by $21.5 at January 1, 2008 and to increase property, plant and equipment by the same amount. Since there was no difference in the measurement of the assets, no adjustment to opening retained earnings was necessary.

Panel B—Indigo Books & Music Inc.

3. ACCOUNTING CHANGES

Gift cards

Effective in the third quarter of fiscal 2007, the Company changed its accounting policy relating to gift cards. This policy change was made based on the Company's review of the gift card accounting clarifications provided by the Securities and Exchange Commission ("SEC") and the introduction of legislation by the Ontario government banning gift card expiry dates and excessive service charges. The Company sells gift cards to its customers and recognizes the revenue as the gift cards are redeemed. The Company also recognizes revenue from unredeemed gift cards (gift card breakage) if the likelihood of the gift card being redeemed by the customer is considered to be remote. Based on historical information, the likelihood of a gift card remaining unredeemed is reasonably certain 24 months after the gift card is issued. The Company now determines its average gift card breakage rate based on redemption rates for all gift cards more than two years old. Once the breakage rate is determined, the resulting revenue is recognized over a 24-month period, commencing when the gift cards are sold, based on historical redemption patterns.

In addition, the Company has reclassified gift card breakage from "Cost of sales, operations, selling and administration" to "Revenues" in the comparative consolidated statements of earnings. In fiscal 2007, the Company recorded $1.2 million in gift card breakage and reclassified $2.2 million of gift card breakage in last year's consolidated statements of earnings. As at March 31, 2007, the provision for unredeemed gift card liability is $27.3 million and is included in accounts payable and accrued liabilities (April 1, 2006 – $19.7 million). There was no material impact to the Company's net earnings and net earnings per share in prior periods as a result of this change in accounting policy.

ning of 2013 would be depreciated over the remaining three years on a straight-line basis, so the depreciation expense in 2013, 2014, and 2015 would be $10,000 ($30,000 ÷ 3). Retained earnings isn't adjusted because the depreciation expense in previous years isn't restated. The year-by-year depreciation expense and accumulated depreciation for each year is shown in Table 10.3.

IFRS require disclosure of changes in accounting policies and estimates. This type of information is very important for stakeholders' understanding of financial statements because it helps explain statement changes that aren't the result of operations.

Exhibit 10.6 gives two examples of changes in accounting policies.[6] In Panel A, Potash Corporation of Saskatchewan Inc. describes how it changed its accounting for inventories in

TABLE 10.3	Aubigny Ltd.: Change in Accounting Estimate					
	2010	**2011**	**2012**	**2013**	**2014**	**2015**
Depreciation expense	$6,000	$ 6,000	$ 6,000	$10,000	$10,000	$10,000
Accumulated depreciation	$6,000	$12,000	$18,000	$28,000	$38,000	$48,000

Current
year

response to a new accounting standard. Notice that the dollar impact on the financial statements is disclosed. Panel B describes the change in how Indigo Books & Music Inc. accounts for gift cards.

LEVERAGE

Leverage is the use of debt in the capital structure of an entity. Leverage can increase the return earned on the equity investment because profits earned from investing borrowed money, above the cost of borrowing, go to the owners. Leverage also adds risk because interest on borrowed money must be paid, regardless of how well or poorly the entity performs.

Let's look at an example. Four Friends Partnership (FFP) was formed to operate a one-year business venture. The four friends decided that $100,000 of invested capital is required to safely launch the venture, but they aren't sure how much debt and how much equity to use. They are considering three possible financing arrangements:

1. one hundred percent equity financing: $100,000 of their own money and no bank borrowing

2. fifty percent debt and 50 percent equity: $50,000 of their own money and $50,000 borrowed from the bank

3. ninety percent debt and 10 percent equity: $90,000 borrowed from the bank and $10,000 of their own money

The friends have predicted two possible outcomes for their venture: a good news outcome where revenues will be $80,000 and expenses $60,000 (excluding interest), and a bad news outcome where revenues will be $50,000 and expenses $48,000 (excluding interest). If the friends decide to borrow, the bank will charge an interest rate of 10 percent. At the completion of the venture, the friends will have to repay any money borrowed from the bank.

We will examine the effect of leverage by using return on equity (ROE). ROE was introduced in Chapter 3 and is defined as

$$\text{Return on equity} = \frac{\text{Net income} - \text{Preferred dividends}}{\text{Average common shareholder's equity}}$$

ROE is a measure of an entity's profitability and effectiveness in using the assets provided by the owners to generate net income. The effects of leverage on FFP's venture are shown in Table 10.4. When 100 percent equity is used, the friends simply earn what the venture earns. If the good news outcome occurs, they earn $20,000, which is a 20 percent ROE ($20,000 ÷ $100,000). If the bad news outcome occurs, they earn $2,000, a 2 percent ROE ($2,000 ÷ $100,000). With both outcomes, the friends get their original investment back.

If FFP borrows to finance its venture, it must pay interest on the borrowed money, but anything earned in excess of the interest cost belongs to the venturers. When 50 percent debt is used, FFP must pay $5,000 ($50,000 × 10%) in interest, so net income is $15,000 in the good news outcome (see Table 10.4). FFP earned 20 percent or $10,000 on the borrowed money, of which $5,000 was paid in interest, leaving $5,000 for the friends. In other words, the friends earned an extra $5,000 without having to invest their own money. As a result, the ROE increases to 30 percent, even though the income of the venture decreased. With ROE, we look at the return on the equity investment. In this situation, the friends invested half as much money but profit decreased by only 25 percent. This is the effect of leverage: using "someone else's" money can increase equity investors' returns.

TABLE 10.4	Scenarios Showing the Effect of Leverage on Performance		
Four Friends Partnership (FFP) **Information regarding new venture**			
Financing alternatives			
	100% equity	**50% debt and 50% equity**	**90% debt and 10% equity**
Debt	$ 0	$50,000	$90,000
Equity	100,000	50,000	10,000
Projected performance outcomes			
Good news outcome			
Revenue	$80,000	$80,000	$80,000
Expenses	60,000	60,000	60,000
	20,000	20,000	20,000
Interest expense	0	5,000	9,000
Net income	$20,000	$15,000	$11,000
Return on equity	20%	30%	110%
Bad news outcome			
Revenue	$50,000	$50,000	$50,000
Expenses	48,000	48,000	48,000
	2,000	2,000	2,000
Interest expense	0	5,000	9,000
Net income	$ 2,000	$(3,000)	$(7,000)
Return on equity	2%	–6%	–70%

But there's a dark side to leverage. While leverage makes good news better, it also makes bad news worse. If the bad news outcome occurs on their 100 percent equity, $100,000 investment option, the four friends earn a small return of 2 percent. The friends take home $2,000 in profit and their initial investment is intact. With the 50 percent equity, 50 percent debt financing option, the cost of borrowing is more than what FFP earned. The four friends must pay $3,000 of their own money to cover the interest. (The venture earned $2,000 before interest, so that plus $3,000 of the friend's money is used to pay the bank.) The $3,000 loss means that the friends lose some of their initial investment. In this scenario, the ROE is −6 percent (−$3,000 ÷ $50,000).

The effect of leverage in the 10 percent equity, 90 percent debt alternative is even more dramatic. In the good news outcome the four friends earn 110 percent on their $10,000 investment. On the other hand, in the bad news outcome their ROE is −70 percent and they have to pay $7,000 of their own money (plus the $2,000 the venture earned before interest) to pay the bank. The loss on the venture is $7,000, and 70 percent of the friends' original $10,000 investment is lost.

How, you might ask, can the friends' return be increasing when the net income of the venture is decreasing? The amount of income being earned as a proportion of the equity investment is increasing, even though the actual dollar amount of net income is decreasing. The friends will have more profit from the venture if only equity is used, but if the bank finances part of the venture, the friends will have a higher return and be able to keep some of their money for other purposes.

From a practical perspective, leverage is useful for a variety of reasons: (a) it allows for more investment or a larger venture; (b) it allows investors to diversify—instead of investing all their money in one project, investors can "spread the money around" which reduces risk; and (c) it allows a project to go ahead even if the investors don't have enough of their own money.

It's important to recognize that the difference in net income of each scenario is due to the cost of financing. In all three financing alternatives, the performance of the business activity itself, the operating income, was the same. (Operating income was $20,000 in the good news outcome and $2,000 in the bad news outcome.) What differed in the income statements was the amount of interest. When analyzing financial statements, separating an entity's business performance from the cost of financing it can provide valuable insights. Entities that go into bankruptcy protection are often viable if the debts are reorganized.

It's also important to remember that there are limits to the amount of money that an entity can borrow. It's possible that if FFP wanted to borrow $90,000 when the owners were investing only $10,000, the bank might charge a higher interest rate or not lend at all because of the investment's risk. Note that the FFP example ignores income taxes. This approach is sensible because FFP is a partnership and partnerships don't pay taxes. Taxes are important, though. The tax implications of any decisions must be taken into consideration. Finally, an entity's balance sheet is an important source of information about leverage. Examination of the debt-to-equity ratio gives insight into the amount of leverage an entity has and is a basis for evaluating the risk the entity is taking on.

www.mcgrawhill
connect.ca

KNOWLEDGE CHECK

❑   What is leverage?

❑   What are the advantages and disadvantages of using leverage when financing a business?

❑   For a given total amount of debt and equity financing, why does the return on equity to the owners increase as the proportion of equity financing and the amount of net income decrease?

EMPLOYEE STOCK OPTIONS

Employees can be compensated in many ways. Salary, bonus, shares in the company, and stock options are common ones. In this section, we will describe employee stock options and discuss the accounting issues surrounding this form of compensation.

Let's begin by covering some stock option basics:

- An **employee stock option** is the right to purchase a specified number of shares of the employer's stock at a specified price over a specified period of time. Employee stock options represent the right to purchase shares, not shares themselves.

- The price at which the employee may purchase the shares is called the **exercise price**. For tax reasons, the exercise price of a stock option is usually the same as or greater than the market price of the shares on the date it's granted.

- The final date an option can be exercised is called the **expiry date**. If the employee has not exercised or used the option by its expiry date, it can't be used to purchase shares. An employee will exercise an option only if the exercise price is less than the market price because otherwise they would be buying shares for more than they are worth in the open market.

Stock options can be an attractive way of compensating employees because they don't cost the entity any cash. This can be very important for entities that are short of cash or are trying to conserve cash, as is common in growing or new businesses. Stock options give the employees the opportunity to make lots of money if the company is successful. However, don't interpret the fact that stock options don't cost the entity any cash to mean that they aren't costly. In fact, stock options have a significant economic cost. They are exercised when the exercise price is below the market value of the shares, which dilutes the value of the shares of other shareholders. This means the wealth of existing shareholders is transferred to the employees exercising the options.

The significance of stock options as a form of compensation for senior executives can be seen in Table 10.5, which shows the compensation earned by the CEOs of seven Canadian companies.[7] The table breaks down the CEOs' compensation into salary and bonus, options (the change in value of the options), and other compensation. Aside from the fact that these CEOs earn a lot of money, notice how significant a role stock options play in compensation.

TABLE 10.5	Compensation of CEOs of Major Canadian Companies, 2007					
Company	Executive	Salary	Bonus	Options[a]	Other[b]	Total
Astral Media Inc.	Ian Greenberg	$780,000	$1,155,000	$3,712,000	$1,391,000	$7,038,000
Indigo Books & Music Inc.	Heather Reisman	300,000	0	0	8,000	308,000
Manulife Financial Corp	Dominic D'Alessandro	1,922,000	5,000,000	34,960,000	1,240,000	43,122,000
Nova Chemicals Inc.	Jeff Lipton	1,284,000	3,909,000	17,222,000	6,621,000	29,036,000
Potash Corp. of Saskatchewan Inc.	William Doyle	1,113,000	0	310,183,000	9,091,000	320,387,000
Royal Bank of Canada	Gordon Nixon	1,400,000	4,000,000	12,609,000	3,367,000	21,376,000
Saputo Inc.	Lino Saputo Jr.	800,000	800,000	1,695,000	0	3,295,000
WestJet Airlines Ltd.	Sean Duffy/Clive Beddoe[c]	$379,000	96,000	2,378,000	326,000	3,179,000

[a]Total annual increase or decrease in value of options, both exercised and exercisable.
[b]Other compensation includes long-term incentive payments, deferred shares, car allowances, pensions, insurance, interest free loans, etc.
[c]Duffy succeeded Beddoe during 2007. Amounts shown are what was paid to both during the year.

Exhibit 10.7 describes the stock option plan of Astral Media Inc. (Astral).[8] The first part of Note 12(c) describes the terms of the plan. Here are some key aspects of the plan:

- The company can grant stock options to employees to purchase Class A shares of the company.
- The number of options issued can't be greater than 10 percent of the number of Class A and B shares outstanding.
- The option exercise price is the closing price for Class A shares on the TSX on the last business day before the options are granted.

Note the following about the outstanding options:

- At the end of fiscal 2008 there were 3,104,096 options outstanding with an average exercise price of $28.55.
- Exercise prices range from $10.96 to $43.76. A table in Exhibit 10.7 breaks the options into different exercise price categories, including 66,576 options with prices between $10.96 and $16.25 (average price $12.76).
- If these 66,576 options were exercised, Astral would receive $849,509.76 (66,576 × $12.76) in cash in exchange for 66,576 shares of Astral's Class A stock. If the market price per share on the date they were exercised was $30, Astral would be giving up shares worth $1,997,280 ($30 × 66,576) for $849,509.76 in cash. The difference of $1,147,770 is the cost borne by the existing shareholders.

Now, how should employee stock options be accounted for? For many years the treatment was to ignore them, and no expense was recorded for stock options granted to or exercised by employees. IFRS require that the value of stock options granted to employees be expensed as part of the compensation expense. Note 12(d) shows that the value of the options granted in

EXHIBIT 10.7

Astral Media Inc.:
Stock Option Plan

12. Capital Stock (continued)

C) STOCK OPTION PLAN, RESTRICTED SHARE UNIT PLAN AND DEFERRED SHARE UNIT PLAN

Under the provisions of the Company's employee stock option plan, the Company may grant options to key employees to purchase a maximum number of Class A shares equal to 10% of the aggregate number of outstanding Class A and Class B shares on a non-diluted basis, when combined with the number of shares reserved for issuance under the Company's other stock-based compensation arrangements (the "Rolling maximum"). The option exercise price is set at the closing price for the Class A shares on the Toronto Stock Exchange on the last business day before the date on which the options are granted. Under the stock option plan, approximately 30% of the stock options vest progressively over 4 or 5 years from the date of granting and approximately 70% vest on the basis of the level of achievement of certain financial performance targets measured over a period of three fiscal years beginning with the fiscal year of their grant. Options have a term of 5 or 10 years.

The status of the Company's employee stock option plan as at August 31 is summarized as follows:

	2008		2007	
	NUMBER OF OPTIONS OUTSTANDING	WEIGHTED AVERAGE EXERCISE PRICE ($)	NUMBER OF OPTIONS OUTSTANDING	WEIGHTED AVERAGE EXERCISE PRICE ($)
Beginning of year	2,979,397	26.24	2,840,297	24.70
Granted	344,732	43.76	320,732	39.75
Exercised	(184,190)	18.09	(128,152)	24.11
Cancelled/Expired	(35,843)	36.34	(53,480)	30.51
End of year	3,104,096	28.55	2,979,397	26.24
Exercisable – end of year	2,228,314	24.61	2,106,341	23.17

The following table summarizes information relating to the outstanding stock options:

RANGE OF EXERCISE PRICES ($)		NUMBER OF OPTIONS OUTSTANDING AT AUGUST 31, 2008	WEIGHTED AVERAGE REMAINING LIFE (YEARS)	WEIGHTED AVERAGE EXERCISE PRICE ($)	NUMBER OF OPTIONS EXERCISABLE AT AUGUST 31, 2008	WEIGHTED AVERAGE EXERCISE PRICE ($)
10.96	- 16.25	66,576	1.33	12.76	66,576	12.76
16.26	- 24.25	1,006,620	3.02	22.81	1,006,620	22.81
24.26	- 36.25	1,395,471	2.93	27.37	1,132,649	26.61
36.26	- 43.76	635,429	3.82	41.89	22,469	39.75
10.96	- 43.76	3,104,096	3.11	28.55	2,228,314	24.61

fiscal 2008 was $8.41 each. This amount is expensed over the period that employees are allowed to exercise them. Astral expensed $6,270,000 in fiscal 2008 for stock-based compensation, which includes plans in addition to the stock option plan discussed here.

This treatment makes good economic sense. Some people argue that, since stock options are usually issued at an exercise price that is less than the market value when they are granted, they have no value. This is clearly false. As long as there is time before the stock option expires, it has an economic value. Indeed, if stock options have no value, why would employees negotiate for and accept them as compensation? The entity granting the option is giving something valuable: the opportunity to purchase stock at below-market prices.

A main objection to expensing the value of stock options is that doing so would significantly lower net income. As has been mentioned several times in the book, accounting has economic consequences and people will respond when they see themselves being disadvantaged by an accounting standard (or anything else). Some readers may find it surprising, but accounting standard setting can be very political and occurs in an environment of conflicting interests.

EXHIBIT 10.7

(continued)
**Astral Media Inc.:
Stock Option Plan**

D) STOCK-BASED COMPENSATION COSTS

During the second quarter of Fiscal 2008, the Company granted 344,732 options to key employees to purchase Class A shares of the Company (320,732 options to purchase Class A shares were granted in the second quarter of Fiscal 2007). The fair value of options granted was determined using the Black-Scholes option pricing model and the following assumptions:

	FISCAL 2008 GRANT	FISCAL 2007 GRANT
Assumptions:		
Risk-free interest rate	3.98%	3.86%
Expected volatility in the market price of the shares	17.80%	22.30%
Expected dividend yield	1.15%	1.01%
Expected life	4.5 years	5 years
Fair value per option:	$ 8.41	$ 9.66

The compensation costs related to stock options and RSUs granted to employees are recorded in operating expenses on the consolidated statements of earnings over their expected vesting period for stock options, and over a three-year vesting period for RSUs. Such compensation costs are credited to contributed surplus on the consolidated balance sheets. For the year ended August 31, 2008, stock-based compensation costs amounted to $6.3 million ($6.1 million for the year ended August 31, 2007) (see Note 13).

ECONOMIC CONSEQUENCES

Accounting matters. The discussion in the previous section about employee stock options and the controversy surrounding how to account for them emphasizes that accounting does matter. If accounting didn't matter, why would people get so excited about new accounting standards?

But why does accounting matter? This theme has been emphasized throughout the book. Accounting matters because it has economic consequences for an entity and its stakeholders. Economic consequences mean the wealth of an entity's stakeholders is affected by how the entity accounts for various transactions and economic events. Many decisions and outcomes, such as those following, can be affected by an entity's choices in how it represents its economic circumstances in the financial statements:

- management compensation

- compliance with debt covenants based on accounting measurements

- selling price of an entity when the price is based on net income or other accounting measurements

- amount of tax an entity pays

- rate changes for regulated companies when the rate is based on accounting measurements

- ability of an entity to receive subsidies from government

- ability of an entity to raise capital (some entities have argued that their ability to raise capital has been adversely affected by certain accounting standards)

This list doesn't include the effect accounting choices might have on decisions made by individual stakeholders—such as buying shares of a particular entity, selling shares already owned, or lending money. But remember, while different accounting choices have economic consequences for stakeholders, the underlying economic activity isn't affected by how an entity accounts. Whether employee stock options are accrued, disclosed, or ignored doesn't change the economic cost of those options. What is affected is the representation of that economic activity in the financial statements.

FINANCIAL STATEMENT ANALYSIS ISSUES

Price-to-Book Ratio

The equity section of an entity's balance sheet represents the book value of its equity. **Book value** (or carrying amount) is the amount recorded in the accounting records for the assets, liabilities, and equities—it's the accounting value of these elements. The **book value of equity** is the balance sheet or accounting value of an entity's equity and is equal to assets minus liabilities as reported on the balance sheet. It's is also referred to as the net assets or net worth of the entity.

The book value of equity isn't a measure of its market value. As we have discussed throughout the text, there are many reasons why book values and market values don't correspond. One is that IFRS rely on historical cost to measure many assets and liabilities—they aren't designed or intended to measure market values. For example, property, plant, and equipment is recorded at its cost and isn't adjusted for changes in market value (although IFRS allows the use of net realizable value), and not all assets are even recorded on the balance sheet (for example, research and development, advertising, and human resources). However, book value is sometimes viewed as what would be left over for shareholders if a company shut down its operations, paid off all of its creditors, collected from all of its debtors, and liquidated itself. From this view, book value can be seen as the minimum amount an entity is worth. This interpretation makes more sense for entities that reflect most of their assets on the balance sheet (like manufacturers and retailers) but less sense for knowledge-based entities that have many unrecorded assets.

The **market value of equity** is the market price of an entity's shares multiplied by the number of common shares outstanding. For public companies, the shares trade publicly so a market price is readily available. There is no readily available market price for private companies.

The **price-to-book ratio** (PB ratio) is often examined by investors and analysts when considering a stock's desirability. The PB ratio is a measure of the stock market's valuation of a company's equity relative to its book value and it indicates if the shares are reasonably valued. If the market expects a company to have higher earnings, its PB ratio will rise because the market value of the equity will increase.

TABLE 10.6	Price-to-Book Ratios for Selected Companies, 2002–2008						
Industry	2008	2007	2006	2005	2004	2003	2002
Corus Entertainment Inc.	1.7	2.0	1.6	1.3	1.3	1.0	1.4
Gildan Activewear Inc.	4.6	6.1	5.0	3.9	2.8	3.0	2.9
Indigo Books & Music Inc.	1.8	2.4	2.2	1.4	1.2	1.7	1.6
Leon's Furniture Limited	2.1	3.1	2.7	2.6	2.4	2.2	2.4
Potash Corporation of Saskatchewan Inc.	9.5	8.3	4.2	4.7	3.0	2.0	1.5
Saputo Inc.	3.4	2.7	2.7	2.7	2.5	2.8	2.8
Transat A.T. Inc.	2.5	4.0	2.5	2.5	2.0	1.1	1.7
WestJet Airlines Inc.	1.8	2.6	2.0	2.6	3.3	3.1	3.9

The PB ratio can be stated as

$$\text{Price-to-book ratio} = \frac{\text{Market value of equity}}{\text{Book value of equity}}$$

A lower PB ratio could indicate that a stock is undervalued and, therefore, an attractive investment. It could also indicate significant problems with the company. Like most of the ratios we have considered in the book, how meaningful a particular amount is varies with the industry. For example, one would expect a software company to have a higher PB ratio than a steelmaker or bank because the software company has many assets that aren't captured on the balance sheet.

For example, the market value of Leon's equity on December 31, 2008 was $636,706,251 ($9 per share $\times$ 70,745,139 shares) and its book value on December 31, 2008 was $353,358,000 (see Leon's balance sheet in Exhibit 10.3) for a PB ratio of 1.8. Table 10.6 provides the PB ratios for the same period for some of the companies we've discussed in the book.[9]

Earnings per Share

One of the most often quoted financial ratios is **earnings per share (EPS)**. EPS is the amount of net income attributable to each individual common share. The investing public pays close attention to and anxiously awaits the announcement of companies' quarterly and annual earnings and EPS. Analysts project EPS, and whether an entity has had a successful quarter or year is often measured by whether it met the analysts' forecasts.

EPS comes in a number of variations. We will look at two of them. The first and most straightforward is **basic earnings per share (basic EPS)**, which is calculated using the following formula:

$$\text{Basic EPS} = \frac{\text{Net income} - \text{Preferred dividends}}{\text{Weighted-average number of common shares outstanding during the period}}$$

Preferred dividends are deducted from net income in the numerator because they aren't available to common shareholders, but they aren't deducted in the calculation of net income. The denominator is the weighted-average number of shares that were outstanding during the year, which is the average number of shares outstanding during the period, taking into consideration when changes in the number of shares outstanding occurred during the period. An example of how to calculate the weighted-average number of shares outstanding is available at the text's companion website: www.mcgrawhillconnect.ca.

We can calculate basic EPS for Leon's from the information in Exhibit 10.3:

$$\begin{aligned} \text{Basic EPS} &= \frac{\text{Net income} - \text{Preferred dividends}}{\text{Weighted-average number of common shares outstanding during the period}} \\ &= \frac{\$63,390,000 - 0}{70,729,548} \\ &= \$0.90 \end{aligned}$$

EPS is reported at the bottom of Leon's statement of income and retained earnings (only net income is shown from the income statement) in Exhibit 10.3. A second EPS measure is called fully diluted EPS. In this chapter and in Chapter 9, we discussed securities such as convertible bonds, convertible preferred shares, and stock options that can be converted into or exchanged for common shares. If these securities are converted or exercised, they may dilute an entity's earnings—they will increase the number of common shares, thereby lowering EPS because earnings would be spread over a larger number of shares. **Fully diluted earnings per share** is designed to show the effect these dilutive securities would have on EPS if all of the securities had been converted or exchanged for common shares during the year. The actual calculations can get complicated and won't be shown here, but fully diluted EPS can be thought of as a worst-case scenario of EPS. You can find Leon's fully diluted EPS in Exhibit 10.3.

Despite all the attention it receives in the media, EPS has significant limitations:

- Like any ratio, EPS has no inherent meaning and must be considered in relation to some benchmark. For example, current EPS could be compared with previous years' EPS to observe trends, or compared with analysts' forecasts of EPS.

- EPS depends on the accounting policies and estimates used in the financial statements.

- EPS may be affected by changes in the number of shares outstanding during a period. For example, if an entity repurchases some of its shares, EPS will increase.

- EPS gives no indication of the entity's ability or willingness to pay dividends. It is simply the earnings attributable to each common share. It doesn't mean cash is on hand.

- It can be very difficult to compare the EPS figures of different entities. Aside from the effect of different accounting choices, EPS is also affected by financing. Entities with identical assets and operating performance will have different EPS if they are financed differently—that is, if they have different proportions of debt and equity.

CANADIAN GAAP FOR PRIVATE ENTERPRISES

Canadian GAAP for Private Enterprises doesn't require companies to calculate and present earnings per share.

INSIGHT

In Canada, the activities and performance of public companies get a lot of attention. This is understandable, as many members of the public have an interest in these companies, either directly or indirectly through pension plans and mutual funds.

However, most corporations and businesses in Canada are private. That means there is no market price on which to base a reasonable estimate of their market values. This is one of the reasons why accounting information is so important for evaluating an entity. For example, how much would you pay to buy a small business in your community? How much would you pay to join a partnership of accountants? Without a market-determined measure of value, it's difficult to know. It's why accounting information is relied on for determining the value of a private company for purposes of a purchase and sale, or in a divorce.

Return on Shareholders' Equity

In Chapter 8, **return on assets (ROA)** was introduced as a measure of the performance and operating efficiency of an entity. ROA provides a measure of the return the entity earns regardless of how it's financed. **Return on equity (ROE)** is a measure of return earned by resources invested only by common shareholders.

$$\text{Return on equity} = \frac{\text{Net income} - \text{Preferred dividends}}{\text{Average common shareholders' equity}}$$

Because ROE measures return to the common shareholders, preferred dividends are deducted from net income. These dividends aren't available to the common shareholders, but the amount isn't deducted in the calculation of net income. The denominator, average common shareholders' equity, excludes equity contributed by the preferred shareholders. As was discussed in the section in this chapter on leverage, ROE will be affected by how the entity is financed. The more leverage or debt that an entity uses, the more volatile ROE will be.

For Leon's, ROE for 2008 was

$$
\begin{aligned}
\text{Return on equity} &= \frac{\text{Net income} - \text{Preferred dividends}}{\text{Average common shareholders' equity}} \\[6pt]
&= \frac{\$63,390,000 - \$0}{(\$353,358,000 + \$322,005,000) \div 2} \\[6pt]
&= \frac{\$63,390,000}{\$337,681,500} \\[6pt]
&= 18.8\%
\end{aligned}
$$

Leon's common shareholders earned an 18.8 percent return on their investment in the company. Investors can compare the ROEs of different entities as part of their evaluation of investment alternatives.

Higher ROEs mean an investment is more attractive, but risk must be considered as well. Generally, the higher the risk of an investment, the higher the return investors expect. Thus, a higher return may indicate more risk, and investors must decide if they willing to accept the additional risk in exchange for the higher return. This risk-return relationship, the trade-off between risk and return, explains why interest rates that banks pay to depositors tend to be low, whereas expected returns on speculative investments tend to be high.

Tables 10.7 provides ROEs for some of the companies we have examined so far in the book.[10] Like other ratios, notice the variation across companies and over time. Leon's and Saputo have both provided very stable returns to their investors over the period shown, while the Potash Corporation and Indigo have steadily improved.

TABLE 10.7	Return on Equity for Selected Companies, 2002–2008						
Industry	2008	2007	2006	2005	2004	2003	2002
Corus Entertainment Inc.	13.30%	11.30%	3.84%	7.94%	(2.65)%	4.61%	(16.41)%
Gildan Activewear Inc.	19.59	21.77	22.46	23.00	20.81	24.78	28.37
Indigo Books & Music Inc.	29.96	22.69	24.78	12.82	4.72	1.85	(61.85)
Leon's Furniture Limited	18.77	19.19	19.56	19.19	18.92	16.52	17.09
Potash Corporation of Saskatchewan Inc.	65.90	25.08	25.72	24.03	13.70	(6.21)	2.57
Saputo Inc.	18.29	16.25	14.13	18.78	19.54	18.12	19.43
Transat A.T. Inc.	(16.01)	27.81	19.98	15.97	24.92	(5.67)	3.41
WestJet Airlines Inc.	17.50	21.96	15.54	3.81	(2.93)	12.93	17.92

Solved Problem

This case is designed to make you think about financial statements from the perspective of a particular stakeholder. The main theme is the problems a buyer of a small business has with a set of financial statements for that business. As usual, you should try to work through the case before looking at the solution.

Kenaston Convenience Store

The Kenaston Convenience Store (KCS) is located near a subdivision in Regina. KCS offers food staples, basic household goods, newspapers and magazines, candy, drinks, and snacks. KCS opened several years ago and is owned and operated by the Wu family. The store has been very successful and now that the neighbourhood has matured and the population is large enough, a major chain of convenience stores, Community Mart Ltd. (CML), is interested in buying KCS to establish a presence in the area. It's CML's usual practice to only move into an area once the population density has reached a certain level. It prefers to buy out an existing convenience store in an area because it gets the benefit of an established location and eliminates a competitor.

You are CML's location evaluator. It's your job to make contact with the owners of established convenience stores and evaluate their suitability for acquisition. Your preliminary evaluation of KCS is that it's a potential candidate for acquisition and your initial discussions with Mr. Wu were favourable. Mr. Wu has agreed to allow you to look at KCS's most recent income statements. The income statements are presented below:

Kenaston Convenience Store Income statements for the years ended March 31,		
	2014	**2013**
Revenue	$417,250	$368,425
Cost of sales	258,695	225,845
Gross margin	158,555	142,580
Expenses		
Depreciation of capital assets	32,000	34,200
Interest	15,200	17,400
Utilities	14,700	13,900
Other	7,500	6,200
Advertising and promotion	6,200	4,500
Salaries and wages	2,000	2,200
Repairs and maintenance	4,150	2,750
Income taxes	12,565	5,400
Total expenses	94,315	86,550
Net income	$ 64,240	$ 56,030

In addition, you obtained the following information from your discussion with Mr. Wu and from observing the business:

- KCS is located in a two-story, 30-year-old building at the edge of the subdivision. The building cost $300,000 and there is a $210,000 mortgage on it. The Wu family lives in a spacious apartment above the store. Mortgage payments, all utilities, and property taxes for the entire building are included in KCS's income statements.

- The store is open seven days a week from 7 a.m. to 11 p.m. The store is always staffed by one of the Wu family and all work is also done by family members. No one gets paid, but money is provided as it is needed, often just taken from the cash register.

- The financial statements are prepared for the bank, which has provided a small loan in addition to the mortgage on the building, and for tax purposes.

- KCS depreciates its capital asset on the same basis as is required for tax purposes, using the rates specified in the *Income Tax Act*.

- All sales are for cash (no credit sales) and are recorded on the cash register. Not all sales are rung up on the register.

- Inventory is counted on the last day of the year. Cost of goods sold is calculated by adding the opening inventory to purchases made during the year and then subtracting ending inventory. Family members often take store items for their own use.

Required:

Prepare a report for your manager, the vice-president of acquisitions, outlining your evaluation of the KCS's income statements. In your report, identify and discuss whether the statements are representative of KCS's activity and whether they give a good indication of how the store would perform if CML purchased and operated it. Be sure to identify and discuss any adjustments you would recommend to make the financial statements more useful.

Report to the controller:

I have examined the income statements for the Kenaston Convenience Store (KCS) and additional information related to the potential purchase of the business. There are many complications with using these income statements as an indicator of the profit our company will earn as operators of the business. I propose that we revise these income statements to approximate ones that would have resulted had the store been owned and operated by our company for the last two years. This will be most useful for determining an appropriate price to pay for KCS. For some of the issues, the amount of adjustment needed is fairly clear but for others further information is needed. I will indicate how each issue should be handled.

1. The fact that the business has been almost exclusively staffed by family members without explicit compensation means the wages expenses is significantly understated and profitability overstated. It should be easy to estimate the staffing costs based on our experience and given the level of sales. The staff costs should include at least one employee at the manager level in accordance with our normal staffing policies.

2. KCS's building is owned by the Wu's, which means CML has to purchase the building or be the Wu's tenants. If we rent, the income statements should reflect a fair rent for the building. It is possible that the building depreciation expense offsets rent, but the amount has to be confirmed. If we buy the building, we must consider the purchase price and any financing costs, as well as any rent earned from the apartment unit. We also need to determine the building's market value. Since CML is purchasing KCS's location, it is important for the store to remain where it is.

3. The cost of merchandise sold is overstated as the family consumed some of the merchandise, so it is included in cost of goods sold but not in sales.

4. The revenues reported on the income statement are understated, but we don't have an estimate of by how much. Some sales aren't rung up, presumably to avoid paying income taxes. We could estimate sales by determining KCS's inventory purchases during the year and applying an appropriate margin. However, the ability to do this is impeded by the fact that cost of sales is also misstated through the Wu's personal use of inventory. Assuming that the personal use inventory is small compared to the inventory actually sold, we can use this estimation technique.

5. The amounts reported for utilities and supplies on the income statements are too high because they include the electricity, heat, and telephone costs for the family home as well as those of the business. We will have to estimate the business's portion of the costs.

6. The advertising and promotion budget may be a fairly accurate representation of the costs incurred but aren't relevant since our approach to promotion may be quite different. Again, we are better served by estimating the budget we would normally follow for a store of this size.

7. The depreciation of capital assets has been based on CCA rates and may not be relevant for our purposes. We should revise the estimated depreciation cost to reflect our normal depreciation policies, based on the market values of the assets required to operate this business. That may require replacement of some equipment and fixtures that aren't in good condition. Our inventory management and reporting requirements may require more sophisticated cash registers and other computers, costs that need to be taken into consideration when estimating the possible profit of acquiring this company.

8. We need to find out what "other expenses" are. These may or may not be incurred under our ownership. They could represent personal expenses or legitimate business expenses.

9. Interest costs likely apply to the entire building, and bank loans may be personal as well as business. We need to determine the purpose of the loans. The cost of the debt we will incur to operate the business needs to be included in the income statement.

In summary, KCS's income statements are a good starting point for analysis, but significant adjustments are needed to make them representative of how the store will perform if owned by CML. Our experience in the industry may help us overcome the problems with the sales and cost of sales, though there is room for significant error. The maximum price we are willing to pay for the business should be based on the expected future profits and the value we place on eliminating the competition.

APPENDIX: THE AUDIT ENVIRONMENT AND THE AUDITORS' REPORT

In Chapter 1, the external auditor was introduced as an independent person adding credibility to an entity's financial information by assessing the information in relation to some standard, such as GAAP or IFRS, and expressing an opinion on it. Auditors provide their opinion on an entity's financial statements in the **auditors' report**.

Audited information is essential in an economy like Canada's, where the management of an entity is often separate from the owners and other stakeholders. Problems result when information produced by management pursues its own interests rather than the interests of the stakeholders. An audit provides assurance that the financial statements are a reasonable representation of the entity's underlying economic activity. Without an external audit, information would be less reliable and stakeholders would have less confidence in it.

In recent years, steps have been taken in Canada to improve investor confidence and protect the public interest by making sure that financial information meets the highest possible standards. The Ontario government passed legislation that increased the power and authority of the Ontario Securities Commission, the body that oversees the sale of securities to the public. The Canadian Public Accountability Board (CPAB) was created by the Canadian Securities Administrators, Office of the Superintendent of Financial Institutions, and the Canadian Institute of Chartered Accountants (CICA) to provide more control and oversight of auditing firms.

In addition, new rules were established to ensure that Canadian chartered accountants providing assurance services maintain their independence from their clients. Independence means that auditors are free of any conflicts of interest that may impair their ability to do their work without bias or partiality. The rules of auditor independence prohibit auditing firms from offering certain services to clients (before these changes it was common for audit firms to offer IT, bookkeeping, and corporate finance services), requiring that the audit partner in charge of an engagement switch every five years, and restricting an auditor from being employed by a client within a year of leaving the auditing firm.

The Auditors' Report

Auditors examine an entity's financial statements and accounting records to evaluate whether the statements are prepared in accordance with the relevant accounting standards. Based on the audit, an auditor issues an opinion. There are four opinions auditors can give. An unqualified opinion says the financial statements satisfy the standards the auditor is using. There are three opinions that indicate problems with the financial statements or the audit: a qualified opinion, an adverse opinion, and a disclaimer of opinion.

Our discussion will focus on the unqualified opinion because it's the most common. An example is provided in Exhibit 10.8.[11] Refer to it as we proceed through the discussion. An

EXHIBIT **10.8** **Unqualified Auditors' Report**

INDEPENDENT AUDITOR'S REPORT
To the shareholders of XYZ Ltd.

Report on the Financial Statements
We have audited the accompanying financial statements of ABC Company, which comprise the balance sheet as at December 31, 20X1 and the income statement, statement of changes in equity and cash flow statement for the year then ended, and a summary of significant accounting policies and other explanatory information.

Management's Responsibility for the Financial Statements
Management is responsible for the preparation and fair presentation of these financial statements in accordance with International Financial Reporting Standards and for such internal control as management determines is necessary to enable the preparation of financial statements that are free from material misstatement, whether due to fraud or error.

Auditor's Responsibility
Our responsibility is to express an opinion on these financial statements based on our audit. We conducted our audit in accordance with Canadian generally accepted auditing standards. Those standards require that we comply with ethical requirements and plan and perform the audit to obtain reasonable assurance about whether the financial statements are free from material misstatement.

An audit involves performing procedures to obtain audit evidence about the amounts and disclosures in the financial statements. The procedures selected depend on the auditor's judgment, including the assessment of the risks of material misstatement of the financial statements, whether due to fraud or error. In making those risk assessments, the auditor considers internal control relevant to the entity's preparation and fair presentation of the financial statements in order to design audit procedures that are appropriate in the circumstances, but not for the purpose of expressing an opinion on the effectiveness of the entity's internal control. An audit also includes evaluating the appropriateness of accounting policies used and the reasonableness of accounting estimates made by management, as well as evaluating the overall presentation of the financial statements.

We believe that the audit evidence we have obtained is sufficient and appropriate to provide a basis for our audit opinion.

Opinion
In our opinion, the financial statements present fairly, in all material respects, the financial position of ABC Company as at December 31, 20X1 and its financial performance and its cash flows for the year then ended in accordance with International Financial Reporting Standards.

[Auditor's signature]

[Date of the auditor's report]

[Auditor's address]

unqualified opinion means the auditors are satisfied that the financial statements present the financial situation of the entity fairly and that they are consistent with the appropriate set of accounting standards such as Canadian GAAP for Private Enterprises or IFRS.

The auditors' report is always addressed to the entity that appointed the auditor—in the case of a public company, the shareholders. The report is broken down into a number of sections. The first tells what the auditor did. It names the entity that was audited, identifies the financial statements, including the notes, and the periods that were audited. The second section explains that management is responsible for the preparation and fair presentation of the financial statements, including the internal controls needed to enable preparation of financial statements that are free of material misstatements.

The third section explains that the auditors' responsibility is to express an opinion on the financial statements based on their audit, and it describes the nature of an audit. The auditors don't have the authority to change the financial statements, they will discuss any concerns they have with management, but it's up to management to make any changes. Ultimately, if the auditors aren't satisfied that the financial statements meet the appropriate standards, they express their dissatisfaction in the auditors' report.

The third section also explains that the auditors conducted their audit in accordance with **generally accepted auditing standards (GAAS),** which is a set of principles developed by the International Auditing and Assurance Standards Board (IAASB). GAAS don't provide extensive detail about how to do an audit, but they offer principles for an approach to engagements that ensures they will be done properly and with enough evidence to provide an opinion.

The section provides some valuable insights into the nature of an audit and the meaning of an audit opinion. The paragraph says that GAAS require that an audit be planned and performed to obtain "reasonable assurance" that the financial statements are free of "material misstatement." The term reasonable assurance means that there is still the possibility of material error or misstatement in the financial statements. It offers a very good chance that the statements are free of material errors, but it isn't a guarantee. The term "material misstatements" means the financial statements can't be considered precise or exact and the auditors' report acknowledges that there may be errors that aren't material in the statements. Immaterial errors, by definition, shouldn't be a concern, but what is immaterial to some stakeholders may be material to others.

The third section also states that "an audit involves performing procedures to obtain audit evidence about the amounts and disclosures in the financial statements. The procedures selected depend on the auditor's judgment...." This usually means that auditors will examine a sample of transactions, and not all of them. Auditors use their professional judgment in deciding how many and which transactions and economic events should be examined.

The section also explains that auditors assess the accounting principles used, estimates made by management, and overall financial statement presentation. Within GAAP or IFRS, auditors must evaluate whether the choices made result in a fair representation of the entity's economic activity. In other words, simply because an entity chooses an alternative that is in accordance with GAAP or IFRS doesn't automatically mean the choice results in fair financial statements.

Finally, the third section indicates that the auditors have obtained enough evidence to support their opinion.

The fourth section expresses the auditors' opinion on the financial statements. It's important to emphasize that the auditor is offering an opinion, not a guarantee. In an unqualified opinion, the auditor states the financial statements present fairly, in all material respects, the financial situation of the entity, in accordance with the appropriate accounting standards (Canadian GAAP or IFRS). There *appear* to be two elements to the opinion—that the financial statements present the financial situation fairly and that the financial statements comply with GAAP or IFRS. In fact, there is only one element. In almost all circumstances, financial statements must comply with GAAP or IFRS to be fair. If they don't comply, they aren't fair.

Other Auditors' Reports

As mentioned, there are three other opinions that auditors provide on financial statements:

Qualified Opinion A **qualified opinion** is used when, overall, the financial statements present an entity's situation fairly but there are material deviations from GAAP or IFRS. A qualified audit opinion always contains the term "except for," in the opinion paragraph. The reason for the qualified opinion is given in the auditors' report.

Adverse Opinion An **adverse opinion** is given when the financial statements are so materially misstated or misleading that they don't fairly present an entity's financial situation. Adverse opinions are rare and would never be given to a public company because it would be unacceptable to the securities regulators. If an adverse opinion were expressed on the financial statements of a private entity, stakeholders receiving them would likely see them as having limited usefulness.

Disclaimer of Opinion When auditors can't obtain enough evidence to support an opinion, they don't give one. This is a **disclaimer of opinion**. Instead, the auditors state in their report that they are unable to express an opinion as to whether the financial statements are fair and in accordance with GAAP or IFRS.

Other Assurance Accountants Can Provide

Audits are only one form of assurance that accountants can provide. A **review engagement** provides less assurance than an audit does about whether an entity's financial statements are in accordance with the standards. The benefit of a review is that it's less expensive than an audit. When an accountant performs a review, the report prepared is called a review engagement report. Review engagements are never performed on public companies because securities laws require audits. A review will be done for private companies when external stakeholders require some assurance, but not the assurance provided by an audit.

Accountants can also provide reports on financial information other than financial statements (for example, a shopping mall may want a report on the amount of sales a store made, because the rent the mall receives is based on sales) or if an entity is in compliance with an agreement or regulations (for example, to determine whether an entity has met the current-ratio requirement of a lending agreement).

? QUESTION FOR CONSIDERATION

You are the property manager for a large mall. Most of the tenants in the mall pay a fixed amount of rent each month plus a percentage of sales made in the store each year. Would you require the stores in the mall to have their sales audited by an independent auditor? Explain.

Answer: An audit would be essential. Since the people managing and owning the stores in the mall prepare the accounting information, there is a possibility that some might understate sales to make a smaller rent payment. An audit would add reliability to the accounting information and sales figures presented by the store.

SUMMARY OF KEY POINTS

▶ **LO 1** A corporation is a separate legal and taxable entity. The shareholders of a corporation aren't liable for the obligations of and losses suffered by the corporation, beyond what they have invested.

Partnerships and proprietorships aren't incorporated. They don't pay income tax or file tax returns—earnings are taxed in the hands of the proprietor or partners. Partners only have limited liability in the case of limited and limited liability partnerships. The equity section of a partnership has a separate account for each partner, to keep track of the capital contributed by, the share of the partnership's earnings of, and the drawings made by each partner.

Not-for-profit organizations (NFPOs) are economic entities whose objective is to provide services and not to make a profit. NFPOs don't have owners or ownership shares that can be traded or sold.

▶ **LO 2** Common shares represent the residual ownership in an entity. Common shareholders are entitled to whatever earnings and assets are left after obligations to creditors and preferred shareholders have been satisfied. Preferred shareholders' rights pertaining to the payment of dividends and/or to the distribution of assets must be satisfied before common shareholders' rights in the event of liquidation. Dividends aren't deductible for tax purposes or expensed for accounting purposes. Shareholders aren't entitled to dividends or any other type of payments from the corporation and no return of principal is guaranteed.

▶ **LO 3** Retained earnings represents the accumulated earnings of an entity over its entire life, less all dividends paid to shareholders over the entity's life. Retained earnings represents an indirect investment by shareholders. Dividends are distributions of a corporation's earnings to its shareholders. There are three types of dividends: cash, property, and stock. Dividends are discretionary and are declared by the board of directors. They are declared on a per share basis and every share of a specific class must receive the same dividend. Once a dividend is declared, it's classified as a liability on the balance sheet. Contributed surplus captures equity transactions that don't fit into the other equity accounts. A stock split divides an entity's shares into a larger number of units, each with a smaller value.

▶ **LO 4** There are two categories of accounting changes—changes in policies and changes in estimates. If a company decides to change an accounting policy, the change is applied retroactively. A change in an accounting estimate is adjusted from the period of the change onward.

▶ **LO 5** Leverage is the use of debt to attempt to increase the return earned on an equity investment. Leverage is attractive because any profits earned from investing borrowed money, above the cost of borrowing, go to the owners. It is risky because the cost of borrowing must be paid, regardless of how well or how poorly the entity performs.

▶ **LO 6** Employee stock options give employees the right to purchase a specified number of shares of the employer's stock at a specified price over a specified period of time. Stock options are an important way of compensating employees. In Canada, the economic value of stock options on the date they are granted to employees must be estimated and the amount expensed as a compensation expense.

▶ **LO 7** The equity section of an entity's balance sheet represents the book value of its equity. The book value of equity is the balance sheet or accounting value of equity and is equal to assets minus liabilities as reported on the balance sheet. It isn't a measure of the market value of the equity. The price-to-book ratio is a measure of the stock market's valuation of a company's equity relative to its book value.

Earnings per share is the amount of net income attributable to each individual common share. Basic earnings per share equals net income less preferred dividends divided by the weighted-average number of common shares outstanding during the period. Fully diluted EPS shows the effect that dilutive securities would have on EPS if the securities were converted or exchanged for common shares. Return on equity provides a measure of the return earned by resources invested by the common shareholders.

▶ **LO 8** (Appendix) An audit adds credibility to information that could be biased by the managers who prepare it. Without an external audit, information would be less reliable and stakeholders would have less confidence in it. However, an audit isn't a guarantee that the financial statements are true, exact, precise, or correct.

There are four opinions that auditors can give on financial statements. The most common is an unqualified opinion, which says the financial statements satisfy the standards used. The three other opinions indicate that there are problems with the financial statements or the audit. These opinions are a qualified opinion, an adverse opinion, and a disclaimer of opinion.

FORMULA SUMMARY

$$\text{Assets} = \text{Liabilities} + \text{Owners' (shareholders') equity}$$

$$\begin{array}{l} \text{Net income} \\ + \text{ Other comprehensive income} \\ \hline \text{Comprehensive income} \end{array}$$

$$\text{Basic EPS} = \frac{\text{Net income} - \text{Preferred dividends}}{\text{Weighted-average number of common shares outstanding during the period}}$$

$$\text{Return on equity} = \frac{\text{Net income} - \text{Preferred dividends}}{\text{Average common shareholder's equity}}$$

$$\text{Price-to-book ratio} = \frac{\text{Market value of equity}}{\text{Book value of equity}}$$

KEY TERMS

accounting estimates, p. 574
accounting policies, p. 574
accumulated other comprehensive income/loss, p. 573
adverse opinion, p. 591
auditors' report, p. 588
authorized capital stock, p. 562
basic earnings per share (basic EPS), p. 583
book value, p. 582
book value of equity, p. 582
Canada Business Corporations Act, p. 564
cash dividend, p. 568
common shares, p. 564
comprehensive income, p. 571
contributed surplus, p. 574
convertible preferred share, p. 565
cumulative preferred share, p. 565

date of declaration of a dividend, p. 568
date of payment of a dividend, p. 568
date of record of a dividend, p. 568
disclaimer of opinion, p. 591
earnings per share (EPS), p. 583
employee stock option, p. 578
exercise price, p. 578
expiry date, p. 578
fully diluted earnings per share, p. 583
generally accepted auditing standards (GAAS), p. 590
general partner, p. 558
hybrid security, p. 566
issued shares, p. 564
leverage, p. 576
limited liability partnership (LLP), p. 558
limited partner, p. 558

limited partnership, p. 558

market value of equity, p. 582

no par value share, p. 565

other comprehensive income, p. 571

outstanding shares, p. 564

par value, p. 565

participating preferred share, p. 565

preferred shares, p. 565

price-to-book ratio, p. 582

property dividend, p. 569

qualified opinion, p. 591

redeemable preferred share, p. 565

retractable preferred share, p. 565

return on assets (ROA), p. 584

return on equity (ROE), p. 584

reverse stock split, p. 570

review engagement, p. 591

stock dividend, p. 569

stock split, p. 570

treasury stock, p. 565

unqualified opinion, p. 590

SIMILAR TERMS

The left column gives alternative terms that are sometimes used for the accounting terms introduced in this chapter, which are listed in the right column.

additional paid-in capital	**contributed surplus, p. 574**
authorized share capital, authorized shares	**authorized capital stock, p. 562**
denial of opinion	**disclaimer of opinion, p. 591**
dividend in kind	**property dividend, p. 569**
net assets, net worth	**book value of equity, p. 582**

ASSIGNMENT MATERIALS

Questions

Q10-1. Explain the difference between common and preferred shares.

Q10-2. Explain the following features sometimes associated with preferred shares:
   a. cumulative
   b. retractable
   c. redeemable
   d. participating
   e. convertible

Q10-3. What does it mean when an entity uses leverage to finance itself? What are the advantages and disadvantages of using leverage?

Q10-4. Describe and explain the characteristics that distinguish corporations from partnerships and proprietorships.

Q10-5. Why are common shares said to represent the residual interest in an entity?

Q10-6. Why is it important that contributed capital be separated from retained earnings in a corporation's financial statements?

Q10-7. Explain the differences between debt and equity. What are the advantages and disadvantages of each? Which do you think is preferable for an entity to use? Explain.

Q10-8. What is a not-for-profit organization? If their objective is not to make a profit, what is it? Why is a traditional income statement not appropriate for a not-for-profit organization?

Q10-9. Explain why not-for-profit organizations don't have an owners' equity section on their balance sheets. What do they have instead? What does that section of the balance sheet represent? How should it be interpreted?

Q10-10. Consider two types of not-for-profit organizations: a charity and a golf course operated for the enjoyment of its members (who must pay to belong to the club). Explain how the natures of these two organizations differ.

Q10-11. What is a limited partnership? What is the difference between limited partners and general partners? Why must a limited partnership have at least one general partner?

Q10-12. What are dividends? Why are dividends not expensed when calculating net income, whereas interest is expensed?

Q10-13. What does par value mean? How does the entry to record the issuance of common shares differ depending on whether the shares have a par value? Provide an example.

Q10-14. Grosvenor Ltd. has the following securities outstanding:
  i. $1,000,000 bond with 10 percent coupon rate.
  ii. $1,000,000 of cumulative preferred shares with a 6.5 percent dividend rate.
  What effect would payments to investors for each security have on the income statement? What would be the net cash cost of each security? Assume that Grosvenor has a tax rate of 30 percent.

Q10-15. Over the last six months, the price of Ixworth Inc.'s (Ixworth) shares has fallen from a high of $32 per share to its current price of $18. Ixworth doesn't plan to issue common shares in the foreseeable future, yet management has expressed concern about the falling share price. Explain why Ixworth's management might be concerned about its share price.

Q10-16. How are changes in the price of shares traded on stock exchanges such as the TSX reflected in an issuing entity's financial statements?

Q10-17. Distinguish between stock splits and stock dividends. How is each accounted for? What is the economic significance of each?

Q10-18. What is retained earnings? What transactions and economic events have an effect on retained earnings? Why is retained earnings considered an indirect investment in an entity?

Q10-19. What are property dividends? How are they accounted for?

Q10-20. You are a shareholder in a public company. The company is proposing to introduce an employee stock option program for its senior executives. Do you think that this proposal is a good idea? In your response, focus on the incentives the stock option plan would create for the executives.

Q10-21. Why do employee stock options impose a cost on shareholders?

Q10-22. Car prices tend to increase over time. One car manufacturer has offered students the opportunity to lock in the price of a new car for when they graduate. By paying $500 today, a student can purchase any car made by the manufacturer at today's price at any time over the next three years. The $500 fee isn't refundable.

Required:

Do you think it's worthwhile to spend $500 to lock in the price of a car for three years? Explain. What are the risks associated with purchasing this price guarantee? Suppose you could sell the price guarantee to somebody else. What would happen to the amount you could sell the price guarantee for if the price of cars increased? If the price of cars decreased? Explain.

Q10-23. What is meant by the term "economic consequence"? Why does accounting have economic consequences?

Q10-24. Since the underlying economic activity of an entity isn't affected by accounting choices such as when revenue is recognized or how capital assets are amortized, why does anyone care what accounting choices an entity makes?

Q10-25. Distinguish between the book value and market value of equity. Why are the two amounts usually different? How is book value per share calculated?

Q10-26. A business owner shows you his balance sheet and points out that the total amount of equity reported is $4,567,000. He says that is the price a buyer should pay for the business. Do you agree? Explain.

Q10-27. Corporations disclose the number of shares authorized and the number of shares outstanding. Explain what these terms mean.

Q10-28. How are preferred shares "preferred"? Are dividends on preferred shares guaranteed? If the preferred shares have a cumulative feature, are the dividends guaranteed? Explain.

Q10-29. Would you rather receive a cash dividend or a stock dividend from a corporation? Explain.

Q10-30. Why do most companies not pay out 100 percent of their earnings each year in dividends?

Q10-31. Why are preferred dividends deducted from net income when calculating earnings per share? Explain. Does earnings per share give an indication of the amount of dividends shareholders can expect to receive? Explain.

Q10-32. Explain why changes in accounting policies and corrections of errors have an effect on retained earnings.

Q10-33. Why might a loan agreement limit or prevent the payment of dividends by the borrower?

Q10-34. Why do you think property dividends are accounted for at their market value instead of their carrying amount? Why are property dividends relatively uncommon?

Q10-35. What are hybrid securities? Why do they sometimes pose a difficult accounting problem?

Q10-36. Explain the difference between a change in accounting policy and a change in accounting estimate. How is each accounted for in the financial statements?

Q10-37. (Appendix) Despite what some people think, an audit does not provide a guarantee that the financial statements are perfect, correct, or exact. Explain.

Q10-38. (Appendix) Identify and explain each of the audit opinions an auditor could express on an entity's financial statements.

Exercises

E10-1. (**Preparing journal entries, LO 2, 3, 5, 6**) For each of the following transactions or economic events, prepare the journal entry that would be required. Assume the year-end in each case is December 31:
a. On April 2, 2015 Barthel Inc. issued 500,000 common shares for $12 per share.
b. On May 17, 2015 Cayley Corp. announced a four-for-one stock split.
c. On June 7, 2015 Duro Ltd. declared a $0.11 per share cash dividend. The dividend was paid on July 4, 2015. Duro had 250,000,000 shares outstanding on June 7, 2015.
d. On August 17, 2015 Gullies Inc. issued 2,000,000 common shares with a par value of $0.01 for $7.50 per share.

e. On April 21, 2015 Quimper Corp. declared and distributed an 8 percent common stock dividend. On April 21, 2015 Quimper had 20,000,000 common shares outstanding and the market price per share was $4.20. The balance in the common shares account on April 21, 2015 was $87,000,000.

f. On December 4, 2015 Yarrow Ltd. declared a property dividend of some of the company's products. Each shareholder received an identical case of products that was taken directly from inventory. The carrying amount of the inventory on December 4, 2015 was $2,100,000 and its market value, based on the most recent selling price to customers, was $3,700,000. The dividend was distributed to the shareholders on December 21, 2015.

E10-2. **(Accounting for equity transactions and preparing the shareholders' equity section of the balance sheet, LO 2, 3)** You are provided with the following information from the equity section of Aurora Ltd.'s balance sheet on December 31, 2014:

Preferred shares—authorized, 1,000,000 shares; outstanding 700,000 shares	$ 3,500,000
Common shares—authorized, unlimited; outstanding 6,000,000 shares	18,000,000
Retained earnings	11,500,000

During the year ended December 31, 2015 the following occurred (events are recorded in the order they occurred during the year):

i. Semi-annual dividend on common shares of $0.25 per share was declared and paid.

ii. 1,000,000 commons shares were issued for $8,000,000.

iii. 50,000 shares of preferred shares were issued for $250,000.

iv. 10,000 common shares were issued in exchange for new equipment. The equipment had a list price on the vendor's price list of $92,000.

v. Preferred dividends of $2 per share were declared and paid.

vi. 10 percent stock dividend was declared on the outstanding common shares.

vii. Semi-annual dividend on common shares of $0.25 was declared. The dividend will be paid in January 2016.

viii. Net income was $5,250,000.

Required:

a. Prepare the journal entries required to record the above events.

b. Prepare the shareholders' equity section of Aurora balance sheet on December 31, 2015.

E10-3. **(Accounting for equity transactions and preparing the shareholders' equity section of the balance sheet, LO 2, 3)** You are provided with the following information from the equity section of Tingwick Ltd.'s balance sheet on December 31, 2013:

Preferred shares—authorized, 2,500,000 shares; outstanding 1,000,000 shares	$ 22,000,000
Common shares—authorized, 200,000,000; outstanding 75,000,000 shares	360,000,000
Accumulated other comprehensive income	1,750,000
Retained earnings	218,500,000

During the year ended December 31, 2014 the following occurred (events are recorded in the order they occurred during the year):

i. Semi-annual dividend on common shares of $0.80 per share was declared and paid.

ii. Issued 4,000,000 common shares for $11 per share.

iii. Issued 500,000 preferred shares for $23 per share.

iv. Issued 1,000,000 common shares in exchange for all the common shares of another company. The estimated value of the acquired company was $12 million.

v. Preferred dividends of $3 per share were declared and paid.

vi. Declared a 5 percent stock dividend on the outstanding common shares.

vii. Net income was $42,000,000.

viii. Comprehensive income for 2014 was $41,200,000.

ix. Semi-annual dividend on common shares of $0.85 was declared. The dividend will be paid in January 2015.

Required:

Prepare the shareholders' equity section of Tingwick balance sheet on December 31, 2014.

E10-4.   **(Correction of an accounting error, LO 3)** In fiscal 2013, Upshall Ltd. (Upshall) purchased land for $510,000. For some reason, the land was expensed when it was purchased. A new employee in the accounting department who was asked to review the company's property, plant, and equipment discovered the error in 2015. Retained earnings on December 31, 2014, Upshall's last year-end, was $3,250,000.

Required:

Prepare the journal entry that must be made in Upshall's books to correct the error. What would retained earnings be on December 31, 2015 after the error had been corrected? Explain why the error is corrected in this way.

E10-5.   **(Correction of an accounting error, LO 3)** In fiscal 2010, Ioco Inc. (Ioco) purchased equipment for $5,000,000. The equipment was supposed to be depreciated over eight years on a straight-line basis. However, for some reason, it wasn't. Ioco's new controller discovered the error in late 2013. Retained earnings on December 31, 2012, Ioco's last year-end, was $17,800,000.

Required:

Prepare the journal entry that must be made in Ioco's books to correct the error. What would retained earnings be on December 31, 2013 after the error had been corrected? Explain why the error is corrected in this way.

E10-6.   **(Accumulated other comprehensive income, LO 3)** On December 31, 2014 Palmarolle Ltd. reported net income of $2,750,000 and comprehensive income of $2,500,000. Accumulated other comprehensive income on December 31, 2013 was $100,000.

Required:

Determine accumulated other comprehensive income on December 31, 2014.

E10-7.   **(Equity section amounts, LO 3)** Determine the missing amounts in 2013 through 2016 for the shaded areas in the table below:

	2012	2013	2014	2015	2016
Net income	$	$75,000	$ 74,300	$ 95000	$101,000
Other comprehensive income		(10000)	3700	20000	(6000)
Comprehensive income		65,000	78600	115000	95,000
Retained earnings	250,000	315000	377,300	457,300	538,300
Accumulated other comprehensive income	(8,000)	(18000)	(14,300)	5,700	(300)
Dividends		10,000	1280	15,000	20000

E10-8.   **(Equity transactions, LO 2, 3, 7)** The shareholders' equity section of Fogo Ltd.'s balance sheet is shown below:

Fogo Ltd.
Extracts from the November 30, 2014 balance sheet

Shareholders' equity

Preferred shares (authorized 100,000; outstanding 75,000)	$1,500,000
Common shares (authorized 10,000,000; outstanding 6,000,000)	3,000,000
Retained earnings	615,000
Total shareholders' equity	$5,115,000

During fiscal 2015 the following occurred:
  i. On January 31, 500,000 common shares were issued for $2 per share.
  ii. On July 31, 1,000,000 common shares were issued for $2.25 per share.
  iii. On October 31, dividends on preferred shares of $2 per share were declared and paid.
  iv. On October 31, dividends on common shares of $.02 per share were declared and paid.
  v. Net income for fiscal 2015 was $400,000.

Required:

a. Calculate the weighted-average number of common shares outstanding during fiscal 2015. (Learn how to calculate the weighted-average number of shares outstanding in the Online Learning Centre for this textbook at www.mcgrawhillconnect.ca.)
b. Calculate basic earnings per share for the year ended November 30, 2015.
c. Calculate return on shareholders' equity for the year ended November 30, 2015.
d. Prepare the shareholders' equity section for Fogo's November 30, 2015 balance sheet.

E10-9. (**Calculating earnings per share, LO 7**) For each of the following situations calculate basic earnings per share for the year ended December 31, 2014:

	Situation A	Situation B	Situation C	Situation D	Situation E
Shares outstanding on December 31, 2013	500,000	2,500,000	10,000,000	5,000,000	100,000,000
Shares issued on June 30, 2014	0	500,000	0	0	20,000,000
Shares repurchased on June 30, 2014			1,000,000	700,000	
Net income for 2014	$400,000	$1,525,000	($ 2,000,000)	$ 400,000	$ 45,000,000
Preferred shares outstanding during 2014	0	500,000	1,000,000	1,000,000	10,000,000
Preferred dividends per share paid	$0	$2	$0	$1	$3

E10-10. (**Accounting for equity transactions, LO 2, 3**) On December 31, 2014 Oyama's equity section of its balance sheet appeared as follows:

Preferred shares (1,000,000 shares authorized, none outstanding) $ 0
Share capital (10,000,000 shares authorized, 2,400,000 outstanding)   8,400,000
Retained earnings   4,850,000

During the year ended December 31, 2015 Oyama Corp. (Oyama) had the following equity-related transactions and economic events.
  i. On January 2, Oyama issued 500,000 common shares for $8 each.
  ii. On February 28, Oyama issued 100,000 preferred shares for $100 each.
  iii. On June 30, Oyama paid a dividend of $0.25 per common share.
  iv. On September 30, Oyama declared a reverse stock split whereby the number of common shares outstanding was reduced by half. A shareholder that had 1,000 shares before the reverse stock split would have 500 after the split.
  v. On December 31, Oyama declared and paid a dividend to preferred shareholders of $5 per share.
  vi. On December 31, Oyama declared and paid a dividend of $0.30 per common share.
  vii. Net income for 2015 was $750,000.

Required:

a. Prepare the journal entries required to record items (i) through (vi).
b. Prepare the equity section of Oyama's balance sheet on December 31, 2015 and provide comparative information for December 31, 2014.
c. Show the equity section of Oyama's balance sheet on December 31, 2014 as it would have been reported in the 2014 annual report. Explain the difference between the equity section for 2014 as reported in the 2015 annual report versus the 2014 annual report.
d. Calculate earnings per share and return on shareholders' equity for the year ended December 31, 2015. If earnings per share for 2014 had been reported as $0.50 per share, what amount would be reported for the year ended December 31, 2014 in the 2015 annual report?
e. How did the reverse stock split affect the performance of Oyama?

E10-11. (Reporting shareholders equity and assessing the ability to pay dividends, LO 2, 3, 7) Kamsack Inc. (Kamsack) was formed in July 2014 to distribute imports from China. During its first year Kamsack had the following equity transactions:

i.   Issued 500,000 common shares to its two shareholders for $15 per share.
ii. Issued 100,000 common shares to the owner of a Chinese company for the exclusive distribution rights in Canada for certain products made by companies she owned. The value of the shares and the exclusive rights is estimated to be about $750,000.
iii. Issued 5,000 preferred shares for $75 each. The preferred shares pay no dividends but must be repurchased by Kamsack within five years for $120 per share.
iv. For the year ended June 30, 2015, Kamsack reported a net loss of $250,000.

Required:

a. Prepare the journal entries need to recorded events (i), (ii), and (iii).
b. Prepare Kamsack's equity section as it should be reported on its June 30, 2015 balance sheet.
c. Can Kamsack pay a dividend on June 30, 2015? Explain your answer. (Think carefully; this question is tricky.)

E10-12. (Accounting for equity transactions, LO 2, 3) On June 30, 2014, Utusivik's equity section was as follows:

Preferred shares (500,000 shares authorized, 25,000 outstanding)	$ 2,000,000
Share capital (5,000,000 shares authorized, 1,000,000 outstanding)	8,000,000
Accumulated other comprehensive income	85,000
Retained earnings	11,900,000

During the year ended June 30, 2015, Utusivik Inc. (Utusivik) had the following equity-related transactions and economic events.

i.   On August 1, 2014 Utusivik issued 500,000 common shares for $22 each.
ii.   On November 30, 2014 Utusivik issued 50,000 preferred shares for $80 each.
iii. On December 31, 2014 Utusivik declared and paid a dividend of $0.75 per common share.
iv.   On April 30, 2015 Utusivik declared a three-for-one stock split.
v.   On June 29, 2015 Utusivik obtained the rights to a patent in exchange for 60,000 Utusivik common shares. The market value of Utusivik stock on June 30, 2015 was $16 per share.
vi.   On June 30, 2015 Utusivik declared and paid a dividend to preferred shareholders of $1.50 per share.
vii. On June 30, 2015 Utusivik declared and paid a dividend of $0.85 per common share.
viii. Net income for 2015 was $4,500,000.
ix.   Comprehensive income for 2015 was 4,600,000.

Required:

    a. Prepare the journal entries required to record items (i) through (vii).

    b. Prepare the equity section of Utusivik's balance sheet on June 30, 2015 and provide comparative information for June 30, 2014.

    c. Show the equity section of Utusivik's balance sheet as it would have been reported in the June 30, 2014 annual report. Explain the difference between the equity section for 2014 as reported in the 2015 annual report versus the 2014 annual report.

    d. Calculate earnings per share and return on shareholders' equity for the year ended June 30, 2015. If earnings per share for 2014 had been reported as $1.80 per share, what amount would be reported for 2014 in the 2015 annual report?

    e. How did the stock split affect the performance of Utusivik?

E10-13. **(Calculating earnings per share, LO 2, 3, 7)** For the year ended September 30, 2014 Queylus Inc. (Queylus) reported net income of $1,278,000. On September 30, 2013 Queylus had the following capital stock outstanding:

Preferred shares, no par, $1 annual dividend, cumulative, 100,000 shares authorized; shares issued, and 75,000 shares issued and outstanding	$1,500,000
Common shares, no par, authorized 10,000,000 shares authorized; 4,800,000 shares issued and outstanding	6,000,000

On January 31, 2014 Queylus issued 500,000 common shares for $12 per share and on June 30, 2014 it issued 250,000 common shares for $11.75 per share.

Required:

    a. Calculate Queylus's basic earnings per share for the year ended September 30, 2014.

    b. How much of a dividend should Queylus's shareholders expect to receive in 2015?

E10-14. **(Calculating earnings per share, LO 2, 3, 7)** For the year ended December 31, 2013, Wabush Inc. (Wabush) reported net income of $11,700,000. On December 31, 2012, Wabush had the following capital stock outstanding:

Preferred shares, no par, $2 annual dividend, cumulative, authorized 1,000,000 shares, and 800,000 shares outstanding	$ 20,000,000
Common shares, no par, authorized: 50,000,000 shares; issued and outstanding: 32,000,000 shares	128,000,000

On June 30, 2013 Wabush repurchased 2,000,000 common shares for $9 per share.

Required:

    a. Calculate Wabush's basic earnings per share for the year ended December 31, 2013.

    b. How much of a dividend should Wabush's shareholders expect to receive in 2014?

E10-15. **(Impact of equity transactions on the statement of cash flows, LO 2, 3, 7)** Indicate if each of the following transactions and economic events would appear in the cash flow statement. If it does appear in the cash flow statement, would it be reported as cash from operations, an investing cash flow, or a financing cash flow? Explain your reasoning.

    a. Conversion of preferred shares into common.

    b. Issuance of common shares for capital assets.

    c. Stock split of 3:1.

    d. Payment of cash dividends on common shares.

    e. Payment of cash dividends on preferred shares.

    f. Declaration of cash dividends on common shares.

    g. Issuance of common shares for cash.

    h. Issuance of preferred shares for cash.

    i. Distribution of a stock dividend.

    j. Payment of a property dividend

    k. Repurchase of common shares for cash.

    l. Exercise of stock options by employees.

E10-16. **(The difference between par and no par value shares, LO 2, 7)** What is the required journal entry for each of the following transactions?

    a. Issued 50,000 shares of no par value shares for $10 per share.

    b. Issued 50,000 shares of $0.10 par value shares for $10 per share.

    c. Issued 50,000 shares of $1.00 par value shares for $10 per share.

    d. What effect does par value have on the financial statements? Does par value affect any ratios or the interpretation of the financial statements? Explain.

E10-17. **(Accounting for dividends, LO 3, 7)** Gogama Ltd. (Gogama) is planning on declaring a dividend for its common shareholders and is considering three alternatives:

    i. Declare a cash dividend of $5 per share.

    ii. Declare a property dividend. Shareholders would receive two common shares of Judson Inc. (Judson) for each share of Gogama stock owned. Judson's common shares have a market value of $2.50 per share and were originally purchased by Gogama for $1 per share.

    iii. Declare a 5 percent stock dividend. Shareholders would receive one Gogama common share for each 20 shares of Gogama stock owned. The current market value of Gogama's stock is $100.

Gogama's year-end is December 31. The balances in the common shares and retained earnings accounts on December 31, 2014 are $7,500,000 and $12,500,000 respectively, after accounting for net income for the year but before accounting for the dividend. Gogama currently has 500,000 common shares outstanding and net income for 2014 is $1,750,000.

Required:

    a. Prepare the journal entries required to record each of the dividends. State any assumptions you make.

    b. How would the equity section of Gogama's December 31, 2014 balance sheet be affected by the three dividends? Show the effect of each dividend separately.

    c. What would basic earnings per share be under each dividend alternative?

    d. What difference does it make which dividend alternative Gogama chooses? Is there an economic difference among the three? Explain. Under what circumstances might one dividend alternative be preferred over the others?

    e. Suppose that instead of paying a property dividend, Gogama sold its shares in Judson and used the proceeds of the sale to pay a cash dividend. Prepare the journal entries required to record the sale of the Judson shares and the declaration and payment of the dividend. What is the difference between paying a property dividend and selling the shares and using the proceeds to pay a dividend?

E10-18. **(Accounting for a partnership, LO 1)** In July 2014, Mr. Irving and Ms. Ruth formed a partnership offering consulting services. Mr. Irving contributed $100,000 in cash to the partnership and Ms. Ruth contributed non-cash assets with a market value of $70,000. During its first year of operations, the partnership earned revenues of $265,000 and incurred expenses of $130,000. Mr. Irving and Ms. Ruth agreed to divide the profits of the partnership in proportion to the value of their initial contributions. During the year, Mr. Irving withdrew $18,000 in cash from the partnership and Ms. Ruth withdrew $21,000 in cash. The partnership's first year-end is December 31, 2014.

Required:

    a. Record the journal entries required for formation of the partnership.

    b. Prepare the statement of partners' capital on December 31, 2014.

E10-19. (**Change in accounting estimate, LO 4**) On November 12, 2009, Griffon Inc. (Griffon) purchased five new forklifts for $380,000. Management estimated that the forklifts would have useful lives of 10 years and a residual value of $60,000. Near the end of fiscal 2016, management reassessed the useful life of the forklifts and decided that their useful life would probably be about 15 years and the residual value would be about $25,000. Griffon's year-end is October 31 and the company uses straight-line depreciation for this type of asset.

Required:

   a. Prepare the journal entry to record the purchase of the forklifts in 2009.
   b. What journal entry would be made in 2016 to reflect the change in the estimated useful lives of the forklifts?
   c. What would be the depreciation expense for the forklifts in fiscal 2010? Prepare the journal entry to record the depreciation expense.
   d. What would be the depreciation expense for the forklifts in fiscal 2018? Prepare the journal entry to record the depreciation expense.
   e. Suppose the forklifts were sold in on January 31, 2021 for $25,000. Prepare the journal entry to record the sale.

E10-20. (**Unit-of-production amortization and change in accounting estimate, LO 4**) Grindstone Corp. (Grindstone) produces fad toys for children. In 2014, Grindstone purchased a new stamping machine to produce the latest fad toy. The machine cost $75,000 plus taxes of $9,750 and delivery and installation was $2,500. Grindstone's management estimates that the market for the toy is about 520,000 units and demand will last seven years. Management expects it will be able to produce and sell 70,000 units in 2014; 100,000 units in 2015 through 2018; 45,000 units in 2019; and 5,000 units in 2020. Once the fad dies, the machine won't be useful and will be sold for scrap, for about $2,000. Grindstone will use unit-of-production depreciation for the machine.

Required:

   a. Prepare the journal entry to record the purchase of the new machine.
   b. Prepare a schedule showing the depreciation expense for each year and the carrying amount of the machine at the end of each year.
   c. Suppose that early in 2016 Grindstone's management realized that the fad would be shorter than it expected and sales would end in 2018. Management estimated it would sell 150,000 units in 2016; 90,000 in 2017; and 20,000 in 2018, at which time the machine would be scrapped for $1,000. Prepare a schedule showing the depreciation expense for 2016, 2017, and 2018, and the carrying amount of the machine at the end of each year. Assume Grindstone's original estimates for 2014 and 2015 were correct.
   d. What entry would be made in 2016 to reflect the change in the number of units of the toy that would be sold?

E10-21. (**Calculate financial ratios, LO 7**) Utterson Inc. (Utterson) is a small manufacturing company in northern Ontario. Utterson's owner has approached you to take an equity position in the company. The owner has provided the balance sheets for the last two years. In addition, you have learned that net income in 2014 was $135,000, interest expense was $28,000, $15,000 in dividends was paid on the preferred shares, and $100,000 was paid on the common shares. Utterson's tax rate is 15.5 percent. The estimated market value of Utterson's shares on December 31, 2014 was $26 per share, the weighted-average number of shares outstanding during 2014 was 50,000, and there were 55,000 shares outstanding on December 31, 2014.

Utterson Inc. Balance sheets as of December 31,					
	2014	**2013**		**2014**	**2013**
Assets			**Liabilities and shareholders' Equity**		
Current assets	$210,000	$202,500	Current liabilities	$168,750	$164,250
Non-current assets	575,000	540,000	Long-term debt	248,750	285,750
			Preferred shares	56,250	56,250
			Common shares	155,500	103,500
			Accumulated other comprehensive income	12,000	9,000
			Retained earnings	143,750	123,750
Total assets	$785,000	$742,500	Total liabilities and shareholders' equity	$785,000	$742,500

Required:

Calculate the following ratios for 2014: current ratio, debt-to-equity ratio, return on assets, return on equity, basic earnings per share, and price-to-book ratio.

Problems

P10-1. **(Effect of transactions and economic events on ratios, LO 2, 3, 5, 6, 7)** Complete the following table by indicating whether the listed transactions or economic events would increase, decrease, or have no effect on the financial ratios listed. Explain your reasoning and state any assumptions that you make.

	Debt-to-equity ratio	Current ratio	Return on equity	Basic earnings per share	Price-to-book ratio	Return on assets
Ratio/amount before taking the transaction/economic event into account	**0.9:1**	**1.3**	**11.5%**	**$3.42**	**1.8**	**7.1%**
1. Issuance of common shares for cash	↓	↑	↓	↓	↓	↓
2. Granting of stock options to employees	—	—	↓	↓	—	↓
3. Stock dividend	—	—	—	↓	—	—
4. Issuance of common shares in exchange for capital assets	↓	—	↓	↓	↓	↓
5. Declaration of a cash dividend on common shares	↑	↓	↑	—	↑	—

P10-2. **(Effect of transactions and economic events on ratios, LO 2, 3, 5, 6, 7)** Complete the following table by indicating whether the listed transactions or economic events would increase, decrease, or have no effect on the financial ratios listed. Explain your reasoning and state any assumptions that you make.

	Debt-to-equity ratio	Current ratio	Return on equity	Basic earnings per share	Price-to-book ratio	Return on assets
Ratio/amount before taking the transaction/economic event into account	**1.8:1**	**1.6**	**9.8%**	**$1.82**	**2.5**	**6.5%**
1. Three-for-one stock split						
2. Payment of a cash dividend that was declared in the previous fiscal year						
3. Repurchase of common shares for cash						
4. Issuance of preferred shares for cash						
5. Declaration of a property dividend; the property being distributed has a carrying amount that is greater than its market value						

P10-3. **(The effects of leverage, LO 5)** Chitek Inc. (Chitek) is an oil and gas exploration company operating in northern Canada. Chitek has not yet begun extracting oil or gas from the ground, but it's close to that stage. When Chitek was formed about 18 months ago, shareholders contributed $12,000,000 in exchange for 6,000,000 common shares in the company. Chitek now requires $8,000,000 of additional capital to exploit the resources it believes it has discovered.

Chitek's CEO is considering two options: sell additional shares in the company or borrow the required funds. If the company borrows, it will have to pay 9 percent interest per year. If it uses equity, it will have to sell 2,000,000 shares to raise the money.

Oil and gas exploration is a risky business. Performance is subject to many factors, including the quantity of oil and gas that can be economically extracted, the market price of the resource, and the ability to control costs. Chitek's CEO has projected two possible outcomes: a good outcome and a poor outcome. Under the good outcome, the CEO estimates that income from operations (income before financing costs) will be $2,000,000 in the first year. Under the poor outcome, the CEO estimates that income from operations will be $500,000 in the first year.

Assume Chitek has a tax rate of 16 percent, and all tax effects are reflected in operating income except for the tax effect of the additional debt or equity.

Required:

a. Prepare partial income statements for Chitek assuming:
   i.   Equity financing of the additional $8,000,000 and the good outcome.
   ii. Equity financing of the additional $8,000,000 and the poor outcome.
   iii. Debt financing of the additional $8,000,000 and the good outcome.
   iv. Debt financing of the additional $8,000,000 and the poor outcome.

b. Calculate basic earnings per share and return on shareholders' equity for the four scenarios described in (a).

c. Explain the advantages and disadvantages of Chitek using debt and the advantages and disadvantages of using equity.

d. If you were a prospective lender, would you lend $8,000,000 to Chitek? Explain.

e. Would you advise Chitek to use debt or equity to raise the additional $8,000,000? Explain.

P10-4. **(The effects of leverage, LO 5)** Greenway Television (Greenway) was recently granted the licenses by the CRTC to operate eight new digital specialty television channels. Greenway plans to begin broadcasting within six to eight months. It already has agreements in principle with cable and satellite operators to include Greenway's channels on their systems (although these agreements aren't binding).

When Greenway was organized two years ago with the purpose of developing specialty channels, the company raised $5,000,000 by selling 2,000,000 common shares to investors. Now that Greenway has received its licenses from the CRTC, it's in need of an additional $5,000,000 to go on air. Greenway's CEO is considering two options: sell additional shares in the company or borrow the required funds. If the company borrows, it will have to pay 10 percent interest per year. If it uses equity, it will have to sell 1,000,000 shares to raise the money.

The success of Greenway has two main elements—subscribers and advertising revenues. The more subscribers it has and the more money advertisers are prepared to spend buying advertising time, the more successful Greenway will be. Once the channels are operating, Greenway will receive a fixed fee for each person who subscribes to a channel. Cable and satellite operators sometimes bundle channels, so if a channel is bundled with other channels that are attractive to viewers, the channel in question will generate revenues regardless of how many people watch it.

Greenway's CEO has projected two possible outcomes: a good outcome and a poor outcome. Under the good outcome, the CEO estimates that income from operations (income before considering financing costs) will be $1,500,000 in the first year. Under the poor outcome, the CEO estimates that income from operations will be $300,000 in the first year.

Assume that Greenway has a tax rate of 28 percent, and all tax effects are reflected in operating income except for the tax effect of the additional debt or equity.

Required:

a. Prepare partial income statements for Greenway assuming:
   i.   Equity financing of the additional $5,000,000 and the good outcome.
   ii. Equity financing of the additional $5,000,000 and the poor outcome.
   iii. Debt financing of the additional $5,000,000 and the good outcome.
   iv. Debt financing of the additional $5,000,000 and the poor outcome.

b. Calculate basic earnings per share and return on shareholders' equity for the four scenarios described in (a).

c. Explain the advantages and disadvantages of Greenway using debt and the advantages and disadvantages of it using equity.

d. If you were a prospective lender, would you lend $5,000,000 to Greenway? Explain.

e. Would you advise Greenway to use debt or equity to raise the additional $5,000,000? Explain.

P10-5. **(Effect of employee stock options, LO 6, 7)** At its annual meeting in March 2014, the shareholders of Jasper Inc. (Jasper) approved a plan allowing the company's board of directors to grant stock options to certain employees as part of their compensation packages. During the year ended December 31, 2014, the board granted 200,000 options to its senior executives. The stock options were issued when Jasper's shares had a market price of $22 per share. The exercise price of the options is $24 per share.

During fiscal 2014, Jasper earned revenues of $37,345,000 and had cost of sales of $18,525,000; selling, general, and administrative expenses of $4,560,000; interest expense of $3,535,000; other expenses of $5,700,000; and an income tax expense of $1,340,000. The economic value of the stock options when they were issued was $1,200,000.

On December 31, 2013 the equity section showed the following:

Capital stock (unlimited number of common shares authorized; 7,000,000 outstanding)	$21,500,000
Retained earnings	18,950,000

During fiscal 2014, Jasper didn't issue or repurchase any common shares. Dividends of $0.10 were declared and paid during the year.

Required:

    a. Prepare Jasper's income statement for the year ended December 31, 2014.

    b. Calculate basic earnings per share and return on shareholders' equity assuming the value of the stock options is expensed when granted and assuming they aren't expensed.

    c. What effect do the two treatments for employee stock options have on cash flow?

    d. Which accounting approach do you think Jasper's managers would prefer? Explain.

    e. Which approach do you think gives a better representation of Jasper's economic performance?

    f. If Jasper didn't accrue the cost of the options in its financial statements, what information would you want disclosed about them? Explain.

P10-6. **(Stock splits and dividends, LO 3, 7)** During the year ended June 30, 2014, Ingonish Inc. (Ingonish) reported the following equity events:

September 15, 2013	5 percent stock dividend
December 15, 2013	Two-for-one stock split
May 15, 2014	$0.60 dividend per share

The equity section of Ingonish's balance sheet on June 30, 2013 was as follows:

Common shares (unlimited number of shares authorized; 10,000,000 issued and outstanding)	$ 87,525,000
Retained earnings	115,200,000

Net income for fiscal 2014 was $38,500,000. In previous years, Ingonish paid its shareholders annual dividends of $1 per share.

Required:

    a. Prepare Ingonish's shareholders' equity section on June 30, 2014.

    b. Calculate basic earnings per share for fiscal 2014. What would EPS have been if the stock split and stock dividend had not occurred?

    c. As an Ingonish shareholder, what is your reaction to the reduction in the per share dividend from $1 per share to $0.60 per share?

    d. The market value of Ingonish's shares on June 30, 2014 was $37.75 per share. What do you estimate the market price of the shares would have been had the stock dividend and stock split not occurred? Explain your answer.

    e. Calculate Ingonish's price-to-book ratio on June 30, 2014. What would the price-to-book ratio have been had the stock split and stock dividend not occurred?

P10-7. **(Stock splits and dividends, LO 3, 7)** During the year ended November 30, 2014 Aguanish Inc. (Aguanish) reported the following equity events:

February 15, 2014	10 percent stock dividend
March 15, 2014	Annual preferred dividend of $2 per share
May 15, 2014	Five-for-one stock split
August 15, 2014	$0.20 dividend per common share

The equity section of Aguanish's balance sheet on November 30, 2013, was as follows:

Preferred shares (authorized, issued, and outstanding: 500,000)	$ 8,000,000
Common shares (unlimited number of shares authorized; 3,000,000 issued and outstanding)	8,750,000
Retained earnings	10,420,000

Net income for fiscal 2014 was $6,500,000. In previous years, Aguanish paid its common shareholders annual dividends of $1 per share.

Required:

a. Prepare Aguanish's shareholders' equity section on November 30, 2014.

b. Calculate basic earnings per share for fiscal 2014. What would EPS have been had the stock split and stock dividend not occurred?

c. As an Aguanish shareholder, what is your reaction to the reduction in the per share dividend from $5 per share to $1 per share?

d. The market value of Aguanish's shares on November 30, 2014 was $120 per share. What do you estimate the market price of the shares would have been had the stock dividend and stock split not occurred? Explain your answer.

e. Calculate Aguanish's price-to-book ratio on November 30, 2014. What would the price-to-book ratio have been had the stock split and stock dividend not occurred? Explain your answer.

P10-8. **(Effect of employee stock options, LO 6, 7)** At its annual meeting in June 2012, the shareholders of Rusylvia Ltd. (Rusylvia) approved a plan allowing the company's board of directors to grant stock options to certain employees as part of their compensation packages. During the year ended March 31, 2013 the board granted 200,000 options to its senior executives. The stock options were issued when Rusylvia's shares had a market price of $10 per share. The exercise price of the options is $10.25 per share.

During fiscal 2013, Rusylvia earned revenues of $17,250,000, and had cost of sales of $7,600,000; selling, general, and administrative expenses of $2,400,000; interest expense of $1,750,000; other expenses of $2,950,000; and an income tax expense of $610,000. The economic value of the stock options when they were issued was $900,000.

On March 31, 2012 the equity section showed the following:

Capital stock:

Preferred shares (unlimited number authorized; 400,000 outstanding, $3 annual dividend, cumulative)	$8,000,000
Common shares (unlimited number authorized; 8,000,000 outstanding)	4,500,000
Retained earnings	7,425,000

On February 1, 2013 Rusylvia issued 600,000 common shares for $10 per share. In March 2013, Rusylvia declared and paid the dividend on the preferred shares and declared and paid a cash dividend of $0.25 per share on the common shares.

Required:

a. Prepare Rusylvia's income statement for the year ended March 31, 2013,
   i. assuming that the options are expensed.
   ii. assuming that the options aren't expensed.

b. Calculate basic earnings per share and return on shareholders' equity, assuming the value of the stock options is expensed when granted, and assuming it isn't expensed.

c. What effect do the two treatments for employee stock options have on cash flow?

d. Which accounting approach do you think Rusylvia's managers would prefer? Explain.

e. Which approach do you think gives a better representation of Rusylvia's economic performance?

f. If Rusylvia didn't accrue the cost of the options in its financial statements, what information would you want disclosed about them? Explain.

P10-9. **(Hybrid securities, LO 2)** In May 2014, Kugluktuk Ltd. (Kugluktuk) sold $200,000 in convertible bonds to investors. The bonds have a coupon rate of 9 percent and mature in May 2024. The bonds are convertible into common shares at the option of the company. The terms of the bond agreement make it highly likely that the bonds will be converted before they mature. Kugluktuk's summarized balance sheet just before the convertible bonds were sold is shown:

Kugluktuk Ltd. Summarized balance sheet (just before the sale of convertible bonds)			
Assets	$2,400,000	Liabilities	$1,000,000
		Shareholders' equity	1,400,000
Total assets	$2,400,000	Total liabilities and shareholders' equity	$2,400,000

Required:

a. Do you think that the convertible bonds are debt or equity? Explain. (Consider the characteristics of debt and equity in your response.)

b. Prepare the journal entry to record the issuance of the convertible bond and calculate the resulting debt-to-equity ratio, assuming that the bonds are classified as debt.

c. Prepare the journal entry to record the issuance of the convertible bond and calculate the resulting debt-to-equity ratio, assuming that the bonds are classified as equity.

d. How do you think Kugluktuk's management would want to classify the convertible bonds for accounting purposes? Explain.

e. How do you think Kugluktuk's management would want to classify the convertible bonds for tax purposes? Explain.

f. How do you think Kugluktuk's management would account for the convertible bonds if the classification for tax purposes had to be the same as the classification for accounting purposes?

g. Does it matter how the convertible bonds are classified? Explain.

P10-10. **(Hybrid securities, LO 2)** In August 2013, Ethelbert Ltd. (Ethelbert) issued 10,000 shares of cumulative, redeemable preferred shares to investors for $500,000. The preferred shares pay an annual dividend of $4 per share and are redeemable beginning in 2015. Ethelbert must redeem the preferred shares before September 1, 2027. Ethelbert's summarized balance sheet just before the preferred shares were sold Is shown:

Ethelbert Ltd. Summarized balance sheet (just before the sale of preferred shares)			
Assets	$4,400,000	Liabilities	$2,000,000
		Shareholders' equity	2,400,000
Total assets	$4,400,000	Total liabilities and shareholders' equity	$4,400,000

Required:

a. Do you think that the preferred shares are really debt or equity? Explain. (Consider the characteristics of debt and equity in your response.)

b. Prepare the journal entry to record the issuance of the preferred shares and calculate the resulting debt-to-equity ratio, assuming that the shares are classified as debt.

c. Prepare the journal entry to record the issuance of the preferred shares and calculate the resulting debt-to-equity ratio, assuming that the shares are classified as equity.

d. How do you think Ethelbert's management would want to classify the preferred shares for accounting purposes? Explain.

e. How do you think Ethelbert's management would want to classify the preferred shares for tax purposes? Explain.

f. How do you think Ethelbert's management would account for the preferred shares if the classification for tax purposes had to be the same as the classification for accounting purposes?

g. Does it matter how the preferred shares are classified? Explain.

P10-11. **(Analyzing the effects of different financing alternatives, LO 2, 7)** Owakonze Inc. (Owakonze), a privately owned corporation, is in need of $1,000,000 to finance an expansion of its operations. Management is considering three financing alternatives:

   i. Issue 100,000 common shares to a group of private investors for $10 per share. In recent years, dividends of $0.65 per share have been paid on the common shares.

   ii. Issue 40,000 cumulative preferred shares with an annual dividend of $2 per share for $25 per share. The preferred shares are redeemable after eight years for $27 per share.

   iii. Issue a $1,000,000 bond with a coupon rate of 7 percent per year and maturity in 12 years.

It's now late July 2014. Owakonze's year-end is July 31. Owakonze plans to raise the needed money at the beginning of its 2015 fiscal year, but management wants to know the financial statement effects and implications of each alternative. Owakonze's accounting department has provided the right-hand side of the balance sheet as of July 31, 2014 and a summarized projected income statement for the year ended July 31, 2015. The projected statements don't reflect any of the proposed financing alternatives. One of Owakonze's existing loans has a covenant that requires the debt-to-equity ratio be below 1:1. Owakonze has a tax rate of 15 percent.

Owakonze Ltd. Summarized projected income statement as of July 31, 2015	
Revenue	$1,900,000
Expenses	1,400,000
Income tax expense	150,000
Net income	$ 350,000
Owakonze Ltd. Liabilities and shareholders' equity as of July 31, 2014	
Liabilities	$ 750,000
Shareholders' equity:	
Preferred shares (200,000 shares authorized, 0 issued)	0
Common shares (unlimited number of shares authorized, 200,000 outstanding)	950,000
Retained earnings	800,000
Total liabilities and shareholders' equity	$2,500,000

Required:

a. Calculate projected net income for Owakonze under the three financing alternatives.

b. Calculate basic earnings per share and return on shareholders' equity under the three financing alternatives.

c. Prepare a report to Owakonze's management explaining the effect of each of the financing alternatives on the financial statements. Include in your report a discussion of the pros and cons of each financing alternative. Also, make a recommendation as to which alternative it should choose. Support your recommendation.

P10-12. (**Different ways of looking at income, LO 2, 7**) In the traditional approach to financial reporting in Canada, net income is thought of as the increase of wealth that belongs to the owners of the entity. In this view, interest is an expense, whereas dividends are a reduction of retained earnings. However, this is only one way to view an entity and its financial statements. Net income could also be calculated by expensing both interest and dividends. An alternative would not treat interest, dividends, or income taxes as expenses.

During the year ended December 31, 2014 Atnarko Ltd. (Atnarko) had revenues of $2,450,000, expenses of $1,400,000, and income taxes of $115,000. In addition, Atnarko incurred interest costs of $170,000, and it declared and paid preferred share dividends of $75,000 and common share dividends of $150,000.

Required:

a. Prepare an income statement for Atnarko using the traditional approach. Explain why the measure of income is useful from the perspective of shareholders.
b. Devise three alternative measures of net income and prepare income statements on these bases. Explain which users of the income statement would find your alternative measures useful.

P10-13. (**Assessing the payment of dividends, LO 7**) Dunsinane Ltd. (Dunsinane) is a publicly traded manufacturing company that makes computer components for sale to end-product manufacturers. Extracts from the last five years' financial statements are shown below.

Dunsinane completed an expansion in 2014 that was financed by a share issuance made in late 2013. Management believes that cash from operations should now be fairly stable and the net cash outflows on investing activities should range between $900,000 and $1,500,000 per year. To date, Dunsinane has not faced the effects of any economic slowdowns. There is concern of the effects of a prolonged slowdown on Dunsinane's revenues, income, and cash flow. Dunsinane has access to a $1,000,000 line of credit secured against accounts receivable that it hasn't used to date. After two years of satisfactory and steady performance since the expansion was completed, the board of directors is considering a proposal to implement an annual common share dividend. Dunsinane has never paid dividends before.

	2016	2015	2014	2013	2012
Assets					
Cash	$ 512,000	$ 375,000	$ 430,000	$1,900,000	$ 175,000
All other assets	8,908,000	7,710,000	6,775,000	4,500,000	3,050,000
Total assets	$9,420,000	$8,085,000	$7,205,000	$6,400,000	$3,225,000
Liabilities	$2,900,000	$2,600,000	$2,400,000	$2,200,000	$1,400,000
Shareholders' equity					
Capital stock (unlimited number of common shares authorized, 1,000,000 outstanding)	3,765,000	3,625,000	3,560,000	3,425,000	1,200,000
Retained earnings	2,755,000	1,860,000	1,245,000	775,000	625,000
Total shareholders' equity	6,520,000	5,485,000	4,805,000	4,200,000	1,825,000
Total liabilities and shareholders' equity	$9,420,000	$8,085,000	$7,205,000	$6,400,000	$3,225,000
Extracts from the cash flow statement					
Cash from operations	$1,130,000	$975,000	($250,000)	($75,000)	$225,000
Cash spent on investing activities	(765,000)	(600,000)	(1,550,000)	(1,200,000)	(900,000)

Required:

Prepare a report to Dunsinane's board of directors, assessing the pros and cons of implementing an annual common share dividend. Identify additional information needed to make a definitive decision. If you recommend that a dividend should be paid, what amount per share should be paid? Provide support for your positions.

P10-14. **(Accounting changes, LO 4, 7)** On October 1, 2010 Independent Manufacturing Inc. (Independent) purchased a state-of-the-art mould-casting machine for $2,500,000. Independent's management estimated the machine would be useful for seven years, at which time it could be sold for $400,000. Independent uses straight-line depreciation on all its capital assets. In September 2013, management realized that because of rapid technological changes, the machine would not likely be useful beyond fiscal 2015. Therefore, Independent decided to shorten its estimate of the machine's useful life to five years and reduce the estimated residual value to zero. Independent's year-end is September 30.

Required:

a. Is the change being made by Independent considered a change in accounting policy or a change in accounting estimate? Explain. How would the change be accounted for?
b. What depreciation expense would Independent have originally reported in fiscal 2011 and 2012 for the machine? What would the carrying amount of the machine have been on September 30, 2012?
c. What depreciation expense would Independent have reported in fiscal 2011 and 2012 for the machine after the accounting change had been made?
d. What depreciation expense will Independent report for the years ended September 30, 2013, 2014, and 2015? What would the carrying amount of the machine have been on September 30, 2013?
e. What are the implications of this change to users of the financial statements? Explain.
f. Do you think this type of change can be objectively made? Explain. What possible motivations could Independent's managers have for making the change? Explain.

P10-15. **(Earnings per share, LO 7)** Nisku Inc. (Nisku) and Grimsby Ltd. (Grimsby) are similar companies. You are considering investing in one of them and have received information about each for the year ended December 31, 2014.

	Nisku Inc. income statement	Grimsby Ltd. income statement
	For the year ended December 31, 2014	For the year ended December 31, 2014
Revenue	$1,250,000	$1,250,000
Cost of sales	475,000	475,000
Gross margin	775,000	775,000
Other expenses	562,500	562,500
Income before taxes	212,500	212,500
Income tax expense	31,875	31,875
Net income	$ 180,625	$ 180,625
	Shareholders' equity Common shares: Authorized: unlimited Outstanding: 1,000,000	Shareholders' equity Common shares: Authorized: unlimited Outstanding: 4,000,000
Share capital*	$ 250,000	$ 250,000
Retained earnings	1,350,000	1,350,000
Shareholders' equity	$1,600,000	$1,600,000

*During 2014 no new shares were issued during the year and each company paid dividends of $75,000.

Required:

Calculate EPS and ROE for both companies and decide which one you would invest in. Explain your conclusion.

P10-16. **(Auditor independence, LO 8, Appendix)** Etna and Partners (Etna) is a firm of accountants in a medium-sized town in Quebec. Recently, the senior partner of the firm was approached by the CEO of Dyment Inc. (Dyment) to discuss the possibility of becoming Dyment's auditor. Dyment is a private corporation with about 150 shareholders, none of whom are involved in the management of the company. In addition, the company has several large loans from banks and other private lenders. Management has recently come under criticism from shareholders about the poor performance of the company and the CEO has assured the shareholders that a turnaround plan is in place. In the meeting with Etna, the CEO offered that, in addition to the audit engagement, Dyment could benefit from Etna's expertise in a number of other areas. In particular, as part of the turnaround plan, the CEO said there was a need for a complete review and overhaul of Dyment's accounting systems. The CEO also felt that Etna could provide expert advice on the turnaround plan itself and ongoing financial and management advice in the future. The audit fee for this client is estimated to be $40,000 per year, which would make Dyment one of Etna's largest clients. The additional work in the first three years could be as much as $100,000 per year.

Required:

The senior partner will be meeting with his partners to discuss the Dyment engagement. Prepare a report that discusses the appropriateness of accepting the audit engagement and the consulting engagement.

Using Financial Statements

CORUS ENTERTAINMENT INC.

Corus Entertainment, Inc. (Corus), a media and entertainment company, engages in the radio and television broadcasting business in Canada. The company operates 53 radio stations, various specialty television networks focused on children and adult genres, and three broadcast television stations. It also produces and distributes children's programming and merchandise products, offers cable advertising and digital audio services, and publishes children's books in English. The company was founded in 1998 and is based in Toronto. Corus's Class B common shares trade on the TSX and the New York Stock Exchange.[12]

www.corusent.com

Corus's consolidated balance sheets, statements of income and comprehensive income and shareholders' equity, and extracts from the statements cash flows and the notes to the financial statements are provided in Exhibit 10.9. Use this information to answer questions FS10-1 to FS10-8.[13]

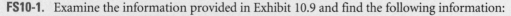

FS10-1. Examine the information provided in Exhibit 10.9 and find the following information:
   a. Retained earnings on August 31, 2007 and 2008.
   b. Dividends paid on common and preferred shares in 2007 and 2008.
   c. Total shareholders' equity on August 31, 2007 and 2008.
   d. Balance in share capital on August 31, 2007 and 2008.
   e. Net income for the years ended August 31, 2007 and 2008.
   f. Net assets on August 31, 2007 and 2008.
   g. Contributed surplus on August 31, 2007 and 2008.
   h. Comprehensive earnings for fiscal 2007 and 2008.
   i. Number of Class A voting shares outstanding on August 31, 2007 and 2008.
   j. Number of Class B non-voting shares issued under the stock option plan during fiscal 2007 and 2008.

EXHIBIT 10.9 Corus Entertainment Inc.

Consolidated balance sheets

As at August 31
(in thousands of Canadian dollars)

	2008	2007
Liabilities and shareholders' equity		
Current		
Accounts payable and accrued liabilities *(note 7)*	196,026	166,083
Income taxes payable	–	1,474
Total current liabilities	196,026	167,557
Long-term debt *(note 8)*	692,750	610,697
Other long-term liabilities *(note 9)*	59,936	64,773
Future tax liability *(note 13)*	87,699	102,851
Total liabilities	1,036,411	945,878
Non-controlling interest	20,237	15,196
Shareholders' equity		
Share capital *(note 10)*	848,257	882,244
Contributed surplus	17,304	10,250
Retained earnings	131,594	95,568
Accumulated other comprehensive loss *(note 20)*	(20,150)	(12,169)
Total shareholders' equity	977,005	975,893
	2,033,653	1,936,967

Consolidated statements of income and comprehensive income

For the years ended August 31
(in thousands of Canadian dollars, except per share amounts)

	2008	2007	2006
Revenues (notes 22 and 24)	787,156	768,743	726,270
Direct cost of sales, general and administrative expenses *(notes 10, 19, 23 and 24)*	535,026	527,822	512,151
Depreciation	22,054	21,556	21,302
Amortization	–	1,555	2,872
Interest expense *(notes 8 and 11)*	41,313	35,838	43,105
Disputed regulatory fees *(notes 7 and 23)*	10,936	–	–
Debt refinancing loss *(note 8)*	–	–	131,951
Other expense, net *(notes 12 and 19)*	7,853	9,800	11,667
Income before income taxes and non-controlling interest	169,974	172,172	3,222
Income tax expense (recovery) *(note 13)*	35,519	59,813	(36,005)
Non-controlling interest	4,620	5,341	3,756
Net income for the year	129,835	107,018	35,471
Earnings per share (note 10)			
Basic	$1.57	$1.27	$0.42
Diluted	$1.54	$1.23	$0.41
Net income for the year	129,835	107,018	35,471
Other comprehensive loss, net of tax			
Unrealized foreign currency translation adjustment	(23)	(641)	(1,519)
Unrealized change in fair value of available-for-sale investments	(1,114)	–	–
Unrealized change in fair value of cash flow hedges	(13,851)	–	–
	(14,988)	(641)	(1,519)
Comprehensive income for the year	114,847	106,377	33,952

EXHIBIT 10.9 (continued) Corus Entertainment Inc.

Consolidated statements of changes in shareholders' equity

For the years ended August 31
(in thousands of Canadian dollars)

	2008	2007	2006
Share capital			
Balance, beginning of year	882,244	870,563	885,911
Issuance of shares under Stock Option Plan	12,338	27,676	6,109
Shares repurchased	(46,555)	(16,229)	(21,687)
Repayment of executive stock purchase loans	230	234	230
Balance, end of year	848,257	882,244	870,563
Contributed surplus			
Balance, beginning of year	10,250	6,878	3,558
Stock-based compensation	7,904	4,133	3,448
Exercise of stock options	(850)	(761)	(128)
Balance, end of year	17,304	10,250	6,878
Retained earnings			
Balance, beginning of year	95,568	51,585	50,802
Cumulative impact of accounting changes *(note 2)*	(1,594)	–	–
Adjusted opening balance	93,974	51,585	50,802
Net income for the year	129,835	107,018	35,471
Dividends *(note 10)*	(47,326)	(42,842)	(19,586)
Share repurchase excess *(note 10)*	(44,889)	(20,193)	(15,102)
Balance, end of year	131,594	95,568	51,585
Accumulated other comprehensive loss			
Balance, beginning of year	(12,169)	(11,528)	(10,009)
Cumulative impact of accounting changes *(note 2)*	7,007	–	–
Adjusted opening balance	(5,162)	(11,528)	(10,009)
Other comprehensive loss, net of tax	(14,988)	(641)	(1,519)
Balance, end of year	(20,150)	(12,169)	(11,528)

Consolidated statements of cash flows

For the years ended August 31
(in thousands of Canadian dollars)

	2008	2007	2006
Operating activities			
Net income for the year	129,835	107,018	35,471
Add (deduct) non-cash items:			
Depreciation	22,054	21,556	21,302
Amortization of program and film rights	145,661	138,711	124,327
Amortization of film investments	28,393	38,781	39,450
Future income taxes	(7,321)	16,295	(74,232)
Non-controlling interest	4,620	5,341	3,756
Stock-based compensation	7,971	13,066	12,137
Debt refinancing loss	–	–	131,951
Imputed interest and other	8,593	2,404	5,950
Net change in non-cash working capital balances related to operations	(11,018)	(27,810)	(9,898)
Payment of program and film rights	(141,917)	(156,220)	(134,751)
Net additions to film investments	(56,293)	(56,069)	(44,445)
Cash provided by operating activities	130,578	103,073	111,018
Financing activities			
Increase in bank loans	85,594	14,388	592,687
Notes repurchase and swap termination	–	(634)	(727,829)
Issuance of shares under stock option plan	11,488	26,915	5,981
Shares repurchased	(91,444)	(36,422)	(36,789)
Dividends paid	(46,284)	(44,845)	(10,547)
Dividend paid to non-controlling interest	(1,742)	(1,524)	(5,304)
Other	(375)	(442)	(6,418)
Cash used in financing activities	(42,763)	(42,564)	(188,219)
Net decrease in cash and cash equivalents during the year	(13,705)	(10,289)	(94,450)
Cash and cash equivalents, beginning of year	33,347	43,636	138,086
Cash and cash equivalents, end of year	19,642	33,347	43,636

EXHIBIT 10.9 (continued) Corus Entertainment Inc.

Consolidated statements of changes in shareholders' equity

For the years ended August 31
(in thousands of Canadian dollars)

	2008	2007	2006
Share capital			
Balance, beginning of year	882,244	870,563	885,911
Issuance of shares under Stock Option Plan	12,338	27,676	6,109
Shares repurchased	(46,555)	(16,229)	(21,687)
Repayment of executive stock purchase loans	230	234	230
Balance, end of year	848,257	882,244	870,563
Contributed surplus			
Balance, beginning of year	10,250	6,878	3,558
Stock-based compensation	7,904	4,133	3,448
Exercise of stock options	(850)	(761)	(128)
Balance, end of year	17,304	10,250	6,878
Retained earnings			
Balance, beginning of year	95,568	51,585	50,802
Cumulative impact of accounting changes *(note 2)*	(1,594)	–	–
Adjusted opening balance	93,974	51,585	50,802
Net income for the year	129,835	107,018	35,471
Dividends *(note 10)*	(47,326)	(42,842)	(19,586)
Share repurchase excess *(note 10)*	(44,889)	(20,193)	(15,102)
Balance, end of year	131,594	95,568	51,585
Accumulated other comprehensive loss			
Balance, beginning of year	(12,169)	(11,528)	(10,009)
Cumulative impact of accounting changes *(note 2)*	7,007	–	–
Adjusted opening balance	(5,162)	(11,528)	(10,009)
Other comprehensive loss, net of tax	(14,988)	(641)	(1,519)
Balance, end of year	(20,150)	(12,169)	(11,528)

FS10-2. Use the information provided in Exhibit 10.9 and calculate the following ratios for the years ended August 31, 2007 and 2008. Interpret and explain your findings. Assume that shareholders' equity on August 31, 2006 was $1,842,209,000:

a. earnings per share

b. return on shareholders' equity

c. debt-to-equity ratio

FS10-3. Examine Corus's statement of shareholders' equity and Note 10 to the financial statements and answer the following questions:

a. Describe the different types of shares that Corus is authorized to issue. How do the classes differ and how are they the same?

b. How many shares of each class were outstanding on August 31, 2008?

c. How much capital (cash and property) was contributed by each class of share?

d. How many shares of each class were issued during fiscal 2008?

e. Why do you think Corus has these different classes of common shares?

FS10-4. Corus's Class A voting shares aren't traded publicly. Who do you think owns these shares and why do you think they exist? Why do you think there are so many fewer Class A than Class B shares?

FS10-5. Use the information in Exhibit 10.9 to answer the following questions:

a. How many of its shares were repurchased by Corus during fiscal 2008? What type of shares were repurchased?

EXHIBIT ⟨ 10.9 ⟩ (continued) Corus Entertainment Inc.

Note 2. Significant accounting policies
Earnings per share
Basic earnings per share are calculated using the weighted average number of common shares outstanding during the year. The computation of diluted earnings per share assumes the basic weighted average number of common shares outstanding during the year is increased to include the number of additional common shares that would have been outstanding if the dilutive potential common shares had been issued. The dilutive effect of stock options is determined using the treasury stock method.

Note 10. Share capital
Authorized
The Company is authorized to issue, upon approval of holders of no less than two-thirds of the existing Class A shares, an unlimited number of Class A participating shares ("Class A Voting Shares"), as well as an unlimited number of Class B non-voting participating shares ("Class B Non-Voting Shares"), Class A Preferred Shares and Class 1 and Class 2 Preferred Shares.

Class A Voting Shares are convertible at any time into an equivalent number of Class B Non-Voting Shares. The Class B Non-Voting Shares are convertible into an equivalent number of Class A Voting Shares in limited circumstances.

The Class A Preferred Shares are redeemable at any time at the demand of Corus and retractable at any time at the demand of a holder of a Class A Preferred Share for an amount equal to the consideration received by Corus at the time of issuance of such Class A Preferred Shares. Holders of Class A Preferred Shares are entitled to receive a non-cumulative dividend at such rate as Corus' Board of Directors may determine on the redemption amount of the Class A Preferred Shares. Each of the Class 1 Preferred Shares, the Class 2 Preferred Shares, the Class A Voting Shares and the Class B Non-Voting Shares rank junior to and are subject in all respects to the preferences, rights, conditions, restrictions, limitations and prohibitions attaching to the Class A Preferred Shares in connection with the payment of dividends.

The Class 1 and Class 2 Preferred Shares are issuable in one or more series with attributes designated by the Board of Directors. The Class 1 Preferred Shares rank senior to the Class 2 Preferred Shares.

In the event of liquidation, dissolution or winding-up of Corus or other distribution of assets of Corus for the purpose of winding up its affairs, the holders of Class A Preferred Shares are entitled to a payment in priority to all other classes of shares of Corus to the extent of the redemption amount of the Class A Preferred Shares, but will not be entitled to any surplus in excess of that amount. The remaining property and assets will be available for distribution to the holders of the Class A Voting Shares and Class B Non-Voting Shares, which shall be paid or distributed equally, share for share, between the holders of the Class A Voting Shares and the Class B Non-Voting Shares, without preference or distinction.

Effective on February 1, 2008, the Class A Voting Shares and Class B Non-Voting Shares were split on a two-for-one basis. Accordingly, the comparative number of shares and per share amounts have been retroactively adjusted to reflect the two-for-one split.

    b. What was the total amount paid by Corus to repurchase its shares? What was the average price paid for each share repurchased?

    c. What is the journal entry that Corus would have made to record the repurchase of shares in fiscal 2008 (be careful in looking for the amounts)?

    d. How would you expect the repurchase of shares to appear in the cash flow statement? Explain.

    e. What do you think the impact of repurchasing shares would have on the share price of the remaining outstanding shares?

FS10-6. Examine the information in Note 10 to Corus's financial statements pertaining to the company's stock option plan and answer the following questions:

    a. Describe the terms of the share compensation plan.

    b. How many employee stock options were outstanding on August 31, 2008? How many of the stock options could be exercised on August 31, 2008?

    c. How many options were granted during fiscal 2008? What was the average exercise price of the options granted during fiscal 2008?

    d. How many options were exercised during fiscal 2008? What was the average price paid for the shares purchased by the employees?

> **EXHIBIT 10.9** (continued) Corus Entertainment Inc.

Issued and outstanding

The changes in the Class A Voting Shares and Class B Non-Voting Shares since August 31, 2006 are summarized as follows:

	Class A Voting Shares		Class B Non-Voting Shares		Total
	#	$	#	$	$
Balance as at August 31, 2006	3,447,858	26,700	80,563,058	843,863	870,563
Conversion of Class A Voting Shares to Class B Non-Voting Shares	(2,000)	(16)	2,000	16	–
Issuance of shares under Stock Option Plan	–	–	1,997,736	27,676	27,676
Shares repurchased	–	–	(1,538,200)	(16,229)	(16,229)
Repayment of executive stock purchase loans	–	–	–	234	234
Balance as at August 31, 2007	3,445,858	26,684	81,024,594	855,560	882,244
Issuance of shares under Stock Option Plan	–	–	725,384	12,338	12,338
Shares repurchased	–	–	(4,388,400)	(46,555)	(46,555)
Repayment of executive stock purchase loans	–	–	–	230	230
Balance as at August 31, 2008	3,445,858	26,684	77,361,578	821,573	848,257

There are no Class A Preferred Shares, Class 1 Preferred Shares or Class 2 Preferred Shares outstanding as at August 31, 2008.

Stock Option Plan

Under the Company's Stock Option Plan (the "Plan"), the Company may grant options to purchase Class B Non-Voting Shares to eligible officers, directors and employees of or consultants to the Company. The number of Class B Non-Voting Shares which the Company is authorized to issue under the Plan is 10% of the issued and outstanding Class B Non-Voting Shares. All options granted are for terms not to exceed ten years from the grant date. The exercise price of each option equals the market price of the Company's stock on the date of grant. Options vest 25% on each of the first, second, third and fourth anniversary dates of the date of grant.

As a result of the two-for-one stock split, the number of outstanding options was adjusted in accordance with existing plan provisions. All prior period option numbers as well as weighted average exercise prices and fair values per option have been retroactively adjusted to reflect the two-for-one stock split.

A summary of the changes to the stock options outstanding since August 31, 2006, is presented as follows:

	Number of options (#)	Weighted average exercise price ($)
Outstanding as at August 31, 2006	6,869,284	13.99
Forfeited	(98,046)	15.62
Exercised	(1,997,736)	13.47
Outstanding as at August 31, 2007	4,773,502	14.18
Granted	255,800	22.45
Forfeited	(434,630)	19.18
Exercised	(725,384)	15.84
Outstanding as at August 31, 2008	3,869,288	13.85

EXHIBIT 10.9 (continued) Corus Entertainment Inc.

As at August 31, 2008, the options outstanding and exercisable consist of the following:

	Options outstanding			Options exercisable	
Range of exercise price ($)	Number outstanding (#)	Weighted average remaining contractual life (years)	Weighted average exercise price ($)	Number outstanding (#)	Weighted average exercise price ($)
9.53–12.48	2,184,060	2.6	11.49	1,972,260	11.44
13.50–16.50	1,130,968	2.2	15.45	880,968	15.26
17.25–22.65	554,260	3.5	19.92	288,460	17.74
9.53–22.65	3,869,288	2.6	13.85	3,141,688	13.09

The fair value of each option granted since September 1, 2003 was estimated on the date of the grant using the Black-Scholes option pricing model. The estimated fair value of the options is amortized to income over the options' vesting period on a straight-line basis. The Company has recorded stock-based compensation expense for the year ended August 31, 2008 of $1,917 (2007 – $3,003; 2006 – $2,915). This charge has been credited to contributed surplus.

The fair value of each option granted in fiscal 2008 was estimated on the date of the grant using the Black-Scholes option pricing model with the following assumptions:

Fair value	$4.32
Expected life	Five years
Risk-free interest rate	3.80%
Dividend yield	2.75%
Volatility	22.6%

On October 22, 2008, the Company granted a further 464,500 options for Class B Non-Voting Shares to eligible officers and employees of the Company. These options are exercisable at $17.62 per share.

Dividends

The holders of Class A Voting Shares and Class B Non-Voting Shares are entitled to receive such dividends as the Board of Directors determines to declare on a share-for-share basis, as and when any such dividends are declared or paid. The holders of Class B Non-Voting Shares are entitled to receive during each dividend period, in priority to the payment of dividends on the Class A Voting Shares, an additional dividend at a rate of $0.005 per share per annum. This additional dividend is subject to proportionate adjustment in the event of future consolidations or subdivisions of shares and in the event of any issue of shares by way of stock dividend. After payment or setting aside for payment of the additional non-cumulative dividends on the Class B Non-Voting Shares, holders of Class A Voting Shares and Class B Non-Voting Shares participate equally, on a share-for-share basis, on all subsequent dividends declared.

The total amount of dividends declared in fiscal 2008 was $47,326 (2007 – $42,842; 2006 – $19,586).

Earnings per share

The following is a reconciliation of the numerator and denominators (in thousands) used for the computation of the basic and diluted earnings per share amounts:

	2008	2007	2006
Net income for the year (numerator)	129,835	107,018	35,471
Weighted average number of shares outstanding (denominator)			
Weighted average number of shares outstanding – basic	82,944	84,561	84,921
Effect of dilutive securities	1,575	2,095	1,572
Weighted average number of shares outstanding – diluted	84,519	86,656	86,493

Diluted earnings per share for fiscal 2008 excluded 171,581 weighted average Class B Non-Voting Shares (2007 – nil; 2006 – 862,262) issuable under the Company's Stock Option Plan because these options were not "in-the-money."

Note 20. Accumulated other comprehensive losses

	2008	2007
Foreign currency translation adjustment	(12,192)	(12,169)
Unrealized loss on available-for-sale investments, net of tax	(1,297)	–
Unrealized loss on cash flow hedge, net of tax	(6,661)	–
	(20,150)	(12,169)

EXHIBIT 10.9 (continued) **Corus Entertainment Inc.**

From Corus's Managment Discussion and Analysis

Cash dividends declared per share

Class A Voting	$0.570015	$0.501250	$0.22625
Class B Non-Voting	$0.574995	$0.506655	$0.23250

In addition, in order to maintain eligibility under the *Broadcasting Act* and the *Radiocommunications Act*, there are limitations on the ownership by non-Canadians of Corus Class A Voting Shares. Under certain circumstances, Corus' Board of Directors may refuse to issue or register the transfer of Corus Class A Voting Shares to any person that is a non-Canadian or may sell the Corus Class A Voting Shares of a non-Canadian as if they were the owner of such Corus Class A Voting Shares.

    e. How many options expired during fiscal 2008? Why would an employee allow an option to expire without exercising it?

    f. What amount did Corus expense in fiscal 2008 as a result of granting stock options to employees? Why is the stock option expense added back to net income in the calculation of cash from operations?

    g. What do you think is the purpose of Corus's share compensation plan?

FS10-7. Examine the information in Exhibit 10.9 and answer the following questions:

    a. What was Corus's comprehensive income in fiscal 2007 and 2008?

    b. What are the sources of the other comprehensive loss in 2008?

    c. What is the accumulated other comprehensive loss on August 31, 2007 and 2008?

    d. Why do you think other comprehensive income isn't just included in the calculation of net income?

FS10-8. During fiscal 2008, Corus completed a stock split. Answer the following questions about the stock split.

    a. Describe the stock split.

    b. What effect did the stock split have on the financial statements?

    c. What journal entry would Corus have recorded as a result of the stock split?

    d. If you looked at the August 31, 2007 annual report, how many shares of each class of Corus's common stock would you expect to see outstanding on August 31, 2007. Explain your answer.

    e. What impact, if any, do you think the stock split would have on Corus's earnings per share? Explain.

    f. What impact, if any, do you think the stock split would have had on Corus's stock price? Explain.

ENDNOTES

1. Extracted from 2100 Bloor Street Limited Partnership's 2007 financial statements.

2. Extracted from the University of Ontario Institute of Technology's 2008 annual report.

3. Extracted from Leon's Furniture Limited's 2008 annual report.

4. Extracted from TransCanada Pipelines Limited's 2008 annual report.

5. Extracted from WestJet Airlines Inc.'s 2008 annual report.

6. Extracted from Potash Corporation of Saskatchewan Inc.'s and Indigo Books & Music Inc.'s 2008 annual reports.

7. *Financial Post Magazine*, November 2008.

8. Extracted from Astral Media Inc.'s 2008 annual repot.

9. Data obtained from *The Financial Post*, "2009 Industry Reports."

10. Data obtained from *The Financial Post*, "2009 Industry Reports."

11. CICA, *Canadian Audit Standards 700*, "Forming an Opinion and Reporting on Financial Statements."

12. Extracted from Yahoo! Finance's website at http://sg.finance.yahoo.com/q/pr?s=CJR.

13. Extracted from Corus Entertainment Inc.'s 2008 annual report.

INVESTMENTS IN OTHER COMPANIES

Mark Powell didn't know he was going to be an accountant back when he worked as a carhop carrying Triple "O" burgers to customers at a White Spot restaurant in his hometown of Richmond, B.C. It was a later job at a steel plant "in a dangerous environment" that did the trick.

"Doing that for seven hours a day was pretty inspirational as far as wanting to get back to schooling and wanting to get a nice comfy office job one day," Powell explained in an interview from his Richmond, B.C., corporate head office.

After receiving his diploma in financial management from the British Columbia Institute of Technology, Powell's first accounting job was

A Boston Pizza location in Quebec, photo courtesy of CPI/The Canadian Press/ Mario Beauregard

at a hotel chain, Town and Country Inns. He earned his certified management accountant (CMA) designation in 1986, and moved on to comptroller positions in various local Vancouver golf and ski resorts, including Grouse Mountain. A leap to a real estate firm as vice-president of finance helped Powell land his "coolest" job: for two years he was based in Aruba, part of a team developing an 18-hole Robert Trent Jones–designed golf resort and housing project.

"That was pretty neat, going to work, and then being able to go windsurfing after, and go to the beach," Powell said.

He chose the CMA route over other designations because he enjoys "making things happen in the future" rather then auditing and reporting about past periods' financial record keeping.

Since 2001, as Chief Financial Officer of the Boston Pizza restaurant empire, and of its parent company T & M Management Services, Powell oversees the core Boston Pizza business as well as the publicly traded Boston Pizza Royalties Income Fund, and other retail and real estate interests in North America.

On a given day, Powell's schedule might include talking to investors or designing an option plan for senior management. He regularly uses financial statements, calling them "tools that you refer to, to help impact the business."

"At the CFO level, we marry finance skills—which is all about maximizing shareholder wealth—with accounting knowledge," Powell explained. "The review is directed at optimizing the operating performance of the business and managing the capital structure."

In his view, accounting students who aim for careers as CFOs or CEOs require "passion for the business that goes far beyond the numbers." "They will draw on knowledge of business, including economics, law, marketing and many other disciplines in the course of completing their work—meaning that the work can be much more interesting than is generally portrayed in the media," Powell said.

With over 100 items on the Boston Pizza menu, Powell's favourite pizza is Hawaiian. But he fights the calories by combining his job overseeing the $800 million company with a different kind of spreadsheet: his golf scorecard.

Powell has boasted a handicap as low as eight, and plays on trips and at charity tournaments. The numbers he remembers best? Hitting an incredibly lucky four holes-in-one in three years.

"I think I can go the rest of my life without having [another] one," he chuckled.

—E.B.

INTRODUCTION

One of the first things I pointed out when we looked at Leon's Furniture Limited's (Leon's) financial statements in Chapter 2 was that the statements are consolidated. This means the single set of statements are an aggregation of more than one corporation's financial information. The financial statements of most public companies are consolidated. Consolidated financial statements are required under IFRS when one company (the parent) controls other companies (subsidiaries). For example, the consolidated financial statements of Rogers Communications Inc. aggregate those of several separate, well-known companies, including Rogers Wireless, Rogers Sportsnet, and the Toronto Blue Jays. An overview of the Rogers' corporate group is shown in Figure 11.1.[1]

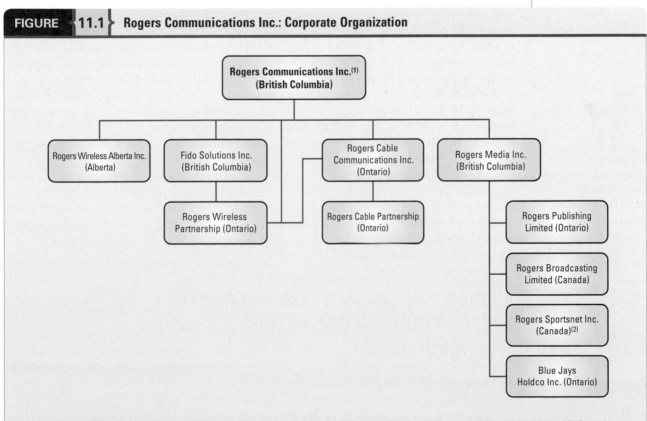

FIGURE 11.1 Rogers Communications Inc.: Corporate Organization

(1) Unless otherwise noted ownership is 100% with the exception of (i) 1 partership unit of RWP is held by Fido, 70,745,778 units of RWP are held by RCI, and 30,319,000 units of RWP are held by RCCI; (ii) Fido holds 2,657,000 First Preferred shares of RCCI and 1,000,000 Series XXXIV Preferred shares of RCI; and (iii) 1 partnership unit of Rogers Cable Partnership is held by RCI and 100,000,001 units are held by RCCI.

(2) Directly and indirectly Rogers Broadcasting Limited holds 100% of Rogers Sportsnet Inc. through its subsidiary Rogers Sports Group Inc.

The idea behind consolidated financial statements is to provide financial information about an entire economic entity, rather than just about the individual pieces. While the concept of consolidated financial statements is straightforward, it's among the most complicated topics in accounting. People studying to become accountants can spend an entire course on the subject.

Gaining control of another company is only one outcome of investment by one corporation in another. Some investments allow the investing corporation to influence the decisions of those companies, but not to control them. Other investments, usually small ones, give the investing corporation no more influence than any small investor would have. These investments, with their different degrees of influence, are each accounted for differently.

In many ways, this topic, particularly consolidation itself, is beyond the scope of an introductory accounting course. However, because consolidated financial statements are encountered so frequently, and because investment-related accounts like goodwill and non-controlling interest are so commonly seen in financial statements, it's important, even for the accounting novice, to be familiar with the subject. To that end, this chapter will provide a discussion of how corporations account for investment in other corporations and how those investments affect the financial statements. The intent is to provide just enough insight into accounting for investments that you can understand and interpret financial statement information relating to it. The appendix to this chapter will address some of the more complex aspects of this topic.

WHY DO COMPANIES INVEST IN OTHER COMPANIES?

There are many reasons why one company invests in another. The reason can be as simple as needing to find a place to invest a temporary surplus of cash. For example, seasonal businesses may have excess cash during certain times of the year. Companies may be accumulating cash for future expansion or acquisitions and invest to earn a reasonable return on it in the meantime. This can be achieved by purchasing the debt or equity of other companies. These investments might provide opportunities to earn dividend, interest, and capital gains income for the investing company.

Other investments are strategic. Companies might purchase competing companies to reduce competition and expand their presence in a market. They might purchase their customers to provide markets for their products or their suppliers to ensure the availability of inputs.

www.saputo.com
www.weston.ca
www.neilsondairy.com
www.rogers.com
www.poolexpert.com
www.onex.com

For example, in 2008 Saputo Inc. purchased Neilson Dairy from George Weston Limited (which also owns Loblaw) for $465 million. By purchasing Neilson Dairy, Saputo increased its presence in Ontario. Also in 2008, Rogers Communications Inc. acquired PoolExpert Inc., a leading website for fantasy sports. By acquiring PoolExpert, Rogers obtained an established sports fantasy business that ties in with its other sports business.

Companies might also purchase all or part of other companies to diversify. Some businesses are cyclical—their performance depends on where the economy is in the business cycle. Cyclical businesses will be profitable in some years and not in others. By diversifying their investments in different businesses and geographic areas, companies try to mitigate the effect of the business cycle. For example, Onex Corporation has major investments in heath care, entertainment, electronics, and financial services.

ACCOUNTING FOR INVESTMENTS IN OTHER CORPORATIONS: INTRODUCTION

How an **investor corporation**, or *investor* (a corporation with an investment in another corporation), accounts for its investment in an **investee corporation**, or *investee* (a corporation in which an investor corporation has invested), depends on the influence it has over the investee corporation. For accounting purposes, there are three levels of influence:

1. **Control** An investor controls an investee and can make all its important decisions. An investee that is controlled is called a subsidiary of the investor, and the financial statements of the investor and investee are aggregated into a single set of consolidated financial statements.

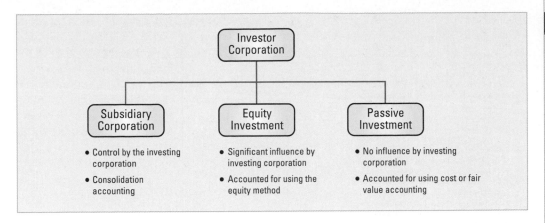

FIGURE **11.2**

Types of Investments in Other Corporations

2. Significant influence—The investor doesn't control an investee but can affect its important decisions. The investor corporation should use the equity method of accounting.

3. Passive investment—The investor has no influence over the decision making of the investee (or at least no more influence than any other small investor). The investment is accounted for at cost or fair value, depending on the type of investment.

These different types of investments in other corporations are summarized in Figure 11.2. We will discuss the methods of accounting for investments in other corporations in detail in the following sections.

CONTROL: ACCOUNTING FOR SUBSIDIARIES

An investor is said to **control** an investee if it is able to make the important decisions of the investee and determine its strategic operating, financing, and investing policies on an ongoing basis, without the support of other shareholders. In other words, the managers of the investor can set the key policies of the investee.

Control usually means the investor owns more than 50 percent of the votes of the investee. Note that 50 percent of votes isn't necessarily the same as 50 percent of common shares. For example, Onex Corporation (Onex) controls a number of companies, despite owning less than 50 percent of the common shares of each. Onex owns 13 percent of the outstanding common shares of Celestica Inc. but has 79 percent of the votes. This is because each of Onex's common shares has 25 votes, whereas those held by other shareholders have only one vote each. Exhibit 11.1 lists the companies that Onex controls, the percentage of the common shares that it owns, and the percentage of the votes that it has.[2] This type of arrangement is quite common in Canada but is far less so in other countries.

An investor with control is referred to as the **parent corporation** (parent) and the investee is called a **subsidiary corporation** (subsidiary). IFRS require parent corporations to prepare **consolidated financial statements**, which aggregate the accounting information of a parent corporation and all of its subsidiaries into a single set of statements. This means that each line in the consolidated financial statements reflects the assets, liabilities, revenues, expenses, and cash flows of the parent and all its subsidiaries. Figure 11.1 shows the corporate structure of Rogers. You can see that there are ten separate corporations and partnerships that are 100 percent owned and controlled by Rogers Communications Inc., and all of these are consolidated into a single set of financial statements.

Consolidated financial statements apply the entity assumption: the consolidated entity is a group of corporations under the control of a parent. The consolidated statements are intended to provide stakeholders interested in the parent—for example, shareholders—with a single set of financial statements that reflect the assets, liabilities, equity, revenues, and expenses of all the corporations controlled by the parent.

As we proceed through this discussion, it's important to keep in mind that consolidated financial statements are an accounting creation. The individual subsidiaries and the parent are

	December 31, 2008		December 31, 2007	
	Onex Ownership	Voting	Onex Ownership	Voting
Investments made through Onex				
Celestica Inc. ("Celestica")	13%	79%	13%	79%
Cineplex Entertainment	23%	(a)	23%	(a)
Sitel Worldwide Corporation ("Sitel Worldwide")	66%	88%	66%	88%
Investments made through Onex and Onex Partners I				
Center for Diagnostic Imaging, Inc. ("CDI")	19%	100%	19%	100%
Cosmetic Essence, Inc. ("CEI")	21%	100%	21%	100%
Emergency Medical Services Corporation ("EMSC")	29%	97%	29%	97%
Res-Care, Inc. ("ResCare")	6%	(a)	6%	(a)
Skilled Healthcare Group, Inc. ("Skilled Healthcare")	9%	89%	9%	90%
Spirit AeroSystems, Inc. ("Spirit AeroSystems")	7%	76%	7%	76%
Investments made through Onex and Onex Partners II				
Allison Transmission, Inc. ("Allison Transmission")	15%	(a)	15%	(a)
Carestream Health, Inc. ("Carestream Health")	39%	100%	39%	100%
Hawker Beechcraft Corporation ("Hawker Beechcraft")	20%	(a)	20%	(a)
RSI Home Products, Inc. ("RSI")	20%	50%[a]	–	–
Tube City IMS Corporation ("Tube City IMS")	35%	100%	35%	100%
Investments made through Onex, Onex Partners I and Onex Partners II				
Husky Injection Molding Systems Ltd. ("Husky")	36%	100%	36%	100%
The Warranty Group, Inc. ("The Warranty Group")	29%	100%	30%	100%
Other invesments				
ONCAP II L.P.	44%	100%	44%	100%
Onex Real Estate Partners ("Onex Real Estate")	86%	100%	86%	100%

(a) Onex exerts significant influence over these equity-accounted investments through its right to appoint members to the Board of Directors (or Board of Trustees) of the entities.

all separate legal entities; each has its own limited legal liability and each must file its own tax return. The consolidated group isn't a legal entity and doesn't file a tax return.

In the consolidated balance sheet, a subsidiary's assets and liabilities are recorded at the amount the parent paid for them on the date the subsidiary was purchased. This is no different than if the parent purchased the assets and liabilities separately. What's different is that the subsidiary continues to own the assets and liabilities and to report them on its own balance sheet so that these assets and liabilities are reported in two places—the subsidiary's balance sheet and the consolidated balance sheet. The amounts reported for the same assets and liabilities may be different on the two balance sheets. Assets and liabilities accounted for at cost (for example, inventory; property, plant, and equipment; and unearned revenue) are reported on the subsidiary's balance sheet at their cost when the subsidiary purchased them; on the consolidated balance sheet, they are recorded at the cost to parent when the subsidiary was purchased. For example, a piece of land purchased by the subsidiary for $1,000 in 1990 but valued at $2,000 when the subsidiary was acquired by the parent in 2013 would be reported on the subsidiary's balance sheet at $1,000 and on the consolidated balance sheet at $2,000. If fair value was used instead of cost, the valuations could be the same. Because the valuations on the subsidiary and consolidated balance sheets may be different, the two can't simply be added together to get the consolidated amount.

We will examine the accounting for the purchase of a subsidiary with an example. Throughout this chapter, the examples assume the investor uses cash to make the investment. Investments can also involve shares of the parent, debt, and non-cash assets. On June 30, 2014, Pefferlaw Ltd. (Pefferlaw) bought 100 percent of the shares of Schuler Corp. (Schuler) from its shareholders for $20,000,000. Pefferlaw would make the following journal entry in its accounting records (not the consolidated statements) to record the investment in Schuler:

Dr. Investment in Schuler (asset +)   20,000,000
    Cr. Cash (asset −)   20,000,000
To record the purchase of 100 percent of the shares of Schuler Corp on June 30, 2014

The investment has no effect at all on Schuler's accounting records or its financial statements because Pefferlaw purchased the shares from Schuler's shareholders, not from the corporation itself.

To prepare consolidated financial statements, Pefferlaw must identify the assets and liabilities it purchased and determine the amount it paid for each. This can be difficult because Pefferlaw purchased the entire company, not individual assets and liabilities, so the purchase price must be allocated to the individual assets and liabilities. To accomplish this, the market or fair values of all of Schuler's identifiable assets and liabilities must be determined as of the date of the purchase. These are the amounts that are reported in the consolidated financial statements. **Identifiable assets and liabilities** are tangible and intangible assets and liabilities that can be specifically identified and measured with some objectivity. Also remember that an asset or liability's cost is its market value on the date it was acquired.

This process of determining the fair value of the assets and liabilities of a subsidiary occurs only once—when the subsidiary is purchased. (Throughout this chapter, the term **fair value** refers to the estimated market value of the subsidiary's assets and liabilities on the date the subsidiary was purchased.) From that point on, the consolidated financial statements are based on the amounts determined as of the date of the purchase. Of course, assets and liabilities normally valued at fair value would be restated each time the consolidated statements are prepared. Table 11.1 summarizes the book and fair values of Schuler's assets and liabilities on June 30, 2014.

TABLE 11.1	Schuler Corp.: Net Asset Fair Values and Carrying Amounts		
	Fair value on June 30, 2014	**Carrying amount on June 30, 2014**	**Difference**
Current assets	$ 5,500,000	$ 5,000,000	$ 500,000
Capital assets	21,500,000	14,000,000	7,500,000
Liabilities	(9,000,000)	(8,000,000)	(1,000,000)
	$18,000,000	$11,000,000	$7,000,000

There are a couple of things to notice in Table 11.1:

- First, there are two measurements of Schuler's assets and liabilities. The carrying amounts appear in Schuler's own financial statements. The fair values on June 30 are the amounts Pefferlaw paid for Schuler's assets and liabilities. The fair values appear on Pefferlaw's consolidated balance sheet.

- Second, only $18,000,000 of the purchase price has been attributed to specific assets and liabilities. The remaining $2,000,000 is **goodwill**. (Remember that goodwill = purchase price − fair value of identifiable assets and liabilities purchased.)

KNOWLEDGE CHECK

www.mcgrawhill
connect.ca

- ❏ Identify and explain the three levels of influence that an investor corporation can have over an investee corporation.

- ❏ What are consolidated financial statements, and under what circumstances are they prepared?

- ❏ In consolidated financial statements, what is the basis of valuing a subsidiary's assets and liabilities?

The Consolidated Balance Sheet on the Date the Subsidiary Is Purchased

We now have the information needed to prepare Pefferlaw's consolidated balance sheet on June 30, 2014, the date Pefferlaw purchased the shares of Schuler. Pefferlaw's consolidated balance sheet includes the following:

a. The amounts reported on Pefferlaw's own balance sheet on June 30, 2014.

    b. The fair value of Schuler's assets and liabilities (not the amounts on Schuler's own balance sheet) on June 30, 2014.

    c. The goodwill from the acquisition of Schuler.

Pefferlaw's consolidated balance sheet *doesn't* include these items:

    a. The "investment in subsidiary account" on the balance sheet, which is replaced by the actual assets and liabilities of the subsidiary.

    b. The shareholders' equity of the subsidiary, which is reflected in the shareholders' equity of the parent.

The contents of Pefferlaw's consolidated balance sheet on June 30, 2014, the date Pefferlaw purchased the shares of Schuler, is shown in Table 11.2.

> The fair value of Schuler's assets and liabilities on the date of purchase, not the carrying amounts on Schuler's own balance sheet, are used in the consolidated balance sheet.

> Notice that the fair value of Schuler's $20,000,000 net assets (assets − liabilities = $29,000,000 − $9, 000,000) is the same amount as in the Investment in Schuler account. Schuler's net assets replace the investment account in the consolidated statements.

> The shareholders' equity section of the subsidiary's balance sheet isn't included in the consolidated financial statements.

TABLE 11.2   Pefferlaw: Consolidated Balance Sheet

	Column 1	Column 2	Column 3
	Balance sheet of Pefferlaw Ltd., June 30, 2014	**Fair value of Schuler Corp.'s assets and liabilities, June 30, 2014**	**Consolidated balance sheet, June 30, 2014**
Current assets	$ 29,000,000	$ 5,500,000	$ 34,500,000
Capital assets	52,000,000	21,500,000	73,500,000
Investment in Schuler	20,000,000		
Goodwill		2,000,000	2,000,000
	$101,000,000	$29,000,000	$110,000,000
Liabilities	$ 38,000,000	$ 9,000,000	$ 47,000,000
Capital stock	22,000,000		22,000,000
Retained earnings	41,000,000		41,000,000
	$101,000,000		$110,000,000

- Column 1 shows Pefferlaw's balance sheet (this information has not been shown before). Notice that this isn't the same as Pefferlaw's consolidated balance sheet. Unconsolidated financial statements reporting on the parent alone are also prepared. In its unconsolidated balance sheet, all that is reported about a parent's subsidiaries is the single line, investment in the subsidiaries (the investment in Schuler account). These unconsolidated statements are required for tax purposes and may be provided to other stakeholders, such as bankers, but aren't usually widely distributed.

- Column 2 shows the fair value of the Schuler's assets and liabilities on June 30, 2014. These are the amounts included on the consolidated balance sheet, but *not* on Schuler's own balance sheet (shown in Table 11.1). Schuler's capital stock and retained earnings aren't shown because they aren't included in consolidated shareholders' equity.

- Column 3 is the consolidated balance sheet. The goodwill only appears on the consolidated balance sheet. Goodwill is calculated as

$$\text{Goodwill} = \text{Purchase price} - \text{Fair value of identifiable assets and liabilities purchased}$$

$$\$2,000,000 = \$20,000,000 - \$18,000,000$$

The purchase of Schuler doesn't affect the consolidated income statement for the year ended June 30, 2014 because the purchase took place on the last day of Schuler's fiscal year. The revenues and expenses of a subsidiary are incorporated into the consolidated income statement only after the date of the purchase. The income statement effects of consolidation are discussed in the appendix.

QUESTION FOR CONSIDERATION

When an entity purchases a subsidiary, the amounts included in the consolidated balance sheet are the fair value of the subsidiary's assets and liabilities on the date of the purchase, not the amounts reported in the subsidiary's own balance sheet. Explain why this treatment isn't a violation of historical cost accounting.

Answer: Recording a subsidiary's assets and liabilities at their fair values in the consolidated balance sheet on the date of the purchase isn't a violation of the historical cost accounting because the subsidiary's assets and liabilities are purchased when the parent purchases the subsidiary. Assigning fair values to these assets and liabilities occurs only once—when the subsidiary is actually purchased. The fair values assigned on that date form the basis of valuing those assets and liabilities in the consolidated financial statements from then on.

Non-controlling Interest

When a parent controls a subsidiary but owns less than 100 percent it, "non-controlling interest" (or minority interest) accounts appear in the consolidated financial statements. IFRS require that the consolidated balance sheet include 100 percent of the fair value of a subsidiary's assets and liabilities, even if the parent owns less than 100 percent of them. IFRS also require the consolidated income statements to include 100 percent of the revenues and expenses of a subsidiary, even if it isn't 100 percent owned.

The rationale for this approach is that even if it doesn't own 100 percent of the subsidiary's net assets, the parent nevertheless controls 100 percent of them, and the consolidated statements should report what the parent controls. The problem is that the consolidated statements then contain assets, liabilities, revenues, and expenses that don't belong to the parent shareholders. What's to be done with the amounts not owned by the parent?

The answer is **non-controlling interest**. On the consolidated balance sheet, non-controlling interest is reported in the equity section that represents the net assets of a subsidiary that are owned by the non-parent shareholders of the subsidiary. On the consolidated income statement, non-controlling interest represents the portion of net income of the subsidiary that belongs to the non-parent shareholders. Net income is calculated as it normally is and then allocated between the parent's shareholders and the non-controlling shareholders. The parent's share of net income goes to retained earnings, and the non-controlling interest's share is closed to non-controlling interest on the balance sheet.

INSIGHT

Non-controlling Interest

Non-controlling interest appears in consolidated financial statements only because 100 percent of a subsidiary's net assets, revenues, and expenses are reported even if the parent owns less than 100 percent of the subsidiary. If only the percentage of the subsidiary's net assets, revenues, and expenses owned by the parent was included, there would be no non-controlling interest.

> ## ✓ KNOWLEDGE CHECK
>
> ❑ What is goodwill and how is it calculated?
>
> ❑ What is non-controlling interest and why does it appear in some entities' consolidated financial statements?

Are Consolidated Financial Statements Useful?

Now that we've looked at the basics of accounting for subsidiaries (which aren't all that basic!), we can consider the usefulness of consolidated financial statements. Consolidated statements provide, in a single set of financial statements, financial information about a group of corporations under the control of a parent. This information might be useful to stakeholders who want stewardship information about the entire economic entity or to evaluate the performance of the corporate group as a whole. Consolidated financial statements may be an effective way for a corporate group to communicate the "big picture" to various stakeholders. With control over its subsidiaries the parent controls the operations of the subsidiaries and can move assets from corporation to corporation. For example, a parent company that is short of cash could have a subsidiary declare a dividend, make a loan, or pay management fees to the parent to help it meet its cash needs. Consolidated statements allow users to see all the resources available to the corporate group.

Consolidated financial statements do not include transactions and profits generated among entities in the corporate group. This means that revenue and profit from exchanges between a parent and a subsidiary, or among the subsidiaries in a consolidated group, aren't included in the consolidated financial statements (this topic is explored in the appendix to this chapter). These **intercompany transactions** and profits aren't meaningful (it would be like selling your computer to yourself and saying you have revenue and profit) and they can be misleading because they make it look like there is more economic activity than there really is. The financial statements of the individual corporations in a consolidated group do include intercompany transactions.

For many stakeholders, however, consolidated financial statements are an obstacle to effective decision making because they aggregate information about the individual corporations in the consolidated group. The details about the different businesses of the parent and its subsidiaries are lost in consolidated financial statements; it's virtually impossible to determine the companies, lines of business, and geographical areas in the group that are doing well and those are doing poorly.

The interests of financial analysts and other sophisticated stakeholders who want to use financial statements as a starting point for predicting future earnings or cash flows may not be served by consolidated statements. For example, the statements can significantly limit the usefulness of ratio analysis. Combining the accounting information of several companies, often those in different industries, results in ratios that aren't representative of any industry. Onex Corporation, mentioned earlier, controls businesses in electronics manufacturing, aerostructures, health care, financial services, customer support services, and metal services. What sense can be made of financial ratios that comprise information about companies in all these very different industries?

IFRS try to help stakeholders by requiring that public companies provide information about the different business activities and the different geographic areas they operate in. This disaggregation of information by types of products and services, geographic location, and major customers is called **segment disclosure**. Onex Corporation's segment information note is shown in Exhibit 11.2.[3] Onex identifies seven industry segments and five geographic segments. For each industry segment, a complete income statement is provided along with selected information from the balance sheet. Revenue and selected balance sheet information is provided for each geographic segment. However, a complete set of financial statements for each segment isn't provided. Stakeholders can gain some very useful insights from the segment disclosure. Onex's segment information can be used to determine which segments generate the most revenue, which is the most profitable, and which requires the largest investment in assets.

29. INFORMATION BY INDUSTRY AND GEOGRAPHIC SEGMENTS (cont'd)

2008 Industry Segments

	Electronics Manufacturing Services	Aero-structures	Healthcare	Financial Services	Customer Support Services	Metal Services	Other	Consolidated Total
Revenues	$ 8,220	$ 3,965	$ 6,152	$ 1,388	$ 1,856	$ 3,112	$ 2,188	$ 26,881
Cost of sales	(7,556)	(3,215)	(4,504)	(665)	(1,197)	(2,932)	(1,650)	(21,719)
Selling, general and administrative expenses	(274)	(188)	(740)	(460)	(520)	(71)	(491)	(2,744)
Earnings before the undernoted items	390	562	908	263	139	109	47	2,418
Amortization of property, plant and equipment	(97)	(117)	(186)	(12)	(64)	(65)	(83)	(624)
Amortization of intangible assets and deferred charges	(16)	(5)	(229)	(19)	(19)	(13)	(65)	(366)
Interest expense of operating companies	(53)	(42)	(255)	(9)	(69)	(41)	(81)	(550)
Interest income (expense)	16	20	10	–	2	–	(13)	35
Earnings (loss) from equity-accounted investments	–	–	13	–	–	–	(335)	(322)
Foreign exchange gains (loss)	(19)	(6)	(9)	–	10	–	107	83
Stock-based compensation recovery (expense)	(25)	(17)	(5)	(1)	–	–	190	142
Other income (expense)	–	4	(1)	(16)	–	–	1	(12)
Gains on sales of operating investments, net	–	–	–	–	–	–	4	4
Acquisition, restructuring and other expenses	(39)	–	(92)	(7)	(36)	–	(46)	(220)
Writedown of goodwill, intangible assets and long-lived assets	(1,061)	–	(142)	–	(129)	(1)	(316)	(1,649)
Earnings (loss) before income taxes, non-controlling interests and discontinued operations	$ (904)	$ 399	$ 12	$ 199	$ (166)	$ (11)	$ (590)	$ (1,061)
Recovery of (provision for) income taxes	(6)	(137)	(108)	(65)	(3)	4	63	(252)
Non-controlling interests	791	(245)	34	(94)	(1)	5	531	1,021
Earnings (loss) from continuing operations	(119)	17	(62)	40	(170)	(2)	4	(292)
Earnings from discontinued operations	–	–	–	–	–	–	9	9
Net earnings (loss)	(119)	17	(62)	40	(170)	(2)	13	(283)
Total assets	$ 4,612	$ 4,821	$ 6,660	$ 6,095	$ 1,020	$ 1,026	$ 5,498	$ 29,732
Long-term debt[a]	$ 892	$ 697	$ 3,367	$ 237	$ 796	$ 519	$ 1,167	$ 7,675
Property, plant and equipment additions	$ 124	$ 299	$ 225	$ 21	$ 67	$ 73	$ 50	$ 859
Goodwill additions	$ –	$ –	$ 64	$ –	$ 7	$ 4	$ 96	$ 171
Goodwill	$ –	$ 3	$ 1,398	$ 419	$ 199	$ 355	$ 572	$ 2,946

(a) Long-term debt includes current portion, excludes capital leases and is net of deferred charges.

Geographic Segments

	2008						2007					
	Canada	U.S.	Europe	Asia and Oceania	Other	Total	Canada	U.S.	Europe	Asia and Oceania	Other	Total
Revenue	$ 1,346	$ 13,259	$ 4,412	$ 5,978	$ 1,886	$ 26,881	$ 1,619	$ 11,235	$ 3,607	$ 5,358	$ 1,614	$ 23,433
Property, plant and equipment	$ 363	$ 2,583	$ 506	$ 467	$ 147	$ 4,066	$ 337	$ 2,301	$ 459	$ 325	$ 67	$ 3,489
Intangible assets	$ 432	$ 1,766	$ 408	$ 108	$ 41	$ 2,755	$ 434	$ 1,638	$ 458	$ 118	$ 44	$ 2,692
Goodwill	$ 212	$ 2,224	$ 357	$ 117	$ 36	$ 2,946	$ 191	$ 1,853	$ 441	$ 930	$ 28	$ 3,443

Revenues are attributed to geographic areas based on the destinations of the products and/or services.

For some stakeholders, even consolidated financial statements with segment information aren't adequate. Lenders are concerned that the legal entities they lend to can make interest and principal payments. The lender is only interested in consolidated statements if a loan is being made to the parent, or if the parent is guaranteeing a loan to a subsidiary. Otherwise, a lender needs the financial statements of the corporation actually borrowing the money.

Consolidated financial statements are intended for stakeholders of the consolidated entity and are of little interest to the non-controlling shareholders or those of a subsidiary. The non-controlling interest on the consolidated statements provides little useful information to stakeholders interested in subsidiaries, who would want to see the financial statements of the subsidiary itself. Shareholders are entitled to receive financial statements of the subsidiaries in which they own shares.

Consolidated financial statements are also not relevant for tax purposes. Each individual corporation is required to file tax returns with the Canada Revenue Agency and provincial taxation authorities. This means that each corporation must prepare financial statements for tax purposes regardless of ownership.

It's important to note that the problems we're discussing aren't caused by consolidated financial statements but by the fact that the companies involved are in many different businesses. Consolidated financial statements are the accounting effect of this situation.

INSIGHT

Accounting for subsidiaries provides managers with significant opportunities to make choices that will influence the consolidated financial statements for many years. When a new subsidiary is acquired, management must allocate the purchase price to the identifiable assets and liabilities and to goodwill. Because the process of assigning market values is imprecise, management can make choices that satisfy its reporting objectives. Different managers could come up with very different reasonable amounts of goodwill for the same acquisition, and different reasonable valuations for the same identifiable assets and liabilities. Because goodwill doesn't have to be amortized, managers concerned about net income might allocate less of the purchase price to depreciable assets and inventory so that more would be included in goodwill.

SIGNIFICANT INFLUENCE

When an investor corporation has **significant influence**, it can impact the strategic operating, investing, and financing decisions of the investee corporation, even though it doesn't have control. IFRS suggest that owning between 20 percent and 50 percent of the votes of an investee company is an indication of significant influence. However, judgment must be used to determine whether significant influence exists in a particular situation. An investor corporation could own 30 percent of the voting shares of an investee but not have significant influence because another investor has control. On the other hand, an investment of less than 20 percent could provide significant influence if, for example, the investor has representation on the investee corporation's board of directors.

When a corporation has significant influence over another entity, the equity method of accounting should be used. The **equity method of accounting** is essentially the same as the consolidation method of accounting for subsidiaries; however, the information appears in the financial statements in a very different way. Instead of aggregating the financial statement of the investee line by line, information about investees subject to significant influence is presented on a single line on the balance sheet and a single line on the income statement.

Using the equity method, an investment is initially recorded on the investor's balance sheet at cost. The balance sheet amount is then adjusted each period by the investor's share of the investee's net income, less dividends declared by the investee. The income statement reports the investor's share of the investee's net income, which is determined by multiplying the investee's net income by the percentage of the investee that the investor owns. The amount is then adjusted for intercompany transactions and other adjustments.

The rationale for using the equity method is that a significant investor can influence important policies of the investee, such as the timing and amount of dividends, which can allow the investor to manage its own earnings. Under the equity method, dividends from an investment aren't considered income and, thus, this type of income manipulation isn't possible. A few points about the equity method of accounting are worth noting:

1. While an equity investment account changes to reflect the earnings of an investee and the dividends it declares, the amount reported on the balance sheet doesn't reflect the market value of the investment. The changes to the balance sheet amount are based on IFRS net income, not on changes in the investee's market value.

2. The income reported from an investment accounted for using the equity method isn't an indication of the amount of dividends or cash that will be forthcoming from the investee. It is simply

an allocation of the investor's share of the investee's income. An equity investment may not be very liquid and the investor may be limited in its ability to obtain cash from the investee.

3. The equity investment account on the investor's balance sheet provides virtually no information about the investee corporation. Information about investments the investor has significant influence over is usually not included in the segment disclosures described earlier. If the investee corporation is public, the financial statements of the investee can be examined. If the investee is private, then little will be known about it.

EXHIBIT 11.3

**Enbridge Inc.:
Equity Accounting**

www.enbridge.com

ENBRIDGE INC.

CONSOLIDATED STATEMENTS OF FINANCIAL POSITION

December 31,	2008	2007
(millions of Canadian dollars)		
Assets		
Current Assets		
Cash and cash equivalents	541.7	166.7
Accounts receivable and other (Note 6)	2,322.5	2,388.7
Inventory (Note 7)	844.7	709.4
	3,708.9	3,264.8
Property, Plant and Equipment, net (Note 8)	16,389.6	12,597.6
✱ Long-Term Investments (Note 10)	2,491.8	2,076.3
Deferred Amounts and Other Assets (Note 11)	1,318.4	1,182.0
Intangible Assets (Note 12)	225.3	212.0
Goodwill (Note 13)	389.2	388.0
Future Income Taxes (Note 24)	178.2	186.7
	24,701.4	19,907.4

CONSOLIDATED STATEMENTS OF EARNINGS

Year ended December 31,	2008	2007	2006
(millions of Canadian dollars, except per share amounts)			
Revenues			
Commodity sales	13,431.9	9,536.4	8,264.5
Transportation and other services	2,699.4	2,383.0	2,380.0
	16,131.3	11,919.4	10,644.5
Expenses			
Commodity costs	12,792.0	9,009.5	7,824.6
Operating and administrative	1,312.2	1,163.7	1,084.2
Depreciation and amortization	658.4	596.9	587.4
	14,762.6	10,770.1	9,496.2
	1,368.7	1,149.3	1,148.3
✱ Income from Equity Investments	177.1	167.8	180.3
Other Investment Income (Note 26)	202.7	195.1	107.8
Interest Expense (Note 15)	(550.8)	(550.0)	(567.1)
Gain on Sale of Investment in CLH (Note 5)	694.6	–	–
	1,892.3	962.2	869.3
Non-Controlling Interests	(55.7)	(45.9)	(54.7)
	1,836.6	916.3	814.6
Income Taxes (Note 24)	(508.9)	(209.2)	(192.3)
Earnings	1,327.7	707.1	622.3

EXHIBIT 11.3

(continued)
Enbridge Inc.:
Equity Accounting

10. LONG-TERM INVESTMENTS

December 31, (millions of Canadian dollars)	Ownership Interest	2008	2007
✳ Equity Investments			
Liquids Pipelines			
Chicap Pipeline	–	–	17.2
Sponsored Investments			
The Partnership	27.0%	2,013.2	944.8
Gas Distribution and Services			
Noverco Common Shares	32.1%	10.8	11.6
Other		–	1.5
International			
Compañía Logística de Hidrocarburos CLH, S.A.	–	–	626.4
Corporate	10%–35%	9.1	16.1
Other Investments			
Gas Distribution and Services			
Noverco Preferred Shares		181.4	181.4
Fuel Cell Energy		25.0	25.0
International			
Oleoducto Central S.A.		223.3	223.3
Corporate			
Value Creation		29.0	29.0
		✳ 2,491.8	2,076.3

An example of equity accounting can be seen in Exhibit 11.3, which shows how Enbridge Inc. reports its investments accounted for using the equity method.[4] Enbridge reports long-term investments of $2,491,800,000 on its December 31, 2008, balance sheet. Note 10 provides a description of these investments, including $2,033,100,000 of investments accounted for using the equity method (these are the ones at the top of Note 10). The note also shows the ownership interest Enbridge has in each equity investment. On the income statement, Enbridge reports $177.1 million in income from equity investments. The items to examine in Exhibit 11.3 are identified with a ✳.

CANADIAN GAAP FOR PRIVATE ENTERPRISE

Consolidation and equity accounting are mostly relevant for public companies. Companies that follow Canadian GAAP for Private Enterprises can elect not to consolidate or equity account even if they control or have significant influence over an investee corporation. These companies can record subsidiaries using the equity method or simply at cost, and they can account for investees over which they have significant influence at cost. Accounting at cost means the investment remains on the balance sheet at the original amount paid, until it's sold. Private companies may choose to avoid consolidation and equity accounting because it's costly and in many cases doesn't provide useful information to stakeholders.

PASSIVE INVESTMENTS

Financial instruments are assets and liabilities that represent the contractual rights or obligations of the entity to receive or pay cash or other financial assets. We have discussed several financial instruments so far in the book, including accounts receivable, accounts payable, bank loans, and bonds. Financial instruments also include derivative securities—assets or liabilities that derive their value from another asset or liability, such as bonds, shares, or commodities. In this section we'll discuss a category of investments referred to as **passive investments**—investments for which the investor corporation can't influence the strategic decision making of the investee corporation. These investments don't give the investor corporation control or significant influence.

All investments in non-voting securities—securities such as debt, preferred shares, or non-voting common shares—are classified as passive investments because without voting power it isn't possible to have influence. Voting shares are passive investments when the investor corporation holds a relatively small proportion of the investee's shares. IFRS suggest that holdings of less than 20 percent of the voting shares of an investee is a passive investment; however, 20 percent is only a guideline. A 10 percent investment that includes representation on the board of directors could give the investor corporation significant influence.

We'll look at three categories of passive investments, each with a different accounting treatment:

- **Held-to-maturity investments** are those with a maturity date, fixed or determinable payments (like interest payments), and intent and ability on the part of management to hold the investment to maturity. Because of the maturity date requirement, common shares and any other investments that don't have a specified life are excluded from this category.

- **Trading investments** are any investments that management designates as a trading investment. Investments in this category are actively bought and sold for profit making.

- **Available-for-sale investments** is the default category. Any investment that doesn't give control or significant influence to the investor corporation or that doesn't meet the criteria for classification as a held-to-maturity or trading investment is considered part of this group.

Management intent plays an important role in the classification of investments. This requirement provides management with the opportunity to use this flexibility to achieve its reporting objectives. This is especially relevant because each of the types of investments is accounted for differently. The accounting treatments for the different categories of investment are summarized in Figure 11.3.

Held-to-maturity investments are accounted for at cost; changes in the market value are ignored. The investment is reported on the balance sheet at cost and gains and losses on the income statement would only be recognized if the investment were sold (which normally shouldn't occur since they are supposed to be held to maturity). Held-to-maturity investments can be written down if they are permanently impaired. Impairment would reduce the amount that the investor could expect to receive at maturity, so a writedown would be an appropriate conservative action to take.

Trading and available-for-sale investments are reported on the balance sheet at their market value. Changes in the market value of these investments while they are owned by an investor are called **unrealized holding gains or losses**—a change in the market value not supported by a transaction as the investments in question aren't sold. **Realized holding gains and losses** occur when there is a sale. The accounting for unrealized gains and losses is different for trading and available-for-sale investments.

For trading investments, unrealized (and realized) gains and losses are recognized in income in the period they occur. If the market value of a trading investment increases by $100,000 during the year, a $100,000 gain is reported on the income statement, regardless of whether the

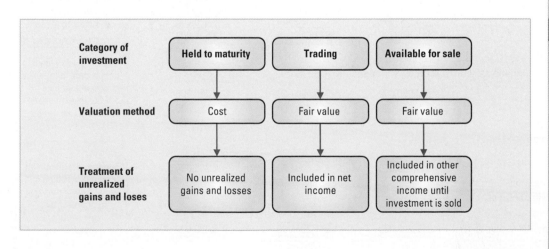

FIGURE 11.3

Accounting for Investments

investment is sold. This treatment makes sense for trading investments because the investing entity is buying and selling investments so it can profit from changes in their value. By recognizing the changing market value as income, economic gains and losses are being reflected as they occur, and income is a better indicator of performance. However, recognizing unrealized gains and losses can add significant variability to reported income.

For available-for-sale investments, unrealized gains and losses are included in other comprehensive income in the calculation of comprehensive income. They aren't included in the calculation of net income. Because available-for-sale investments can be sold if management decides to do so, the market value gives stakeholders an idea of how much would be realized from the sale. When the gain or loss is realized by selling the investment, the full amount of the unrealized gains and losses that were included in other comprehensive income (and are in accumulated other income/loss) are recognized in net income.

For all these investment categories, interest revenue is accrued as it's earned and dividend revenue is recognized when it's declared. There are no differences among the methods.

We can compare the accounting for the different methods with an example. On November 1, 2014 Elko Inc. (Elko) purchased $1,000,000 in corporate bonds as an investment. The bonds had a face value of $1,000,000 and a coupon rate of 7 percent, with interest paid semi-annually on April 30 and October 31. Recording the initial purchase of the bonds is the same with the three methods:

Dr. Investment in bonds	1,000,000	
Cr. Cash		1,000,000

Because of changes in the economy and a change in the issuing company's credit rating, the market value of the bonds on April 30, 2015 was $1,025,000. The balance sheet and income statement for Elko on April 30, 2014 using the three categories of passive investments is shown in Table 11.3. Key differences to note in the statements are shaded in the table.

TABLE 11.3   Elko Inc.: Financial Statements

Elko Inc.
Balance sheet as of April 30, 2014

	Hold to maturity	Trading	Available for sale
Assets			
All other assets	$11,500,000	$11,500,000	$11,500,000
Investment in bonds	1,000,000	1,025,000	1,025,000
	$12,500,000	$12,525,000	$12,525,000
Liabilities and Shareholders' Equity			
All liabilities	$ 7,000,000	$ 7,000,000	$ 7,000,000
Shareholders' equity:			
Capital stock	2,000,000	2,000,000	2,000,000
Retained earnings	3,500,000	3,525,000	3,500,000
Accumulated other comprehensive income: unrealized holding gains			25,000
Total shareholders' equity	5,500,000	5,525,000	5,525,000
	$12,500,000	$12,525,000	$12,525,000

> The investments are carried at cost if classified as hold to maturity and at market if classified as trading or available for sale.

> The unrealized holding gain is included in retained earnings if the investment is classified as trading and in accumulated other comprehensive income if classified as available for sale.

Elko Inc.
Income statement for the year ended April 30, 2014

	Hold to maturity	Trading	Available for sale
Revenue	$ 8,000,000	$ 8,000,000	$ 8,000,000
Expenses	6,870,000	6,870,000	6,870,000
Interest income from bonds	70,000	70,000	70,000
Unrealized holding gain on bond investment		25,000	
Net income	$ 1,200,000	$ 1,225,000	$ 1,200,000
Other comprehensive income:			
Unrealized holding gains on available for trade investments			25,000
Comprehensive income	$ 1,200,000	$ 1,225,000	$ 1,225,000

> The unrealized holding gain is only recognized in net income if the investment is classified as trading.

> The unrealized holding gain is included in other comprehensive income if the investment is classified as available for sale.

Notice that the balance sheet valuation of Elko's bonds is the market value if the bonds are classified as trading or available-for-sale investments. The gain is reflected in retained earnings if the bonds are classified as a trading investment because the unrealized gain is included in net income. Total equity is the same for both trading and available-for-sale investments, but the available-for-sale balance sheet includes the increase in market value as accumulated other comprehensive income. On the income statement, the unrealized gain is included in the calculation of net income when the bond is classified as a trading investment, whereas if it's classified as available for sale, the unrealized gain is classified as other comprehensive income.

If Elko sold the bonds on May 1, 2014 for $1,025,000, the financial statements would be as shown in Table 11.4. (Table 11.4 assumes a one-day period [May 1, 2014] and no economic activity on May 1 except the sale of the bonds.) There are a few key points to notice in Table 11.4:

- The investment in bonds account is now zero because the bonds have been sold.
- Retained earnings is the same for all three classifications of the investment. This is because once gains are realized there is no difference between the methods.
- There are no unrealized gains or losses reported on the income statement; the bonds were sold so the gain was realized.
- There is no gain reported when the bonds are classified as trading investments because the gain was recognized in the year ended April 30, 2014.
- The gain in available-for-sale net income is offset by a decrease in other comprehensive income. The balance in "accumulated other comprehensive income: unrealized holding gains" is now zero. Once gains or losses are realized, the previously unrealized amount is included in income and closed to retained earnings.

TABLE 11.4 Elko Inc.: Financial Statements after the Sale of Bonds			
Elko Inc. **Balance sheet as of May 1, 2014**			
	Hold to maturity	**Trading**	**Available for sale**
Assets			
All other assets	$12,525,000	$12,525,000	$12,525,000
Investment in bonds	0	0	0
	$12,525,000	$12,525,000	$12,525,000
Liabilities and Shareholders' Equity			
All liabilities	$ 7,000,000	$ 7,000,000	$ 7,000,000
Shareholders' equity			
Capital stock	2,000,000	2,000,000	2,000,000
Retained earnings	3,525,000	3,525,000	3,525,000
Accumulated other comprehensive income: unrealized holding gains			0
Total shareholders' equity	5,525,000	5,525,000	5,525,000
	$12,525,000	$12,525,000	$12,525,000
Elko Inc. **Income Statement for the one day period ended May 1, 2014**			
Revenue			
Expenses			
Interest income from bonds			
Gain on the sale of bonds	25,000		25,000
Unrealized holding gain on bond investment			
Net income	$ 25,000	$ 0	$ 25,000
Other comprehensive income:			
Unrealized holding gains on available for trade investments			(25,000)
Comprehensive income	$ 25,000	$ 0	$ 0

Once the gain is realized, the balance sheets under the three classifications are identical.

The gain is included in net income on the hold-to-maturity and available-for-sale income statements when it's realized. The gain was recognized on the trading income statement in the year ended April 30, 2014.

When the bond is classified as available for sale, the gain must be reclassified from other comprehensive income to gain on the sale of bonds on the income statement.

KNOWLEDGE CHECK

☐ What are the three categories of passive investments and what are the characteristics of each?

☐ What is the basis of valuation on the balance sheet for each category of investment?

☐ For each category of passive investment, explain how unrealized gains and losses are accounted for.

Solved Problem

Tecumseh Inc. (Tecumseh) is a small diversified company in eastern Canada. The company is owned and operated by the Doh family. Tecumseh operates a restaurant in Moncton, New Brunswick, a potato farm in Prince Edward Island, a fish processing plant in Newfoundland, and a trucking company operating throughout the Maritime provinces. The president of Tecumseh, Mark Doh, has approached your aunt Meaghan for a $250,000 loan to update the potato farm operations. Your aunt recently won a lottery and she has set up an investment fund to invest in small Canadian businesses. She thinks it would be fun to be involved in these businesses and hopes that it will be a good way for her to make some money from her winnings.

As part of the preliminary investigation, Tecumseh has provided a consolidated balance sheet for the two years ended December 31, 2014. The balance sheet consolidates all of Tecumseh's activities. This is the first time your aunt has ever seen a consolidated balance sheet (the other companies she has considered were not consolidated) and she's not sure what to make of it. She has asked you to write a report identifying the key aspects of the consolidated balance sheet she should be aware of when deciding whether to grant the loan to the potato farm. She would also like any other general observations you can make about the balance sheet. Tecumseh's consolidated balance sheets and some additional information are provided below.

Tecumseh Inc.
Consolidated balance sheets for the years ended December 31

	2014	2013		2014	2013
Cash	$ 55,000	$ 85,000	Bank loan	$ 125,000	$ 25,000
Accounts receivable	1,250,000	850,000	Accounts payable	1,110,000	985,000
Inventory	850,000	800,000	Unearned revenue	125,000	99,000
Other current assets	35,000	45,000		1,360,000	1,109,000
	2,190,000	1,780,000	Long-term debt	2,300,000	1,900,000
Plant, property, and equipment	4,285,000	4,021,000	Future income taxes	310,000	275,000
Goodwill	900,000	900,000		3,970,000	3,284,000
			Share capital	2,000,000	2,000,000
			Accumulated other comprehensive income	(25,000)	5,000
			Retained earnings	1,180,000	1,137,000
			Non-controlling interest	250,000	275,000
Total assets	$7,375,000	$6,701,000	Total liabilities and shareholders' equity	$7,375,000	$6,701,000

Additional Information

- Tecumseh Inc. has four operations: a restaurant, a potato farm, a fish processing plant, and a trucking company. Each operation is organized as a separate corporation.

- The non-controlling interest relates to the potato farm. The farmer who operates the farm owns 25 percent of the shares of the farm.

- The goodwill arose when Tecumseh purchased the trucking company.

Solution:

Dear Aunt Meaghan:

Thank you for the opportunity to prepare this report for you. Based on my review of Tecumseh's balance sheets for the years ended December 31, 2014 and 2013, I offer the following points for your consideration:

1. The first and most important point to remember is that you are being asked to lend money to the potato farm and these financial statements apply to the entire corporate group. That is, the assets and liabilities reported in the balance sheet belong to all of Tecumseh's operations, not just to the potato farm, which is a separate legal entity. This balance sheet doesn't give you much insight into the assets and liabilities of the farm itself. You must obtain the financial statements of the potato farm. Will your loan be guaranteed by the parent company or will the obligation to repay be limited to the farm? If only the farm is on the hook then the relevance of these consolidated statements is limited.

2. The goodwill on the balance sheet is a large asset but it is not clear what it represents. The goodwill arose when Tecumseh bought the trucking company and means it paid $900,000 more than could be attributed to specifically identifiable net assets. Thus, you can't tell what the goodwill represents or if it represents anything at all. In addition, this goodwill is not related to the potato farm, the company to which you are being asked to lend.

3. The non-controlling interest on the liability side of the balance sheet represents the fact that Tecumseh does not own 100 percent of the potato farm. The consolidated balance sheet reports 100 percent of the net assets controlled by Tecumseh, even though it doesn't own 100 percent of the farm's net assets. The additional information states that 25 percent of the farm is owned by the potato farmer. The non-controlling interest account reflects this fact. This account doesn't mean that money, goods, or services are owed to a third party but simply show the potato farmer's "equity" in the assets and liabilities reported in the consolidated balance sheet.

4. The non-controlling interest does provide a small clue about how the potato farm is doing. The non-controlling interest decreased from 2013 to 2014, which means that the farm suffered a loss in 2014. You will have to get financial statements for the farm itself before making a decision about whether to make a loan to it, but this piece of information gives some insight about what to expect.

5. In general, the ability to analyze consolidated financial statements is quite limited. Tecumseh's balance sheet combines the assets and liabilities of four very different types of businesses, so it's very difficult to make much sense of any type of ratio analysis.

6. I notice from the balance sheet that Tecumseh's overall debt has increased significantly in 2014 over 2013. Long-term debt increased by $400,000 and the bank loan by $100,000. As a result, the debt-to-equity ratio has increased from 1.13 to 1.34—not alarming (though consideration of the individual business lines is necessary), but you should investigate the need for such a large increase in debt, especially in light of a much smaller increase in property, plant, and equipment. In addition, you should find out whether the new debt is for the farm or for another part of the operation. You should also find out what security has been provided for the existing debt and whether the owners have personally guaranteed it. This is important

information because it will give you some insight into how much protection (through collateral and personal guarantees) you can obtain if you decided to lend money to the farm.

7. Liquidity on the consolidated balance sheet seems strong (the current ratio is 1.61, which is about the same as in 2013), but I am very concerned about the large increase in accounts receivable. Not much analysis of receivables is possible without the income statement and other information, but this could be a concern if the increase is not matched by increases in revenues. Tecumseh may be having trouble collecting its receivables or, perhaps, there is a receivable to a manager or shareholder in the reported balance. Once again, you need to find out whether this increase in receivable pertains to the farm.

8. As I have indicated throughout this report, you do not have nearly enough information to make a lending decision. You need the farm's financial statements and you must obtain additional information. It is always important to remember that these are historical financial statements; they report past transactions. Ultimately, a lending decision should be based on the ability of an entity to generate cash flows to pay the interest on the loan and the principal.

Best wishes and thanks for letting me do this report for you.

Your nephew,
John

APPENDIX

The Consolidated Financial Statements in Periods after a Subsidiary Is Purchased

In periods after the acquisition of a subsidiary, the consolidated financial statements are more than the sum of the lines on the income statements and balance sheets of the parent and subsidiaries. Three adjustments are described below.

Fair Value Adjustments Remember that consolidated financial statements report the assets and liabilities of the subsidiary at their fair values on the date the subsidiary was acquired. This treatment has consequences for later periods. When the inventory that was on hand at acquisition is sold, cost of goods sold is the cost of the inventory as reported on the consolidated balance sheet, not the cost on the subsidiary's balance sheet. Similarly, the depreciation and amortization of capital assets is calculated using their fair values on the acquisition date. Recall the Pefferlaw-Schuler example from the main part of the chapter. In that example, the $21.5 million fair value of Schuler's capital assets included in Pefferlaw's consolidated balance sheet is what is depreciated (see Table 11.2). It doesn't matter that these same assets are recorded at $14 million on Schuler's own balance sheet. For the purpose of preparing the consolidated financial statements, it's the $21.5 million that matters. It isn't even necessary for the same depreciation method to be used on both the consolidated and subsidiary's statements.

Remember, the fair value of a subsidiary's assets and liabilities isn't determined each time consolidated financial statements are prepared (unless IFRS require the asset or liability to be fair valued each period). Fair valuing is done once, when the subsidiary is acquired, and those values become the historical costs for use in the preparation of future consolidated financial statements.

Goodwill As mentioned earlier, goodwill doesn't have to be amortized. Management must regularly evaluate the goodwill and write it down if it's impaired. The writedown would reduce the amount of goodwill on the consolidated balance sheet and the reduction would be expensed on the consolidated income statement.

Intercompany Transactions For the most part, a consolidated income statement can be prepared by adding together the income statements of the parent and the subsidiaries. Some adjustments are needed, two of which we just discussed. It may also be necessary to adjust the consolidated financial statements for intercompany transactions.

It's important and useful that intercompany transactions are eliminated when consolidated financial statements are prepared. This means that revenues and expenses and changes in the value of assets and liabilities that result from transactions between subsidiaries and with the parent aren't reflected in the consolidated statements. These have no economic significance to the consolidated entity. Only transactions with entities external to the consolidated group have economic significance. Transactions between corporations within the group are part of the financial statements each corporation prepares but are eliminated on consolidation. After all, have there been any economic gains to the consolidated entity if a subsidiary sells merchandise to its parent at a profit? If sales among entities in a corporate group aren't eliminated, revenues and expenses in the consolidated income statement will be overstated, and receivables, inventory, and payables on the balance sheet may also be overstated.

Let's use an example to examine the effect of intercompany transactions. Seech Inc. (Seech) is a 100-percent-owned subsidiary of Pitaga Ltd. (Pitaga). During the year ended December 31, 2014, Seech sold merchandise costing $2,000,000 to Pitaga for $4,500,000. This is the only transaction that Pitaga and Seech entered into during 2014. Seech recorded the sale with the following journal entries:

Dr. Accounts receivable (asset +)	4,500,000	
Cr. Revenue (revenue +, shareholders' equity +)		4,500,000
To record the sale of merchandise to Pitaga		

Dr. Cost of sales (expense +, shareholders' equity −)	2,000,000	
Cr. Inventory (asset −)		2,000,000
To record the cost of the merchandise sold to Pitaga		

Pitaga recorded its purchase of the merchandise from Seech with the following journal entry:

Dr. Inventory (asset −)	4,500,000	
Cr. Accounts payable (liability −)		4,500,000
To record the purchase of merchandise from Seech		

Notice the effect of this transaction. Seech has earned a profit of $2,500,000 ($4,500,000 − $2,000,000) and the inventory it sold to Pitaga is now valued at $4,500,000 on Pitaga's balance sheet. There are receivables and payables of $4,500,000. In the context of historical cost, transactions-based accounting, nothing has happened to justify reporting the revenue and profit and the increase in the value of inventory, accounts receivable, and accounts payable in the consolidated statements. From the perspective of the consolidated entity, this is like recognizing a profit, increasing the value of inventory, and reporting payables and receivables when moving goods from one warehouse to another. Table 11.5 sets out the effect of intercompany transactions between Pitaga and Seech.

TABLE 11.5	Effect of Intercompany Transactions: Scenario 1 (Seech's sale of merchandise to Pitaga—merchandise held by Pitaga at year-end)			
	Column 1		Column 2	Column 3
	Accounting information for the year ended December 31, 2014		Pitaga Ltd. consolidated statements (intercompany transactions not eliminated)	Pitaga Ltd. consolidated statements (intercompany transactions eliminated)
	Pitaga Ltd.	Seech Inc.		
Revenue	$ 0	$4,500,000	$4,500,000	$ 0
Cost of sales	0	2,000,000	2,000,000	0
Net income	0	$2,500,000	$2,500,000	0
Accounts receivable	0	$4,500,000	$4,500,000	$ 0
Inventory	$4,500,000	0	$4,500,000	$2,000,000
Accounts payable	$4,500,000	0	$4,500,000	$ 0

- Column 1 shows the summarized income statements and extracts from the balance sheets of the two companies. (These statements would be used for tax purposes and perhaps by a banker who loaned money to these entities.)

- Column 2 shows Pitaga's consolidated financial statements if the intercompany transactions aren't eliminated. In this column, Pitaga appears to be an active, perhaps successful enterprise with sales of $4,500,000 and net income of $2,500,000. It isn't possible to tell from these statements that no real economic activity has occurred.

- Column 3 shows the consolidated statements if the intercompany transactions are eliminated. These statements show no activity: no revenues, no expenses, inventory reported at its cost to Seech, and no receivables or payables.

This example demonstrates how intercompany transactions can impact the financial statements and the potential difficulties for stakeholders who interpret and analyze financial statements that include intercompany transactions. When the financial statements of a subsidiary are being examined (not the consolidated financial statements), it's important to be aware that intercompany transactions can have a significant effect.

? QUESTION FOR CONSIDERATION

Explain why including intercompany transactions in consolidated financial statements can make those statements misleading to users.

Answer: If intercompany transactions aren't eliminated from consolidated financial statements, a number of problems exist that can mislead stakeholder:

1. Revenue from sales by one member of the consolidated entity to another will be included in consolidated revenue. This will overstate the economic activity of the entity, making it appear the entity is generating more revenue than it really is.

2. If an entity purchases inventory from another entity in the consolidated group at a profit, the value of the inventory on the balance sheet is increased, which violates historical cost accounting.

3. If the transactions between the corporations in the consolidated entity aren't settled in cash, receivables and payables will be increased by the amounts owing between the entities, thereby overstating current assets and payables will be increased by the amounts owing between the entities, thereby overstating current liabilities.

4. As a result of the effects in (1) to (3), financial ratios will be distorted from the amounts that would be reported if intercompany transactions were eliminated.

EXAMPLE OF ACQUIRING LESS THAN 100 PERCENT OF A SUBSIDIARY—NON-CONTROLLING INTEREST

Now let's look at a situation where a parent acquires control of a subsidiary but owns less than 100 percent of it. On January 31, 2014, Padlei Ltd. (Padlei) purchased 80 percent of the common shares of Schyan Inc. (Schyan) for $900,000 cash. On January 31, 2014, Schyan's balance sheet reported net assets of $1,000,000. The fair value of Schyan's identifiable net assets on January 31, 2014 was $1,125,000. There is no goodwill in this acquisition. The effects of this acquisition are shown in Table 11.6.

Notice the following:

❶ Consolidated assets is the sum of the amount on Padlei's balance sheet plus the fair value of Schyan's assets on the date of acquisition. The valuation of Padlei's assets on its own balance sheet isn't relevant to the consolidated balance sheet.

❷ The investment in Schyan account on Padlei's balance sheet doesn't appear on the consolidated balance sheet. The account is replaced by Schyan's actual net assets.

❸ Consolidated liabilities is the sum of the amount on Padlei's balance sheet plus the fair value of Schyan's liabilities on the date of acquisition. The valuation of Padlei's liabilities on its own balance sheet isn't relevant to the consolidated balance sheet.

❹ Schyan's shareholders' equity (as it appears on its own balance sheet) doesn't appear on the consolidated balance sheet.

❺ The non-controlling interest is equal to 20 percent of the fair value of Schyan's identifiable net assets on the date of acquisition.

❻ The non-controlling interest is included in the equity section of the consolidated balance sheet, but it's the equity of the non-controlling shareholders, not the shareholders of Padlei.

Now let's look at the income statement. The summarized income statements of Padlei and Schyan and the summarized consolidated income statement for fiscal 2015 are shown in Table 11.7. Notice that 100 percent of Schyan's revenues and expenses are included in the consolidated income statement, even though 20 percent of those revenues and expenses belong to the non-controlling interest. Net income is calculated in the usual way, but it's then allocated between Padlei's shareholders and the non-controlling interest. Schyan's "other" shareholders

TABLE 11.6	The Effect of Non-controlling Interest			
	Summarized balance sheets January 31, 2014		Fair value of Schyan's net assets January 31, 2014	Padlei Ltd. summarized consolidated balance sheet January 31, 2014
	Padlei Ltd.	Schyan Inc.		
Assets other than the investment	$ 9,400,000	$2,500,000	$2,725,000	$12,125,000 ❶
Investment in Schyan (at cost)	900,000			0 ❷
Total assets	$10,300,000	$2,500,000		$12,125,000
Total liabilities	$ 4,000,000	$1,500,000	1,600,000	$ 5,600,000 ❸
Shareholders' equity				
Share capital	2,000,000	750,000		2,000,000 ❹
Accumulated other comprehensive income	100,000			100,000 ❹
Retained earnings	4,200,000	250,000		4,200,000 ❹
Total Padlei Ltd. shareholders' equity	6,300,000	1,000,000		6,300,000 ❹
Non-controlling interest ❻				225,000 ❺
Total liabilities and shareholders' equity	$10,300,000	$2,500,000		$12,125,000

TABLE 11.7	Non-controlling Interest and the Income Statement		
	Summarized income statement for the year ended January 31, 2015		Padlei Ltd. consolidated income statement for the year ended January 31, 2015
	Padlei Ltd.	Schyan Inc.	
Revenues	$1,000,000	$750,000	$1,750,000
Expenses	700,000	500,000	1,200,000
Net income	$ 300,000	$250,000	$ 550,000
Attributable to:			
Padlei Ltd. shareholders			$ 500,000
Non-controlling interest			50,000*
			$ 550,000
Earnings per share:			
Basic			$1.25
Diluted			1.20

*The non-controlling interest's share of Padlei's net income is equal to 20 percent of Schyan Inc.'s net income ($250,000 × 20 percent).

are entitled to 20 percent of Schyan's net income or $50,000 ($250,000 × 20%). The $500,000 of income that belongs to Padlei's shareholders is closed to retained earnings and the $50,000 that belongs to the non-controlling shareholders is closed to non-controlling interest on Padlei's consolidated balance sheet. In the example, non-controlling interest on the balance sheet would increase by $50,000 in 2015. Also, the earnings per share is calculated on the net income that belongs to Padlei's shareholders. It doesn't include the non-controlling interest.

This example focuses on the presentation of the non-controlling interest in the income statement. In a more comprehensive example there would be adjustments for intercompany transactions and adjustments for differences between the carrying amount and fair value of certain assets and liabilities.

One final note: You may notice in Enbridge's income statement in Exhibit 11.3 that the non-controlling interest is presented differently than shown in Table 11.7. The reason is that Enbridge's statements were prepared before the requirement to present non-controlling interest in shareholders' equity shown in Table 11.7 came into effect.

SUMMARY OF KEY POINTS

▶ **LO 1** There are many reasons why one company invests in another: earning a return on idle cash; strategic moves such as purchasing a competitor, supplier, or customer; and to diversify.

▶ **LO 2** When an investor has control of an investee, the investor prepares consolidated financial statements. Consolidated financial statements aggregate the accounting information of a parent corporation and all of its subsidiaries into a single set of financial statements. On the consolidated balance sheet, the assets and liabilities of a subsidiary are reported at their fair value on the date the subsidiary was purchased.

Goodwill arises when a parent pays more than the fair value of the subsidiary's identifiable assets and liabilities on the date the subsidiary is purchased. Goodwill isn't amortized.

Non-controlling interest arises when a parent company owns less than 100 percent of the shares of a subsidiary it controls. It arises because the consolidated balance sheet includes 100 percent of a subsidiary's assets and liabilities and the income statement includes 100 percent of its revenues and expenses, even though the parent owns less than 100 percent of those assets and liabilities.

▶ **LO 3** When one corporation has significant influence on the decision making of another, the equity method of accounting is used. The equity method is essentially the same as accounting for subsidiaries using the consolidation method, except that the information about equity-accounted-for investments is presented on a single line on the balance sheet and a single line on the income statement. An investment accounted for using the equity method is initially recorded on the investor's balance sheet at cost. The balance sheet amount is then adjusted each period by the investor's share of the investee's net income, less dividends declared by the investee.

▶ **LO 4** Passive investments are those for which the investor corporation can't influence the strategic decision making of the investee corporation. All investments in non-voting securities are passive. Voting shares are accounted for as passive investments when the investing company holds a relatively small proportion of the voting shares.

Passive investments can be classified as held to maturity, trading, and available for sale. Held-to-maturity investments are held until they mature and are accounted for at cost. Trading investments are designated as such by management and are typically securities actively bought and sold for profit. Available for sale is the default category. Any investment that doesn't give control or significant influence to the investing corporation, or that doesn't meet the criteria for classification as a held-to-maturity or trading investment, is classified as available for sale. Trading and available-for-sale investments are valued at market value. Gains and losses on trading investments are recognized in the income statement in the period they occur, regardless of whether they are realized. Unrealized gains and losses on available-for-sale investments are classified as other comprehensive income.

▶ **LO 5** (Appendix) In periods after the acquisition of a subsidiary, the consolidated financial statements are more than the sum of the lines on the income statements and the balance sheets of the parent and subsidiaries. Three adjustments that must be considered are fair value adjustments of assets and liabilities, possible impairment of goodwill, and the elimination of intercompany transactions.

KEY TERMS

available-for-sale investments, p. 635
consolidated financial statement, p. 625
control, p. 625
equity method of accounting, p. 632
fair value, p. 627
financial instruments, p. 634
held-to-maturity investments, p. 635
goodwill, p. 627
identifiable assets and liabilities, p. 627
intercompany transaction, p. 630
investee corporation, p. 624

investor corporation, p. 624
non-controlling interest, p. 629
parent corporation, p. 625
passive investment, p. 635
realized holding gains and losses, p. 635
segment disclosure, p. 630
significant influence, p. 632
subsidiary corporation, p. 625
trading investments, p. 635
unrealized holding gains or losses, p. 635

SIMILAR TERMS

The left column gives alternative terms that are sometimes used for the accounting terms introduced in this chapter, which are listed in the right column.

minority interest **non-controlling interest, p. 629**
market value **fair value, p. 627**

ASSIGNMENT MATERIALS

Questions

Q11-1. What is goodwill? Under what circumstances is it recorded on financial statements?

Q11-2. Why is understanding the extent that one corporation influences another important for accounting purposes? What impact does an entity's degree of influence have on the accounting for investments?

Q11-3. Explain the following degrees of influence that one corporation can have over another and the implications of each for financial reporting:
a. control
b. significant influence
c. no influence

Q11-4. What are consolidated financial statements? What are some of the benefits and limitations of them?

Q11-5. Why do companies invest in other companies?

Q11-6. What are intercompany transactions? Why are the effects of intercompany transactions eliminated when consolidated financial statements are prepared?

Q11-7. What is a subsidiary? How are subsidiaries accounted for? Explain.

Q11-8. What is meant by "non-controlling interest"? What does the non-controlling interest on a company's balance sheet represent? What does it represent on the income statement?

Q11-9. Explain how a non-controlling shareholder in a subsidiary would use the non-controlling interest accounts on the parent's consolidated balance sheet and income statement.

Q11-10. When a subsidiary is acquired, the managers of the parent must allocate the purchase price to the subsidiary's identifiable assets and liabilities. Because the subsidiary's assets and liabilities are bought as a bundle, management has some flexibility in how it allocates the purchase price. Given this flexibility, how do you think the objectives of financial reporting would affect management's allocation of the purchase price? Explain.

Q11-11. What is segment disclosure? Why is segment information required in the financial statements of public companies?

Q11-12. Explain the usefulness of the consolidated financial statements of a parent corporation for the following stakeholders:
a. shareholder of the parent corporation
b. major supplier of one of the subsidiaries
c. Canada Revenue Agency (for income tax determination)

Q11-13. What are the three categories of passive investments? Explain the differences in how the categories are accounted for.

Q11-14. Explain why consolidated financial statements aren't just the sum of the amounts reported on the parent's and subsidiaries' financial statements.

Q11-15. Explain the following terms:
a. investor corporation
b. investee corporation
c. parent corporation
d. subsidiary corporation

Q11-16. When the equity method of accounting for investments is used, dividends received from the investee corporation reduce the balance in the investment account on the investor's balance sheet. The dividends aren't treated as investment income on the income statement. Explain.

Q11-17. Explain the difference between the parent's consolidated financial statements and the financial statements of the parent alone.

Exercises

E11-1. **(Accounting for different types of investments in securities, LO 2, 3, 4)** How should an investor corporation account for the following investments?
   a. Ownership of 51 percent of the voting shares of a company.
   b. Ownership of 20 percent of the outstanding common shares of a company. These common shares represent 60 percent of the votes.
   c. Ownership of 25 percent of the shares of a company.
   d. Ownership of 0.05 percent of the shares of a company.

E11-2. **(Accounting for different types of investments in securities, LO 2, 3, 4)** State how the investor corporation would account for the following investments. Explain your choice.
   a. Purchase of $1,000,000 of bonds that management intends to hold until they mature in three years.
   b. Investment in non-voting shares of a private corporation. Management hopes to sell the shares within six months.
   c. Investment representing 15 percent of the voting shares of a private corporation. One person owns the remainder.
   d. Investment in 52 percent of the voting shares of a private corporation. One person owns the remaining shares.
   e. Investment in 30 percent of the voting shares of a public corporation. The investor corporation is the largest single investor in the public corporation and it has five representatives on its board of directors. The board has 15 members.
   f. Investment in 60 percent of the voting shares of a public corporation. The investor corporation intends to sell its investment within six months.

E11-3. **(Non-controlling interest, LO 2)** On December 31, 2014, Kootuk Inc. (Kootuk) purchased 75 percent of the common shares of Grimmer Ltd. (Grimmer) for $3,500,000. At the time of the purchase, Kootuk's management made the following estimates of the fair values of Grimmer's assets and liabilities:

	Carrying amount of Grimmer's assets and liabilities on December 31, 2014	Fair value of Grimmer's assets and liabilities on December 31, 2014
Assets	$5,000,000	$6,000,000
Liabilities	2,000,000	2,400,000

Required:

   a. Calculate the amount of non-controlling interest that Kootuk would report on its December 31, 2014, consolidated balance sheet as a result of its purchase of Grimmer.
   b. What amount would be included in the assets and liabilities on the Kootuk's December 31, 2014 consolidated balance sheet as a result of the purchase of Grimmer?

E11-4. **(Non-controlling interest, LO 2)** On August 31, 2015, Hoselaw Inc. (Hoselaw) purchased 60 percent of the common shares of Upsalquitch Ltd. (Upsalquitch) for $8,000,000. At the time of the purchase, Upsalquitch's management made the following estimates of the fair values of it's assets and liabilities:

	Carrying amount of Upsalquitch's assets and liabilities on August 31, 2015	Fair Value of Upsalquitch's assets and liabilities on August 31, 2015
Current assets	$1,000,000	$1,250,000
Tangible capital assets	3,000,000	3,600,000
Patents	100,000	1,000,000
Current liabilities	875,000	900,000
Long-term debt	2,125,000	2,000,000

Required:

a. Calculate the amount of non-controlling interest that Hoselaw would report on its August 31, 2015 consolidated balance sheet as a result of its purchase of Upsalquitch.

b. What amount would be included in each asset and liability account on the August 31, 2015 consolidated balance sheet as a result of the purchase of Upsalquitch?

c. What does non-controlling interest on the balance sheet represent? Explain why it appears. How should users of financial statements interpret non-controlling interest?

E11-5. **(Accounting for passive investments, LO 4)** Chockpish Inc. (Chockpish) has provided you with the following list of transactions and economic events that involved its investment portfolio in 2015. For each of the items, prepare any journal entries required. Explain your entries fully. Chockpish's year-end is December 31.

a. On January 15, 2,000 shares of Inwood Corp. were purchased at $37 per share.

b. On February 12, a cheque for $10,000 was received from Guthrie Inc. for dividends.

c. At the close of trading on December 31, bonds of Hydraulic Corp. were priced $980 per thousand-dollar bond. Chockpish's 100 bonds have a carrying amount of $1,000 per bond and the company plans to hold the bonds until they mature in 2018.

d. At the close of trading on December 31, shares of Kynoch Ltd. were priced at $12 per share. Chockpish's 5,000 shares of Kynoch Ltd. have a carrying amount of $15 per share. Chockpish plans to continue holding these shares for the foreseeable future.

e. At the close of trading on December 31, shares of Jobrin Inc. were priced at $19 per share. Chockpish's 3,000 shares of Jobrin have a carrying amount of $22 per share. Chockpish plans to sell the shares by March 31, 2016.

E11-6. **(Accounting for passive investments, LO 4)** Yellek Inc. (Yellek) is a private corporation owned by the Yellek family. Yellek maintains a significant investment portfolio of publicly traded shares as a method of maximizing the return on surplus cash that the family keeps in the company. In March 2014, Yellek purchased 50,000 shares of Viking Corp. (Viking), a public company that trades on the TSX, for $20 per share. Then in May 2014, Yellek purchased an additional 20,000 shares of Viking for $23 per share. During 2014, Viking declared and paid a dividend of $0.12 a share on April 30 and a dividend of $0.12 a share on September 30. On November 12, 2014, Yellek sold 15,000 of its Viking shares for $25 per share because it needed cash to pay dividends to members of the family.

On December 12, 2014, Viking made an announcement that stunned the investment community. Viking was being forced to close one of its operating facilities permanently because of environmental concerns. The facility was responsible for about 20 percent of its annual production and the company said that it didn't think it would be able to make up the lost production in the short term. Immediately after the announcement, Viking's share price fell to $13 per share. On December 31, 2014, Viking's shares closed at $13.25.

Required:

a. Prepare the journal entries to record the purchase of Viking shares during 2014.

b. Prepare the journal entries to account for the dividends declared and paid by Viking during 2014.

c. Prepare the journal entry to record the sale of Viking shares on November 12, 2014. Explain your entry.

d. How would you account for the effects of the announcement made by Viking on December 12, 2014? Explain. Prepare any journal entries required. Indicate the amount that would be reported on Yellek's balance sheet for its investment in Viking.

E11-7. **(Consolidation accounting, LO 2)** In order to expand its market penetration in the retail clothing market, Balmoral Designs Ltd. (Balmoral) purchased 100 percent of the outstanding shares of Chipman Fine Clothiers Inc. (Chipman). Balmoral paid $4,200,000 cash for the shares and its management determined that at the time of acquisition the fair value of Chipman's identifiable assets and liabilities was $2,400,000. The following information was obtained as of the date Chipman was acquired and was prepared before the purchase occurred:

	Balmoral	Chipman (carrying amounts)	Chipman (fair values)		Balmoral	Chipman (carrying amounts)	Chipman (fair values)
Current assets	$ 7,000,000	$1,900,000	$2,400,000	Current liabilities	$ 5,000,000	$ 750,000	$750,000
Non-current assets	5,000,000	1,050,000	1,170,000	Non-current liabilities	2,000,000	400,000	420,000
				Shareholders' equity	5,000,000	1,800,000	
Total assets	$12,000,000	$2,950,000		Total liabilities and shareholders' equity	$12,000,000	$2,950,000	

Required:

Calculate the amounts that would appear on Balmoral's consolidated balance sheet on the date it acquired Chipman.

E11-8. **(Consolidation accounting, LO 2)** In order to expand its product line, Dorchester Manufacturing Ltd. (Dorchester) purchased 100 percent of the outstanding shares of Hardisty Inc. (Hardisty). Dorchester paid $3,500,000 cash for the shares. The following information was obtained as of the date Hardisty was acquired and was prepared before the purchase occurred:

	Dorchester	Hardisty (carrying amounts)	Hardisty (fair values)		Dorchester	Hardisty (carrying amounts)	Hardisty (fair values)
Current assets	$ 4,250,000	$1,500,000	$1,900,000	Current liabilities	$ 3,250,000	$1,250,000	$1,350,000
Non-current assets	16,250,000	5,000,000	6,000,000	Non-current liabilities	9,000,000	3,150,000	3,550,000
				Shareholders' equity	8,250,000	2,100,000	
Total assets	$20,500,000	$6,500,000		Total liabilities and shareholders' equity	$20,500,000	$6,500,000	

Required:

Calculate the amounts that would appear on Dorchester's consolidated balance sheet on the date it acquired Hardisty.

E11-9. **(The equity method of accounting, LO 3)** On January 1, 2014, Fletwode Corp. (Fletwode) purchased 2,250,000 common shares of Irvine Ltd. (Irvine) for $10,000,000. The investment represents a 30 percent interest in Irvine and gives Fletwode significant influence over Irvine. For 2014, Fletwode's share of Irvine's net income was $390,000, and during the year Irvine paid dividends of $100,000 to all shareholders. Both companies have December 31 year-ends.

Required:

a. Prepare Fletwode's journal entry to record its investment in Irvine.
b. What amount would be reported on Fletwode's December 31, 2014 balance sheet for this investment? How much would Fletwode report on its December 31, 2014 income statement from its investment in Irvine?

E11-10. **(The equity method of accounting, LO 3)** On June 1, 2014, Wostok Corp. (Wostok) purchased 1,000,000 common shares of Griffin Ltd. (Griffin) for $2,000,000. The investment represents a 40 percent interest in Griffin and gives Wostok significant influence. During fiscal 2015, Wostok's share of Griffin's net income was $440,000. Also, Griffin paid dividends during the year of $0.50 per share. Both companies have May 31 year-ends.

Required:

a. Prepare Wostok's journal entry to record its investment in Griffin.
b. How much would Wostok report on its May 31, 2015 income statement from this investment?
c. What amount would be reported on Wostok's May 31, 2015 balance sheet for its investment in Griffin?

E11-11. **(Consolidated income statement, LO 2, 5)** Explain how the following items would affect consolidated net income in the year a subsidiary is purchased and in the year after:

a. Impairment of the value of goodwill.
b. Land with a carrying amount of $2,000,000 on the subsidiary's balance sheet on the date the subsidiary was purchased has a fair value of $5,000,000.
c. Equipment with a carrying amount of $1,000,000 on the subsidiary's balance sheet on the date the subsidiary was purchased has a fair value of $1,500,000. The equipment had a remaining useful life of five years on the date of acquisition.
d. Inventory with a carrying amount of $200,000 on the subsidiary's balance sheet on the date the subsidiary was purchased has a fair value of $230,000.
e. Dividends paid by the subsidiary to the parent.
f. Services sold at a profit by the subsidiary to the parent.
g. The subsidiary is 80 percent owned by the parent.

Problems

P11-1. **(Accounting for passive investments, LO 4)** In June 2013, Jolicure Inc. (Jolicure) and Horsefly Inc. (Horsefly) each began operations. Each company was formed with an initial capital contribution of $100,000. During the year ended May 31, 2014, each company had revenue of $225,000 and total expenses of $175,000. In addition, during the first year of operations, each company purchased 1,000 shares of Nictaux Ltd. (Nictaux), a public company, for $12 per share. In May 2014, Horsefly sold its shares in Nictaux for $20 per share and immediately repurchased them at the same price. Jolicure didn't sell its shares during fiscal 2014. On May 31, 2014, each company had total assets (excluding the shares in Nictaux) of $168,000 and total liabilities of $30,000. For both companies, the investment was considered as available for sale. Assume that the market value of the investment on May 31, 2014 was $20 per share.

Required:

    a. Prepare summarized balance sheets and income statements for Jolicure and Horsefly as of May 31, 2014.

    b. Which company performed better in fiscal 2014?

    c. Why do you think Horsefly sold and repurchased the shares in Nictaux? Do you think that this was a wise transaction to enter into? Explain.

P11-2. **(Accounting for passive investments, LO 4)** On August 1, 2014, Lourdes Inc. (Lourdes) purchased 20,000 preferred shares of Matagami Ltd. for $120 per share. The shares have a dividend of $12 per share and must be repurchased by Matagami on or before November 30, 2020 for $120 per share. On December 31, 2014, Lourdes' year-end, the market value of the shares was $95 per share. On December 31, 2014, Lourdes had total assets (excluding the investment in the preferred shares) of $35 million, total liabilities of $25 million and share capital of $4 million. In addition, Lourdes' revenues and expenses for 2014 (excluding all income statement effects related to the preferred shares) were $8,200,000 and $6,100,000 respectively. Retained earnings on January 1, 2014 was $6,060,000.

Required:

    a. Prepare a summarized balance sheet and income statement on December 31, 2014, assuming that Lourdes accounts for the shares as a (i) trading investment, (ii) held-to-maturity investment, and (iii) available-for-sale investment, assuming that Lourdes owned the shares on December 31, 2014.

    b. Prepare a summarized balance sheet and income statement on December 31, 2014, assuming that Lourdes accounts for the shares as a (i) trading investment, (ii) held-to-maturity investment, and (iii) available-for-sale investment, assuming that Lourdes sold the shares on December 31, 2014, for $95 per share.

P11-3. **(Preparation of a consolidated balance sheet on the date a subsidiary is purchased, LO 2)** On August 31, 2014, Pacquet Inc. (Pacquet) purchased 100 percent of the common shares of Schwitzer Ltd. (Schwitzer) for $2,000,000 cash. Pacquet's and Schwitzer's balance sheets on August 31, 2014 just before the purchase are shown:

Balance Sheets as of August 31, 2014		
	Pacquet Inc.	**Schwitzer Ltd.**
Current assets	$3,500,000	$ 625,000
Capital assets	3,250,000	1,250,000
Total assets	$6,750,000	$1,875,000
Current liabilities	$1,350,000	$ 375,000
Non-current liabilities	1,250,000	500,000
Capital stock	2,000,000	250,000
Retained earnings	2,150,000	750,000
Total liabilities and shareholders' equity	$6,750,000	$1,875,000

Management determined that the fair values of Schwitzer's assets and liabilities were as follows:

	Fair value of Schwitzer's identifiable assets and liabilities on August 31, 2014
Current assets	$ 875,000
Capital assets	1,950,000
Current liabilities	375,000
Non-current liabilities	550,000

Required:

    a. Prepare Pacquet's balance sheet immediately following the purchase.

    b. Calculate the amount of goodwill that would be reported on Pacquet's consolidated balance sheet on August 31, 2014.

    c. Prepare Pacquet's consolidated balance sheet on August 31, 2014.

    d. Calculate the current ratios and debt-to-equity ratios for Pacquet, Schwitzer, and for the consolidated balance sheet on August 31, 2014. Interpret the differences between the ratios. When calculating the ratios, use Pacquet and Schwitzer's balance sheets after the purchase had been made and recorded.

    e. You are a lender who has been asked to make a sizeable loan to Schwitzer. Which balance sheets would you be interested in viewing? Explain. How would you use Pacquet's consolidated financial statements in making your lending decision?

P11-4. **(Preparation of a consolidated balance sheet on the date a subsidiary is purchased, LO 2)** On January 31, 2015, Paju Inc. (Paju) purchased 100 percent of the common shares of Shellmouth Ltd. (Shellmouth) for $6,250,000 in cash. Paju's and Shellmouth's balance sheets on January 31, 2015, just before the purchase are shown:

Balance Sheets as of January 31, 2015		
	Paju Inc.	**Shellmouth Ltd.**
Current assets	$ 7,500,000	$5,625,000
Capital assets	14,687,500	1,875,000
Total assets	$22,187,500	$7,500,000
Current liabilities	$ 1,500,000	$1,875,000
Non-current liabilities	7,500,000	625,000
Capital stock	9,375,000	3,750,000
Retained earnings	3,812,500	1,250,000
Total liabilities and shareholders' equity	$22,187,500	$7,500,000

Management determined that the fair values of Shellmouth's assets and liabilities were as follows:

	Fair value of Shellmouth's identifiable assets and liabilities on January 31, 2015
Current assets	$4,875,000
Capital assets	2,375,000
Current liabilities	2,000,000
Non-current liabilities	937,500

Required:

    a. Prepare Paju's balance sheet immediately following the purchase.

    b. Calculate the amount of goodwill to be reported on Paju's consolidated balance sheet on January 31, 2015.

    c. Prepare Paju's consolidated balance sheet on January 31, 2015.

    d. Calculate the current ratios and debt-to-equity ratios for Paju, Shellmouth, and for the consolidated balance sheet on January 31, 2015. Interpret the differences between the ratios. When calculating the ratios, use Paju's and Shellmouth's balance sheets after the purchase has been made and recorded.

e. You are a potential investor who has been asked to purchase a 25 percent equity interest in Shellmouth (you would purchase the shares from Shellmouth, not from Paju). Which balance sheets would you be interested in viewing? Explain. How would you use Paju's consolidated financial statements in making your investment decision? What concerns would you have about making an equity investment in Shellmouth?

P11-5. **(Preparation of a consolidated balance sheet on the date a subsidiary is purchased when less than 100 percent of the subsidiary is purchased, LO 5, Appendix)** On March 31, 2015, Popkum Inc. (Popkum) purchased 65 percent of the common shares of Saguay Ltd. (Saguay) for $1,200,000. Popkum's and Saguay's balance sheets on March 31, 2015 just before the purchase were:

Balance Sheets as of March 31, 2015		
	Popkum Inc.	Saguay Ltd.
Current assets	$2,625,000	$ 468,750
Capital assets	2,437,500	937,500
Total assets	$5,062,500	$1,406,250
Current liabilities	$1,012,500	$ 281,250
Non-current liabilities	937,500	375,000
Capital stock	1,500,000	187,500
Retained earnings	1,612,500	562,500
Total liabilities and shareholders' equity	$5,062,500	$1,406,250

Management determined that the fair values of Saguay's assets and liabilities were as follows:

	Fair value of Saguay's identifiable assets and liabilities on March 31, 2015
Current assets	$ 656,250
Capital assets	1,462,500
Current liabilities	281,250
Non-current liabilities	412,500

Required:

a. Calculate the amount of goodwill to be reported on Popkum's consolidated balance sheet on March 31, 2015.
b. Calculate the amount of non-controlling interest to be reported on the consolidated balance sheet on March 31, 2015.
c. Prepare Popkum's consolidated balance sheet on March 31, 2015.
d. Calculate the current ratios and debt-to-equity ratios for Popkum, Saguay, and for the consolidated balance sheet on March 31, 2015. Interpret the differences between the ratios.
e. Explain what the non-controlling interest on the balance sheet represents. How would you interpret it from the perspective of a shareholder of Popkum? How would you interpret it from the perspective of a shareholder in Saguay? How would you interpret it from the perspective of a lender?

www.mcgrawhillconnect.ca

P11-6. **(Preparation of a consolidated balance sheet on the date a subsidiary is purchased when less than 100 percent of the subsidiary is purchased, LO 5, Appendix)** On October 31, 2014, Pahonan Inc. (Pahonan) purchased 75 percent of the common shares of Seebe Ltd. (Seebe) for $1,500,000. Pahonan's and Seebe's balance sheets on October 31, 2014, just before the purchase are shown:

Balance Sheets as of October 31, 2014		
	Pahonan Inc.	Seebe Ltd.
Current assets	$2,000,000	$2,250,000
Capital assets	6,875,000	750,000
Total assets	$8,875,000	$3,000,000
Current liabilities	$ 600,000	$ 750,000
Non-current liabilities	3,000,000	250,000
Capital stock	3,750,000	1,500,000
Retained earnings	1,525,000	500,000
Total liabilities and shareholders' equity	$8,875,000	$3,000,000

Management determined that the fair values of Seebe's assets and liabilities were as follows:

	Fair value of Seebe's assets and liabilities on October 31, 2014
Current assets	$1,950,000
Capital assets	950,000
Current liabilities	800,000
Non-current liabilities	375,000

Required:

a. Prepare the journal entry that Pahonan would make to record its purchase of Seebe's shares.

b. Prepare the journal entry that Seebe would make to record its purchase by Pahonan.

c. Calculate the amount of goodwill to be reported on Pahonan's consolidated balance sheet on October 31, 2014.

d. Calculate the amount of non-controlling interest to be reported on the consolidated balance sheet on October 31, 2014.

e. Prepare Pahonan's consolidated balance sheet on October 31, 2014.

f. Calculate the current ratios and debt-to-equity ratios for Pahonan and Seebe, and for the consolidated balance sheet on October 31, 2014. Interpret the differences between the ratios.

g. Explain what the non-controlling interest on the balance sheet represents. How would you interpret it from the perspective of a shareholder of Pahonan? How would you interpret it from the perspective of a shareholder in Seebe? How would you interpret it from the perspective of a lender?

P11-7. **(Intercompany transactions, LO 5, Appendix)** Vonda Inc. (Vonda) is a 100-percent-owned subsidiary of Atik Ltd. (Atik). During the year ended March 31, 2014, Vonda sold, on credit, merchandise costing $500,000 to Atik for $1,000,000. These were the only transactions that Atik and Vonda entered into during fiscal 2014 (with each other or with third parties) and there were no other costs incurred.

Required:

    a. Prepare an income statement for Vonda for the year ended March 31, 2014.

    b. What amount of accounts receivable would Vonda report on its March 31, 2014 balance sheet?

    c. What amount of inventory and accounts payable would Atik report on its March 31, 2014 balance sheet?

    d. Prepare Atik's March 31, 2014 consolidated income statement assuming that intercompany transactions aren't eliminated. How much would be reported for accounts receivable, inventory, and accounts payable on the March 31, 2014 consolidated balance sheet?

    e. Prepare Atik's March 31, 2014 consolidated income statement, assuming that intercompany transactions are eliminated. How much would be reported for accounts receivable, inventory, and accounts payable on the March 31, 2014 consolidated balance sheet?

    f. Discuss the differences in the information you prepared in parts (d) and (e). Which information is more useful to stakeholders? Explain.

P11-8. **(Intercompany transactions, LO 5, Appendix)** Guilds Inc. (Guilds) is a 100-percent-owned subsidiary of Nutak Ltd. (Nutak). During the year ended August 31, 2014, Guilds sold merchandise costing $300,000 to Nutak for $750,000. These were the only transactions that Nutak and Guilds entered into during 2014 (with each other or with third parties) and there were no other costs incurred. The sale was on credit.

Required:

    a. Prepare an income statement for Guilds for the year ended August 31, 2014.

    b. What amount of accounts receivable would Guilds report on its August 31, 2014 balance sheet?

    c. What amount of inventory and accounts payable would Nutak report on its August 31, 2014 balance sheet?

    d. Prepare Nutak's August 31, 2014 consolidated income statement assuming that intercompany transactions aren't eliminated. How much would be reported for accounts receivable, inventory, and accounts payable on the August 31, 2014 consolidated balance sheet?

    e. Prepare Nutak's August 31, 2014 consolidated income statement assuming that intercompany transactions are eliminated. How much would be reported for accounts receivable, inventory, and accounts payable on the August 31, 2014 consolidated balance sheet?

    f. Discuss the differences in the information you prepared in parts (d) and (e). Which information is more useful to stakeholders? Explain.

P11-9. **(Intercompany transactions, LO 5, Appendix)** Dozois Inc. (Dozois) is a 100-percent-owned subsidiary of Yarbo Ltd. (Yarbo). During the year ended July 31, 2015, Dozois sold merchandise costing $1,100,000 to Yarbo for $1,500,000. During fiscal 2015, Yarbo sold, on credit, the merchandise it had purchased from Dozois to third parties for $1,600,000. These were the only transactions that Yarbo and Dozois entered into during 2015 (with each other or with third parties) and there were no other costs incurred.

Required:

    a. Prepare an income statement for Dozois for the year ended July 31, 2015.

    b. What amount of accounts receivable would Dozois report on its July 31, 2015 balance sheet?

    c. What amount of inventory and accounts payable would Yarbo report on its July 31, 2015 balance sheet?

d. Prepare Yarbo's July 31, 2015 consolidated income statement assuming that intercompany transactions aren't eliminated. How much would be reported for accounts receivable, inventory, and accounts payable on the July 31, 2015 consolidated balance sheet?

e. Prepare Yarbo's July 31, 2015 consolidated income statement assuming that intercompany transactions are eliminated. How much would be reported for accounts receivable, inventory, and accounts payable on the July 31, 2015 consolidated balance sheet?

f. Discuss the differences in the information you prepared in parts (d) and (e). Which information is more useful to stakeholders? Explain.

P11-10. **(Passive investments, LO 4)** In July 2014, Roddickton Ltd. (Roddickton) purchased 50,000 shares of Kola Inc. (Kola), a publicly traded company, for $22 per share. Roddickton received dividends of $1.10 per share from its investment in Kola. On December 31, 2014, the closing price for Kola's shares was $29. There were 100,000,000 shares of Kola's common stock outstanding during 2014.

Required:

a. Prepare the journal entry that would be made to record the purchase of the shares.

b. Prepare the journal entry to record the dividends received by Kola during 2014.

c. How would you classify this investment for financial reporting purposes? How would you decide? Does it matter how the investment is accounted for?

d. If the investment in Kola were classified as available for sale, what amount would be reported on Roddickton's December 31, 2014 balance sheet? Explain. Would there be any impact on the income statement/statement of comprehensive income? Explain.

e. If the investment in Kola were classified as a trading investment, what amount would be reported on Roddickton's December 31, 2014 balance sheet? Explain. Would there be any impact on the income statement/statement of comprehensive income? Explain.

f. Do you think a management cares whether its investments are classified as available for sale or trading? Explain.

Using Financial Statements

BROOKFIELD ASSET MANAGEMENT LTD.

www.brookfield.com

Brookfield Asset Management Inc. (Brookfield) is a global asset management company focused on property, power, and other infrastructure assets. The company has approximately $80 billion under management. Brookfield owns and manages one of the largest portfolios of premier office properties and hydroelectric power generation facilities as well as transmission and timberland operations, located in North and South America and Europe. The company is listed on the New York and Toronto stock exchanges.[5]

Brookfield's consolidated balance sheets, statements of income and comprehensive income, and extracts from the statements of cash flows, notes to the financial statements, and annual information form are provided in Exhibit 11.4. Use this information to respond to questions FS11-1 to FS11-5.[6]

FS11-1. What companies/industries does Brookfield account for using the equity method? What was Brookfield's ownership interest in each of these on December 31, 2008? Why are these companies accounted for using the equity method? What is the carrying amount (book value) of each of the equity-accounted-for investments? Why is Norbord Inc. no longer accounted for using the equity basis?

FS11-2. Examine Note 28 to Brookfield's financial statements and answer the following questions on segment disclosure:

a. Identify the business segments in which Brookfield operates. Which segment has the most revenues? Which has the most assets? Which has the most income?

EXHIBIT 11.4	Brookfield Asset Management Corp.: Financial Statement Extracts

SUBSIDIARIES

The following is a list of the Corporation's main active subsidiaries, indicating the jurisdiction of incorporation and the percentage of voting securities owned, or over which control or direction is exercised directly or indirectly, by the Corporation:

Name	Jurisdiction of Incorporation	Percentage of Voting Securities Owned, Controlled or Directed
Property Operations		
Brookfield Homes Corporation	Delaware	58.2
Brookfield Properties Corporation	Canada	51.4
BPO Properties Limited	Canada	89.7
Power Generating Operations		
Brookfield Renewable Power Inc.	Ontario	100.0
Great Lakes Hydro Income Fund	Quebec	50.0
Other		
Brascan Brasil, S.A.	Brazil	100.0
Brookfield Investments Corporation	Ontario	100.0
Norbord Inc.	Ontario	60.3 [a]
Fraser Papers Inc.	Ontario	75.3

(a) The Corporation's direct and indirect ownership in Norbord Inc. increased to 75% in January 2009.

CONSOLIDATED BALANCE SHEETS

AS AT DECEMBER 31 (MILLIONS)	Note	2008	2007
Assets			
Cash and cash equivalents		$ 1,242	$ 1,561
Financial assets	3	787	1,529
Investments	4	890	1,352
Accounts receivable and other	5	7,310	7,139
Intangible assets	6	1,632	2,026
Goodwill	2	2,011	1,528
Operating assets			
Property, plant and equipment	7	36,375	37,725
Securities	8	1,303	1,828
Loans and notes receivable	9	2,061	909
		$ 53,611	$ 55,597
Liabilities and shareholders' equity			
Corporate borrowings	10	$ 2,284	$ 2,048
Non-recourse borrowings			
Property-specific mortgages	11	22,889	21,644
Subsidiary borrowings	11	5,102	7,076
Accounts payable and other liabilities	12	8,903	9,863
Intangible liabilities	13	891	1,112
Capital securities	14	1,425	1,570
Non-controlling interests in net assets	15	6,329	4,770
Shareholders' equity			
Preferred equity	16	870	870
Common equity	17	4,918	6,644
		$ 53,611	$ 55,597

b. Identify the geographic segments that Brookfield reports in Note 28. Which segment has the most revenues? Which has the most assets? Why do you think segment income information isn't provided for the geographic segments?

c. Is the segmented information provided only for the entities that are consolidated into Brookfield's consolidated financial statements? Explain.

EXHIBIT ⟨11.4⟩ (continued) Brookfield Asset Management Corp.: Financial Statement Extracts

CONSOLIDATED STATEMENTS OF INCOME

YEARS ENDED DECEMBER 31 (MILLIONS, EXCEPT PER SHARE AMOUNTS)	Note	2008	2007
Total revenues		$ 12,868	$ 9,343
Fees earned		449	415
Revenues less direct operating costs	21		
Commercial properties		1,831	1,548
Power generation		886	611
Infrastructure		196	290
Development and other properties		240	418
Specialty funds		304	370
		3,906	3,652
Investment and other income		903	857
		4,809	4,509
Expenses			
Interest		1,984	1,786
Current income taxes	23	(7)	68
Asset management and other operating costs		640	464
Non-controlling interests in net income before the following	22	791	636
		1,401	1,555
Other items			
Equity accounted loss from investments	24	(46)	(72)
Depreciation and amortization		(1,330)	(1,034)
Provisions and other		(267)	(112)
Future income taxes	23	461	(88)
Non-controlling interests in the foregoing items	22	430	538
Net income		$ 649	$ 787
Net income per common share	17		
Diluted		$ 1.02	$ 1.24
Basic		$ 1.04	$ 1.27

CONSOLIDATED STATEMENTS OF COMPREHENSIVE (LOSS) INCOME

YEARS ENDED DECEMBER 31 (MILLIONS)	Note	2008	2007
Net income		$ 649	$ 787
Other comprehensive (loss) income	3		
Foreign currency translation		(780)	410
Available-for-sale securities		(277)	(79)
Derivative instruments designated as cash flow hedges		(45)	(73)
Future income taxes on above items		(113)	44
		(1,215)	302
Comprehensive (loss) income		$ (566)	$ 1,089

d. Why is segment disclosure required under IFRS? As a user of Brookfield's annual report, how would your ability to use the financial statements be impaired by not having the segmented information?

e. What are the limitations of Brookfield's segment disclosure?

FS11-3. The following questions pertain to Brookfield's non-controlling interest:

a. What amount of non-controlling interest is reported on Brookfield's December 31, 2008 balance sheet? What does this amount represent?

b. What amount of non-controlling interest is reported on Brookfield's statement of income for the year ended December 31, 2008? What does this amount represent?

c. Which companies in Brookfield's portfolio gave rise to the non-controlling interest?

EXHIBIT 11.4 (continued) Brookfield Asset Management Corp.: Financial Statement Extracts

CONSOLIDATED STATEMENTS OF CASH FLOWS

YEARS ENDED DECEMBER 31 (MILLIONS)	Note	2008	2007
Operating activities			
Net income		$ 649	$ 787
Adjusted for the following non-cash items			
Depreciation and amortization		1,330	1,034
Future income taxes and other provisions		(194)	200
Realization gains		(164)	(231)
Non-controlling interest in non-cash items	22	(430)	(538)
Equity accounted loss and dividends received from investments		68	93
		1,259	1,345
Net change in non-cash working capital balances and other		(279)	1,472
Undistributed non-controlling interests in cash flows		587	467
		1,567	3,284

NOTES TO CONSOLIDATED FINANCIAL STATEMENTS

1. SUMMARY OF ACCOUNTING POLICIES

(a) Basis of Presentation

All currency amounts are in United States dollars ("U.S. dollars") unless otherwise stated. The consolidated financial statements include the accounts of Brookfield Asset Management Inc. (the "company") and the entities over which it has voting control, as well as Variable Interest Entities ("VIEs") for which the company is considered to be the primary beneficiary.

The company accounts for investments over which it has significant influence using the equity basis. Interests in jointly controlled partnerships and corporate joint ventures are proportionately consolidated. Measurement of investments in which the company does not have a significant influence depends on the financial instrument classification.

(d) Operating Assets
(v) Financial Assets, Investments and Securities

Financial Assets include securities that are not an active component of the company's asset management operations and are designated as either held-for-trading or available-for-sale. Investments in securities that are actively deployed in the company's operations are classified as securities and are designated as either held-for-trading or available-for-sale. Financial Assets and Securities are recorded at fair value, with changes in fair value accounted for in net income or other comprehensive income as applicable. Equity instruments designated as available-for-sale financial assets and securities that do not have a quoted market price from an active market are carried at cost.

4. INVESTMENTS

Equity accounted investments include the following:

(MILLIONS)	% of Investment 2008	% of Investment 2007	Book Value 2008	Book Value 2007
Chile Transmission	17%	28%	$ 324	$ 330
Property funds	20 - 25%	20 - 25%	233	382
Brazil Transmission	3 - 10%	7.5 - 25%	207	205
Norbord Inc.	—	41%	—	180
Real Estate Finance Fund	—	27%	—	148
Other			126	107
Total			$ 890	$ 1,352

On March 12, 2008, following a change in the ownership structure of the Real Estate Finance Fund, the company commenced accounting for its investment on a consolidated basis. During the fourth quarter of 2008, the company increased its ownership interest in Norbord Inc. and began accounting for its investment on a consolidated basis.

EXHIBIT ⟨11.4⟩   (continued) Brookfield Asset Management Corp.: Financial Statement Extracts

8.   SECURITIES

(MILLIONS)	2008	2007
Government bonds	$ 381	$ 465
Corporate bonds	344	670
Fixed income securities	408	449
Common shares	27	62
Canary Wharf Group common shares	143	182
Total	$ 1,303	$ 1,828

Securities represent holdings that are actively deployed in the company's financial operations and include $954 million (2007 – $1,638 million) owned through the company's insurance operations.

Corporate bonds include fixed-rate securities totalling $340 million (2007 – $634 million) with an average yield of 6.1% (2007 – 5.2%) and an average maturity of approximately three years. Government bonds and fixed-income securities include predominantly fixed-rate securities.

During the fourth quarter of 2008, the company transferred its investment in Canary Wharf Group to a pound sterling self-sustaining subsidiary.

15.   NON-CONTROLLING INTERESTS IN NET ASSETS

Non-controlling interests in net assets represent the common and preferred equity in consolidated entities that is owned by other shareholders.

(MILLIONS)	2008	2007
Common equity	$ 5,883	$ 4,232
Preferred equity	446	538
Total	$ 6,329	$ 4,770

22.   NON-CONTROLLING INTERESTS IN INCOME

Non-controlling interests of others in income is segregated into the non-controlling share of income before certain items and their share of those items, which include depreciation and amortization, income taxes and other provisions.

(MILLIONS)	2008	2007
Non-controlling interests' share of income prior to the following	$ 791	$ 636
Non-controlling interests' share of depreciation and amortization, and future income taxes and other provisions	(430)	(538)
Non-controlling interests in income	$ 361	$ 98
Distributed as recurring dividends		
Preferred	$ 2	$ 5
Common	203	169
Undistributed (Overdistributed)	156	(76)
Non-controlling interests in income	$ 361	$ 98

24.   EQUITY ACCOUNTED LOSS FROM INVESTMENTS

Equity accounted loss from investments includes the following:

(MILLIONS)	2008	2007
Norbord	$ (46)	$ (17)
Fraser Papers [1]	—	(23)
Stelco Inc. [2]	—	(32)
Total	$ (46)	$ (72)

1 During 2007, the company increased its ownership in Fraser Papers to 56% and started to account for the investment on a consolidated basis

2 During 2007, the company sold its 23% common equity interest in Stelco

EXHIBIT 11.4 (continued) Brookfield Asset Management Corp.: Financial Statement Extracts

28.   SEGMENTED INFORMATION

| AS AT AND FOR THE YEARS ENDED DECEMBER 31 | 2008 | | | 2007 | | |
| | Revenue | Net Income | Assets | Revenue | Net Income | Assets |
(MILLIONS)						
Commercial properties	$ 3,075	$ 203	$ 23,699	$ 2,891	$ 24	$ 23,571
Power generation	1,286	328	6,778	971	106	7,106
Infrastructure	616	37	4,414	622	4	4,230
Development and other properties	3,654	(7)	9,822	1,751	138	12,115
Specialty funds	2,139	126	3,943	1,368	187	2,676
Cash, financial assets, fee revenues and other	2,098	(38)	4,955	1,740	328	5,899
	$ 12,868	$ 649	$ 53,611	$ 9,343	$ 787	$ 55,597

Revenue and assets by geographic segments are as follows:

| AS AT AND FOR THE YEARS ENDED DECEMBER 31 | 2008 | | 2007 | |
| | Revenue | Assets | Revenue | Assets |
(MILLIONS)				
United States	$ 5,617	$ 27,220	$ 4,844	$ 27,156
Canada	3,005	11,755	2,604	12,248
Australia	1,826	6,031	622	8,323
Brazil	1,092	5,749	636	5,648
Europe	543	1,901	251	1,154
Other	785	955	386	1,068
	$ 12,868	$ 53,611	$ 9,343	$ 55,597

d. Why is the non-controlling interest added back to income from continuing operations when calculating cash from operations?

e. How much of the non-controlling interest was distributed as dividends?

f. If you were an investor in Brookfield Properties Corporation, a company 51.4 percent owned by Brookfield, how would you use the non-controlling interest information included in Brookfield's financial statements?

FS11-4. How much does Brookfield report on its December 31, 2008 balance sheet for securities? What categories of securities does Brookfield own? Which category do you think is most risky and which do you think is least risky? Explain. How are the securities valued?

FS11-5. What are the problems and limitations of analyzing financial ratios based on Brookfield's consolidated financial statements? Explain your reasons.

ENDNOTES

1. Extracted from Rogers Communications Inc.'s 2008 annual information form.

2. Extracted from Onex Corporation's 2008 annual report.

3. Ibid.

4. Extracted from Enbridge Inc.'s 2008 annual report.

5. Adapted from Brookfield Asset Management Inc.'s website at http://www.brookfield.com/content/corporate_info-16.html.

6. Extracted from Brookfield Asset Management Inc.'s 2008 annual report.

CHAPTER 12

ANALYZING AND INTERPRETING FINANCIAL STATEMENTS

At this 44th-floor office high atop First Canadian Place in the heart of Toronto's financial district, lawyer Robin Schwill has just returned from court where he updated a bankruptcy court judge about his client's latest negotiations with potential lenders. Schwill is a partner with the Bay Street law firm Davies Ward Phillips & Vineberg and has worked on some of the most high-profile corporate turnarounds and bankruptcies in recent Canadian business history.

These include Eddie Bauer, Nortel, Quebecor World, Ivaco, Air Canada, and Coventree Capital, an investment firm killed by its exposure to the North American sub-prime mortgage market collapse in 2007. In 2003, he helped a London, Ontario, candy maker that manufactured Life Savers restructure its secured debt before being sold.

Robin Schwill, BBA, MBA, LLB
Partner, Davies Ward Phillips &
Vineberg LLP
Financial Restructuring and Insolvency

Armed with both an MBA and a law degree from York University, Schwill's expertise in accounting and finance makes him one of the country's most sought-after insolvency and restructuring lawyers.

"Accounting is really the language of business," Schwill said in an interview. "If you really want to have a career within the business world or something that even relates to business or even journalism, reporting on business events, you cannot operate, to my mind, at any real, high level without understanding the language of business, which is twofold: accounting and legal."

After Schwill's first exposure to accounting courses in his Sutton West, Ontario high school, his father quickly put the teenager to work keeping the books for the family's small picture framing business. Schwill did journal entries, trial balances, and the closing off.

"I liked the accounting, I was good at accounting; it certainly helped at business school," Schwill recalled.

"And no, the framing business didn't ever go bankrupt," Schwill said, chuckling.

Although the soft-spoken Schwill might look like the typical mild-mannered accountant, he always planned to practice corporate law. It was while articling at law firm Osler Hoskin & Harcourt LLP that Schwill became interested in the bankruptcy and restructuring side of the profession.

"It had a lot more to do with the business aspect, the financial practicalities, then securities law and mergers and acquisitions," Schwill said. "As a legal advisor on the restructuring side, I think you actually get a lot closer to the numbers a lot faster than you would doing other standard public company work like takeover bids."

On any given day, he might be helping an Ontario auto parts supplier secure $5 million in loans in order to survive a few extra months and prevent layoffs at General Motors or Chrysler plants. Or he could be drafting an affidavit for a court to permit a company to enter bankruptcy protection under the *Companies Creditors' Arrangement Act (CCRA)*.

For that second case, he regularly analyzes companies' financial statements to write the legal documents covering a projected 13-week cash flow forecast for the court, or to decide how a company might later meet deadlines to pay back its creditors.

According to Schwill, this requires careful interpretation of the accounting numbers in financial statements, because creditors, bankers, lawyers, and accountants all have different uses for that information.

"I don't really care about the accounting rules," Schwill explained. "What I care about is understanding the underlying economics of the transaction, and once I understand, I can choose to characterize it as 'How would I report that—as an expense, or as an asset?' [because] those things will have different meanings to a user who's looking for value."

—E.B.

INTRODUCTION

After working your way through 11 chapters of this book you should have a good idea about how to read and interpret financial statement information. But now what? This chapter pulls together what's been covered so far. A useful analogy is to compare accounting information to a mystery. The reader of an accounting report, like the reader of a good mystery, must sort through clues, interpret and analyze information, exercise judgment, decide which information is relevant and which should be ignored, and use the information to come to a conclusion. Solving an accounting mystery requires detective work. The numbers tell a story, but it's usually necessary to read between the lines.

This chapter begins by providing some perspective on how different stakeholders approach the task of analyzing financial statements. It discusses the importance of having a good understanding of an entity and explains the concepts of permanent and transitory earnings, which are valuable for understanding how current earnings is useful for predicting future earnings.

Throughout the book, tools for analyzing and interpreting financial statements were discussed. This chapter reviews those analytical tools and offers additional methods for interpreting financial statements. Two techniques for restating the financial statement numbers as proportions and eliminating the impact of their size are introduced: common size financial statements and trend statements. The analytical tools and ratios are grouped into four themes:

1. evaluating performance
2. liquidity
3. solvency and leverage
4. other common ratios

WHY ANALYZE AND INTERPRET FINANCIAL STATEMENTS?

Analysis and interpretation of financial information isn't an end in itself. People analyze financial statements to help them make better decisions. The type of analysis done by stakeholders depends on the decisions they have to make. Different stakeholders need to resolve different questions. As a result, each stakeholder group will approach their analysis differently. Let's look at some stakeholders and discuss reasons why they would want to analyze financial statements.

Creditors Creditors come in many shapes and sizes. They may be suppliers of goods and services that get paid sometime (usually in a short time) after supplying the goods or services. They may be banks providing short term or permanent working capital loans, or suppliers of long-term financing through notes payable, bonds, debentures, or mortgages. Creditors may be public or private investors.

Creditors have two broad concerns:

- *Ability to pay*. To assess this concern, creditors consider the resources the entity has and the reliability, timing, and stability of its future cash flows. Creditors are particularly concerned about a borrower's ability to make payments as economic conditions change; for example, if the economy enters a recession.

- *Value of security*. Security is assets a creditor can sell if the borrower is unable to meet its obligations. For this reason, a creditor will want to know the net realizable value of the assets provided as security. Security can also come through restrictions on certain behaviours of the borrower: payment of dividends, additional borrowing, and sale of certain assets. The borrower might be asked to comply with specified accounting measures, such as the current ratio or the debt-to-equity ratio, and to remain within specified levels of these measures.

Restrictions limiting the actions of borrowers are known as **covenants**. Violating covenants can have significant economic consequences for the borrower, such as immediate repayment of the loan or an increase in the interest rate charged on the loan.

The type of analysis a creditor requires depends on the nature of the credit being provided. Short-term creditors will be concerned about an entity's financial situation at the time the credit is offered, liquidity of current assets, and how quickly the current assets turn over. Long-term creditors will want to forecast future cash flows and evaluate the borrower's ability to generate earnings.

Equity Investors In many ways, equity investors need to know everything and there are many questions they (or prospective equity investors) can ask. The value of the entity or its shares is extremely important information for people considering investing in or purchasing a private company. Private companies don't have prices set on a stock exchange, so a reasonable price is determined through financial statement analysis. Public companies are also thoroughly analyzed by individual investors, analysts for investment bankers, and mutual and pension fund managers to determine the attractiveness of investing in a particular company.

Other stakeholders and their interests include the following:

- Employees and their representatives analyzing the financial statements of the employer to determine the employer's ability to pay increased wages.

- The Canada Revenue Agency (CRA) analyzing financial statements to assess the reasonableness of amounts reported in tax returns.

- Regulators using financial information to evaluate requests by regulated companies for permission to increase their prices.

There are other stakeholders as well. The point is that while stakeholders use financial accounting information in their decision making, in most cases the financial statements don't present the answers to their questions "on a silver platter." Usually, the information in the financial statements must be analyzed, massaged, evaluated, and interpreted before it can provide insights about the entity.

KNOW THE ENTITY

Financial statements are only one source of information about an entity, albeit an important one. The successful analysis of an entity can't be achieved only by examining its financial statements. In fact, the analysis of an entity shouldn't even begin with the financial statements.

Financial statements are nothing more than numbers on pages. An understanding of what those numbers are saying requires an understanding of the entity's business, industry, and environment. Information can be obtained from many sources: the media, brokerage firms, and online services such as Globeinvestor.com, Bloomberg.com, Morningstar.ca, and The Motley Fool (www.fool.com).

www.statcan.gc.ca

What does one need to know about an entity, its industry, and environment? The list could be endless and much depends on the entity being investigated. The following are some possible questions:

- What does the entity do—what business or businesses is it in?

- What strategies does the entity use to make money?

- What are the entity's key success factors?

- What is the entity's competitive environment? (Are there many competitors? Is it easy for new competitors to enter the market?)

- What are the entity's competitive advantages?

- Who are the managers of the entity? What experience do they have? What has their performance been?

- What are the risks faced by the entity?

- Is the entity regulated? How does regulation affect the way it can conduct business?

- How do economic conditions and changes in economic conditions affect the entity?

- What are the conditions in the entity's businesses?

- How does the entity produce, market, and distribute its products?

- What are the key inputs for the entity and how does it obtain them? What are the conditions in the supplier market?

- Who are the entity's customers?

While one should examine sources besides the annual report to learn about an entity, its industry, and its environment, the sections of annual reports of public companies beyond the financial statements and notes can provide considerable useful information. One very valuable section is the **management discussion and analysis (MD&A)**, something that all publicly traded companies, but not private ones, must provide. The MD&A is prepared by an entity's managers and gives them the opportunity to discuss its financial results, position, and future prospects. The MD&A is intended to provide readers with a view of the entity through the eyes of management, but the quality of them varies widely from entity to entity and depends on what management puts into it. Some entities provide very informative MD&As, whereas others do little more than state the obvious.

While the MD&A can be a very valuable source of information about an entity, it's important to remember that management prepares it. This is an interesting paradox. Management is, for the most part, the best source of information and insight about the entity. But management is likely biased in how it presents information about the entity. That's not to say that the information they provide is false. Rather, management is likely to focus on positive aspects of the entity, its performance, and its prospects, and to provide favourable and optimistic interpretations of events.

Private companies aren't required to provide a MD&A. In general, one can expect to find far less information about private companies than about public ones, both from the companies themselves and from other sources. To begin with, private companies aren't required to disclose their financial statements to the public, and the investment community has little interest in them.

Of course, stakeholders should evaluate all information for its usefulness and credibility. Just because information is provided by a source other than the entity itself doesn't mean it's unbiased. For example, information from industry associations might support the interests of that industry. Also, research by brokerages and investment bankers may not want to offend companies that might use their services in the future, so they may be reluctant to make negative statements about potential future clients. There are many Internet discussion boards where investors exchange information about investment opportunities. Information from these sources is highly unreliable since it's usually very difficult to verify.

PERMANENT EARNINGS AND EARNINGS QUALITY

Permanent Earnings

One of the themes emphasized throughout this book is that net income isn't an absolute or true number. It is a measure of the economic gain or loss of the owners of the entity—a representation of the entity's underlying economic performance, albeit not a complete or comprehensive one. We have seen that measuring economic gains and losses is extremely complex. As a result, it isn't possible to determine an entity's "true" net income. The amount of income an entity reports is a function of the accounting policies it chooses and the estimates it makes. Despite all the difficulties that exist in measuring income, the measurement of income is important because it provides information to stakeholders for decision making.

Many stakeholders use current earnings to forecast future earnings. Their decisions are helped by knowing an entity's future net income. IFRS acknowledge the importance of future-oriented information but don't, however, require or support providing forecasted financial statements. As a result, stakeholders are left to their own devices to make these forecasts.

For forecasting future earnings, historical earnings can be used as a starting point. An important aspect of interpreting historical earnings is determining the components of earnings that can be expected to recur in future periods. These **permanent earnings**—earnings that are expected to be repeated in the future—are a good indicator of future earnings. In contrast, **transitory earnings** are earnings that aren't expected to be repeated. The net income of an entity can have both permanent and transitory components.

The distinction between permanent and transitory earnings and their impact on forecasting future earnings can be shown with an example. In mid-2014, Rusagonis Ltd. (Rusagonis) signed a $100,000 contract with a customer. After considering all costs, Rusagonis' management expects to earn $31,000 from the contract. If the revenue and earnings associated with this contract are to repeat year after year, the contract will increase permanent earnings. Measuring the value of a company as the present value of its future earnings, we would expect the value of Rusagonis to increase by the present value of a series of $31,000 payments to be received for the foreseeable future. As a result of the new contract, lenders would conclude that Rusagonis could support more debt, shareholders might anticipate increased dividends, and unions and employees might argue for increased wages and salaries.

In contrast, if the contract is just a one-time event, Rusagonis is clearly better off, but only by $31,000. A stakeholder would ignore the contract when estimating future earnings because it wouldn't be relevant—it was simply a one-time event and the effect on earnings is transitory. Everything else being equal, earnings would be expected to return to the pre-2014 level in the next year.

This discussion should highlight the importance to stakeholders of understanding the sources of an entity's earnings and the reason for changes in earnings. Permanent and transitory earnings should be interpreted differently, and financial statements should provide information that helps users distinguish them.

IFRS provide some help by requiring disclosure of events when they are significant and necessary for fair presentation. The language in the accounting standards is somewhat vague, so whether a transaction or economic event should be separately disclosed in the income statement or notes is often a matter of judgment. Managers may have incentives to highlight bad news as unusual and non-recurring but not to emphasize good news as unusual. Unusual items are more likely to be interpreted as transitory. For public companies, a transitory event should have less of an effect on the stock price, so managers might prefer to classify bad news as unusual. The logic is opposite for good news. If a good news event is classified as usual rather than unusual, the stock market may include its impact in permanent earnings. Similarly, if managers' bonuses are based on earnings before unusual items, there would be incentives for them to classify bad news as unusual and good news as part of "ordinary" operations.

Separate disclosure of events isn't uncommon. *Financial Reporting in Canada,* 33rd edition, reports that in 2007 there were 132 items disclosed separately on the income statement of the 200 companies surveyed.[1] The following types of items were identified:

- restructuring costs
- gains and losses on the disposal of capital assets
- gains and losses on the disposal of long-term investments
- impairment or writeoff of assets

An example of an unusual item can be found Enbridge's income statement in Exhibit 11.3 of Chapter 11. In 2008, the company reported a $694.6 million gain from the sale of an investment, which resulted in a significant increase in earnings over the previous year. Without the gain, earnings would have been about the same as the previous two years. If stakeholders focused only on the bottom line, they wouldn't see that the increase in earnings was likely temporary, caused by an unusual item.

 QUESTION FOR CONSIDERATION

Explain the difference between transitory and permanent earnings. Why is it important for users of financial statements to distinguish between them?

Answer: Permanent earnings are expected to be repeated in the future, whereas transitory earnings aren't expected to be repeated. Forecasting future earnings and cash flows depends on distinguishing between permanent and transitory earnings. For example, a lender trying to determine whether a prospective borrower will be able to meet interest and principal payments will want information about the entity's earnings and cash flows that are likely to occur in the future. Permanent earnings provide information in this regard, whereas transitory earnings don't. This isn't to say that transitory earnings aren't important—they can provide useful insights about the performance of the entity and management, but truly transitory events aren't useful for predictive purposes.

 INSIGHT

Our discussion in this section has focused on the reporting requirements of IFRS. It's important to recognize that the interpretation of transactions and other economic events as permanent or transitory isn't just an IFRS issue. Regardless of the accounting basis being used, stakeholders should distinguish between events that have permanent and transitory implications for the financial statements. Stakeholders should also be aware of any information that will affect their predictions. Information about commitments, contingencies, subsequent events, off-balance-sheet financing, and environment changes such as the economy, labour issues, regulation, competition, and so on should also be taken into consideration.

Earnings Quality

Earnings quality is another indicator of the usefulness of current earnings for predicting future earnings. Earnings quality is high if current and future earnings are highly correlated and low if current and future earnings aren't correlated. For example, earnings quality is low if there are a lot of transitory earnings in the income statement that can't be easily identified. Earnings quality is high if earnings are mainly permanent or it's easy to separate permanent and transitory earnings.

But earnings quality is much more than separating permanent and transitory earnings. Managers affect earnings quality with their accounting policies, estimates, and accruals. Earnings quality is impacted by earnings management when managers move earnings among periods to achieve their reporting objectives. This distorts the relationship between current and future earnings and impairs the usefulness of the financial statements for predicting future earnings and cash flow.

As we know, accounting doesn't affect an entity's cash flows (at least not directly, although there can be secondary cash flow effects caused by taxes, bonus plans, and so on). Earnings during a period can be thought of as being comprised of two elements: cash flow and accruals. These components can be expressed as an equation:

$$\text{Earnings} = \text{Cash from operations} + \text{Accruals}$$

Cash from operations is real. An entity collects and spends a specific number of dollars during the period. Accounting can do nothing to change that. Accruals represent the non-cash part of earnings. Accruals include things like depreciation, bad debt expense, accrued liabilities, provisions for losses, writedowns of assets, and allowances for returns, to name a few. Accruals require judgment as managers must estimate accrual amounts because the actual amounts aren't usually known.

Consider the bad debt expense. An accrual of a little too much bad debt expense this year means that, at some time in the future, a little bit less of an expense will be required. In other words, if managers make accruals that lower earnings in one period, earnings will be higher in another period to compensate. At the end of the life of an entity, collections are known with certainty, but during an entity's life it has to be estimated. Managers can use the uncertainty surrounding estimates and accruals to shift earnings among periods and possibly lower earnings quality.

Earnings quality can also be affected by an entity's operating decisions—the timing of its actual transactions. For example, if an entity wants to increase its income in a period, it can defer discretionary expenditures to a later period. Expenditures on items such as research and development, advertising, and repairs and maintenance are candidates for this type of treatment. However, cutting these expenditures just to boost the bottom line can be counterproductive, because while the cuts may provide a short-term increase to net income, they may reduce future earnings. An accounting impact of this is that the relationship between current and future earnings is weakened and earnings quality is reduced.

There are a number of ways to evaluate discretionary spending. One way is to look at an expenditure in relation to the sales of the entity. For example, for research and development costs, the following ratio could be calculated:

$$\text{Ratio of research and development expense to sales} = \frac{\text{Research and development expense}}{\text{Sales}}$$

Similar ratios can be calculated for other discretionary expenses. A significant decrease in the ratio in a period could indicate an attempt by management to bolster earnings by cutting discretionary spending. But there could be legitimate business reasons for the decrease. Remember, the ratios usually give clues, not definite answers.

Earnings management will be further discussed later in the chapter, once the different analytical tools have been discussed. However, below are some additional points to consider:

- Disclosure is one of the most effective ways of achieving understanding of the effects of an entity's accounting choices on its financial statements. If stakeholders were informed about the impact of accounting choices and estimates, they would be better able to assess the quality of an entity's earnings and then make better forecasts and assessments of the quality of information that management is providing. Disclosure requirements have been improving but it isn't practical to disclose every detail of an entity's economic activity, so there will always be limitations to comprehensive analyses.

- Accounting choices often have implications beyond the period of the choice. For example, when an entity takes a big bath by writing off or writing down some of its assets, earnings in later periods will be higher than they would have been had the big bath not occurred, because there are fewer costs to expense. If an entity wrote down equipment with a carrying amount of $10,000,000 to $4,000,000, income would be reduced by $6,000,000, but then there would be $6,000,000 less equipment to depreciate over the remaining useful life. The big bath itself would likely be interpreted as a transitory item, but the effect in subsequent years could be viewed as permanent.

www.mcgrawhill
connect.ca

KNOWLEDGE CHECK

- ❑ Why is it useful to stakeholders for entities to provide separate information about unusual items?

- ❑ What is meant by the term *earnings quality*? Give examples of how managers' accounting choices and operating decisions can affect an entity's earnings quality.

USING RATIOS TO ANALYZE ACCOUNTING INFORMATION

Throughout this book we have discussed using financial statement information to analyze entities. In most chapters, ratios and other analytical tools were introduced. In this chapter, some of the same ratios and analytical tools are discussed, but they are grouped into four analytical themes:

1. evaluating performance
2. liquidity
3. solvency and leverage
4. other common ratios

The material from earlier chapters isn't repeated in its entirety here, so you may find it helpful to review the earlier part of the book where the ratio or tool was initially introduced. Table 12.1 summarizes the financial statement analysis material covered in each chapter.

TABLE 12.1	Summary of Financial Statement Analysis Coverage in Chapters 2 through 11
Chapter	**Coverage**
Chapter 2	• Current ratio, page 42. • Debt-to-equity ratio, pages 43–44.
Chapter 3	• Profit margin ratio, page 110. • Return on equity, page 110.
Chapter 4	• The effect of accounting choices on financial statement numbers, pages 170ff.
Chapter 5	• Interpreting the cash flow statement, pages 257–265. • The effect of accrual accounting choices on the cash flow statement, pages 265–266.
Chapter 6	• Hidden reserves, pages 316–319. • Quick ratios and limitations of the current ratio for measuring liquidity, pages 319–322. • Accounts receivable turnover ratio and average collection period of accounts receivable—limitations of these measures, pages 322–323.
Chapter 7	• Inventory turnover ratio and average number of days inventory on hand—evaluation of inventory management, pages 378–380. • A banker's view of inventory, page 381.
Chapter 8	• Limitations to using historical information about capital assets for decision making, pages 413–414. • The effect of accounting policy choices on the cash flow statement, pages 439–440. • The effect of accounting policy choice on ratios, pages 441–442. • Return on assets—measurement of performance and operating efficiency of an entity, pages 441–443.
Chapter 9	• Debt-to-equity ratio—measure of risk and debt carrying ability, pages 511–512. • Interest coverage ratio—ability to cover fixed financing charges, pages 512–513.
Chapter 10	• Leverage, pages 576–578. • Carrying amount versus market value of equity—why the accounting value of equity can differ from the market value, pages 582–583. • Earnings per share (basic and fully diluted)—summary measure of performance, pages 583–584. • Return on shareholders' equity—measure of return earned by common shareholders, pages 584–585.
Chapter 11	• Limitations of consolidated financial statements for ratio analysis, pages 630–631.

Before we begin our discussion, here are a few points to keep in mind:

- There are no accounting standards for ratio or financial statement analysis; a person can modify or create any ratios appropriate for the analysis. What is important is making sure that the right tool is used.

- While many of the topics, ratios, and tools are presented separately, they can't be considered independently. Integrating information from different analyses will give the most informed insights.

- Financial information has to be integrated with information from other sources for a more complete picture of the entity and its circumstances.

- Materiality is important. Small percentage changes in some accounts (such as gross margin) can be very significant whereas large percentage changes in other accounts may be unimportant.

- Financial statement information can't be interpreted in a vacuum; it must be compared to previous years' information for the same entity and information for other entities, industry standards, forecasts, and other benchmarks.

Common Size Financial Statements and Trend Analysis

Interpreting raw numbers—the numbers presented in a set of financial statements—can be challenging. It can be difficult to make sense of trends and relationships among the numbers in the statements. It can also be difficult to compare the raw numbers of different entities. In this section we will discuss two tools that make this type of analysis easier:

- common size financial statements or vertical analysis

- trend or horizontal analysis

These tools eliminate the impact of size from the financial statement numbers by restating them as proportions. They also create many of the ratios we examine.

Common Size Financial Statements or Vertical Analysis **Common size financial statements**, or **vertical analysis**, express the amounts on the balance sheet and income statement as percentages of other elements in the same year's statements. On the balance sheet the amounts are stated as a percentage of total assets and on the income statement they are a percentage of revenue.

If the balance sheet amounts are percentages of total assets, the common size balance sheet will show the percentage each item is of total assets. This gives a good view of the asset and liability composition of the entity and of how it has changed over time. Similarly, if income statement amounts are stated as percentages of revenues, the stakeholder can see what proportion of sales each expense represents. This type of analysis shows the relative importance of different expenses and allows comparisons over time and with other entities. For example, comparing common size income statements allows stakeholders to see the percentage of each sales dollar spent on advertising, research and development, or wages. Examining the common size financial statements over a number of years may make it possible to explain things like changes in profitability. It might also help identify problem areas by highlighting expenses that have changed significantly relative to sales.

Table 12.2 provides partial balance sheet (Panel A) and complete income statement (Panel D) information about Leon's Furniture. Panels B and E provide common size information for the balance sheet and income statement. The common size amounts on the balance sheet are calculated by dividing each line by that year's total assets so that each amount is stated as a proportion of the total. For example, inventory for 2008 on the common size balance sheet is calculated as

$$\text{Common size inventory}_{2008} = \frac{\text{Inventory}_{2008}}{\text{Total assets}_{2008}}$$

$$= \frac{\$92,904,000}{\$513,408,000}$$

$$= 0.181$$

This means that on December 31, 2008, inventory represented 18.1 percent of Leon's assets. The same approach is used for the income statement except that the denominator is the year's sales. For example, for salaries and commissions for 2008,

$$\text{Common size salaries and commissions}_{2008} = \frac{\text{Salaries and commissions}_{2008}}{\text{Sales}_{2008}}$$

$$= \frac{\$112,270,000}{\$740,376,000}$$

$$= 0.152$$

Before reading on, take a few minutes to examine the common size statements and try to interpret them.

TABLE 12.2 Leon's Furniture Ltd.: Common Size and Trend Financial Statements

Panel A—Leon's Furniture Ltd.: Selected balance sheet accounts on December 31 ($000s),

	2008	2007	2006	2005	2004	2003	2002
Assets:							
Accounts receivable	$ 30,291	$ 33,684	$ 26,319	$ 20,705	$ 17,763	$ 18,602	$ 31,221
Inventory	92,904	75,640	74,733	72,644	71,279	58,841	55,047
Property, plant & equipment, net	219,813	211,619	207,066	182,023	170,022	150,468	136,584
Total assets	$513,408	$475,226	$438,997	$381,702	$368,121	$334,578	$320,439
Liabilities:							
Accounts payable and accrued liabilities	$ 95,247	$ 92,051	$ 94,023	$ 75,485	$ 79,451	$ 77,566	$ 73,151
Customers' deposits	14,119	13,533	12,887	9,496	9,896	7,217	6,664
Total liabilities	160,050	153,221	151,422	121,264	118,254	96,969	87,804
Shareholders' equity:							
Total shareholders' equity	353,358	322,005	287,575	260,438	249,867	237,609	232,635
Total liabilities and shareholders' equity	$513,408	$475,226	$438,997	$381,702	$368,121	$334,578	$320,439

Note: Only selected lines from the balance sheet are included. Some information is omitted.

Panel B—Leon's Furniture Ltd.: Common size balance sheets on December 31,

	2008	2007	2006	2005	2004	2003	2002
Assets:							
Accounts receivable	0.059	0.071	0.060	0.054	0.048	0.056	0.097
Inventory	0.181	0.159	0.170	0.190	0.194	0.176	0.172
Property, plant & equipment, net	0.428	0.445	0.472	0.477	0.462	0.450	0.426
Total assets	1.000	1.000	1.000	1.000	1.000	1.000	1.000
Liabilities:							
Accounts payable and accrued liabilities	0.186	0.194	0.214	0.198	0.216	0.232	0.228
Customers' deposits	0.028	0.028	0.029	0.025	0.027	0.022	0.021
Total liabilities	0.312	0.322	0.345	0.318	0.321	0.290	0.274
Shareholders' equity:							
Total shareholders' equity	0.688	0.678	0.655	0.682	0.679	0.710	0.726
Total liabilities and shareholders' equity	1.000	1.000	1.000	1.000	1.000	1.000	1.000

TABLE 12.2 (continued) Leon's Furniture Ltd.: Common Size and Trend Financial Statements

Panel C—Leon's Furniture Ltd.: Trend balance sheets on December 31,

	2008	2007	2006	2005	2004	2003	2002
Assets:							
Accounts receivable	0.970	1.079	0.843	0.663	0.569	0.596	1.000
Inventory	1.688	1.374	1.358	1.320	1.295	1.069	1.000
Property, plant & equipment, net	1.609	1.549	1.516	1.333	1.245	1.102	1.000
Total assets	1.602	1.483	1.370	1.191	1.149	1.044	1.000
Liabilities:							
Accounts payable and accrued liabilities	1.302	1.258	1.285	1.032	1.086	1.060	1.000
Customers' deposits	2.119	2.031	1.934	1.425	1.485	1.083	1.000
Total liabilities	1.823	1.745	1.725	1.381	1.347	1.104	1.000
Shareholders' equity:							
Total shareholders' equity	1.519	1.384	1.236	1.120	1.074	1.021	1.000
Total liabilities and shareholders' equity	1.602	1.483	1.370	1.191	1.149	1.044	1.000

Panel D—Leon's Furniture Ltd.: Income statement for the years ended December 31 ($000s),

	2008	2007	2006	2005	2004	2003	2002
Sales	$740,376	$637,456	$591,286	$547,744	$504,591	$456,352	$449,693
Cost of sales	440,360	363,261	341,403	323,629	295,241	267,323	261,265
Gross profit	300,016	274,195	249,883	224,115	209,350	189,029	188,428
Salaries & commissions	112,270	99,461	89,413	81,364	75,394	69,433	66,610
Advertising expense	33,752	32,008	32,326	30,494	29,492	27,193	27,306
Rent & property taxes	11,268	10,486	10,656	9,518	9,579	9,213	7,316
Amortization	16,253	14,034	13,348	11,892	10,412	9,881	8,552
Employee profit sharing	4,321	4,200	3,645	3,105	2,870	2,441	2,483
Other operating expenses	46,447	39,251	35,913	33,675	30,558	26,993	25,807
Interest income	(4,836)	(4,695)	(3,539)	(2,857)	(3,083)	(3,390)	(2,650)
Other income	(13,595)	(11,573)	(13,380)	(17,801)	(16,609)	(13,737)	(10,727)
Income before taxes	94,136	90,580	79,491	74,725	70,737	61,002	63,731
Current income taxes	29,396	31,122	27,287	24,646	23,389	26,541	19,461
Future income taxes	1,350	1,407	612	1,115	1,244	(4,391)	5,750
Net income	$ 63,390	$ 58,494	$ 53,602	$ 48,964	$ 46,104	$ 38,852	$ 38,520

TABLE 12.2 (continued) Leon's Furniture Ltd.: Common Size and Trend Financial Statements

Panel E—Leon's Furniture Ltd.: Common size income statement for the years ended December 31,*

	2008	2007	2006	2005	2004	2003	2002
Sales	1.000	1.000	1.000	1.000	1.000	1.000	1.000
Cost of sales	0.595	0.570	0.577	0.591	0.585	0.586	0.581
Gross profit	0.405	0.430	0.423	0.409	0.415	0.414	0.419
Salaries & commissions	0.152	0.156	0.151	0.149	0.149	0.152	0.148
Advertising expense	0.046	0.050	0.055	0.056	0.058	0.060	0.061
Rent & property taxes	0.015	0.016	0.018	0.017	0.019	0.020	0.016
Amortization	0.022	0.022	0.023	0.022	0.021	0.022	0.019
Employee profit sharing	0.006	0.007	0.006	0.006	0.006	0.005	0.006
Other operating expenses	0.063	0.062	0.061	0.061	0.061	0.059	0.057
Interest income	(0.007)	(0.007)	(0.006)	(0.005)	(0.006)	(0.007)	(0.006)
Other income	(0.018)	(0.018)	(0.023)	(0.032)	(0.033)	(0.030)	(0.024)
Income before taxes	0.127	0.142	0.138	0.136	0.140	0.134	0.142
Current income taxes	0.040	0.049	0.046	0.045	0.046	0.058	0.043
Future income taxes	0.002	0.002	0.001	0.002	0.002	(0.010)	0.013
Net income	0.086	0.092	0.091	0.089	0.091	0.085	0.086

*Columns may not add exactly due to rounding.

Panel F—Leon's Furniture Ltd.: Trend income statement for the years ended December 31,

	2008	2007	2006	2005	2004	2003	2002
Sales	1.646	1.418	1.315	1.218	1.122	1.015	1.000
Cost of sales	1.685	1.390	1.307	1.239	1.130	1.023	1.000
Gross profit	1.592	1.455	1.326	1.189	1.111	1.003	1.000
Salaries & commissions	1.685	1.493	1.342	1.221	1.132	1.042	1.000
Advertising expense	1.236	1.172	1.184	1.117	1.080	0.996	1.000
Rent & property taxes	1.540	1.433	1.457	1.301	1.309	1.259	1.000
Amortization	1.900	1.641	1.561	1.391	1.217	1.155	1.000
Employee profit sharing	1.740	1.692	1.468	1.251	1.156	0.983	1.000
Other operating expenses	1.800	1.521	1.392	1.305	1.184	1.046	1.000
Interest income	1.825	1.772	1.335	1.078	1.163	1.279	1.000
Other income	1.267	1.079	1.247	1.659	1.548	1.281	1.000
Income before taxes	1.477	1.421	1.247	1.173	1.110	0.957	1.000
Current income taxes	1.511	1.599	1.402	1.266	1.202	1.364	1.000
Future income taxes	0.235	0.245	0.106	0.194	0.216	(0.764)	1.000
Net income	1.646	1.519	1.392	1.271	1.197	1.009	1.000

The common size statements make year-to-year comparisons very convenient. By comparing each row, we see how each amount has changed over time. For example, the common size income statements show that in 2008 Leon's gross profit (gross margin), as a proportion of sales, is the lowest it's been over the seven years, and there has been a significant decrease from 2007 to 2008. It's difficult see this just from looking at Leon's actual statements of earnings.

There are some items that stand out from the seven-year analysis:

- Inventory has ranged from 19.4 percent of total assets in 2004 to 15.9 percent in 2007. There has been a significant jump in 2008 from 2007, following a downward trend from 2004 through 2007.

- In 2008, accounts payable and total liabilities are at their lowest as a proportion of total assets in the seven-year period.

- Leon's performance has been very stable over the period shown. Net income as a percentage of sales has varied only slightly, ranging from a low 8.5 percent to a high of 9.1 percent.

- Most expenses have varied little over the seven years. However, the increase in cost of sales in 2008 is cause for concern. This is by far Leon's largest expense and a small percentage decrease in the gross profit percentage can have a significant effect on the bottom line. For example, if cost of sales as a percentage of sales remained the same in 2008 as it was in 2007, everything else remaining the same, gross profit would have been have been $18.4 million higher. Net income would have increased by the same amount or 29 percent.

- Dollar spending on advertising has increased over the period, but as a percentage of sales it has decreased steadily by about 25 percent since 2002.

Though this point has been made many times in the book, it bears repeating: *Financial statement analysis may help identify problems, but it won't usually explain them.* For example, why did gross profit decrease by so much in 2008? Perhaps it was due to foreign currency fluctuations that increased the cost of imported merchandise, poor purchasing decisions or inventory management, or a toughening competitive environment. Simply looking at the data doesn't give us the answer. Leon's MD&A explains that the decrease is due to the company's acquisition of Appliance Canada, which has lower margins than the typical Leon's store. In many cases, though, explanations aren't found in the annual report, MD&A, or anywhere else, and stakeholders have to rely on their own analysis for answers.

Common size financial statements allow stakeholders to compare entities that are different in size by eliminating the effects of size and presenting the financial statement components on a common basis. Of course, differences between entities have to be interpreted carefully because they can be due to different accounting choices as well as to differences in the economic performance and nature of the entities.

Horizontal Analysis or Trend Statements   **Horizontal analysis**, or **trend statements**, is another analytical tool that eliminates the effects of size from financial statements. Trend statements restate the financial statements with each account amount presented as a percentage of a base year amount. This shows the change in each account over time. To construct trend statements, it's first necessary to specify a base year.

Panel C of Table 12.2 provides Leon's 2002 through 2008 trend amounts for selected balance sheet accounts, and Panel F provides trend income statements. The general formula for calculating trend amounts is

$$\text{Trend statement amount} = \frac{\text{Current year amount}}{\text{Base year amount}} \times 100\%$$

For sales in 2008 the calculation is

$$\text{Trend statement sales} = \frac{\text{Sales}_{2008}}{\text{Sales}_{2002}} \times 100\%$$

$$= \frac{\$740,376,000}{\$449,693,000} \times 100\%$$

$$= 164.6\%$$

This means that Leon's sales in 2008 were 164.6 percent of sales in 2002, or sales grew by 64.6 percent between 2002 and 2008. The trend data allows the user to see the change in each account over time relative to the base year.

Notice that for calculating trend data, a base year is chosen for each line in the financial statements and the amounts for other years are stated as a percentage of the base. If trend cost of sales for 2007 was calculated, the numerator would be cost of sales in 2007 and the denominator would be cost of sales in 2002. When the trend statement amount is calculated for another line on the financial statements, the amounts from that line are used. To see the percentage change from a time other than the selected base year, the calculation must be redone with a different denominator.

Examination of Leon's trend data yields some observations:

- Sales and cost of sales have grown similarly over the seven years. By 2008, growth of cost of sales was slightly higher than sales, which implies a decreasing gross profit.

- Advertising expense has grown much more slowly than sales and the other expenses.

- Through 2008, net income had grown by the same percent as sales, although in the previous five years it had been growing faster than sales.

- Over the period shown, inventory and sales have grown at about the same rate, although in any given year there have been variations. This suggests that Leon's inventory management is reasonable.

Some interpretational issues associated with using trend statements should be noted:

- When the balance in an account changes from positive to negative, or from negative to positive, the change can't be interpreted simply by looking at the percentage change relative to the base year.

- If the balance in an account in the base year is zero, it isn't possible to calculate a trend number for subsequent years. In addition, very small balances in the base year can result in huge percentage changes that may not be meaningful.

- Trend information gives no perspective on materiality. Without reference to the actual numbers, it's possible to spend time worrying about an account that isn't material.

Evaluating Performance

Many stakeholders want to evaluate the performance of entities. This is often easier said than done because performance is a multi-faceted concept that can be measured in different ways, and different performance indicators can often tell conflicting stories about how an entity is doing. In this section, we discuss different ways of evaluating the performance of an entity. As we do, remember that we can't claim that IFRS or any accounting system can provide an entity's true income. Accounting measurements are representations of an entity's economic activity and are subject to the accounting policies and estimates the managers make. Thus, while there might be a "true" income or economic reality out there, it isn't possible to know what it is. At the same time, while there are many problems associated with measuring performance, those problems don't take away the need to measure it so that stakeholders can make decisions about how to invest their resources, evaluate how well managers have done their jobs, and address many other performance-related questions. How then, does one approach this task?

A logical place to start is with the income statement. In accrual accounting, the income statements provide an indication of an entity's economic benefits (revenues) and the economic sacrifices (expenses) that were incurred to generate those benefits. Net income is a representation of the net economic benefit or sacrifice of the owners of the entity over a period. We can also look at subtotals within the income statement to get different indicators of performance. Gross margin (sales − cost of sales), operating income, and income before taxes are examples of different, potentially informative measures that are reported on an income statement. Ratios are among the most commonly used tools for analyzing financial statements and examining the relationships between the numbers. Also, like common size financial statements and trend statements, ratios eliminate the effect of size from the data. Let's examine some common income statement performance measures.

Gross Margin Gross margin is the difference between sales and cost of sales. It's often stated as a percentage of sales and called the gross margin percentage, which is the percentage of each dollar of sales that is available to cover other costs and return a profit to the entity's owners. The gross margin percentage is defined as

$$\text{Gross margin percentage} = \frac{\text{Sales} - \text{Cost of sales}}{\text{Sales}} \times 100\% = \frac{\text{Gross margin}}{\text{Sales}} \times 100\%$$

Continuing with Leon's as our example, Leon's gross margin is reported on the gross profit line of its income statement shown in Panel B of Table 12.2. For 2008, Leon's gross margin was $300,016,000 and its gross margin percentage 40.5 percent. Leon's gross margin percentage can be found on the common size income statements in Panel D of the table. As we discussed earlier, Leon's gross margin slipped in 2008, which could be an indicator of problems, although the MD&A attributed the decrease to an acquisition.

An entity's gross margin percentage can be improved in two ways:

1. Increase the price charged for goods or services. It isn't always possible for a business to raise its price without sales decreasing. Some companies might be willing to accept lower sales for higher margins while others accept small margins and try to make money on volume (the gross margin percentage will be lower but increased sales will provide a higher gross margin).

2. Cost control and efficiency. If an entity can obtain the inputs it requires at a lower cost, or use those inputs more efficiently, the entity will have a higher gross margin percentage.

Gross margin percentages can vary dramatically from entity to entity and industry to industry as is seen in Table 12.3. Notice that The Brick Group Income Fund, which is in the same industry as Leon's, has a gross margin for 2008 that is almost identical to Leon's. Some companies like Magna International Inc. and Loblaw Companies Limited have relatively "thin" or small margins. This doesn't mean those companies don't perform well. It's important to consider the nature of the business. For example, some businesses make a small amount of money on each transaction but earn a profit by having a lot of sales.

Some industries don't lend themselves to determining a gross margin. Service businesses, like law or accounting firms, don't have costs that would typically be included in cost of sales.

TABLE 12.3	Gross Margin Percentages for Selected Companies		
Company	**Industry**	**2008**	**2007**
The Brick Group Income Fund	Furniture retailing	40.6%	40.1%
Canfor Corporation	Forestry	25.2	21.1
High Liner Foods Inc.	Food processing	21.9	26.2
Indigo Books & Music Inc.	Book retailing	43.1	
Leon's Furniture Limited	Furniture retailing	40.5	43.0
Loblaw Companies Limited	Grocery	22.4	
Research In Motion Limited	Computer hardware	46.1	51.3
Tim Hortons Inc.	Food service	42.2	42.0

Note: Gross margins for Indigo and Loblaw aren't available for 2007 because these companies didn't begin disclosing cost of inventory sold separately until 2008.

Profit Margin Ratio The profit margin ratio is a bottom-line measure of performance. It indicates the percentage of each sales dollar that the entity earns in profit. The ratio is defined as

$$\text{Profit margin ratio} = \frac{\text{Net income}}{\text{Sales} \times 100\%}$$

A higher profit margin ratio indicates greater profitability because a larger proportion of each dollar of sales is profit. Leon's profit margin for the fiscal year ended December 31, 2008 is calculated as

$$\text{Profit margin ratio} = \frac{\text{Net income}}{\text{Sales} \times 100\%}$$

$$= \frac{\$63,390,000}{\$740,376,000} \times 100\%$$

$$= 8.6\%$$

The profit margin ratio of 8.6 percent means that Leon's made $0.086 for every dollar of sales. Leon's profit margin in 2007 was 9.1 percent.

There are some variations of the profit margin ratio. The numerator can be defined as operating income or income before non-controlling interest. These provide measures of profitability that reflect ongoing operations rather than overall profitability. Table 12.4 shows the profit margin ratios for some Canadian companies for the years 2005 through 2008.[2] The table shows that there is a wide variation of profit margin among companies and over time.

TABLE 12.4	Profit Margin Ratios for Selected Canadian Companies			
Company	**Profit margin for:**			
	2008	**2007**	**2006**	**2005**
The Brick Group Income Fund	−14.1%	0.3%	2.8%	2.6%
Canfor Corporation	−12.3	−9.0	12.9	2.7
High Liner Foods Inc.	2.3	2.5	2.0	−15.5
Indigo Books & Music Inc.	3.3	5.7	3.4	3.0
Leon's Furniture Limited	8.6	9.1	8.7	8.9
Research In Motion Limited	17.1	21.5	20.8	18.5
Tim Hortons Inc.	13.9	14.2	15.6	12.9
WestJet Airlines Limited	7.0	9.1	6.5	1.7

We create variations on the profit margin ratio by moving up the income statement a bit. For example, operating profit margin is income before financing costs (interest), unusual items, and other non-operating costs. This is a measure of performance for the actual business activities of the entity.

Return on Investment Our discussion of performance to this point has focused on the income statement. We have looked at two measures of performance, each calculated as a percentage of sales. These provide some insight into an entity's profitability, but they ignore the cost to generate those sales and earn those profits. An entity could have a high gross margin and profit margin, but the amount of investment required to earn those margins, the amount of assets or equity required, might indicate that performance wasn't very good. In other words, a profit of $1,000,000 will be evaluated differently depending on whether the investment required to earn it was $5,000,000 or $50,000,000.

This is where our measures of return on investment come in. Earlier in the book, two measures of return on investment—return on assets (ROA) and return on equity (ROE)—allowed us to assess the performance of an entity in relation to the investment made. They differ in the investment base that each uses. ROA uses all investment, debt and equity, to determine the return. It measures the entity's performance independent of how its assets were financed. In contrast, ROE determines the common equity investor's return on the investment. Both are valid and widely used measures. Here are the definitions of ROA and ROE in equation form:

$$\text{Return on assets} = \frac{\text{Net income} + \text{After-tax interest expense}}{\text{Average total assets}} = \frac{\text{Net income} + \text{Interest expense} \times (1 - \text{Tax rate})}{\text{Average total assets}}$$

$$\text{Return on equity} = \frac{\text{Net income} - \text{Preferred dividends}}{\text{Average common shareholders' equity}}$$

The numerator in ROA has after-tax interest expense added back because the ratio is a measure of return that is independent of how the assets are financed. If the interest expense were included in the numerator, ROA would be affected by the amount of debt because the interest expense would increase with the amount of debt. When calculating ROE, preferred dividends are deducted from net income because it's a measure of return to the common shareholders, and preferred dividends are paid to the preferred shareholders. ROA and ROE for Leon's, The Brick, and the retailing industry they are a part of are shown in Table 12.5.[3] Leon's outperforms The Brick and the retailing industry in every year shown. In addition, Leon's returns are consistent over the five-year period.

TABLE 12.5	Return on Assets and Return on Equity for Leon's, The Brick, and the Retailing Industry			
	2008	**2007**	**2006**	**2005**
Leon's ROA	12.82%	12.80%	13.06%	13.06%
ROE	18.77	19.19	19.56	19.19
The Brick ROA	(22.96)	0.62	4.67	4.20
ROE	(75.87)	1.18	8.08	6.47
Retailing ROA	6.92	8.35	9.17	9.54
ROE	10.64	14.38	15.36	17.63

TABLE 12.6	Return on Equity and Assets for Selected Companies				
		2008	**2007**	**2006**	**2005**
Canfor Corporation	ROE	(20.85)%	(17.83)%	22.26%	5.07%
	ROA	(8.78)	(6.61)	12.54	3.84
High Liner Foods Inc.	ROE	11.21	8.66	7.84	(55.61)
	ROA	6.01	3.46	4.74	(27.54)
Indigo Books & Music Inc.	ROE	29.96	22.69	24.78	12.82
	ROA	13.14	8.33	7.45	4.34
Leon's Furniture Limited	ROE	12.82	12.80	13.06	13.06
	ROA	18.77	19.19	19.56	19.19
Research In Motion Limited	ROE	38.59	40.33	28.18	19.19
	ROA	27.81	30.09	23.39	15.49
WestJet Airlines Ltd.	ROE	17.50	21.96	15.54	3.81
	ROA	7.39	8.89	6.62	2.43

Returns on equity and assets for some of the companies we've looked at in the book are shown in Table 12.6. Note the variation between the companies as well as from company to company. Also notice the difference between ROE and ROA. Large differences indicate companies using a lot of debt for financing (leverage). Of the firms listed, Leon's seems to be the one that provides the most consistent returns.

Keep in mind that these measures of return on investment are affected by managers' accounting choices. This means that comparisons among firms may not be valid, though it might be possible to interpret trends among different firms. Also, remember that returns are related to risk; the higher the risk, the higher the return should be. Therefore, differences in returns may reflect differences in risk as well as different performance levels.

It's common to break down ROA into components—profit margin and asset turnover—to understand how an entity is generating its returns and to help identify how its performance can be improved. ROA can then be stated as

$$\text{Return on assets} = \text{Asset turnover ratio} \times \text{Profit margin ratio} \times 100\%$$
$$= \frac{\text{Sales}}{\text{Average total assets}} \times \frac{\text{Net income} + \text{Interest expense} \times (1 - \text{Tax rate})}{\text{Sales}} \times 100\%$$
$$= \frac{\text{Net income} + \text{Interest expense} \times (1 - \text{Tax rate})}{\text{Average total assets}} \times 100\%$$

TABLE 12.7	Combinations of Profit Margin and Asset Turnover for Generating a Specific ROA		
	Company A	**Company B**	**Company C**
Sales	$8,000,000	$1,000,000	$4,000,000
Net income	640,000	20,000	40,000
Average assets	8,000,000	250,000	500,000
Profit margin ratio	8%	2%	1%
Asset turnover ratio	1	4	8
Return on assets	8%	8%	8%

Remember that profit margin indicates the amount of each sales dollar the entity earns as profit. **Asset turnover** is a measure of how effectively an entity can generate sales from its asset base. The more sales an entity can generate from its asset base, the higher its asset turnover ratio and the higher its ROA. An entity that produces the same amount of sales but carries less inventory than its competitors, everything else being equal, will have a higher asset turnover ratio and a higher ROA.

An entity can generate a given ROA through different combinations of profit margin and asset turnover. The objective for any entity is to maximize its ROA. It's up to management to design strategies that achieve this objective. A business or industry might pursue a strategy of accepting a low profit margin but compensate by having a high asset turnover ratio—make a small amount of money on each sale, but make a lot of sales. Those with a relatively low asset turnover ratio would try to compensate with a higher profit margin.

In Table 12.7, three combinations for earning an 8 percent ROA are shown. Company A generates its ROA with a relatively high profit margin (8 percent) but a relatively low asset turnover ratio (1 percent). Company C does the opposite: a very small profit margin ratio but its assets turn over quickly. Company B is in between.

By breaking down ROA into its components, it's possible to identify sources of an entity's performance problems. A low profit margin requires different corrective steps than a low asset turnover ratio. An entity with a low profit margin might focus on product pricing (it might try to increase its prices) or find ways of controlling or reducing costs. A company with a low asset turnover ratio might look for unproductive or idle assets that could be sold, or for assets that could be managed more efficiently and effectively (inventory or receivables levels that could be lowered).

Of course, there are limits to the improvements management can make. If an entity is already performing well in either profit margin or asset turnover, there is only so much the managers can do to make improvements. Also, the nature of an industry imposes limits on these ratios. For example, industries requiring very large capital investments tend to have lower asset turnover ratios.

Now let's examine the components of Leon's ROA. The information needed from Leon's financial statements to do the analysis is shown in Table 12.8.

TABLE 12.8	Return on Investment for Leon's Furniture Ltd., 2004–2008				
	2008	**2007**	**2006**	**2005**	**2004**
Revenue	$740,376,000	$637,456,000	$591,286,000	$547,744,000	
Net income (loss)	63,390,000	58,494,000	53,602,000	48,964,000	
Total assets	513,408,000	475,226,000	438,997,000	381,702,000	368,121,000
Interest expense	0	0	0	0	
Tax rate	32.7%	35.9%	35.1%	34.5%	

For 2008, the breakdown of ROA is calculated as follows:

$$
\begin{aligned}
\text{Return on assets}_{2008} &= \text{Asset turnover ratio} \times \text{Profit margin ratio} \times 100\% \\
&= \frac{\text{Sales}}{\text{Average total assets}} \times \frac{\text{Net income} + [\text{Interest expense} \times (1 - \text{Tax rate})]}{\text{Sales}} \times 100\% \\
&= \frac{\$740,376,000}{(\$513,408,000 + \$475,226,000)/2} \times \frac{\$63,390,000 + [\$0 \times (1 - 0.327)]}{\$740,376,000} \times 100\% \\
&= 1.498 \times 0.086 \times 100\% \\
&= 12.8\%
\end{aligned}
$$

Note that in this calculation we use profit margin after adding back the after-tax cost of interest. This makes the calculation consistent with the definition of return on assets. We can use the information in Table 12.8 to calculate return on assets and its components for the fiscal years 2005 through 2008. The results are shown in Table 12.9.

TABLE 12.9	Return on Assets for Leon's Furniture Limited, 2005–2008				
	Return on assets	**=**	**Asset turnover ratio**	**×**	**Profit margin percentage**
2008	12.82%	=	1.498	×	8.56%
2007	12.80%	=	1.395	×	9.18%
2006	13.06%	=	1.441	×	9.07%
2005	13.06%	=	1.461	×	8.94%

As mentioned, Leon's ROA has been very stable over recent years, as have been the components of it. We could further break down the asset turnover ratio into additional component parts, such as receivables turnover (see Chapter 6) and inventory turnover (see Chapter 7), to gain further insight into changes in the asset turnover ratio. We can find additional information about the profit margin percentage by examining the common size financial statements (see Table 12.2) to see changes in the income statement components.

Earnings per Share Earnings per share (EPS) is the amount of net income that is attributable to each individual share of common stock. EPS comes in a number of variations, but the most straightforward is basic EPS, which is calculated using the following formula:

$$
\text{Basic EPS} = \frac{\text{Net income} - \text{Preferred dividends}}{\text{Weighted-average of common shares outstanding during the period}}
$$

Preferred dividends are deducted from net income in the numerator because the amount isn't available to common shareholders, but they aren't deducted in the calculation of net income. The denominator is the weighted-average number of shares that were outstanding during the year (see the text website at www.mcgrawhillconnect.ca for an explanation of the weighted-average number of shares).

Another EPS measure is fully diluted EPS, which shows the effect that dilutive securities (convertible bonds, convertible preferred shares, and stock options that can be converted into common stock) would have on EPS if they were converted or exchanged for common stock. Fully diluted EPS can be thought of as a worst-case scenario of EPS. It's given because predicting future earnings is an important use of financial statements.

 CANADIAN GAAP FOR PRIVATE ENTERPRISES

Canadian GAAP for Private Enterprises doesn't require companies to calculate and present earnings per share.

INSIGHT

Financial Ratios and Market Values

IFRS allows companies to value certain capital assets at their fair value. This will create problems interpreting many ratios (including return on assets and equity and debt-to-equity ratio). Comparability will be impaired unless all the companies being compared use the same valuation method. Also, if the fair value of the assets being revalued fluctuates by a significant amount the ratios will also fluctuate. This situation adds another challenge for stakeholders evaluating financial statements.

www.mcgrawhill
connect.ca

KNOWLEDGE CHECK

- ☐ What is gross margin? What is gross margin percentage? What does gross margin percentage mean?
- ☐ Distinguish return on assets from return on equity. How is each calculated?

Liquidity

Liquidity is the availability of cash and near-cash resources, which are necessary for meeting payments as they come due. Lenders and creditors assess an entity's liquidity to ensure it will be able to pay amounts owed. If there is concern the entity won't be able to meet its obligations, lenders and creditors may not want to provide credit, or they may attach terms to any credit offered that will reflect the level of risk associated with the entity.

In Chapter 6, the current and quick (acid test) ratios were introduced. The current ratio is a measure of the resources an entity has to meet its short-term obligations. The higher the current ratio, the more likely an entity will be able to meet its current obligations. It also indicates greater protection in the event the entity's cash flow somehow becomes impaired. The ratio assumes that inventory, receivables, and other current assets can be converted to cash on a timely basis. The current ratio is defined as

$$\text{Current ratio} = \frac{\text{Current assets}}{\text{Current liabilities}}$$

The quick ratio is a stricter test of an entity's ability to meet its obligations because it excludes less liquid assets such as inventory and prepaids. Inventory can take a fairly long time to convert into cash because it has to be sold and the purchase price collected before cash is realized. For businesses in which inventory turns over relatively slowly, a lot of time can pass before the inventory is realized in cash. In these cases, inventory can't be considered very liquid. Other current assets (for example, prepaids) will never be realized in cash, so it makes sense to exclude them from an assessment of liquidity. The quick or acid test ratio is defined as follows:

$$\text{Quick ratio acid test ratio} = \frac{\text{Quick assets}^*}{\text{Current liabilities}}$$

*Quick assets include cash, temporary investments, accounts receivable, and any other current assets that can be quickly converted to cash.

A major problem with both the current and quick ratios is that they are static measures. They reflect the existing current resources available to meet existing obligations but say nothing about the entity's ability to generate cash flow. Ultimately, an entity's liquidity depends on its ability to generate cash flows, so paying attention to cash from operations is important. As long as an entity has a steady and reliable flow of cash coming in, a low current ratio isn't a concern. However, if cash flow is unpredictable—for example, if an entity is sensitive to economic changes or competitive changes in the industry—then the current ratio indicates an entity's ability to weather any cash flow disturbances in the short term. A higher current (or quick) ratio means an entity has more insurance in the event that cash flow becomes impaired.

It's important to understand that many liquidity problems arise because of changes in the environment. If an entity's environment remains stable and predictable, it's unlikely to face liquidity problems (assuming that it doesn't already have liquidity problems). However, a changing environment can create significant liquidity pressures. Change can take many forms. It can be economy-wide (an economic slowdown) or specific to the entity (growth) or to an industry (competition). Change in the environment can affect the timing and amount of cash flows. An economic slowdown might reduce an entity's sales, force a reduction in prices, increase the amount of uncollectible accounts receivable, increase the time it takes to collect receivables, and make inventory less saleable. Regardless of these problems, suppliers would still have to be paid the full agreed-upon amount.

The turnover of receivables and inventory gives additional insight into an entity's liquidity. Receivables and inventory can represent important parts of the cash cycle, so understanding how long it takes to realize them in cash can help a stakeholder predict cash flows and identify liquidity problems. The accounts receivable turnover ratio indicates how quickly an entity collects its receivables. The larger the ratio, the more quickly receivables are being collected. The average collection period is the number of days, on average, it takes to collect receivables. A decrease in the receivables turnover ratio (or an increase in the average collection period) relative to previous years or a deterioration relative to similar firms or industry benchmarks may suggest a liquidity problem. Receivables may have become less collectable (uncollectibles increase) and/or the period of time it takes to collect receivables has increased. As a result, the entity has less cash to meet its obligations. The following are formulas for the accounts receivable turnover ratio and the average collection period for accounts receivable:

$$\text{Accounts receivable turnover ratio} = \frac{\text{Credit sales}}{\text{Average accounts receivable}}$$

$$\text{Average collection period of accounts receivable} = \frac{365}{\text{Accounts receivable turnover ratio}}$$

The inventory turnover ratio indicates the number of times during a period the entity is able to purchase and sell (or use) its stock of inventory. The average number of days inventory on hand indicates the number of days, on average, it takes to sell or use inventory. A high turnover rate (or low average number of days inventory on hand) indicates a more liquid inventory that is sold more quickly so less cash is invested in inventory. A decreasing inventory turnover ratio (or increasing average number of days inventory on hand) relative to previous years, or one that is deteriorating relative to similar firms or industry benchmarks, may suggest a liquidity problem. Inventory may not be selling well or some could be obsolete. Following are the formulas for the inventory turnover ratio and the average number of days inventory on hand:

$$\text{Inventory turnover ratio} = \frac{\text{Cost of sales}}{\text{Average inventory}}$$

$$\text{Average number of days inventory on hand} = \frac{365}{\text{Inventory turnover ratio}}$$

A third turnover ratio can be added, one we haven't examined before. The **accounts payable turnover ratio** provides information about how quickly an entity pays its accounts payable. This ratio is calculated using the following formula:

$$\text{Accounts payable turnover ratio} = \frac{\text{Credit purchases}}{\text{Average accounts payable}}$$

IFRS requires disclosure of the cost of inventory expensed during the year so purchases can be estimated using the following equation:

$$\text{Purchases} = \text{Cost of sales} - \text{Beginning inventory} + \text{Ending inventory}$$

This ratio focuses on amounts owed to suppliers of inventory. The fact that accounts payable usually includes amounts owed to many different types of suppliers, including employees, is a problem. A better ratio would be to consider all purchases on credit and all amounts owed to all suppliers.

In its December 31, 2014 financial statements, Bawlf Ltd. (Bawlf) reported beginning inventory of $190,000, ending inventory of $225,000, and cost of sales of $1,100,000. Accounts payable on December 31, 2013 and 2014 were $127,000 and $135,000, respectively. All of Bawlf's accounts payable pertain to the purchase of inventory. The first step is to calculate the amount of inventory purchased during 2014:

$$
\begin{aligned}
\text{Purchases} &= \text{Cost of inventory expensed} - \text{Beginning inventory} + \text{Ending inventory} \\
&= \$1,100,000 \qquad\qquad - \qquad \$190,000 \quad + \quad \$225,000 \\
&= \$1,135,000
\end{aligned}
$$

$$
\begin{aligned}
\text{Accounts payable turnover ratio} &= \frac{\text{Purchases}}{\text{Average accounts payable}} \\
&= \frac{\$1,135,000}{[(\$127,000 + \$135,000) \div 2]} \\
&= 8.66
\end{aligned}
$$

The accounts payable turnover ratio can also be stated as the number of days that the entity takes to pay its accounts payable. This ratio, the **average payment period for accounts payable**, is calculated as follows:

$$\text{Average payment period for accounts payable} = \frac{365}{\text{Accounts payable turnover ratio}}$$

Bawlf's average payment period for accounts payable can be calculated:

$$
\begin{aligned}
\text{Average payment period for accounts payable} &= \frac{365}{\text{Accounts payable turnover ratio}} \\
&= \frac{365}{8.66} \\
&= 42.1 \text{ days}
\end{aligned}
$$

This amount means that, on average, Bawlf takes just over 42 days to pay its suppliers.

Examining these amounts over time for an entity may provide some useful insights. A decreasing accounts payable turnover ratio or increasing average payment period may indicate that the entity is having cash flow problems and extending the time it takes to pay its accounts payable.

Taken together, these three turnover ratios, when expressed in number of days, give an idea of how well operating cash inflows and outflows are matched. Recall that in Chapter 5 we discussed the lag that exists between the expenditure of cash and the receipt of cash. The three turnover ratios allow us to estimate the lag using the following equation:

$$
\text{Cash lag} = \frac{\text{Average collection period of}}{\text{accounts receivable}} + \frac{\text{Average number of}}{\text{days inventory on hand}} - \frac{\text{Average payment period}}{\text{for accounts payable}}
$$

The larger the cash lag, the longer the period of time the entity must self-finance its inventory and accounts receivable. The lag length will likely increase during periods of financial distress. This information can be important to stakeholders such as lenders, who want to predict cash flows and assess the risk associated with a loan.

However, analyzing liquidity isn't only a matter of using ratios. The notes to the financial statements often provide information that is useful, information that isn't reflected in the financial statements themselves. For example, many entities have access to lines of credit that they can borrow from as needed. If the available lines of credit have not yet been fully used, the unused amount isn't reported on the balance sheet. That available credit can be an important source of liquidity for the entity and should be taken into consideration when its liquidity position is analyzed.

Exhibit 12.1 provides part of Note 10 from Maple Leaf Foods Inc. (Maple Leaf), the meat processing company, which describes credit available to the company to use as it's needed.[4] Maple Leaf can borrow up to $870 million under the terms of the borrowing arrangement, of which $559.8 million had been utilized as of December 31, 2008, an increase of $423.5 million over 2007. The $310.2 million that hasn't been used isn't reflected on the balance sheet but represents a source of liquidity if and when needed. Given the large amount of the credit facility used in 2008, some stakeholders might wonder if there would be enough credit available for 2009 or if new arrangements would be required.

www.mapleleaf.com

Entities sometimes make commitments that require them to make cash payments in the future. These were described earlier in the book as executory contracts—contract arrangements for which neither party has performed its side of the arrangement, so there are no financial statement effects. These commitments, such as payments required under operating leases, have implications for an entity's liquidity because they commit an entity to expend cash.

---

10. Long-Term Debt

(e)   The Company has an unsecured revolving debt facility with a principal amount of $870.0 million. The maturity date is May 31, 2011. This facility can be drawn in Canadian dollars, U.S. dollars, or British pounds, and bears interest based on bankers' acceptance rates for Canadian dollar loans and LIBOR for U.S. dollar and British pound loans. As at December 31, 2008, $559.8 million of the revolving facility was utilized (2007: $136.3 million), of which $119.8 million was in respect of letters of credit and trade finance (2007: $111.3 million). The Company uses interest rate swaps to mitigate the risk from variable cash flows by effectively converting certain variable rate borrowings to fixed-rate borrowings. Through the use of an interest rate swap (Note 12), the Company has effectively fixed the interest rate on $200.0 million of variable rate debt under this facility, at 3.1%. The notional amount of the swap is $200.0 million, maturing in August 2009. This swap had a negative fair value of $2.5 million as at December 31, 2008, which was recorded in other current liabilities.

EXHIBIT 12.1

Maple Leaf Foods Inc.: Credit Facility

 KNOWLEDGE CHECK

www.mcgrawhill connect.ca

☐   What is liquidity? Why are creditors very interested in the liquidity of entities they provide credit to?

☐   Explain the difference between quick ratio and the current ratio. How is each calculated?

Solvency and Leverage

In the last section, liquidity was defined as the availability of cash and near-cash resources to meet obligations as they come due. In contrast, **solvency** refers to its ability to meet its long-term obligations—the financial viability of an entity.

One of the important sources of insight into an entity's solvency is its capital structure. **Capital structure** refers to an entity's sources of financing—its relative proportions of debt and equity. This is important in assessing solvency because the more debt an entity has, the more risk there is to its long-term solvency. A common tool for evaluating capital structure is the debt-to-equity ratio.

The debt-to-equity ratio is a measure of the relative amount of debt to equity an entity is using. It indicates the riskiness of the entity and its ability to carry more debt. More debt increases risk because if interest and principal payments aren't made when required, the entity faces significant economic and legal consequences.

There are many variations of the debt-to-equity ratio. The debt-to-equity ratio discussed so far in the book is defined as

$$\text{Debt-to-equity ratio} = \frac{\text{Total liabilities}}{\text{Total shareholders' equity}}$$

This ratio includes all liabilities and all equity. Other variations on the debt-to-equity ratio include

$$\text{Long-term debt-to-equity ratio} = \frac{\text{Long-term debt}}{\text{Total shareholders' equity}}$$

$$\text{Debt-to-total assets ratio} = \frac{\text{Total liabilities}}{\text{Total liabilities} + \text{Total shareholders' equity}} = \frac{\text{Total liabilities}}{\text{Total assets}}$$

We won't discuss these alternatives further, but recognize that these are different ways of measuring the same concept, although they are measuring slightly different things. For example, the long-term debt-to-equity ratio excludes working capital (which is used to finance operations) and focuses on the long-term financing of the entity.

Simply using the numbers on the balance sheet to calculate at the debt-to-equity ratio can provide misleading results and interpretations. Leases, pensions, and future income taxes can all impair the interpretation of the debt-to-equity and other ratios that incorporate liabilities. If an entity extensively uses operating leases, a form of off-balance-sheet financing, then liabilities and the debt-to-equity ratio will be understated. If this is the case, stakeholders might want to incorporate the operating lease "liability" into their assessment of the entity's capital structure.

Because interest has to be paid regardless of whether an entity is performing well or poorly, debt makes an entity riskier. That doesn't mean entities should carry no debt. While debt does add risk, it offers some benefits as well:

- Debt is usually less costly than equity because the payments to debt holders are specified and debt-holders are entitled to be paid before equity investors. The lower risk means a lower expected return.

- Interest on debt is tax-deductible, whereas dividends to shareholders are not.

An entity needs a balance between debt and equity financing. Too much debt may result in an inability to pay obligations. Also, debt becomes more expensive as the relative amount of it increases because lenders charge higher interest rates as their risk increases. An entity's optimal amount of debt depends on the entity. An entity with reliable cash flows can afford to carry more debt than one with less predictable cash flows. Factors affecting the reliability of cash flows include competition, threat of technological change, sensitivity to economic cycles, and predictability of capital expenditures.

An entity's solvency can also be assessed by its ability to generate cash from operations. An entity that can reliably generate cash is best equipped to meet its obligations. Earnings are often used instead of cash flow to assess cash flow generating ability. While earnings aren't cash flow and the two can differ significantly in the short term, earnings tend to be a good indicator of long-term cash flow. A reliable flow of earnings or cash assures creditors that the entity will be able to meet its obligations.

The **interest coverage ratio (accrual basis)** is one of a number of ratios designed to measure the ability of an entity to meet its fixed financing charges—its interest payments in particular. The interest coverage ratio is defined as

$$\text{Interest coverage ratio (accrual basis)} = \frac{\text{Net income} + \text{Interest expense} + \text{Tax expense}}{\text{Interest expense}}$$

The larger the ratio, the better able the entity is to meet its interest payments. However, the interest coverage ratio is limiting in that it ignores the fact that entities have fixed charges other than interest. Other fixed charges can include debt repayment and lease payments on operating leases. This ratio can be modified to include these other charges.

Some stakeholders prefer a cash-based interest coverage ratio because debt holders have to be paid in cash, not in earnings. The **interest coverage ratio (cash basis)** shows the number of dollars of cash from operations for each dollar of interest that had to be paid, and is calculated as

$$\text{Interest coverage ratio (cash basis)} = \frac{\text{Cash from operations excluding interest paid}}{\text{Interest paid}}$$

In Chapter 9, we calculated the accrual interest coverage ratio for WestJet. (WestJet is used because Leon's has no debt.) Here we'll do the cash-basis interest coverage ratio calculation for WestJet for the year ended December 31, 2008:

$$\text{Interest coverage ratio (cash basis)} = \frac{\text{Cash from operations + Interest paid}}{\text{Interest paid}}$$
$$= \frac{\$460,586,000 + \$76,604,000}{\$76,604,000}$$
$$= 7.01$$

This means that WestJet generated $7.01 of cash from operations for every dollar of interest paid. Thus lenders can have some confidence that WestJet will be able to make its interest payments. A summary of the accrual and cash basis interest coverage ratios for WestJet for the period 2002 through 2008 is shown in Table 12.10. The cash-basis measures are consistently higher than the accrual ones but they have a similar pattern. (This shouldn't be surprising because WestJet's cash from operations is consistently higher than its net income.) Since 2004, the interest coverage ratios have improved, suggesting that WestJet's credit risk is decreasing.

TABLE 12.10	Accrual and Cash-Basis Interest Coverage Ratios for WestJet Airlines Ltd.				
	2008	**2007**	**2006**	**2005**	**2004**
Accrual basis	4.35	4.15	3.34	1.94	0.64
Cash basis	7.01	8.15	6.04	5.54	4.44

The interest coverage ratio and other measures of an entity's ability to meet its fixed charges are very important indicators for creditors. A higher coverage ratio is more assurance that creditors will be paid. The level of a coverage ratio considered acceptable depends on the entity. A creditor can accept a lower coverage ratio for an entity with more reliable earnings and cash flows, and they would want a higher level for an entity in a cyclical industry or with highly variable earnings and cash flows.

It's important to remember that the interest coverage and similar ratios are historical measures showing what has happened, not necessarily what will happen. Examining historical trends can help give insight into an entity's ability to generate adequate earnings to cover current and future obligations, but it's also important to consider any changes that may affect that ability. For example, increasing competition or changing economic conditions could impair an entity's ability to generate earnings and cash flow in the future, despite its historical success in doing so.

Accounting ratios are often used as covenants in loan agreements. Exhibit 12.2 provides a summary of the financial covenants that Denison Mines Corp., a uranium mining company, has as part of some of its lending agreements.[5] The covenants are based on financial statement measures such as tangible net worth (assets [excluding intangibles] − liabilities), total net debt to earnings, interest coverage ratio, and current ratio. In the exhibit, management notes that it's possible that one of the covenants will be violated by the fourth quarter of 2009. As a result, Note 1 to Denison's financial statements (note shown) calls into question whether the company is a going concern.

DENISON MINES

MANAGEMENT'S DISCUSSION AND ANALYSIS
Year Ended December 31, 2008

LIQUIDITY AND CAPITAL RESOURCES
The Company is required to maintain the following financial covenants on a consolidated basis:

- Minimum tangible net worth of $450,000,000 plus 50% of positive quarterly net income and 50% of net proceeds of all equity issues after December 31, 2007;

- Maximum ratio of total net debt to earnings before interest, taxes, depreciation and amortization and other allowed adjustments as defined in the credit agreement ("EBITDA"), of 3.5 to 1.0 for each fiscal quarter starting with the fiscal quarter ending December 31, 2008 and including the fiscal quarter September 30, 2009 and 3.0 to 1.0 for each fiscal quarter thereafter. EBITDA is calculated on a rolling four quarters' basis commencing with the third quarter 2008;

- Minimum interest coverage ratio of 3.0 to 1.0 using rolling EBITDA and rolling interest expense for each fiscal quarter starting with the fiscal quarter ending December 31, 2008; and

- Minimum current ratio of 1.1 to 1.0.

In addition to the financial covenants, there was a one-time only production covenant for 2008 production which was met.

Interest payable under the facility is bankers' acceptance rate or London Interbank Offered Rate ("Libor") plus a margin or prime rate plus a margin. The margin used is between 75 and 275 basis points depending on the credit instrument used and the magnitude of the net total debt to EBITDA ratio (the "ratio"). The facility is subject to a standby fee of 60 to 75 basis points depending upon the ratio. A standby fee of 75 basis points applies in all circumstances where the amounts drawn under the facility are less than $62,500,000.

As of the date hereof, the Company is in compliance with all covenants.

Based on the Company's current financial projections, a breach of the total net debt to EBITDA covenant is possible by the fourth quarter of 2009 (see Note 1 to the consolidated financial statements).

Other Common Ratios

Price-to-Earnings Ratio   It's common to hear discussion of an entity's **price-to-earnings** or **P/E ratio**. Stock market listings in newspapers and online usually provide entities' P/E ratios. The P/E ratio is defined as

$$\text{P/E ratio} = \frac{\text{Market price per share}}{\text{Earnings per share}}$$

Conceptually, the P/E ratio indicates how the market values an entity's earnings and what it sees as its growth prospects. The higher the P/E ratio, the more the market expects earnings to grow. Another way of thinking about this is that the higher an entity's P/E ratio, the more sensitive its share price is to changes in earnings. For example, a P/E ratio of 10 means a $1 increase in EPS will result in a $10 increase in share price.

The P/E ratio is also an indicator of the risk associated with future earnings. The higher an entity's risk, the lower its P/E ratio will be for a given level of earnings. (The reason for this is that when risk is higher, future cash flows are discounted at a higher rate to reflect the risk.)

For a number of reasons, the P/E ratio must be interpreted carefully. Remember from our discussion of earnings quality that earnings in any given period will contain both permanent and transitory components. These two will have different effects on the market price of shares, which in turn will have implications for the P/E ratio.

Also, conceptually, the market price of a share represents the present value of the cash flows that will be received by shareholders—a future-oriented perspective. Earnings, on the other hand, is largely a historically focused measure. As a result, the link between earnings and share price isn't perfect. Current information is immediately reflected in the entity's share price; earnings won't be affected until the next set of financial statements is issued.

If an entity has very low but positive earnings in a period, the P/E ratio will be very large. In that case, the P/E ratio is simply the mathematical result of division by a small number. In addition, a P/E ratio isn't meaningful if an entity has a loss, and it isn't possible to determine the

P/E ratios of private companies because the market price for their shares isn't readily available. Finally, earnings are affected by the accounting choices an entity makes, so the P/E ratio will vary with different accounting choices for the same underlying economic activity.

Recent P/E ratios for some of the companies we've examined throughout the book are shown in Table 12.11.[6]

TABLE 12.11	Average P/E Ratios for Selected Companies			
	2008	**2007**	**2006**	**2005**
Canfor Corporation	n.m.	n.m.	3.7	21.0
High Liner Foods Inc.	9.1	16.8	23.8	n.m.
Indigo Books & Music Inc.	11.1	7.0	11.9	10.1
Leon's Furniture Limited	11.6	17.1	14.4	14.1
Loblaw Companies Limited	15.6	35.7	n.m.	23.8
Potash Corporation of Saskatchewan Inc.	12.7	26.7	18.7	18.4
Research In Motion Limited	26.3	36.2	30.8	34.6
WestJet Airlines Ltd.	11.2	12.6	13.8	70.1

Note: n.m indicates that the P/E ratio isn't measurable because net income was negative.

Dividend Payout Ratio The **dividend payout ratio** shows the proportion of earnings being paid to common shareholders as dividends. It's defined as

$$\text{Dividend payout ratio} = \frac{\text{Common dividends declared}}{\text{Net income}}$$

A dividend payout ratio of 0.25 means that 25 percent of earnings is paid in dividends; the rest is retained. An entity with a net loss can still pay a dividend. If the losses continue, however, it's likely that eventually it won't have the resources to sustain the dividend. Having cash to pay dividends is necessary. With a net loss, the dividend payout ratio isn't meaningful. A dividend payout ratio greater than 1.0 is also possible.

An entity's dividend payout ratio can vary quite a bit from period to period if it pays the same dividend every year, regardless of the amount of earnings. For public companies, dividends tend to be constant over time, increasing when the managers feel there will be adequate future cash flow to permanently support that level of dividends. Managers of public companies are very reluctant to decrease dividends because this suggests to investors that current and future cash flows are declining, and that the decline is expected to be permanent. This usually causes stock prices to fall significantly.

Private companies are much less concerned about maintaining dividends. The shareholders of private companies will likely consider tax issues, their personal cash needs, and the cash requirements of the entity in any dividend decisions.

Leon's dividend payout ratio for 2008 was

$$\begin{aligned}
\text{Dividend payout ratio} &= \frac{\text{Common dividends declared}}{\text{Net income}} \\
&= \frac{\$26,873,000}{\$63,390,000} \\
&= 42.4\%
\end{aligned}$$

QUESTION FOR CONSIDERATION

Zehner Ltd. (Zehner) is a publicly traded Canadian company. On December 31, 2014, the last day of its fiscal year, Zehner's management signed a new, long-term contract with a customer. The contract will increase Zehner's revenue significantly and management and financial analysts agree that the contract, to begin mid-2015, will be very profitable.

Required: How do you think Zehner's share price will be affected by the announcement of the new contract? How will Zehner's December 31, 2014, earnings be affected? Explain.

Answer: Zehner's share price should increase. The new contract is expected to be very profitable, which means the company is now more valuable. Larger earnings mean investors can expect more cash in the future. In contrast, the announcement will have no effect on Zehner's December 31, 2014 earnings as earnings represent economic activity that has already occurred. As of December 31, 2014, Zehner has earned no revenue and would report no profits as a result of the new contract. Earnings will only be affected when the contract comes into effect in the middle of 2015, so the full effect won't be reflected in earnings until 2016.

SOME LIMITATIONS AND CAVEATS ABOUT FINANCIAL STATEMENTS AND FINANCIAL STATEMENT ANALYSIS

Financial ratios are powerful tools for analyzing and evaluating entities, providing valuable insights into their performance and prospects. However, ratio analysis has limitations, some of them quite severe. Analysis of IFRS-based information is largely constrained by the limitations of the information itself. The existence of these limitations and caveats don't mean that financial statement and ratio analysis isn't useful or shouldn't be done. But to get the most out of financial statement and ratio analysis, it's important to understand the strengths and limitations of these tools. Let's examine some of the limitations and the caveats associated with financial statement and ratio analysis.

- *IFRS financial statements are historical.* In most cases, financial statements can be used as a starting point of an analysis, but the user has to incorporate his or her own future-oriented information to project the future.

- *IFRS financial statements have limitations because things change.* Economic conditions, technology, and the marketplace change. Entities themselves change. As a result, the future may be different from the past, which may limit the usefulness of historical financial statements analyses (especially in industries subject to rapid and unpredictable change such as entities in high-technology industries).

- *Managers prepare financial statements.* This is both good and bad news. Managers are the best equipped to prepare financial statements because they are the ones who know and understand the entity best. However, managers' self-interests can influence the accounting choices they make. Also, because an entity can only prepare one set of general purpose financial statements, managers often have to choose among the competing information needs of the different stakeholders when deciding how to orient the financial statements.

- *Financial statements are not comprehensive.* Financial statements don't reflect all of an entity's assets and liabilities, or all of its economic activity. Many valuable resources and important obligations are not reported. For example, spending on human resources and research is expensed as incurred, not classified as assets. There are also off-balance-sheet obligations such as commitments and operating leases. In addition, traditional financial statements provide little information about market values or changes in market values. For the most part, assets are recorded at their cost and are left at cost, even though their market values may change, often significantly. (IFRS allows entities to report the market values of certain assets, if they choose to.)

- *Accounting policy choices and estimates affect ratios.* Entities can often choose from alternative acceptable accounting policies, so different policies used for similar economic activity can result in different financial statements. To know if differences among entities are due to real economic activity or accounting policy choices, it's important to carefully read the note describing the significant accounting policies. Also, accrual accounting requires managers to make estimates of future, uncertain events when they prepare their financial statements, which requires judgment. All accounting choices can be affected by the assumptions, information, biases, and self-interests of the managers.

- *Comparing financial statements can be difficult to do.* Accounting is used to compare entities. Tools such as common size financial statements and financial ratios allow these comparisons. However, comparisons should be done cautiously and steps should be taken to ensure that comparisons are valid (for example, by adjusting for differences in accounting policies and estimates).

- *Financial statements are not the only source of information.* It isn't possible to analyze an entity only by its financial statements. A comprehensive analysis will integrate information from many sources.

- *Financial analysis is a diagnostic tool. It doesn't necessarily provide explanations for problems that are identified.* Accounting information reflects the economic activity of an entity—the entity's strategies, management, operations, and environment. Problem areas identified through financial analysis reflect these factors, but understanding the root of the problem requires knowledge of the entity's strategies, operations, and environment.

EARNINGS MANAGEMENT

This last section returns to one of the themes we examined throughout the book: earnings management. Managers often have choices when deciding how to account for, disclose, and present information in their financial statements. These choices can create significant economic consequences for stakeholders.

The term *earnings management* isn't limited to making choices that affect net income. It also applies to choices that affect other lines on the income statement and the balance sheet, and it applies to how management discloses information in the notes to the financial statements.

The flexible nature of accounting rules gives managers the ability to manage accounting numbers. The economic consequences of accounting information offer them the motivation. The earnings of public companies are carefully studied by investors and analysts, and the managers of these companies are under pressure to meet investors' expectations and to maintain the stock price. Managers can help achieve these objectives by using accounting choices to increase or smooth earnings. Also, managers' compensation, opportunities in the job market, and job security can be affected by the results reported in the financial statements. Managers may also have an incentive to pursue any number of objectives: sell company shares for as high a price as possible, obtain the best terms for a loan, avoid violation of debt covenants, obtain financial support from government, minimize taxes, or generally influence the outcome of decisions that rely on accounting information.

Many accounting scandals are the result of using accounting rules to achieve management objectives. Some are clear cases of fraud. However, it's a mistake to think that most or even many of the situations of earnings management are fraudulent. In fact, most cases of earnings management occur within the rules. For example, when a manager decides that the useful life of a new piece of equipment is 10 years rather than eight years, she is making a choice that will affect assets, net income, and any ratios that rely on these measures (e.g., profit margin or return on assets). But there is nothing fraudulent about her choice, unless 10 years isn't a reasonable estimate of the equipment's useful life. However, just because the choices managers make can be said to be "within the rules" doesn't make this approach to financial reporting right, but it is reality.

Table 12.12 identifies some of the techniques that managers have to manage earnings. The table shows the different financial accounting reporting areas and identifies the techniques as policies, estimates, or other. All of the techniques in the table have been addressed in this book.

TABLE 12.12	Earnings Management Opportunities		
	Policies	**Estimates**	**Other**
Revenue recognition	• When to recognize revenue	• Bad debts • Returns • Discounts	
Inventory	• Inventory valuation method (FIFO, average cost, specific identification) • Costs included in inventory	• Writedowns of obsolete and damaged inventory	
Capital assets	• Depreciation method	• Useful lives • Timing and amount of writedowns and writeoffs	
Liabilities	• Leases	• Warranty provisions • Pensions • Accrued liabilities	
Assets versus expenses	• Capitalization policies		
Other			• Big baths • Income statement classifications as ordinary versus unusual • Off-balance-sheet financing • Non-recurring items • Disclosure of commitments and contingencies

A FINAL THOUGHT

Accounting is often characterized as dull and boring. And it can be—if all you think about is the mechanics: journal entries, preparing financial statements in good form, and getting the calculations right. But you've now seen what makes accounting interesting. Accounting is about high-level thinking skills, about human nature, and about judgment. If you've worked with the material presented in the book you should be on your way to being a sophisticated and savvy user of financial statements.

Good luck!

Solved Problem

Esperanza Stores Corp. (Esperanza) operates two small retail stores in malls in Charlottetown. The two stores were opened in late 2008 and, according to Minh Tran, the president and majority shareholder, they have grown spectacularly over the last few years. To provide customers with the merchandise they want, Esperanza has moved into larger locations and further increased the floor space of its stores by taking over adjacent retail space as it became available. Ms. Tran is currently thinking about opening additional stores.

Ms. Tran has approached the bank for an expanded line of credit. Esperanza's current line of credit is $30,000 and as of December 31, 2014 the line of credit has almost been fully used. Ms. Tran has provided the bank with Esperanza's financial statements for 2011 through 2014. The statements are available in Table 12.13. Additional information provided by Ms. Tran accompanies the financial statements.

TABLE 12.13	Esperanza Stores Corp.: Financial Statements

Esperanza Stores Corp.
Balance Sheets as of December 31,

	2014	2013	2012	2011
Assets				
Cash	$ 10,000	$ 25,000	$ 50,000	$ 75,000
Inventory	200,000	160,000	125,000	78,000
Other current assets	16,298	17,322	8,440	6,000
Total current assets	226,298	202,322	183,440	159,000
Capital assets	182,000	151,000	110,000	75,000
Accumulated depreciation	(75,530)	(60,400)	(41,800)	(22,500)
	$332,768	$292,922	$251,640	$211,500
Liabilities and Shareholders' equity				
Bank loan	$ 29,371	$ 23,821	$ 11,966	$ 0
Accounts payable	101,000	81,500	65,000	45,000
Other payables	3,000	13,000	19,000	24,000
Current portion of long-term debt	20,000	5,000	5,000	5,000
Total current liabilities	153,371	123,321	100,966	74,000
Long-term debt	20,000	40,000	45,000	50,000
Capital stock	50,000	50,000	50,000	50,000
Retained earnings	109,397	79,601	55,674	37,500
	$332,768	$292,922	$251,640	$211,500

Esperanza Stores Corp.
Income Statements for the years ended December 31,

	2014	2013	2012	2011
Revenue	$535,000	$485,000	$450,000	$350,000
Cost of sales	299,600	264,325	238,500	182,000
Gross margin	235,400	220,675	211,500	168,000
Selling, general, and administrative costs	180,000	170,000	165,000	140,000
Interest expense	6,200	6,000	5,200	5,000
Other expenses	11,000	14,000	18,000	20,000
Income before taxes	38,200	30,675	23,300	3,000
Income taxes	8,404	6,748	5,126	660
Net income	$ 29,796	$ 23,927	$ 18,174	$ 2,340

Ms. Tran provides additional information:

- All sales of merchandise to customers are for cash or major credit card. No credit terms are offered. Esperanza recognizes revenue at the time of sale.

- All inventory is purchased on credit.

- The long-term loan is from a private lender and must be repaid in full by 2012. Esperanza has been making payments on the loan since cash has been available to do so.

- Esperanza has never paid dividends.

Required:

You are Ms. Tran's banker. Review the information provided and prepare a report for your manager assessing whether Esperanza should receive a larger credit line.

Solution:

Comment: The response below attempts to analyze and interpret the information provided by Esperanza from the perspective of a lender. The analysis relies exclusively on tools introduced in this chapter and elsewhere in the book. In an actual analysis of this type, additional information about the entity, the economy, and the market place would be available and incorporated in the report.

Report on Esperanza Stores Corp.

I have completed my examination of Esperanza Stores Corp. (Esperanza) and while, on the surface, the stores appear to be performing well, there are some concerns. In essence, it appears that Esperanza is facing a serious liquidity problem and may have difficulty generating the cash flows to support a significant loan. This is not to say that Esperanza is a lost cause, and some improvements could make Esperanza a more viable candidate for a loan. As my report details, there are many positive accomplishments. The data I refer to in my report are presented in Tables 12.14 through 12.17.

Performance

Esperanza has performed well over the last four years. Net income has significantly improved each year, from $2,340 in 2011 to $29,796 in 2014. In addition, Esperanza's profit margin (Tables 12.14 or 12.16), return on assets (Table 12.16), and return on equity (Table 12.16) have all increased in each reported year. Sales have also been growing, with 2014 results almost 53 percent greater than they were in 2011. In absolute numbers, sales have grown from $350,000 in 2011 to $535,000 in 2014. Clearly, the company has done a good job building its business.

On the other hand, gross margin percentage (Table 12.16) has declined steadily from 48 percent in 2011 to 44 percent in 2014—a significant and alarming drop. Had Esperanza been able to maintain its 48 percent gross margin in 2014, net income would have been more than $21,000 higher and there would have been significantly more cash coming in.

Further information is needed to explain the decline. Is it due to increased competition or a pricing strategy that tried to increase sales by lowering prices? And what is the gross margin percentage likely to be in future, as this will have significant implications for cash flows?

Despite the decline in the gross margin percentage, the gross margin has increased each year because of the increase in sales. Also, despite the gross margin percentage decline, the profit margin percentage has increased each year. Esperanza has achieved this improvement through cost control. Selling, general, and administrative costs have increased at a much slower rate than sales, and the proportion of these costs as a percentage of revenue has fallen over the four-year period.

An important question is whether spending has been permanently reduced or only deferred. Also, will the reduction in spending will have implications for Esperanza's ability to maintain and increase sales in the future.

Overall, Esperanza has performed well. The company has grown its business with sales, profits, and improving profitability. The company's liquidity is another matter.

Liquidity

While Esperanza's performance has been fine, I have serious concerns about its liquidity. All liquidity indicators have been deteriorating over the past four years and the company is in danger of running out of cash. The current ratio decreased from 2.15 in 2011 to 1.48 in 2014. While a current ratio of 1.48 in and of itself isn't a problem, the significant decline is.

The current ratio also masks the fact that an increasing proportion of Esperanza's assets is inventory. Since 2011, the proportion of total assets represented by inventory has increased from 36.9 percent to 60.1 percent. In addition, the amount of inventory on hand has increased much more rapidly than revenues. While one would expect inventory to grow at a rate similar to sales, over the period 2011 to 2014 the amount of inventory on hand has increased 256 percent, while revenues have grown by only about 53 percent. It is possible Esperanza may be carrying significant amounts of unsalable inventory. If the inventory cannot be sold or can only be sold at a discount, the current ratio overstates the company's liquidity. Other possible explanations for the large increase in inventory are failure to meet expected sales forecasts or a wider range of merchandise being carried in the stores. The increase could also be the result of poor inventory management.

The quick ratio, the availability of very liquid current assets to cover current liabilities, supports a liquidity problem. Esperanza's only quick asset is cash, and over the last four years the amount of cash it is holding has declined significantly—only $10,000 as of December 31, 2014. If, for example, the current portion of long-term debt had to be paid immediately, Esperanza would not have the resources to do so.

The inventory turnover and accounts payable turnover ratios raise similar concerns. Since 2011, Esperanza has been taking much longer to sell its inventory and to pay suppliers. The average number of days inventory is held before being sold has increased by over 40 percent, from 155 days in 2012 to 219 days in 2014. The average number of days the company takes to pay its suppliers has increased from 70 days in 2012 to 98 days in 2014. This suggests that Esperanza is responding to its liquidity problems by delaying payments to suppliers for as long as possible. Taking the average number of days inventory and the average payment period for accounts payable together, the period over which Esperanza is self-financing its inventory has increased from 85 days in 2012 (155 − 70) to 121 days in 2014 (219 − 98).

From the information provided, I constructed cash flow statements for 2012 through 2014. These statements are rough because of missing information, particularly the depreciation expense. It seems likely that, given the small change in accumulated depreciation year to year, some capital assets were sold over these years. Therefore, using change in the accumulated depreciation account as an estimate of the depreciation expense may be in error. If assets are actually being sold, actual cash from operations is likely greater than I calculated.

Cash from operations in each of the three years has been positive and growing, but it is still quite small. Depending on sales in 2015, the company might not have enough cash to make its planned payment on the long-term debt. The company's operating cash flow is crucial for assessing a loan. While the current and quick ratios suggest liquidity problems, the problems could be mitigated with enough cash flow. At this point, the cash flow statement and my interpretation of the turnover ratios do not relieve my uneasiness. Even so, Esperanza has been able to reduce its long-term debt over the last three years, although it was achieved by increasing its bank loan each year.

There is also potential for trouble if suppliers more aggressively try to collect amounts owing to them or if they stop providing credit. If this happens, any loan our bank makes could be in jeopardy. Esperanza has little to offer in the way of security. There are no receivables, and it is probable that capital assets and inventory will not produce much cash if they had to be sold.

Because of expansion over the last three years, Esperanza has made significant investments in capital assets. An important question is whether additional expenditures for capital assets will be required. The depletion of the company's cash can be largely attributed to the purchases of capital assets each year.

Overall, Esperanza seems to be an attractive and successful business. Its challenge is to survive its liquidity problems. At this point I do not recommend extending additional credit to the company. I think that Esperanza should take immediate steps to reduce its inventory levels to free up cash and reduce its investment in working capital. Also, the company should limit its spending on capital assets until its liquidity position becomes more solid.

TABLE 12.14   Common Size Financial Statements

Esperanza Stores Corp.
Common Size Balance Sheets as of December 31,

	2014	2013	2012	2011
Cash	0.030	0.085	0.199	0.355
Inventory	0.601	0.546	0.497	0.369
Other current assets	0.049	0.059	0.034	0.028
Total current assets	0.680	0.691	0.729	0.752
Capital assets	0.547	0.515	0.437	0.355
Accumulated depreciation	(0.227)	(0.206)	(0.166)	(0.106)
	1.000	1.000	1.000	1.000
Bank loan	0.088	0.081	0.048	0.000
Accounts payable	0.304	0.278	0.258	0.213
Other payables	0.009	0.044	0.076	0.113
Current portion of long-term debt	0.060	0.017	0.020	0.024
Total current liabilities	0.461	0.421	0.401	0.350
Long-term debt	0.060	0.137	0.179	0.236
Capital stock	0.150	0.171	0.199	0.236
Retained earnings	0.329	0.272	0.221	0.177
	1.000	1.000	1.000	1.000

Esperanza Stores Corp.
Common Size Income Statements for the Years Ended December 31, 2011–2014

Revenue	1.000	1.000	1.000	1.000
Cost of sales	0.560	0.545	0.530	0.520
Gross margin	0.440	0.455	0.470	0.480
Selling, general, and administrative costs	0.336	0.351	0.367	0.400
Interest expense	0.012	0.012	0.012	0.014
Other expenses	0.021	0.029	0.040	0.057
	0.071	0.063	0.052	0.009
Income tax expense	0.016	0.014	0.011	0.002
Net income	0.056	0.049	0.040	0.007

TABLE 12.15 Trend Financial Statements

Esperanza Stores Corp.
Trend Balance Sheets as of December 31,

	2014	2013	2012	2011
Cash	0.133	0.333	0.667	1.000
Inventory	2.564	2.051	1.603	1.000
Other current assets	2.716	2.887	1.407	1.000
Total current assets	1.423	1.272	1.154	1.000
Capital assets	2.427	2.013	1.467	1.000
Accumulated depreciation	3.357	2.684	1.858	1.000
	1.573	1.385	1.190	1.000
Bank loan	n/a	n/a	n/a	n/a
Accounts payable	2.244	1.811	1.444	1.000
Other payables	0.125	0.542	0.792	1.000
Current portion of long-term debt	4.000	1.000	1.000	1.000
Total current liabilities	2.073	1.667	1.364	1.000
Long-term debt	0.400	0.800	0.900	1.000
Capital stock	1.000	1.000	1.000	1.000
Retained earnings	2.917	2.123	1.485	1.000
	1.573	1.385	1.190	1.000

Esperanza Stores Corp.
Trend Income Statements for the Years Ended December 31,

	2014	2013	2012	2011
Revenue	1.529	1.386	1.286	1.000
Cost of sales	1.646	1.452	1.310	1.000
Gross margin	1.401	1.314	1.259	1.000
Selling, general, and administrative costs	1.286	1.214	1.179	1.000
Interest expense	1.240	1.200	1.040	1.000
Other expenses	0.550	0.700	0.900	1.000
	12.733	10.225	7.767	1.000
Income tax expense	12.733	10.225	7.767	1.000
Net income	12.733	10.225	7.767	1.000

TABLE ⟨ 12.16 ⟩ Financial Ratios

Esperanza Stores Corp.
Selected Financial Ratios

	2014	2013	2012	2011
Current ratio	1.475	1.641	1.817	2.149
Quick ratio	0.065	0.203	0.495	1.014
Inventory turnover ratio	1.664	1.855	2.350	
Average number of days inventory on hand	219.3	196.8	155.3	
Accounts payable turnover ratio	3.722	4.086	5.191	
Average payment period for accounts payable	98.1	89.3	70.3	
Purchases (cost of sales − beginning inventory + ending inventory)	$339,600	$299,325	$285,500	
Gross margin percentage	0.440	0.455	0.470	0.480
Profit margin percentage*	0.065	0.059	0.049	0.018
Asset turnover	1.710	1.781	1.943	
Return on assets	0.111	0.106	0.096	
Return on equity	0.206	0.203	0.188	
Debt-to-equity ratio (liabilities ÷ shareholders' equity)	1.088	1.260	1.381	1.417

*Profit margin is calculated as net income + after-tax cost of interest/sales.

TABLE ⟨ 12.17 ⟩ Cash Flow Statements

Esperanza Stores Corp.
Cash Flow Statements for the Years Ended December 31,

	2014	2013	2012
Net income	$29,796	$23,927	$18,174
Add: depreciation expense	15,130	18,600	19,300
	44,926	42,527	37,474
Adjustments for changes in current operating accounts			
Increase in inventory	(40,000)	(35,000)	(47,000)
Decrease/(increase) in other current assets	1,024	(8,882)	(2,440)
Increase in accounts payable	19,500	16,500	20,000
(Decrease) in other payables	(10,000)	(6,000)	(5,000)
Cash from operations	15,450	9,145	3,034
Investing activities—purchase of capital assets	(31,000)	(41,000)	(35,000)
Financing activities			
Repayment of long-term debt	(5,000)	(5,000)	(5,000)
Bank loan	5,550	11,855	11,966
	550	6,855	6,966
Decrease in cash during year	(15,000)	(25,000)	(25,000)
Cash balance at beginning of year	25,000	50,000	75,000
Cash balance at end of year	$10,000	$25,000	$50,000

SUMMARY OF KEY POINTS

▶ **LO 1** Current income is important for forecasting future earnings. Permanent earnings are expected to repeat in the future and are a useful indicator of future earnings. Earnings that are not considered permanent are called transitory. An entity's net income can have both permanent and transitory components. IFRS require disclosure of information that is helpful for understanding the components of earnings.

Earnings quality refers to the usefulness of current earnings for predicting future earnings. Earnings quality is high if there is a close relationship between current earnings and future earnings and low if that relationship isn't close. Another way of thinking about earnings quality is the extent to which reported earnings are permanent. Managers lower earnings quality when they manage earnings through their accounting policies, estimates, and accruals, and through the timing of actual transactions, such as discretionary expenditures and sales.

▶ **LO 2** Financial ratios are a common tool used for examining, evaluating, and assessing an entity. A vast number of different ratios have been developed for various purposes. In this chapter, ratios and analytical tools are grouped into four analytical themes: (1) evaluating performance, (2) liquidity, (3) solvency and leverage, and (4) other common ratios. Two tools that make this type of analysis easier are common size financial statements and trend analysis, which eliminate the impact of size from the financial statement numbers and restate them as proportions.

▶ **LO 3** Financial ratios are a powerful and informative tool for analyzing and evaluating entities. However, ratio analysis has limitations, some of them quite severe. To get the most out of financial statement analysis, it's important to understand the strength and limitations of the tools being used. The limitations include the following:

- IFRS financial statements are mainly historical.

- Managers prepare financial statements.

- Financial statements are not comprehensive.

- Accounting policy choices and estimates affect ratios.

- Comparing financial statements can be difficult to do.

- Financial statements are not the only source of information.

- Financial analysis is a diagnostic tool. It doesn't necessarily provide explanations for problems that are identified.

▶ **LO 4** Managers often have choices when deciding how to account for, disclose, and present information about their entity's transactions and economic events. These choices can have a significant impact on the numbers and disclosures in the financial statements and notes, which in turn can have economic consequences for stakeholders. The economic consequences of accounting information provide managers with incentives to make particular accounting choices that will allow them to meet their objectives of financial reporting—something known as earnings management.

FORMULA SUMMARY

$$\text{Common size amount}_{year} = \frac{\text{Income statement account}_{year}}{\text{Sales}_{year}}$$

$$\text{Common size amount}_{year} = \frac{\text{Balance sheet account}_{year}}{\text{Total assets}_{year}}$$

Performance

$$\text{Trend statement amount}_{\text{current year}} = \frac{\text{Current year amount}}{\text{Base year amount}} \times 100\%$$

$$\text{Gross margin percentage} = \frac{\text{Sales} - \text{Cost of sales}}{\text{Sales}} \times 100\% = \frac{\text{Gross margin}}{\text{Sales}} \times 100\%$$

$$\text{Profit margin ratio} = \frac{\text{Net income}}{\text{Sales}} \times 100\%$$

$$\text{Return on assets} = \frac{\text{Net income} + \text{After-tax interest expense}}{\text{Average total assets}} = \frac{\text{Net income} + \text{Interest expense} \times (1 - \text{Tax rate})}{\text{Average total assets}}$$

OR

$$\text{Return on assets} = \text{Asset turnover ratio} \times \text{Profit margin ratio} \times 100\%$$

$$\text{Return on equity} = \frac{\text{Net income} - \text{Preferred dividends}}{\text{Average common shareholders' equity}}$$

$$\text{Basic EPS} = \frac{\text{Net income} - \text{Preferred dividends}}{\text{Weighted-average of common shares outstanding during the period}}$$

Liquidity

$$\text{Current ratio} = \frac{\text{Current assets}}{\text{Current liabilities}}$$

$$\text{Quick ratio (acid test ratio)} = \frac{\text{Quick assets}}{\text{Current liabilities}}$$

$$\text{Accounts receivable turnover ratio} = \frac{\text{Credit sales}}{\text{Average accounts receivable}}$$

$$\text{Average collection period of accounts receivable} = \frac{365}{\text{Accounts receivable turnover ratio}}$$

$$\text{Inventory turnover ratio} = \frac{\text{Cost of sales}}{\text{Average inventory}}$$

$$\text{Average number of days inventory on hand} = \frac{365}{\text{Inventory turnover ratio}}$$

$$\text{Accounts payable turnover ratio} = \frac{\text{Credit purchases}}{\text{Average accounts payable}}$$

$$\text{Average payment period for accounts payable} = \frac{365}{\text{Accounts payable turnover ratio}}$$

$$\text{Cash lag} = \begin{array}{c}\text{Average collection} \\ \text{period of accounts} \\ \text{receivable}\end{array} + \begin{array}{c}\text{Average number} \\ \text{of days inventory} \\ \text{on hand}\end{array} - \begin{array}{c}\text{Average payment} \\ \text{period for accounts} \\ \text{payable}\end{array}$$

Solvency and Leverage

$$\text{Debt-to-equity ratio} = \frac{\text{Total liabilities}}{\text{Total shareholders' equity}}$$

$$\text{Interest coverage ratio (accrual basis)} = \frac{\text{Net income} + \text{Interest expense} + \text{Tax expense}}{\text{Interest expense}}$$

$$\text{Interest coverage ratio (cash basis)} = \frac{\text{Cash from operations excluding interest paid}}{\text{Interest paid}}$$

Other Common Ratios

$$\text{P/E ratio} = \frac{\text{Market price per share}}{\text{Earnings per share}}$$

$$\text{Dividend payout ratio} = \frac{\text{Common dividends declared}}{\text{Net income}}$$

KEY TERMS

accounts payable turnover ratio, p. 683

asset turnover, p. 680

average payment period for accounts payable, p. 684

capital structure, p. 685

common size financial statement (vertical analysis), p. 670

covenant, p. 664

dividend payout ratio, p. 689

earnings quality, p. 667

horizontal analysis (trend statements), p. 674

interest coverage ratio (accrual basis), p. 686

interest coverage ratio (cash basis), p. 687

management discussion and analysis (MD&A), p. 665

permanent earnings, p. 666

price-to-earnings (P/E) ratio, p. 688

solvency, p. 685

transitory earnings, p. 666

trend statements (horizontal analysis), p. 674

vertical analysis (common size financial statement), p. 670

SIMILAR TERMS

The left column gives alternative terms that are sometimes used for the accounting terms introduced in this chapter, which are listed in the right column.

horizontal analysis	**trend statements, p. 674**
sustainable earnings, recurring earnings, core earnings, persistent earnings	**permanent earnings, p. 666**
vertical analysis	**common size financial statements, p. 670**

ASSIGNMENT MATERIALS

Questions

Q12-1. What is gross margin? Why can it be important to determine an entity's gross margin? Why is it difficult to determine gross margin from some entity's financial statements?

Q12-2. What is the difference between permanent and transitory earnings? Why might it be important to distinguish between these types of earnings?

Q12-3. Suppose you were considering making an investment in one of Canada's major grocery chains, Loblaw Companies Ltd. or Sobeys Inc. As part of your research, you obtained each company's annual report. What concerns would you have in comparing the information presented in each company's financial statements when making your decision? What steps could you take to overcome these concerns?

Q12-4. Why is it important to learn as much as you possibly can about an entity when doing an analysis of it? Explain.

Q12-5. Is it advisable to make a decision to lend money to an entity by looking *only* at its financial statements? Explain.

Q12-6. Identify and explain the limitations and caveats associated with using financial ratio analysis on IFRS-based financial statements.

Q12-7. What are the implications for financial statement analysis of the fact that managers can often choose among different, acceptable accounting methods? Provide examples of some of the accounting choices that preparers have to make.

Q12-8. Explain how the following events would affect the usefulness of current earnings as a basis for predicting future earnings if information about each wasn't separately disclosed:
a. An entity has a two-month strike during the year.
b. An entity writes off a significant amount of capital assets.
c. An entity signs a contract with its employees for an increase in wages.
d. An entity records a gain on the disposal of one of its vehicles.

Q12-9. Is it possible for an entity to be too liquid? Explain.

Q12-10. Explain why the quick ratio might be a better indicator of an entity's liquidity than the current ratio.

Q12-11. Describe a situation where a user of a private corporation's financial statements would be interested in segregating permanent and transitory earnings. Explain why the separation of the two types of earnings would be important in the situation.

Q12-12. Explain the concept of quality of earnings. What distinguishes high-quality earnings from low-quality earnings?

Q12-13. Explain how each of the following would affect the quality of an entity's earnings:
a. Management decides to increase advertising in the current period as part of a special event. Management expects the increase to occur only in the current year and spending levels will return to historical levels in the future.
b. Management increases the estimated useful life of some of the entity's capital assets.
c. Management decides to write down certain capital assets to reflect changes in market conditions.

Q12-14. What are common size financial statements? Explain why they can be useful for analyzing an entity over and above the actual financial statements of the entity.

Q12-15. What are trend financial statements? Explain why they can be useful for analyzing an entity over and above the actual financial statements of the entity.

Q12-16. What is liquidity? Why are suppliers concerned about the liquidity of an entity?

Q12-17. Why isn't it adequate for stakeholders to focus their analyses of entities only on the financial statements? What type of information about an entity that's not included in financial statements might be useful for a stakeholder? What other sources of information might a stakeholder turn to?

Q12-18. What are covenants? Why are covenants often included in lending agreements? What purpose do they serve? Why are covenants often stated in accounting terms?

Q12-19. Explain the two broad concerns that creditors have about the credit they provide to entities. Describe the different types and sources of information that creditors require to evaluate these concerns.

Q12-20. What is the difference between short-term and long-term creditors? Why would each approach financial statement analysis differently? What type of information would each require for making a decision to supply credit to a prospective borrower? Explain.

Q12-21. In many ways equity investors need to know everything. Explain why this is true.

Q12-22. Would information about each of the following be useful to a prospective long-term creditor of an entity? Would information about each item be available from the financial statements? Explain your answers.
a. competitive advantages and disadvantages
b. risks faced by the entity
c. source of supplies and conditions in the supplier market
d. regulatory environment

Q12-23. Would information about each of the following be useful to a prospective equity investor in an entity? Would information about each item be available from the financial statements? Explain your answers.
a. quality, experience, and performance of the managers
b. strategies for making money
c. competitive environment
d. lines of business

Q12-24. What is the management discussion and analysis (MD&A)? Why do you think public companies are required to provide an MD&A, whereas private companies are not?

Q12-25. Contrast the benefits and limitations of information provided to stakeholders by management versus information from a financial analyst who is independent of the entity.

Q12-26. What are the characteristics of accrual accounting that allow managers to manage earnings? Why do these characteristics allow earnings to be managed?

Q12-27. Explain the difference between return on assets and return on equity. Which measure is a more useful measure of the performance of an entity? Explain.

Q12-28. Why is it necessary to evaluate financial ratios on a comparative basis rather than in absolute terms? What bases of comparison can be used?

Q12-29. You have been asked to do an in depth analysis of a company's financial statements but you haven't been told what the purpose of the analysis is—that is, what decision the person has to make. Is it possible for you to effectively proceed with this assignment? Explain.

Exercises

E12-1. (**Classifying transactions and economic events as permanent or transitory, LO 1**) Would you classify each of the following as transitory or permanent in the entity's financial statements? Explain your reasoning.
  a. severance pay to a number of executives who were fired during a reorganization
  b. increase in the selling price of an entity's products
  c. writedown of inventory
  d. loss on the sale of land

E12-2. (**Classifying transactions and economic events as permanent or transitory, LO 1**) Would you classify each of the following as transitory or permanent in the entity's financial statements? Explain your reasoning.
  a. increase in raw materials costs
  b. payment of fines for violating environmental laws
  c. revenues associated with a division the entity has sold
  d. damage caused by an earthquake

E12-3. (**Usefulness of information for decision making, LO 1**) For each of the following situations, explain why IFRS financial statements would be of limited use for predicting the entity's future performance:
  a. The entity purchases a major new operating division near its year end in a new line of business.
  b. A large and successful U.S. firm in the same line of business enters the Canadian market late in the fiscal year.
  c. The entity just began operations and is growing rapidly.
  d. The entity is in a declining industry and has just closed down a number of its plants.
  e. The entity is a producer of software.

E12-4. **(Preparing common size financial statements, LO 2)** Examine the balance sheets and income statements for Amqui Inc. (Amqui).

Amqui Inc. Balance Sheets as of December 31,			
	2014	**2013**	**2012**
Cash	$ 9,000	$ 12,000	$ 10,000
Accounts receivable	52,600	46,400	35,000
Inventory	59,250	46,000	45,000
Other current assets	12,000	11,000	8,000
Total current assets	132,850	115,400	98,000
Property, plant, and equipment (net of depreciation)	255,000	210,000	185,000
Total assets	$387,850	$325,400	$283,000
Bank loans	$ 48,310	$ 27,400	$ 23,000
Accounts payable and accrued liabilities	45,900	41,000	38,000
Total current liabilities	94,210	68,400	61,000
Long-term liabilities	70,000	62,000	50,000
Capital stock	125,000	125,000	125,000
Retained earnings	98,640	70,000	47,000
Total liabilities and shareholders' equity	$387,850	$325,400	$283,000

Amqui Inc. Income Statements For the Years Ended December 31,			
	2014	**2013**	**2012**
Revenue	$520,128	$481,600	$430,000
Cost of sales	246,068	228,900	210,000
Gross margin	274,060	252,700	220,000
Selling and marketing expenses	88,127	80,850	77,000
General and administrative expenses	37,769	34,650	33,000
Depreciation	30,000	28,000	23,000
Miscellaneous expenses	63,245	58,560	48,000
Interest expense	15,000	12,000	8,000
Income before taxes	39,919	38,640	31,000
Income tax expense	8,783	10,000	8,000
Net income	$ 31,136	$ 28,640	$ 23,000

Additional information:
- All sales are on credit.
- All purchases of inventory are on credit.
- Amqui must begin repaying its long-term debt in 2016.

Required:

a. Prepare common size balance sheets and income statements for 2012, 2013, and 2014.
b. Analyze and interpret the common size financial statements you prepared.
c. How are these common size statements more useful than the statements originally prepared by Amqui?
d. Why would it be unwise to examine the common size financial statements without considering the financial statements originally prepared by Amqui?

E12-5. (**Preparing trend financial statements, LO 2**) Use the financial statements for Amqui Inc. provided in Exercise E12-4 to respond to the following:

a. Prepare trend balance sheets and income statements for 2012, 2013, and 2014. Use 2012 as the base year.
b. Analyze and interpret the trend financial statements you prepared.
c. How are these trend statements more useful than the statements originally prepared by Amqui?
d. Why would it be unwise to examine the trend financial statements without considering the financial statements originally prepared by Amqui?

E12-6. (**Calculating liquidity ratios, LO 2**) Use the information provided about Amqui Inc. in Exercise E12-4 to respond to the following.

a. Calculate the following for 2013 and 2014:
   i.   current ratio
   ii.   quick ratio
   iii.   accounts receivable turnover ratio
   iv.   average collection period of accounts receivable
   v.   inventory turnover ratio
   vi.   average number of days inventory on hand
   vii.   accounts payable turnover ratio
   viii. average payment period for accounts payable
   ix.   cash lag
b. Assume the role of an important new supplier to Amqui. Use the amounts calculated in (a) to prepare a report assessing whether Amqui should be granted credit terms for purchases from your company. Explain the conclusions you make.

E12-7. (**Using common size and trend statements to evaluate performance, LO 2**) The income statements of Lameque Corp. (Lameque) for the years ended March 31, 2013 through 2015, are shown below:

Lameque Corp. Income Statements For the Years Ended March 31			
	2015	2014	2013
Sales	$5,750,000	$5,225,000	$4,850,000
Cost of sales	3,150,000	2,750,000	2,561,000
Gross margin	2,600,000	2,475,000	2,289,000
Expenses:			
Selling and marketing	405,000	333,500	344,410
Advertising and promotion	607,500	494,500	477,730
General and administrative	258,000	210,000	190,000
Depreciation	300,000	275,000	260,000
Interest	405,000	333,500	344,410
Unusual income (gain)	(500,000)	—	—
Income before income taxes	1,124,500	828,500	672,450
Income tax expense	200,000	160,000	150,000
Net income	$ 924,500	$ 668,500	$ 522,450

Required:

    a. Prepare common size and trend financial statements for Lameque. (For the trend statements, use 2013 as the base year.)

    b. Use the information from (a) to evaluate the performance of Lameque. Explain fully. Your evaluation should include a comparison of Lameque's performance from year to year.

    c. How does the unusual income affect your ability to evaluate Lameque's performance and to interpret your common size and trend financial statements?

E12-8. **(Calculating accounts payable turnover, LO 2)** You have been provided with the following information from the balance sheets and income statements of Batchawana Inc. (Batchawana). Accounts payable and inventory are from the balance sheet as of December 31 of the stated year and cost of sales is for the stated year ended December 31. Assume that all purchases of inventory are made on credit and cost of sales includes only the cost of inventory sold.

Batchawana Inc. Financial Statement Information				
	2014	**2013**	**2012**	**2011**
Accounts payable	$1,125,000	$ 966,410	$ 859,769	$ 667,815
Inventory	1,630,980	1,578,287	1,449,251	1,136,366
Cost of sales	5,056,038	5,208,356	4,811,514	3,613,645

Required:

    a. Calculate the accounts payable turnover ratio for 2014, 2013, and 2012.

    b. Calculate the average payment period for accounts payable for 2014, 2013, and 2012.

    c. Interpret your results from (a) and (b).

    d. What circumstances could explain a declining accounts payable turnover ratio (or increasing average payment period for accounts payable)?

E12-9. **(Determining the effects of transactions on ratios, LO 2)** Complete the following table by indicating whether the transactions or economic events would increase, decrease, or have no effect on the financial ratios listed. Consider each item independently. State any assumptions you make. Explain your reasoning.

	Quick ratio	Inventory turnover ratio	Return on assets	Profit margin percentage	Debt-to-equity ratio
Ratio before the transactions/ economic events	**0.85**	**3.5**	**12%**	**8%**	**1.5:1**
a. Accrual of wages owed to employees at the end of a period					
b. Writedown of inventory to net realizable value					
c. Payment of a previously declared dividend					
d. Purchase of land in exchange for a long-term note payable					
e. Depreciation of equipment					
f. Repurchase of common shares for cash					

E12-10. **(Determining the effects of transactions on ratios, LO 2)** Complete the following table by indicating whether the transactions or economic events would increase, decrease, or have no effect on the financial ratios listed. Consider each item independently. State any assumptions you make. Explain your reasoning.

	Interest coverage ratio	Accounts receivable turnover	Price-to-earnings ratio	Return on equity	Gross margin percentage
Ratio before the transactions/ economic events	4.12	4.75	22.7	12%	61%
a. Unexpected announcement by a public company of a new long-term contract with a new customer					
b. Accrual of a warranty liability					
c. Declaration of a cash dividend					
d. Sale of inventory for cash					
e. Sale of common shares for cash					
f. Payment of an obligation by supplying inventory instead of paying cash					

E12-11. **(Determining the effects of transactions on ratios, LO 2)** Complete the following table by indicating whether the transactions or economic events would increase, decrease, or have no effect on the financial ratios listed. Consider each item independently. State any assumptions you make. Explain your reasoning.

	Current ratio	Average payment period for accounts payable	Return on assets	Gross margin percentage	Earnings per share
Ratio before the transactions/ economic events	1.3	38	12.5%	48%	$1.75
a. Early retirement of long-term debt (classified as long-term when retired)					
b. Writedown of impaired property, plant, and equipment					
c. 2 for 1 stock split					
d. Repayment of the current portion of a long-term liability					
e. Payment of an amount owing to a supplier					
f. Credit sale of merchandise to a customer					

E12-12. **(Evaluating accounts receivable, LO 2)** Oungre Inc. (Oungre) is a small printing business that provides a wide range of printing services to retail and commercial clients. Retail customers pay cash, while Oungre offers its commercial customers 30 days from the delivery date to pay amounts owing. You have been provided with the following information from Oungre's accounting records (Oungre's year-end is December 31):

	2011	2012	2013	2014
Accounts receivable (on December 31)	$336,250	$ 425,250	$ 355,600	$ 322,000
Sales (for the year ended)		3,325,000	3,521,875	3,828,125
Percentage of sales to commercial customers		70%	72%	64%

Required:

    a. Calculate Oungre's accounts receivable turnover ratio and average collection period of accounts receivable for 2012, 2013, and 2014.

    b. Assess how well Oungre managed its accounts receivable over the three-year period.

    c. What are some possible explanations for why Oungre's collection isn't less than 30 days? What steps might Oungre's management take to reduce the collection period?

    d. Suppose you did not know what the proportion of Oungre's sales to commercial customers was. How would your calculation of the accounts receivable turnover ratio and the average collection period of accounts receivable be affected? How would your interpretation of the performance of Oungre's management be affected?

E12-13. **(Evaluating inventory management, LO 2)** Zawale Ltd. (Zawale) is a wholesaler of fresh fruits and vegetables. Zawale purchases fruits and vegetables from growers and supplies them to small grocery stores. You have been provided with the following information from Zawale's accounting records (Zawale's year-end is December 31):

	2012	2013	2014	2015
Inventory (on December 31)	$109,688	$ 123,188	$ 121,500	$ 141,375
Cost of sales (for the year ended)		7,087,500	7,969,500	9,463,781

Required:

    a. Calculate Zawale's inventory turnover ratio and average number of days inventory on hand for 2013, 2014, and 2015.

    b. Evaluate how well Zawale's management is managing the inventory. Explain.

    c. What are some possible explanations for the results you found in (a) and (b)?

    d. What are the implications for Zawale's performance of the results you found in (a)? Explain.

E12-14. **(Evaluating accounts payable management, LO 2)** Guisachan Books Inc. (Guisachan) is a small book retailer. Guisachan has approached your company, a large publishing house, requesting credit terms on purchases. Guisachan has never purchased from your company. If credit is approved, Guisachan would be given 60 days to pay outstanding amounts. You have been provided with the following information from Guisachan's accounting records (Guisachan's year-end is March 31):

	2012	2013	2014	2015
Accounts payable (on March 31)	$201,600	$ 218,400	$ 256,200	$ 302,400
Credit purchases (for the year ended)		1,344,000	1,386,000	1,365,000

Required:

    a. Calculate Guisachan's accounts payable turnover ratio and average payment period for accounts payable for 2013, 2014, and 2015.

    b. Assume you are the publishing house credit manager. How would you interpret the information about Guisachan's accounts payable? How would this information influence your decision about offering credit to Guisachan? Explain. What additional information would you request before making a final decision? Explain.

    c. What effect will the results you calculated in (a) have on Guisachan's cash from operations? Explain. Is this a good situation? Explain. How might Guisachan's suppliers respond? Explain.

E12-15. **(Calculating EPS, price-to-earnings ratio, and dividend ratios, LO 2)** Junor Inc. (Junor) is a publicly traded company. During its year ended July 31, 2015, Junor reported net income of $22,750,000; declared and paid quarterly dividends of $0.08 per share on its 25,000,000 outstanding common shares; and paid $2,000,000 in preferred dividends. During the year, no shares were issued and none were repurchased from investors. On July 31, 2015, Junor's share price was $8.75.

Required:

Calculate the following ratios for 2015. Explain and interpret the meaning of each ratio:

    a. basic earnings per share for fiscal 2015

    b price-to-earnings ratio on July 31, 2015

    b. dividend payout ratio for fiscal 2015

E12-16. **(Calculating EPS, price-to-earnings ratio, and dividend ratios, LO 2)** Kovach Ltd. (Kovach) is a publicly traded company. During its year ended March 31, 2014, Kovach reported a net loss of $12,000,000; declared and paid quarterly dividends of $0.12 per share on its 120,000,000 outstanding common shares; and paid $5,000,000 in preferred dividends. During the year no shares were issued and none were repurchased from investors. On March 31, 2014, Kovach's share price was $3.22.

Required:

    a. Calculate the following ratios for 2014. Explain and interpret the meaning of each ratio:

        i. basic earnings per share for fiscal 2014

        ii. price-to-earnings ratio on March 31, 2014

        iii. dividend payout ratio for fiscal 2014

    b. Explain how it's possible for Kovach to pay a dividend when it reported a loss during fiscal 2014.

    c. Explain why Kovach would have a share price greater than zero when the company is losing money.

E12-17. (**Examining the effect of debt covenants on debt and dividends, LO 2**) During fiscal 2014, Husavick Inc. (Husavick) borrowed $250,000 from a private lender. The loan agreement requires that Husavick's debt-to-equity ratio not exceed 1.8:1 at any time. The loan is repayable in 2020. You have been provided with the following information from Husavick's accounting records:

Husavick Inc.
Summarized Balance Sheet
For the Year Ended July 31, 2014

Assets:	
Current assets	$ 630,000
Non-current assets	2,583,000
Total assets	$3,213,000
Liabilities and shareholders' equity:	
Current liabilities	$ 368,000
Non-current liabilities	1,690,000
Shareholders' equity	1,155,000
Total liabilities and shareholders' equity	$3,213,000

Required:

a. Calculate Husavick's debt-to-equity ratio on July 31, 2014.

b. How much additional debt could Husavick carry without violating the debt covenant on July 31, 2014?

c. How much could Husavick have paid in dividends during fiscal 2014 without violating the debt covenant?

d. What would be the effect on Husavick's debt-to-equity ratio if it declared a $150,000 dividend on July 31, 2014 that was to be paid on August 15, 2014? What could be done to solve the problem that is created by the dividend declaration?

E12-18. (**Computing ratios, LO 2**) Hurstwood Wineries Ltd. (Hurstwood) produces and markets wines from its vineyards in Ontario and B.C. You have been provided with the following income statements and balance sheets for Hurstwood:

Hurstwood Wineries Ltd.
Income Statements for the Years Ended March 31
(in thousands of dollars)

	2014	2013
Credit sales	$43,667	$43,433
Cost of goods sold	27,732	27,408
Gross profit	15,935	16,025
Selling and administration	11,281	10,647
Earnings before interest and depreciation	4,654	5,378
Interest	717	781
Depreciation	1,350	1,241
Earnings before unusual items	2,587	3,356
Unusual items (loss)	(485)	3,125
Earnings before income taxes	2,102	6,481
Provision for (recovery of) income taxes:		
Current	1,084	1,817
Future	(147)	232
	937	2,049
Net earnings for the year	1,165	4,432
Retained earnings—beginning of year	20,453	16,985
Dividends on common shares	964	964
Retained earnings—end of year	$20,654	$20,453

Hurstwood Wineries Ltd.
Balance Sheets as of March 31
(in thousands of dollars)

	2014	2013
Assets		
Current assets:		
Accounts receivable	$ 3,771	$ 3,922
Inventories	15,368	15,621
Prepaid expenses	351	278
	19,490	19,821
Property, plant, and equipment, and goodwill	22,546	20,177
Investment	1,783	1,782
	$43,819	$41,780
Liabilities		
Current liabilities:		
Bank indebtedness	$ 8,942	$ 6,833
Accounts payable and accrued liabilities	4,274	3,431
Dividends payable	241	241
Income and other taxes payable	464	1,004
Current portion of long-term debt	776	685
	14,697	12,194
Long-term debt	5,673	6,191
Future income taxes	1,358	1,505
	21,728	19,890
Shareholders' equity		
Capital stock (weighted average number of shares outstanding during 2014 was 3,953,050 and during 2013 was 3,875,200)	1,437	1,437
Retained earnings	20,654	20,453
	22,091	21,890
	$43,819	$41,780

Required:

a. Compute the following ratios and amounts for Hurstwood for 2014 and 2013:
   i.   gross margin percentage
   ii.   profit margin percentage
   iii. earnings per share
   iv.   working capital
   v.   current ratio
   vi.   quick ratio
   vii. debt-to-equity ratio
   viii. interest coverage ratio
   ix.   dividend payout ratio

b. Compute the following ratios and amounts for Hurstwood for 2014:
   i.   asset turnover
   ii.   return on equity
   iii. return on assets
   iv.   inventory turnover ratio
   v.   average number of days inventory on hand
   vi.   accounts receivable turnover ratio
   vii. average collection period of accounts receivable
   viii. accounts payable turnover ratio
   ix.   average payment period for accounts payable
   x.   cash lag

c. How do the unusual items reported on the 2014 and 2013 income statements affect your ability to predict Hurstwood's future performance?

d. Comment on Hurstwood's liquidity, based on amounts you calculated in (a) and (b). Be sure to consider the nature of Hurstwood's business in your response.

E12-19. **(Understanding return on assets, LO 2)** You are provided with the following information about Unwin Corp. (Unwin), a small manufacturing company:

	2013	2012	2011	2010	2009
Sales	$3,273,600	$3,059,440	$2,913,750	$2,625,000	$
Net income (before interest, after taxes)	133,750	128,495	110,725	91,875	
Total liabilities (at year-end)	865,685	816,685	735,750	681,250	625,000
Shareholders' equity (at year-end)	954,200	813,440	684,940	574,220	482,345
Interest expense	87,500	75,000	37,500	87,500	
Tax rate	16%	16%	16%	16%	

Required:

a. Calculate Unwin's return on assets by determining its profit margin and asset turnover ratio.

b. Calculate Unwin's return on equity.

c. Assess the Unwin's profitability. In your response, explain the reasons for any changes in it.

E12-20. **(Understanding return on assets, LO 2)** You are provided with the following information about Louisbourg Inc. (Louisbourg), a vehicle repair company:

	2014	2013	2012	2011	2010
Sales	$1,903,844	$1,673,075	$1,467,031	$1,296,875	$
Net income	80,584	78,278	73,881	70,169	
Total liabilities (at year-end)	408,954	391,861	375,582	360,079	345,313
Shareholders' equity (at year-end)	666,902	641,518	568,442	499,761	434,792

Required:

a. Calculate Louisbourg's return on assets by determining its profit margin and asset turnover ratio. Assume that profit margin equals net income divided by sales.

b. Calculate Louisbourg's return on equity.

c. Assess Louisbourg's profitability. In your response, explain the reasons for any changes in it.

E12-21. **(Interpreting ratios, LO 2)** You have been provided with the following ratios for two retail business. Use the ratios to evaluate and compare the liquidity situations of the two.

	Business A	Business B
Current ratio	1.26	1.75
Quick ratio	0.75	0.38
Inventory turnover ratio	3.1	2.6
Accounts payable turnover ratio	4.56	3.65

E12-22. (**Interpreting ratios, LO 2**) You have been provided with the following ratios for two retail business. Use the ratios to evaluate and compare the performance of the two businesses.

	Business A	Business B
Gross margin	40%	33%
Profit margin	5%	6.2%
Return on assets	3.1%	5.1%

Problems

P12-1. (**Find the missing information, LO 2**) Use the information provided about Foxwarren Inc. (Foxwarren) to determine the information missing from its December 31, 2015 balance sheet and income statement for the year ended December 31, 2015. For all final amounts determined, round to the nearest thousands of dollars.

Foxwarren Inc.
Balance Sheets for the Years Ended December 31,

	2015	2014
Cash	$	$ 125,000
Accounts receivable		500,000
Inventory		750,000
Capital assets (net)		2,150,000
Total assets	$	$3,525,000
Accounts payable	$	$ 680,000
Long-term debt		1,250,000
Capital stock		1,000,000
Accumulated other comprehensive income		25,000
Retained earnings		570,000
Total liabilities and shareholders' equity	$	$3,525,000

Foxwarren Inc.
Income Statement for the Year Ended December 31, 2015

Revenue	$
Cost of sales	3,500,000
Gross margin	
Selling, general, and administrative expenses	
Interest expense	
Income before taxes	
Income tax expense	
Net income	
Other comprehensive income	
Comprehensive income	
Number of common shares outstanding during 2015	$

Additional information for the year:
- dividends of $150,000 were paid
- there are no preferred shares outstanding
- all sales and purchases of inventory are on credit
- no new common shares were issued and no common shares were repurchased
- comprehensive income was $340,000
- tax rate = 20 percent
- gross margin percentage = 50.0 percent
- profit margin percentage = 4.0 percent
- interest coverage ratio = 4
- EPS = $0.28

- ROA = 9.92 percent
- days inventory = 82.125
- days receivable = 25.94
- days payable = 68.41
- debt-to-equity ratio = 1.244
- current ratio = 2.076

P12-2. (**Find the missing information, LO 2**) Use the information provided about Voligny Inc. (Voligny) to determine the information missing from its December 31, 2014 balance sheet and income statement for the year ended December 31, 2014. For all final amounts determined, round to thousands of dollars.

Voligny Ltd.
Balance Sheets as of the Years Ended December 31,

	2014	2013
Cash	$	$ 1,250,000
Accounts receivable		2,000,000
Inventory		1,500,000
Capital assets (net)		12,250,000
	$	$17,000,000
Accounts payable	$	$ 1,000,000
Long-term debt		6,000,000
Share capital		2,500,000
Retained earnings		7,500,000
	$	$17,000,000

Voligny Ltd.
Income Statement for the Year Ended December 31, 2014

Revenue	$
Cost of sales	
Gross margin	
Selling general and administrative expenses	
Interest expense	
Income before taxes	
Income tax expense	
Net income	$1,000,000

Additional information for the year:
- no dividends were paid
- there are no preferred shares outstanding
- all sales and purchases of inventory are on credit
- no new common shares were issued and no common shares were repurchased
- tax rate = 20 percent
- gross margin percentage = 60 percent
- profit margin percentage = 12.5 percent
- interest coverage ratio = 2.1
- EPS = $0.75
- inventory turnover ratio = 1.828
- accounts receivable turnover ratio = 3.333
- accounts payable turnover ratio = 2.467
- debt-to-equity ratio = 0.827
- current ratio = 3.25

P12-3. **(Considering the current ratios of different industries, LO 2)** Consider the following industries and indicate whether you think each would have a low or high current ratio (e.g., above or below 1.25). Explain your thinking.
   a. telecommunications (like Rogers Communications)
   b. airline (like WestJet)
   c. retail furniture store (like Leon's)
   d. software developer
   e. real estate developer (builds and operates apartment buildings)
   f. car manufacturer (like General Motors)

P12-4. **(Considering the debt-to-equity ratios of different industries, LO 2)** Consider the following industries and indicate whether you think the debt-to-equity ratios of entities in the industry would tend to be high or low (e.g., above one or below one). Consider whether you would want to lend money to an entity in the industry. Explain your answer.
   a. oil and gas exploration company
   b. software developer
   c. auto parts manufacturer
   d. cattle farmer
   e. biotechnology company
   f. electricity utility
   g. furniture retailer

P12-5. **(Determining the effect of a big bath on future earnings and financial ratios, LO 1, 2, 4)** Lucknow Ltd. (Lucknow) is a public company manufacturing casings for electronic equipment. Recently, the board of directors replaced management because it was felt the company was underperforming. The new management team undertook a major restructuring of the company that included a $21,000,000 writedown of property, plant, and equipment and intangibles as well as $5,000,000 in severance and related costs. The written-down assets will continue to be used. The restructuring is reported separately in Lucknow's income statement as a "non-recurring" item and isn't included in the calculation of operating income. In addition, Lucknow wrote down its inventory in fiscal 2014 by $1,000,000. The amount is included in cost of sales.

Lucknow's summarized income statement for the year ended December 31, 2014 is as follows:

Lucknow Ltd.
Summarized Income Statement for the Year Ended December 31, 2014
(000s)

Revenue		$142,000
Operating expenses:		
Cost of sales	$82,000	
Depreciation	26,000	
Selling general and administrative costs	32,000	140,000
Operating income		2,000
Other expenses:		
Non-recurring items:		
Writedown of property, plant, and equipment	21,000	
Other restructuring costs	5,000	
Interest expense	12,500	
Income tax expense	0	38,500
Net income		($ 36,500)

The writedowns will reduce the depreciation expense by $3,000,000 per year for each of the next seven years, beginning in fiscal 2015. After the announcement and release of the income statement, analysts revised their forecasts of earnings for the next three years to:

Year ended December 31, 2015	$ 2,000,000
Year ended December 31, 2016	$ 8,500,000
Year ended December 31, 2017	$12,000,000

You also obtained the following information from Lucknow's December 31, 2013 and 2014 balance sheets:

Lucknow Ltd.
Summarized Balance Sheet Information
as of December 31, 2013 and 2014
(000s)

	2014	2013
Current assets	$ 32,975	$ 37,500
Total assets	142,767	151,597
Current liabilities	41,720	28,150
Non-current liabilities	47,250	33,150
Shareholders' equity	53,797	90,297

Required:

a. What would net income be in each of 2014 through 2017 had Lucknow not written off the assets but continued to depreciate them? Assume Lucknow's operations of don't change regardless of the accounting method used? Interpret the differences in net income under the two scenarios. Use the analysts' forecasts to determine net income. Ignore the impact of taxes.

b. What would Lucknow's gross margin percentage, profit margin ratio, debt-to-equity ratio, return on assets, and return on equity be in 2014 assuming (i) that the assets had been written off and (ii) assuming that the assets had not been written off and they were continuing to be depreciated. Interpret the results under each assumption.

c. How would the writedowns in 2014 affect Lucknow's gross margin percentage, profit margin ratio, debt-to-equity ratio, return on assets, and return on equity in 2015 through 2017? How is your ability to analyze and interpret the financial statements affected?

P12-6. **(Evaluating the effect of R&D accounting on financial statement analysis, LO 1, 2, 3)** One controversial accounting issue is accounting for research costs. IFRS require research costs to be expensed as incurred. Some people argue that research is a legitimate asset and expensing it results in an understatement of assets and income, violates matching, making companies that invest heavily in research appear less successful than they actually are.

Chortitz Ltd. (Chortitz) is a large and successful software development company. You have been provided with Chortitz's balance sheets for 2012 through 2015 and income statements for 2013 through 2015. Chortitz expensed (and expended) $7,906,000 for research in 2011 and $6,612,000 in 2012.

Chortitz Ltd.
Summarized Balance Sheet Information as of June 30,
(000s)

	2015	2014	2013	2012
Current assets	$47,953	$51,563	$41,102	$34,815
Total assets	90,923	92,441	76,024	70,589
Current liabilities	32,154	33,220	22,233	18,569
Non-current liabilities	11,550	9,240	6,188	4,331
Shareholders' equity	47,219	49,981	47,603	47,689

Chortitz Ltd.
Income Statements for the Years Ended June 30,
(000s)

	2015	2014	2013
Revenues	$ 121,852	$ 93,180	$ 76,343
Cost of revenues:			
License & networking	4,849	2,215	1,501
Customer support	6,296	4,728	2,600
Service	20,596	18,975	12,255
Total cost of revenues	31,741	25,918	16,356
	90,111	67,262	59,987
Operating expenses:			
Research and development	20,057	14,638	9,383
Sales and marketing	42,337	35,416	30,064
General and administrative	10,883	16,361	4,885
Depreciation	5,178	4,586	4,225
Total operating expenses	78,455	71,001	48,557
Income (loss) from operations	11,656	(3,739)	11,430
Interest expense	1,005	765	498
Income before income taxes	10,651	(4,504)	10,932
Provision for (recovery of) income taxes	2,115	(854)	1,995
Net income for the year	$ 8,536	$ (3,650)	$ 8,937
Weighted average number of common shares outstanding during the year	20,032,092	22,349,268	20,914,365

Required:

a. Recalculate Chortitz's net income in 2013, 2014, and 2015, assuming research is capitalized and amortized over three years. Also calculate total assets and shareholders' equity, assuming research is capitalized and amortized. What amount would be reported on the balance sheet for research in this case? (Assume that one-third of the amount expended on research is expensed each year, including the year of the expenditure, and that the accounting for research and development has no effect on income taxes.)

b. Calculate Chortitz's profit margin ratio, interest coverage ratio, earnings per share, debt-to-equity ratio, ROA, and ROE for 2013, 2014, and 2015 using the information as presented in the company's financial statements. Calculate the same ratios, assuming that Chortitz capitalizes and amortizes its research costs over three years.

c. Evaluate the performance and solvency of Chortitz under the "expense" and "capitalize" scenarios. What are the implications of the differences between the two scenarios? Do you think there is merit in the criticisms some people have expressed about the current IFRS treatment of research costs? Explain fully.

P12-7. **(Evaluating performance, LO 2)** Nywening Ltd. (Nywening) operates in a highly competitive industry. Price is very important to most customers and it's very difficult for small operators such as Nywening to differentiate themselves on product quality. It's possible to differentiate based on service, but most competitors offer reasonably comparable service packages. The president of Nywening is reviewing the company's performance in 2014. During 2014, sales increased by 12 percent to $3,500,000. Average total assets for the year were $1,950,000, net income was $200,000, and interest expense was $60,000. Nywening's tax rate is 20 percent.

The president believes that Nywening can improve its performance in 2015. She would like to see a 15 percent growth in sales in 2015 and a return on assets of 20 percent. The president estimates that it will be necessary to increase assets by 10 percent in 2015. The president doesn't think that any additional borrowing will be required and, as a result, the interest expense for 2015 will be the same as for 2014. The tax rate is expected to stay the same.

Required:

    a. Calculate Nywening's profit margin, asset turnover, and return on assets for 2014.

    b. What asset turnover ratio in 2015 will achieve the president's objectives? What net income is needed? What would the profit margin be if the objectives are achieved? For purposes of this question use net income plus the after tax cost of interest to calculate profit margin.

    c. Do you think the president's objectives are reasonable?

P12-8. **(Evaluating liquidity, LO 2)** You have been provided with the following information about Marquis Inc. (Marquis):

	2012	2013	2014	2015
Accounts receivable	$ 150,000	$ 157,500	$ 165,375	$ 173,644
Inventory	100,000	105,000	110,250	115,763
Accounts payable	75,000	78,750	82,688	86,822
Revenue	1,000,000	1,050,000	1,155,000	1,270,500
Cost of sales	550,000	577,500	641,025	711,538

Required:

    a. Calculate the accounts receivable, inventory, and accounts payable turnover ratios for 2013 through 2015 (assume that all sales and purchases are on credit).

    b. Calculate the average collection period of accounts receivable, average number of days inventory on hand, and average payment period for accounts payable for 2013 through 2015.

    c. Determine Marquis's cash lag for 2013 through 2015.

    d. Interpret the results you obtained in (a) through (c). What do these results tell you about Marquis's liquidity over the last three years? What are some possible explanations for the results?

    e. Suppose you are a banker Marquis's management has approached about an expanded line of credit. How would the results you obtained in (a) through (c) affect your decision? Explain.

P12-9. **(Evaluating liquidity, LO 2)** You have been provided with the following information about Yarker Ltd. (Yarker).

	2012	2013	2014	2015
Accounts receivable	$ 1,125,000	$ 1,215,000	$ 1,275,750	$1,339,538
Inventory	2,500,000	2,600,000	2,730,000	2,593,500
Accounts payable	100,000	101,920	104,876	97,639
Revenue	10,000,000	10,500,000	10,290,000	9,775,500
Cost of sales	4,000,000	4,179,000	4,074,943	3,851,840

Required:

    a. Calculate the accounts receivable, inventory, and accounts payable turnover ratios for 2013 through 2015.

    b. Calculate the average collection period of accounts receivable, average number of days inventory on hand, and average payment period for accounts payable for 2013 through 2015.

    c. Determine Yarker's cash lag for 2013 through 2015.

    d. Interpret the results you obtained in (a) through (c). What do these results tell you about Yarker's liquidity over the last three years? What are some possible explanations for the results?

    e. Suppose you are a banker Yarker's management approached about an expanded line of credit. How would the results you obtained in (a) through (c) affect your decision? Explain.

P12-10. (**The effect of leverage on ROA and ROE, LO 2**) Three companies, Company A, Company B, and Company C, are identical in every respect except for how they are financed. You are provided with the following information about each company.

	Company A			Company B			Company C		
	Jan. 1, 2015	Dec. 31, 2015	Dec. 31, 2016	Jan. 1, 2015	Dec. 31, 2015	Dec. 31, 2016	Jan. 1, 2015	Dec. 31, 2015	Dec. 31, 2016
Income before interest and taxes		$ 28,000	$ 3,000		$ 28,000	$ 3,000		$ 28,000	$ 3,000
Interest expense		0	0		3,000	3,000		7,000	7,000
Income tax expense (recovery)		4,480	480		4,000	0		3,360	(640)
Net income		23,520	2,520		21,000	0		17,640	(3,360)
Dividends paid (on common stock)		10,000	5,880		7,480	3,360		4,120	0
Total assets	100,000	113,520	110,160	100,000	113,520	110,160	100,000	113,520	110,160
Shareholders' equity	100,000	113,520	110,160	70,000	83,520	80,160	30,000	43,520	40,160
Tax rate		0.16	0.16		0.16	0.16		0.16	0.16

Required:

a. Calculate ROA and ROE for each company for the years ended December 31, 2015 and 2016.
b. Explain the differences in performance among the three companies.
c. Explain the effect of leverage on the performance measures.
d. Which company is the best investment? Explain.

P12-11. (**The effect of leasing on ratios, LO 2, 4**) Plevna Inc. (Plevna) is a small, publicly owned manufacturing company in eastern Canada. In 2014, Plevna's management decided to acquire additional manufacturing equipment to meet increasing demand for its products. However, instead of purchasing the equipment, Plevna arranged to lease the equipment. The lease came into effect on December 1, 2013. In its 2014 financial statements, Plevna accounted for the leases as operating leases. You have obtained Plevna's summarized balance sheets and income statements for 2013 and 2014.

Plevna Inc.
Summarized Balance Sheets as of November 30,

	2014	2013
Cash	$ 212	$ 276
Accounts receivable	695	608
Inventory	1,825	1,547
Capital assets (net)	2,895	2,652
Other non-current assets	375	442
Total assets	$6,002	$5,525
Current liabilities	$1,728	$1,823
Long-term debt	990	950
Share capital (1,000,000 shares outstanding)	1,200	1,200
Retained earnings	2,084	1,552
Total liabilities and shareholders' equity	$6,002	$5,525

Plevna Inc.
Income Statements for the Years Ended November 30,

	2014	2013
Revenue	$17,250	$14,500
Cost of sales	9,402	7,996
Selling, general, and administrative expenses	6,512	5,550
Depreciation expense	310	275
Lease expense for equipment	75	
Interest expense	92	86
Income tax expense	177	148
Net income	$ 682	$ 445

Had Plevna accounted for the equipment leases as capital leases, the following differences would have occurred in the 2014 financial statements:
- No lease expense would have been recorded.
- The leased equipment would have been recorded on the balance sheet as capital assets for $460,000. The equipment would have been depreciated straight line over 10 years.
- A liability of $460,000 would have been recorded at the inception of the lease. On November 30, 2014, the current portion of the liability would have been $75,000. The interest expense arising from the lease would have been $46,000. On November 30, 2014, the remaining liability, including the current portion would have been $431,000.
- There would be no effect on the tax expense for the year.

Required:

a. Prepare revised financial statements, assuming that Plevna treated the leases as capital leases instead of as operating leases.
b. Calculate the following ratios, first using the financial statements as initially prepared by Plevna and then using the revised statements you prepared in part (a):
   i.   debt-to-equity ratio
   ii. return on assets
   iii. return on equity
   iv. profit margin ratio
   v.   current ratio
   vi. asset turnover
   vii. earnings per share
   viii. interest coverage ratio
c. Discuss the differences between the two sets of ratios you calculated in (b). Why are the ratios different? How might users of the financial statements be affected by these differences? Which set of ratios gives a better perspective on the performance, liquidity, and leverage of Plevna? Explain.

P12-12. (**Determining the effect of a big bath on future earnings, LO 1, 2, 4**) Oromocto Inc. (Oromocto) is a large mining company. In 2011, it wrote down $20,000,000 in costs that it incurred finding and developing certain mining properties. If Oromocto had not written down these costs, $4,000,000 more in depreciation would have been expensed in each year from 2011 through 2015. The summarized financial statement information for the years 2011 through 2014 are given:

Oromocto Inc.
Summarized Financial Statement Information
(000s)

	2010	2011	2012	2013	2014
Revenue		$140,300	$128,800	$142,600	$151,800
Operating expenses		71,553	66,332	74,295	80,150
Depreciation expense		32,200	33,120	34,040	35,880
Interest expense		5,520	5,520	5,520	5,520
Income tax expense		4,654	3,574	4,312	4,537
Net income		$ 26,373	$ 20,254	$ 24,433	$ 25,713
Total assets	$170,200	$197,922	$228,106	$247,695	$270,395
Total shareholders' equity	$115,000	$141,373	$161,627	$186,060	$211,773

Additional information:
- Oromocto has no preferred shares outstanding.
- The depreciation expense doesn't include the depreciation of the written-down assets and the writedown isn't reflected in the presented information.
- Oromocto's tax rate is 15 percent.
- Assume that the writedown and any additional depreciation expense don't affect Oromocto's tax expense.

Required:

a. Determine Oromocto's net income for 2011 through 2014, assuming that the $20,000,000 writedown (i) occurred and (ii) didn't occur. For (ii), depreciation of the assets must be expensed each year.
b. Calculate Oromocto's profit margin, return on assets, and return on equity, assuming the writedown (i) occurred and (ii) didn't occur.
c. Should the writedown be considered permanent or transitory? Explain.
d. As an equity investor in Oromocto, how would your evaluation of the company be affected by whether the writedown occurred versus if the assets were depreciated over their remaining life? In responding you should consider permanent versus transitory earnings.

P12-13. (Forecasting future earnings, LO 1) You have been presented with Everell Ltd.'s income statement for the year ended September 30, 2015.

Everell Ltd.
Income Statement for the Year Ended September 30, 2015

Sales	$12,750,000
Cost of sales	5,737,500
Gross margin	7,012,500
Expenses:	
Salaries and wages	2,754,000
Depreciation	987,000
Selling and administrative	1,450,000
Interest	500,000
Other	325,000
Unusual item—lawsuit	(3,000,000)
Income before income taxes	3,996,500
Income tax expense	599,475
Net income	$ 3,397,025

In addition, you have learned the following:

- Cost of sales in 2015 includes a writedown of inventory of $295,000. The amount of the writedown is about three times larger than the usual yearly amount to account for non-saleable inventory or inventory that will have to be sold at a deep discount.
- Sales includes $1,250,000 for a one-time sale to a foreign government. The gross margin percentage on this sale was 60 percent, which is significantly higher than what Everell normally experiences.
- Selling and administrative costs includes a $200,000 retirement bonus to the former CEO.
- Everell signed a contract with its employees, effective October 1, 2015. The contract increases union wages and benefits by 5 percent. Wages to union employees represent 70 percent of salary and wage expense in 2015. Wages to other employees are not expected to change during 2016.
- During 2015 Everell won a lawsuit against a former employee for divulging confidential information to her new employer. The employee and her new employer are required to pay damages to Everell of $3,000,000.
- Sales (excluding the one-time sale note above) are expected to grow by 8 percent during 2016. Inventory costs are expected to increase by 9 percent, selling and administrative expenses to decrease by 2 percent, interest expense isn't expected to change, depreciation expense to increase by 2 percent, and other expenses to increase by 4 percent.

Required:

a. Use Everell's 2015 income statement and the additional information to forecast an income statement for 2016.
b. Explain and interpret Everell's actual performance in 2015 and the performance you forecast for 2016.
c. Discuss the difficulties with forecasting the future performance of an entity and the problems with using IFRS financial statements for forecasting.

P12-14. (**Evaluating liquidity and solvency, LO 2**) Galahad Inc. (Galahad) is a small manufacturer of customized car parts designed for people who want to accessorize their cars. Galahad's products are sold to retailers across Canada and about 20 percent of its sales are outside of Canada, mainly in the United States. The president of Galahad feels that the company has a good product and established markets, and has performed well over the last few years. However, she is concerned that Galahad is chronically tight on cash. She has approached your organization for a significant loan to provide the company with additional working capital, as well as to purchase capital assets that need to be replaced. The president has provided income statements and balance sheets for recent years.

Galahad Inc.
Income Statements for the Years Ended July 31,

	2014	2013	2012
Sales	$1,852,000	$1,981,640	$1,961,823
Cost of sales	1,038,973	1,099,810	1,075,079
Selling, general, and administrative expenses	652,053	670,757	656,211
Depreciation	110,000	102,000	98,000
Research and development	45,000	88,000	125,000
Gain on sale of investment	(63,000)		
Income tax expense	13,000	3,000	1,000
Net income	$ 55,974	$ 18,073	$ 6,533

Galahad Inc.
Balance Sheets for the Years Ended July 31,

	2014	2013	2012	2011
Cash	$ 5,580	$ 26,606	$ 28,533	$ 40,000
Receivables	275,000	215,000	200,000	145,000
Inventory	315,000	210,000	200,000	165,000
Prepaid expenses	51,000	28,000	20,000	15,000
Current assets	646,580	479,606	448,533	365,000
Capital assets	1,109,000	960,000	788,000	560,000
Accumulated depreciation	(460,000)	(350,000)	(248,000)	(150,000)
Investment, at cost	0	75,000	75,000	0
	$1,295,580	$1,164,606	$1,063,533	$775,000
Bank loans	$ 125,000	$ 92,000	$ 47,000	$ 0
Accounts payable and accrued liabilities	350,000	308,000	270,000	210,000
Current liabilities	475,000	400,000	317,000	210,000
Long-term debt	175,000	175,000	175,000	0
Capital stock	500,000	500,000	500,000	500,000
Retained earnings	145,580	89,606	71,533	65,000
	$1,295,580	$1,164,606	$1,063,533	$775,000

Additional information:
- The long-term debt is due to be repaid in early 2016. The amount is owed to a large bank and is secured against certain capital assets.
- Galahad has a $130,000 line of credit available from another bank. Bank loans represent the amount borrowed against the line of credit.
- All sales to customers and purchases of inventory are made on credit.
- Interest expense is included in selling, general, and administrative expenses. Interest expense was $26,000 in 2014, $28,000 in 2013, and $10,000 in 2012.

Required:

Prepare a report to the corporate lending department evaluating the liquidity and solvency of Galahad. Provide a preliminary recommendation, with support, on whether the loan should be made. What additional information would you want before reaching a final decision on the loan application? In your analysis consider Galahad's cash flow.

P12-15. (**Evaluating an equity investment, LO 2**) Refer to the information about Galahad provided in Problem P12-14. You are an investment analyst for Qualicum Investment Group, Inc. (Qualicum). Qualicum raises capital from individual investors and invests in promising small businesses, with the expectation that the businesses will grow and that it will ultimately be able to sell the investments at a profit. The president of Galahad has approached your organization to make a significant equity investment in the company.

Required:

Prepare a report to Qualicum's executive board analyzing Galahad's performance over the last few years and assessing its attractiveness as an investment. What additional information would you want before reaching a final decision on whether to invest? In your analysis consider Galahad's cash flow.

P12-16. (**Assessing inventory and performance, LO 1, 2**) Bold! Ltd. is a men and women's retail clothing chain with stores located across Canada. The company is looking for new equity investment to help finance a major expansion. A private investment fund is looking to place some money in the Canadian retail industry and is considering Bold! Ltd. You are an analyst for a private investment fund and your manager has asked you to analyze some the company's information for trends and insights. You have information relevant to inventory and Bold!'s performance for the last seven years as well as other financial statement information that might be useful.

Periods ended:	2015	2014	2013	2012	2011	2010	2009
	$000s	$000s	$000s	$000s	$000s	$000s	$000s
Operating revenue	$163,550	$158,099	$148,351	$166,350	$178,115	$175,487	$179,977
General and administrative expenses	72,428	69,777	71,741	69,669	74,439	71,394	64,195
Cost of sales	87,365	79,565	76,953	82,863	90,060	88,788	92,098
Net income	12,892	1,653	(5,503)	(185)	(7,097)	5,394	10,725
Cash and equivalents	19,882	20,579	11,833	21,193	23,000	7,254	3,777
Inventories	27,404	28,561	32,348	29,031	29,915	37,029	38,662
Accounts receivable	755	724	402	594	634	600	484
Accounts payable and accrued liabilities	9,845	9,387	10,708	8,170	9,425	10,559	10,472

*All purchases and sales are on credit.

Required:

Prepare the report requested by your manager. Provide any ratios that you think appropriate. Be sure to interpret your results and explain the tools that you use to do the analysis.

Using Financial Statements

THE FORZANI GROUP LTD.

The Forzani Group Ltd. is Canada's largest sporting goods retailer, offering brand-name and private-brand products. It operates stores across the country, under the following corporate and franchise banners: Sport Chek, Coast Mountain Sports, Sport Mart, National Sports, Athletes World, Sports Experts, Tech Shop, Nevada Bob's Golf, Hockey Experts, and The Fitness Source. The company also retails online at www.sportmart.ca and offers a sporting goods information site, www.sportchek.ca. At the end of fiscal 2009, Forzani Group operated 337 corporate stores and was franchisor/licensor of 227 stores.[7]

www.forzanigroup.com

Forzani's consolidated balance sheets, statements of operations, comprehensive earnings, and cash flows, and extracts from the notes to the financial statements are provided in Exhibit 12.3.[8] Use this information to respond to questions FS12-1 to FS12-9.

FS12-1. Prepare common size and trend statements from Forzani's balance sheets and statements of operations for fiscal 2007 through 2009. Analyze the statements you prepared to identify any issues you think might require additional explanation. Explain why you identified these issues.

EXHIBIT ⟨ 12.3 ⟩ The Forzani Group Ltd.: Extracts from the Financial Statements

The Forzani Group Ltd.
Consolidated Balance Sheets
(in thousands)

As at	Febuary 1, 2009	February 3, 2008	January 28, 2007
ASSETS			
Current			
Cash	$ 3,474	$ 47,484	$ 22,758
Accounts receivable	84,455	75,506	65,543
Inventory (Note 3)	291,497	319,445	302,207
Prepaid expenses (Note 4)	2,827	14,501	2,688
	382,253	456,936	393,196
Capital assets (Note 5)	196,765	188,621	191,146
Goodwill and other intangibles (Note 6)	91,481	89,335	90,238
Other assets (Note 7)	9,280	3,863	8,011
Future income tax assets (Note 12)	9,681	16,209	
	$ 689,460	$ 754,964	$ 682,591
LIABILITIES			
Current			
Indebtedness under revolving credit facilities	$ 17,130	$ —	$ —
Accounts payable and accrued liabilities	277,820	279,910	230,977
Current portion of long-term debt (Note 8)	7,501	51,863	1,163
	302,451	331,773	232,140
Long-term debt (Note 8)	126	6,586	58,303
Deferred lease inducements	47,811	55,089	58,543
Deferred rent liability	5,893	6,033	5,737
Future income tax liability	—	—	55
	356,281	399,481	354,778
SHAREHOLDERS' EQUITY			
Share capital (Note 11)	147,161	157,105	148,424
Contributed surplus	6,401	7,210	8,294
Accumulated other comprehensive earnings (loss)	863	(8)	—
Retained earnings	178,754	191,176	171,095
	333,179	355,483	327,813
	$ 689,460	$ 754,964	682,591

Additional information from Forzani's January 29, 2006 financial statements:	
Accounts receivable	$ 68,927
Inventory	278,002
Total assets	653,206
Accounts payable and accrued liabilities	244,293
Total shareholders' equity	278,280

EXHIBIT 12.3 **(continued) The Forzani Group Ltd.: Extracts from the Financial Statements**

The Forzani Group Ltd.
Consolidated Statements of Operations
(in thousands, except per share data)

	For the 52 weeks ended February 1, 2009	For the 53 weeks ended February 3, 2008	For the 52 weeks ended January 28, 2007
Revenue			
Retail	$ 994,043	$ 969,256	$ 925,443
Wholesale	352,715	361,753	338,512
	1,346,758	1,331,009	1,263,955
Cost of sales	863,239	852,608	812,363
Gross margin	483,519	478,401	451,592
Operating and administrative expenses			
Store operating	277,089	251,630	236,870
General and administrative	109,328	103,801	107,462
	386,417	355,431	344,332
Operating earnings before undernoted items	97,102	122,970	107,260
Amortization of capital assets	47,613	44,468	43,410
Interest	5,175	5,797	7,354
Loss on sale of investment (Note 21)	-	864	-
	52,788	51,129	50,764
Earnings before income taxes	44,314	71,841	56,496
Income tax expense (recovery) (Note 12)			
Current	6,273	27,439	19,897
Future	8,716	(3,049)	1,382
	14,989	24,390	21,279
Net earnings	$ 29,325	$ 47,451	$ 35,217
Earnings per share (Note 11(c))	$ 0.94	$ 1.40	$ 1.06
Diluted earnings per share (Note 11(c))	$ 0.93	$ 1.39	$ 1.04

FS12-2. Compute and interpret the following ratios for Forzani for fiscal years 2008 and 2009. Use these ratios to assess Forzani's liquidity. Be sure to use the information provided from Forzani's January 28, 2007, balance sheet.
   a. current ratio
   b. quick ratio
   c. accounts receivable turnover ratio
   d. average collection period of accounts receivable
   e. inventory turnover ratio
   f. average number of days inventory on hand
   g. accounts payable turnover ratio
   h. average payment period for accounts payable

FS12-3. Compute and interpret the following ratios for Forzani for fiscal 2009, 2008, and 2007. Use these ratios to assess Forzani's performance:
   a. gross margin
   b. profit margin
   c. return on assets
   d. return on equity

EXHIBIT 12.3 (continued) The Forzani Group Ltd.: Extracts from the Financial Statements

Consolidated Statements of Comprehensive Earnings

Net earnings	$	29,325	$	47,451
Other comprehensive earnings (loss):				
Unrealized foreign currency gains and (losses) on cash flow hedges		1,340		(138)
Tax impact		(469)		51
Other comprehensive earnings (loss)		871		(87)
Comprehensive earnings	$	30,196	$	47,364

Consolidated Statements of Accumulated Other
Comprehensive Earnings (Loss) ("AOCE")

Accumulated other comprehensive earnings (loss), beginning of period	$	(8)	$	-
Transitional adjustment upon adoption of new financial instruments standard		-		79
Accumulated other comprehensive earnings (loss), beginning of period, as restated		(8)		79
Other comprehensive earnings (loss)		871		(87)
Accumulated other comprehensive earnings (loss), end of period	$	863	$	(8)

The Forzani Group Ltd.
Consolidated Statements of Cash Flows
(in thousands)

		For the 52 weeks ended February 1, 2009		For the 53 weeks en February 3, 2008
Cash provided by (used in) operating activities				
Net earnings	$	29,325	$	47,451
Items not involving cash:				
Amortization of capital assets		47,613		44,468
Amortization of deferred finance charges		377		738
Amortization of deferred lease inducements		(11,500)		(11,109)
Rent expense (Note 9)		152		524
Stock-based compensation (Note 11(d))		(174)		2,756
Future income tax expense (recovery)		8,716		(3,049)
Loss on sale of investment (Note 21)		-		864
Unrealized loss on ineffective hedges		321		44
		74,830		82,687
Changes in non-cash elements of working capital related to operating activities (Note 9)		20,913		23,737
		95,743		106,424
Cash provided by (used in) financing activities				
Net proceeds from issuance of share capital (Note 11(b))		2,384		13,273
Share repurchase via normal course issuer bid (Note 11(e))		(44,027)		(33,331)
Long-term debt		(51,199)		(19,198)
Revolving credit facility		17,130		-
Lease inducements received		4,221		7,648
Dividends paid (Note 11(f))		(9,327)		(2,472)
		(80,818)		(34,080)
Changes in non-cash elements of financing activities (Note 9)		(1,121)		(1,698)
		(81,939)		(35,778)
Cash provided by (used in) investing activities				
Capital assets		(52,139)		(40,660)
Other assets		(2,998)		2,151
Acquisition of wholly-owned subsidiaries (Note 17)		-		(8,774)
		(55,137)		(47,283)
Changes in non-cash elements of investing activities (Note 9)		(2,677)		1,363
		(57,814)		(45,920)
Increase (decrease) in cash		(44,010)		24,726
Net cash position, opening		47,484		22,758
Net cash position, closing	$	3,474	$	47,484

EXHIBIT 12.3 (continued) The Forzani Group Ltd.: Extracts from the Financial Statements

2. Significant Accounting Policies

(b) Inventory valuation

Inventory is valued at the lower of laid-down cost and net realizable value. Laid-down cost is determined using the weighted average cost method and includes invoice cost, duties, freight, and distribution costs. Net realizable value is defined as the expected selling price.

Under the prior guidance, the Company included storage costs in the cost of inventory. This is no longer permitted, resulting in a $1,357,000 adjustment to opening inventory for the year and a corresponding adjustment to opening retained earnings. Prior periods have not been restated.

(h) Revenue recognition

Revenue includes sales to customers through corporate stores operated by the Company and sales to, and service fees from, franchise stores and others. Sales to customers through corporate stores operated by the Company are recognized at the point of sale, net of an estimated allowance for sales returns. Sales of merchandise to franchise stores and others are recognized at the time of shipment. Royalties and administration fees are recognized when earned, in accordance with the terms of the franchise/license agreements.

(i) Store opening expenses

Operating costs incurred prior to the opening of new stores, other than rent incurred during the fixturing period, are expensed as incurred.

(j) Fiscal year

The Company's fiscal year follows a retail calendar. The fiscal years for the consolidated financial statements presented are the 52-week period ended February 1, 2009 and the 53-week period ended February 3, 2008.

3. Inventory

Included within cost of sales for the period ended February 1, 2009, are normal course charges to inventory made throughout the year, of $12,265,000 (2008 – $12,514,000). These charges include the disposal of obsolete and damaged product, inventory shrinkage and permanent markdowns to net realizable values.

8. Long Term Debt

	2009	2008
G.E. term loan	$ -	$ 49,744
Mortgage with monthly payments of $58,000 and an interest rate of 6.2% compounded semi-annually, secured by land and building, expiring October 2009.	5,458	5,782
Vendor take-back, unsecured with implied interest rate of 4.8% and payments due March 2009	2,043	2,792
Asset retirement obligation	126	113
Other	-	18
	7,627	58,449
Less current portion	7,501	51,863
	$ 126	$ 6,586

Principal payments on the above, due in the next five years, are as follows:

2010	$	7,501
2011	$	-
2012	$	-
2013	$	-
2014	$	-

EXHIBIT 12.3 (continued) The Forzani Group Ltd.: Extracts from the Financial Statements

9.   Supplementary Cash Flow Information

	For the 52 weeks ended February 1, 2009	For the 53 weeks ended February 3, 2008
Rent expense		
Straight-line rent expense	$ (140)	$ 228
Non-cash free rent	292	296
	$ 152	$ 524
Change in non-cash elements of working capital related to operating activities		
Accounts receivable	$ (11,137)	$ (9,963)
Inventory	21,753	13,772
Prepaid expenses	11,674	(11,813)
Financial Instruments	764	-
Accounts payable and accrued liabilities	(2,141)	31,741
	$ 20,913	$ 23,737
Change in non-cash elements of financing activities		
Lease inducements	$ (907)	$ (1,115)
Long-term debt	-	(568)
Change in fair value of cash flow hedge	871	-
Net financial assets	(1,085)	(15)
	$ (1,121)	$ (1,698)
Change in non-cash elements of investing activities		
Capital assets	$ 668	$ 795
Other assets	(3,345)	568
	$ (2,677)	$ 1,363
Net cash interest paid	$ 4,648	$ 5,017
Net cash taxes paid	$ 26,109	$ 29,509

11.   Share Capital

(a)   Authorized

An unlimited number of Class A shares (no par value)

An unlimited number of Preferred shares, issuable in series

(f)   Dividends

On April 7, 2009 the Company declared a dividend of $0.075 per Class A common share, payable on May 4, 2009 to shareholders of record on April 20, 2009. The Company's stated intention is to declare annual dividends of $0.30 per share, payable quarterly, subject to the Board of Directors discretion.

13.   Commitments

(a)   The Company is committed, at February 1, 2009, to minimum payments under long-term real property and data processing hardware and software equipment leases, for future years, as follows:

Year	Gross
2010	$ 87,523
2011	$ 77,283
2012	$ 65,083
2013	$ 52,753
2014	$ 40,403
Thereafter	$ 86,471

In addition, the Company may be obligated to pay percentage rent under certain of the leases.

EXHIBIT 12.3 (continued) The Forzani Group Ltd.: Extracts from the Financial Statements

18. Segmented Financial Information

The Company operates principally in two business segments: corporately-owned and operated retail stores and as a wholesale business selling to franchisees and others. Amortization and interest expense are not disclosed by segment as they are substantially retail in nature.

In determining the reportable segments, the Company considered the distinct business models of the retail and wholesale operations, the division of responsibilities, and the reporting to the CEO and Board of Directors.

	For the 52 weeks ended February 1, 2009	For the 53 weeks ended February 3, 2008
Revenues:		
Retail	$ 994,043	$ 969,256
Wholesale	352,715	361,753
	1,346,758	1,331,009
Operating Profit:		
Retail	115,431	143,517
Wholesale	37,229	35,296
	152,660	178,813
Non-segment specific administrative expenses	55,558	55,843
Operating profit before under noted items	97,102	122,970
Amortization of capital assets	47,613	44,468
Interest expense	5,175	5,797
Loss on sale of investment	-	864
	52,788	51,129
Earnings before income taxes	44,314	71,841
Income tax expense	14,989	24,390
Net earnings	$ 29,325	$ 47,451

FS12-4. Compute and interpret the following ratios for Forzani for fiscal years 2009, 2008, and 2007. Use these ratios to assess Forzani's solvency and liquidity. Don't restrict your evaluation to the ratios you are required to calculate.
   a. debt-to-equity ratio
   b. interest coverage ratio (earnings based)
   c. interest coverage ratio (cash based) (for 2009 and 2008 only)

FS12-5. Does Forzani have any off-balance-sheet liabilities? Describe these liabilities. What impact do the off-balance-sheet liabilities have on your ability to evaluate Forzani's capital structure and risk? Calculate Forzani's debt-to-equity ratio on February 1, 2009, using only the amounts reflected in the balance sheet, and compare that amount with the ratio taking into consideration the off-balance-sheet amounts. Don't forget to discount the amounts where appropriate. Assume a discount rate of 15 percent.

FS12-6. Forzani's cash position is significantly lower at the end of fiscal 2009 than the year before. Explain the reason for the decrease. Is this something you are concerned about? Explain. Why is Forzani's cash from operations so much greater than its net income?

FS12-7. Fozani's net income in fiscal 2009 is almost $15 million, or about 61 percent lower than fiscal 2008. Net income in 2009 is also much lower than in fiscal 2007. Analyze Forzani's income statements and explain the decrease.

FS12-8. You are the credit analyst for a company that Forzani has approached to become a major supplier of hockey equipment. Prepare a report to the manager of the credit department assessing the credit-worthiness of Forzani and recommending whether the company should extend credit. Be sure to consider the information provided in the notes to the financial statements provided in Exhibit 12.3.

FS12-9. You are considering purchasing some of Forzani's common shares. Use the information provided in Exhibit 12.3 to assess the attractiveness of such an investment. What additional information would you want to make a decision?

ENDNOTES

1. Andree Lavigne, Diane Paul, John Tang, Jo-Ann Lempert, Helene Marcil, and Louise Overbeek, *2008 Financial Reporting in Canada*, 33rd ed., Federal Publications Inc., 2008.

2. Data from the *Financial Post*, "2009 Industry Reports," at http://www.fpinfomart.ca (accessed August 2009).

3. Data from the *Financial Post*, "2009 Industry Reports," at http://www.fpinfomart.ca (accessed May 2009).

4. Extracted from Maple Leaf Foods Inc.'s 2008 annual report.

5. Extracted from Denison Mines Corp. 2008 annual report.

6. Data from the *Financial Post*, "2009 Industry Reports," at http://www.fpinfomart.ca (accessed May 2009).

7. Adapted from The Forzani Group Ltd.'s fiscal 2007 and 2008 annual report.

8. Adapted from The Forzani Group Ltd.'s annual reports.

APPENDIX

COMPREHENSIVE CASES

CASE 1: ALPHA INC.

In November 2014, Allison Chhor, the sole shareholder of Alpha Inc. (Alpha), agreed to sell 100 percent of her shares to Denis Sonin. Ms. Chhor and Mr. Sonin agreed the selling price would be equal to four times Alpha's net income for the year ended December 31, 2014. The final selling price would be determined once the financial statements were issued, at which time Mr. Sonin would pay the agreed selling price to Ms. Chhor and take over management and ownership of Alpha. The contract of sale stipulated that Mr. Sonin could challenge any of the accounting that Alpha used in the financial statements and if the parties could not agree on acceptable accounting for any issue, the disputed issues would be turned over to an arbitrator for resolution.

Alpha manufactures precision tools for high-tech companies. The tools must meet exact specifications otherwise they are not useful to the customer. Alpha usually conducts extensive testing of its tools and submits the results to the customer for approval. If the test results are approved by the customer, Alpha ships the tools.

In late January 2015, Ms. Chhor delivered Alpha's financial statements to Mr. Sonin. Overall, he was satisfied with the statements but several items caught his eye and he wants to follow up on them. Mr. Sonin has asked you to prepare a report discussing the items he is concerned about, described below:

1. In late 2014, Alpha received a large order from a new customer. Alpha had never made tools of this type before but believed it had the ability to do so, so it accepted the order. Because the tools are unusual, Alpha does not have the equipment necessary to properly test them, and the customer will test them instead. The customer is not required to accept or pay for the tools until it decides that they meet specifi-

cations. If the tools do not meet specifications they can be returned to either be remade or reworked. Alpha recognized revenue on this order when the tools were shipped to the customer, the usual point it recognizes revenue, on December 20, 2014.

2. In early 2014, Alpha received an order for tools from a customer. The tools are specialized and have very little application beyond the customer and other companies in the same industry. When the tools were in the testing stage, the customer announced that it was filing for bankruptcy and unable to take delivery of the order. At year-end, those tools were recorded at cost and included in inventory.

3. In 2014, Alpha purchased new equipment for its testing lab. The equipment was installed and running on May 15, 2014 but a safety ruling from a building inspector in early June required that the equipment be moved to another part of the building. The cost of the relocation was included in the cost of the equipment and the amount is being amortized over five years, the estimated useful life of the equipment.

4. The notes to the financial statements disclosed that Alpha purchased a significant amount of consulting services from a company that is owned by Ms. Chhor.

Required:

Prepare a report to Mr. Sonin analyzing the issues that he has brought to your attention. Your report should clearly explain your role and how you are approaching your task. You should provide a full explanation of each issue, identifying alternative treatments where appropriate. You should recommend an appropriate treatment for each issue, keeping in mind your role. Your recommendations should be well supported.

CASE 2: ANGELA KELLETT, BARRISTER AND SOLICITOR

Angela Kellett is a recent law school graduate. She opened her practice six months ago and her client base has been growing steadily over that time. Ms. Kellett was approached by a new client, Ferdinand Jones, who wanted advice about selling his business. Mr. Jones and the buyer are in the final stages of negotiations. So far they have agreed on all terms except the final selling price. The buyer has proposed an earnout arrangement whereby Mr. Jones would receive a fixed payment plus a share of net income for one or two years after the sale is complete. The buyer has stipulated that for purposes of the earnout arrangement, the financial statements would be prepared in accordance with GAAP consistently applied and that the financial statement would have to receive an unqualified audit opinion from an independent auditor.

Ms. Kellett took some business courses while in law school, including a course in financial accounting, and she's very worried about the earnout arrangement. She remembers from her accounting courses that managers have a lot of leeway when it comes to preparing the financial statements, and she thinks that her client may be significantly disadvantaged by the earnout arrangement. Ms. Kellett has come to see you for information and advice about the earnout. She would like you to review the information she has about her client's business and provide advice about terms that should be included in the sale agreement to minimize the risks to her client of being affected by accounting choices made by the new owner of the company.

Mr. Jones' company, Inuvik Technologies Inc. (Inuvik), manufactures sophisticated components for heavy equipment. The company is small but well-known in the industry for producing high-quality, reliable components. Mr. Jones believes Inuvik's success lies the extensive testing the company does before components are shipped to customers, the warranty and after sales support provided, and the ongoing investment in research and development.

Ms. Kellett provided you with the following additional information about Inuvik and its operations:

- One of the reasons the buyer is buying Inuvik is because it is complementary to other businesses he owns. The buyer expects that Inuvik will be a major supplier to some of these businesses.

- Inuvik values its inventory at the lower of FIFO cost and net realizable value. It uses specific identification for components that are specially designed for customers. The company has a large inventory of parts used to construct its products and for repairs and maintenance of products sold. Some of the inventory is quite old but kept to ensure that Inuvik can support older products still in use.

- A new generation of production equipment will be introduced within the next six to 12 months and, to remain competitive, Mr. Jones thinks that Inuvik will have to make a significant investment in new equipment. The existing equipment would still be usable (in fact Mr. Jones says it has another three years of life left), but it will not produce output of the same quality as the new equipment. The old equipment would only be useable on a limited basis, and its value in the used-equipment market would be very low.

- Inuvik generally recognizes its revenue on delivery. However, customers have the right to return components that do not meet specifications. Returns have never been a large problem, though from time to time a major order will require modification. The company offers customers 45 days to pay. Most customers pay on time, and bad debts have been predictable in each of the past five years at about 1 to 1.5 percent of revenues.

- Inuvik reports significant development costs, which are being amortized over five years, on its balance sheet. The costs relate to new technologies that Inuvik has developed for integration into its products.

- Inuvik provides a five-year warranty on all its products. The warranty covers all repairs required as a result of manufacturer's defects. Warranty costs have averaged about 4 percent of sales over the last five years and have been relatively stable. Last year, the company utilized a new technology in some of its components, and Mr. Jones is unsure what warranty costs will be for that line.

- Ten years ago, Inuvik purchased a competitor and merged its operations with its own. As a result of the purchase, $250,000 of goodwill is reported on Inuvik's balance sheet as of the most recent year-end. The company no longer amortizes its goodwill in accordance with GAAP. Inuvik evaluates the goodwill annually to ensure that it is not overvalued.

- Inuvik will be managed by the son of the new owner. To date, the amount of compensation taken by Mr. Jones in any year was determined by the amount of cash available in the company and his personal needs. The form of the compensation also varied, sometimes paid in salary and bonus and other times as a dividend. The way compensation was paid usually depended on tax cost and benefits.

Required:

Prepare the report requested by Angela Kellett.

CASE 3: BATTLEFORD BATTLESHIPS

The Battleford Battleships is a minor league hockey team that played in a town in the midwestern United States since 1988. For many years the team was very successful, usually playing to capacity crowds and winning the league championship several times. In recent years the team has fallen on hard times. As a result, the owners of the Battleships, the Battleford family, sold the team to a wealthy investor and hockey enthusiast from a Canadian city on the prairies. The deal was finalized on May 15, 2013 and it was immediately announced that the team would be moving to a new city.

The team will play in a new arena in the city's downtown. The arena, which is owned by the municipal government, has a capacity of 11,500 people and has 30 luxury boxes. The terms of the sale had the investor paying $2 million plus two times the profits earned by the Battleships in its fiscal year ended July 31, 2014, as reported in the annual audited financial statements. The hockey season runs from October through early May each year.

The Battleford family recently received the financial statements for the year ended July 31, 2014 and they have a number of concerns regarding them, so they have approached you for advice. They would like you to prepare a report that addresses the following concerns they have identified:

- In June 2014, in an effort to put a winning team on the ice for the 2014–2015 season, the Battleships signed two star players to four-year contracts. The contracts paid the players signing bonuses of $225,000 each (signing bonuses are amounts paid only when a contract is signed by a player) plus $250,000 per season. The Battleships expensed the signing bonuses at the time the contracts were signed and the players received their money.

- In September 2013, a number of former employees launched a $500,000 lawsuit against the Battleships for damages suffered because of their loss of employment when the team moved. The Battleships' lawyers have indicated that, while it is likely the team will have to pay something to the employees, the amount will be nowhere near the amount stated in the lawsuit. However, to be conservative, the new owners of the team have accrued an expense for the full amount of the lawsuit.

- Fans can purchase full and partial season ticket packages for all games. These packages allow fans to obtain tickets at discounted prices and ensure that they can get the seats they want. Packages are purchased in the summer months, before the season begins, and cash must be paid at the time of purchase. Revenue from ticket sales is recognized when a game is actually played.

- From May through July 2014 the Battleships launched an aggressive marketing campaign to sell tickets for the 2014–2015 season. The team used local television, radio, Internet, and newspapers to get its message out. The campaign was successful with a significant increase in tickets sold. All advertising amounts were expensed as incurred.

Required:

Prepare the report requested by the former owners of the Battleships. Be sure to provide a complete explanation and analysis along with appropriate recommendations for each accounting issue you identify.

CASE 4: BN DESIGN AND MAINTENANCE LIMITED

Recently, Anton Ellino agreed to purchase a 25 percent interest in BN Design and Maintenance Limited (BNL) from its founder and sole shareholder, Bess Nnerdium. BNL's financial statements have been prepared mainly for tax purposes in previous years. Ms Nnerdium is selling part of her stake in BNL because she requires cash for personal and other business uses. She believes that Mr. Ellino will be a good investor because his considerable experience in BNL's business will be helpful for the planned growth and expansion of the company.

Founded in 1992, BNL provides landscape design and maintenance as well as lawn care and snow removal services to commercial and government clients on a contract basis. Landscape maintenance, lawn care, and snow removal contracts are usually for a year and payments are made on a predetermined schedule. Periodically, there are disputes with customers and payment in full is not received, or some customers default on the payments even though services have been provided.

For landscape design projects BNL contracts with clients to landscape areas around buildings and in parks. A fixed fee is negotiated with the client for the work. BNL also charges for plants and other materials used in implementing the design and for the labour involved. BNL has a group of professional landscape architects who do the design work. Most landscape design projects are completed within one year, but at the present time the company has three large projects that are expected to take three years to complete. Initial design work on all of the projects began in autumn 2013. BNL is paid quarterly by the clients, based on the negotiated fee.

In July 2014, BNL signed a five-year contract with a municipality to provide snow removal from city parking lots. Because snowfall is unpredictable, the contract stipulates that BNL will receive a minimum payment each year of $30,000 regardless of the amount of snow (even if there is no snow). Otherwise, the amount BNL receives is based on the amount of snow that falls, as measured by Environment Canada.

Many of the plants and trees that BNL uses in its landscape design are grown on a farm it owns. Plants are planted from seed or as tree saplings and grown until ready for use in a landscaping project. It often takes many years before a plant is ready for use. The farm is tended by a small group of horticulturists who also work on developing new species of plants. In the last 12 months, $100,000 was spent on this development work.

BNL owns a small building in Richmond Hill that houses BNL's office as well as offices of other businesses operated by Bess Nnerdium and her family. Office space is also rented out to other businesses. The building was purchased in 1994 for $350,000 and was recently appraised at $975,000. The building is financed through a mortgage provided by a relative of Bess Nnerdium, with an interest rate that is significantly below the market rate.

Anton Ellino and Bess Nnerdium have agreed in principle to sell the shares of BNL based on the net income of the company, but they are unable to decide on appropriate accounting policies for determining the selling price. They have come to you for help in selecting accounting policies. They would also like your advice on other financial statement issues they should consider regarding the selling price of BNL. They ask that you explain your reasoning fully so that they can understand it and be able to ask questions.

Required:

Prepare the report.

CASE 5: CHAMPION HARDWARE LIMITED

Champion Hardware Ltd. (Champion) is a retailer of hardware and home renovations in a medium-sized Canadian city. The store has been in business for many years and has grown along with the community. Recently, Champion's owner decided to sell the store because he felt he was too old for the rigours of operating it. Desji Osisanya has expressed interest in buying Champion and they have been negotiating for several months. Mr. Osisanya has been working for Champion as a marketing manager and he is confident it will continue to be successful. Buying Champion will also fulfill Mr. Osisanya's lifelong ambition of owning his own business. The current owner and Mr. Osisanya have agreed in principle to base the selling price on Champion's net income before unusual items for the two most recent fiscal years.

Mr. Osisanya has just received the Champion's 2014 financial statements. For the most part he's satisfied with the statements, but he has some concerns and he has approached you for advice regarding these. He would like a report evaluating how these items should be accounted for in the year-end income statements for purposes of determining the price he should pay for Champion.

1. As a primary supplier of construction materials in the area, Champion offers credit terms to builders and contractors, allowing them up to 90 days to pay. About four months ago a large home builder indicated it was in serious financial trouble. The builder is one of Champion's largest customers and a major employer in the area. Champion agreed to allow this builder more time to pay. Informally, the builder has agreed to pay what it can each time it sells a home and Champion has agreed to accept these payments. At the end of fiscal 2014, amounts owed by this builder represented 11 percent of accounts receivable. Champion recognizes revenue when the customer takes delivery of goods purchased. Sales of homes has slowed down in recent months.

2. During fiscal 2014, Champion sold some vacant land adjacent to its store. A family-owned grocery chain purchased the land to build a large new store. Champion believes that the new store will attract new business. Champion originally paid $500,000 for the land and the grocery chain will pay $2,000,000 for it—$550,000 in cash and the remainder in five years. The amount owing is secured by the land and personal guarantees of the grocery chain's owners.

3. Four years ago, Champion obtained an exclusive dealership for a line of high-quality kitchen cabinets. The dealership rights were for an initial five-year period, with five-year renewals

possible, at the option of the manufacturer. Champion was assured at the time of signing the initial agreement that a renewal was virtually certain. Champion spent $160,000 to setup displays promoting the line. These costs were capitalized and are being depreciated over 10 years. Just before the end of fiscal 2014, Champion learned that the exclusive dealership won't be renewed and Champion won't be selling the products beyond the end of the first five-year term, which expires in three months.

4. Early in fiscal 2014, a customer was injured in the store and is suing Champion for $250,000. Champion has offered $30,000 but that has been rejected. An initial court date of May 2015 has been set. The lawsuit has been disclosed in a note to the financial statements.

5. As the community grows, it is increasingly likely that large national chains of hardware and home renovation stores will open in the area. To strengthen customer loyalty, Champion implemented a rewards program early in the fiscal 2014. The program awards points for every dollar spent in the store and these can be redeemed for merchandise. During the year, merchandise costing $25,000 was obtained by customers redeeming their points. Goods acquired through the rewards program are expensed when the customer takes delivery.

Required:

Prepare the report requested by Mr. Osisanya.

CASE 6: DAPHNE'S CATERING LTD.

Daphne's Catering Ltd. (DCL) provides catering services to people living in Durham region and the eastern part of Metro Toronto. The company is owned and operated by Daphne Flatt, who founded the business in 1998. DCL can provide meals for groups as small as two and as large as 500. DCL operates out of its state of the art commercial kitchen located in Ajax. The meals are prepared in the kitchen and delivered to the site of the event. DCL's kitchen is adjacent to a banquet hall it also owns. DCL also generates revenue by renting out the banquet hall for functions and catering them.

The company has been very successful over the years and Daphne has made a lot of money. Recently, Daphne decided that she would like to slow down the pace of her life and has decided to sell her shares (she owns 100 percent of the company). Joe Insalacco expressed interest in buying DCL and has been in negotiations with Daphne for several months. The parties have agreed that Joe will purchase Daphne's shares for $550,000 plus five times average net income for the last two fiscal years.

Two days ago, Daphne couriered DCL's September 30, 2015 year-end financial statements to Joe. Joe is not very knowledgeable about accounting matters so he has engaged you to examine the statements and raise any issues of concern as they pertain to his agreement to buy DCL. You review the financial statements, have a conversation with Joe and a brief chat with Daphne, and you discover the following:

a. DCL's net income for the years ended September 30, 2015 and 2014 respectively, was $275,000 and $160,000.

b. In October 2014, DCL printed several thousand brochures for distribution to businesses and homes in areas of Durham and Toronto. The brochures were designed to promote DCL's services over the 2014 Christmas and New Year's period, emphasizing the 2014 holiday meals. Because of bad weather and problems with the distributor, only about 40 percent of the brochures were distributed. The brochures remain safely stored at the DCL kitchen. A prepaid expense for $19,000 is reported on the September 30 balance sheet for the undistributed brochures.

c. A large corporate function scheduled for September 18, 2015 had to be cancelled by the customer on short notice. The customer asked whether the event could be rescheduled for October 2, 2015. DCL's banquet hall was available on October 2 and DCL was happy to reschedule. On August 31, the customer paid $45,000 (75 percent of the agreed price) as the original contract stipulated. DCL recognized the amount received in August as revenue in its

2015 fiscal year. The customer paid the remaining $15,000 owing on October 4, 2015. DCL incurred $44,000 in costs for meals, entertainment, and labour and these were expensed at the time of the event.

d. Each year during the last week of September, DCL has a major maintenance program on its kitchen and banquet hall. Late September is usually a quiet time and Daphne has found it more efficient to do all the maintenance work at once. The banquet hall is closed for several days and the kitchen can have only limited operations. This year the maintenance program was delayed into October because of the corporate function held on October 2. The cost of the maintenance program in 2015 was $18,000. In fiscal 2014, the maintenance program was carried out and completed in late September.

e. DCL is in the process of developing a line of packaged foods for sale in grocery stores so customers can bring to their homes the taste and convenience of a high-quality catered meal. Over the last 18 months, DCL has invested $55,000 in the development of the product. Daphne is confident that the product will be successfully and profitably brought to grocery stores but she realizes there are significant development, production, and marketing obstacles that will have to be overcome before that occurs. The $55,000 is reported on the balance sheet as a product development cost on September 30, 2015.

Joe wants a report discussing issues pertaining to the purchase of DCL. He would like full explanations of your recommendations and the reasoning behind them so that he can have a full understanding when he meets with Daphne. He would also like you to quantify the impact of the any adjustments you make on the final selling price of DCL.

Required:

Prepare the report requested by Joe Insalacco.

CASE 7: EXTREME SPORTING GOODS INC.[1]

Paul Pistone was delighted when he was offered a position as president of Extreme Sporting Goods Inc. (Extreme), a small manufacturer of sporting goods. The company had a long history and once dominated its market. Unfortunately, increased competition had resulted in declining profitability. Paul believed that with the marketing skills he gained as product manager with a major consumer products company he could easily turn the company around. He was so confident of his ability that he agreed to a rather unusual contract with the company at the request of Gil Gerrard, the president of Acme Industries Corporation (Acme), the company that owns Extreme. The contract specified that Paul would resign after one year if he did not increase the company's return on assets to at least 10 percent.

After one year, Paul has made many changes at Extreme with many positive results. Revenues have increased significantly without adding staff, and inventory turnover has increased. However, Paul has just had a meeting with Gil Gerrard, who presented him with the Extreme financial statements for the year ending December 31, 2013. Those statements, which are attached, show that Extreme didn't achieve the return on asset target of 10 percent. Gil has given Paul an ultimatum. Paul must resign or accept a 40 percent salary cut.

Paul is puzzled by this outcome. He knows that he and Gil have not gotten along very well recently. In fact, a meeting a few months ago ended in a shouting match. Paul has discussed his situation with his lawyer and believes that legal action against Acme may be appropriate. He has asked you to prepare a briefing memo for the lawyer on the accounting treatment of the following transactions. Paul would also like your memo to include an analysis of the performance of Extreme over the past year.

Required:

Provide the memo to Paul's lawyer.

Extreme Sporting Goods, Inc.
Income Statements
For the years ending December 31,

	2013	2012	2011
Revenues	$17,437,400	$13,712,500	$14,535,250
Cost of sales	11,334,310	9,461,625	9,883,970
Gross profit	6,103,090	4,250,875	4,651,280
Selling, general, and administrative expenses	5,754,342	4,662,250	4,651,280
Operating profit	348,748	(411,375)	0
Other income (expense):			
Interest expense	(110,000)	0	0
Other income, net	156,000	197,000	71,000
	46,000	197,000	71,000
Income before income taxes	394,748	(214,375)	71,000
Income taxes	157,899	(85,750)	28,400
Net income	$ 236,849	($ 128,625)	$ 42,600

Extreme Sporting Goods Inc.
Balance Sheets
As of December 31,

	2013	2012	2011
ASSETS			
Current Assets			
Cash and cash equivalents	$ 224,324	$ 495,000	$ 210,000
Accounts receivable	4,625,900	3,892,000	3,954,100
Inventories	6,041,000	5,642,000	5,152,000
Loan due from parent	2,000,000	0	0
Other current assets	275,000	591,000	475,000
Total current assets	13,166,224	10,620,000	9,791,100
Property, Plant, and Equipment			
Land	900,000	650,000	650,000
Buildings and improvements	5,450,000	3,950,000	3,950,000
Machinery and equipment	6,245,000	5,885,000	5,525,000
	12,595,000	10,485,000	10,125,000
Less accumulated depreciation	7,990,000	7,240,000	6,125,000
Total property, plant, and equipment, net	4,605,000	3,245,000	4,000,000
Other assets	1,250,000	906,375	785,000
Total assets	$19,021,224	$14,771,375	$14,576,100

LIABILITIES AND SHAREHOLDERS' EQUITY

	2013	2012	2011
Current liabilities			
Bank loan	$ 2,000,000	$ 0	$ 0
Accounts payable	2,875,000	2,050,000	1,802,100
Accrued liabilities	2,163,000	975,000	899,000
Total current liabilities	7,038,000	3,025,000	2,701,100
Shareholders' equity			
Common stock	3,750,000	3,750,000	3,750,000
Retained earnings	8,233,224	7,996,375	8,125,000
Total shareholders' equity	11,983,224	11,746,375	11,875,000
Total liabilities and shareholders' equity	$19,021,224	$14,771,375	$14,576,100

Notes to the Financial Statement

1. The warehouse that Extreme has used for 20 years, originally purchased for $1,000,000, was reported on the December 31, 2012 balance sheet at $400,000 net of accumulated depreciation. In early January, shortly after Paul took over as president, Acme insisted that Extreme sell the warehouse to another Acme subsidiary for $400,000 and purchase a virtually identical warehouse one block away for $2,500,000. The property was purchased on January 11, 2013. All related depreciation is recorded (at CCA rates) in selling and administrative expenses. (The CCA rate for buildings is 4 percent per year, declining balance.)

2. Paul replaced several senior managers with some colleagues from his former employer. Generous settlements, including two years of salary and beginning July 1, 2013 were arranged with the replaced managers. On the December 31, 2013 balance sheet, there is a liability for the remaining 18 months, and the full $900,000 expense for the two years was included in selling and administrative expense.

3. Acme needed cash for expansion and "arranged" an interest-free loan from Extreme for $2,000,000. Since Extreme needed cash at certain times of the year, an operating loan was required that would not have been otherwise necessary. The interest incurred was $110,000 and Paul estimates the Extreme could have earned an additional $160,000 of interest on the surplus funds if Acme had not "borrowed" them.

4. One of Paul's first decisions was to drop several poorly performing product lines. The remaining inventory of those products that was reported on the December 31, 2012 balance sheet at $1,050,000 was sold on January 20, 2013 for $255,000. The $255,000 is in 2013 revenue and the $1,050,000 is in cost of goods sold.

5. Paul spent $300,000 on a new information system. $14,000 of the cost was for computer hardware and the remainder was for software. It is Acme's policy to use CCA rules for all assets. As a result, 50 percent of the cost of software is expensed in the year it's purchased (the remainder expensed in the subsequent year) and all computer hardware on the financial statement is depreciated at the maximum CCA rate of 30 percent declining balance.

6. Paul was so excited by the successes of the first year that he took a number of key employees to Aruba for a training session. Any employee who met his or her goals for 2013 was included. The trip occurred on January 20, 2014, but the resort required payment on November 2013. The full amount of $100,000 was included in selling and administrative expense for 2013.

CASE 8: FAMILY BOOKS LTD.

Family Books Ltd. (FBL) is a three-store chain of booksellers operating in three small communities in Ontario. These communities don't have stores operated by the well-known large booksellers. FBL is owned and operated by Mr. Dickens, whose father started the stores 45 years ago. FBL sells a wide range of books, CDs, and related items to retail customers. Books not carried by FBL can be special-ordered.

Recently, Mr. Dickens decided to sell FBL and a friend of yours who has known Mr. Dickens for a few months is considering buying it. She examined FBL's financial statements and identified some issues that she has concerns about, and she has asked for your opinion on them. She wants to know the impact these issues will have on her ability to assess FBL's performance. She has also given you FBL's most recent balance sheet and would like your thoughts on it.

- The stores maintain a fairly large inventory, considering the small size of the communities. Once in stock, FBL will keep a book on hand indefinitely. Book publishers allow bookstores to return up to 20 percent of books purchased for any reason, but FBL often doesn't take advantage of this because it's records are disorganized.

- FBL tries to encourage reading in its communities. Late in 2013 it started the Family Book Club. By joining the club, members receive a series of books at a significant discount. For example, the best seller series costs members $250 per year and they receive 10 best-sellers over the year. Members must pay the full amount when they join the club. FBL recognizes the revenue when a person pays their membership.

- Customers may return purchases if the items are unused. Customers receive a credit note that must be used in the store. FBL only accounts for returns when they occur.

- Two of the stores are housed in buildings owned by FBL, one of which was acquired 40 years ago. One of the stores has a large apartment that is occupied by the family of one of Mr. Dickens' children, and they don't pay rent.

- The third store occupies a rented space in the downtown area. Rent is $3,200 per month plus 1 percent of gross annual sales. The sales-based portion of the rent is expensed when paid, within 60 days of year-end.

Required:

Prepare a report to your friend providing the requested analysis.

Family Bookstores Ltd.
Balance Sheet
As at December 31, 2014

Cash	$ 10,000		Bank loan	$ 25,000
Accounts receivable	55,000		Accounts payable and other	
Inventory	425,000		current liabilities	265,000
Prepaids	5,000			
			Mortgage payable	95,000
Property, plant, and equipment				
(net of accumulated deprecation)	135,000		Common stock	40,000
			Retained earnings	240,000
Start-up costs				
(net of amortization)	35,000			
			Total liabilities and	
Total assets	$ 665,000		shareholders' equity	$665,000

CASE 9: GOOD QUALITY AUTO PARTS LIMITED[2]

Good Quality Auto Parts Limited (GQAP) is a medium-sized, privately owned producer of auto parts that are sold to car manufacturers, repair shops and retail outlets. In March 2014, the union negotiated a new three-year contract with the company for the 200 shop-floor employees. At the time, GQAP was in financial difficulty and management felt unable to meet the union contract demands. Management also believed any strike would force the company into bankruptcy.

The company proposed that, in exchange for wage concessions, it would implement a profit-sharing plan whereby the shop-floor employees would receive 10 percent of the company's annual after-tax profit as a bonus in each year of the contract. Although the union generally finds this type of contract undesirable, it believed that insisting on the prevailing industry settlement would jeopardize GQAP's survival. As a result, the contract terms were accepted.

The contract specifies that (a) no major changes in accounting policies may be made without approval by GQAP's auditor, (b) the union may engage an accountant to examine the accounting records of the company and meet with GQAP's management and auditor to discuss any issues, and (c) any controversial accounting issues are to be negotiated by the union and management to arrive at a mutual agreement. If the parties cannot agree, the positions of the parties are to be presented to an independent arbitrator for resolution.

On April 10, 2015, GQAP's management presented to the union its annual financial statements and the unqualified audit report for the year ended February 28, 2015, the first year that the profit sharing plan was in effect. The union engaged you to examine these financial statements and determine whether there are any controversial accounting issues. As a result of your examination, you identified a number of issues that are of concern to you. You met with the GQAP's controller and obtained the following information:

1. GQAP wrote off $250,000 of inventory manufactured between 2006 and 2014. There have been no sales from this inventory in over two years. The controller explained that up until this year she had some hope that the inventory could be sold as replacement parts. However, she now believes that the parts can't be sold.

2. GQAP's contracts with the large auto manufacturers allow them to return items for any reason. The company has increased the allowance for returned items by 10 percent in the year just ended. The controller contends that, because of stiff competition faced by these auto manufacturers, there will likely be a significant increase in the parts returned.

3. GQAP has a policy of writing off any small tool acquisitions, even though the tools will be used over several periods. For the year just ended, small tools costing $170,000 were acquired.

4. In April 2014, GQAP purchased $500,000 of new manufacturing equipment. To reduce the financial strain of the acquisition, the company negotiated a six-year payment schedule. GQAP decided to use accelerated depreciation at a rate of 40 percent for the new equipment. The controller argued that because of rapid technological changes in the industry, equipment is more likely to become technologically, rather than operationally, obsolete. The straight-line depreciation method applied to the existing equipment has not been changed. Similar existing equipment is depreciated over 10 years.

5. In 2007, GQAP purchased a small auto parts manufacturer and merged it into its own operation. At the time of acquisition, $435,000 of goodwill was recorded. The company has written off the goodwill in the year just ended. The controller explained that GQAP's poor performance, in particular, has made the goodwill worthless.

6. In February 2015, the president and the chairman of the board, who between them own 75 percent of the voting shares of the company, received bonuses of $250,000 each. GQAP did not pay any dividends during the current year. In the prior year, dividends amounting to $650,000 were paid. The controller said that the board of directors justified the bonuses as a reward for keeping the company afloat despite extremely difficult economic times.

The union has asked you to prepare a report on the position it should take on the issues identified when discussing them with management. The union also wants to know what additional information you require in order to support this position.

Required:

Prepare the report.

CASE 10: JEREMY LANGER

Jeremy Langer is a young entrepreneur who lives in a large Canadian city. In early 2014, he saw a good opportunity to make some money selling souvenirs designed especially for the upcoming International World Festival, a six-week event to be held in June and July 2014. The International World Festival is held every three years in a different city. The Festival has never been held in Canada and it was last held in North America in 1982. The city was expecting a large influx of tourists for the event. You obtain the following information on Jeremy's venture:

- In January, Jeremy opened a bank account in the name of his business venture and deposited $15,000 of his own money. Jeremy also developed a number of designs for the souvenirs he plans to sell. The designs cost $1,200 and he paid cash from the venture's bank account.

- In early February, Jeremy presented his designs to the Festival organizing committee. Use of the Festival name or logos on souvenirs required approval by the committee if they were to be legally sold. Jeremy's designs were approved and he paid a licensing fee of $2,000 to legally sell the souvenirs.

- In late February, Jeremy borrowed $30,000 from the bank and agreed to pay the bank its money back plus $1,000 in interest on August 1, 2014.

- In May, Jeremy signed a contract with a company to produce the souvenirs. Because of the nature of the souvenirs, it's necessary to produce them all before the Festival begins. Jeremy had 5,000 souvenirs produced at a cost of $10 each. It won't be possible to produce additional souvenirs. Jeremy paid the producer $40,000 in cash and agreed to pay an additional $5,000 on June 30 and the remainder at the end of the festival.

- Jeremy purchased an old van to transport the souvenirs for $5,000 in cash.

- Jeremy hired a number of vendors who operate street carts to sell merchandise. He agreed to pay the vendors $5 for each souvenir sold. The selling price of Jeremy's souvenirs is $19 each. The vendors will pay Jeremy $14 for each souvenir they sell.

- On June 30, Jeremy makes the $5,000 payment to the producer of the souvenirs.

- On July 3, Jeremy has 3,500 unsold souvenirs.

- Jeremy has incurred other costs of $1,000 to date, all in cash.

It's July 3, 2014. The festival has been under way for three and half weeks and Jeremy hasn't had a chance to sit down and take stock of how his venture is doing. He asks you to help him.

Required:

a. Prepare an income statement and balance sheet for Jeremy's venture as of July 3, 2014. Explain the accounting choices you made and why you made them. Be sure to discuss the users and uses of the income statement in your response.

b. Assume the role of Jeremy's banker. Jeremy has provided you with the statements that were prepared in (a). Are these statements useful to you? Explain. What concerns do you have about the venture at this point? Explain. What suggestions would you give to Jeremy?

c. Use the statements you prepared in (a) to advise Jeremy about how his venture has performed to date. What suggestions would you give to Jeremy for operating the venture for the remainder of the Festival? Jeremy has asked whether he can withdraw money from the venture for some personal needs. What would you advise Jeremy?

CASE 11: ONTARIO PRINTING LIMITED

In September 2014, Alex Jesse and Evan Shayne decide to end their 10-year business relationship as owners of Ontario Printing Limited (OPL). OPL is a commercial printing business that Alex and Evan organized in 2004. They each own 50 percent of the common shares of OPL, but Alex operates and manages it. Evan participates in major decisions but, for the most part, is not involved in day-to-day operations. Alex and Evan agree that Alex will purchase the shares of OPL from Evan at fair market value. They agree that fair market value will be equal to five times average net income for the past two years, including the fiscal year ending October 31, 2014. Alex and Evan also agree that the accounting policies should be in accordance with Generally Accepted Accounting Principles for Private Enterprises. Alex and Evan recognize that adjustments to the final selling price might be necessary to take specific circumstances into consideration. Since their decision to part ways, Evan has not been involved in any way in the activities and operation of OPL.

You obtain the following information about OPL:

1. OPL has used its financial statements primarily for tax purposes. The company writes off any expenditure that can be justified for tax purposes, regardless of whether they have any future benefit.

2. The company owns a small building in the north end of the city. Its offices occupy the ground floor and the rest of the building is leased to tenants. Since the building was acquired, its market value has increased from $800,000 to $1,750,000, based on increases in neighbouring property values.

3. Alex and Evan have charged many personal expenses to the business over the years.

4. Alex took a salary of $125,000 during the year. A manager doing Alex's work at a competitor would be paid between $50,000 and $75,000, depending on the size of the company and responsibilities. Evan agreed to this salary several years ago.

5. In mid-October 2014, Alex launched a major advertising campaign. Alex hopes the advertising will allow OPL to increase utilization of its equipment and expand capacity in the near future. During the last two weeks of October, OPL spent several thousand dollars for media and direct contact with potential clients.

6. In early October 2014, OPL shut down for two days for annual maintenance of equipment. The work is done each year to ensure equipment operates at maximum efficiency and to avoid costly breakdowns. The annual maintenance was last done in November 2013.

7. In late October 2014, Alex sold some equipment at a loss of $37,000.

8. During the summer of 2014, Evan negotiated a contract with a customer on behalf of OPL to produce instruction manuals for its products. The contract begins in January 2015. In exchange for lower printing rates, the customer has guaranteed a minimum of $200,000 of work over two years. The customer will pay as work is done. Any shortfall from the $200,000 will be paid at the end of the contract term.

Required:

Alex and Evan have engaged you to prepare a report they can use to determine the selling price of Evan's shares. The report should state the accounting policies that should be used for preparing the financial statements to be used specifically to set the selling price of OPL, as well as any adjustments that should be made to the final price as a result of other information and concerns you have. You should explain your reasoning fully so that lawyers for the respective parties will have a basis for discussion.

CASE 12: RICHIBUCTO RATTLESNAKES AND SPORTS COMPLEX, LTD.

Max Lee is a successful dentist in southern Ontario. He began his practice fifteen years ago. Recently, Max has been looking for an investment to indulge his lifelong interest in sports. He and a group of like-minded people are looking for a minor league sports franchise to purchase. All members of the group are mainly interested in the fun and excitement of owning a sports team, but they don't want to spend much of their own money, beyond the initial amount they pay for the franchise. None of them has experience in business, accounting, or operating a sports franchise. All members of the group will continue in their present occupations after a team is purchased.

The group has begun preliminary discussions with the owner of a hockey franchise in Atlantic Canada, the Richibucto Rattlesnakes (Rattlesnakes). The owner of the franchise, Jane Bowen, says the franchise has been quite successful but she wants to sell the Rattlesnakes because of her failing health. Bowen has owned and operated the team since its formation in 1985, when she purchased the franchise rights for the city from the league. In 1994, Jane built a 6,000-seat arena in the city to house the team. The arena is also used for other events promoted by Jane or by third parties who rent the facility. Revenue is also generated from concessions (food, souvenirs, and parking).

The group has obtained the Rattlesnakes' most recent year's financial statements. Jane has indicated that the statements are prepared strictly for tax purposes as there are no other users. The statements are, by and large, prepared according to GAAP for Private Enterprises, but not exclusively.

Max Lee has come to you for advice on interpreting the financial statements. He has indicated that he does not understand them very well and wants to get some insights into what they do and do not tell. He would also like your advice on what additional accounting and financial information he should request from Jane Bowen before deciding on how much he and his group are prepared to pay for the team and its facility.

Required:

Prepare a report to Max Lee providing the advice he requested. Be specific and provide full explanations.

Richibucto Rattlesnakes and Sports Complex, Ltd.
Balance Sheet
As at July 30, 2014

Cash	$ 125,000	Bank loan	$ 225,000
Accounts receivable	5,000	Accounts payable	100,000
Prepaids and other assets	15,000		
Capital assets	8,450,000		
Less: Accumulated amortization	(6,337,500)		
	2,112,500	Common stock	1,100,000
Hockey team franchise	400,000	Retained earnings	1,232,500
		Total liabilities and	
Total assets	$2,657,500	shareholders' equity	$2,657,500

Richibucto Rattlesnakes and Sports Complex, Ltd.
Income Statement
For the year ended July 30, 2014

Revenue		
Hockey	$3,200,000	
Concessions and parking	1,200,000	
Other events	1,500,000	
Other revenue	210,000	$6,110,000
Expenses		
Hockey operations	1,760,000	
Concessions and parking	540,000	
Other events	1,125,000	
Building costs	2,550,000	5,975,000
Expansion fee revenue		250,000
Income tax expense		77,000
Net income		$ 308,000

Richibucto Rattlesnakes and Sports Complex, Ltd.
Notes to the Financial Statements

1. Fixed assets include the arena and land, along with the equipment necessary to operate the arena and hockey team.

2. The hockey team franchise account is the original cost of the franchise. The amount is not amortized.

3. Hockey revenue includes $355,000 for the radio broadcast rights to the team's home games. The radio network is also owned, separately, by Bowen and her family.

4. Revenue is recognized for hockey games and other events when the event occurs.

5. During fiscal 2014, the league expanded by two teams. The Rattlesnakes' share of the expansion fee is $250,000.

6. The team has a working arrangement with a major league professional hockey team. The major league team supplies players and pays their salaries, but is entitled to use those players at its discretion. Approximately 60 percent of the players used by the Rattlesnakes are supplied by the major league team. The contract with the major league team expires in two years.

7. The bank loan is personally guaranteed by Jane Bowen and is secured against company assets as well as Jane's personal assets.

CASE 13: SHMEVAN STORES LTD[3]

Shmevan Stores Ltd. (Shmevan) is a national chain of franchised business supplies stores. Currently, there are 75 stores in the chain, each store owned and operated by people who live in the communities where the stores operate. The stores sell a complete line of business supplies, office furniture, computer hardware and software, and other business-related products. Shmevan supplies all merchandise to the stores. Shmevan is able to obtain lower prices because of its significant buyer power. Shmevan receives a royalty on all sales made by the franchise stores.

In May 2013, in response to the tough and increased competition in the business supplies market, Shmevan's management introduced a contest to motivate franchise store owners and encourage innovation of new and profitable business practices. The winner of the contest is to receive a cash prize of $150,000. The prize is to be awarded to the store reporting the highest percentage increase in net income before taxes for the year ended October 31, 2014.

On a preliminary review of the financial statements by Shmevan's management, the franchise store in Saskatoon was the winner. The Saskatoon store reported a percentage increase in income before taxes of 278 percent using the formula used for the contest. However, the panel made up of Shmevan's management along with five people representing the owners of the franchise stores has concerns about the results reported by the Saskatoon store. Some believe that Saskatoon has misrepresented its financial position. As a result of the concerns, a number of stores have protested awarding the prize to the Saskatoon store. The second-place finisher in the contest, the store in Fredericton, reported a percentage increase in income before taxes of 201 percent.

You have been engaged by Shmevan to review the financial information prepared by the Saskatoon store. Shmevan would like a report assessing the appropriateness of the accounting methods Saskatoon used and whether these accounting methods were "fair in the context of the contest." In preparing to write your report, you have gathered the following information:

1. The formula used to calculate the percentage increase in net income before taxes is

$$\frac{\text{Income before taxes in 2014} - \text{Income before taxes in 2013}}{\text{Income before taxes in 2013}}$$

In the event that income before taxes in 2013 is below $100,000, for purposes of the formula, net income before taxes in 2013 is assumed to be $100,000.

2. For the year ended October 31, 2013, the Saskatoon store reported income before taxes of $42,000.

3. The Saskatoon store normally recognizes revenue when goods are delivered to customers.

4. During 2014, the Saskatoon store changed its inventory valuation method from average cost to FIFO. Saskatoon's owner explained that the change was to make the store's accounting records consistent with other stores in the chain. As of October 31, 2014, 58 of the Shmevan stores use FIFO. The effect of the change was to increase income by $18,000 in 2013 and by $21,000 in 2014 versus the amount that would have been reported using average cost.

5. During the fiscal year ended October 31, 2013, the Saskatoon store wrote off $50,000 of inventory because management deemed that it could not be sold. In February 2014, the inventory was sold to three separate customers for $72,000.

6. In October 2014, the president of the Saskatoon store made three television commercials that are to be broadcast in the Saskatoon area beginning in December. As of October 31, the commercials have been completed but not shown on television. The commercials cost $15,000 to produce and the amount has been capitalized and is reported on the October 31, 2014, balance sheet.

7. In September and October 2014, the Saskatoon store ran a promotion that offered significant discounts to customers who made large purchases. These customers were assured that they could return any purchases after 90 days for a full refund for any reason. Sales in September and October 2014 were significantly higher than the same months the year before, and preliminary evidence suggests that sales in November 2014 have declined from 2013.

8. In October 2013, the Saskatoon store paid employees $22,000 in advances against commissions that would be earned in fiscal 2014. The advances were accounted for as wage expenses in 2013. The amount was paid because some employees were facing financial difficulties and the owner of the store wanted to help them out.

9. During fiscal 2014, the Saskatoon store sold a delivery vehicle, some furniture and fixtures, and a number of miscellaneous other assets. Most items were sold for more than their net book values (gains), but some were sold at a loss. Overall, the sales produced a gain of $17,000.

Required:

Prepare the report requested by Shmevan.

ENDNOTES

1. This case was written by Daniel Armishaw.

2. Adapted from the 1991 Uniform Final Examination, Canadian Institute of Chartered Accountants.

3. Adapted from the 2000 Uniform Final Examination, Canadian Institute of Chartered Accountants.

GLOSSARY

Accelerated depreciation (page 422) Allocates more of the cost of a capital asset to expense in the early years of its life and less in the later years.

Account (page 96) A category of asset, liability, or owners' equity.

Accounting (page 3) A system for producing information about an entity and communicating that information to people who want or need the information for making decisions.

Accounting cycle (page 89) The process by which data about economic events are entered into an accounting system, processed, organized ,and used to produce information such as financial statements.

Accounting equation (page 37) The conceptual foundation of modern accounting that states assets = liabilities + owners' equity.

Accounting estimates (pages 119, 574) Estimated amounts that must be used when financial statements are prepared because the actual amounts pertaining to many economic events and transactions are not known with certainty at the time. Examples include the amount of accounts receivable that will not be collected, the useful lives of capital assets, and the cost of warranty services that have not yet been provided.

Accounting policies (pages 54, 574) The methods, principles, and practices used by an entity to report its financial results.

Accounts payable turnover ratio (page 683) A ratio that provides information about how quickly an entity pays its accounts payable; defined as credit purchases ÷ average accounts payable.

Accounts receivable turnover ratio (page 322) A measure of how well an entity's credit program is being managed. Gives an idea of how quickly the entity is collecting its receivables. The ratio is defined as credit sales divided by average receivables.

Accrual accounting (page 45) A system of accounting that measures the economic performance of an entity rather than just its cash flows. Under the accrual system, revenue is recognized when it is earned and expenses matched to revenue, regardless of when the cash is received or spent.

Accrued expense (page 116) An expense that is recognized and recorded in the financial statements before the cash payment is made.

Accrued liability (page 116) A liability that is recognized and recorded in the financial statements but the recording is not triggered by an external event such as receipt of a bill or invoice.

Accrued revenue (page 118) Revenue that is recorded before cash is received.

Accumulated other comprehensive income (or **loss**) (page 573) An equity account that accumulates other comprehensive income from the statement of comprehensive income.

Acid test ratio (page 319) A measure of an entity's liquidity. Defined as an entity's most liquid assets (cash, cash equivalents, temporary investments, receivables) divided by current liabilities.

Adjusting entry (page 112) Journal entries recorded at the end of a reporting period that reflect economic changes that may have occurred during the period but that have not been recorded in the accounting system. Adjusting entries are not triggered by exchanges with outside entities.

Adverse opinion (page 591) The audit opinion given when the financial statements are so materially misstated or misleading that they do not present fairly the financial position, results of operations, and/ or cash flows of the entity.

After-tax cost of borrowing (page 511) The interest rate an entity pays after taking into consideration the tax-deductibility of interest. The after-tax cost of borrowing is calculated as: actual interest rate × (1 − tax rate).

Aging schedule (page 310) A schedule that classifies accounts receivable by the length of time they have been outstanding.

Allowance for uncollectible accounts (page 309) A contra asset account to accounts receivable or other receivables account that represents the portion of the receivables that management estimates will not be collected.

Amortization (page 418) The process of allocating the cost of intangible asset to expense over time.

Annuity (page 304) A series of equal cash flows (inflows or outflows), usually made at equally spaced time intervals.

Asset turnover (page 680) A measure of how effectively an entity can generate sales from its asset base; defined as sales ÷ average total assets.

Asset (page 37) Economic resources, for carrying out its business activities, that provide future benefits to an entity.

Authorized capital stock (page 562) The maximum number of each type of share that can be issued by a corporation.

Available-for-sale investments (page 635) Any investment that doesn't give control or significant influence to the investing corporation, or that doesn't meet the criteria for classification as a held-to-maturity or trading investment.

Average collection period of accounts receivable (page 322) A measure of how well an entity's credit program is being managed by giving the number of days receivables are outstanding before they are collected. The average collection period of accounts receivable is calculated by dividing the accounts receivable turnover ratio into 365.

Average cost method (page 362) An inventory cost flow assumption that determines the average cost of all goods on hand during the period and uses that average to calculate cost of sales and the balance in ending inventory.

Average number of days inventory on hand ratio (page 379) A ratio used to evaluate the efficiency of inventory management. The average number of days inventory on hand ratio indicates the number of days it takes an entity to sell its inventory. The ratio is defined as 365 divided by the inventory turnover ratio.

Average payment period for accounts payable (page 684) The average number of days that the entity takes to pay its accounts payable.

Balance sheet (page 37) The financial statement that provides information about the financial position—its assets, liability and owners' equity—of an entity at a moment in time.

Bank overdraft (page 242) Occurs when an entity removes more money from their bank account than there is in the bank account, effectively creating an amount owing to the bank. The amount of the overdraft is treated as a liability.

Bank reconciliation (page 298) Examining the differences between an entity's accounting records and its bank account.

Basic earnings per share (**basic EPS**) (page 583) Net income minus preferred share dividends divided by the weighted-average number of shares outstanding during the period.

Betterment (page 416) An expenditure made that improves an existing capital asset, thereby making it more valuable to the entity. A betterment might increase a capital asset's useful life or improve its efficiency.

Big bath (page 195) The expensing of a significant amount of assets that would normally have been amortized or otherwise expensed in future periods.

Bond (page 485) A formal borrowing arrangement in which a borrower agrees to make periodic interest payments to lenders as well as repay the principal at a specified time in the future.

Book value (page 582) The amount shown in the accounting records for an asset, liability, or equity item.

Book value of equity (page 582) The balance sheet value of the equity section of the balance sheet and is equal to assets − liabilities from the balance sheet. Book value of equity is also referred to as the net assets or net worth of the entity.

Callable bond (page 487) A bond that gives the bond issuer the option to repurchase the bond from investors at a time other than the maturity date under conditions that are specified in the bond agreement.

Canada Business Corporations Act (page 564) The federal legislation that governs federally incorporated companies.

Canada Revenue Agency (CRA) (page 9) The Canadian government department responsible for administration and enforcement of the Canadian federal tax laws.

Capital assets (pages 39, 412) Resources that contribute to the earning of revenue over more than one period by helping an entity to produce, supply, support, or make available the goods or services it offers to its customers. Capital assets are not bought and sold in the ordinary course of business.

Capital cost allowance (page 449) Amortization for tax purposes.

Capital expenditure (page 260) Money spent to purchase capital assets.

Capital lease (page 498) A lease that transfers the benefits and risks of ownership to the lessee. Assets associated with a capital lease are capitalized on the balance sheet of the lessee along with liability representing the lease payments to be made over the life of the lease.

Capital structure (pages 511, 685) The term used to describe how an entity is financed—the amount of debt and equity the entity has.

Capitalize (page 413) An amount expended or accrued that is recorded on the balance sheet as an asset.

Carrying amount (page 115) The cost of capital assets less the accumulated depreciation.

Cash accounting (page 45) A system of accounting where revenue is recognized when cash is received and expenses recognized when cash is spent.

Cash cycle (page 234) The cycle by which an entity begins with cash, invests in resources, provides goods or services to customers using those resources, and then collects cash from customers.

Cash dividend (page 568) A distribution in cash of a corporation's earnings to its shareholders.

Cash flow statement (page 242) The financial statement that shows how cash was obtained and used during a period and classifies cash flows as operating, investing or financing.

Cash from/used in financing activities (pages 52, 261) The cash an entity raises and pays to equity investors and lenders.

Cash from/used in investing activities (pages 52, 261) The cash an entity spent buying capital and other long-term assets and cash received from selling those assets.

Cash from/used in operations (pages 52, 261) The cash an entity generates from or uses in its regular business activities.

Cash lag (page 235) The delay between the expenditure of cash and the receipt of cash.

Closing journal entry (page 126) The journal entry required for resetting temporary account balances to zero and transferring the balances in the temporary accounts to retained earnings or owners' equity.

Commitment (page 509) A contractual agreement to enter into a transaction in the future.

Common shares (pages 43, 562) Shares representing the residual ownership in an entity. Common shareholders are entitled to whatever earnings and assets are left after obligations to debt holders and preferred shareholders have been satisfied.

Common size financial statement (**vertical analysis**) (page 670) An analytical tool in which the amounts in the balance sheet and income statement are expressed as percentages of other elements in the same year's statements

Comparability (page 172) The qualitative characteristic of accounting information under Canadian GAAP that states that users should be able to compare the accounting information provided by different entities and the information of a particular entity from period to period.

Completed-contract method (page 184) A critical-event approach to revenue recognition that recognizes revenue in full when a contract is completed.

Componentization (page 418) When an item acquired is made up of parts or components for which different useful lives or depreciation methods are appropriate, IFRS requires each component to be accounted for separately.

Compound interest (page 299) Interest that is calculated on the principal amount and on interest accumulated in previous periods.

Comprehensive income (pages 50, 571) The change in equity from transactions and economic events from all sources that don't involve owners.

Conservatism (page 371) A fundamental GAAP accounting concept that serves to ensure that assets, revenue, and net income are not overstated and that liabilities and expenses are not understated. The implication is that when preparers are faced with reasonable alternative accounting treatments, they should choose the one that is more conservative.

Consignment sale (page 177) A transaction in which the producer or distributor of goods transfers the goods to another entity for sale but for which the rights and risks of ownership do not transfer. The producer or distributor recognizes revenue when the other entity actually sells the merchandise to somebody else.

Consolidated financial statements (pages 34, 625) A single set of financial statements that aggregate the accounting information of a parent corporation and all of its subsidiaries.

Contingent liability (page 508) A liability that may arise in the future if future events occur.

Contra-asset account (page 114) An account that is used to accumulate subtractions from a related asset account.

Contributed surplus (page 574) A shareholders' equity account that shows amounts received by the entity from the sale of shares that are greater than the par value of the shares.

Control (page 625) When an investor is able to make the important decisions of the investee and determine its strategic operating, financing, and investing policies on an ongoing basis, without the support of other shareholders.

Convertible bond (page 487) May be exchanged by the investor for other securities of the issuing entity, such as common stock.

Convertible preferred shares (page 565) Preferred shares that shareholders can choose to exchange for a specified number of common shares for each preferred share that they convert.

Corporation (page 6) A separate legal entity created under the corporation laws of Canada or of a province. A corporation has many of the rights and responsibilities of an individual.

Cost of sales (page 47) The cost of an entity's inventory that was sold during a period.

Cost-recovery method (page 184) Revenue in a period is recognized up to the amount of costs incurred during the period (except for the last year of the project).

Cost-benefit trade-off (page 5) The concept of comparing the benefits of an action with the costs of the action, and taking action only if the benefits exceed the costs.

Coupon rate (page 487) The percentage of the face value that the issuer pays to investors each year as interest.

Covenant (page 664) Restrictions that impose limits on the actions of borrowers.

Credit (page 97) An entry to an account that has the effect of decreasing assets and expenses, and increasing liabilities, owners' equity, and revenues.

Creditor (page 37) An entity to whom the reporting entity has an obligation to provide cash or other assets in the future.

Critical-event approach (page 171) A revenue recognition approach where an entity recognizes revenue when a specified instant in the earnings process, called the critical event, occurs. When the critical event occurs, 100 percent of the revenue is recognized.

Cumulative preferred shares (page 565) Preferred shares that require payment of any dividends on the shares that have not been paid, in respect of the current year or previous years, before the common shareholders can receive any dividends.

Current assets (page 39) Assets that will be used up, sold, or converted to cash within one year or one operating cycle.

Current liability (page 40) Liabilities that will be paid or satisfied within one year or one operating cycle.

Current ratio (page 42) A measure of entity's liquidity; defined as current assets divided by current liabilities.

Date of declaration of a dividend (page 568) The date when the board of directors of a corporation declares a dividend.

Date of payment of a dividend (page 568) The date when the dividends are actually paid to shareholders.

Date of record of a dividend (page 568) The registered owner of shares on the date of record is entitled to receive a dividend declared by a corporation.

Debenture (page 485) A bond with no collateral provided to the lenders.

Debit (page 97) An entry to an account that has the effect of increasing assets and expenses, and decreasing liabilities, owners' equity, and revenues.

Debit card (page 102) A method of payment that allows a customer to pay for goods and services by transferring money directly from the customer's bank account to the vendor's bank account. Payment by debit card is equivalent to payment by cash.

Debt (page 484) Amounts borrowed and owed by an entity.

Debt-to-equity ratio (page 43) A ratio that provides a measure of the amount of debt relative to equity an entity uses for financing. The ratio gives an indication

of the riskiness of the entity and its ability to carry more debt; defined as total liabilities ÷ total shareholders' equity.

Declining balance (page 422) An accelerated method of amortization. The method applies an amortization rate to the NBV of the asset at the beginning of the year to calculate the amortization expense.

Deferred expense (page 113) Assets that are acquired in one period but not expensed, at least in part, until a later period.

Deficit (page 43) When retained earnings is negative.

Defined-benefit plan (page 504) A pension plan in which the employer promises to provide employees certain specified benefits in each year they are retired.

Defined-contribution plan (page 504) A pension plan in which the employer makes a cash contribution to the pension fund as specified in the agreement with the employees. The pension benefits received at retirement depend on the amount contributed on behalf of the individual (by the employer and the employee) and on how well investments made with the funds in the fund perform.

Deflation (page 296) A period when, on average, prices in the economy are falling.

Demand loan (page 479) A loan that must be repaid whenever the lender requests or demands repayment.

Depletion (page 418) The term used to describe the amortization of the cost of natural resources.

Depreciable amount (page 421) The amount of a capital asset that will be depreciated.

Depreciation (pages 46, 418) Amortization of the cost of tangible capital assets. The expensing of the cost of capital assets in a period.

Derecognition (page 490) When a bond or other liability is removed from the balance sheet.

Development stage companies (page 262) Companies that are in the process of developing their products and markets, and have not yet begun its planned business activity.

Direct method of calculating cash from operations (page 248) A method of calculating/reporting cash from operations by showing cash collections and cash disbursements from operations during the period.

Direct writeoff method (page 308) A method of accounting for uncollectible receivables where the receivable is removed from the list of accounts receivable and an expense is recorded when management decides that a receivable will not be collected.

Disclaimer of opinion (page 591) When auditors can't obtain enough evidence to support an opinion they don't give one but instead they state in their report that they are unable to express an opinion as to whether the financial statements are fair and in accordance with GAAP or IFRS.

Discount (on debt) (page 490) When a bond is sold to investors for less than its face value. This occurs when the coupon rate is greater than the effective rate of interest for the bond.

Discount rate (page 302) The rate used to calculate the present value of future cash flows.

Dividend (page 43) Distributions of a corporation's earnings to shareholders.

Dividend payout ratio (page 689) The proportion of earnings that is being paid to common shareholders as dividends.

Double-entry bookkeeping (page 94) An accounting system in which each transaction or economic event is recorded in two places in the accounts.

Earnings management (page 113) Managers' use of accounting choices to achieve their own objectives.

Earnings per share (EPS) (page 583) The amount of net income that is attributable to each individual share of common stock.

Earnings quality (page 667) The usefulness of current earnings for predicting future earnings.

Economic consequences (page 4) The effect of actions and decisions on people's wealth.

Effective interest rate (page 487) The real or market rate of interest that is paid or earned on debt.

Employee stock option (page 578) A right granted to an employee to purchase a specified number of shares of the employer's stock at a specified price over a specified period of time.

Entity (page 3) An economic unit such as an individual, proprietorship, partnership, corporation, government, not-for-profit organization, etc. In an accounting environment, an entity is an economic unit that a stakeholder wants accounting information about.

Entity concept (page 241) Assumes that information can be provided for an entity of interest (corporation, partnership, proprietorship, division of a corporation, etc.), separate from the owners or other entities.

Entity-specific value (page 414) Also known as value-in-use, which is the net present value of the cash flow the asset will generate or save over its life or the net present value of the cash the asset would allow the entity to avoid.

Equity method of accounting (page 632) An investment accounted for using the equity method is initially recorded on the balance sheet at cost. The balance sheet amount is adjusted each period for the investor's share of the investee company's income, less dividends declared. The income statement reports the investor company's share of the investee's net income.

Event after the reporting period (subsequent event) (page 509) An economic event that occurs after an entity's year end, but before the financial statement are released.

Exchange rate (page 297) The price to buy one currency stated in terms of another currency.

Executory contract (page 102) An exchange of promises where one party promises to supply goods or services and the other party promises to pay for them, but neither side has fulfilled its side of the bargain.

Exercise price (page 578) The price at an employee holding an employee stock option is allowed to purchase the shares.

Expense (page 45) Economic sacrifices made to earn revenue. Sacrifices can be the result of using up an asset or incurring a liability. Expenses result in a decrease in owners' equity.

Expiry date (page 578) The final date that an option can be exercised. After an option expires, it cannot be used to purchase shares.

External audit (page 12) The process of examining, on behalf of stakeholders who are external to the entity, an entity's financial statements and the data supporting the information in the financial statements for the purpose of determining whether the statements adhere to principles such as fairness and GAAP.

External auditors (page 12) The people who examine entities' financial information on behalf of stakeholders who are external to the entity.

Face value of a bond (page 487) The amount that the holder of the bond, the investor, will receive when the bond matures.

Fair value (page 627) In accounting for a subsidiary, the estimated market value of the subsidiary's assets and liabilities on the date the subsidiary was purchased.

Financial accounting (page 4) The field of accounting that provides information to people who are external to an entity—people who do not have direct access to an entity's information.

Finance lease (page 498) A lease that transfers the risks and rewards of ownership to the lessee. Assets associated with a capital lease are capitalized on the balance sheet of the lessee along with liability representing the lease payments to be made over the life of the lease

Financial flexibility (page 257) Reserves giving an entity the ability to react and adjust to threats and opportunities.

Financial instruments (page 634) Assets and liabilities that represent the contractual rights or obligations of the entity to receive or pay cash or other financial assets.

Finished goods inventory (page 356) Inventory that has been completed and is ready for sale.

First-in, first-out (FIFO) (page 361) An inventory cost flow assumption in which the cost of inventory that is purchased or produced first is expensed first. For raw materials that are used in a manufacturing process, the cost of the raw materials that were purchased first is the cost that is used in the production process first. With a FIFO system, the cost of inventory reported on the balance sheet represents the cost of inventory that was purchased or produced most recently.

Fiscal year (page 35) The 12-month period over which performance is measured and at the end of which a balance sheet is prepared.

Fixed-rate loan (page 485) A loan whose interest rate does not change.

Free cash flow (page 260) The cash that is remaining after reducing cash from operations by cash spent on capital expenditures and dividends.

Fully diluted earnings per share (page 583) An earnings per share measure that reflects the effect that dilutive securities would have on basic EPS if the dilutive securities were converted or exchanged for common shares.

Future income tax assets and liabilities (page 519) Assets and liabilities that arise because the accounting methods used to prepare the general purpose financial statements are sometimes different from the methods used to calculate taxable income and the amount of income tax an entity must pay.

Future income tax expense (page 519) Also called deferred income tax. The temporary difference between the accounting value of assets and liabilities and the tax value of assets and liabilities on the balance sheet date, multiplied by the entity's tax rate.

Future value (FV) (page 299) The amount of money you will receive in the future by investing it today at a given interest rate.

General journal (page 119) The chronological record of the journal entries that have been entered into the accounting system.

General ledger (page 121) A record of all the accounts of an entity.

General partner (page 558) Member of a limited partnerships who does not have limited liability and is liable for all debts and obligations of the partnership. A limited partnerships must have at least one general partner.

General purpose financial statements (page 33) Financial statements that are prepared for a wide range of stakeholders, but not necessarily tailored to the needs of any or all of them.

Generally Accepted Accounting Principles for Private Enterprises (GAAP) (page 14) The broad principles and conventions that provide guidance to accountants and managers for making accounting choices as well as rules and procedures that are established as accepted accounting practices at a particular time.

Generally accepted auditing standards (GAAS) (page 590) A set of general guidelines, stated in the *CICA Handbook*, that provide guidance to auditors in the conduct of their audits.

Going concern (page 241) An entity that will be continuing its operations for the foreseeable future.

Goodwill (pages 434, 627) The amount that a parent pays for a subsidiary over and above the fair value of the subsidiary's identifiable assets and liabilities on the date the subsidiary is purchased.

Gradual approach (page 171) A revenue recognition approach that results in revenue being recognized gradually over a period of time.

Gross margin (page 48) Sales minus cost of goods sold.

Gross margin percentage (page 48) Gross margin divided by sales.

Half-year rule (page 449) A requirement in the *Income Tax Act* that allows an entity to deduct for tax purposes, in the year an asset is purchased, only one-half the amount of CCA that would otherwise be allowable.

Held-to-maturity investments (page 635) An investment with a maturity date, fixed or determinable payments (like interest payments), and management must have the ability and intention to hold the investment to maturity.

Hidden reserves (page 316) Undisclosed accounting choices used to manage earnings and other financial information with the intention of satisfying the self-interests of the preparers.

Holding gain or loss (page 373) A change in the value of inventory or some other asset while the asset is owned by the entity. A holding gain or loss is called a realized holding gain or loss if the asset is sold before the financial statement date, and the holding gain or loss is called an unrealized holding gain or loss if the asset is still owned by the entity on the financial statement date.

Horizontal analysis (trend statement) (page 674) An analytical tool in which the amounts in the balance sheet and income statement are expressed as percentages of a base year set of financial statements.

Hybrid securities (page 566) Securities that have characteristics of debt and equity.

Identifiable assets and liabilities (pages 434, 627) Tangible or intangible assets and liabilities that can be specifically identified and measured with some objectivity.

Income statement (page 44) The financial statement that provides a measure of the economic performance of an entity over a period of time. The income statement summarizes an entity's revenues and expenses for a period.

Indirect method of calculating cash from operations (page 248) A method of calculating/reporting cash from operations by reconciling from net income to cash from operations by adjusting net income for non-cash amounts that are included in the calculation of net income and for operating cash flows that are not included in the calculation of net income.

Inflation (page 296) A period when, on average, prices in the economy are rising.

Intangible asset (page 412) A capital asset that does not have physical substance, such as patents, copyrights, trademarks, brand names and goodwill.

Intercompany transactions (page 630) Transactions among the corporations in a consolidated group. Intercompany transactions are eliminated when preparing consolidated financial statements. This means that sales and expenses, and changes in the value of assets and liabilities that occur as a result of transactions among subsidiaries and with the parent are not reflected in the consolidated statements.

Interest (page 43) The cost of borrowing money.

Interest coverage ratio (accrual basis) (page 686) A ratio that measures the ability of an entity to meet its fixed financing charges. Defined as (net income + interest expense + tax expense) ÷ interest expense.

Interest coverage ratio (cash basis) (page 687) A ratio that measures the ability of an entity to meet its fixed financing charges. Defined as cash from operations excluding interest paid ÷ interest paid.

Internal control (page 297) The processes that management implements to provide reasonable assurance that that an entity will be able to achieve its objectives regarding the reliability of financial reporting, the effectiveness and efficiency of its operations, and compliance with relevant laws and regulations.

International Financial Reporting Standards (page 14) A set of globally accepted, high-quality accounting standards produced by the International Accounting Standards Board and mandatory for Canadian public companies.

Inventory (page 355) Goods that are available for sale by an entity, or goods that will be used to produce goods that will be sold when they are completed. Inventory can also include materials used in supplying a service to customers.

Inventory conversion period (page 235) The average length of time between receiving inventory from a supplier and selling it to a customer.

Inventory self-financing period (page 235) The average number of days between date inventory is paid for and the date it's sold to a customer.

Inventory turnover ratio (ITO) (page 378) Provides information on how efficiently inventory is being managed by measuring how quickly the entity is able to sell its inventory. The inventory turnover ratio is defined as cost of sales divided by average inventory.

Investee corporation (page 624) A corporation that an investor corporation has invested in.

Investor corporation (page 624) A corporation that has an investment in another company.

Issued shares (page 564) The number of authorized shares that have been distributed to shareholders.

Journal entry (page 96) The method used to enter information about economic events into the accounting system.

Just-in-time (JIT) inventory (page 380) A system where the manufacturer orders materials or produces parts or finished goods only when they are required rather than holding stock of items for production or sale.

Last-in, first-out (LIFO) (page 368) An inventory cost flow assumption in which the cost of inventory that was purchased or produced most recently is matched to revenue first. For raw materials that are used in a manufacturing process, the cost of the raw materials that were purchased last or most recently is the cost that is used in the production process first. With LIFO, the cost of inventory reported on the balance sheet represents the cost of old, sometimes very old inventory.

Lease (page 497) A contractual arrangement where one entity (the lessee) agrees to pay another entity (the lessor) a fee in exchange for the use of an asset.

Lessee (page 497) An entity that leases an asset from the asset's owner.

Lessor (page 497) An entity that leases assets that it owns to other entities.

Letter of credit (page 496) A guarantee from a bank that a customer will pay amounts owed to a seller.

Leverage (page 576) The use of debt to increase the return earned on the equity investment of the owners.

Liability (page 37) Obligations an entity has to pay debts or provide goods or services.

Limited liability (page 7) Shareholders of a corporation are not liable for the obligations of and losses suffered by the corporation.

Limited liability partnership (LLP) (page 558) An ordinary partnership in which innocent partners are shielded from personal liability for malpractice liabilities of the firm. An individual partner of the LLP would not be liable for claims against the firm arising from negligence or other forms of malpractice unless the partner was personally involved in the negligence or malpractice.

Limited partner (page 558) Members of a limited partnership who have limited liability protection and as a result are not personally liable for the debts and obligations of the partnership.

Limited partnership (page 558) Partnerships in which some of the partners have limited liability protection.

Line of credit (pages 242, 480) An arrangement with a lender that allows an entity to borrow up to a specified maximum amount when and if the entity requires the money.

Liquidity (page 41) An entity's ability to make payments as they come due.

Lower of cost and market (LCM) rule (page 369) Requires that when the market value of inventory at the end of a reporting period is lower than the cost of the inventory, the inventory must be reported on the balance sheet at its market value. The amount of the writedown, the difference between the cost of the inventory and its market value, is reported as a loss in the income statement. The loss is recorded in the period the inventory decreases in value, not when the inventory is sold.

Maintenance (page 416) Expenditures that allow an asset to operate as intended—to do what it is designed to do. Maintenance costs should be expensed when incurred.

Management discussion and analysis (MD&A) (page 665) Prepared by an entity's managers, it provides them the opportunity to discuss its financial results, position, and future prospects. It is intended to provide readers with a view of the entity through the eyes of management.

Managerial accounting (page 4) The field of accounting that provides information to the managers of the entity and others decision makers who work for the entity, to assist them in making decisions related to operating the entity.

Market value of equity (page 582) The market price of an entity's shares multiplied by the number of shares outstanding.

Matching (matching concept) (page 93) The process of recording and reporting expenses in the period that the revenue those expenses help earn is recorded and reported.

Materiality (page 37) The significance of financial information to stakeholders. Information is material if its omission or misstatement would affect the judgment of a user of the information.

Maturity date of a bond (page 487) The date that the borrower or bond issuer has agreed to pay back the principal (the face value of the bond) to the bondholders.

Mortgage (page 485) A loan that provides the borrower's property as collateral.

Net assets (page 46) These are assets minus liabilities.

Net realizable value (NRV) (page 369) The amount of cash that is expected to be received from the sale or realization of an asset after taking into consideration any additional costs.

No par value share (page 565) Shares that do not have a par value assigned to them.

Non-controlling interest (page 629) An account on a consolidated balance sheet that represents the net assets of a subsidiary that are owned by entities other than the shareholders of the parent corporation. This arises when a parent owns less than 100 percent of the commons shares of a subsidiary, because GAAP requires that the consolidated statements include 100 percent of the subsidiary's assets, liabilities, revenues, and expenses.

Non-current assets (page 40) Assets that will not be used up, sold, or converted to cash within one year or one operating cycle.

Non-current liability (page 40) Liabilities that will be paid or satisfied in more than one year or one operating cycle.

Note payable (page 485) A formal obligation signed by the borrower promising to repay a debt.

Not-for-profit organization (page 8) An entity whose objective is to provide services and not to make a profit. Examples include hospitals, charities, churches, mosques and synagogues, unions, clubs, daycare centres, and universities.

Off-balance-sheet financing (page 497) A financing arrangement that occurs when an entity can borrow money without a liability appearing on its balance sheet.

Operating cycle (page 39) The time it takes from the initial investment an entity makes in goods and services until cash is received from customers.

Operating lease (page 498) A lease that does not transfer the rights and risks of ownership to the lessee. Assets associated with an operating lease remain on the books of the lessor, the lessor recognizes revenue from the lease when payments are received or receivable, and the lessee recognizes an expense when the payment to the lessor is paid or payable.

Other comprehensive income (pages 50, 571) Those transactions and economic events that involve non-owners and affect equity but that remain, for various reasons, excluded from the calculation of net income.

Outstanding shares (page 564) The number of shares of a corporation currently in the hands of shareholders.

Overhead (page 357) The costs in a manufacturing process other than direct labour and direct materials. Overhead costs are more difficult or even impossible to associate directly with the product being made.

Owners' equity (page 37, 43) The investment the owners of an entity have made in the entity.

Par value (page 565) A value assigned to each share of common stock in the articles of incorporation. The *Canada Business Corporations Act* and the corporations acts of a number of provinces do not permit par value shares.

Parent corporation (page 625) An investor corporation that controls an investee corporation.

Participating preferred shares (page 565) The amount of the preferred share dividend increases above the stated amount if certain conditions are met. The amount of the preferred dividend is often tied to the dividend paid on the common shares.

Partner (page 8) An entity that is one of two or more owners of a partnership.

Partnership (page 8) An unincorporated business owned by two or more entities. (Partners can be corporations or individuals.) A partnership is not legally separate from the partners who own it.

Passive investments (page 635) Investments where the investor corporation cannot influence the strategic decision making of the investee corporation.

Payables deferral period (page 235) The average number of days between receipt of goods or services from a supplier to payment of the supplier.

Pension (page 503) Income provided to a person after they retire.

Percentage-of-completion method (page 184) A method of revenue recognition used with the gradual approach to revenue recognition. It allocates revenues and related expenses among more than one reporting period based on a measure of the effort completed in each period.

Percentage-of-credit-sales method (page 312) A method of estimating uncollectible receivables that is based on management's estimate of the percentage of credit sales that will not be collected in a period.

Percentage-of-receivables method (page 309) An amount of uncollectible receivables based on management's estimate of the percentage of period ending receivables balance that will not be collected.

Period costs (page 187) Costs that are expensed in the period that in which they are incurred.

Periodic inventory control system (page 358) An inventory control system where the inventory account is not adjusted whenever a transaction affects inventory. The balance in the inventory account at the end of period and cost of goods sold for the period are determined by counting the inventory on hand on the period ending date.

Periodic-reporting assumption (page 241) One of the basic assumptions underlying GAAP that states that meaningful financial information about an entity can be provided for periods of time that are shorter than the life of an entity.

Permanent accounts (page 126) Balance sheet accounts carried forward from one period to the next.

Permanent differences (page 519) Revenues and expenses that are recognized for tax purposes but never recognized for financial reporting purposes, or are recognized for financial reporting purposes but never recognized for tax purposes.

Permanent earnings (page 666) Earnings that are expected to be repeated in the future.

Perpetual inventory control system (page 358) A system of inventory control that keeps an ongoing record of purchases and sales of inventory. When inventory is purchased or sold, the inventory account is immediately debited or credited to record the change. When inventory is sold, cost of sales is immediately debited.

Posting (page 121) The process of transferring each line of a journal entry to the corresponding account in the general ledger.

Preferred shares (page 565) Shares of a corporation that have rights that must be satisfied before common shareholders'. These preferred rights pertain to the payment of dividends and/or to the distribution of assets in the event of liquidation.

Premium (on debt) (page 493) When a bond is sold to investors for more than its face value. Occurs when the coupon rate is greater than the effective rate of interest for the bond.

Prepaid expenses (page 113) Assets that are acquired in one period but not expensed, at least in part, until a later period or periods.

Preparers (page 11) The people responsible for deciding what, how, and when information is going to be presented in an entity's financial statements and other accounting information are presented. The preparers are the people who make the decisions—senior managers such as controllers, chief financial offers and even chief executive officers—not to the people who do the physical preparation of the statements.

Present value (page 299) The worth today of money that will be received in the future.

Price-to-book ratio (page 582) A measure of the stock market's valuation of a company's equity relative to its book value. Used as an indication of whether the shares are reasonably valued.

Price-to-earnings (P/E) ratio (page 688) Conceptually, the P/E ratio gives an indication of how the market values an entity's earnings. It is seen as indicator of the growth prospects of an entity. Defined as market price per share ÷ earnings per share.

Principal (page 43) The amount borrowed from a lender.

Private corporation (page 8) A corporation whose shares and other securities are not available for purchase without agreement with the private corporation or its shareholders.

Proceeds (page 487) The amount of money a bond issuer receives from selling bonds to investors.

Product costs (page 187) Costs that can be matched to specific revenues and that are expensed when the revenue they help generate is recognized.

Profit margin ratio (page 110) A measure of how effective the entity is at controlling expenses and reflects the amount of income earned for each dollar of sales. Equal to net income/revenue.

Property dividend (page 569) Dividends paid with property instead of cash.

Property, plant, and equipment (page 39) Tangible capital assets that are used on an ongoing basis to earn revenue, but that are not sold in the ordinary course of business.

Proprietor (page 8) A person who owns a proprietorship.

Proprietorship (page 8) An unincorporated business owned by one person. Not legally separate from the person who owns it.

Prospectus (page 181) A legal document that provides detailed information about a company that is offering its shares for public sale.

Provision (page 481) Similar to an accrued expense and liability, except there is uncertainty about the timing and amount of the liability.

Prudence (page 371) A fundamental GAAP accounting concept that serves to ensure that assets, revenue, and net income are not overstated and that liabilities and expenses are not understated. The implication is that when preparers are faced with reasonable alternative accounting treatments, they should choose the one that is more conservative.

Public corporation (page 7) A corporation whose shares or other securities are available for purchase by any entity that has an interest in owning the securities and money to buy them. The securities of public corporations are usually traded on a stock exchange.

Qualified opinion (page 591) The audit opinion given when, overall, the financial statements present the entity's situation fairly, but the statements do deviate from GAAP (or from whatever set of accounting standards the auditor is auditing to). A qualified audit opinion always contains the term "except for," which prefaces the explanation why the qualified audit report was given.

Quick ratio (page 319) A measure of entity's liquidity. Defined as an entity's most liquid assets (cash, cash equivalents, temporary investments, receivables) divided by current liabilities.

Raw materials inventory (page 356) The inputs into the production process of a manufacturer or processor.

Realized holding gain or loss (page 635) A holding gain or loss that has been realized because the asset has been sold before the financial statement date.

Receivables (page 306) Amounts owed to an entity. The amounts can be due from customers (accounts receivable), taxation authorities (taxes receivable), investments (interest and dividends receivable), shareholders or employees (shareholder/employee loans receivable), etc.

Receivables conversion period (page 235) The average length of time between delivery of goods to a customer and receipt of cash.

Recognition (page 188) The process whereby any financial statement element—asset, liability, equity, expense or revenue—is entered into the accounting system and reported in the financial statements.

Recoverable amount (page 438) The greater of the net realizable value (NRV) less cost to sell and value-in-use (defined as the present value of the asset's future cash flows).

Redeemable preferred shares (page 565) Preferred shares that that the issuer can purchase back from investors if it chooses, according to specified terms.

Relevance (page 178) The qualitative characteristic of accounting information under Canadian GAAP that states that the information provided to users must be relevant or useful for the decisions they have to make.

Reliability (page 178) The qualitative characteristic of accounting information under Canadian GAAP that states that the information provided to users must be a reasonable measure of what it is intended to measure.

Repairs (page 416) Expenditures that allow an asset to operate as intended—to do what it is designed to do. Repair costs should be expensed when incurred.

Replacement cost (page 373) The current price that would have to be paid to purchase an identical or equivalent asset.

Residual value (page 418) The amount a capital asset can be sold for at the end of its useful life.

Retained earnings (page 43) A balance sheet account that shows the amount of earnings a corporation has earned over its life less the amount of dividends paid to shareholders over the corporation's life.

Retractable bond (page 487) A bond that gives the investor the option to cash in the bond before the maturity date under certain conditions.

Retractable preferred shares (page 565) Preferred shares that shareholders can require the issuer to purchase the preferred shares from them, if they choose, according to specified terms.

Return on assets (ROA) (pages 441, 584) A measure of the performance and operating efficiency of an entity. Defined as net income + after tax interest expense/total assets.

Return on equity (ROE) (pages 110, 584) A measure of the profitability of an entity and its effectiveness in using the assets provided by the owners of the entity to generate net income. Equal to net income/owners' equity. owners' equity can be the period end amount or the average for the period.

Revenue (page 45) Economic benefits earned by providing goods or services to customers. Revenue results in an increase in owners' equity.

Revenue recognition (page 92) The point in time when revenue is recorded in the accounting system and is reported in the income statement.

Reverse stock split (page 570) A reduction in the number of shares.

Review engagement (page 591) A form of assurance that provides less assurance to users than an audit does about whether an entity's financial statements are in accordance with GAAP. Review engagements are never performed on public companies because securities laws require audits. A review will be done for private companies when external stakeholders are satisfied with less assurance than is provided by an audit.

Segment disclosure (page 630) Disaggregations of information about an entity by types of products and services, geographic location, and major customers.

Segregation of duties (page 298) An internal control procedure that requires that people who handle an asset should not be responsible for the record keeping for the asset.

Share (page 6) A unit of ownership in a corporation.

Shareholder (page 6) An entity that owns shares of a corporation and that is therefore an owner of the corporation.

Shareholders' equity (page 43) The owners' equity of a corporation.

Significant influence (page 632) An ownership interest in an investee corporation that allows the investor corporation to affect the strategic operating, investing, and financing decisions of the investee corporation even though it does not have control.

Simple interest (page 299) Interest that is paid or earned on the principal amount only.

Solvency (page 685) The financial viability of an entity—its ability to meet its long-term obligations.

Special purpose report (page 57) Accounting reports that are prepared to meet the needs of specific stakeholders and/or a specific purpose.

Specific identification method (page 362) An inventory valuation method that assigns the actual cost of a unit of inventory to that unit of inventory.

Stakeholder (page 10) A group or individual that is interested in or has a "stake" in an entity.

Start-up company (page 262) Companies that are in the process of developing their products and markets, and have not yet begun its planned business activity.

Statement of cash flows (page 52) Shows how an entity obtained and used cash during a period and provides information about how cash was managed. It's also an important source of information about an entity's liquidity.

Statement of retained earnings (page 50) The financial statement that summarizes the changes to retained earnings during a period.

Statement of shareholders' equity (page 50) Presents changes during a period in each account in the equity section of the balance sheet.

Stock dividend (page 569) The distribution of a corporation's own shares to its existing shareholders.

Stock exchange (page 7) A place (physical or virtual) where entities can trade securities of publicly traded entities.

Stock split (page 570) The division of an entity's shares into a larger number of units, each with a smaller value.

Straight-line depreciation (pages 106, 421) The method that depreciates an equal amount of the cost of an asset each period.

Subsequent event (page 509) An economic event that occurs after an entity's year-end, but before the financial statement are released.

Subsidiary corporation (page 625) An investee corporation that is controlled by an investor corporation.

T-account (page 122) An accounting textbook device used to represent general ledger accounts. Each T-account corresponds with a general ledger account.

Tangible asset (page 412) A capital asset with physical substance, such as land, buildings, equipment, vehicles, and furniture.

Taxable income (page 511) The measure of income that is used, as defined by the *Income Tax Act*, to calculate the amount of tax an entity must pay.

Temporary account (page 126) Accounts whose balances are reset to zero at the end of a period by closing them to retained earnings or owners' equity. All income statement accounts are temporary accounts. The balances in temporary accounts are not carried forward from one period to the next.

Temporary differences (page 519) Revenues and expense that are fully recognized for both tax and financial reporting purposes, but the recognition happens at different times.

Time value of money (page 299) The concept that people would prefer to receive a given amount of money sooner rather than later.

Trading investments (page 635) Any investment that management designates as a trading investment. Investments in this category are actively bought and sold for profit making. All gains and losses (realized and unrealized) are recognized in the income statement in the period in which they occur.

Transactional entry (page 112) An entry that is triggered by an exchange with another entity.

Transitory earnings (page 666) Earnings that are not expected to be repeated in future periods.

Treasury stock (page 565) Shares that were previously sold to investors and that the issuing corporation has repurchased but not retired.

Trend statements (horizontal analysis) (page 674) An analytical tool in which the amounts in the balance sheet and income statement are expressed as percentages of a base year set of financial statements.

Trial balance (page 125) A listing of all the accounts in the general ledger by their balances. The main purpose of the trial balance is to ensure that the debits equal the credits.

Unearned revenue (page 116) A liability that results from receiving cash before the recognition of revenue.

Unit-of-measure assumption (page 241) One of the basic assumptions underlying GAAP that states that economic activity of an entity can be effectively stated in terms of a single unit of measure. The unit of measure that is almost always used is money, and in Canada the monetary unit used is usually the Canadian dollar.

Unit-of-production depreciation (page 423) A usage-based method of depreciation used when consumption can be readily associated with an assets use, not to the passage of time or obsolescence.

Unqualified opinion (page 590) The audit opinion that is given when the auditors are satisfied that the financial statements present the financial situation of the entity fairly and that statements follow GAAP.

Unrealized holding gain or loss (page 635) Increases or decreases in the market value of assets that are not supported by a transaction with an outside party.

Value-in-use (page 414) The net present value of the cash an asset would generate over its life or the net present value of the cash the asset would allow the entity to avoid. Also known as *entity-specific value*.

Variable rate loan (page 485) A loan whose interest rate changes with market conditions.

Vertical analysis (common size financial statements) (page 670) An analytical tool in which the amounts in the balance sheet and income statement are expressed as percentages of other elements in the same year's statements.

Warranty (page 176) A promise by a seller or producer of a product to correct specified problems with the product.

Working capital (page 41) Current assets minus current liabilities.

Working capital ratio (page 42) A measure of entity's liquidity. Defined as current assets divided by current liabilities.

Work-in-process inventory (WIP) (page 356) Inventory that is partially completed on the financial statement date.

Writedown (page 369) A reduction in the net book value of an asset to some measure of the market value of the asset. A writedown is achieved by debiting an expense and crediting the asset.

Writeoff (page 369) The writedown of an asset to zero.

Zero-profit method (page 184) Revenue in a period is recognized up to the amount of costs incurred during the period (except for the last year of the project).

PHOTO CREDITS

Chapter 1
Page 1, Special Thanks to Ian Clarke

Chapter 2
Page 32, Special Thanks to Sheila Fraser

Chapter 3
Page 88, Special Thanks to Craig Hannaford,
photo courtesy of The Canadian Press/
Frank Gunn

Chapter 4
Page 169, Special Thanks to Hélène Fortin

Chapter 5
Page 233, Special Thanks to Navdeep Bains

Chapter 6
Page 293, Special Thanks to Frances Horodelski

Chapter 7
Page 354, Special Thanks to Jacek Surma

Chapter 8
Page 411, Special Thanks to Al Rosen

Chapter 9
Page 477, Special Thanks to Hedley and
Katherine Chan

Chapter 10
Page 556, Special Thanks to Chris Lovell

Chapter 11
Page 622, Photo courtesy of CPI/The Canadian
Press/Mario Beauregard

Chapter 12
Page 662, Special Thanks to Robin Schwill

Also, thanks to Kyle Schruder, Sheena Brennan, and Meaghan Trewin.

INDEX